T0388465

ROUTLEDGE HANDBOOK OF THE INTERNATIONAL RELATIONS OF SOUTH ASIA

This handbook offers a comprehensive overview of the international relations of South Asia.

South Asia as a region is increasingly assuming greater significance in global politics for a host of compelling reasons. This volume offers the most comprehensive collection of perspectives on the international politics of South Asia, and it covers an extensive range of issues spanning from inter-state wars to migration in the region. Each contribution provides a careful discussion of the four major theoretical approaches to the study of international politics: Realism, Constructivism, Liberalism, and Critical Theory. In turn, the chapters discuss the relevance of each approach to the issue area addressed in the book. The volume offers coverage of the key issues under four thematic sections:

- Theoretical Approaches to the Study of the International Relations of South Asia
- Traditional and Emerging Security Issues in South Asia
- The International Relations of South Asia
- Cross-cutting Regional Issues

Further, every effort has been made in the chapters to discuss the origins, evolution, and future direction of each issue.

This book will be of much interest to students of South Asian politics, human security, regional security, and international relations in general.

Šumit Ganguly is a Distinguished Professor of Political Science and holds the Rabindranath Tagore Chair in Indian Cultures and Civilizations at Indiana University, Bloomington, USA. He is an author or editor of over 20 books, including the *Routledge Handbook of Asian Security Studies* (2009; 2019).

Frank O'Donnell is the Deputy Director of the South Asia Program at the Henry L. Stimson Center in Washington, DC. He publishes and comments widely on Southern Asian security issues, including co-authoring *India and Nuclear Asia: Forces, Doctrine, and Dangers* (Washington, DC: Georgetown University Press, 2018).

'This is, hands down, the most comprehensive volume on South Asia's geostrategy, security, and international relations published to date. Juxtaposing leading IR theories with essays by noted country experts, it is an indispensable resource for scholars, policymakers, and students seeking to understand a complex and increasingly important region.'

—**Neil DeVotta,** *Wake Forest University, USA*

'Enriched by the four theoretical approaches to the study of International Relations of South Asia, the articles included in the book provide a variety of perspectives on aspects of traditional and non-traditional securities besides raising the agenda of redefinition of security. The book is immensely useful to the serious scholars, policy makers and students of international relations of South Asia.'

—**Lok Raj Baral,** *Former Professor Political Science, Tribhuvan University, Kathmandu, and Former Ambassador of Nepal to India*

'This intellectually rigorous and comprehensive handbook is a significant contribution to the understanding of South Asia's dealings with the world and to IR studies in general. Presenting the views of preeminent scholars and applying IR theory to south Asian practice, the 34 chapters of the book reveal the strengths and limitations of different theoretical approaches, examine strategic culture, illuminate the international relationships of major actors, and describe the longer term implications of trans-national issues like terrorism, climate change and outer space. Its writing makes it accessible to the informed layman. This is a book to savour, to return to often, and is destined to become a standard work of reference, setting a high standard for future scholars of South Asian IR.'

—**Shivshankar Menon,** *Centre for China Studies, Ashoka University, India*

'This is an extraordinarily comprehensive, up to date, and high-quality volume on South Asia's international relations. Its 34 chapters cover the four major theoretical approaches – realism, liberalism, constructivism and critical theory – and the entire gamut of issues from longstanding security issues within the region to emerging security issues like cybersecurity, space and refugees, to political economy, to country-specific international relations, perspectives from major world capitals and cross-national issues such as climate change and Covid. It will be a vital reference point for scholars of IR working on South Asia for a long time to come.'

—**Eswaran Sridharan,** *Academic Director and Chief Executive Officer, University of Pennsylvania Institute for the Advanced Study of India, New Delhi, India*

ROUTLEDGE HANDBOOK OF THE INTERNATIONAL RELATIONS OF SOUTH ASIA

*Edited by
Šumit Ganguly and Frank O'Donnell*

LONDON AND NEW YORK

Cover image: © Getty Images

First published 2022
by Routledge
4 Park Square, Milton Park, Abingdon, Oxon OX14 4RN

and by Routledge
605 Third Avenue, New York, NY 10158

Routledge is an imprint of the Taylor & Francis Group, an informa business

© 2023 selection and editorial matter, Šumit Ganguly and Frank O'Donnell;
individual chapters, the contributors

The right of Šumit Ganguly and Frank O'Donnell to be identified as the authors of the
editorial material, and of the authors for their individual chapters, has been asserted
in accordance with sections 77 and 78 of the Copyright, Designs and Patents Act 1988.

All rights reserved. No part of this book may be reprinted or reproduced or utilised
in any form or by any electronic, mechanical, or other means, now known or
hereafter invented, including photocopying and recording, or in any information
storage or retrieval system, without permission in writing from the publishers.

Trademark notice: Product or corporate names may be trademarks or registered trademarks,
and are used only for identification and explanation without intent to infringe.

British Library Cataloguing-in-Publication Data
A catalogue record for this book is available from the British Library

Library of Congress Cataloging-in-Publication Data
Names: Ganguly, Šumit, editor. | O'Donnell, Frank, 1985- editor.
Title: Routledge handbook of the international relations of South Asia /
edited by Šumit Ganguly and Frank O'Donnell.
Description: Abingdon, Oxon ; New York, NY : Routledge, 2022. |
Includes bibliographical references and index. | Identifiers: LCCN 2022019605 (print) |
LCCN 2022019606 (ebook) | ISBN 9781032159881 (hardback) |
ISBN 9781032159898 (paperback) | ISBN 9781003246626 (ebook)
Subjects: LCSH: South Asia--Relations. | National security--South Asia. |
Geopolitics--Indo-Pacific Region.
Classification: LCC DS341 .R683 2022 (print) | LCC DS341 (ebook) |
DDC 327.54--dc23/eng/20220428
LC record available at https://lccn.loc.gov/2022019605
LC ebook record available at https://lccn.loc.gov/2022019606

ISBN: [978-1-032-15988-1] (hbk)
ISBN: [978-1-032-15989-8] (pbk)
ISBN: [978-1-003-24662-6] (ebk)

DOI: 10.4324/9781003246626

Typeset in Bembo
by KnowledgeWorks Global Ltd.

Sumit Ganguly dedicates this book to his daughter, Tara.
Frank O'Donnell dedicates this book to his parents, Dominic and Kathy,
and his wife Kim.

CONTENTS

Acknowledgments	xi
Contributors	xii
Introduction	1

PART I
Theoretical Approaches to the Study of the International
Relations of South Asia   **5**

1 Realist Approaches to the Study of International Relations of South Asia   7
  Rajesh Rajagopalan

2 Liberal Approaches to the International Relations of South Asia   20
  Ian Hall

3 Constructivist Approaches to the International Relations of South Asia   32
  Aditi Malhotra

4 Critical Theory Approaches to the International Relations of South Asia   46
  Shibashis Chatterjee

PART II
Traditional and Emerging Security Issues in South Asia   **61**

5 Indian Strategic Culture   63
  Rajesh Basrur

Contents

6 Pakistan's Strategic Culture 79
Jamison C. Heinkel

7 The Evolution of the Sino-Indian Rivalry 92
Manjeet S. Pardesi

8 The Evolution of the India-Pakistan Rivalry 104
Mahesh Shankar

9 India's Nuclear Weapons Program 116
Yogesh Joshi

10 Pakistan's Nuclear Weapons Program 130
Hannah Haegeland and Arzan Tarapore

11 Terrorism and Counter-Terrorism in South Asia: Government
Support for Militant Groups in South Asia 142
Tricia Bacon

12 Insurgencies and Counterinsurgencies in South Asia 158
Subhasish Ray

13 Indian and Pakistani Conventional Military Doctrines 170
Frank O'Donnell

14 Track Two Diplomacy and the India-Pakistan Conflict 184
Peter Jones

15 Human Security in South Asia 197
Swarna Rajagopalan

16 South Asia: States of Cyber(In)Security 213
Trisha Ray

PART III
The International Relations of South Asia **229**

17 Afghanistan's Relations with South Asia: Diplomacy Amid Conflict 231
Michael Kugelman

18 Sri Lanka and South Asia 245
Nilanthi Samaranayake

Contents

19 Bangladesh's International Relations with South Asia and Beyond 258
Ali Riaz

20 Domestic Politics and Structural Constraints: Pakistan and
its South Asian Neighbors 275
Ryan Brasher

21 India's Relations with Her Neighbors 289
Chris Ogden

22 Reinventing Non-Alignment in South Asia: The Foreign Policies
of Nepal and the Maldives 301
Nicolas Blarel and Constantino Xavier

23 Trends in US Policy Toward South Asia 314
Jeff Smith

24 China and South Asia: Beijing Builds Influence 330
Andrew Scobell

25 Russia and South Asia 341
Vidya Nadkarni

26 Japan's Relations with South Asia 354
Monika Chansoria

27 The UK and South Asia 369
David Scott

28 France and South Asia 383
Gilles Boquérat

29 Germany's South Asia Policy 395
Christian Wagner

PART IV
Cross-Cutting Regional Issues 409

30 The Politics of Climate Change in South Asia 411
Dhanasree Jayaram

31 Polycentric versus State-Led Responses to the COVID-19 Pandemic 425
Dinsha Mistree

Contents

32 Refugees and Migration in South Asia 439
Kavita R. Khory

33 Space Programs, Policies, and Diplomacy in South Asia 454
Ajey Lele

34 Regional Trade and Investment in South Asia 470
Surupa Gupta

Index 483

ACKNOWLEDGMENTS

The editors would like to thank Spenser Warren, a doctoral candidate in Political Science at the Indiana University Bloomington, for his valuable research assistance. They are also grateful to the contributors and anonymous reviewers in helping deliver this volume.

CONTRIBUTORS

Tricia Bacon is Associate Professor at American University's School of Public Affairs and Director of the Policy Anti-Terrorism Hub at American University. She is the author of *Why Terrorist Organizations Form International Alliances*, published by University of Pennsylvania Press. Bacon previously worked on counterterrorism for over ten years at the Department of State.

Rajesh Basrur is Senior Fellow, S. Rajaratnam School of International Studies, Nanyang Technological University, Singapore; and concurrently Research Associate, Contemporary South Asian Studies Programme, Oxford School of Global and Area Studies, University of Oxford. He is the author of *Subcontinental Drift: Domestic Politics and India's Foreign Policy* (Georgetown University Press, forthcoming) and five other books.

Nicolas Blarel is Associate Professor of International Relations at the Institute of Political Science, Leiden University. He is the author of *The Evolution of India's Israel Policy: Continuity, Change, and Compromise since 1922* (Oxford University Press) and has co-edited the *Oxford Handbook of India's National Security*. Blarel has a forthcoming co-edited book, *The South Asia to Gulf Migration Governance Complex* (Bristol University Press).

Gilles Boquérat holds a Ph.D. in History from the University of Paris 1-Panthéon-Sorbonne, specializes in contemporary South Asia. He has been a doctoral research fellow at SIS, JNU, and a resident scholar at the French Centre for Human Sciences, New Delhi, and at the Institute of Strategic Studies, Islamabad. He is currently a senior research associate at the Foundation for Strategic Research in Paris.

Ryan Brasher is a political scientist at Simpson University in northern California. He taught at Forman Christian College in Lahore, Pakistan, from 2014 to 2021, and previously worked for a development organization in Afghanistan as well. His research has focused on ethno-federalism, the construction of ethnic identity, religious minorities, and religious fundamentalism in South and Central Asia.

Monika Chansoria is Senior Fellow at Japan Institute of International Affairs in Tokyo. Her research interests include contemporary Asian security, weapons proliferation, and great power

Contributors

politics in the Indo-Pacific. She has authored five books on Asia's security affairs. Previously, she has held senior research positions at Fondation Maison des Sciences de l'Homme, Paris, and at Hokkaido University, Sapporo, Japan.

Shibashis Chatterjee is Professor at the Department of International Relations and Governance Studies, Shiv Nadar University, India. He is the author of *India's Spatial Imaginations of South Asia* (OUP, 2019) and the co-editor of *Peace and Conflict Studies: Perspectives from South Asia* (Routledge). A recipient of the Fulbright Award twice, he has taught at Yale, Indiana, and Makerere University.

Surupa Gupta is Professor of Political Science and International Affairs at the University of Mary Washington. Her research focuses on Indian foreign economic policy, India's role in global governance in economic issues, politics of trade liberalization and agricultural policy reform in India. Her research has been published in scholarly journals such as *International Studies Perspectives*, *International Negotiations*, and *Contemporary South Asia* (forthcoming).

Ian Hall is Professor of International Relations and the Deputy Director (Research) at the Griffith Asia Institute at Griffith University, Queensland, Australia. He is Academic Fellow of the Australia India Institute at the University of Melbourne and a co-editor of the *Australian Journal of International Affairs*. His publications include *Modi and the Reinvention of Indian Foreign Policy* (2019).

Hannah Haegeland is Senior Member of the Technical Staff at Sandia National Laboratories CMC with expertise in nuclear issues, cross-domain escalation, risk reduction, and regional security. She manages cooperative security portfolios with Southern Asia and the Middle East, promoting global security in the 21st century through science-oriented research and engagement.

Jamison C. Heinkel is Ph.D. Candidate at the Department of Political Science, South Asia Institute, Heidelberg University, Germany. An analyst with the US Department of Defense, his research interests include South Asia, West Africa, and the Middle East. He obtained masters' degrees from the National Intelligence University and the Josef Korbel School of International Studies, University of Denver.

Dhanasree Jayaram is Assistant Professor, Department of Geopolitics and International Relations, and Co-coordinator, Centre for Climate Studies at Manipal Academy of Higher Education (MAHE), India. She is also Research Fellow at Earth System Governance; Research Fellow at Centre Marc Bloch; and Guest Researcher at Freie Universität Berlin, pursuing the Alexander von Humboldt Foundation's International Climate Protection Fellowship 2022–23.

Peter Jones is Associate Professor in the Graduate School of Public and International Affairs at the University of Ottawa. He is also Executive Director of the Ottawa Dialogue, an NGO which runs Track 2 and Track 1.5 dialogues, including an extensive program of dialogues in South Asia. His publications include *Track Two Diplomacy: In Theory and Practice*.

Yogesh Joshi is Research Fellow at the Institute of South Asian Studies (ISAS) at the National University of Singapore. He is also a non-resident Global Policy Fellow with

Contributors

the Woodrow Wilson Center for Scholars, Washington, DC. Before joining ISAS, he was MacArthur and Stanton Nuclear Postdoctoral Fellow at the Centre for International Security and Cooperation, Stanford University, United States.

Kavita Khory is Ruth Lawson Professor of Politics and Director of the McCulloch Center for Global Initiatives at Mount Holyoke College. A specialist on South Asia, she focuses on foreign policy, nationalism, and migration. She is the editor of *Global Migration: Challenges in the 21st Century.*

Michael Kugelman is Asia Program Deputy Director and Senior Associate for South Asia at the Woodrow Wilson Center in Washington, DC. He also writes the weekly South Asia Brief for *Foreign Policy* magazine. His main specialty is Afghanistan, Pakistan, and India, including their relations with the broader region and with the United States.

Ajey Lele is Security Analyst based in New Delhi, India. He has obtained a Masters in Physics and his Ph.D. is in International Relations. His specific areas of research include issues related to Weapons of Mass Destruction (WMD), Space Security and Strategic Technologies. He is the author of a book *Asian Space Race: Rhetoric or Reality* (Springer, 2013).

Aditi Malhotra is the Editor-in-Chief of the *Canadian Army Journal* (CAJ). Before joining CAJ, she was the co-editor of the *Journal for Intelligence, Propaganda and Security Studies* (Austria). Malhotra holds a Ph.D. in Political Science from the University of Muenster, Germany. Formerly, she held appointments at the National Institute of Advanced Studies and the Centre for Land Warfare Studies in India.

Dinsha Mistree is Research Fellow in the Program on Strengthening US-India Relations at the Hoover Institution and Research Fellow in the Rule of Law Program at Stanford Law School. He studies the political economy of development, with a special focus on South Asia. He holds an MA and Ph.D. in Politics from Princeton, and an SB and SM in Political Science from MIT.

Vidya Nadkarni is Professor of Political Science at the University of San Diego. Nadkarni's research interests cover the foreign policies of rising (China), resurgent (Russia), and aspiring (India) powers. She is the author of *Strategic Partnerships in Asia: Balancing without Alliances* (2010); co-editor of *Emerging Powers in Comparative Perspective* (2012) and *Challenge and Change* (2016); and co-author of *The Foreign Policy of Russia* (2019).

Frank O'Donnell is Deputy Director of the South Asia Program at the Stimson Center. His research explores nuclear doctrine and posture development, conventional military modernization, and national security policymaking processes in Southern Asia. He is the co-author of *India in Nuclear Asia: Evolution of Regional Forces, Perceptions, and Policies* (Georgetown University Press, 2018).

Chris Ogden is Senior Lecturer in Asian Security at the University of St Andrews, where he teaches International Relations of India and China. His research interests concern the interplay between foreign and domestic policy influences in South Asia (primarily India) and East Asia (primarily China), Hindu nationalism, authoritarianism, and great powers. For more information, see http://chris-ogden.org.

Contributors

Manjeet S. Pardesi is Senior Lecturer in the Political Science and International Relations Programme and Asia Research Fellow at the Centre for Strategic Studies at Victoria University of Wellington. His research interests include historical international relations, great power politics, Asian security, and the Sino-Indian rivalry.

Rajesh Rajagopalan is Professor of International Politics at Jawaharlal Nehru University, New Delhi. His research and publications focus on international political theory and India's foreign and security policies.

Swarna Rajagopalan works as an independent scholar, writer, consultant, and activist. She trained as a political scientist at the University of Illinois at Urbana-Champaign and is Visiting Professor of Politics at Krea University. Her portfolio is at swarnar.com and she tweets @ swarraj.

Subhasish Ray is Professor at the Jindal School of Government and Public Policy at O.P. Jindal Global University. His research interests fall in the area of civil conflict, broadly construed. He serves as an editor for the *Journal of Genocide Research*. His most current line of research examines how a legacy of conflict shapes elections, public opinion, and voting.

Trisha Ray is Associate Fellow with the Observer Research Foundation in India. Her research centers on geopolitics, international security, and emerging technologies. She co-chairs ORF's flagship technology conference, CyFy, and she is also a member of UNESCO's Working Group on Information Accessibility. Trisha completed her master's degree at the Walsh School of Foreign Service, Georgetown University.

Ali Riaz is Distinguished Professor of Political Science at Illinois State University, and Nonresident Senior Fellow of Atlantic Council. His primary areas of interest are South Asian politics, democratization, violent extremism, political Islam, and Bangladeshi politics. His recent publications include *Voting in a Hybrid Regime: Understanding the 2018 Bangladeshi Election* (2019), and an edited volume *Religion and Politics in South Asia* (2021).

Nilanthi Samaranayake is Director of the Strategy and Policy Analysis Program at CNA. She studies Indian Ocean regional security and the smaller South Asian countries. Samaranayake's analysis has been published in *Asian Security* and *Journal of Indo-Pacific Affairs*, among other outlets. She holds an MSc in International Relations from the London School of Economics and Political Science. The views expressed are those of the author.

Andrew Scobell is the Distinguished Fellow for China at the United States Institute of Peace (USIP) and an adjunct professor in the Edmund A. Walsh School of Foreign Service at Georgetown University. Prior to joining USIP, he spent 11 years as a senior political scientist at the RAND Corporation. He earned a doctorate in Political Science from Columbia University.

David Scott is a member and writer for the Center for International Maritime Security (CIMSEC). An Indo-Pacific national strategies expert, especially China and India, Scott's publications include the UK relationship with India, UK role in the Indian Ocean, and UK maritime deployments to the Indo-Pacific. His publications are available at www.d-scott. com/publications, and he can be contacted at davidscott366@outlook.com.

Contributors

Mahesh Shankar is Associate Professor and Director of the International Affairs Program at Skidmore College in Saratoga Springs, New York. He holds a Ph.D. in Political Science from McGill University, and is the author of *The Reputational Imperative: Nehru's India in Territorial Conflict* with Stanford University Press.

Jeff M. Smith is Research Fellow at the Heritage Foundation in Washington, DC. He is the author of *Cold Peace: China-India Rivalry in the 21st Century* and the author/editor of *Asia's Quest for Balance: China's Rise and Balancing in the Indo-Pacific*. He has testified before multiple congressional committees and served as an advisor on several presidential campaigns.

Arzan Tarapore is the South Asia Research Scholar at the Shorenstein Asia-Pacific Research Center at Stanford University, where his research focuses on Indian military strategy and regional security. He is also Senior Non-resident Fellow at the National Bureau of Asian Research. Prior to his scholarly career, he served in the Australian Defence Department.

Christian Wagner is Senior Fellow at the German Institute for International and Security Affairs (SWP) in Berlin. His main areas of research are India, South Asia, and the Indo-Pacific with a special focus on democracy, foreign policy, and security issues.

Constantino Xavier is Fellow in Foreign Policy at the Centre for Social and Economic Progress (CSEP) in New Delhi. At CSEP, he leads the Sambandh Initiative on Regional Connectivity focused on South Asia. Xavier is Non-resident Fellow at the Brookings Institution and holds a Ph.D. in South Asian studies from the Johns Hopkins University.

INTRODUCTION

The international relations of South Asia provide an extraordinary canvas for both students and scholars. Every conceivable issue in international relations can be studied in the region, and its dynamics pose stern tests for each major theoretical paradigm. The region has witnessed inter-state and intra-state conflicts; is riven with endemic class, ethnic, and politico-religious strife; continues to host massive refugee movements across national borders; is both a significant driver and victim of climate change effects; and faces major challenges with regional economic integration. It is home to two nuclear-armed rivals, India and Pakistan, with a third one, China, increasingly interwoven in this nuclear competition. Indeed, China has cast a long shadow over the region for several decades. Since the early 1960s, it has built a strategic nexus with Pakistan. More recently it has sought to enhance its footprint through the ambitious Belt and Road Initiative (BRI) strategic infrastructure project, while its invasion of sections of Indian-claimed Kashmir in 2020 generated a rare, and dangerous, occurrence of military fatalities between nuclear adversaries. This would have been the first such occurrence in decades, if not for the Pulwama-Balakot militarized crisis between India and Pakistan setting that record the previous year.

China's global rival, the US, remains engaged in the region. However, Washington's recalibration of its South Asia strategy has ended 20 years of military commitment to supporting democratization in Afghanistan, in favor of a more singular focus on leveraging regional relationships against Chinese influence. The US withdrawal from Afghanistan—and the swift collapse of the US-backed Ghani government and resumption of power by the Taliban—has generated regional ripple effects that will likely persist through much of the 21st century. Nevertheless, the US dedication to improving relations with significant South Asian states, especially India, is clear, as is the underlying rationale behind this diplomacy. Other world and major powers—including Russia, France, Germany, and the United Kingdom—are also deepening their engagement with the region, recognizing both its human and economic potential and its geostrategic significance as the likely center of great power competition.

South Asia faces multiple security and human development challenges, many of which are transregional in nature. The COVID-19 pandemic, climate change, and refugee crises are perhaps the most obvious in terms of the necessity for regional as opposed to separate state domestic responses. Yet, they are overlaid upon a persisting failure of regionalism in general,

DOI: 10.4324/9781003246626-1

Introduction

as documented by the weaknesses of the regional institutions that exist and of cross-border trade and investment. Still more pressures weigh upon the region and demand a South Asian collective response, including growing cybersecurity threats and poor progress on improving human security as the human population continues to boom. As the region grapples with these multiple and often interrelated challenges—and is increasingly subject to intense pressures from world and major powers to align with one against others—this volume offers a thorough analysis of the international relations of South Asia.

The volume is divided into four distinct sections. The first spells out four major theoretical approaches—Realism, Liberalism, Constructivism, and Critical Theory—to the study of international relations. South Asia poses distinct challenges to each school. The focus of many regional states upon strengthening state sovereignty and seeking military solutions offers strong supporting evidence for Realist arguments. However, these are challenged by notable imbalances of power, which have existed for decades and remain uncorrected. India's rival, if we use rational metrics such as population and military sizes, is China. However, India remains preoccupied with Pakistan, a materially weaker state, in its security planning and strategic thought. India should be the regional hegemon of South Asia by the same metrics, but has been unable to exert its influence across the region accordingly.

South Asia also provides effective evidence for Liberal arguments, in that its conflict-prone and unstable political nature dovetails with its variable record of democratization and weak regional trade and institutions. Still, both Realist and Liberal arguments are challenged by the visibility of ideological competition as a driver of South Asian politics and conflict. Powerful identities and ideologies are at play, ranging from Sinhala nationalism in Sri Lanka, to Hindu supremacism in India, to Islamist actors throughout the region.

As Constructivists argue, these ideological clashes underpin the ongoing persistence of the India-Pakistan conflict and decades-long Sri Lankan civil war. However, Constructivist scholarship on the region has not significantly explored non-security issues, which can still substantially shape domestic and thus regional politics.

Finally, Critical Theory draws our attention to the fact that the above characteristics of the region are not immutable, and that domestic civil society actors have indeed highlighted an alternative set of priorities for leaders, recognizing and addressing "shared culture, economic plights of the masses, a common hydrological, energy, and climate cartography, and the need for a political transformation that would assuage sovereign anxieties, allow reconciliation of communities, and invest in substantial democratization."[1] The redefinition of security along these lines is conceptually possible; however, it remains a distant prospect at the time of writing, as South Asian leaders remain focused upon building and maintaining Westphalian sovereignty structures instead.

The second section deals with both traditional and emerging security issues in South Asia. The region plays host to a multiplicity of insecurities. The 2020 Chinese Ladakh incursion and 2019 India-Pakistan militarized crisis indicate growing appetites among these three states for conventional conflict. At the conventional level, military planning across these three states increasingly emphasizes rapid strikes and thrusts into adversary territory, with declining concern for the unplanned escalatory consequences such actions might incur. This trend continues at the nuclear level, with new doctrinal interpretations and platforms which generate security dilemma effects and heighten nuclear risk. Moreover, terrorism and insurgencies remain persistent threats throughout South Asia. The danger of a major attack by a Pakistan-sponsored terrorist group leading to an India-Pakistan war is unabated. Meanwhile, ISIS-affiliated groups are present in several South Asian states, while Pakistan struggles to contain the Tehrik-e-Taliban group which operates out of Afghanistan.

Introduction

These traditional, military-centric security challenges both exist alongside and intersect with relatively understudied security concerns. South Asian states, militaries, businesses, and citizens are increasingly exposed to cyberattacks. In what emerges as a persisting theme of this volume, this transregional threat has not motivated a regional response. Instead, South Asian governments have adopted patchwork and halting regulatory and cyber strategy policies, which run behind the ever-evolving range and sophistication of dangers from the cyber domain. This in turn only exacerbates the insecurities experienced at the level of the individual in South Asia: The level of human security. The chapter on this topic establishes four categories of human insecurity experienced across the region, namely "structural inequalities; governance failures; climate change, and a changing citizenship context where belonging is defined by exclusions and citizen agency is limited."[2] The extraordinary human potential of the region can only be delivered if outcomes improve at this level of individual security.

The third section focuses on the international relations of the region as seen from the vantage point of all the regional capitals. It also includes chapters from the perspectives of several world and major powers involved in the region.

At the outset, despite significant economic setbacks primarily due to the impact of the COVID-19 pandemic, India remains an economic power of some consequence. While still sandbagged with substantial rural and urban poverty, it is nevertheless the sixth largest economy in the world. If it makes sound economic choices in a post-COVID era, there is every reason to believe that it can place itself on a path of sustained economic growth that can address questions of endemic poverty.

It is also embroiled in an intractable rivalry with China. Yet, on its own, it is incapable of effectively competing with the China given the growing discrepancies in their relative capabilities—economic, military, and diplomatic. Without a doubt this realization has led India to gradually warm up to the Quadrilateral Security Dialogue even as it insists on maintaining its "strategic autonomy."

Apart from the dominant power, India, there are other consequential actors in the region. For the past two decades, Pakistan has played an oversize role in world politics largely because of its proximity to Afghanistan and the American presence in the country. Even after the American withdrawal from Afghanistan in August 2021, Pakistan's importance, while diminished, has not been entirely erased. As a nuclear-armed state with significant sectarian conflicts which are virtually endemic, it will remain a country of concern to the major powers.

The other, smaller states, while not as consequential for world politics, are nevertheless of importance in the region and beyond. Sri Lanka, which has long had a fraught relationship with India, is now the site of significant Sino-Indian competition for influence. Furthermore, its strategic significance may grow in the foreseeable future as the Peoples Liberation Army Navy (PLAN) enhances its presence in the Indian Ocean.

Bangladesh, which Henry Kissinger had long callously and sardonically written off as a "basket case," has demonstrated that it is a viable state. More to the point, today it enjoys better social indicators than those of India. It has emerged as a major hub for the global supply chain in the production of garments. Despite its achievements on both fronts, its future remains at risk especially as it confronts the existential threat of climate change.

Afghanistan is now a year into Taliban rule, after 20 years of US-backed regimes and counterinsurgency efforts. While a more inclusive Afghan government might unlock greater regional diplomatic recognition and support, there is little sign of the Taliban yielding such control at the time of writing. Its lack of political inclusion elevates the risk that non-state actors, such as ISIS-K and the TTP, will continue to pose a regional threat from within

Introduction

Afghanistan's borders. This in turn reduces the attractiveness of Afghanistan to China as a new foreign investment target, as China suffers similar extremist attacks on its projects within Pakistan.

Nepal and Bhutan seek to maintain a modicum of independence in their foreign and domestic policies. These tasks are not made easy as they face the pressures of the two behemoth powers that surround it. Finally, the Maldives, an archipelagic country in the Indian Ocean, is now entirely at the mercies of climate change. Ironically, this comes at a time when its geostrategic significance has dramatically increased owing to the PLAN's expanding interest in the Indian Ocean leading to growing misgivings on the part of India, the United Kingdom, France, and the United States.

China and the United States are engaging in new diplomatic, economic, and military outreach initiatives toward South Asia to avert regional states drifting into their global rival's sphere of influence. While China's efforts are hindered by its intensifying rivalry with India, American initiatives are limited by the comparatively low financial assistance it offers vis-à-vis China, alongside weaker engagement with the smallest South Asian states. Russia's diplomacy is primarily focused upon maintaining a strong political and military supply arrangement with India, while establishing ties with Pakistan in an effort to strengthen its influence in Afghanistan and to reduce the impacts of the solidifying US-India strategic partnership.

Following the end of their military involvement in Afghanistan, the United Kingdom and France have curtailed their relations with Pakistan and not recognized the Afghan Taliban government. Both powers are refocusing their attentions on defense partnerships with India, as they look to China's rise as the new defining challenge of the 21st century. German engagement with the region has tended to focus on developmental support, but its Indo-Pacific Guidelines of 2020 highlight an increasing interest in building regional security presence to address the Chinese challenge.

The fourth and final section tackles issues that are genuinely cross-national. At the time of writing in March 2022, an average of three people in South Asia died of COVID every minute.[3] Aside from limited Indian efforts to distribute vaccines, there has not been a truly regional collective response to this deadly pandemic; instead, states have preferred to prioritize national responses. This dynamic of primarily national responses to transregional and transnational challenges also characterizes South Asian climate change mitigation, even though the region is one of the most vulnerable to climate change effects. It is further demonstrated in the absence of any regional framework for refugee management. The chapters on economic relations and regionalism further elucidate how the paucity of regional cooperation and state preferences for securitizing these issues deepen the insecurities which their citizens face.

The region is thus theoretically contested, while its societies face a diversity of transformational challenges and its states simultaneously attempt to manage the growing centrality of South Asia as the crucible of 21st century geopolitics. South Asia is only increasing in global importance and complexity, rendering this volume essential to both scholars and students.

Notes

1 See Chapter 4.
2 See Chapter 15.
3 "Racing to Respond to the COVID-19 Crisis in South Asia," UNICEF, accessed March 20, 2022, https://www.unicef.org/rosa/racing-respond-covid-19-crisis-south-asia.

PART I

THEORETICAL APPROACHES TO THE STUDY OF THE INTERNATIONAL RELATIONS OF SOUTH ASIA

1
REALIST APPROACHES TO THE STUDY OF INTERNATIONAL RELATIONS OF SOUTH ASIA

Rajesh Rajagopalan

Despite Realism's centrality in the study of international politics, the approach has not been used to explain the international politics of South Asia. While it may be tempting to justify this by dismissing Realism as a Western import, there is also a local political philosophical tradition that can be identified with Realism in the form of Kautilya's *Arthashastra*, which makes the absence of Realist academic work even more puzzling.[1] Even a recent surge of academic interest in this historical tradition has not yet translated into applying Realism to contemporary international politics of the region.[2] Realism as an approach cannot entirely be absolved for this particular state of affairs because much of it is explicitly focused on great power politics and the state of the international system rather than on regional international politics.

Nevertheless, Realism can provide important insights into international politics of the region. Though Realism does not claim to provide much focus on regional international politics and generally has not been employed in this manner, basic Realist concepts and ideas about international politics can be utilized for this purpose. As an example, Stephen Walt has used such Realist principles to explain international politics in the Middle East.[3] Though he focused more on developing a general alternative to balance of power theory by theorizing about the importance of threat perceptions and did not develop a theory of regional international politics itself, his use of Realism in a non-great power context suggests that the approach can be successfully used in such a context. This chapter will similarly use Realism to provide a broad explanation of international politics in South Asia. Specifically, Realism in this chapter refers to Structural Realism, which is the basis of most of the current variants of contemporary Realism.

The next section will briefly outline the dearth of Realism in explaining South Asian international politics. The third section will set out the key structural conditions that are relevant to explaining South Asian international politics. This includes two broad sets: The regional structural condition and the global structural condition. Within the regional structure, two key variables are important: Most importantly and obviously, the regional balance of power which impacts all South Asian states, and its consequences for their behavior. Simply stated, India's overwhelming dominance in material power within the region is the single most relevant factor that needs to be considered in understanding South Asian international politics from a Realist standpoint. The second variable is geography, in particular the peculiar

DOI: 10.4324/9781003246626-3

7

situation in which India is a neighbor to all the countries in the region (except, of course, Afghanistan) but none of the others are neighbors to each other (again, with the exception of Afghanistan and Pakistan). The global structural condition of Cold War bipolarity and post-Cold War unipolarity is the other relevant structural condition that impacted the region's international politics. One of the problems here, however, is that the global-regional nexus is neither easy nor straightforward. How these two structural conditions interact is complicated, especially given the persistence of the regional structure and the relative variability of the global structure.

The subsequent section will examine the effects of these structural conditions. India's choice of internal balancing and its antipathy toward security partnerships and alliances flow from these structural conditions, as does the choice of external balancing of the other South Asian states, the relative ineffectiveness (so far at least) of such efforts, and even the similarity in the behavior of polar powers toward the region. But Realism, especially the structural variant used in this chapter, has well-known limitations, and these are outlined in the penultimate section. These include India's focus on Pakistan rather than China as the primary security concern, Pakistan's insistence on balancing a much larger and stronger India, and India's failure to generate regional dominance and leadership. The concluding section outlines why, despite these difficulties, a structural Realist approach still has important insights to offer on international politics of the region.

Studying South Asian IR: The Dearth of Realism

The limited use of Realism in studying Indian foreign policy has been commented upon by other scholars.[4] Though there are a few academic efforts that attempt to provide explanations of Indian foreign policy from variations of Realist theory, such analyses become even scarcer when the focus moves from Indian foreign policy to the region itself.[5]

On the one hand, this is the understandable consequence of Realism being largely dominated by American scholars who tend to focus on the global polar system in which, by happy coincidence, the US happens to be the dominant power. The logic that Realists explicitly use to justify this focus—that the study of the most powerful actors is likely to tell us more about the international system than studying weaker states—is internally con-sistent, but not of much use to those wanting to go beyond questions of system stability.[6] The consequence has been, as Dale Copeland notes, that "(W)hen it comes to the study of regional conflicts, realists as a group have been loath to put forward a clear and generaliz-able theory."[7]

Despite this, scholars have used Realist principles to examine regional international pol-itics. An early example is the concept of "regional security complex," developed by Barry Buzan and Ole Wæver.[8] Though it also includes non-Realist variables, Buzan and Wæver's work is useful because of its focus on international politics within regions, and in particular on the importance of regional balance of power, independent of great power politics. However, Buzan and Wæver's effort at shoehorning polarity into regional international relations is flawed because it remains a descriptive rather than an explanatory variable. In addition, their application of this insight to South Asia is marred by their characterization of the region as bipolar, which is difficult to square with the enormous imbalance of power in the region, espe-cially between India and Pakistan. Nevertheless, their work is important for being a useful and rare effort to use Realist concepts to examine regional international politics, including in South Asia. A more recent effort uses Realism to look at regional international order and problematically transposes the Neorealist view of systemic order to that of regions. In doing so, it ignores the global-regional nexus, which recognizes that regional orders exist not in isolation but within a global systemic order, with which it interacts.[9]

These problems with the limited previous Realists efforts to examine regional, especially South Asian international politics, need not suggest that Realism is inherently unsuitable for the purpose. This chapter outlines some key Realist variables that can be used to examine regional international politics, and how these can be applied to understand South Asian international politics. As the next section suggests, these variables encompass both those at the local level—the distribution of power, the effects of proximity, and the persistence of these two variables—as well as those at the global systemic level, such as international structural polarity, the global-regional nexus, and the malleability of the global structure.

Understanding South Asian International Politics: Key Variables

From a Realist perspective, both the regional distribution of power and the global balance are important considerations in the foreign policy and international politics of regions.

Regional Variables

The Regional Distribution of Power

The most important variable that impacts regional international politics and the states in the region is the regional distribution of power. As mentioned earlier, the distribution of power does not necessarily have to be categorized into polarities, as is the standard Realist approach when examining the global system. The reason is that when Realists use systemic polarity, polarity has an explanatory role, even if Realists do not agree about its specific effects. Thus, Waltz and other Realists have argued that bipolarity is more stable than multipolarity or unipolarity.[10] In turn, this has influenced Realists to argue that the end of bipolarity would lead to greater instability and that unipolarity would be a short-lived phenomenon.[11] Other Realists have pushed back on at least the latter notion, arguing that a unipolar order is likely to be much more stable.[12] The relative merits of these arguments are less relevant here than the fact that polarity plays an important explanatory and predictive role when used in this global context. But transposing this to regions is problematic because regional polarity cannot be considered in isolation. Stronger external powers can intrude and potentially alter the effects of polarity in a manner that is not a problem in the global system. That is why the characterization of South Asia as either unipolar or bipolar makes little sense because South Asia cannot exclude external influences, unlike the global system.

Nevertheless, the distribution of power within South Asia is an important consideration for any Realist analysis because it does affect the choices of both regional and external states. Even a cursory examination of this distribution will illustrate the huge imbalance in the region in favor of India. India accounts for about 66% of the total area of South Asia, 72% of its population, and 80% of GDP.[13] This overwhelming imbalance in raw resources also gives India a military that dwarfs its neighbors. The only country in the region that even attempts to maintain a military balance with India is Pakistan, but India outspends Islamabad six-fold, giving India military forces that are more than twice as large as Pakistan.[14] India's military also has to cater to the requirements of defending its border with China, but this is a requirement that has become pressing only recently. Going forward, this could complicate the military balance from New Delhi's perspective, but this does not necessarily refute the larger point about the imbalance within South Asia itself. The only area where Pakistan matches India is in the balance of nuclear forces, where the smaller power has built a capability that matches India.

India's material superiority within the region is huge. For comparison, note that US GDP immediately after the Second World War was only about 50% of world GDP, which was the highest point it ever reached. During the last few decades of American unipolarity, US GDP has been hovering at about a quarter of global GDP. Similarly, despite China's economic strength, it still has less than half of the total GDP of Asia. If wealth or even concentration of power were key variables in determining polarity, South Asia could clearly be characterized as unipolar rather than bipolar, as Buzan and Wæver do.[15] But the question is whether such characterizations matter at all: Can the expectations of Realist systemic theorizing about polarity be transposed to South Asia, as T.V. Paul does, in any meaningful way?[16] The answer clearly has to be no: None of the expectations that can be derived from Realist theorizing about polarity and global politics can be seen in South Asia, including the region banding together against India, or the expected instability of a unipolar system. The primary reason for this is not hard to find, which is that the South Asian region exists within a global system rather than being insular. This means that though India's material superiority does matter, it can also be balanced and countered by powers and politics external to the region itself. Thus, external powers and global politics external to the region, specifically bipolarity until 1991 and unipolarity subsequently, have had an effect on international politics within the region as well as on the foreign policy choices of all South Asian states.

Geography and Proximity Effects

Though difficult to theorize except in the broadest terms, geography has played a role in Realist theories. Largely absent in much of Waltzian Structural Realism, geography and proximity were recognized as important variables in both balance of threat theory and Offensive Realism.[17] In the former, all else being equal, proximity increases the perception of threat and, hence, balancing. In the latter, again, distance and other factors such as the stopping power of water play an important role. Though neither of these analyses are specifically about regional international politics, the role that proximity and power balances play have important consequences for a Realist approach to regional international politics. Specifically, they both suggest that states consider those powers that are proximate to them to be a greater source of insecurity than those farther away. Thus, they are more likely to balance against the proximate powers, and likely to see those farther away as potential security partners in these efforts.

South Asia's geography thus plays a part in the international politics of the region. India's central position, with various neighbors situated around its periphery means that none of India's neighbors are neighbors to each other, thus reducing the likelihood that they would be security concerns to each other.[18] The exception—Pakistan and Afghanistan—provide further validation to this proposition because the fact that they are neighbors make them a security concern to each other in a manner that neither is to any of the other smaller states in the region. Though Afghanistan is a security concern to India, this is related not to any intrinsic Indian concern about Afghanistan as much as an extension to New Delhi's security concerns regarding Pakistan.[19] It is the possibility of Pakistan using Afghanistan against India that concerns New Delhi. For Pakistan, it is concern about India flanking Pakistan through Afghanistan that represents a worry, though Pakistan and Afghanistan also have mutual security concerns because they are also neighbors.[20]

If India's neighbors are not security concerns to each other because they are not neighbors, they all share security concerns about India because they are all neighbors to India (except Afghanistan). In addition, they are not even proximate to each other, being considerably far from each other. But because they are all neighbors to India, they have either political and/or territorial disputes, of varying intensity, with India. Thus, though the most powerful by far, India is politically isolated within the region because of its difficult relations with each of its South Asian neighbor. This has secondary effects: For example, despite its power, the wariness of its neighbors prevents India from playing any leadership role within the region and contributes to the difficulty of creating an effective regional institutional order. An additional important feature of regional structures, relevant to South Asia, is that regional structures tend to be much more persistent than global structures. This is because the local distribution of power is based much more on natural endowments of states, such as land and population size. These are unlikely to alter sharply over the short or medium terms as a consequence of economic growth rates. Thus, in South Asia, the imbalance of power has lasted longer than either the global bipolar period or the post-Cold War unipolar period and appears set to continue for decades more. Thus, the consequences of regional power and geography are likely to be much more long-lasting than that of global systemic balances, which can be altered by varying rates of economic growth among a much larger set of states.

Global Systemic Variables

Polarity

Though global polarity may matter in systemic stability and other effects, it is not particularly helpful when considering regional international politics. Regional powers and even weak states have greater interest and agency in regional international politics that allows them greater influence in local settings. Thus, global powers have often found that the balance of influence in regional international politics does not follow the global balance of power. During the Cold War, both the US and the Soviet Union frequently found themselves following the dictates of their local clients than the other way around. Thus, though global systemic politics does have an impact on regional international politics, it can do so in much more surprising ways than might be assumed by the disparity in power between polar powers and weaker regional states.

South Asian international politics during the Cold War illustrates this dynamic well. Though both superpowers sought to get India and Pakistan to focus on the global conflict, it was the regional conflict between these two that determined the interaction between the two regional powers and their superpower partners. The most obvious example is the US-Pakistan mutual defense agreement (1954), which Pakistan used as a ploy to get military assistance from Washington to counter India rather than counter international communism. The US was similarly frustrated that India, despite being a democracy, would not join US efforts to counter the Soviet Union.[21] Even after the US came to Indian assistance during the 1962 Sino-Indian war, India remained unwilling to give in to US pressures to resolve the Kashmir dispute with Pakistan.

Such treatment was, of course, not reserved for Washington alone. The Soviet Union faced similar difficulties with both India and Pakistan, after it stepped in to attempt to resolve the South Asian conflict. After the 1965 India-Pakistan war, Moscow sought a position as an honest broker between the two sides, taking a more neutral position between India and Pakistan, much like the US had earlier in the decade. This effort was no more successful than the Washington's, with the two South Asian powers resolutely continuing their local conflict irrespective of the inconvenience it caused to the ambitions of polar powers. Moreover, just as Pakistan used the US alliance for helping it counter India, India hurriedly negotiated a friendship treaty in August 1971 in order to force Moscow to support India in the developing crisis in East Pakistan, despite Moscow's disagreement about India's approach to the crisis.[22] In essence, both India and Pakistan repeatedly used the global bipolar competition to their ends, twisting the polar powers into supporting India's and Pakistan's local interests.

This dynamic was in important part the consequence of a global bipolar competition in which there were, as Waltz has noted, "no peripheries," forcing both global powers to exaggerate the importance of smaller and weaker powers beyond any intrinsic value they added in material power to either of the poles.[23] But because this was a specific feature of bipolarity, this also ended with the end of the bipolar competition. In a unipolar world system, with only one polar power, the tables turned, with both India and Pakistan competing for the affections of the US, a logic that Realists have noted and explained.[24] Nevertheless, developments specific to South Asia gave both India and Pakistan some greater influence. In Pakistan's case, the US war in Afghanistan and Pakistan's territorial advantage allowed it a great amount of influence in a way that could not have been predicted by the logic of systemic unipolarity and the US's role as the unipole. Similarly, the developing competition with a fast-rising China has given India greater importance in US strategy. If, as appears probable, the international system becomes a bipolar one, it will increase the importance of the region to both the US and China. However, the region's proximity to China also means some of its choices are much more predetermined than was the case in the last Cold War. For example, India will not be able to maintain the kind of neutrality between the two polar powers as it did then because New Delhi itself is in conflict with China. Similarly, Pakistan will have little choice but to partner with China, reducing its capacity also to play the two poles against each other.

But in a new systemic bipolar competition, the smaller states in South Asia will likely gain greater attention than they did during the last Cold War. Then, these smaller states could be ignored in favor of India and Pakistan. Now, China's interest in balancing India, and its material capacity to offer its support, means that it is likely to pay much greater attention to these smaller states. Indeed, this has already begun, with Chinese investment push into every small South Asian state, and Indian efforts to counter that with economic and infrastructural assistance. A more powerful China thus changes the dynamic of South Asian international politics, forcing India to improve its diplomatic game in the region, but also making for much more intense competition and insecurity across the region.

The Consequences of Structural Conditions

India's Focus on Internal Balancing

One of the key consequences of the regional structural condition of India's material superiority is that it allows India to emphasize internal over external balancing. Though India has fought three full-scale conventional wars with Pakistan and one with China and was engaged in security competition with both, India has had sufficient material capability on its own to balance against both with its own resources. India's material superiority was so great that though Pakistan consistently spent roughly twice as much on its defense (proportionately) than India did, in absolute terms, India spends four to six times as much as Pakistan.[25] This gross imbalance was of course far worse in the case of India's other smaller South Asian neighbors.

On the surface, India's focus on internal balancing might seem odd in the context of its security competition with China. After all, India suffered a grievous defeat at China's hands in the 1962 border war. But though China has traditionally been considered a great power, and

Realist Approaches

was allotted a UN Security Council seat for this reason, the actual material balance between India and China was fairly even, at least until China began to grow at much faster rates in the 1980s. In fact, Indian and Chinese GDP was roughly the same in 1962, at US $42 billion for India and US $47 for China.[26] And though India did receive some US and Soviet assistance in the 1960s, India had sufficient domestic material wherewithal to build an entire army for the China border, a task it largely completed by the end of the 1960s. In short, even against China, India was not in such a relatively weak material position that it required external assistance. Seen in this light, India's nonalignment, and Pakistan's alignment strategies, are clear responses to their respective structural conditions. Obviously, with the changing relative material fortunes, India's position vis-à-vis China has dramatically worsened. Not surprisingly, even though India is still not ready for a military alliance, it has become much more accepting of security cooperation with others, as can be seen in its vastly improved relations with the US, Japan, and Australia (the other members of the Quad) as well as other powers in the region.

The Rest of South Asia: External Balancing—or Hiding

The huge imbalance of power in South Asia also had consequences for the strategies of the smaller states. Absent sufficient domestic capacities for balancing India, and too weak and geographically apart even to combine together against India, they had to look outside the region for help to counter India. But even this was rarely forthcoming for any of them, with the exception of Pakistan. In varying degrees, therefore, the South Asian strategic response to India was the same: External balancing or hiding.

Pakistan had the benefit of somewhat greater domestic capacity to balance India. In addition, at least until the 1965 India-Pakistan war, Pakistan resorted to unhelpful psychological bolstering—such as that one Pakistani equals ten Indians—to convince itself that it could match Indian material power.[27] More pragmatically, Pakistan also resorted to external balancing. Pakistan's greater material capacity (relative to the other, smaller South Asian states) made it attractive to external powers such as the US because Pakistan could play a potentially useful role in the bipolar competition. Pakistan's geopolitical location was an added attraction, which Islamabad skillfully exploited. Still, this partnership was a troubled one because the partners differed on the purpose: For the US, the purpose was to counter the Soviet Union and China, while for Pakistan, it was India. It was only in China that Pakistan could find an external power that agreed with its strategic objectives. Thus, despite the oddity of a revolutionary Maoist communist state partnering with a feudal, religious one, it became a deep and abiding relationship that was far more stable than the US-Pakistan relationship. Nuclear weapons became the other source of Pakistan's security. The clarity of the defeat in the December 1971 war with India, and the ascension of Zulfiqar Ali Bhutto as prime minister, led to the launching of a determined quest for nuclear weapons.[28]

For the other smaller South Asian states, the choice was even more constrained. Their domestic capacities were a fraction of even Pakistan's, which also made them unattractive to external powers, especially as the external powers also did not want to hurt their much more valuable ties with India. Thus, though some of these states periodically flirted with external powers, they never found sufficient or consistent support. For example, both Nepal and Sri Lanka sought such external ties but were ultimately disappointed. Nepal struggled in trying to develop relationships with external powers, especially China, to balance both its dependence on India as well as India's power.[29] Most of this time, Nepal's China relations have been "a 'card' against India than an actual hand."[30] Sri Lanka, similarly, "has taken every opportunity of strengthening her position through every counterpoise available to her."[31] Even Bangladesh, which Indian military action contributed to creating, worries about Indian power and has sought to balance the generally favorable relations between the two countries by simultaneously balancing India with the help of both Pakistan and China.[32]

As stated previously, these structural conditions have been changing more recently as a consequence of China's rise. For the first time, the smaller regional states have a potential external partner that has both the power and the desire to assist them in balancing against India. For example, China officials signaled that Beijing would oppose any Indian interference in the Maldives, backing up an editorial in *Global Times*.[33] The competition between India and China gives smaller powers considerable leeway and they will likely use it to bargain for benefits from both New Delhi and Beijing.

Polar Power Behavior in South Asia

Another Realist expectation is about the behavior of polar powers, which should be visible in many aspects of their behavior, including their regional policies. Of relevance here are expectations of such behavior in bipolarity and unipolarity. In bipolarity, Realism expects that the two polar powers would pursue similar objectives and policies. This broad expectation has much to support it considering how the US and the Soviet Union behaved in South Asia during the Cold War.

From the 1950s up to 1971, the two superpowers sought to resolve the India-Pakistan conflict so that both regional powers could be enlisted to their side of the bipolar competition. Both polar powers saw the Kashmir dispute as a distraction from their larger global contest and were frustrated at the intransigence of the two regional adversaries in persisting with it. Though the US signed a mutual defense treaty with Pakistan in 1954, it did not give up on India or in seeking to find a solution to the Kashmir dispute or at least minimize its effects.[34] In the aftermath of the 1962 Sino-Indian war, Washington sought to leverage the temporary Indian need for US support to find such a solution.[35] When this effort proved fruitless, the US withdrew, eventually settling down to having a closer relationship with Pakistan, while maintaining a working relationship with India. Moscow followed a similar trajectory, broadly. Starting with a closer relationship with India, the Soviet Union also attempted to settle the Kashmir dispute in the aftermath of the 1965 India-Pakistan war.[36] But this effort, just as in the US case, proved unsuccessful, and the Soviet Union reverted to a policy that tilted toward India while maintaining a modicum of civil relations with Pakistan. Both the US and the Soviets found that their greater power did not necessarily translate into greater regional influence: What Mastny noted about the Soviet-Indian dynamic—that "India usually took the initiative, whereas the Soviet Union mainly reacted"—could as well describe the dilemma that both superpowers found themselves in.[37]

Unipolarity changed this dynamic. One of the effects of unipolarity is that it changes the balance of influence between the (now sole) polar power and others, giving the former far greater freedom of action and reducing the options of others.[38] This dynamic can be seen in South Asia too, as all the regional states sought better ties with the US, understanding that Washington was the only game in town. The most dramatic illustration of this is in the changed nature of US-India relations, which now bears little relationship to the Cold War years.[39]

If, as seems likely now, the global system should move toward bipolarity, would South Asian international politics return to the imperatives of the past? This is unlikely because of one crucial difference with the Cold War bipolarity: China is a neighbor to the region and its proximity makes both its interest in the region far greater and its power much more relevant. This makes it difficult, at least for India, to return to nonalignment in a new bipolar distribution of global power.

Unresolved Puzzles for Realist Approaches to South Asian IR

Realism, especially the structural neorealist variant employed in this chapter, provides only a broad account of the pressures that states face and its consequences on international politics. Waltz was very clear about its limitations.[40] Thus, Realist approaches are not always useful in explaining the details of foreign policy. But even beyond this major drawback, there are some puzzles for Realism in the international politics of South Asia.

An important one is India's choice to focus much of its balancing efforts on Pakistan rather than China, a tendency that was dominant from the 1950s until recently. Realist theory expects states to balance against the greatest threats, defined in terms of power, that they face. By any measure, Pakistan was far weaker than China, which should have been the primary focus of India's balancing efforts. Even if there was some misperception of the China threat in the 1950s, India's clear defeat in the 1962 war should have disabused India of its choice. But though India started paying greater attention to balancing China, it was still disproportionately focused on Pakistan, the lesser threat. At best, India did just enough, building a large enough army to defend its northern border but refusing to match China's nuclear capability until decades later.[41] None of the existing Realist explanations—of underbalancing, or balance of threat—explain India's choices.[42] None of the variables in the underbalancing literature are relevant to the choice India made, while balance of threat includes "hostile intent" as a variable, which only raises more questions about the source of the perception that Pakistan's hostile intent was greater than China's. While a Neoclassical Realist account may potentially provide some answers, it uses variables, including ideational and domestic political ones, that do not sit well with Realism.[43]

Another puzzle for Realism is Pakistan's insistence on balancing against the much larger India to the extent that is detrimental to Pakistan itself. While states have been known to "overbalance" to such an extent that they collapse—the Soviet Union being a prominent example—its logic itself is unclear from a Realist perspective. The Soviet collapse has been explained as the consequence of Moscow trying to reform to better compete with the US but losing control of the reform process itself.[44] While Pakistan is far from collapse, its balancing effort cannot be characterized as the normal response to a security threat that it faces from India. The threat to Pakistan from India's greater power is irrefutable, as is the need to balance against the threat. The puzzle, thus, is not Pakistan's balancing but its overbalancing, especially considering both that Pakistan has nuclear weapons to ensure its survival (at the very least) and that the growing economic disparity with India means that Pakistan's more strenuous efforts are unlikely to bear much fruit.

A third puzzle for the Realist approach to South Asian international politics is why India has not managed to develop any dominance in the region, despite the overwhelming power disparity between India and the rest of South Asia.[45] While one answer might be that more powerful external actors may have stymied India's effort, it is not clear that India even attempted to generate such a leadership position for itself in the region. This is surprising considering India's decades-long effort to seek better global status and position, such as through a UN Security Council permanent membership. While India has attempted to exclude external powers from the region, this has not been accompanied by any effort to exercise regional leadership itself.

Conclusion

Despite the dearth of Realist explanations for South Asian international politics, the approach itself is useful for understanding some of the dynamics that shape both foreign policies and outcomes in the region. Any effort to apply a Realist approach must begin with the balance of power in the region and India's overwhelming dominance in material power. This impact all the states in the region—India, as the dominant power, and also its neighbors, who must grapple with how to manage this giant in their midst. Realists must also consider the weaknesses of the theory itself: The approach has been developed largely by American scholars, but this has also skewed the focus of the theory toward systemic concerns, leading to the underdevelopment of its potential for explaining regional international political dynamics or the imperatives facing non-polar powers. This does not mean that the theory is useless in addressing such concerns but it does mean that the insights of the theory must be adapted to explain non-polar politics. While some well-known weaknesses of the theory probably cannot be fixed—its indeterminism and inability to explain foreign policies in detail, for example—the question of the focus of the theory is not one such. China's rise and its impact on the Asian region hopefully provides sufficient incentive to undertake this task.

Notes

1 George Modelski, "Kautilya: Foreign Policy and International System in the Ancient Hindu World," *The American Political Science Review*, 58, no. 3 (September 1964): 549–560, https://doi.org/10.2307/1953131; Roger Boesche, *The First Great Political Realist: Kautilya and His Arthashastra* (Lanham: Lexington Books, 2002).

2 These include Boesche, *First Great Political Realist*; Roger Boesche, "Kautilya's Arthashastra on War and Diplomacy in Ancient India," *The Journal of Military History*, 67, no. 1 (January 2003): 9–37, https://doi.org/10.1353/jmh.2003.0006; Rashad Uz Zaman, "Kautilya: The Indian Strategic Thinker and Indian Strategic Culture," *Comparative Strategy*, 25, no. 3 (2006): 231–247, https://doi.org/10.1080/01495930600956260; Pradeep Kumar Gautam, Saurabh Mishra, and Arvind Gupta (editors), *Indigenous Historical Knowledge: Kautilya and His Vocabulary, Volumes 1–3* (New Delhi: Institute for Defence Studies and Analyses/Pentagon Press, 2016); Subrata K. Mitra and Michael Liebig, *Kautilya's Arthashastra: An Intellectual Portrait: The Classical Roots of Modern Politics in India* (New Delhi: Rupa, 2017); Deepshika Shahi, *Kautilya and Non-Western IR Theory* (Cham: Palgrave Pivot, 2019), https://doi.org/10.1007/978-3-030-01728-6.

3 Stephen M. Walt, *Origins of Alliances* (Cornell: Cornell University Press, 1987).

4 Pratap Bhanu Mehta, "Still Under Nehru's Shadow? The Absence of Foreign Policy Frameworks in India," *India Review*, 8, no. 3 (2009): 209–233, https://doi.org/10.1080/14736480903116750.

5 See, for example, Šumit Ganguly, "India's National Security: A Neo-classical Realist Account," in *The Oxford Handbook of India's National Security*, eds. Šumit Ganguly, Nicolas Blarel and Manjeet Pardesi (New Delhi: Oxford University Press, 2018): 25–41.

6 For examples of this explicit justification, see Kenneth N. Waltz, *Theory of International Politics* (New York: Addison-Wesley, 1979): 72; and John J. Mearsheimer, *The Tragedy of Great Power Politics* (New York: W.W. Norton & Co, 2001): 5.

7 Dale C. Copeland, "Realism and Neorealism in the Study of Regional Conflict," in *International Relations Theory and Regional Transformation*, ed. T.V. Paul (Cambridge: Cambridge University Press, 2012): 49.

8 Barry Buzan and Ole Wæver, *Regions and Powers: The Structure of International Society* (Cambridge: Cambridge University Press, 2003).

9 T.V. Paul, "Regional Transformation in International Relations," in *International Relations Theory and Regional Transformation*, ed. T.V. Paul (Cambridge: Cambridge University Press, 2012): 3–21.

10 Kenneth N. Waltz, "The Stability of A Bipolar World," *Daedalus* 93, no. 3 (1964): 881–909, http://www.jstor.org/stable/20026863.

11 John J. Mearsheimer, "Back to the Future: Instability in Europe After the Cold War," *International Security*, 15, no. 1 (Summer 1990): 5–56, https://doi.org/10.2307/2538981; Kenneth N. Waltz, "Structural Realism After the Cold War," *International Security*, 25, no. 1 (Summer 2000): 5–41, https://doi.org/10.1162/016228800560372.

12 William C. Wohlforth, "The Stability of A Unipolar World," *International Security*, 24, no. 1 (Summer 1999): 5–41, https://www.jstor.org/stable/2539346.

13 Calculated from data in Central Intelligence Agency, *The World Factbook: South Asia*, https://www.cia.gov/the-world-factbook/south-asia/.

14 Calculated from "Chapter 6: Asia," *The Military Balance*, 120, no. 1 (2020): 220–323, https://doi.org/10.1080/04597222.2020.1707967.

15 Buzan and Wæver, *Regions and Powers*, 101.

16 Paul, "Regional Transformation in International Relations."

17 Walt, *Origins of Alliances*; Mearsheimer, *The Tragedy of Great Power Politics*.

18 This aspect has been noted earlier. See Gowher Rizvi, "The Role of Smaller States in the South Asian Complex," in *South Asian Insecurity and the Global Powers*, eds. Barry Buzan and Gowher Rizvi (New York: Palgrave Macmillan, 1986): 129.

19 "India at UNSC: Afghanistan Shouldn't be Used by Pakistan-based Terrorists," *Times of India*, August 25, 2021, https://timesofindia.indiatimes.com/india/india-at-unsc-afghanistan-shouldnt-be-used-by-pakistan-based-terrorists/articleshow/85608528.cms.

20 Tom Wheeldon, "Pakistan Cheers Taliban Out of 'Fear of India'—Despite Spillover Threat," *France24*, August 18, 2021, https://www.france24.com/en/asia-pacific/20210818-pakistan-cheers-taliban-out-of-fear-of-india-%E2%80%93-despite-spillover-threat.

21 On the evolution of US-India relations during the cold war, see Harold A. Gould and Šumit Ganguly (eds.), *The Hope and the Reality: U.S.-India Relations from Roosevelt to Reagan* (New York: Routledge, 2019); and Tanvi Madan, *Fateful Triangle: How China Shaped U.S.-Indian Relations During the Cold War* (Washington: Brookings Institution Press, 2020).

22 Srinath Raghavan, *1971: A Global History of the Creation of Bangladesh* (Cambridge: Harvard University Press, 2013); and Rudra Chaudhuri, *Forged in Crisis: India and the United States Since 1947* (New York: Oxford University Press, 2014).

23 Waltz, "The Stability of Bipolarity."

24 Stephen M. Walt, "Alliances in A Unipolar World," *World Politics*, 61, no. 1 (January 2009): 86–120, https://doi.org/10.1017/S0043887109000045.

25 Rajesh Rajagopalan, "Neorealist Theory and the India-Pakistan Conflict," in *International Relations in India: Theorising the Region and Nation*, eds. Kanti Bajpai and Siddharth Mallavarapu (New Delhi: Orient Longman, 2004): 142–172.

26 In current US $. The World Bank, "GDP: Current US $: China, India," https://data.worldbank.org/indicator/NY.GDP.MKTP.CD?locations=CN-IN.

27 Šumit Ganguly, "Deterrence Failure Revisited: The Indo-Pakistani War of 1965," *Journal of Strategic Studies*, 13, no. 4 (1990): 77–93, https://doi.org/10.1080/01402399008437432.

28 Feroz Hassan Khan, *Eating Grass: The Making of the Pakistani Bomb* (Stanford: Stanford University Press, 2012).

29 For an early account of this struggle, see Leo Rose, *Nepal: Strategy for Survival* (Berkeley: University of California Press, 1971).

30 Amish Raj Mulmi, *All Roads Lead North: Nepal's Turn to China* (Chennai: Context, 2021): 209.

31 Rizvi, "The Role of Smaller States in the South Asian Complex," 140.

32 Anindya Jyoti Majumdar, "Making Sense of India-Bangladesh Relations," *India Quarterly*, 70, no. 4 (December 2014): 327–340, https://doi.org/10.1177/0974928414545919.

33 Atul Aneja, "China Will Take Action If India Sends Troops to Maldives: Global Times," *The Hindu*, February 13, 2018, https://www.thehindu.com/news/national/china-will-take-action-if-india-sends-troops-to-maldives-global-times/article22738864.ece.

34 Madan, *Fateful Triangle*.

35 Timothy W. Crawford, "Kennedy and Kashmir, 1962-63: The Perils of Pivotal Peacemaking in South Asia," *India Review*, 1, no. 3 (2002): 1–38, https://doi.org/10.1080/14736480208404632.

36 On the evolution of Soviet-Indian relations, see Vojtech Mastny, "The Soviet Union's Partnership with India," *Journal of Cold War Studies*, 12, no. 3 (Summer 2010): 50–90, https://doi.org/10.1162/JCWS_a_00006.

37 Mastny, "The Soviet Union's Partnership with India," 51.

38 Walt, "Alliances in A Unipolar World."
39 Šumit Ganguly, "India's Foreign Policy Grows Up," *World Policy Journal*, 20, no. 4 (Winter 2003/2004): 41–47.
40 See, for example, Kenneth N. Waltz, "International Politics is Not Foreign Policy," *Security Studies*, 6, no. 1 (1996): 54–57, https://doi.org/10.1080/09636419608429298.
41 Ganguly, "India's National Security: A Neo-Classical Realist Account," 26–28.
42 On underbalancing, see Randall L. Schweller, "Unanswered Threats: A Neoclassical Realist Theory of Underbalancing," *International Security*, 29, no. 2 (Fall 2004): 159–201, https://doi.org/10.1162/0162288042879913.
43 Ganguly, "India's National Security: A Neo-Classical Realist Account."
44 William Wohlforth, "Realism and the End of the Cold War," *International Security*, 19, no. 3 (Winter 1994–1995): 91–129, https://doi.org/10.2307/2539080.
45 Subrata K. Mitra, "The Reluctant Hegemon: India's Self-Perception and the South-Asian Strategic Environment," *Contemporary South Asia*, 12, no. 3 (September 2003): 399–417, https://doi.org/10.1080/0958493032000175914.

Bibliography

"India at UNSC: Afghanistan Shouldn't be Used by Pakistan-based Terrorists." *Times of India*, August 25, 2021. https://timesofindia.indiatimes.com/india/india-at-unsc-afghanistan-shouldnt-be-used-by-pakistan-based-terrorists/articleshow/85608528.cms.

Aneja, Atul. "China Will Take Action If India Sends Troops to Maldives: Global Times." *The Hindu*, February 13, 2018. https://www.thehindu.com/news/national/china-will-take-action-if-india-sends-troops-to-maldives-global-times/article22738864.ece.

Barry, Buzan, and Ole, Wæver. *Regions and Powers: The Structure of International Society*. Cambridge: Cambridge University Press, 2003.

Boesche, Roger. "Kautilya's Arthashastra on War and Diplomacy in Ancient India." *The Journal of Military History*, 67, no. 1 (January 2003): 9–37. https://doi.org/10.1353/jmh.2003.0006.

Boesche, Roger. *The First Great Political Realist: Kautilya and His Arthashastra*. Lanham: Lexington Books, 2002.

Central Intelligence Agency. *The World Factbook: South Asia*. https://www.cia.gov/the-world-factbook/south-asia/.

Choudhury, Rudra. *Forged in Crisis: India and the United States Since 1947*. New York: Oxford University Press, 2014.

Copeland, Dale C. "Realism and Neorealism in the Study of Regional Conflict." In *International Relations Theory and Regional Transformation*, edited by T.V. Paul, 49–73. Cambridge: Cambridge University Press, 2012.

Crawford, Timothy W. "Kennedy and Kashmir, 1962-63: The Perils of Pivotal Peacemaking in South Asia." *India Review*, 1, no. 3 (2002): 1–38. https://doi.org/10.1080/14736480208404632.

Ganguly, Šumit. "Deterrence Failure Revisited: The Indo-Pakistani War of 1965." *Journal of Strategic Studies*, 13, no. 4 (1990): 77–93. https://doi.org/10.1080/01402399008437432.

Ganguly, Šumit. "India's Foreign Policy Grows Up." *World Policy Journal*, 20, no. 4 (Winter 2003/2004): 41–47.

Ganguly, Šumit. "India's National Security: A Neo-Classical Realist Account." In *The Oxford Handbook of India's National Security*, edited by Šumit Ganguly, Nicolas Blarel, and Manjeet Pardesi, 25–41. New Delhi: Oxford University Press, 2018.

Gautam, Pradeep K., Saurabh Mishra, and Arvind Gupta (Eds.). *Indigenous Historical Knowledge: Kautilya and His Vocabulary, Volumes 1–3*. New Delhi: Institute for Defence Studies and Analyses/Pentagon Press, 2016.

Gould, Harold A., and Šumit Ganguly (Eds.). *The Hope and the Reality: U.S.-India Relations from Roosevelt to Reagan*. New York: Routledge, 2019.

International Institute for Strategic Studies. "Chapter 6: Asia." *The Military Balance*, 120, no. 1 (2020): 220–323. https://doi.org/10.1080/04597222.2020.1707967.

Khan, Feroz Hassan. *Eating Grass: The Making of the Pakistani Bomb*. Stanford: Stanford University Press, 2012.

Madan, Tanvi. *Fateful Triangle: How China Shaped U.S.-Indian Relations During the Cold War*. Washington: Brookings Institution Press, 2020.

Majumdar, Anindya Jyoti. "Making Sense of India-Bangladesh Relations." *India Quarterly*, 70, no. 4 (December 2014): 327–340. https://doi.org/10.1177/0974928414545919.

Mastny, Vojtech. "The Soviet Union's Partnership with India." *Journal of Cold War Studies*, 12, no. 3 (Summer 2010): 50–90. https://doi.org/10.1162/JCWS_a_00006.

Mearsheimer, John J. "Back to the Future: Instability in Europe After the Cold War." *International Security*, 15, no. 1 (Summer 1990): 5–56. https://doi.org/10.2307/2538981.

Mearsheimer, John J. *The Tragedy of Great Power Politics*. New York: W.W.Norton & Co, 2001.

Mehta, Pratap Bhanu. "Still Under Nehru's Shadow? The Absence of Foreign Policy Frameworks in India." *India Review*, 8, no. 3 (2009): 209–233. https://doi.org/10.1080/14736480903116750.

Mitra, Subrata K. "The Reluctant Hegemon: India's Self-Perception and the South-Asian Strategic Environment." *Contemporary South Asia*, 12, no. 3 (September 2003): 399–417. https://doi.org/10.1080/0958493032000175914.

Mitra, Subrata K., and Liebig, Michael. *Kautilya's Arthashastra: An Intellectual Portrait: The Classical Roots of Modern Politics in India*. New Delhi: Rupa, 2017.

Modelski, George. "Kautilya: Foreign Policy and International System in the Ancient Hindu World." *The American Political Science Review*, 58, no. 3 (September 1964): 549–560. https://doi.org/10.2307/1953131.

Mulmi, Amish Raj. *All Roads Lead North: Nepal's Turn to China*. Chennai: Context, 2021.

Paul, T.V. Paul. "Regional Transformation in International Relations." In *International Relations Theory and Regional Transformation*, edited by T.V. Paul, 3–21. Cambridge: Cambridge University Press, 2012.

Raghavan, Srinath. *1971: A Global History of the Creation of Bangladesh*. Cambridge: Harvard University Press, 2013.

Rajagopalan, Rajesh. "Neorealist Theory and the India-Pakistan Conflict." In *International Relations in India: Theorising the Region and Nation*, edited by Kanti Bajpai, and Siddharth Mallavarapu, 142–172. New Delhi: Orient Longman, 2004.

Rizvi, Gowher. "The Role of Smaller States in the South Asian Complex." In *South Asian Insecurity and the Global Powers*, edited by Barry Buzan, and Gowher Rizvi, 127–156. New York: Palgrave Macmillan, 1986.

Rose, Leo. *Nepal: Strategy for Survival*. Berkeley: University of California Press, 1971.

Schweller, Randall L. "Unanswered Threats: A Neoclassical Realist Theory of Underbalancing." *International Security*, 29, no. 2 (Fall 2004): 159–201. https://doi.org/10.1162/0162288042879913.

Shahi, Deepshika. *Kautilya and Non-Western IR Theory*. Cham: Palgrave Pivot, 2019. https://doi.org/10.1007/978-3-030-01728-6.

Walt, Stephen M. *Origins of Alliances*. Cornell: Cornell University Press, 1987.

Waltz, Kenneth N. "International Politics is Not Foreign Policy." *Security Studies*, 6, no. 1 (1996): 54–57. https://doi.org/10.1080/09636419608429298.

Waltz, Kenneth N. "Structural Realism After the Cold War," *International Security*, 25, no. 1 (Summer 2000): 5–41. https://doi.org/10.1162/016228800560372.

Waltz, Kenneth N. "The Stability of a Bipolar World." *Daedalus*, 93, no. 3 (1964): 881–909. http://www.jstor.org/stable/20026863.

Waltz, Kenneth N. *Theory of International Politics*. New York: Addison-Wesley, 1979.

Wheeldon, Tom. "Pakistan Cheers Taliban Out of 'Fear of India'—Despite Spillover Threat." *France24*, August 18, 2021. https://www.france24.com/en/asia-pacific/20210818-pakistan-cheers-taliban-out-of-fear-of-india-%E2%80%93-despite-spillover-threat.

Wohlforth, William C. "The Stability of a Unipolar World." *International Security*, 24, no. 1 (Summer 1999): 5–41. https://www.jstor.org/stable/2539346.

Zaman, Rashad Uz. "Kautilya: The Indian Strategic Thinker and Indian Strategic Culture." *Comparative Strategy*, 25, no. 3 (2006): 231–247. https://doi.org/10.1080/01495930600956260.

2
LIBERAL APPROACHES TO THE INTERNATIONAL RELATIONS OF SOUTH ASIA

Ian Hall

Liberal analysts argue that explaining international relations of any region requires knowledge of the domestic politics that shape the foreign policies of states, as well as the pressures exerted by other governments, international organizations, corporations and financial institutions, and non-state actors on those states.[1] They hold that some political ideas and some types of government, supported by international institutions, may tend towards more peaceful and prosperous regions, but most liberals are not naïve idealists. They recognize that there are costs as well as benefits to democratic governance or economic openness, especially where governments lack capacity and societies are vulnerable to exploitation.

Liberals reject the realist assumption that there is little need to examine domestic politics or international institutions to explain what states do, because international anarchy and the uneven distribution of power compel states to behave as security-maximizing rational actors.[2] They counter that there is ample empirical evidence to show that states do not behave as realists assume they should. Liberals also reject the constructivist argument that foreign and security policies are primarily functions of the identities of societies.[3] They acknowledge that socially constructed ideas, rules, and institutions matter, but insist that bargaining between political, economic, and social groups with different interests and varying levels of power also shapes state behavior. Finally, liberals reject the Marxist argument that foreign and security policies are determined by the nature of a state's economy and its position within a global economic system divided between dominant advanced capitalist societies and dependent and less-developed suppliers of human or natural resources.[4]

Instead, liberals argue that explaining why states do what they do requires, as Stephan Haggard puts it, a "bottom-up rather than a top-down approach."[5] Liberalism demands that scholars open up the state and look inside to explore how policies are formulated by governments contending with a range of different ideas about what should be done, with the demands of various competing interest groups, and with the expectations of other states and non-state actors in international relations.

South Asia is a region of conflict and competition, with great disparities of power between states. It is a region where identity politics are never far from public life. It is also a region deeply marked by historical and ongoing economic inequality and exploitation, some justified by liberal ideologies. Finally, it is a region with weak regional institutions and very low levels of economic integration.[6] Perhaps for these reasons, realist, constructivist, and Marxist

DOI: 10.4324/9781003246626-4

Liberal Approaches

approaches have been—and remain—more popular than liberalism among scholars of the region's international relations.[7]

Nevertheless, this chapter argues that liberalism is more useful to scholars working on South Asia's international relations than commonly recognized. It suggests that the region offers a testing ground for a set of theories developed in the very different contexts of the Atlantic and East Asian worlds.[8] It contends that liberalism helps us to explain why South Asia has low levels of economic interdependence, relatively frequent conflict between states, and weak regional institutions. To make these arguments, it looks in turn at the main factors that liberals think shape the international relations of states: Political ideas, regime types and societal actors, and international institutions.

Political Ideas

The eight modern states of South Asia—Afghanistan, Bangladesh, Bhutan, India, Maldives, Nepal, Pakistan, and Sri Lanka—are the inheritors of a rich and varied set of ideas about social organization deriving from multiple religious traditions—including Buddhist, Christian, Hindu, Muslim, Parsi, and Sikh—and multiple traditions of political thought, both local and imported under European colonial rule and afterwards. These various sets of ideas address the challenges of relations between different cultural groups and between independent polities.[9]

South Asia's elites have picked and chosen from this broad menu of political ideas to craft their domestic and foreign policies. Although scarred by the impact of successive waves of invasion and long periods of colonial rule, all have adopted or adapted models of governance from outside the region. India's founders borrowed both from the British and the Soviet Union, opting for a liberal constitution, neutrality in matters of religious practice, and a quasi-socialist, centrally planned development strategy that aimed at self-reliance. Over time, however, their preferred variety of liberalism, secularism, and socialism has been challenged or replaced by other ideas—by authoritarianism, majoritarianism, and economic liberalism, in particular. Pakistan's founders also adopted and modified a British model, but their successors have often drawn inspiration from Islamist ideologies from the Arab states. In both cases, the impact of their ideas is clear in their foreign policies—in India's liberal-inflected support for international law and the United Nations and in its suspicion of Western capitalism, and in Pakistan's Islamist brand of *Realpolitik*.[10]

In Afghanistan, Bhutan, Maldives, and Nepal, the impact of European imperialism was less severe than it was elsewhere in South Asia, with a more limited effect on local political ideas. The British repeatedly tried and failed to exert control over successive Afghan kings, eventually acknowledging the country's independence in 1926. The Kingdoms of Bhutan and Nepal also clashed with the British but retained much formal and informal autonomy. Once a Buddhist kingdom, the Maldives was converted to Islam in the 12th century and became a British protectorate in 1796, which it remained until 1965.

As a result, the political ideologies of modern Afghanistan, Bhutan, Maldives, and Nepal have arguably been influenced more by their dominant religions (Islam, Buddhism, Islam, and Hinduism, respectively), traditions of statecraft inherited from past rulers, and imported, rather than imperially implanted, modern ideologies. The influence of these different sets of ideas varies widely, however, both between these states and over time, as circumstances change. Afghanistan is a classic case: During the past century, it has been a constitutional monarchy (1926–1973), then a modernizing republic (1973–1978), a Soviet-aligned socialist republic (1978–1992), a putative Salafist emirate (1992–2001), and a Western-backed democratic republic (2004–2021), until the Taliban resumed control.

Maldives and Nepal have also seen much ideological contention. In Maldives, a long-standing monarchy was replaced soon after independence with a democratic republic led by a president that soon deteriorated into a quasi-autocracy, then a prolonged struggle for power between conservative Islamic and more liberal, pro-democracy forces.[11] In Nepal, the instability has been even more pronounced. From the 1930s onwards, an absolutist monarchy that claimed to govern according to Hindu *dharma* was challenged by both social democratic and communist movements, resulting in changes of regime and civil conflict, including the eventual abolition of the monarchy in 2008. Today, liberal, social democratic, Marxist, and Maoist ideas, as well as identity politics, all contend to shape Nepal's domestic and foreign policies.[12] By contrast, Bhutan has experienced more ideational and institutional stability, with an absolute monarchy evolving into a constitutional system guided by elite interpretations of local traditions of rule and Buddhist ethics.[13]

In Bangladesh, India, Pakistan, and Sri Lanka, the picture is even more complex. At independence, all inherited a rich set of Hindu, Buddhist, and Muslim ideas about statecraft, as well as modern Western theories left by the British. Local nationalist activists also imported a wider variety of ideas from elsewhere—from the German Empire, post-Meiji Restoration Japan, the United States, and the Soviet Union—to make the case for self-determination.[14]

These ideas matter to scholars of international relations because Bangladesh, India, and Pakistan are all invented states, carved out of the pre-existing polity of British India after intense ideological conflict, and designed to realize their founders' visions. Working with local leaders, the British created the two states of India and Pakistan to help manage tensions between the majority Hindu and minority Muslim populations. This act of Partition was a response to the "Two Nation Theory" advanced from the 1920s onwards by Muhammed Iqbal and Muhammed Ali Jinnah. That theory held that despite shared languages, histories, and cultural practices, the peoples of British India would not be able to live with equal dignity in a single postcolonial state because they were divided by religion. Such a state would be dominated by the Hindu majority; Muslims would be rendered second class citizens. The "Two Nations" must therefore have two states, even if it meant dividing and dislocating communities, and binding populations with different languages, histories, and cultures into new polities.[15]

Partition based on the Two Nation Theory had lasting consequences for South Asia's international relations, especially for relations between India and Pakistan. The first was the creation of a new state—Pakistan—that claimed and still claims, in effect, to represent the interests of Muslims across the subcontinent, putting it at odds with India from the start.[16] The second was the design of a Constitution for India that attempted to refute the claim that Muslims would be second class citizens, and a political order that aimed at keeping the state out of matters of religion. The third was the emergence in India of an explicitly Hindu nationalism, mirroring Muslim nationalism. That ideology offers an alternative vision to the liberal, secular, socialist society envisaged by India's postcolonial elite—a vision of a Hindu *Rashtra* (loosely, "state") in which the interests of the majority take priority over the interests of minorities, including Muslims.[17] And the fourth was lasting tension between different parts of Pakistan, especially between the dominant Punjabi elite in the West and Bengalis in the East, which led to the creation of Bangladesh, with India's assistance, in 1971.[18] That act of secession represented an effective rejection of Two Nation Theory and the associated idea that Muslim solidarity on the subcontinent trumped linguistic, historical, and cultural ties.

The international relations of Sri Lanka have also been deeply affected by ethnic and religious division. Three quarters of its citizens are Sinhalese and mostly Buddhist, with

Liberal Approaches

the remainder Tamil Hindus and Christians or Muslim Moors. After independence in 1948, Sinhalese majoritarianism, underpinned by the belief that Sinhalese culture was under threat, led to peaceful protests by minority groups and then, in 1976, to the outbreak of civil war, with the so-called Liberation Tigers of Tamil Eelam (LTTE) fighting for a separate Tamil state. Inevitably, the conflict drew in other actors, notably India, which first backed the LTTE in response to Tamil concern, then intervened militarily to keep a fragile peace in Sri Lanka, then turned on and fought the insurgents, and finally abandoned the war altogether.[19]

Across South Asia, then, an array of locally created and imported ideologies have shaped forms of government and distributions of resources, redrawn borders, and generated internal and inter-state conflicts, all affecting the international relations of the region. They have also helped to generate different national security and development strategies. Conscious of their weakness relative to the developed world and keen to maintain national independence, most South Asian states have pursued forms of "nonalignment," involving a refusal to ally with any major power and an attempt to maintain beneficial relations with all, so as to avoid entanglements in others' conflicts and the costs that they would impose. India pioneered this approach; Bangladesh, Maldives, Nepal, and Sri Lanka all adopted it, to varying degrees, after independence.[20] And although India has lately forged a strong partnership with the United States to manage China's assertiveness across the Indo-Pacific, New Delhi remains committed to maintaining its strategic autonomy and avoiding formal alliances.[21]

Afghanistan and especially Pakistan have used different strategies, driven by different nationalist agendas, as well as the belief that the benefits that can be extracted from allies outweigh the costs, including the possibility that limits might be placed on their freedom of action. Afghanistan has been nonaligned at times, but at others forged close ties with the Soviet Union between 1979 and 1989, and with the United States between 2001 and 2021. Pakistan has been more consistent in its approach, formally allying with the United States and the United Kingdom during the Cold War, as well as agreeing major security pacts with China and Saudi Arabia, to offset India's power.[22]

In sum, potent ideas about how best to manage cultural and religious differences within and between states and how best to maintain national independence given limited power and resources have shaped and continue to shape the international relations of South Asia.

Regime Types and Societal Actors

Liberals have long argued that the character of a state's political institutions shapes its international behavior. In particular, they maintain that—as Immanuel Kant famously suggested—states with republican systems of government, in which the people determine domestic and foreign policy, are less prone to belligerence than autocracies, in which the rulers rarely bear the costs of war.[23] They point to the extensive evidence that appears to confirm the view that democracies, in particular, tend not to fight one another, though they regularly go to war with non-democracies.[24]

Exactly why democracies are less bellicose, at least with similar regimes, is debated. Kant's argument—that the people, having to bear the costs of war in blood and taxes, are less likely to support it—is still favored by some liberal theorists. They argue that political systems that faithfully reflect the views of citizens in their foreign and security policies tend to be more peaceable in their international relations.[25] They commonly point to checks and balances within those systems—including regular elections, the oversight of executive action by legislatures, a free media, and robust civilian control of armed forces—that reduce the risk of a reckless or opportunistic leader launching military action.[26] Others argue that democracies fight less because their policies are often aligned, or that democratic governments are acculturated into settling disputes without the threat or use of violence.[27] Still others argue that democracies tend not to go to war because they are economically interdependent, making conflict costly and non-violent forms of dispute management more attractive.[28]

South Asia offers a useful test of these theories. Today, the eight states in the region have a variety of different forms of government and—outside India, barring a short period of authoritarianism in the mid-1970s—those forms have also often changed.

India's founders created a constitutional federal republic with regular competitive elections, and a bicameral legislature charged with the responsibility of making laws and—together with the judiciary—holding the executive to account. They created a space for a free media, albeit one bounded by restrictive laws inherited from the British authorities regarding the handling of sensitive information, libel, the maintenance of public order, and sedition. Recognizing the relative weakness of the new state, they also imposed strict civilian control over the military, effectively excluding the armed forces from the highest levels of decision-making on foreign and security policy.[29]

In this system, modelled on British parliamentary democracy, responsibility for formulating and implementing foreign and security policy is vested in part of the core executive, including Prime Minister and their office; the External Affairs Minister (EAM) and their Ministry, headed by the Foreign Secretary; and the Defence Minister and their officials. They manage the day-to-day business, but are—in theory, at least—bound by the Constitution, which explicitly directs India's governments to adhere to the principles of the United Nations Charter in their conduct of international relations, to parliament and the courts, and ultimately to the electorate.[30]

In practice, however, India's core executive has often been able to make and implement foreign and security policy without much scrutiny. Under Jawaharlal Nehru, the first prime minister, who also served as his own foreign minister, few politicians had the will or knowledge to challenge the government's line. The parliamentary committee charged with oversight provided little—and continued to neglect their duties long after Nehru.[31] And the electorate took little interest either, beyond cheering the efforts of successive prime ministers to defend India's status as a great nation and aspiring major power.[32]

The de facto autonomy enjoyed by India's core executive, combined with the lack of like-minded democracies on its borders and very low levels of regional economic independence, as well as the country's relative power compared to its neighbors might have combined to allow it to test the limits of liberal theories about the behavior of democracies. But for most of India's history, its leaders have adhered to what has been termed "strategic restraint," refraining from the overt threat or use of force, even when provoked.[33] When India has fought—against China in 1962 and against Pakistan in 1947, 1965, 1971, and 1999—it has almost always done so in response to an armed attack.[34] And where India has deployed troops elsewhere, in Maldives, Seychelles, and Sri Lanka, it has been by invitation, or at the behest of the UN, for peacekeeping operations.

Like India, Pakistan also provides a test of liberal theories—and evidence of their usefulness. Also founded as a federal parliamentary republic, Pakistan's experiment with democracy has been more troubled.[35] The country has endured long periods of military rule—from 1958 to 1971, from 1977 to 1988, and from 1999 to 2007—and the armed forces have arguably never been fully under civilian control.[36] Even under civilian rule, the military—especially the powerful Inter-Services Intelligence agency—has strongly influenced foreign and security policy. Pakistan is also home to many competing Islamist movements, some supportive of

Liberal Approaches

democratic politics, like Jama'at-i Islam, and some, like Tehrik-i-Taliban Pakistan, that want to impose a theocratic system of government.[37] Several of these movements are vehemently hostile to India, partly (but not wholly) due to the longstanding dispute over Kashmir, and back insurgent and terrorist activities, sometimes with tacit or active support from parts of the state.[38]

Some thus argue that Pakistan's tendency to resort to force to try to settle disputes is best explained by incomplete democratization—in particular, by the unwillingness of the elite to set aside ambitious ideological goals and curb the power of both the military and armed non-state actors.[39] Pakistan offers evidence to support the liberal theory that powerful interests within states can distort their foreign and security policy preferences, affecting their international relations. In this case, the armed forces' political influence and significant economic interests have shaped Pakistan's strategic behavior, pushing it to seek foreign allies that can provide the funds and materiel, American, Chinese, or Saudi, the generals want to pursue their regional ambitions.[40]

Armies do not play a similar role anywhere else in South Asia. Bangladesh has spent periods under military rule (1975–1979; 1982–1986) and has experienced several attempted coups. It does suffer from dynastic politics and widespread corruption, but its system of government—constitutionally-bounded, democratic, and parliamentary—has proved reasonably robust, despite challenges from militant Islamists, as well as the generals. Bangladesh's international relations have been and continue to be shaped by other domestic interests. During the 1970s and 80s, securing food and other aid for a large and vulnerable population was a major concern, opening Bangladesh to pressure from major donors and international organizations. So too was the fate of Bangladeshis stuck in dozens of enclaves within India and the challenge of managing the water that runs through India. Bangladesh's emergence as a major garment manufacturer in the 2000s has helped to reduce poverty, but also generates other issues, creating powerful economic lobbies allied to foreign multinationals and drawing attention to local labor rights from other governments and non-governmental organizations.[41]

Sri Lanka has experienced similar tensions—and others. Since 1972, it has been governed by a hybrid presidential-parliamentary system, in which the president heads the executive and the prime minister leads the ruling party. However, the long-running civil war, pitting the Sinhalese-dominated government against Tamil separatists, boosted the influence of armed forces in Sri Lankan politics and complicated its relations with India and the rest of the world.[42] More recently, Sri Lanka's economic success has enhanced the influence of local business interests and international investors, both state and private, giving rise to fears that parts of its political elite and its foreign policy can be corrupted by domestic and outside actors, especially China.[43]

In Maldives and Nepal, both fragile democracies, fears have also arisen that local political elites can be—and have been—captured by local business interests or foreign money. But in Nepal, as in Bhutan and especially Afghanistan, ethnic divisions also loom large, and affect international relations as well as domestic politics. The condition of the Madheshi people who straddle the border between India has contributed to civil conflict within Nepal and to disputes with New Delhi, including the 2015 informal blockade imposed by Indian sympathizers that caused a significant bilateral dispute and a tilt toward China by Kathmandu.[44] In parallel, the condition of the Nepali-speaking Lhotshampa by the Ngalung-dominated government of Bhutan has caused tensions with both Kathmandu and New Delhi, who have had to accept refugees from that community.[45]

With Afghanistan, the inability of elites to construct and maintain inclusive representative governments has of course had even more serious effects on its international relations.

It is home to four major ethnic groups—Pashtuns, Tajiks, Hazaras, and Uzbeks—all overlapping its borders, and while the majority are Sunni Muslims, a sizable minority are Shia. A quarter of the population is urban and much of that well-educated; the rest is rural, with varying levels of economic and social development. Power struggles between these groups have occurred since the Kingdom of Afghanistan was established in 1926, drawing in outside forces, notably Pakistan, home to about 30 million Pashtuns, and the Central Asian states.[46]

Regime types and societal actors play important roles in shaping the international relations of South Asia, enabling certain behaviors and imposing costs on others. There is some evidence to suggest that democratic governments are more restrained in this region as in others, but that powerful actors within states, notably the armed forces and business interests, can dominate foreign and security policy, and societal divisions can spill over into international disputes.

International Institutions

Liberals maintain that international institutions shape the behavior of states, restricting their choices, modifying incentives, and providing forums for diplomatic action. They point to classic examples like the European Union (EU), which has played a key role in transforming Western Europe—and latterly, after the absorption of several former communist states, Central Europe—from a region of endemic conflict to one of peace and prosperity. Liberals argue the EU succeeded in this task by restructuring incentives. In particular, the EU has facilitated a high level of economic interdependence that has raised the cost of military conflict beyond what any member state would likely be willing to tolerate, since attacking a neighbor would plunge the aggressor into economic crisis. As a result, EU members have been able to reduce their defense expenditure and focus instead on social welfare.

Of course, liberals recognize that these benefits of peace and prosperity have a price—and indeed that other factors, including superpower management, have contributed to Europe's success. EU membership places effective limits on the exercise of state sovereignty, domestically and internationally. Member states must adhere to certain rules and standards in their internal governance, for example, and subject themselves to EU law, made by the European Commission, Council, and Parliament, as well as the European Court of Justice.[47]

South Asia has no regional institution comparable to the EU. A South Asian Association for Regional Cooperation (SAARC) was founded in 1985 by Bangladesh, Bhutan, India, the Maldives, Nepal, Pakistan, and Sri Lanka; Afghanistan joined in 2007. Its Charter is wide-ranging, committing member states to hold annual leader summits, a council of ministers, a secretariat, based in Kathmandu, and a series of technical committees, and to cooperate to boost regional economic, social, and cultural development. Since 1985, SAARC has also established a limited free trade area and a plethora of other initiatives, from a development fund and a set of information-sharing centers to a literary award and a dedicated South Asian University, in New Delhi.[48]

Yet, SAARC has fallen far short of playing a transformative role in the international relations of South Asia. Progress toward deeper economic integration, with freer flows of goods and services, has been painfully slow, even after the conclusion of the agreement to create South Asia Free Trade Area in 2004. The World Bank estimates that regional trade is only a third of what it could be, if restrictions were eased or lifted, and infrastructure improved.[49] Some argue that SAARC has proved useful in facilitating the exchange of data and expertise through its technical centers.[50] But SAARC has done little, if anything, to mitigate tensions

Liberal Approaches

between members, especially between India and Pakistan. Indeed, the organization has been held hostage when bilateral disputes flare, as the frequent postponements and cancellations of SAARC summits demonstrate.[51]

Worse still, in recent years, SAARC has been increasingly circumvented by the use of minilateral and multilateral initiatives by some South Asia states. India has favored the Bay of Bengal Initiative for Multi-Sectoral Technical and Economic Cooperation (BIMSTEC), which also counts Bangladesh, Bhutan, Myanmar, Nepal, Sri Lanka, and Thailand as members, to further regional trade facilitation and infrastructure development.[52] In parallel, Bangladesh, Bhutan, India, and Nepal have used the so-called BBIN initiative to try to boost road connectivity and trade electricity, with mixed results.[53] Pakistan, for its part, has chosen to deepen its economic relationship with China, through the China Pakistan Economic Corridor (CPEC), a major component of the Belt and Road Initiative (BRI).[54] So too, to a lesser degree, have Nepal and Sri Lanka, as Kathmandu and Colombo look to Beijing to improve their infrastructure and find new markets.[55]

South Asian states have also been prone to engage in mini- and multilateral initiatives beyond the immediate region. Afghanistan, Bangladesh, and Pakistan are members of the Organization of Islamic Cooperation. India is a member of the East Asia Summit and other Association of Southeast Asian Nations-centered organizations and mechanisms. Both India and Pakistan are now full members of the China- and Russia-led, security-focused Shanghai Cooperation Organization. India works with Australia, Japan, and the US under the auspices of the Quad and with Russia and China in another minilateral.[56] And all South Asian states belong to the Non-Aligned Movement.

Moreover, the relative failure of inclusive regional institutions in South Asia should not be taken as evidence of hostility to multilateralism in general. Bangladesh, India, Pakistan, and Sri Lanka, in particular, have long been strong supporters of the UN system—the first three as major contributors to peacekeeping operations. In this context, South Asian states clearly perceive the benefits of active participation outweigh the costs. The UN Charter provides a strong set of norms concerning sovereignty and non-intervention that they value; the organization provides a platform to defend their interests against regional and extra-regional challengers. It also allows South Asian states to gather information, as well as shape international discussion on a range of issues in global governance—from climate change to nuclear proliferation—with which they are concerned.

Conclusion

Taking a liberal approach to the international relations of South Asia has advantages: It provides a useful toolkit for exploring how foreign and security policies are formulated and implemented by states. It allows analysts to explore the dominant ideas held by elites about relations with other social and political communities, as well as the influence of powerful state and societal actors, from militaries to multinationals. And it focuses attention on the pressures imposed from outside, from other states and non-state actors, including international institutions. In this regional context, the liberal approach draws attention to debates about the relations between different ethnic and religious groups, and how they have sustained animosities between states, as well as between communities. It also highlights the ways in which different regime types can and do shape international behavior, curbing or permitting belligerence, in particular. Finally, the liberal approach helps to explain the failure of regional multilateralism and push for greater economic openness, in terms of the calculations South Asian states have made and continue to make about their costs and benefits.

Notes

1 Andrew Moravscik, "Taking Preferences Seriously: A Liberal Theory of International Politics," *International Organization* 51, no. 4 (1997): 513–553.
2 See especially Kenneth N. Waltz, *Theory of International Politics* (Reading, Mass.: Addison Wesley, 1979). It should be noted that Waltz held that a theory of international politics was not a theory of foreign policy, acknowledging that states did not always behave as realists expect them to.
3 See Paul A. Kowert, "Foreign Policy and the Social Construction of State Identity," in *Oxford Research Encyclopedia of International Studies* (Oxford: Oxford University Press, 2010), https://doi.org/10.1093/acrefore/9780190846626.013.397.
4 See Benno Teschke and Steffan Wyn-Jones, "Marxism in Foreign Policy," in *Oxford Research Encyclopedia of Politics* (Oxford: Oxford University Press, 2017), https://doi.org/10.1093/acrefore/9780190228637.013.372.
5 Stephan Haggard, "The Liberal View of the International Relations of Asia," in *The Oxford Handbook of the International Relations of Asia*, ed. Saadia M. Pekkanen, John Ravenhill, and Rosemary Foot (Oxford: Oxford University Press, 2014), 45.
6 For a primer, see Sugata Bose and Ayesha Jalal, *Modern South Asia: History, Culture, Political Economy*, 4th ed. (London and New York: Routledge, 2017).
7 For a useful survey, see E. Sridharan, ed., *International Relations Theory and South Asia: Security, Political Economy, Domestic Politics, Identities, and Images*, 2 vols. (New Delhi: Oxford University Press, 2014).
8 See, for example, Bhumitra Chakma, "Liberal Peace and South Asia," *India Quarterly* 70, no. 3 (2014): 187–205.
9 On local ideologies, see Rochana Bajpai and Carlo Bonura, "South Asian and Southeast Asian Ideologies," in *The Oxford Handbook of Political Ideologies*, ed. Michael Freeden and Marc Stears (Oxford: Oxford University Press, 2013).
10 For helpful overviews, see Stephen Philip Cohen's *India: Emerging Power* (Washington, DC: Brookings, 2001) and his *The Idea of Pakistan* (Washington, DC: Brookings, 2004).
11 Azim Zahir, *Islam and Democracy in the Maldives: Interrogating Reformist Islam's Role in Politics* (London and New York: Routledge, 2021).
12 Mahendra Lawoti, ed., *Contentious Politics and Democratization in Nepal* (New Delhi: SAGE, 2007).
13 Mark Turner, Sonam Chuki, and Jit Tshering, "Democratization by Decree: The Case of Bhutan," *Democratization* 18, no. 1 (2011): 184–210.
14 Tim Harper, *Underground Asia: Global Revolutionaries and the Assault on Empire* (Cambridge, Mass.: Harvard University Press, 2021).
15 For a short account of Two Nation Theory, see C. Christine Fair, *Fighting to the End: The Pakistan Army Way of War* (New York: Oxford University Press, 2014), 41–46.
16 Šumit Ganguly, *Deadly Impasse: Indo-Pakistani Relations at the Dawn of a New Century* (Cambridge: Cambridge University Press, 2016).
17 Christophe Jaffrelot, *The Hindu Nationalist Movement in India* (New York: Columbia University Press, 1996).
18 For a helpful survey, see Craig Baxter, *Bangladesh: From a Nation to a State* (London and New York: Routledge, 2018).
19 Sandra Destradi, "India and Sri Lanka's Civil War: The Failure of Regional Conflict Management in South Asia," *Asian Survey* 52, no. 3 (2012): 595–616.
20 The best study of non-alignment remains A. P. Rana, *The Imperatives of Nonalignment: A Conceptual Study of India's Foreign Policy Strategy in the Nehru Period* (Delhi: Macmillan, 1976).
21 S. Jaishankar, *The India Way: Strategies for an Uncertain World* (New Delhi: HarperCollins, 2020).
22 For a useful discussion, see T. V. Paul, *The Warrior State: Pakistan in the Contemporary World* (New York: Oxford University Press, 2014).
23 Michael Doyle, "Liberalism and World Politics," *American Political Science Review* 80, no. 4 (1986): 1151–1169.
24 On these arguments, see Nils Petter Gleditsch, "Democracy and Peace," *Journal of Peace Research* 29, no. 4 (1992): 369–376.
25 Rudolph J. Rummel, "Libertarianism and International Violence," *Journal of Conflict Resolution* 27, no. 1 (1983): 27–71.
26 David Leblang and Steve Chan, "Explaining Wars Fought by Established Democracies: Do Institutional Constraints Matter?" *Political Research Quarterly* 56, no. 4 (2003): 385–400.

Liberal Approaches

27 Thomas Risse-Kappen, "Democratic Peace-Warlike Democracies? A Social Constructivist Interpretation of the Liberal Argument," *European Journal of International Relations* 1, no. 4 (1995): 491–517.

28 Mark J. Gasiorowski, "Economic Interdependence and International Conflict: Some Cross-National Evidence," *International Studies Quarterly* 30, no. 1 (1986): 23–38.

29 Anit Mukherjee, *The Absent Dialogue: Politicians, Bureaucrats, and the Military in India* (New Delhi: Oxford University Press, 2020).

30 Rajendra M. Abhyankar, *Indian Diplomacy: Beyond Strategic Autonomy* (New Delhi: Oxford University Press, 2018), xix.

31 Jayantanuja Bandyopadhyaya, *The Making of India's Foreign Policy: Determinants, Institutions, Processes and Personalities* (New Delhi: Allied Publishers, 1991), 159–178.

32 Devesh Kapur, "Public Opinion and Indian Foreign Policy," *India Review* 8, no. 3 (2009): 286–305.

33 Stephen P. Cohen and Sunil Dasgupta, *Arming without Aiming: India's Military Modernization* (Washington, DC: Brookings, 2010), 1–28.

34 The arguably exception being 1971, as India's covert involvement in conflict in East Pakistan predates the attack on its airfields by Pakistani aircraft that provided the formal *casus belli*.

35 Maya Tudor, *The Promise of Power: The Origins of Democracy in India and Autocracy in Pakistan* (Oxford: Oxford University Press, 2013).

36 Paul Staniland, "Explaining Civil-Military Relations in Complex Political Environments: India and Pakistan in Comparative Perspective," *Security Studies* 17, no. 2 (2008): 322–362.

37 Vali Nasr, "Military Rule, Islamism and Democracy in Pakistan," *The Middle East Journal* 58, no. 2 (2004): 195–209.

38 C. Christine Fair, "The Militant Challenge in Pakistan," *Asia Policy* 11 (2011): 105–138.

39 See, for example, Paul, *Warrior State*.

40 Hoo Tiang Boon and Glenn K. H. Ong, "Military Dominance in Pakistan and China–Pakistan Relations," *Australian Journal of International Affairs* 75, no. 1 (2021): 80–102. See also Fair, *Fighting to the End*.

41 Marilyn Rock, "Globalisation and Bangladesh: The Case of Export-Oriented Garment Manufacture," *South Asia: Journal of South Asian Studies* 24, no. 1 (2001): 201–225.

42 Neil DeVotta, "Parties, Political Decay, and Democratic Regression in Sri Lanka," *Commonwealth & Comparative Politics* 52, no. 1 (2014): 139–165.

43 For a discussion, see Darren J. Lim and Rohan Mukherjee, "What Money Can't Buy: The Security Externalities of Chinese Economic Statecraft in Post-War Sri Lanka," *Asian Security* 15, no. 2 (2019): 73–92.

44 Dhananjay Tripathi, "Influence of Borders on Bilateral Ties in South Asia: A Study of Contemporary India–Nepal Relations," *International Studies* 56, no. 2–3 (2019): 186–200.

45 Bhakta Raj Giri, "Bhutan: Ethnic Policies in the Dragon Kingdom," *Asian Affairs* 35, no. 3 (2004): 353–364.

46 Abubakar Siddique, *The Pashtun Question: The Unresolved Key to the Future of Pakistan and Afghanistan* (London: Hurst, 2014).

47 Mark A. Pollack, "Theorizing the European Union: International Organization, Domestic Polity, or Experiment in New Governance?" *Annual Review of Political Science* 8 (2005): 357–398.

48 Lawrence Saez, *The South Asian Association for Regional Cooperation (SAARC): An Emerging Collaboration Architecture* (London and New York: Routledge, 2012).

49 World Bank, "Why #OneSouthAsia?" https://www.worldbank.org/en/programs/south-asia-regional-integration/overview, accessed: December 15, 2021.

50 Zahid Shahab Ahmed, *Regionalism and Regional Security in South Asia: The Role of SAARC* (London and New York: Routledge, 2016).

51 Only 18 of the nominally annual summits were held between 1985 and 2021. In the 2010s, only three summits were convened—in 2011, 2014, and 2015—before a boycott of a Pakistan-hosted event by Afghanistan, Bangladesh, Bhutan, and India in the aftermath of the Uri terrorist attack.

52 See Constantino Xavier, *Bridging the Bay of Bengal: Toward a Stronger BIMSTEC* (Washington: Carnegie Endowment for International Peace, 2018). BIMSTEC's origins lie in a grouping called BIST-EC (Bangladesh, India, Sri Lanka, and Thailand Economic Cooperation) formed in 1997 and subsequently expanded to include Myanmar, Nepal, and Bhutan. Its secretariat is in Dhaka.

53 Parthapratim Pal, "Intra-BBIN Trade: Opportunities and Challenges," *Observer Research Foundation Issue Brief* 135 (2016).

54 Andrew Small, "First Movement: Pakistan and the Belt and Road Initiative," *Asia Policy* 24, no. 1 (2017): 80–87.
55 Jingdong Yuan, "China's Belt and Road Initiative in South Asia and the Indian Response," *Issues & Studies* 55, no. 2 (2019): 1–27.
56 Frank O'Donnell and Mihaela Papa, "India's Multi-Alignment Management and the Russia–India–China (RIC) Triangle," *International Affairs* 97, no. 3 (2021): 801–822.

Bibliography

Abhyankar, Rajendra M. *Indian Diplomacy: Beyond Strategic Autonomy*. New Delhi: Oxford University Press, 2018.

Ahmed, Zahid Shahab. *Regionalism and Regional Security in South Asia: The Role of SAARC*. London and New York: Routledge, 2016.

Bajpai, Rochana, and Carlo Bonura. "South Asian and Southeast Asian Ideologies." In *The Oxford Handbook of Political Ideologies*, edited by Michael Freeden and Marc Stears. Oxford: Oxford University Press, 2013.

Bandyopadhyaya, Jayantanuja. *The Making of India's Foreign Policy: Determinants, Institutions, Processes and Personalities*. New Delhi: Allied Publishers, 1991.

Baxter, Craig. *Bangladesh: From a Nation to a State*. London and New York: Routledge, 2018.

Boon, Hoo Tiang, and Glenn K. H. Ong. "Military Dominance in Pakistan and China–Pakistan Relations." *Australian Journal of International Affairs* 75, no. 1 (2021): 80–102.

Sugata, Bose, and Ayesha Jalal. *Modern South Asia: History, Culture, Political Economy*. 4th ed. London and New York: Routledge, 2017.

Chakma, Bhumitra. "Liberal Peace and South Asia." *India Quarterly* 70, no. 3 (2014): 187–205.

Cohen, Stephen Philip. *India: Emerging Power*. Washington, DC: Brookings, 2001.

Cohen, Stephen Philip. *The Idea of Pakistan*. Washington, DC: Brookings, 2004.

Cohen, Stephen P., and Sunil Dasgupta. *Arming Without Aiming: India's Military Modernization*. Washington, DC: Brookings, 2010.

Destradi, Sandra. "India and Sri Lanka's Civil War: The Failure of Regional Conflict Management in South Asia." *Asian Survey* 52, no. 3 (2012): 595–616.

DeVotta, Neil. "Parties, Political Decay, and Democratic Regression in Sri Lanka." *Commonwealth & Comparative Politics* 52, no. 1 (2014): 139–165.

Doyle, Michael. "Liberalism and World Politics." *American Political Science Review* 80, no. 4 (1986): 1151–1169.

Fair, C. Christine. "The Militant Challenge in Pakistan." *Asia Policy* 11 (2011): 105–138.

Fair, C. Christine. *Fighting to the End: The Pakistan Army Way of War*. New York: Oxford University Press, 2014.

Ganguly, Šumit. *Deadly Impasse: Indo-Pakistani Relations at the Dawn of a New Century*. Cambridge: Cambridge University Press, 2016.

Gasiorowski, Mark J. "Economic Interdependence and International Conflict: Some Cross-National Evidence." *International Studies Quarterly* 30, no. 1 (1986): 23–38.

Giri, Bhakta Raj. "Bhutan: Ethnic Policies in the Dragon Kingdom." *Asian Affairs* 35, no. 3 (2004): 353–364.

Gleditsch, Nils Petter. "Democracy and Peace." *Journal of Peace Research* 29, no. 4 (1992): 369–376.

Haggard, Stephan. "The Liberal View of the International Relations of Asia." In *The Oxford Handbook of the International Relations of Asia*, edited by Saadia M. Pekkanen, John Ravenhill, and Rosemary Foot, 45–63. New Delhi: Oxford University Press, 2014.

Hall, Ian. "India's National Security: A Liberal Account." In *The Oxford Handbook of India's National Security*, edited by Šumit Ganguly, Nicolas Blarel, and Manjeet S. Pardesi, 42–59. Oxford: Oxford University Press, 2018.

Harper, Tim. *Underground Asia: Global Revolutionaries and the Assault on Empire*. Cambridge, Mass: Harvard University Press, 2021.

Jaffrelot, Christophe. *The Hindu Nationalist Movement in India*. New York: Columbia University Press, 1996.

Jaishankar, S. *The India Way: Strategies for an Uncertain World*. New Delhi: HarperCollins, 2020.

Kapur, Devesh. "Public Opinion and Indian Foreign Policy." *India Review* 8, no. 3 (2009): 286–305.

Liberal Approaches

Kowert, Paul A. "Foreign Policy and the Social Construction of State Identity." In *Oxford Research Encyclopedia of International Studies*. Oxford: Oxford University Press, 2010. https://doi.org/10.1093/acrefore/9780190846626.013.397.

Lawoti, Mahendra, ed. *Contentious Politics and Democratization in Nepal*. New Delhi: SAGE, 2007.

Leblang, David, and Steve Chan. "Explaining Wars Fought by Established Democracies: Do Institutional Constraints Matter?" *Political Research Quarterly* 56, no. 4 (2003): 385–400.

Lim, Darren J., and Rohan Mukherjee. "What Money Can't Buy: The Security Externalities of Chinese Economic Statecraft in Post-War Sri Lanka." *Asian Security* 15, no. 2 (2019): 73–92.

Moravcsik, Andrew. "Taking Preferences Seriously: A Liberal Theory of International Politics." *International Organization* 51, no. 4 (1997): 513–553.

Mukherjee, Anit. *The Absent Dialogues: Politicians, Bureaucrats, and the Military in India*. New Delhi: Oxford University Press, 2020.

Nasr, Vali. "Military Rule, Islamism and Democracy in Pakistan." *The Middle East Journal* 58, no. 2 (2004): 195–209.

O'Donnell, Frank, and Mihaela Papa. "India's Multi-Alignment Management and the Russia–India–China (RIC) Triangle." *International Affairs* 97, no. 3 (2021): 801–822.

Pal, Parthapratim. "Intra-BBIN Trade: Opportunities and Challenges." *Observer Research Foundation Issue Brief* 135 (2016).

Pollack, Mark A. "Theorizing the European Union: International Organization, Domestic Polity, or Experiment in New Governance?" *Annual Review of Political Science* 8 (2005): 357–398.

Rana, A. P. *The Imperatives of Nonalignment: A Conceptual Study of India's Foreign Policy Strategy in the Nehru Period*. Delhi: Macmillan, 1976.

Risse-Kappen, Thomas. "Democratic Peace—Warlike Democracies? A Social Constructivist Interpretation of the Liberal Argument." *European Journal of International Relations* 1, no. 4 (1995): 491–517.

Rock, Marilyn. "Globalisation and Bangladesh: The Case of Export-Oriented Garment Manufacture." *South Asia: Journal of South Asian Studies* 24, no. 1 (2001): 201–225.

Rummel, Rudolph J. "Libertarianism and International Violence." *Journal of Conflict Resolution* 27, no. 1 (1983): 27–71.

Saez, Lawrence. *The South Asian Association for Regional Cooperation (SAARC): An Emerging Collaboration Architecture*. London and New York: Routledge, 2012.

Siddique, Abubakar. *The Pashtun Question: The Unresolved Key to the Future of Pakistan and Afghanistan*. London: Hurst, 2014.

Small, Andrew. "First Movement: Pakistan and the Belt and Road Initiative." *Asia Policy* 24, no. 1 (2017): 80–87.

Sridharan, E., ed. *International Relations Theory and South Asia: Security, Political Economy, Domestic Politics, Identities, and Images*. 2 Vols. New Delhi: Oxford University Press, 2014.

Staniland, Paul. "Explaining Civil-Military Relations in Complex Political Environments: India and Pakistan in Comparative Perspective." *Security Studies* 17, no. 2 (2008): 322–362.

Teschke, Benno, and Steffan Wyn-Jones. "Marxism in Foreign Policy." In *Oxford Research Encyclopedia of Politics*. Oxford: Oxford University Press, 2017. https://doi.org/10.1093/acrefore/9780190228637.013.372.

Tripathi, Dhananjay. "Influence of Borders on Bilateral Ties in South Asia: A Study of Contemporary India–Nepal Relations." *International Studies* 56, no. 2–3 (2019): 186–200.

Tudor, Maya. *The Promise of Power: The Origins of Democracy in India and Autocracy in Pakistan*. Oxford: Oxford University Press, 2013.

Turner, Mark, Sonam Chuki, and Jit Tshering. "Democratization by Decree: The Case of Bhutan." *Democratization* 18, no. 1 (2011): 184–210.

Waltz, Kenneth N. *Theory of International Politics*. Reading, Mass: Addison Wesley, 1979.

World Bank. "Why #OneSouthAsia?" https://www.worldbank.org/en/programs/south-asia-regional-integration/overview, accessed: December 15, 2021.

Xavier, Constantino. *Bridging the Bay of Bengal: Toward a Stronger BIMSTEC*. Washington: Carnegie Endowment for International Peace, 2018.

Yuan, Jingdong. "China's Belt and Road Initiative in South Asia and the Indian Response." *Issues & Studies* 55, no. 2 (2019): 1–27.

Zahir, Azim. *Islam and Democracy in the Maldives: Interrogating Reformist Islam's Role in Politics*. London and New York: Routledge, 2021.

3
CONSTRUCTIVIST APPROACHES TO THE INTERNATIONAL RELATIONS OF SOUTH ASIA

Aditi Malhotra

Introduction

This chapter aims to assess how scholars have utilized the lens òf constructivism to enrich one's understanding of modern South Asian international relations (IR), particularly over the last decade. The theory of constructivism surfaced in the late 1980s and became a popular alternative to the previously dominant theories in the post-Cold War era. Before the emergence of constructivism as a theory of IR, the discipline was dominated by the lenses of (neo) realism and (neo)liberalism, particularly during the Cold War. The "neo-neo" approaches were relatively similar in their ontological and epistemological claims with different theoretical perspectives of inter-state behavior. According to Realism, states compete to secure their interests in an anarchic world. Liberalism contested this view by claiming that self-serving states are not always interested in conflict but also value international cooperation achieved through positive linkages between institutions and groups. The Constructivist approach emerged as a viable "middle ground between the two schools of thought centered on the 'conflictual relations' or the 'cooperative tendencies in human nature.'"[1]

Constructivism in its early days began as an "interpretive meta-theory," which questioned the reliance of Neorealism on material forces to explain IR.[2] Nicholas G. Onuf—one of the founders of constructivism—underlined the importance of revisiting the fundamentals of IR in his book, *World of Our Making*.[3] He highlighted the need to understand global politics as a function of human actions and social interactions. Contrary to traditional assumptions, Constructivism propounds that the international system is not a result of material forces and their distribution alone. The ontological foundation of Constructivism is based on the claim that "social reality is constructed."[4] The epistemological outlook is that "knowledge is constructed," followed by the understanding that reality and knowledge are "mutually constitutive."[5] The fundamental tenets of the Constructivist approach include the relevance and importance of "identity," "norms" and "ideas" in international politics.

The theory claims that anarchy, cooperation, or even the international system do not exist in nature as a physical form and, therefore, should not be viewed as reality by default. Instead, these are "socially constructed" realities that have emerged from social interactions between actors and agents of the state.[6] For example, the term "South Asia" is a socially constructed concept or a "mental map" defined or conceptualized based on a specific geopolitical and

DOI: 10.4324/9781003246626-5

historical emphasis.[7] There is a shared agreement among some scholars and practitioners that eight countries (Afghanistan, Bangladesh, Bhutan, India, Maldives, Nepal, Pakistan, and Sri Lanka) can be clubbed together (metaphorically) as a legitimate sub-region. Constructivism's construction of reality enables one to separate South Asia as a conceptual sub-unit of the massive landmass of Asia. In short, the concept of South Asia is a constructed reality infused by regional geopolitics and historical associations.

As the subsequent sections demonstrate, the understanding of South Asian IR is enhanced considerably by utilizing constructivism because it offers an in-depth and holistic explanation of issues and concepts overlooked by traditional theories. The theory can identify and unravel the nuances of inter-state and intra-state relations in South Asia by peeking inside the "black box" model of a state. It values the influence of material factors and combines them with ideational and non-material determinants to portray a complete picture of real-world developments in South Asia without compromising on the finer details such as the state's experiential reality and sub-state identities. Because constructivism factors in the local factors, it does greater justice to explaining policy changes (including of smaller states) compared to mainstream theories that tend to apply a set of western concepts to non-western settings.

Constructivist Explanations of International Relations

One of the fundamental propositions is the role of identity in international politics. Constructivism understands identity as an actors' self-representation of who they are and how they relate to external actors. The fundamental questions pertaining to identity include, "Who am I in the socially interactive international system? What role do I play in relation to the Others?" Alexander Wendt argues that "actors acquire identities—relatively stable, role-specific understandings and expectations about self, by participating in collective meanings."[8] They form "the basis of interests."[9] The self-conception of a state determines what its interests would be and how would it pursue those interests. This also implies that the type of international system that exists (for example, anarchic or cooperative) is based on how the actors identify themselves, how they perceive others, and what they consider to be their self-interest and interest vis-à-vis others.

Based on a state's social interaction with outside actors, it can acquire multiple identities such as a sovereign country, peaceful state, ally, great power, or imperial power.[10] These identities then shape the interests, determining external behavior and policy choices. Hill and Wallace shed light on the link between national identity and foreign policy. According to them,

> the foreign policy rests upon a shared sense of national identity, of a nation-state's 'place in the world', its friends and enemies, its interests and aspirations. These underlying assumptions are embedded in national history and myth, changing slowly over time as political leaders reinterpret them and external and internal developments reshape them.[11]

Aspects such as historical, cultural, and political contexts also influence national identity and thereby the actor's interests.[12] Because states have distinct histories, cultures, social landscapes, or domestic political systems, their external behavior is bound to differ from one another. By grasping the unique experiential realities of the states or sub-systemic factors, Constructivism peeks into the "black box" model of the state and offers explanations of state behavior that other conventional IR theories tend to overlook. This explains why countries such as Brazil, Russia, India, China, and the United States have different foreign policy attributes and do not always act like each other in the international system.

When states choose their identities, they tend to adhere to the associated norms. Norms can be described as "a standard of appropriate behavior for actors with a given identity."[13] Therefore, if a state assumes the identity of a sovereign state, it will comply with norms that are appropriate and associated with it. Norms are intersubjective and connected with actions. They serve as frameworks for expected or most appropriate behavior. Finnemore and Sikkink divide norms into three broad categories: Regulative, constitutive, and prescriptive norms.[14] While regulative norms tend to "order and constrain behavior," constitutive norms "create new actors, interests, or categories of action."[15] Prescriptive or evaluative norms "involve standards of 'appropriate' or 'proper' behavior" and provide a sense of "oughtness," which differentiates norms from rules.[16] Given the varying functions of the norms, they have varied influences on the actor's actions. Having noted that, it is equally important to note that norms do not determine actions directly. Norms along with identities shape interests, which in turn shape actions and policy choices.[17]

In addition to identity and norms, constructivism also places great emphasis on ideas. Ideas are mental frames or constructs widely shared among people or groups. From the gamut of ideas that exist, Tannenwald focuses on four types: "Ideologies, normative beliefs, cause-effect beliefs and policy prescriptions," which she explains deftly:[18]

a. Ideologies are related to doctrines, philosophies, or beliefs that a group of people share and stand by. Examples include political doctrines such as liberalism and Marxism.
b. Normative ideas deal with what is considered right and wrong or just and unjust—for instance, human rights violations or invasions.
c. Cause-effect ideas deal with understanding what means one should choose to achieve a specific end or objective.
d. Policy prescription ideas relate to shared beliefs on "causal ideas" or specific strategies and policy actions that effectively address policy issues or challenges.[19]

Given this understanding, it is worth noting that while Constructivism regards the state as a crucial actor, it also acknowledges other actors and their agential value in international politics. Additional actors may include "states' agencies, social community, international organizations, think tanks" that shape ideas, norms, and the identity of a state.[20] Constructivism breaks the tradition of state-centric approaches by factoring in non-state actors of varying types. It also enables one to analyze the role played by sub-national actors in IR.

Constructivism claims that identities, ideas, norms, and interests are not static or fixed as assumed under other conventional IR approaches. Because these aspects are "constructed," they are subject to changes primarily as a function of social interactions (including the processes of socialization and internalization).[21] This does not mean that identities, ideas, and norms are fluid and ever-changing. Broadly, they are stable but may evolve or change over long stretches of time. Constructivists posit that changes in identity, norms, or ideas can affect a state's interests, thereby spurring a change in actions and patterns of behavior.

Given this theoretical backdrop, it is crucial to understand that constructivism is not a monolithic school of thought (like any other IR theory) and has many variants. Despite the ontological and epistemological outlooks, there is a range of variants of Constructivism—such as Social Constructivism and Critical Constructivism[22]—that emphasize some concepts more than others and have nuanced understandings of pertinent concepts. Needless to state, the school of thought and its variants are continuously experiencing conceptual development through scholarly debates within the discipline of IR and infusion with other approaches.[23]

One of the strengths of the Constructivist approach lies in its treatment of the agent-structure dilemma in IR, whether the agent influences the structure or vice-versa. Constructivism goes beyond the conventional assumptions in IR theories that the structure and agents are ontologically distinct. They also believe that the structure is dominant and can significantly shape the agent's behavior. One of the basic premises of the Constructivist approach is that the agency and structure are "mutually constituted" and ontologically equal.[24] This implies that both the structure and the agency hold equal precedence and are interconnected. They influence each other in the process of their social interactions.

For instance, one can refer to the shared understanding of an "international system" as the structure and associate the states as "agents," i.e., entities that operate within the structure. According to Constructivists, the conduct of the state or states can shape the notion and concept of the international system. Similarly, the international system can socialize states or influence them to adjust their behavior to align with the constructed reality of the structure. The ongoing interaction between the two within the social context can lead to their reconstruction or redefinition. In short, both entities can influence and co-determine the other.

It is crucial to note that despite the ideational focus of constructivism, it does not disregard the relevance of power or interests as one of the explanatory variables. Instead, it propounds that ideational and non-material factors interact with structural and material determinants, and sub-national aspects to construct "reality" or multiple realities.

Constructivism and South Asian IR

In previous decades, the literature on South Asia IR gave the impression that regional issues were best explained through structural approaches. Despite the Eurocentric conceptions of global politics, these theories were used to describe regional interactions in non-western settings, including South Asia. Materialistic factors and the logic of balance of power (BoP) were projected as the primary determinants of South Asian affairs.[25] Notwithstanding their valuable contributions, recent works have highlighted some of the weaknesses in traditional theoretical approaches, leading to insufficient insights on regional affairs and inter-state interactions.

Over the last decade, many scholars have opted for constructivism and associated approaches to examine empirical puzzles of South Asia. This is a marked change from the previous works that generally relied on the concepts of BoP and the security dilemma to explain regional politics and inter-state relations. With new literature, there is greater cognizance of the complexities in South Asia's inter-state relations and intra-state affairs. At the same time, there is a greater acknowledgement that endogenous and ideational factors augment one's understanding of regional politics. The following section provides an overview of Constructivism-guided studies over the last decade and their contributions to explaining South Asian IR. The larger section is sub-divided into smaller sections, based on the fundamental tenets of constructivism: Identity, norms, and ideas. These sub-sections demonstrate how scholars and analysts have used each concept to explain contemporary South Asian IR comprehensively.

Identity

In the last ten years, the concept of identity has gained considerable attention from the community of IR scholars and foreign policy analysts. That noted, a great deal of the emerging literature concentrates on security issues. This is an expected trend considering most constructivism-centric studies on South Asian IR begin by challenging existing Realist accounts on regional security issues and offering better explanations.[26] Another aspect of constructivism-driven studies is the lopsided attention toward India and Pakistan with limited attention on other states in the region. This practice persists despite some recent works that break the tradition and analyze the policies of Bhutan, Maldives, and Sri Lanka. Nevertheless, by studying ideational determinants of state behavior, contemporary works have provided new insights on previously analyzed issues and explored new areas of inquiry.

As stated, the lens of constructivism is widely employed in the area of Indian foreign policy. Many scholars have used the concept of identity to explain the dichotomies in New Delhi's external policy and regional interactions. Chacko's work on India's national identity deserves mention as it heavily draws from Constructivism as a theory and methodology.[27] In her book on Indian foreign policy, Chacko argues that realist or liberal accounts tend to confine India to either a Realist power, an Idealist power, or a mix of the two.[28] Apart from broad-level analysis, there is little thought on the changes in Indian policy despite no substantial changes in official rhetoric. She argues that India's post-colonial identity, including "civilizational exceptionalism," infuses an element of morality in Indian foreign policy.[29] At the same time, its experiential reality of invasions and conquest has shaped India's foreign relations.[30]

In her more recent research, Chacko uses the framework of Constructivism to address a prominent empirical puzzle that has received inadequate theoretical attention. She identifies the reason for a change in India's strategic posture toward Pakistan from 2008 to 2016. India has practiced strategic restraint toward Pakistan after the 2008 terrorist attacks in Mumbai but chose to conduct surgical strikes in disputed Kashmiri territory under Pakistan's control in the 2016 Uri attack. In the mid-2000s, as Chacko argues, India's choices were shaped by a "transformational" identity that adopted an economic growth-centric outlook. New Delhi's attention centered on economic growth, thus favoring a policy of restraint (focusing on back-channel talks and people-to-people ties). India's identity steadily turned more "aspirational" in the following years.

The identity shift culminated with the change in government in 2014 from a Congress-led alliance to a Bharatiya Janata Party (BJP)-led alliance. Under Prime Minister Modi, India's identity was influenced by the tenets of "aspirational Hindu nationalism" and the leadership's "desire to appease the neo-middle class."[31] The new identity is also connected to "zero tolerance" toward Pakistan, as promised in BJP's manifesto. As posited by the logic of constructivism, the change in identity resulted in changed policy actions, hence the contrasting responses to Pakistan-supported attacks on India. If the traditional IR approaches analyzed this issue, there is a high likelihood of partial explanation given their inability to analyze endogenous factors.

Theoretical and conceptual nuances of constructivism have enabled researchers to understand the idiosyncrasies of regional interactions at the systemic and sub-systemic levels. Ali, Haider, and Ali study India-Pakistan relations through the lens of contested identities.[32] Their study makes an interesting observation that Islamabad is supportive of the Chinese military might but is threatened by Indian military capabilities, which are comparatively weaker. India and Pakistan have fought three wars, one conflict, and are involved in a protracted dispute over Jammu and Kashmir. Without disregarding the relevance of material factors, the authors argue that other variables also determine bilateral relations. They claim that the India-Pakistan rivalry is greatly determined by their hostile "socio-cognitive identities" shaped by social institutions in their countries. The study identifies four important institutions—education, media, religion, and politics—which create hostile and incompatible national, ideological, and religious identities through socialization and internalization. These identities create adversarial interests, which support and facilitate the creation of confrontational policies toward the Other.

The finding implies that even if material determinants became irrelevant, the ideational clashes between the countries would continue to shape an adversarial equation between the neighbors. This understanding opens avenues for possible conflict resolution because conflictual ideas of today can be replaced by more cooperative ideas through socialization and internalization. It would not be an exaggeration to state that constructivist approaches present the scope for conflict resolution instead of Neorealism, which is mainly concerned about the prospects of war/conflict in an anarchic environment and thereby paints a doomsday picture. In contrast to this practice, Mario Carranza analyzes the possibilities of nuclear arms control in South Asia with insights from Constructivism. He stresses three aspects, namely, international social environment, domestic opinion, and identity-based India-Pakistan conflict, to enhance the prospects of nuclear arms control and disarmament.[33] Although the study presents an idealistic scenario, Carranza makes valuable contributions by introducing innovative ways to address the traditional security problems of the region.

Apart from investigating inter-state security issues, the concept of identity has contributed considerably to the understanding of ethnic conflicts in South Asia. The region has diverse populations with different cultures, religions, and ethnicities. While there is relative regional stability, there is no denying that South Asia is home to many ethnic and religious conflicts. Chatterjee argues that ethno-linguist-religious nationalist movements have questioned the "constitutional legitimacy" of almost all states in South Asia.[34] Mainstream IR theories have largely failed to account for this phenomenon, particularly in South Asia. This is primarily due to their systemic outlook and inability to account for sub-state factors and actors. Although still limited, there has been an uptick of studies that delve into the issue of ethnocentric or religious conflict.

Interestingly, most of such studies are conducted by South Asian scholars. According to Mir and Ahmed, ethnic or religious nationalism movements emerge due to strong affiliation based on ethnicity, language, or religion.[35] These distinct community identities separate them from Others that are likely to belong to the majority community. Making a similar argument, Chatterjee claims that the combination of "dialectical interaction between homogenizing state nationalism(s)" and sub-nationalism obstructs the possibility of cultural assimilation.[36] According to Chatterjee, all South Asian states use "territorial nationalism" to undermine the perceived threat of such movements. They also carve a "monolith construction of nationhood" to counter the perceived threats from specific identity-based groups.[37] This tends to threaten the distinct identities of the minority community along with fears of majoritarianism.

Many studies have argued that the assertion of ethnic, religious, or linguistic identity and nationalism transform into conflicts. Some movements remain confined to the borders of a state. For instance, intra-state problems such as the Chakma community in Bangladesh, the Hindu-Muslim divide in India, the Mohajir community in Pakistan, and the Dravidian identity in India. Some forms of nationalism spill over to neighboring states, adding complications in inter-state relations. In this context, Mir and Ahmed argue that "states with hostile relations exploit internal fault-lines of other countries to further their own diplomatic and national interests."[38] Instances include the Kashmir dispute between India and Pakistan, Pakistani assistance to the Khalistan movement in Indian Punjab, and Indian support to *Mukti Bahini* in East Pakistan.

Pathak adds to the debate by highlighting the relevance of "identity" as a crucial factor in the creation of Bangladesh. He claims that the identity associated with the Muslim League's understanding of a Pakistani Muslim (largely Urdu speaking) clashed with the distinct identity of Bengali-speaking people in East Pakistan.[39] The prolonged identity clash (based on ethnicity and linguistics) interacted with other pertinent (structural and material) factors to result in the partition of Pakistan and the creation of Bangladesh.[40] A similar argument has emerged in studies that have analyzed the Dravidian movement in India, which emerged in opposition to the North Indian Hindi identity[41] and the Kachin ethno-religious-linguistic identity that stood in opposition to the Bamar ethnic majority in Myanmar.[42] Interestingly, in some instances, despite the non-dilution of identities, some identity-based conflicts have witnessed resolution. Utilizing Wendt's understanding of identity change, Chatterjee argues that ethnic-religious-linguistic conflicts can transform into cooperative accommodation with changes in the conception of self and the Other, as seen with the Khalistan nationalism movement and the Dravidian movement in India.[43]

Identity-based explanations have contributed considerably to the subject of intra-state violence and conflicts in South Asia. Recent years have witnessed an emergence of valuable studies on intra-state ethnic alliances and how identities affect them. One such example is Hasangani's research on the de-facto ethnic alliance of the Sinhalese and Muslims against the Liberation Tigers of Tamil Eelam (LTTE) in Sri Lanka.[44] Realist accounts would have explained the Sinhalese-Muslim alliance as a function of the "enemy of my friend is my enemy" thinking. However, they are likely to falter in explaining why Sri Lanka witnessed Sinhalese-Muslim riots despite their cordial associations during the Sri Lankan Civil War.

Offering answers to this phenomenon, Hasangani studies the behavior of Sinhalese and Muslims between 1983 and 2015. She finds irregular patterns of convergence and divergence between the two ethnicities during the Civil War.[45] There were periods of cooperation and phases of disengagement despite a common "enemy." She argues that ethnic relations remain in "flux due to unfixed, multiple ethnic identities."[46] She also shows that ethnic identities comprise multiple constitutive elements and plural identities within.[47] Changes in the constitutive elements of the identity are reflected in their interests, thereby actions. Hasangani concludes that the fluctuations in Sinhalese-Muslim de-facto alliance were connected to the "activation/deactivation of certain constitutive elements of ethnic identities."[48]

Norms and Ideas

Unlike the concept of identity, which has been heavily employed in Constructivism-guided studies, there is limited application of norms and ideas in the context of South Asian IR. Nevertheless, existing studies contribute considerably to the field by focusing on smaller states in the region. Current studies push the envelope in the research area and underscore the explanatory value of its application in explaining South Asian IR. While some studies employ "ideas" as an explicit explanatory factor, others rely on it implicitly. Regardless, their contribution to the field remains notable.

In a seminal study on Bhutan, Theys explains Bhutan's norm creation through the process of *Bhutanisation* since the 1980s. Through royal edicts, Bhutan introduced the concepts of *tha damtshig* (loyalty and respect for other community members, especially elders) and driglam namzha (official dress code of the traditional dress) and emphasized Dzongkha as the national language.[49] This norm creation and its internalization among the populace have steadily shaped Bhutan's national identity, which is also connected to the concept of Gross National Happiness (GNH). The GNH—a counter to the concept of Gross Domestic Product (GDP)—prioritizes the pursuit of happiness and sustainable development over pure monetary measures. The norms created by Bhutan contribute to the identity of the citizenry and allow the leadership to introduce new ideas and shape international norms.

This is addressed in a study by Theys and Rietig. They argue that Bhutan has effectively utilized its national identity and associated ideas to create a unique international identity, accentuate its regional status, and impact global sustainability governance.[50] The authors argue that Bhutan challenged the "fundamental ideas about what constitutes development and placed happiness on the global agenda."[51] Thimphu depended on a "policy entrepreneur" who implemented numerous strategies to spread the idea, gain mass appeal, and socialize the United Nations into factoring happiness as an indicator of development. The change in international norms was reflected in the adoption and implementation of UN Resolutions, which encourage member states to prioritize the pursuit of happiness. This study challenges the notion of traditional IR theories that small states have limited capacity to shape norms or influence regional/international policies. In their words, Bhutan has exemplified that "a small developing country with structural weaknesses" possesses the ability to "exert global influence."[52] Notably, the study demonstrates the value of the blend of norms and ideas in reshaping international political norms.

In a similar vein, Jaschik employs the case of Maldives to argue that small states shape international agendas by effectively framing ideas rather than relying on economic or military power.[53] He examines Maldives' success in generating international influence on the issue of climate change. Malé resorted to many strategies to promote ideas on climate change, strategically frame the ideas, and lead to a greater internalization of those ideas. Some of the strategies and tactics included setting up informal dialogues, strategic framing in the media, consistent interaction with a range of state and non-state actors (especially like-minded actors), and reliance on symbolism such as participation in an underwater cabinet meeting.[54] Adding more context to the broader argument, Rasheed studies the Maldives' "island vulnerability identity," which is associated with the idea of its vulnerability in the face of climate change.[55] Although limited in number, such studies underline the importance of "ideas" in shaping regional and international norms and constructing reality in an interactive setting.

David Scott contributes to this debate by connecting New Delhi's changing involvement in regional integration to changes in its idea of "region."[56] Post-independence, India's understanding of the region was limited to the geographical region of South Asia, which determined its South Asia-centric foreign and security policy. This explains why Indian leaderships asserted dominance in South Asia while forgoing any substantial involvement in farther regions. However, in recent decades, India's conception and the idea of the region (from a policy point-of-view) has expanded beyond the confines of a "subcontinental mindset" and embraced the regions of the Indian Ocean, Southeast Asia, and Pacific Asia.[57] The changing idea and understanding of the region have expectedly shaped India's outlook and external policy.[58]

In contrast to the works mentioned above, scholars (albeit very few) have also used "norms" to explain the failure of regional cooperation. The influence of norms in inter-state relations has added to the ongoing debate on the failure of multilateralism in South Asia. Michael utilized the constructivist framework of "norm localization" to analyze regional multilateralism, focusing on the South Asian Association for Regional Cooperation (SAARC) and the Indian Ocean Rim (IORA).[59] Despite the presence of such institutions, he argues that there is an absence of cooperation, integration (economically and politically) and multilateralism in South Asia. According to Michael, when multilateralism is localized and implemented in South Asian settings, it is primarily shaped to align with the "ideational orthodoxy" of Indian foreign policy.[60]

The study examines India's role in shaping the norms of multilateralism during discussions before establishing SAARC and IORA. The author claims that New Delhi successfully diffused the original concept of multilateralism and customized it to align with the core principles of its foreign policy approach: "Focus on bilateralism and independence," wariness toward discussing contentious issues or strategic and security matters in multilateral settings, non-alignment, and reluctance to pool resources.[61] Such norm localization and grafting (connecting new ideas with existing ones) resulted in the "under-institutionalization" of SAARC and IORA.[62] By leading the norm-shaping process and diffusing the original norm of multilateralism, India was instrumental in creating weak institutions, thereby hampering the potential of multilateralism in South Asia. This is a novel finding, which challenges the assumption of Neorealism that multilateralism in South Asia suffers primarily due to India-Pakistan power politics and a security dilemma.[63]

Furthermore, the Constructivist turn in South Asian IR has brought the utility of "norms" in explaining issues unique to South Asia. In this context, a study by Maley (although not recently published) examines the contestation between international and domestic norms and their consequences on the Taliban in Afghanistan. While Maley does not explicitly use Constructivism when analyzing the foreign policy of the Taliban (from 1996–2001), he examines the tensions that existed between the international norms and the Taliban's national norms.[64] Specifically, he posits that the clash between international norms on women's basic rights and the Taliban's contrarian norms and perspectives on the issue became a serious impediment to the Taliban's international isolation. In a more recent study, Kristensen makes a similar argument in her work that identifies obstacles to the peace process before the Taliban's recent takeover of Afghanistan.[65] She notes the "colliding ideational and relation norms" on the issues of democracy (considered a foreign concept), peace talks (contrasting procedures of negotiations), and gender rights (anti-women views) remained the most prominent challenge to negotiations and the peace process.[66] Despite the limited studies in this area, some of the stated findings confirm that some unique issues in South Asia boil down to the question of norms and ideas and not simply materialist variables that traditional neo-neo theories heavily depend on.

Conclusion

The chapter provided a broader overview of Constructivism and demonstrated its utility in advancing the understanding of South Asia's IR. First, Constructivism has provided theoretical diversity in South Asian IR and effectively showed that inter-state and intra-state relations in the region are greatly influenced by sub-systemic factors and ideational determinants such as identity, norms, and ideas. Second, constructivism (through the concept of identity change) has helped identify reasons for policy changes, especially in the absence of a significant change in material or structural factors. Third, it has challenged the conventional wisdom of traditional IR theories and presented nuanced alternate (ideational) explanations of South Asian issues. Fourth, it made valuable contributions by examining and analyzing the foreign policy of small South Asian states with structural weaknesses. Because Realism or Neoliberalism have remained concerned with bigger powers and their interactions, most of their accounts neglect states that are smaller in terms of geography, economy, or political influence. This gap is somewhat plugged by Constructivism in South Asian IR. Fourth, identity shed light on the inter-state security problem in South Asia and explained the complexities of intra-state conflicts that plague the region. Fifth, in stark contrast with structural explanations, constructivism remains an appropriate framework to explore possibilities of conflict resolution in South Asia.

Despite the stated contributions to South Asian IR, some weaknesses in current literature need to be plugged in by future research. Primarily, many Constructivist accounts have fallen into the neo-neo "trap" by concentrating on security issues. It would be theoretically

Constructivist Approaches

and empirically rewarding to have more studies examining non-security issues of South Asia. Further, current studies utilize norms and ideas without distinct conceptualization and operationalization. There is an urgent need for more studies that apply norms and ideas to analyses. At the same time, it is crucial to offer clarity when utilizing constructivist concepts and methodologies. Regardless of the weaknesses, Constructivism-guided studies have proved their merit in analyzing South Asian issues. The ground is fertile for future research endeavors and analyses of issues that remain untouched by other conventional IR theories.

Notes

1 Emanuel Adler, "Seizing the Middle Ground: Constructivism in World Politics," *European Journal of International Relations* 3, no. 3 (September 1997): 319–363. https://doi.org/10.1177/1354066197003003003.
2 Maysam Behravesh, "Constructivism: An introduction," *E-International Relations*, February 3, 2011, https://www.e-ir.info/2011/02/03/constructivism-an-introduction/#_edn1.
3 Nicholas G. Onuf, *World of Our Making: Rules and Rule in Social Theory and International Relations* (Columbia, NC: University of South Carolina Press, 1989).
4 Hoyoon Jung, "The Evolution of Social Constructivism in Political Science: Past to Present," *SAGE Open* 9, no. 1 (January 2019): 1–10. https://doi.org/10.1177/2158244019832703, 2.
5 *Ibid.*
6 Sarina Theys, "Constructivism," in *International Relations Theory*, eds. Stephen Mcglinchey, Rosie Walters and Christian Scheinpflug (Bristol, UK: E-International relations, 2017), 36–41, 36.
7 See, Albert Tzeng, William L. Richter and Ekaterina Koldunova, *Framing Asian Studies: Geopolitics and Institutions* (Singapore: ISEAS–Yusof Ishak Institute, 2018).
8 Alexander Wendt, "Anarchy is What States Make of it: The Social Construction of Power Politics," *International Organization* 46, no. 2 (1992): 391–425. https://doi.org/10.1017/s0020818300027764, 397.
9 *Ibid.*, 398.
10 *Ibid.*
11 Christopher Hill and William Wallace, "Introduction: Actors and Actions," in *The Actors in Europe's Foreign Policy* (London, UK: Routledge, 1996), 1–18, 8.
12 See, Jutta Weldes, "Constructing National Interests," *European Journal of International Relations* 2, no. 3 (September 1996): 275–318. https://doi.org/10.1177/1354066196002003001; Peter J. Katzenstein, *The Culture of National Security: Norms and Identity in World Politics* (New York: Columbia University Press, 1996).
13 Martha Finnemore and Kathryn Sikkink, "International Norm Dynamics and Political Change," *International Organization* 52, no. 4 (1998): 887–917. http://www.jstor.org/stable/2601361, 891.
14 *Ibid.*
15 *Ibid.*
16 *Ibid.*
17 Nilüfer Karacasulu and Elif Uzgören, "Explaining Social Constructivist Contributions to Security Studies," *Perceptions: Journal of International Affairs* 12 (Summer-Autumn 2007): 27–48. http://sam.gov.tr/pdf/perceptions/Volume-XII/summer-autumn-2007/KaracasuluUzgoren.pdf.
18 Nina Tannenwald, "Ideas and Explanation: Advancing the Theoretical Agenda," *Journal of Cold War Studies* 7, no. 2 (2005): 13–42. https://doi.org/10.1162/1520397053630619. 15–16.
19 *Ibid.*
20 Martin Weber, "Constructivism and Critical theory," in *An Introduction to International Relations: Australian perspectives*, eds. Richard Devetak, Anthony Burke, and Jim George (Cambridge, UK: Cambridge University Press, 2007), 96–108, 98.
21 Ian Hurd, "Legitimacy and Authority in International Politics," *International Organization* 53, no. 2 (1999): 379–408. http://www.jstor.org/stable/2601393.
22 This variant falls within the framework of "Critical Theory," which is discussed in more detail in Chapter 4.
23 Priya Chacko, "Constructivism and Indian Foreign Policy," in *New Directions in Indian Foreign Policy: Theory and Praxis*, ed. Harsh Pant (Cambridge, UK: Cambridge University Press, 2018), 48–66.

24 Audie Klotz and Cecilia Lynch, *Strategies for Research in Constructivist International Relations* (Armonk, NY M.E. Sharpe, 2007), 3.

25 Bharat Karnad, *Nuclear Weapons and Indian Security: The Realist Foundations of Strategy* (New Delhi, India: Macmillan India, 2002); Šumit Ganguly, "Indian Security Policy," in *Routledge Handbook of Security Studies*, eds. Myriam Dunn Cavelty and Thierry Balzacq, 2nd. Edition (London, UK: Routledge, 2017); George J. Gilboy and Eric Heginbotham, "Double Trouble: A Realist View of Chinese and Indian Power," *The Washington Quarterly* 36, no. 3 (2013): 125–142. https://doi.org/10.1080/0163660X.2013.825554; Rajesh Rajagopalan, "Neorealist Theory and the India-Pakistan Conflict-II," *Strategic Analysis* 22, no. 10 (1999): 1525–1536. https://doi.org/10.1080/09700169908458901; Shakthi De Silva, "Balancing, Bandwagoning, or Hedging? Independent Ceylon's reaction to Regional Hegemony," *South Asian Survey* 22, no. 2 (September 2015): 189–209. https://doi.org/10.1177/0971523117753929.

26 See Muhammad Shoaib Pervez, *Security Community in South Asia: India – Pakistan* (Oxon, UK: Routledge, 2013); Chacko, "Constructivism and Indian Foreign Policy," 48–66; Ahmad Ali, Syed Imran Haider, and Muhammad Ali, "Role of Identities in the Indo-Pak Relations: A Study in Constructivism," *Global Regional Review* 2, no. 1 (2017): 305–319. http://dx.doi.org/10.31703/grr.2017 (II-I).21

27 See Priya Chacko, *Indian Foreign Policy: The Politics of Postcolonial Identity from 1947 to 2004* (Oxon, UK: Taylor & Francis, 2013); Chacko, "Constructivism and Indian Foreign Policy," 48–66.

28 Chacko, *Indian Foreign Policy.*

29 *Ibid.*

30 *Ibid.*

31 Chacko, "Constructivism and Indian Foreign Policy," 12.

32 Ali, Ali, and Haider, "Role of Identities," 305–319.

33 Mario E. Carranza, *India Pakistan Nuclear Diplomacy: Constructivism and the Prospects for Nuclear Arms Control and Disarmament in South Asia* (London, UK: Rowman & Littlefield, 2016).

34 Shibashis Chatterjee, "Ethnic Conflicts in South Asia: A Constructivist Reading," *South Asian Survey* 12, no. 1 (March 2005): 75–89. https://doi.org/10.1177/097152310501200106. 81.

35 Mir and Ahmed, "Ethnic Conflicts in South Asia," 10–19.

36 Chatterjee, "Ethnic Conflicts in South Asia," 85.

37 *Ibid.*

38 Mir and Ahmed, "Ethnic Conflicts in South Asia," 15.

39 Pathak, "Constructivist Analysis," 245–250.

40 *Ibid.*

41 Kunal Debnath, "Populist Mobilization, Role of Political Elites and Anti-Centre Campaign in Recent Tamil Politics in India," *Advance* (2019): 1–19. https://doi.org/10.31124/advance.8063051.v1.

42 Alexandre Pelletier, "Identity Formation, Christian Networks, and the Peripheries of Kachin Ethnonational Identity," *Asian Politics & Policy* 13 (2021): 72–89. https://doi.org/10.1111/aspp.12571.

43 Chatterjee, "Ethnic Conflicts in South Asia," 75–89.

44 Sandunika Hasangani, "The Making and Breaking of (De-Facto) Ethnic Alliances: A Constructivist Reading of Sinhalese-Muslim Relations in Sri Lanka During 1983–2015," *Journal of Language, Area and Cultural Studies* 25 (January 2019): 187–204. https://ssrn.com/abstract=3656846.

45 Hasangani, "The Making and Breaking," 187–204.

46 *Ibid.*, 196.

47 *Ibid.*

48 *Ibid.*

49 Heidi Karst, "Protected areas and ecotourism: Charting a path toward social-ecological wellbeing" (PhD diss., University of Waterloo, 2017).

50 Sarina Theys, and Katharina Rietig, "The Influence of Small States: How Bhutan Succeeds in Influencing Global Sustainability Governance," *International Affairs* 96, no. 6 (November 2020): 1603–1622. https://doi.org/10.1093/ia/iiaa157.

51 *Ibid.*, 1604.

52 *Ibid.*, 1603.

53 Kevin Jaschik, "Small States and International Politics: Climate Change, the Maldives and Tuvalu," *International Politics* 51, no. 2 (2014): 272–293. doi:10.1057/ip.2014.5.

54 *Ibid.*

55 Athaulla A. Rasheed, "Small Island Climate Diplomacy in the Maldives and Beyond," *E-International Relations*, June 16, 2019, https://www.e-ir.info/2019/06/16/small-island-climate-diplomacy-in-the-maldives-and-beyond/.
56 David Scott, "India and Regional Integration," in *Handbook of India's International Relations*, ed. David Scott (London, UK: Routledge, 2011), 118–128.
57 *Ibid.*
58 *Ibid.*
59 Arndt Michael, "Cooperation is What India Makes of It – A Normative Inquiry into the Origins and Development of Regional Cooperation in South Asia and the Indian Ocean," *Asian Security* 14, no. 2 (2018): 119–135. https://doi.org/10.1080/14799855.2017.1347636, 121.
60 *Ibid.*, 121.
61 *Ibid.*
62 *Ibid.*
63 Saqib Ullah Khan, Sabira Iqbal, and Atta Ullah Jan, "Neo-Realist Paradigm and the Fragile State of Regional Cooperation in South Asia: Prospects and Challenges," *Sir Syed Journal of Education & Social Research* 4, no. 2 (2021): 160–166. https://doi.org/10.36902/sjesr-vol4-iss2-2021.
64 William Maley, "The Foreign Policy of the Taliban," *Council on Foreign Relations*, September, 2005, https://www.cfr.org/sites/default/files/pdf/2005/08/ForeignPolicy_Taliban_Paper.pdf.
65 Sofie Bøgelund Kristensen, "Afghanistan Peace and Reconcilation" (Master diss., Aalborg University, 2012) https://projekter.aau.dk/projekter/files/65540158/Master_thesis_Afghanistan_peace_and_reconciliation_1_.docx.
66 *Ibid.*, 59.

Bibliography

Adler, Emanuel. "Seizing the Middle Ground: Constructivism in World Politics." *European Journal of International Relations* 3, no. 3 (September 1997): 319–363. https://doi.org/10.1177/1354066197003003003.

Ali, Ahmad, Syed Imran Haider, and Muhammad Ali. "Role of Identities in the Indo-Pak Relations: A Study in Constructivism." *Global Regional Review* 2, no. 1 (2017): 305–319. http://dx.doi.org/10.31703/grr.2017(II-I).21.

Behravesh, Maysam. "Constructivism: An introduction." *E-International Relations*, February 3, 2011, https://www.e-ir.info/2011/02/03/constructivism-an-introduction/#_edn1.

Carranza, Mario E. *India Pakistan Nuclear Diplomacy: Constructivism and the Prospects for Nuclear Arms Control and Disarmament in South Asia*. London: Rowman & Littlefield, 2016.

Chacko, Priya. "Constructivism and Indian Foreign Policy." In *New Directions in Indian Foreign Policy: Theory and Praxis*, edited by Harsh Pant, 48–66. Cambridge: Cambridge University Press, 2018.

Chacko, Priya. *Indian Foreign Policy: The Politics of Postcolonial Identity from 1947 to 2004*. Oxon: Taylor & Francis, 2013.

Chatterjee, Shibashis. "Ethnic Conflicts in South Asia: A Constructivist Reading." *South Asian Survey* 12, no. 1 (March 2005): 75–89. https://doi.org/10.1177/097152310501200106.

De Silva, Shakthi. "Balancing, Bandwagoning or Hedging? Independent Ceylon's Reaction to Regional Hegemony." *South Asian Survey* 22, no. 2 (September 2015): 189–209. https://doi.org/10.1177/0971523117753929.

Debnath, Kunal. "Populist Mobilization, Role of Political Elites and Anti-Centre Campaign in Recent Tamil Politics in India." *Advance* (2019): 1–19. https://doi.org/10.31124/advance.8063051.v1.

Finnemore, Martha, and Kathryn Sikkink. "International Norm Dynamics and Political Change." *International Organization* 52, no. 4 (1998): 887–917. http://www.jstor.org/stable/2601361.

Ganguly, Šumit. "Indian Security Policy." In *Routledge Handbook of Security Studies*, edited by Myriam Dunn Cavelty and Thierry Balzacq, 2nd. Edition. London: Routledge, 2017.

Gilboy, George J., and Eric Heginbotham. "Double Trouble: A Realist View of Chinese and Indian Power." *The Washington Quarterly* 36, no. 3 (2013): 125–142. https://doi.org/10.1080/0163660X.2013.825554.

Hasangani, Sandunika. "The Making and Breaking of (De-Facto) Ethnic Alliances: A Constructivist Reading of Sinhalese-Muslim Relations in Sri Lanka During 1983–2015." *Journal of Language, Area and Cultural Studies* 25 (January 2019): 187–204. https://ssrn.com/abstract=3656846.

Hill, Christopher, and William Wallace. "Introduction: Actors and Actions." In *The Actors in Europe's Foreign Policy*, edited by Christopher Hill, 1–18. London: Routledge, 1996.

Hurd, Ian. "Legitimacy and Authority in International Politics." *International Organization* 53, no. 2 (1999): 379–408. http://www.jstor.org/stable/2601393.

Jaschik, Kevin. "Small States and International Politics: Climate Change, the Maldives and Tuvalu." *International Politics* 51, no. 2 (2014): 272–293. https://doi.org/10.1057/ip.2014.5.

Jung, Hoyoon. "The Evolution of Social Constructivism in Political Science: Past to Present." *SAGE Open* 9, no. 1 (January 2019): 1–10. https://doi.org/10.1177/2158244019832703.

Karacasulu, Nilüfer, and Elif Uzgören. "Explaining Social Constructivist Contributions to Security Studies." *Perceptions: Journal of International Affairs* 12 (Summer-Autumn 2007): 27–48. http://sam. gov.tr/pdf/perceptions/Volume-XII/summer-autumn-2007/KaracasuluUzgoren.pdf.

Karnad, Bharat. *Nuclear Weapons and Indian Security: The Realist Foundations of Strategy*. New Delhi: Macmillan India, 2002.

Karst, Heidi. "*Protected areas and ecotourism: Charting a path toward social-ecological wellbeing.*" PhD diss., University of Waterloo, 2017.

Katzenstein, Peter J. *The Culture of National Security: Norms and Identity in World Politics*. New York: Columbia University Press, 1996.

Khan, Saqib Ullah, Sabira Iqbal, and Atta Ullah Jan. "Neo-Realist Paradigm and the Fragile State of Regional Cooperation in South Asia: Prospects and Challenges." *Sir Syed Journal of Education & Social Research* 4, no. 2 (2021): 160–166. https://doi.org/10.36902/sjesr-vol4-iss2-2021.

Kipgen, Nehginpao. "Politics of Ethnic Conflict in Manipur." *South Asia Research* 33, no. 1 (February 2013): 21–38. https://doi.org/10.1177/0262728013475541.

Klotz, Audie, and Cecilia Lynch. *Strategies for Research in Constructivist International Relations*. Armonk, N.Y: M.E. Sharpe, 2007.

Kristensen, Sofie Bøgelund. "Afghanistan Peace and Reconcilation." Master diss., Aalborg University, 2012.

Maley, William. "The Foreign Policy of the Taliban." *Council on Foreign Relations*, September, 2005, https://www.cfr.org/sites/default/files/pdf/2005/08/ForeignPolicy_Taliban_Paper.pdf.

Michael, Arndt. "Cooperation is What India Makes of It – A Normative Inquiry into the Origins and Development of Regional Cooperation in South Asia and the Indian Ocean." *Asian Security* 14, no. 2 (2018): 119–135. https://doi.org/10.1080/14799855.2017.1347636.

Mir, Mohm Amin, and Zulafqar Ahmed. "Ethnic Conflicts in South Asia: Impediments to Regional Integration." *World Affairs: The Journal of International Issues* 24, no. 3 (2020): 10–19. https://www.jstor.org/stable/48590640.

Onuf, Nicholas G. *World of Our Making: Rules and Rule in Social Theory and International Relations*. Columbia, NC: University of South Carolina Press, 1989.

Pathak, Tripuresh. "Constructivist Analysis of Independence of Bangladesh." *Research Journal of Humanities and Social Sciences* 12, no. 4 (2021): 245–250. https://doi.org/10.52711/2321-5828.2021.00044.

Pelletier, Alexandre. "Identity Formation, Christian Networks, and the Peripheries of Kachin Ethnonational Identity." *Asian Politics & Policy* 13 (2021): 72–89. https://doi.org/10.1111/aspp.12571.

Pervez, Muhammad Shoaib. *Security Community in South Asia: India – Pakistan*. Oxon: Routledge, 2013.

Rajagopalan, Rajesh. "Neorealist Theory and the India-Pakistan Conflict-II." *Strategic Analysis* 22, no. 10 (1999): 1525–1536. https://doi.org/10.1080/09700169908458901.

Rasheed, Athaulla A. "Small Island Climate Diplomacy in the Maldives and Beyond." *E-International Relations*, June 16, 2019, https://www.e-ir.info/2019/06/16/small-island-climate-diplomacy-in-the-maldives-and-beyond/.

Scott, David. "India and Regional Integration." In *Handbook of India's International Relations*, edited by David Scott, 118–128. London: Routledge, 2011.

Tannenwald, Nina. "Ideas and Explanation: Advancing the Theoretical Agenda." *Journal of Cold War Studies* 7, no. 2 (2005): 13–42. https://doi.org/10.1162/1520397053630619.

Theys, Sarina. "Constructivism." In *International Relations Theory*, edited by Stephen Mcglinchey, Rosie Walters, and Christian Scheinpflug, 36–41. Bristol: E-International Relations, 2017.

Theys, Sarina, and Katharina Rietig. "The Influence of Small States: How Bhutan Succeeds in Influencing Global Sustainability Governance." *International Affairs* 96, no. 6 (November 2020): 1603–1622. https://doi.org/10.1093/ia/iiaa157.

Tzeng, Albert, William L. Richter, and Ekaterina Koldunova. *Framing Asian Studies: Geopolitics and Institutions*. Singapore: ISEAS–Yusof Ishak Institute, 2018.

Weber, Martin. "Constructivism and Critical Theory." In *An Introduction to International Relations: Australian Perspectives*, edited by Richard Devetak, Anthony Burke, and Jim George, 96–108. Cambridge: Cambridge University Press, 2007.

Weldes, Jutta. "Constructing National Interests." *European Journal of International Relations* 2, no. 3 (September 1996): 275–318. https://doi.org/10.1177/1354066196002003001.

Wendt, Alexander. "Anarchy is What States Make of It: The Social Construction of Power Politics." *International Organization* 46, no. 2 (1992): 391–425. https://doi.org/10.1017/S0020818300027764.

4
CRITICAL THEORY APPROACHES TO THE INTERNATIONAL RELATIONS OF SOUTH ASIA

Shibashis Chatterjee

Introduction

South Asia, consisting of India, Pakistan, Bangladesh, Nepal, Bhutan, Sri Lanka, Maldives, and Afghanistan, is one of the most important regions of the world while also being fraught with numerous paradoxes. While the geographical landmass denoted by the term South Asia is home to one of the world's oldest civilizations, dating back to the 26th century BCE, modern South Asia is very much a post-1945 construct. The expression "South Asia" was coined by the US State Department for strategic or geopolitical purposes and gained acceptance and traction partly as it appeared far more neutral than the term "Indian subcontinent" or variations thereof.[1] Yet, this neutrality is entirely superficial. The religious, cultural, and historical references to South Asia do not match with the geographies of the contemporary South Asian states. In a sense, it is an empty geographical expression, one that is attractive for its innate ambiguities, openness, and remarkable diversity. Even as a region, it shows significant divergent tendencies. Pakistan and Afghanistan have increasingly sought to claim attachments to West and Central Asia, Nepal and Bhutan are culturally divided between Indian and Tibetan influences, Sri Lanka and Maldives draw upon wider Asia-Pacific cultural roots, and India has increasingly looked at Southeast Asia and beyond. Bangladesh is possibly the only state in South Asia that culturally relates to eastern India and not beyond (despite sharing a 270-km-long border with Myanmar, there are few cultural linkages). The central point here is that South Asia is a divided subcontinent. The political identities that constitute it share little with its cultural, historical, sociological, and anthropological roots.[2] Hence, the politics of South Asia has witnessed an extraordinary sensitivity to difference, a project fraught with anomalies that often spills over into violence since national and cultural boundaries are not coincidental.

Realism, Liberalism, Constructivism, and Critical Theory remain the four major theoretical approaches to the study of International Relations (IR). Realism offers a statist explanation of IR in terms of power and security. Notwithstanding certain in-house differences concerning the motivations of state action and the relationship between security and power, Realists agree on the centrality of states, a view of politics that emphasizes mistrust, insecurity, and power, and the unchanging nature of international politics.[3] Liberalism is the other dominant approach in IR that emphasizes the role of transactions, markets and

46

DOI: 10.4324/9781003246626-6

institutions, democracy, and the possibility of corrigibility in IR.[4] Constructivists recognize the attractions of both power and interests but add that identities provide the explanation of international phenomena at the deepest level. They contend that both material and ideational factors matter in world politics, and find it difficult to choose between either agency-centric or structural explanations.[5] Critical theorists build on the Marxist heritage, although two distinctive branches have emerged in IR. Robert Cox developed the initial variant taking a cue from Antonio Gramsci's idea of hegemony, understood as the extension of the dominant liberal capitalist worldview as the hegemonic perspective undergirding world politics and drew attention to the political role of theory as a justificatory discourse.[6] The other branch builds closely on the ideas of Jurgen Habermas, such as discourse ethics, communicative action, and the relations between modes of knowledge and human interests.[7] Taking a cue from Habermas's insistence on the need to create a radical democracy based on deliberation and the universal principle of reason to find solutions to our social and political problems under late modernity, theorists like Andrew Linklater developed normative arguments questioning the state as a political community and redirected attention to the Kantian idea of a cosmopolitan ethics.[8] Both traditions share a number of commitments—the idea of critique in the widest possible sense (not limited to the economy as Marx argued), politically engaged rather than neutral theory, and, most importantly, emancipation in a progressive direction. We will return at the end of this study to the discussion regarding which of these approaches explain South Asian IR best.

Regional/International Context

South Asia is one of the world's fastest growing regions with a demographic dividend that promises sustained economic development over several generations, is home to a large and growing middle class that is promising for the prospects of both economic vitality and democracy, and is the connector linking the West Asian, Central Asian, and Southeast Asian regional sub-systems. Yet, it is also one of the least internally integrated economies of the world, and its IR are marred by an intense geopolitical rivalry between India and Pakistan, the growing economic and strategic footprint of China leading to a rivalry with India, and intermittent problems of cross-border terrorism, domestic insurgencies, and the failure of states to create institutions to regulate clandestine movement of people, contraband items, and unofficial or illegal trade across borders. The developments in Afghanistan since the Soviet invasion of 1979 have fundamentally changed the political dynamics of the western region of the subcontinent. This, together with the extraordinary involvement of the great powers in the wake of the Afghan crisis, and China's fledging military and infrastructural ties with most South Asian states, automatically dilates the geopolitical significance of the subcontinent and the concomitant dominance of realist discourses in the international affairs of the subcontinent.[9]

From a critical IR theory perspective, this reading of the subcontinent is problematic in many ways. It encourages arms race and military alliances, accentuates competitive dynamics and restrictive trade practices, and prioritizes military security over human security needs. We argue, on the contrary, that the significance of South Asia lies in its potential to tackle the challenges to the democratic process, its project of carving out a political community amidst inevitable sociocultural heterogeneity, its fight against environmental degradation and the loss of habitat for the vulnerable sections of the population, and its response to the political problems stemming out of people's urge to uplift their standards of living. In a sense, the political and anthropological duality of the subcontinent is central to how critical theory understands the interrelations of the region. From this vantage point, unless one engages with the structural contradictions of the region, the politics of transformation remains stillborn.

This draws attention to the fact that there are many ways to imagine South Asia and these imaginations affect the way its IR are described. The dominant reading is political and state-centric. It has led to the popular realist framing of the subcontinent. This is the vision held by the ruling elites of South Asia who valorize competitive nationalism, securitize borders and territory, and create the template for the national-security state. This also explains why regionalism has hobbled in South Asia. Its refusal to accommodate the "political" has resulted in a highly conservative mindset on mobility and connectivity. This view militates against the possibility of change owing to South Asia's socioeconomic, political, locational, and territory-driven predispositions to violence. Yet, South Asia has been imagined differently by civil society groups and radicals who build on shared culture, economic plights of the masses, a common hydrological, energy, and climate cartography, and the need for a political trans-formation that would assuage sovereign anxieties, allow reconciliation of communities, and invest in substantial democratization.[10]

History and Existing Tracks

The overwhelming dominance of India in South Asian affairs conditions the history of the subcontinent and it is impossible to tell a cohesive story of the place otherwise. Modern South Asia is very much a creation of British colonialism. India, Pakistan (eventually Bangladesh), and Sri Lanka were crown colonies, while Nepal, Bhutan, Afghanistan, and the Maldives were British protectorates. As David Ludden puts it, "The partition of British India resulted in a broad demolition of old cultural spaces including South Asia, the Indian Ocean coastal regions, and West, Central, and South-East Asia."[11] The colonial experience nationalized a hitherto shared cultural space, and this left South Asia permanently divided on the question of political community. All states were forced to undertake nation-building projects, and this invariably proved problematic since cultural, religious, and linguistic markers were shared across sovereign spaces. The sovereign lives of South Asian states were, therefore, doubly fraught. While states sought to achieve the ideal trinity of territory-language-people, it was evidently an impossible quest owing to extraordinary ethnic and religious diversity.

Second, the problems of domestic political communities spilled over across national bound-aries and created tensions between states. India and Pakistan have territorial disputes over Kashmir, and their national imaginations have also clashed over the relations between faith and citizenship. Bangladesh remains divided over the dual bases of its national identity—religion and language, and both ethnic and communal tensions have often permeated into the bordering Indian provinces. India-Sri Lanka relations soured over the Tamil minority question in the island, and although Colombo militarily defeated the Liberation Tigers of Tamil Eelam (LTTE) in 2009, the plight and political marginalization of the Tamils continue to mar the bilateral relations. The lack of political and cultural integration between the hills and the plains in Nepal has repeatedly drawn in India, creating political tensions and bilateral discords. Ethnic tensions have also bedeviled relations between Nepal and Bhutan from time to time and created refugees flows.[12]

A more familiar way to tell the history of South Asia is to view it through the lens of geo-politics, although it partly distorts the narrative by collapsing it into the bilateral tensions between India and Pakistan. The enmity between India and Pakistan can be explained in various ways.[13] In a nutshell, the conflict is a product of history, divergent national imagin-ations and political values, territory, power asymmetry, Pakistan's irredentism and predatory behavior, and persistence of weak institutions and hostile domestic politics, which makes it virtually impossible to build a meaningful political consensus on peace deals. At the heart of the conflict remains the territorial conflict over Kashmir, which has resulted in three wars (1948, 1965, and 1999). The two states also fought a war in 1971 over the genocide in East Pakistan that led to the creation of the new sovereign state of Bangladesh. The protracted rivalry between the two states has acquired a nuclear dimension. Four major crises—the Kargil War in 1999, the border standoff in 2001-02, the crisis following the Mumbai terror attacks in 2008, and the surgical strikes in 2016—took place under the nuclear shadow and has spawned a sizeable literature on crisis escalation or stability under deterrence.[14] Pakistan has consistently drawn in the US and China to counterbalance Indian dominance while India has generally tried to limit the influence of external powers in South Asia (except for the Treaty of Peace, Friendship and Cooperation in 1971 with the Soviet Union to balance a Pakistan-China-US military build-up against it). Since 2010, with the ascent of China, Beijing's strategic and economic footprint has steadily grown in South Asia, and while India has tried to offset this tendency, it has failed to dissuade its South Asian neighbors from warming up to China. Overall, India has dominated the subcontinent but could neither hegemonize nor lead it.

Religious extremism and terrorism have substantially influenced South Asian politics,[15] particularly after General Zia turned Pakistan into a full-fledged religious state with his backing for Wahabi Sunni fundamentalist Islam since the middle of the 1980s. The abortive Soviet invasion of Afghanistan and the disastrous American response to it ultimately brought the Taliban to power. They ruled the state from 1996 until 2001 when it was militarily removed from power by the American-led coalition forces. As the coalition troops ultimately withdrew in 2021, the Taliban reestablished their control. Taliban's success has greatly motivated and bolstered the fundamentalist Islamist forces across South Asia. While the rise of Hindu and Buddhist right-wing forces in India, Sri Lanka, and Myanmar (which remains an in-between state) have indigenous roots, the role of Islamist radicalism and terrorism also contributed handsomely to it.[16]

Political authoritarianism has grown in South Asia. India has taken a decidedly right-wing turn. Its commitment to civil liberties, secularism, and minority rights stand contested, and political institutions like the judiciary, the Election Commission, and central investigative services are under significant institutional scrutiny, much of the media and the press muzzled and bruised, and political dissent is alarmingly criminalized.[17] In Bangladesh, successive regimes have been using "state institutions for the persecution and even annihilation of opponents."[18] In Pakistan, a structural shift to right-wing Islamist politics combined with high inflation and low economic growth has created an increasingly volatile political environment, which has been further complicated by the developments in Afghanistan.[19] India and China loom large on Maldives' domestic politics. In 2021, the "India Out" campaign led by former President Yameen fueled political unrest and India interfered adroitly to neutralize it.[20] In Nepal, the old divide between factions of Maoists close to China and parties loyal to India has kept the nation politically divided, and the border dispute since 2015 has further complicated matters.[21] Political authoritarianism is on the rise in Sri Lanka, leading to a highly personalized and kinship-oriented rule. The UN Office Human Rights High Commission finds "deepening impunity, increasing militarization of governmental functions, ethno-nationalist rhetoric, and intimidation of civil society" in Sri Lanka.[22]

The subcontinent also remains divided by Sino-Indian rivalry. While Maldives, Sri Lanka, and Nepal show increasing support for Beijing's perspectives, Dhaka and Thimphu remain closer to New Delhi, even though Chinese strategic and economic influences are growing in Bhutan and Bangladesh. Pakistan's growing economic crisis has turned the security inter-dependence between Islamabad and Beijing utterly asymmetric.[23] More recently, although India, Bangladesh, and Bhutan have started recovering from the economic downturn following the pandemic, Pakistan, Nepal, and Sri Lanka face acute economic hardships, and Afghanistan is on the verge of an economic collapse.[24]

Continuity and Change

Politics and IR in South Asia have largely remained unchanged in paradigmatic terms. The subcontinent continues to demonstrate three major trends. First, nation-building in South Asia betrays the contradictions of territory and culture. Second, the geopolitical conflict between India and Pakistan, increasingly overlain by an interventionist China, sets the overall parameter of IR in South Asia. Third, the projects of democracy in South Asia remain fraught, elite-driven, and essentially ethnicized. The chapter argues that the affairs of the subcontinent are dominated by elite-driven defensive realist discourses that dilate the claims of sovereignty and fail to overcome the need for communication, open frontiers, and free movement of all factors of production. *From a critical theory perspective, this is both an affirmation and a negation.* It affirms the Coxian dictum that theories are always partisan, and the dominant groups decide the nature of politics. It is a negation inasmuch as, judging by empirical trends, there is no politically potent and discursive politics of transformation at play in South Asia. From the perspectives of Linklater and Habermas, this confirms the absence of strong deliberative guarantees to democracy and no immediate possibility of an emancipatory project of transforming the nature of political community in South Asia.

Politics of Nation-Building

The defining feature of South Asia remains its contested nation-building project. As post-colonial societies, South Asian states suffer from economic challenges, authoritarian political practices, poor human development indicators, major climate challenges, and a rather unusual anxiety over territorial control. What explains this predicament? From a critical theory stand-point, two immediate explanations are available. First, the political imagination of South Asian elites is virtually hegemonized by the Westphalian international order that builds on exclusivity, territoriality, and sovereignty.[25] Postcolonial vulnerability highlights the pangs of sovereignty, and it becomes exceedingly difficult to imagine boundaries of political community beyond the existing borders. This also explains why citizenship remains the most vulnerable political enterprise in the subcontinent and elites cannot risk upscaling no matter how constricting boundaries become.[26]

Second, nationalism in South Asia was always a paradoxical project. As Partha Chatterjee has shown, in postcolonial South Asia, the political elite accepted Western science and technology but rejected its cultural idioms, and accordingly created the dichotomy between the private/spiritual and the public/material.[27] However, and far more crucially, Western technologies of modern statecraft had socialized the elites into mapping the demographics by caste, religion, tribes, and linguistic groups, and yet at the same time, aggregate these categories into the national body. The nation was, therefore, both disaggregated and united at the same time. The gradual introduction of representative democracy politicized the enumerated communities. In British India, this sowed the seeds of Muslim fear of a Hindu majority; elsewhere, similar problems were created vis-à-vis ethnicity and language. The intrinsic problems of the nation turned political authoritarianism into a resource that the elite wielded freely and justified it by the insecurities of the state.

Geopolitics

The centrality of geopolitics in the making of modern South Asia and the meaning of security as framed by state both show remarkable continuity.[28] Geopolitics and nationalism decide how elites think of security across South Asia as a whole. This becomes, in the language of critical theory, the performativity of security—the idea that the nation is imperiled from outside unless the state guarantees the border against possible incursions which are not necessarily military. People's movements are potentially securitized in this imagination since the insecurity of the national form inheres in the inauthenticity of its culture.[29] The demographic anxiety is not merely economic; it is primarily cultural—deliberately demonizing the "other," effacing shared cultures and heightening the sense of absolute differences between "national" communities. In this imagination, adversarial neighborly relations become the very precondition of security.

This discourse has gained further legitimacy in the absence of a shared sense of security community in the subcontinent. This also explains why South Asia remains one of the least integrated regions of the world. While the relatively smaller neighbors like Bangladesh, Sri Lanka, and Nepal have often bandwagoned with India (the predominant power within the region), they have also engaged in hedging and soft balancing to counter undesirable Indian political influence by moving closer to China.[30] This automatically makes it an imperative for New Delhi to leverage every opportunity to reverse Chinese inroads in its immediate neighborhood.[31] What underlies this dynamic, however, is the way domestic politics ultimately decides the security codes amongst South Asian states. All smaller South Asian states share something in common vis-à-vis India—their politics are invariably polarized into forces favorable and hostile to India. These ties, again, are not purely political; they build on centuries of old and unshakeable cultural links. With China, the political is independent of the social; with India, in contrast, the political is constitutive of the social.

The intractable conflict between India and Pakistan, however, is the stronger explanation for the failure of regionalism in South Asia. Both Indian and Pakistani IR scholars reflect these perceptions. According to Šumit Ganguly, for instance, Pakistan is a predatory state that is unreconciled to the regional distribution of power.[32] Similarly, from a Pakistani standpoint, Moonis Ahmar attributes the conflict to security perceptions, arms build-up, and mutual suspicion which has its roots in historical legacy of the subcontinent.[33] Especially after the loss of Bangladesh in 1971, Pakistan's vulnerability and insecurity has largely been responsible for sustaining the political values of praetorianism and the reification of a national security state at all costs. Likewise, India's mistrust of Pakistan has multiplied with Islamabad's adoption of sub-conventional warfare strategies in Kashmir, primarily through aiding and abetting terror strikes, deepening of Pakistan's all-purpose relations with China, and gaining a natural strategic depth in Taliban-controlled Afghanistan. All of this has resulted in an intense security competition between the two states, their differences in national capabilities notwithstanding, and beleaguered the prospects of a transformative regionalism in South Asia.

Democracy and Authoritarianism

The constrictions of the political community and the fraught nature of regional geopolitics have not only encouraged political authoritarianism but also cast a shadow on the projects of democratization in South Asia. While the record of democratization in South Asia is mixed, there is ample evidence of majoritarianism in virtually every state.[34] This is largely a structural problem built into the nature of political community and citizenship arising out of the numerical logic of electoral democracy itself. In South Asia, over the decades, ethnic membership has become the chief determinant of democratic outcomes (I use ethnicity very broadly to include religious groups, linguistic communities, tribes, and caste groups). This is explained by a range of factors. First, ethnic groups often dictate patterns of resource allocation and control key political positions in the state thereby keeping rival communities at bay. Invariably, when they lose power to the other group, the same dynamic is perpetuated.[35] Second and relatedly, the state suffers from intense competitive bidding for benefits by groups which immediately enhances the value of group membership as a bargaining strategy encouraging group leaders to invest in the subjective awareness of the "group." Techniques of group consolidation and boundary making become central to the democratic process itself.[36]

In nearly every South Asian state, political consciousness runs along community lines. In India, despite the manifest strength of its democratic structures and practices, political identities formed along the lines of caste, religion, ethnicity, and language, which decided electoral outcomes. "The Congress system"[37] that ruled India for the most part evolved as a horizontal strategy of complex group representations that could be equilibrated from above. Over the years, a distinctive politics of recognition took hold in India, creating politicized social categories like Dalits and Other Backward Castes (OBCs), ethnic groups in the volatile northeastern states, and linguistic groups that perceived economic and political disadvantage in relative terms. With the rise of the BJP, religious affiliation has emerged as the dominant collective identity in the state, although, on closer analysis, the significance of caste mobilization and ethnic positioning remains as critical to democratic outcomes as ever.[38]

Sri Lanka evolved a parliamentary democracy that quickly succumbed to ethnic majoritarianism and pitted the weaker Tamil minorities against the deliberately discriminatory Sinhala-majority state, which resulted in the long Civil War.[39] Bangladesh, a state blessed with remarkable ethnic (linguistic) homogeneity, has also failed to normalize its democracy since the dual bases to its national identity—the Islamic lineage on one hand and the linguistic heritage on the other, have become the determinants of its polarized political culture, with the Awami League claiming a greater affinity for the linguistic heritage and the Bangladesh Nationalist Party (broadly in league with Jamat) mobilizing primarily on behalf of the Muslim nationalist identity.[40] Pakistan remains fragmented by rival ethnic identities, with the Baluch, Pushto, and Sindhi communities challenging the economic and political dominance of the Punjabis.[41] Afghanistan struggles to evolve a political identity over and above allegiance to tribal chieftains and kinship groups. The history of the state is a living testimony to its limited efficacy as ethnic groups relentlessly bargain for largesse and privilege from Kabul.[42] In Nepal, the political dynamic is divided primarily between the Hill and the Terai plains, with caste and ethnic groups like Chhetri, Bahun, Megar, Tharu, Gurung, Limbu, Newar, Rai, and Tamang, among many others, attempting to establish their control over the administrative apparatus as a way of guaranteeing more resources. Tibetan cultural heritage has powerful attractions in Bhutan that partly explains the exclusions of groups that do not "belong."[43] In many of these South Asian states, politics is not seen as sufficiently "autonomous" since India often looms large in their political outcomes. In Afghanistan, Pakistan substitutes for India. This has tended to securitize the polity itself as the continuity of regimes often takes priority over developmental needs and the security of the "nation" is articulated precisely along lines of affiliation and independence vis-à-vis the neighboring state.

There are two additional factors to consider here. First, South Asia has never been a liberal political order;[44] its ethos and constitutive norms are quintessentially communitarian in impulse.[45] While South Asia is deeply communitarian, there is no agreement in society about which community is politically relevant. This right, by default, has been arrogated by the state. Automatically, security in South Asia is collapsed into dominant statehood. South

Asian states, therefore, hold on to their sectarian geopolitical self-identities and cannot evolve a regional approach that enables them to resolve collective action problems in domains like health, ecology and environment, migration, and livelihood. From the perspective of critical theory, a solution to South Asia's long-term problems, premised on reconciliation, democracy, participation or justice, cannot even start unless the lens shifts. Will the narrative change in South Asia? Critical theory says that while the possibility of change remains, the material conditions at present are unconducive to any radical transformation of trends.

Theoretical Explanations

South Asian IR and domestic politics are inextricably intertwined. While political realism certainly explains the endurance of India-Pakistan rivalry and the alliance patterns in the subcontinent, it cannot fully account for the role of domestic variables. The argument here is that South Asia is too complex a space to allow any easy theoretical explanation and no one theory explains all the trends satisfactorily. Realism certainly is the preferred lens of the South Asian elites since there has not been any fundamental transformation in the international politics of the region. When it comes to India-Pakistan relations, this certainly holds true.[46] Political realism provides a credible explanation of what causes the conflict and the persistence of the rivalry. The conflict is explained either in terms of security dilemma or predation on the part of Pakistan. However, what is it that triggers predatory behavior on the part of Pakistan? Most studies on India-Pakistan conflict draw upon a range of deeper structural factors—the territorial dispute over and the clash of national imaginations centered on Kashmir, the historical memory of the Partition, Hindu-Muslim religious differences, to name a few. Hence, while political realism provides a powerful causal account of the conflict, it has limitations. An adequate theoretical exposition of the conflict awaits a proper accounting of for the role of identity, historical memory, and domestic politics. Critical theorists are far better placed to provide such a holistic account.

We find that South Asia's predicament goes beyond India-Pakistan rivalry and is largely the result of peculiar constructions of the political community, the insecurity of nationalism, and the persistence of the postcolonial anxiety over borders, sovereignty, and citizenship. While the behavior of the relatively smaller South Asian states can be explained in terms of balance of power, bandwagoning, hedging, hiding, and soft balancing, such descriptions tell us little about the role that domestic politics plays in conditioning such strategic choices or why nationalism and ethnic identities are securitized in the subcontinent. Monika Barthwal-Datta and Soumita Basu have rightly concluded that regional security studies on South Asia have remained fixated on elite perceptions regarding state survival and the preservation of borders, and this has tied most academic analysis to the level of the state, severely neglecting alternative possibilities, actors, social forces, and practices.[47] South Asian politics, domestic and international, require coming to terms with its postcolonial anxieties and problems of nation-building, and exploring the politics of transformation.

Conclusion

Our forecast for the region is rather bleak, both in terms of empirics and theory. With China's increasing involvement and aggressive posturing in the region, the competitive dynamics will trump the cooperative possibilities. India has little option but to balance China more actively near home. This will intensify Pakistan's security dilemma and will encourage it to try altering the status quo in the region by taking calibrated risks. The Talibanization of Afghanistan would impact political trends across South Asia negatively by invigorating radical fundamentalist forces in different states. The economic crisis in Afghanistan and Pakistan makes the situation potentially even more explosive as unemployed, radicalized youth in large numbers would be motivated to join terror organizations. This can adversely affect the situation in the Kashmir Valley where, despite the massive political changes ushered in by the present political dispensation in India, a groundswell of support exists for radical Islam. The withdrawal of the US from Afghanistan and its declining ties with Pakistan would worsen the situation in the region as Islamabad would have little restraint in its strategic choices. Further, the domestic political trends are also not encouraging in the subcontinent and a quick reversal is unlikely. Political polarization and authoritarianism are growing and the prospects of reviving liberal policies remain bleak. Finally, the ongoing pandemic has caused a significant economic slowdown in South Asia. Protracted economic crises may either encourage ultra-nationalist elements or force states to explore economic regionalism seriously. This, however, would not be easy. Regionalism has collapsed in the last decade due to the deterioration in India-Pakistan relations, infrastructural bottlenecks, the emergence of the PRC's Belt and Road Initiative (BRI) as an alternative, and little economic incentives amongst the stakeholders. State-led regionalism has little prospects of success in the region for political and historical reasons. However, a revamped regionalism that would include private actors and civil society groups might prove to be a game changer. With the deepening of the economic crisis, states may ultimately be forced to entertain this possibility seriously.

Realists argue that South Asia is a fraught subcontinent with the geopolitical confrontation between India and Pakistan, increasingly affected by China's growing footprints. Moreover, India has had varied problems with all its South Asian neighbors. South Asia, in a nutshell, remains a contested space, where divergent notions of politics, cultural imaginations and fundamental economic divisions convulse all states from time to time. Realists see no possibility of South Asia escaping from this cycle of gloom. Liberalism never took root in the region and India's right-wing shift since 2014 has made it even more unattractive as a paradigm for politics at large. The domestic-international intertwining makes constructivism and critical theory meaningful theoretical vantage points, since there are multiple imaginations of South Asia that indicate the possibilities of transformation at least in conceptual terms.

Can South Asia achieve turnaround any time soon? Can meaningful economic, political, and security integration happen here under conditions of plurality and diversity? From a critical theory standpoint, we argue that such a transformation is challenging but not impossible to achieve. First, the region must come to terms with its formative dissonance between the logic of sovereignty and culture. Second, nationalism needs to mature so that domestic challenges are not conflated into international disputes as it often happens in South Asia. Third, South Asia's IR need to be thoroughly democratized. Realists may have won the day so far. The future may well be with critical theory.

Notes

1 In the words of Sudipta Kaviraj, "South Asia emerged in the 1950-60s as an academic-governmental term of American coinage designating a spatial area of concern for American strategy and foreign policy. This was a typical external term: i.e. a term by which outsiders designated a territory for purposes significant to them, but devoid of any affective significance for its inhabitants." See Sudipta Kaviraj, "A Strange Love of the Land: Identity, Poetry and Politics in the (Un)making of South Asia," *South Asia Multidisciplinary Academic Journal* 10 (2014): 1.
2 For details, see Kaviraj, "A Strange Love," 1–4. Also, see Shibashis Chatterjee, *India's Spatial Imaginations of South Asia: Power, Commerce, and Community* (New Delhi: Oxford University Press, 2018), Chapter 1.

Critical Theory Approaches

3 William Wohlforth, "Realism," in *The Oxford Handbook of International Relations*, eds. Christian Reus-Smit and Duncan Snidal (Oxford: Oxford University Press, 2008), 132–133.

4 Michael W. Doyle, "Liberalism and World Politics," *American Political Science Review* 80, no. 4 (December 1986): 1151–1169.

5 Alexander Wendt, *Social Theory of International Politics* (Cambridge: Cambridge University Press, 1999).

6 Robert W. Cox and Timothy J. Sinclair, *Approaches to World Order* (Cambridge: Cambridge University Press, 1996).

7 For an excellent survey, see Jurgen Haacke, "Theory and Praxis in International Relations: Habermas, Self-reflection, Rational Argumentation," *Millennium Journal of International Studies* 25, no. 2 (1996): 255–289.

8 See Andrew Linklater, *Men and Citizens in the Theory of International Relations* (London: Macmillan, 1990) and *Beyond Realism and Marxism: Critical Theory and International Relations* (London: Macmillan, 1989).

9 Sandy Gordon explains why South Asia captivates global attention for reasons both good and bad. South Asia's "poverty and instability" causes a substantial drain on global collective resources and development assistance and contributes to regional dissonance that "washes back and forward across borders, feeding from internal instability and in turn contributing to international tension" (Gordon 2012: 53). Yet, South Asia is economically attractive for its "labour-intensive manufacturing potential," proximity to energy resources, and the centrality of the Indian economy and its control of the sea-lanes for massive energy flows critical to China's economic rise. Sandy Gordon, "Why South Asia Matters in World Affairs," *Policy* 28, no. 1 (Autumn 2012): 53–54.

10 Aminah Mohammad-Arif, "Introduction. Imaginations and Constructions of South Asia: An Enchanting Abstraction?" *South Asia Multidisciplinary Academic Journal* 10 (2014): 15. Chaturvedi and Tripathi write, "This dichotomy of strength and weakness, security and insecurity, hope and fear with connections and disconnects is a remarkable, if not unusual, feature of South Asia and gives birth to borders and boundaries with different kinds of territoriality." Dhananjay Tripathi and Sanjay Chaturvedi, "South Asia: Boundaries, Borders and Beyond," *Journal of Borderlands Studies* 35, no. 2 (2020): 173.

11 David Ludden, *India and South Asia: A Short History* (Short Histories) (Oxford: Oneworld Publications, 2013). Kindle Edition.

12 For the Nepalese refugee crisis in Bhutan, see Rosalind Evans, "The Perils of Being a Borderland People: On the Lhotshampas of Bhutan," *Contemporary South Asia* 18, no. 1 (2010): 25–42.

13 Šumit Ganguly, *Deadly Impasse: Indo-Pakistani Relations at the Dawn of a New Century* (New York: Cambridge University Press, 2016). Atul Mishra, *Sovereign Lives of India and Pakistan: Post-partition Statehood in South Asia* (New Delhi: Oxford University Press, 2021).

14 Karthika Sasikumar, "India-Pakistan Crises under the Nuclear Shadow: The Role of Reassurance," *Journal for Peace and Nuclear Disarmament* 2, no. 1 (2019): 151–169.

15 Atul Mishra, *Sovereign Lives of India and Pakistan: Post-partition Statehood in South Asia* (New Delhi: Oxford University Press, 2021).

16 See the essays in Imran Ahmed, et al., eds., *Religion, Extremism and Violence in South Asia* (London: Palgrave Macmillan, 2022).

17 Christophe Jaffrelot, *Modi's India: Hindu Nationalism and the Rise of Ethnic Democracy* (Princeton N.J.: Princeton University Press, 2021).

18 Ali Riaz, "Three Issues at Centre of Bangladesh Politics," *New Age*, February 17, 2022, https://www.newagebd.net/article/157461/three-issues-at-centre-of-bangladesh-politics.

19 Uzair Younus, "Pakistan's Shifting Political and Economic Winds," United States Institute of Peace, October 27, 2021, https://www.usip.org/publications/2021/10/pakistans-shifting-political-and-economic-winds.

20 Rangoli Mitra, "The China–India Cold War in Maldives," *The Diplomat*, January 19, 2022, https://thediplomat.com/2022/01/the-china-india-cold-war-in-maldives/.

21 Peter Gill, "Nepal's Democracy in Crisis," *The Diplomat*, February 6, 2021, https://thediplomat.com/2021/02/nepals-democracy-in-crisis/. Also, Santosh Sharma Poudel, "India–Nepal Territorial Dispute Flares up Again," *The Diplomat*, February 9, 2022, https://thediplomat.com/2022/02/india-nepal-territorial-dispute-flares-up-again/.

22 UNHCR, "Promotion Reconciliation, Accountability and Human Rights in Sri Lanka," Report of the Office of the High Commissioner for Human Rights, A/HRC/46/20, January 27, 2021, https://www.ohchr.org/Documents/Countries/LK/Sri_LankaReportJan2021.docx.

23 Tara Kartha, "Pakistan is Sinking into its Own Jihadi Strategy – 2022 Will be No Different," *ThePrint*, January 3, 2022, https://theprint.in/opinion/pakistan-sinking-into-jihadi-strategy-2022-no-different/793130/.

24 See the various World Bank Country Overviews.

25 Ranabir Samaddar, "The Failed Dialectic of Territoriality and Security, and the Imperatives of Dialogue," *International Studies* 35, no. 1 (1998): 107–122.

26 Shibashis Chatterjee and Udayan Das, "Refugees in South Asia: Political Membership, Nation-Building Projects and Securitisation of Human Flows," in *Internal Migration Within South Asia*, ed. Ujjaini Mukhopadhyay (Springer, Singapore, 2022), 27–49.

27 Partha Chatterjee, *The Nation and Its Fragments* (Princeton N.J: Princeton University Press, 2020).

28 Shibashis Chatterjee, "Deconstruction and Double Reading of the South Asian Security Order," in *International Relations Theory and South Asia 2*, ed. E. Sridharan (New Delhi: Oxford University Press, 2011), 318–327.

29 For an intriguing analysis, see Ashis Nandy, "The Idea of South Asia: A Personal Note on Post-Bandung Blues," *Inter-Asia Cultural Studies* 6, no. 4 (2005): 541–545.

30 E. Sridharan, "India and South Asia: From Balancing to Bandwagoning?," *India in Transition*, October 24, 2011, https://casi.sas.upenn.edu/iit/essridharan.

31 Tanvi Madan, "Major Power Rivalry in South Asia," Discussion Paper Series on Managing Global Disorder No. 6, October, 2021, https://www.cfr.org/report/major-power-rivalry-south-asia.

32 Ganguly, *Deadly Impasse*, 19–21.

33 Moonis Ahmar, "Security Perceptions in the Indo-Pakistan Relationship," *Pakistan Horizon* 37, no. 1 (1984): 100–119.

34 See the various essays in Sten Widwalm, *Routledge Handbook of Autocratization in South Asia* (London: Routledge, 2021).

35 Shibashis Chatterjee and Sulagna Maitra, "Identity, Conflicts and Security," in *Peace and Conflict Studies: Perspectives from South Asia*, eds. Anindya Jyoti Majumdar and Shibashis Chatterjee (London: Taylor & Francis, 2020), 112.

36 Chatterjee and Sulagna Maitra, *Identity, Conflicts and Security*, 113.

37 The Indian political scientist, Rajini Kothari, developed the idea of the "Congress System," which denoted "a well-oiled party machinery, party-government interlinkage, and the facilitative factors" that sustained the "system." Ritabrata Chakraborty, "An Enduring System," *The Telegraph* (Kolkata), October 12, 2021, https://www.telegraphindia.com/opinion/an-enduring-congress-system/cid/1834303. The "Congress system" denoted a flexible political space that allowed variegated interests broadly committed to nationalism and secularism to cohabit, a kind of a political "thermostat" as Kothari described it. In Kothari's words, "In the Indian system, however, where a strong and potentially monolithic party must provide its own correctives to its power if it is to function democratically, the positive role of the party organization becomes a necessity." Rajni Kothari, "The Congress 'System' in India," *Asian Survey* 4, no. 12 (1964): 1172.

38 John Harriss, "Political Change, Political Structure, and the Indian State since Independence," in *Routledge Handbook of South Asian Politics*, ed. Paul R. Brass (London and New York: Routledge, 2010), 274–290.

39 Ahilan Kadirgamar, "Polarization, civil war, and persistent majoritarianism in Sri Lanka. Political polarization in south and Southeast Asia: Old divisions, new dangers," Carnegie Endowment for International Peace, 2020, https://carnegieendowment.org/2020/08/18/polarization-civil-war-and-persistent-majoritarianism-in-sri-lanka-pub-82437. Also, Jayadeva Uyangoda, "Ethnic Politics in Sri Lanka: Changing Dynamics," *Policy Studies* no. 32 (2007), https://www.eastwestcenter.org/system/tdf/private/PS032.pdf?file=1&type=node&id=32178.

40 Akhand Akhtar Hossain, "Islamic Resurgence in Bangladesh's Culture and Politics: Origins, Dynamics and Implications," *Journal of Islamic Studies* 23, no. 2 (2012): 165–198.

41 Veena Kukreja, "Ethnic Diversity, Political Aspirations and State Response: A Case Study of Pakistan," *Indian Journal of Public Administration* 66, no. 1 (2020): 28–42.

42 James F. Dobbins, *After the Taliban: Nation-building in Afghanistan* (Washington D.C: Potomac Books, Inc., 2008).

43 Mona Chetri, *Ethnicity and Democracy in Eastern Indian Borderland* (Amsterdam: Amsterdam University Press, 2017). Also, Prashant Jha, *Battles of the New Republic: A Contemporary History of Nepal* (Oxford: Oxford University Press, 2014).

Critical Theory Approaches

44 Bhumitra Chakma, "Liberal Peace and South Asia," *India Quarterly* 70, no. 3 (2014): 187–205, https://doi.org/10.1177%2F0974928414535290.
45 Chatterjee and Das, "Refugees," 33–35.
46 Ganguly, *Deadly Impasse*, 19–27; Thazha V. Paul, "Why has the India-Pakistan Rivalry Been So Enduring? Power Asymmetry and an Intractable Conflict," *Security Studies* 15, no. 4 (2006): 600–630.
47 Monika Barthwal-Datta and Soumita Basu, "Reconceptualizing Regional Security in South Asia: A Critical Security Approach," *Security Dialogue* 48, no. 5 (2017): 395.

Bibliography

Ahmar, Moonis. "Security Perceptions in the Indo-Pakistan Relationship." *Pakistan Horizon* 37, no. 1 (1984): 100–119. http://www.jstor.org/stable/41403911.

Ahmed, Imran, Shahab Zahid, Brasted Howard, and Akbarzadeh Shahram (Eds.). *Religion, Extremism and Violence in South Asia.* London: Palgrave Macmillan, 2022.

AkhtarHossain, Akhand. "Islamic Resurgence in Bangladesh's Culture and Politics: Origins, Dynamics and Implications." *Journal of Islamic Studies* 23, no. 2 (2012): 165–198.

Barthwal-Datta, Monika, and Soumita Basu. "Reconceptualizing Regional Security in South Asia: A Critical Security Approach." *Security Dialogue* 48, no. 5 (2017): 393–409.

Chakma, Bhumitra. "Liberal Peace and South Asia." *India Quarterly* 70, no. 3 (2014): 187–205. https://doi.org/10.1177%2F0974928414535290.

Chakraborty, Ritabrata. "An enduring system." *The Telegraph* (Kolkata), October 12, 2021. https://www.telegraphindia.com/opinion/an-enduring-congress-system/cid/1834303.

Champakalakshmi, R., Stanley A. Wolpert, Muzaffar Alam, T.G. Percival Spear, Frank Raymond Allchin, Joseph E. Schwartzberg, Philip B. Calkins, Romila Thapar, Sanjay Subrahmanyam, K.R. Dikshit, and A.L. Srivastava. "India". Encyclopaedia Britannica, February 2, 2022, https://www.britannica.com/place/India [Accessed 2 February 2022].

Chatterjee, Partha. *The Nation and Its Fragments.* Princeton, N.J: Princeton University Press, 2020.

Chatterjee, Shibashis. *India's Spatial Imaginations of South Asia: Power, Commerce, and Community.* New Delhi: Oxford University Press, 2018.

Chatterjee, Shibashis, and Udayan Das. "Refugees in South Asia: Political Membership, Nation-Building Projects and Securitisation of Human Flows." In *Internal Migration Within South Asia*, edited by Ujjaini Mukhopadhyay, 27–49. Singapore: Springer, 2022.

Chatterjee, Shibashis, and Sulagna Maitra. "Identity, Conflicts and Security." In *Peace and Conflict Studies: Perspectives from South Asia*, edited by Anindya Jyoti Majumdar, and Shibashis Chatterjee, 95–119. London: Taylor & Francis, 2020.

Chetri, Mona. *Ethnicity and Democracy in Eastern Indian Borderland.* Amsterdam: Amsterdam University Press, 2017.

Cox, Robert, W., and Sinclair, Timothy J. *Approaches to World Order.* Cambridge: Cambridge University Press, 1996.

Destradi, Sandra. "India and Sri Lanka's Civil War: The Failure of Regional Conflict Management in South Asia." *Asian Survey* 52, no. 3 (2012): 595–616.

Dobbins, James F. *After the Taliban: Nation-Building in Afghanistan.* Washington D.C: Potomac Books, Inc, 2008.

Doyle, Michael W. "Liberalism and World Politics." *American Political Science Review* 80, no. 4 (December 1986): 1151–1169.

Evans, Rosalind. "The Perils of Being a Borderland People: On the Lhotshampas of Bhutan." *Contemporary South Asia* 18, no. 1 (2010): 25–42.

Ganguly, Šumit. *Deadly Impasse: Indo-Pakistani Relations at the Dawn of a New Century.* New York: Cambridge University Press, 2016.

Gill, Peter. "Nepal's Democracy in Crisis." *The Diplomat*, February 6, 2021. https://thediplomat.com/2021/02/nepals-democracy-in-crisis/.

Gordon, Sandy. "Why South Asia Matters in World Affairs." *Policy* 28, no.1 (Autumn 2012): 53–56.

Gostoli, Ylenia. "Is a New Draft Law in the Maldives Aimed at Muzzling Criticism of India?" *TRT World*, February 4, 2022. https://www.trtworld.com/magazine/is-a-new-draft-law-in-the-maldives-aimed-at-muzzling-criticism-of-india-54390.

Haacke, Jurgen. "Theory and Praxis in International Relations: Habermas, Self-Reflection, Rational Argumentation." *Millennium Journal of International Studies* 25, no. 2 (1996): 255–289.

Harriss, John. "Political Change, Political Structure, and the Indian State Since Independence." In *Routledge Handbook of South Asian Politics*, edited by Paul R. Brass, 274–290. London and New York: Routledge. 2010.https://www.eastwestcenter.org/system/tdf/private/PS032.pdf?file=1&type=node&id=32178.

Jaffrelot, Christophe. *Modi's India: Hindu Nationalism and the Rise of Ethnic Democracy.* Princeton N.J: Princeton University Press, 2021.

Jha, Prashant. *Battles of the New Republic: A Contemporary History of Nepal.* Oxford: Oxford University Press, 2014.

Kadirgamar, Ahilan. "Polarization, civil war, and persistent majoritarianism in Sri Lanka. Political polarization in south and Southeast Asia: Old divisions, new dangers." Carnegie Endowment for International Peace, 2020. https://carnegieendowment.org/2020/08/18/polarization-civil-war-and-persistent-majoritarianism-in-sri-lanka-pub-82437.

Kaviraj, Sudipta. "A Strange Love of the Land: Identity, Poetry and Politics in the (un) Making of South Asia." *South Asia Multidisciplinary Academic Journal* 10 (2014): 1–16. http://journals.openedition.org/samaj/3756.

Kothari, Rajni. "The Congress 'System' in India." *Asian Survey* 4, no. 12 (1964): 1161–1173. https://doi.org/10.2307/2642550.

Kukreja, Veena. "Ethnic Diversity, Political Aspirations and State Response: A Case Study of Pakistan." *Indian Journal of Public Administration* 66, no. 1 (2020): 28–42.

Linklater, Andrew. *Beyond Realism and Marxism: Critical Theory and International Relations.* London: Macmillan, 1990.

Linklater, Andrew. *Men and Citizens in the Theory of International Relations.* London: Macmillan, 1990.

Ludden, David. *India and South Asia: A Short History (Short Histories).* Kindle ed. Oxford: Oneworld Publications, 2013.

Madan, Tanvi. "Major Power Rivalry in South Asia." Discussion Paper Series on Managing Global Disorder No. 6, October, 2021. https://www.cfr.org/report/major-power-rivalry-south-asia.

Mishra, Atul. "In South Asia, the Politics of Religious Extremism." *Hindustan Times*, November 4, 2021. https://www.hindustantimes.com/opinion/in-south-asia-the-politics-of-religious-extremism-101635928797317.html.

Mishra, Atul. *Sovereign Lives of India and Pakistan: Post-Partition Statehood in South Asia.* New Delhi: Oxford University Press, 2021.

Paul, Thazha V. "Why Has the India-Pakistan Rivalry Been so Enduring? Power Asymmetry and an Intractable Conflict." *Security Studies* 15, no. 4 (2006): 600–630.

Poudel, Santosh Sharma. "India-Nepal Territorial Dispute Flares up Again." *The Diplomat*, February 9, 2022. https://thediplomat.com/2022/02/india-nepal-territorial-dispute-flares-up-again/.

Riaz, Ali. "Three Issues at the Centre of Bangladesh Politics." *New Age*, February 17, 2022. https://www.newagebd.net/article/157461/three-issues-at-centre-of-bangladesh-politics.

Samaddar, Ranabir. "The Failed Dialectic of Territoriality and Security, and the Imperatives of Dialogue." *International Studies* 35, no. 1 (1998): 107–122.

Mitra, Rangoli. "The China-India Cold War in Maldives." *The Diplomat*, January 19, 2022. https://thediplomat.com/2022/01/the-china-india-cold-war-in-maldives/.

Sridharan, E. "India and South Asia: From Balancing to Bandwagoning?" October 24, 2011. https://casi.sas.upenn.edu/iit/essridharan.

The World Bank. "Bangladesh Overview: Development news, research, data." World Bank Bangladesh Overview. Last modified October 3, 2021. https://www.worldbank.org/en/country/bangladesh/overview#1.

The World Bank. "India Overview: Development news, research, data." World Bank India Overview. Last modified October 4, 2021. https://www.worldbank.org/en/country/india/overview#1.

The World Bank. "Nepal Overview: Development news, research, data." World Bank Nepal Overview. Last modified October 7, 2021. https://www.worldbank.org/en/country/nepal/overview#1.

The World Bank. "Pakistan Overview: Development news, research, data." World Bank Pakistan Overview. Last modified October 6, 2021. https://www.worldbank.org/en/country/pakistan/overview#1.

The World Bank. "South Asia Overview: Development news, research, data." World Bank South Asia Overview. Last modified October 6, 2021. https://www.worldbank.org/en/region/sar/overview#1.

The World Bank. "Sri Lanka Overview: Development news, research, data." World Bank Sri Lanka Overview. Last modified October 7, 2021. https://www.worldbank.org/en/country/srilanka/overview#1.

Tripathi, Dhananjay, and Sanjay Chaturvedi. "South Asia: Boundaries, Borders and Beyond." *Journal of Borderlands Studies* 35, no. 2 (2020): 173–181.

Uyangoda, Jayadeva. "Ethnic Politics in Sri Lanka: Changing Dynamics." East – West Center, *Policy Studies* No. 32, 2007.

Wendt, Alexander. *Social Theory of International Politics*. First ed. Cambridge: Cambridge University Press, 1999.

Widwalm, Sten. *Routledge Handbook of Autocratization in South Asia*. London: Routledge, 2021.

Wohlforth, William. "Realism." In *The Oxford Handbook of International Relations*, edited by Christian Reus-Smit, and Duncan Snidal, 132–149. Oxford: Oxford University Press, 2008.

Younus, Uzair. "Pakistan's Shifting Political and Economic Winds." United States Institute of Peace, October 27, 2021. https://www.usip.org/publications/2021/10/pakistans-shifting-political-and-economic-winds.

PART II

TRADITIONAL AND EMERGING SECURITY ISSUES IN SOUTH ASIA

5
INDIAN STRATEGIC CULTURE

Rajesh Basrur

Introduction

A thorough exploration of India's foreign policy requires that we recognize the ways in which it conforms to the broadly predictable patterns of all states that theoretical paradigms highlight, but also the ways in which it exhibits unique elements peculiar to it. In general, India does display a substantial number of foreign policy behaviors that are readily identifiable as realist, such as military preparedness for optimizing national security and the prioritization of national interests over collective interests, which is visible in its policies on international trade and climate change. But most states do this as best as they can. Hence, it is not particularly helpful to think of a realist or realpolitik approach as a special characteristic of Indian strategy except to correct analytical errors that argue to the contrary. The study of Indian strategic culture needs to focus on those elements of India's foreign policy thinking and behavior that are both *distinctive* in relation to theoretical expectations and *sustained* over time.

The concept of strategic culture occupies a significant place among international relations scholars.[1] It is succinctly defined by one of its early contemporary exponents, Colin Gray, as "the socially constructed and transmitted assumptions, habits of mind, traditions, and preferred methods of operation—that is, behavior—that are more or less specific to a particular geographically based security community."[2] This remains the essence of strategic culture even as it has evolved over time to reflect refinements relating to continuity and change,[3] the significance of domestic politics,[4] and the behavior patterns of an ever widening assortment of states.[5] One area I try to refine is with respect to change. While some aspects of strategic culture do change—either over time or owing to shock—others remain unchanging (as I show below). I classify these as "Mutable" and "Deep" Strategic Culture respectively.

Theoretically, strategic culture can be accommodated within diverse school of international relations theory. Liberal theories focus on subsystemic levels of analysis,[6] classical realism and neoclassical realism (but not neorealism) do the same,[7] and constructivism is rooted in the power of ideas.[8] Hence, debates over the place of strategic culture in scholarly analysis are at least bridgeable,[9] if not superficial.

There is also a considerable literature on strategic culture with respect to India.[10] As is evident from the works cited here, there is much variety in this scholarship, which encompasses diverse time frames from the *longue durée* to post-independence history and spans the strategic,

DOI: 10.4324/9781003246626-8

economic, and other domains. A number of studies explore similar policy territory[11] without necessarily dwelling on strategic culture *per se*. Some of the features of Indian strategic culture identified are a realist predisposition since ancient times, an idealist bent in the first decades of the postcolonial era, a defensive mindset, and a tendency to neglect strategic planning.

In the pages that follow, I focus on three aspects of Indian strategic culture. First, I examine the definition, including some distortions, in the conceptualization of strategic culture in writings about India. Second, I try and introduce greater clarity about change and continuity in the analysis of independent India's external history. I first identify issues that fall under Mutable Strategic Culture, which is sustained over considerable periods of time, but is subject to change. I then turn to Deep Strategic Culture, which I argue is unchanging in the long term.

Myths and Clarifications

It is important first to contest a myth that drew much attention and even approval in early writings about Indian strategic culture. Some writers conflate societal culture and strategic culture. While in principle there is room for identifying the societal roots of strategic culture, it is important to be clear that societal-cultural attributes do not necessarily generate strategy, and at the same time, strategy may or may not be rooted in cultural life. A case in point is George Tanham's crude generalization about the world view of Indians and its alleged effects on strategic thinking:

> The acceptance of life as a mystery and the inability to manipulate events impedes preparation for the future in all areas of life, including the strategic. The Indian belief in life cycles and repetitions, in particular, limits planning in the Western sense.[12]

Similarly, Sandy Gordon makes the sweeping and untenable generalization that the caste system in India produces a "propensity towards compartmentalization and exclusivity" that militates against planning.[13] These and other errors built on ignorance of Indian history have been pointed out elsewhere.[14] Their persistence reflects a deeper problem. That such distorted perspectives should be taken seriously at all reflects the weak conceptualization of strategic culture in India. Fortunately, recent scholarship has been less prone to facile generalizations. It bears repetition, nevertheless, that a nation's strategic culture is fundamentally a pattern of preferences both in thinking and in policy action that shapes the making of foreign policy. This may or may not have something to do with societal culture. Importantly, a critique of strategic culture should not be expressed as an *absence* of strategic culture, as is periodically asserted.[15] All states, for better or worse, have a strategic culture, i.e. a pattern of thinking and acting in a strategic context, even if it is suboptimal. What critics who say this clearly mean is the (alleged) absence of a culture of strategic thinking and planning. This too is problematic as a meaningful generalization over time, but at least has the merit of being definitionally clear.

A second aspect of strategic culture that needs to be borne in mind is the frequent reference to realism and realpolitik that we find in the literature.[16] This does not always illuminate the concept very well since a realist approach is commonplace in relations between states. Still, if substantial evidence is available to show a *lack* of realism over time, then identifying a shift to realism might be useful in order to show the reorientation of strategic culture. I will discuss this point further below and show that realism has been more pervasive in post-independence India's strategic behavior than is commonly thought, which undercuts claims about India's shift to realism and pragmatism in the 1990s.

This brings up the question of continuity and change. While some scholars have focused on changes in strategic culture, mainly arising from some sort of shock (see endnote 3), the literature for the most part emphasizes continuity. But it is important to recognize that strategic culture is not immutable. On the contrary, changes may appear suddenly or incrementally, as will be shown below. The point is to bear in mind that strategic culture is not impervious to change, but that, even where it does undergo alteration, it generally influences policy by acting as a constraint on state behavior.

Contemporary Indian Strategic Culture: A Second Look

The focus in this chapter is on post-independence strategic culture. Longer-term assessments have certainly been made, but these are hard to sustain without meticulously accumulated and consistent evidence from Indian history, which is difficult to do. For instance, the notion that Indian elites have a defensive mindset has little empirical basis given the history of conquests in South Asia and beyond by Indian rulers. Besides, as mentioned above, the contention that Indian strategic thinking has been permeated by a tradition of realpolitik dating back to ancient times, including the ideas of Kautilya, is interesting, but not particularly enlightening since realist strategy is commonplace in the history of *all* states. It is more useful to try and gauge (a) how strategic culture produces a behavior pattern that is different from standard theoretical expectations, and (b) how strategic culture itself is affected by—and responds to—pressures for change.

The main focus of scholars with respect to foundational change in contemporary India's foreign policy preferences centers on the 1990s, when three major policy shifts occurred. Two of them resulted from exogenous shock. First, the end of the Cold War rendered the centerpiece of Indian foreign policy—the Nonaligned Movement (NAM)—outmoded and propelled India to reframe its strategic orientation from being wary of the major powers, especially the United States, to building strong linkages with them. Second, the onset of a severe balance-of-payments crisis forced Indian policymakers to rethink their commitment to a policy of autarky held dear since independence and look to integrate the country with the global economy. And third, growing pressure from nuclear-armed adversaries as well as the nonproliferation regime triggered a series of nuclear tests in 1998, which reflected a shift from reluctant to affirmative nuclearization. Taken together, these changes are often said to have marked a paradigm shift in India's strategic culture from a moralist to a more realist one.[17] To a substantial degree, though realist elements of foreign policy in the first postcolonial decades under Nehru and especially Indira Gandhi have been widely recognized, this is true. But a more careful look shows we need to qualify this view.

During the period when India stressed the centrality of principles such as decolonization, disarmament, and equity in economic relations, it did so primarily in the context of its relationship with the global power structure. At the regional level, its approach was a much more hard-headed realist one. To clarify this, it is helpful to examine the broad policy orientations that states tend to adopt within a broad realist framework.[18] Strong states tend to leverage their power advantages vis-à-vis smaller ones, while weak ones try to offset these. The former prefer to negotiate disputes bilaterally, seek closer economic linkages with weak interlocutors, and periodically employ—or threaten to employ—coercive material power in the pursuit of strategic objectives. The latter tend to do the opposite: Seek strength in numbers by taking disputes to multilateral forums, adopt moat-building strategies to try and keep the economic power and cultural intrusiveness of big powers at bay, and try to resist big powers' intervention by means of balancing, both internal (building their own strength) and external (drawing on others' strength through alliances or like arrangements).

In the South Asian region, postcolonial India exhibited all the strong-state behaviors listed above.[19] First, it insisted on negotiating its disputes with Bangladesh, Nepal, and Pakistan bilaterally. Second, it welcomed economic closeness with its small neighbors (notably, all except landlocked Bhutan and Nepal have low levels of trade with it). And third, it repeatedly projected coercive power in its neighborhood, including the breakup of Pakistan in 1971, unwelcome military intervention in Sri Lanka in 1987, and the virtual blockading of Nepal in 1989.

At the global level, India demanded systemic change in world politics and employed the language of principle, but its actual behavior was typical of all weak states. It minimized its relations with the United States and leaned on the United Nations and on NAM and the Group of 77 developing nations (G77); kept the global economy at arm's length; and steadily built up its military capacities with help from the Soviet Union (though shying away from an alliance). Regardless of the language of Indian diplomacy, India's strategic orientation was fundamentally in accord with realist expectations and varied with its relative position in differing international contexts. It follows that, notwithstanding the postcolonial emphasis on principles for changing the world, the foundations of Indian strategic thinking and behavior have always been realist.

This brings us back to the problem of definition. First, much that is said to constitute contemporary Indian strategic culture, particularly the supposed novelty of its pragmatism, is illusory. To be meaningful, the term strategic culture must identify patterns that constitute a *departure* from theoretically expected uniformity. Second, and more important, while the changes identified by scholars are indeed correct, the question of a change in strategic culture needs to be considered in a more nuanced way than has hitherto been the case. One way of doing this is to posit a "deep" strategic culture—a deeply embedded ideational structure—that persists even as day-to-day habits of thought and action are altered. How exactly a deep strategic culture is to be defined is tricky, perhaps tautological since it is a recognition that is *post facto* (a long-term attribute is deep until it is not!). But it nevertheless facilitates our ability to explain and anticipate critically important aspects of Indian strategic behavior.

Accordingly, in the discussion that follows, I shall attempt to gauge critically important facets of Indian strategic thinking and practice that can be classified as (a) "Level 2 Strategic Culture" or strategic culture in the ordinarily used sense of the term, which is sustained over considerable time frames measurable in decades, but is also subject to change; and (b) "Deep Strategic Culture" or those patterns that are sustained unchanged over a long period of time (in the present context, since independence) irrespective of changing circumstance and shifts in level 2 strategic culture.

Level 2 Strategic Culture

Though this level of strategic culture is subject to change, it is not malleable, but retains a significant measure of resistance to change under much pressure. It is liable to collapse or be transformed if subject to shock. But it is also subject to incremental pressure over time that, while enabling it to resist change better, can nevertheless reach a tipping point leading to its disintegration.

Intervention and Employment of Force

There has been some discussion over the kind of state that India is likely to become as its material power grows. Will it behave like other major powers have historically and project its military force in the self-interested pursuit of "order"? A leading Indian analyst puts it bluntly:

> As India rises on the world stage, its interests become global and it is called on to contribute to regional and international peace and security, the real question before India is not whether to intervene, but when, where and how.[20]

From independence in 1947 till the late 1980s, India did use force from time to time in its neighborhood, ousting the Portuguese from Goa in 1961, fostering the breaking away of Bangladesh from Pakistan in 1971, averting a coup in the Seychelles in 1986, sending an uninvited peacekeeping force into Sri Lanka in 1987, and defeating a brief coup in the Maldives in 1988. Arguably, this was a strategic culture of forceful intervention that came to the foreground periodically over four decades.

But since the last event, India has followed instead an opposite policy of strategic restraint and refrained from military intervention even when invited. It ignored Sri Lanka's call for military assistance against the Tamil Tigers in 2000, declined an American invitation to deploy a peacekeeping force in Iraq in 2003, weighed the possibility of—but refrained from—military action in or even extending substantial assistance to an Afghanistan torn by civil war in the 2000s, gave no more than limited military support to Sri Lanka's government in the final phase of its civil war (2006–09), ignored a call for intervention from the Maldives (2012), and subsequently rejected domestic demands for military intervention to pressurize an unfriendly Maldivian government.[21]

Clearly, there is a case for the argument that, contrary to realist expectations, India has exhibited a shift in its strategic culture from military intervention (the first four decades after independence) to non-intervention (the three decades from 1990). The reasons for this shift have yet to be examined in depth. Possible explanations include the lessons of the failed Sri Lanka intervention in 1987 and, more broadly, a new confidence arising from economic growth and expanded military capability, including the crossing of the nuclear threshold, which regards intervention as unnecessary.

Nuclear Restraint

A somewhat different case is that of Indian nuclear strategy. After independence, there was a constant thread of nuclear reluctance that produced what was viewed as a strategic culture of nuclear restraint.[22] The use of "strategic culture" to label Indian thought and practice is appropriate because the whole process of acquiring nuclear weapons capability was marked by a deviation from the expectations of realist analysis. Despite Prime Minister Jawaharlal Nehru's moral reservations about nuclear weapons, India had strong incentives for going nuclear when India suffered a serious military defeat at the hands of China in 1962, followed by China's first nuclear test two years later. Yet Nehru and his successors adhered to a policy of restraint: Research and development aimed at acquiring nuclear capability proceeded incrementally; Indira Gandhi authorized a single test in 1974, but eschewed an active weapons program thereafter; Rajiv Gandhi ordered assembling of the bomb in the late 1980s, but kept the program small and secret; and it was only 24 years after the first test that Prime Minister Atal Bihari Vajpayee carried out a second series of tests in 1998.

Nuclear restraint continued thereafter. India's strategic elite swore by a doctrine of "minimum deterrence," which was never fleshed out in public, but came to encompass the idea of assured retaliation based on a small number of weapons. The chief components of this nuclear doctrine and posture were: A declaration that additional tests are not essential; adherence to the principle of No First Use (NFU); rejection of tactical weapons for small-scale nuclear warfighting; the concomitant threat of massive retaliation against any sort of enemy nuclear first strike (modified in 2003 to include a strike with biological or chemical weapons); a non-deployed posture, i.e. a weapons system consisting of unassembled devices for safety and security; and an understanding that deterrence operates at fairly low qualitative as well as quantitative levels.

Following the operationalization of nuclear capability, contradictions began to appear in the framework of nuclear restraint.[23] Pressures to enhance capabilities based on more testing were expressed in occasional statements from members of the strategic elite. The push for a wider assortment of weapons based on a triad (land-, air-, and sea-based) produced a growing variety of platforms and missiles of different ranges that went well beyond the requirements of minimum deterrence. Questions were raised about the efficacy of NFU and non-deployed weapons, and some advocated the acquisition of tactical weapons. Over time, it became clear that the old minimalist strategic culture had split into two. Minimalist preferences were retained in the form of non-deployment, but the launching of the first nuclear weapons-carrying submarine undercut this as it makes no sense to have submarines that can travel far and deep without weapons on board. Policymakers also held on to minimalism against pressures for testing and a shift to accepting tactical weapons, but the appearance of an ever-widening range of missiles and the quest for more capabilities in such technologies as multiple warhead missiles took a part of nuclear strategy away from minimalism toward an open-ended maximalism.

Has nuclear restraint crumbled? Certainly, India has come a long distance from the minimalism expressed in the early days after the 1998 tests. But arguably, its strategic culture has constrained an arms racing tendency and prevented (thus far) shifts to active deployment and warfighting doctrine. A fundamental reason for the steady drift is that the meaning of "minimum deterrence" has yet to be clearly grasped. In part, it reflects the failure of the political elite to come to grips with the complex reality of nuclear weapons—a failure that has left it unable to provide the intellectual ballast for nuclear minimalism.[24] At this juncture, it is difficult to say how far this shift will go, but it would seem fair to say that a tipping point signifying radical change is not yet in sight.

This section has identified change, both complete and partial, in India's strategic culture. I turn now to those facets that have shown resilience and continuity over the entire period from 1947 till today.

Deep Strategic Culture

While I do not make the claim that Deep Strategic Culture is unshakeable, I do believe that with respect to the two aspects discussed here—a preference for strategic autonomy and the determination to pursue higher international status—there is a case for asserting that no substantial change in strategic culture has occurred or is likely.

Strategic Autonomy

Scholars writing about the changes in India's foreign policy have noted the passing of non-alignment, which stressed autonomy in decision-making and had long been a cornerstone of postcolonial Indian foreign policy.[25] The centrality of nonalignment rested on the colonial experience of economic exploitation and political repression for two centuries. Nehru and his successors wished to avoid integration with the global economy and with the major military powers for fear that the end result might be the same. The end of the Cold War, the reference point of the movement, appeared to have rendered nonalignment obsolete. Indeed, a glance at major foreign policy speeches by Indian prime ministers and foreign ministers from the 1990s onward illustrates the downgrading of NAM. But the conceptual basis of nonalignment nevertheless remained central to the foreign policy thinking of

Indian elites.[26] Its essence—strategic autonomy—continues to attract support from leading Indian intellectuals today.[27]

What exactly *was* nonalignment from New Delhi's standpoint?[28] Apart from refusal to choose between Cold War camps, its key characteristics were (a) the preservation of India's independence in decision-making, which would have been undermined had India joined one camp or the other; and (b) the exercising of leverage by India to try and play off the United States and the Soviet Union in order to extract gains from both sides. These two central tenets of Indian foreign policy remain in place today despite talk of an alliance between India and the United States.[29] Joining an alliance against the looming threat from China is not on the menu of strategic options. Elite opinion instead leans toward a more cautious "alignment" rather than a full-fledged alliance.[30]

The term "multialignment," which carries a strong resemblance to nonalignment, expresses the current foreign policy perspective.[31] More widely used—and best capturing an enduring feature of Indian strategic culture since independence—is the term "strategic autonomy."[32] The arrangement for putting this in place is the signing of multiple "strategic partnerships." These allow for varying degrees of cooperation, including defense cooperation, which encompasses arms transfers, military exercises and logistics sharing, without involving joint planning or joint operations.[33] India has entered into a number of strategic partnerships—with France, Japan, Russia, and the United States, among others—that involves defense cooperation of this nature.[34] This enables it to avoid dependence on major powers and to obtain military and economic gains from all its partners. In effect, the foundational principle of nonalignment—strategic autonomy—remains unchanged. Any calculus aimed at anticipating future Indian strategy will have to bear in mind this entrenched facet of Indian strategic culture.

The Pursuit of Status

An enduring feature of India's strategic culture is the pursuit of status. To be sure, the acquisition of status is hardly unique to India. Many states seek status and prestige, which makes the study of status an important component of international relations scholarship.[35] A number of studies on India have also recognized the centrality of status seeking to Indian foreign policy over the years.[36] From Nehru onward, political leaders have seen India as a "civilizational power" with the right to a place under the sun of world politics.[37] Consequently, independent India has consistently attempted to attain a level of prestige for itself that is, arguably, beyond its actual capacity to back with material power. In the early decades, Nehru attempted to elevate India's status through his efforts to project its leadership as a state focused on moral principles (egalitarianism, non-violence), but defeat in the war against China in 1962 exposed the superficiality of such claims in the absence of material power. Gradually, his successors from Indira Gandhi onward altered the balance between material power and normative claims, focusing on the former without downsizing the latter. Over the decades, though, India's material capabilities did not measure up to its claims to be acknowledged as a major power in the making. In particular, India remained on the defensive as it shunned integration with the world economy and continued to fend off the nuclear nonproliferation regime. This changed following the end of the Cold War.

The material bases of India's claim to higher status began to grow rapidly from the 1990s. Between 1991 and 2019, India's economy grew (in constant 2010 US$) from $512.92 billion in 1991 to $2.96 trillion, while its military spending concomitantly rose (in current US$) from

$8.62 billion to $66.51 billion.[38] Though few in Washington and elsewhere might admit it, India's image shifted from that of an "emerging economy" to that of a "rising power" after its 1998 nuclear tests, a reassessment highlighted by the US willingness to assist India in bypassing the rules of the nonproliferation regime by allowing it access to civilian nuclear trade. India's newfound status brought it a number of status benefits: Membership of the Group of Twenty major economies (G20); entry into components of the nuclear nonproliferation regime such as the Missile Technology Control Regime and the Wassenaar Arrangement (though not the Nuclear Suppliers Group); membership of major multilateral groupings such as the Quadrilateral Security Dialogue (Australia, India, Japan, the US), BRICS (Brazil, Russia, India, China, South Africa), and IBSA (India, Brazil, South Africa); inclusion in the Shanghai Cooperation Organization; and the prestige associated with the major-power strategic partnerships discussed in the preceding section. All of this underscored the claim that India is a "leading power."[39]

The argument that status seeking is a characteristic of India's deep strategic culture is a strong one since India has pursued it over the decades regardless of its ups and downs in material terms. From time to time, it has been willing to drop its own principles for the sake of status attainment. For instance, India had long been critical of the Antarctic Treaty as a cartel that overriding the world's claims to a common space, but dropped its criticisms once it was allowed to join the treaty in 1983. Similarly, in its drive for admission into the nonproliferation regime, of which it had been a trenchant critic, India has been vocal in claiming that it is a "responsible" nuclear power in abiding by the rules of the regime. At the most difficult of moments, while struggling to respond to the Covid-19 pandemic, it has still tried to display leadership in distributing vaccines, medicines, and protective equipment. In short, India has over 75 years held fast to the pursuit of status and is unlikely to shed its keenness to attain higher rank and prestige in the world of states. This represents a characteristic of its Deep Strategic Culture—one that is unlikely to fade in the foreseeable future.

Conclusion

In this chapter, I have first clarified the often confused understanding of the concept of strategic culture, especially in relation to its relationship with the realist paradigm. Thereafter, I have sought to refine the concept by distinguishing between two subcategories. Mutable Strategic Culture is a source of foreign policy uniqueness over time, but subject to incremental and sometimes sudden change, though it does play a significant role in constraining change. In contrast, Deep Strategic Culture consists of core attributes that retain a high degree of continuity over an extended period of time and are able to resist shocks. In the Indian context, I have illustrated Mutable Strategic Culture with respect to military intervention/non-intervention, where two distinct (successive) strategic cultures are identified; and nuclear restraint, where a long-standing strategic culture shows significant cracks under pressure. Deep Strategic Culture is then highlighted with respect to two areas that have remained fundamentally unchanged over 75 years: A preference for strategic autonomy and the desire for status.

Constraints of space preclude discussion of a number of important aspects of Indian strategic culture. Attention needs to be given to strategic culture in relation to economic policy and environmental policy. The question of competing subcultures and how they shape the overarching strategic culture merits examination. This again is closely related to the ways in which India's domestic politics shapes its strategic culture. It is hoped that future scholarship will attend to these facets.

Notes

1 Alan Bloomfield, "Time to Move On: Reconceptualizing the Strategic Culture Debate," *Contemporary Security Policy* 33, no. 3 (2012): 437–461; Antulio J. Echevarria II, "Colin Gray and the Paradox of Strategic Culture: Critical But Unknowable," *Comparative Strategy* 40, no. 2 (2021): 174–178; Colin S. Gray, "National Style in Strategy: The American Example," *International Security* 6, no. 2 (Fall, 1981): 21–47; Colin S. Gray, *Nuclear Strategy and National Style* (Lanham, MD: Hamilton Press, 1986); Patrick Hinton, "Strategic Culture," *RUSI Journal* 165, no. 4 (2020): 80–87; Alastair Iain Johnston, *Cultural Realism: Culture and Grand Strategy in Chinese History* (Princeton, NJ: Princeton University Press, 1995); Tamir Libel, "Rethinking Strategic Culture: A Computational (Social Science) Discursive-Institutionalist Approach, *Journal of Strategic Studies* 43, no. 5 (2020): 686–709; Edward Lock, "Refining Strategic Culture: Return of the Second Generation," *Review of International Studies* 36, no. 3 (2010): 685–708; Jack L. Snyder, *The Soviet Strategic Culture: Implications for Limited Nuclear Options* (Santa Monica, CA: the Rand Corporation, 1977).
2 Colin S. Gray, *Modern Strategy* (Oxford: Oxford University Press, 1999), 28.
3 Bloomfield, "Time to Move On"; Michael Liebig, "India's Strategic Culture and its Kautilyan Lineage," *Journal of the United Service Institution of India* 150, no. 622 (October–December 2020), https://usiofindia.org/publication/usi-journal/indias-strategic-culture-and-its-kautilyan-lineage/; David McCraw, "Change and Continuity in Strategic Culture: The Cases of Australia and New Zealand," *Australian Journal of International Affairs* 65, no. 2 (2011): 167–184.
4 Shaiel Ben-Ephraim, "From Strategic Narrative to Strategic Culture: Labor Zionism and the Roots of Israeli Strategic Culture," *Comparative Strategy* 39, no. 2 (2020): 145–161; McCraw, "Change and Continuity in Strategic Culture."
5 Some notable studies from a growing literature (India excepted, since they are cited separately) are: Dmitry (Dima) Adamsky, "From Israel with Deterrence: Strategic Culture, Intra-war Coercion and Brute Force," *Security Studies* 26, no. 1 (2017): 157–184; Dmitry (Dima) Adamsky, "Russian Campaign in Syria – Change and Continuity in Strategic Culture," *Journal of Strategic Studies* 43, no. 1 (2020): 104–125; Mark Beeson, Alan Bloomfield, and Wahyu Wicaksana, "Unlikely Allies? Australia, Indonesia and the Strategic Cultures of Middle Powers," *Asian Security* 17, no. 2 (2021): 178–194; Alessia Biava, Margriet Drent, and Graeme P. Herd, "Characterizing the European Union's Strategic Culture: An Analytical Framework," *Journal of Common Market Studies* 49, no. 6 (2011): 1227–1248; Mohammad Eslami and Alena Vysotskaya Guedes Vieira, "Iran's Strategic Culture: The 'Revolutionary' and 'Moderation' Narratives on the Ballistic Missile Programme," *Third World Quarterly* 42, no. 2 (2021): 312–328; Huiyun Feng and Kai He, "A Dynamic Strategic Culture Model and China's Behaviour in the South China Sea," *Cambridge Review of International Affairs* 34, no. 4 (2021): 510–529; David G. Haglund, "What Can Strategic Culture Contribute to Our Understanding of Security Policies in the Asia-Pacific Region?" *Contemporary Security Policy* 35, no. 2 (2014): 310–328; Jeannie L. Johnson, Kerry M. Kartchner, and Jeffrey A. Larsen, *Strategic Culture and Weapons of Mass Destruction: Culturally Based Insights into Comparative National Security Policymaking* (New York: Palgrave Macmillan, 2009); Xiaobing Li, *China's War in Korea: Strategic Culture and Geopolitics* (Singapore: Palgrave Macmillan, 2019); Christoph O. Meyer, *The Quest for a European Strategic Culture: Changing Norms on Security and Defence in the European Union* (Basingstoke and New York: Palgrave Macmillan, 2006); Malik Mufti, *Daring and Caution in Turkish Strategic Culture: Republic at Sea* (Basingstoke and New York: Palgrave Macmillan, 2009); Vipin Narang, *Nuclear Strategy in the Modern Era: Regional Powers and International Conflict* (Princeton and Oxford: Princeton University Press, 2014); Andrea Passeri, "'A Tender Gourd among the Cactus': Making Sense of Myanmar's Alignment Policies through the Lens of Strategic Culture," *Pacific Review* 33, no. 6 (2020): 931–957; Gregory V. Raymond, "Strategic Culture and Thailand's Response to Vietnam's Occupation of Cambodia, 1979–1989: A Cold War Epilogue," *Journal of Cold War Studies* 22, no. 1 (2020): 4–45; Po P. Shang, "Myanmar's Foreign Policy: Shifting Legitimacy, Shifting Strategic Culture," *Journal of Current Southeast Asian Affairs* (October 22, 2021): 1–18; Mette Skak, "Russian Strategic Culture: The Role of Today's Chekisty," *Contemporary Politics* 22, no. 3 (2016): 324–341; Rashed Uz Zaman, "Strategic Culture: A 'Cultural' Understanding of War," *Comparative Strategy* 28, no. 1 (2009): 68–88.
6 David L. Rousseau and Thomas C. Walker, "Liberalism," in *The Routledge Handbook of Security Studies*, eds. Victor Mauer and Myriam Dunn Cavelty (Abingdon: Routledge, 2009), 21–33.
7 Hans J. Morgenthau, *Politics among Nations*, 7th ed., revised by Kenneth W. Thompson and W. David Clinton (Boston: McGraw Hill, 2006); Norrin Ripsman, Jeffrey W. Taliaferro, and Steven E. Lobell, *Neoclassical Realist Theory of International Politics* (New York: Oxford University Press, 2016).

For a neorealist perspective that tends to treat the internal characteristics of states as irrelevant, see Kenneth N. Waltz, *Theory of International Politics* (Reading, MA: Addison-Wesley, 1979); and John J. Mearsheimer, *The Tragedy of Great Power Politics* (New York: Norton, 2001).

8 Alexander Wendt, *Social Theory of International Politics* (Cambridge: Cambridge University Press, 1999).

9 John Glenn, "Realism versus Strategic Culture: Competition and Collaboration?" *International Studies Review* 11, no. 3 (2009): 523–551.

10 Kanti Bajpai, "Indian Strategic Culture," in *Asia in 2020: Future Strategic Balances and Alliances*, ed. Michael R. Chambers (Carlisle, PA: Strategic Studies Institute, U.S. Army War College, 2002), 245–303; Rajesh M. Basrur, "Nuclear Weapons and Indian Strategic Culture," *Journal of Peace Research* 38, no. 2 (2001): 181–198; Bernhard Beitelmair-Berini, "Theorizing Indian Strategic Culture(s): Taking Stock of a Controversial Debate," in *Theorizing Indian Foreign Policy*, eds. Misha Hansel, Raphaelle Khan, and Melissa Levaillant (Routledge, 2016); Runa Das, "The Prism of Strategic Culture and South Asian Nuclearization," *Contemporary Politics* 15, no. 4 (2009): 395–411; Runa Das, "Strategic Culture, Identity and Nuclear (In)security in Indian Politics: Reflections from Critical Constructivist Lenses," *International Politics* 47, no. 5 (2010): 472–496; Ian Hall, "The Persistence of Nehruvianism in India's Strategic Culture," in *Strategic Asia 2016-17*, eds. Ashley J. Tellis, Alison Szalwinski, and Michael Wills (Seattle: National Bureau of Asian Research, 2016), 141–167; Rodney W. Jones, *India's Strategic Culture* (Washington, DC: Defense Threat Reduction Agency, 2006); Rohan Mukherjee, "Statuspolitik as Foreign Policy: Strategic Culture and India's Nuclear Behavior," (unpublished), accessed December 17, 2021, https://www.academia.edu/14464145/Statuspolitik_as_Foreign_Policy_Strategic_Culture_and_Indias_Nuclear_Behavior; Harsh V. Pant, "Indian Strategic Culture: The Debate and Its Consequences," in *Handbook of India's International Relations*, ed. David Scott (London and New York: Routledge, 2011), 14–22; Shrikant Paranjpe, *India's Strategic Culture: The Making of National Security Policy* (London: Routledge, 2013); Adil Rasheed, "Influence of Vedanta on Indian Strategic Culture," *Journal of Defence Studies* 15, no. 3 (July–September 2021): 69–91; Sarang Shidore, "India's Strategic Culture and Deterrence Stability on the Indian Subcontinent," in *Deterrence Instability and Nuclear Weapons in South Asia*, eds. Michael Krepon, Joshua T. White, Julia Thompson, and Shane Mason (Washington, DC: Stimson Center, 2015), 119–147; Constantino H. Xavier, *From Inaction to Intervention: India's Strategic Culture of Regional Involvement (Nepal, Sri Lanka and Myanmar, 1950s-2000s)*, PhD diss., Johns Hopkins University, 2016; Rashed Uz Zaman, "Kautilya: The Indian Strategic Thinker and Indian Strategic Culture," *Comparative Strategy* 25, no. 3 (2006): 231–247.

11 See, e.g. Amrita Narlikar, "Peculiar Chauvinism or Strategic Calculation? Explaining the Negotiating Strategy of a Rising India," *International Affairs* 82, no. 1 (2006): 59–76; Deepa Ollapally and Rajesh Rajagopalan, "India: Foreign Policy Perspectives of an Ambiguous Power," in *Worldviews of Aspiring Powers: Domestic Foreign Policy Debates in China, India, Iran, Japan and Russia*, eds. Henry R. Nau and Deepa Ollapally, Oxford Scholarship Online, 2012, https://doi.org/10.1093/acprof:oso/9780199937479.003.0003; Rahul Sagar, "State of Mind: What Kind of Power Will India Become?" *International Affairs* 85, no. 4 (2009): 801–816; Teresita C. Schaffer and Howard B. Schaffer, *India at the Global High Table: The Quest for Regional Primacy and Strategic Autonomy* (Washington, DC: Brookings Institution Press, 2016).

12 George K. Tanham, *Indian Strategic Thought: An Interpretive Essay* (Santa Monica, CA: RAND, 1992), 17.

13 Sandy Gordon, *India's Rise to Power* (Basingstoke and London: Macmillan), 7.

14 Pant, "Indian Strategic Culture."

15 Indrani Bagchi, "Why India Does Not Have a Vibrant Strategic Culture," *Times of India*, October 21, 2012, https://economictimes.indiatimes.com/news/politics-and-nation/why-india-does-not-have-a-vibrant-strategic-culture/articleshow/16894467.cms; "Can India Become a Great Power?" *The Economist*, March 30, 2013, https://www.economist.com/leaders/2013/03/30/can-india-become-a-great-power; V. P. Malik, "Missing a Strategic Culture," *Indian Express*, June 23, 2017, https://indianexpress.com/article/opinion/columns/missing-a-strategic-culture-pakistan-terrorism-geo-political-security-china-obor-4717549/; Arjun Subramaniam, "Does India Have a Strategic Culture? Yes, it is Slowly Beginning to Have One," *Times of India*, February 4, 2016, https://timesofindia.indiatimes.com/blogs/toi-edit-page/does-india-have-a-strategic-culture-yes-it-is-slowly-beginning-to-develop-one/.

16 See, e.g. Paranjpe, *India's Strategic Culture; Xavier, From Inaction to Intervention.*

17 Šumit Ganguly, "India's Foreign Policy Grows Up," *World Policy Journal* 20, no. 4 (2003–4): 41–47; Šumit Ganguly and Manjeet Pardesi, "Explaining Sixty Years of India's Foreign Policy," *India Review* 8, no. 1 (January 2009): 4–49; Deepa Ollapally and Rajesh Rajagopalan, "The Pragmatic Challenge to Indian Foreign Policy," *Washington Quarterly* 34, no. 2 (2011): 145–162; C. Raja Mohan, *Crossing the Rubicon: The Shaping of India's New Foreign Policy* (New York: Palgrave Macmillan, 2003).

18 Michael Mandelbaum, *The Fate of Nations* (New York: Cambridge University Press, 1988).

19 This section draws from Rajesh Basrur, "Paradigm Shift: India during and after the Cold War," in *The Engagement of India*, ed. Ian Hall (Washington, DC: Georgetown University Press, 2014), 169–183.

20 C. Raja Mohan, "How to Intervene," *Indian Express*, March 7, 2011, http://archive.indianexpress. com/news/how-to-intervene/758818/0. See also Walter C. Ladwig III, "India and Military Power Projection: Will the Land of Gandhi Become a Conventional Great Power?" *Asian Survey* 50, no. 6 (November/December 2010): 1162–1183.

21 Rajesh Basrur, unpublished book manuscript on Indian foreign policy, Chapter 6.

22 Basrur, "Nuclear Weapons and Indian Strategic Culture." For useful histories, see Šumit Ganguly, "India's Pathway to Pokhran II: The Prospects and Sources of New Delhi's Nuclear Weapons Program," *International Security* 23, no. 4 (1999): 148–177; George Perkovich, *India's Nuclear Bomb: The Impact on Global Proliferation* (Berkeley, CA: University of California Press, 1999); and K. Subrahmanyam, "Indian Nuclear Policy–1964-98 (A Personal Recollection)," *Strategic Analysis* 42, no. 3 (2018): 293–311.

23 See, e.g. Rajesh M. Basrur, *Minimum Deterrence and India's Nuclear Security* (Stanford, CA: Stanford University Press, 2006); Christopher Clary and Vipin Narang, "India's Counterforce Temptations: Strategic Dilemmas, Doctrine, and Capabilities," *International Security* 43, no. 3 (Winter 2018/19): 7–52; Yogesh Joshi and Frank O'Donnell, *India and Nuclear Asia: Forces, Doctrine, and Dangers* (Washington, DC: Georgetown University Press, 2018); Frank O'Donnell, "India's Nuclear Counter-revolution: Nuclear Learning and the Future of Deterrence," *Nonproliferation Review* 26, nos. 5–6 (2019): 407–426.

24 For a broader view of this intellectual failure extending to other aspects of Indian military organization and strategy, see Anit Mukherjee, *The Absent Dialogue: Politicians, Bureaucrats, and the Military in India* (New York: Oxford University Press, 2020).

25 Pieter-Jan Dockx, "India's Choice: The United States and the End of Non-alignment," *South Asia @LSE*, August 7, 2017, https://blogs.lse.ac.uk/southasia/2017/08/07/indias-choice-the-united-states-and-the-end-of-non-alignment/; Šumit Ganguly, "India after Nonalignment: Why Modi Skipped the Summit," *Foreign Affairs*, September 19, 2016, https://www.foreignaffairs.com/articles/india/2016-09-19/india-after-nonalignment; Harsh V. Pant, "The End of Non-Alignment?" *Orbis* 61, no. 4 (2017): 527–540.

26 Rajen Harshe, "India's Non-Alignment: An Attempt at Conceptual Reconstruction," *Economic and Political Weekly* 25, no. 7/8 (February 17–24, 1990): 399–405; M. S. Rajan, "India's Foreign Policy: The Continuing Relevance of Nonalignment," *International Studies* 30, no. 2 (1993): 141–150.

27 Sunil Khilnani, Rajiv Kumar, Pratap Bhanu Mehta, Prakash Menon, Nandan Nilekani, Srinath Raghavan, Shyam Saran, and Siddharth Varadarajan, *NonAlignment 2.0: A Foreign and Strategic Policy for India in the Twenty First Century* (New Delhi: Center for Policy Research, 2012) https://cprindia. org/research/reports/nonalignment-20-foreign-and-strategic-policy-india-twenty-first-century.

28 Cecil V. Crabb, Jr., *The Elephants and the Grass: A Study of Nonalignment* (New York: Praeger, 1965); A. P. Rana, *The Imperatives of Non-Alignment: A Conceptual Study of India's Foreign Policy Strategy in the Nehru Period* (New Delhi: Macmillan, 1976).

29 Nikki Haley and Mike Waltz, "It's Time to Formalize an Alliance With India," *Foreign Policy*, October 25, 2021, https://foreignpolicy.com/2021/10/25/us-india-alliance-military-economy-biden-china-afghanistan/; Yusuf T. Unjhawala, "Why India Should Align with the US," Observer Research Foundation, May 16, 2020, https://www.orfonline.org/expert-speak/why-india-should-align-us-66233/.

30 For a widely circulated view on this, see *Khilnani* et al., *NonAlignment 2.0*.

31 Ian Hall, "Multialignment and Indian Foreign Policy under Narendra Modi," *Round Table* 105, no. 3 (2016): 271–286; M. K. Narayanan, "Non-alignment to Multi-alignment," *Hindu*, January 5, 2021, https://www.thehindu.com/opinion/lead/indian-diplomacy-non-alignment-to-multi-alignment/article13982580.ece.

32 Alexey D. Muraviev, Dalbir Ahlawat, and Lindsay Hughes, "India's Security Dilemma: Engaging Big Powers While Retaining Strategic Autonomy," *International Politics*, 2021, https://doi.org/10.1057/s41311-021-00350-z; Jeff M. Smith, "Strategic Autonomy and U.S.-Indian Relations," *War on the Rocks*, November 6, 2020, https://warontherocks.com/2020/11/strategic-autonomy-and-u-s-indian-relations/.

33 Rajesh Basrur and Sumitha Narayanan Kutty, "Modi's India and Japan: Nested Strategic Partnerships," *International Politics*, Forthcoming, https://doi.org/10.1057/s41311-021-00288-2.

34 Meredith Roaten, "India Manages Diverse Arms Sources for Military Modernization," *National Defense*, December 9, 2021, https://www.nationaldefensemagazine.org/articles/2021/12/9/india-manages-diverse-arms--sources-for-military-modernization.

35 Joshua Freedman, "Status Insecurity and Temporality in World Politics," *European Journal of International Relations* 22, no. 4 (2015): 797–822; T. V. Paul, Deborah Welch Larson, and William C. Wohlforth, eds. *Status in World Politics* (New York: Cambridge University Press, 2017); Thomas J. Volgy, Renato Corbetta, Keith A. Grant, and Ryan G. Baird, eds. *Major Powers and the Quest for Status in International Politics: Global and Regional Perspectives* (New York: Palgrave Macmillan, 2011).

36 Rajesh Basrur and Kate Sullivan de Estrada, *Rising India: Status and Power* (Abingdon and New York: Routledge, 2017); Baldev Raj Nayar and T. V. Paul, *India in the World Order: Searching for Major-Power Status* (Cambridge: Cambridge University Press, 2003); T. V. Paul and Mahesh Shankar "Status Accommodation through Institutional Means: India's Rise in the Global Order," in *Status in World Politics*, eds. T. V. Paul, Deborah Welch Larson, and William C. Wohlforth (New York: Cambridge University Press, 2017), 165–191.

37 Deepa Ollapally, "India: The Ambivalent Power in Asia," *International Studies* 48, nos. 3 & 4 (2011): 201–222.

38 World Bank, "GDP (constant 2010 US$) – India," accessed September 12, 2020, https://data.worldbank.org/indicator/NY.GDP.MKTP.KD?end=2019&locations=IN&start=1991&year_low_desc=true; World Bank, "Military expenditure (current USD) – India," accessed September 12, 2020, https://data.worldbank.org/indicator/MS.MIL.XPND.CD?end=2018&locations=IN&start=1991.

39 "IISS Fullerton Lecture by Dr. S. Jaishankar, Foreign Secretary in Singapore," Ministry of External Affairs, India, July 20, 2015, http://mea.gov.in/Speeches-Statements.htm?dtl/25493/IISS_Fullerton_Lecture_by_Foreign_Secretary_in_Singapore.

Bibliography

"Can India Become A Great Power?" *The Economist*, March 30, 2013. https://www.economist.com/leaders/2013/03/30/can-india-become-a-great-power.

"GDP (constant 2010 US$) – India." World Bank. Accessed September 12, 2020. https://data.worldbank.org/indicator/NY.GDP.MKTP.KD?end=2019&locations=IN&start=1991&year_low_desc=true.

"Military expenditure (current USD) – India." World Bank. Accessed September 12, 2020. https://data.worldbank.org/indicator/MS.MIL.XPND.CD?end=2018&locations=IN&start=1991.

Adamky, Dmitry (Dima). "Russian Campaign in Syria – Change and Continuity in Strategic Culture." *Journal of Strategic Studies* 43, no. 1 (2020): 104–125.

Adamsky, Dmitry (Dima). "From Israel with Deterrence: Strategic Culture, Intra-War Coercion and Brute Force." *Security Studies*, 26, no. 1 (2017): 157–184.

Bagchi, Indrani. "Why India Does Not Have A Vibrant Strategic Culture." *Times of India*, October 21, 2012. https://economictimes.indiatimes.com/news/politics-and-nation/why-india-does-not-have-a-vibrant-strategic-culture/articleshow/16894467.cms.

Bajpai, Kanti. "Indian Strategic Culture." In *Asia in 2020: Future Strategic Balances and Alliances*, edited by Michael R. Chambers, 245–303. Carlisle, PA: Strategic Studies Institute, U.S. Army War College, 2002.

Basrur, Rajesh M. "Nuclear Weapons and Indian Strategic Culture," *Journal of Peace Research* 38, no. 2 (2001): 181–198.

Basrur, Rajesh M. *Minimum Deterrence and India's Nuclear Security*. Stanford, CA: Stanford University Press, 2006.

Basrur, Rajesh. "Paradigm Shift: India during and after the Cold War." In *The Engagement of India*, edited by Ian Hall, 169–183. Washington, DC: Georgetown University Press, 2014.

Basrur, Rajesh, and Sumitha Narayanan Kutty. "Modi's India and Japan: Nested Strategic Partnerships." *International Politics, Forthcoming.* https://doi.org/10.1057/s41311-021-00288-2.

Basrur, Rajesh, and Kate Sullivan de Estrada. *Rising India: Status and Power.* Abingdon and New York: Routledge, 2017.

Beeson, Mark, Alan Bloomfield, and Wahyu Wicaksana. "Unlikely Allies? Australia, Indonesia and the Strategic Cultures of Middle Powers." *Asian Security* 17, no. 2 (2021): 178–194.

Beitelmair-Berini, Bernhard. "Theorizing Indian Strategic Culture(s): Taking Stock of a Controversial Debate." In *Theorizing Indian Foreign Policy,* edited by Misha Hansel, Raphaelle Khan and Melissa Levaillant. Abingdon and New York: Routledge, 2016: 91–111.

Ben-Ephraim, Shaiel. "From Strategic Narrative to Strategic Culture: Labor Zionism and the Roots of Israeli Strategic Culture." *Comparative Strategy* 39, no. 2 (2020): 145–161.

Biava, Alessia, Margriet Drent, and Graeme P. Herd. "Characterizing the European Union's Strategic Culture: An Analytical Framework." *Journal of Common Market Studies* 49, no. 6 (2011): 1227–1248.

Bloomfield, Alan. "Time to Move On: Reconceptualizing the Strategic Culture Debate." *Contemporary Security Policy* 33, no. 3 (2012): 437–461.

Clary, Christopher, and Vipin Narang. "India's Counterforce Temptations: Strategic Dilemmas, Doctrine, and Capabilities." *International Security* 43, no. 3 (Winter 2018/19): 7–52.

Crabb, Cecil V. Jr. *The Elephants and the Grass: A Study of Nonalignment.* New York: Praeger, 1965.

Das, Runa. "Strategic Culture, Identity and Nuclear (In)Security in Indian Politics: Reflections from Critical Constructivist Lenses." *International Politics* 47, no. 5 (2010): 472–496.

Das, Runa. "The Prism of Strategic Culture and South Asian Nuclearization." *Contemporary Politics* 15, no. 4 (2009): 395–411.

Dockx, Pieter-Jan. "India's Choice: The United States and the End of Non-alignment." *South Asia @LSE,* August 7, 2017. https://blogs.lse.ac.uk/southasia/2017/08/07/indias-choice-the-united-states-and-the-end-of-non-alignment/.

Echevarria, Antulio J. "Colin Gray and the Paradox of Strategic Culture: Critical but Unknowable." *Comparative Strategy* 40, no. 2 (2021): 174–178.

Eslami, Mohammad, and Alena Vysotskaya Guedes Vieira. "Iran's Strategic Culture: The 'Revolutionary' and 'Moderation' Narratives on the Ballistic Missile Programme." *Third World Quarterly* 42, no. 2 (2021): 312–328.

Feng, Huiyun, and Kai He. "A Dynamic Strategic Culture Model and China's Behaviour in the South China Sea." *Cambridge Review of International Affairs* 34, no. 4 (2021): 510–529.

Freedman, Joshua. "Status Insecurity and Temporality in World Politics." *European Journal of International Relations* 22, no. 4 (2015): 797–822.

Ganguly, Šumit. "India after Nonalignment: Why Modi Skipped the Summit." *Foreign Affairs,* September 19, 2016. https://www.foreignaffairs.com/articles/india/2016-09-19/india-after-nonalignment.

Ganguly, Šumit. "India's Foreign Policy Grows Up." *World Policy Journal* 20, no. 4 (2003-4): 41–47.

Ganguly, Šumit. "India's Pathway to Pokhran II: The Prospects and Sources of New Delhi's Nuclear Weapons Program." *International Security* 23, no. 4 (1999): 148–177.

Ganguly, Šumit, and Manjeet Pardesi. "Explaining Sixty Years of India's Foreign Policy," *India Review* 8, no. 1 (January 2009): 4–49.

Glenn, John. "Realism Versus Strategic Culture: Competition and Collaboration?" *International Studies Review* 11, no. 3 (2009): 523–551.

Gordon, Sandy. *India's Rise to Power.* Basingstoke and London: Macmillan, 1995.

Gray, Colin S. "National Style in Strategy: The American Example." *International Security* 6, no. 2 (Fall, 1981): 21–47.

Gray, Colin S. *Nuclear Strategy and National Style.* Lanham, MD: Hamilton Press, 1986.

Gray, Colin S. *Modern Strategy.* Oxford: Oxford University Press, 1999.

Haglund, David G. "What Can Strategic Culture Contribute to Our Understanding of Security Policies in the Asia-Pacific Region?" *Contemporary Security Policy* 35, no. 2 (2014): 310–328.

Haley, Nikki, and Mike Waltz. "It's Time to Formalize an Alliance with India." *Foreign Policy,* October 25, 2021. https://foreignpolicy.com/2021/10/25/us-india-alliance-military-economy-biden-china-afghanistan/.

Hall, Ian. "Multialignment and Indian Foreign Policy Under Narendra Modi." *Round Table* 105, no. 3 (2016): 271–286.

Hall, Ian. "The Persistence of Nehruvianism in India's Strategic Culture." In *Strategic Asia 2016–17*, edited by Ashley J. Tellis, Alison Szalwinski, and Michael Wills, 141–167. Seattle: National Bureau of Asian Research, 2016.

Harshe, Rajen. "India's Non-Alignment: An Attempt at Conceptual Reconstruction." *Economic and Political Weekly* 25, no. 7/8 (February 17–24, 1990): 399–405.

Hinton, Patrick. "Strategic Culture." *RUSI Journal* 165, no. 4 (2020): 80–87.

Jaishankar, S. "IISS Fullerton Lecture by Dr. S. Jaishankar, Foreign Secretary in Singapore." Ministry of External Affairs (India). July 20, 2015. http://mea.gov.in/Speeches-Statements.htm?dtl/25493/ IISS_Fullerton_Lecture_by_Foreign_Secretary_in_Singapore.

Johnson, Jeannie L., Kerry M. Kartchner, and Jeffrey A. Larsen. *Strategic Culture and Weapons of Mass Destruction: Culturally Based Insights into Comparative National Security Policymaking*. New York: Palgrave Macmillan, 2009.

Johnston, Alastair Iain. *Cultural Realism: Culture and Grand Strategy in Chinese History*. Princeton, NJ: Princeton University Press, 1995.

Jones, Rodney W. *India's Strategic Culture*. Washington, DC: Defense Threat Reduction Agency, 2006.

Joshi, Yogesh, and Frank O'Donnell. *India and Nuclear Asia: Forces, Doctrine, and Dangers*. Washington, DC: Georgetown University Press, 2018.

Khilnani, Sunil, Rajiv Kumar, Pratap Bhanu Mehta, Prakash Menon, Nandan Nilekani, Srinath Raghavan, Shyam Saran, and Siddharth Varadarajan *NonAlignment 2.0: A Foreign and Strategic Policy for India in the Twenty First Century* New Delhi: Center for Policy Research, 2012) https://cprindia.org/ research/reports/nonalignment-20-foreign-and-strategic-policy-india-twenty-first-century.

Ladwig, Walter C. III. "India and Military Power Projection: Will the Land of Gandhi Become a Conventional Great Power?" *Asian Survey* 50, no. 6 (November/December 2010): 1162–1183.

Li, Xiaobing. *China's War in Korea: Strategic Culture and Geopolitics*. Singapore: Palgrave Macmillan, 2019.

Libel, Tamir. "Rethinking Strategic Culture: A Computational (Social Science) Discursive-Institutionalist Approach." *Journal of Strategic Studies* 43, no. 5 (2020): 686–709.

Liebig, Michael. "India's Strategic Culture and Its Kautilyan Lineage." *Journal of the United Service Institution of India* 150, no. 622 (October-December 2020). https://usiofindia.org/publication/ usi-journal/indias-strategic-culture-and-its-kautilyan-lineage/.

Lock, Edward. "Refining Strategic Culture: Return of the Second Generation." *Review of International Studies* 36, no. 3 (2010): 685–708.

Malik, V. P. "Missing a Strategic Culture." *Indian Express*, June 23, 2017. https://indianexpress.com/ article/opinion/columns/missing-a-strategic-culture-pakistan-terrorism-geo-political-security-china-obor-4717549/.

Mandelbaum, Michael. *The Fate of Nations*. New York: Cambridge University Press, 1988.

McCraw, David. "Change and Continuity in Strategic Culture: The Cases of Australia and New Zealand." *Australian Journal of International Affairs* 65, no. 2 (2011): 167–184.

Mearsheimer, John J. *The Tragedy of Great Power Politics*. New York: Norton, 2001.

Meyer, Christoph O. *The Quest for a European Strategic Culture: Changing Norms on Security and Defence in the European Union*. Basingstoke and New York: Palgrave Macmillan, 2006.

Mohan, C. Raja. "How to Intervene." *Indian Express*, March 7, 2011. http://archive.indianexpress.com/ news/how-to-intervene/758818/0.

Mohan, C. Raja. *Crossing the Rubicon: The Shaping of India's New Foreign Policy*. New York: Palgrave Macmillan, 2003.

Morgenthau, Hans J. *Politics Among Nations*. 7th ed. Boston: McGraw Hill, 2006.

Mufti, Malik. *Daring and Caution in Turkish Strategic Culture: Republic at Sea*. Basingstoke and New York: Palgrave Macmillan, 2009.

Mukherjee, Anit. *The Absent Dialogue: Politicians, Bureaucrats, and the Military in India*. New York: Oxford University Press, 2020.

Mukherjee, Rohan. "Statuspolitik as Foreign Policy: Strategic Culture and India's Nuclear Behavior." (Unpublished), accessed December 17, 2021. https://www.academia.edu/14464145/ Statuspolitik_as_Foreign_Policy_Strategic_Culture_and_Indias_Nuclear_Behavior.

Muraviev, Alexey D., Dalbir Ahlawat, and Lindsay Hughes. "India's Security Dilemma: Engaging Big Powers While Retaining Strategic Autonomy." *International Politics, Forthcoming*, https://doi. org/10.1057/s41311-021-00350-z.

Narang, Vipin. *Nuclear Strategy in the Modern Era: Regional Powers and International Conflict*. Princeton and Oxford: Princeton University Press, 2014.

Narayanan, M. K. "Non-alignment to Multi-alignment." *Hindu*, January 5, 2021. https://www.thehindu.com/opinion/lead/indian-diplomacy-non-alignment-to-multi-alignment/article13982580.ece.

Narlikar, Amrita. "Peculiar Chauvinism or Strategic Calculation? Explaining the Negotiating Strategy of a Rising India." *International Affairs* 82, no. 1 (2006): 59–76.

Nayar, Baldev Raj, and T. V. Paul. *India in the World Order: Searching for Major-Power Status*. Cambridge: Cambridge University Press, 2003.

O'Donnell, Frank. "India's Nuclear Counter-Revolution: Nuclear Learning and the Future of Deterrence." *Nonproliferation Review* 26, nos. 5–6 (2019): 407–426.

Ollapally, Deepa. "India: The Ambivalent Power in Asia." *International Studies* 48, nos. 3 & 4 (2011): 201–222.

Ollapally, Deepa, and Rajesh Rajagopalan. "India: Foreign Policy Perspectives of an Ambiguous Power." In *Worldviews of Aspiring Powers: Domestic Foreign Policy Debates in China, India, Iran, Japan and Russia*, edited by Henry R. Nau and Deepa Ollapally. Oxford Scholarship Online, 2012. https://doi.org/10.1093/acprof:oso/9780199937479.003.0003.

Ollapally, Deepa, and Rajesh Rajagopalan. "The Pragmatic Challenge to Indian Foreign Policy." *Washington Quarterly* 34, no. 2 (2011): 145–162.

Pant, Harsh V. "Indian Strategic Culture: The Debate and Its Consequences." In *Handbook of India's International Relations*, edited by David Scott, 14–22. London and New York: Routledge, 2011.

Pant, Harsh V. "The End of Non-Alignment?" *Orbis* 61, no. 4 (2017): 527–540.

Paranjpe, Shrikant. *India's Strategic Culture: The Making of National Security Policy*. London: Routledge, 2013.

Passeri, Andrea. "'A Tender Gourd Among the Cactus': Making Sense of Myanmar's Alignment Policies Through the Lens of Strategic Culture." *Pacific Review* 33, no. 6 (2020): 931–957.

Paul, T. V., and Mahesh Shankar. "Status Accommodation Through Institutional Means: India's Rise in the Global Order." In *Status in World Politics*, edited by T. V. Paul, Deborah Welch Larson, and William C. Wohlforth, 165–191. New York: Cambridge University Press, 2017.

Paul, T. V., Deborah Welch Larson, and William C. Wohlforth, eds. *Status in World Politics*. New York: Cambridge University Press, 2017.

Perkovich, George. *India's Nuclear Bomb: The Impact on Global Proliferation*. Berkeley, CA: University of California Press, 1999.

Rajan, M. S. "India's Foreign Policy: The Continuing Relevance of Nonalignment." *International Studies* 30, no. 2 (1993): 141–150.

Rana, A. P. *The Imperatives of Non-Alignment: A Conceptual Study of India's Foreign Policy Strategy in the Nehru Period*. New Delhi: Macmillan, 1976.

Rasheed, Adil. "Influence of Vedanta on Indian Strategic Culture." *Journal of Defence Studies* 15, no. 3 (July–September 2021): 69–91.

Raymond, Gregory V. "Strategic Culture and Thailand's Response to Vietnam's Occupation of Cambodia, 1979–1989: A Cold War Epilogue." *Journal of Cold War Studies* 22, no. 1 (2020): 4–45.

Ripsman, Norrin, Jeffrey W. Taliaferro, and Steven E. Lobell. *Neoclassical Realist Theory of International Politics*. New York: Oxford University Press, 2016.

Roaten, Meredith. "India Manages Diverse Arms Sources for Military Modernization." *National Defense*, December 9, 2021. https://www.nationaldefensemagazine.org/articles/2021/12/9/india-manages-diverse-arms–sources-for-military-modernization.

Rousseau, David L., and Thomas C. Walker. "Liberalism." In *The Routledge Handbook of Security Studies*, edited by Victor Mauer, and Myriam Dunn Cavelty, 21–33. Abingdon: Routledge, 2009.

Sagar, Rahul. "State of Mind: What Kind of Power Will India Become?" *International Affairs* 85, no. 4 (2009): 801–816.

Schaffer, Teresita C., and Howard B. Schaffer. *India at the Global High Table: The Quest for Regional Primacy and Strategic Autonomy*. Washington, DC: Brookings Institution Press, 2016.

Shang, Po P. "Myanmar's Foreign Policy: Shifting Legitimacy, Shifting Strategic Culture." *Journal of Current Southeast Asian Affairs* (October 22, 2021): 1–18.

Shidore, Sarang. "India's Strategic Culture and Deterrence Stability on the Indian Subcontinent." In *Deterrence Instability and Nuclear Weapons in South Asia*, edited by Michael Krepon, Joshua T. White, Julia Thompson, and Shane Mason, 119–147. Washington, DC: Stimson Center, 2015.

Skak, Mette Skak. "Russian Strategic Culture: The Role of Today's *Chekisty*." *Contemporary Politics* 22, no. 3 (2016): 324–341.

Smith, Jeff M. "Strategic Autonomy and U.S.-Indian Relations." *War on the Rocks*, November 6, 2020. https://warontherocks.com/2020/11/strategic-autonomy-and-u-s-indian-relations/.

Snyder, Jack L. *The Soviet Strategic Culture: Implications for Limited Nuclear Options*. Santa Monica, CA: the Rand Corporation, 1977.

Subrahmanyam, K. "Indian Nuclear Policy–1964-98 (A Personal Recollection)." *Strategic Analysis* 42, no. 3 (2018): 293–311.

Subramaniam, Arjun. "Does India Have a Strategic Culture? Yes, it is Slowly Beginning to Have One." Times of India, February 4, 2016. https://timesofindia.indiatimes.com/blogs/toi-edit-page/does-india-have-a-strategic-culture-yes-it-is-slowly-beginning-to-develop-one/.

Tanham, George K. *Indian Strategic Thought: An Interpretive Essay*. Santa Monica, CA: RAND, 1992.

Unjhawala, Yusuf T. "Why India Should Align with the US." Observer Research Foundation, May 16, 2020. https://www.orfonline.org/expert-speak/why-india-should-align-us-66233/.

Volgy, Thomas J., Renato Corbetta, Keith A. Grant, and Ryan G. Baird, eds. *Major Powers and the Quest for Status in International Politics: Global and Regional Perspectives*. New York: Palgrave Macmillan, 2011.

Waltz, Kenneth N. *Theory of International Politics*. Reading, MA: Addison-Wesley, 1979.

Wendt, Alexander Wendt. *Social Theory of International Politics*. Cambridge: Cambridge University Press, 1999.

Xavier, Constantino H. *"From Inaction to Intervention: India's Strategic Culture of Regional Involvement (Nepal, Sri Lanka and Myanmar, 1950s-2000s)."* PhD diss., Johns Hopkins University, 2016.

Zaman, Rashed Uz Zaman. "Kautilya: The Indian Strategic Thinker and Indian Strategic Culture." *Comparative Strategy* 25, no. 3 (2006): 231–247.

Zaman, Rashed Uz. "Strategic Culture: A 'Cultural' Understanding of War." *Comparative Strategy*, 28, no. 1 (2009): 68–88.

6

PAKISTAN'S STRATEGIC CULTURE*

Jamison C. Heinkel

Introduction

In early September 2021, Lieutenant General Faiz Hamid, head of Pakistan's spy agency, the Inter-Services Intelligence (ISI), arrived in Kabul, Afghanistan, to meet with the Taliban only a few days after the United States and other countries evacuated forces and civilians from Hamid Karzai International Airport.[1] Pakistan and the ISI, after 20 years of providing support and safe havens to the Taliban, apparently emerged victorious with the return of the Taliban to power and India's departure from Afghanistan.[2] The Taliban's return, however, threatens Pakistan's internal and external security interests with the Taliban's close ties to anti-Pakistan and anti-Chinese militant groups.[3] Why would Pakistan choose a policy that worsens Pakistan's internal security situation and strains its relationship with close ally China, which Pakistan aligns itself to balance against Pakistan's perceived greatest external threat India (Parkes 2019)?

This chapter seeks to explain Pakistan's seemingly acting against its best interests through the lens of strategic culture. Aside from Afghanistan's instability, Pakistan's myriad problems include Islamic extremism, ethno-sectarian violence, insurgencies and separatist movements, a lack of human and civil rights enforcement, a dysfunctional economy, underdeveloped government institutions and government instability, the absence of a public consensus on what Pakistan stands for as a nation and a state, and a powerful military bureaucracy that controls Pakistan's foreign and security policy (Heinkel and deVillafranca 2016). Moreover, Pakistan has the sixth largest nuclear arsenal in the world, the most for a non-signatory to the Nuclear Proliferation Treaty.[4] As these problems have compounded over the years, Pakistan's foreign and security policy toward its neighbors has grown both increasingly defensive and aggressive, marked by consistently fractious relations with Afghanistan and, particularly, with the much larger and more powerful India, with whom it has fought four wars. Understanding Pakistan's behavior toward real or perceived external and internal threats is thus critical in attempting to mitigate Pakistan's instability and its impact on South Asia and the international community.

---

* **Disclaimer:** *The views/statements of fact, opinion, or analysis expressed in this book are strictly my own and do not reflect the official policy or position of the Department of Defense (DoD), or the U.S. Government. Review of the material does not imply DoD or U.S. Government endorsement of factual accuracy or opinion.*

DOI: 10.4324/9781003246626-9

This chapter reviews the conceptual history and debates on state strategic culture in international relations. This follows with analyzing strategic culture and applying it to Pakistan's decision-making on the wars it fought against India, the use of proxy militants, and nuclear weapons development. I argue that within the Pakistan military, the anti-India Pakistani nationalist subculture remains dominant and will likely do so for at least another decade, absent a shock to its ingrained threat perceptions or a generational shift. Finally, this chapter concludes with the implications of strategic culture on Pakistan and areas for future study.

Theorizing Strategic Culture

There have been differences in the approaches taken toward strategic culture because of its abstract nature (Anand V. 2020). By the late 1940s and the early 1950s, culture as a central variable made its way into political science from anthropology and psychology (Desch 1998). Leites (1948) conceptualized a psychocultural construct that influences the behavior of individuals known as an operational code (Feng 2007). Operational code was further refined by George (1969; Leites 1953). The first generation of strategic culture scholarship emerged round the late 1970s and the early 1980s, with scholars arguing that structural realism failed to explain differences in behavioral patterns among nations. Snyder (1977) introduced the term strategic culture with his argument that the Soviet Union may not necessarily subscribe to American norms of rationality in nuclear strategy but because of its own distinct strategic culture. In sum, the Soviet Union may not adopt the similar rationale and exercise restrained retaliation as per game theory. Instead, Snyder proposed that Soviet strategic culture may be having a predisposition toward unrestrained counterforce strikes. The emergence of the term strategic culture led to a discourse assessing a variety of strategic issues with four generations of scholarship (Anand V. 2020).

This first generation of strategic culture scholars (Booth 1979; Gray 1981) regard the concept as independent catch-all variables, which explains that differences in strategic behavior of states are caused by the dissimilarities in such items as their geography, historical experience, and political culture (Beitelmair-Berini 2021; Anand V. 2020). Booth defined strategic culture as a "nation's traditions, values, attitudes, patterns of behavior, habits, symbols, achievements and particular ways of adapting to the environment and solving problems with respect to the threat and use of force" (Booth 1990). Gray (1981) posits that strategic culture "provides the milieu within which strategy is debated" and represents a semi-permanent influence on security policy (Lantis 2014). The second generation (Klein 1988) appeared in the mid-1980s as a critique to the first generation's deterministic view on strategic culture, with scholars considering strategic culture to be mainly instrumental (Beitelmair-Berini 2021; Anand V. 2020).

The rise of constructivism in the post-Cold War era influenced theoretical work on strategic culture, paying particular attention to identity formation (Lantis 2002). Desch (1998) posits that cultural theories might supplement neorealism by helping to explain time lags between structural change and alterations in state behavior, by accounting for seemingly "irrational" state behavior, and in helping to explain state actions in "structurally indeterminate situations" (Lantis 2002). The school of liberalism in international relations is less applicable to Pakistan's strategic culture, which assumes that progress in world affairs is possible with the international system and not necessarily stuck in an endless cycle of conflict, war, and balance-of-power politics (Dueck 2016). The third and most influential generation emerged during this period with constructivism's influence and in response to the lack of methodological rigor of the first generation with a desire to build a falsifiable theory. According to Johnston (1995), strategic culture is an "ideational milieu that limits behavioral choices, from which one could derive predictions about strategic choice." This milieu is shaped by "shared assumptions and decision rules that impose a degree of order on individual and group conceptions of their relationship to their social, organizational or political environment." Furthermore "strategic culture is an integrated system of symbols (e.g., argumentation structures, languages, analogies, metaphors) which acts to establish pervasive and long-lasting strategic preferences by formulating concepts of the role and efficacy of military force in interstate political affairs, and by clothing these conceptions with such an aura of factuality that the strategic preferences seem uniquely realistic and efficacious" (Johnston 1995).

The fourth generation emerged by the end of the first decade of the 21st century, suggesting a solution to the Johnston (third generation)-Gray (first generation) debate, by proposing a strategic cultural model featuring competing subcultures (Anand V. 2020). These subcultures each present a different interpretation of a state's international social/ cultural context—who a state's "friends" and "foes" are—which in turn affects how that state interprets the material variables—geography, relative power, technological change, etc.—relevant to strategic decision-making. These different paradigms compete in public discourse for influence over strategic decision-making (Bloomfield 2012). According to this view, only those strategic subcultures which could provide an answer to the challenges thrown up by the strategic environment get selected as the dominant ones influencing policy (Anand V. 2020).

What Is Pakistan's Strategic Culture?

To understand Pakistan's strategic culture, we will need to go back to at least the creation of Pakistan. Pakistan's creation was predicated on the two-nation theory of a homeland for the Muslims in South Asia, separate from the Hindu majority in India. Pakistan's Muslim League party founders envisioned Pakistan as a homeland for India's Muslims—a secure place where they could fulfill their cultural and civilizational destiny (Cohen 2004). Soon after partition in August 1947, Pakistan engaged in the first war over Kashmir with India from 1947 to 1948. Pakistan fought three additional wars with India, two more over Kashmir (1965 and 1999) and the 1971 war that resulted in the bifurcation of Pakistan. Fair (2014) and Ganguly (2016) argue that Pakistan is a revisionist state. This stems from Pakistan's irredentist claim and commitment to incorporate the Muslim-majority state of Jammu and Kashmir beginning with Pakistan's initiation of the 1947–1948 war with India over Kashmir. Pakistan revisionism includes undermining the territorial status quo of Kashmir and in undermining India's position in the region and across the world. This claim draws from Glaser (2010), suggesting that Pakistan may be a purely greedy state, defined as "fundamentally dissatisfied with the status quo, desiring additional territory even when it is not required for security." Glaser uses the term greed to describe nonsecurity motives. Purely greedy states pursue revisionist policies to increase their prestige, to spread their ideology, or to propagate their religion (Fair 2014). Greedy states are different from states that are motivated only by security, which Glaser calls "security seekers" (2010). Moreover, Ganguly (2016) argues that the Indo-Pakistani relationship is not a security dilemma as Pakistan's fundamental goal of wresting Kashmir from India undermines Pakistan's own security in provoking a much more powerful neighbor. In short, Pakistan's apprehensions about India are more ideological than security driven (Fair 2014; Ganguly 2016). Pakistan, weak in the ability to control its people, territory, and ability to project legitimacy, is also ideological in responding to perceived internal and external threats.

Rizvi (2002) sums up Pakistan's strategic culture as: (a) An acute insecurity developed in the early years of independence due to troubled relations with India and problems with Afghanistan. (b) A strong distrust of India and a history of acrimonious Indo-Pakistani relations reinforced by the historical narratives of the pre-independence period and the troubled bilateral interaction in the post-independence period. (c) Aversion to an India-dominated regional power arrangement for South Asia. (d) An active search for security to maintain its independence in deciding about foreign policy options and domestic policies. (e) A close nexus between Islam and strategic thinking, leading to connections between Islamic militancy and foreign policy. Islam figures prominently in political and military discourse.

"The Pakistan Army controls most levers of power with respect to national security and foreign policy, as well as domestic policies that influence these domains" (Fair 2016). Thus, in the study of the strategic culture of Pakistan, "... the army, which for the vast majority of the country's history has directly and indirectly influenced defense policy toward India and Afghanistan as well as military alliances with the United States and China, among others, is the most appropriate institution to study" (Fair 2014; Cohen 2004; Schaffer and Schaffer 2011). Shah (2014) examines the Pakistan military as an institution of the state. Within that institution, it is the officer corps and its senior leadership that make the most important institutional decisions during both war and peace, which the rank and file are, at least in theory, duty bound to carry out. Further, the high command is the public face and voice of the institution. David O. Smith (2018), in a study on Pakistan Army officers who served at the Pakistan Army Command and Staff College[5] between 1977 and 2014, finds that the Army's ideology, ethos, or organizational culture can be briefly summarized as: (a) The Army is the custodian of Pakistani nationalism; (b) It guarantees Pakistani sovereignty viz its principal existential threat, India; (c) It is the only national institution that is competent and honest; (d) It is the only national institution that can be trusted to safeguard the national interest; (e) It is a vehicle for social mobility because promotion is based solely on merit and demonstrated good performance. In the 37 years of this study, the Pakistan Army's attitudes and values changed very little.

C. Christine Fair (2014) in one of the most extensive examinations of Pakistan's strategic culture reviewed a variety of Pakistani military publications. This culture is characterized by four beliefs: (1) that Pakistan is an insecure and incomplete state, (2) that Afghanistan is a source of instability, (3) that India rejects the two-nation theory and seeks to dominate or destroy Pakistan, and (4) that India is a regional hegemon that must be resisted. The army operationalizes these strategic concepts as well as the tools that it has developed over time to context with respect to national security and foreign policy (Fair 2016).

Strategic Culture Impact on Policies

Several scholars posit that Pakistan's behavior can be explained by the strategic culture of the Pakistan Army (Fair 2014). These attributes of Pakistan's strategic culture noted earlier shaped Pakistan's security and foreign policy options. Defying rationalist expectations, national security policies endure despite their failure to address Pakistan's strategic goals. This section first examines the import of strategic culture on the wars Pakistan has fought with India, secondly, Pakistan's use of proxies to advances its strategic goals, and finally, Pakistan's nuclear strategy.

First, Pakistan, despite initiating several wars against India, has failed to complete its objectives. Reviewing Pakistan's decision to initiate hostilities in 1965, in spite of clear signals from India with its much larger armed forces that it would respond aggressively, Ganguly

Pakistan's Strategic Culture

(1990) found Pakistan's behavior as contradicting the hypothesis of rational utility maximization. Except for the 1971 war, Pakistan does not see itself as ever having been defeated militarily. For the Pakistan Army, defeat comes only when it can no longer resist India. Pakistan's defense establishment holds the conviction that India is fundamentally opposed to Pakistan's existence, rejects the two-nation theory, seeks every opportunity to undo history, and numerous Pakistan domestic threats are the result of external foes, primarily India. Pakistan's strategic culture means that it is "willing to take considerable risks in relations with India" such as the use of militant proxies "because doing nothing is the sine qua non of defeat for the army" (Fair 2016).

Second, employing religiously motivated militant groups to offset conventional military weakness toward India has long been a tool used by the Pakistan Army. Smith (2018) notes the irony of the Kashmir situation is that the danger posed by groups like Lashkar-e-Tayyiba in provoking military confrontation with India will always be offset by their perceived utility in tying down large numbers of Indian military and security forces in the non-strategic Kashmir area in peacetime and in mounting behind-the-lines operations against the Indian Army in the event of future war (Smith 2018).

Pakistan's instrumentalization of Islamist groups such as the Taliban has historically been the principal strategic method employed by the military to minimize Indian influence in Afghanistan (Parkes 2019). Pakistan helped the Taliban consolidate power in Afghanistan in the mid-to-late 1990s. Viewing the Taliban as a friendly regime that could stabilize Pakistan's often unruly ethnic Pushtun population and provide much-needed "strategic depth" in Afghanistan in Pakistan's military competition with India, Pakistani leaders were loath to see the return of instability, and possibly hostility, on their western flank. Scholars (Khan 2012; Lavoy 2005) ask why Pakistan did an about face from supporting the Taliban to siding with the United States after 9/11 as this reversed Pakistan's policy and countered its strategic culture. Faced with intense pressure from the United States, Pakistan's President Pervez Musharraf agreed to break relations with the Taliban, provide basing and over-flight permission for all US and coalition forces, deploy along the Afghanistan border, and provide intelligence support to the international counterterrorism coalition. "While most of Pakistan's mainstream political parties supported the government's decision to join the international coalition against terrorism, the country's Islamic groups and parties were outraged" (Lavoy 2005). Musharraf survived several assassination attempts by Islamic extremists. Despite this formal policy reversal of siding with the United States, Pakistan continued to support the Taliban (Kugelman 2021; Perlez 2021).

Many experts point to strategic culture in explaining Pakistan's behavior, but for Afghanistan, the concept is more instructive in highlighting how policy flexibility is reduced. This literature emphasizes strategic culture's significant constraints on the freedom of choice for decision-makers, reducing policy flexibility (Aldrich 2017; Booth 1979; Lavoy 2005; Parkes 2019). Lavoy (2005) posits an explanation that the behavior of key strategic elites, known as mythmakers, is free to accept some constraints and yet ignore or overcome others. These strategic mythmakers operate within the confines of both the international environment and their nation's political culture, but they sometimes have some degrees of freedom to reorient and expand the internal and external boundaries of their behavior. However, the more a mythmaker tries to extend either of these boundaries of traditional behavior, the greater the risk they run domestically and internationally. Leadership entails knowing one's limits, but also knowing how to take advantage of rare opportunities for change, when they present themselves.

The myth-making approach points analysts to examine strategic elites as well as their beliefs about national security. It further calls attention to the institutionalization of these beliefs, or myths, in the rules, values, and beliefs of key national security institutions. As organization theorists would understand, the more national security myths become institutionalized, the greater the hold of culture takes over strategic elites (Lavoy 2005). Parkes (2019) notes that Pakistan's strategy supporting militants risks jeopardizing Pakistan's strategic partnership with China, which is another method used by Pakistan to counterbalance India. Beijing's growing strategic interests in the region require stability in South Asia, whereas Pakistan's strategic method in Afghanistan indicates a preference for instability. The destabilizing effect of Pakistan's support for Islamist groups, and China's desire for political and economic stability in South Asia, indicate latent divergent interests in the Sino-Pakistan strategic partnership, potentially factoring China as a looming constraint on Pakistan's Afghanistan policy. If China's economic interests in South Asia in theaters such as the China–Pakistan Economic Corridor (CPEC) are threatened, Pakistan faces a potential dilemma between its support for Islamist groups and its desire to deepen its relationship with China. China and Pakistan are indispensable allies in competition with India, and the CPEC strategically complements this partnership. However, the CPEC is a specific locus of strategic tension between Pakistan's support for Islamist groups and the potential security risk for China's economic aspirations and highlights a paradox in Pakistan's grand strategy.

Finally, scholars have proffered the influence of strategic culture in Pakistan's development of nuclear weapons in response to India's nuclear explosions (Rizvi 2002, F.H. Khan 2005; Lavoy 2005). Neorealism, which posits that countries generally try to balance against security threats first by developing their own military might and only secondly by forming alliances, would suggest that Pakistan should have launched a nuclear weapons program when it learned that India had initiated its own program to make nuclear bombs shortly after China's nuclear test in October 1964 (Lavoy 2005). However, Pakistan's quest for nuclear weapons began in 1972 after Pakistan's loss of East Pakistan following the 1971 Bangladesh Liberation War and India's intervention. India's 1974 "peaceful nuclear experiment" then jostled Pakistan out of its nuclear complacency (F.H. Khan 2005). Lavoy (2005) argues that a strategic culture approach to this policy change would hypothesize that because the dominant national security organization in the country was the armed forces, and because this institution was very conservative and pro-Western, Pakistan would continue to rely on conventional weapons and a close strategic relationship with the United States to meet its security needs.[6] Coming so close after its defeat in East Pakistan and reeling under domestic pressures, Pakistan had a severe shock. Failing to find support from allies and international institutions, Pakistan determined that only by matching India's conventional and nuclear development could its security be ensured (F.H. Khan 2005). Feroz Hassan Khan (2005) argues that in a mix of realism and strategic culture, Pakistan's behavior is predictable in many ways. It will not seek parity with India but will do its utmost to balance and retain initiative; it will seek external alliances with outside powers (the United States or China) but will not sacrifice its regional objectives. Pakistan will be cognizant of "emerging India" in partnership with the United States but will never assume that this rise will be benign. The most rational path that might be suggested for Pakistan is to accept this reality, give up its claims, and bandwagon with emerging India. But realism and strategic culture will predict that Pakistan will never accept hegemony. Strategic culture explains that Pakistan will work relentlessly to develop responses and countervailing strategies to ensure that India has a high cost to pay for any adventure (F.H. Khan 2005).

Some observers predicted that nuclear weapons would stabilize India-Pakistan relations and make war less likely because any conflict now could escalate to nuclear use.[7] This logic caused earlier nuclear powers to act cautiously with one another; however, the advent of nuclear weaponry has not diminished the violence in Indian-held Kashmir or along the Kashmir

Line of Control, where Indian and Pakistani forces have routinely traded fire. The continued border skirmishing and Pakistan's use of guerilla proxies creates strong pressures for conventional warfare (Lavoy 2005).

Pakistan's policy options further shaped by strategic culture include an advocacy of a pluralist power arrangement for South Asia, greater attention to external security, acquisition of military capacity to raise the cost of war for the adversary, liberal allocation of resources to defense, weapons procurement from abroad, and the use of diplomacy and alliance-building with other states, especially with the United States, for strengthening its position in the region (Rizvi 2002). Shah (2014) argues that the Pakistan military's tutelary beliefs and norms, a legacy of its formative experience under conditions of geopolitical insecurity with the perceived security threat from India combined with the internal conflict arising from nation-state building have profoundly shaped its political interventions and influence by justifying the authoritarian expansion of its role in state and society, to include the military's outright rule of the state for over 30 years, at the expense of civilian political institutions.

Is strategic culture alone enough to explain variation in Pakistan's behavior? The emphasis on strategic culture does not totally exclude the role of other considerations, such as realism, professionalism, and organizational imperatives. Many of Pakistan's security-related decisions involve the elements of more than one approach. At times, the dictates of different approaches conflict with each other and the policymakers may be unwilling or unable to make a clear-cut choice. This is the case with the approach of Pakistan's security managers toward the militant Islamic groups in the post-9/11 period (Rizvi 2002). The next section examines strategic subcultures.

Pakistan's Strategic Subcultures

Does Pakistan have strategic subcultures?[8] Strategic subcultures "contain an integrated mix of social/cultural and material/technical concepts. These are then promoted by various domestic groups competing against one another to offer the 'most accurate' interpretation of their states' international context" (Bloomfield 2012; Lantis 2014). There have been little scholarly attempts to identify Pakistan's competing strategic subcultures.[9] For one, there are several limitations to the current study of Pakistan's national security and the military. Pakistan has sought to limit critiques of the government and, more specifically, the military. This is likely part of its strategy to counter questions of legitimacy and thus challenges to the government's writ and regime's control in the pursuit of Pakistan's continued nation-building project. This strategy uses disinformation, disruption, and denial tactics to minimize international and domestic criticism to the regime. Islamabad often uses disinformation to delegitimize political challengers as treasonous, foreign conspiracies, or attempting to link these persons or groups to Islamic terrorism (Grare 2013). The state further attempts to disrupt the discussion by intimidating, threatening, or sometimes killing journalists, academics, activists, and nationalists, as well as protesting events, conferences, and pressuring foreign governments (Walsh 2020, The Economist 2014). Denial refers to the domestic media pressure and international media blackouts, denying foreign access to issues pertaining to military and security forces activities, human rights, and Baloch nationalism (Zurutuza 2014). Thus, this chapter relies on available official documents, scholarly research, journalistic accounts, human rights organization reports, and narratives from multiple actors in Pakistan.

Pakistan's military subcultures include Islamist, pro-Western, and anti-Indian/Pakistani nationalist, which are not mutually exclusive and can overlap within one another. With the danger of radical religious thought spreading in Pakistani society, army officials have noted an increasing trend of Islamization in the army, despite the various "filters" used to vet officers for future promotions (Nawaz 2020; Smith 2018). In 2018, then US President Donald Trump's administration suspended security assistance to Pakistan as well as its military training and education program. This brought comparisons to the 1990's when the United States refused to certify that Pakistan did not have nuclear weapons, triggering the "Pressler Amendment" that required cutting off all military assistance. This period brought about a generation of Pakistan military leadership that the US did not know as well, and thus could not engage as effectively with them when needed. Furthermore, Pakistani officials warned it could push their military to further look to China or Russia for leadership training (Ali and Stewart 2018).

In 2018, the world's top antiterrorism monitoring group, the Financial Action Task Force (FATF), placed Pakistan on its gray list for failing to adequately crack down on terrorism financing and money laundering. The listing made it more expensive for Pakistan to raise money on the international bond market, further exacerbating Pakistan's debt crisis and weakening its economy. To comply with the FATF's demands, Pakistani officials said they banned militant groups in the country, their bank accounts frozen and assets confiscated. Hafiz Muhammad Saeed, the founder of Jamaat-ud Dawa and another outlawed militant group, Lashkar-e-Tayyiba, was arrested and convicted for terrorism financing charges; however, he had been arrested and freed by local courts several times in the past, leading to accusations that Pakistan's action against militant leaders has been superficial and meant only to temporarily placate Western concerns (Masood and Abi-Habib 2019; George & Hussain 2020). Moreover, the flagship publication of the Pakistan Army characterized the FATF's pressure on Pakistan as a direct economic threat from hostile states (India) that impacts Pakistan's national security, making the local environment non-conducive for international investments.[10] In 2021, senior Pakistani government and military officials announced a desire to shift the narrative of geo-political contestation into geo-economic integration (Tariq 2021).

Does this represent a shift in Pakistan's long-standing policy of supporting militants? If so, is a change in strategic culture? Or does this represent potential multiple competing subcultures and what is the likelihood that a new subculture will become dominant? Lantis (2002) finds that a country's strategic culture can change, contending that at least two conditions during a crisis caused "strategic cultural dilemmas" and produced changes in national security policy. First, external shocks may serve to fundamentally challenge existing beliefs and undermine past historical narratives. Second, foreign policy behavior may break the traditional bounds of strategic cultural orientations when primary tenets of strategic thought directly conflict with one another, in a strategic cultural dissonance. Thus, strategic cultural dilemmas define new directions for policy and demand the reconstruction of historical narratives. However, like paradigm shifts, these changes take time and energy for common acceptance.

Has Pakistan's strategic culture changed? One argument is that "Pakistan's reliance on nonstate actors evolved considerably with the introduction of nuclear weapons, or at least the introduction of nuclear overhang. Pakistan's fusing of its nonstate actor policy with its concepts of nuclear deterrence has created a strategy that is very difficult to defeat without accepting extreme risk. Similarly, Pakistan's perceptions of the Afghan threat quickly became imbricated with its concerns about India" (Fair 2016). Ijaz Khan (2012) argues that a change in the foreign policy decision-making process requires a new look at Pakistan's memory. He suggests a reevaluation of Pakistan's identity and moving beyond its ideological underpinnings, the military removing Islamic politicization and reasserting professionalism, and reforming Pakistan's education system and school syllabi. Pakistani strategic culture peace is not a choice and a thorough and fundamental change in self-identity as well as world view is required. The author argues that a plural democratic Pakistan is the only way toward that change (I. Khan 2012).

Fair, however, argues that these strategic cultural perceptions leave very little room for reforming Pakistan. "The traditional US approach toward the country has involved financial and military assistance, ostensibly guided by the logic that such aid could help it feel less insecure and thus resolve its conflicts with India and Afghanistan. This would permit Pakistan to put down the Islamic extremist proxies and roll back its policy of nuclear proliferation. However, such optimism is ill-founded as Pakistan's apprehensions about India and Afghanistan are ideological as well as material. Eliminating Pakistan's material sources of disquiet cannot address the ideological concerns about its environment and even rewards Pakistan for the behaviors it has adopted to manage these perceived threats." Moreover, "... even if Pakistan were to be truly governed by civilians, it is unlikely that the country would behave differently because the army has effectively ensured that its core strategic beliefs and the tools to manage them are also embraced by ordinary Pakistanis. This implies that a more genuinely democratic structure would not necessarily result in Pakistan abandoning its revisionism toward India in Kashmir or beyond" (Fair 2016).

An anti-Indian-focused subculture will likely continue to dominate the Pakistan military's thinking over the next decade, to include its policy of supporting militant groups, absent a shock that shifts the military's threat perception. The India-centric threat perception, however, may lessen over time as younger generations of officers rise through the ranks who have grown up professionally fighting Islamist militants, such as Tehrik-e Taliban Pakistan (Smith 2018). The next section explores additional questions, implications, and areas for future research.

Conclusion

Rizvi summarizes strategic culture as an "... approach [that] helps us understand the historical and psychological dynamics of decision-making. It highlights the impact of ideological and other societal variables on policymaking and offers a better understanding of the sociocultural and political context within which the policymakers function. Any study of a state's strategic profile and the possible reaction to security pressures requires, inter alia, a good appreciation of the strategic culture of the country concerned. This facilitates communication between the security policymakers and the outside actors, i.e., individuals, states, and organizations, on security-related issues and helps to identify ways and means to change their policy outputs" (Rizvi 2002). Aqil Shah notes that unless one builds an informed understanding of how members of the military think, perceive, judge, evaluate, and choose one course of action over another, any analysis of the military in politics will be insufficient (Shah 2014). Fair (2014) argues that understanding the strategic culture of the Pakistan Army "... is the key to understanding what, if any, options the international community has for influencing this strategic culture and the strategic preferences it wields."

"Pakistan has adopted several strategies to manage its security environment, including ideological tools, the pursuit of strategic depth in Afghanistan, and the use of proxy fighters under its expanding nuclear umbrella" (Fair 2016). Faruqui notes that "Pakistan's preoccupation with seeking a military solution to its conflict with India is strategically myopic on three counts. First, it has not been militarily successful. Second, it has failed to achieve Pakistan's stated political aims. Third, it has been costly, in terms of the benefit foregone by not spending enough on raising the people's standard of living" (Faruqui 2003). "Pakistan continues to pursue these strategies even though they are very unlikely to succeed and have imposed a high cost on the state" (Fair 2016).

The Pakistan Army's "strategic culture is enduring and unlikely to change," especially in the near term (Fair 2016). Thus, if Pakistan appears to break in long-standing policies that counter the military's strategic culture, it must be viewed with deep skepticism as this potential subculture is unlikely to become the dominant view of the Pakistan military. "Any perceived change in Pakistani policy in response to the application of carrots or sticks by the international community will almost certainly be tactical and temporary" (Smith 2018).

Further, Parkes (2019) suggests further research in conceptualizing how China factors in Pakistan's strategic culture given their "all-weather" friendship and variables such as grand strategy, history, and geography. The Sino-Pakistan strategic partnership is a locus of geopolitical power that is unlikely to pale in significance to strategic scholarship as China's rise challenges global order and redefines post–Cold War security structures.

In sum, strategic culture plays an important role in shaping policies but is not the lone determinant. Strategic culture can change although likely not instantaneous, occurring over time, or due to an exogenous shock. Understanding Pakistan's strategic culture, the constraints it poses, and role of key individuals and elites within its key strategic institutions may help policymakers as they formulate relationships with Pakistan amidst continued instability in South Asia.

Notes

1 Naveed Siddiqui, "'Don't worry, everything will be okay': ISI chief during Kabul visit," *Dawn*, September 4, 2021, https://www.dawn.com/news/1644463.
2 Jane Perlez, "The Real Winner of the Afghan War? It's Not Who You Think," *New York Times*, August 26, 2021, https://www.nytimes.com/2021/08/26/world/asia/afghanistan-pakistan-taliban.html.
3 Mercy A. Kuo, "Pakistan-China Relations and the Fall of Afghanistan," *The Diplomat*, August 31, 2021, https://thediplomat.com/2021/08/pakistan-china-relations-and-the-fall-of-afghanistan/.
4 Hans M. Kristensen and Matt Korda, "Nuclear Notebook: How Many Nuclear Weapons Does Pakistan Have in 2021?" *Bulletin of the Atomic Scientists*, September 7, 2021, https://thebulletin.org/premium/2021-09/nuclear-notebook-how-many-nuclear-weapons-does-pakistan-have-in-2021/; "Nuclear Weapons: Who Has What at a Glance." *Arms Control Association*, October 2021, https://www.armscontrol.org/factsheets/Nuclearweaponswhohaswhat.
5 The Pakistan Army Command and Staff College is located in Quetta, the capital of Balochistan Province. The students at Quetta are generally considered to be the very best and brightest of the Pakistan Army, and selection to the Staff College is their first major step toward upward mobility in the Army (Smith 2018).
6 Lavoy (2005) finds his myth-making model performs better than realism or strategic culture in explaining Pakistan's policy change toward developing nuclear weapons.
7 See Šumit Ganguly and S. Paul Kapur, *India, Pakistan, and the Bomb: Debating Nuclear Stability in South Asia* (New York: Columbia University Press, 2012).
8 See Beitelmair-Berini (2021), Hall (2016), and Bajpai (2002) for an analysis of strategic subcultures in India.
9 A notable exception, Heuser (2000) suggests three subcultures in Pakistan's foreign policy. One fiercely anti-Indian, anti-colonial, and nationalistic, another pro-Western and liberal, and a third radical Islamist (Bloomfield 2012). However, this does not address Pakistan's most powerful institution, the military.
10 Pakistan Army General Headquarters, *Pakistan Army Green Book 2020* (Rawalpindi: Crystal, 2020).

Bibliography

"Nuclear Weapons: Who Has What at a Glance." *Arms Control Association*, October 2021. https://www.armscontrol.org/factsheets/Nuclearweaponswhohaswhat.
"Pakistan: Escalating Attacks on Journalists Authorities Should Stop Stifling Dissent, Protect the Media." *Human Rights Watch*, June 3, 2021. https://www.hrw.org/news/2021/06/03/pakistan-escalating-attacks-journalists#.

"Pakistan: Surge in Harassment of Journalists Who "Criticize" on Social Media." *Reporters Without Borders*, September 17, 2017. https://rsf.org/en/news/pakistan-surge-harassment-journalists-who-criticize-social-media.

"Read: Full Text of Gen Bajwa's Speech at the Islamabad Security Dialogue." *Dawn*, March 18, 2021. https://www.dawn.com/news/1613207.

Ahmed, Munir. "Pakistani Journalists' Group Vows to Fight for Press Freedom." *Associated Press*, May 3, 2021. https://apnews.com/article/pakistan-business-journalists-89ab9083a0ba7602f1c7591b587386f6.

Aldrich, Richard J. "Strategic Culture as a Constraint: Intelligence Analysis, Memory and Organizational Learning the Social Sciences and History." *Intelligence and National Security* 32, no. 5 (2017): 625–635. https://doi.org/10.1080/02684527.2017.1310977.

Ali, Idrees, and Phil Stewart. "Exclusive: As Trump Cracks Down on Pakistan, U.S. Cuts Military Training Programs." *Reuters*, August 10, 2018. https://www.reuters.com/article/us-pakistan-usa-military-exclusive/exclusive-as-trump-cracks-down-on-pakistan-u-s-cuts-military-training-programs-idUSKBN1KV166.

Anand V. "Revisiting the Discourse on Strategic Culture: An Assessment of the Conceptual Debates." *Strategic Analysis* 44, no. 3 (2020): 193–207. https://doi.org/10.1080/09700161.2020.1787684.

Beitelmair-Berini, Bernhard. *India's Grand Strategy and Foreign Policy: Strategic Pluralism and Subcultures.* New York: Routledge, 2021.

Bloomfield, Alan. "Time to Move On: Reconceptualizing the Strategic Culture Debate." *Contemporary Security Policy* 33, no. 3 (2012): 437–461. https://doi.org/10.1080/13523260.2012.727679.

Booth, Ken, and Russell Trood, eds. *Strategic Cultures in the Asia-Pacific Region.* London: Macmillan Press, 1999.

Booth, Ken. "The Concept of Strategic Culture Affirmed." In *Strategic Power: USA/USSR*, edited by C.G. Jacobsen, 121–135. New York: St. Martin's Press, 1990.

Booth, Ken. *Strategy and Ethnocentrism.* New York: Holmes & Meier, 1979.

Cohen, Stephen P. *The Idea of Pakistan.* Washington DC: Brookings, 2004.

Das, Runa. "The Prism of Strategic Culture and South Asian Nuclearization." *Contemporary Politics* 15, no. 4 (2009): 395–411. https://doi.org/10.1080/13569770903416463.

Desch, Michael C. "Culture Clash: Assessing the Importance of Ideas in Security Studies." *International Security* 24, no. 1 (Summer 1998): 141–170.

Dueck, Colin. "U.S. Strategic Culture: Liberalism with Limited Liability." In *Understanding Strategic Cultures in the Asia-Pacific*, edited by Ashley J. Tellis, Alison Szalwinski, and Michael Wills, 194–218. Seattle: The National Bureau of Asian Research, 2016.

The Economist. "Journalism in Pakistan: The Silencing of the Liberals," April 26, 2014. https://www.economist.com/asia/2014/04/26/the-silencing-of-the-liberals.

Fair, C. Christine. "Pakistan's Strategic Culture: Implications for How Pakistan Perceives and Counters Threats." *The National Bureau of Asian Research* 61 (2016).

Fair, C. Christine. *Fighting to the End: The Pakistan Army's Way of War.* New York: Oxford University Press, 2014.

Faruqui, Ahmad. *Rethinking the National Security of Pakistan: The Price of Strategic Myopia.* New York: Routledge, 2003.

Feng, Huiyun. *Chinese Strategic Culture and Foreign Policy Decision-Making: Confucianism, Leadership, and War.* New York: Routledge, 2007.

Ganguly, Šumit. "Deterrence Failure Revisited: The Indo-Pakistani Conflict of 1965." *Journal of Strategic Studies* 13, no. 4 (December 1990): 77–93. https://doi.org/10.1080/01402399008437432.

Ganguly, Šumit. *Deadly Impasse: Indo-Pakistani Relations at the Dawn of a New Century.* Cambridge: Cambridge University Press, 2016.

Ganguly, Šumit, and S. Paul Kapur. *India, Pakistan, and the Bomb: Debating Nuclear Stability in South Asia.* New York: Columbia University Press, 2012.

George, Alexander L. "The 'Operational Code': A Neglected Approach to the Study of Political Leaders and Decision-Making." *International Studies Quarterly* 13, no. 2 (June 1969): 190–222.

George, Susannah, and Shaiq Hussain. "Pakistan Hopes Its Steps to 'Eradicate' Terrorism will Keep it Off a Global Blacklist." *Washington Post*, February 20, 2020. https://www.washingtonpost.com/world/asia_pacific/pakistan-fatf-terrorism-blacklist/2020/02/20/df67602c-51e4-11ea-80ce-37a8d4266c09_story.html.

Grare, Frederic. "Balochistan: The State Versus the Nation." Carnegie Papers, April 11, 2013. https://carnegieendowment.org/2013/04/11/balochistan-state-versus-nation-pub-51488.

Gray, Colin S. "National Style in Strategy: The American Example." *International Security* 6, no. 2 (Fall 1981): 21–47. https://doi.org/10.2307/2538645.

Hall, Ian. "The Persistence of Nehruvianism in India's Strategic Culture." In *Understanding Strategic Cultures in the Asia-Pacific*, edited by Ashley J. Tellis, Alison Szalwinski, and Michael Wills, 140–167. Seattle: The National Bureau of Asian Research, 2016.

Heinkel, Jamison C., and Richard deVillafranca. "Could Pakistan Lose Balochistan? Balochistan's Insurgency and Its Implications for Pakistan and the Region." *Journal of Strategic Intelligence* 1, no. 1 (Summer 2016): 62–72.

Heuser, Beatrice. "Beliefs, Culture, Proliferation and Nuclear Weapons." *Journal of Strategic Studies* 23, no. 1 (2000): 75–100. https://doi.org/10.1080/01402390008437779.

Johnston, Alastair Iain. "Thinking about Strategic Culture." *International Security* 19, no. 4 (Spring 1995): 32–64. https://doi.org/10.2307/2539119.

Khan, Feroz Hassan. "Comparative Strategic Culture: The Case of Pakistan." *Strategic Insights* 4, no. 10 (October 2005). https://calhoun.nps.edu/bitstream/handle/10945/11241/khan2Oct05.pdf?sequence=1&isAllowed=y

Khan, Ijaz. *Pakistan's Strategic Culture and Foreign Policy Making: A Study of Pakistan's Post 9/11 Afghan Policy Change.* New York: Nova Science, 2012.

Klein, Bradley S. "Hegemony and Strategic Culture: American Power Projection and Alliance Defence Politics." *Review of International Studies* 14, no. 2 (1988): 133–148. https://doi.org/10.1017/S026021050011335X.

Kristensen, Hans M., and Matt Korda, "Nuclear Notebook: How Many Nuclear Weapons Does Pakistan Have in 2021?" *Bulletin of the Atomic Scientists*, September 7, 2021. https://thebulletin.org/premium/2021-09/nuclear-notebook-how-many-nuclear-weapons-does-pakistan-have-in-2021/.

Kugelman, Michael. "Pakistan's Friendship with the Taliban Is Changing." *Foreign Policy*, September 13, 2021. https://foreignpolicy.com/2021/09/13/pakistan-taliban-ties-afghanistan/.

Kuo, Mercy A. "Pakistan-China Relations and the Fall of Afghanistan." *The Diplomat*, August 31, 2021. https://thediplomat.com/2021/08/pakistan-china-relations-and-the-fall-of-afghanistan/.

Lantis, Jeffrey S., ed. "Strategic Cultures and Security Policies in the Asia-Pacific." *Contemporary Security Policy* 35, no. 2 (August 2014): 165–328.

Lantis, Jeffrey S. "Strategic Culture and National Security Policy." *International Studies Review* 4, no. 3 (Fall 2002): 87–113. https://doi.org/10.1111/1521-9488.t01-1-00266.

Lantis, Jeffrey S. "Strategic Culture: From Clausewitz to Constructivism." *Strategic Insights* 4, no. 10 (October 2005). https://calhoun.nps.edu/bitstream/handle/10945/11257/lantisOct05.pdf?sequence=1&isAllowed=y

Lavoy, Peter. "Pakistan's Strategic Culture: A Theoretical Excursion." *Strategic Insights* 4, no. 10 (November 2005). ttps://calhoun.nps.edu/bitstream/handle/10945/11264/lavoyOct05.pdf?sequence=1&isAllowed=y

Leites, Nathan. "Psycho-Cultural Hypotheses about Political Acts." *World Politics* 1, no. 1 (October 1948): 102–119.

Leites, Nathan. *A Study of Bolshevism.* Glencoe, Illinois: The Free Press, 1953.

Masood, Salman, and Maria Abi-Habib. "Pakistan Avoids Terrorism Blacklist and Sanctions." *New York Times*, October 18, 2019. https://www.nytimes.com/2019/10/18/world/asia/pakistan-terrorism-blacklist-sanctions.html.

Nawaz, Shuja. *The Battle for Pakistan: The Bitter US Friendship and a Tough Neighborhood.* Lanham: Rowman & Littlefield, 2020.

Parkes, Aidan. "Pakistan's Strategic Culture and Its Gordian Knot in Afghanistan." *Journal of Asian Security and International Affairs* 6, no. 3 (2019): 254–274. https://doi.org/10.1177/2347797019885728.

Perlez, Jane. "The Real Winner of the Afghan War? It's Not Who You Think." *New York Times*, August 26, 2021. https://www.nytimes.com/2021/08/26/world/asia/afghanistan-pakistan-taliban.html.

Rizvi, Hasan-Askari. "Pakistan's Strategic Culture." In *South Asia in 2020: Future Strategic Balances and Alliances*, edited by Michael R. Chambers, 305–328. US Army War College Press, 2002.

Sayeed, Saad. "In Pakistan's Once-Vibrant Media, Some Journalists View Intimidation as the New Normal." *Reuters*, October 9, 2018. https://www.reuters.com/article/us-pakistan-media/in-pakistans-once-vibrant-media-some-journalists-view-intimidation-as-the-new-normal-idUSKCN1MJ0DX.

Schaffer, Howard B., and Teresita C. Schaffer. *How Pakistan Negotiates with the United States: Riding the Roller Coaster.* Washington DC: United States Institute for Peace, 2011.

Shah, Aqil. *The Army and Democracy: Military Politics in Pakistan*. Cambridge: Harvard University Press, 2014.

Siddiqui, Naveed. "'Don't Worry, Everything will be Okay': ISI Chief during Kabul Visit." *Dawn*, September 4, 2021. https://www.dawn.com/news/1644463.

Smith, David O. *The Quetta Experience: A Study of Attitudes and Values within the Pakistan Army*. Washington DC: Wilson Center, 2018.

Snyder, Jack. *The Soviet Strategic Culture: Implications for Limited Nuclear Operations. R-2154-AF*. Santa Monica: Rand Corporation, 1977.

Tariq, Hamna. "Realizing the U.S.-Pakistan Geoeconomic Pivot." *South Asian Voices*, June 14, 2021. https://southasianvoices.org/realizing-the-u-s-pakistan-geoeconomic-pivot/.

Tellis, Ashley J., Alison Szalwinski, and Michael Wills, eds. *Understanding Strategic Cultures in the Asia-Pacific*. Seattle: The National Bureau of Asian Research, 2016.

Walsh, Declan. *The Nine Lives of Pakistan: Dispatches from a Precarious State*. New York: W.W. Norton & Company, 2020.

Zurutuza, Karlos. "A Black Hole for Media in Balochistan." *Al Jazeera*, February 5, 2014. https://www.aljazeera.com/features/2014/2/5/a-black-hole-for-media-in-balochistan.

7

THE EVOLUTION OF THE SINO-INDIAN RIVALRY

Manjeet S. Pardesi

China and India have been locked in a "strategic rivalry"[1] since the late 1940s. Strategic rivalries are long-term contests over specific issues in international relations in which the two sides compete over shared goals, and view each other as hostile and threatening, thereby raising the probability of conflict. There are two issues in contention in the Sino-Indian rivalry.[2] This contest began as a *positional* rivalry in the late 1940s as China and India competed for leadership in Asian strategic affairs in the postwar/postcolonial period. However, the People's Liberation Army's (PLA's) invasion of eastern Tibet in October 1950 followed by the annexation of all of Tibet by mid-1951 added a *spatial/territorial* dimension to the Sino-Indian rivalry.

The incorporation of Tibet made China and India contiguous states. However, given the unsettled India-Tibet frontier and China's rejection of colonial-era treaties meant that the entire Sino-Indian frontier—approximately 3,500 km long—was now contested, and involved disputes over two chunks of territories in particular: Aksai Chin in the west (approximately 38,000 square km) and most of the area corresponding with what is the Indian state of Arunachal Pradesh today in the east (approximately 90,000 square km).[3]

These *positional* and *spatial* dimensions notwithstanding, the Sino-Indian rivalry is asymmetrical.[4] While India's elites view China as their most consequential rival (ranked above India's subcontinental rival, Pakistan), China's elites perceive India as a "lesser" rival (ranked below China's other rivals since the late 1940s: The United States, the Soviet Union, and Japan). This asymmetry is not simply a function of material power disparity that favors China in the Sino-Indian dyad. Instead, it is rooted in historically informed cognitive biases.

Modern China had encountered modern India as an agent of British colonialism during its "century of humiliation" as the British Empire had used British Indian troops during the Opium Wars and the Boxer Rebellion. Ethnic Indians were also employed in the police services in Britain's "treaty ports" in China, including in Shanghai and Hong Kong. Furthermore, China wanted to be wealthy and powerful like the western states and Japan, while consciously avoiding India's status as a formal colony. The Chinese disdain for India continued even after India's independence because the Indian state was seen as "a creation of British colonialism,"[5] and China (erroneously) viewed Anglo-American power lurking behind India's ambitions for leadership in Asia. China was also concerned about Indian and Anglo-American designs on Tibet.

By contrast, the Indian leadership believed that China and India would build the postwar/postcolonial order in Asia together. This thinking was the outcome of a very different set of

DOI: 10.4324/9781003246626-10

interactions with China on the part of independent India's leaders.[6] After the Japanese invasion of China in 1937, both the Communists and the Nationalists had sought help from India. While their outreach to India is best explained by wartime exigencies, India's leaders (erroneously) viewed this gesture as an expression of the Chinese desire to work with India to end colonialism as well as the era of western hegemony in Asia. However, the PLA's invasion of eastern Tibet in 1950 led to fears of Chinese expansionism and hegemony in India.[7]

In other words, China and India were suspicious of each other's intentions in the late 1940s and early 1950s. This distrust emerged out of their historical interactions over the preceding decades. Four distinct phases of the Sino-Indian rivalry can be identified in the ensuing decades: The first phase leading up to the 1962 Sino-Indian War when each side tried to unsuccessfully assuage the fears of the other; the second phase after the war characterized by balance-of-power politics (that ended in December 1988 before the end of the Cold War); the third phase when the two sides decided to shelve contentious issues while seeking cooperative avenues (that ended sometime in the first decade of the 21st century); and the fourth and current phase when Sino-Indian tensions are on the rise yet again. Each of these four phases is discussed in the following four sections. The chapter concludes by noting that the Sino-Indian rivalry has become more complex as it is now intertwined with their other rivalries: The India-Pakistan and the US-China rivalries.

Phase 1—The Run-Up to 1962

The 1950s began with India's bid to seek leadership in Asia, albeit in partnership with China.[8] This was most vividly on display at the 1955 Bandung Conference. While Indonesia was the host, the backing of the Indian Prime Minister Jawaharlal Nehru was crucial. In fact, it was Nehru who made China's participation at this conference possible.[9] The People's Republic of China (PRC) was not yet a member of the United Nations (UN), and there was apprehension in several Asian states about China's ambitions. Not surprisingly, the PRC leadership had made a conscious decision to not compete with Nehru for Asian leadership at Bandung.

India and China were upset with America's Southeast Asian Treaty Organization (SEATO) that was announced in 1954.[10] While China viewed this alliance as a part of America's containment strategy of the PRC, India thought of it as the continuation of western military dominance in Asia. Even as their motivations were different, India had China had reasons to work together to create an "Asian" order (at least for now). A few years earlier, India had also sought to mediate between China and the United States during the 1950–53 Korean War in the absence of direct diplomatic links between them, and played an important (if often overlooked) role in paving the way to armistice. Notably, India also advocated for the PRC's admission into the UN (instead of the Republic of China), and even turned down an American offer made in 1950 for India to assume the Chinese seat at the UN Security Council. China found India's advocacy of its cause useful, while India continued to believe that the two countries could work together in Asia.

However, developments related to Tibet complicated Sino-Indian relations.[11] India was the only country that officially protested to the PRC after the PLA invaded eastern Tibet in 1950. In the protest notes, India also stated its intention of continuing its British-era privileges there, which included the stationing of a small contingent of troops. While China's leaders were upset with India's complaints and with its desire to continue colonial-era privileges, they did not raise this issue in their response to India. Tibet was commercially oriented toward India then, and Lhasa was more easily accessible via eastern India than overland from China directly. The first roads linking Tibet with China (the Qinghai-Tibet and Sichuan-Tibet

Highways) were only built in 1954. Furthermore, there was the issue of feeding the PLA troops in Tibet who had to be supplied via India. Consequently, the Chinese leader Mao Zedong was aware that good relations with India were important for Tibet's integration with the PRC.

The Seventeen Point Agreement that formalized the PRC's annexation of Tibet in 1951 allowed for considerable autonomy as Tibet retained its small military and currency, while the Dalai Lama's "local" government continued to collect taxes there and engaged in commercial activities with India.[12] The Indian rupee also circulated in the Tibetan economy (albeit unofficially). India's main concern was the maintenance of Tibetan "autonomy" and a degree of Indian influence there to prevent any Chinese military pressure on India's northern frontiers.

Given that the PLA troops were not deployed along the Sino-Indian frontier, India believed that an implicit understanding with China on the Tibetan issue was in place. Consequently, they signed an agreement in 1954 related to Tibetan trade through which India recognized Tibet as a part of China while agreeing to end all its British-era privileges there. Furthermore, the preamble to this agreement included *Panchsheel* (or the Five Principles of Peaceful Coexistence). India and China approached *Panchsheel* as the Asian response to America's SEATO and tried to extend it to others in the region, especially in the Himalayas (Nepal) and in Southeast Asia (Burma and Cambodia).

However, two developments related to Tibet brought Sino-Indian differences to the fore in the second half of the 1950s. First, as China began implementing communist "reforms" in eastern Tibet (especially in Kham and Amdo), it led to several local protests and insurgencies against Chinese rule. Chinese reforms that included land reforms were viewed as attacks on the Tibetan identity itself as Buddhist monasteries were the biggest landowners in Tibet. The PRC responded to this violence militarily and the PLA aerially bombed several monasteries. As the Khampas tried to organize and respond to the PLA's assault, the Kalimpong/India-based Gyalo Thondup (the Dalai Lama's brother) became the liaison between the Khampas and the American Central Intelligence Agency (CIA). When the Dalai Lama visited India in 1956–57, China unsuccessfully tried to prevent him from visiting Kalimpong (where he spent a month). China also complained to India about the activities of the spies in Kalimpong.[13]

Second, in late 1957, China announced the creation of the Xinjiang-Tibet Highway, a section of which passed through the disputed Aksai Chin region.[14] Notably, Khampa activities were concentrated near the two other China-Tibet highways, thereby raising the importance of the Xinjiang-Tibet Highway for the PLA now that Tibet was facing unrest. Furthermore, this highway through Aksai Chin was the only route that was traversable throughout the year given the more forbidding topography of the regions that the Qinghai-Tibet and Sichuan-Tibet Highways passed through, especially during the winter months. As India complained to China about this road that passed through what it deemed to be Indian territory, the Sino-Indian border dispute came to the fore and was inextricably linked with the Tibetan issue (when seen from Beijing).

This was the larger geopolitical context when the 1959 Lhasa Revolt against the authority of the PRC in Tibet broke out.[15] Notably, this revolt was the largest organized opposition against the rule of the PRC since its creation, which resulted in the dramatic escape of the Dalai Lama to India. The Dalai Lama denounced the Seventeen Point Agreement from India and announced the creation of a Tibetan government-in-exile. The Dalai Lama was followed by several thousand Tibetans (including Khampas) into India where they were given refuge. While India did not (and still does not) recognize the Tibetan government-in-exile, China blamed India for the 1959 Lhasa Revolt even as there is no evidence of India's involvement in it.

The suppression of the Tibetan revolt required a large-scale military operation that resulted in the deaths of 87,000 Tibetans. The "entire PLA establishment, except one branch (the navy) and one military region (Inner Mongolia), joined the rebellion suppression in Tibet"[16] that lasted well into 1961. As the PLA rushed to seal China's borders with India (to capture the rebels and to prevent them from returning into Tibet/China from India), Chinese and Indian troops clashed briefly in late 1959 (at Longju and Kongka). Simultaneously, the PLA sought to provide "defense in depth for the Aksai Chin Road" after 1959 by moving the PLA posts deeper into contested territory. Not surprisingly, India responded with its "forward policy" in late 1961.[17] India's forward policy aimed to capture the no-man's land between Indian and Chinese positions in the disputed frontier, and to politically dominate the PLA positions in this region (even as Indian forces were ill-equipped for the task).

India was working under the erroneous assumption that even as Indian and Chinese troops may clash locally at certain points, a Sino-Indian war was unlikely because it would escalate into a major war involving the superpowers.[18] In the meanwhile, China believed (erroneously as well) that India wanted nothing short of restoring Tibet to its pre-1950/51 status as a "buffer" between India and China, and that India's forward policy in Aksai Chin had its sights on the crucial segment of the Xinjiang-Tibet Highway passing through that region (even as India had no such plans).[19]

In addition to these concerns related to Tibet, larger Asian strategic issues were also lurking in the background through issue-linkage. The PLA believed that India desired hegemony in the Himalayan states of Nepal, Bhutan, and Sikkim. Furthermore, the 1954 *Panchsheel* agreement between India and China lapsed in June 1962 as India declined to renew it after imposing economic sanctions on Tibet. In fact, India declined to renew this agreement by arguing that these principles were not just about Tibet but that they were also about peace in Asia, especially in Southeast Asia. Consequently, China attacked India in October 1962 for a complex mix of reasons: The border issue which was linked to the Tibetan issue and matters pertaining to Tibet/*Panchsheel* also impinged on larger Asian strategic affairs.

In other words, both *positional* and *spatial* issues were at stake in the run-up to the 1962 Sino-Indian War. China justified its actions in 1962 by not only complaining about the border dispute, but also noting that India had larger ambitions in Asia and designs on Tibet after having learned from the British colonial experience.[20] As India's under-equipped forces crumbled against the massive Chinese assault, New Delhi turned toward Washington for help (despite prior misgivings related to SEATO). So grave was the situation for India that Nehru requested America's intervention in the form of a defensive air war against China.[21] On its part, Beijing had carefully planned the attack to overlap with the Cuban Missile Crisis, and unilaterally declared a ceasefire after besting Indian forces and reaching its claimed lines in the eastern and western sectors of the border before the United States had the chance to formally respond to India.

Phase 2—Balance-of-Power Politics (1962–1988)

India's defeat in 1962 and turn toward the United States meant that India's quest for Asian leadership was hollow. The war changed India's approach toward international relations as India briefly "aligned" with the United States (the rhetoric of non-alignment notwithstanding). In the meanwhile, China and Pakistan were in the process of forging an entente during the Sino-Indian War itself and resolved their territorial dispute in 1963. As China threatened to open a second front during the 1965 India-Pakistan War, the United States also issued implicit threats to the PRC to deter China from doing so.[22] At the same time, the United States imposed sanctions on both India and Pakistan. Given Indian criticism of American policies in Vietnam (when the scale of US involvement was expanding), the nascent India–US alignment ended in 1965. India then began to look toward the Soviet Union to help balance China. The Sino-Soviet split had become public by 1963.

As America sought to forge a tacit alliance with the PRC against the Soviet Union in the Cold War, a process in which Pakistan played an important role behind-the-scenes,[23] India feared the emergence of US-China-Pakistan alignment. Consequently, on the eve of the 1971 Bangladesh War, India and Soviet Union entered into a "treaty of peace, friendship and cooperation" with security undertones. So dramatically had the US-India relationship deteriorated that the United States encouraged China to open a second front against India if New Delhi escalated the war by attacking West Pakistan.[24] Meanwhile, the Soviets deployed forces along their frontier with China to signal that they may intervene in the event of a Chinese attack on India.

While the threat of a larger war passed in 1971, the Soviet-India relationship did not transform into one that promoted a common vision of regional order in Asia. In fact, India did not endorse the Soviet Union's Asian Collective Security Proposal. India's victory in 1971 and the vivisection of Pakistan (and the creation of Bangladesh) also partly reversed India's humiliating defeat in 1962.[25] In fact, it was India's military modernization after 1962 that made the victory of 1971 possible, thereby inadvertently setting India on the path toward primacy in South Asia. The Sino-Indian positional rivalry had been transformed by this time as India became more focused on subcontinental affairs instead of competing with China for leadership at the pan-Asian level. But this did not imply Chinese leadership in Asia. The non-communist Southeast Asian states remained suspicious of Maoist China and its attempt to export its ideology (while relations between China and North Vietnam also deteriorated in the 1970s).

Meanwhile, China had become a nuclear power in 1964. Therefore, the Chinese threat to open a second front during the 1965 India-Pakistan War led India down the nuclear path (as India wanted to avoid coercion—whether nuclear or non-nuclear—by a nuclear-armed China).[26] At the same time, other considerations, including an attempt at status parity with China, were also involved in India's decision to test a nuclear device in 1974. India also absorbed Sikkim in 1975 even as China complained about Indian expansionism and hegemonism.

The Sino-Pakistani entente continued to deepen, and China began to share nuclear technology with Pakistan in the late 1970s. China's extensive nuclear assistance to Pakistan included the enrichment of uranium to weapon-grade, nuclear warhead design, and help with nuclear-capable ballistic missiles.[27] China and Pakistan also formally inaugurated the Karakorum Highway in 1978 that connected Xinjiang with Pakistan after traversing through Gilgit-Baltistan that India claimed (and continues to claim) as a part of Kashmir.[28]

During the visit of the Chinese foreign minister Huang Hua to India in 1981, India and China agreed to reopen their border talks (that had been suspended since 1962). During the 1960s and 1970s, China had consolidated its control over Tibet politically as well through connectivity and infrastructure. India also undertook the modernization of its military in the 1980s and captured the Siachen Glacier (disputed with Pakistan) in 1984. Siachen gave India the ability to monitor the Aksai Chin road as well as the Karakoram Highway.[29] These larger developments were looming in the background when the 1986–87 Sumdorong Chu crisis emerged between India and China that raised the possibility of a second war between them.[30]

This crisis that saw the deployment of thousands of troops along the Sino-Indian border in the eastern sector—estimates vary from 50,000 to 400,000 troops—was a major turning point in Sino-Indian relations. The crisis passed due to a combination of factors that included military deterrence as well as the lack of Soviet support for India in its contest with China (as the Soviet leader Mikhail Gorbachev sought to mend Sino-Soviet ties). Consequently, when protests began in Tibet in late 1987 (for reasons unrelated to the Sumdorong Chu Crisis), India temporarily sealed its borders with Tibet.

A year later when the unrest in Tibet was still ongoing, the Indian Prime Minister Rajiv Gandhi visited Beijing (in what was the first Prime Ministerial visit since the 1962 war). During his visit, Gandhi and the Chinese leader Deng Xiaoping decided that India and China would seek to foster new venues of cooperation, especially in the economic domain, while postponing the settlement of more contentious issues. China was more than a decade into its economic reforms that had been launched in 1978, while India was also trying to go down that path (albeit in fits and starts). Their common desire for stability launched a new phase in Sino-Indian relations.

Phase 3—Cooperation Amidst Tensions (~1988–2008)

Three months after Gandhi's visit in March 1989, China declared martial law in Tibet and deployed 170,000 PLA troops and 30,000 personnel of the People's Armed Police to calm the unrest.[31] Unlike the 1950s, India did not formally complain about this (nor did India offer any support to the Tibetans via the exiled community living in India). Later, as many Western democracies raised concerns about the Tiananmen Square massacre in June 1989, India officially remained silent. India's silence was a politico-strategic calculation given the domestic challenges that New Delhi was facing in the Punjab and Kashmir. As the Cold War ended, China and India were inwardly focused (politically and economically). These domestic priorities allowed them to de-escalate their rivalry.

In 1993 and 1996, China and India signed two agreements to stabilize their frontiers. They agreed to avoid large-scale military exercises involving more than 15,000 troops along their borders, while providing prior notification for exercises involving more than 5,000 troops.[32] However, as China acceded to the Nuclear Non-Proliferation Treaty in 1992 and signed the Comprehensive Test Ban Treaty in 1996, India began to feel global pressure (including from China) to formally join the global nuclear order after giving up its quest for nuclear weapons. Meanwhile, the strategic relationship between China and Pakistan continued.

Not surprisingly, India openly went nuclear in 1998 by tacitly justifying its actions after blaming China and the China-Pakistan strategic collusion.[33] Although China was more upset with India's justification of its nuclear tests than by the tests themselves, the Chinese foreign ministry did announce that China may consider resuming nuclear tests depending upon the developments in the subcontinent.[34] (Pakistan had responded to India's nuclear tests with its own tests later in May 1998).

Despite these tensions, Sino-Indian economic ties dramatically took off after 1988. Bilateral trade that stood at barely $100 million in 1988 expanded to over $50 billion by 2008.[35] In the first decade of the 21st century, China and India were being hailed as rising powers that were en route to emerging as the three largest economies in the world (along with the United States but with China in the vanguard) by the middle of the century. Such long-term prognosis not-withstanding, China was rapidly climbing the technological ladder even as India struggled with a sluggish manufacturing base that was neither globally competitive nor integrated with the East Asian production networks that were increasingly oriented toward China. The bilateral Sino-Indian commercial relationship remained lopsided as India exported raw materials to China while importing manufactured products. Their commercial relationship remained imbalanced as India's trade deficit with China increased on an annual basis.

Manjeet S. Pardesi

Table 7.1 China and India (Basic Indicators of Material Power)

	1988		2008		2020	
	GDP (US$ trillion)	Military Expenditure (US$ billion)	GDP (US$ trillion)	Military Expenditure (US$ billion)	GDP (US$ trillion)	Military Expenditure (US$ billion)
CHINA	0.312	11.3 (1989)	4.59	78.84	14.72	252.3
INDIA	0.297	11.35	1.199	33	2.66	72.89

Source: World Development Indicators, The World Bank, https://databank.worldbank.org/source/world-development-indicators

The most notable feature over these two decades (1988–2008) was not the simultaneous rise of China and India as hailed in many media commentaries. From a strategic perspective, what mattered the most was that India was in relative decline vis-à-vis China (even as India was rising in absolute terms). Although the Indian and Chinese economies were of the same size and spent more or less the same amount on their militaries in 1988, the Chinese economy was almost four times larger than the Indian economy while China's defense expenditure was two-and-a-half times India's by 2008 (see Table 7.1).[36] In other words, China and India were rising asymmetrically with China rising faster and developing more comprehensively. As this asymmetry became stark, the Sino-Indian rivalry entered its fourth and current phase.

Phase 4—Asymmetry and Rising Tensions

It remains unclear what prompted the tempo of Sino-Indian rivalry to escalate in the first decade of the 21st century as the 1988 consensus to shelve the contentious issues began to erode. While this issue and its timing deserve further analysis, the year 2008 is being noted as the turning point for heuristic purposes in this chapter.[37] Tensions were already budding in Sino-Indian relations by 2008. After a lull in militarized disputes post-Sumdorong Chu, there were two militarized disputes of short intensity and duration between them in 2003 and 2007 followed by a third one in 2009.[38] What is noteworthy is that tensions were rising in the Sino-Indian relationship before the emergence of President Xi Jinping in China (in 2012–13) or that of Prime Minister Narendra Modi in India (in 2014). The gradual escalation of Sino-Indian tensions in the current phase of their rivalry predates the emergence of nationalist leaders in these countries.

China had already hardened its position on Arunachal Pradesh in 2006.[39] Whether coincidentally or not, 2006 also witnessed the opening of the Qinghai-Tibet high-speed railway (that carried PLA troops to Lhasa for the first time in 2007).[40] India had also begun the process of modernizing its border infrastructure along the Chinese frontier in 2005.[41] By 2010, India was referring to Kashmir as a "core" issue for New Delhi on a par with Tibet and Taiwan for China.[42] In 2010, India also publicly expressed "genuine concerns" about "China's role in POK (Pakistan-Occupied Kashmir), China's J&K (Jammu & Kashmir) policy, and the Sino-Pak security and nuclear relationship."[43]

Since then, there have been five major militarized crises along the Sino-Indian frontier: In 2013, 2014, 2015, 2017, and 2020.[44] The 2017 Doklam Crisis is noteworthy because it was the Bhutan-China territorial dispute that led Indian troops to cross the international boundary into this disputed region given the India-Bhutan security relationship.[45] On the other hand, the 2020 Ladakh Crisis (that has simmered down but is not yet over) saw the loss of life for the first time since 1975 as tensions escalated along the Sino-Indian frontier. Even as the overall military balance favors China, Sino-Indian military power in the localized Himalayan context remains balanced for now (although there are signs that even the local balance may be shifting in China's favor).[46] However, these crises have not only raised concerns about the status of the 1993 and 1996 agreements between China and India, but they have also led India to put restrictions on Chinese economic investments in critical sectors in the Indian economy.

Additionally, there are two other issues that may escalate tensions in the Sino-Indian rivalry. First, while China's control over Tibet is no longer in doubt (unlike in the 1950s), the Tibetans remain unreconciled with their current political status. More than 157 Tibetans in the PRC have self-immolated since 2009 (in addition to ten in exile in India and Nepal since 1998).[47] In 2011, the Dalai Lama relinquished his political role to the democratically elected Tibetan government-in-exile. China's refusal to recognize this government is a cause of concern given the Dalai Lama's advanced age. (The Dalai Lama turned 86 in 2021). In fact, the issue of the Dalai Lama's reincarnation may itself precipitate a crisis in Sino-Indian relations (especially if his reincarnation is born in exile in India).[48] Given that the Dalai Lama and the Tibetan government-in-exile back the Indian position on the Sino-Indian territorial dispute, all these issues are connected to each other.

Second, as India's strategic ties with the United States have deepened over the past two decades, they have raised Chinese suspicions. In fact, this issue is directly related to the Sino-Indian positional rivalry. While India was actively competing with China for leadership in Asia in the 1950s, India's current strategy revolves around preventing Chinese dominance in Asia, a goal that New Delhi shares with Washington. India is one of the central pillars of the United States approach to the Indo-Pacific, and India has partnered with Japan, Australia, and the United States in the so-called Quad.[49] In fact, President Donald Trump's Indo-Pacific strategy specifically called for Indian preeminence and leadership in South Asia and the Indian Ocean while promoting India's engagement with Southeast Asia.[50] Whether or not this specific approach survives in the post-Trump era, India is determined to "Act East." China's leading scholars of India are aware of India's eastern ambitions and believe that "the core demand of India has always been to merge into the Asia-Pacific region," and that India aims to "contain" China through its Indo-Pacific strategy.[51]

Conclusion

China and India's strategic rivalry with its positional and spatial dimensions remains unresolved even as it has escalated and de-escalated over the decades. In other words, it has remained a carefully "managed" rivalry.[52] While spatial issues persist, the positional dimension of the Sino-Indian rivalry has been transformed over the decades. India is no longer in competition with China for Asian leadership. Instead, India seeks to prevent Chinese domination in Asia. India seems to be willing to work with the United States in this endeavor given the growing asymmetry in material capabilities between India and China. On its part, the Sino-Pakistani entente persists and is likely to strengthen as the China-Pakistan Economic Corridor develops.

The Sino-Indian rivalry has become complex as it overtly interacts with the India-Pakistan and the US-China rivalries now. These changes notwithstanding, the fundamental asymmetry in the Sino-Indian rivalry also continues: While India seeks some notion of "equality" in its relations with China,[53] Beijing continues to focus on the United States and Japan and does not think of New Delhi as a peer. In fact, the growing material power asymmetry between them may further entrench these divergent perceptions, thereby exacerbating their already fraught relations.

Notes

1 Michael P. Colaresi, Karen Rasler, and William R. Thompson, *Strategic Rivalries in World Politics* (New York: Cambridge University Press, 2007).

2 Manjeet S. Pardesi, "The Initiation of the Sino-Indian Rivalry," *Asian Security* 15, no. 3 (2019): 253–284.

3 The PLA had used the western "route" through Aksai Chin in 1951 to consolidate its position in Tibet, and the current boundary in that region reflects the position established by China during the 1962 Sino-Indian War that India lost. The boundary in the eastern sector corresponds with the line established by the 1914 Simla Agreement between British India and Tibet.

4 Manjeet S. Pardesi, "Explaining the Asymmetry in the Sino-Indian Strategic Rivalry," *Australian Journal of International Affairs* 75, no. 3 (2021): 341–365. Also see Andrew Scobell, "Himalayan Standoff: Strategic Culture and the China-India Rivalry," in T. V. Paul, ed., *The China-India Rivalry in the Globalization Era* (Washington: Georgetown University Press, 2018), 165–186.

5 Harold C. Hinton, *China's Turbulent Quest" An Analysis of China's Foreign Relations since 1949* (Bloomington: Indiana University Press, 1972), 244.

6 The British Indian Army—the army of the Raj—did not play any role in India's freedom movement.

7 A. S. Bhasin, *Nehru, Tibet, and China* (Gurugram: Penguin, 2021).

8 Francine R. Frankel, *When Nehru Looked East: Origins of India-US Suspicion and India-China Rivalry* (New York: Oxford University Press, 2020).

9 Amitav Acharya, *East of India, South of China: Sino-Indian Encounters in Southeast Asia* (New Delhi: Oxford University Press, 2017).

10 Acharya, *East of India, South of China*, especially Chapters 3 and 4.

11 On Tibet's historical status before 1950–51, see Melvyn C. Goldstein, *A History of Modern Tibet, 1913–1951, Volume 1* (Berkeley: University of California Press, 1989). This paragraph draws from Goldstein's work.

12 On Tibetan issues (as they pertained to Sino-Indian relations before 1959), see Melvyn C. Goldstein, *A History of Modern Tibet, 1951–1955, Volume 2* (Berkeley: University of California Press, 2007); Melvyn C. Goldstein, *A History of Modern Tibet, 1955–1957, Volume 3* (Berkeley: University of California Press, 2014); and Melvyn C. Goldstein, *A History of Modern Tibet, 1957–1959, Volume 4* (Berkeley: University of California Press, 2019).

13 Carole McGranahan, *Arrested Histories: Tibet, the CIA, and Memories of a Forgotten War* (Durham: Duke University Press, 2010).

14 Mahnaz Z. Ispahani, *Roads and Rivals: The Politics of Access in the Borderlands of Asia* (Ithaca: Cornell University Press, 1989), 157–180.

15 Tsering Shakya, *The Dragon in the Land of the Snows* (New York: Penguin, 1999), 197–276.

16 Xiaoyuan Liu, *To the End of Revolution: The Chinese Communist Party and Tibet, 1949–1959* (New York: Columbia University Press, 2020), 383.

17 Allen S. Whiting, *The Chinese Calculus of Deterrence: India and Indochina* (Ann Arbor: The University of Michigan Press, 1975), 11.

18 Steven A. Hoffmann, *India and the China Crisis* (Berkeley: University of California Press, 1990); and Srinath Raghavan, *War and Peace in Modern India* (Ranikhet: Permanent Black, 2010), 227–310.

19 John W. Garver, "China's Decision for War with India in 1962," in Alastair Iain Johnston and Robert S. Ross, eds., *New Directions in the Study of China's Foreign Policy* (Stanford: Stanford University Press, 2006), 86–130.

20 "More on Nehru's Philosophy in the Light of the Sino-Indian Boundary Question," *Renmin Ribao*, October 27, 1962.

21 Bruce O. Riedel, *JFK's Forgotten War: Tibet, the CIA, and Sino-Indian War* (Washington: Brookings, 2015).

22 John W. Garver, *Protracted Contest: Sino-Indian Rivalry in the Twentieth Century* (Seattle: University of Washington Press, 2001), 194–204.

23 F. S. Aijazuddin, *From a Head, Through a Head to a Head: The Secret Channel between the US and China through Pakistan* (Karachi: Oxford University Press, 2000).

24 Srinath Raghavan, *1971: A Global History of the Creation of Bangladesh* (Cambridge: Harvard University Press, 2013).

25 Steven A. Hoffmann, "Anticipation, Disaster, and Victory: India 1962—71," *Asian Survey* 12, no. 11 (1972): 960–979.

The Evolution of the Sino-Indian Rivalry

26 Manjeet S. Pardesi, "China's Nuclear Forces and their Significance to India," *The Nonproliferation Review* 21, no. 3–4 (2014): 337–354.

27 Henrik Stålhane Hiim, *China and International Nuclear Weapons Proliferation: Strategic Assistance* (New York: Routledge, 2019), 50–84.

28 Ispahani, *Roads and Rivals*, 145–213.

29 Georges Eng Bok Tan, "How Does the PLA Cope with 'Regional Conflict' and 'Local War'?," in Richard H. Yang, ed., *China's Military: The PLA in 1990/1991* (Kaohsiung: National Sun Yat-sen University, 1991), 151.

30 Manjeet S. Pardesi, "Managing the 1986-87 Sino-Indian Sumdorong Chu Crisis," *India Review* 18, no. 5 (2019): 534–551.

31 John Tkacik, Maryanne Kivelhan, and Joseph Fewsmith, "Who's Hu? Assessing China's Heir Apparent," The Heritage Foundation, April 19, 2002, https://www.heritage.org/asia/report/whos-hu-assessing-chinas-heir-apparent-hu-jintao.

32 Waheguru Pal Singh Sidhu and Jing Dong Yuan, *China and India: Cooperation or Conflict?* (New Delhi: India Research Press, 2003), 113–140.

33 Šumit Ganguly, "India's Pathway to Pokhran II: The Prospects and Sources of New Delhi's Nuclear Weapons Program," *International Security* 23, no. 4 (1999): 148–177.

34 "China to Consider Resuming Tests If Nuclear Arms Tensions Between India and Pakistan Worsens," *South China Morning Post*, June 2, 1998.

35 Jingdong Yuan, "Sino-Indian Economic Ties since 1988: Progress, Problems, and Prospects for Future Development," *Journal of Current Chinese Affairs* 45, no. 3 (2016): 36, 40.

36 In fact, the asymmetry is even more marked in terms of defense spending because China had consistently outspent India through most of the Cold War by a significant margin (the equivalent figures for 1988 and 1989 notwithstanding).

37 Although the issue continues to be debated, some scholars believe that Chinese foreign policy became more assertive after the 2008 Global Financial Crisis. China managed the 2008 crisis better than all the other major powers. See Kenneth Lieberthal and Wang Jisi, "Addressing U.S.-China Strategic Distrust," John L. Thornton China Center Monograph Series, Number 4, March 2012, https://www.brookings.edu/wp-content/uploads/2016/06/0330_china_lieberthal.pdf.

38 Paul F. Diehl, "Whither Rivalry or Withered Rivalry?," in T. V. Paul, ed., *The China-India Rivalry in the Globalization Era* (Washington: Georgetown University Press, 2018), 262.

39 John W. Garver, *China's Quest: The History of the Foreign Relations of the People's Republic of China* (New York: Oxford University Press, 2016), 749.

40 "Tibet Train Carries China Troops," *BBC News*, December 1, 2007, http://news.bbc.co.uk/2/hi/asia-pacific/7122433.stm.

41 Shivshankar Menon, *Choices: Inside the Making of India's Foreign Policy* (Washington: Brookings, 2016), 24.

42 Indrani Bagchi, "China Must Treat Kashmir on a Par with Taiwan-Tibet," *Times of India*, November 16, 2010.

43 "Address by the Foreign Secretary at the ORF Conference on China," *The Hindu*, December 3, 2010.

44 Will Green, "Conflict on the Sino-Indian Border: Background for Congress," U.S.-China Economic and Security Review Commission Issue Brief, July 2, 2020.

45 Šumit Ganguly and Andrew Scobell, "The Himalayan Impasse: Sino-Indian Rivalry in the Wake of Doklam," *The Washington Quarterly* 41, no. 3 (2018): 177–190.

46 Frank O'Donnell and Alex Bollfrass, "The Strategic Postures of China and India: A Visual Guide," Project on Managing the Atom, Belfer Center for Science and International Affairs, March 23, 2020.

47 Self-Immolation Fact Sheet, International Campaign for Tibet, last updated January 13, 2021, https://savetibet.org/tibetan-self-immolations/.

48 Iskander Rehman, "After His Holiness: Tibet, Reincarnation Politics, and the Future of Sino-Indian Relations," *Survival* 61, no. 4 (2019): 131–156.

49 Rajesh Rajagopalan, "Evasive Balancing: India's Unviable Indo-Pacific Strategy," *International Affairs* 96, no. 1 (2020): 75–93.

50 "U.S. Strategic Framework for the Indo-Pacific," The White House, January 5, 2021, https://trumpwhitehouse.archives.gov/wp-content/uploads/2021/01/IPS-Final-Declass.pdf.

51 Li, "India's Advance East Strategy and Its Indo-Pacific Diplomacy," *Contemporary International Relations* 28, no. 3 (2018): 28, 52.

52 T. V. Paul, "Explaining Conflict and Cooperation in the China-India Rivalry," in Paul, *The China-India Rivalry in the Globalization Era*, 6.

53 Prior to becoming the Indian Foreign Minister, S. Jaishankar stated the following in a conversation with Professor Wang Gungwu in Singapore: "A country like India would not be able to deal with China except on a basis of equality." "Asia in the New World Order," *Channel News Asia*, May 2, 2018, https://www.channelnewsasia.com/watch/asia-new-world-order-1545236. Quote at 14m 15s.

Bibliography

"Address by Foreign Secretary at ORF Conference on China." *The Hindu*, December 3, 2010.

"Asia in The New World Order." *Channel News Asia*, May 2, 2018. https://www.channelnewsasia.com/watch/asia-new-world-order-1545236.

"China to Consider Resuming Tests if Nuclear Arms Tensions Between India and Pakistan Worsens." *South China Morning Post*, June 2, 1998.

"More on Nehru's Philosophy in the Light of the Sino-Indian Boundary Question." *Renmin Ribao*, October 27, 1962.

"Tibet Train Carries China Troops," *BBC News*, December 1, 2007. http://news.bbc.co.uk/2/hi/asia-pacific/7122433.stm.

Acharya, Amitav. *East of India, South of China: Sino-Indian Encounters in Southeast Asia*. New Delhi: Oxford University Press, 2017.

Aijazuddin, F. S. *From a Head, through a Head to a Head: The Secret Channel between the US and China through Pakistan*. Karachi: Oxford University Press, 2000.

Bagchi, Indrani. "China Must Treat Kashmir on a Par with Taiwan-Tibet." *Times of India*, November 16, 2010.

Bhasin, A. S. *Nehru, Tibet, and China*. Gurugram: Penguin, 2021.

Colaresi, Michael P., Karen Rasler, and William R. Thompson. *Strategic Rivalries in World Politics*. New York: Cambridge University Press, 2007.

Diehl, Paul F. "Whither Rivalry or Withered Rivalry?" In *The China-India Rivalry in the Globalization Era*, edited by T. V. Paul, 253–272. Washington: Georgetown University Press, 2018.

Frankel, Francine R. *When Nehru Looked East: Origins of India-US Suspicion and India-China Rivalry*. New York: Oxford University Press, 2020.

Ganguly, Šumit. "India's Pathway to Pokhran II: The Prospects and Sources of New Delhi's Nuclear Weapons Program." *International Security* 23, no. 4 (1999): 148–177.

Ganguly, Šumit, and Andrew Scobell. "The Himalayan Impasse: Sino-Indian Rivalry in the Wake of Doklam." *The Washington Quarterly* 41, no. 3 (2018): 177–190.

Garver, John W. "China's Decision for War with India in 1962." In *New Directions in the Study of China's Foreign Policy*, edited by Alastair Iain Johnston, and Robert Ross, 86–130. Stanford: Stanford University Press, 2006.

Garver, John W. *China's Quest: The History of the Foreign Relations of the People's Republic of China*. New York: Oxford University Press, 2016.

Garver, John W. *Protracted Contest: Sino-Indian Rivalry in the Twentieth Century*. Seattle: University of Washington Press, 2001.

Goldstein, Melvyn C. *A History of Modern Tibet, 1913–1951, Volume 1*. Berkeley: University of California Press, 1989.

Goldstein, Melvyn C. *A History of Modern Tibet, 1951–1955, Volume 2*. Berkeley: University of California Press, 1989.

Goldstein, Melvyn C. *A History of Modern Tibet, 1955–1957, Volume 3*. Berkeley: University of California Press, 1989.

Goldstein, Melvyn C. *A History of Modern Tibet, 1957–1959, Volume 4*. Berkeley: University of California Press, 1989.

Green, Will. "Conflict on the Sino-India Border: Background for Congress." U.S.-China Economic and Security Review Commission Issue Brief, July 2, 2020.

Hiim, Henrik Stålhane. *China and International Nuclear Weapons Proliferation: Strategic Assistance*. New York: Routledge, 2019.

Hinton, Harold C. *China's Turbulent Quest: An Analysis of China's Foreign Relations Since 1949*. Bloomington: Indiana University Press, 1972.

Hoffmann, Steven A. "Anticipation, Disaster, and Victory." *Asian Survey* 12, no. 11 (1972): 960–979.

Hoffmann, Steven A. *India and the China Crisis*. Berkeley: University of California Press, 1990.

Ispahani, Mahnaz Z. *Roads and Rivals: The Political Uses of Access in the Borderlands of Asia*. Ithaca: Cornell University Press, 1989.

Li, Li. "India's Advance East Strategy and Its Indo-Pacific Diplomacy." *Contemporary International Relations* 28, no. 3 (2018): 28–52.

Lieberthal, Kenneth, and Wang Jisi. "Addressing U.S.-China Strategic Distrust." John L. Thornton China Center Monograph Series, Number 4, March 2012. https://www.brookings.edu/wp-content/uploads/2016/06/0330_china_lieberthal.pdf.

McGranahan, Carol. *Arrested Histories: Tibet, the CIA, and Memories of a Forgotten War*. Durham: Duke University Press, 2010.

Menon, Shivshankar. *Choices: Inside the Making of India's Foreign Policy*. Washington: Brookings, 2016.

O'Donnell, Frank, and Alex Bollfrass. "The Strategic Postures of China and India: A Visual Guide." Project on Managing the Atom, Belfer Center for Science and International Affairs, 2020.

Pardesi, Manjeet S. "China's Nuclear Forces and Their Significance to India." *The Nonproliferation Review* 21, nos. 3–4 (2014): 337–354.

Pardesi, Manjeet S. "Explaining the Asymmetry in the Sino-Indian Strategic Rivalry." *Australian Journal of International Affairs* 75, no. 3 (2021): 341–365.

Pardesi, Manjeet S. "Managing the 1986-87 Sino-Indian Sumdorong Chu Crisis." *India Review* 18, no. 5 (2019): 534–551.

Pardesi, Manjeet S. "The Initiation of the Sino-Indian Rivalry." *Asian Security* 15, no. 3 (2019): 253–284.

Paul, T. V. "Explaining Conflict and Cooperation in the China-India Rivalry." In *The China-India Rivalry in the Globalization Era*, edited by T. V. Paul, 3–23. Washington: Georgetown University Press, 2018.

Raghavan, Srinath. *1971: A Global History of the Creation of Bangladesh*. Cambridge: Harvard University Press, 2013.

Raghavan, Srinath. *War and Peace in Modern India*. Ranikhet: Permanent Black, 2010.

Rajagopalan, Rajesh. "Evasive Balancing: India's Unviable Indo-Pacific Strategy." *International Affairs* 96, no. 1 (2020): 75–93.

Rehman, Iskander. "After His Holiness: Tibet, Reincarnation Politics, and the Future of Sino-Indian Relations." *Survival* 61, no. 4 (2019): 131–156.

Riedel, Bruce O. *JFK's Forgotten War: Tibet, the CIA, and Sino-Indian War*. Washington: Brookings, 2010.

Scobell, Andrew. "Himalayan Standoff: Strategic Culture and the China-India Rivalry." In *The China-India Rivalry in the Globalization Era*, edited by T. V. Paul, 165–186. Washington: Georgetown University Press, 2018.

Self-Immolation Fact Sheet. International Campaign for Tibet. Last updated January 13, 2021. https://savetibet.org/tibetan-self-immolations/.

Shakya, Tsering. *The Dragon in the Land of Snows*. New York: Penguin, 1999.

Sidhu, Waheguru Pal Singh, and Jing Dong Yuan. *China and India: Cooperation or Conflict?* New Delhi: India Research Press, 2003.

Tan, Georges Eng Bok. "How Does the PLA Cope With 'Regional Conflict' and 'Local War'?." In *China's Military: The PLA in 1990/1991*, edited by Richard H. Yang. Kaohsiung: National Sun Yat-sen University, 1991.

Tkacik, John, Maryanne Kivelhan, and Joseph Fewsmith. "Who's Hu? Assessing China's Heir Apparent, Hu Jintao." The Heritage Foundation, April 19, 2002. https://www.heritage.org/asia/report/whos-hu-assessing-chinas-heir-apparent-hu-jintao.

U.S. Strategic Framework for the Indo-Pacific. The White House. January 5, 2021.

Whiting, Allen S. *The Chinese Calculus of Deterrence: India and Indochina*. Ann Arbor: The University of Michigan Press, 1975.

Yuan, Jingdong. "Sino-Indian Economic Ties Since 1988: Progress, Problems, and Prospects for Future Development." *Journal of Current Chinese Affairs* 45, no. 3 (2016): 31–71.

8

THE EVOLUTION OF THE INDIA-PAKISTAN RIVALRY

Mahesh Shankar

Introduction

In October 1947, a mere few months after Partition, and the coming into being of the newly independent states of India and Pakistan, the two countries fought their first war. Since then they have fought three more wars—in 1965, 1971, and 1999—with the intervening periods characterized for large parts by hostility, crises, and preparation for war. In recent years and decades, the rivalry and its implications for the broader South Asian region, and indeed the world at large, have only acquired more complexity and danger. The India-Pakistan rivalry has been one of the most intractable for the best part of seven decades, and has seemingly only become further so.

This chapter discusses various aspects of the India-Pakistan relationship that have made it so conflict prone over the years. It begins with a brief overview of the oft-told story of origins of, and prominent explanations for, the rivalry and why it has remained so intractable. The remainder of the chapter focuses on exploring its nature and how its contours have shifted in recent times. It argues that while dramatic changes have characterized the context surrounding the rivalry in the last two decades—owing primarily to the introduction of nuclear weapons, the emergence of terrorism as a more prominent means of war, and significant domestic political developments in both countries—the practical effect of these transformations has been to, at best, freeze the conflict in its current state, and at worst to render it all the more difficult to resolve, while introducing the prospect of catastrophic nuclear annihilation. It argues that a mix of strategic and ideological factors that the Realist and Constructivist theoretical frameworks emphasize continue to structure the relationship, while Liberalism's focus on domestic political and institutional considerations has become increasingly salient to the dynamics of the rivalry. In short, in India-Pakistan relations, the more things change, the more they do in fact stay the same. Conflict will continue to animate the India-Pakistan relationship for some time to come, with negative implications for the broader regional context, while continuing to generate global concerns.

Origins of the India-Pakistan Rivalry

The roots of the India-Pakistan rivalry lie in the waning periods of British colonial rule in South Asia, and the successful call by the Muslim League party for a new state for the Muslims of the subcontinent, leading to the decision to partition undivided India. Soon after it was clear

DOI: 10.4324/9781003246626-11

that there would be two new successor states, the sides had begun bickering over the division of military and financial resources.[1] Even more consequential was the immediate contestation over territory, and especially the fate of the more than 500 princely states, which had been more indirectly ruled by the British during colonial rule. Their future—whether they would remain independent or joint one or the other of the newly formed dominions—was up for grabs.[2]

By the time of Britain's exit in August 1947, fortunately, rulers of *most* of the states had either convinced themselves or been persuaded or coerced to abandon any thoughts of independence, and had agreed to accede to India or Pakistan.[3] The fate of three states—Jammu and Kashmir (J&K), Junagadh, and Hyderabad—however, would continue to be unresolved and contentious for a longer time. This was due, in part, to the fact that the ruler in each of these states was of a different religion from the majority of the population,[4] which brought up the complicated question of majority will vs. ruler's prerogative. The rulers of Hyderabad and Junagadh would eventually be coerced into acceding to India—the fact that these were Hindu majority states surrounded by Indian territory made the outcome for the only viable option in a logistical sense, as well as a strategic imperative to Indian leaders. Kashmir, however, with its majority Muslim population living under a Hindu ruler, and importantly its geographical contiguity to both India and Pakistan, became the first major bone of contention between the two new countries.

By October 1947, the first war between the two countries, over Kashmir, had already broken out as tribal invaders swiftly descended toward Srinagar, with the encouragement and material support of Pakistan.[5] In response, the Maharaja immediately sought India's military intervention, and Indian troops soon entered the war, but only after Delhi had received an official instrument from the Maharaja confirming Kashmir's accession to India.[6] By the time the two sides had agreed to a UN-brokered ceasefire that came into effect on January 1, 1949, India had successfully managed to establish physical control over some two-thirds of the disputed territory, with the rest—what would come to be described in India as Pakistan-Occupied Kashmir (POK) and in Pakistan as "Azad Kashmir"—in Pakistan's control.

In the years that followed, this has remained the status quo, a status quo that India has sought to preserve, and Pakistan to overturn. More dramatically, from a regional security perspective, the rivalry has manifested itself in growing hostility between the two sides, and more importantly, periodic wars. In 1965, and again in 1999 (albeit at a more limited level), Pakistan attempted to fulfill its revisionist goals in Kashmir through military means. The war of 1971 had as its underlying cause a domestic rift between East and West Pakistan, which prompted India's military intervention, eventuating in the dismemberment of Pakistan and the formation of Bangladesh. Apart from the wars themselves, of course, the rivalry has also been the spark for numerous crises, diplomatic and military, and since the 1980s, the emergence of terrorism as a sustained phenomenon. This history, along with the acquisition of nuclear weapons by the primary state protagonists in the conflict, has led to increasing concerns about the implications of the rivalry from a regional and global security perspective.

Why then has the rivalry remained so intractable, war prone and resistant to compromise? How have things changed in recent decades—especially since the 1990s and to what effect? It is to those questions that the remainder of this chapter turns.

Explaining the India-Pakistan Rivalry

The extensive literature on the India-Pakistan rivalry has offered robust theoretical explanations for its origins and intractability, explanations that have stood the test of time. For many scholars and observers of the region, Realism, with its focus on military-strategic considerations, offers the most persuasive account of the relationship. From this perspective, the very structural asymmetry of power created with Partition means that even if ideological concerns were nonexistent, both sides would have incentives to fight for purely strategic reasons, either to maintain or expand the asymmetry (in the case of India) or to overturn it (in the case of Pakistan).[7] These military-strategic material concerns have been animating more specific disagreements as well, from the time of Partition when the two sides bitterly argued over the relative share of the resources inherited by each. In the case of the Kashmir dispute, the vital geo-strategic location of state only heightened the salience of the territory to the two sides.[8] For India, an ideologically hostile Pakistan in possession of Kashmir was feared to pose a much bigger threat to mainland India than it would otherwise. For Pakistan, the strategic stakes have arguably been even higher, given the presence in Kashmir of the headwaters of three major rivers that serve as the lifeline of Pakistan's agricultural economy and the fact of major Pakistani road and rail arteries running in proximity to the border with the state.[9]

Other scholars, by contrast, point to the Constructivist school of thought's emphasis on ideational factors as a more persuasive explanation for the rivalry. In this telling of the story, the underlying cause of the animosity in the relationship is primarily ideological, the roots of which—as noted above—lie in Partition. Both countries have been engaged since then in seeking to establish the validity of their respective and contrasting national ideologies; for Pakistan that of the two-nation theory and an idea of the country as the necessary homeland of the subcontinent's Muslims, and for the Indian leadership, it was the conception of the country as a secular and inclusive state.[10] The two sides holding thoroughly incompatible guiding ideologies has rendered, in this view, the contest of ideas as essentially zero-sum, making hostility an inevitable feature of their relationship. This ideological competition has manifested itself in, for instance, the dispute over Kashmir, where winning over a Muslim-majority state becomes key to each side establishing the validity of their respective nationalisms.

Resultantly, on both sides, there have been incentives to pursue conflict and intransigence, both because of ideological commitments as well as military-strategic considerations. If this were not enough, however, in keeping with the expectations of Liberalism, domestic political imperatives have increasingly served as yet another factor driving political-military elites in each of the countries toward the path of rivalry. For one, in both countries, leaders have increasingly viewed compromise on any significant matter with the other side, Kashmir being the most obvious example, as politically risky if not suicidal. What room might have been available on both sides to make concessions soon after independence has likely evaporated. For another group of scholars focused on domestic politics, it is the institutional structures in the two countries that equally animate the incentives political elites confront with regard to the rivalry. Especially in the case of Pakistan, the civil-military relationship, and the Army's domination of the political realm since the 1960s, has been identified as a key driver of policy vis-à-vis India. By this logic, the military's outsized position in domestic politics in Pakistan—from which come not only political, but very real economic and material benefits for the institution and its leadership[11]—necessitates the existence of external threats and revisionist goals that legitimize such a role. The cultivation of India as an ideological and military-strategic threat, and perennially keeping the Kashmir dispute on the front burner, therefore serves a crucial organizational interest for the Army.[12]

In summary, the India-Pakistan rivalry has proved as complex and intractable as it is due precisely to the fact that it is fueled by a multiplicity of factors, systemic and domestic, strategic and ideational. While the origins of the rivalry itself can be traced to ideological contestation that led to the partition of undivided India in the first place, it is undeniable that the asymmetry in size, power, and resources that followed created additional military-strategic imperatives for the pursuit of rivalry, especially in Pakistan. Over time, domestic

The Evolution of the India-Pakistan Rivalry

political and institutional structures have developed—as a consequence, in part, of the ideological and strategic rivalry—to contribute to the intensity of the rivalry. Finally, the failure to engender Liberal mechanisms such as economic interdependence and/or regional institutions in the region means that there are few (if any) factors that might otherwise incentivize and encourage cooperation over conflict.[13] Analytical eclecticism, in other words, is a necessity in making sense of the India-Pakistan relationship in a comprehensive manner. The intersection of these three frameworks—Realism, Constructivism, and Liberalism—in any account of this rivalry becomes more apparent as one considers its evolution in recent decades.

The India-Pakistan Rivalry Since the 1990s

The last two to three decades have seen dramatic changes in the military-strategic and political contexts that surround the India-Pakistan rivalry, with major implications for both the nature of the relationship. Three of them have been particularly noteworthy: Acquisition of nuclear weapons by both sides, the growing reliance on terrorism as means of effecting revisionist goals, and the changing nature of domestic politics. The rest of this chapter describes these more recent developments and evaluates their impact on the nature and prospects of war and peace in South Asia. The examination suggests that, on the whole and in combination, these shifts have added significantly to the complexity and challenges of managing the competition and moved it in the direction of, at best, a long-term freeze, and more likely increasing intractability, and growing risk of crises and catastrophic war.

Nuclear Weapons

Perhaps the most important of these developments, one that can be linked causally to some of the other changes described below, is the acquisition of nuclear weapons by both India and Pakistan. While both countries dramatically declared themselves nuclear weapon states with back-to-back tests in 1998, it is well understood that they had both functioned since at least the 1980s under the reasonable assumption that the other had these capabilities.[14] While nuclearization in South Asia led to global outrage and concern, it immediately led to a robust debate—based on a shared understanding that this was a dramatic and consequential event—on the effects it had on the prospects of crises and wars in South Asia.

Optimists argued that the introduction of nuclear deterrence would stabilize the region by reducing incentives on either side for full-scale war—a not infrequent occurrence in previous decades—and with major changes in the status quo through military means no longer practical, perhaps even create conditions for a negotiated resolution to major outstanding disputes.[15] Pessimists, on the other hand, offered the logic of the stability-instability paradox, the idea that even if deterrence prevented larger wars, it would paradoxically create more room for the revisionist side, Pakistan, to support more limited or asymmetric means of conflict. They portended that nuclear weapons would offer an umbrella under with Islamabad could ratchet up terrorism in India, something it already had a record of encouraging in the past. Conflict would not diminish, but rather just adopt a different shape, with unpredictable consequences.[16]

What then has been the record since nuclear weapons were introduced into the relationship? With the caveat that we are dealing with a very limited time period of two decades, a case could be made that, as optimists expected, full scale wars have indeed become less imaginable. Critics often point to the 1999 Kargil War as an immediate rebuttal to this argument, but the fact that the two sides managed to limit a war that would have perhaps expanded in the past suggests that nuclear weapons might have introduced some modicum of caution in both sides, the dangerous rhetoric surrounding the war notwithstanding.[17] There is also evidence of the two sides having attempted to resolve the Kashmir issue via back channel discussions, first in 1998–1999 (prior to the Kargil War), and then in 2004–2007,[18] with both sides reportedly coming very close to a solution in the second instance. The fact that the Hindu nationalist Bharatiya Janata Party (BJP) was in power in India in 1999 and a military regime ruled Pakistan in 2004–2007 might suggest that even the most unlikely of protagonists had been encouraged toward peace in part by the new structural context imparted by nuclear weapons.[19]

Terrorism

Despite such seemingly hopeful signs, however, the unfortunate reality over the last two decades has been the fact that while full-scale wars have been avoided, major political efforts toward peace have been clearly infrequent, inconsistent, and unsuccessful, while violence itself has been less absent, and more just shifted form.

As pessimists had portended, Pakistani revisionism has—not surprisingly, given the stakes at play—far from dissipated. It has, instead, simply adjusted to the realities of nuclear deterrence, and found expression in lower intensity and more asymmetric forms of coercion such as terrorism. Such tactics are of course not new to the region and have been used since as early as the first Kashmir War which began with a tribal invasion from Pakistan, and have since featured in the lead up to the 1965 and 1971 wars. The 1999 Kargil War was, of course, the clearest expression of it immediately after the nuclear tests. This low-intensity form of warfare has, however, manifested itself in a more sustainable manner and become a more integral part of Pakistan's strategy for revisionism under the cover of nuclear weapons, most notably in the form of terrorism.

Insurgency and terrorism emerged as a major phenomenon in Kashmir in the late 1980s and the early 1990s, first indigenously in response to severe political missteps, including electoral corruption, on the part of India that marginalized and alienated many in the state. By the mid-1990s, however—by when, importantly, both sides were known to have nuclear weapons, only undeclared—Pakistan had begun to exploit the tumult in Kashmir by actively raising and sponsoring terrorist groups to attack targets in Kashmir.[20] The period since 1998 has not only seen a continuance of those tactics, but an emboldening and broadening of them, with a string of high-profile attacks by terrorist groups operating out of Pakistan, not only inside but outside Kashmir as well. Some of the most prominent of these, to name just a few, include the 2001 attacks on J&K Legislative Assembly and the Indian Parliament in New Delhi, major attacks in Mumbai in 2006 and 2008, and more recently the 2019 attack in Pulwama in J&K.

Nuclear weapons have arguably allowed Pakistan more freedom to more effectively and brazenly pursue this form of low-intensity conflict, in the not unreasonable expectation that the risk of nuclear escalation severely diminishes India's retaliatory options in response to such attacks that would be sufficient to deter Pakistan from this seemingly low-cost option of coercion. The fact that India has indeed struggled to find an appropriate mechanism to help deter Pakistan's incentives to sponsor cross-border terrorism[21]—even the attack on Parliament only prompted massive military mobilization, but no retaliatory action—perhaps only validates such thinking on the other side. In effect then, while nuclear weaponization in the subcontinent has reduced the *conventional* military means available to Pakistan, it has simultaneously increased the *unconventional/low-intensity* options available to it to pursue its revisionist goals, options that are perhaps more appropriate and practical for a relatively weaker revisionist actor in any case.

Nuclear weapons, in short, have had the limited effect of preventing all-out war, while effectively freezing the dispute and shifting conflict and instability to lower but, by no means, inconsequential levels. They have, in that sense, substantively changed—for the worse—the strategic context in the region and incentive structures for each side, affecting how the rivalry is addressed and the tactics that are deployed.

Confronting Terrorism in a New Nuclear Context

The original question scholars, analysts, and practitioners of the region grappled with after 1998 was that of whether the effects of nuclear weapons would be largely stabilizing or desta-bilizing. As discussed above, the answer to that is complicated, but not especially encour-aging. In recent years, however, questions have arisen about what these low-intensity tactics of coercion, including terrorism, utilized by Pakistan in pursuit of its revisionist goals, mean for the nature of the nuclear balance in the region and the prospects of catastrophic war. While the basis for deterrence optimism is the idea that both sides will be rational enough to be satisfied with adequate second strike capabilities for situations of last resort and adopt rea-sonable doctrinal positions—such as India's no-first-use policy—there is growing recognition and evidence for the fact that each side's response to the other's choices in a tit-for-tat manner has complicated such thinking and created a more permissive and destabilizing context for escalation toward even nuclear first use.

As the status quo actor, terrorism presents India with an ongoing security challenge, one that also directly impacts its ability to impart any kind of normality or stability to the internal situation in Kashmir. To the extent that the presence of nuclear weapons magnifies the escal-ation risks of any kind of military response on India's part to acts of terror, the last two decades have been a constant struggle for the country's leadership in finding effective yet safe ways of countering the challenge. As discussed in more detail elsewhere in this volume, India has consequently explored limited conventional military options of various kinds—such as the *Cold Start Doctrine*—that can potentially achieve its retaliatory and deterrence goals in future scenarios of major terrorist attacks.[22] In the last decade, India has begun implementing such options, most notably in the reported "surgical strikes" against militant launch pads across the India-Pakistan Line of Control (LoC) in September 2016, and in the even more audacious airstrikes on alleged terrorist infrastructure in Balakot in February 2019.

Pakistan's response to these—not unexpected—moves on India's part has consisted of adopting a much more ambiguous, and importantly more ambitious, doctrinal role for its nuclear weapons, involving the development of low-yield nuclear weapons capability, which can conceivably be used on the battlefield against Indian troops, while still keeping the con-flict limited rather than sparking outright nuclear war.[23] These developments have serious risks attached to them, including emboldening Pakistan toward increasing and more ambi-tious support for terrorist attacks on Indian targets, while exacerbating preexisting concerns about an already loose and delegative command and control structure for nuclear weapons in Pakistan. As the country becomes increasingly reliant on tactical nuclear weapons, the possibilities of inadvertent nuclear war due to miscalculation and communication failures or rogue radicalized actors deliberately initiating a nuclear attack on India become increasingly less farfetched.[24]

In New Delhi, this new straightjacket—in addition to the fear of potential chemical and biological terrorist attacks[25]—has seemingly led to a reconsideration of India's own previous commitment to a minimal nuclear deterrent and nuclear no-first-use posture.[26] Clary and Narang make this case in most detail in their 2019 article, where they suggest that India might be moving toward a nuclear doctrine that is increasingly tempted by the prospect of first use of nuclear weapons and counter-force targeting. They see as evidence for this the development of technological capabilities that would be appropriate for such a role—a "combination of more weapons, a greater number of accurate delivery vehicles at higher state of readiness and responsiveness, precise warheads, multiple independently targetable reentry vehicles (MIRVs), and a layered ballistic missile defense system...."[27] These technological shifts have been matched by rhetorical ones, with an increasing number of high-ranking officials, especially retired ones, civilian and military, making statements in recent years that call for a loosening of India's existing nuclear doctrine.

While perhaps understandable on their own terms, these developments in India (or even the perception that they are in the works) risk having the practical effect in Pakistan of reinforcing pre-existing fears about Indian intentions, and an already destabilizing nuclear doctrine, encouraging further expansion, diversification, and greater dispersal of the nuclear arsenal to meet the new challenge. In sum, nuclear weapons have not only had the effect of complicating the India-Pakistan contest by facilitating Pakistan's use of terrorism as a sustained means of pursuing revisionist goals. In fact, in a far from ideal feedback loop, the phenomenon of terrorism has itself encouraged both actors to increasingly adopt nuclear doctrines and postures that take the rivalry into more destabilizing and dangerous directions.

Domestic Politics

The fact that domestic politics has become increasingly important to the dynamics of the relationship is of course not surprising. As noted above, internal politics has never been absent as a variable affecting this rivalry, and it is only obvious that with building hostility over several decades, punctuated with wars and crises, public opinion was destined to become only increasingly hardened and salient to decision-making on both sides.

Yet, shifts in both the strategic and domestic landscapes in recent times have contributed to domestic politics acquiring growing centrality in shaping the future of the India-Pakistan rivalry. One such strategic shift, as discussed above, is the increasing reliance on and incidence of terrorism emanating from Pakistan. In India, the increasing targeting of the civilian population, inside and increasingly outside Kashmir, has inevitably led to a public opinion more engaged about India-Pakistan relations than they were perhaps in previous decades when the two countries were known to meticulously avoid civilian casualties in even wars and crises.[28] In Pakistan, on the other hand, incubating terrorism has required an accelerated radicalization (often religious) of pockets of the country's population, as well as the continued framing of India as an existential threat. This process has been facilitated with the support of the dominant military, which itself has been argued to have been undergoing a similar religious turn in the last few decades.[29]

The Islamization of political culture in Pakistan has of course been long in the making, with its antecedents in the Zia era of the 1980s. The dramatic domestic shift in India has, however, been much more recent, especially with the ascendance to a position of near political hegemony of the ruling Hindu nationalist BJP under Narendra Modi and Amit Shah. This dispensation has shown itself to be ideologically inclined toward both a more muscular national security posture—not least because Modi himself has spent significant effort to build up such an image, of a "56-inch chest" leader[30]—as well as an overtly unapologetic Hindu nationalism, that is less sympathetic, if not completely hostile, to both the Muslim minority in India, and to what is in this worldview their natural extension, Pakistan.[31] The fact that BJP has found it increasingly politically profitable to mobilize public support on these lines has further incentivized the current leadership in New Delhi to bind itself and its electoral fortunes to this hard-line stance.

These domestic changes have manifested themselves in dramatic ways in the Indian government's policies and actions in the last several years, both independent of and in response to Pakistan. Two of these are particularly noteworthy, for their sheer unprecedentedness. The first was India's response to a spate of terrorist strikes leading up to the February 2019 suicide bomber attack in Pulwama (J&K), claimed by Pakistan-based Jaish-e-Mohammed group, which killed about 40 Indian paramilitary personnel. India's response was unprecedented, especially considering the challenges described earlier in the chapter.[32] On February 26, New Delhi launched airstrikes on suspected Jaish camps in Balakot, deep in Pakistan's Khyber-Pakhtunkhwa province, the first time India had carried out military action that far inside Pakistan without being in war. Pakistan responded the next day with airstrikes of its own, with the consequent dogfight resulting in an Indian aircraft being brought down in Pakistani territory and its pilot captured alive. The Indian pilot was eventually released, and the crisis managed, but the brief period did display the Modi government's willingness to take a more muscular approach toward Pakistan, despite the risks of rapid escalation.[33]

A second, equally dramatic development with major consequences for the India-Pakistan rivalry was the scrapping by the Indian Parliament of Article 370 of the Constitution in August 2019, thereby revoking the special position and autonomy that Jammu and Kashmir state had enjoyed as part of the Indian Union since the 1950s. The act also demoted the territory from a State to a Union Territory, bringing it more directly under the control of the central government. This step, dramatic in itself, was accompanied—ostensibly to maintain public order and prevent violence—by months-long draconian measures (even by Kashmir's standards) involving restrictions on local political activity (with many leaders arrested) and a sharp clampdown on all freedom of movement or communication of the civilian population, including a complete cutting off of internet and mobile services.[34]

Both cases demonstrate the intersection and complementarity for the current regime of their military-strategic and ideological proclivities and domestic mobilizational and electoral interests. In either case, an argument could be made—as the government did—that a more assertive policy was necessary from the perspective of maintaining territorial integrity and ensuring national security in the face of domestic threats in Kashmir, as well as those that were emanating from Pakistan. Such action was, however, also in perfect consonance with the BJP's ideological predilection of hostility toward Pakistan and suspicion of Muslim population and leadership in Kashmir. Finally, these actions, independent of the military-strategic and ideological motivations, served an equally important domestic mobilizational purpose for Modi and Shah. Revoking Article 370 and the Balakot strikes served the purely domestic political goal of establishing the party's ideological bona fides, and by providing a "win" on these fronts, played a signaling role for the domestic audience.[35]

Indeed, the fact that these actions have thus far shown little in terms of the real impact in either changing the local situation in Kashmir or Pakistani incentives or behavior—and in the case of Kashmir, have instead exacerbated grievances in the population[36]—suggests that the strategic dimension might have been secondary to the domestic political motives driving these decisions. The Balakot strikes were fully exploited by the BJP to burnish Modi's image on the way to a comprehensive win in the 2019 national elections. Indeed, the political rewards that have seemingly flowed from these actions have arguably moved even other, more "secular" parties in the political arena toward a "Soft Hindutva" stance, as evidenced in their fairly muted reactions to the scrapping of Article 370, or their hesitancy to debate the veracity of the narrative that was built around the Balakot strikes.[37]

Conclusion

In recent decades, related developments of the introduction of nuclear weapons, a growing reliance in Pakistan on terrorism, and the shifting nature of domestic politics in both countries have only further complicated the dynamics of the India-Pakistan rivalry. These factors indicate that the immediate future of the India-Pakistan relation is bleak, as structural conditions, both domestic and international, have shifted in ways that have only reduced any opportunities and incentives on either side to make any substantive gestures to ending the rivalry.

Any hopes for peace are therefore unlikely to emerge from conditions as they currently are. Rather, they will require some dramatic shift or crisis—domestic or international—which would push one or both sides to change course. This could be, unlikely as it potentially seems, domestic political developments in India that significantly assuage anxieties of the Kashmiri people and successfully convince them to throw in their lot with the Indian union. Or change could come in response to an international crisis involving the two countries, which takes the two countries to the precipice of (but hopefully not over it) nuclear war, forcing a reconsideration of the rivalry. Similarly, economic and other domestic crises are known to incentivize countries to seek peace externally; perhaps something of that nature in either or both countries will push them toward serious engagement.

While unlikely and even undesirable, were such crises come to pass, the good news may be the fact that ironically the military in Pakistan and the BJP in India, both entities that have benefited from fueling the conflict, will also be in the best position given their political hegemony and hawkish credentials to make tough compromises. As some political science theories have proposed, given the right structural circumstances, foreign policy hawks are better able to pursue the path of compromise than their dovish counterparts. While the military has dominated Pakistani politics for decades now, observers have always pointed to the fact that, since Nehru and maybe Indira Gandhi, there has been "no sign that any Indian leader or party...has the courage and persuasive powers to change the public's mind."[38] In a dominant Narendra Modi, India at least has the latter.

Notes

1 Ayesha Jalal, *The State of Martial Rule: The Origins of Pakistan's Political Economy of Defence* (Cambridge: Cambridge University Press, 1990), 22–48.
2 Ramachandra Guha, *India after Gandhi: The History of the World's Largest Democracy* (New York: Harper Collins, 2007), 51–73.
3 V.P. Menon, *The Story of the Integration of the Indian States* (Calcutta: Orient Longmans, 1956).
4 In Hyderabad and Junagadh, the rulers were Muslim while the majority of the population was Hindu, and the reverse situation obtained in Jammu and Kashmir.
5 Shuja Nawaz, *Crossed Swords: Pakistan, Its Army, and the Wars Within* (Karachi: Oxford University Press, 2008), 43–53.
6 Šumit Ganguly, *The Crisis in Kashmir: Portents of War, Hopes of Peace* (Cambridge Cambridge University Press, 1997), 9–10.
7 See, for example, Paul, T. V., "Why Has the India-Pakistan Rivalry Been So Enduring? Power Asymmetry and an Intractable Conflict," *Security Studies* 15, no. 4 (2006): 600–630; Rajesh Rajagopalan, "Neorealist Theory and the India–Pakistan Conflict," (in two parts) *Strategic Analysis* 22, no. 9 and 10 (December 1998 and January 1999).
8 Victoria Schofield, *Kashmir in Conflict: India, Pakistan and the Unfinished War* (New York: I.B. Tauris, 2000), 10.

The Evolution of the India-Pakistan Rivalry

9 Zafrullah Khan, Pakistan's Foreign Minister after independence, argued that if Kashmir ended up with India, "Pakistan might as well, from both the economic and strategic points of view, become a feudatory of India or cease to exist as an independent sovereign State." Quoted in Mujtaba Razvi, *The Frontiers of Pakistan: A Study of Frontier Problems in Pakistan's Foreign Policy* (Karachi: National Pub. House, 1971), 95.

10 Šumit Ganguly, *The Origins of War in South Asia: The Indo-Pakistani Conflicts since 1947* (Boulder: Westview Press, 1994), 19; Ashutosh Varshney, "India, Pakistan, and Kashmir: Antinomies of Nationalism," *Asian Survey* 31, no. 11 (1991): 997–1007.

11 Ayesha Siddiqa, *Military Inc.: Inside Pakistan's Military Economy* (Pluto Press, 2017).

12 Husain Haqqani, *Pakistan: Between Mosque and Military* (Washington D.C.: Carnegie Endowment for International Peace, 2005); Aqil Shah, *The Army and Democracy: Military Politics in Pakistan* (Cambridge, MA: Harvard University Press, 2014).

13 Kishore C. Dash, "The Political Economy of Regional Cooperation in South Asia," *Pacific Affairs* 69, no. 2 (Summer 1996), 185–209.

14 S. Paul Kapur, *Dangerous Deterrent: Nuclear Weapons Proliferation and Conflict in South Asia* (Stanford, CA: Stanford University Press, 2007).

15 Šumit Ganguly and Devin T. Hagerty, *Fearful Symmetry: India-Pakistan Crises in the Shadow of Nuclear Weapons* (New Delhi: Oxford University Press, 2005); Šumit Ganguly, "Nuclear Stability in South Asia," *International Security* 33, no. 2 (Fall 2008), 45–70.

16 S. Paul Kapur, "Ten Years of Instability in a Nuclear South Asia," *International Security* 33, no. 2 (Fall 2008), 71–94.

17 Rajesh M. Basrur, *Minimum Deterrence and India's Nuclear Security* (Stanford, CA.: Stanford University Press, 2006), 73–74.

18 These "back channel" talks are recounted in detail in Steve Coll, "The Back Channel: India and Pakistan's Secret Kashmir Talks," *The New Yorker*, March 2, 2009, http://www.newyorker.com/magazine/2009/03/02/the-back-channel.

19 Robert Wirsing, *Kashmir in the Shadow of War: Regional Rivalries in a Nuclear Age* (Armonk, NY: M. E. Sharpe, 2003), 35.

20 See Šumit Ganguly, "Explaining the Kashmir Insurgency: Political Mobilization and Institutional Decay," *International Security* 21, no. 2 (Fall 1996), 76–107.

21 India has been largely restricted to diplomatic lobbying seeking to isolate Pakistan regionally and globally, via for instance the Financial Action Task Force (FATF) mechanism, in its counter-terrorism efforts. Frank O'Donnell and Mihaela Papa, "India's Multi-Alignment Management and the Russia-India-China (RIC) Triangle," *International Affairs* 97, no. 3 (2021), 801–822.

22 Walter C. Ladwig III, "Cold Start for Hot Wars? The Indian Army's New Limited War Doctrine," *International Security* 32, no. 3 (2008), 158–190.

23 Vipin Narang, "Posturing for Peace? Pakistan's Nuclear Postures and South Asian Stability," *International Security* 34, no. 3 (Winter 2009–10), pp. 74–76.

24 Mahesh Shankar and T.V. Paul, "Nuclear Doctrines and Stable Strategic Relationships: The Case of South Asia," *International Affairs* 91, no. 1 (2016), 14–15.

25 Rajesh M. Basrur, *Minimum Deterrence and India's Nuclear Security* (Stanford, CA: Stanford University Press, 2006), chapter 6.

26 Sanjeev Miglani and John Chalmers, "BJP Puts 'No First Use' Nuclear Policy in Doubt," *Reuters*, April 7, 2014, https://www.reuters.com/article/india-election-bjp-manifesto/bjp-puts-no-first-use-nuclear-policy-in-doubt-idINDEEA3605820140407.

27 Christopher Clary and Vipin Narang, "India's Counterforce Temptations: Strategic Dilemmas, Doctrine, and Capabilities," *International Security* 43, no. 3 (2019), 25.

28 On how domestic politics affects foreign policy in India, see Vipin Narang and Paul Staniland, "Democratic Accountability and Foreign Security Policy: Theory and Evidence from India," *Security Studies* 27, no. 3 (2018), 410–447.

29 For a historical overview, see C. Christine Fair, "The Militant Challenge in Pakistan," *Asia Policy* 11 (January 2011), 105–138.

30 Amit Shah used this phrase in April 2019 to convey the muscular policy of the Modi government in the direct context of Indian strikes on terrorist targets in Pakistan. "Modi is the Man with 56-inch Chest: Amit Shah," *The Hindu*, April 28, 2019, https://www.thehindu.com/elections/loksabha-2019/modi-is-the-man-with-56-inch-chest/article26973945.ece.

31 For a recent account of the ideological underpinnings of Modi's rise, see Christophe Jaffrelot, *Modi's India: Hindu Nationalism and the Rise of Ethnic Democracy* (Princeton: Princeton University Press, 2021).

32 "Kashmir Attack: Tracing the Path that Led to Pulwama," *BBC News*, May 1, 2019, https://www.bbc.com/news/world-asia-india-47302467.

33 On this and implications of the strikes, see Arzan Tarapore, "Balakot, Deterrence, and Risk: How this India-Pakistan Crisis Will Shape the Next," *War of the Rocks*, March 11, 2019, https://warontherocks.com/2019/03/balakot-deterrence-and-risk/.

34 "Article 370: What Happened with Kashmir and why it Matters," *BBC News*, August 6, 2019, https://www.bbc.com/news/world-asia-india-49234708.

35 On security-related themes in the 2019 election campaign, see Christophe Jaffrelot and Gilles Verniers, "The BJP's 2019 Election Campaign: Not Business as Usual," *Contemporary South Asia* 28, no. 2 (2020), 155–177.

36 Šumit Ganguly, "Kashmir's Year of Hopelessness," *Foreign Policy*, August 5, 2020, https://foreignpolicy.com/2020/08/05/kashmirs-year-of-hopelessness.

37 See for example, "Delhi CM Arvind Kejriwal Dismissed 'Soft Hindutva' Allegations…," *Outlook India*, November 11, 2021, https://www.outlookindia.com/website/story/india-news-arvind-kejriwal-responds-to-soft-hindutva-allegations-gives-true-version/400467.

38 "Šumit Ganguly and Kanti Bajpai, "India and the Crisis in Kashmir," *Asian Survey* 34, no. 5 (1994), 413.

Bibliography

"Article 370: What Happened with Kashmir and Why It Matters." *BBC News*, August 6, 2019. https://www.bbc.com/news/world-asia-india-49234708.

"Delhi CM Arvind Kejriwal Dismissed 'Soft Hindutva' Allegations." *Outlook India*, November 11, 2021. https://www.outlookindia.com/website/story/india-news-arvind-kejriwal-responds-to-soft-hindutva-allegations-gives-true-version/400467.

"Kashmir Attack: Tracing the Path that Led to Pulwama." *BBC News*, May 1, 2019. https://www.bbc.com/news/world-asia-india-47302467.

"Modi is the Man with 56-inch Chest: Amit Shah." *The Hindu*, April 28, 2019. https://www.thehindu.com/elections/lok-sabha-2019/modi-is-the-man-with-56-inch-chest/article26973945.ece.

Basrur, Rajesh M. *Minimum Deterrence and India's Nuclear Security*. Stanford: Stanford University Press, 2006.

Clary, Christopher, and Vipin Narang. "India's Counterforce Temptations: Strategic Dilemmas, Doctrine, and Capabilities." *International Security* 43, no. 3 (2019): 7–52.

Coll, Steve. "The Back Channel: India and Pakistan's Secret Kashmir Talks." *The New Yorker*, March 2, 2009. http://www.newyorker.com/magazine/2009/03/02/the-back-channel.

Dash, Kishore C. "The Political Economy of Regional Cooperation in South Asia." *Pacific Affairs* 69, no. 2 (Summer 1996): 185–209.

Fair, C. Christine. "The Militant Challenge in Pakistan." *Asia Policy* 11 (January 2011): 105–138.

Ganguly, Šumit. "Explaining the Kashmir Insurgency: Political Mobilization and Institutional Decay." *International Security* 21, no. 2 (Fall 1996): 76–107.

Ganguly, Šumit. "Kashmir's Year of Hopelessness." *Foreign Policy*, August 5, 2020. https://foreignpolicy.com/2020/08/05/kashmirs-year-of-hopelessness.

Ganguly, Šumit. "Nuclear Stability in South Asia." *International Security* 33, no. 2 (Fall 2008): 45–70.

Ganguly, Šumit. *The Crisis in Kashmir: Portents of War, Hopes of Peace*. Cambridge: Cambridge University Press, 1997.

Ganguly, Šumit. *The Origins of War in South Asia: The Indo-Pakistani Conflicts Since 1947*. Boulder: Westview Press, 1994.

Ganguly, Šumit, and Kanti Bajpai. "India and the Crisis in Kashmir." *Asian Survey* 34, no. 5 (1994): 401–416.

Ganguly, Šumit, and Devin T. Hagerty. *Fearful Symmetry: India-Pakistan Crises in the Shadow of Nuclear Weapons*. New Delhi: Oxford University Press, 2005.

Guha, Ramachandra. *India after Gandhi: The History of the World's Largest Democracy*. New York: Harper Collins, 2007.

Haqqani, Husain. *Pakistan: Between Mosque and Military*. Washington D.C: Carnegie Endowment for International Peace, 2005.

Jaffrelot, Christophe. *Modi's India: Hindu Nationalism and the Rise of Ethnic Democracy*. Princeton: Princeton University Press, 2021.

Jaffrelot, Christophe, and Gilles Verniers. "The BJP's 2019 Election Campaign: Not Business as Usual." *Contemporary South Asia* 28, no. 2 (2020): 155–177.

Jalal, Ayesha. *The State of Martial Rule: The Origins of Pakistan's Political Economy of Defence.* Cambridge: Cambridge University Press, 1990.

Kapur, Paul S. "Ten Years of Instability in a Nuclear South Asia." *International Security* 33, no. 2 (Fall 2008): 71–94.

Kapur, Paul S. *Dangerous Deterrent: Nuclear Weapons Proliferation and Conflict in South Asia.* Stanford: Stanford University Press, 2007.

Ladwig III, Walter C. "Cold Start for Hot Wars? The Indian Army's New Limited War Doctrine." *International Security* 32, no. 3 (2008): 158–190.

Menon, V.P. *The Story of the Integration of the Indian States.* Calcutta: Orient Longmans, 1956.

Miglani, Sanjeev, and John Chalmers. "BJP Puts 'No First Use' Nuclear Policy in Doubt." *Reuters,* April 7, 2014. https://www.reuters.com/article/india-election-bjp-manifesto/bjp-puts-no-first-use-nuclear-policy-in-doubt-idINDEEA3605820140407.

Narang, Vipin. "Posturing for Peace? Pakistan's Nuclear Postures and South Asian Stability." *International Security* 34, no. 3 (Winter 2009–10): 74–76.

Narang, Vipin, and Paul Staniland. "Democratic Accountability and Foreign Security Policy: Theory and Evidence from India." *Security Studies* 27, no. 3 (2018): 410–447.

Nawaz, Shuja. *Crossed Swords: Pakistan, Its Army, and the Wars Within.* Karachi: Oxford University Press, 2008.

O'Donnell, Frank, and Mihaela Papa. "India's Multi-Alignment Management and the Russia-India-China (RIC) Triangle." *International Affairs* 97, no. 3 (2021): 801–822.

Paul, T. V. "Why Has the India-Pakistan Rivalry Been So Enduring? Power Asymmetry and an Intractable Conflict." *Security Studies* 15, no. 4 (2006): 600–630.

Rajagopalan, Rajesh. "Neorealist Theory and the India–Pakistan Conflict." *Strategic Analysis* 22, no. 9 and 10 (December 1998 and January 1999).

Razvi, Mujtaba. *The Frontiers of Pakistan: A Study of Frontier Problems in Pakistan's Foreign Policy.* Karachi: National Publishing House, 1971.

Schofield, Victoria. *Kashmir in Conflict: India, Pakistan and the Unfinished War.* New York: I.B. Tauris, 2000.

Shah, Aqil. *The Army and Democracy: Military Politics in Pakistan.* Cambridge, MA: Harvard University Press, 2014.

Shankar, Mahesh, and T.V. Paul. "Nuclear Doctrines and Stable Strategic Relationships: The Case of South Asia." *International Affairs* 91, no. 1 (2016): 1–20.

Siddiqa, Ayesha. *Military Inc.: Inside Pakistan's Military Economy.* Pluto Press, 2017.

Tarapore, Arzan. "Balakot, Deterrence, and Risk: How this India-Pakistan Crisis Will Shape the Next." *War of the Rocks,* March 11, 2019. https://warontherocks.com/2019/03/balakot-deterrence-and-risk.

Varshney, Ashutosh. "India, Pakistan, and Kashmir: Antinomies of Nationalism." *Asian Survey* 31, no. 11 (1991): 997–1007.

Wirsing, Robert. *Kashmir in the Shadow of War: Regional Rivalries in a Nuclear Age.* Armonk, NY: M. E. Sharpe, 2003.

9
INDIA'S NUCLEAR WEAPONS PROGRAM

Yogesh Joshi

India's first Prime Minister, Jawaharlal Nehru, and his chief nuclear scientist Homi Bhabha laid the foundation of an elaborate nuclear science program in 1948, just a year after India's independence. For almost 50 years until 1998, India demurred from fully embracing the logic of nuclear deterrence. India's atomic reluctance is highly puzzling. After China went nuclear in October 1964, India took almost a decade to conduct a peaceful nuclear explosion (PNE) in May 1974 but abstained from weaponizing its nascent nuclear capability. In response to the Pakistani nuclear program, it finally decided to covertly build a small nuclear arsenal in 1989 but desisted from declaring its nuclear intentions for another decade.[1] India's nuclear weapons program was the most debated and discussed nuclear program in the history of all nuclear-weapon states. As George Perkovich writes in his defining account of India's nuclear program: "No nation has debated more democratically than India whether to acquire or give-up nuclear weapons."[2] The policy of nuclear ambiguity where India maintained the appearance of a peaceful nuclear program while developing threshold nuclear capability neither helped its security requirements nor fulfilled its quest for major power status. Its nuclear reluctance was in part inspired by a sense of moral superiority and to prove that it was an exceptional major power.[3] Yet, in the realm of international politics, where military power remained the ultima ratio in inter-state interaction, such nuclear morality found no takers.

India's nuclear ambivalence neither served India's material interests nor its ideological aspirations. It only symbolized India's inability to behave like a normal state in international politics, an unwillingness to prioritize power over principles. Therefore, scholars often attributed India's nuclear program to its quest for prestige or the pulls and pressures of bureaucratic actors within the Indian state. However, beginning with the threat posed by Pakistan in the mid-1980s, India's nuclear program was primarily driven by its security requirements. If May 1998 socialized India into a competitive arena of inter-state politics, within a decade of going overtly nuclear, the Indo–US civilian nuclear agreement of 2008 forced the world to accept India's nuclear weapons status. Since then, India has emerged as one of the world's major nuclear powers with the wherewithal to deliver atomic weapons through land, air, sea, and inter-continental distances.[4]

This chapter examines the origins and evolution of India's nuclear weapons program. Understanding the origins and development of India's nuclear weapons program is essential for three reasons. First, India is the only country facing two nuclear-armed adversaries with

DOI: 10.4324/9781003246626-12

major territorial disputes at stake: Pakistan and China. Yet, India's perception of the nuclear threat from Pakistan and China is markedly different, and so are its deterrent requirements. Facing two unique nuclear adversaries engenders a lot of pressure on India's nuclear weapons program and posture.[5]

Second, India's atomic arsenal is undergoing massive technological updates. In the last decade, India has successfully incorporated Intercontinental Range Ballistic Missiles (ICBMs) and nuclear submarines (SSBNs) into its nuclear delivery vectors and developed Ballistic Missile Defence (BMD) and Multiple Independent Reentry Vehicle (MIRV) capabilities. India's rapidly growing technological profile and changing military ambitions of its nuclear managers signal an aggressive shift in India's nuclear posture.[6]

Lastly, the subcontinent's evolving nuclear dynamics and India's growing nuclear profile have stoked heated doctrinal debates amongst the Indian strategic community.[7] From a purely deterrence-based nuclear strategy of no-first-use (NFU), New Delhi, many contend, is or should shift toward nuclear coercion by embracing the possibility of the first use of nuclear weapons against Pakistan and China.[8] Today, India's nuclear doctrinal debate stands at a crucial juncture.

This chapter undertakes the following path. The first section provides a brief history of India's nuclear program and policy until 1989, when India began weaponizing its nuclear capability. The chapter then divides the evolution of India's nuclear program into three distinct periods. Between 1989 and 1998, the Indian nuclear weapons program entered a phase of "reserved arsenal," whose primary objective was deterring Pakistan. Its chief characteristics were absolute secrecy around weaponization, minimalism regarding the size of the arsenal and delivery methods, and ad hocism concerning use doctrine and command and control. After the 1998 tests, India's nuclear weapons program evolved into a "responsible arsenal," where the primary aim was to build a credible nuclear deterrent and get accommodated in the global nuclear order. Therefore, the period was characterized by an explicit restraint in the size of the arsenal and behavior vis-à-vis nuclear adversaries. The last and ongoing phase in the evolution of India's nuclear program is one of a "resurgent arsenal." In the post-2008 period, India's nuclear weapons program has expanded dramatically. Likewise, the responsible nuclear posture has shifted toward a ready arsenal. Finally, a coercion-heavy first-use-centric preemptive doctrine appears to be replacing the earlier purely deterrent retaliation-centric doctrine. The penultimate section discusses how international relation (IR) theories have made sense of India's nuclear weapons program. It concludes by surmising some possible futures of India's atomic arsenal.

Origins and Brief History of India's Nuclear Weapons Program

India's nuclear weapons program has been an offshoot of its atomic energy program.[9] India's atomic journey began with establishing the Indian Atomic Energy Establishment (IAET) at Trombay in 1948. Nehru and Bhabha aimed to place India at the vanguard of atomic science in the developing world. India's ambitious plans and its growing nuclear infrastructure also gave her a greater voice in global nuclear politics, evident in its status as a founding member of the International Atomic Energy Agency (IAEA).

India faced its first nuclear threat after China went nuclear in October 1964.[10] It created a demand for the bomb, both in India's noisy political landscape and its scientific enclave. To deflect criticism, Prime Minister Shastri allowed the nuclear scientists to theoretically investigate the possibility of conducting a subterranean nuclear explosion for peaceful purposes (SNEPP).[11] Shastri also appealed to the established nuclear powers such as the US, Soviet

Union, and Britain to provide security guarantees for non-nuclear-weapon states against the threat or use of atomic weapons.[12] Only disappointments came in India's way. Nuclear Non-proliferation Treaty (NPT) not only legitimized China's nuclear weapons program, but other nuclear-weapon states also declined to offer positive security guarantees to the non-nuclear-weapon states.[13] As a state with an advanced nuclear energy program, New Delhi considered NPT a humiliation.[14]

India did not accelerate its nuclear weapons program, however.[15] The SNEPP was buried by India's new atomic chief Vikram Sarabhai, who replaced Homi Bhabha after his accidental death in early 1966. Indian decision-makers believed that China would not dare use its nuclear weapons given the inherent risk of retaliation by great powers such as the US and USSR. The extant condition of international politics provided India with a minimum deterrent against China.[16] Even when US-China relations improved under President Nixon, the Soviet Union remained adamantly on India's side.

India's deft realpolitik was evident during the 1971 Bangladesh war when India neutralized both China and the US through its treaty of friendship with the USSR. It squarely defeated Pakistan and established its military hegemony in Asia. After the war, Indira Gandhi gave the go-ahead to conduct a peaceful nuclear test. Though Indira's domestic political compulsions drove the exact timing of the test in May 1974, the overall decision appeared to be inspired by the Prime Minister's desire to opportunistically use the most momentous period in India's military history to consolidate its newfound strength. Yet, the test had no medium-to-long-term military consequence. The PNE remained non-weaponized, and the Prime Minister declined to follow it up with more nuclear tests or any efforts to build prototype weapons and concomitant delivery systems.

Post-PNE, India's nuclear program faced global sanctions.[17] New Delhi also remained oblivious of the Pakistani nuclear weapons program, particularly the AQ Khan proliferation network. It was only in 1979 that Indian intelligence agencies confirmed New Delhi's worst fears: Pakistan's ability to process uranium enrichment.[18] For the next decade, Pakistan received China's warhead design and missile technology assistance. By the late 1980s, Pakistani nuclear weapons almost neutralized India's conventional military edge, evident in the Brasstacks military crisis of late 1987.[19] Therefore, in 1989, Rajiv Gandhi decided to weaponize India's threshold nuclear capability.[20] This "bomb-in-basement" approach braved the end of the Cold War, immense pressure from the US against India's nuclear weapons program, and the tightening noose of the nonproliferation regime in the form of Comprehensive Test Ban Treaty.[21] However, it was only under the new hawkish BJP government elected in 1998 that New Delhi took the risk of conducting a series of nuclear tests and declaring its nuclear weapons status.

Ever since Prime Minister Rajiv Gandhi took the fateful decision to weaponize India's nuclear capability in 1989, India's nuclear weapons program has evolved through three distinct phases.

A Reserved Arsenal, 1989–1999

Reacting to the confirmation of Pakistan's possession of nuclear weapons by Indian intelligence agencies in March 1988, Prime Minister Rajiv Gandhi remarked, "We co-existed with the Chinese bomb for 20 years but a Pakistani bomb? I don't know that we will be able to co-exist with it."[22] Pakistan had preempted India in acquiring a nuclear arsenal in the subcontinent. As K. Subrahmanyam later confirmed, "in the period between 1987–1990, India was totally vulnerable to the Pakistani nuclear threat."[23]

Out of this existential threat, Rajiv Gandhi ordered the weaponization of India's nuclear capability in early 1989. New Delhi's objectives were highly limited: Deter Pakistan from nuclear blackmailing or, worse, use nuclear weapons in an actual conflict without the fear of nuclear retaliation. This narrow security objective had to be achieved under an enormously complex geopolitical environment of US hegemony in the post-Cold War period and growing American interests in global nuclear non-proliferation. Therefore, as Gaurav Kampani argues, the need for secrecy and speed drove India's nuclear weapons program during this period.[24] The combination of limited strategic objectives and an equally limiting strategic environment resulted in a reserved arsenal characterized by three major features.

First, the size of the arsenal was kept very small. Based on the modernization of the device's design tested in 1974, the Indian scientific enclave built aircraft-delivered fission devices by 1993–1994. However, boosted fission devices, tested in 1998, took several more years to finish. Even when international analysts estimated the availability of enough plutonium to produce over 60 nuclear weapons by 1991,[25] the actual number of nuclear devices India developed over this period hardly exceeded a count of two dozen in total.[26] Such low quantities of atomic weapons, even when the Indian nuclear energy program boasted of vast amounts of fissile material, reflected a desire to develop a limited arsenal for the specific purpose of deterring Pakistan.

Second, the deployment of the arsenal relied on a few delivery platforms, primarily fighter aircraft.[27] India had initiated a ballistic missile program and a nuclear submarine program in the mid-1980s; however, the only platform fully developed for nuclear delivery was the Mirage-2000 fighter aircraft obtained from France in the late-1980s. Between 1994 and 1996, the Indian Air Force and the scientific enclave were tasked to develop technological and operational solutions to deliver gravity-based nuclear weapons. Several reasons drove India's initial reliance on the air vector. First, fighter aircraft provided a speedy resolution to the immediate requirement of building a deliverable nuclear arsenal in the face of the challenge posed by Pakistan's already operational nuclear arsenal. Second, the nuclear devices developed by Indian nuclear scientists were too bulky to be delivered by ballistic missiles. Lastly, India's ballistic missile program and its nuclear submarine program were far too underdeveloped to share the burden of nuclear delivery at this stage.

Lastly, the operationalization of the arsenal remained ad hoc with hardly any effort to build elaborate institutional structures of command and control and define the boundaries of nuclear weapons use through nuclear doctrines.[28] First, nuclear weapons were maintained in a de-mated and de-alerted state. Nuclear cores were the responsibility of the Bhabha Atomic Research Center (BARC). The trigger assemblies were under the Defence Research and Development Organisation (DRDO) jurisdiction, with the Indian Air Force controlling delivery vehicles. Second, the efficient deployment of India's nuclear arsenal under such a diffused network of actors required an elaborate command and control system. However, all nuclear decision-making remained under the firm control of the Prime Minister's office without the formation of a dedicated organization that could develop the necessary technological, organizational, and procedural capabilities and routines for a flawless deployment of India's nuclear deterrent. The role of the Indian military, except that as a final user of nuclear weapons, in India's nuclear weapons program was therefore negligible. Lastly, the credibility of nuclear deterrence depends on its terms of use and its effective communication to the adversary. At this stage, three factors contributed to the lack of doctrinal clarity in India's slowly consolidating but reserved arsenal: India's limited objectives vis-à-vis deterring Pakistan, the relatively simple managerial problems associated with small nuclear arsenals, and the need to maintain secrecy in the face of tightening nuclear non-proliferation regime.

India's nuclear weapons program during the crucial decade between 1989 and 1998 was reserved for the twin tasks of developing an existential deterrent vis-à-vis Pakistan while escaping the pulls and pressures of the global non-proliferation regime. Therefore, such a reserved arsenal resulted in a "recessed deterrent" based upon few nuclear weapons, limited delivery vectors, and ad hocism in operational issues concerning readiness, employment, and use of its atomic arsenal.[29]

A Responsible Arsenal, 1998–2008

The May 1998 nuclear weapons tests had two significant implications for India's nuclear weapons program.[30] First, by embracing its nuclear weapons status, India's nuclear arsenal finally escaped the highly constraining burden of secrecy. India's nuclear weapons program could now be pursued openly even when it would invite punitive sanctions from Western countries and their allies. As Indian Prime Minister Vajpayee argued then, there was no rationale to shroud India's nuclear status in "needless ambiguity."[31] Second, India's open defiance of the nuclear non-proliferation regime was a signal to the rest of the world of its intention to become a major power in global politics, not on Nehruvian idealism of yesteryears but by accumulating material power. India's nuclear weapons program, therefore, stood at a significant crossroad. On the one hand, New Delhi could run with its nuclear weapons program, develop a maximalist nuclear arsenal, and continue to openly challenge the established nuclear order and the Western stranglehold on the global nuclear nonproliferation regime.[32] On the other, it could voluntarily embrace constraints on its nuclear arsenal, exhibit responsible nuclear behavior by adopting a deterrent-only nuclear use doctrine, and develop excellent command and control mechanisms to reduce global skepticism over its capability to manage its nuclear power arsenal.[33]

As former Foreign Secretary Shyam Saran argues, India opted for "responsibility" and "restraint."[34] A few days after the tests, Vajpayee declared in the Parliament that India's nuclear weapons will never be "weapons of aggression."[35] He also offered a NFU pledge to Pakistan, declared a moratorium on nuclear testing, declined to "subscribe" to the Cold War nuclear doctrines, and assured the world that India's nuclear weapons would remain firmly under civilian control. Officially, the Indian government labeled this "responsible arsenal" as the pursuit of a "minimum credible deterrent."[36]

Its first significant feature was the explicit enunciation of a nuclear doctrine detailing the conditions under which India would deploy and employ nuclear weapons.[37] The National Security Advisory Board first presented India's nuclear doctrine in August 1999, and the Government officially granted its imprimatur to a revised version in March 2003. The doctrine eschewed any war-fighting role for nuclear weapons: India's nuclear weapons were solely dedicated to deterring the use or threat of use of nuclear weapons and other weapons of mass destruction by its adversaries. To this end, the doctrine promised a NFU of nuclear weapons. The credibility of India's nuclear deterrent rested on India's ability to retaliate massively against any use of nuclear weapons. The doctrine, therefore, demanded a secure second-strike capability based on a triad of nuclear delivery systems. Survivability rather than the absolute credibility of a response was the focus. In so far, survivability ensured the risk of retaliation against an adversary, the risk of retaliation rather than its absolute certainty provided India the element of deterrence. Lastly, obtaining the prerequisite of survivability and the complexity of managing a sophisticated nuclear arsenal required an elaborate command and control mechanism. The ad hocism of yesteryears paved the way for an efficient, secure, and redundant command and control system.

To a large extent, the growth of India's nuclear arsenal followed the mandates of minimalism laid down in India's nuclear doctrine. The decade following the 1998 tests saw a very modest but secular increase in India's nuclear arsenal and delivery capabilities. If India had only a dozen atomic warheads developed during the previous decade, between 1998 and 2008, the nuclear arsenal grew by an average of five warheads a year.[38] By the year 2008, India's nuclear weapons stockpile amounted to a total of 70 warheads, even when India's fissile material stockpile was sufficient for a couple of hundred nuclear weapons. Given the emphasis on survivability and a triadic delivery structure, India's ballistic missile program gained some pace with maturing of the Prithvi and Agni class of ballistic missiles. The nuclear-capable short-range Prithvi missile was operationalized soon after the 1998 tests. Yet, in terms of longer-range missiles, only Agni I of 700 km range and Agni II of 2000 km range were inducted for nuclear delivery by 2008.[39] More extended range Agni missiles and India's nuclear submarine program remained under development and shrouded in secrecy. To complete its requirement for a nuclear triad, however, India developed naval versions of Prithvi missiles called Dhanush and emplaced them in the Indian Navy's missile boats for a sea-based deterrent.[40] In all, India's technological force development saw modest growth during this period.

The last major characteristic of India's responsible arsenal was the creation of a wide-ranging institutional and bureaucratic machinery to build an elaborate command and control system guiding India's nuclear program from cradle to use.[41] Following the Kargil war of June–July 1999 and the recommendation made in the Draft Nuclear Doctrine of August 1999, the Indian Government quickly established a Strategic Forces Command (SFC) to oversee the employment and deployment of nuclear weapons during situations ranging from peace, crisis, and war. It also developed a Nuclear Command Authority (NCA) to establish political control over the SFC. Even while developing such institutional structures for command and control, India maintained its nuclear arsenal in the de-mated and de-alerted state with warheads kept separate from delivery vehicles.[42] India's relaxed approach reassured the world of its responsible attitude toward nuclear risk management.

India's choice for a responsible arsenal was motivated by two factors. First, a minimal arsenal not only satisfied India's deterrent requirements vis-à-vis Pakistan, but it also signaled India's intentions not to enter a nuclear arms race with Beijing, at least during the developmental phase of India's nuclear capabilities. Second, India's responsible nuclear behavior, particularly regarding nonprovocative nuclear doctrines and non-use of nuclear weapons, allowed her to gain greater trust and confidence from the US and its western allies. The process started with India's tactical restraint vis-à-vis Pakistan during the Kargil war and was followed by the promulgation of an NFU doctrine. New Delhi also drastically shifted policy regarding the Non-Proliferation Treaty and supported US-led counterproliferation initiatives such as UNSC Resolution 1540,[43] Container, and Proliferation Security Initiatives.[44] India's nuclear minimalism combined with its embrace of the US-led non-proliferation order paid rich dividends in the form of the Indo-US Civilian Nuclear Agreement. The primary objective of the agreement was to cement a closer Indo-US strategic partnership to balance China's rise. However, India's responsible nuclear behavior greatly assisted the change in the US domestic laws and the exception provided to New Delhi both in the IAEA and the NSG.[45] In the decade following the 1998 nuclear tests, India's nuclear arsenal served to deter its adversaries and help realize India's foreign policy priorities.[46]

A Resurgent Arsenal, 2008 Onwards

The period after the Indo-US nuclear deal represents India's resurgence as a nuclear weapon state that increasingly resembles the established nuclear powers in terms of its nuclear force structure and its operational philosophy of using nuclear weapons. As Kampani argues, "Today India can be classified as a conventional nuclear weapons power...following pattern of nuclear arsenal development, command control and use doctrines similar to those developed by legally recognized nuclear weapons powers during the 'first nuclear age.'"[47] The value of nuclear restraint, in the post-2008 period, as a foundational principle guiding the evolution of India's nuclear arsenal seems to have lost much of its worth.

The current phase of nuclear resurgence is driven mainly by India's emerging security requirements, particularly the need for deterrence stability vis-à-vis China and crisis stability vis-à-vis Pakistan.[48] Though achieving a credible second-strike capability against China was a long-term goal of India's nuclear weapons program, the need of attaining deterrence vis-à-vis Beijing has gained significant traction in India's nuclear policy in the last decade.[49] Much of it owes to the growing Sino-Indian dissonance over the boundary dispute and increasing militarization of the Himalayan frontier. India's deterrence objectives vis-à-vis Pakistan have also changed. Through a series of Pakistan-sponsored conventional and sub-conventional crises beginning with the Kargil war in 1999 to the 2008 terrorist attacks in Mumbai, New Delhi believes that it can only deter Islamabad's penchant for risk-taking by dominating the escalation ladder during crises.[50] Such escalation dominance requires greater conventional military resources and options to dominate the nuclear spectrum of the escalation ladder. Of course, India's nuclear resurgence is helped by India's growing strategic closeness with the US and the recognition of its nuclear weapons status. Unlike the 1990s and the early 2000s, India's expanding nuclear force structure hardly evinces any concern from major nuclear weapons powers today.

India's twin requirements of attaining deterrence stability vis-à-vis China and crisis stability vis-à-vis Pakistan are evident in the ongoing technological force development, the debate around its increasingly contested nuclear doctrine, and the evolving dynamics of its command-and-control mechanisms. India's nuclear weapons inventory today consists of almost 150 nuclear warheads.[51] In terms of the size of the nuclear arsenal, this increase is still quite conservative. However, significant strides have been made in terms of delivery vehicles. Compared to the first two decades of weaponization, when most of its warheads were deployed on fighter jets, the current inventory is increasingly being deployed on land-based and sea-based delivery vectors. Since 2011, India has inducted Intermediate Range Ballistic Missiles such as Agni II (2000 km), Agni III (2500 km), Agni IV (3500 km), and the Intercontinental Range Ballistic Missile Agni V (5200 km) missiles in its nuclear force structure.[52] Today, half of India's nuclear weapons inventory is deployed on these missiles. If the expanding range of India's missiles allows deterrence to be projected deep inside Chinese territory, deployment on rail or road-mobile launchers ensures greater survivability.

India's sea-based deterrence has also come of age. India's first SSBN, INS Arihant, conducted its maiden deterrent patrol in late 2018.[53] Equipped with only 700-km-range missiles, Arihant is still considered a technology demonstrator and has very little utility against China. Yet, India aims to induct six SSBNs in the next decade, progressively increasing the lethality and range of its underwater nuclear vector. The diversity of delivery vehicles is further augmented by increasing India's land-based and sea-based missiles' lethality and accuracy. Agni-IV and Agni-V have been deployed with the MIRV technologies to facilitate greater penetration of enemy airspace and saturation of the target. The newer missiles in India's inventory have far

India's Nuclear Weapons Program

greater accuracy than the first-generation Prithvi and Agni missiles. Some contend that this focus on accuracy and saturation, combined with the development of localized ballistic missile defense, is evidence of India's efforts to dominate future crises with Pakistan.[54] Analysts contend that such technological accretion may provide India with a first-strike advantage and signal New Delhi's willingness to dominate the escalation ladder.[55]

A passionate debate also accompanies the ongoing resurgence in force development on India's nuclear use doctrine.[56] If nuclear warfighting and the first use of atomic weapons were anathema to India's nuclear thinking in the first two decades of weaponization, these first principles have now come under severe scrutiny from India's strategic community. Pakistan's full spectrum deterrence and it's very low nuclear thresholds, including tactical nuclear weapons, have rendered India's stated doctrine of massive retaliation incredulous.[57] Moreover, the growing conventional military gap with China and the fear of two-front war resulting from the strengthening Sino-Pak military collusion have raised the utility of the first use of nuclear weapons as a stop-gap arrangement for conventional deterrence India-China border. Consequently, the Indian nuclear doctrine faces tremendous pressure to shift from a strictly retaliatory posture to a more flexible use posture, including preemption of adversary's nuclear capabilities and use of tactical nuclear weapons on the conventional battlefield. As far as China is concerned, New Delhi has remained steadfastly committed to the NFU of nuclear weapons. However, vis-à-vis Pakistan, analysts contend that India's policy is subtly shifting in favor of conventional or nuclear preemption.[58]

The last characteristic of India's nuclear resurgence is the growing complexity of its command-and-control infrastructure. The SFC has grown in size, mandate, and complexity of operations. From a small nucleus within the Integrated Defense Staff (IDS) in 2002, the SFC is now staffed with more than a 100 personnel. It has expanded into several departments dedicated to operational necessities such as logistics, infrastructure, technical section to oversee force development, separate departments for developing guidelines for the operational readiness of the land, air, and sea vectors, and an electronics group to spearhead the development of release codes and maintaining communications network.[59] The appointment of a Chief of Defence Staff has further streamlined the institutional interaction between the SFC and NCA headed by the Prime Minister. A significant development in India's Command and Control mechanism has been the shift away from the negative controls employed by separating nuclear cores from delivery vehicles to the "positive action links" or technical controls.[60] The use of positive controls along with canisterization of missiles have greatly facilitated the readiness of India's nuclear arsenal. India is slowly moving toward a launch-on-command nuclear posture from a de-alerted and de-mated nuclear arsenal. This is particularly true for India's sea-based nuclear forces.[61]

IR Theory and Explaining India's Nuclear Weapons Trajectory

Scholars have approached India's nuclear program through three major theoretical schools with the discipline of IR: Constructivism, which privileges identity and role construction; Liberalism, which focuses on domestic politics; and lastly, Realism, where security threats and national interests dominate decision-making.

The long trajectory of its nuclear program and ambivalence in its nuclear decision-making have rendered identity and prestige a dominant variable in explaining India's nuclear journey. As Karsten Frey has argued, "in India's nuclear policy formulation, status-seeking became a national interest in its own right."[62] Postcolonial scholars situate India's nuclear policy and weapons program in the anxieties of a newly independent India to emerge as a modern state among their technologically advanced Western peers.[63] The uniqueness of India's experiment as a nation and the experience of its founding fathers also created a sense of moral-politico exceptionalism, driving its quest for a nuclear weapons status.[64] Certain groups within domestic politics also viewed nuclear weapons as the symbol of India's emergence and cultural resurgence as a Hindu nation. For example, the right-wing political parties such as the forerunner to the BJP, the Bharatiya Jans Sangh, and the now-defunct Swatantra Party and progenies such as the Bharatiya Janata Party (BJP) have always been pro-bomb. These pro-nuclear parties remained on the margins of political power during the first fifty years of India's independence. That, in considerable measure, is critical to understanding India's nuclear ambivalence.[65] Lastly, India's nuclear weapons program and policy have been explained from the rising powers' perspective. India's nuclear weapons program is also seen as a revisionist strategy of rising powers to get accommodated in the international order.[66]

Organizational and bureaucratic politics are also held responsible for India's fitful nuclear journey and the evolution of its nuclear weapons program. A significant part of India's decision to conduct nuclear tests both in 1974 and 1998 is attributed to the organizational interests of nuclear scientists at the Bhabha Atomic Research Center.[67] India's nuclear scientists failed in civilian nuclear science; they made up by exploring its military applications. Similarly, the bureaucratic interests of the DRDO are fundamental to understanding the origins of India's ballistic missile program and the nuclear submarine program.[68] If scientific lobbies prodded India down the nuclear path, the tense civil-military relations contributed to the delay in weaponization of India's nuclear capability. Distrust of the military by the civilian decision-makers was also responsible for India's war-averse nuclear strategy, the delay in developing effective operational routines, and command and control mechanisms.[69]

Both prestige and bureaucratic politics answer parts of the Indian nuclear puzzle. However, India's threat perceptions and security requirements still offer the most holistic explanation for the origins of India's nuclear weapons program and its evolving trajectory in the last three decades.[70] India's atomic ambivalence defined by moralistic repugnance for nuclear weapons and a vicarious desire for status accruing from nuclear weapons did engender an impression that New Delhi's security anxieties were manageable without recourse to nuclear weapons. India's rather meek response to the Chinese nuclear threat in the 1960s and 1970s justifies such a reading. Yet, new historiography shows how India's security requirements singularly came to occupy its nuclear decision-making in the 1980s and 1990s due to Pakistan's nuclearization and China's technical support to Islamabad.[71] The threat perception vis-à-vis Pakistan was acute: Islamabad's nuclear ambitions posed an existential threat given its historical penchant for revisionism in South Asia. Pakistan had consistently challenged the territorial status quo even when it was an inferior military power in the Indo-Pak dyad. In New Delhi's thought process, therefore, nuclear weapons in Pakistani possession would have only exacerbated the latter's inclination for a military resolution of the territorial conflict. Therefore, to deter Pakistan, an indigenous nuclear capability was a must. Thus, India's decision to weaponize its nuclear capability shows an evident appreciation of its security requirements and the constraints and opportunities provided by its external environment.

Conclusion

As this chapter shows, the pursuance of national interests against the opportunities and challenges offered by external conditions informed the three phases of India's nuclear evolution. The "reserved arsenal" phase balanced the need to deter the Pakistani atomic threat under the constraints imposed by tightening the nuclear nonproliferation regime. India's "responsible arsenal" was a balance between New Delhi's quest to maintain a minimum credible deterrent on the one hand and its desire to get accommodated in the global nuclear order on the other. The ongoing phase of resurgent arsenal is based upon India's recalibration of its security requirements against China and Pakistan.

Two factors will define the shape and form of India's nuclear arsenal in the coming times. First, the stability of the India-China nuclear relationship is increasingly threatened by the asymmetry of their conventional military balance. In case this asymmetry aggravates, New Delhi may bolster its conventional deterrence through the threat of early use of nuclear weapons in a major Sino-Indian conflict. Second, in the last decade, India has adopted an uncompromising posture toward Pakistan's support for terrorism. India will leverage emerging technologies such as drones, cyber weapons, hypersonics, and space and ground-based surveillance to dominate the escalation ladder. These developments promise to augment the lethality and readiness of India's nuclear arsenal, decrease the use thresholds in its nuclear posture and shift its doctrine away from the objective of deterrence to nuclear coercion.

Notes

1 Šumit Ganguly, "India's Pathway to Pokhran II: The Prospects and Sources of India's Nuclear Weapons Test," *International Security* 23, no. 4 (1999): 148–177.
2 George Perkovich, *India's Nuclear Bomb: The Impact on Global Nuclear Nonproliferation* (Los Angeles: University of California Press, 2002), 447.
3 C. Raja Mohan, "India's Nuclear Exceptionalism," in *Nuclear Proliferation and International Security*, eds. Sverre Lodgaard and Bremer Maerli (London: Routledge, 2007).
4 Gaurav Kampani, "Why India's Post-1998 Evolution as a Conventional Nuclear Weapons Power Evokes Surprise," *Journal of Peace and Nuclear Disarmament* 2, no. 1 (2019): 170–183.
5 Yogesh Joshi and Frank O'Donnell, *India and Nuclear Asia: Forces, Doctrines and Dangers* (Washington, DC: Georgetown University Press, 2018).
6 Vipin Narang, "Five Myths About India's Nuclear Posture," *The Washington Quarterly* 36, no. 3 (2013): 143–157.
7 Frank O'Donnell, "India's Nuclear Counter-Revolution: Nuclear Learning and the Future of Deterrence," *The Nonproliferation Review* 26, no. 5–6 (2019): 407–426.
8 Christopher Clary and Vipin Narang, "India's Counterforce Temptations: Strategic Dilemma, Doctrines and Capabilities," *International Security* 43, no. 3 (Winter 2018/19): 7–52.
9 Harsh V. Pant and Yogesh Joshi, *Indian Nuclear Policy: Oxford India Short Introduction* (New Delhi: Oxford University Press, 2018).
10 John Garver, *Protracted Contest: Sino-Indian Rivalry in the Twentieth Century* (Seattle: University of Washington Press, 2001).
11 Raj Chengappa, *Weapons of Peace: The Secret Story of India's Quest to be a Nuclear Power* (New Delhi; HarperCollins, 2002).
12 Andrew B. Kennedy, "India's Nuclear Odyssey: Implicit Umbrellas, Diplomatic Disappointments, and the Bomb," *International Security* 36, no. 2 (2011): 120–153.
13 Jayita Sarkar, "The Making of Non-Aligned Nuclear Power: India's Proliferation Drift," *International History Review* 37, no. 5: 933–950.
14 Rohan Mukherjee, "Nuclear Ambiguity and International Status: India in the Eighteen-Nation Committee on Disarmament, 1962–1969," in *India and the Cold War*, ed. Manu Bhagvan (Chapel Hill: University of North Carolina Press, 2019), 126–150.
15 Yogesh Joshi, "Perceptions and Purpose of the Bomb: Explaining India's Nuclear Restraint against China," *Modern Asian Studies*, November 16, 2021, doi: 10.1017/S0026749X21000329.
16 Ibid.
17 Yogesh Joshi, "Between Principles and Pragmatism: India and the Nuclear Non-Proliferation Regime in the Post-PNE Era, 1974–1980," *The International History Review* 40, no. 5 (2018): 1073–1093.
18 K. Subrahmanyam, "India's Nuclear Policy: 1964–1998," in *Nuclear India*, ed. J. Singh (New Delhi: Knowledge World, 1998), 26–53.

19 Kanti Bajpai, P.R. Chari, Pervez Iqbal Cheema, Stephen Cohen, and Šumit Ganguly, *Brasstacks and Beyond: Perception and Management of Crisis in South Asia* (New Delhi: South Asia Books, 1997).

20 Subrahmanyam, "India's Nuclear Policy."

21 Perkovich, *India's Nuclear Bomb.*

22 Quoted in Jasjit Singh, "India's Nuclear Policy: A Perspective," *Strategic Analysis*, November 1989, p. 799.

23 Subrahmanyam, "India's Nuclear Policy," 45.

24 Gaurav Kampani, "New Delhi's Long Nuclear Journey: How Secrecy and Institutional Roadblocks Delayed India's Weaponsiation," *International Security* 38, no. 4 (2014): 79–114.

25 George Perkovich, "A Nuclear Third Way in South Asia," *Foreign Policy* 91 (1993): 85–104.

26 Vipin Narang, "Strategies of Nuclear Proliferation: How States Pursue the Bomb," *International Security* 41, no. 3 (2016): 110–150.

27 Kampani, "New Delhi's Long Nuclear Journey."

28 Ibid.

29 Perkovich, "A Nuclear Third Way in South Asia."

30 C. Raja Mohan, *Crossing the Rubicon: Shaping of India's New Foreign Policy* (New Delhi: Viking, 2003).

31 *India Today*, "Interview with Prime Minister Atal Bihari Vajpayee, March 15, 1998.

32 Bharat Karnad, *Nuclear Weapons and Indian Security: Realist Foundations of Strategy* (New Delhi: Macmillan, 2002).

33 Rajesh Basrur, *Minimum Deterrence and India's National Security* (Stanford, CA: Stanford University Press, 2006).

34 Shyam Saran, "The Dangers of Nuclear Revisionism," *Business Standard*, April 22, 2014, https://www.business-standard.com/article/opinion/shyam-saran-the-dangers-of-nuclear-revisionism-114042201335_1.html.

35 Press Information Bureau, "Evolution of India's Nuclear Policy," Paper Laid on the Table of the Lok Sabha, May 27, 1998.

36 P. R. Chari, "India's Nuclear Doctrine: Confused Ambitions," *The Nonproliferation Review* 7, no. 3 (2000): 123–135.

37 Basrur, *Minimum Deterrence.*

38 Robert S. Norris and Hans M. Kristensen, "Indian Nuclear Forces, 2008," *Bulletin of the Atomic Scientists* 64, no. 5 (2008): 38–41.

39 *Ibid.*

40 Yogesh Joshi, "Samudra: India's Convoluted Path to Undersea Nuclear Weapons," *The Non-Proliferation Review* 26, no. 5–6 (2019): 481–497.

41 Joshi and O'Donnell, *India and Nuclear Asia.*

42 Ashley J. Tellis, *India's Emerging Nuclear Posture: Between Recessed Deterrent and Ready Arsenal* (Santa Monica: RAND Corporation, 2001).

43 UNSC Resolution 1540 requires states to establish appropriate export control laws to arrest proliferation of nuclear technology to non-state actors.

44 Joshi and O'Donnell, *India and Nuclear Asia.*

45 Karthika Sasikaumar, "India's Emergence as a Responsible 'Nuclear' Power," *International Journal* 52, no. 4 (2007): 825–844.

46 Joshi and O'Donnell, *India and Nuclear Asia.*

47 Gaurav Kampani, "Why India's Post-1998 Evolution."

48 Joshi and O'Donnell, *India and Nuclear Asia.*

49 Rajesh Basrur, "India and China: A Managed Nuclear Rivalry?" *The Washington Quarterly* 42, no. 3 (2019): 151–170.

50 Clary and Narang, "India's Counterforce Temptations."

51 Hans M. Kristensen and Matt Korda, "Nuclear Notebook: Indian Nuclear Forces, 2020," *Bulletin of Atomic Scientists*, July 1, 2020, https://thebulletin.org/premium/2020-07/nuclear-notebook-indian-nuclear-forces-2020/.

52 Ibid.

53 Joshi, "Samudra."

54 Clary and Narang, "India's Counterforce Temptations."

55 Ibid.

56 Joshi and O'Donnell, *India and Nuclear Asia.*

57 S. Paul Kapur, *Dangerous Deterrent: Nuclear Weapons Proliferation and Conflict in South Asia* (New Delhi: Oxford University Press, 2008).
58 Clary and Narang, "India's Counterforce Temptations."
59 Gaurav Kampani, "India: The Challenges of Nuclear Operationalization and Strategic Stability," in *Strategic Asia 2013-14: Asia in the Second Nuclear Age*, eds. Ashley Tellis, Abraham M. Denmark, and Travis Tanner (Washington, DC: National Bureau of Asian Research, 2013): 100–128.
60 Ibid.
61 Joshi, "Samudra."
62 K. Frey, *India's Nuclear Bomb and National Security* (New York: Routledge, 2006).
63 Itty Abraham, *The Making of the Indian Atomic Bomb: Science, Secrecy and the Postcolonial State* (London: Zed Books, 1998).
64 P. Malik, *India's Nuclear Debate: Exceptionalism and the Bomb* (New Delhi: Routledge, 2010).
65 K. Bajpai, "The BJP and the Bomb," in *Inside Nuclear South Asia*, ed. S. D. Sagan (Stanford, CA: Stanford University Press, 2009), 25–67.
66 T.V. Paul, "The Systemic Bases of India's Challenge to the Global Nuclear Order," *The Nonproliferation Review* 6, no. 1 (1998): 1–11.
67 Ashok Kapur, *Pokhran and Beyond: India's Nuclear Behaviour* (New Delhi: Oxford University Press, 2001).
68 Frank O'Donnell and Harsh V. Pant, "Evolution of India's Agni-V Missile: Bureaucratic Politics and Nuclear Ambiguity," *Asian Survey* 54, no. 3 (2014): 584–610.
69 S. P. Rosen, *Societies and Military Power: India and Its Armies* (Ithaca, NY: Cornell University Press, 1996).
70 Ganguly, "India's Pathways to Pokhran II."
71 Joshi, "Perceptions and Purpose of the Bomb."

Bibliography

Abraham, Itty. *The Making of the Indian Atomic Bomb: Science, Secrecy and the Postcolonial State*. London: Zed Books, 1998.
Bajpai, K. "The BJP and the Bomb." In *Inside Nuclear South Asia*, edited by S. D. Sagan, 25–67. Stanford, CA: Stanford University Press, 2009.
Bajpai, Kanti, P.R. Chari, Pervez Iqbal Cheema, Stephen Cohen, and Šumit Ganguly. *Brasstacks and Beyond: Perception and Management of Crisis in South Asia*. New Delhi: South Asia Books, 1997.
Basrur, Rajesh. "India and China: A Managed Nuclear Rivalry?" *The Washington Quarterly* 42, no. 3 (2019): 151–170.
Basrur, Rajesh. *Minimum Deterrence and India's National Security*. Stanford, CA: Stanford University Press, 2006.
Chakma, B. "Towards Pokhran-II: Explaining India's Nuclearisation Process." *Modern Asian Studies* 39, no. 1 (2005): 189–236.
Chari, P.R. "India's Nuclear Doctrine: Confused Ambitions." *The Nonproliferation Review* 7, no. 3 (2000): 123–135.
Chengappa, Raj. *Weapons of Peace: The Secret Story of India's Quest to Be a Nuclear Power*. HarperCollins: New Delhi, 2002.
Clary, Christopher, and Vipin Narang. "India's Counterforce Temptations: Strategic Dilemma, Doctrines and Capabilities." *International Security* 43, no. 3 (Winter 2018/19): 7–52.
Frey, K. *India's Nuclear Bomb and National Security*. New York: Routledge, 2006.
Ganguly, Šumit. "India's Pathway to Pokhran II: The Prospects and Sources of India's Nuclear Weapons Test." *International Security* 23, no. 4 (1999): 148–177.
Garver, John. *Protracted Contest: Sino-Indian Rivalry in the Twentieth Century*. Seattle: University of Washington Press, 2001.
India Today. "Interview with Prime Minister Atal Bihari Vajpayee, March 15, 1998.
Joshi, Yogesh. "Perceptions and Purpose of the Bomb: Explaining India's Nuclear Restraint against China." *Modern Asian Studies* 56, no. 4 (2021). doi: 10.1017/S0026749X21000329.
Joshi, Yogesh. "Between Principles and Pragmatism: India and the Nuclear Non-Proliferation Regime in the Post-PNE Era, 1974–1980." *The International History Review* 40, no. 5 (2018): 1073–1093.

Joshi, Yogesh. "Samudra: India's Convoluted Path to Undersea Nuclear Weapons." *The Non-Proliferation Review* 26, no. 5–6 (2019): 481–497.

Joshi, Yogesh, and Frank O'Donnell. *India and Nuclear Asia: Forces, Doctrines and Dangers.* Washington, DC: Georgetown University Press, 2018.

Kampani, Gaurav. "India: The Challenges of Nuclear Operationalization and Strategic Stability." In *Strategic Asia 2013–14: Asia in the Second Nuclear Age,* edited by Ashley Tellis, Abraham M. Denmark, and Travis Tanner, 100–128. Washington, DC: National Bureau of Asian Research, 2013.

Kampani, Gaurav. "New Delhi's Long Nuclear Journey: How Secrecy and Institutional Roadblocks Delayed India's Weaponsiation." *International Security* 38, no. 4 (2014): 79–114.

Kampani, Gaurav. "Why India's Post-1998 Evolution as a Conventional Nuclear Weapons Power Evokes Surprise." *Journal of Peace and Nuclear Disarmament* 2, no. 1 (2019): 170–183.

Kapur, Ashok. *Pokhran and Beyond: India's Nuclear Behaviour.* New Delhi: Oxford University Press, 2001.

Kapur, S. Paul. *Dangerous Deterrent: Nuclear Weapons Proliferation and Conflict in South Asia.* New Delhi: Oxford University Press, 2008.

Karnad, Bharat. *Nuclear Weapons and Indian Security: Realist Foundations of Strategy.* New Delhi: Macmillan, 2002.

Kennedy, Andrew B. "India's Nuclear Odyssey: Implicit Umbrellas, Diplomatic Disappointments, and the Bomb." *International Security* 36, no. 2 (2011): 120–153.

Kristensen, Hans M., and Matt Korda. "Nuclear Notebook: Indian Nuclear Forces, 2020." *Bulletin of Atomic Scientists,* July 1, 2020. https://thebulletin.org/premium/2020-07/nuclear-notebook-indian-nuclear-forces-2020/.

Malik, P. *India's Nuclear Debate: Exceptionalism and the Bomb.* New Delhi: Routledge, 2010.

Mohan, C. Raja. "India's Nuclear Exceptionalism." In *Nuclear Proliferation and International Security,* edited by Sverre Lodgaard and Bremer Maerli, 152–171. London: Routledge, 2007.

Mohan, C. Raja. *Crossing the Rubicon: Shaping of India's New Foreign Policy.* New Delhi: Viking, 2003.

Mukherjee, Rohan. "Nuclear Ambiguity and International Status: India in the Eighteen-Nation Committee on Disarmament, 1962–1969." In *India and the Cold War,* edited by Manu Bhagvan, 126–150. Chapel Hill: University of North Carolina Press, 2019.

Narang, Vipin. "Five Myths About India's Nuclear Posture." *The Washington Quarterly* 36, no. 3 (2013): 143–157.

Narang, Vipin. "Strategies of Nuclear Proliferation: How States Pursue the Bomb." *International Security* 41, no. 3 (2016): 110–150.

Norris, Robert S., and Hans M. Kristensen. "Indian Nuclear Forces, 2008." *Bulletin of the Atomic Scientists* 64, no. 5 (2008): 38–41.

O'Donnell, Frank. "India's Nuclear Counter-Revolution: Nuclear Learning and the Future of Deterrence." *The Nonproliferation Review* 26, no. 5–6 (2019): 407–426.

O'Donnell, Frank, and Harsh V. Pant. "Evolution of India's Agni-V Missile: Bureaucratic Politics and Nuclear Ambiguity." *Asian Survey* 54, no. 3 (2014): 584–610.

Pant, Harsh V. "India's Nuclear Doctrine and Command Structure: Implications for Civil-Military Relations in India." *Armed Forces & Society* 33, no. 2 (2007): 238–264.

Paul, T.V. "The Systemic Bases of India's Challenge to the Global Nuclear Order." *The Nonproliferation Review* 6, no. 1 (1998): 1–11.

Perkovich, George. "A Nuclear Third Way in South Asia." *Foreign Policy* 91 (1993): 85–104.

Perkovich, George. *India's Nuclear Bomb: The Impact on Global Nuclear Nonproliferation.* Los Angeles: University of California Press, 2002.

Press Information Bureau. "Evolution of India's Nuclear Policy." *Paper Laid on the Table of the Lok Sabha,* May 27, 1998.

Rajagopalan, Rajesh. "India Now Controls the Escalation Ladder." *Observer Research Foundation,* October 5, 2016. https://www.orfonline.org/expert-speak/india-now-controls-the-escalation-ladder/.

Rosen, S.P. *Societies and Military Power: India and Its Armies.* Ithaca, NY: Cornell University Press, 1996.

Saran, Shyam. "The dangers of nuclear revisionism." *Business Standard,* April 22, 2014. https://www.business-standard.com/article/opinion/shyam-saran-the-dangers-of-nuclear-revisionism-114042201335_1.html.

Sarkar, Jayita. "The Making of Non-Aligned Nuclear Power: India's Proliferation Drift." *International History Review* 37, no. 5 (2015): 933–950.

Sasikumar, Karthika. "India's Emergence as a Responsible 'Nuclear' Power." *International Journal* 52, no. 4 (2007): 825–844.

Singh, Jasjit. "India's Nuclear Policy: A Perspective." *Strategic Analysis*, November 1989, p. 799.

Subrahmanyam, K. "India's Nuclear Policy: 1964–1998." In *Nuclear India*, edited by J. Singh, 26–53. New Delhi: Knowledge World, 1998.

Tellis, Ashley J. *India's Emerging Nuclear Posture: Between Recessed Deterrent and Ready Arsenal.* Santa Monica: RAND Corporation, 2001.

10
PAKISTAN'S NUCLEAR WEAPONS PROGRAM

Hannah Haegeland and Arzan Tarapore

The India-Pakistan strategic rivalry has produced four conventional wars (in 1947–48, 1965, 1971, and 1999), fueled several internal insurgencies, and inhibited economic and diplomatic cooperation across the region. For decades after independence, India held clear and growing strategic advantages in this rivalry—underscored by the 1971 war, when it sliced Pakistan in half. In response to this lopsided equation, Pakistan's leaders hoped that the acquisition of nuclear weapons would guarantee the state's survival and place it on more equal political and military footing. So important was this capability that Pakistan's then-Foreign Minister, Zulfikar Ali Bhutto, famously swore that already-impoverished Pakistanis would "eat grass" if necessary to acquire it.

While several motivations coincided in this major national commitment, the origins and evolution of Pakistan's nuclear weapons program can best be explained through the lens of realist international relations. Nuclear weapons were primarily a tool to promote national security and political interests. Pakistan's leaders expected nuclear weapons would limit the threat of Indian military power, allow it to more freely pursue its policy goals in contesting control of Kashmir, and cement its leadership in the Islamic world.

We argue in this chapter that the actual record has been decidedly more mixed. India has likely been deterred from using military force above a limited threshold because of Pakistani nuclear weapons. But Pakistan is no closer to realizing or legitimizing its claims on Kashmir, and the evolution of its nuclear posture, interacting with changes in India's approach to the use of military force, has created a range of new risks for strategic stability. And even after establishing nuclear deterrence, the Pakistani state continues to expend scarce resources on security against India—including continued development of its nuclear arsenal—at the expense of economic prosperity.

This chapter traces the origins and evolution of Pakistan's nuclear weapons program in three sections. First, we argue that Pakistan pursued a nuclear weapons capability primarily for security reasons. Second, we argue Pakistani nuclear capability has iteratively interacted with Indian military developments, lowering the threshold for nuclear use. And finally, briefly, we outline a range of new strategic conditions that will have unpredictable consequences for the program.

130   DOI: 10.4324/9781003246626-13

Motivations and Origins

The creation of a nuclear weapons program requires both means and motives. While materials, technology, and scientific and engineering expertise are critical among the necessary means, empowered and motivated stakeholders set possessor states apart. Study of the history of Pakistan's nuclear weapons program has been limited by data access challenges, but enough is known to identify key players and strategies.[1] The roles and preeminence of different drivers shifted as Pakistan moved from exploratory stages in the 1960s to active pursuit including espionage, technology acquisition, and enrichment in the 1970s and 1980s, and eventually to overt testing in 1998. Key domestic stakeholders for the origins of Pakistan's program include Foreign Minister and later Prime Minister, Z.A. Bhutto; the infamous spy, engineer, and proliferator, Abdul Qadeer Khan; and the Pakistan Army. Driving external forces at play included India, the United States, China, and Saudi Arabia, among other international players, with roles ranging from technical collaborators and political and financial patrons to potential adversaries.

Why did Pakistan pursue nuclear weapons and how did it go about it? Like all nuclear states, there were multiple, overlapping motivations including traditional models of security, domestic politics, and the pursuit of international prestige.[2] The bomb was a key element in Bhutto's nation-building efforts as the country's first civilian leader and an early and prolific communicator on postcolonial "third world" geopolitics.[3] While the Pakistan Army has pur-view over the nuclear weapons program today, its early champions were civilians. Domestic competition among scientists and laboratories and among technocrats, scientists, and the mili-tary also impacted program development.[4] And even the Pakistani public played an important role, providing consensus support for the nuclear weapons program, enabling alternating military and civilian leadership of the country to prioritize it over other national interests.[5] The most common underlying thread in these different motivations is Pakistan's perceptions of a powerful and hostile India.

Pakistan's pursuit of nuclear weapons, therefore, can be explained broadly in realist terms: That is, Pakistan was responding to interstate competition for power and security. But, as we note above, Pakistan's response was not perfectly rational and it was not a unitary actor. Its interpretation of the international environment was filtered through a lens that magnified Indian power and perfidy, and its early nuclear program was subject to the interaction of mul-tiple, often competing domestic actors. In that way, Pakistan's nuclear program can best be explained in a neoclassical realist paradigm, which sees states behaving in accordance with their relative power and security, albeit in ways mediated and distorted through the state's particular perceptions and domestic constraints.[6]

The literature on key security motivations for Pakistan developing nuclear weapons can be summarized in two broad categories. Initially, Pakistan worked toward a credible deterrent to create opportunities for favorably shifting its position vis-à-vis India, preventing or at least ensuring it would not lose a future conflict, and perhaps even to redraw territorial boundaries in Kashmir. Later (post-1971) security concerns were more urgently motivated by perceived existential threats, to secure Pakistan's survival as a state and safeguard against regime change.

Pakistan played a unique and pivotal role for the United States during the Cold War, and for a time the partnership had critical utility for the security and foreign policies of both countries. During the war, US nonproliferation objectives came into tension with strategic cooperation with Pakistan on other foreign policy issues, particularly related to the Soviet invasion of Afghanistan and the Iranian revolution.[7] Pakistan leveraged this to adopt what one scholar labels a "sheltered" strategy to develop its program,[8] using competing US policy priorities to covertly develop its program without fear of reprisal, so long as it refrained from full weaponization. From 1986 to 1998, Pakistan then utilized its ambiguous nuclear capability to induce American intervention in its disputes with India.[9]

It is now clear that previous arguments about Pakistan's bomb being a simple response to India's 1974 "peaceful nuclear explosion" (PNE) are lacking. Before the Indian 1974 PNE, notably after incurring crippling losses in the 1971 India-Pakistan war, Pakistani decision-makers moved beyond exploring dual-use nuclear technologies and capabilities to covertly pursuing weaponization.[10] Pakistan and India had recurring crises and two wars in the 1960s and 1970s, but it was the 1971 war resulting in the creation of Bangladesh that changed the equation for Pakistan, establishing an enduring and defining existential security concern. Not long after this pivot toward weaponization, Pakistani leaders began to credit their latent nuclear weapons capability with having bolstered Pakistan's position during crises, including the 1986–87 Brasstacks crisis.[11]

Since Pakistan had not yet tested, ambiguity about how far along in the weaponization process its program was and associated warfighting capabilities posed planning problems for a potential adversary, in this case India. It is unclear whether or how Pakistan's recessed capability may have played a role in India's calculus during Operation Brasstacks and the crisis it prompted, or if there was any observable nuclear signaling. Practically, Pakistani signaling of its nearly complete nuclear weapons capability may have been aimed more at the United States than at India. Pakistan employed a tactic of drawing US attention to nuclear risks, inducing American crisis management involvement while still ensuring the United States would not impose sanctions under the "Pressler Amendment." Versions of this Pakistani tactic of drawing US attention to nuclear risks on the subcontinent have proven effective for over 40 years and still work during bilateral crisis to a more limited extent today. Ultimately, though, the fact that Pakistani leaders believed their nuclear capabilities successfully helped deter Indian aggression is salient to the origins of Pakistan's later declared nuclear doctrine which similarly relies on ambiguity, as well as for broader study of latent nuclear deterrence.[12]

Another important element of Pakistan's nuclear weapons program has to do with its history of what scholars call "horizontal proliferation," spreading nuclear technologies and science and engineering to other states. Pakistan's proliferation beneficiaries included Iran, Libya, and North Korea, largely through the illicit nuclear supplier network of A.Q. Khan operating from the 1980s through 2002.[13] Historical accounts of A.Q. Khan highlight the sometimes defining role of actions by motivated individuals, state challenges to control all aspects of nuclear programs, and the potential for costly consequences of civilian-military leadership divides on critical national security issues.[14] There is some debate over a "double standard" criticism that the United States treated Pakistan's development of nuclear weapons more harshly than it did India's. Both states after all broke the foundational understanding captured under the US "Atoms for Peace" program and related efforts by other supplier states like Canada that nuclear energy knowledge and technology would be shared but ought not to be used for nuclear weapons production. One response to this criticism rests on Pakistan's history with horizontal proliferation—both on the receiving and on the giving ends—namely assistance received from the United States and France and then importantly from China, and sales by A.Q. Khan's proliferation network. Discovering the exact details of how each country's program came about, what science and technologies were domestic versus imported or stolen, and US and other third-party responses to development is the work of future historians with better data access, but horizontal proliferation is a defining characteristic of Pakistan's nuclear history.[15]

Pakistan's Nuclear Weapons Program

In terms of military tactics, Pakistan's program is aimed at India. However, Pakistan is part of a markedly asymmetric nuclear triad in Asia. Pakistan is most concerned with deterring India, which seeks to deter China, which in turn seeks to deter the United States and Russia. In 1998, Pakistan's May tests were in direct response to India's overt tests that same month, but India was responding in part to perceived threats posed by China. This chain reaction is relevant to early nuclear history in Asia, but it has come to bear even more heavily on post-1998 developments in proliferation, competition, and nuclear strategy.[16]

Effects on Security Policy and Regional Stability

What effect did Pakistan's declared nuclear weapons status have on its security policy? A body of international relations scholarship suggests that states may be emboldened by nuclear weapons acquisitions to pursue more expansive or aggressive policies. This may be especially true in the case of Pakistan because it is both weaker in aggregate conventional military power than India, and because it has revisionist territorial claims against India.[17] In that sense, Pakistan is the type of state with the most to gain from nuclear weapons, because they buttress its security against a stronger rival and offer a tool for long-thwarted policy goals.[18] In this way, nuclear weapons acquisitions may not only fail to prevent conflict through deterrence, but may actually hasten conflict through emboldenment.

Just one year after the nuclear tests, Pakistan appeared to test this proposition in the Kargil conflict.[19] Pakistani forces (specifically members of the Northern Light Infantry), dressed in civilian attire, surreptitiously established lodgments across several peaks in and around the Kargil sector of the Line of Control. Beyond its long-standing goals of revising the territorial status quo and "unfreezing" the Kashmir dispute, Pakistan was probably keen to avenge India's 1984 seizure of the Siachen glacier, and threaten a key Indian supply route. Thus, although the underlying motivations for seizing control of Kargil long predated the nuclear tests, the Pakistan Army probably gained some confidence from its newfound status as a declared nuclear weapons state. It likely judged that its new demonstrated deterrent would reduce the chances of an escalatory Indian response and increase the chances of international diplomatic intervention to spotlight the Kashmir dispute. It remains unclear if this confidence was decisive in triggering the Kargil campaign; the Pakistan Army arguably could have attempted the fait accompli even in absence of its declared nuclear capability.

Beyond the Kargil conflict, Pakistan also escalated its unconventional campaign against India. It used irregular forces to press its territorial claims in Kashmir since literally the first Kashmir conflict in 1947. Throughout the 1990s, it had sustained an insurgency in the Indian-controlled state of Jammu and Kashmir, where Indian security forces were struggling to suppress a separatist movement. After the nuclear tests and Kargil war, Pakistan widened and escalated that campaign to support terrorist attacks beyond Kashmir, in major Indian cities. An attack on the Indian Parliament in December 2001 triggered a massive Indian mobilization—significantly larger than during the Kargil war—which lasted most of a year and twice came close to open war. India accused Pakistan of sponsoring a string of other attacks across Indian cities—and produced clear evidence that the perpetrators of the "26/11" complex attack in Mumbai in 2008 were being directed, during the attack itself, from Pakistan.

Throughout this campaign, Pakistan used its nuclear weapons and posture to deter India from responding. It has issued preemptive threats of nuclear strike during crises, even in the 1980s, when its nuclear capability was recessed and ambiguous. These threats were made credible by its nuclear posture after the 1998 tests, designed to quickly escalate to nuclear use in case of an Indian attack. This posture was manifested in both declaratory policy—with frequent nuclear threats—and capability development—with a growing suite of dispersed and short-range delivery systems, as we discuss below.[20]

These deterrent threats apparently worked. Even in the Kargil war, when India had to respond to Pakistan's military encroachments, it placed strict limits on the scale and scope of force its military could use—for example, restricting its aircraft to flying only on its own side of the LoC. In the 2001–02 mobilization, India held back from launching major conventional operations because they carried the risk of uncontrollable escalation to Pakistan's nuclear red lines. After the 2008 Mumbai attacks, India had no good retaliatory options short of major conventional operations, which it again ruled out as unduly risky.[21] By effectively deterring India, therefore, Pakistan's post-1998 declared nuclear capability served its security strategy by reducing the potential costs of Pakistan's unconventional campaign of sponsoring cross-border terrorism in India.

Nuclear weapons not only added an important dimension to Pakistan' security strategy, they undermined strategic stability in the region. The India-Pakistan dyad has become more unstable in at least three ways. First, Pakistan's posture of rapid escalation, for the sake of credibility, requires riskier command and control arrangements. During a crisis or wartime, its threat of rapid first use of nuclear weapons could involve dispersed deployment of weapons and possibly delegated authority to use the weapons. During a crisis, Pakistan likely keeps warheads and delivery systems in close proximity so they can be mated and deployed quickly. These steps may weaken peacetime safeguards against accidental or unauthorized use. The recurring crises and wars between India and Pakistan since 1947 pose concerning questions about how often the Pakistan military may invoke such heightened nuclear status decisions.[22]

Second, Pakistan's nuclear posture enables it to be more aggressive in its sub-conventional attacks against India. Pakistan's posture threatens rapid escalation to the nuclear threshold—promising asymmetric escalation when compared to India's posture of massive but delayed retaliation. India designed its capability to be used only in response to a nuclear strike, ostensibly guaranteeing that it would not escalate to the nuclear threshold first in a crisis. With this credible guarantee in place, Pakistani leaders could be confident that their threat of asymmetric escalation to nuclear use would deter Indian conventional reprisal attacks, and accordingly grow increasingly emboldened and aggressive in their sub-conventional campaign against India, progressively raising the level of violence and risk in the region.[23]

Third, this increased instability at sub-conventional and possibly conventional levels may then filter up to the nuclear level. Some scholars have argued that the introduction of nuclear weapons in the long-standing rivalry between India and Pakistan has helped to stabilize the historically war-prone dyad. In this "stability-instability paradox," as it is known, declared nuclear powers like Pakistan may indeed be emboldened to pursue their revisionist aims more aggressively, but mutual deterrence ensures that low-level violence does not escalate. Both sides in a mutual-deterrence rivalry understand the catastrophic costs of potential nuclear war and accordingly act with greater caution, and may even seek to improve their long-term relationship while sub-conventional instability continues.[24]

In contrast, other scholars have suggested that sub-conventional instability cannot be reliably contained. As one actor—in this case, Pakistan—grows more aggressive under its nuclear umbrella, the other actor—in this case, India—grows increasingly likely to respond with force. Even if both sides would prefer to avoid escalation to nuclear use, the cycle of incrementally escalating force may paint each side into a corner. For a multitude of reasons—including safeguarding territorial integrity, perceptions of international credibility, or pressure from domestic audiences—both sides may judge that backing down in a crisis is more politically

Pakistan's Nuclear Weapons Program

costly than continuing to escalate. In this sense, there are no reliable firebreaks between sub-conventional instability and strategic instability.[25]

Does the stability-instability paradox apply in South Asia, or is the nuclear rivalry fundamentally unstable? The historical record provides evidence for both arguments. On one hand, India and Pakistan have endured several intense security crises—including an open conventional conflict in 1999 and general mobilization in 2001–02—which have not escalated to the nuclear level. Several other incidents of cross-border terrorist provocation—especially in 2008—did not even elicit any military response from India. Deterrence has worked, and strategic stability has survived, so far. On the other hand, political pressure has been growing in India to mount a military response to Pakistan-based terrorism. India did strike back at Pakistan with special forces in 2016, and an air strike in 2019—each time an escalation on its previous response. And following the 2019 air strike at Balakot, Pakistan responded with air incursions of its own against India, which briefly raised the prospects of rapidly escalating instability. This recent trend suggests the Indian government is taking increasingly escalatory steps to punish Pakistan and accept greater risks of further instability.

While South Asia has not yet suffered a nuclear exchange, the doctrines and capabilities on both sides are setting the conditions that make nuclear use more likely. India and Pakistan have engaged in an action-reaction cycle in which each sides seeks the capacity to gain some military advantage, which spurs its adversary to counter with its own doctrinal or capability innovation. With each iteration of this cycle, the two sides have created more options for using and escalating military force quickly, before either the other side or the international community can respond.

This action-reaction cycle gathered momentum after the 2001–02 crisis.[26] The ponderously large Indian military took several weeks to mobilize—that is, to create a viable option to retaliate against Pakistan. In that time, Pakistan was able to make effective defensive preparations and the US led an intense diplomatic intervention to urge restraint and make an Indian military offensive politically untenable. The Indian military's overarching lesson learned from the crisis, then, was the need to be able to mobilize and strike Pakistan quickly, before Pakistan or the United States could thwart it. It thus set about developing a new doctrine for conventional operations, known as Cold Start. One key feature of Cold Start was the aim of compressing the timeframe required for deploying and using force.[27]

Another key feature of Cold Start was setting more modest operational objectives—so that India could impose some punitive costs without triggering a Pakistani nuclear response. For years, some Indian strategic thinkers had harbored fantasies of slicing through Pakistani territory with deep penetrating offensives. This was the putative objective of the Indian Army's doctrine for mechanized operations. Pakistan lacks strategic depth, so invading Indian forces could seize control of key north-south lines of communication in Pakistan, or encircling major cities like Lahore, with relatively modest incursions. The prospect of Indian invaders in effect splitting Pakistani territory played directly into the Pakistani establishment's fears that India would again seek to dismember the Pakistani state as it had done in 1971. For Pakistan, this was precisely the type of Indian military threat that necessitated a nuclear deterrent.

Thus, at the height of the 2001–02 crisis, as India's three strike corps prepared for battle, Pakistan issued a blunt warning. The director of Pakistan's Strategic Plans Division, which controls its nuclear arsenal, publicly signaled Pakistan's nuclear red lines. He asserted that Pakistan would retaliate with nuclear weapons if India crossed any of four thresholds: Conquering a large part of Pakistani territory, destroying a large part of the Pakistani military, strangulating Pakistan economically, or provoking large-scale political destabilization or subversion inside Pakistan.[28] The specific scale of these red lines—for example, how much territory was too much?—was left deliberately ambiguous, to increase the doubt and therefore deterrent effect in India. But the underlying message was clear: Pakistan was willing to use nuclear weapons first, when faced with conventional military or even unconventional or non-military threats from India.

Cold Start, accordingly, sought to bypass this nuclear threat. It proposed making shallow incursions—again, the specific scale remained unstated—so that Indian forces would not approach Pakistani red lines. But this of course left Cold Start mired in a strategic dilemma. If India's punitive response was deliberately calibrated to avoid triggering a Pakistani nuclear response—setting aside the difficulty of making that calibration accurately—that punitive response would by definition impose only tolerable, or relatively minor, costs on Pakistan. India was thus seeking to develop military options against Pakistan that *by design* would be strategically inconsequential. India's military response would be less about imposing sufficient costs on Pakistan to dissuade it from its sub-conventional campaign and more about catalyzing international pressure on Pakistan and satiating Indian domestic pressure to act.

For years, Cold Start was a declaratory doctrine that was constantly disputed, often disavowed, and shrouded in doubt.[29] The Indian military made negligible apparent headway in changing its force structure, organization, or dispositions to implement the doctrinal change. Thus, a series of cross-border terrorist provocations—most notably in Mumbai in 2008—went unanswered in the apparent absence of viable military options.

Nevertheless, Pakistan reacted to Cold Start with its own nuclear evolution. To deter the possibility of shallow Indian incursions, Pakistan began to expand its program with the development of tactical nuclear weapons.[30] The majority of Pakistan's nuclear arsenal is deliverable by surface-to-surface missiles; the remainder by air-launched cruise missiles and aircraft-dropped bombs. By 2013, it had introduced tactical Nasr missiles, with a low yield and a range of about 60 km. These short-range missiles are designed to interdict invading Indian forces, including those already on Pakistani territory.

In 2015, the Pakistan Army began referring to these tactical weapons as the centerpiece of its new "full spectrum deterrence" posture. Whereas its earlier minimum credible deterrent was designed to deter existential threats to the country, full spectrum deterrence was being developed to deter any military threats, including the less-than-existential threats posed by the erstwhile Cold Start doctrine. Pakistan's nuclear posture had evolved to be an integral part of Pakistan's military strategy—a tool of warfighting, not only deterrence. Tactical nuclear weapons lowered the threshold for nuclear use and multiplied demands for rigorous command and control and security of the weapons.

Other elements of full-spectrum deterrence are designed to offer Pakistan more delivery options from the ground and sea. As India began fielding long-range and more-survivable missiles—mostly to deter China—Pakistan followed suit. Academic and policy assessments note the road-mobile Shaheen-3 ballistic missile, whose 2,750 km range could target all of the Indian mainland—and could even range Israel—and the Ababeel, with multiple warheads designed to overcome ballistic missile defense systems. Galvanized by India's nascent triad, Pakistan is also developing naval nuclear capabilities. For example, it is developing a sea-based delivery option with the Babur-3 cruise missile, likely designed to be launched from submarines for a credible second-strike capability. Although these missiles are still being tested and not yet in service, strategic delivery systems still account for the bulk of Pakistan's nuclear arsenal.[31]

Meanwhile, India began reacting to Pakistan's full-spectrum deterrence—especially its tactical nuclear weapons—with new conventional options. If major Cold Start-type operations would be targeted with nuclear attack, India sought to further reduce the scale of its retaliatory strike. In 2016, following a Pakistan-based terrorist strike at Uri, Indian special forces launched a raid against terrorist camps just over the Line of Control in Kashmir, and in 2019, Indian fighter aircraft went much further, targeting—with dubious effects—what India claimed was a terrorist facility at Balakot, in Pakistan proper, rather than disputed Kashmir.

In no way did these Indian reprisals approach Pakistan's nuclear red lines—they did not, as some Indian commentators claimed, call Pakistan's nuclear bluff. They did reveal that some military action could remain below the threshold of nuclear retaliation, but India had again revised downward its military ambitions, from deep penetrating attacks prescribed by mechanized force doctrine, to shallow incursions prescribed by Cold Start, to single ground and air raids. India had found an option for military action—largely as a signal to Pakistan and domestic Indian audiences—but Pakistan's nuclear deterrent forced that action to be strategically negligible.

Despite the shrinking scale of Indian military ambitions, the Balakot crisis also offered a glimpse into how that relatively modest military action could still generate crisis instability. In part this was likely intentional—New Delhi probably judged that its threshold-busting air strike would show India to be unpredictable and highly resolved, deliberately raising the risk of conflict to compel Pakistan to back down. In part, however, neither side could control escalation reliably—the crisis was mitigated after Pakistan made the conciliatory gesture of returning a captured Indian pilot, but could have spun out of control had the aerial skirmish claimed more lives or accidentally caused significant damage. New Delhi probably judged the Balakot crisis to validate its claim that it can find space for conventional operations, and that offramps exist even after a crisis escalates. But a similar crisis in the future, featuring a Pakistan primed to show its redoubled resolve, and subject to the vagaries of operational chance, would have no reliable firebreaks before approaching Pakistan's threshold for nuclear use.[32]

Other potential sources of crisis instability are on the horizon. Developments in India may prompt Pakistan to react again with yet-unknown changes to its posture. On the conventional level, the Indian Army has finally begun to reorganize into Integrated Battle Groups— in other words, after years of apparent inaction, the Army is taking tangible steps to actualize Cold Start. On the nuclear level, meanwhile, some scholars have suggested that India is at least considering and creating the option for a counterforce posture. Such a posture would seek to eliminate Pakistan's nuclear capability preemptively, to deny Pakistan its deterrent and leave it exposed to India's conventional military.[33] Both of these developments would again challenge Pakistan's existing nuclear capability and concepts, and may prompt the next round of Pakistan's nuclear evolution, with unknown consequences for regional stability.

Implications for Future Regional Security and Global Nuclear Dynamics

Discerning strategic turning points is difficult except in hindsight, but the 2019 Balakot crisis may prove to be a key milestone in ushering in a "third nuclear age" in South Asia, marked by renewed nuclear competition among great powers, new nuclear-armed states, and a greater willingness to escalate and take risks.[34] Consistent with the realist account in this chapter, Pakistan's nuclear program will continue to be shaped by the action-reaction cycle of evolution with India, mediated through the prisms of its military-dominated establishment. In the coming years, it will also face four new sets of issues, related to this evolving nuclear age, which will have unpredictable consequences.

First, near-term prospects for crisis prevention and crisis management mechanisms in South Asia are weak. The United States has long played the key third-party role in encouraging nuclear risk reduction, crisis management, and strategic stability in South Asia. Considering growth of the US-India strategic partnership, cooling of ties between the United States and Pakistan, and strengthening of the Sino-Pakistani relations, the US role in diffusing a future India-Pakistan crisis may be necessarily limited. Compounding these shifts in bilateral relationships is the challenge of simultaneous crisis management. During the 2019 Balakot crisis, US policymaker resources were divided between South Asia, North Korea, and Iran. The United States and other potential third-party managers may face these conditions again in a future crisis and meet with less luck in terms of the readily available offramps from conflict escalation present in 2019.

Second, "strategic chain" dynamics remain active and are likely to remain so for the foreseeable future. Chinese, Russian, and US efforts to modernize and/or expand nuclear forces are having cascading effects on India and therefore Pakistan, resulting in continued development of Pakistan's nuclear arsenal and posture. An unfolding and understudied aspect of these developments in South Asia is the impact of military technologies that are "emerging" for the region and the capabilities they facilitate. For Pakistan's defense calculus, the salient newer technologies include submarines, armed and unarmed drones, ballistic, cruise, and hypersonic missiles, ballistic missile defense, satellites for intelligence surveillance and reconnaissance, and anti-satellite capabilities. These newly developed and deployed technologies and capabilities will impact cross domain deterrence, crisis onset scenarios, and escalation dynamics in unpredictable ways.

Consider, for example, the challenge of defining proportional responses amidst increasing asymmetry in the China-India-Pakistan triad. How will asymmetry between China and India, and between India and Pakistan, compound blurry red lines, signaling, and escalation control strategies, especially given the other nuclear-armed states operating forces in the Indian Ocean Region (IOR)? For example, what happens to Pakistan's operational and strategic calculi if India were to deploy a modified Heron medium-altitude long-endurance, unmanned aerial vehicle on the line of control during a crisis? Is the use of a drone modified to carry conventional munitions instead of typical cross-border firing and mortar shells inherently more destabilizing? Similarly, could we envision a future crisis where one state destroys another's satellite for signaling reasons? What would a proportional response look like to such an event if the victim of the attack lacks anti-satellite weapons? The uncertainty inherent in these newer technologies being asymmetrically deployed in Asia will prove destabilizing in future nuclear crises yielding increasingly gray cross-domain conventional and dual-use system escalation that will be harder to prevent and control.

Third, as a middle power focused almost entirely on India, Pakistan is sometimes overlooked as a nuclear-armed state in assessments of large power defense planning. Yet, Pakistan will be a key player—whether as a passive or active third party or as a direct actor—in any IOR conflict involving China, for example. This has key implications for not just Indian but also US national security priorities in Asia. India's ability to partner with the United States in a hypothetical future IOR conflict will be affected by the status of Pakistani nuclear capabilities and its stance on the conflict. Pakistan would have the ability to take advantage of such a conflict with minimal effort and incurring limited risks. Even if Pakistan were to remain a declared neutral party, its presence would still likely weaken India's utility as a US partner to some extent given its two-front war concerns. Because of this dynamic nuclear multipolarity, middle powers like Pakistan will become increasingly important for future nuclear crises between large powers.

Fourth, South Asia's regional security environment faces renewed sources of instability with dangerous implications for counterterrorism and nuclear security. South Asia's nuclear-armed militaries are expanding their warfighting capabilities in an environment that became much more unstable with the withdrawal of US and coalition forces from Afghanistan in 2021. The region is home to porous underregulated borders, entrenched illicit economies, two nuclear weapons programs, and at least one nascent nuclear energy program (in Bangladesh). Violent nonstate actor groups with various levels of sophistication have a long history of operating across South Asia. These include groups with international agendas and historically expressed interests in chemical, biological, radiological, and nuclear weapons. The regional challenges of counterterrorism and securing sensitive nuclear materials, facilities, and equipment are likely to become more entwined. With the right policy will, this development could helpfully prompt regional and international cooperation on efforts such as border security measures to interdict radiological and nuclear materials and technologies. New research and policy attention is required to assess how nonstate actors may exacerbate regional security in this nuclearized environment.

Notes

1 See Feroz Khan, *Eating Grass: The Making of the Pakistani Bomb* (Stanford University Press, 2012); Rabia Akhtar, *The Blind Eye: U.S. Non-Proliferation Policy towards Pakistan from Ford to Clinton* (University of Lahore Press, 2018); Hassan Abbas, *Pakistan's Nuclear Bomb: A Story of Defiance, Deterrence, and Deviance* (Oxford University Press, 2018).

2 Scott Sagan, "Why Do States Build Nuclear Weapons? Three Models in Search of a Bomb," *International Security* 21, no. 3 (Winter 1996/1997): 54–86.

3 See, for example, Bhutto's writing—couched in Islamicate political rhetoric—on nuclear weapons and small state politics in the face of post-Cold War imperialism, arguing against costly alignment with the United States. Zulfiqar Ali Bhutto, *The Myth of Independence* (London and Lahore: Oxford University Press, 1969).

4 Khan, *Eating Grass*, 68–94.

5 *Ibid*; Christopher Clary, "Pakistan: The Nuclear Consensus," in *Nuclear Debates in Asia: The Role of Geopolitics and Domestic Processes*, eds. Mike M. Mochizuki and Deepa M. Ollapally (Lanham: Rowman and Littlefield, 2016), 221–243.

6 Gideon Rose, "Neoclassical Realism and Theories of Foreign Policy," *World Politics* 51, no. 1 (October 1998): 144–172.

7 For U.S. government accounts of this tension, see Burr's primary source summary and analysis: William Burr, "The Carter Administration's 'Damnable Dilemma': How to Respond to Pakistan's Secret Nuclear Weapons Program, 1978–1979," *Journal of Cold War Studies* 23, no. 1 (2021): 4–54.

8 See Akhtar, *The Blind Eye*; Narang, *Nuclear Strategy in the Modern Era*; and Vipin Narang, "Strategies of Nuclear Proliferation: How States Pursue the Bomb," *International Security* 41, no. 3 (Winter 2016/17): 110–150.

9 Narang, *Nuclear Strategy in the Modern Era*, 55–93.

10 Khan, *Eating Grass*, 95–123.

11 C. Christine Fair, *Fighting to the End: The Pakistan Army's Way of War* (New Delhi: Oxford University Press, 2014), 221.

12 Michael Krepon and Liv Dowling, "Crisis Intensity and Nuclear Signaling in South Asia," in *Investigating Crises: South Asia's Lessons, Evolving Dynamics, and Trajectories*, eds. Sameer Lalwani and Hannah Haegeland (Washington, DC: Stimson Center, 2018), 195–197; Narang, *Nuclear Strategy in the Modern Era*, 57–65; *Matthew* Fuhrmann and Benjamin Tkach, "Almost Nuclear: Introducing the Nuclear Latency Dataset," *Conflict Management and Peace Science* 32, no. 4 (2015): 443–461; Matthew Fuhrmann, "The Logic of Latent Nuclear Deterrence," Working Paper (September 8, 2017), SSRN: https://ssrn.com/abstract=3052231.

13 For an authoritative summary, see Richard Cronin, Alan Kronstadt, and Sharon Squassoni, *Pakistan's Nuclear Proliferation Activities and the Recommendations of the 9/11 Commission: U.S. Policy Constraints and Options*, report Congressional Research Service, May 24, 2005. Updated May 24, 2005.

14 Abbas, *Pakistan's Nuclear Bomb*.

15 Akhtar, *Blind Eye*; Gordon Corera, *Shopping for Bombs: Nuclear Proliferation, Global Insecurity, and the Rise and Fall of the A.Q. Khan Network* (Oxford: Oxford University Press, 2006).

16 Robert Einhorn and Waheguru Pal Singh Sidhu, "The Strategic Chain: Linking Pakistan, India, China, and the United States," report Brookings Institution, 2017.

17 While the balance of aggregate military power is lopsided in India's favor, the balance of usable power is much closer—see Arzan Tarapore, "Almost Parity: Understanding the India-Pakistan Conventional Military Balance," in *Routledge Handbook on South Asian Foreign Policy*, ed. Aparna Pande (London: Routledge, 2021).

18 S. Paul Kapur, *Dangerous Deterrent: Nuclear Weapons Proliferation and Conflict in South Asia* (Stanford, Calif.: Stanford University Press, 2007). See also Šumit Ganguly and S. Paul Kapur, *India, Pakistan, and the Bomb: Debating Nuclear Security in South Asia* (New York: Columbia University Press, 2010).

19 For background, see Peter R. Lavoy, ed., *Asymmetric Warfare in South Asia: The Causes and Consequences of the Kargil Conflict* (Cambridge: Cambridge University Press, 2009).

20 See Vipin Narang, "Posturing for Peace? Pakistan's Nuclear Postures and South Asian Stability," *International Security* 34, no. 3 (Winter 2009/10): 38–78.

21 Sandeep Unnithan, "Why India Didn't Strike Pakistan After 26/11," *India Today*, October 26, 2015.

22 Narang, "Posturing for Peace."

23 C. Christine Fair, *Fighting to the End: The Pakistan Army's Way of War* (New Delhi: Oxford University Press, 2014).

24 Šumit Ganguly, "Nuclear Stability in South Asia," *International Security* 33, no. 2 (Fall 2008): 45–70.

25 S. Paul Kapur, "Ten Years of Instability in a Nuclear South Asia," *International Security* 33, no. 2 (Fall 2008): 71–94.

26 For background, see V. K. Sood and Pravin Sawhney, *Operation Parakram: The War Unfinished* (New Delhi: Sage, 2003).

27 Walter C. Ladwig III, "A Cold Start for Hot Wars? The Indian Army's New Limited War Doctrine," *International Security* 32, no. 3 (2007–2008): 158–190.

28 Lt. Gen. Khalid Kidwai, quoted in Paolo Cotta-Ramusino and Maurizio Martellini, "Nuclear Safety, Nuclear Stability, and Nuclear Strategy in Pakistan," Landau Network – Centro Volta, January 2002. https://pugwash.org/2002/01/14/report-on-nuclear-safety-nuclear-stability-and-nuclear-strategy-in-pakistan/.

29 Shashank Joshi, "India's Military Instrument: A Doctrine Stillborn," *Journal of Strategic Studies* 36, no. 4 (2013): 512–540.

30 Khalid Kidwai and Peter Lavoy, "A Conversation with Gen. Khalid Kidwai," *Carnegie Endowment for International Peace*, March 23, 2015. https://carnegieendowment.org/files/03-230315carnegie KIDWAI.pdf.

31 Hans M. Kristensen and Matt Korda, "Nuclear Notebook: How Many Nuclear Weapons Does Pakistan Have in 2021?" *Bulletin of the Atomic Scientists*, September 7, 2021. https://thebulletin.org/premium/2021-09/nuclear-notebook-how-many-nuclear-weapons-does-pakistan-have-in-2021/.

32 Arzan Tarapore, "Balakot, Deterrence, and Risk: How this India-Pakistan Crisis will Shape the Next," *War on the Rocks*, March 11, 2019.

33 Christopher Clary and Vipin Narang, "India's Counterforce Temptations: Strategic Dilemmas, Doctrine, and Capabilities," *International Security* 43, no. 3 (Winter 2018–2019): 7–52. For a counterargument, see Rajesh Rajagopalan, "India and Counterforce: A Question of Evidence," Occasional Paper no. 247, Observer Research Foundation, New Delhi, May 2020.

34 Nicholas L. Miller and Vipin Narang, "Is a New Nuclear Age Upon Us?" *Foreign Affairs*, December 30, 2019.

Bibliography

Abbas, Hassan. *Pakistan's Nuclear Bomb: A Story of Defiance, Deterrence, and Deviance*. Oxford: Oxford University Press, 2018.

Akhtar, Rabia. *The Blind Eye: U.S. Non-Proliferation Policy Towards Pakistan from Ford to Clinton*. Lahore: University of Lahore Press, 2018.

Bhutto, Zulfiqar Ali. *The Myth of Independence*. London and Lahore: Oxford University Press, 1969.

Burr, William. "The Carter Administration's 'Damnable Dilemma': How to Respond to Pakistan's Secret Nuclear Weapons Program, 1978–1979." *Journal of Cold War Studies* 23, no. 1 (2021): 4–54.

Clary, Christopher, and Vipin Narang. "India's Counterforce Temptations: Strategic Dilemmas, Doctrine, and Capabilities." *International Security* 43, no. 3 (Winter 2018–2019): 7–52.

Clary, Christopher. "Pakistan: The Nuclear Consensus." In *Nuclear Debates in Asia: The Role of Geopolitics and Domestic Processes*, edited by Mike M. Mochizuki and Deepa M. Ollapally, 221–243. Lanham: Rowman and Littlefield, 2016.

Cotta-Ramusino, Paolo, and Maurizio Martellini. "Nuclear Safety, Nuclear Stability, and Nuclear Strategy in Pakistan." Landau Network – Centro Volta, January 2002. https://pugwash.org/2002/01/14/report-on-nuclear-safety-nuclear-stability-and-nuclear-strategy-in-pakistan/.

Cronin, Richard, Alan Kronstadt, and Sharon Squassoni. *Pakistan's Nuclear Proliferation Activities and the Recommendations of the 9/11 Commission: U.S. Policy Constraints and Options.* Report Congressional Research Service, May 24, 2005.

Einhorn, Robert, and Waheguru Pal Singh Sidhu. "The Strategic Chain: Linking Pakistan, India, China, and the United States." Report, Brookings Institution, 2017.

Fair, C. Christine. *Fighting to the End: The Pakistan Army's Way of War.* New Delhi: Oxford University Press, 2014.

Fuhrmann, Matthew, and Benjamin Tkach. "Almost Nuclear: Introducing the Nuclear Latency Dataset." *Conflict Management and Peace Science* 32, no. 4 (2015): 443–461.

Fuhrmann, Matthew. "The Logic of Latent Nuclear Deterrence." Working Paper, September 8, 2017. SSRN: https://ssrn.com/abstract=3052231.

Ganguly, Šumit, and S. Paul Kapur. *India, Pakistan, and the Bomb: Debating Nuclear Security in South Asia.* New York: Columbia University Press, 2010.

Ganguly, Šumit. "Nuclear Stability in South Asia." *International Security* 33, no. 2 (Fall 2008): 45–70.

Joshi, Shashank. "India's Military Instrument: A Doctrine Stillborn." *Journal of Strategic Studies* 36, no. 4 (2013): 512–540.

Kapur, S. Paul. "Ten Years of Instability in a Nuclear South Asia." *International Security* 33, no. 2 (Fall 2008): 71–94.

Kapur, S. Paul. *Dangerous Deterrent: Nuclear Weapons Proliferation and Conflict in South Asia.* Stanford: Stanford University Press, 2007.

Khan, Feroz. *Eating Grass: The Making of the Pakistani Bomb.* Stanford, CA: Stanford University Press, 2012.

Kidwai, Khalid, and Peter Lavoy. "A Conversation with Gen. Khalid Kidwai." *Carnegie Endowment for International Peace*, March 23, 2015. https://carnegieendowment.org/files/03-230315carnegie KIDWAI.pdf.

Krepon, Micahel, and Liv Dowling. "Crisis Intensity and Nuclear Signaling in South Asia." In *Investigating Crises: South Asia's Lessons, Evolving Dynamics, and Trajectories*, edited by Sameer Lalwani, and Hannah Haegeland, 187–218. Washington, D.C: Stimson Center, 2018.

Kristensen, Hans M., and Matt Korda. "Nuclear Notebook: How Many Nuclear Weapons Does Pakistan Have in 2021?" *Bulletin of the Atomic Scientists*, September 7, 2021. https://thebulletin.org/premium/2021-09/nuclear-notebook-how-many-nuclear-weapons-does-pakistan-have-in-2021/.

Ladwig, Walter C. III. "A Cold Start for Hot Wars? The Indian Army's New Limited War Doctrine." *International Security* 32, no. 3 (2007–2008): 158–190.

Lavoy, Peter R., ed. *Asymmetric Warfare in South Asia: The Causes and Consequences of the Kargil Conflict.* Cambridge: Cambridge University Press, 2009.

Miller, Nicholas L., and Vipin Narang. "Is a New Nuclear Age Upon Us?" *Foreign Affairs*, December 30, 2019.

Narang, Vipin. "Posturing for Peace? Pakistan's Nuclear Postures and South Asian Stability." *International Security* 34, no. 3 (Winter 2009/10): 38–78.

Narang, Vipin. "Strategies of Nuclear Proliferation: How States Pursue the Bomb." *International Security* 41, no. 3 (Winter 2016/17): 110–150.

Narang, Vipin. *Nuclear Strategy in the Modern Era: Regional Powers and International Conflict.* Princeton: Princeton University Press, 2014.

Rajagopalan, Rajesh. "India and Counterforce: A Question of Evidence." Occasional Paper no. 247, Observer Research Foundation, New Delhi, May 2020.

Rose, Gideon. "Neoclassical Realism and Theories of Foreign Policy." *World Politics* 51, no. 1 (October 1998): 144–172.

Sagan, Scott. "Why Do States Build Nuclear Weapons? Three Models in Search of a Bomb." *International Security* 21, no. 3 (Winter 1996/1997): 54–86.

Sood, V. K., and Pravin Sawhney. *Operation Parakram: The War Unfinished.* New Delhi: Sage, 2003.

Tarapore, Arzan. "Balakot, Deterrence, and Risk: How This India-Pakistan Crisis Will Shape the Next." *War on the Rocks*, March 11, 2019.

11

TERRORISM AND COUNTER-TERRORISM IN SOUTH ASIA

Government Support for Militant Groups in South Asia

Tricia Bacon

Introduction

South Asia, primarily Afghanistan and Pakistan, is home to over 25 US-designated terrorist organizations, the largest concentration in the world (see Table 11.1).[1] It is not simply the total number of resident groups that is noteworthy. This tally includes branches of the two groups that seek to lead the Sunni jihadist movement, al-Qaida and the Islamic State.[2] Moreover, senior al-Qaida leaders have operated in the region for decades. The effects of this concentration are clear. South Asia is one of the regions most afflicted by terrorism.[3] There are a myriad of reasons why South Asia has proven so ripe for militant groups, both indigenous and foreign. But one important reason is the presence of governments that support them: Pakistan and Afghanistan under Taliban rule.[4]

Principal-agent theory provides a rational choice framework to analyzing these relationships. Approaches to militant group clients and reasons for these relationships differ, with Pakistan having a clear policy agenda driving its actions while the persistence of the Taliban's commitment to militant partners is less straightforward. Consequently, the theory has more explanatory power for the Pakistani government's behavior than the Afghan Taliban's. Both the de facto Taliban regime and the Pakistani government experience the pitfalls predicted by principal-agent theory. Nonetheless, neither is inclined to sever ties with their militant group clients.

This chapter proceeds in five sections. First, it discusses the implications for the Afghan Taliban and Pakistani government's support for militant groups. Second, it provides an empirical history of the Pakistani government and Afghan Taliban regime's support for militant groups. Third, it describes principal-agent theory as a framework to examine state sponsorship. Fourth, it applies principal-agent theory to both governments. Finally, it concludes by looking forward into the future.

DOI: 10.4324/9781003246626-14

Terrorism and Counter-Terrorism in South Asia

Table 11.1 US-designated Organizations

US-designated Organizations*	
Group Name	Designation**
Haqqani Network	Foreign Terrorist Organization
Harakat ul-Jihad Islami	Foreign Terrorist Organization
Harakat ul-Mujahidin	Foreign Terrorist Organization
Hizbul Mujahidin	Foreign Terrorist Organization
Indian Mujahedeen	Foreign Terrorist Organization
Islamic Jihad Union	Foreign Terrorist Organization
Islamic Movement of Uzbekistan	Foreign Terrorist Organization
Islamic State in Bangladesh	Foreign Terrorist Organization
Islamic State in Khorasan	Foreign Terrorist Organization
Jaish-e-Mohamed	Foreign Terrorist Organization
Jundallah	Foreign Terrorist Organization
Lashkar-e-Tayyiba	Foreign Terrorist Organization
Lashkar-e-Jhangvi	Foreign Terrorist Organization
Liberation Tigers of Tamil Eelam	Foreign Terrorist Organization
Al-Qaida	Foreign Terrorist Organization
Al-Qaida in the Indian Subcontinent	Foreign Terrorist Organization
Tehrik-e-Taliban Pakistan	Foreign Terrorist Organization
Balochistan Liberation Army	Executive Order 13224
Eastern Turkistan Islamic Movement	Executive Order 13224
Jamaat-ul-Ahrar	Executive Order 13224
Jama'at ul Dawa al-Qu'ran	Executive Order 13224
Tariq Gidar Group	Executive Order 13224
Commander Nazir Group	Executive Order 13224
Babbar Khalsa International	Executive Order 13224
International Sikh Youth Foundation	Executive Order 13224

*This list does not include the Terrorist Exclusion List

**Most groups designated as FTOs are also designated under Executive Order 13224

Regional and International Implications

Government support for militant groups has had major consequences for South Asia. State sponsorship of militant groups has aggravated conflicts and heightened the terrorist threat in the region for decades. It has stoked inter-state conflict, particularly because of Pakistani support for groups that contest India's control over Kashmir.[5] These relationships have even caused substantial harm to the sponsoring governments. Pakistan experienced such backlash after it acquiesced to US pressure to support the war in Afghanistan, to the violent dismay of groups it had long nurtured.[6] Similarly, members of groups once allied with the Taliban joined the Islamic State in the Khorasan, which became the Taliban's violent challenger.[7] In addition, the Taliban's refusal to break ties with militant groups has caused states to impose sanctions that have crippled its ability to govern and exacerbated the humanitarian crisis in Afghanistan.[8]

The effects reach beyond the region. Sponsored groups have struck elsewhere. Most notably, al-Qaida used its haven under the Taliban to plan the 9/11 attacks. The US invasion of Afghanistan in 2001 was a response to the Taliban's insistence on protecting al-Qaida after 9/11. Post-2001, many of the most serious international plots had roots in Pakistan.[9] In addition, attacks in India by Pakistan-sponsored groups have brought the two countries to the brink of war, raising the prospect of miscalculation or escalation that could lead to nuclear war.[10]

143

Overview of Two State Sponsors

South Asia is home to two governments that aid an array of militant groups (see Table 11.2) and have so since their formation. The Pakistani government and Afghan Taliban regime even support several of the same organizations, and the Afghan Taliban was one of Pakistan's clients during its time as an insurgent group.

Pakistan

The Pakistani government, primarily the Pakistani Army and its Inter-Service Intelligence (ISI), has sponsored militant groups as an instrument of national security since the Partition.[11] Its support for militant groups has been driven by, though not limited to, its sense of insecurity vis-à-vis India and a desire to challenge India's control of Kashmir.[12] Its sponsorship grew in scale and sophistication in the 1980s, during the anti-Soviet war in Afghanistan, with Saudi and American largesse at its disposal. In addition to its support for Afghan *mujahideen*, General Muhammad Zia-ul-Haq's government nurtured Pakistani groups. After the *mujahideen* ousted the Soviet forces, these Pakistani groups turned their sights to Kashmir and stoked the insurgency there throughout the 1990s. In 2000, they expanded their attacks beyond Kashmir.[13] The Pakistani security establishment's support for anti-India militant groups was substantial, hands-on, and systematic, such as instruction in training facilities.

Table 11.2 Status of Sponsorship of Militant Groups

Status of Sponsorship of Militant Groups	
Group Name	*State Sponsor*
Haqqani Network	Part of Afghan Taliban Regime
Harakat ul-Jihad Islami	Pakistan & Afghan Taliban Sponsored
Harakat ul-Mujahidin	Pakistan & Afghan Taliban Sponsored
Hizbul Mujahidin	Pakistan Sponsored
Indian Mujahedeen	Pakistan Sponsored
Islamic Jihad Union	Afghan Taliban Sponsored
Islamic Movement of Uzbekistan	Afghan Taliban Sponsored
Islamic State in Bangladesh	None
Islamic State in Khorasan	None
Jaish-e-Mohamed	Pakistan & Afghan Taliban Sponsored
Jundallah	None
Lashkar-e-Tayyiba	Pakistan & Afghan Taliban Sponsored
Lashkar-e-Jhangvi	Afghan Taliban Sponsored
Liberation Tigers of Tamil Eelam	None
Al-Qaida	Afghan Taliban Sponsored
Al-Qaida in the Indian Subcontinent	Afghan Taliban Sponsored
Tehrik-e-Taliban Pakistan	Afghan Taliban Sponsored
Balochistan Liberation Army	None
Eastern Turkistan Islamic Movement	Afghan Taliban Sponsored
Jamaat-ul-Ahrar	Afghan Taliban Sponsored
Jama'at ul Dawa al-Qu'ran	Afghan Taliban Sponsored
Tariq Gidar Group	Afghan Taliban Sponsored
Commander Nazir Group	Afghan Taliban Sponsored (sometimes Pakistan Sponsored)
Babbar Khalsa International	Pakistan Sponsored
International Sikh Youth Foundation	Pakistan Sponsored

Meanwhile, a civil war had engulfed Afghanistan after the government collapsed in 1992. When the Taliban mobilized in response to the lack of security and order, Pakistan found a new client in its quest to install a friendly government and avoid a hostile encirclement. It helped the Taliban to come to power in 1996. As in Kashmir, the Pakistan's support for the Taliban was institutionalized and expansive.[14]

However, the fallout from 9/11 put immense pressure on Pakistan's sponsorship policies. Pervez Musharraf's government acceded to the US invasion of Afghanistan.[15] Immediately following the Taliban's collapse, Pakistan's support for its client was circumscribed, in part because the group appeared to be defeated. However, when a government emerged in Afghanistan that the Pakistan saw as antithetical to its interests, it re-commenced support, particularly for the Haqqani Network, but sought to hide its actions and make them more deniable.[16]

It faced a backlash for capitulating to the US war in Afghanistan and counter-terrorism actions at home, including among groups it supported against India. Secretary of State Hillary Clinton famously said that "It's like that old story—you can't keep snakes in your backyard and expect them only to bite your neighbors. Eventually those snakes are going to turn on whoever has them in the backyard."[17] Compounding Pakistan's woes, one of those groups, Jaish-e-Mohamed, attacked the Indian Parliament in December 2001, bringing the two nuclear-armed countries to the brink of war. Musharraf came under massive international pressure to cease support for anti-India militant groups.[18] Instead, in a pattern that repeated itself, its assistance grew more covert, and it undertook symbolic actions to assuage international demands.[19] Even these limited measures, coupled with military operations in the Federally Administered Tribal Areas, further infuriated once-friendly militants and produced a new anti-government organization, the Pakistani Taliban. By 2007, Pakistan faced a full-fledged insurgency at home.[20]

But one client, Lashkar-e-Tayyiba, remained loyal, and the Pakistani government used it to counter hostile groups at home and continue to clandestinely support attacks against India.[21] However, ISI's support for the group's attack in Mumbai in 2008 was publicly revealed when one of the attackers survived and a plotter was arrested in the United States, destroying any deniability. India showed restraint, opting not to respond militarily. International pressure on the Pakistani government once again mounted, to no avail. The Pakistani government simply undertook another faux crackdown.[22]

By 2015, the Pakistani military had brought the internal insurgency to a manageable level.[23] Ultimately, the deterioration of internal security did not cause it to reevaluate proxy relationships. Instead, the Pakistani government became *more* resistant to relinquishing proxies, lest those groups create internal insecurity if they were not tethered to the state. It repaired its relationship with Jaish-e-Mohamed and reinforced its ties with Lashkar-e-Tayyiba. Both groups grew more circumspect about attacks outside of Kashmir. While plots have been disrupted, there has not been a large-scale terrorist attack by either group in India outside of Kashmir since 2008.

However, India's tolerance for attacks within Kashmir diminished under Prime Minister Narendra Modi.[24] Thus, when Jaish-e-Mohamed operatives attacked an Indian Army facility in Uri in 2016,[25] India reacted by claiming that it conducted "surgical strikes" against militant camps in Pakistan-Administered Kashmir.[26] Then in 2019, a Jaish-e-Mohamed suicide bomber struck a paramilitary convoy near Pulwama. This time, India conducted a cross-border strike on a purported terrorist facility near Balakot, in Pakistan's Khyber Pakhtunkhwa province, striking beyond Pakistan-Administered Kashmir for the first time since the war in 1971. Pakistan launched retaliatory strikes that resulted in an air battle that ended in the downing of an Indian aircraft and Pakistan's capture of the pilot. Pakistan released the pilot, and tensions de-escalated. But India's willingness to retaliate militarily was clear.[27] That year, India revoked Article 370, stripping Kashmir of its degree of autonomy. The move, among its many effects, injected a greater sense of urgency among Pakistan's clients dedicated to uniting Kashmir with Pakistan.[28]

Meanwhile, as the United States' commitment to Afghanistan waned, the Taliban and the subsidiary Haqqani Network, both Pakistani clients, made gains. After a US agreement with the Taliban to withdraw its forces from Afghanistan in exchange for assurances that terrorists finding haven there would not conduct external attacks, the fate of the war was sealed.[29] The Taliban seized power in 2021, in a victory not only for the group but for Pakistan's sponsorship policies.[30]

Afghanistan under the Taliban Regime

The Afghan Taliban is now the de facto government of Afghanistan, though it has not been recognized by the international community. It initially swept through Afghanistan between 1994 to 1996 on a campaign of providing order and security, an antidote to devastating civil war. In 1996, it gained control of most of Afghanistan, with a pocket of resistance in the north under a coalition of ethnic minorities known as the Northern Alliance, and imposed a rigid code of Islamic law.[31]

During the 1990s, a host of foreign militant groups found haven in Afghanistan. The Taliban inherited some of these "guests," most notably al-Qaida, when it came to power, but more arrived under the Taliban regime. Afghanistan became the epicenter of Sunni jihadism.[32] Dozens of Sunni militant groups received sanctuary, trained, raised funds, and regrouped from losses.[33] In return, these organizations, most notably al-Qaida, provided the Taliban with badly needed finances amid an economic crisis in Afghanistan. They also offered the Taliban an alternative form of legitimacy at a time when it was shunned by the international community. In addition, some participated in the Taliban's war with the Northern Alliance.

While the Taliban did not use any of these groups for external conflicts, the resident organizations used their sanctuary in Afghanistan for their external agendas. Most notably, al-Qaida used its haven in Afghanistan to plan attacks in East Africa in 1998, in Yemen in 2000, and then in the United States in 2001.[34] The Taliban discouraged al-Qaida and others from conducting external operations because they resulted in further international pressure on the Taliban, but it proved unable or unwilling to marshal the requisite disincentives. That failure proved fatal for the regime after 9/11 when the Taliban refused to relinquish al-Qaida.[35]

The US and Northern Alliance quickly overthrew the Taliban regime, and for several years there was limited violence in Afghanistan. But the Taliban reemerged as an insurgent force in 2006 on the back of an increasing aggrieved population and renewed support from the Pakistani government.[36] As the Taliban regenerated into a viable insurgent force, government support from Pakistan and then Iran outstripped what foreign militants could provide, but they persisted as a force multiplier in the insurgency. Foreign militants played only a support role in the conflict, but they maintained alliances with the Taliban, particularly the Haqqani Network faction.[37]

In 2015, the Islamic State in Khorasan emerged as a rival to the Taliban, attracting members of Taliban allies, like the Pakistani Taliban and Islamic Movement of Uzbekistan, as well as disaffected Afghan Taliban. Since the Taliban took power in 2021, the Islamic State in Khorasan has become the main opposition to the Taliban. Should the Taliban turn on foreign militant groups or alienate hardliners, the Islamic State of Khorasan offers an alternative, a threat Taliban leaders recognize.

As discussed, in 2020, the United States struck a deal with the Taliban to withdraw its military forces in exchange for assurances that the Taliban would not allow its territory to be used for terrorism outside of Afghanistan.[38] The Taliban undertook steps to bring foreign militants under closer monitoring. But it did not oust them. Soon after taking power, the Taliban faced a humanitarian and economic crisis that outstripped its capability, hindering its ability to supervise the groups for which it provides haven.

Principal-Agent Theory

Principal-agent theory comes out of rational choice approaches, originally developed to examine economic problems. It was adapted to illuminate political dilemmas,[39] and in the past decade, principal-agent theory has also been applied to states' relationships with militant groups.[40] At its core is the idea of delegation; a principal offers "conditional authority" to an agent to act on its behalf.[41] The principal provides resources or assistance, and the agent implements the policy set by the principal. In the context of states sponsoring militant groups, the government is generally the principal, and the militant group is the client.[42]

A core contention of principal-agent theory is that principals are interested in reducing transaction costs and thereby turn to delegation to yield economic utility. There can also be legitimization benefits for a principal. Moreover, principals can signal the credibility of their commitments, gain specialized expertise, and ensure continued commitment to the policy.

Thus, government support for militant groups is a form of policy delegation, wherein the principal has a goal and uses a militant agent to achieve it.[43] Militant groups may have greater asymmetric capabilities or an ability to act in a geographic location.[44] As Byman and Kreps point out, "Delegating can be a signal of credible commitment since an agent might have fewer incentives to change or renege on policies than the principal …. Whereas a state such as Iran cannot credibly suggest that it will retaliate militarily for every perceived Israeli transgression, it can use its agents' actions to signal commitment to engage in tit-for-tat retaliation."[45] By delegating to a militant group, governments can act without the cost of a military confrontation with a potentially more powerful state and with some veneer of plausible deniability.[46] Sponsoring a client can also be a way for a regime to bolster legitimacy at home.[47] Importantly, some governments seek to export an ideological movement and have a genuine ideological commitment.[48] The main incentive for a militant client is the resources a principal provides, which is particularly important because it is usually at a disadvantage vis-à-vis its adversaries.[49]

But the arrangement comes with pitfalls. Sometimes plausible deniability fails, and targeted governments retaliate directly against the principal. Moreover, actions by clients like international terrorist attacks can draw broader censure.[50] In delegating to an agent, principals give up some control over how their objectives are pursued, though the amount of control relinquished varies. In particular, principals' ability to manage their agents can diminish if the agents have other principals. In addition, adverse selection can occur if principals "do not have adequate information about the competence or reliability of agents" when selecting a client.[51] Principals also experience agency costs because preferences can diverge between the principal and the agent.[52] Governments may find the resources they supply are being used for other activities and struggle to monitor their clients. As Salehyan, Gleditsch, and Cunningham explained, "rebels can devote suboptimal effort to the conflict with the resources provided; engage in unwelcome or egregious behavior such as war crimes; they may divert resources toward other, undesired, objectives; or in some cases, the agent may use the resources supplied against the patron itself."[53]

For the clients, the arrangement results in a loss of autonomy, though like the principals, the degree of that loss varies. As Salehyan, Siroky, and Wood argued, "sponsors expect returns on their 'investment,' and they often attempt to influence the actions of their clients."[54] In so doing, state sponsorship can substitute for constituent support or result in unpopular violence, creating dependence on the principal and further reducing the group's autonomy.[55] Clients can also lose support from principals when a more desirable agent emerges or when the principal's calculus changes.[56] Finally, agents can face punishment from the principal when they undertake actions that diverge from principals' preference or are perceived as slacking.[57]

Principal-Agent Theory and State Sponsorship in South Asia

How well does the principal-agent theory explain Pakistan and the Afghan Taliban's behavior? Have they maximized the benefits? How much have they been able to avoid the pitfalls?

Pakistan has delegated to multiple militant groups to pursue its policies in Afghanistan, India, and even at home. Its policy goals in these relationships have been to secure a friendly government to the west, challenge India's control of Kashmir to the east, and counter hostile groups at home. Indeed, that has largely but not entirely been the outcome of these principal-agent relationships. Its agent is now in power in Afghanistan and the threat at home has diminished from its peak.[58] Though Pakistan is no closer to gaining control of Kashmir, its use of militant groups has helped to keep the issue alive.

Consistent with principal-agent theory, Pakistan's investment in agent relationships has indeed cost less than direct wars in India or Afghanistan, wars it would not be well positioned to win. Agent groups have been able to operate where the Pakistani military is constrained. Rather than its agents providing asymmetric capability the government does not have, for many years Pakistan actively imparted such capability through its role in training. As principal-agency theory predicts, it has used its support for militant groups as a form of costly signaling, demonstrating its commitment to Kashmir, and to avoiding hostile encirclement in Afghanistan. At times, support for militant groups has offered some legitimacy to the government at home, particularly by signaling a commitment to Kashmir.

Pakistan has also incurred the costs of principal-agent relationships. Admittedly, it is not often clear when an agent for Pakistan has taken unauthorized risks. The Pakistani security establishment tries to portray itself as experiencing the pitfalls of principal-agent relationships when it is actually supporting actions, like the 2008 Mumbai attacks. For many years, Pakistan largely avoided direct retaliation by targeted states. While it had been on the precipice of war with India because of the actions of its agents, like the 2001 Parliament attack, it is only in recent years that India has more directly targeted Pakistan in response to the actions of its militant clients.

Pakistan has given up some control for how its objectives are pursued in exchange for principal-agent relationships. However, the Pakistani security establishment has been adept at managing clients, including using coercion or punishment when a client is insufficiently responsive. But the Taliban also attracted other sponsors, such as Iran, making it less responsive to Pakistan.[59] The main asset Pakistan still provides for its agents is safe haven. None of its clients depend on the Pakistani government for resources or training anymore. Thus, making that safe haven more or less comfortable is the main leverage to exert control over them. Pakistan has had less trouble than other principals in monitoring its clients because a significant subset of them reside or operate in Pakistan. By providing safe haven, the Pakistani security establishment enhances its ability to monitor many of its clients. While some of Pakistan's agents may shirk at times, because it has multiple clients, it can focus assistance on the ones that are more active at any given time.

Pakistan has suffered from some adverse selection, meaning its selected clients without adequate knowledge about their reliability. For example, the Pakistani government supported the rise of the Afghan Taliban between 1994 and 1996, only to find that it was not as pliable as Pakistan wished once in power. But those frustrations were not enough to cause Pakistan to sever the relationship, which persists today.

Finally, Pakistan has experienced perhaps the most significant pitfall of principal-agent relationships: Blowback. Some of its clients turned against the state in the aftermath of Pakistan's acquiescence to the US war in Afghanistan. But while some argued that Pakistan would have to relinquish its militant proxies in order to substantially reduce the terrorist threat within, the Pakistani government managed to do so while repairing ties with the most affected clients, particularly Jaish-e-Mohamed, the group that has been responsible for a number of major attacks in Kashmir in recent years.

For their part, Pakistan's clients have experienced the predicted loss of autonomy as a result of their relationship with the Pakistani security establishment. Perhaps most notably, their freedom to engage in operations in Kashmir or in India outside of Kashmir has fluctuated based on the calculations of the Pakistani government. However, most, though not all, have avoided the pitfall of allowing sponsorship to substitute for constituent support. Over time, its major agent groups have become largely self-sufficient, depending on the Pakistani security establishment primarily for sanctuary. But they have been subjected to varying levels of support from Pakistan, as its most favored client changes over time and some agent groups have been abandoned and become defunct, like Harakat ul-Mujahideen. The degree to which they have been punished by Pakistan for undertaking actions that diverge from the principal's preference is hard to assess because the Pakistani government undertakes faux crackdowns in response to international pressure. But it has also arrested members of its client groups to express dissatisfaction.

The ability of principal-agent theory to explain the Afghan Taliban regime's behavior is more limited. The Afghan Taliban is not delegating any policy to the foreign militant groups finding haven in Afghanistan. With aims limited to Afghanistan, the Taliban does not have a motive to support such groups as an alternative to direct war. It has employed foreign militants in its internal conflicts, but they supplemented the Afghan Taliban's fighting power, rather than behaving as a substitute. The sponsored militant groups in Afghanistan are not generally providing significant asymmetric capability that the Taliban regime does not have, given the number of years the Taliban functioned as an insurgent force, though select ones can provide specialized expertise. Sponsored organizations are also not capable of operating in places the Taliban wants to operate but cannot, given that the Taliban is the indigenous entity, and its aims are limited to Afghanistan. Furthermore, they do not offer the Taliban plausible deniability for actions because they are pursuing their own agendas. The Taliban does receive some legitimacy through its sponsorship, specifically legitimacy within the Sunni jihadist movement and hardliners within the Taliban. The Taliban's sponsorship has often been attributed to ideological commitment,[60] but there is debate about how wide and deep that ideological commitment is.[61]

The Taliban has incurred significant costs because of these relationships. When agent groups have taken risks, the Taliban has borne the brunt of the fallout. That risk continues to loom large now that the Taliban is back in power and maintaining its relationships with the foreign militant groups. Not only has it been the target of direct retaliation, but it has been isolated from the international community because of its relationships with militant groups. It also experiences preference divergence with agent organizations because most, if not all, the foreign militant groups receiving haven have external ambitions that the Taliban does not share and have a history of defying orders not to conduct attacks outside of Afghanistan. The Taliban is providing a fundamental resource, safe haven, that groups can use for goals other than the Taliban's, but its ability and commitment to monitoring them is limited, especially given the enormity of the governance challenges. The Taliban also faces a reality that should it seek to oust the foreign militant groups or restrain them too harshly, they could turn their guns on the Afghan regime.

The Taliban has experienced adverse selection. It inherited relationships with al-Qaida and some of the other foreign militant groups, meaning they were already present when the Taliban took power. The Taliban credited them for their participation in the anti-Soviet war but did not have adequate information about these agents when the relationship formed, such as al-Qaida's determination to pursue global jihad. However, it has that information now and maintains the relationship.

For the agency organizations, living under the Taliban regime in the 1990s and now has resulted in only limited losses of autonomy. In the current environment, that loss of autonomy comes in the form of the Taliban's commitment in its agreement with the United States not to allow groups receiving sanctuary to conduct external attacks. But at present, the larger hurdle for most of those groups is their capability. When they develop the requisite capability, it is unclear whether the Taliban's pledge will deter them from engaging in external attacks. It is more likely that they will seek to hide any operations connection to Afghanistan than abstain from pursing their causes. They certainly fear the Taliban abandoning them, as most have few viable alternatives of places to find sanctuary. Moreover, they face the hazard of living in exile, which can make it difficult to garner support from their constituencies.

Though the central asset both governments currently provide their agents is safe haven, overall, principal-agent theory sheds more light on Pakistan and its agents' behavior. It does not offer as persuasive an explanation of the Taliban's behavior, which does not have a clear policy rationale. The Afghan regime has received little benefit and borne enormous costs. This difference may reflect that Pakistan has been more of an active sponsor, providing more resources, training, and material, and it has a more expansive policy agenda for its clients. The Taliban is more than a passive sponsor, meaning a government that turns a blind eye to militant groups, as it deliberately cooperates with the resident groups. But it has not actively provided assistance the way Pakistan has, nor does it have a policy that it seeks to delegate to militant groups. Thus, while principal-agent theory has utility in understanding state sponsorship of militant groups, it can also fall short in illuminating why some regimes choose to do so.

Future Outlook: Limited Opportunities, Ample Danger

Both the Pakistani and Afghan Taliban governments have incurred tremendous costs as a result of their sponsorship of militant groups. The Afghan Taliban was overthrown in 2001. Its unwillingness to break ties with militant partners, specifically al-Qaida, then prolonged the subsequent war, which claimed an estimated 176,000 lives.[62] Now that it is back in power, these relationships have resulted in continued sanctions and limits on badly needed economic and humanitarian assistance. In Pakistan, militant clients have brought the country to the brink of war with India on multiple occasion. Moreover, over 66,000 people have been killed during the conflict within Pakistan since 2001.[63] Pakistan has also come under tremendous international pressure because of these relationships, such as a "grey list" designation by the Financial Action Task Force in 2018 because of "strategic deficiencies" in countering "money laundering, terrorist financing, and proliferation funding."[64] A grey list designation "serves as a signal to the global financial and banking system about heightened risks in transactions with the country in question."[65] It has resulted an estimated $38 billion in losses to Pakistan's GDP.[66] However, neither the Pakistani government nor the Afghan Taliban sees these costs as a result of their sponsorship policies, instead portraying themselves as victims of unjust actions by international actors.

Thus, neither government is likely to abandon their militant agents. The type of support or amount a given client gets may change, but the fundamental underlying policies will not. Pakistan's sense of insecurity and dissatisfaction with the status quo virtually guarantees the continued cultivation of militant clients. Despite the problems with the Afghan Taliban as a client, its proxy victory in Afghanistan reinforces this long-standing policy. The Afghan Taliban is a much less active sponsor than Pakistan, but it has resisted enormous pressures to relinquish these relationships. Moreover, the enormity of the governance challenges facing the regime means that the Taliban will have little capacity or interest in monitoring resident groups. Its preoccupation with preserving internal unity also deters major change on its policy toward foreign militant groups. The challenge from the Islamic State in Khorasan reinforces its continued sponsorship because ceasing support risks these groups cooperating with the Islamic State or members defecting to it.

Thus, the specter of terrorist attacks emanating from Pakistan or Afghanistan and the ensuing fallout looms large. The Pakistani government has become more cautious about supporting attacks in India, but with the Taliban victory in Afghanistan, it has lost an outlet it used to manage the level of militant group activity in Kashmir. It will be under increasing pressure from its militant agents to support activities in Kashmir. At the same time, India has grown more emboldened to respond to provocations even in Kashmir, creating the potential for conflict between the two states as the result of militant group actions. For the Taliban, its provision of haven without sufficient monitoring capabilities provides breathing room for those groups to rebuild and pursue their external agendas. Safe haven is a hugely important commodity for terrorist groups' longevity and ability to recover. Safe haven does not translate directly into external capability, but it allows groups to grow stronger in ways that help enable more effective attacks.[67]

While inter-state war has become rarer since World War II, state support for militants is a common, albeit uneven, feature in international relations. Over a dozen governments have forged six or more such relationships.[68] On average, conflicts with state sponsors typically last longer, cause more fatalities, and are more difficult to end through negotiations.[69] Governments that sponsor militant groups accrue benefits and experience an array of risks. The Afghan Taliban and Pakistan are no exception, though principal-agent theory and its rationalist framework vary in how well it can explain their behavior. Having a state sponsor is not necessarily entirely positive for militant groups either, but it provides an array of advantages, which agent groups in Afghanistan and Pakistan have demonstrated.

Notes

1 Brian Dodwell and Don Rassler, "A View from the CT Foxhole: General John W. Nicholson, Commander, Resolute Support and U.S. Forces-Afghanistan," *Combating Terrorism Center at West Point* 10, no. 2 (February 22, 2017), https://ctc.usma.edu/a-view-from-the-ct-foxhole-general-john-w-nicholson-commander-resolute-support-and-u-s-forces-afghanistan/. There are terrorist

actors in South Asia which are not those officially recognized by the US. For reasons of space, the actors and states discussed are the most impactful for the region, and the chapter will predominantly focus on them.

2 "Al-Qaeda in the Indian Subcontinent (AQIS): The Nucleus of Jihad in South Asia," The Soufan Center, January 23, 2019, https://thesoufancenter.org/research/al-qaeda-in-the-indian-subcontinent-aqis-the-nucleus-of-jihad-in-south-asia/; Amira Jadoon, "Allied and Lethal: Islamic State Khorasan's Network and Organizational Capacity in Afghanistan and Pakistan," December 3, 2018, https://www.ctc.usma.edu/allied-lethal-islamic-state-khorasans-network-organizational-capacity-afghanistan-pakistan/.

3 "Global Terrorism Index 2020: Measuring the Impact of Terrorism," Sydney: Institute for Economics & Peace, November 2020, http://visionofhumanity.org/reports.

4 Both governments primarily support Sunni jihadist groups, though Pakistan has also assisted Sikh militant organizations. Iran also supports an array of militant groups, but its activities are beyond the scope of this chapter.

5 Owen L. Sirrs, *Pakistan's Inter-Services Intelligence Directorate: Covert Action and Internal Operations* (London: Routledge, 2016), https://doi.org/10.4324/9781315559711.

6 S. Paul Kapur and Šumit Ganguly, "The Jihad Paradox: Pakistan and Islamist Militancy in South Asia," *International Security* 37, no. 1 (July 1, 2012): 111–41, https://doi.org/10.1162/ISEC_a_00090.

7 Amira Jadoon, Nakissa Jahabani, and Charmaine Willis, "Challenging the ISK Brand in Afghanistan-Pakistan: Rivalries and Divided Loyalties," *Combating Terrorism Center at West Point Sentinel* 11, no. 4 (April 26, 2018): 23–29.

8 Erica Moret, "The Role of Sanctions in Afghanistan's Humanitarian Crisis," *IPI Global Observatory* (blog), October 14, 2021, https://theglobalobservatory.org/2021/10/the-role-of-sanctions-in-afghanistans-humanitarian-crisis/.

9 Šumit Ganguly and S. Paul Kapur, "The Sorcerer's Apprentice: Islamist Militancy in South Asia," *The Washington Quarterly* 33, no. 1 (January 1, 2010): 47–59, https://doi.org/10.1080/01636600903418686.

10 Robert Wirsing, *Kashmir in the Shadow of War: Regional Rivalries in a Nuclear Age* (Armonk, N.Y: MESharpe, 2003); S. Paul Kapur, "India and Pakistan's Unstable Peace: Why Nuclear South Asia Is Not like Cold War Europe," *International Security* 30, no. 2 (2005): 127–152; Steve Coll, "The Stand-Off," *The New Yorker*, February 6, 2006, https://www.newyorker.com/magazine/2006/02/13/the-stand-off.

11 C. Christine Fair, "The Militant Challenge in Pakistan," *Asia Policy* 11, no. 1 (February 2, 2011): 105–137, https://doi.org/10.1353/asp.2011.0010.

12 See C. Christine Fair and Šumit Ganguly, "Five Dangerous Myths about Pakistan," *The Washington Quarterly* 38, no. 4 (October 2, 2015): 73–97, https://doi.org/10.1080/0163660X.2015.1125830 for a challenge to the idea that India is actually an existential threat to Pakistan.

13 Aparna Rao, Michael Bollig, and Monika Böck, *The Practice of War: Production, Reproduction and Communication of Armed Violence* (Berghahn Books, 2008), 138.

14 Ahmed Rashid, *Taliban: Militant Islam, Oil and Fundamentalism in Central Asia*, 2nd ed. (New Haven, CT: Yale University Press, 2010).

15 Pervez Musharraf, *In the Line of Fire: A Memoir* (New York: Free Press, 2006).

16 Steve Coll, *Ghost Wars: The Secret History of the CIA, Afghanistan, and Bin Laden, from the Soviet Invasion to September 10, 2001* (New York: Penguin Press, 2004).

17 "Snakes in Your Backyard Won't Bite Only Neighbours: Hillary to Pak," NDTV, October 21, 2011, https://www.ndtv.com/world-news/snakes-in-your-backyard-wont-bite-only-neighbours-hillary-to-pak-573412.

18 Sharon LaFraniere, Rajiv Ch, and Rasekaran, "Musharraf Pledges to Rein in Militants," *Washington Post*, May 28, 2002, https://www.washingtonpost.com/archive/politics/2002/05/28/musharraf-pledges-to-rein-in-militants/b5656ec2-e0c1-4c10-95f6-348839c95921/.

19 Ashley J. Tellis, "Pakistan and the War on Terror: Conflicted Goals, Compromised Performance" (Carnegie Endowment for International Peace, January 18, 2008), https://carnegieendowment.org/2008/01/18/pakistan-and-war-on-terror-conflicted-goals-compromised-performance-pub-19848.

20 Marvin G. Weinbaum, "Insurgency and Violent Extremism in Pakistan," *Small Wars & Insurgencies* 28, no. 1 (January 2, 2017): 34–56, https://doi.org/10.1080/09592318.2016.1266130.

21 C. Christine Fair, "Lashkar-e-Tayiba and the Pakistani State," *Survival* 53, no. 4 (September 1, 2011): 29–52, https://doi.org/10.1080/00396338.2011.603561.

22 Stephen Tankel, *Storming the World Stage: The Story of Lashkar-e-Taiba* (New York: Columbia University Press, 2011); Tricia Bacon, "The Evolution of Pakistan's Lashkar-e-Tayyiba Terrorist Group," *Orbis* 63, no. 1 (2019): 27–43, https://doi.org/10.1016/j.orbis.2018.12.003.

23 Sameer Lalwani, "Actually, Pakistan Is Winning Its War on Terror," *Foreign Policy* (blog), December 10, 2015, https://foreignpolicy.com/2015/12/10/actually-pakistan-is-winning-its-war-on-terror/.

24 Ankit Panda, "Gurdaspur, Pathankot, and Now Uri: What Are India's Options?" accessed December 16, 2021, https://thediplomat.com/2016/09/gurdaspur-pathankot-and-now-uri-what-are-indias-options/.

25 "Militants Attack Indian Army Base in Kashmir 'Killing 17,'" BBC News, September 182016, sec. India, https://www.bbc.com/news/world-asia-india-37399969.

26 "Reversing Roles," *The Economist*, October 6, 2016, https://www.economist.com/asia/2016/10/06/reversing-roles?zid=306&ah=1b164dbd43b0cb27ba0d4c3b12a5e227.

27 Rohan Mukherjee, "Climbing the Escalation Ladder: India and the Balakot Crisis," *War on the Rocks* (blog), October 2, 2019, https://warontherocks.com/2019/10/climbing-the-escalation-ladder-india-and-the-balakot-crisis/.

28 Šumit Ganguly, "Modi Crosses the Rubicon in Kashmir," *Foreign Affairs*, April 16, 2020, https://www.foreignaffairs.com/articles/india/2019-08-08/modi-crosses-rubicon-kashmir.

29 Carter Malkasian, *The American War in Afghanistan: A History* (New York, NY: Oxford University Press, 2021).

30 Javid Ahmad, "Opinion | How Pakistan Won in Afghanistan," *Wall Street Journal*, October 26, 2021, sec. Opinion, https://www.wsj.com/articles/how-pakistan-won-in-afghanistan-taliban-india-borders-11635263372.

31 Rashid, *Taliban*.

32 Tricia Bacon, *Why Terrorist Groups Form International Alliances* (University of Pennsylvania Press, 2018).

33 Steve Coll, *Ghost Wars: The Secret History of the CIA, Afghanistan, and Bin Laden, from the Soviet Invasion to September 10, 2001* (New York: Penguin Press, 2004).

34 Lawrence Wright, *The Looming Tower: Al-Qaeda and the Road to 9/11*, 1st ed. (New York: Knopf, 2006).

35 National Commission on Terrorist Attacks upon the United States, "The 9/11 Commission Report: Final Report of the National Commission on Terrorist Attacks Upon the United States (9/11 Report)," (National Commission on Terrorist Attacks Upon the United States, July 22, 2004), https://www.govinfo.gov/app/details/GPO-911REPORT/https%3A%2F%2Fwww.govinfo.gov%2Fapp%2Fdetails%2FGPO-911REPORT%2Fcontext.

36 Tricia Bacon and Daniel Byman, "De-Talibanization and the Onset of Insurgency in Afghanistan," *Studies in Conflict & Terrorism* (January 14, 2021): 1–25, https://doi.org/10.1080/1057610X.2021.1872159.

37 Vahid Brown and Don Rassler, *Fountainhead of Jihad: The Haqqani Nexus, 1973–2012* (Oxford; New York: Oxford University Press, 2013).

38 Lindsay Maizland, "U.S.-Taliban Peace Deal: What to Know," Council on Foreign Relations, accessed December 14, 2021, https://www.cfr.org/backgrounder/us-taliban-peace-deal-agreement-afghanistan-war.

39 Thomas G. Weiss and Rorden Wilkinson, *International Organization and Global Governance* (London: Routledge, 2013), 134, http://ebookcentral.proquest.com/lib/aul/detail.action?docID=1480757.

40 Daniel Byman and Sarah E. Kreps, "Agents of Destruction? Applying Principal-Agent Analysis to State-Sponsored Terrorism," *International Studies Perspectives* 11, no. 1 (February 1, 2010): 1–18, https://doi.org/10.1111/j.1528-3585.2009.00389.x.

41 Byman and Kreps.

42 There is an increasing recognition that non-state actors can also be principals. See Assaf Moghadam and Michel Wyss, "The Political Power of Proxies: Why Nonstate Actors Use Local Surrogates," *International Security* 44, no. 4 (April 1, 2020): 119–57, https://doi.org/10.1162/isec_a_00377.

43 Idean Salehyan, Kristian Skrede Gleditsch, and David E. Cunningham, "Explaining External Support for Insurgent Groups," *International Organization* 65, no. 4 (2011): 709–44; Jeremy M. Berkowitz, "Delegating Terror: Principal–Agent Based Decision Making in State Sponsorship of Terrorism," *International Interactions* 44, no. 4 (July 4, 2018): 709–48, https://doi.org/10.1080/03050629.2017.1414811.

44 Salehyan, Gleditsch, and Cunningham.

45 Byman and Kreps, "Agents of Destruction?"
46 Berkowitz, "Delegating Terror," 716.
47 Brandon Ives, "Religious Institutionalism: A Domestic Explanation for External Support of Rebel Groups," *International Interactions* 45, no. 4 (July 4, 2019): 693–719, https://doi.org/10.1080/030506 29.2019.1621309.
48 Byman and Kreps, "Agents of Destruction?"
49 Salehyan, Gleditsch, and Cunningham, "Explaining External Support for Insurgent Groups," 716.
50 Berkowitz, "Delegating Terror," 714.
51 Salehyan, "The Delegation of War to Rebel Organizations," 495.
52 Weiss and Wilkinson, *International Organization and Global Governance*, 135.
53 Salehyan, Gleditsch, and Cunningham, "Explaining External Support for Insurgent Groups," 2011, 714.
54 Idean Salehyan, David Siroky, and Reed M. Wood, "External Rebel Sponsorship and Civilian Abuse: A Principal-Agent Analysis of Wartime Atrocities," *International Organization* 68, no. 3 (July 2014): 638, https://doi.org/10.1017/S002081831400006X.
55 Salehyan, Gleditsch, and Cunningham, "Explaining External Support for Insurgent Groups," 2011, 717; Salehyan, Siroky, and Wood, "External Rebel Sponsorship and Civilian Abuse," 657.
56 David B. Carter, "A Blessing or a Curse? State Support for Terrorist Groups," *International Organization* 66, no. 1 (January 2012): 129–151, https://doi.org/10.1017/S0020818311000312.
57 Salehyan, "The Delegation of War to Rebel Organizations," 506.
58 However, the Taliban's victory in Afghanistan has bolstered the Pakistani Taliban as well, raising concerns about a resurgence.
59 Tricia Bacon, "Slipping the Leash? Pakistan's Relationship with the Afghan Taliban," *Survival* 60, no. 5 (September 3, 2018): 159–180, https://doi.org/10.1080/00396338.2018.1518379. It will probably be even less responsive now that it is in power.
60 Byman and Kreps, "Agents of Destruction?"
61 Ashley Jackson and Rahmatullah Amiri, "Taliban Narratives on Al Qaeda in Afghanistan" (Centre for the Study of Armed Groups, September 13, 2021), https://odi.org/en/publications/taliban-narratives-on-al-qaeda-in-afghanistan/.
62 "Human Costs of U.S. Post-9/11 Wars: Direct War Deaths in Major War Zones," The Costs of War, accessed December 15, 2021, https://watson.brown.edu/costsofwar/figures/2021/WarDeathToll.
63 "Human Costs of U.S. Post-9/11 Wars."
64 "Jurisdictions under Increased Monitoring – October 2021," accessed December 15, 2021, https://www.fatf-gafi.org/publications/high-risk-and-other-monitored-jurisdictions/documents/increased-monitoring-october-2021.html.
65 "Economic Consequences of FATF 'Grey Listing,'" Economist Intelligence Unit, October 20, 2018, https://www.eiu.com/industry/article/377308821/economic-consequences-of-fatf-grey-listing/2018-10-30.
66 Naafey Sardar, "Bearing the Cost of Global Politics: The Impact of FATS Grey-Listing on Pakistan's Economy" (Islamabad: Tabadlab, 2021), https://www.tabadlab.com/wp-content/uploads/2021/02/Tabadlab-Working-Paper-07-Bearing-the-Cost-of-Global-Politics.pdf. This estimate dates back to 2008, reflecting a previous period during which Pakistan was on the FATF grey list.
67 Elizabeth Grimm Arsenault and Tricia Bacon, "Disaggregating and Defeating Terrorist Safe Havens," *Studies in Conflict & Terrorism* 38, no. 2 (February 1, 2015): 85–112, https://doi.org/10.108 0/1057610X.2014.977605.
68 Idean Salehyan, "The Delegation of War to Rebel Organizations," *The Journal of Conflict Resolution* 54, no. 3 (2010): 493–515.
69 David E. Cunningham, "Blocking Resolution: How External States Can Prolong Civil Wars," *Journal of Peace Research* 47, no. 2 (2010): 115–27.

Bibliography

Ahmad, Javid. "Opinion | How Pakistan Won in Afghanistan." *Wall Street Journal*, October 26, 2021, sec. Opinion. https://www.wsj.com/articles/how-pakistan-won-in-afghanistan-taliban-india-borders-11635263372.
"Al-Qaeda in the Indian Subcontinent (AQIS): The Nucleus of Jihad in South Asia." The Soufan Center, January 23, 2019. https://thesoufancenter.org/research/al-qaeda-in-the-indian-subcontinent-aqis-the-nucleus-of-jihad-in-south-asia/.

Arsenault, Elizabeth Grimm, and Tricia Bacon. "Disaggregating and Defeating Terrorist Safe Havens." *Studies in Conflict & Terrorism* 38, no. 2 (February 1, 2015): 85–112. https://doi.org/10.1080/1057 610X.2014.977605.

Bacon, Tricia. "Slipping the Leash? Pakistan's Relationship with the Afghan Taliban." *Survival* 60, no. 5 (September 3, 2018): 159–180. https://doi.org/10.1080/00396338.2018.1518379.

———. "The Evolution of Pakistan's Lashkar-e-Tayyiba Terrorist Group." *Orbis* 63, no. 1 (2019): 27–43. https://doi.org/10.1016/j.orbis.2018.12.003.

———. Why Terrorist Groups Form International Alliances. Philadelphia: University of Pennsylvania Press, 2018.

Bacon, Tricia, and Daniel Byman. "De-Talibanization and the Onset of Insurgency in Afghanistan." *Studies in Conflict & Terrorism*, (January 14, 2021): 1–25. https://doi.org/10.1080/10576 10X.2021.1872159.

Berkowitz, Jeremy M. "Delegating Terror: Principal–Agent Based Decision Making in State Sponsorship of Terrorism." *International Interactions* 44, no. 4 (July 4, 2018): 709–748. https://doi.org/10.1080/ 03050629.2017.1414811.

Brown, Vahid, and Don Rassler. *Fountainhead of Jihad: The Haqqani Nexus, 1973–2012.* Oxford; New York: Oxford University Press, 2013.

Byman, Daniel, and Sarah E. Kreps. "Agents of Destruction? Applying Principal-Agent Analysis to State-Sponsored Terrorism." *International Studies Perspectives* 11, no. 1 (February 1, 2010): 1–18. https://doi.org/10.1111/j.1528-3585.2009.00389.x.

Carter, David B. "A Blessing or a Curse? State Support for Terrorist Groups." *International Organization* 66, no. 1 (January 2012): 129–151. https://doi.org/10.1017/S0020818311000312.

Coll, Steve. *Ghost Wars: The Secret History of the CIA, Afghanistan, and Bin Laden, from the Soviet Invasion to September 10, 2001.* New York: Penguin Press, 2004.

———. "The Stand-Off." *The New Yorker*, February 6, 2006. https://www.newyorker.com/magazine/ 2006/02/13/the-stand-off.

Cunningham, David E. "Blocking Resolution: How External States Can Prolong Civil Wars." *Journal of Peace Research* 47, no. 2 (2010): 115–127.

Dodwell, Brian, and Don Rassler. "A View from the CT Foxhole: General John W. Nicholson, Commander, Resolute Support and U.S. Forces-Afghanistan." *Combating Terrorism Center at West Point* 10, no. 2 (February 22, 2017). https://ctc.usma.edu/a-view-from-the-ct-foxhole-general-john-w-nicholson-commander-resolute-support-and-u-s-forces-afghanistan/.

Economist Intelligence Unit. "Economic Consequences of FATF 'Grey Listing.'" October 20, 2018. https://www.eiu.com/industry/article/377308821/economic-consequences-of-fatf-grey-listing/2018-10-30.

Fair, C. Christine. "Lashkar-e-Tayiba and the Pakistani State." *Survival* 53, no. 4 (September 1, 2011): 29–52. https://doi.org/10.1080/00396338.2011.603561.

———. "The Militant Challenge in Pakistan." *Asia Policy* 11, no. 1 (February 2, 2011): 105–137. https:// doi.org/10.1353/asp.2011.0010.

Fair, C. Christine, and Šumit Ganguly. "Five Dangerous Myths About Pakistan." *The Washington Quarterly* 38, no. 4 (October 2, 2015): 73–97. https://doi.org/10.1080/0163660X.2015.1125830.

Ganguly, Šumit. "Modi Crosses the Rubicon in Kashmir." April 16, 2020. https://www.foreignaffairs. com/articles/india/2019-08-08/modi-crosses-rubicon-kashmir.

Ganguly, Šumit, and S. Paul Kapur. "The Sorcerer's Apprentice: Islamist Militancy in South Asia." *The Washington Quarterly* 33, no. 1 (January 1, 2010): 47–59. https://doi.org/10.1080/ 01636600903418686.

"Global Terrorism Index 2020: Measuring the Impact of Terrorism." Sydney: Institute for Economics & Peace, November 2020. http://visionofhumanity.org/reports.

The Costs of War. "Human Costs of U.S. Post-9/11 Wars: Direct War Deaths in Major War Zones." Accessed: December 15, 2021. https://watson.brown.edu/costsofwar/figures/2021/ WarDeathToll.

Ives, Brandon. "Religious Institutionalism: A Domestic Explanation for External Support of Rebel Groups." *International Interactions* 45, no. 4 (July 4, 2019): 693–719. https://doi.org/10.1080/0305 0629.2019.1621309.

Jackson, Ashley, and Rahmatullah Amiri. "Taliban Narratives on Al Qaeda in Afghanistan." Centre for the Study of Armed Groups, September 13, 2021. https://odi.org/en/publications/ taliban-narratives-on-al-qaeda-in-afghanistan/.

Jadoon, Amira. "Allied and Lethal: Islamic State Khorasan's Network and Organizational Capacity in Afghanistan and Pakistan." December 3, 2018. https://www.ctc.usma.edu/allied-lethal-islamic-state-khorasans-network-organizational-capacity-afghanistan-pakistan/.

Jadoon, Amira, Nakissa Jahabani, and Charmaine Willis. "Challenging the ISK Brand in Afghanistan-Pakistan: Rivalries and Divided Loyalties." *Combating Terrorism Center at West Point Sentinel* 11, no. 4 (April 26, 2018): 23–29.

"Jurisdictions under Increased Monitoring - October 2021." Accessed: December 15, 2021. https://www.fatf-gafi.org/publications/high-risk-and-other-monitored-jurisdictions/documents/increased-monitoring-october-2021.html.

Kapur, S. Paul. "India and Pakistan's Unstable Peace: Why Nuclear South Asia Is Not like Cold War Europe." *International Security* 30, no. 2 (2005): 127–152.

Kapur, S. Paul, and Šumit Ganguly. "The Jihad Paradox: Pakistan and Islamist Militancy in South Asia." *International Security* 37, no. 1 (July 1, 2012): 111–141. https://doi.org/10.1162/ISEC_a_00090.

LaFraniere, Sharon, Rajiv Ch, and Rasekaran. "Musharraf Pledges to Rein in Militants." *Washington Post*, May 28, 2002. https://www.washingtonpost.com/archive/politics/2002/05/28/musharraf-pledges-to-rein-in-militants/b5656ec2-e0c1-4c10-95f6-348839c95921/.

Lalwani, Sameer. "Actually, Pakistan Is Winning Its War on Terror." *Foreign Policy* (blog), December 10, 2015. https://foreignpolicy.com/2015/12/10/actually-pakistan-is-winning-its-war-on-terror/.

Maizland, Lindsay. "U.S.-Taliban Peace Deal: What to Know." Council on Foreign Relations. Accessed: December 14, 2021. https://www.cfr.org/backgrounder/us-taliban-peace-deal-agreement-afghanistan-war.

Malkasian, Carter. *The American War in Afghanistan: A History*. New York, NY: Oxford University Press, 2021.

"Militants Attack Indian Army Base in Kashmir 'Killing 17.'" *BBC News*, September 18, 2016, sec. India. https://www.bbc.com/news/world-asia-india-37399969.

Moghadam, Assaf, and Michel Wyss. "The Political Power of Proxies: Why Nonstate Actors Use Local Surrogates." *International Security* 44, no. 4 (April 1, 2020): 119–157. https://doi.org/10.1162/isec_a_00377.

Moret, Erica. "The Role of Sanctions in Afghanistan's Humanitarian Crisis." *IPI Global Observatory* (blog), October 14, 2021. https://theglobalobservatory.org/2021/10/the-role-of-sanctions-in-afghanistans-humanitarian-crisis/.

Mukherjee, Rohan. "Climbing the Escalation Ladder: India and the Balakot Crisis." *War on the Rocks* (blog), October 2, 2019. https://warontherocks.com/2019/10/climbing-the-escalation-ladder-india-and-the-balakot-crisis/.

Musharraf, Pervez. *In the Line of Fire: A Memoir*. New York: Free Press, 2006.

Panda, Ankit. "Gurdaspur, Pathankot, and Now Uri: What are India's Options?" Accessed: December 16, 2021. https://thediplomat.com/2016/09/gurdaspur-pathankot-and-now-uri-what-are-indias-options/.

Rao, Aparna, Michael Bollig, and Monika Böck. *The Practice of War: Production, Reproduction and Communication of Armed Violence*. Oxford, NY: Berghahn Books, 2008.

Rashid, Ahmed. *Taliban: Militant Islam, Oil and Fundamentalism in Central Asia*. 2nd ed. New Haven, CT: Yale University Press, 2010.

"Reversing Roles." *The Economist*, October 6, 2016. https://www.economist.com/asia/2016/10/06/reversing-roles?zid=306&ah=1b164dbd43b0cb27ba0d4c3b12a5e227.

Salehyan, Idean. "The Delegation of War to Rebel Organizations." *The Journal of Conflict Resolution* 54, no. 3 (2010): 493–515.

Salehyan, Idean, Kristian Skrede Gleditsch, and David E. Cunningham. "Explaining External Support for Insurgent Groups." *International Organization* 65, no. 4 (2011): 709–44.

———. "Explaining External Support for Insurgent Groups." *International Organization* 65, no. 4 (October 2011): 709–44. https://doi.org/10.1017/S0020818311000233.

Salehyan, Idean, David Siroky, and Reed M. Wood. "External Rebel Sponsorship and Civilian Abuse: A Principal-Agent Analysis of Wartime Atrocities." *International Organization* 68, no. 3 (July 2014): 633–61. https://doi.org/10.1017/S002081831400006X.

Sardar, Naafey. "Bearing the Cost of Global Politics: The Impact of FATS Grey-Listing on Paksitan's Economy." Islamabad: Tabadlab, 2021. https://www.tabadlab.com/wp-content/uploads/2021/02/Tabadlab-Working-Paper-07-Bearing-the-Cost-of-Global-Politics.pdf.

Sirrs, Owen L. *Pakistan's Inter-Services Intelligence Directorate: Covert Action and Internal Operations.* London: Routledge, 2016. https://doi.org/10.4324/9781315559711.

"Snakes in Your Backyard Won't Bite Only Neighbours: Hillary to Pak." *NDTV,* October 21, 2011. https://www.ndtv.com/world-news/snakes-in-your-backyard-wont-bite-only-neighbours-hillary-to-pak-573412.

Commission on Terrorist Attacks upon the United States. "The 9/11 Commission Report: Final Report of the National Commission on Terrorist Attacks Upon the United States (9/11 Report)." Government. July 22, 2004. https://www.govinfo.gov/app/details/GPO-911REPORT/https%3A%2F%2Fwww.govinfo.gov%2Fapp%2Fdetails%2FGPO-911REPORT%2Fcontext.

Tankel, Stephen. *Storming the World Stage: The Story of Lashkar-e-Taiba.* New York: Columbia University Press, 2011.

Tellis, Ashley J. "Pakistan and the War on Terror: Conflicted Goals, Compromised Performance." Carnegie Endowment for International Peace, January 18, 2008. https://carnegieendowment.org/2008/01/18/pakistan-and-war-on-terror-conflicted-goals-compromised-performance-pub-19848.

Weinbaum, Marvin G. "Insurgency and Violent Extremism in Pakistan." *Small Wars & Insurgencies* 28, no. 1 (January 2, 2017): 34–56. https://doi.org/10.1080/09592318.2016.1266130.

Weiss, Thomas G., and Rorden Wilkinson. *International Organization and Global Governance.* London: Routledge, 2013. http://ebookcentral.proquest.com/lib/aul/detail.action?docID=1480757.

Wirsing, Robert. *Kashmir in the Shadow of War: Regional Rivalries in a Nuclear Age.* Armonk, N.Y.: MESharpe, 2003.

Wright, Lawrence. *The Looming Tower: Al-Qaeda and the Road to 9/11.* 1st ed. New York: Knopf, 2006.

12
INSURGENCIES AND COUNTERINSURGENCIES IN SOUTH ASIA

Subhasish Ray

Introduction

On the eve of Partition, even in the places where there was a heightened sense of difference, there were many countervailing forces. Mercantile and manufacturing communities from sari weavers to tea planters depended on pragmatic co-operation for their livelihoods, while festivals and holidays were flamboyantly celebrated across the board. Class, as ever, acted as a social gel and rich Hindus, Sikhs and Muslims of the same social standing partied together in gilded hotels, irrespective of religion; university friends of various backgrounds attended the same classes; and poor agriculturalists relaxed together on charpois at the end of a day's work. Above all, it was a very long jump from a sense of difference, or lack of social cohesion, to mass slaughter and rape. There was nothing "inevitable" about Partition and nobody could have predicted, at the end of the Second World War, that half a million people or more were going to die because of these differences.[1]

The Sepoy Mutiny of 1857 in undivided India was a turning point for the British Empire, and for European colonial rule more generally. Prior to the mutiny, colonial empires in Asia and Africa had followed a familiar script. The European powers, it was claimed, had a universal mandate to bring "civilization" to subject populations in these regions. The mutiny turned this claim on its head. The post-mutiny regime that emerged was a severely diminished entity, with an almost manic obsession for "law and order" (Mamdani 1996). However, this sudden shift in European self-understanding was entirely divorced from the diversity and fluidity of social relations that colonial administrators encountered on the ground. Here, ethnicity proved to be a useful tool for mapping social realities into easily identifiable and manipulable categories, and very soon, colonial social policy came to be articulated exclusively in terms of "community," "caste," "tribe," etc. Thus emerged the so-called ethnographic state (Dirks 2001).

Innovated in British South Asia, it subsequently diffused to Africa via transferred administrators (Kirk-Greene 1980), and also made the leap to French colonies, even though the official French policy of "assimilation" precisely disavowed the use of ethnic markers (Echenberg 1991).

158

DOI: 10.4324/9781003246626-15

Yet, as the passage cited above from Yasmin Khan's authoritative study of the 1947 interregnum shows, deep as the sense of ethnic difference in British India was in the aftermath of World War II, there were enough signs of civic vitality to indicate that a bright post-war future was still possible. Moreover, this was the case even beyond the subcontinent, the focus of her study. In Sri Lanka, for example, the British had deliberately pursued a policy of empowering a coalition of moderate Sinhalese and Sri Lankan Tamil elites to take over the reins of power after dominion status was granted. Nonetheless, political order fell apart in the subcontinent between 1945 and 1947 and within a decade from Sri Lanka gaining dominion status. Most importantly, developments during this period were instrumental in the onset of ethnic insurgencies across the major states of the region.

As a voluminous body of research attests, political order, when it unravels, is difficult to rebuild in most circumstances. In South Asia, however, this problem is magnified by the region's sheer size—it is home to roughly one-fifth of the world's population—and its continuously evolving social heterogeneity. As a result, state control over society is always in the making.

This chapter maps this history of contention, focusing, in particular, on the experiences of India, Pakistan, and Bangladesh.[2] The analysis is divided into two parts. The first section traces the roots of the subcontinent's most significant insurgency movements to the circumstances of the transition from colonial to post-colonial rule. The next section assesses the current state of these movements, why they are active, where they persist, and why they have been rendered inactive elsewhere.

Onset of Insurgencies

To see why the circumstances of decolonization are so critical for understanding insurgency movements in South Asia, let us begin by considering the most protracted and the most recently active ethnic insurgency in the region, namely the Naga insurgency and the Tehreeke-Taliban Pakistan (TTP) or Pakistani Taliban insurgency.

The Naga National Council (NNC) initiated armed operations in 1956 to assert Naga sovereignty over the Naga-dominated areas of Northeastern India. The group had been spearheading a movement since the end of the war for creating an autonomous zone comprised of these areas within an autonomous province of Assam, in line with the autonomy they enjoyed under colonial rule. The Nagas, it claimed, had achieved a sense of separateness from the rest of India under indirect colonial rule, and hence, if independence were granted sans autonomy, they would be "swamped" by the demographically dominant Assamese and the culturally dominant Bengalis of the region. Incidentally, the NNC's demands were not unique in any sense. Similar claims had been advanced on behalf of other smaller, but influential, minority groups as well—most prominently, by the Akali Dal, which spoke on behalf of the Sikhs (Bal Riar 2006)—during the negotiations leading up to independence.[3] All these demands, however, fell on deaf ears, since the Cabinet Mission—a three-member team appointed by the Labor government to negotiate a peaceful transfer of power in "consultation" with Indian leaders—was fixated, as previous negotiating teams appointed by London had been, on the so-called Muslim question. Settling the concerns of the largest minority group, its members surmised, whether by keeping India united with a provision of grouping of Muslim-majority provinces within a broader union of all erstwhile provinces—Assam and Bengal were to be fused for this purpose—or through a planned partition—hiving off the Muslim-majority areas of Punjab, Bengal, and Assam to create a new independent state alongside India—was the precondition for settling the claims of all other disaffected minorities.

In the event, the Mission failed, triggering a British scuttle from the subcontinent, and in its wake, a *de facto* partition ensued, enforced by uncontrolled migration and ethnic cleansing, which claimed nearly a quarter of a million lives.[4] Importantly for the current discussion, even though the partition seemed to have, at least temporarily, settled the Sikh question,[5] the Naga question festered. Although Assam emerged from the partition cauldron as a separate province minus the portions that were annexed to Pakistan, the new government in Delhi, in line with its colonial predecessors, avoided direct engagement with the question of Naga autonomy. Instead, the onus for settling the issue was shifted to the provincial governor, and herein was the context of a series of face-offs between the Assam government and the NNC, which eventually escalated into armed confrontations after a brutal crackdown on the group by the Assam police in 1953.

According to the South Asia Terrorism Portal (SATP), a web platform that monitors insurgency-related fatalities in South Asia, the TTP is the "deadliest" among all indigenous insurgency outfits that operate today in Pakistan. The formation of the TTP was announced after the infamous Lal Masjid (literally "red mosque" in Urdu) incident in Islamabad in July 2007, when the Pakistani army laid a siege on the mosque and its residents, who had been persistently and violently protesting the country's participation in the US-sponsored "war on terror" in Afghanistan in the capital's streets since January 2006. The group claimed that it was launching an armed struggle against the Pakistani state to establish an Islamic political system in Pakistan based on its interpretation of Sharia (Sayed 2021). Incidentally, this was not the first time that an anti-systemic group had demanded the replacement of Pakistan's semi-democratic regime by a theological elite. The demand was as old as the state of Pakistan itself. No sooner had the partition violence subsided that a section of the new political elite started challenging Muhammad Ali Jinnah's vision of an independent Pakistan as a secular entity along the lines of Kemal Atatürk's Turkey or Reza Shah's Iran.[6] The most prominent voice in this regard was Abul Maududi, founder of the Jamaat-e-Islami, currently South Asia's largest Islamic organization. Maududi debunked comparisons between Pakistan and other Muslim countries since "it has been achieved exclusively with the objective of becoming the homeland of Islam."[7] Although Jinnah's immediate successors managed to put a lid on these aspirations,[8] the balance of power swung again in favor of the latter when general Zia-ul-Haq assumed power after deposing the charismatic Zulfiqar Ali Bhutto in a military coup in 1977. Lacking an independent basis of legitimacy, Zia formed an alliance with the ulema. The alliance gave the Pakistan army the ideological scaffolding to train mujahideen (literally "those engaged in jihad" in Arabic) in ethnic Pashtun areas bordering Afghanistan and Pakistan to fight against the Soviet Union-propped regime in Kabul. It was precisely from these radicalized sections among the Pashtuns that the Afghan Taliban, and subsequently, the TTP, was formed, thus opening a new chapter in the partition-inscribed tussle between the secular and theological strands of Muslim nationalism.

If South Asia's most protracted and its most recent ethnic insurgencies bear the heavy burden of the circumstances under which India and Pakistan were created, so too does its most successful ethnic insurgency movement, the Bangladesh liberation struggle. Here, another adverse colonial legacy that had been lurking under the surface as the primary Muslim-non-Muslim contradiction played itself out, bursting into the open once Pakistan was declared an independent state. The armed forces of the new state were almost entirely constituted of Punjabis and Pashtuns, a product of the colonial "martial race" doctrine,[9] which conferred on the inhabitants of the northwestern regions of undivided India the status of being "eminently suitable" for military service.[10] Complementing such acute imbalances in the ethnic composition of the armed forces was the dominance of Muhajirs (literally "immigrant" in Urdu) in the political and bureaucratic structures of the new nation. A key contradiction within the Pakistan movement was that the demand for an independent Muslim nation-state in the Indian subcontinent resonated more deeply in the Muslim-minority provinces of British India rather than the Muslim-majority provinces of Punjab and Bengal, whose Muslim-majority districts were partitioned to create the new state (Noman 1990, 4–5). This was the source of the dominance of a figure like Jinnah, who was a native of the erstwhile Bombay Presidency, within the Pakistan Muslim League, which spearheaded the Pakistan movement. None of these imbalances would have been fatal, though, had the three groups, independently or collectively, constituted a demographic majority. That status, however, belonged to Bengali Muslims, who had the clear preponderance of numbers. Yet, instead of settling for a power-sharing arrangement with Bengali Muslims, Pakistan's new civilian and military elites prevaricated on the question of holding democratic elections for nearly a decade after the country's independence, a period that eventually ended with the military coup of 1958, led by General Ayub Khan, an ethnic Pashtun. Furthermore, they anointed Urdu, the mother tongue of the Muhajirs, who constituted roughly 8% of the country's population, as the national language of Pakistan. Worse still, when a language movement naturally crystallized among Bengali Muslims in opposition to this move, the Punjabi and Pashtun-dominated armed forces responded with a brutal crackdown on February 21, 1952—subsequently commemorated in Bangladesh as the Language Martyrs Day—in which several student activists were killed. These two developments—the monopolization of political, military, and bureaucratic power by West Pakistani elites and the growing consciousness among East Pakistanis of their ethnic separateness—both of which continued apace in the first era of military rule, set the stage for the bloody liberation struggle that followed in 1971.

The neo-realism school in international relations applies the lens of the ethnic security dilemma to explain ethnic conflicts during the breakdown of imperial regimes. The theory, originally developed by Posen (1993), connects these conflicts to the fear of group extinction amidst a rapidly changing political environment. Starting from the premise that inter-ethnic relations in newly independent countries resemble inter-state relations in the anarchic international system, Posen argues that the temporary absence of an overarching centralized authority in the new state will trigger a deadly pattern of mobilization and counter-mobilization among groups because of the inability of group members on all sides to distinguish between defensive and offensive motivations. Under the circumstances, groups that sense the slightest offensive advantage will exploit it at the first available opportunity.

Posen's formulation is indispensable for understanding the emotions that engulf individuals and groups when a highly centralized polity collapses, as did the British Empire over undivided India. Consider another passage from Khan's (2017, 84) study describing the fraught state of Punjabi society before it was engulfed by violence in 1947:

> Security was the paramount need of the hour. Anxious families acquired basic arms or barricaded in their allies but this had an escalating effect as it made other neighbouring communities feel more insecure.

It is easy to see that without explicitly invoking the term "ethnic security dilemma," Khan is clearly referring to a similar dynamic.

An important substantive question that arises here is whether the structure of the ethnic security dilemma makes ethnic partitions unavoidable in the interests of lasting peace. In an influential study, Kaufmann (1996) concurs, positing that conflicts rooted in the ethnic security dilemma cannot be resolved through power-sharing mechanisms since the latter will only harden ethnic differences and magnify the advantages of striking first. Instead, they can either be resolved through planned or *de facto* ethnic partitions as neither of the parties involved in the conflict will stop until each has secured a piece of territory from which "the other" has been cleansed or reduced to the status of second-class citizens.

As the cases of insurgency discussed thus far show, however, *contra* Kaufmann, the first partition of the Indian subcontinent clearly did not bring inter-group conflict to a full stop. But, perhaps 1947 was an anomalous conjuncture, coming as it did in the wake of a great international crisis. Yet, as we discuss below, neither did the second partition of the subcontinent have the effects predicted by Kaufmann.

The case of Bangladesh after 1971 offers the most compelling evidence against the ethnic partition=ethnic peace thesis. The new state that emerged after another round of mass migrations, this time to India and Pakistan, was far more ethnically homogeneous than any other state in South Asia. Roughly 90% of the country's population is currently comprised of Muslims. Nonetheless, within three decades of its independence, the country witnessed two insurgency uprisings. The first uprising, in the mold of the "sons of the soil" rebellion, occurred in the Chittagong Hill Tracts (CHT), where the Shanti Bahini (literally "peace force" in Bengali), a militant outfit, was formed to challenge Bengali encroachment into tribally owned land in the region. The uprising ended when the CHT Peace Accord was signed in 1997 between the Bangladesh government and tribal representatives. The second uprising involved Islamist militant organizations. The emergence of these groups was coterminous with the intensification of an ideological conflict that was birthed by the liberation struggle itself, between those who fought on the side of the liberationists and were committed to the idea of secular Bangladesh and elements aligned with Maududi's Jamaat-e-Islami in East Pakistan, who collaborated with the Pakistani army. This schism was subsequently manifested in the country's party system, which devolved into a no holds barred winner-takes-all contest between the Awami League, which counted the secularists on its side, and the Bangladesh National Party, which allied with what had by then become the Jamaat-e-Islami Bangladesh.

Although several Islamic militant groups had emerged in Bangladesh from 1986 to 2001— described by Mostofa (2021, 2039–2040) as the "formation period" of Islamic militancy in the country—these operated at low levels of intensity as long as political power alternated between the two umbrella alliances as part of an invisible, but commonly understood "rules of the game" (Blair 2010). This consensus broke down prior to the 2006 general election, starting a political crisis that lasted until a fresh election was held in 2008. It was during this period that some of the militant groups that had surfaced earlier came to the foreground. Chief among them were the Jaggrata Muslim Janata Bangladesh (literally "awakened Muslims of Bangladesh" in Bengali, henceforth JMJB) and the Jamaat-ul-Mujahideen (literally "assembly of martyrs" in Bengali, henceforth JMB). The JMJB showed its operational prowess when it simultaneously launched 459 non-fatal demonstration bomb attacks on August 17, 2005 across 63 of Bangladesh's 64 districts. On November 29, 2005, the organization mounted the first ever suicide bomb attack in Bangladesh, in Gazipur district, in which seven individuals, including the bomber, were killed. The attacks brought a swift response from the Bangladesh armed forces. Bangla Bhai (alias for Siddique ul-Islam, literally "Brother of Bangla" in Bengali), the military commander of the JMJB and the mastermind behind the attacks, was arrested and executed on March 29, 2007. Though the execution led to a temporary lull in the militancy and regular electoral politics resumed, this "silent phase" was superseded by a "violent phase" from 2013 onwards. The backdrop to this shift was the ruling Awami League's decision to constitute an International Crimes Tribunal (ICT) in 2009 to try the so-called war criminals of 1971. When the ICT sentenced one of the accused, Abdul Quader Mollah,

Insurgencies and Counterinsurgencies in South Asia

to life imprisonment, a popular, but peaceful protest by secularists erupted in Dhaka's streets on February 5, 2013, demanding capital punishment for Mollah.[11] The Shahbag movement, which got its name from the city's Shahbag Square, where the protestors had gathered, took a step further and also started demanding a complete ban on the Jamaat-e-Islami Bangladesh and boycott of all institutions that supported the party. These events had a galvanizing effect on the militancy, culminating in Bangladesh's worst ever hostage crisis, when Islamists attacked a café in Dhaka, frequented by foreigners, on July 1, 2016, which led to the killings of 20 hostages. The main perpetrators behind the attack were members of the neo-JMB, an offshoot of the JMB that had established links with the Islamic State (IS) and al-Qaida (AQ).

The central challenge that the South Asian experience poses for pro-partition arguments is this. In polities riven with complex ethnic divisions, such as the ones that emerged from decolonization, ethnic security dilemmas cannot be addressed through partition since the very criteria used to separate two warring groups will produce new security dilemmas for hitherto unmobilized ethnic groups. Most importantly, the latter *cannot be anticipated at the outset of partition* since the process of partition itself produces new social realities. The conflict between Islamists and secularists in Bangladesh, for example, was largely unarticulated from 1947 to 1971, when the Bengali-non-Bengali cleavage provided the master narrative for politics in undivided Pakistan. Yet, it was fully formed and articulated by the time the liberation war ended. Indeed, it was being shaped and forged in the midst of the war itself,[12] thus pointing toward a more contingent and conflict-sensitive understanding of ethnic identity than afforded by the pro-partition view.

While the ethnic security dilemma is clearly important for explaining insurgency onsets in South Asia, not all ethnic insurgencies in the region can be explained using this logic. Take, for example, the Sri Lankan civil war. In this case, a key precondition for the ethnic security dilemma, namely, the sudden breakdown of imperial authority, simply did not exist. Nor can the theory satisfactorily explain the onsets of the Kashmir insurgency or the Sikh insurgency in the 1980s in India. Moreover, an entire class of insurgency, Maoist rebellions in India and Nepal, had non-ethnic origins. In the remainder of this section, I discuss these cases in more detail.

State collapse was a *non-sequitur* for the onset of an ethnic insurgency in Indian Kashmir. As noted by Ganguly (1996), the preconditions for a classic ethnic security dilemma more likely existed in the region in 1965, when the insurgency did not materialize, than in 1989, when it did materialize. In 1965, the Indian state had been considerably weakened, via external conflict with Pakistan, and through internal conflicts, primarily the language riots in southern India. Moreover, a siege mentality had taken hold in Kashmir Valley as furious protests broke out over an alleged sacrilege committed at the famous Hazratbul shrine, and to make matters worse, the region was flush with infiltrators ready to escalate the unrest to the next level. Yet, no such escalation took place.

Moving across to Indian Punjab, one notes a similar setting. The mostly rural Sikhs had been agitating since 1947 for a separate Sikh-majority state within India. Although the national government prevaricated on this issue for a period of time, risking escalation of the conflict at various points, the matter was eventually settled with the creation of the state of Punjab in 1966. Statehood and the so-called Green Revolution in Indian agriculture combined to transform Punjab into one of India's most economically prosperous states. Yet, by the 1970s, a view had taken hold among the Sikh peasantry that they were victims of internal colonialism—the disproportionate contributions by the community to the country's military and economic security had not translated into commensurate political influence nationally—and in 1984, a full-fledged movement for an independent Sikh nation-state was formed.

The Khalistan (literally "land of the Sikh brethren" in Punjabi) movement was brutally crushed by the Indian armed forces by 1993—one of the few examples of a successful counterinsurgency (COIN) campaign in South Asia—but as in the case of the Sri Lankan Tamil and Kashmiri insurgencies, the movement took root in a state that was intact and whole, both at the local and the national level.

If the experiences of the first and the second partition in South Asia engage us to complicate the neo-realist understanding of ethnic groups, the Sri Lankan Tamil, Kashmiri, Sikh, and Maoist insurgencies, all of which took off in the 1980s, enjoin us to look toward theories of international security that take the domestic politics of states seriously for potential clues to their origins. Here, Ganguly's (1996) explanation for the onset of the Kashmiri insurgency offers us a unified framework for thinking about these various insurgencies. According to the study, the Kashmiri insurgency took off in 1989 because of the deepening of two trends in the local political environment. *Contra* to the 1960s, when structural conditions were much more permissive for insurgency, Kashmiris had become more politically conscious due to the education initiatives of earlier Kashmiri governments. Importantly, the growth in political consciousness occurred in tandem with the *deinstitutionalization* of both the national and local political systems, wherein dynastic tendencies within the major political parties—the Rajiv Gandhi-led Congress in Delhi and the Farooq Abdullah-led National Conference in Kashmir—had choked all pathways to political mobility for young and ambitious Kashmiris. Under the circumstances, a would-be-political entrepreneur, such as Yasin Malik, who had watched from close quarters as the two big parties rigged the 1987 state assembly election—he was serving as an election agent for one of the smaller parties in the fray—had few qualms in joining the Jammu and Kashmir Liberation Front, an insurgent outfit, when security forces cracked down on popular protests against the glaringly obvious electoral wrongdoings.

The contradictions of illiberal governance within a formally democratic political system were also at play in the onset of the Sikh insurgency in 1984. Indira Gandhi's response to the Anandpur Sahib Resolution[13] of the Akali Dal was in the spirit of shooting the messenger without heeding the message as she sought to undercut the party's support among the Sikh peasantry by nurturing an extremist faction within the party, led by Jarnail Singh Bhindranwale. The move backfired as a political cult developed around Bhindranwale, who began to espouse the idea of a militant Sikh movement. In 1982, Bhindranwale and his followers moved into the Golden Temple complex, the preeminent spiritual site of the Sikh religion, from wherein they ran what appeared to be a "parallel government" for a separate nation-state. Matters came to a head when the group inhabited and fortified the sacred Akal Takht, at which point, the Indian army initiated Operation Bluestar to eject the group from the Takht. Although the operation succeeded in its objective—Bhindranwale was killed in the exchange of fire that ensued and the area was secured—the damages to the Takht from the army's shelling scarred the Sikh psyche deeply, eventually galvanizing communitywide support for the Khalistan project that had hitherto eluded its proponents.

Notwithstanding their class politics rhetoric, the Maoist insurgencies in Nepal and India too can be traced back to the pathologies of democratic practice in the two contexts. The current phase of the Maoist insurgency in India, ongoing since the 1980s,[14] has been primarily concentrated in the country's centrally located states in districts with large tribal populations (Kennedy and King 2013). This association is typically attributed to tribal grievances related to the post-colonial state's voracious appetite for controlling their forest homelands and the tactical success of Maoist leaders in framing the insurgency in terms that are meaningful to these groups. What has been underscored much less is the experience of political parties, such as the Jharkhand Mukti Morcha (literally "Jharkhand Freedom Rally" in Hindi; henceforth

JMM), that have sought to pursue a politics of tribal autonomy within India's parliamentary system. Here, Basu (2012) observes a schism between the "politics of recognition" and the "politics of redistribution." While parties like the JMM, which currently runs the state government of Jharkhand, have succeeded in the politics of recognition, they have failed to use it as leverage in redistributive politics. Indeed, according to Chandra (2013), it might be more productive to conceptualize the Maoist insurgency through the lens of intergenerational conflict within India's tribal communities, wherein an older generation remains tethered to the systemic politics of tribal autonomy, whereas a younger and more restive generation has gravitated toward the Maoists for substantive gains.

Persistence of Insurgencies

Irrespective of their origins, whether in the politics of decolonization or in post-colonial democratic failures, insurgencies in South Asia have been notoriously persistent. Table 12.1 summarizes the insurgency onsets discussed in the previous section and their current status using data from the UCDP/PRIO Armed Conflict Dataset version 21.1. As the table indicates, the only conflict in the list that subsided within five years of onset is the Bangladesh freedom struggle, which was also rare in that the rebel side emerged victorious in the conflict.

Before proceeding further, it is worth noting that the overall trend in South Asia since the 2000s has been in the direction of fewer insurgency-related incidents and fatalities. In general, South Asian states have been able to gain greater control over their citizens during this period (Staniland 2020). That being said, what is striking is how many insurgencies continue to perpetuate at low intensity levels, with no serious signs of an imminent closure. Take, for instance, Kashmiri insurgents. Their numbers have shrunk sharply from the heights seen in the 1990s, and the alarming possibility of the movement linking up with IS or AQ has subsided (Siyech 2018). Yet, at the same time, the region has seen an equally sharp rise in what Lalwani and Gayner (2020) denote as "quasi-violence," i.e., "resistance by civilians rather than armed militants," involving "semi-organized, nonlethal pressure"—such as stone-pelting of security personnel by young Kashmiris—"to directly or indirectly compel shifts in state behavior." More importantly for our purposes, they argue that this strategy appealed to the

Table 12.1 Timing of Select Insurgency Onsets in South Asia and Their Current Status

Rebel Organization	Location	Start Year	End Year
Naga Nationalist Council, Naga Socialist Council of Nagaland-Isaac-Muivah faction, Naga Socialist Council of Nagaland-Khaplang faction	India	1956	Active
Tehreek-e-Taliban	Pakistan	2003	Active
Mukti Bahini	Pakistan	1971	1971
Chittagong Hill Tracts People's Coordination Association, Shanti Bahini	Bangladesh	1974	1991
Islamic State	Bangladesh	2016	Active
Liberation Tigers of Tamil Elam	Sri Lanka	1984	2009
Sikh insurgents	India	1983	1993
Kashmir insurgents	India	1989	Active
Communist Party of Nepal-Maoist	Nepal	1996	2006
People's War Group, Maoist Communist Centre, Communist Party of India-Maoist	India	1990	Active

Source: UCDP/PRIO Armed Conflict Dataset version 21.1.

region's activists since "the appeal of overt militancy diminished…owing to one of the world's densest intelligence networks and battle-hardened security forces, but participation in corrupt, delegitimized, and impotent politics proved equally unsatisfying." In other words, the Indian state's success in containing overt insurgency has produced a shift toward covert violence. Indeed, according to the study, the shift to a more all-pervasive form of violence may have triggered the momentous decision by the incumbent Bharatiya Janata Party (BJP) government in Delhi to suspend Articles 370 and 35A of the Indian constitution immediately after its reelection in 2019.[15] In one fell sweep, the two important constants of India's strategic approach to Kashmir since independence were removed, giving fresh ballast to overt insurgency.

The key to understanding why this is the case is to recognize that South Asian states lack the capacity and the will to evolve coherent COIN doctrines. Instead, as noted by Staniland (2018) in the context of India, COIN policymaking tends to vary across and within insurgency theaters depending on the centrality/peripherality of the conflict from the point of view of national and sub-national elites. The result being that at any given point of time, internal security resembles a patchwork of "armed orders." A clear manifestation of this is the proclivity of national governments to hold elections in insurgency-affected areas, but then to undermine the same using "exceptions" for "disturbed areas." Baruah (2005), for example, points to the practice of "counterinsurgency constitutionalism" in India's Northeastern states, wherein, *contra* to practice elsewhere in India, ex-military administrators were appointed as governors, and further still, the latter were given extraordinary leeway to intervene in local administration in the interests of COIN even though the Indian Constitution is explicit that they only have ceremonial authority. Naseemullah (2014) identifies similar forms of "hybrid governance" in Pakistan's ethnic Pashtun-dominated Northwestern regions bordering Afghanistan. Moving across to Kashmir, Chowdhary (2015) offers how the People's Democratic Party in Jammu and Kashmir had contested the 2014 state assembly election on a platform of everyday governance-related matters and stayed away from the "politics of conflict resolution."[16] Waterman (2021) pushes these readings further by documenting a variety of political orders even within a particular type of "armed order," ceasefires in parts of India's Northeastern region with substantial Naga populations.

A growing body of research also documents the complicated effects of the developmental initiatives of South Asian states in insurgency-affected areas. Kaila, Singhal, and Tuteja (2020) perform a structural break analysis using time series data on violence from Jammu and Kashmir in the period 1998–2017 and identify a transition from a "high violence" to a "low violence" regime that coincided with the implementation of a large-scale development program and the phasing in of the Mahatma Gandhi National Rural Employment Guarantee Scheme. Using an ethnographic approach, Kamra (2018) finds that another national government scheme, the Prime Minister's Rural Development Fellowship, had helped to rebuild the state's legitimacy in the Maoist-affected Junglemahal area of the state of West Bengal in India. Another ethnographic study, also conducted in Junglemahal, however, points to the pitfalls of "securitized development," which may prevent genuine buy-in for top-down developmental initiatives in these settings (Ray and Dutta 2018).

Conclusion

At the time of the writing of this chapter, India has recorded four major insurgency events in 2021 alone—resumption of ethnic cleansing by terror groups in Kashmir; killings of 22 Central Reserve Police Force personnel in an ambush by Maoists in Chattisgarh; killings of seven Assam Rifles personnel, including a Commanding Officer (and his wife and six-year-old child), in an ambush by the People's Liberation Army in Manipur; and killings of six civilians in an ambush by the Assam Rifles in Nagaland. Add to this Fair, Ashkenaze, and Batchelder's (2021) findings that an apparently "closed" case—the Khalistan movement—is showing signs of reemergence, and the diagnosis seems obvious—nation-building remains a fraught project in the world's largest democracy, and in South Asia, more generally.

My burden in this chapter has been to use existing research in this area to outline some potential causes for these nation-building struggles and for their persistence over time. One area in which this research has been lacking is in offering a theoretical framework that integrates the political and developmental aspects of COIN with the motivations of insurgent groups into a synthetic explanation for the persistence of insurgencies. Venugopal's (2011) "military fiscalism" thesis in the context of the Sri Lankan civil war is a step in this direction. The study demonstrates how the protracted war served an important social function by absorbing large number of Sinhalese youth in the armed forces, who would otherwise have swelled the ranks of the "lumpen proletariat" on the account of the market-oriented economic reforms that had been initiated since the 1980s, shrinking the state's ability to maintain a social security net at the pre-1980 levels. While this political economy perspective does capture important aspects of the interconnectedness of the actions of states and insurgents in persistent insurgencies, it falls short of a synthetic explanation. Here, a logical next step would be to adopt a "complex systems" approach. Keen's (2012) "war systems" theory, subsequently extended by Keen and Andersson (2018) using the concept of "double games," is a useful intervention in this context, helping us to see that the aim of either side in a protracted insurgency is rarely ever to "win" the conflict. New research applying these ideas can make important contributions to our understanding of the complicated and ever-dynamic international and comparative politics of internal security in South Asia.

Notes

1 Khan (2017, 22).
2 I focus on these three countries purely in the interests of brevity.
3 Interestingly, even sub-groups advanced such claims. For example, spokesmen on behalf of Mazhbi Sikhs sought safeguards for the community against potential domination by Jat Sikhs in an independent India. On this, see Ray (2017, 395).
4 Brass (2003, 75).
5 Once the migrations to and from the newly created nations and the violence subsided, a new demographic reality emerged: Almost the entire Sikh community was now concentrated in India over a geographically contiguous area. Indeed, in some districts of eastern Punjab, group members constituted a majority of the population, a status that they did not have in *any* district of undivided Punjab. Thus, the political project that a section of the Sikh leadership had pursued single-mindedly throughout the long 1940s, namely, to achieve a "politically effective concentration" of the group's population (Brass 2003, 86), had come to fruition.
6 In her important study of Jinnah's politics in the long 1940s, Jalal (1985) argues that the founder of Pakistan was minimally interested in creating an autonomous power center for the Muslims of undivided India within a united India. Indeed, this was the logic behind Plan A in the Cabinet Mission's policy statement of May 16, 1946 of keeping India united through a grouping of Muslim and non-Majority provinces below the union level. Having achieved his minimal aims, however, Jinnah made the tactical mistake of pressing the negotiators for more concessions, which led him to eventually reject the statement—no further concessions were forthcoming and he could not afford to be seen as backing down by his constituents—leaving Plan B—partition—as the only option on the table.
7 As cited in Noman (1990, 6).
8 Ibid, p. 7. A mixture of means was used to contain the movement. On the one hand, the Objectives Resolution was promulgated, which included a vague commitment to include Islamic principles in

Pakistan's future constitution. On the other hand, violent mobilizations, such as attacks on the supposedly heretical Qadiani sect, were put down with an iron fist.

9 The doctrine justified the over-representation of select communities in the colonial security apparatus on the grounds that "one of the essential differences between the East and West" is "in the East, with certain exceptions, only certain clans and classes can bear arms" whereas "The others have not the physical courage for the warrior" [General Sir George MacMunn as cited in Kirk-Greene (1980, 395)].

10 Incidentally, the Sikhs were beneficiaries of this doctrine as well, a position they continued to hold in the post-colonial armed forces in India, though their dominance was considerably whittled down due to the partition. For data on post-colonial recruitment patterns in India, see Khalidi (2003).

11 See D'Costa (2015) for a critical analysis of the Tribunal's functioning.

12 Kalyvas (2008) denotes this phenomenon as "ethnic defection."

13 The resolution evolved from deliberations within the Akali Dal. It was a list of the various concerns that ailed the Sikh peasantry.

14 An earlier uprising in the Naxalbari area of the state of West Bengal in 1967, under the banner of the Communist Party of India (Marxist-Leninist), was quickly stamped out through brutal police action by successive state governments, including one led by the parliamentary Left.

15 Article 370 assured Jammu and Kashmir's autonomous status within the Indian Union and Article 35A restricted property ownership in the region to those of indigenous origins. They were enduring reminders that a political resolution to the Kashmir insurgency was yet possible. No less dramatic and unprecedented was the manner in which the abrogation was carried out. Kashmiris were subjected to a prolonged internet shutdown. This was accompanied by the suspension of party politics, with even moderate Kashmiri leaders being placed under detention, a move that has only recently been rescinded, and that too with several caveats.

16 See Ray (2018) for analysis of how the BJP has exploited a similar schism in India's northeastern states to emerge as the dominant political party in that region.

Bibliography

Bal Riar, Sukhmani. *The Politics of the Sikhs: 1940–47.* Chandigarh: Unistar Books Pvt. Ltd, 2006.

Baruah, Sanjib. *Durable Disorder: Understanding the Politics of Northeast India.* Delhi: Oxford University Press, 2005.

Basu, Ipshita. "The Politics of Recognition and Redistribution: Development, Tribal Identity Politics and Distributive Justice in India's Jharkhand." *Development and Change* 43, no. 6 (2012): 1291–1312.

Blair, Harry. "Party Overinstitutionalization, Contestation and Democratic Degradation in Bangladesh." In *Routledge Handbook of South Asian Politics: India, Pakistan, Bangladesh, Sri Lanka, and Nepal,* edited by Paul R. Brass. Florence, KY: Routledge, 2010, 98–117.

Brass, Paul R. "The Partition of India and Retributive Genocide in the Punjab, 1946-47: Means, Methods, and Purposes." *Journal of Genocide Research* 5, no. 1 (2003): 71–101.

Chandra, Uday. "Beyond Subalternity: Land, Community, and the State in Contemporary Jharkhand." *Contemporary South Asia* 21, no. 1 (2013): 52–61.

Chowdhary, Rekha. "Democratic Processes in the Context of Separatism and Political Divergence: A Analysis of 2014 Assembly Elections in Jammu and Kashmir." *Studies in Indian Politics* 3, no. 2 (2015): 164–178.

D'Costa, Bina. "Of Impunity, Scandals, and Contempt: Chronicles of the Justice Conundrum." *International Journal of Transitional Justice* 9 (2015): 357–366.

Dirks, Nicholas B. *Castes of Mind: Colonialism and the Making of Modern India.* Princeton: Princeton University Press, 2001.

Echenberg, Myron. *Colonial Conscripts: The Tirailleurs Senegalais in French West Africa, 1857–1960.* London: James Currey Ltd, 1991.

Fair, C. Christine, Kerry Ashkenaze, and Scott Batchelder. "'Ground Hog Da Din' for the Sikh Insurgency?" *Small Wars & Insurgencies* 32, no. 2 (2021): 344–373.

Ganguly, Šumit. "Explaining the Kashmir Insurgency." *International Security* 21, no. 2 (1996): 76–107.

Jalal, Ayesha. *The Sole Spokesman: Jinnah, the Muslim League and the Demand for Pakistan.* Cambridge: Cambridge University Press, 1985.

Kaila, Heidi, Saurabh Singhal, and Divya Tuteja. "Development Programs, Security, and Violence Reduction: Evidence from an Insurgency in India." *World Development* 130 (2020): 104911.

Kalyvas, Stathis. "Ethnic Defection in Civil War." *Comparative Political Studies* 41, no. 8 (2008): 1043–1068.

Kamra, Lipika. "The Expanded State in Contemporary India: Counterinsurgency and the Prime Minister's Rural Development Fellowship." *Contemporary South Asia* 27, no. 1 (2018): 1–14.

Kaufmann, Chaim. "Possible and Impossible Solutions to Ethnic Civil War." *International Security* 20, no. 4 (1996): 136–175.

Keen, David. *Useful Enemies: When Waging Wars Is More Important Than Winning Them*. New Haven: Yale University Press, 2012.

Keen, David, and Ruben Andersson. "Double Games: Success, Failure and the Relocation of Risk in Fighting Terror, Drugs and Migration." *Political Geography* 67 (2018): 100–110.

Kennedy, Jonathan, and Lawrence King. "Adivasis, Maoists and Insurgency in the Central Indian Tribal Belt." *European Journal of Sociology* LIV, no. 1 (2013): 1–32.

Khalidi, Omar. *Khaki and Ethnic Violence in India: Army, Police and Paramilitary Forces during Communal Riots*. New Delhi: Three Essays Collective, 2003.

Khan, Yasmin. *The Great Partition: The Making of India and Pakistan, New Edition*. New Haven: Yale University Press, 2017.

Kirk-Greene, Anthony H. M. "'Damnosa Hereditas': Ethnic Ranking and the Martial Races Imperative in Africa." *Ethnic and Racial Studies* 3, no. 4 (1980): 393–414.

Lalwani, Sameer P., and Gillian Gayner. *India's Kashmir Conundrum: Before and After the Abrogation of Article 370*. Washington, DC: United States Institute of Peace, 2020.

Mamdani, Mahmood. *Citizen and Subject: Contemporary Africa and the Legacy of Late Colonialism*. Princeton: Princeton University Press, 1996.

Mostofa, Shafi Md. "Understanding Islamist Militancy in Bangladesh." *Journal of Asian and African Studies* 56, no. 8 (2021): 2036–2051.

Naseemullah, Adnan. "Shades of Sovereignty: Explaining Political Order and Disorder in Pakistan's Northwest." *Studies in Comparative International Development* 49 (2014): 501–522.

Noman, Omar. *Pakistan: A Political and Economic History since 1947*. London: Kegan Paul International, 1990.

Posen, Barry R. "The Security Dilemma and Ethnic Conflict." *Survival* 35, no. 1 (1993): 27–47.

Ray, Subhasish. "Intra-Group Interactions and Inter-Group Violence: Sikh Mobilization during the Partition of India in a Comparative Perspective." *Journal of Genocide Research* 19, no. 3 (2017): 382–403.

Ray, Subhasish. "The Second Dominant Party System and India's COIN Strategy." *Indian Politics & Policy* 1, no. 1 (2018): 131–161.

Ray, Subhasish, and Mohan J. Dutta. "Insecure Peace: Understanding Citizen-Local Government Relations in a Maoist-Affected Region in India." *Critical Asian Studies* 50, no. 1 (2018): 37–57.

Sayed, Abdul. *The Evolution and Future of Tehrik-e-Taliban Pakistan*. Washington, DC: Carnegie Endowment for International Peace, 2021.

Siyech, Mohammed Sinan. "Why Has the Islamic State Failed to Grow in Kashmir?" *Counter Terrorist Trends and Analyses* 10, no. 5 (2018): 11–15.

Staniland, Paul. "Internal Security Strategy in India." *India Review* 17, no. 1 (2018): 142–158.

Staniland, Paul. *Political Violence in South Asia; The Triumph of the State?* Washington, DC: Carnegie Endowment for International Peace, 2020.

Venugopal, Rajesh. "The Politics of Market Reform at a Time of Civil War: Military Fiscalism in Sri Lanka." *Economic and Political Weekly* (December 3, 2011): 67–75.

Waterman, Alex. "Ceasefires and State Order-Making in Naga Northeast India." *International Peacekeeeping* 28, no. 3 (2021): 496–525.

13

INDIAN AND PAKISTANI CONVENTIONAL MILITARY DOCTRINES

Frank O'Donnell

Introduction

Contemporary debates on Indian and Pakistani military doctrines and operations tend to focus upon nuclear policy. However, nuclear operations in both New Delhi and Rawalpindi are also predicated upon a breakdown in conventional deterrence. Conventional rungs on the escalation ladder are those in which previous India-Pakistan conflicts have been fought. After each clash, both states also consistently seek to revise conventional force planning to reflect perceived lessons learnt. Investigating how these states conceptualize their use of conventional forces is therefore essential to understand the nature of their military competition and the emerging shape of South Asian security more generally.

This chapter contends that India and Pakistan are continuing a post-2002 trend of seeking conventional limited war options that can achieve two objectives. First, to deliver decisive conventional strike(s) to compel the rival to cease intolerable behavior. Second, to ensure that the strikes are nevertheless sufficiently escalatory to force the adversary to choose between either expanding the conflict toward conventional war (with the attendant risk of nuclear escalation) or entering de-escalation negotiations. As interested third parties recognize that the adversary is now at this stage, they will also intervene to compel a freeze to hostilities and mutual de-escalation.

There are certain tensions between these objectives. Neither state has been able to develop a concept of conventional operations that is destructive enough to fundamentally alter rival foreign and defense policy behavior, and yet not threaten a nuclear response from the rival. Both states seek to avoid the binary choice of conventional war actions or de-escalation, while still imposing this choice on the rival. This leads to both states continually exploring new upward rungs on the conventional escalation ladder, testing mutual escalation thresholds in real time.

These dynamics are exacerbated by the introduction of new technologies. New standoff precision-strike capabilities within Indian and Pakistani arsenals are engendering greater policymaker confidence in their abilities to issue decisive strikes yet manage the escalation ladder. These include air-delivered precision-guided munitions, such as the Indian SPICE-2000 and Pakistani LS-6 bombs.[1] These developments also feature a growing range of ballistic and cruise missiles, as variably launched from the air, ground, and sea. These states can exploit

170   DOI: 10.4324/9781003246626-16

the dual-use nature of many of its aircraft platforms and missiles to terminate the conflict through either adversary self-deterrence or third-party perception that war is imminent. Both states are therefore conceptualizing limited war approaches that intentionally test thresholds for conventional or nuclear war.

These developments are critical to global security and our theoretical understanding of the region. The Pulwama-Balakot conflict of February–March 2019, as the most recent episode in this iterative process of limited war planning and action, formed only the second instance of direct conventional conflict between major lethal platforms of nuclear-armed rivals in history.[2] The progressive learning by each capital of strategic lessons from previous conflicts and enactment of new conventional concepts most closely supports the constructivist school of international relations. The constructivist school especially captures the nature of policy "learning" in the Indo-Pakistani context, in that the perceived lessons and solutions are placing national security and strategic stability at greater risk.

While conventional air and naval doctrinal and posturing developments are significant to the contours of Indo-Pakistani competition, most official conventional planning focuses on ground forces. This chapter reflects this reality, while still discussing the most impactful air and naval developments in the section exploring new technologies. The first section of this chapter will analyze the relative explanatory value of constructivist, realist, liberal, and critical theories for this strategic context. It will next provide an overview of the concept of limited war and the core elements of its practice to be managed and communicated to the adversary in ensuring it does not escalate to major war. It will then explore the conventional strategy development in India and Pakistan since 1998, highlighting how securing near-term military advantages are taking precedence over the escalation management practices essential to ensuring that conflicts remain limited. The following section will examine how key technology acquisitions are enabling these developments, before the chapter concludes with policy recommendations for India and Pakistan to stabilize their conventional competition.

This chapter recommends that both states focus on developing conventional deterrence-by-denial postures, rather than the cross-border strike packages that currently test conflict thresholds. This will demonstrate to the adversary that any attempted military solutions to their disputes will end in failure. To further avert the risk of unintended escalation, confidence-building measures should be more robustly built into their military deployments.

Theories of International Relations and India-Pakistan Military Posturing

The school of constructivism is most closely associated with the concept of iterative policy learning by decision-makers and strategic communities. This conceptualizes the process by which national security communities draw certain lessons from their strategic context and past incidents, and implement policy solutions intended to address these perceived lessons. Crucially, the solution need not be one that actually promotes national security or strategic stability, and can indeed worsen the strategic context. This is because the lesson itself is drawn from subjective perceptions of the strategic environment. Since Kargil, India and Pakistan have gradually learned that conventional operations that manipulate their rival's nuclear threshold deliver the greatest potential security benefits.[3] Alternative or parallel options that could be adopted have not been pursued with the same consistent commitment. These include diplomatic dialogue to resolve their underlying political disputes; bilateral economic liberalization to elevate the economic costs of war; and, for Pakistan, an end to hosting and sponsoring anti-India terrorist groups on its soil. An attack by these groups against Indian targets remains the most likely cause of a conflict between India and Pakistan.

Critical theory approaches to international relations seek to discern "the prospects for realizing higher levels of human freedom across the world society as a whole."[4] As such, critical theorists can describe concepts such as the sovereign state, politicization of territory, conventional militaries, and nuclear deterrence as structures that can be replaced with more pacific relationships built upon alternative concepts. However, these structures are also used by national leaders to exercise power over humans, and inhibit their abilities to begin constructing these alternative relationships.[5] As applied toward this topic, critical theory highlights that India-Pakistan military posturing is built upon perceptual constructs, and different approaches exist which would reduce the risk of conflict. However, this is highly similar to the constructivist contribution. The deeper interest of critical theory in theoretically interrogating the processes for the creation and potential dismantlement of concepts as fundamental as the sovereign state or standing military is beyond the scope of this chapter.

The position of provocative military planning at the foreground of the Indo-Pakistani relationship is further explained by the liberal school of international relations. This school holds that economic interdependence and regional institutions can reduce the possibility and scope of conflict, through the trust developed by routinization of dialogue within an institution and the greater economic costs of politico-military tensions. Liberal theory highlights the absence of these factors as reasons for the persisting Indo-Pakistani mutual desire for militarized solutions to their disputes.[6]

By contrast, the realist school of international relations is most challenged by these developments. The nuclear revolution thesis, as advanced by realist scholars, attests that the introduction of nuclear deterrence to a bilateral rivalry will deter both parties from seeking military solutions to their disputes, through fear of starting a potentially atomic escalation spiral; "states are not likely to run major risks for minor gains."[7] The 1999 Kargil war, 2019 India-Pakistan near-war, and continuing trend of Indo-Pakistani conventional military planning contradict these assumptions. Indeed, a central theme of their planning is to test and manipulate the nuclear threshold of the rival.

Limited War in Theory and South Asian Practice

For a limited war to remain such, adversaries must tacitly cooperate in agreeing to respect certain boundaries to the conflict, even as they are engaged in hostilities. There are three elements of a conflict around which these boundaries are set: Political aims, means, and geographic scope. Political aims form the most important of these three. As it contains the motivations and objectives of the state in the conflict, it determines the other two elements. Varying aims could, for example, include compelling an adversary to cease military encroachments on a segment of disputed territory or to permanently annex adversary territory. Means refers to the qualitative and quantitative characteristics of the military capabilities employed by the state, as defined in destructive potential. Geographic scope involves the tacitly agreed theater of conflict.[8]

The tacit boundaries in each dimension have been termed "focal points" by Schelling.[9] The belligerents must be able to mutually recognize these boundaries without directly communicating them to each other; such direct communication could carry implications of state weakness, in that it may be physically unable to expand the war past these agreed limits, incentivizing the adversary to escalate the conflict to achieve its preferred outcome. For these boundaries to have the greatest chance of mutual recognition, they must form natural Rubicons. Indeed, Schelling famously highlighted the example of a river bisecting a conflict theater as an example of a focal point, in which the river would form the natural boundary.

Crossing it would be independently seen by both parties as deliberately escalatory, with few or no other natural Rubicons to limit further escalation.[10]

As well as an explanation of the focal point concept, this river analogy serves as an example of the geographic scope element of limited war. Between nuclear rivals, the clearest focal point in the means category is the threshold between conventional and nuclear war, as opposed to thresholds within "limited" nuclear wars.[11] Finally, the geographic scope and means elements must correspond to the political objective. If the political aim is to compel an adversary to retreat from a few kilometers of occupied border territory, then a mass mobilization of ground, air, naval, and nuclear forces, across multiple theaters, will strongly suggest to the adversary that this declared political aim is a ruse and the real goal is much more ambitious.

India-Pakistan relations since 1998 have supplied much of the corpus of modern case studies on limited wars.[12] Following their nuclear tests and declaration of overt nuclear weapons states in 1998, New Delhi and Islamabad publicly affirmed that military solutions were no longer possible to their political disputes, due to the mutually perceived risk of any level of conflict spiraling to nuclear war. However, on Pakistan's side, this statement later turned out to have only reflected the sentiments of the civilian political leadership. A cabal of senior Pakistani military officers took the different view that mutually assured destruction could enable Pakistani conventional adventurism. In this reading, India would concede Pakistani occupation attempts rather than risk war in a nuclear environment.

Upon discovery of the Pakistani incursions, however, Indian decision-makers resolved to forcibly evict the intruders and restore the *status quo ex ante*. In doing so, they ordered Indian military leaders not to cross the Line of Control (LoC), as this was the clearest focal point that Pakistan would implicitly recognize as a sign of the limited Indian scope of the conflict. Indian forces were also concentrated on the areas of incursion, and nuclear weapons did not play a meaningful part in Indian war planning. New Delhi thus successfully signaled to Islamabad its focal points in political objective, geographic scope, and means, permitting the war to be concluded without significant escalation.[13]

Indian Conventional Doctrine toward Pakistan

Since the Kargil conflict, Indian dissatisfaction with its preparedness for short-notice, high-intensity limited conventional conflicts has become a principal theme of its doctrinal thinking and planning. This discomfort was compounded by the outcomes of subsequent incidents. In the 2001–2002 crisis, a Pakistan-sponsored terrorist attack on the Indian Parliament led to a massive Indian military buildup along Pakistan border areas. The length of time it took the Indian armed forces to mobilize permitted a sufficient Pakistani counter-mobilization, forcing a stalemate and mutual demobilization. In 2004, the Indian Army released details of a new "Cold Start" operational concept, featuring new "integrated battle group" (IBG) formations.[14] The design and functioning of an IBG has been reported as "self-contained and highly-mobile 'battle groups,' with Russian-origin T-90S tanks and upgraded T-72 M1 tanks at their core, adequately backed by air cover and artillery fire assaults, for rapid thrusts into enemy territory within 96 hours."[15]

These IBGs would be supported by reorganizations of the existing larger Army formations. As facing Pakistan, these consist of three "strike corps" designated as the I, II, and XXI corps, respectively. Comprising around 45,000–50,000 personnel each, these corps were designed for the initial breakthrough role now being assigned to IBGs. However, the extended timeframe for mobilizing such a large formation, as evidenced in the 2001–2002 crisis, meant that Army planners looked to IBG-like formations for a more agile alternative. The other legacy formation was seven defensive or holding corps of similar size. These were intended to block Pakistani invasion attempts and then shift to supporting the strike corps as necessary.

Under the IBG reforms, these holding corps would receive additional offensive capabilities, and now provide the initial breakthrough role under a new title of "pivot" corps. The Indian Army would next release IBGs to exploit the gaps generated by the pivot corps, and then rapidly proceed among multiple vectors with enough firepower, defensive capabilities, and mobility to act as autonomous divisions potentially separated from the main force. The destabilization in enemy lines caused by the unpredictable IBG vector lines, plus their role in widening the conventional breakthrough areas, would then permit follow-on Indian strike corps to pour through these gaps to ensure local enemy organizational collapse.

The next, and most recent, iteration of Indian land warfare operational art has been delivered through the Indian Army Land Warfare Doctrine, produced in November 2018. This builds upon the thinking of the IBG concept, to the extent that it plans reformation of all existing divisions into IBGs. The doctrine states that, in conventional war, "all combat operations will be as Integrated Battle Groups (IBGs)."[16] In operations against Pakistan, IBGs will be tasked "with the aim of destroying the centre of gravity of the adversary and securing spatial gains."[17]

The IBG model itself will also be revised. Firstly, the standard base model IBG will be reduced in size. The previous size of around 15,500 troops, around that of a division, will be reduced to a maximum of under 10,000.[18] The composition of forces will remain largely the same, incorporating "infantry, armoured, artillery, air-defence, and support units, all of which would be backed by attack helicopters."[19] Secondly, there will be variability in IBG structures depending upon their mission.[20] Examples could be IBGs with a greater concentration of heavy armor and air assault elements for initial breakthrough operations, and light mechanized infantry-focused IBGs for follow-on forces.

The overarching vision is of a higher number of smaller and inherently more mobile IBGs, to serve as both the leading edge and follow-on forces for a cross-border assault. The increased number of IBGs could theoretically promise a similar greater number of breakthrough points and axes of advance, further confusing enemy strategic planners as per the logic of the 2004 Cold Start Concept. This objective would be further complemented by the compression of operation sequencing, from the three stages of Cold Start (pivot corps breakthrough, IBG follow-on forces, and then commitment of strike forces to consolidate gains) to effectively a single indistinguishable stage of IBG breakthrough/follow-on forces; as the doctrine states, "all combat operations will be as IBGs."[21]

At the same time, the 2018 doctrine strongly implies deeper operations inside Pakistan and Pakistan-administered Kashmir than the 50–80 km limit of Cold Start. With regard to operations across the Line of Control, the doctrine-led modernization will "enhance our punitive response options to greater depth, effect, sophistication and precision."[22] Whereas securing and defending limited spatial gains inside Pakistan was the intent behind Cold Start, the new formulation of "destroying the centre of gravity of the adversary and securing spatial gains" is more ambitious; it is difficult to imagine that Pakistan's ultimate military integrity, or "centre of gravity," would be destroyed by the 50–80 km gains of the past.[23] Moreover, Army briefings on likely axes of advance now feature an intention to "penetrate towards the large towns and cities in Pakistan's heartland."[24] While the doctrine does not specifically state that territory seized will still be toward a political objective of near-term withdrawal in return for Pakistani concessions on supporting terrorist actors, the directions and extended depth of this planned operation will raise questions as to whether this objective still applies. India's conventional war planning, therefore, is steadily departing from the limited war principles evidenced in the Kargil war of seeking the most obvious focal points to signal the limitation of political objective, geographic scope, and means to Pakistan.

Indian Conventional Doctrine toward China

Since 2004, Indian conventional planning toward China has been shifting from a posture of deterrence-by-denial toward one of deterrence-by-punishment. The pre-2004 approach involved deliberate underinvestment in Indian transport links near the border with China. This followed an Indian assumption that Indian forces would be quickly overrun in any conflict with China, and that China could be more credibly delayed by the poor quality of Indian border roads. This delay would provide sufficient time for Indian forces to be mobilized from its interior to push back the Chinese incursions.

However, since then, India has gradually shifted its doctrinal approach to China to deterrence-by-punishment. New Delhi is gradually increasing its ground and air forces along its land border with China. Two new divisions—the Fifty-Sixth and Seventy-First Mountain Divisions, which encompass around 35,000 troops—were raised for Arunachal Pradesh defense missions in 2009–2010. The divisions have been equipped with artillery and T-90 tanks, matériel normally used for penetrating assaults. Moreover, the establishment of the Seventeenth Mountain Strike Corps adds approximately another 24,000 troops to India's ground posture against China.[25] This new corps will be India's first China-specific strike corps built to launch forward offensives into Chinese territory.

The IBG concept is also being applied within the China theater, although the restructuring process is reportedly now on hold due to Covid-19 restrictions.[26] In addition, in August 2016, the Indian Army positioned 120 T-72M1 tanks in the plains of Ladakh in eastern Kashmir, an area that witnessed Chinese advances in the 1962 war between the two countries. Once these new formations are fully raised, India will be able to draw on an estimated 200,000 forces in the Western, Central, and Eastern Army Commands close to China border areas.[27]

However, there are significant challenges to this Indian effort. The overall Army staffing shortfall has meant that most of these new forces have been reallocated from those facing Pakistan or other theaters.[28] China has not been deterred by these upgrades, as evidenced by its successful army occupation of areas of Indian-administered Ladakh since April 2020.[29] Moreover, it is continuing to strengthen its permanent army, air force, and logistics position in border areas facing India.[30] This further reduces the likelihood of the Indian Army's ability to achieve a surprise breakthrough to seize limited tracts of Chinese-administered Tibet, as the organizing purpose of the Mountain Strike Corps. While the quality of India's border roads is improving, their condition still affects Indian Army mobilization and deployment timeframes.

Finally, in the event of escalation with either Pakistan or China, the Indian Army only had sufficient munitions for around ten days of "intense" conflict as of 2020.[31] This could moderate the ambitions of decision-makers in choosing whether to risk valuable ammunition on a limited salient into adversary territory or devote it to blocking operations instead. However, the increased propensity of Indian decision-makers toward risk-taking behavior— as evidenced in the Pulwama-Balakot crisis—means an IBG-led conflict cannot be ruled out.

Pakistani Conventional Doctrine

The Pakistan Army is already largely organized around a deterrence-by-denial concept.[32] Of its nine corps, up to seven are dedicated to India-centric missions, and 80% of Pakistan's army divisions are positioned close to border areas with India. The IV, XXX, and XXXI

Corps are headquartered in Lahore, Gujranwala, and Bahawalpur respectively, and mandated with blocking early Indian incursions in their respective areas across Punjab. The X Corps is assigned a similar mission for defending the LoC and Siachen, while the V Corps is tasked with preventing potential further-reaching Indian advances to cut off Lahore-Karachi transport and communications links.[33] Since 1989, Pakistan planning for a major Indian incursion has also involved launching counterattacks nearly simultaneously with blocking operations.[34] The I and II Corps are "armour-heavy strike corps, intended to implement the doctrine of the 'riposte' by penetrating Indian territory and, if possible, occupying limited areas."[35] These Corps face northwest India and Indian-administered Kashmir respectively. Elements of the IV, XXX, and XXXI Corps could also support these counterattack formations.[36]

Despite these seemingly robust conventional deterrence-by-denial capabilities, Pakistan has adopted two further measures in response to the Indian Cold Start concept from 2004 to the present. The first is intensified conventional war planning to block or quickly evict these potential Indian intrusions. Pakistan's military adopted a policy in 2012 mandating the deployment of a quarter of battalion reserves immediately after any significant terrorist atrocity in India.[37] To ensure its forces adequately meet the specific IBG threat, Pakistan also instituted a series of "Azm-e-Nau" (New Resolve) military exercises from 2009 to 2013. A new doctrinal approach was conceptualized from the experience of these exercises, and was tested in the final Azm-e-Nau IV exercise in 2013. This operation integrated armor, artillery, air defense, and civil aviation capabilities, alongside deployment of F-7P, F-16, JF-17, and Mirage aircraft. Pakistani officials claimed that they were able to mobilize forces in a shorter timeframe than envisioned by India for IBGs.[38] Moreover, an assessment published on a Pakistan military website claimed that Azm-e-Nau proved that Pakistan was able to conduct these major operations against India despite simultaneously deploying significant forces to pacifying Afghanistan border areas.[39]

The trends in Indian and Pakistani threat assessments and accompanying force positioning also favor Pakistani deterrence-by-denial. Overall, both states field roughly 270,000 Army personnel against each other. However, these include all Pakistani armored formations. By contrast, some of India's armored formations are necessarily tasked for China-centric missions, reducing its qualitative capabilities vis-à-vis Pakistan.[40] Moreover, the Taliban's assumption of power in Afghanistan means that Pakistan will likely not require its existing heavy military presence in its western theater, freeing up even more Pakistani forces for the Indian theater. India has further retasked its I Corps, one of its three strike corps, toward more China-centric missions in Ladakh.[41] The Indian Army also had a staffing shortage of nearly 28,000 personnel, or close to two divisions, as of 2019.[42] This reduction in India's forces dedicated for Pakistan-centric missions further improves Pakistan's chances in blocking the kind of rapid cross-border operations which Indian Army conventional planning is increasingly being organized around.

The second major Pakistani response to Cold Start has certain parallels with India, in attempting to manipulate their mutual conventional-nuclear threshold. Just as India's IBG conceptual development aims to raise the nuclear threshold by creating room on the escalation ladder for ambitious conventional ground incursions, Pakistan seeks to lower the threshold by including Nasr tactical nuclear weapons within its planning for an IBG-led Indian incursion. The role of Nasr in Pakistan's nuclear doctrine preceded the Cold Start concept, and is discussed in more detail in Chapter 10. Nevertheless, it forms part of an overall conventional and nuclear concept publicly outlined by a leading Pakistani official and in the *Pakistan Army Green Book* as "Quid Pro Quo Plus."[43] This specifies that any Indian attack will be met with a more escalatory Pakistani response. This Pakistani response need not be nuclear.

The *Green Book* author cited the February 2019 Indian airstrike on one target in Pakistan, and the Pakistani conventional air attack on six targets in India in response, as an example of this calculated escalation.[44] Moreover, the precise scenario in an Indian cross-border attack at which Pakistani decision-makers would contemplate using tactical nuclear weapons appears to be an open debate among its officials and experts.[45]

In their conventional doctrinal development, both states are therefore seeking to rapidly escalate to gain the initiative. Within these concepts, these states are discarding key focal point tenets of escalation control in limited war, especially that of geographic scope in crossing the border or LoC and seizing adversary territory. The risk of unplanned escalation is elevated by this departure from the Kargil war adherence to ensuring the limited political objective, geographic scope, and means were consistent with each other and clear to the adversary. This point is especially underlined by mutual intentions to test the nuclear threshold of their rival. India's plans to quickly cross the border and seize an unclear volume of territory of a rival with very little strategic depth would likely prompt early Pakistani discussions on nuclear options. Pakistani intentions to involve the Nasr in its response to a major Indian incursion would heighten the pre-existing Indian debate on its nuclear no-first-use commitment. Recent serving Indian officials and experts have suggested that the doctrine is now one of ambiguity or that adversary nuclear preparations could qualify as first-use.[46]

Conventional Technological Transformation

The similar intentions of Indian and Pakistani conventional planning to quickly enter adversary territory and terminate the conflict just short of nuclear escalation is further evidenced by their key technology acquisitions. Both states are investing in precision-guided munitions (PGMs) to rapidly overwhelm local defenses, regardless of the risk that these weapons could be misinterpreted as constituting a nuclear attack. This danger is further amplified by the fact that several of these technologies are custom-designed for destroying targets relevant to adversary nuclear forces, such as hardened shelters and command-and-control bunkers. Relatedly, as these technologies reach maturity and full integration into national armed forces, the increased level of military accuracy which decision-makers can expect may incentivize conventional strikes on adversary military dual-use or nuclear bases. Attacking adversary military nuclear platforms and bases are categorized as "counterforce" operations, as distinguished from population centers under "countervalue" operations.[47] Both of these terms normally assume nuclear strikes on these targets. There is a variety of rival assets that could qualify as counterforce targets, including "hard" counterforce targets like "reinforced missile silos and command-and-communication bunkers" and "soft" targets such as "airfields, submarine bases, and military posts."[48]

However, the direction of Indo-Pakistani doctrinal and technology development suggests that limited *conventional* counterforce attacks could be perceived as an increasingly viable option by its decision-makers. Using such an operation to escalate an existing crisis would align with Pakistan's Quid Pro Quo Plus concept. It would similarly dovetail with India's longstanding efforts to elevate the nuclear threshold with Pakistan, through developing consequential conventional attack options that leave Pakistan with a binary response of concession or conventional war potentially leading to nuclear escalation.

India and Pakistan are integrating a wide variety of PGMs into their defense planning. In December 2021, India tested the 700-km-range Pralay conventional ballistic missile, which Indian officials portrayed as being the first ballistic missile tasked for long-range conventional strike operations.[49] India is also fielding multiple variants of the Pinaka conventional multi-barrel rocket launch (MBRL) system, with a maximum reach of 75 km. Pinakas are tasked with artillery-type functions of bombarding adversary positions before the primary armored offensive.[50] The Prahaar, as a third conventional ballistic missile model, has a range of 150 km.[51]

India is also investing in cruise missiles, including the Brahmos supersonic cruise missile with air-, sea-, and ground-launched variants. From an initial claimed range of 290 km, India is working to progressively extend the range of new Brahmos models to 1,500 km.[52] New Delhi is developing other PGMs, such as a 1000-kg conventional air-delivered glide bomb, and a separate 450-kg laser-guided bomb. Indian officials have indicated that they view these munitions as key to achieving consequential conventional strikes; for example, the Brahmos-II (K) variant and the laser-guided bomb are both designed to destroy hardened targets, such as sensitive command-and-control bunkers.[53]

Pakistan's PGMs feature a stronger concentration on cruise missile platforms. These include C-802 antiship missiles; the 450-km-range Babur 1A and 700-km-range Babur 1B cruise missiles; and the 350-km-range Ra'ad and 600-km-range Ra'ad-II cruise missiles. Each of these models is potentially nuclear-capable, and the Nasr could also be employed for conventional bombardment.[54] As the comparative army deployments of India and Pakistan and India and China appear likely to produce stalemate rather than the limited and defensible breakthrough which India and Pakistan plan around, this incentivizes decision-makers to view standoff PGMs as the way to attain the impactful conventional blows they desire in a conflict. As Indian and Pakistani strategic communities tend to distrust stated conventional designations for PGMs, and assume that they hold secret nuclear missions, PGM launch preparations could prompt unplanned escalation in a crisis. The dangers from these developments are only intensified by the increasing reliance of both states on these types of munitions and concepts of conventional operations.

Conclusion

India and Pakistan are deliberately moving away from conventional military planning that seeks to identify focal points that would signal the limited scope of any conflict to each other, and thus safeguard against escalation approaching the nuclear level. Their conventional army planning focuses on rapidly seizing narrow tracts of adversary territory, breaking with one of the key focal points of the Kargil war. Steadily improving PGMs offer another dangerous option of deep conventional strikes that pinpoint potentially nuclear or dual-use bases. Moreover, many of these PGM platforms are also assigned to nuclear strike missions and more are perceived to be by the rival. The goal of conventional military planning, as most recently evidenced in the 2019 near-war, is to push the adversary into self-deterrence against escalating to the level of conventional or nuclear war. As dangerous as this is, developments in Indian and Pakistani strategic thought include targeting nuclear or dual-use facilities in conventional counterforce operations. They also feature treating nuclear *signaling*, such as adversary nuclear force preparations, as equivalent to first use. These trends significantly threaten regional and global security.

To reduce the dangers emanating from these developments, India and Pakistan should properly employ some of their existing CBMs. These include using the crisis hotline between Indian and Pakistani director-general of military operations (DGMOs) to clarify conditions and organize climbdowns, as opposed to trading insults. Pakistan and India should also develop new CBMs, such as visible demarcation of conventional from nuclear platforms, through physical separation and distinguishing livery. The most ambitious measure would be agreeing quantitative limits to deployment of conventional platforms against each other, similar to the conventional forces in Europe treaty. However, such an agreement would have to be necessarily asymmetric, for India to be able to sustain adequate defenses against both China and Pakistan. Moreover, it would require binding guarantees from Pakistan, as potentially verified by international third parties, that it was no longer hosting and sponsoring anti-India terrorist groups. This initiative would demonstrate to India that Pakistan was not seeking to use these groups as a loophole to the agreement.

Finally, reflecting the principally constructivist nature of these conventional military risks, both states would need to internally inculcate new "lessons" about their strategic past. These would primarily include recognizing that deterrence-by-denial, rather than seizure of tracts of land, is the most realistic and responsible conventional concept to apply. There is scope for optimism: The rivals have been able to strike important CBMs in their past, which have held throughout crises to the current day.

Notes

1 Sameer Joshi, "How Pakistan Planned to Hit India Back for Balakot—The Mission, the Fighters, the Tactics," *The Print*, September 14, 2019, https://theprint.in/defence/how-pakistan-planned-to-hit-india-back-for-balakot-the-mission-the-fighters-the-tactics/291522/. All chapter hyperlinks are accessed December 27, 2021, unless otherwise stated.

2 The 1969 Sino-Soviet border war formed the first example. See Michael S. Gerson, *The Sino-Soviet Border Conflict: Deterrence, Escalation, and the Threat of Nuclear War in 1969* (Arlington, VA: Center for Naval Analyses, 2010). The existing scholarship does recognize that the 1999 Kargil War and the 1969 Sino-Russian War were qualitatively different from other crises/incidents between nuclear-armed rivals. See, for example, Abhijnan Rej, "S(c)helling in Kashmir: Bargaining under the Nuclear Shadow," *Washington Quarterly* 42, no. 2 (2019): 179.

3 Frank O'Donnell, "India's Nuclear Counter-revolution: Nuclear Learning and the Future of Deterrence," *Nonproliferation Review* 26, no. 5–6 (2019): 407–426.

4 Andrew Linklater, *Beyond Realism and Marxism: Critical Theory and International Relations* (New York: St. Martin's Press, 1990), 7.

5 Richard Shapcott, "Critical Theory," in *Oxford Handbook of International Relations*, eds. Christian Reus-Smit and Duncan Snidal (Oxford: Oxford University Press, 2008): 327–345.

6 Michael W. Doyle, "Three Pillars of the Liberal Peace," *American Political Science Review* 99, no. 3 (August 2005): 463–466.

7 Scott D. Sagan and Kenneth N. Waltz, *The Spread of Nuclear Weapons: A Debate Renewed* (New York: W.W. Norton, 2003), 6–7.

8 Jeffrey A. Larsen, "Limited War and the Advent of Nuclear Weapons," in *On Limited Nuclear War in the 21st Century*, eds. Jeffrey A. Larsen and Kerry M. Kartchner (Stanford, CA: Stanford University Press, 2014), 8–10.

9 Thomas C. Schelling, *The Strategy of Conflict* (Cambridge, MA: Harvard University Press, 1960), 57.

10 Thomas C. Schelling, "Bargaining, Communication and Limited War," *Conflict Resolution* 1, no. 1 (March 1957): 19–36.

11 Thomas C. Schelling, *Arms and Influence (2008 Edition, orig. 1966)* (New Haven: Yale University Press, 2008), 130–141.

12 See, for example, Walter C. Ladwig III, "A Cold Start for Hot Wars? The Indian Army's New Limited War Doctrine," *International Security* 32, no. 3 (Winter 2007/8): 158–190; and Peter R. Lavoy, ed., *Asymmetric Warfare in South Asia: The Causes and Consequences of the Kargil War* (Cambridge: Cambridge University Press, 2009).

13 Šumit Ganguly, *Deadly Impasse: Indo-Pakistani Relations at the Dawn of a New Century* (Cambridge: Cambridge University Press, 2016), 31–42.

14 Ali Ahmed, *India's Doctrine Puzzle: Limiting War in South Asia* (New Delhi: Routledge, 2014), 58; Ladwig, "A Cold Start for Hot Wars?," 158–190.

15 Ahmed, *India's Doctrine Puzzle*, 58.

16 Indian Army, *Land Warfare Doctrine – 2018* (New Delhi: Indian Army, 2018), 4, https://www.indianarmy.nic.in/Site/NewsDetail/frmNewsDetails.aspx?n=bniEtbbo9LN7kb4q3kupGg==&NewsID=aa9ndruuIAhHn3Le4Tp7sA==.

17 *Ibid.*, 5.

18 The scale reduction is magnified by the fact that this 15,500 calculation excludes non-combat support forces, which when included brings the average division to around 20,000. The calculation of new IBGs amounting to less than 10,000 *includes* these support forces. See Rahul Bedi, "Indian Army Announces New Land Warfare Doctrine," *Jane's Defence Weekly*, December 21, 2018, https://www.janes.com/article/85381/indian-army-announces-new-land-warfare-doctrine; and Franz-Stefan Gady, "Is the Indian Military Capable of Executing the Cold Start Doctrine?," *The Diplomat*, January 29, 2019, https://thediplomat.com/2019/01/is-the-indian-military-capable-of-executing-the-cold-start-doctrine/.

19 Bedi, "Indian Army Announces New Land Warfare Doctrine." See also Gady, "Is the Indian Military Capable of Executing the Cold Start Doctrine?"

20 Indian Army, *Land Warfare Doctrine*, 5.

21 *Ibid.*, 4.

22 *Ibid.*, 3.

23 *Ibid.*, 5.

24 Ajai Shukla, "Army Chief says Military must Prepare for Cold Start," *Business Standard*, January 14, 2017, https://www.business-standard.com/article/current-affairs/army-chief-says-military-must-prepare-for-cold-start-117011301174_1.html.

25 Pradip R. Sagar, "India Needs a Dedicated Mountain Strike Corps to Tackle China," *The Week (India)*, July 4, 2021, https://www.theweek.in/theweek/cover/2021/06/25/india-needs-a-dedicated-mountain-strike-corps-to-tackle-china.html.

26 Press Trust of India, "Roll out of Integrated Battle Groups Delayed due to Covid-19: Army Chief," *Business Standard*, May 10, 2020, https://www.business-standard.com/article/current-affairs/roll-out-of-integrated-battle-groups-delayed-due-covid-19-army-chief-120051000597_1.html.

27 Frank O'Donnell, *Stabilizing Sino-Indian Security Relations: Managing the Strategic Rivalry after Doklam* (Beijing: Carnegie-Tsinghua Center for Global Policy, 2018), 6, https://carnegieendowment.org/files/CP335_ODonnell_final.pdf. See also Sagar, "India Needs a Dedicated Mountain Strike Corps."

28 Sagar, "India Needs a Dedicated Mountain Strike Corps."

29 Ajai Shukla, "Playing into Chinese Hands in Ladakh," *Business Standard*, August 7, 2020, https://www.business-standard.com/article/opinion/playing-into-china-s-hands-in-ladakh-120080700061_1.html; Sushant Singh, "From Ladakh to Eastern Sector, Latest Satellite Imagery Shows Additional Chinese Pressure on India," *The India Cable*, December 21, 2021, https://www.theindiacable.com/p/from-ladakh-to-eastern-sector-latest.

30 Singh, "From Ladakh to Eastern Sector."

31 Rajat Pandit, "Army Stocking up Munitions for 40-day War," *Times of India*, January 27, 2020, https://timesofindia.indiatimes.com/india/army-stocking-up-munitions-for-40-day-war/articleshow/73647518.cms.

32 Maimuna Ashraf, "Pakistan's Consolidating Conventional Deterrence: An Assessment," *South Asian Voices*, December 7, 2018, https://southasianvoices.org/pakistan-conventional-deterrence-assessment/.

33 "Pakistan Army Order of Battle," *GlobalSecurity.Org*, November 7, 2011, http://www.globalsecurity.org/military/world/pakistan/army-orbat.htm; "Pakistan – Army," *Jane's Sentinel Security Assessment – South Asia*, May 21, 2021, https://customer-janes-com.ezproxy.library.tufts.edu/Janes/Display/JWARA216-SAS.

34 Francisco Aguilar et al., *An Introduction to Pakistan's Military* (Cambridge, MA: Belfer Center for Science and International Affairs, 2011), 10, https://www.belfercenter.org/sites/default/files/legacy/files/Pakistan-Military-final-B.pdf.

35 "Pakistan – Army," *Jane's Sentinel Security Assessment – South Asia*.

36 *Ibid.*

37 Walter C. Ladwig III, "Indian Military Modernization and Conventional Deterrence in South Asia," *Journal of Strategic Studies* 38, no. 5 (2015), 746.

38 "Pakistan Develops New War Doctrine to Counter India," *India Today*, June 17, 2013, http://indiatoday.intoday.in/story/pakistan-develops-new-war-doctrine-to-counter-india/1/280569.html.

39 Muhammad Khan, "From Cold Start to Cold Storage!" *Hilal*, November 2013, https://www.ispr.gov.pk/front/t-article.asp?id=87. This article link is now inactive, but the article text is now available at https://www.thefreelibrary.com/From+Cold+Start+to+Cold+Storage!-a0353399765.

40 Ladwig, "Indian Military Modernization," 755–756.

41 Ajai Shukla, "Army's Pivot to the North," *Business Standard*, January 7, 2021, https://www.business-standard.com/article/opinion/army-s-pivot-to-the-north-121010701572_1.html.

42 Press Trust of India, "Armed Forces Facing Shortage of Nearly 60,000 Personnel, says Govt," *Hindustan Times*, December 27, 2017, https://www.hindustantimes.com/india-news/armed-forces-facing-shortage-of-nearly-60-000-personnel-says-govt/story-0Uc1XYkmLgBmMSOY0QDLZO.html.

43 "Keynote Address and Discussion Session with Lieutenant General (Retd.) Khalid Kidwai, Advisor, National Command Authority; and former Director-General, Strategic Plans Division, Pakistan," International Institute for Strategic Studies, London, February 6, 2020, https://www.iiss.org/-/media/files/events/2020/transcript-of-lt-general-kidwais-keynote-address-as-delivered—iiss-ciss-workshop-6feb20.pdf?la=en&hash=4EB4E4D0D7BFA4A0551AF178BA23357929BD42E5; Maria Sultan, "Cross Domain Deterrence - The Pulwama Attack: Limited War & Nuclear Implications Reestablishing Deterrence & High Order War," in *Pakistan Army Green Book 2020*, ed. Maj. Gen. Fida Hussain Malik (Rawalpindi: Pakistan Army General Headquarters, 2020): 75–91.

44 Sultan, "Cross Domain Deterrence," 78.

45 Zafar Khan, "Pakistan's Nuclear First Use Doctrine: Obsessions and Obstacles," *Contemporary Security Policy* 36, no. 1 (2015): 149–170.

46 O'Donnell, "India's Nuclear Counter-revolution," 416–419.

47 Dennis M. Drew and Donald M. Snow, *Making Strategy: An Introduction to National Security Processes and Problems* (Maxwell AFB, AL: Air University Press, 1988), 129, https://media.defense.gov/2017/Apr/06/2001728005/-1/-1/0/B_0023_DREW_SNOW_MAKING_STRATEGY.PDF.

48 *Ibid.*, 129. See also Christopher Clary and Vipin Narang, "India's Counterforce Temptations: Strategic Dilemmas, Doctrine, and Capabilities," *International Security* 43, no. 3 (Winter 2018/19): 7–52.

49 Shishir Gupta, "'Pralay', India's First Conventional Ballistic Missile, Test-fired Again," *Hindustan Times*, December 23, 2021, https://www.hindustantimes.com/india-news/pralay-india-s-second-conventional-ballistic-missile-testfired-101640235805392.html.

50 Sushant Kulkarni, "Developed by Two Pune-based Facilities of DRDO, Pinaka-ER Missile and Ancillary Systems Tested Successfully," *Indian Express*, December 16, 2021, https://indianexpress.com/article/cities/pune/pune-drdo-pinaka-er-missile-ancillary-systems-tested-7675366/.

51 Hemant Kumar Rout, "India Successfully Test Fires Short-range Tactical Ballistic Missile Prahaar," *New Indian Express*, September 20, 2018, https://www.newindianexpress.com/nation/2018/sep/20/india-successfully-test-fires-short-range-tactical-ballistic-missile-prahaar-1874747.html.

52 Snehesh Alex Philip, "India Now Working on 1,500-km Range BrahMos Supersonic Cruise Missile," *The Print*, November 24, 2020, https://theprint.in/defence/india-now-working-on-1500-km-range-brahmos-supersonic-cruise-missile/550924/.

53 Frank O'Donnell and Debalina Ghoshal, "Managing Indian Deterrence: Pressures upon Credible Minimum Deterrence and Nuclear Policy Options," *Nonproliferation Review* 26, nos. 1–2 (2019): 429–430.

54 Usman Ansari, "Pakistan Navy Test-fires Land Attack Missile," *Defense News*, December 21, 2012, https://defenceforumindia.com/threads/pakistan-navy-test-fired-missiles.45465/#post-640848; "Pakistan Conducts Successful Test of Enhanced Version of Home-grown Cruise Missile: ISPR," *Dawn*, December 21, 2021, https://www.dawn.com/news/1665039; Gabriel Dominguez, "Pakistan Test-launches Longer-range Variant of Ra'ad II ALCM," *Jane's Defence Weekly*, February 19, 2020, https://www.janes.com/defence-news/news-detail/pakistan-test-launches-longer-range-variant-of-raad-ii-alcm.

Bibliography

"Keynote Address and Discussion Session with Lieutenant General (Retd.) Khalid Kidwai, Advisor, National Command Authority; and former Director-General, Strategic Plans Division, Pakistan." International Institute for Strategic Studies, London, February 6, 2020. https://www.iiss.org/-/media/files/events/2020/transcript-of-lt-general-kidwais-keynote-address-as-delivered—iiss-ciss-workshop-6feb20.pdf?la=en&hash=4EB4E4D0D7BFA4A0551AF178BA23357929BD42E5.

"Pakistan – Army." *Jane's Sentinel Security Assessment – South Asia*, May 21, 2021, https://customer-janes-com.ezproxy.library.tufts.edu/Janes/Display/JWARA216-SAS.

"Pakistan Army Order of Battle." *GlobalSecurity.Org*, November 7, 2011. http://www.globalsecurity.org/military/world/pakistan/army-orbat.htm.

"Pakistan Conducts Successful Test of Enhanced Version of Home-grown Cruise Missile: ISPR." *Dawn*, December 21, 2021. https://www.dawn.com/news/1665039.

Aguilar, Francisco, Randy Bell, Natalie Black, Sauce Falk, Sasha Rogers, and Aki Peritz. *An Introduction to Pakistan's Military*. Cambridge, MA: Belfer Center for Science and International Affairs, 2011. https://www.belfercenter.org/sites/default/files/legacy/files/Pakistan-Military-final-B.pdf.

Ahmed, Ali. *India's Doctrine Puzzle: Limiting War in South Asia*. New Delhi: Routledge, 2014.

Ansari, Usman. "Pakistan Navy Test-fires Land Attack Missile." *Defense News*, December 21, 2012. https://defenceforumindia.com/threads/pakistan-navy-test-fired-missiles.45465/#post-640848.

Ashraf, Maimuna. "Pakistan's Consolidating Conventional Deterrence: An Assessment." *South Asian Voices*, December 7, 2018. https://southasianvoices.org/pakistan-conventional-deterrence-assessment/.

Bedi, Rahul. "Indian Army Announces New Land Warfare Doctrine." *Jane's Defence Weekly*, December 21, 2018. https://www.janes.com/article/85381/indian-army-announces-new-land-warfare-doctrine.

Clary, Christopher, and Vipin Narang. "India's Counterforce Temptations: Strategic Dilemmas, Doctrine, and Capabilities." *International Security* 43, no. 3 (Winter 2018/19): 7–52.

Dominguez, Gabriel. "Pakistan Test-launches Longer-range Variant of Ra'ad II ALCM." *Jane's Defence Weekly*, February 19, 2020. https://www.janes.com/defence-news/news-detail/pakistan-test-launches-longer-range-variant-of-raad-ii-alcm.

Doyle, Michael W. "Three Pillars of the Liberal Peace." *American Political Science Review* 99, no. 3 (August 2005): 463–466.

Drew, Dennis M., and Donald M. Snow. *Making Strategy: An Introduction to National Security Processes and Problems*. Maxwell AFB, AL: Air University Press, 1988. https://media.defense.gov/2017/Apr/06/2001728005/-1/-1/0/B_0023_DREW_SNOW_MAKING_STRATEGY.PDF.

Gady, Franz-Stefan. "Is the Indian Military Capable of Executing the Cold Start Doctrine?" *The Diplomat*, January 29, 2019. https://thediplomat.com/2019/01/is-the-indian-military-capable-of-executing-the-cold-start-doctrine/.

Ganguly, Šumit. *Deadly Impasse: Indo-Pakistani Relations at the Dawn of a New Century*. Cambridge: Cambridge University Press, 2016.

Gerson, Michael S. *The Sino-Soviet Border Conflict: Deterrence, Escalation, and the Threat of Nuclear War in 1969*. Arlington, VA: Center for Naval Analyses, 2010.

Gupta, Shishir. "'Pralay', India's First Conventional Ballistic Missile, Test-fired Again." *Hindustan Times*, December 23, 2021. https://www.hindustantimes.com/india-news/pralay-india-s-second-conventional-ballistic-missile-testfired-101640235805392.html.

Joshi, Sameer. "How Pakistan Planned to Hit India Back for Balakot — The Mission, the Fighters, the Tactics." *The Print*, September 14, 2019. https://theprint.in/defence/how-pakistan-planned-to-hit-india-back-for-balakot-the-mission-the-fighters-the-tactics/291522/.

Khan, Zafar. "Pakistan's Nuclear First Use Doctrine: Obsessions and Obstacles." *Contemporary Security Policy* 36, no. 1 (2015): 149–170.

Khan, Muhammad. "From Cold Start to Cold Storage!" *Hilal*, November 2013. https://www.ispr.gov.pk/front/t-article.asp?id=87.

Kulkarni, Sushant. "Developed by Two Pune-Based Facilities of DRDO, Pinaka-ER Missile and Ancillary Systems Tested Successfully." Indian Express, December 16, 2021. https://indianexpress.com/article/cities/pune/pune-drdo-pinaka-er-missile-ancillary-systems-tested-7675366/.

Ladwig, Walter C, III. "A Cold Start for Hot Wars? The Indian Army's New Limited War Doctrine." *International Security* 32, no. 3 (Winter 2007/8): 158–190.

Ladwig, Walter C, III. "Indian Military Modernization and Conventional Deterrence in South Asia." *Journal of Strategic Studies* 38, no. 5 (2015): 729–772.

Larsen, Jeffrey A. "Limited War and the Advent of Nuclear Weapons." In *On Limited Nuclear War in the 21st Century*, edited by Jeffrey A. Larsen, and Kerry M. Kartchner, 3–20. Stanford, CA: Stanford University Press, 2014.

Lavoy, Peter R., ed. *Asymmetric Warfare in South Asia: The Causes and Consequences of the Kargil War*. Cambridge: Cambridge University Press, 2009.

Linklater, Andrew. *Beyond Realism and Marxism: Critical Theory and International Relations*. New York: St. Martin's Press, 1990.

O'Donnell, Frank. "India's Nuclear Counter-Revolution: Nuclear Learning and the Future of Deterrence." *Nonproliferation Review* 26, nos. 5–6 (2019): 407–426.

O'Donnell, Frank. *Stabilizing Sino-Indian Security Relations: Managing the Strategic Rivalry after Doklam.* Beijing: Carnegie-Tsinghua Center for Global Policy, 2018. https://carnegieendowment.org/files/CP335_ODonnell_final.pdf.

O'Donnell, Frank, and Debalina Ghoshal. "Managing Indian Deterrence: Pressures upon Credible Minimum Deterrence and Nuclear Policy Options." *Nonproliferation Review* 26, nos. 1–2 (2019): 419–436.

Pandit, Rajat. "Army Stocking up Munitions for 40-day War." *Times of India*, January 27, 2020. https://timesofindia.indiatimes.com/india/army-stocking-up-munitions-for-40-day-war/articleshow/73647518.cms.

Philip, Snehesh Alex. "India Now Working on 1,500-km Range BrahMos Supersonic Cruise Missile." *The Print*, November 24, 2020. https://theprint.in/defence/india-now-working-on-1500-km-range-brahmos-supersonic-cruise-missile/550924/.

Press Trust of India. "Roll out of Integrated Battle Groups Delayed due to Covid-19: Army Chief." *Business Standard*, May 10, 2020. https://www.business-standard.com/article/current-affairs/roll-out-of-integrated-battle-groups-delayed-due-covid-19-army-chief-120051000597_1.html.

Press Trust of India. "Armed Forces Facing Shortage of Nearly 60,000 Personnel, says Govt." *Hindustan Times*, December 27, 2017. https://www.hindustantimes.com/india-news/armed-forces-facing-shortage-of-nearly-60-000-personnel-says-govt/story-0Uc1XYkmLgBmMSOY0QDLZO.html.

Rej, Abhijnan. "S(c)Helling in Kashmir: Bargaining under the Nuclear Shadow." *Washington Quarterly* 42, no. 2 (2019): 163–186.

Rout, Hemant Kumar. "India Successfully Test Fires Short-range Tactical Ballistic Missile Prahaar." *New Indian Express*, September 20, 2018. https://www.newindianexpress.com/nation/2018/sep/20/india-successfully-test-fires-short-range-tactical-ballistic-missile-prahaar-1874747.html.

Sagan, Scott D., and Kenneth N. Waltz. *The Spread of Nuclear Weapons: A Debate Renewed.* New York: W.W. Norton, 2003.

Sagar, Pradip R. "India Needs a Dedicated Mountain Strike Corps to Tackle China." *The Week (India)*, July 4, 2021. https://www.theweek.in/theweek/cover/2021/06/25/india-needs-a-dedicated-mountain-strike-corps-to-tackle-china.html.

Schelling, Thomas C. "Bargaining, Communication and Limited War." *Conflict Resolution* 1, no. 1 (March 1957): 19–36.

Schelling, Thomas C. *Arms and Influence (2008 Edition, Orig. 1966).* New Haven: Yale University Press, 2008.

Schelling, Thomas C. *The Strategy of Conflict.* Cambridge, MA: Harvard University Press, 1960.

Shapcott, Richard. "Critical Theory." In *Oxford Handbook of International Relations*, edited by Christian Reus-Smit, and Duncan Snidal, 327–345. Oxford: Oxford University Press, 2008.

Shukla, Ajai. "Army Chief says Military must Prepare for Cold Start." *Business Standard*, January 14, 2017. https://www.business-standard.com/article/current-affairs/army-chief-says-military-must-prepare-for-cold-start-117011301174_1.html.

Shukla, Ajai. "Army's Pivot to the North." *Business Standard*, January 7, 2021. https://www.business-standard.com/article/opinion/army-s-pivot-to-the-north-121010701572_1.html.

Shukla, Ajai. "Playing into Chinese Hands in Ladakh." *Business Standard*, August 7, 2020. https://www.business-standard.com/article/opinion/playing-into-china-s-hands-in-ladakh-120080700061_1.html.

Singh, Sushant. "From Ladakh to Eastern Sector, Latest Satellite Imagery Shows Additional Chinese Pressure on India." *The India Cable*, December 21, 2021. https://www.theindiacable.com/p/from-ladakh-to-eastern-sector-latest.

Sultan, Maria. "Cross Domain Deterrence - The Pulwama Attack: Limited War & Nuclear Implications Reestablishing Deterrence & High Order War." In *Pakistan Army Green Book 2020*, edited by Fida Hussain Malik Maj. Gen., 75–91. Rawalpindi: Pakistan Army General Headquarters, 2020.

14
TRACK TWO DIPLOMACY AND THE INDIA-PAKISTAN CONFLICT

Peter Jones[1]

Introduction

The India-Pakistan relationship has seen a significant number and variety of unofficial peace-making efforts over many decades. This chapter will examine those efforts and place them in the context of the literature on what is broadly known as "Track Two Diplomacy." The first part will briefly explore what Track Two Diplomacy is, or rather, the variety of things that it is. The second part will outline a representative sampling of the dialogues that have existed at different levels of interaction in an effort to illustrate the breadth and depth of these activities. The third part will identify the lessons or ideas that emerge from all of these dialogues, both for India-Pakistan relations and also for the field of Track Two. The conclusion will suggest questions that the field may wish to consider going forward. It should be noted that there is a significant amount of Track Two activity in South Asia beyond the India-Pakistan relationship. For reasons of space, it will not be discussed in detail in this chapter.

Track Two Diplomacy

Before exploring how Track Two diplomacy has been active in the India-Pakistan context, it would be useful to consider briefly the history of the field and its key issues. Informal discussions between influential private citizens who seek to move official diplomacy toward peace and the resolution of conflicts have been around for many years.[2] The forerunner of what we today call "Track Two Diplomacy" began in the 1960s, and is largely credited to John Burton, a former diplomat who became disenchanted with traditional diplomacy and sought to explore others means whereby conflicts might be resolved. Burton sought a conflict resolution method that would bring together influential, but non-official, citizens of countries in conflict for a special kind of facilitated dialogue.[3] These workshops are not simply well-intentioned attempts to stimulate dialogue, as most private diplomacy initiatives had been, but the application of a social science-based facilitative methodology by a trained practitioner. Instead of proposing solutions, the role of the facilitator is to help the parties in conflict come up with proposals and solutions, based on a joint analysis. A key element of this is to shift the discourse from a bargaining one to a "problem-solving" approach, a discussion in which the participants take the view that the issue between them is not a difference in

184

DOI: 10.4324/9781003246626-17

Track Two Diplomacy and the India-Pakistan Conflict

positions to be bargained over, but rather a mutually held "problem" that they have to try to resolve together. These dialogues gave birth to a field that has gone by several names over the decades, but the one that stuck was given by Joseph Montville: "Track Two Diplomacy."[4] In terms of international relations (IR) theory, these processes are generally reckoned to be an attempt to shift the discourse away from realist-inspired, zero-sum bargaining behavior and toward a constructivist dialogue aimed at encouraging a search for sum-sum outcomes.[5] In recent years, the field has grappled with a series of issues relating to diversity, inclusion, local ownership of such dialogues, and whether those running them should use their agency in the service of advocacy of norms such as human rights, as opposed to being impartial facilitators of dialogue.[6]

There are now many different kinds of Track Two, each with its methodologies and adherents. One area in which the field has seen much growth and debate is over the question of the "levels" of Track Two and the appropriate uses of each. Briefly, there are generally acknowledged to be three "levels" of dialogues that take place under the broad rubric of "Track Two."[7] These levels are not absolute; dialogues can exhibit elements of more than one, and dialogues may also drift between them over time. Also, some authors have posited the existence of more than three, though they are in some ways talking about the same thing with different names.[8]

The first level (though this is not meant in hierarchically) includes dialogues involving officials acting in their "private capacity," or other very closely connected people who are present with the knowledge of their authorities.[9] Such "Track 1.5" dialogues usually take place under an academic or other non-official body in order to create a level of deniability and intellectual freedom. An example of Track 1.5 would be the Oslo talks at which Israelis and Palestinians met under the auspices of a Norwegian Government-supported NGO and which began as a Track 2 process, but evolved to Track 1.5, and then Track 1, as officials joined.[10] Another example is the dialogue between leaders of the African National Congress and influential Afrikaner South African citizens, which helped produce the formula that led to beginning of the formal transition to majority rule in South Africa.[11]

The second generally acknowledged "level" of Track Two are dialogues involving influential, but non-official participants. They are somewhat more "removed" from official diplomacy than Track 1.5, and therefore afford greater freedom. Whereas Track 1.5 dialogues are usually intended primarily, if not solely, for official audiences, Track Two dialogues can be directed at officials, or at the public opinion, or both. They can involve a wider range of people, including those who have never held official positions but are influential more broadly within their societies. They may be intended to explore and comment on proposals and ideas known to be close to official positions, in order to see if movement may be possible, or they may be intended to see if entirely new approaches to the conflict can be developed, which will influence a broader re-thinking of attitudes. Dialogues of this type may be thought of as existing on a spectrum, and many different types have been suggested over the years, ranging from "Inter-active Problem Solving" to "Inter-active Conflict Resolution," to "Soft Track Two," to "Circum-negotiation."[12]

Finally, there are activities at a level known as "Track Three."[13] These engage civil society and other advocacy groups in activities aimed at developing their capacity to challenge prevailing interests. This can take many forms, for example, capacity-building and training to enable disenfranchised groups in conflict-prone societies to participate more effectively in peace processes, with the intent of broadening these processes away from their "elite" level bias. Importantly, there is an element of advocacy about the facilitator's role in Track Three that is usually absent from Track 1.5 and Track Two. Whereas the latter levels of dialogue generally take the view that it is for the participants in the dialogues to develop ideas, and that the facilitator is not there to inject imperatives into the discussions, Track Three is significantly oriented toward a more activist role.

Another way to categorize different types of Track Two dialogues is to speak in terms of the influence they seek to have on the conflict itself; whether they seek to manage, resolve or transform it. Conflict management takes the view that the dispute is not ripe to be ended. Instead, the focus is on engaging in a long-term process to "managing" the conflict in hopes that this will reduce violence and lay the stage over time for efforts to end it. "Conflict resolution" dialogues take the view that the time has come to develop proposals aimed at bringing about a resolution of the conflict. It is important to note that the participants in Track Two dialogues can be well ahead of official positions; in other words, they can take the view that the time has come to begin developing resolution proposals even if the official positions are not close to this. Finally, there is a type of dialogue known as "conflict transformation." Such dialogues often seek to empower groups, views, and interests who are not represented in their societies as a means of laying the stage for the transformation of the underlying situation. In many respects, while Track 1.5 and Track Two recognize that the structure of the conflict (the governing elites and their preferences) is a given which must be worked with over time, Track Three dialogues seek to change that structure through projects aimed as much at advocacy as at dialogue.[14]

India-Pakistan Track Two

As this general review of the field demonstrates, the term "Track Two Diplomacy" covers a multitude of different types of dialogues. In turning to the India-Pakistan case, we see that all of these different types of dialogue have been active over a long time.[15] Some dialogues have been at Track 1.5 or Track Two levels and aimed, often, at trying to manage the relationship, or, more rarely, develop proposals to resolve differences. Others have been at the Track Three level and have been aimed at promoting broader civil society and "people-to-people" contacts with the hope of affecting a transformation in attitudes. For the purposes of this chapter, the dialogues that will be considered are those that have achieved an ongoing series of meetings over a period of time, rather than those that are, or were, "one-off" conferences or interactions with no follow-up.

There are numerous examples of Track 1.5 or Track Two dialogues aimed at bilateral/security issues. The *Neemrana dialogue,* launched in 1991, brings together senior, retired officials, and other influential people for regular dialogues about bilateral relations. The discussions are confidential and there is no foreign facilitator. Funding comes from within the region and meetings are held in each country, on a rotating basis. The Neemrana dialogue does not seem to now be regularly active, but rather meets intermittently when the two governments believe it might be useful. The last such meeting publicly known to have taken place was in 2018.[16] The *Chao Track* (formerly the Chaophrya Dialogue) was launched in 2008 and convenes regular meetings on a variety of different bilateral topics. It has been run by institutes on both sides, and it is presently conducted by the Council for Strategic Defence Research (CDSR) in India. Australia was active in supporting its launch, and it receives funding from outside the region. Meetings are held outside of the region. The discussions are confidential, but the Chao Track regularly publishes working papers and other documents that are the result of its meetings.[17] The *Ottawa Dialogue* began its work in the late 1990s. It brings together influential, usually retired senior officials. The Ottawa Dialogue has a number of different working groups looking at specific bilateral issues. The discussions are confidential and held outside the region. Public documents on the content of the discussions are rarely issued, but policy papers and proposals are prepared and passed to the two governments. The Dialogue is facilitated by a group from out of the region, and funding also comes from outside the region. In addition to its work facilitating dialogues, the Ottawa Dialogue maintains an active research program into Track Two itself and seeks to develop the field of unofficial dialogue through research and publishing.[18] The London-based *International Institute for Strategic Studies* (IISS) holds a variety of annual workshops and sponsors joint research into India-Pakistan issues.[19] *South Asian Voices* is a largely online process run by the Stimson Center in Washington. It has convened some in-person meetings, but its work is mostly done by various authors and analysts from India and Pakistan, and elsewhere, who collaborate online to produce papers and analyses. These are then published on the SAV website.[20]

Of course, other institutions have been active in promoting India-Pakistan dialogue on bilateral and security issues. The *Pugwash Conferences on Science and World Affairs* have been active, off and on, both on various India-Pakistan issues and also on Afghanistan.[21] An organization called the BALUSA Group ran such dialogues between 1995 and 2003.[22] The *Kashmir Study Group* was formed in 1996 and produced a number of studies on how that conflict could be resolved. It was funded by a Kashmiri-born US business leader, Farooq Kathwari. Study efforts that bring together individuals from the two sides to jointly examine particular issues include efforts by *The Cooperative Monitoring Center* at the Sandia National Laboratory in the US, which has brought together senior Indian and Pakistani experts to examine possibilities for arms restraint and confidence-building in various contexts.[23]

Meanwhile, Track Three civil society dialogues are also active. Most aim to open up spaces for dialogue between civil society groups who seek to explore whether the barriers erected after the bloody Partition of 1947 can be breeched to allow more normal relationships to develop between the peoples of the two countries. Many such initiatives take the form of advocacy for particular causes or courses of action. As a former Pakistani High Commissioner to India, who has played an extensive role in bilateral relations, has said of Track Three interactions; "The underlying idea was to promote goodwill on both sides, and it always worked well. This was instrumental in putting across the broad sentiments of the people on both sides of the divide to the policy makers. The role of such interaction at the grassroots level is significant."[24]

Examples of such dialogues are numerous. *The Pakistan-India Peoples' Forum for Peace and Democracy* (PIPFPD) is one of the oldest civil-society organizations working for dialogue and reconciliation between the two sides and has held a series of meetings and working groups since 1995.[25] In the youth dialogue space, organizations have existed over the years to encourage youth dialogue, such as the *Indo-Pak Youth Forum for Peace* and *Youth for Peace's* India-Pakistan dialogue project, "Guftagu."[26] The US-based group *Seeds of Peace* runs a summer camp that brings together youths from the two countries with the objective that they should return and become advocates of greater dialogue and understanding.[27] In the cultural and artistic space, annual events such as the *Lahore Literary Festival*[28] and the *Jaipur Literature Festival*[29] have made consistent efforts to showcase authors from the other side and have invited them to participate, when visas have been forthcoming. Musical, film, and other artistic endeavors have also been active in promoting such exchanges over the years. In the space of encouraging dialogue between women from the two countries, groups such as *Women in Security, Conflict Management and Peace* (WISCOMP)[30] have conducted training for women in conflict resolution and peacebuilding between the two sides. The UK-based NGO *Conciliation Resources* has supported the work of individual women from across the divide in Kashmir to promote dialogue and training for women from either side of the Line of Control.[31] On sectoral issues, such as water, organizations such as the *Atlantic Council of the United States* have sponsored Track Two work.[32] In the trade and economics space, institutions such as the *Federation of Indian Chambers of Commerce and Industry*[33] and the *Federation of Pakistan Chambers of Commerce and Industry*[34] have held regular events and sponsored studies devoted to encouraging trade and commerce between the two countries and the lowering of barriers to such trade, as have individual business sectors.

More broadly, and although it falls beyond the scope of this chapter, there is a history of regional dialogues incorporating all of the countries of South Asia, in which Indian and Pakistani scholars and institutes participate.[35] These dialogues have sought, variously, to explore on a multilateral basis security, economic, and foreign policy issues, and also civil-society connections across the region. Many of these dialogues are associated with, or support various aspects of, the regional multilateral Track One process, known as the South Asia Association for Regional Cooperation (SAARC). These Track Two dialogues thus involve participants from all eight member nations of SAARC.[36] Topics for these regional Track Two dialogues range widely over issues such as environmental cooperation, food security, economic cooperation, and so forth. While these dialogues are often consciously aimed at issues beyond the specific difficulties of the India-Pakistan relationship, that dynamic affects them, as it affects the work of SAARC overall—when relations between Islamabad and Delhi are particularly bad, it spills over into the region's multilateral diplomacy, whether at the official or unofficial level.

Lessons

In looking at India–Pakistan Track Two in the whole, eight general ideas or "lessons" emerge.

Firstly, there is a major issue of the sustainability of these dialogues. Financially, they rely, for the most part, on funds received from foundations, individuals, or governments who are well-disposed toward this sort of activity. This makes them vulnerable to changes in policy or priority on the part of these donors. Most dialogues have existed for a few years and then dissolved. Dialogues that have gone on for a decade or more, such as Chao, IISS, and Ottawa, are quite rare, and even they are subject to ongoing financial pressure and stress. Other dialogues, such as PIPFPD, are able to "maintain" themselves in being, in terms of a web-page and the occasional meeting, but do not appear to have a sustained program of work. This is problematic, as it is well-established in the Track Two literature that it takes time to effect change and to see that change is transmitted to intended audiences. Perhaps it is time for a coalition of those who undertake and those who support these efforts at all levels, whether in the region or outside it, to consider whether a broader sustaining strategy might be possible, or even a set of such strategies given the different levels of dialogue. A separate but equally important aspect of the sustainability of these dialogues is that of "participant fatigue;" finding and keeping engaged high-level participants. Repeated meetings over time, sometimes in the face of criticism by opponents of dialogue and reconciliation at home, can be wearing on participants.[37]

Secondly, and following on from the point made above, it is difficult to gauge the extent of support for these dialogues among "the people" on either side as there are few reliable indicators of broader public sentiment toward this sort of activity. There is, however, an active segment of the press and of the political spectrum that views it all with great suspicion. This opposition ranges from groups and individuals who are convinced that any form of talking to "the other side" is treason, to those who believe that however well-intentioned all this may be, the participants in these dialogues are naïve and are being duped. Given the tendencies of much of the press in the region to favor controversy, ringing statements of opposition to these dialogues are likely to be picked up and amplified with the objective of stirring up an exchange that will attract attention. The space for more nuanced reporting on them thus becomes limited as a result, leading to breathless stories, instead of quiet and thoughtful analysis. In cases of dialogues at the Track 1.5 level, where discretion is necessary to allow new ideas to be carefully developed and considered, angry revelations of "secret talks" and "back-channel deals" can undermine years of work. Even in Track Two and Three, where the dialogues are meant to be open, there is a constant backdrop of voices who stridently question the utility of dialogue. There seems to be little in the way of a coordinated effort to point out the benefits of this sort of interaction and to make the case to the public on each side that talking is better than fighting. Those engaged in these efforts, and those who support them, whether they are working at the confidential or open levels, perhaps need to consider the benefits of working together to develop and promulgate a set of arguments in support of this kind of work that can be deployed in response to those whose instinctive reaction to any dialogue is dismissive or even hostile.

Thirdly, it is difficult to assess the impact of all this.[38] Rarely do such dialogues have a direct and immediate impact on the conflict. Rather, it seems that the manner in which they impact official policy, or public opinion, may be more likened to "seepage" over time, than to direct transfer of proposals in the short term; an exercise in perception shaping. Simply put, useful ideas arising from such dialogues can make it onto the policy or public agenda of the two countries, but they will do so indirectly, over time, and usually with little or no acknowledgement from governments as to where they originated. At the Track 1.5, security-oriented level of dialogues, this transfer is often accomplished through confidential briefings for officials given by participants from the dialogues, or confidential policy papers given to the governments. Another form of seepage has been when participants in a Track Two dialogue process have gone into government service and taken the ideas they have learned from Track Two sessions, and the contacts they have made, with them. Either way, the seepage in question can take time, and the results may not be apparent until after a particular Track Two dialogue has moved on.[39] In terms of the more civil society-oriented dialogues at the Track Three level, the question of how their results are transferred is more difficult to measure. As these dialogues are intended to influence broader public opinion, it becomes even more difficult to understand in a systematic way how public views are being affected against the general backdrop of negative publicity about the bilateral relationship. The anecdotal comments of individuals who believe that these interactions have a positive impact are important, but it is simply the case that we have very little understanding of whether and how these dialogues influence the broad mass of civil society on each side.

Fourthly, in terms of the security or foreign policy-oriented dialogues at Track 1.5 and Two levels, the two governments, like many others around the world, tend to jealously guard their prerogatives as the custodians of their nations' foreign and security policy. While this does not mean that there is no scope for useful ideas emerging from these dialogues to be of interest to both governments, Delhi and Islamabad are, in principle, suspicious that private citizens, even retired officials, have a significant role to play in the policy or diplomatic process over issues perceived to be critical to national security. This is perhaps slightly more the case in terms of India, as Pakistan has a general goal, at a declaratory level at least, of "internationalizing" the bilateral dispute. That being said, elements of the Pakistani government can be just as resistant as those in Delhi to what they perceive to be "meddling," when the results of dialogue discussions are not consistent with their views and desires.

Fifthly, those running dialogues in the India-Pakistan context, whether they be at the Track 1.5/Two levels or Track Three or someplace in between, need to have a high degree of patience and persistence. They must also develop a subtle definition of "success." At the Track 1.5 level, those running such dialogues must accept that they are working in the "conflict management" space; thoughts of "resolving," much less "transforming," the conflict as a direct result of these dialogues must be kept in check. Moreover, those running these dialogues also need to know how to keep quiet and not claim parental ownership of ideas that do make it to the policy process. Finally, it means that those who support these efforts financially require a willingness to fund them quietly and over a long period of time. This does not mean, of course, that some dialogues active in this space have not made the decision to make their ideas public and advocate them. The Pugwash Conferences, South Asian Voices, and the Kashmir Study Group have had this as part of their model from the beginning and they sought to stimulate public discussion of alternative ideas. But dialogues such as Neemrana and Ottawa have consciously adopted a quiet approach. Meanwhile, those working at the Track Three civil-society level are, by definition, geared toward public dissemination and advocacy of their results, but must also accept that sudden breakthroughs are unlikely in terms of influencing public opinion toward the conflict.

Sixthly, there is a degree of opinion, particularly, though not exclusively, in India that dialogues on sensitive issues run by "outsiders" are less welcome than those run indigenously.[40] This is not uniformly so, but is a broad trend. Practically, this means that dialogues that are run by outside institutions are rarely able to get permission to hold their meetings in either India or Pakistan—visas are not forthcoming. However, this does *not* mean that such dialogues cannot play a constructive role. It does mean that they need to keep quiet and not overtly discuss their results. In addition, Track 1.5 dialogues being run by outsiders should be open about their sources of funding as a level of trust needs to be built up with the two governments that those running these dialogues are not serving other agendas or will seek cheap headlines. A reality of this situation is thus that regional governments can exercise a degree of "control" over what should be independent processes; that those who run these types of dialogues will come to (consciously or unconsciously) display a degree of self-censorship in order to remain acceptable to Delhi and Islamabad as players. This has the effect of limiting the extent to which those who participate in such dialogues, and who value continued access to the government on each side, are prepared to engage in some of the practices that are held to be the emerging standards of the field, such as using their agency to promote various norms of behavior.[41] In the case of Track Two and especially Track Three dialogues, the reality is different as they are not dependent on "access" to officials. Indeed, their objectives are to influence the broader society.

Seventh, if outside actors are subject to a degree of influence from the two governments, this can be even more the case for local organizations that can be subject to pressures over their personal security and over the sources of their funding.[42] This turns on its head the debate over the benefits of "local ownership." As a general rule, advocates of ever-increasing local ownership of unofficial dialogue processes believe that locally-run dialogues are more authentic and effective, while those run by outsiders are subject to pressures and biases that are detrimental.[43] In the India-Pakistan context, with the two governments firmly in control of the space and determined to remain so, it is questionable as to whether exclusively foreign or local actors are able to run dialogues that escape the pressures that the governments can bring to bear on them. In theory, the answer may lie in increased partnerships between local dialogue leaders and those from outside the region to run dialogue projects, though it must be recognized that these relationships can also bring risks, particularly to the local actors who can be accused by their governments as acting in the service of "foreign agendas." Equally prone to pressures are the participants in such dialogues, who can be excoriated for their willingness to talk to the "other side" by those in their own societies for whom any form of dialogue is unacceptable.

Finally, and following on from the above, there seems to have been little effort over the years to coordinate between the various tracks to see if they can strengthen and provide impetus to each other. This is the so-called "multi-track" approach, whereby an effort is made to harness the different inherent strengths of the different levels of dialogue into a more concerted effort.[44] In fairness, South Asia is not alone here. Though it is increasingly spoken of in the conflict resolution literature as the way the field must progress, there are few if any examples in practice of the actual application of the multi-track approach anywhere; no one seems to know how to bring together for maximum effect a disparate set of dialogues intended to influence different audiences in different ways. But it is striking that all of this effort, on all of these different levels of dialogue, does not seem to have produced a discussion of whether the Tracks could somehow work together to push change on a more systemic level. Despite the inherent difficulties of bringing together many actors who are working at different levels and with different objectives, perhaps this may be an area where those working on the India-Pakistan conflict at different levels need to consider whether something can be done to increase their effectiveness.

Conclusion

The India-Pakistan relationship offers one of the most active and well-documented case studies of the application of Track Two, in all its levels, to a major conflict over a long period. For all this effort, it must be admitted that the India-Pakistan relationship is as fraught as ever and the danger of serious conflict remains. That being acknowledged, expectations that unofficial dialogue should have somehow resolved this conflict are not reasonable—after all, official diplomacy, has not resolved it either. These dialogues have helped to manage the relationship. They have opened spaces for discussion, on different levels, which could not be opened by governments and may be useful if the sides decide to change their relationship. However, it is incumbent on those active in the field to ask themselves some critical questions about whether and how they have had an impact, and could have one in the future. These include questions as to whether their dialogue efforts have become an end in themselves, rather than pushing the sides to explore new ways forward, and questions as to whether there are new and novel ways to work with others active at different levels in the field to try to change the ground in ways that will shake up the conflict and produce circumstances in which fundamental change might be encouraged.

Notes

1 Executive Director of the Ottawa Dialogue and Professor in the Graduate School of Public and International Affairs at the University of Ottawa. The author wishes to thank several participants in these dialogues for their comments on previous drafts. Unless they are specifically quoted in the chapter, all of those consulted have preferred to remain anonymous. The author is solely responsible for the contents of this chapter.
2 S.E. Cooper, *Patriotic Pacifism: Waging War on War in Europe, 1815–1914* (New York: Oxford University Press, 1991); L. Lehrs, "A Last-Minute Private Peace Initiative: Albert Ballin's Mediation Efforts between Germany and Britain, 1908–1914," *Hague Journal of Diplomacy* 13, no. 3 (2018): 297–332.

3 For more on Burton's ideas and their contribution to the conflict resolution field, see the collection of articles in the special themed edition in honor of John W. Burton of the *International Journal of Peace Studies* 6, no. 1 (2001), online journal accessed on February 13, 2022 at: https://www3.gmu.edu/programs/icar/ijps/vol6_1/cover6_1.htm.

4 For general histories of Track Two, see P. Jones, *Track Two Diplomacy in Theory and Practice* (Palo Alto, CA: Stanford University Press, 2015), 7–53; R.J. Fisher, "Historical Mapping of the Field of Inter-active Conflict Resolution," in *Second Track/Citizen's Diplomacy: Concepts and Techniques for Conflict Transformation*, eds. J. Davies and E. Kaufman (Lanham, MD: Rowman & Littlefield, 2002), 61–80; and C.R. Mitchell, "From Controlled Communication to Problem Solving: The Origins of Facilitated Conflict Resolution," *The International Journal of Peace Studies* 6, no. 1 (Spring 2001).

5 Jones, *Track Two Diplomacy*, 34–42.

6 J. Palmiano Federer, "Toward a Normative Turn in Track Two Diplomacy? A Review of the Literature," *Negotiation Journal* 37, no. 4 (2021): 427–450.

7 For more on the "levels" idea, see Jones, *Track Two Diplomacy*, 7–31; J.P. Lederach, *Building Peace: Sustainable Reconciliation in Divided Societies* (Washington DC: United States Institute of Peace, 1997); and J. Palmiano Federer, J. Pickhardt, C. Altpeter, K. Abatis, and P. Lustenburger, *Beyond the Tracks? Reflections on Multitrack Approaches to Peace Processes* (Swisspeace, 2019), accessed December 14, 2021, https://www.swisspeace.ch/assets/publications/a879843a62/Multi-Track-01-block.pdf.

8 For example, L. Diamond, and J. MacDonald, *Multitrack Diplomacy: A Systems Approach to Peace, 3rd Ed.* (West Hartford CT: Kumarian Press, 1996).

9 S.A. Nan, D. Druckman, and J.E. Horr, "Unofficial International Conflict Resolution: Is There a Track One and A Half? Are There Best Practices?" *Conflict Resolution Quarterly* 27, no. 1 (2009): 65–82.

10 J. Egeland, "The Oslo Accord: Multiparty Facilitation through the Norwegian Channel," in *Herding Cats: Multiparty Mediation in a Complex World*, eds. C.A Crocker, F.O. Hampson, and P. Aall (Washington, DC: United States Institute of Peace press, 2003), 527–546.

11 D. Lieberfield, "Evaluating the Contributions of Track Two Diplomacy to Conflict Termination in South Africa, 1984–90," *Journal of Peace Research* 39, no. 3 (2002): 355–372.

12 H.C. Kelman, "Interactive Problem-solving: Informal Mediation by the Scholar Practitioner," in *Studies in International Mediation: Essays in Honor of Jeffrey Z. Rubin*, ed. J. Bercovitch (New York: Palgrave MacMillan, 2002), 167–193; Fisher, "Historical Mapping;" and H. Saunders, "Pre-negotiation and Circum-negotiation: Arenas of the Peace Process," in *Managing Global Chaos: Sources of and Responses to International Conflict*, eds. C. Crocker, F.O. Hampson, and P. Aall (Washington, DC: U.S. Institute of Peace, 1996), 419–432.

13 Lederach, *Building Peace*.

14 P. Jones, *Track Two Diplomacy*, 61–71; P. Gamaghelyan, "Towards an Inclusive Conception of Best Practices in Peace and Conflict Initiatives: The Case of the South Caucasus," *International Negotiation* 26, no. 1 (2021): 125–150.

15 See, for example, A.S. Shah, "Non-Official Dialogue between India and Pakistan: Problems and Prospects," *ACDIS Occasional Paper*, University of Illinois, August 1997; S. Chakrabarti, "The Relevance of Track II Diplomacy in South Asia," *International Studies* 40, no. 3 (2003): 265–276; B.M. Kutty, "Pakistan-India Relations: Non-Governmental Initiatives for Peace," *Pakistan Horizon* 57, no. 3 (2004): 41–53; Centre for Humanitarian Dialogue and Delhi Policy Group, *Conflict Resolution: Learning Lessons from Dialogue Processes in India*, July 2011, especially 33–35, accessed December 9, 2021, https://www.files.ethz.ch/isn/131093/Conflict%20resolution%20in%20India.pdf; T.S. Maini, and Hamdani, Y.L., "A New Face for India and Pakistan's Track Two Diplomacy," *The Diplomat*, October 20, 2014, accessed December 3, 2021, https://thediplomat.com/2014/10/a-new-face-for-india-and-pakistans-track-ii-diplomacy/; M. Bornstein, *et al.*, "Civil Societies: Empowering Peace Constituencies in India and Pakistan," School of International and Public Affairs, Columbia University, 2015; and Tahir Ashraf, Md. Akhir Nasrudin, and Javaid Akhtar Salyana, "Mapping of Track Two Initiatives: A Case of Pakistan-India Conflict (1988–2001)," *Pakistan Journal of Social Sciences* 37, no. 1 (2017), 16–29.

16 "Neemrana Dialogue: India-Pakistan Revive Track II Diplomacy Talks after Three Years, But Major Outcomes Unlikely," *Firstpost*, May 1, 2018, accessed December 5, 2021, https://www.firstpost.com/india/neemrana-dialogue-india-pakistan-revive-track-ii-diplomacy-talks-after-three-years-but-major-outcomes-unlikely-4451887.html.

17 Council for Strategic Defense and Research, "The Chao Track," accessed December 7, 2021, https://csdronline.org/dialogue.

18 The Ottawa Dialogue, accessed December 7, 2021, https://ottawadialogue.ca/. In the interest of full disclosure, the author of this chapter is the Executive Director of the Ottawa Dialogue.

19 The International Institute for Strategic Studies, "South Asia," accessed December 7, 2021, https://www.iiss.org/research/south-asia.

20 The Stimson Centre, "South Asian Voices," accessed December 7, 2021, https://southasianvoices.org/.

21 Pugwash Conferences on Science and World Affairs, "South Asia," accessed December 8, 2021, https://pugwash.org/category/south-asia/.

22 Foreign Policy Research Institute, "Track II Indo-Pakistani Diplomacy (1995–2003): The BALUSA Group," accessed December 7, 2021, https://www.fpri.org/article/2017/08/track-ii-indo-pakistani-diplomacy-1995-2003-balusa-group/.

23 For a list of publications, see "Sandia National Laboratories, Publications Database," accessed December 10, 2021, https://sandia.prod.acquia-sites.com/publications?fulltext=South+Asia.

24 Personal correspondence with Shahid Malik, December 6, 2021.

25 S. Banerjee, "Two Decades of an Indo-Pak Collaborative Experiment – Pakistan India People's Forum for Peace and Democracy," *Countercurrents.org*, February 26, 2021, accessed December 11, 2021, https://countercurrents.org/2021/03/two-decades-of-an-indo-pak-collaborative-experiment-pakistan-india-peoples-forum-for-peace-and-democracy/.

26 Both of these organizations seem to no longer be active, at least under these names. For more on them, see https://www.peaceinsight.org/en/articles/youth-for-peace-in-pakistan/?location=pakistan&theme= and https://www.yourcommonwealth.org/youth-networks/guftagu-idp2016/.

27 Seeds of Peace, South Asia Programs, accessed December 12, 2021, https://www.seedsofpeace.org/programs/developing-leaders/south-asia/.

28 Lahore Literary Festival website, accessed December 10, 2021, http://www.lahorelitfest.com/.

29 Jaipur Literary Festival website, accessed December 10, 2021, https://jaipurliteraturefestival.org/.

30 WISCOMP website, accessed December 12, 2021, https://wiscomp.org/.

31 Conciliation Resources, "Empowering Women across Divided Kashmir" website, accessed December 11, 2021, https://www.c-r.org/news-and-views/stories/empowering-women-across-divided-kashmir. Conciliation Resources is also more broadly engaged in promoting people-to-people contacts in Kashmir: https://www.c-r.org/programme/south-asia.

32 F. Nabeel, "Recasting Pakistan's Water Scarcity Challenge," Atlantic Council website, accessed December 11, 2021, https://www.atlanticcouncil.org/in-depth-research-reports/issue-brief/recasting-pakistans-water-scarcity-challenge/.

33 The FICCI's page on South Asia, accessed December 12, 2021, https://ficci.in/international.asp?deskid=54522.

34 The FPCCI's webpage, accessed December 12, 2021, http://fpcci.org.pk/.

35 For a discussion of regional Track Two in South Asia, see D.D. Kaye, *Talking to the Enemy: Track Two Diplomacy in the Middle East and South Asia* (Santa Monica: Rand Corp., 2007).

36 The webpage of the SAARC Secretariat, accessed December 11, 2021, https://www.saarc-sec.org/.

37 G. Kanwal., "India-Pakistan Track II Peacemaking Efforts," posted on the website of the Centre for Land Warfare Studies, December 27, 2011, accessed December 10, 2021, https://archive.claws.in/748/india-pakistan-track-ii-peace-making-efforts-brig-gurmeet-kanwal.html.

38 The question of measuring the impact of Track Two dialogues consumes much energy in the field. See P. Jones, "Talking for the Sake of it, or Making a Difference? Measuring and Evaluating Track Two Diplomacy," in *New Directions in Peacebuilding Evaluation*, ed. T.P. D'Estree (New York: Roman and Littlefield, 2019), 69–90.

39 These findings are consistent with experience in other regions: E. Cuhadar, "Assessing Transfer from Track Two Diplomacy: The Cases of Water and Jerusalem," *Journal of Peace Research* 46, no. 5 (2009): 641–658. For more on transfer and Track Two, see T.P. D'Estrée, and B.B. Fox, "Incorporating Best Practices into Design and Facilitation of Track Two Initiatives," *International Negotiation* 26, no. 1 (2021), 5–38; and P. Jones, *Track Two Diplomacy in Theory and Practice* (Palo Alto, CA: Stanford University Press, 2015), 136–164.

40 Although there is also a, perhaps, counter-argument that at least *some* foreign-run Track Two dialogues have in the past been tolerated by authorities in the region as a way of "mollifying" the foreigners and allowing them a sense of productive involvement. Personal communication with Jack Gill, Washington, December 5, 2021.

41 S. Hellmüller, J. Pring, and O. Richmond, "How Norms Matter in Mediation: An Introduction," *Swiss Political Science Review* 26, no. 4 (2020): 345–363; and J. Palmiano Federer, "Cowboys or

Mavericks? The Normative Agency of NGO Mediators," in *Rethinking Peace Mediation: Challenges of Contemporary Peacemaking Practice*, eds. C. Turner and M. Wählisch (Bristol: Bristol University Press, 2021), 71–91.

42 In 2020, for example, India toughened laws concerning the "foreign funding" of NGOs in, what opponents argued, is an effort to silence dissent. See, for example, D. Ghoshal, "NGOs Say India's New Rules on Foreign Funding Will Hit Operations," *Reuters*, October 1, 2020, accessed December 3, 2021, https://www.reuters.com/article/india-ngo-idINKBN26M5PG. Pakistan has long had such laws and also toughened them recently. See H. Janjua, "Why is the Pakistan Government Cracking Down on NGOs?" *Die Welt*, February 11, 2021, accessed December 3, 2021, https://www.dw.com/en/why-is-the-pakistani-government-cracking-down-on-ngos/a-56537755.

43 For more on this debate, see S. Hellmüller, "Owners or Partners? A Critical Analysis of the Concept of Local Ownership," In *Is Local Beautiful? Peacebuilding between International Interventions and Local Led Initiatives*, eds. S. Hellmüller and M. Sachsi (New York: Springer, 2014), 3–14; A. Boutellis, D. Mechoulan, and M-J. Zahar, *Parallel Tracks or Connected Pieces? UN Peace Operations, Local Mediation, and Peace Processes* (New York: United Nations, 2020); S. Allen, "Evolving Best Practices: Engaging the Strengths of Both External and Local Peacebuilders in Track Two Dialogues through Local Ownership," *International Negotiation* 26, no. 1 (2021), 67–84.

44 For more, see J.P. Lederach, *Building Peace*; and J. Palmiano Federer, J. Pickhardt, C. Altpeter, K. Abatis, and P. Lustenburger, *Beyond the Tracks?*

Bibliography

Allen, S. "Evolving Best Practices: Engaging the Strengths of Both External and Local Peacebuilders in Track Two Dialogues through Local Ownership." *International Negotiation* 26, no. 1 (2021): 67–84.

Ashraf, Tahir, Md. Akhir Nasrudin, and Javaid Akhtar Salyana. "Mapping of Track Two Initiatives: A Case of Pakistan-India Conflict (1988–2001)." *Pakistan Journal of Social Sciences* 37, no. 1 (2017): 16–29.

Banerjee, S. "Two Decades of an Indo-Pak Collaborative Experiment – Pakistan India People's Forum for Peace and Democracy," *Countercurrents.org*, February 26, 2021, accessed December 11, 2021. https://countercurrents.org/2021/03/two-decades-of-an-indo-pak-collaborative-experiment-pakistan-india-peoples-forum-for-peace-and-democracy/.

Bornstein, M. *et al.* "Civil Societies: Empowering Peace Constituencies in India and Pakistan." *School of International and Public Affairs*, Columbia University, 2015.

Boutellis, A., D. Mechoulan, and M-J. Zahar. *Parallel Tracks or Connected Pieces? UN Peace Operations, Local Mediation, and Peace Processes*. New York: United Nations, 2020.

Centre for Humanitarian Dialogue and Delhi Policy Group. *Conflict Resolution: Learning Lessons from Dialogue Processes in India*. July 2011.

Chakrabarti, S. "The Relevance of Track II Diplomacy in South Asia." *International Studies* 40, no. 3 (2003): 265–276.

Conciliation Resources. "Empowering Women across Divided Kashmir." Accessed December 11, 2021. https://www.c-r.org/news-and-views/stories/empowering-women-across-divided-kashmir.

Cooper, S.E. *Patriotic Pacifism: Waging War on War in Europe, 1815–1914*. New York: Oxford University Press, 1991.

Council for Strategic Defense and Research. "The Chao Track." Accessed December 7, 2021. https://csdronline.org/dialogue.

Cuhadar, E. "Assessing Transfer from Track Two Diplomacy: The Cases of Water and Jerusalem." *Journal of Peace Research* 46, no. 5 (2009): 641–658.

D'Estrée, T. P., and B.B. Fox. "Incorporating Best Practices into Design and Facilitation of Track Two Initiatives." *International Negotiation* 26, no. 1 (2021).

Diamond, L., and J. MacDonald. *Multitrack Diplomacy: A Systems Approach to Peace*. 3rd ed. West Hartford, CT: Kumarian Press, 1996.

Egeland, J. "The Oslo Accord: Multiparty Facilitation through the Norwegian Channel." In *Herding Cats: Multiparty Mediation in a Complex World*, edited by C.A. Crocker, F.O. Hampson, and P. Aall. Washington, DC: United States Institute of Peace Press, 2003.

FICCI. Accessed December 12, 2021. https://ficci.in/international.asp?deskid=54522.

"Neemrana Dialogue: India-Pakistan Revive Track II Diplomacy Talks After Three Years, But Major Outcomes Unlikely," *Firstpost*, May 1, 2018, accessed December 5, 2021.https://www.firstpost. com/india/neemrana-dialogue-india-pakistan-revive-track-ii-diplomacy-talks-after-three-years-but-major-outcomes-unlikely-4451887.html.

Fisher, R.J. "Historical Mapping of the Field of Inter-Active Conflict Resolution." In *Second Track/ Citizen's Diplomacy: Concepts and Techniques for Conflict Transformation*, edited by J. Davies, and E. Kaufman. Lanham, MD: Rowman & Littlefield, 2002.

Foreign Policy Research Institute. "Track II Indo-Pakistani Diplomacy (1995–2003): The BALUSA Group." Accessed December 7, 2021. https://www.fpri.org/article/2017/08/track-ii-indo-pakistani-diplomacy-1995-2003-balusa-group/.

FPCCI. Accessed December 12, 2021. http://fpcci.org.pk/.

Gamaghelyan, P. "Towards an Inclusive Conception of Best Practices in Peace and Conflict Initiatives: The Case of the South Caucasus." *International Negotiation* 26, no. 1 (2021).

Ghoshal, D. "NGOs say India's New Rules on Foreign Funding will Hit Operations." *Reuters*, October 1, 2020, accessed December 3, 2021. https://www.reuters.com/article/india-ngo-idINKBN26M5PG.

Hellmüller, S. "Owners or Partners? A Critical Analysis of the Concept of Local Ownership." In *Is Local Beautiful? Peacebuilding between International Interventions and Local Led Initiatives*, edited by S. Hellmüller, and M. Sachsi. New York: Springer, 2014.

Hellmüller, S., J. Pring, and O. Richmond. "How Norms Matter in Mediation: An Introduction." *Swiss Political Science Review* 26, no. 4 (2020).

Jaipur Literary Festival. Accessed December 10, 2021. https://jaipurliteraturefestival.org/.

Janjua, H. "Why is the Pakistan Government Cracking Down on NGOs?" *Die Welt*, February 11, 2021, accessed December 3, 2021. https://www.dw.com/en/why-is-the-pakistani-government-cracking-down-on-ngos/a-56537755.

Jones, P. "Talking for the Sake of It, or Making a Difference? Measuring and Evaluating Track Two Diplomacy." In *New Directions in Peacebuilding Evaluation*, edited by T.P. D'Estree. New York: Roman and Littlefield, 2019.

Jones, P. *Track Two Diplomacy in Theory and Practice*. Palo Alto CA: Stanford University Press, 2015.

Kanwal, G. "India-Pakistan Track II Peacemaking Efforts." Centre for Land Warfare Studies, December 27, 2011, accessed December 10, 2021. https://archive.claws.in/748/india-pakistan-track-ii-peace-making-efforts-brig-gurmeet-kanwal.html.

Kaye, D.D. *Talking to the Enemy: Track Two Diplomacy in the Middle East and South Asia*. Santa Monica: Rand Corp, 2007.

Kelman, H.C. "Interactive Problem-Solving: Informal Mediation by the Scholar Practitioner." In *Studies in International Mediation: Essays in Honor of Jeffrey Z. Rubin*, edited by J. Bercovitch. New York: Palgrave MacMillan, 2002.

Kutty, B.M. "Pakistan-India Relations: Non-Governmental Initiatives for Peace." *Pakistan Horizon* 57, no. 3 (2004).

Lahore Literary Festival. Accessed December 10, 2021. http://www.lahorelitfest.com/.

Lederach, J.P. *Building Peace: Sustainable Reconciliation in Divided Societies*. Washington, DC: United States Institute of Peace, 1997.

Lehrs, L. "A Last-Minute Private Peace Initiative: Albert Ballin's Mediation Efforts between Germany and Britain, 1908–1914." *Hague Journal of Diplomacy* 13, no. 3 (2018).

Lieberfeld, D. "Evaluating the Contributions of Track Two Diplomacy to Conflict Termination in South Africa, 1984–90." *Journal of Peace Research* 39, no. 3 (2002).

Maini, T.S., and Y.L. Hamdani. "A New Face for India and Pakistan's Track Two Diplomacy." *The Diplomat*, October 20, 2014, accessed December 3, 2021. https://thediplomat. com/2014/10/a-new-face-for-india-and-pakistans-track-ii-diplomacy/.

Mitchell, C.R. "From Controlled Communication to Problem Solving: The Origins of Facilitated Conflict Resolution." *The International Journal of Peace Studies* 6, no. 1 (Spring 2001).

Nabeel, F. "Recasting Pakistan's Water Scarcity Challenge." Atlantic Council. Accessed December 11, 2021. https://www.atlanticcouncil.org/in-depth-research-reports/issue-brief/recasting-pakistans-water-scarcity-challenge/.

Nan, S.A., D. Druckman, and J.E. Horr. "Unofficial International Conflict Resolution: Is There a Track One and a Half? Are There Best Practices?" *Conflict Resolution Quarterly* 27, no. 1 (2009).

Palmiano Federer, J. "Cowboys or Mavericks? The Normative Agency of NGO Mediators." *In Rethinking Peace Mediation: Challenges of Contemporary Peacemaking Practice*, edited by C. Turner, and M. Wählisch. Bristol: Bristol University Press, 2021.

Palmiano Federer, J. "Toward a Normative Turn in Track Two Diplomacy? A Review of the Literature." *Negotiation Journal* 37, no. 4 (2021).

Palmiano Federer, J., J. Pickhardt, C. Altpeter, K. Abatis, and P. Lustenburger. Beyond the Tracks? Reflections on Multitrack Approaches to Peace Processes. Swisspeace, 2019.

Pugwash Conferences on Science and World Affairs. "South Asia." Accessed December 8, 2021. https://pugwash.org/category/south-asia/.

SAARC Secretariat. Accessed December 11, 2021. https://www.saarc-sec.org/.

Sandia National Laboratories, Publications Database. Accessed December 10, 2021. https://sandia.prod.acquia-sites.com/publications?fulltext=South+Asia.

Saunders, H. "Pre-Negotiation and Circum-Negotiation: Arenas of the Peace Process." In *Managing Global Chaos: Sources of and Responses to International Conflict*, edited by C.A. Crocker, F.O. Hampson, and P. Aall. Washington, DC: U.S. Institute of Peace, 1996.

Seeds of Peace, South Asia Programs. Accessed December 12, 2021. https://www.seedsofpeace.org/programs/developing-leaders/south-asia/.

Shah, A.S. "Non-Official Dialogue between India and Pakistan: Problems and Prospects." *ACDIS Occasional Paper*, University of Illinois, August 1997.

The International Institute for Strategic Studies. "South Asia." Accessed December 7, 2021. https://www.iiss.org/research/south-asia.

The Ottawa Dialogue. Accessed December 7, 2021. https://ottawadialogue.ca/.

The Stimson Centre. "South Asian Voices." Accessed December 7, 2021. https://southasianvoices.org/.

WISCOMP website. Accessed December 12, 2021. https://wiscomp.org/.

15
HUMAN SECURITY IN SOUTH ASIA

Swarna Rajagopalan

The idea of "human security" is intuitively appealing in South Asia, which in 2020 was home to 1,856,882.40 humans,[1] living in eight states, with several million of those humans being displaced within their states and many others elsewhere (estimate: 2.5 million)[2], stateless— that is, without entitlements. Of the internally displaced, 4,578,000 were displaced by conflict or violence[3] and 9,241,120 by disasters that occur more frequently due to climate change.[4] The precarity of their everyday survival lends an obviousness to this idea, while the traditional academic and policy discourse on security feels distant, hollow, and esoteric.

South Asian Snapshots

In South Asia, millions still live in poverty, meaning they live in conditions that might include poverty, homelessness, lack of access to safe drinking water and sanitation, lack of access to healthcare and education. These translate into lack of political agency and, therefore, lack of a voice in policymaking. The overlay of deprivation, conflict, climate change, and development projects that are predatory and/or unsustainable creates the condition of a permanent complex emergency for most ordinary South Asians. Life remains precarious, and for those further marginalized by structural inequalities related to caste, race, class, disability, gender, and sexual orientation, the availability of food, shelter, and clothing are no guarantee of a good life.

As Figure 15.1 shows, there are still significant numbers of South Asians living in poverty. While absolute incomes may have gone up and, therefore, the numbers of those living below the poverty line gone down, in terms of household deprivations in health, education, and standard of living, we are still looking at significant percentages of the population. Being employed may still only mean a hand-to-mouth existence for almost 40% of South Asians. The precarity of economic growth and progress in the region was evident with the onset of the COVID-19 pandemic.

Another way of assessing the well-being of a society is to look at how women fare (see Table 15.1). While most South Asian women can expect to live up to 65 years, if you look at their access to contraceptives, their chances of getting pregnant in their teens and surviving childbirth, it does not reflect the advances of modern medicine or the so-called advantages of modernity. They are still essentially reproductive machines. Apart from Bhutan and Nepal,

DOI: 10.4324/9781003246626-18

197

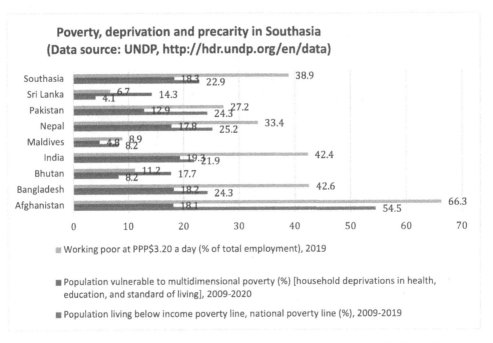

Figure 15.1 Poverty, deprivation, and precarity in South Asia. (Data source: UNDP, http://hdr.undp.org/en/data)

labor force participation rates are low; that is, paid work outside the home. Intimate partner violence rates are high across the region, with India and Sri Lanka approaching the "one in three women are abused" statistic level and Afghanistan and Bangladesh reporting that half the female population has experienced violence.

Before the pandemic, almost half the world's child marriages were reported to take place in South Asia, with one in three child brides being Indian.[5] In times of crisis, young girls below 18 are almost twice as likely to be married.[6] Early marriage puts an end to education for girls, limits their livelihood options, and makes them more vulnerable to domestic and intimate partner violence and at risk for HIV/AIDS.[7]

A penchant for secretive decision-making and sudden announcements, such as the Indian decision to demonetize large currency notes in 2016[8] or, in 2020, impose a total lockdown with four hours' notice, undermines any hard-built resilience in households and communities. Rather than meet an existing challenge, this creates a massive humanitarian crisis. When lockdowns came into effect, migrant workers lost their jobs and began to walk home across India. Urban women work largely in the informal sector; domestic workers were barred from entering housing societies where they worked, and street vendors could not sell their wares. Household incomes plummeted, resulting in debt, tensions, and violence within the home. Across the region, rising levels of domestic violence, elder abuse, child sexual abuse, forced marriage, and child marriage have been reported. It is hard to write today without writing about the pandemic, but the most important lesson of this time has been how poorly this region has journeyed toward giving its denizens a better life.

The reality of forced displacement defies the traditional security fiction that states are made up of people who have always lived and will always live in one place. Of the almost 8 billion

Table 15.1 Gender Indicators for South Asia

		Afghanistan	Bangladesh	Bhutan	India	Maldives	Nepal	Pakistan	Sri Lanka	South Asia
a)	Contraceptive prevalence, any methods (% of women ages 15–49)	19	63	66	54	19	47	34	65	52
b)	Survival to age 65 (% of cohort)	69	80	72	75	92	79	73	91	75
c)	Adolescent fertility rates (births per 1000 women ages 15–19)	61	82	18	11	7	64	38	20	23
d)	Labor force participation rate (% ages 15 and older), female	21.6	36.3	58.9	20.5	41.6	82.8	21.9	35.4	23.2
e)	Maternal mortality ratio (deaths per 100,000 live births)	638	173	183	133	53	186	140	36	149
f)	Violence against women ever experienced, intimate partner (% of female population ages 15 and older)	50.8	54.2	15.1	28.8	16.3	25	24.5	31	Not available

Sources: a–c: The World Bank, Data, accessed at https://data.worldbank.org on November 5, 2021

d–f: UNDP, Database, accessed at http://hdr.undp.org/en/data on November 5, 2021

Swarna Rajagopalan

Table 15.2 Internal Displacement in South Asia (2020)

	Conflict New Displacement	Conflict Total Number of Internally Displaced Persons (IDPs)	Disaster New Displacement	Disaster Total Number of IDPs	Total New Displacement	Total Number of IDPs
Afghanistan	404,000	3,547,000	46,000	1,117,000	450,000	4,664,000
Bangladesh	230	427,000	4,443,000	345,000	4,443,230	772,000
Bhutan			120		120	
India	3900	473,000	3,856,000	929,000	3,859,900	1,402,000
Nepal			48,000	28,000	48,000	28,000
Pakistan	390	104,000	829,000	806,000	829,390	910,000
Sri Lanka		27,000	19,000	1400	19,000	28,400

Source: Internal Displacement Monitoring Centre, Dataset, Global Internal Displacement Database, accessed at https://www.internal-displacement.org/database/displacement-data on November 5, 2021.

people on the earth in 2020, almost 8 million are internally displaced persons in South Asia alone (see Table 15.2).[9]

United Nations High Commissioner for Refugees (UNHCR) estimated that 11.2 million people fled their countries in 2020 alone. Afghanistan produces among the largest number of refugees while Pakistan and Bangladesh ranked among the host countries taking in most refugees.[10] If 86% of the world's refugees are hosted by developing countries, South Asian states hosted 2,593,748 in 2020 (see Table 15.3).[11] These estimates are based on those forcibly displaced who are registered in some way. Many are displaced without any records or registration, and for them, access to the most basic benefits becomes impossible.[12]

The Hobbesian nature of life for the average South Asian is hard to deny as this is written at the end of 2021. The case for paradigms and frameworks that place this human life at the center of both study and policy is an ethical one and a practical one.

The Evolving Discourse on Human Security

The antecedents of "human security" lie in initiatives like the World Order Models Project[13] and in three Global Commission reports by Willy Brandt, Olof Palme, and Gro Harlem Brundtland.[14] These found expression in the contributions by two South Asian intellectuals, Mahbub ul Haq and Amartya Sen, both economists, who became early architects of the human security discourse.

Mahbub ul Haq and Amartya Sen's work on poverty, deprivation, and development led them to the conclusion that we are not secure by virtue of armies and arsenals alone, as

Table 15.3 Refugees Hosted in 2020

Afghanistan	72,278
Bangladesh	866,534
India	195,403
Nepal	19,565
Pakistan	1438,955
Sri Lanka	1013

Source: World Bank, 2021

much as in the absence of hunger, illness, and daily intimidation. The first articulation of the term appeared in a United Nations Development Programme (UNDP) report rather than a security policy document.

Mahbub ul Haq was a founder of UNDP's human development reports. The first report in 1990 defined human development thus: "Human development is a process of enlarging people's choices. The most critical of these wide-ranging choices are to live a long and healthy life, to be educated and to have access to resources needed for a decent standard of living. Additional choices include political freedom, guaranteed human rights and personal self-respect."[15] Four years later, the 1994 UNDP Human Development Report used the term human security, putting people rather than states at the heart of how we define security and insecurity. "For most people today, a feeling of insecurity arises more from worries about daily life than from the dread of a cataclysmic world event. Job security, income security, health security, environmental security, security from crime-these are the emerging concerns of human security all over the world."[16]

Launched in 1990, the UNDP Human Development Report began to relate and measure development in terms that related not just to macroeconomic measures but to the actual quality of life and welfare of human beings. The Human Development Index measures how states are doing in these terms by measuring indicators along three dimensions: A long and healthy life, being knowledgeable, and having a decent standard of living.[17] UNDP's 1994 report, which introduced the term "human security," identified seven areas in which humans experienced threats to their security: Economic security, food security, health security, environmental security, personal security, community security, and political security.

In 2000, at a conference on human security, the Secretary-General Kofi Annan spoke of "freedom from fear" and "freedom from want."[18] He also mentioned the "freedom of future generations to inherit a healthy natural environment." Working from 2001 to 2003, the Commission on Human Security, which was co-chaired by Sadako Ogata, and Amartya Sen added, "freedom to live in dignity."[19] Tadjbakhsh and Chenoy point out that the Commission's definition of human security combined "the necessity to protect vital freedoms by building on people's strengths and aspirations (Sen's approach to capabilities) and protecting them from critical and pervasive threat situations (Ogata's approach)."[20] The idea of security was thus anchored in the well-being of humans living in interdependent states rather than the survival of states within an anarchical system.

In the decade after the UNDP report first talked about "human security," the idea was implicit or explicated in other speeches and reports.[21] One of these was the final report of the International Commission on Intervention and State Sovereignty, which advocated a "Responsibility to Protect," whereby humanitarian interventions were justified to protect human beings if their own states were failing to do so. In 2005, "In Larger Freedom," a progress report on the Millennium Development Goals, was divided into three parts—freedom from want (a commitment to the Goals); freedom from fear (a new security consensus), and freedom to live in dignity (human rights, and the Responsibility to Protect).[22] The idea of human security changed the answers to the three key questions in security studies: Whose security? security from what? security by what means?

"Human security" came to be adopted by a few states primarily as a foreign policy value. Japan has supported the Commission on Human Security and made development assistance a central part of its foreign policy—addressing "freedom from want." Canada has focused on "freedom from fear," with its support for humanitarian interventions, for instance.

There has been a great deal of writing and thinking on this subject, both conceptual discussions: Is a broad definition useful or analytically profligate? Human security has been critiqued as a concept, for its analytical utility, for political reasons (for its sidelining of the state), for imposing one culturally bound set of values on the world, and because it would be hard to implement.[23] In just 2020–2021, a Google Scholar search[24] showed pages of publications relating the concept to climate change, COVID-19 and biosecurity, racism, human rights, terrorism, economic precariousness, food and energy security, and gender—and the studies involved cases from around the world.

The extension of the idea of security, as human security, to include a host of issues is a tempting proposition, and not just for activists. Identifying any issue as a security issue is an argument for raising its priority level, increasing its resource allocation, and escalating decision-making levels.[25] This speech act of securitization, however, has the concomitant effect of requiring citizens to surrender agency to technocrats or experts and decision-makers who are allowed to be less accountable in the interests of security. Security concerns are insulated from public discussion and by extension, critique. Thus, by securitizing the well-being of humans, we ironically increase the insecurity of those who wish to engage critically with how it is being served. If the idea of human security enables the securitization of everyday life, then ironically it could reinforce the militarization that is a side-effect of statist security projects.

The Human Security Bottom-line in South Asia

A summary of the human security challenges in South Asia might include a very long litany of woes. Four background conditions underpin this litany: Structural inequalities, governance failures, climate change, and a changing citizenship context where belonging is defined by exclusions and citizen agency is limited.

Structural Inequalities

As a region, South Asia is marked by great deprivation but also pockets of immense affluence and privilege. In the year before the pandemic disrupted economies around the world, the South Asia Alliance for Poverty Eradication released a report, Growing Inequality in South Asia.[26] The report points to three standard measures of inequality—the Gini Coefficient, the Palma Ratio, and the Income Quintile Share Ratio—to show that the gap between the richest and poorest is growing at an alarming rate. The report observes that "the relationship between economic growth and inequality has been directly proportional."[27]

A World Bank study on inequality in the states that it is a function of circumstances at birth (gender and caste), opportunities during youth (health and education), and through a life-time, mobility (the potential to move for a job or to a city) as well as socio-economic support systems set up by the state.[28] In South Asia, social exclusion extends beyond gender and caste, though. States have sought to restrict access to rights and opportunities for linguistic, religious, and ethnic minorities. The lack of facilities and provisions to include people with disabilities makes them unequal citizens. Class barriers are almost insurmountable for most, and in the aftermath of the pandemic, it will be hard for working class communities to recover. A 2021 Oxfam briefing paper stated that while it took just nine months for the world's 1000 richest people to recover, the poorest may take over a decade to recover from the impact of COVID-19.[29]

The abstraction "structural inequalities" is a composite of daily human experiences of uncertainty about survival. When her supervisor routinely grazes her bottom on his inspection of the factory work floor, the worker must choose between asserting her right not to be touched without consent and earning a living. When one caste builds a wall in the middle of the village, restricting access to the bus stand, young people from the other caste must risk lynching to go to their college. When a mob sets fire to a place of worship belonging to a different community or beats a man to death because he may have eaten beef, what should be a matter of individual preference or belief becomes a matter of life and death. When middle class housing complexes terminate the services of domestic helpers during a pandemic arguing that they come from less hygienic surroundings, what they see as a safety measure throws entire families into chronic hunger, especially in the absence of a social safety net.

Governance Failure

Strictly, "governance" simply means the act or process of governing, but since the 1980s, the term has come to be used to evoke certain norms that governments are expected to adhere to. There are two dimensions to governance.[30] The first relates to service delivery and resource allocation. The second relates governance to democratic norms—rule of law, human rights, transparency, accountability, institutional integrity, and public participation. Both contribute to the insecurity and survival challenges of citizens. Good governance enables citizens to transcend the survival and security challenges posed by structural inequalities, by providing services and ensuring access to them, in a transparent and fair manner. South Asian governments have by and large fared poorly on both dimensions.

The new Taliban government in *Afghanistan* has imposed curbs on citizens leaving the country.[31] Reprisals have followed for members of the old government, raids on the homes of journalists and human rights defenders have been carried out, and the access of women and girls to education, livelihoods, and the public sphere are once more being restricted. Citizenship rules in *Bhutan* are strict and many Nepali speakers are not citizens, depriving them of the right to vote, and thereby, representation.[32] In one of *India*'s most developed states, Tamil Nadu, data gathered through Right to Information petitions showed that 300 people from Scheduled Caste/Scheduled Tribe communities were killed in caste murders just between 2016 and 2020.[33] The State Vigilance Monitoring Committee, which is meant to investigate this, has met thrice in 30 years.

It has been reported that chronic hunger and malnutrition, unresolved over the decades, still result in stunting and low weight among children in *Nepal*.[34] Lack of access to food is a function of poverty, structural inequalities, and governance failures and has long-term consequences for the country. The Rohingya exodus from *Myanmar* has created great economic pressure for *Bangladesh*.[35] The costs of supporting the refugees, who are able to intermingle with locals and the pressure on land, ecology, and infrastructure pose a humanitarian and governance challenge. The *Maldives*' dependence on luxury tourism had provided a basis for growth, but first the tsunami in 2004 and then the pandemic in 2020–2021 have shown that tourism can be a precarious foundation for economic well-being.[36] Successive governments have failed to diversify the country's economic bases. The massive protests underway in Gwadar, *Pakistan,* illustrate how geopolitical choices have an impact on local living conditions. One of the key issues has been the intrusion and poaching by Chinese trawlers in the waters where, traditionally, locals have fished.[37]

Sri Lanka's incomplete transition from conflict to peace leaves many human security challenges unresolved, including the return of refugees and the internally displaced as well as the location of the thousands of those "disappeared" during and after the war ended. This leaves many households in limbo, not just emotionally but also economically as without proof of death, families are unable to claim "widow benefits" or property rights.[38]

The failure to address foundational problems—from historical iniquities to providing the basics—in ways that are fair-handed, transparent, responsive, and sustainable, results sooner or later, in damaging people's life-chances and their security.

Climate Change

Commenting on South Asia's vulnerability to climate change, a recent World Bank report stated, "The region is living through a 'new climate normal' in which intensifying heat waves, cyclones, droughts, and floods are testing the limits of government, businesses, and citizens to adapt."[39] While people struggle to make sense of unseasonal extreme weather that destroys harvests and disrupts urban infrastructure, the governments of the region represent a spectrum of positions on the climate crisis. If the Maldives, as a small island developing state whose existence is imperiled by rising sea levels, has been a leading advocate of climate action, then India, which claims to speak for other emerging economies, is focused on an apportionment of responsibilities that will not penalize some countries for the emissions of others. What South Asians are experiencing everyday suggests that the time for this negotiation may now be past.[40]

Human security during the climate emergency depends on three inter-related responses.[41] The first is to prevent a further degradation of the environment and to roll-back whatever damage is remediable. The second is to build community resilience. The third is to factor climate change into development plans and projects.

At the 2021 United Nations Climate Change Conference (COP26), South Asian governments drew attention to the specific climate change challenges that they faced.[42] Their commitments were focused largely on rolling back emissions and adoption of renewable fuels. The phasing out of coal was a contentious issue for India, among other larger developing countries. A sticking point for all the countries is the cost of adaptation—who will pay for the transition to cleaner energy?[43]

The challenge of community resilience seemed to have been a peripheral concern at the COP26, though Bangladesh and Maldives both raised the question of preparing for climate change refugees. Progress on the Sustainable Development Goals as well as Disaster Risk Reduction best practices is undermined by climate change, which is the major driver of risk at this moment. Climate-smart disaster risk management entails taking into account the changing nature of weather and climate extremes, that "disasters are primarily caused by processes that lead vulnerable people and assets to be in locations which are exposed to hazards," and working to reduce emissions.[44] Preparing communities to cope and survive increasingly frequent disasters requires that we recognize that inequality exacerbates their impact, and that building resilience involves not just mortar and bricks infrastructure but an understanding of and the courage to tackle those hierarchies.

The accelerating climate crisis does not just undermine progress on the Sustainable Development Goals, but also makes it imperative that we re-think "development" itself. What will it mean to develop backward areas or communities? What will be the measures of our progress? We have already learned to question development projects that replace marshlands with industrial estates or displace communities. It is important that our projects now anticipate climate disasters, extreme weather events, and the depredation these will cause. For instance, while tourism might seem viable in a hill-side town, frequent landslides and flash floods not only disrupt trade but also destroy infrastructure. Having a back-up revenue source would be climate-smart and would reinforce community resilience and security.

Citizenship

Writing in the early 1990s, Mohammed Ayoob stated that it was the state-building process that was the source of most insecurity in the "Third World."[45] This is taken to refer to the consolidation of physical borders and to institutions. Equally, if not more, central, however, are questions relating to citizenship and belonging. There are two dimensions, not unrelated, to this. One relates to ethnicity or other identity markers (faith, language, caste). The other relates to the relationship between citizen and state.

Citizenship has been contentious for the better part of a century in South Asia. Whether states should be defined by ethnic or communal markers and who therefore belongs more rightfully than others is a familiar contest. The formation of Pakistan in 1947 was based on one differentiation between the Muslims of the subcontinent and others. The formation of Bangladesh in 1971 marked ethnolinguistic distinctions within the category of South Asian Muslims. Majoritarian impulses persist in both countries till date, expressed as political domination. In Pakistan, it takes the form of Punjabi domination over national politics but also more conservative and radical forms of Islam over other sects. In Bangladesh, it was manifest in the difficult history of the Chittagong Hill Tracts communities with the mainstream.

In Sri Lanka, the decades-long war originated in a majoritarian drive to identify the state as Sinhala Buddhist, with a bid to rectify what was seen as a colonial partiality toward minorities. While the war ended in 2009, the underlying issues remain unresolved, and the stalled transitional justice process is evident.

India, which began with an inclusive ideology and a pluralistic vision, has followed its neighbors by repeatedly voting into power a party whose ideology favors one faith community over others, that seeks to identify India with the Hindu community—in discourse and in law. The Citizenship (Amendment) Act 2019 made it possible for non-Muslim refugees from Afghanistan, Pakistan, and Bangladesh to become citizens. The law has faced criticism and massive protests for its discrimination against Muslims and has been read along with the project to create a National Register of Citizens, which would render stateless those who cannot provide birth or identity proofs.

Citizenship matters because citizenship is what entitles people to the protection and services of a state. Between governance failures that are reflected in inadequate and/or inefficient delivery of services relating to nutrition, health, sanitation, education, and even safety, and deliberate exclusions from access to these services, South Asian states are reinforcing vulnerabilities rather than alleviating them. When citizenship is denied, and a person is rendered stateless, the very foundations of their "freedom from fear," "freedom from want," and "freedom to live with dignity" are shaken.

The other dimension of citizenship is the relationship between the citizen (or collectives of citizens, that is, civil society) and the state. Freedom of expression and assembly are key. While all South Asian constitutions recognize these,[46] in reality, governments have a less than smooth relationship with civil society organizations, especially those that are human rights advocates or that mobilize public opinion around foundational issues—such as citizenship. Most South Asian constitutions also have emergency provisions, and their statute books hold on to an anti-sedition law. In an annual report, CIVICUS, a global civil society alliance ranked civic space in Afghanistan, Bangladesh, India, and Pakistan as "Repressed" while Bhutan, Maldives, Nepal, and Sri Lanka are "Obstructed."[47]

> Across South Asia, civil society is being increasingly constrained ... Anti-democratic authoritarian tendencies and greater securitization of laws and practices appears to be the main drivers of this narrowing trend, with the mid-2010s appearing to be

the period of convergence for this constriction in many of the countries. Democracy champions, human rights defenders (HRDs), and activists have been in the crosshairs of authorities everywhere for challenging state actions and speaking out. A great deal of the narrowing of space for civil society concerns minorities, which is also due to the hardening of majoritarianism across the region.[48]

Country by country, the report found that freedom of expression, association, and assembly were being curtailed across the region. The targeting of human rights defenders, especially women and minorities, was common across regimes. Increasing regulation and financial constraints on civil society organizations hampered their ability to function, especially if they work on civil rights, labor, or environment. Finally, the pandemic has served as an excuse to increase both policing and surveillance, with the use of apps for contact tracing, mapping isolation areas or vaccination registrations.[49] Governments have been cladding their emergency responses in militaristic terms, waging "war" on the virus,[50] policing lockdowns,[51] and raising and allocating resources without transparency or accountability.[52] Despite this, the virus has torn through populations, leaving them devastated. The result was an aggregation of data without clear privacy regulations.

Summary: Defining the Bottom-line

In South Asia, as perhaps it does elsewhere, the academic discourse on human security captures the reality of everyday life. For people trapped in historically hierarchical social relationships by growing economic inequality and forceful political gatekeeping, unable to access the bare minimum survival necessities, in a deteriorating ecological crisis, without being able to hold anyone accountable, insecurity is reality. The infinite potential of humans as creative agents in their own lives is limited by systems that constrain without offering much in return. The power of the idea of human security has lain in its ability to capture lived reality.

Conclusion

The account in this chapter locates the origins of human insecurity in four structural, systemic factors: Structural inequalities, governance failure, climate change, and citizenship. The road to "freedom from fear," "freedom from want," and "freedom to live in dignity" begins with opening the discussion of security beyond policy board rooms and academic conferences to take cognizance of everyday reality.

When you juxtapose the reality of the woman locked down with her three-generational family into a two-room home, with mouths to feed, mounting debt, arguments about money and violent abuse, who is also trying to protect her teenage daughter from the roaming hands of other family members, against that of South Asia's massive armies and nuclear arsenals—it may be a false dichotomy, but it is also true that the latter is of no use to the former. Making the political choice to speak of human security is not to reject the traditional focus on state security but to enhance and, therefore, to ground the security of states in the everyday security of the humans who make up the states.

Notes

1 The World Bank, "Population, Total – South Asia," World Bank Open Data, accessed December 15, 2021, https://data.worldbank.org/indicator/SP.POP.TOTL?locations=8S.

Human Security in South Asia

2 Nafees Ahmad, "Options for Protecting Refugees in South Asia," *Harvard International Law Journal*, 2019, https://harvardilj.org/2019/09/options-for-protecting-refugees-in-south-asia/.

3 The World Bank, "Internally Displaced Persons, Total Displaced by Conflict and Violence (Number of People)—South Asia," World Bank Open Data, accessed December 15, 2021, https://data.worldbank.org/indicator/VC.IDP.TOCV?locations=8S.

4 The World Bank, "Internally Displaced Persons, New Displacement Associated with Disasters (Number of Cases) – South Asia," World Bank Open Data, accessed December 15, 2021, https://data.worldbank.org/indicator/VC.IDP.NWDS?locations=8S.

5 UNICEF, "Towards Ending Child Marriage, Global Trends and Profiles of Progress" (2021), 12, https://data.unicef.org/wp-content/uploads/2021/10/Towards-Ending-Child-Marriage-Global-trends-and-profiles-of-progress-report.pdf.

6 UNICEF, 15.

7 UNICEF India, "Ending Child Marriage and Adolescent Empowerment," accessed November 5, 2021, https://www.unicef.org/india/what-we-do/end-child-marriage.

8 Krishna Veera Vanamali, "Demonetisation, 5 Years on: Key Economic Indicators Paint a Mixed Picture," *Business Standard*, November 8, 2021.

9 Internal Displacement Monitoring Centre, "2020 Internal Displacement, Global Internal Displacement Database," accessed November 5, 2021, https://www.internal-displacement.org/database/displacement-data.

10 UNHCR, "Global Trends in Forced Displacement 2020" (2020), 18–19, https://www.unhcr.org/60b638e37/unhcr-global-trends-2020.

11 The World Bank, "Refugee Population by Country or Territory of Asylum – South Asia," World Bank Open Data, accessed November 5, 2021, https://data.worldbank.org/indicator/SM.POP.REFG.

12 Women's Regional Network, "Women's Regional Network Publications," Publications, accessed December 18, 2021, https://www.womensregionalnetwork.org/publications. (In community-based research among IDP women in Afghanistan, Pakistan, and India, women repeatedly spoke about this.)

13 Amanda Dugan, "The World Order Models Project," *World Policy*, March 7, 2012, http://worldpolicy.org/2012/03/07/the-world-order-models-project/.

14 Independent Commission on International Development Issues, "North-South: A Programme for Survival" (1980), https://books.google.co.in/books/about/North_South_a_Programme_for_Survival.html?id=yS-7AAAAIAAJ&redir_esc=y; The Independent Commission on Disarmament and Security Issue, "Common Security: A Blueprint for Survival" (1982), https://www.foreignaffairs.com/reviews/capsule-review/1982-09-01/common-security-blueprint-survival; World Commission on Environment and Development, "Our Common Future" (1987), https://sustainabledevelopment.un.org/content/documents/5987our-common-future.pdf.

15 United Nations Development Programme (UNDP), "Human Development Report 1990" (1990), 1, http://hdr.undp.org/sites/default/files/reports/219/hdr_1990_en_complete_nostats.pdf.

16 United Nations Development Programme (UNDP), "Human Development Report 1994" (1994), 3, http://hdr.undp.org/sites/default/files/reports/255/hdr_1994_en_complete_nostats.pdf.

17 United Nations Development Programme (UNDP), "Human Development Index (HDI)," Human Development Reports, accessed November 21, 2021, http://hdr.undp.org/en/content/human-development-index-hdi.

18 United Nations, "Secretary-General Salutes International Workshop on Human Security in Mongolia," May 8, 2000, Press Release SG/SM/7382, https://www.un.org/press/en/2000/20000508.sgsm7382.doc.html.

19 Commission on Human Security, "Human Security Now" (2003), https://reliefweb.int/sites/reliefweb.int/files/resources/91BAEEDBA50C6907C1256D19006A9353-chs-security-may03.pdf.

20 Shahrbanou Tadjbakhsh and Anuradha Chenoy, *Human Security: Concepts and Implications*, 1st ed. (Routledge India, 2008), 28, https://www.routledge.com/Human-Security-Concepts-and-implications/Tadjbakhsh-Chenoy/p/book/9780415473385.

21 Tadjbakhsh and Chenoy, *Human Security: Concepts and Implications*.

22 Report of the Secretary-General, "In Larger Freedom: Towards Development, Security and Human Rights for All" (United Nations General Assembly, March 21, 2005), https://documents-dds-ny.un.org/doc/UNDOC/GEN/N05/270/78/PDF/N0527078.pdf?OpenElement.

23 Tadjbakhsh and Chenoy, *Human Security: Concepts and Implications*, 58.

24 "Google Scholar Search for Academic Work on 'Human Security,'" accessed November 21, 2021, https://scholar.google.com/scholar?as_ylo=2020&q=Human+Security&hl=en&as_sdt=0,5.

25 Ole Waever, "Securitization and Desecuritization," in *On Security*, ed. Ronnie D. Lipschutz (New York: Columbia University Press, 1995).

26 South Asia Alliance for Poverty Eradication (SAAPE) Secretariat, "'Growing Economies, Growing Inequalities,' Growing Inequality in South Asia - South Asia Inequality Report 2019" (Kathmandu, 2019), 7–14, https://saape.org/wp-content/uploads/2019/10/SA-report.pdf.

27 South Asia Alliance for Poverty Eradication (SAAPE) Secretariat, "'Growing Economies, Growing Inequalities,' Growing Inequality in South Asia - South Asia Inequality Report 2019" (Kathmandu, 2019), 13, https://saape.org/wp-content/uploads/2019/10/SA-report.pdf.

28 Martín Rama *et al.*, "Addressing Inequality in South Asia" (The World Bank, 2015), 92, https://openknowledge.worldbank.org/bitstream/handle/10986/20395/9781464800221.pdf?sequence=5&isAllowed=y.

29 Oxfam International, "The Inequality Virus" (January 2021), 8.

30 "UN System Task Team on the Post-2015 Development Agenda" (UNDESA, UNDP, UNESCO, May 2012), 3–4, https://www.un.org/millenniumgoals/pdf/Think%20Pieces/7_governance.pdf.

31 Human Rights Watch, "Afghanistan," 2021, https://www.hrw.org/asia/afghanistan.

32 Freedom House, "Freedom in the World 2021: Bhutan," 2021, https://freedomhouse.org/country/bhutan/freedom-world/2021.

33 Lalitha Ranjani, "300 Caste Killings in TN, 13 Convictions in Five Years: RTI Data," *The New Indian Express*, September 13, 2021, https://www.newindianexpress.com/states/tamil-nadu/2021/sep/15/300-caste-killings-in-tn-13-convictions-in-five-years-rti-data-2358885.html.

34 "Hunger for Governance," *Nepali Times*, June 17, 2021, sec. Editorial, https://www.nepalitimes.com/editorial/hunger-for-governance/.

35 Mohammad Sajedur Rahman and Nurul Huda Sakib, "Statelessness, Forced Migration and the Security Dilemma along Borders: An Investigation of the Foreign Policy Stance of Bangladesh on the Rohingya Influx," *SN Social Sciences* 1, no. 6 (June 30, 2021), https://doi.org/10.1007/s43545-021-00173-y.

36 The World Bank, "Overview: The World Bank in Maldives," accessed December 15, 2021, https://www.worldbank.org/en/country/maldives/overview#1.

37 Arif Rafiq, "Pakistan Wanted Gwadar to Be the Next Singapore. China's Role Didn't Help," *Foreign Policy*, December 14, 2021, https://foreignpolicy.com/2021/12/14/pakistan-gwadar-port-protests-china-belt-and-road-cpec/.

38 Suryanarayan V., "Continuing Tragedy of War Widows in Sri Lanka," *The New Indian Express*, April 20, 2021, https://www.newindianexpress.com/opinions/2021/apr/20/continuingtragedy-of-war-widows-insri-lanka-2292240.html.

39 The World Bank, "South Asia Climate Roadmap," October 28, 2021, https://www.worldbank.org/en/region/sar/publication/south-asia-climate-roadmap.

40 Michael Kugelman, "Climate-Induced Displacement: South Asia's Clear and Present Danger," Wilson Center, September 30, 2020, https://www.wilsoncenter.org/article/climate-induced-displacement-south-asias-clear-and-present-danger; Chirag Dhara and Roxy Mathew Koll, "How and Why India's Climate Will Change in the Coming Decades," *The India Forum*, August 20, 2021, https://www.theindiaforum.in/article/how-and-why-india-s-climate-will-change-coming-decades?utm_source=website&utm_medium=organic&utm_campaign=category&utm_content=Environment.

41 Indrani Phukan, "The Process of the Climate Smart Disaster Risk Management Approach (CSDRM)," Southasiadisasters.net, Towards Climate Smart Disaster Risk Reduction in India, no. 88 (November 2012): 2. (This is similar to what Disaster Risk Reduction experts refer to as a 'Climate Smart Disaster Risk Management Approach.')

42 Aakriti Ghimire, "COP26 and Nepal's Climate Commitments," *The Kathmandu Post*, November 12, 2021, https://kathmandupost.com/climate-environment/2021/11/12/cop26-and-nepal-s-climate-commitments; Tribune Desk, "COP 26: National Statement by Prime Minister Sheikh Hasina," *Dhaka Tribune*, November 2, 2021, https://www.dhakatribune.com/bangladesh/2021/11/02/cop-26-national-statement-by-prime-minister-sheikh-hasina; Sam Meredith, "'We Are Not Drowning, We Are Fighting': Countries Vulnerable to Climate Disaster Issue Rallying Cry," *CNBC*, November 2, 2021, https://www.cnbc.com/2021/11/02/cop26-maldives-barbados-and-climate-activists-issue-warrior-cry-to-world.html; Aron White, "'We Don't Believe in Net Zero at the Moment' – Pakistan's

Top Climate Official at COP26," *The Third Pole*, November 4, 2021, https://www.thethirdpole.net/en/climate/we-dont-believe-in-net-zero-pakistan-top-climate-official-at-cop26/.

43 Santosh Sharma Poudel, "COP26 Finds Its Scapegoats – India and China," *The Diplomat*, November 17, 2021, https://thediplomat.com/2021/11/cop26-finds-its-scapegoats-india-and-china/; Michael Kugelman, "Can South Asia Get Serious about Climate Change?" *Foreign Policy*, November 4, 2021, https://foreignpolicy.com/2021/11/04/south-asia-cop26-climate-change-modi-pledge/.

44 Tom Mitchell, "CSDRM: Agenda for Action in Asia," Southasiadisasters.net, Towards Climate Smart Disaster Risk Reduction in India, no. 88 (November 2012): 10.

45 Mohammed Ayoob, *The Third World Security Predicament: State Making, Regional Conflict, and the International System* (Boulder: Lynne Rienner Publishers, 1995), https://www.rienner.com/title/The_Third_World_Security_Predicament_State_Making_Regional_Conflict_and_the_International_System.

46 Constitute website, accessed December 16, 2021, https://www.constituteproject.org/constitutions?lang=en&status=in_force&status=is_draft.

47 CIVICUS: World Alliance for Citizen Participation, "People Power Under Attack 2020: A Report Based on Data from the CIVICUS Monitor" (2020), https://civicus.contentfiles.net/media/assets/file/GlobalReport2020.pdf.

48 The South Asia Collective, "South Asia State of Minorities Report 2020: Minorities and Shrinking Civic Space," vii, accessed December 16, 2021, https://ruralindiaonline.org/en/library/resource/south-asia-state-of-minorities-report-2020-minorities-and-shrinking-civic-space/.

49 Radhika Radhakrishnan, "How Covid-19 Helped Govt Control Your Data & You," *Article 14*, March 3, 2021, https://www.article-14.com/post/how-covid-19-helped-govt-control-your-data-you.

50 Cynthia Enloe, "COVID-19: 'Waging War' Against a Virus is NOT What We Need to Be Doing," Women's International League for Peace and Freedom, accessed November 21, 2021, https://www.wilpf.org/covid-19-waging-war-against-a-virus-is-not-what-we-need-to-be-doing/.

51 Common Cause *et al.*, "Status of Policing in India Report 2020-21: Policing in the Covid-19 Pandemic" (Common Cause & Lokniti – Centre for the Study Developing Societies (CSDS), 2021), https://www.commoncause.in/wotadmin/upload/SPIR%202020-2021%20Vol.%20II%20Policing%20in%20the%20Covid-19%20Pandemic.pdf.

52 World Justice Project, "Accountable Governance and the COVID-19 Pandemic" (July 2020), https://worldjusticeproject.org/sites/default/files/documents/Accountable%20Governance-10.20.20.pdf. (This is just one of many INGO documents urging transparency and accountability in pandemic responses.)

Bibliography

Ahmad, Nafees. "Options for Protecting Refugees in South Asia." *Harvard International Law Journal*, 2019. https://harvardilj.org/2019/09/options-for-protecting-refugees-in-south-asia/.

Ayoob, Mohammed. *The Third World Security Predicament: State Making, Regional Conflict, and the International System*. Boulder: Lynne Rienner Publishers, 1995. https://www.rienner.com/title/The_Third_World_Security_Predicament_State_Making_Regional_Conflict_and_the_International_System.

CIVICUS: World Alliance for Citizen Participation. "People Power Under Attack 2020: A Report Based on Data from the CIVICUS Monitor." 2020. https://civicus.contentfiles.net/media/assets/file/GlobalReport2020.pdf.

Commission on Human Security. "Human Security Now." 2003. https://reliefweb.int/sites/reliefweb.int/files/resources/91BAEEDBA50C6907C1256D19006A9353-chs-security-may03.pdf.

Common Cause, Centre for the Study of Developing Societies, Programme for Comparative Democracy, TATA Trusts, and LAL Family Foundation. "Status of Policing in India Report 2020-21: Policing in the Covid-19 Pandemic." Common Cause and Lokniti – Centre for the Study Developing Societies (CSDS), 2021. https://www.commoncause.in/wotadmin/upload/SPIR%202020-2021%20Vol.%20II%20Policing%20in%20the%20Covid-19%20Pandemic.pdf.

Constitute website. Accessed December 16, 2021. https://www.constituteproject.org/constitutions?lang=en&status=in_force&status=is_draft.

Dhara, Chirag, and Roxy Mathew Koll. "How and Why India's Climate Will Change in the Coming Decades." *The India Forum*, August 20, 2021. https://www.theindiaforum.in/article/how-and-why-india-s-climate-will-change-coming-decades?utm_source=website&utm_medium=organic&utm_campaign=category&utm_content=Environment.

Dugan, Amanda. "The World Order Models Project." *World Policy*, March 7, 2012. http://worldpolicy.org/2012/03/07/the-world-order-models-project/.

Enloe, Cynthia. "COVID-19: 'Waging War' Against a Virus is NOT What We Need to Be Doing." Women's International League for Peace and Freedom. Accessed November 21, 2021. https://www.wilpf.org/covid-19-waging-war-against-a-virus-is-not-what-we-need-to-be-doing/.

Freedom House. "Freedom in the World 2021: Bhutan." 2021. https://freedomhouse.org/country/bhutan/freedom-world/2021.

Ghimire, Aakriti. "COP26 and Nepal's Climate Commitments." *The Kathmandu Post*, November 12, 2021. https://kathmandupost.com/climate-environment/2021/11/12/cop26-and-nepal-s-climate-commitments.

"Google Scholar Search for Academic Work on 'Human Security.'" Accessed November 21, 2021. https://scholar.google.com/scholar?as_ylo=2020&q=Human+Security&hl=en&as_sdt=0,5.

Human Rights Watch. "Afghanistan." 2021. https://www.hrw.org/asia/afghanistan.

"Hunger for Governance." *Nepali Times*, June 17, 2021, sec. Editorial. https://www.nepalitimes.com/editorial/hunger-for-governance/.

Independent Commission on International Development Issues. "North-South: A Programme for Survival." 1980. https://books.google.co.in/books/about/North_South_a_Programme_for_Survival.html?id=yS-7AAAAIAAJ&redir_esc=y.

Internal Displacement Monitoring Centre. "2020 Internal Displacement, Global Internal Displacement Database." Accessed November 5, 2021. https://www.internal-displacement.org/database/displacement-data.

Kugelman, Michael. "Can South Asia Get Serious About Climate Change?" *Foreign Policy*, November 4, 2021. https://foreignpolicy.com/2021/11/04/south-asia-cop26-climate-change-modi-pledge/.

———. "Climate-Induced Displacement: South Asia's Clear and Present Danger." Wilson Center, September 30, 2020. https://www.wilsoncenter.org/article/climate-induced-displacement-south-asias-clear-and-present-danger.

Meredith, Sam. "'We Are Not Drowning, We Are Fighting': Countries Vulnerable to Climate Disaster Issue Rallying Cry." *CNBC*, November 2, 2021. https://www.cnbc.com/2021/11/02/cop26-maldives-barbados-and-climate-activists-issue-warrior-cry-to-world.html.

Mitchell, Tom. "CSDRM: Agenda for Action in Asia." *Southasiadisasters.net*, Towards Climate Smart Disaster Risk Reduction in India, no. 88 (November 2012): 10.

Oxfam International. "The Inequality Virus." January 2021.

Phukan, Indrani. "The Process of the Climate Smart Disaster Risk Management Approach (CSDRM)." *Southasiadisasters.net*, Towards Climate Smart Disaster Risk Reduction in India, no. 88 (November 2012): 2.

Radhakrishnan, Radhika. "How Covid-19 Helped Govt Control Your Data & You." *Article 14*, March 3, 2021. https://www.article-14.com/post/how-covid-19-helped-govt-control-your-data-you.

Rafiq, Arif. "Pakistan Wanted Gwadar to Be the Next Singapore. China's Role Didn't Help." *Foreign Policy*, December 14, 2021. https://foreignpolicy.com/2021/12/14/pakistan-gwadar-port-protests-china-belt-and-road-cpec/.

Rama, Martín, Tara Béteille, Yue Li, Pradeep K. Mitra, and John Lincoln Newman. "Addressing Inequality in South Asia." The World Bank, 2015. https://openknowledge.worldbank.org/bitstream/handle/10986/20395/9781464800221.pdf?sequence=5&isAllowed=y.

Ranjani, Lalitha. "300 Caste Killings in TN, 13 Convictions in Five Years: RTI Data." *The New Indian Express*, September 13, 2021. https://www.newindianexpress.com/states/tamil-nadu/2021/sep/15/300-caste-killings-in-tn-13-convictions-in-five-years-rti-data-2358885.html.

Report of the Secretary-General. "In Larger Freedom: Towards Development, Security and Human Rights for All." United Nations General Assembly, March 21, 2005. https://documents-dds-ny.un.org/doc/UNDOC/GEN/N05/270/78/PDF/N0527078.pdf?OpenElement.

Sajedur Rahman, Mohammad, and Nurul Huda Sakib. "Statelessness, Forced Migration and the Security Dilemma along Borders: An Investigation of the Foreign Policy Stance of Bangladesh on the Rohingya Influx." *SN Social Sciences* 1, no. 160 (June 30, 2021). https://doi.org/10.1007/s43545-021-00173-y.

Sharma Poudel, Santosh. "COP26 Finds Its Scapegoats – India and China." *The Diplomat*, November 17, 2021. https://thediplomat.com/2021/11/cop26-finds-its-scapegoats-india-and-china/.

"'Growing Economies, Growing Inequalities,' Growing Inequality in South Asia – South Asia Inequality Report 2019." Kathmandu: South Asia Alliance for Poverty Eradication (SAAPE) Secretariat, 2019. https://saape.org/wp-content/uploads/2019/10/SA-report.pdf.

Suryanarayan, V. "Continuing Tragedy of War Widows in Sri Lanka." *The New Indian Express*, April 20, 2021. https://www.newindianexpress.com/opinions/2021/apr/20/continuingtragedy-of-war-widows-insri-lanka-2292240.html.

Tadjbakhsh, Shahrbanou, and Anuradha Chenoy. *Human Security: Concepts and Implications*. 1st ed. Routledge India, 2008. https://www.routledge.com/Human-Security-Concepts-and-implications/Tadjbakhsh-Chenoy/p/book/9780415473385.

The Independent Commission on Disarmament and Security Issue. "Common Security: A Blueprint for Survival." 1982. https://www.foreignaffairs.com/reviews/capsule-review/1982-09-01/common-security-blueprint-survival.

The South Asia Collective. "South Asia State of Minorities Report 2020: Minorities and Shrinking Civic Space." Accessed December 16, 2021. https://ruralindiaonline.org/en/library/resource/south-asia-state-of-minorities-report-2020-minorities-and-shrinking-civic-space/.

The World Bank. "Internally Displaced Persons, New Displacement Associated with Disasters (Number of Cases) – South Asia." World Bank Open Data. Accessed December 15, 2021. https://data.worldbank.org/indicator/VC.IDP.NWDS?locations=8S.

———. "Internally Displaced Persons, Total Displaced by Conflict and Violence (Number of People)—South Asia." World Bank Open Data. Accessed December 15, 2021. https://data.worldbank.org/indicator/VC.IDP.TOCV?locations=8S.

———. "Overview: The World Bank in Maldives." Accessed December 15, 2021. https://www.worldbank.org/en/country/maldives/overview#1.

———. "Population, Total – South Asia." World Bank Open Data. Accessed December 15, 2021. https://data.worldbank.org/indicator/SP.POP.TOTL?locations=8S.

———. "Refugee Population by Country or Territory of Asylum – South Asia." World Bank Open Data. Accessed November 5, 2021. https://data.worldbank.org/indicator/SM.POP.REFG.

———. "South Asia Climate Roadmap." The World Bank, October 28, 2021. https://www.worldbank.org/en/region/sar/publication/south-asia-climate-roadmap.

Tribune, Desk. "COP 26: National Statement by Prime Minister Sheikh Hasina." *Dhaka Tribune*, November 2, 2021. https://www.dhakatribune.com/bangladesh/2021/11/02/cop-26-national-statement-by-prime-minister-sheikh-hasina.

"UN System Task Team on the Post-2015 Development Agenda." UNDESA, UNDP, UNESCO, May 2012. https://www.un.org/millenniumgoals/pdf/Think%20Pieces/7_governance.pdf.

UNHCR. "Global Trends in Forced Displacement 2020." 2020. https://www.unhcr.org/60b638e37/unhcr-global-trends-2020.

UNICEF. "Towards Ending Child Marriage, Global Trends and Profiles of Progress." 2021. https://data.unicef.org/wp-content/uploads/2021/10/Towards-Ending-Child-Marriage-Global-trends-and-profiles-of-progress-report.pdf.

UNICEF India. "Ending Child Marriage and Adolescent Empowerment." Accessed November 5, 2021. https://www.unicef.org/india/what-we-do/end-child-marriage.

United Nations. "Secretary-General Salutes International Workshop on Human Security in Mongolia." May 8, 2000, Press Release SG/SM/7382. https://www.un.org/press/en/2000/20000508.sgsm7382.doc.html.

United Nations Development Programme (UNDP). "Human Development Index (HDI)." Human Development Reports. Accessed November 21, 2021. http://hdr.undp.org/en/content/human-development-index-hdi.

———. "Human Development Report 1990." 1990. http://hdr.undp.org/sites/default/files/reports/219/hdr_1990_en_complete_nostats.pdf.

———. "Human Development Report 1994." 1994. http://hdr.undp.org/sites/default/files/reports/255/hdr_1994_en_complete_nostats.pdf.

Vanamali, Krishna Veera. "Demonetisation, 5 Years on: Key Economic Indicators Paint a Mixed Picture." *Business Standard*, November 8, 2021.

Waever, Ole. "Securitization and Desecuritization." In *On Security*, edited by Ronnie D. Lipschutz. New York: Columbia University Press, 1995.

White, Aron. "'We Don't Believe in Net Zero at the Moment' – Pakistan's Top Climate Official at COP26." *The Third Pole*, November 4, 2021. https://www.thethirdpole.net/en/climate/we-dont-believe-in-net-zero-pakistan-top-climate-official-at-cop26/.

Women's Regional Network. "Women's Regional Network Publications." Publications. Accessed December 18, 2021. https://www.womensregionalnetwork.org/publications.

World Commission on Environment and Development. "Our Common Future." 1987. https://sustainabledevelopment.un.org/content/documents/5987our-common-future.pdf.

World Justice Project. "Accountable Governance and the COVID-19 Pandemic." July 2020. https://worldjusticeproject.org/sites/default/files/documents/Accountable%20Governance-10.20.20.pdf.

16
SOUTH ASIA: STATES OF CYBER(IN)SECURITY

Trisha Ray

Introduction

The proliferation of digital technologies has triggered a paradigm shift in how governments and businesses operate, and how people work, interact, and consume, and with it an imposition of sovereignty and borders in a space once considered outside the reach of governments, the "weary giants of flesh and steel."[1] In 2020, 3.5 billion people were online, with South Asia alone being home to approximately 990 million internet users. The region has also been home to some of the fastest growing digital economies in the world.[2] From ridesharing and food delivery apps, to booming online businesses and massive multi-year projects to onboard citizens onto e-government services and platforms, South Asia's digital adoption story has been remarkable. Accordingly, many of the governments of the region have articulated national strategies to leverage digital technologies to transform their own functioning and to modernize their economies, such as *Digital Bangladesh*, *Digital India*, the *Digital Nepal Framework*, and *Digital Pakistan*.

Concurrently, the volume of cyberattacks grew exponentially, and the Asia-Pacific region alone witnessed a 168% increase in cyberattacks between 2020 and 2021, with malicious actors targeting utilities, internet service providers, among others.[3] Instances of cyber espionage also continue to grow. Hackers sponsored by the DPRK and Russia, for instance, targeted vaccine researchers in Canada, France, India, South Korea, and the United States.[4]

Securing the digital highways that enable societies and industries to grow and prosper has therefore become an imperative for states, industries, and communities alike, one that crosses the realms of economic growth, national security, sustainable development, and geopolitics. As of 2020, 78 countries have national cybersecurity strategies, 91 have legislation for countering cybercrime, and 63 have outlined strategies for protecting critical infrastructure.[5]

A common refrain in cyberspace is that no one country or entity can solve cybersecurity challenges alone. Yet even as the networked nature of the cybersecurity challenge calls for a coordinated response, the massive strategic and economic benefits states and state-sponsored non-state actors gain from cyber operations has made consensus on *clear and enforceable* rules difficult. China frequently employs cyber espionage for economic and security objectives, including for industrial espionage and theft of information protected by intellectual property rights (IPR) law. Russia "sees activities in cyberspace as a subset to the all-encompassing framework of

DOI: 10.4324/9781003246626-19

'information confrontation.'"[6] In other words, cyberattacks are part of Moscow's information warfare strategy, which seeks to undermine the systems and alliances of its geopolitical rivals.

Many of the capitals of South Asia have in recent years expanded cooperation with partners globally. However, intra-regional cooperation has been limited, in part due to persistent geopolitical tensions. The India–Pakistan rivalry has for instance translated into cyberattacks targeting each other's government websites and critical infrastructure.

This chapter delves into the global status quo on cyber(in)security in South Asia and points to specific drivers of cyber instability in the region. It also highlights three narrative commonalities in how the countries in the region legislate on and engage with global processes in cybersecurity. Despite regional rivalries and other drivers of cyber instability, the capitals of South Asia have outlined similar concerns and priorities: A safe and secure cyberspace for economic prosperity; the need to counter the new challenges posed by the intersection of cyber and existing security threats such as terrorism; and negotiating the contours of sovereignty in a fundamentally borderless cyberspace. The chapter concludes with questions to animate inquiry into the next decade.

In Search of a Theory of Cyberspace

To understand the evolution of cybersecurity, it is imperative first to understand power and influence in cyberspace, and how this exercise is different from conventional conceptions of power in international relations.

Cyberspace is a networked electronic medium through which information is created, stored, processed, modified, exchanged, and eliminated.[7] It cannot be "destroyed" and is simultaneously *virtual* in that one cannot physically interact with it, and *real* in terms of the real-world effects of the flows within in it.

Often, political scientists apply theoretical frameworks based in conventional notions of power relations and conflict or seek precedents in older disruptive technologies.[8] From a neo-realist perspective, power is defined in terms of tangible assets, such as weapons, personnel, technology, and money.[9] Choucri and Clark applied the theory of Lateral Pressure—which refers to the tendency "of individuals and societies to expand their activities and exert influence and control beyond their established boundaries"—to describe state behavior in cyberspace.[10] Some, like China, the United States, and India, have shown lateral expansion in both conventional and cyber domains: Dominance in conventional technologies correlates with dominance in cyber.

An oddity of power in cyberspace, however, is that states can exercise outsized influence with relatively few resources. Chief of the General Staff of the Armed Forces of the Russian Federation, Valery Gerasimov, elucidates in a 2013 article:[11]

> We must acknowledge that, while we understand the essence of traditional military actions carried out by regular armed forces, we have only a superficial understanding of asymmetrical forms and means .... The information space opens wide asymmetrical possibilities for reducing the fighting potential of the enemy.

Power can also be defined in terms of "soft power," the ability (usually of states) to influence outcomes through cooption and "attraction" rather than coercion.[12] Nye defines cyber power as the ability to obtain preferred outcomes both within and outside cyberspace "through use of the electronically interconnected information resources of the cyber domain."[13] Kim for instance, uses Goddard's works on network theories in international relations in his paper describing middle power behavior in cyberspace.[14] Kim further writes about how cybersecurity is as much a battle of narratives as it is of capabilities:[15]

> Cyber security issues are typical examples of securitization in the sense that threats to security in cyberspace, at least so far, tend to be a matter of constituting discourses, rather than that of hunting down real threats.

Theoretical understandings of power in cyberspace are complicated by the sheer number of actors that populate it: Individuals, communities, governments, a panoply of non-state actors, and multinational corporations. States, while they remain a principal player, are not the only ones that can exert power and influence.[16]

It is difficult also to treat cyberspace theoretically as a separate domain.[17] This is true in that cyberspace cannot be treated as a domain separate from air, land, sea, and space. Accordingly, cybersecurity policies and processes cut across several conventional regimes: Space, nuclear, and drones are just some examples. Attempts at adapting existing conventions governing these technologies within the United Nations (UN) and elsewhere have proven challenging, however, given that these conventions govern the actions of states, and the coming decade will continue to see the proliferation of private companies and other non-state actors in these spheres.[18] Some experts also criticize the use of conventional arms control frames in modern thinking of cyberspace.[19] This framing is evident in the first *Tallinn Manual*, and in the fact that the UN's cyber norms process is under the UN Convention on Certain Conventional Weapons.

Cyberspace, and therefore cybersecurity, the security of data, networks, programs, and devices that constitute cyberspace, pertains not just to "security," but to essential systems like health, banking, telecommunications, and electricity, as well as the individuals who rely on them. Malware like 2017's NotPetya, reportedly part of Russia's arsenal in the conflict with Ukraine, and ransomware attacks WannaCry, traced to North Korean hackers, caused major disruptions in essential services, including notably UK's National Health Service.[20] In this sense then, cyberspace is also diffuse in another way and cybersecurity cannot be viewed as a separate, virtual system but rather as something embedded in our real, day-to-day lives.[21]

Cyber Instability in South Asia

South Asia is simultaneously digitally connected and fractured. The countries in the region have varying levels of digital connectivity, institutional capacities, and legislation. Maldives, for instance, has an underdeveloped cybersecurity ecosystem and is the only country in South Asia with neither a cybersecurity strategy nor a dedicated Computer Emergency Response Teams (CERT)/Computer Incident Response Teams (CIRT) as of 2021. Currently, the Penal Code Act 2014 (No. 19/2014) is the primary legal instrument for cybercrimes and the Cybercrime Department of the Maldives Police Service is the enforcing body.

Concurrently, South Asia is one of the least integrated in terms of regional institutions and structures. While an alphabet soup of regional organizations abounds—South Asian Association for Regional Cooperation (SAARC) and Bay of Bengal Initiative for Multi-Sectoral Technical and Economic Cooperation (BIMSTEC) primary among them—cooperation within these structures on cybersecurity is limited. The SAARC members (Afghanistan, Bangladesh, Bhutan, India, the Maldives, Nepal, Pakistan, and Sri Lanka) and the BIMSTEC countries (India, Thailand, Myanmar, Nepal, Bangladesh, Sri Lanka, and Bhutan) for instance have discussed cybercrime within the limited context of countering terrorism, including drug trafficking and human trafficking.[22] The CERTs/CIRTs of the region are part of different

Trisha Ray

Table 16.1 Cybersecurity and Connectivity in South Asia

Country	Cybersecurity Strategy	Privacy and Data Protection Legislation[23]	CERT/ CIRT	Internet Subscribers[24]	Global Cybersecurity Index Rank[25]
Afghanistan	National Cyber Security Strategy of Afghanistan (NCSA) 2014	None	AFCERT	8% (2015)	171
Bangladesh	National Cybersecurity Strategy 2014	None	BGD e-GOV CIRT bdCERT	77.7% (2021)	53
Bhutan	National Cybersecurity Strategy (Draft)	Bhutan Information, Communications and Media Act 2018	BtCIRT	48% (2019)	134
India	National Cybersecurity Policy 2013; 2020 (Draft)	Information Technology Act 2000 Personal Data Protection Bill (Draft)	CERT-In	61.6% (2021)	10
Maldives	None	Privacy and Data Protection Act (Draft)	None	63% (2017)	177
Nepal	National Cybersecurity Policy 2021 (Draft)	The Privacy Act 2018	npCERT	84% (2021)	94
Pakistan	National Cybersecurity Policy 2021	Personal Data Protection Bill (Draft)	Pakistan CERT	17% (2019)	79
Sri Lanka	Information and Cyber Security Strategy of Sri Lanka (2019–2023)	None	Sri Lanka CERT	35% (2020)	83

forums for cooperation, with little overlap. The CERTs of Bangladesh, Bhutan, India, and Sri Lanka are part of the Asia-Pacific CERT. Meanwhile, Pakistan and Bangladesh are part of the Organisation of Islamic Cooperation CERT (OIC-CERT). Deeper regional cooperation at both regional and extra-regional forums has also been confounded by persistent political differences and strategic divergence.

Drivers of Instability

South Asia is marked by fractious security relationships,[26] which in turn have translated into a state of cyber instability. Following the 2008 terrorist attack in Mumbai, for instance, Pakistani and Indian hackers reportedly carried out a series of cyberattacks on government websites of the opposing country.[27] In 2020, amidst border skirmishes in the region, government and military organizations in Nepal and Afghanistan were targeted using phishing attacks.[28] In 2020–2021, in the aftershocks of the border skirmishes between Indian and Chinese forces in Galwan, India's transportation sector as well as, reportedly, its electricity grid were targeted by Chinese hackers.[29]

China's shadow looms large over the region. New Delhi remains wary of the Belt and Road Initiative (BRI), of which Pakistan, Sri Lanka, Nepal, and Bangladesh are all a part.[30] The Digital Silk Road (DSR), a complement to the BRI, has further supported the expansion of Chinese technology companies in South Asia, West Asia, and beyond. DSR encapsulates telecommunications networks, cloud infrastructure, e-commerce, and surveillance technology.

Box 16.1 Major Cybersecurity Incidents in South Asia

South Asia has been hit by several major cybersecurity incidents, growing rapidly since 2014. Banking systems have proven especially vulnerable; however, the region has seen attacks targeting elections, government websites, as well as critical infrastructure like electricity and telecommunications. The relatively low levels of cybersecurity readiness, including of public infrastructure, has resulted in frequent data breaches. This box highlights the range of threat actors and vectors in the region.

Multiple Intrusions Targeting Afghanistan Government (2014 onward)

A Chinese-speaking threat actor, labeled "IndigoZebra," used vulnerabilities in the cloud storage service Dropbox, for cyber espionage operations targeting the National Security Council of Afghanistan. The operations are part of a larger campaign, believed to date back to 2014. Check Point, a software research firm, discovered the operation in 2021.

Bangladesh Bank heist (2016)

North Korean hackers, part of a collective dubbed the "Lazarus Group," used spear-phishing emails to compromise Bangladesh Bank's systems, particularly those that interfaced with the SWIFT communications system. They attempted the theft of USD 1 billion using fraudulent SWIFT messages, of which transactions worth USD 81 million went through.

Multiple DDoS attacks—Maldives (2017)

Dhirragu, Orredoo, and Raajje Online, three internet service providers in Maldives, were subject to distributed denial of service or DDoS attacks lasting a week in January 2017.

Multiple bank data breaches—Pakistan (2018)

150,632 data dumps of 22 Pakistani banks were posted for sale on the dark web in November 2018. The compromised data consisted of card numbers and payment details.

Multiple Chinese state-sponsored intrusions—India (2021)

The UIDAI, the body in charge of India's national biometric ID Aadhaar, was one of many Indian entities targeted by a Chinese state-sponsored group, dubbed TAG-28. TAG-28 also targeted The Times Group, a media house. These attacks, Recorded Future states, were part of an ongoing Chinese cyber campaign against India following border clashes in 2020. Other attacks targeted critical infrastructures and states-owned enterprises in the nuclear, space, and defense sectors.

Lanka Government Cloud Data Loss (2021)

In August 2021, data from National Medicines Regulatory Authority hosted on the Lanka Government Cloud "vanished." Attorney General Sanjay Rajaratnam stated in court that medicine traffickers may have been behind the incident.

Nepal Telecom Breach (2021)

Recorded Future, an American cybersecurity firm, identified a data exfiltration event perpetrated by a Chinese state-sponsored group, labeled TAG-22. The compromised IP was traced to Nepal Telecom, although the NTC denies that such a breach occurred.

In 2017, China and Afghanistan signed an agreement that would link them via a fiber optic connection through the Wakhan Corridor, and in Pakistan, the CPEC Fiber Optic Project will connect Rawalpindi with Khunjrab.[31] China has also been aggressively expanding its BeiDou global navigation satellite system (GNSS), a competitor to the US's GPS and the EU's GALILEO.[32] GNSS is vulnerable to jamming and spoofing attacks, which are forms of radio interference attacks. Attacks on GNSS pose threats to maritime and logistics industries, aviation, as well as motor vehicles. In the future, GNSS vulnerabilities will also implicate both commercial and military autonomous vehicles.[33] T.V. Paul notes how the smaller states of South Asia have benefited from "India–China managed rivalry," partly because Indian strategies to counter China have primarily relied on "soft balancing."[34] Indeed, that appears to be the case in cybersecurity and high technologies as well. New Delhi has, among other actions, expanded relations with the Quad and the EU, has 34 active Memorandums of Understanding (MoUs) on information and communications technology (ICT) and cybersecurity in 2021, and has, especially since the 2010s, actively incorporated cybersecurity issues into its engagement with regional instruments like BIMSTEC and SAARC.[35] At the same time, there is some debate on whether India possesses offensive cyber capabilities, with analysts indicating that it has developed fairly advanced offensive capabilities with a focus on Pakistan, and is likely looking to expand these with an eye toward China.[36]

South Asian Approaches to Cybersecurity

Intersection with "Traditional" Offline Threats

The most developed aspect of cybersecurity policy in South Asia is in relation to combating existing regional security threats, such as terrorism, insurgency, and maritime security.

In 2017, former President Ashraf Ghani of Afghanistan signed into law a Cyber Crime Code that introduced penalties for cyber terrorism and espionage and introduced efforts to control militants' online presence.[37] The Code was likely a reaction to an evolving Taliban that, since the 2010, rapidly grew its online presence: In 2005, the Taliban's online presence centered on its website *Al Emarah*, but by 2014–2015, its presence had expanded to mainstream social media platforms like Twitter.[38]

The National Security Adviser (NSA) Level India, Maldives, Sri Lanka Trilateral was established in 2011 with a focus on maritime security in the Indian Ocean region. It convened three times up till 2015, and then lay dormant till 2021, when it was revived with four pillars: Marine safety; terrorism and radicalization; trafficking and organized crime; and cybersecurity.[39]

Trusted and Secure ICTs for Economic Growth

"Digital advances have generated enormous wealth in record time," stated UN Secretary General António Guterres in a 2019 United Nations Conference on Trade and Development (UNCTAD) report, "but that wealth has been concentrated around a small number of individuals, companies and countries." In other words, data flows and the economic benefits from them accrue to a handful of companies based in developed and large economies.

The economic dimension of cybersecurity—that is, cybersecurity as an enabler for international competitiveness and digital-led economic growth—is a common theme in digital and cybersecurity strategies of South Asia. Both Sri Lanka and Nepal's strategies emphasize the role of cybersecurity in economic and social transformation.[40] India's National Cybersecurity Policy 2013 links cybersecurity with inclusive digital transformation and cites a trusted and secure ICT environment as crucial to India's role in the global IT market.

Promoting indigenous cybersecurity solutions is also a key pillar for a "secure cyber eco-system."[41] Bangladesh's 2014 strategy views cybersecurity as crucial to its "economic security and democratic objectives."[42] Afghanistan's 2014 strategy places itself within the larger context of post-war socio-economic reconstruction.[43]

Sovereign Cyberspace

What does sovereignty mean in cyberspace? In international law, one view is that sovereignty is a fundamental rule of international law ("sovereignty as a rule"). The *Tallinn Manual* for instance defines sovereignty in cyberspace as jurisdiction over cyber infrastructure, people, and activities originating in one's territory or having a *substantial effect* in their territory.[44] In other words, any cyber operations on a country's digital systems and those that have effects within a country's territory are a violation of sovereignty. A second view holds that sovereignty guides state interactions, forming the basis upon which other rules of international law emanate, but is not a rule in itself ("sovereignty as a principle"). What constitutes a violation of sovereignty in cyberspace is therefore context-dependent.[45]

While some South Asian countries, namely India and Pakistan, have all affirmed the applicability of sovereignty and sovereign equality in statements to the UN's Group of Governmental Experts (GGE) on Developments in the Field of Information and Telecommunications in the Context of International Security and its sister process in the Open-ended Working Group (OEWG) format, no country has comprehensively outlined what this would mean in practice.

Pakistan's 2021 Cybersecurity Policy states as one of its guiding principles that "a cyber-attack on Pakistan critical infrastructure as an act of aggression against national sovereignty and will defend itself with appropriate response measures,"[46] a statement that would put it squarely within the "sovereignty as a rule" camp, but there is little clarity on what these "appropriate measures" entail.

India meanwhile has been ambiguous on this issue. At the first meeting of the OEWG, the Indian delegation has sought clarifications on what constitutes a violation of sovereignty in cyberspace and the threshold for invoking the right to self-defense.[47] Subsequent submissions have been somewhat more engaged, and India's comments on the initial pre-draft of the OEWG report in 2020 provide some insight into the administration's evolving understanding of sovereign control:

> Territorial jurisdiction and sovereignty are losing relevance in contemporary (sic) cyberspace discourse ... [It] is important to recommend a new form of sovereignty which should be based on ownership of data i.e. the ownership of the data would be that of the person who has created it and the territorial jurisdiction of a country would be on the data which is owned by its citizens irrespective of the place where the data physically is located .... This new concept of data-oriented sovereignty extends beyond the classical territorial based jurisdiction.[48]

This is supported by a statement from Ravi Shankar Prasad, the former Minister for Electronics and Information Technology, at the 2020 G20 Digital Economy Ministers meeting:[49]

> We understand the issue of data innovation and data cross flow, but we also need to acknowledge the sovereignty of the data... we are very clear that data must belong to the sovereign nation concerned to protect the privacy of its people, to protect the digital concerns of its people.

Therefore, beyond the "rule versus principle" interpretation of sovereignty in cyberspace, a third interpretation has gained traction as well. This third interpretation upholds a state's right to legislate and act on its national and economic security interests, without external interference.

Conclusion: Looking Ahead and Open Questions

In the past decade, cyberattacks perpetrated by state and non-state actors alike have continued to rise, spreading across critical civilian sectors like banking, healthcare, telecommunications, and—especially since 2019—has impacted other basic services like electricity, digital IDs, and more. Cybersecurity preparedness in South Asia is still relatively low. Most countries in the region have yet to either formulate a cybersecurity strategy or need to urgently update their existing frameworks, and there is a similar gap in foundational data protection legislation. The region also sees from cyber instability arising from existing tensions, including fractious border relations and differences over geopolitical alignments. While each country in the region participates at different global technical and norms-making forums on cybersecurity, like the ITU, the UN OEWG on Cyber, the Asia Pacific CERT, and the OIC CERT, South Asia does not act as a region, but as a disparate set of national interests.

Nevertheless, there remain open questions on how state actors in South Asia are likely to develop and refine their stances on cybersecurity issues, both through their domestic legislation and capacities, as well as their engagement in multilateral and multistakeholder forums. Five of these key questions are elucidated below.

First, international relations scholars should keep an eye on the developing foreign policy stances on the question of sovereignty in cyberspace. The cyber threats arising from connectedness grew precipitously over the past decade, but technology fluency—cybersecurity capacity, skills, and literacy—has not grown at the same rate. In the absence of sufficient capacity to manage cybersecurity risk, connectedness itself is seen as undermining national security. Pakistan's National Cybersecurity Policy 2021, for example, frames digital interdependence as a threat, "In [the] absence of adequate local resources, reliance on external resources including skills, hardware, and software, is a direct threat to Cyber Security."[50] Cyber sovereignty in this context, as mentioned in the previous section, has become a narrative tool in norm making to assert a state's autonomy in legislation and control over technology flows.

Second, relating to the evolving debate around cyber sovereignty is the ongoing negotiation of boundaries between national security and individual privacy. How Pakistan, India, and Maldives' draft data protection legislations resolve issues of state access to personal data for instance will be a key development to track in the next half decade. In the case of India's draft Personal Data Protection Bill (2019), the controversial Section 35 grants the Central Government power to exempt agencies from the Bill's provisions. This provision "re-animates India's digital 'trilemma' of simultaneously generating economic growth, protecting individual privacy, and safeguarding national security."[51]

Third, there is an open question about the potential integration of the Taliban-led regime in Afghanistan into cybersecurity dialogues. Cybercrime legislation under the previous civilian administration was framed with the Taliban as a non-state threat actor. With the state apparatus now under its control, how will the new administration legislate on cybersecurity and data protection issues? Will Kabul engage with regional and extra-regional partners, or will it become a rogue cyber state along the lines of North Korea?

Fourth, as cybersecurity is still a nascent area of foreign policy for most of the capitals of South Asia, what patterns of power projection will we see the different countries partake in?

At a regional level, cyber complements other forms of power projection, as seen in the many cases of retaliatory cyberattacks between India and Pakistan, on the heels of border skirmishes. At a global level, India has emerged as a purveyor of cyber sovereignty narratives and continues a pattern of middle power network diplomacy, cooperating on cybersecurity issues at several multilateral forums like the CCW, BRICS, SCO, and BIMSTEC, while building out partnerships underpinned by "democratic values" with the Quad, the EU, and others.

Cybersecurity as an element of foreign policy is at a nascent stage in South Asia, especially compared to the region's rapid digital development. There is still plenty of scope for inquiry into how the trends mentioned in this chapter will develop in the coming decade, as the countries in the region "mainstream" cybersecurity issues into their foreign policy.

Notes

1 John Perry Barlow, "A Declaration of the Independence of Cyberspace," Electronic Frontier Foundation, accessed October 2, 2021, https://www.eff.org/cyberspace-independence.

2 "Global Cybersecurity Index 2020," International Telecommunications Union, accessed September 23, 2021, https://www.itu.int/epublications/publication/global-cybersecurity-index-2020/en/; "Shifting Gears: South Asia Economic Focus, Fall 2021," World Bank, October 7, 2021, https://www.worldbank.org/en/region/sar/publication/shifting-gears-south-asia-economic-focus-fall-2021.

3 "Check Point Research: Asia Pacific Experiencing a 168% Year on Year Increase in Cyberattacks in May 2021," Check Point, May 27, 2021, https://blog.checkpoint.com/2021/05/27/check-point-research-asia-pacific-experiencing-a-168-year-on-year-increase-in-cyberattacks-in-may-2021/.

4 Tom Burt, "Cyberattacks Targeting Health Care Must Stop," Microsoft, November 13, 2020, https://blogs.microsoft.com/on-the-issues/2020/11/13/health-care-cyberattacks-covid-19-paris-peace-forum/?2020-11-12.

5 "Global Cyber Strategies Index," Center for Strategic and International Studies, accessed October 25, 2021, https://www.csis.org/programs/strategic-technologies-program/cybersecurity-and-governance/global-cyber-strategies-index.

6 Janne Hakala and Jazlyn Melnychuk, "Russia's Strategy in Cyberspace," NATO Strategic Communications Centre of Excellence, June 2021.

7 V.Kh. Fedorov, E.G. Baleno, et al., "Cyberspace: Key Properties and Traits," *Journal of Physics: Conference Series*. 2096 012039 (October 2021), https://doi.org/10.1088/1742-6596/2096/1/012039; Stefan Steiger, Sebastian Harnisch, Kerstin Zettl, and Johannes Lohmann, "Conceptualising Conflicts in Cyberspace," *Journal of Cyber Policy* 3, no. 1 (2018): 77–95, https://doi.org/10.1080/23738871.2018.1453526.

8 Daryl Bockett, "Virtual Theory: Integrating Cybersecurity into International Relations Theory," *The International Journal of Interdisciplinary Global Studies* 12, no. 4 (2018): 15–30, https://doi.org/10.18848/2324-755X/CGP/v12i04/15-30; S. Shaheen, "Offense-Defense Balance in Cyber Warfare," in *Cyberspace and International Relations: Theory, Prospects and Challenges* (Berlin Heidelberg: Springer-Verlag, 2013), 77–93, https://doi.org/10.1007/978-3-642-37481-4_5.

9 John J. Mearsheimer, *The Tragedy of Great Power Politics* (2001), 55; Kenneth Waltz, *Theory of International Politics* (1979), 131.

10 Nazli Choucri and David D. Clark, *International Relations in the Cyber Age: The Co-Evolution Dilemma* (MIT Press: 2019).

11 Valery Gerasimov, "The Value of Science is in the Foresight: New Challenges Demand Rethinking the Forms and Methods of Carrying out Combat Operations," *Military-Industrial Kurier*, February 27, 2013. Translated from Russian June 21, 2014 by Robert Coalson, ed., Central News, Radio Free Europe/Radio Liberty,.

12 Joseph S. Nye Jr., "Soft Power," *Foreign Policy*, no. 80, Twentieth Anniversary (Autumn 1990), 153–171.

13 Joseph S. Nye Jr., *Cyber Power* (Belfer Center for Science and International Affairs, May 2010), 3–4.

14 Sangbae Kim, "Cyber Security and Middle Power Diplomacy: A Network Perspective," *The Korean Journal of International Studies* 12, no. 2 (December 2014): 323–352, http://dx.doi.org/10.14731/kjis.2014.12.12.2.323; Stacie E. Goddard, "Brokering Change: Networks and Entrepreneurs in International Politics," *International Theory* 1, no. 2 (2009): 249–281.

15 Kim, "Cyber Security and Middle Power Diplomacy: A Network Perspective."

16 Lucas Kello, *The Virtual Weapon and International Order* (United States: Yale University Press, 2017); Joseph S. Nye, *The Future of Power* (United Kingdom: Public Affairs, 2011).

17 Dan Efrony, "The Cyber Domain, Cyber Security and What about the International Law?" The Federmann Cyber Security Center at The Hebrew University of Jerusalem, accessed September 2, 2021.

18 Rajeswari Pillai Rajagopalan, "Electronic and Cyber Warfare in Outer Space," *UNIDIR Space Dossier* 3 (May 2019), https://www.unidir.org/files/publications/pdfs/electronic-and-cyber-warfare-in-outer-space-en-784.pdf; Clémence Poirier, "Interdependences between Space and Cyberspace in a Context of Increasing Militarization and Emerging Weaponization of Outer Space—A French Perspective," in *Outer Space and Cyber Space: Similarities, Interrelations and Legal Perspectives* (Springer International Publishing, 2021); James M. Acton, "Escalation through Entanglement: How the Vulnerability of Command-and-Control Systems Raises the Risks of an Inadvertent Nuclear War," *International Security* 43, no. 1 (Summer 2018).

19 Pukhraj Singh, "A Death Knell for the International Norms of Cyber Conflict," *Modern War Institute*, August 8, 2019, https://mwi.usma.edu/death-knell-international-norms-cyber-conflict/; Gary Brown, "On the Spectrum of Cyberspace Operations," *Small Wars Journal*, December 11, 2012, https://smallwarsjournal.com/jrnl/art/on-the-spectrum-of-cyberspace-operations.

20 "Six Russian GRU Officers Charged in Connection with Worldwide Deployment of Destructive Malware and Other Disruptive Actions in Cyberspace," US Department of Justice, October 19, 2020, https://www.justice.gov/opa/pr/six-russian-gru-officers-charged-connection-worldwide-deployment-destructive-malware-and; "North Korean Regime-Backed Programmer Charged with Conspiracy to Conduct Multiple Cyber Attacks and Intrusions," US Department of Justice, September 6, 2018, https://www.justice.gov/opa/pr/north-korean-regime-backed-programmer-charged-conspiracy-conduct-multiple-cyber-attacks-and; S. Ghafur, Kristensen, K. Honeyford, et al. "A Retrospective Impact Analysis of the WannaCry Cyberattack on the NHS," *Npj Digital Medicine* 2, no. 98 (2019), https://doi.org/10.1038/s41746-019-0161-6, https://www.nature.com/articles/s41746-019-0161-6.

21 Nazli Choucri, *Cyberpolitics in International Relations* (United Kingdom: MIT Press, 2012).

22 "The SAARC Anti-Terrorism Mechanism," *SAARC Secretariat*, accessed November 3, 2021, https://www.saarc-sec.org/images/areas-of-cooperation/ESC/Security%20Files/The%20SAARC%20Anti%20Terrorism%20Mechanism.docx; "Security," *BIMSTEC*, accessed November 3, 2021, https://bimstec.org/?page_id=6113.

23 Privacy and data protection legislation, as defined by the UN Conference on Trade and Development. Laws pertaining to specific sectors, such as digital transactions, do not qualify.

24 Maldives, Pakistan, Bhutan, Afghanistan: Data compiled from World Bank; "Individuals using the Internet (% of population)," World Bank, https://data.worldbank.org/indicator/IT.NET.USER.ZS; Nepal: Nepal Telecommunications Authority MIS Report Magh, 2077 (14 January 2021–12 February 2021), https://nta.gov.np/wp-content/uploads/2021/03/MIS-2077-MAGH.pdf; India: Total internet subscriber per 100 population from "The Indian Telecom Services Performance Indicators April – June 2021," Telecom Regulatory Authority of India, October 21, 2021, https://www.trai.gov.in/sites/default/files/PIR_21102021_0.pdf; Bangladesh: Bangladesh Telecommunication Regulatory Commission, accessed November 20, 2021, http://www.btrc.gov.bd/content/internet-subscribers-bangladesh-october-2021; Note: Nationally reported data counts total subscriptions, as opposed to unique subscribers. In other words, multiple internet subscriptions owned by the same entity count as multiple connections.

25 Global Cybersecurity Index 2020, *ITU.*

26 Ashley J. Tellis, *Stability in South Asia* (Santa Monica, CA: RAND Corporation, 1997), https://www.rand.org/pubs/documented_briefings/DB185.html; John Garver, *Protracted Contest* (University of Washington Press, 2001); S. Paul Kapur, *Dangerous Deterrent: Nuclear Weapons Proliferation and Conflict in South Asia* (Stanford: Stanford University Press, 2007).

27 SNS, "Pakistan Websites Hacked; Dedicated to Pulwama Martyrs, says Message | Check List," *The Statesman*, February 18, 2019, https://www.thestatesman.com/world/pakistan-websites-hacked-dedicated-to-pulwama-martyrs-says-message-1502733200.html; Sudhi Ranjan Sen, "Indo-Pak Tensions Play Out in Cyberspace, Websites Hit," *Hindustan Times*, March 4, 2019, https://www.hindustantimes.com/india-news/indo-pak-tensions-play-out-in-cyberspace-websites-hit/story-0qj6riwp9ETU6mKQrsjbCN.html.

28 Joseph C. Chen, Jaromir Horejsi, and Ecular Xu, "SideWinder Uses South Asian Issues for Spear Phishing, Mobile Attacks," *Trend Micro*, December 9, 2020, https://www.trendmicro.com/en_us/research/20/l/sidewinder-leverages-south-asian-territorial-issues-for-spear-ph.html.

29 "China-linked Group RedEcho Targets the Indian Power Sector amid Heightened Border Tensions," Recorded Future, February 28, 2021, https://www.recordedfuture.com/redecho-targeting-indian-power-sector/; Press Trust of India, "Highways Ministry asks NHAI, Automakers to Tighten IT Security after Cyber Attack Threats," *Tribune India*, March 21, 2021, https://www.tribuneindia.com/news/nation/highways-ministry-asks-nhai-automakers-to-tighten-it-security-after-cyber-attack-threats-228534.

30 Harsh V. Pant and Premesha Saha, eds., *Mapping the Belt and Road Initiative: Reach, Implications, Consequences* (Observer Research Foundation, February 2021), https://www.orfonline.org/wp-content/uploads/2021/02/BRI-report-FINAL.pdf.

31 Annie Cowan, "Challenges and Opportunities in the Context of China's Belt & Road Initiative," East West Institute, April 9, 2018, https://www.eastwest.ngo/sites/default/files/arp-challenges-andopportunities-in-the-context-of-bri.pdf; "Fiber Optic Project Of CPEC," CPEC Authority at the Ministry of Planning, Development & Special Initiatives, Government of Pakistan, http://cpec.gov.pk/map-single/3.

32 Jun Lu, Xia Guo, et al., "Global Capabilities of BeiDou Navigation Satellite System," *Satellite Navigation* 1, no. 27 (2020), https://doi.org/10.1186/s43020-020-00025-9; Richard Ghiasy and Rajeshwari Krishnamurthy, "China's Digital Silk Road and the Global Digital Order," *The Diplomat*, April 13, 2021, https://thediplomat.com/2021/04/chinas-digital-silk-road-and-the-global-digital-order/.

33 Sagar Dasgupta, Mizanur Rahman, et al., "Prediction-based GNSS Spoofing Attack Detection for Autonomous Vehicles," presented at Transportation Research Board 100th Annual Meeting, Transportation Research Board (Washington, DC, USA, 2010) arXiv:2010.11722 [cs.RO].

34 T.V. Paul, "When Balance of Power Meets Globalization: China, India and the Small States of South Asia," *Sage Journals* 39, no. 1 (2018), 50–63, https://doi.org/10.1177/0263395718779930.

35 "Joint Statement from Quad Leaders," Ministry of External Affairs of the Government of India, September 24, 2021, https://mea.gov.in/bilateral-documents.htm?dtl/34318/Joint+Statement+from+Quad+Leaders; "India-EU Connectivity Partnership," Ministry of External Affairs of the Government of India, May 8, 2021, https://www.mea.gov.in/bilateral-documents.htm?dtl/33854/IndiaEU_Connectivity_Partnership; "Active MoUs," Ministry of Electronics & Information Technology, Government of India, accessed December 1, 2021, https://www.meity.gov.in/content/active-mous.

36 "Cyber Capabilities and National Power: A Net Assessment," International Institute for Strategic Studies, June 28, 2021, https://www.iiss.org/blogs/research-paper/2021/06/cyber-capabilities-national-power.

37 "Afghanistan: Cyber Crime Code Signed into Law," Library of Congress, August 16, 2017, https://www.loc.gov/item/global-legal-monitor/2017-08-16/afghanistan-cyber-crime-code-signed-into-law/.

38 International Crisis Group, "Taliban Propaganda: Winning the War of Words?," *Asia Report* no. 158, July 2008: 15, https://www.justice.gov/sites/default/files/eoir/legacy/2014/09/29/icg_07242008.pdf.

39 Meera Srinivasan, "India, Sri Lanka and Maldives to Collaborate on Security," *The Hindu*, August 6, 2021, https://www.thehindu.com/news/international/india-sri-lanka-maldives-to-collaborate-on-security/article35775231.ece.

40 "राष्ट्रिय साइबर सुरक्षा नीति, २०७८," Ministry of Communication and Information Technology of Nepal, June 2021, https://mocit.gov.np/categorydetail/cybersecuritypolicydraft; "National Information and Cyber Security Strategy of Sri Lanka 2019-2023," Democratic Socialist Republic of Sri Lanka, Sri Lanka CERT, November 2018, https://www.cert.gov.lk/documents/NCSStrategy.pdf.

41 "National Cyber Security Policy – 2013," Ministry of Electronics and Information Technology of India, 2013, https://www.meity.gov.in/content/national-cyber-security-policy-2013-0.

42 "The National Cybersecurity Strategy of Bangladesh, 2014," *Bangladesh Gazette*, March 11, 2014, https://www.dpp.gov.bd/upload_file/gazettes/10041_41196.pdf.

43 National Cybersecurity Strategy of Afghanistan, Islamic Republic of Afghanistan Ministry of Communications and IT, 2014, https://mcit.gov.af/sites/default/files/2020-08/National%20Cybersecurity%20Strategy%20of%20Afghanistan%20%28November2014%29.pdf.

44 Michael N. Schmitt, *Tallinn Manual 2.0 on the International Law Applicable to Cyber Operations* (Cambridge: Cambridge University Press, 2017), https://doi.org/10.1017/9781316822524.

45 Harriet Moynihan, "The Application of International Law to State Cyberattacks," Chatham House, December 2, 2019; Poirier, "Interdependences between Space and Cyberspace in a Context of Increasing Militarization and Emerging Weaponization of Outer Space—A French Perspective."

46 "National Cyber Security Policy 2021," Ministry of Information Technology & Communication of Pakistan, 2021, https://moitt.gov.pk/SiteImage/Misc/files/National%20Cyber%20Security%20Policy%202021%20Final.pdf.

47 Statement delivered by India at the Organisational Session of the Open-Ended Working Group (OEWG) on "Developments in the field of Information and Telecommunications in the Context of International Security," New York, June 3, 2019, http://meaindia.nic.in/cdgeneva/?8251?000.

48 INDIA's comments on the Initial Pre-Draft of the report of the OEWG on developments in the field of information and telecommunications in the context of international security, April 2020, https://ccgdelhi.org/wp-content/uploads/2020/09/india-comments-on-oewg-2020-chair-pre-draft-final.pdf.

49 Karishma Mehrotra, "Need to Acknowledge Sovereignty of Data: Prasad," *Indian Express*, July 23, 2020, https://indianexpress.com/article/india/need-to-acknowledge-sovereignty-of-data-prasad-6519159/.

50 National Cyber Security Policy 2021, Ministry of Information Technology & Communication of Pakistan.

51 ORF Technology and Media Initiative, "The Personal Data Protection Bill 2019: Recommendations to the Joint Parliamentary Committee," Observer Research Foundation, ORF Special Report No. 102, March 2020, https://www.orfonline.org/research/the-personal-data-protection-bill-2019-61915/.

Bibliography

Acton, James M. "Escalation through Entanglement: How the Vulnerability of Command-and-Control Systems Raises the Risks of an Inadvertent Nuclear War." *International Security* 43, no. 1 (Summer 2018).

"The National Cybersecurity Strategy of Bangladesh, 2014." *Bangladesh Gazette*, March 11, 2014. https://www.dpp.gov.bd/upload_file/gazettes/10041_41196.pdf.

Bangladesh Telecommunication Regulatory Commission. Accessed November 20, 2021. http://www.btrc.gov.bd/content/internet-subscribers-bangladesh-october-2021.

Barlow, John Perry. "A Declaration of the Independence of Cyberspace." Electronic Frontier Foundation, accessed October 2, 2021. https://www.eff.org/cyberspace-independence.

BIMSTEC. "Security." Accessed November 3, 2021. https://bimstec.org/?page_id=6113.

Bockett, Daryl. "Virtual Theory: Integrating Cybersecurity into International Relations Theory." *The International Journal of Interdisciplinary Global Studies* 12, no. 4 (2018): 15–30. https://doi.org/10.18848/2324-755X/CGP/v12i04/15–30.

Brown, Gary. "On the Spectrum of Cyberspace Operations." *Small Wars Journal*, December 11, 2012. https://smallwarsjournal.com/jrnl/art/on-the-spectrum-of-cyberspace-operations.

Burt, Tom. "Cyberattacks Targeting Health Care Must Stop." Microsoft, November 13, 2020. https://blogs.microsoft.com/on-the-issues/2020/11/13/health-care-cyberattacks-covid-19-paris-peace-forum/?2020-11-12.

Center for Strategic and International Studies. "Global Cyber Strategies Index." Accessed October 25, 2021. https://www.csis.org/programs/strategic-technologies-program/cybersecurity-and-governance/global-cyber-strategies-index.

Check Point. "Check Point Research: Asia Pacific Experiencing a 168% Year on Year Increase in Cyberattacks in May 2021." May 27, 2021. https://blog.checkpoint.com/2021/05/27/check-point-research-asia-pacific-experiencing-a-168-year-on-year-increase-in-cyberattacks-in-may-2021/.

Chen, Joseph C., and Jaromir Horejsi, et al. "SideWinder Uses South Asian Issues for Spear Phishing, Mobile Attacks." *Trend Micro*, December 9, 2020. https://www.trendmicro.com/en_us/research/20/l/sidewinder-leverages-south-asian-territorial-issues-for-spear-ph.html.

Nazli, Choucri, and David D. Clark. *International Relations in the Cyber Age: The Co-Evolution Dilemma.* Cambridge: MIT Press, 2019.

Nazli, Choucri. *Cyberpolitics in International Relations.* Cambridge: MIT Press, 2012.

Cowan, Annie. "Challenges and Opportunities in the Context of China's Belt & Road Initiative." East West Institute, April 9, 2018. https://www.eastwest.ngo/sites/default/files/arp-challenges-andopportunities-in-the-context-of-bri.pdf.

CPEC Authority at the Ministry of Planning, Development & Special Initiatives, Government of Pakistan. "Fiber Optic Project of CPEC." http://cpec.gov.pk/map-single/3.

Dasgupta, Sagar, and Mizanur Rahman, et al. "Prediction-based GNSS Spoofing Attack Detection for Autonomous Vehicles." *Presented at Transportation Research Board 100th Annual Meeting, Transportation Research Board.* Washington, DC, 2010. arXiv:2010.11722 [cs.RO]. https://arxiv.org/abs/2010.11722.

Democratic Socialist Republic of Sri Lanka, Sri Lanka CERT. "National Information and Cyber Security Strategy of Sri Lanka 2019-2023." November 2018. https://www.cert.gov.lk/documents/NCSStrategy.pdf.

Efrony, Dan. "The Cyber Domain, Cyber Security and What about the International Law?" The Federmann Cyber Security Center at The Hebrew University of Jerusalem, accessed September 2, 2021.

Fedorov, V.Kh., and E.G. Baleno, et al. "Cyberspace: Key Properties and Traits." *Journal of Physics: Conference Series.* 2096 012039 (October 2021). https://doi.org/10.1088/1742-6596/2096/1/012039.

Garver, John. *Protracted Contest.* Seattle: University of Washington Press, 2001.

Gerasimov, Valery. "The Value of Science is in the Foresight: New Challenges Demand Rethinking the Forms and Methods of Carrying Out Combat Operations." *Military-Industrial Kurier* (February 27, 2013).

Ghafur, S., and K. Kristensen, et al. "A Retrospective Impact Analysis of the WannaCry Cyberattack on the NHS." *Npj Digital Medicine* 2, no. 98 (2019). https://doi.org/10.1038/s41746-019-0161-6.

Ghiasy, Richard, and Rajeshwari Krishnamurthy. "China's Digital Silk Road and the Global Digital Order." *The Diplomat,* April 13, 2021. https://thediplomat.com/2021/04/chinas-digital-silk-road-and-the-global-digital-order/.

Goddard, Stacie E. "Brokering Change: Networks and Entrepreneurs in International Politics." *International Theory* 1, no. 2 (2009): 249–281.

Hakala, Janne, and Jazlyn Melnychuk. "Russia's Strategy in Cyberspace." NATO Strategic Communications Centre of Excellence, June 2021.

IBM Security. "Cost of a Data Breach Report 2021." Accessed November 3, 2021. https://www.ibm.com/security/data-breach.

International Crisis Group. "Taliban Propaganda: Winning the War of Words?" *Asia Report* no. 158, July 2008. https://www.justice.gov/sites/default/files/eoir/legacy/2014/09/29/icg_07242008.pdf.

International Institute for Strategic Studies. "Cyber Capabilities and National Power: A Net Assessment." June 28, 2021. https://www.iiss.org/blogs/research-paper/2021/06/cyber-capabilities-national-power.

International Telecommunications Union. "Global Cybersecurity Index 2020." Accessed September 23, 2021. https://www.itu.int/epublications/publication/global-cybersecurity-index-2020/en/.

Islamic Republic of Afghanistan Ministry of Communications and IT. "National Cybersecurity Strategy of Afghanistan, 2014." https://mcit.gov.af/sites/default/files/2020-08/National%20Cybersecurity%20Strategy%20of%20Afghanistan%20%28November2014%29.pdf.

Kapur, S. Paul. *Dangerous Deterrent: Nuclear Weapons Proliferation and Conflict in South Asia.* Stanford: Stanford University Press, 2007.

Kello, Lucas. *The Virtual Weapon and International Order.* New Haven, CT: Yale University Press, 2017.

Kim, Sangbae. "Cyber Security and Middle Power Diplomacy: A Network Perspective." *The Korean Journal of International Studies* 12, no. 2 (December 2014): 323–352. https://doi.org/10.14731/kjis.2014.12.12.2.323.

Library of Congress. "Afghanistan: Cyber Crime Code Signed into Law." August 16, 2017. https://www.loc.gov/item/global-legal-monitor/2017-08-16/afghanistan-cyber-crime-code-signed-into-law/.

Lu, Jun., and Xia Guo, et al. "Global Capabilities of BeiDou Navigation Satellite System." *Satellite Navigation* 1, 27 (2020). https://doi.org/10.1186/s43020-020-00025-9.

Mearsheimer, John J. *The Tragedy of Great Power Politics.* New York: W.W. Norton, 2001.

Mehrotra, Karishma. "Need to Acknowledge Sovereignty of Data: Prasad." *Indian Express,* July 23, 2020. https://indianexpress.com/article/india/need-to-acknowledge-sovereignty-of-data-prasad-6519159/.

Ministry of Communication and Information Technology of Nepal. "राष्ट्रिय साइबर सुरक्षा नीति, २०७८." June 2021. https://mocit.gov.np/categorydetail/cybersecuritypolicydraft.

Ministry of Electronics & Information Technology, Government of India. "Active MoUs." Accessed December 1, 2021. https://www.meity.gov.in/content/active-mous.

Ministry of Electronics and Information Technology of India. "National Cyber Security Policy – 2013." https://www.meity.gov.in/content/national-cyber-security-policy-2013-0.

Ministry of External Affairs of the Government of India. "India-EU Connectivity Partnership." May 8, 2021. https://www.mea.gov.in/bilateral-documents.htm?dtl/33854/IndiaEU_Connectivity_Partnership.

Ministry of External Affairs of the Government of India. "Joint Statement from Quad Leaders." September 24, 2021. https://mea.gov.in/bilateral-documents.htm?dtl/34318/Joint+Statement+from+Quad+Leaders.

Ministry of External Affairs, Government of India. "Statement delivered by India at the Organisational Session of the Open-Ended Working Group (OEWG) on 'Developments in the field of Information and Telecommunications in the Context of International Security." New York, June 3, 2019. https://meaindia.nic.in/cdgeneva/?8251?000.

Ministry of Information Technology & Communication of Pakistan. "National Cyber Security Policy 2021." https://moitt.gov.pk/SiteImage/Misc/files/National%20Cyber%20Security%20Policy%202021%20Final.pdf.

Moynihan, Harriet. "The Application of International Law to State Cyberattacks." Chatham House, December 2, 2019.

Nepal Telecommunications Authority. "Nepal Telecommunications Authority MIS Report Magh, 2077 (14 January 2021–12 February 2021)." https://nta.gov.np/wp-content/uploads/2021/03/MIS-2077-MAGH.pdf.

Nye, Joseph S. "Soft Power." *Foreign Policy*, no. 80, Twentieth Anniversary (Autumn 1990): 153–171.

Nye, Joseph S. *Cyber Power*. Belfer Center for Science and International Affairs, May 2010.

Nye, Joseph S. *The Future of Power*. New York: Public Affairs, 2011.

ORF Technology and Media Initiative. "The Personal Data Protection Bill 2019: Recommendations to the Joint Parliamentary Committee." Observer Research Foundation, ORF Special Report No. 102, March 2020. https://www.orfonline.org/research/the-personal-data-protection-bill-2019-61915/.

Pant, Harsh V., and Premesha Saha, eds. Mapping the Belt and Road Initiative: Reach, Implications, Consequences. Observer Research Foundation, February 2021. https://www.orfonline.org/wp-content/uploads/2021/02/BRI-report-FINAL.pdf.

Paul, T.V. "When Balance of Power Meets Globalization: China, India and the Small States of South Asia." *Sage Journals* 39, no. 1 (2018), 50–63. https://doi.org/10.1177/0263395718779930.

Poirier, Clémence. "Interdependences between Space and Cyberspace in a Context of Increasing Militarization and Emerging Weaponization of Outer Space—A French Perspective." In *Outer Space and Cyber Space: Similarities, Interrelations and Legal Perspectives*. Cham, Switzerland: Springer International Publishing, 2021.

Press Trust of India. "Highways Ministry asks NHAI, Automakers to Tighten IT Security after Cyber Attack Threats." *Tribune India*, March 21, 2021. https://www.tribuneindia.com/news/nation/highways-ministry-asks-nhai-automakers-to-tighten-it-security-after-cyber-attack-threats-228534.

Rajagopalan, Rajeswari. "Electronic and Cyber Warfare in Outer Space." *UNIDIR Space Dossier* 3, May 2019. https://www.unidir.org/files/publications/pdfs/electronic-and-cyber-warfare-in-outer-space-en-784.pdf.

Recorded Future. "China-linked Group RedEcho Targets the Indian Power Sector amid Heightened Border Tensions." February 28, 2021. https://www.recordedfuture.com/redecho-targeting-indian-power-sector/.

SAARC Secretariat. "The SAARC Anti-Terrorism Mechanism." Accessed November 3, 2021. https://www.saarc-sec.org/images/areas-of-cooperation/ESC/Security%20Files/The%20SAARC%20Anti%20Terrorism%20Mechanism.docx.

Schmitt, Michael N. *Tallinn Manual 2.0 on the International Law Applicable to Cyber Operations*. Cambridge: Cambridge University Press, 2017. https://doi.org/10.1017/9781316822524.

Sen, Sudhi Ranjan. "Indo-Pak Tensions Play Out in Cyberspace, Websites Hit." *Hindustan Times*, March 4, 2019. https://www.hindustantimes.com/india-news/indo-pak-tensions-play-out-in-cyberspace-websites-hit/story-0qj6riwp9ETU6mKQrsjbCN.html.

Shaheen, Salma. "Offense-Defense Balance in Cyber Warfare." In *Cyberspace and International Relations: Theory, Prospects and Challenges*, 77–93. Berlin Heidelberg: Springer-Verlag, 2013. https://doi.org/10.1007/978-3-642-37481-4_5.

Singh, Pukhraj. "A Death Knell for the International Norms of Cyber Conflict." Modern War Institute, August 8, 2019. https://mwi.usma.edu/death-knell-international-norms-cyber-conflict/.

SNS. "Pakistan Websites Hacked; Dedicated to Pulwama Martyrs, says Message | Check List." *The Statesman*, February 18, 2019. https://www.thestatesman.com/world/pakistan-websites-hacked-dedicated-to-pulwama-martyrs-says-message-1502733200.html.

Srinivasan, Meera. "India, Sri Lanka and Maldives to Collaborate on Security." *The Hindu*, August 6, 2021. https://www.thehindu.com/news/international/india-sri-lanka-maldives-to-collaborate-on-security/article35775231.ece.

Steiger, Stefan, Sebastian Harnisch, Kerstin Zettl, and Johannes Lohmann. "Conceptualising Conflicts in Cyberspace." *Journal of Cyber Policy* 3, no. 1 (2018): 77–95. https://doi.org/10.1080/23738871.2018.1453526.

Telecom Regulatory Authority of India. "The Indian Telecom Services Performance Indicators April – June 2021." October 21, 2021. https://www.trai.gov.in/sites/default/files/PIR_21102021_0.pdf.

Tellis, Ashley J. *Stability in South Asia*. Santa Monica, CA: RAND Corporation, 1997.

UN Department of Economic and Social Affairs. "UN E-Government Development Index." Accessed August 31, 2021. https://publicadministration.un.org/egovkb/Data-Center.

US Department of Justice. "North Korean Regime-Backed Programmer Charged with Conspiracy to Conduct Multiple Cyber Attacks and Intrusions." September 6, 2018. https://www.justice.gov/opa/pr/north-korean-regime-backed-programmer-charged-conspiracy-conduct-multiple-cyber-attacks-and.

US Department of Justice. "Six Russian GRU Officers Charged in Connection with Worldwide Deployment of Destructive Malware and Other Disruptive Actions in Cyberspace." October 19, 2020. https://www.justice.gov/opa/pr/six-russian-gru-officers-charged-connection-worldwide-deployment-destructive-malware-and.

Waltz, Kenneth. *Theory of International Politics*. New York: McGraw-Hill, 1979.

World Bank. "Individuals using the Internet (% of population)." https://data.worldbank.org/indicator/IT.NET.USER.ZS.

World Bank. "Shifting Gears: South Asia Economic Focus, Fall 2021." October 7, 2021. https://www.worldbank.org/en/region/sar/publication/shifting-gears-south-asia-economic-focus-fall-2021.

PART III

THE INTERNATIONAL RELATIONS OF SOUTH ASIA

17

AFGHANISTAN'S RELATIONS WITH SOUTH ASIA

Diplomacy Amid Conflict

Michael Kugelman

From 1979 to 2021, Afghanistan was a country in conflict. First came the Soviet invasion and a successful anti-Soviet insurgency. Then came a civil war followed by a period of brutal Taliban rule. The final chapter of these bloody 42 years was a US-led war that resulted in another insurgency and the Taliban's return to power.

Unsurprisingly, Afghanistan's diplomacy over the last few decades was directly tied to its war. In the late 1990s, Afghanistan's foreign relations were limited, as only three countries (one of them Pakistan) recognized a Taliban regime that seized power by force and ruled through repression. In the nearly 20-year period between late 2001, when US forces removed the Taliban from power, and August 2021, when the Taliban re-took power, Kabul was led by US-backed governments that emphasized relations with those countries best positioned to help prosecute counterinsurgency efforts against the Taliban. Most of those countries were not in South Asia.

This chapter argues that Afghanistan's relations with South Asia over the last 20 years centered around India and Pakistan, the only two countries in the region with a direct bearing on the war in Afghanistan. Kabul viewed New Delhi as a critical partner because it provided security and economic assistance meant to help Afghanistan fight the Taliban and to support a war-battered economy. Kabul saw Islamabad as an important but problematic neighbor that was the Taliban insurgency's main external sponsor. The chapter argues that these foreign policy choices and behavior over the past 20 years can best be explained by the Realist theory of international relations (IR). It asserts that Afghanistan's foreign relations with South Asia in the future will be informed by three key factors: Regime type, level of stability, and regional dynamics. In particular, if Afghanistan is led by a brutal regime and especially if it suffers from serious instability, it will continue to struggle to build a broader relationship with the region, beyond India and Pakistan.

The chapter begins with a brief review of the current literature on the topic, followed by a discussion of the topic's importance. It then provides a snapshot of Kabul's relations with South Asia over the last 20 years, describes the principle themes of those relations, identifies the IR theories that best explain those relations, and lists several factors that can help predict Kabul's future foreign relations with South Asia.

DOI: 10.4324/9781003246626-21

State of the Literature

Scholarship on Afghanistan's recent relations with its South Asian neighbors is limited. Not surprisingly, what little exists focuses on Afghanistan's relations with India and Pakistan.[1] One reason for this paucity of literature is that, given Afghanistan's limited relations with South Asia on the whole, there's little on which to base scholarly work. There is additional literature on Afghanistan's relations with India and especially Pakistan in works focused on broader issues, such as the war in Afghanistan, US policy in South Asia, and terrorism.[2]

Scholarship produced by Afghans themselves on their country's relations with the region is quite limited; what does exist largely focuses on time periods before 2001.[3] Given concern about the lack of Afghan voices in debates—whether media, policy, or scholarly—on Afghanistan, this is something that deserves attention and improvement. Scholars from Afghanistan—many of whom relocated to the West after the 2021 Taliban takeover—should be given opportunities to pursue research on Afghanistan's relations with South Asia.

A Less-Than-Robust Track Record of Regional Relations

Over the last 20 years, Afghanistan prioritized relations with Washington and other NATO partners fighting the Taliban and providing security assistance, as well as those—from EU nations to wealthy donor countries like Japan—providing aid to bolster an economy buffeted by war. Kabul has long been heavily dependent on international aid. Before the Taliban re-took power in August 2021, about 75% of public spending came from foreign assistance.[4] Kabul emphasized ties with the countries providing this critical support. Most of them were outside South Asia.

Consequently, what stands out about Afghanistan's recent diplomatic history is that relations with its South Asian neighbors were relatively limited. It strengthened ties with India—its closest partner in the region and biggest regional donor. For very different reasons, it also allocated extensive bandwidth to relations with Pakistan, the only South Asian state that borders Afghanistan. Pakistan was the Taliban's biggest wartime backer, which included providing sanctuary for its leaders. Kabul's relations with other South Asian states were more modest. Kabul's attempts to broaden regional ties through trade and connectivity were eclipsed by the exigencies of pursuing diplomacy focused on the war effort and constrained by Afghanistan's security problems.

The Importance of Afghanistan's Relations with South Asia

The fact that Afghanistan's recent relations with South Asia were relatively limited does not mean they are unimportant for study and scholarship. On a basic level, there has been more commentary and scholarship on the war in Afghanistan than on Kabul's foreign relations during the course of that war. As a result, this chapter's topic is understudied.

The topic is also significant because it focuses on how a strategically located country conducts relations with neighbors while suffering through unrelenting war. US officials tend to understate Afghanistan's strategic significance. When he was vice president, Joe Biden told Afghan President Hamid Karzai that "Pakistan is 50 times more important than Afghanistan for the United States."[5] And yet, landlocked Afghanistan serves as a gateway to Central and South Asia and the Middle East. Its geography has produced a centuries-long legacy of foreign interventions and incursions.

Additionally, Afghanistan was convulsed by war for more than 40 years, with few respites other than several brief truces with the Taliban. This raises important questions for study—questions that are addressed in this chapter, but still require further investigation. How does a long period of conflict impact a country's diplomacy with its neighbors, and especially a country so dependent on foreign assistance? Does its diplomacy change over the course of the war it is fighting? How does this diplomacy impact the war effort? Such questions are important, but relatively unexplored in the context of Afghanistan. Some focus on the thinking of Afghan officials about regional diplomacy is also important, given that so much commentary about Afghanistan over the last few decades has revolved around the motivations of the US, or other NATO powers, or donors, or the regional players, as opposed to Afghans themselves. A study of Afghanistan's regional relations that includes perspectives from the Afghans involved in these relations can illuminate the agency of Afghan governments.

The topic is relevant from both regional and broader global contexts. Afghanistan matters for the region. Its chronic instability has produced regional spillover effects, from heightened refugee flows and an intensified drug trade to cross-border terrorism. Several countries in the region have directly confronted at least one of these effects. Pakistan has confronted all three. On the flip side, a more stable Afghanistan provides tantalizing opportunities for the region. These include trade and connectivity projects that crisscross Afghanistan and link South Asia to Central Asia and the Middle East. In this sense, Afghanistan's neighbors—and their relations with Kabul—are impacted by events within Afghan borders.

Seen from a global standpoint, Afghanistan's relations with its neighbors matter because it is internationally consequential. The Taliban takeover and the withdrawal of US forces in 2021 provoked a debate among policymakers and scholars as to whether Afghanistan could become a safe haven for terrorists that plot global attacks, as was the case in the late 1990s and up until 2001. This debate stands unsettled. But there is no doubt that Afghanistan has become a country where the biggest contemporary global threats have converged. One Afghan writer has described this dynamic as "quadruple crises": Conflict, COVID-19, climate change, and economic collapse.[6] Also, Afghanistan's humanitarian crisis could intensify refugee flows that extend to Europe, especially with Pakistan and Iran, the two top traditional destinations for Afghan refugees, taking an increasingly restrictive position on migration from Afghanistan.

Afghanistan's relations with its neighbors will impact its ability to ease these threats, all of which have international implications. Will it cooperate with Pakistan on border security and refugee flows? Will it receive assistance from South Asian countries to address pandemic risks? Will it be a part of any region-wide climate change mitigation efforts? Amid international donor fatigue, the departure of NATO forces, and a lack of a global strategy on how to help Afghanistan, regional actors will become increasingly important interlocutors for Kabul as it confronts its quadruple crises.

Afghanistan's Regional Relations: An Empirical History

Afghanistan's engagement with South Asia over the last 20 years was heavily focused on India and Pakistan. Kabul's foreign relations with other regional actors were more limited. This was largely a strategic choice: Since they weren't well-positioned to help Afghanistan pursue critical war-related aims, they were not viewed as priorities. But the choice was also rooted in state capacity: Afghanistan did not have the resources to maintain a meaningful diplomatic presence in the smaller South Asian states. Afghanistan does not have an embassy in Bhutan, Maldives, or Nepal. It only opened one in Sri Lanka in 2013.

Relations with India and Pakistan: A Tale of Two Very Different Experiences

After the Taliban were removed from power in 2001, India became Afghanistan's closest partner in South Asia, and one of its closest partners overall. The two countries never experienced a crisis in relations during that long period when the Taliban were not in power, until the group once again seized control in August 2021. Kabul prioritized ties with New Delhi because of their shared rivalry with Islamabad, the Taliban's main backer, and because of New Delhi's ability and willingness to provide generous amounts of economic assistance, as well as non-combat security aid, to back the Afghan war effort.

The origin of these strong ties came in the 1990s, when New Delhi backed the anti-Taliban Northern Alliance forces that would eventually work with the United States to overthrow the Taliban. New Delhi quickly established relations with the first post-Taliban government, and served as its advocate regionally, which included lobbying for its membership in the South Asian Association for Regional Cooperation (SAARC), South Asia's main regional organization.[7] Kabul joined SAARC in 2007.

Economic cooperation, both trade and especially development assistance, was the cornerstone of Afghanistan-India partnership. It was cemented in a strategic partnership agreement inked in 2011. But such support began soon after the inauguration of the first post-Taliban government: In 2003, the two concluded a preferential trade agreement. By July 2021, soon before the Taliban re-took power, bilateral trade volume was estimated at $1 billion. This is not an insignificant figure, given that India does not border Afghanistan and lacked direct land access because Pakistan declined to provide transit trade rights. Meanwhile, over the last 20 years, India has provided about $3 billion in development assistance. It developed 400 projects, which included a large dam, a 135-mile highway, a pediatric hospital, and the current Parliament building. New Delhi also provided education opportunities in India to thousands of Afghan students.[8]

India also provided security assistance to Afghanistan. A major component was training for the Afghan security forces, which in its early phases ranged from weapons handling to map-reading. The 2011 strategic partnership agreement scaled up this support, with several hundred Afghan officers receiving training at Indian military academies in the subsequent years. Between 2017 and 2019, India also provided basic weapons training and leadership skills to female Afghan air force and army officers. India's provision of weaponry was largely limited to small arms. In 2013, with the NATO mission in Afghanistan preparing to transition from a combat to a training and advising mission, Karzai—knowing Afghanistan would soon be leading counterinsurgency efforts—made specific requests to the Indian government for fighter aircraft and trucks during a trip to New Delhi.[9] However, New Delhi's main heavy-weaponry contribution amounted to fighter helicopters transferred from Russia.[10] India never put boots on the ground in Afghanistan. This decision, along with its refusal to provide more heavy weaponry, can be attributed in part to a desire not to provoke Pakistan, which worried about Indian influence on Pakistan's western flank and accused India of backing anti-Pakistan militants based in Afghanistan. New Delhi denied these charges.

While Kabul enjoyed warm ties with New Delhi, its relations with Islamabad were rife with tensions. Kabul maintained its official policy, since Pakistan's independence, of refusing to recognize the Afghanistan-Pakistan border, known as the Durand Line. The border issue was magnified starting in 2014, when Pakistan began building a fence along its side of the border, which it claimed was to keep militants from entering Pakistan. For Kabul, this represented an effort to legitimize a border it rejected. The issue was further inflamed during the presidency of Ashraf Ghani, who expressed public support for the Pashtun Tahafuz Movement (PTM), an ethnic Pashtun movement in Pakistan that strongly criticized the Pakistani military and called for greater Pashtun rights.[11] Pakistan's military feared that the PTM's activism was meant to unite Pashtuns on both sides of the border. The open embrace of the PTM by Ghani, himself a Pashtun, heightened Islamabad's anxieties.

Militancy was Kabul's other tension point with Islamabad. Pakistan sheltered the leaders of the Taliban insurgency, and it harbored close ties to the Taliban's brutal Haqqani Network faction. Kabul frequently accused Pakistan of complicity in attacks in Afghanistan. Meanwhile, Pakistan alleged that terrorists used Afghan soil to plot attacks on Pakistan, including one in 2014 that killed nearly 150 schoolchildren. With Afghanistan and Pakistan both convulsed by terrorist violence that each blamed the other for sponsoring, cross-border terrorism was an albatross around the neck of Afghanistan-Pakistan relations. Pakistan periodically carried out cross-border shelling against terrorist targets in Afghanistan, angering Kabul. Such assaults continued in 2021, even after the Taliban takeover.

These tensions, however, did not prevent diplomatic achievements. In 2010, Kabul and Islamabad concluded the Afghanistan-Pakistan Transit Trade Agreement (APTTA), which provided Afghan access to Pakistani ports and Afghanistan-Pakistan border crossings, and Afghan truck access to the India-Pakistan border post at Wagah. Islamabad also provided development assistance to the tune of about $1 billion by 2018. In 2017, the two sides concluded the Afghanistan-Pakistan Action Plan for Peace and Solidarity (APAPPS), which became a basis for structured security and non-security dialogue. Most strikingly, in 2015, the main Pakistani and Afghan intelligence agencies signed an accord focused on counterterrorism and intelligence-sharing.

Kabul's cooperation with Islamabad also played out in multilateral settings. Both worked together in the Heart of Asia-Istanbul Process, an Afghanistan-focused group, and in the Shanghai Cooperation Organization, where Afghanistan has observer status and of which Pakistan became a full member in 2017. A desire for strengthening cross-border connectivity was another motivation fueling Afghanistan-Pakistan cooperation with other countries. They explored prospects for expanding the China-Pakistan Economic Corridor into Afghanistan, and Afghanistan, Pakistan, and Uzbekistan signed a deal in 2021 to develop a transnational railway system. Afghan leaders saw Islamabad as a key part of regional connectivity plans. As far back as 2014, President Ghani described Afghanistan as a land bridge linking Central Asia and Pakistan.[12] Admittedly, the relentless war in Afghanistan limited the viability of these plans.

However, any hope that this cooperation would create a healthier relationship with Pakistan was misplaced. Mohammed Haneef Atmar, Afghanistan's national security adviser from 2014 to 2018 and foreign minister from 2020 to 2021, later described Kabul's relations with Islamabad as "a failure on every aspect," given that constant security tensions militated against the improvement of bilateral ties—even when non-security cooperation was attempted as a confidence-building measure to build more trust for addressing security tensions, especially related to terrorism. "With every CT [counterterrorism] failure," according to Atmar, "all the progress made on the other fronts was washed away."[13] Indeed, diplomatic achievements were often followed by major setbacks. Soon after the finalization of APTTA, Afghanistan signed its strategic partnership accord with India, angering Islamabad. Terrorists attacked Afghanistan's Parliament building several weeks after the signing of the 2015 security accord, prompting Afghan allegations of Pakistani complicity in the attack.[14] Afghanistan's relations with Pakistan over the last two decades were a case of one step forward, two steps back.

Relations with the Rest: Limited Engagement

Afghanistan engaged relatively little with other countries in South Asia. Of its five regional neighbors beyond India and Pakistan, Bangladesh and Sri Lanka received the most attention. Unsurprisingly, the main feature of Kabul's relations with Dhaka over the last few decades has revolved around humanitarian assistance. In early 2021, the large Bangladeshi development organization Building Resources Across Communities (BRAC) was present in nearly half of Afghanistan's provinces over the last two decades.[15] Afghanistan-Bangladesh relations are sensitive, however. Bangladeshi jihadists fought alongside anti-Soviet mujahedeen fighters in the 1980s and returned home to form new terror groups that later carried out attacks in Bangladesh.[16] Dhaka has approached relations with Kabul with caution, so as not to embolden radicals at home, some of whom celebrated the Taliban victory in 2021. This is likely a major reason why Dhaka declined a reported request, in 2010, from Washington to send troops to Afghanistan to help fight the Taliban.[17]

Afghanistan's relations with Sri Lanka, formally established in the 1950s, received a boost in 2013, when Kabul opened an embassy in Colombo. New accords followed that focused on cooperation in areas ranging from defense and legal assistance to air connectivity and investment. In 2020 and early 2021, the two sides inked MOUs to explore greater diplomatic and commercial cooperation. Afghan officials highlighted their shared experiences of prolonged war and viewed Sri Lanka as a model of a successful post-conflict state. This shared experience was a major factor that prompted Kabul to upscale bilateral relations and open its embassy in Colombo.[18] Still, much of the relationship's potential went unfulfilled. The war, and later the COVID pandemic, limited trade and investment opportunities. And then the Taliban takeover froze the relationship's momentum and plunged future relations into uncertainty.

Kabul's relations with Maldives, Nepal, and Bhutan were cordial but minimal. There were some trade and people-to-people successes with Maldives, which in 2019 imported about $2.5 million worth of Afghan horticulture exports and in that same year announced a visa-on-arrival program for Afghan citizens.[19] Relations with Nepal were largely defined by the presence of Nepalese workers in Afghanistan. Nepal's Gurkha fighters provided security at many embassies in Afghanistan. More than 10,000 Nepalese received labor permits to work in Afghanistan between 2015 and 2021, though additional Nepalese workers were there illegally.[20]

Principal Themes

The main trend in Afghanistan's regional relations over the last 20 years is imbalance. Relations with India and Pakistan were more extensive than with other countries. According to Mohammad Ashraf Haidari, who was appointed as Kabul's ambassador to Sri Lanka in 2018, Kabul sought to address this imbalance: President Ghani "wanted to move beyond Pakistan and India," prompting him to charge Haidari with deepening ties with Sri Lanka as a first step toward widening the geographic scope of Kabul's regional relations.[21] Still, on the whole, over the last two decades, Afghanistan deployed relatively little diplomatic capital beyond India and Pakistan.

This was the case for strategic and practical reasons. Kabul's foreign relations were shaped by the war. India was an important partner because it provided large quantities of development assistance to strengthen infrastructure and a broader economy battered by war, as well as security aid to enhance warfighting capacity. Kabul focused ample attention on Islamabad mainly for negative reasons—it was a longstanding rival sponsoring the Taliban—but also to try to ease tensions and promote more opportunities for security and trade cooperation with a bordering state. Given that Afghanistan was at war for the last 20 years, it didn't have the bandwidth or financial resources to establish an on-ground diplomatic presence in, or to focus heavily on, countries further afield, especially because they had less bearing on the war.

According to Atmar, the former Afghan national security adviser and foreign minister, geography was another factor constraining ties with other South Asian states: They lacked a land route to Afghanistan, limiting possibilities for trade cooperation. Over the last few years, annual trade volume was barely $15 million with Bangladesh; $2.5 million with Maldives; and about $700,000 with Sri Lanka, according to official figures from these countries. However, India lacks a direct land route to Afghanistan, but it was Kabul's top regional commercial partner at the time of the Taliban takeover, with annual trade valued at $1.3 billion. Its exports went to Afghanistan via the port of Karachi in Pakistan, where they were offloaded and transferred to trucks that traveled to the Pakistan-Afghanistan border.[22] India's trade successes with Afghanistan, despite geographic constraints, can be attributed to the overall strength of India-Afghanistan relations, which generated incentives to trade a large array of goods, especially fruits, nuts, and garments, despite the non-tariff trade barriers posed by geography.

On the whole, Afghanistan favors trade with countries outside South Asia. Of Afghanistan's top five export and import partners in 2019, only two, India and Pakistan, were in the region.[23] In fairness to Afghanistan, South Asian countries on the whole trade with each other relatively infrequently. Because of poor infrastructure, bad diplomatic relations, and a broader lack of connectivity, South Asia's intraregional trade volume is among the lowest of any region in the world.

Another theme of Afghanistan's relations with South Asia was missed opportunities. Tensions with Pakistan hindered deeper security and trade cooperation. War and violence discouraged more trade and investment with the region. Insecurity and financing constraints inhibited progress on existing transnational infrastructure projects like the Turkmenistan-Afghanistan-Pakistan-India gas pipeline. Recent years did see the emergence of some new connectivity initiatives. These include an Afghanistan-Pakistan-Uzbekistan rail agreement; a connectivity-focused "quad" grouping with Afghanistan, America, Pakistan, and Uzbekistan; and an India-backed transport corridor project in Iran, including the development of the Chabahar port. Future progress with these ventures will require stability in Afghanistan.

These themes and trends were consistent over the last 20 years. This is because the war—to which Afghanistan's diplomacy was tethered—was unrelenting.

Afghanistan's Regional Relations through the Lens of Realism

Kabul's approach to regional relations over the last 20 years reflects the Realist school of IR theory.[24] Afghan governments privileged relations with those countries best positioned to help Kabul achieve its national interests, which included above all state survival in the face of a Taliban insurgency that began in the early 2000s and would gain strength exponentially over the next 20 years. State survival, according to the realist school, is an essential national interest for all states. Kabul also prioritized relations with those countries best equipped to help it achieve another core national interest, that of economic preservation.

Consequently, Afghanistan focused its regional relations on India, which was willing to provide several billion dollars in development assistance as well as multiple forms of security aid—all focused on strengthening infrastructure and development in the face of conflict and on enhancing the capacity of Afghan military forces to fight the Taliban. Afghanistan's other main target of engagement in South Asia was Pakistan, which was the main patron of the Taliban organization that threatened Afghan state survival. Pakistan's sheltering of Taliban leaders for the duration of the US-led war, the assistance it provided to Taliban fighters, and the impact all this had on strengthening the insurgency were constant concerns for Kabul. Its decision to allocate so much policy bandwidth to its relationship with Pakistan can be attributed to a desire to address the Pakistani state policies vis-à-vis the Taliban that threatened the survival of the Afghan state.

Kabul's decision not to pursue extensive relations with countries other than India and Pakistan was also based on calculations about national interest. These other countries could not provide large amounts of security or economic assistance to help Afghanistan tackle the Taliban or bolster its war-battered economy. The main features of these modest regional relations outside of India and Pakistan revolved around what could help Kabul address those national interests. Humanitarian aid from Bangladesh is one example. Kabul's decision to elevate relations with Sri Lanka in 2013 was fueled in part by the belief that Sri Lanka's own experience as a war-torn country that managed to chart a path toward peace could offer lessons to Afghanistan for achieving a peaceful outcome to its war, thereby helping ensure state survival.

Kabul viewed its relations with the United States and other NATO countries, as well as key donor countries like Japan, as priorities because they provided the bulk of military and economic support to Afghanistan. Because they were best placed to help Kabul achieve its national interests of state survival and economic preservation, these were the countries that Afghan officials emphasized the most in their IR, along with its regional neighbors India and Pakistan.

Afghanistan viewed international organizations, such as the United Nations, as important players over the last 20 years, but mainly in terms of aid provision. Kabul did not view them as essential players in peace negotiations with the Taliban, or in talks to reduce tensions with Pakistan. Afghan officials preferred to deal directly with the Taliban and with the Pakistani government. When Kabul did agree to mediation, that role was played by other countries, not international organizations. The British military chief, for example, tried to mediate Afghanistan-Pakistan tensions in 2021 during the final weeks of the US military presence. Kabul also welcomed regional diplomatic efforts focused on pursuing reconciliation in Afghanistan, and it participated in some of these initiatives.

Afghanistan's preference for working with nation states over international organizations to pursue its national interests reflects Realism, which emphasizes the agency of nation states operating in an anarchic international system, more so than it does Liberalism, an IR theory that emphasizes the strong role played by international organizations in pursuing peace and cooperation.[25] To be sure, Kabul's heavy dependence on UN agencies and other international groups for aid does illustrate Afghanistan's recognition of the critical role of international organizations. Liberalism may help explain some of Kabul's behavior, such as its decision to rely on international organizations for aid, but Realist interpretations are more convincing.

Future Drivers of Afghanistan's Relations with South Asia

Making predictions about Afghanistan's future relations with South Asia is risky because of many uncertainties about Afghanistan itself—especially regarding political leadership and stability. This caveat aside, several factors can help predict how Afghanistan's regional relations may look in the coming months and years.

Regime Type

The type of leadership in Kabul will help determine the extent of Afghanistan's future relations with South Asia. If Afghanistan is led by the Taliban or a group like it, relations with the region will have their limits as South Asian countries (with the possible exception of Pakistan) are unlikely to formally recognize Kabul. If the government is led by the Taliban or a similar group, and there are concerns among regional players about its links to international terror groups, or its unwillingness to curb them, then Kabul will struggle to carve out formal relationships with the region. That said, if there is relative stability in Afghanistan and South Asian countries' concerns about security there are properly addressed, then the potential for Afghanistan's regional relations will be higher. However, Bangladesh and the Maldives, which have experiences with Islamist extremism, and are home to radicals that have connections to Afghanistan, may be cautious about engaging with an Afghan government led by jihadists, for fear of the impact this could have on extremists at home. Kabul would also struggle to forge a warm relationship with New Delhi, which would view such a government as a direct threat to its security interests.

However, if Afghanistan is led by a government that emerges from a power-sharing arrangement, or from an election, then Kabul will not be viewed as a pariah regionally and will have more opportunities to pursue more formal and substantive relations with its South Asian neighbors. This will give Kabul a chance to develop a truly regional foreign policy, in which it scales up diplomacy with countries given short shrift over the last 20 years. This represents a best-case scenario for Afghanistan's regional relations, but it is unlikely for the foreseeable future, given the total collapse in 2021 of the Islamic Republic of Afghanistan—a weak and deeply corrupt but nonetheless democratic state.

If Afghanistan's government is led by an entity that is not in full control of the country, then Kabul's regional diplomacy will be fractured and chaotic. Entities in control elsewhere in Afghanistan, which would presumably be opposed to the group in control of Kabul, would likely pursue separate foreign policies meant to undermine the group in charge in Kabul. This may include pursuing relations with countries in South Asia that are rivals of countries engaging closely with the group in control of Kabul. India-Pakistan rivalry could figure heavily in this scenario, with one country backing the regime controlling Kabul and the other backing factions that oppose the regime and exert control outside Kabul. Proxy war would be a possibility.

Level of Stability

If Afghanistan is relatively stable, with no war and minimal terrorism threats, and the government enjoys a monopoly on the use of force, then Kabul will have opportunities to expand relations with the region—both thematically and geographically. It will not need to restrict itself to engaging only with those countries that can help fight a war that is no longer being fought. It can look to scale up trade and investment cooperation with countries around the region that were previously hesitant to ramp up commercial collaborations with a conflicted country. To be sure, these opportunities may be limited by the regime type factor: A brutal, undemocratic Afghan government may struggle to attract close cooperation from some regional players. However, so long as Afghanistan is relatively stable, an undemocratic government won't necessarily be a major obstacle. A country like Pakistan will worry more about assurances of security than human rights. For practical reasons, it will welcome relations with Afghanistan—to enhance border security and trade, among other things. Other South Asian states may also prioritize trade opportunities over rights concerns. India is an exception. Because of major ideological differences with the Taliban and similar violent Islamist groups, which have previously attacked Indian individuals and interests in Afghanistan, New Delhi would be more cautious to engage, even if there is stability.

If Afghanistan reverts to the state of conflict that ended in 2021, Kabul will not have the capacity or bandwidth to focus on pursuing broad-based relationships with the region. It will conduct its regional diplomacy according to its war needs, as it did between 1979 and 2021. The government's main priorities would be the pursuit of economic and military support—though the extent to which it does this, and the countries that it targets for such diplomacy, would depend on regime type.

A destabilized Afghanistan would pose obstacles for its regional relations. Regional players, especially India and Pakistan, may use covert means to back preferred armed factions. Additionally, regional spillover effects could spark tensions between Kabul and its neighbors. Conflict-inducted displacement could cause a fresh refugee crisis for a Pakistani state that wants to limit Afghan refugee flows. If regional terrorists exploit conflict conditions to carve out new sanctuaries in Afghanistan, and use Afghan soil to plot and execute attacks elsewhere in South Asia, Kabul's relations with the region could face major tests.

Regional Dynamics

The geopolitics of South Asia will impact Kabul's future foreign relations. Engaging with the region commercially is difficult even in the best of times, given bad regional relations, an ineffective SAARC, poor infrastructure, and a consequent lack of intraregional trade. This absence of regional cohesion is unlikely to change in the future. New Delhi—motivated by its rivalry with Islamabad—is developing new sub-regional connectivity projects that bypass SAARC and engage members of the Bay of Bengal Initiative for Multisectoral Technical and Economic Cooperation (BIMSTEC). Five SAARC members belong to BIMSTEC, but Pakistan does not—and neither does Afghanistan.

Increasing Chinese investments in South Asia may help bridge South Asia's infrastructure gap, but they could also worsen another longstanding challenge: Geopolitical rivalry. China's deepening presence in South Asia will strengthen its partnership with longtime ally Pakistan, while increasing India-China and India-Pakistan rivalry. This means that even if Afghanistan's regime type and level of stability allow it to pursue deeper relations with the region, it will need to navigate South Asia's lack of regional integration and intensifying regional rivalries.

Regional dynamics do offer opportunities for Kabul. Post-pandemic, growing economies in South Asia—especially Bangladesh, India, and Sri Lanka—will seek new markets for bilateral trade and investment. Additionally, India and Pakistan are keen to scale up relations with Central Asia, and they see Afghanistan as a bridge. Pakistan inked its new rail agreement with Afghanistan and Uzbekistan in 2021. India is a part of the International North-South Transit Corridor (INSTC), a multi-modal transport corridor envisioned to stretch from India through Afghanistan to Russia. Other countries in the region, including Bangladesh, may eventually view INSTC as an initiative worth joining.[26] "There's a huge opportunity if Central Asia is connected by land to South Asia," according to Atmar. "This opportunity will unlock enormous economic potential …. And Afghanistan is that land bridge for South and Central Asia."[27] However, by joining these different connectivity projects, Afghanistan risks getting caught up in India-Pakistan rivalry. More broadly, these possibilities can only fructify if there is enough stability and if regional players are comfortable with the type of regime in power.

Conclusion

The story of Afghanistan's relations with South Asia over the last 20 years is one of limited engagement and missed opportunities. Constant war precluded Kabul from mustering the necessary bandwidth and resources to pursue substantive relations with the wider region. Instead, Afghanistan's foreign relations were driven by wartime considerations. It focused its relations on India, a close partner, and Pakistan, its rival neighbor—the two countries in the region most relevant to the conflict. New Delhi was Kabul's top regional donor, mainly development aid but also security assistance. Islamabad was an indirect party to the war, given its sponsorship of the Taliban. Other countries in the region were given short shrift in Kabul's diplomatic calculations, though it did give some priority to Bangladesh, a key source of humanitarian assistance, and Sri Lanka, which Kabul viewed as a useful model for how to become a post-conflict state. But because of war, the potential for more trade and investment with the region couldn't be met. Deeper cooperation with Pakistan, Afghanistan's only contiguous neighbor in South Asia, was constrained by tensions over Islamabad's role in the war.

In the future, Afghanistan may find itself in a better position to broaden its regional engagement and to capitalize on missed opportunities. But this will require a regime type with which the region is willing to engage closely, and especially a modicum of stability that gives the region assurances about engaging and especially investing in Afghanistan. Given the uncertainties about Afghanistan's future, it is difficult to judge if and when these conditions will be in place—and if they are, whether or not they will endure.

Notes

1 See Avinash Paliwal, *My Enemy's Enemy: India in Afghanistan from the Soviet Invasion to the US Withdrawal* (Oxford: Oxford University Press, 2017); Harsh Pant, *India's Afghan Muddle: A Lost Opportunity* (New York: Harper Collins, 2015); Elizabeth Threlkeld and Grace Easterly, "Afghanistan-Pakistan Ties and Future Stability in Afghanistan," PeaceWorks No. 175, U.S. Institute of Peace, August 2021, https://www.usip.org/sites/default/files/2021-08/pw_175-afghanistan_pakistan_ties_and_future_stability_in_afghanistan.pdf; and Huma Baqai and Nausheen Wasi, eds., *Pakistan-Afghanistan Relations: The Way Forward* (Karachi, Pakistan: Institute of Business Administration, 2021).

2 See Steve Coll, *Directorate S: The C.I.A. and America's Secret Wars in Afghanistan and Pakistan* (New York: Penguin Press, 2018); Carlotta Gall, *The Wrong Enemy: America in Afghanistan, 2001–2014* (Boston: Houghton Mifflin Harcourt, 2014); and Zahid Hussain, *No-Win War: The Paradox of U.S.-Pakistan Relations in Afghanistan's Shadow* (Oxford: Oxford University Press, 2021).

3 One example is Mohammad Hasan Kakar, *A Political and Diplomatic History of Afghanistan, 1863–1901* (Leiden, The Netherlands: Brill Publishers, 2006). There have also been a few recent edited volumes about contemporary Afghanistan-Pakistan relations, including Baqai and Wasi's study, that feature chapters by Afghan writers.

4 "Financing Peace: Fiscal Challenges and Implications for a Post-Settlement Afghanistan," World Bank Policy Note, World Bank, December 2019, https://documents1.worldbank.org/curated/en/776581575555846850/pdf/Financing-Peace-Fiscal-Challenges-and-Implications-for-a-Post-Settlement-Afghanistan.pdf.

5 Coll, *Directorate S*, 352.

6 Saad Mohseni, "It's Getting Dire in Afghanistan. Biden Can't Walk Away," *Politico*, November 5, 2021, https://www.politico.com/news/magazine/2021/11/05/its-getting-dire-in-afghanistan-biden-cant-walk-away-519734.

7 "India to Back Afghan Membership for SAARC," *Outlook*, November 8, 2005, https://www.outlookindia.com/newswire/story/india-to-back-afghan-membership-for-saarc/333666.

8 Nirupama Subramanian, "Explained: What are India's Investments in Afghanistan?" *Indian Express*, July 16, 2021, https://indianexpress.com/article/explained/explained-indias-afghan-investment-7406795/.

9 Ross Colvin, "Afghanistan's Karzai Gives India Military Equipment 'Wish List,'" *Reuters*, May 22, 2013, https://www.reuters.com/article/us-india-afghanistan/afghanistans-karzai-gives-india-military-equipment-wish-list-idUSBRE94L0DQ20130522.

10 Michael Kugelman, "The Most Important Arms Deal You've Never Heard Of," War on the Rocks, December 22, 2015, https://warontherocks.com/2015/12/the-most-important-arms-deal-youve-never-heard-of/.

11 Baqir Sajjad Sayed, "FM Rejects Ghani's Tweets as Gross Interference," *Dawn*, February 8, 2019, https://www.dawn.com/news/1462512.

12 Ishrat Husain and Muhammad Ather Elahi, "The Future of Afghanistan-Pakistan Trade Relations," Peace Brief 191, U.S. Institute of Peace, August 2015, https://www.usip.org/sites/default/files/PB191-The-Future-of-Afghanistan-Pakistan-Trade-Relations.pdf.

13 Mohammad Haneef Atmar, video interview with author, December 24, 2021.

14 Ayesha Tanzeem, "Pakistan Rejects Afghan Allegations on Parliament Attack," Voice of America, June 25, 2015, https://www.voanews.com/a/kabul-blames-haqqani-network-pakistan-for-parliament-attack/2836385.html.

15 BRAC, "Afghanistan," https://bracinternational.org/afghanistan/.

16 Snigdhendu Bhattacharya, "How Afghanistan-trained Mujahideen Brought Terror to Bangladesh in the 1990s," *Outlook*, August 20, 2021, https://www.outlookindia.com/website/story/world-news-how-afghanistan-trained-mujahideen-brought-terror-to-bangladesh-in-the-1990s/392029.

17 Subir Bhaumik, "Taliban Takeover in Afghanistan Stokes Bangladesh's Terrorist Fears," *The Diplomat*, August 26, 2021, https://thediplomat.com/2021/08/taliban-takeover-in-afghanistan-stokes-bangladeshs-terrorist-fears/ and "Bangladesh Would Not Send Troops to Afghanistan: Hasina," *Indian Express*, October 3, 2010, http://archive.indianexpress.com/news/bangladesh-would-not-send-troops-to-afghanistan-hasina/691866/.

18 Mohammad Ashraf Haidari, email interview with author, December 17, 2021.

19 "Ambassador Haidari Meets Maldivian Counterpart to Discuss Afghanistan-Maldives Bilateral Relations," Embassy of Afghanistan in Sri Lanka, Colombo, Sri Lanka, May 26, 2019, https://www.colombo.mfa.af/news/ambassador-haidari-meets-maldivian-counterpart-to-discuss-afghanistan-maldives-bilateral-relations.html.

20 "Nepali Repatriation from Kabul Starts," *Nepali Times*, August 17, 2021, https://www.nepalitimes.com/banner/nepali-repatriation-from-kabul-starts/.

21 Haidari, email interview with author.

22 Aishwarya Paliwal, "Afghanistan Crisis: Indian Trade Worth $1.5 billion Stops Abruptly as Afghans Stare at Bleak Future," *India Today*, August 24, 2021, https://www.indiatoday.in/india/story/afghanistan-crisis-indian-bilateral-trade-stops-abruptly-afghans-bleak-future-1844493-2021-08-24.

23 "Afghanistan Trade," World Bank, World Integrated Trade Solution software, https://wits.worldbank.org/countrysnapshot/en/AFG/textview.

24 See Steven E. Lobell, Norrin M. Ripsman, and Jeffrey W. Taliaferro, eds, *Neoclassical Realism, The State, and Foreign Policy* (Cambridge: Cambridge University Press, 2009) and Kenneth N. Waltz, *Theory of International Politics* (New York: McGraw-Hill, 1979).

25 See Daniel Deudney and G. John Ikenberry, "The Nature and Sources of Liberal International Order," *Review of International Studies* 25, no. 2 (April 1999): 179–196.

26 M.D. Pathik Hasan, "The International North-South Transit Corridor: What is the Potential for Bangladesh?" Silk Road Briefing, August 8, 2021, https://www.silkroadbriefing.com/news/2021/08/08/the-international-north-south-transport-corridor-what-is-the-potential-for-bangladesh/.

27 Atmar, video interview with author.

Bibliography

Atmar, Mohammad Haneef. Video interview with author, December 24, 2021.

Baqai, Huma, and Nausheen Wasi, eds. *Pakistan-Afghanistan-Relations: The Way Forward*. Karachi, Pakistan: Institute of Business Administration, 2021.

Bhattacharya, Snigdhendu. "How Afghanistan-trained Mujahideen Brought Terror to Bangladesh in the 1990s." *Outlook*, August 20, 2021. https://www.outlookindia.com/website/story/world-news-how-afghanistan-trained-mujahideen-brought-terror-to-bangladesh-in-the-1990s/392029.

Bhaumik, Subir. "Taliban Takeover in Afghanistan Stokes Bangladesh's Terrorist Fears." *The Diplomat*, August 26, 2021. https://thediplomat.com/2021/08/taliban-takeover-in-afghanistan-stokes-bangladeshs-terrorist-fears/.

BRAC. "Afghanistan." https://bracinternational.org/afghanistan/.

Coll, Steve. *Directorate S: The C.I.A. and America's Secret Wars in Afghanistan and Pakistan*. New York: Penguin Press, 2018.

Colvin, Ross. "Afghanistan's Karzai Gives India Military Equipment 'Wish List.'" Reuters, May 22, 2013. https://www.reuters.com/article/us-india-afghanistan/afghanistans-karzai-gives-india-military-equipment-wish-list-idUSBRE94L0DQ20130522.

Deudney, Daniel, and G. John Ikenberry. "The Nature and Sources of Liberal International Order." *Review of International Studies* 25, no. 2 (April 1999): 179–196.

Embassy of Afghanistan in Sri Lanka. "Ambassador Haidari Meets Maldivian Counterpart to Discuss Afghanistan-Maldives Bilateral Relations." Colombo, Sri Lanka, May 26, 2019. https://www.colombo.mfa.af/news/ambassador-haidari-meets-maldivian-counterpart-to-discuss-afghanistan-maldives-bilateral-relations.html.

Gall, Carlotta. *The Wrong Enemy: America in Afghanistan, 2001–2014*. Boston: Houghton Mifflin Harcourt, 2014.

Ganguly, Šumit, and Nicholas Howenstein. "India-Pakistan Rivalry in Afghanistan." *Journal of International Affairs* 63, no. 1 (Fall/Winter 2009): 127–140. https://www.jstor.org/stable/24384176.

Government of India. "Text of Agreement on Strategic Partnership between the Republic of India and the Islamic Republic of Afghanistan." Ministry of External Affairs, New Delhi, India, October 4, 2011. https://mea.gov.in/bilateral-documents.htm?dtl/5383/.

Government of Pakistan. "Afghanistan-Pakistan Transit Trade Agreement." Department of Commerce, Islamabad, Pakistan, 2010. https://www.commerce.gov.pk/wp-content/uploads/pdf/APTTA.pdf.

Haidari, Mohammad Ashraf. Email interview with author, December 17, 2021.

Hasan, M.D. Pathik. "The International North-South Transit Corridor: What is the Potential for Bangladesh?" Silk Road Briefing, August 8, 2021. https://www.silkroadbriefing.com/news/2021/08/08/the-international-north-south-transport-corridor-what-is-the-potential-for-bangladesh/.

Husain, Ishrat, and Muhammad Ather Elahi. "The Future of Afghanistan-Pakistan Trade Relations." Peace Brief 191, U.S. Institute of Peace, August 2015. https://www.usip.org/sites/default/files/PB191-The-Future-of-Afghanistan-Pakistan-Trade-Relations.pdf.

Hussain, Zahid. *No-Win War: The Paradox of U.S.-Pakistan Relations in Afghanistan's Shadow*. Oxford: Oxford University Press, 2021.

"Bangladesh Would Not Send Troops to Afghanistan: Hasina." *Indian Express*, October 3, 2010. http://archive.indianexpress.com/news/bangladesh-would-not-send-troops-to-afghanistan-hasina/691866/.

Kakar, Mohammad Hasan. *A Political and Diplomatic History of Afghanistan, 1863–1901*. Leiden, The Netherlands: Brill Publishers, 2006.

Kugelman, Michael. "Danger on the Durand Line." *Foreign Affairs*, March 2, 2017. https://www.foreignaffairs.com/articles/afghanistan/2017-03-02/danger-durand-line.

———. "The Most Important Arms Deal You've Never Heard Of." War on the Rocks, December 22, 2015. https://warontherocks.com/2015/12/the-most-important-arms-deal-youve-never-heard-of/.

———. "The Politics of Taliban Recognition." *South Asian Voices*, November 10, 2021. https://southasianvoices.org/the-politics-of-taliban-recognition/.

Lobell, Steven E., Norrin M. Ripsman, and Jeffrey W. Taliaferro, eds. *Neoclassical Realism, The State, and Foreign Policy*. Cambridge: Cambridge University Press, 2009.

Mohseni, Saad. "It's Getting Dire in Afghanistan. Biden Can't Walk Away." *Politico*, November 5, 2021. https://www.politico.com/news/magazine/2021/11/05/its-getting-dire-in-afghanistan-biden-cant-walk-away-519734.

"Nepali Repatriation from Kabul Starts." *Nepali Times*, August 17, 2021. https://www.nepalitimes.com/banner/nepali-repatriation-from-kabul-starts/.

Paliwal, Aishwarya. "Afghanistan Crisis: Indian Trade Worth $1.5 billion Stops Abruptly as Afghans Stare at Bleak Future." *India Today*, August 24, 2021. https://www.indiatoday.in/india/story/afghanistan-crisis-indian-bilateral-trade-stops-abruptly-afghans-bleak-future-1844493-2021-08-24.

Paliwal, Avinash. *My Enemy's Enemy: India in Afghanistan from the Soviet Invasion to the US Withdrawal.* Oxford: Oxford University Press, 2017.

Pant, Harsh. *India's Afghan Muddle: A Lost Opportunity.* New York: Harper Collins, 2015.

Press Trust of India. "India to Back Afghan Membership for SAARC." *Outlook*, November 8, 2005. https://www.outlookindia.com/newswire/story/india-to-back-afghan-membership-for-saarc/333666.

Sayed, Baqir Sajjad. "FM Rejects Ghani's Tweets as Gross Interference." *Dawn*, February 8, 2019. https://www.dawn.com/news/1462512.

Siddique, Abubakar. *The Pashtun Question: The Unresolved Key to the Future of Afghanistan.* London: Hurst, 2014.

Subramanian, Nirupama. "Explained: What are India's Investments in Afghanistan?" *Indian Express*, July 16, 2021. https://indianexpress.com/article/explained/explained-indias-afghan-investment-7406795/.

Tanzeem, Ayesha. "Pakistan Rejects Afghan Allegations on Parliament Attack." Voice of America, June 25, 2015. https://www.voanews.com/a/kabul-blames-haqqani-network-pakistan-for-parliament-attack/2836385.html.

Threlkeld, Elizabeth, and Grace Easterly. "Afghanistan-Pakistan Ties and Future Stability in Afghanistan." PeaceWorks No. 175. U.S. Institute of Peace, August 2021. https://www.usip.org/sites/default/files/2021-08/pw_175-afghanistan_pakistan_ties_and_future_stability_in_afghanistan.pdf.

Tomsen, Peter. *The Wars of Afghanistan: Messianic Terrorism, Tribal Conflicts, and the Failures of Great Powers.* New York: PublicAffairs, 2013.

Waltz, Kenneth N. *Theory of International Politics.* New York: McGraw-Hill, 1979.

World Bank. "Afghanistan Trade." World Integrated Trade Solution software. https://wits.worldbank.org/countrysnapshot/en/AFG/textview.

———. "Financing Peace: Fiscal Challenges and Implications for a Post-Settlement Afghanistan." World Bank Policy Note, December 2019. https://documents1.worldbank.org/curated/en/776581575555846850/pdf/Financing-Peace-Fiscal-Challenges-and-Implications-for-a-Post-Settlement-Afghanistan.pdf.

18
SRI LANKA AND SOUTH ASIA

Nilanthi Samaranayake

Sri Lanka is an increasingly important country worth studying for its relationships with fellow South Asian countries, as well as its position in the wider context of international politics. As a member of the South Asian Association for Regional Cooperation (SAARC), Sri Lanka continues to deepen its regional relationships, especially with India as its dominant neighbor. Within the global context, Colombo's approach has received increased attention, largely due to the trend of China's deepening ties with the small island nation.[1] As US-China strategic competition casts a shadow over all countries with significant ties to both of these great powers,[2] Sri Lanka is drawing on its experience during the Cold War to navigate this emerging dynamic in the new era. Therefore, this topic is important for students and researchers to examine for its implications in the coming years.

Theory

This volume examines prominent theoretical approaches to the study of international relations in the South Asian region: Realism, liberalism, constructivism, and critical theory.[3] Aspects of each school can be detected when studying the international politics of, and thinking within, Sri Lanka over the years. Yet, realism's attention to power politics and capabilities resonates most prominently among analysts of the country. Going forward, the subfield of research on small states can help provide greater explanatory power to understand Sri Lanka's relations with the region. This section will reference some relevant theoretical and empirical writings as a launch pad for scholars and students wishing to learn more.

Four Theoretical Schools

From a critical theory perspective, Sri Lanka belongs to "a coalition of 'Third World' states which struggles to undo the dominance of 'core' countries" and serve as 'emancipatory counter-hegemonic' forces."[4] Constructivism for its part focuses on concepts such as norms, identity, and ideas—a social interpretation of international politics that goes beyond metrics of hard power such as military capabilities.[5] The application of critical theory and constructivism to the case of Sri Lanka is clear. The country remains proud of its participation in the 1955 Bandung conference of Asian and African nations, which sought to chart a different course

DOI: 10.4324/9781003246626-22

than one of Cold War bipolarity.[6] It served as a precursor to the non-alignment movement. Going further, Sri Lanka's Foreign Ministry emphasizes its role in catalyzing the Bandung conference through the 1954 Colombo Powers Conference.[7] This emphasis on the idea of non-alignment persists in Sri Lanka's international diplomatic identity and talking points to the present day.

Liberalism draws attention to the economic dimension of international relations through the argument for free trade as a means of "integrating the developing world into the wider global economy."[8] Sri Lankan economist Saman Kelegama, for example, wrote about the country's setbacks in pursuing a liberal approach to economic development. Of note, he highlights a challenge that continues to plague Sri Lanka in the present day: The country's foreign-exchange crisis.[9] Economic development is an issue that occupies Sri Lankan decision-makers, as the country seeks to permanently graduate to upper-middle-income country status, but has not sufficiently updated its economic management practices.

While critical theory, constructivism, and liberalism explain Sri Lanka's economic, ideational, and normative outlook into the present day, realism dominates discussions of the country's security outlook. Within this framework, Sri Lanka is largely viewed through the prism of having either balanced against or bandwagoned with the great powers of the United States and the Soviet Union during the Cold War years, as well as India as the dominant country in South Asia since independence. With its emphasis on material capabilities, realism is often used to examine major powers, including India with its nuclear arsenal. Realism as a theory has not historically focused on small states like Sri Lanka; however, Sri Lankan academics writing during the Cold War era can be found to reference realist concepts in understanding the implications for their small state. For example, in the title of their edited volume series *Security Dilemma of a Small State*,[10] Sri Lankan scholars Mahinda Werake and P.V.J. Jayasekera refer to the realist concept of a security dilemma—an idea popularized in international relations literature by Robert Jervis.[11]

Emerging Sri Lankan Scholarship

In contemporary literature, Sandya Nishanthi Gunasekara[12] and Rajni Nayanthara Gamage[13] both reference the structural realist concepts of bandwagoning and balancing in their analyses of Sri Lanka's historical foreign policy approaches. As a middle-option strategy, Chulanee Attanayake (along with co-author Archana Atmakuri)[14] and Shakthi De Silva[15] have examined hedging strategies and applied this analysis to the case of Sri Lanka. As neorealism has gained popularity and more attention over the past 40 years to include variants in building upon this thinking, Sri Lankan scholars have also adopted this thinking into analysis of their country. For example, Shakthi De Silva[16] and Bhagya Senaratne[17] have written about the merits of neoclassical realism in interpreting Sri Lanka's experience, taking into account the role of domestic factors in producing international outcomes.

The Small States Theoretical Subfield

The above theories and work by scholars have been useful to advance rigorous analysis of Sri Lanka and its international relations from the Cold War era to the contemporary period. An emerging analytical lens of relevance to the study of Sri Lanka is the subfield of small states. Scholars are drawing attention to the need to develop more robust theories of small states in international affairs,[18] especially considering they constitute the majority of states in the international community.[19] South Asian regional scholars can examine Sri Lanka functionally as a small state, including the types of metrics and traits that it shares with other smaller South Asian (SSA) countries[20] and Indian Ocean island states.[21]

In fact, small states in these regions have common needs, surprising strengths given their size, and significant concerns due to their relative capabilities.[22] These are all factors that apply to the case of Sri Lanka. For example, Colombo has specific economic development needs as a small state that it seeks to fulfill via external assistance.[23] The intense scrutiny that Sri Lanka has received over its ties with China in the past decade only scratches the surface of this driver. Second, like other small states, Sri Lanka has surprising strengths despite its size. Foremost are its location and status as hosting the busiest container port in South Asia.[24] The former Commander of US Pacific Command, Admiral Harry Harris, spoke about the strategic importance of Sri Lanka's location in the Indian Ocean.[25] Finally, Sri Lanka faces concerns found in other small states, namely its asymmetry in power with its regionally dominant neighbor.[26] This asymmetry is a factor that informs much of Colombo's threat perceptions and thinking about its room for strategic action if the country veers too far from India's interests.

Brief Empirical History

In the modern era, Sri Lanka was known as Ceylon until 1972. Following centuries of Western colonization—first by Portugal, then by the Netherlands, and finally by Great Britain, the country gained independence in 1948. Yet unlike India, which actively sought to evict the British from the subcontinent after it won independence the previous year, Ceylon pursued a defense arrangement with the United Kingdom as a newly independent country with few military capabilities. The leadership felt threat perceptions from the north in India,[27] which were also rooted in what has been called the Sinhalese ethnic majority's historical "minority complex vis-à-vis the Tamils" due to the proximity of the populous Tamil Nadu state in India.[28] It was not until the following decade under new leadership in Colombo that the United Kingdom completed the transfer of its air and naval bases to Ceylon's control in 1957.

In addition to regional threat perceptions, Sri Lanka confronted an environment of great power competition at the dawn of the Cold War between the United States and Soviet Union and observed the risks of being caught in it. Ceylon's early leadership was considered to be "conspicuously pro-Western and openly critical of communism."[29] In the next several years, the country had experienced multiple vetoes by the Soviet Union over admission to the UN and decided to establish diplomatic relations with this superpower in 1956. Yet during this decade, Ceylon also found itself in the crosshairs of the US Battle Act, which prohibited exports of strategic goods such as rubber to the Communist bloc and denied aid to countries engaging in this transfer. Ceylon incurred this ban due to its 1952 Rubber-Rice barter agreement with the People's Republic of China. After Colombo's negotiations with the United States in 1955–1956, US development assistance was eventually granted to Ceylon.

Even two decades later, the effect of great power competition persisted for Colombo. Notably in 1971, Ceylon joined with Tanzania to propose a UN resolution that the Indian Ocean should remain a "Zone of Peace."[30] It was an attempt to call attention to threat perceptions by regional states over the rising military presence of great powers during the Cold War. Fifty years later, this theme of Indian Ocean insecurity is reemerging among resident countries—including Sri Lanka—but with the United States and China as the new great power competitors.[31]

At the national level, the history of internal ethnic strife is well documented. These deep ethnic tensions were exacerbated by leaders' actions in the years after independence to limit the use of the Tamil language by making Sinhala the country's official language, culminating with the onset of Colombo's war in 1983 against the Liberation Tigers of Tamil Eelam (LTTE) insurgency until 2009. The conduct at the end of this war was very controversial, with the 2011 UN Secretary-General's Panel of Experts reporting an estimate of up to 40,000 civilian deaths.[32] Over a decade later, the issue continues to be closely examined by foreign governments and international institutions. Prominent examples are US government sanctions on Sri Lankan military officers for human rights violations, the European Parliament's resolution exploring a temporary withdrawal of Sri Lanka's benefits from having the European Union's Generalised Scheme of Preferences Plus (GSP+) program, and a statement by Michelle Bachelet, UN High Commissioner for Human Rights, on reconciliation, accountability, and human rights in Sri Lanka.

Major Changes in the Past Decade

The past decade witnessed significant change to the study of Sri Lanka compared with the preceding decade. In 2009, Sri Lanka had emerged from nearly 30 years of civil war. The heightened attention to international networks of terrorists in that decade increasingly drew Sri Lanka into the discourse about methods of asymmetric warfare, especially the phenomenon of suicide terrorism conducted by the LTTE.[33] This domestic-level focus on insurgency and ethnic tension has persisted even in international-level analysis.[34]

Yet at the start of the past decade, China's increasing commercial transactions and military capabilities placed greater attention on Sri Lanka in the international context. Beijing's naval presence in the Indian Ocean due to counterpiracy deployments beginning in 2008–2009,[35] combined with its maritime infrastructure investments in South Asia,[36] raised questions about the implications of these activities for each country in the region. Sri Lanka came to be featured in debates about China's ambitions for building commercial ports and military bases in Southeast Asia and South Asian countries, referred to as a "string of pearls."[37] In 2007, the Sri Lankan and Chinese governments acknowledged progress in discussions to build a port in Hambantota, which first opened in 2010 and has remained controversial as a symbol for the overall questions about China's role in this country to the present day.[38] Much writing about Sri Lanka in the past decade has been devoted to evaluating these bilateral relations and assessing the potential implications for China's wider goals in the region.

At the beginning of the 2020s, attention to Sri Lanka's relationship with China has only intensified. For its part, China has increased its Indian Ocean presence through regular naval deployments, including undersea, and the establishment of its first-ever overseas military base in Djibouti. Furthermore, the recent context finds India facing persistent threats, and even casualties, at its border with China. As a result, questions persist over where Colombo stands in its ties with an increasingly assertive Beijing.

Yet, as the preceding decade drew to a close, terrorism once again emerged as a major threat after the 2019 Easter Sunday bombings. Beyond the familiar Tamil-Sinhalese ethnic tension, discrimination against the country's Muslim population and the threat of Islamic extremism[39] have begun to receive greater attention from observers. Despite this significant event, much attention to Sri Lanka continues to reside in questions about the country's geostrategic orientation with regard to China and is likely to continue in the current decade.[40]

At the time of writing, Sri Lanka finds itself in an unprecedented economic, social, and political crisis that has resulted in the country's first-ever default on its debt and resignations from both the president and prime minister. Sri Lanka will face significant challenges in course-correcting its management of the economy and reestablishing the public's access to essentials such as food, fuel, and medical services. A focus on domestic priorities may set back the country's overseas ambitions in the years ahead.

Key Relationships within South Asia

Against this wider geostrategic backdrop, Sri Lanka maintains unique ties with each of its South Asian neighbors. The Ministry of Foreign Affairs has established a South Asia and SAARC Division that is responsible for bilateral and regional ties and maintains the following regional presence:

> Sri Lanka maintains resident missions in 6 South Asian countries i.e. Afghanistan, Bangladesh, India, the Maldives, Nepal and Pakistan, while having one Deputy High Commission in Chennai and two Consulates General in Mumbai and Karachchi.[41]

This section examines key points of Sri Lanka's bilateral relations with each regional country.

Maldives

The South Asian neighbor with which Sri Lanka has the most in common is Maldives. Both countries are island states in the Indian Ocean and their populations share deep historical and cultural bonds. For example, many Maldivian nationals live in Sri Lanka, and Maldives' fish is a staple in Sri Lankan cuisine. Strategically, they also share similar threat perceptions rooted in their smaller size and relationship to India. For example, both have experts who have written about the "security dilemma" that each country faces as a "small state."[42]

From Sri Lanka's perspective, it "nurtured Maldives" and helped boost Maldives' development from a country focused on fishing economically to become a leader in luxury tourism.[43] Colombo has helped enable Maldives' growth in this industry, with airline connectivity to Malé operating through Bandaranaike International Airport. Sri Lanka is also a diplomatic hub where many embassies in Colombo are accredited to Maldives, compared to only a handful in Malé.

Despite occasional fishing disputes, the two countries remain close. They are also collaborating with India in a trilateral security framework via the recently named Colombo Security Conclave. The format originally launched in 2011 as a series of meetings at the National Security Advisor-level with operational-level interactions in the maritime domain. For example, the three countries' coast guards interact via the DOSTI exercise held most recently in 2021.

Bangladesh

Sri Lanka has experienced a somewhat competitive relationship with Bangladesh. Since the 1940s, Colombo has viewed India as on top of the regional hierarchy, followed by Pakistan, Sri Lanka, and then other South Asian countries.[44] Sri Lanka was never a Least Developed Country like Bangladesh, which did not gain independence until 1971. In the subsequent decades, however, Bangladesh built a readymade garment industry that became competitive with Sri Lanka's.

The two countries have different recollections of the Bangladesh War of Independence. From Bangladesh's perspective, Colombo was not favorable to the cause of independence due to its willingness to permit Islamabad's forces to refuel, as Pakistan's "supply chain and air assaults passed through Sri Lanka."[45] From Sri Lanka's perspective, Colombo permitted landing and refueling because Pakistani forces could not conduct long-haul flights over India.[46] New Delhi had banned flights by Pakistani aircraft over Indian territory after the hijacking of an Indian Airlines plane. Colombo's sense of competition with Dhaka and the latter's bitter memory during independence have persisted as themes in bilateral relations to the present day.

Despite Bangladesh's well-known travails in the past 50 years, the country has grown to overtake Sri Lanka on a variety of measures including economic and military capabilities. For example, Bangladeshi military forces delivered relief after Sri Lanka experienced deadly floods in 2016. In 2021, Dhaka has also offered financial assistance via a much-needed currency swap—its first ever—to Sri Lanka, which has seen a significant increase in its debt and diminished foreign exchange reserves. Bangladesh's ascendant role in South Asia is a stark reminder to Sri Lanka about its former advantages and how far it has fallen behind. Yet, Bangladeshi policymakers see room for the bilateral relationship to grow, particularly in terms of trade and maritime shipping.[47] In fact, Bangladesh relies on transshipment from Colombo port within South Asia (as well as Singapore in Southeast Asia) due to the comparatively advanced maritime infrastructure.

India and Pakistan

Sri Lanka has worked to preserve its autonomy in the face of a significantly larger neighbor, India, while trying to avoid becoming ensnared in the India-Pakistan conflict. Both countries are examined together in this section, as Colombo has needed to navigate each with consideration to the other, given their competitive dynamics at the regional level.

Upon independence in 1948, Ceylon signed a defense agreement with the United Kingdom due to its concerns about India's regional intentions. As the new government grew comfortable with New Delhi, Ceylon demonstrated a willingness to alter its stance toward India. For example, Prime Minister S.W.R.D. Bandaranaike entered office in 1956 and viewed India as less threatening than previously. His administration asked British troops to leave Sri Lanka.[48]

On the other hand, Sri Lanka has found it difficult to achieve a balance in its ties with New Delhi and Islamabad, demonstrating an inclination to ultimately comply with India's preferences. For example, despite conveying its neutrality in the 1948 and 1965 wars, Ceylon allowed Pakistani civilian and military aircraft refueling access in 1971 for operational reasons, rather than out of a desire to undercut New Delhi in the East Pakistan conflict.[49] Broadly, Ceylon felt trapped in competitive Cold War politics between the United States and Soviet Union, with regional-level implications for its India and Pakistan policies. Yet, Colombo understood the limits of its foreign policy space and recognized that ultimately India's security preferences could not be denied.[50] For its part, India was displeased by Colombo's actions, which were seen as meddling, and External Affairs Minister Swaran Singh threatened that India may intercept planes traveling to Sri Lanka.[51] As often seen in the country's foreign policy then and through the present day, Sri Lanka agreed to Indian pressure at a high-enough threshold. This pattern was also seen in Sri Lanka's foreign policy outreach to the United States in the 1980s, when the great power's relations with South Asia were not viewed positively by India.[52] These memories inform Sri Lanka's foreign policy in the present day, as the country's diplomats still discuss the perils of using the "Yankee card" in the context of relations with India.[53]

The bilateral relationship in the 1980s was further complicated by military intervention. Ethnic tensions in Sri Lanka had been building for years, resulting in protracted conflict between the LTTE insurgency and Colombo. Concerned about the Tamil population in Sri Lanka, India attempted a naval operation in June 1987 to deliver humanitarian relief to the northern city of Jaffna. This mission was deterred by the Sri Lanka Navy, but Indian military forces entered Sri Lankan airspace without permission and delivered supplies by airdrop. In July 1987, Sri Lanka's president J.R. Jayewardene and India's prime minister Rajiv Gandhi signed a bilateral accord, which discussed bringing about greater governing power to the Northern and Eastern provinces. Furthermore, the accord resulted in the presence of the Indian Peace Keeping Force for the next few years in Sri Lanka. The memories of India's intervention in Sri Lanka and the still-unresolved issue of devolution of power continue to inform Colombo's thinking in the present day about the limits of its room to conduct both domestic and foreign policy.

In the modern era, Pakistan and Sri Lanka enjoy generally positive ties across multiple dimensions. This cooperation spans economic relations and people-to-people contacts, as well as standard naval diplomacy. Still, the same pattern exists where Sri Lanka is viewed to ultimately defer to India's interests as the dominant country in South Asia. This tendency has only been amplified as India has built greater economic, diplomatic, and military capabilities over the past decade. For example, when Pakistan's Prime Minister Imran Khan visited Sri Lanka in 2021, his speech to address Parliament was canceled—a move that was viewed as Colombo seeking to avoid India's ire by giving Khan this platform.[54] More broadly, Sri Lanka now participates in regular bilateral military exercises with India, and has renewed its participation in a trilateral maritime exercise with India and Maldives. By comparison, the room for Sri Lanka-Pakistan relations to grow appears increasingly limited.

Nepal and Bhutan

Sri Lanka's ties with the Himalayan countries of Bhutan and Nepal are not as robust as those with its more proximate neighbors, but they are generally positive. Sri Lankan scholars and diplomats have closely studied Nepal's and Bhutan's complex ties with India to gain insights into their foreign policy approaches toward their giant neighbor.[55]

Sri Lanka and Bhutan share a warm relationship, aided more by cultural and religious ties than indicators such as diplomatic presence. A majority of the population in both countries identifies as Buddhist—Mahayana in Bhutan and Theravada in Sri Lanka. In terms of social development, all Bhutanese medical students receive training in Sri Lanka, Bangladesh, or India.[56] Although as SAARC countries, their diplomats engage with each other, there is no Sri Lankan high commission in Bhutan due to cost,[57] making it the only South Asian country in which Sri Lanka does not have a mission. It is worth noting, however, that Bhutan's first step out of its India-dominant diplomacy and into a multilateral organization occurred when the country joined the Ceylon-hosted Colombo Plan in 1962.[58] In the contemporary era, Bhutan served as Secretary General of the Colombo Plan Secretariat in 2014.

Sri Lanka also has warm relations with Nepal, reinforced by a sense of shared history even if they are geographically distant. Nepal stands out to Sri Lanka's majority Buddhist population as the country where Gautama Buddha was born. In the modern era, Sri Lankan policymakers see Nepal as a country that has underperformed, which is also a view held by Sri Lankan policymakers of their own country.[59] Indeed, they share an identity as post-conflict, lower middle-income countries that seek to recover from instability over many years. Nepal hosts the SAARC Secretariat in Kathmandu, where Sri Lankan diplomats have served as Secretary General as recently as 2021.

Afghanistan

Afghanistan is a frontier South Asian country, having joined SAARC only in 2011. As a result, Sri Lanka's ties with Afghanistan are relatively underdeveloped. The two countries only established diplomatic relations in 2014, largely due to the force of personalities of their presidents at the time. Hamid Karzai and Mahinda Rajapaksa were eager to build the bilateral relationship and also self-identified as fiercely independent from both Pakistan and India. Their push was the catalyst that advanced diplomatic ties and resulted in the establishment of high commissions.[60] Colombo has seen promise in their relationship over the past decade along economic lines, with the goal of augmenting the number of Sri Lankan workers in Afghanistan.

After the fall of Kabul in 2021 and entry of Taliban rule, however, Sri Lanka finds itself in a difficult position of determining next steps in its ties with Afghanistan. It subsequently evacuated all Sri Lankan nationals. Going forward, Colombo still seeks to send an anti-terrorism message internationally, largely due to its war against the LTTE insurgency and more recent experience with the Easter Sunday bombings.[61] Therefore, recognition of Taliban rule remains a controversial prospect. Along with other countries, Sri Lanka continues to monitor the situation in Afghanistan.

Forecast of Sri Lanka's Relations with South Asia

Interest in the study of Sri Lanka and its international relations has grown over the past decade and is likely to expand in the coming years. This is largely due to China's ascendance onto the global stage and escalating great power competition. Beforehand, Sri Lanka was largely viewed through the internal prisms of ethnic strife and terrorism. Now, its ties with China have refocused analytic attention outward on Sri Lanka's foreign relations, raising questions about whether the country may provide preferential commercial and military access to China, ultimately to the detriment of Indian (and US) security interests. In a sense, this contemporary focus on how Sri Lanka navigates great powers, as well as India as the dominant regional country, is a reversion to the situation during the Cold War era at both the regional and international levels.

Future study of Sri Lanka's international relations will need to prioritize better understanding the perspectives of small states in international affairs. Much attention has been paid to explaining the actions of great and major powers, and increasingly even middle powers. Small states, however, tend to be an afterthought. The heightened interest in Sri Lanka is an opportunity for theoretical and empirical analysis of SSA states, their bilateral relationships, and strategic positions within South Asia. Treating these SSA countries as a discrete analytic unit holds potential for the study of the region's international relations and beyond.

Beyond analytical opportunities, the danger of this increased attention to Sri Lanka's international relations is securitization of the topic by policymakers and analysts. Given the wider contemporary focus on threats posed by China's rise, much of the increased attention to Sri Lanka has been driven by questions about the country's relationship with China. Two consecutive US administrations have declared a new era of competition with China and consequently view the actions of third-party countries such as Sri Lanka through this lens. Examining Sri Lanka's geostrategic and regional ties solely along security lines risks overlooking the considerable developmental, diplomatic, and ideological dimensions of this small state's foreign relations. Beyond overlooking these traditional areas, it also risks neglecting non-traditional challenges such as natural and human-made disasters. The impacts

Sri Lanka and South Asia

of the latter gained prominence in 2020–2021 when Sri Lanka suffered two major shipping accidents that damaged the marine environment.

The next ten years are likely to see closer attention to Sri Lanka's international relations in the dynamic South Asian region. The India-Pakistan and US-Soviet Union rivalries once served to focus attention on Colombo's policies at the regional and global levels, respectively. In the contemporary era, the India-China and US-China rivalries appear to be posing similar challenges for Sri Lanka. To understand Sri Lanka's current posture and future trajectory in the region, scholars will need to draw on emerging research on small states as well as the major schools of international relations theory.

Notes

1 Nilanthi Samaranayake, "Are Sri Lanka's Relations with China Deepening? An Analysis of Economic, Military, and Diplomatic Data," *Asian Security* 7, no. 2 (June 22, 2011): 142–143, https://doi.org/10.1080/14799855.2011.581603.
2 White House, *Interim National Security Strategic Guidance*, March 2021, 20, https://www.whitehouse.gov/wp-content/uploads/2021/03/NSC-1v2.pdf.
3 See in this volume Rajesh Rajagopalan's "A Realist Approach to the IR of South Asia;" Ian Hall's "A Liberal Approach to the IR of South Asia;" Ananya Sharma's "A Constructivist Approach to the IR of South Asia;" and Vineet Thakur's "A Critical Approach to IR in South Asia."
4 Richard Devetak, "Critical Theory," in Scott Burchill, Andrew Linklater, Richard Devetak, Jack Donnelly, Matthew Paterson, Christian Reus-Smit, and Jacqui True, *Theories of International Relations*, 3rd ed. (Basingstoke: Palgrave Macmillan, 2005), 153.
5 Chris Brown and Kirsten Ainley, *Understanding International Relations,* 3rd ed. (Basingstoke: Palgrave Macmillan, 2005), 48–51, 93.
6 Government of Sri Lanka, Foreign Ministry, "Bandung Conference," undated, https://mfa.gov.lk/cool_timeline/bandung-conference.
7 Government of Sri Lanka, Foreign Ministry, "Colombo Powers Conference," undated, https://mfa.gov.lk/cool_timeline/colombo-powers-conference.
8 Scott Burchill, "Liberalism," in Scott Burchill, Andrew Linklater, Richard Devetak, Jack Donnelly, Matthew Paterson, Christian Reus-Smit, and Jacqui True, *Theories of International Relations*, 3rd ed. (Basingstoke: Palgrave Macmillan, 2005), 76.
9 Saman Kelegama, "Development in Independent Sri Lanka: What Went Wrong?" *Economic and Political Weekly* 35, no. 17 (Apr. 22–28, 2000): 1477.
10 Mahinda Werake and P.V.J. Jayasekera, eds., *Security Dilemma of a Small State: Internal Crisis and External Intervention in Sri Lanka* (Kandy: Institute for International Studies, 1995).
11 Brown and Ainley, *Understanding International Relations,* 2005, 96.
12 Sandya Nishanthi Gunasekara, "Bandwagoning, Balancing, and Small States: A Case of Sri Lanka," *Asian Social Science* 11, no. 28 (2015): 212, https://doi.org/10.5539/ass.v11n28p212.
13 Rajni Nayanthara Gamage, "Balancing and Bandwagoning: Explaining Shifts in Sri Lankan Foreign Policy," *Journal of the Indian Ocean Region* 13, no. 2 (2017): 133, https://doi.org/10.1080/19480881.2017.1299450.
14 Chulanee Attanayake and Archana Atmakuri, "Navigating the Sino-Indian Power Struggle in the Indian Ocean: The Case of Sri Lanka," *Journal of the Indian Ocean Region* 17, no. 1 (2021): 114, https://doi.org/10.1080/19480881.2021.1878587.
15 Shakthi De Silva, "Making Sense of the Haze: Hedging and Its Attributes," *University of Colombo Review* (Series III) 1, no. 1 (2020): 94.
16 Shakthi De Silva, "Decrypting Sri Lanka's 'Black Box' amidst an Indo–China 'Great Game,'" *Journal of the Indian Ocean Region* 16, no. 2 (2019): 146, https://doi.org/10.1080/19480881.2019.1640575.
17 Bhagya Senaratne, "Chinese Financing in South Asia: The Story of Sri Lanka," *South Asian Voices*, January 21, 2021, https://southasianvoices.org/chinese-financing-in-south-asia-the-story-of-sri-lanka.
18 Baldur Thorhallsson, "Studying Small States: A Review," *Small States & Territories* 1, no. 1 (2018): 17.
19 Matthias Maass, *Small States in World Politics: The Story of Small State Survival, 1648–2016* (Manchester: Manchester University Press, 2017), 34, 152.

20 Nilanthi Samaranayake, *China's Engagement with Smaller South Asian Countries* (Washington: United States Institute of Peace, 2019), 15–16.
21 Nilanthi Samaranayake, "Indian Ocean Island States and the Quad Plus," *Journal of Indo-Pacific Affairs* 3, no. 5 (2020): 231–232.
22 Nilanthi Samaranayake, "Island States in a Region of Great Powers," in *Sea Change: Evolving Maritime Geopolitics in the Indo-Pacific Region*, eds. David Michel and Ricky Passarelli (Washington: Stimson Center, 2014), 61.
23 Samaranayake, "Are Sri Lanka's Relations with China Deepening?" 2011, 142–143.
24 Samaranayake, "Indian Ocean Island States and the Quad Plus," 2020, 233.
25 Adm. Harry B. Harris, Jr. US Pacific Command, "Galle Dialogue," Colombo, Sri Lanka, November 28, 2016, https://www.pacom.mil/Media/Speeches-Testimony/Article/1013623/adm-harry-harris-commander-us-pacific-command-galle-dialogue.
26 Samaranayake, *China's Engagement with Smaller South Asian Countries*, 2019, 15–16.
27 Jeewaka Saman Kumara, "National Security Dilemmas of Developing Small States: A Study of Sri Lanka," *Modern Sri Lanka Studies* 4, no. 2 (2013): 46–47.
28 K.M. de Silva, A History of Sri Lanka (Colombo: Vijitha Yapa Publications, 2005), 629.
29 Amal Jayawardena, "Soviet Involvement in South Asia: The Security Dimension," in *Security Dilemma of a Small State: Sri Lanka in the South Asian Context*, ed. P.V.J. Jayasekera (New Delhi: Institute for International Studies, 1992), 373.
30 Bukar Bukarambe, "Zone of Peace or Strategic Primacy: Politics of Security in the Indian Ocean," *Security Dialogue* 16, no. 1 (January 1985): 51, https://doi.org/10.1177/096701068501600108.
31 P.K. Balachandran, "President Gotabaya Reiterates Lanka's Plea to Make the Indian Ocean a Zone of Peace," *NewsIn.Asia*, October 5, 2020, https://newsin.asia/president-gotabaya-reiterateslankas-plea-to-make-the-indian-ocean-a-zone-of-peace; and Meera Srinivasan, "Indian Ocean Has to Remain a Zone of Peace: Ajit Doval," *The Hindu*, December 1, 2014, https://www.thehindu.com/news/international/south-asia/indian-ocean-has-to-remain-a-zone-ofpeace-ajit-doval/article6651325.ece.
32 UN Internal Review Panel on United Nations Action in Sri Lanka, "Report of the Secretary-General's Internal Review Panel on United Nations Action in Sri Lanka" (Geneva: UN, November 2012), 14, https://digitallibrary.un.org/record/737299.
33 Robert A. Pape, "The Strategic Logic of Suicide Terrorism," *The American Political Science Review* 97, no. 3 (August 2003): 343.
34 Teresita C. Schaffer, "India Next Door, China Over the Horizon: The View from South Asia," in *Strategic Asia 2011–12: Asia Responds to Its Rising Powers—China and India*, eds. Ashley J. Tellis, Travis Tanner, and Jessica Keough (Seattle and Washington, D.C.: The National Bureau of Asian Research, 2011), 302–304.
35 C. Raja Mohan, *Samudra Manthan: Sino-Indian Rivalry in the Indo-Pacific* (Washington: Carnegie Endowment for International Peace, 2012), 146–155.
36 Robert D. Kaplan, *Monsoon: The Indian Ocean and the Future of American Power* (New York: Random House, 2011), 191–212.
37 "China Builds up Strategic Sea Lanes," *Washington Times*, January 17, 2005, https://www.washingtontimes.com/news/2005/jan/17/20050117-115550-1929r.
38 Nilanthi Samaranayake, "Chinese Belt and Road Investment Isn't All Bad—or Good," *Foreign Policy*, March 2, 2021, https://foreignpolicy.com/2021/03/02/sri-lanka-china-bri-investment-debt-trap.
39 A.R.M. Imtiyaz, "The Easter Sunday Bombings and the Crisis Facing Sri Lanka's Muslims," *Journal of Asian and African Studies* 55, no. 1 (2020): 3, 12–13, https://doi.org/10.1177/0021909619868244.
40 Ranga Jayasuriya, "Sleepwalking into a Great Power Rivalry: The Evolution of Sri Lanka's Foreign Policy in the 21st Century," in *Routledge Handbook on South Asian Foreign Policy*, ed. Aparna Pande (Abingdon and New York: Routledge, 2021).
41 Government of Sri Lanka, Foreign Ministry, "South Asia and SAARC Division," undated, https://mfa.gov.lk/south-asia-and-saarc-division.
42 Mahinda Werake and P.V.J. Jayasekera, eds., *Security Dilemma of a Small State: Internal Crisis and External Intervention in Sri Lanka* (Kandy: Institute for International Studies, 1995); Ibrahim Hussain Zaki and Regina Mulay Parakh, *Small State Security Dilemma: A Maldivian Perception* (New Delhi: Lancer Books, 2008).
43 Author's interview with retired senior Sri Lankan official, July 2021.
44 Author's interview with retired senior Sri Lankan official, July 2021.
45 Author's interview with senior Bangladeshi official, August 2021.

46 Author's interview with retired senior Sri Lankan official, July 2021.

47 Author's interview with senior Bangladeshi official, August 2021.

48 Kumara, "National Security Dilemmas of Developing Small States: A Study of Sri Lanka," 2013, 47.

49 Amal Jayawardane, "A Historical Overview of Sri Lanka-Pakistan Relations: A Sri Lankan Perspective," in *Pakistan-Sri Lanka Relations: A Story of Friendship*, eds. Lieutenant Colonel Muhammad Imran and Bhagya Senaratne (Islamabad: National Defence University's Institute for Strategic Studies, Research and Analysis, 2017), 7; author's interview with retired senior Sri Lankan official, July 2021.

50 P.V.J. Jayasekera, "Indo-Sri Lanka Relations: The Security Dimensions," in *Security Dilemma of a Small State: Sri Lanka in the South Asian Context*, ed. P.V.J. Jayasekera (New Delhi: Institute for International Studies, 1992), 492–493.

51 Srinath Raghavan, *1971: A Global History of the Creation of Bangladesh* (Cambridge, MA: Harvard University Press, 2013), 176–178.

52 Tanvi Madan, "India is Not Sitting on the Geopolitical Fence," *War on the Rocks*, October 27, 2021, https://warontherocks.com/2021/10/india-is-not-sitting-on-the-geopolitical-fence.

53 Nilanthi Samaranayake, "China's Relations with the Smaller Countries of South Asia," in *China and International Security: History, Strategy, and 21st-Century Policy*, eds. Donovan Chau and Thomas Kane (Santa Barbara: Praeger Security International, 2014), 228.

54 Riaz Khokhar and Asma Khalid, "Reviewing Pakistan-Sri Lanka Relations," *South Asian Voices*, March 22, 2021, https://southasianvoices.org/reviewing-pakistan-sri-lanka-relations.

55 For analysis of both Nepal and Bhutan, see Amal Jayawardena, "Changes in Power Structure and Security Perceptions in South Asian Sub-System," in *Security Dilemma of a Small State: Sri Lanka in the South Asian Context*, ed. P.V.J. Jayasekera (New Delhi: Institute for International Studies, 1992), 298–301; author's interview with retired senior Sri Lankan official, July 2021.

56 71% in Sri Lanka in one 2020 survey. See Thinley Dorji, Saran Tenzin Tamang, and T.V.S.V.G.K. Tilak, "Self-Learning on COVID-19 among Medical Students in Bhutan: A Cross-Sectional Study," *Heliyon* 7, no. 7 (2021): 3, https://doi.org/10.1016/j.heliyon.2021.e07533.

57 Author's interview with retired senior Sri Lankan official, July 2021.

58 Karma Phuntsho, *The History of Bhutan* (Gurgaon: Random House India, 2013), 575.

59 Author's interview with retired senior Sri Lankan official, July 2021.

60 Author's interview with retired senior Sri Lankan official, July 2021.

61 Asanga Abeyagoonasekera, "Remembering a Military Quagmire: The Exit of the United States in Afghanistan and the Impact on the Small States," *South Asia Journal*, September 5, 2021, http://southasiajournal.net/remembering-a-military-quagmire-the-exit-of-the-united-states-in-afghanistan-and-the-impact-on-the-small-states/.

Bibliography

Abeyagoonasekera, Asanga. "Remembering a Military Quagmire: The Exit of the United States in Afghanistan and the Impact on the Small States." *South Asia Journal*, September 5, 2021. http://southasiajournal.net/remembering-a-military-quagmire-the-exit-of-the-united-states-in-afghanistan-and-the-impact-on-the-small-states/.

Attanayake, Chulanee, and Archana Atmakuri. "Navigating the Sino-Indian Power Struggle in the Indian Ocean: The Case of Sri Lanka." *Journal of the Indian Ocean Region* 17, no. 1 (2021): 114. https://doi.org/10.1080/19480881.2021.1878587.

Author's interview with retired senior Sri Lankan official, July 2021.

Author's interview with senior Bangladeshi official, August 2021.

Balachandran, P.K. "President Gotabaya Reiterates Lanka's Plea to Make the Indian Ocean a Zone of Peace." *NewsIn.Asia*, October 5, 2020. https://newsin.asia/president-gotabaya-reiterateslankas-plea-to-make-the-indian-ocean-a-zone-of-peace.

Brown, Chris, and Kirsten Ainley. *Understanding International Relations*, 3rd ed. Basingstoke: Palgrave Macmillan, 2005, 48–51, 93.

Bukarambe, Bukar. "Zone of Peace or Strategic Primacy: Politics of Security in the Indian Ocean." *Security Dialogue* 16, no. 1 (January 1985): 51. https://doi.org/10.1177/096701068501600108.

Burchill, Scott. "Liberalism." In Scott Burchill, Andrew Linklater, Richard Devetak, Jack Donnelly, Matthew Paterson, Christian Reus-Smit, and Jacqui True, *Theories of International Relations*, 3rd ed. Basingstoke: Palgrave Macmillan, 2005, 76.

"China Builds up Strategic Sea Lanes." *Washington Times*, January 17, 2005. https://www.washingtontimes.com/news/2005/jan/17/20050117-115550-1929r.

de Silva, K.M. *A History of Sri Lanka*. Colombo: Vijitha Yapa Publications, 2005, 629.

De Silva, Shakthi. "Decrypting Sri Lanka's 'Black Box' Amidst an Indo–China 'Great Game.'" *Journal of the Indian Ocean Region* 16, no. 2 (2019): 146. https://doi.org/10.1080/19480881.2019.1640575.

De Silva, Shakthi. "Making Sense of the Haze: Hedging and Its Attributes." *University of Colombo Review* (Series III) 1, no. 1 (2020): 94.

Devetak, Richard. "Critical Theory." In Scott Burchill, Andrew Linklater, Richard Devetak, Jack Donnelly, Matthew Paterson, Christian Reus-Smit, and Jacqui True, *Theories of International Relations*, 3rd ed. Basingstoke: Palgrave Macmillan, 2005, 153.

Dorji, Thinley, Saran Tenzin Tamang, and T.V.S.V.G.K. Tilak. "Self-Learning on COVID-19 among Medical Students in Bhutan: A Cross-Sectional Study." *Heliyon* 7, no. 7 (2021): 3. https://doi.org/10.1016/j.heliyon.2021.e07533.

Government of Sri Lanka, Foreign Ministry. "Bandung Conference." Undated. https://mfa.gov.lk/cool_timeline/bandung-conference.

Government of Sri Lanka, Foreign Ministry. "Colombo Powers Conference." Undated. https://mfa.gov.lk/cool_timeline/colombo-powers-conference.

Government of Sri Lanka, Foreign Ministry. "South Asia and SAARC Division." Undated. https://mfa.gov.lk/south-asia-and-saarc-division.

Harris, Admiral Harry B. Jr. US Pacific Command. "Galle Dialogue." Colombo, Sri Lanka, November 28, 2016. https://www.pacom.mil/Media/Speeches-Testimony/Article/1013623/adm-harry-harris-commander-us-pacific-command-galle-dialogue.

Hussain Zaki, Ibrahim, and Regina Mulay Parakh. *Small State Security Dilemma: A Maldivian Perception*. New Delhi: Lancer Books, 2008.

Imtiyaz, A.R.M. "The Easter Sunday Bombings and the Crisis Facing Sri Lanka's Muslims." *Journal of Asian and African Studies* 55, no. 1 (2020): 3, 12–13. https://doi.org/10.1177/0021909619868244.

Jayasekera, P.V.J. "Indo-Sri Lanka Relations: The Security Dimensions." In *Security Dilemma of a Small State: Sri Lanka in the South Asian Context*, edited by P.V.J. Jayasekera, 492–493. New Delhi: Institute for International Studies, 1992.

Jayasuriya, Ranga. "Sleepwalking into a Great Power Rivalry: The Evolution of Sri Lanka's Foreign Policy in the 21st Century." In *Routledge Handbook on South Asian Foreign Policy*, edited by Aparna Pande. Abingdon and New York: Routledge, 2021.

Jayawardane, Amal. "A Historical Overview of Sri Lanka-Pakistan Relations: A Sri Lankan Perspective." In *Pakistan-Sri Lanka Relations: A Story of Friendship*, edited by Muhammad Imran, and Bhagya Senaratne, 7. Islamabad: National Defence University's Institute for Strategic Studies, Research and Analysis, 2017.

Jayawardena, Amal. "Changes in Power Structure and Security Perceptions in South Asian Sub-System." In *Security Dilemma of a Small State: Sri Lanka in the South Asian Context*, edited by P.V.J. Jayasekera, 298–301. New Delhi: Institute for International Studies, 1992.

Jayawardena, Amal. "Soviet Involvement in South Asia: The Security Dimension." In *Security Dilemma of a Small State: Sri Lanka in the South Asian Context*, edited by P.V.J. Jayasekera, 373. New Delhi: Institute for International Studies, 1992.

Jeewaka Saman Kumara. "National Security Dilemmas of Developing Small States: A Study of Sri Lanka." *Modern Sri Lanka Studies* 4, no. 2 (2013): 46–47.

Kaplan, Robert D. *Monsoon: The Indian Ocean and the Future of American Power*. New York: Random House, 2011, 191–212.

Kelegama, Saman. "Development in Independent Sri Lanka: What Went Wrong?" *Economic and Political Weekly* 35, no. 17 (April 22–28, 2000): 1477.

Khokhar, Riaz, and Asma Khalid. "Reviewing Pakistan-Sri Lanka Relations." *South Asian Voices*, March 22, 2021. https://southasianvoices.org/reviewing-pakistan-sri-lanka-relations.

Maass, Matthias. *Small States in World Politics: The Story of Small State Survival, 1648-2016*. Manchester: Manchester University Press, 2017, 34, 152.

Madan, Tanvi. "India is Not Sitting on the Geopolitical Fence." *War on the Rocks*, October 27, 2021. https://warontherocks.com/2021/10/india-is-not-sitting-on-the-geopolitical-fence.

Nayanthara Gamage, Rajni. "Balancing and Bandwagoning: Explaining Shifts in Sri Lankan Foreign Policy." *Journal of the Indian Ocean Region* 13, no. 2 (2017): 133. https://doi.org/10.1080/1948088 1.2017.1299450.

Nishanthi Gunasekara, Sandya. "Bandwagoning, Balancing, and Small States: A Case of Sri Lanka." *Asian Social Science* 11, no. 28 (2015): 212. https://doi.org/10.5539/ass.v11n28p212.

Pape, Robert A. "The Strategic Logic of Suicide Terrorism." *The American Political Science Review* 97, no. 3 (August 2003): 343.

Phuntsho, Karma. *The History of Bhutan.* Gurgaon: Random House India, 2013, 575.

Raghavan, Srinath. *1971: A Global History of the Creation of Bangladesh.* Cambridge, MA: Harvard University Press, 2013, 176–178.

Raja Mohan, C. *Samudra Manthan: Sino-Indian Rivalry in the Indo-Pacific.* Washington: Carnegie Endowment for International Peace, 2012, 146–155.

Samaranayake, Nilanthi. "China's Relations with the Smaller Countries of South Asia." In *China and International Security: History, Strategy, and 21st-Century Policy,* edited by Donovan Chau, and Thomas Kane, 228. Santa Barbara: Praeger Security International, 2014.

Samaranayake, Nilanthi. "Chinese Belt and Road Investment Isn't All Bad—or Good." *Foreign Policy,* March 2, 2021. https://foreignpolicy.com/2021/03/02/sri-lanka-china-bri-investment-debt-trap.

Samaranayake, Nilanthi. "Indian Ocean Island States and the Quad Plus." *Journal of Indo-Pacific Affairs* 3, no. 5 (2020): 231–233.

Samaranayake, Nilanthi. "Island States in a Region of Great Powers." In *Sea Change: Evolving Maritime Geopolitics in the Indo-Pacific Region,* edited by David Michel, and Ricky Passarelli, 61. Washington: Stimson Center, 2014.

Samaranayake, Nilanthi. *China's Engagement with Smaller South Asian Countries.* Washington: United States Institute of Peace, 2019, 15–16.

Samaranayake, Nilanthi. "Are Sri Lanka's Relations with China Deepening? An Analysis of Economic, Military, and Diplomatic Data." *Asian Security* 7, no. 2 (2011): 142–143. https://doi.org/10.1080/14799855.2011.581603.

Schaffer, Teresita C. "India Next Door, China over the Horizon: The View from South Asia." In *Strategic Asia 2011–12: Asia Responds to Its Rising Powers—China and India,* edited by Ashley J. Tellis, Travis Tanner, and Jessica Keough, 302–304. Seattle and Washington, D.C: The National Bureau of Asian Research, 2011.

Senaratne, Bhagya. "Chinese Financing in South Asia: The Story of Sri Lanka." *South Asian Voices,* January 21, 2021. https://southasianvoices.org/chinese-financing-in-south-asia-the-story-of-sri-lanka.

Srinivasan, Meera. "Indian Ocean Has to Remain a Zone of Peace: Ajit Doval." *The Hindu,* December 1, 2014. https://www.thehindu.com/news/international/south-asia/indian-ocean-has-to-remain-a-zone-ofpeace-ajit-doval/article6651325.ece.

Thorhallsson, Baldur. "Studying Small States: A Review." *Small States & Territories* 1, no. 1 (2018): 17.

UN Internal Review Panel on United Nations Action in Sri Lanka. "Report of the Secretary-General's Internal Review Panel on United Nations Action in Sri Lanka." Geneva: UN, November 2012, 14. https://digitallibrary.un.org/record/737299.

Werake, Mahinda, and P.V.J. Jayasekera, eds. *Security Dilemma of a Small State: Internal Crisis and External Intervention in Sri Lanka.* Kandy: Institute for International Studies, 1995.

White House. *Interim National Security Strategic Guidance.* March 2021, 20. https://www.whitehouse.gov/wp-content/uploads/2021/03/NSC-1v2.pdf.

19

BANGLADESH'S INTERNATIONAL RELATIONS WITH SOUTH ASIA AND BEYOND

Ali Riaz

Introduction

Since its founding in 1971, Bangladesh's international relations have experienced both continuity and changes. Its foreign policy and interactions with regional and global powers as well as with multilateral bodies have been influenced by existing global orders and its domestic political environment. The features and patterns of Bangladesh's foreign relations since its independence can be broadly divided into three phases: The early days after independence between 1972 and 1975, between 1975 and 2009, and post-2009. During these periods, it has interacted and continued to engage with other nations within the imperatives of Cold War bipolar world order, the United States (US)-dominated unipolar world order and the emergent multi-player global order.

Considering the historical linkages and its geographical location, Bangladesh's most important bilateral relationship has been with India. It had played a significant role in the emergence of Bangladesh during its war of independence.[1] Yet, the relationship has not been linear. There has been a fear among some Bangladeshis that India would use its vastly superior strength to intimidate Bangladesh, especially over economic matters.[2] However, others have insisted on a mutually beneficial and unbreakable bond between Bangladesh and India, underpinned by their historical, cultural, and geographic linkages.[3] Among the global powers, the United States has been a key development and security partner, especially since 1975 after the Sheikh Mujib regime was deposed through a bloody coup. This is despite its initial opposition to Bangladesh's emergence as an independent country.[4] Its influence has had its ebbs and flows. This relationship has undergone a transformation at various levels; at times these two countries have worked closely, while at other times tensions have soared.

The Soviet Union (USSR, 1917–1991) was a close ally in the years between 1972 and 1975. Russia, the principal successor state of the Soviet Union, has become an influential actor since 2009. The most dramatic shift of Bangladesh's foreign policy has been in its relationship with China, which took years to recognize the country's independence, but increasingly has become an influential actor, especially since 2011.

This chapter discusses the features of Bangladesh's international relations in these three eras and maps the trajectories focusing on the relationship with global and regional powers.

258

DOI: 10.4324/9781003246626-23

Bangladesh's International Relations with South Asia and Beyond

It explains Bangladesh's foreign policy behavior of the past 50 years using the neo-realist framework. Within this framework, a combination of the state's location within the international system and domestic power dynamics shapes the choices of the foreign policy.[5] As a small state surrounded by a large country, India, and with limited resources, Bangladeshi policymakers had adopted the policies based on neo-realist approach. Bangladesh's foreign policy orientation between 1972 and 1975, that is its alignment with the Indo-Soviet axis, was predicated by the supportive roles of these countries during the war of independence and the cold war contestation. The ideological orientation of the Sheikh Mujib regime, especially its predilection for socialist rhetoric and egalitarianism, served as the justifications. The situation changed after Ziaur Rahman came to power. Bangladesh's economic necessities and the domestic political dynamics influenced the shift in foreign policy. This continued under several governments and due to the hegemonic role of the West, particularly the United States. Bangladesh's growing geopolitical significance due to the increasing importance of the Indo-Pacific region, Bangladesh's economic growth, China's growing assertiveness, and neglect of the US in the region have provided the justifications for the Bangladeshi policymakers to turn toward China since the 2000s. Drawing on the pathway of the past five decades and Bangladesh's growing geopolitical significance due to the increasing importance of the Indo-Pacific region, the concluding section explores the options in the coming years.

Bangladesh in the Indo-Soviet Axis: 1972–1975

Bangladesh emerged as an independent state at the height of the Cold War through a nine-month-long war of independence against Pakistan in 1971. The global political scene, particularly the contestation between the United States and then Soviet Union, shaped Bangladesh's relationship with the major powers and India. Its entrance to various multilateral bodies, including the United Nations, was influenced by the ongoing Cold War.

India, which not only provided shelter to the 10 million Bengalis during the war of independence but also provided moral and material support to the Bengali freedom fighters, became the key actor in Bangladesh's international relations after the country's independence. India's role as the midwife in the independence of Bangladesh put the former in the driver's seat; "in the immediate post-liberation period, Indian influence in major policy-making was a notable feature of Bangladesh foreign policy"[6] and "India [had] more often than not loomed large on Bangladesh's strategic horizon."[7] Several additional factors contributing to the warm relationships, including the personal rapport between Prime Ministers Sheikh Mujibur Rahman of Bangladesh and Indira Gandhi of India, and the ideological affinity between the two incumbent parties, Bangladesh Awami League (BAL) and the Indian National Congress (INC), are worth mentioning.

However, by 1973, signs of differences and strains began to appear. Suspicions regarding the intention of India and impression that India is overwhelmingly influencing Bangladesh's domestic affairs began to feature in public discourse. These impressions were engendered by several issues. Indian training of Jatiyo Rakhi Bahini (JRB—national defense forces) was one of them.[8] The JRB, a paramilitary force, was established in February 1972, was being used against the opposition activists, and viewed as a replacement of the Bangladesh Army. Others include the 10-mile-long free trade zone,[9] the non-requirement of visas just after the liberation of Bangladesh, and the signing of the 1972 Treaty of Friendship.[10] The 25-year "Treaty of Friendship, Co-operation and Peace" signed in 1972, modeled after the Indo-Soviet Treaty of 1971,[11] raised suspicions among many alleging that "various clauses of the treaty undermined Bangladesh's options vis-à-vis India."[12] Signing of the land border demarcation deal in 1974 and negotiations on the maritime boundary demarcation were viewed as positive developments, but unresolved issues such as the sharing of water of common rivers, particularly Ganges, and the Indian decision to unilaterally commission the Farakka Barrage began to cause long-term irritations. Geography and gratitude of the Bangladeshi leadership provided the impetus for the congenial relationship. Bangladesh's unequivocal support to India's nuclear test in 1974, while it was criticized by many, demonstrates the depth of the relationship. However, Sheikh Mujib's decision to join the Organization of Islamic Conference (OIC) summit in 1974 reportedly made India uncomfortable.[13] The OIC, an intergovernmental body of Muslim countries, did not support Bangladesh's independence war and was lukewarm in recognizing the independent Bangladesh. Mujib's decision to join the organization was viewed some in India as abandonment of Bangladesh's commitment to secularism.[14]

India's influence on Bangladesh's foreign policy was not only a part of India's desire to establish the upper hand in South Asia vis-à-vis its archrival Pakistan, but was also tied to the Soviet Union's efforts to keep Bangladesh within its sphere of influence. From the onset of the Bangladesh crisis in 1971, the Soviet Union (USSR) showed its tacit support to India's assistance to the Bangladesh government in exile. The support became explicit as the crisis unfolded.[15] The signing of the defense treaty with India at a time when the US sided with Pakistan was predicated by Cold War imperatives, cementing the Indo-Soviet relationship and bolstering the morale of the Bengali freedom fighters.[16] In December, as the Bangladesh crisis turned into a full-scale war between India and Pakistan, the Soviet Union exercised its veto power in the UN Security Council to stop adopting a ceasefire resolution.[17] The US-sponsored resolution would have compelled the Indian forces to retreat from the Eastern front where it was fighting alongside the Bangladesh forces to defeat the Pakistan Army and ensure the emergence of the independent Bangladesh. Soon after independence, the USSR quickly recognized Bangladesh and became engaged in the reconstruction efforts at the bilateral level. Mujib's first trip abroad was to Moscow in March 1972[18] when the USSR delivered one squadron of MiGs, the first defense cooperation of Bangladesh with any country.[19] Although the Soviet Ambassador to Dhaka was recalled immediately before the 1973 elections, reportedly for meddling in domestic relations,[20] the high-profile relationship continued. In 1974, when Bangladesh faced a famine and the US refused to provide food under PL–480, the USSR diverted some of the food it brought from the US to help Bangladesh. The Public Law 480, also known as Food for Peace, allows the US to provide agricultural products to developing countries in concessional terms and free of cost, under some circumstances.

The United States' stand against the Bangladesh independence movement owed to its long-standing tilt toward Pakistan, including for Pakistan being the US interlocutor for establishing its relationship with China.[21] This US position constrained its influence on Bangladesh. However, the US was engaged in relief operations through the United Nations since January 1972,[22] and recognized Bangladesh in April 1972. Although the US government was unhappy with Bangladesh's alignment with the Soviet axis, it decided to recognize the country and engage for two reasons: The increasing pressure from the US lawmakers who were opposed to the White House policy in 1971 and to curb Soviet influence in the region.[23] Bangladesh's leadership, on the other hand, faced with the need for economic assistance for rebuilding the country after the war, dropped its initial opposition to accept foreign aid and began to embrace the US. US recognition and support paved the way for Bangladesh's admission into various UN bodies.[24] The US used its ties with China in 1974 to prevent it from using its veto power to block Bangladesh's entry to the UN.[25] China blocked Bangladesh's membership in the UN twice, in 1972 and 1973.[26]

However, US-Bangladesh tensions remained. Sources of contention included the Bangladesh government's domestic policies, including nationalization of industries as a part of its socialist policies. Bangladesh also offered foreign policy support for North Vietnam.[27] The relationship soured after the US administration decided to suspend food aid under PL-480 in 1974 when Bangladesh was facing a serious food crisis in the wake of a devastating flood. The suspension was due to Bangladesh's decision to sell jute to Cuba, a country which was under a US embargo. Whether the famine was a result of the distribution policy of the government[28] or due to US suspension remains a matter of controversy,[29] but it quickly contributed to a popular belief that US policies led to thousands of deaths in Bangladesh. During this period, although Bangladesh reportedly reached out to China through unofficial channels seeking recognition, there was lukewarm response, at its best.

Bangladesh's Westward Shift: 1979–2009

Bangladesh's foreign policy experienced a dramatic shift after the military coup in 1975, which saw the assassination of Sheikh Mujibur Rahman and the displacement of the Bangladesh Awami League from power. General Ziaur Rahman emerged as the strongman and at the helm of power by 1977 after a series of coups and counter-coups. Domestic political changes, particularly the nationalist posture of the Zia regime, the adoption of a territoriality-based national identity, the encouragement of religion in the public sphere, and the elimination of secularism as a state principle created a different political terrain.[30] The government adopted market-based economic policies and embarked on the privatization of nationalized entities. Concurrently, a significant shift in the foreign policy orientation of the country, closer relationships with the United States, China, and the Muslim countries of the Middle East on the one hand and downturn in the influence of India and the Soviet Union characterized this phase until 1996.

Improvements in the relationship with the US under the Zia regime (1975–1981) was reflected in Bangladesh's position on the Iran crisis in 1979, and its unequivocal condemnation of the Soviet invasion of Afghanistan. Increased US aid to Bangladesh, expanded trade ties, and closer cooperation between the two countries in international forums became easily discernable.[31] This was furthered in the subsequent years, under the military regime of Ershad (1982–1990). Indicative of the continuity of the closer relationship was demonstrated in Bangladesh's desire to join the coalition forces in 1990 ahead of the First Gulf War. Bangladesh agreed to the request of the US. Cooperation on security, which began under the Zia regime, flourished in the subsequent decades.

The continuity of the Bangladesh-US relationship not only under the military regimes of Rehman and subsequently Hussain Mohammed Ershad but also after Bangladesh embarked on democratization in 1991 is evident. The governments headed by Khaleda Zia (1991–1996, 2001–2006) and Sheikh Hasina (1996–2001, 2009–) did not break away from the path of close cooperation. Instead the relationship was further strengthened, despite some occasional divergence. In the post-9/11 era, on the one hand, security cooperation increased as Bangladesh was viewed by US policymakers as a potential recruiting ground for militants.[32] On the other hand, frustration was growing as the Bangladesh Nationalist Party (BNP) government was denying the existence of Islamist militant groups and was initially unwilling to confront the menace.[33] The presence of Islamists in the ruling coalition was also making the US uncomfortable. Since the 1990s, smaller nations like Bangladesh received less attention from the US. This is due to two factors: A closer relationship between the US and India, and US intervention in Afghanistan which shifted its focus to Afghanistan-Pakistan theatre. In post-2001,

India became the US linchpin to South Asia, which had impacted the India–Bangladesh relationship.

As mentioned previously, Bangladesh's most important bilateral relationship is with its neighbor India, which is also the bellwether of the nature and alignment of Bangladesh's international relations. The India–Bangladesh relationship began to show serious strains under the Zia regime. The factors that perpetrated the strains were sharing of Ganges water[34] and India's unwillingness to ratify the Land Boundary Agreement (LBA) demarcating the borders between the two countries signed in 1974. The LBA was signed between Sheikh Mujib and Indira Gandhi, and ratified by Bangladesh, but the Indian parliament was unable to ratify it because of domestic political opposition until 2015.[35] India's support for the rebels of Chittagong Hill Tracts became one of the principal irritants.[36] Bangladesh's attempt to internationalize the water sharing by raising it in OIC Foreign Ministers Conference in May 1976, Non-aligned countries' summit in August 1976, and at the UN General Assembly in September 1976 exasperated India the most.[37] Ziaur Rahman's proposal in 1979 to create a regional forum of South Asian countries (emerged as the South Asian Association of Regional Cooperation – SAARC in 1985) was viewed by India as an effort to create a bloc against India to regionalize bilateral issues. While both India and Bangladesh continued a normal diplomatic and economic relationship, it was far from the heyday of the Mujib era.

There was very little change under the Ershad regime. In some measures, except Sheikh Hasina's first term in power between 1996 and 2001, the Bangladesh–India relationship remained cold and formal. Khaleda Zia's first term (1991–1996) showed some signs of improvement. The two countries signed a deal that provided Bangladesh a 999-year lease of a narrow corridor, which allows access to a small piece of land (enclave) located within the boundaries of India[38] and concluded agreements regarding repatriation of Chakma refugees and Indian investment in Bangladesh's railway sector. But the relationship soon lost momentum due to lack of enthusiasm on the part of both parties. When Bangladesh ditched the bilateral path to push the water-sharing issue to the Commonwealth in 1993 and to the UN General Assembly in 1995, the relationship returned to the Ziaur Rahman era.

With Sheikh Hasina's assumption of power in 1996, the relationship began to warm up. The signing of the 30-year Ganges Water Sharing Treaty (December 12, 1996) with India and signing of a peace treaty with the Chittagong Hill Tracts rebels with the blessings of India (December 2, 1997) exemplified the change. Bangladesh's decision to deny space to Indian rebels was welcomed by the Indian government while the issue of alleged illegal migration from Bangladesh, politicized by the Bharatiya Janata Party (BJP), created some dissonance. The killing of 16 Indian soldiers in 2001 in a border clash, the first in the history of the two nations, was the lowest point of the relationship. In the following five years, during the second term of Khaleda Zia, accusations and counteraccusations between Bangladesh and India about harboring Indian insurgents in Bangladesh, illegal migration from Bangladesh, and India's reluctance to resolve land and maritime border disputes made the relationship tense. The presence of an Islamist party, the Bangladesh Jamaat-i-Islami (BJI), in the ruling coalition and proliferation of Islamist militant groups in Bangladesh lessened India's trust on the ruling BNP.

Turning to China

While the Bangladesh–India relationship oscillated, Bangladesh's relationship with China took on a firmer footing. After its recognition of Bangladesh in 1975, China gradually moved closer, thanks to the Ziaur Rahman regime, which cultivated the relationship as a counterweight to Indian influence. Beginning in 1977, China became the principal supplier of light weapons,[39] and its investments in infrastructure development began to outstrip other development partners. The volume of trade between two countries increased with the balance of trade in favor of China. In 2005, China became the largest source of Bangladesh's imports.[40] The changes in the governments—from Zia to Ershad to Khaleda to Hasina—had not dampened relations. A defense cooperation treaty was signed in 2002 during a visit of Prime Minister Khaleda Zia,[41] and several economic cooperation agreements were signed during Sheikh Hasina's visit in 1996. Stronger economic cooperation was largely viewed as Bangladesh's successful economic diplomacy in securing development financing while maintaining its leaning toward the West and India.

As such, between 1975 and 2009, Bangladesh's international relations were largely guided by pragmatism and economic considerations, instead of idealism and ideology. Its domestic economic policies allowing foreign direct investment facilitated the pursuit of such a pragmatic foreign policy. Its leaning toward the West remained constant although Bangladesh adopted a policy of "Look East" in 2002, which engendered economic cooperation with China. Post-1975 Russia featured very little in Bangladesh's international relations; this was due to two factors—first the ideological shift of the ruling parties in Bangladesh and second the downfall of the Soviet Union in 1991. The progressively weakening relationship between the USSR and Bangladesh can be understood from the actions of the latter in 1980 and 1983. Bangladesh expelled four Soviet diplomats in 1980 alleging that the Embassy had brought spying equipment, and in 1983, the government expelled 18 diplomats for engaging in un-diplomatic activities.[42]

Bangladesh-Pakistan Relations: Fluctuations

Bangladesh's relations with Pakistan have fluctuated since the 1971 war. The formal recognition of Bangladesh's independence came in February 1974, which allowed Sheikh Mujib to travel to Pakistan to attend the OIC summit held in Lahore that month. In July 1974, Pakistani Prime Minister Zulfikar Ali Bhutto visited Bangladesh. Relations between the two countries improved following the collapse of the Mujib regime in 1975, and full diplomatic relations were established in 1976. Three issues remained unresolved; they were: Receiving an official apology from Pakistan for the genocide in 1971, repatriation of Pakistanis stranded in Bangladesh, and the division of assets held by Pakistani authorities before the war. Diplomatic relationship continued with occasional spat between these two countries. For example, in 2000[43] and 2015,[44] Bangladesh expelled Pakistani diplomats from Dhaka, and Pakistan retaliated in 2016.[45] Despite visits of Bangladeshi leaders to Pakistan (Ziaur Rahman in 1977, Sheikh Hasina in 1999, and Khaleda Zia in 2006) and Pakistani leaders to Bangladesh (Pervez Musharraf in 2002), the relationship has remained strained. It has further deteriorated since 2009, as reflected in Hasina's decision not to join the D8 summit in 2012 in Pakistan[46] and Bangladesh pulling out of the SAARC Summit in 2016 scheduled in Islamabad.[47] In 2013, adoption of a resolution by the Pakistani parliament after the execution of Bangladesh Jamaat-i-Islami leader Abdul Quader Mollah was condemned by Bangladesh as an interference in its domestic affairs.[48] Similar reactions were expressed in 2016 after Pakistan angrily reacted to the execution of BJI leader Motiur Rahman Nizami.[49] Signs of improvement in the relationship began to appear in 2019. Bangladesh, after more than 20 months of delay, accepted the Pakistani High Commissioner in Dhaka.[50] In 2020, Pakistani Prime Minister Imran Khan called Hasina and urged for "closer ties."[51] Prime Minister Hasina gave an audience to Pakistani envoy in Dhaka in December 2020,[52] and the message from PM Khan on Bangladesh's Independence Day in March 2021 was far more conciliatory than ever before.[53]

Economic consideration was also the key in Bangladesh's relationship with the Islamic countries in the Gulf and the Middle East after 1978. Short-term migration of low-skilled labor in the Middle East and Gulf created a source of remittances, which later became one of the two key sources of its revenue. In similar vein, since the mid-1970s, Bangladesh cultivated its relationship with European countries and Japan, which has been the largest development partner.

In the Midst of a Tug-of-War: 2009–2021

After a two-year rule by a military-backed administration (2007–2008), elections held in December 2008 became a watershed moment in the history of the country not only because of the return of an elected civilian government or a landslide victory of the Bangladesh Awami League but also as the beginning of a new phase of international relations of Bangladesh. By 2021, the country was thrust into a tug-of-war between the US and China. Increased Sino-American competition in the Indian Ocean region, the United States' efforts to confront China's growing assertiveness through building various alliances, and the Sino-Indian rivalry in South Asia placed the country amidst the competition, thanks to the BAL's short-sighted foreign policy.

Immediately after the 2008 election, it became obvious that the BAL would pick up the relationship with India where it had left off in 2001. It remained unclear what future course it would pursue with other major actors, for example, the United States, Russia, and China.

By early 2010, following Hasina's visit to New Delhi and the warm reception she received, a new era of Indo-Bangladesh relations was in the offing. In the subsequent years, security cooperation was strengthened, trade increased, more than 100 treaties and memoranda of understandings were signed, cooperation in the energy sector ensued, and India received the transit facility it asked for and gained access to the ports. Also, Bangladesh enabled New Delhi to set up a coastal surveillance system radar in the Bay of Bengal. These cooperative ties were described by both Bangladesh and India as a golden age. While both governments were quite pleased, discontent began to simmer among the public at large as India continued to ignore Bangladesh's legitimate claims. The signing of a water-sharing treaty of the Teesta River was deferred, Bangladesh's access to the Indian market was restricted, and killings by the Indian border security force continued unabated.[54] India moved forward with the construction of the Tipaimkh dam on the Barak River in the Indian state of Manipur, upstream of the Meghna river in Bangladesh, and went ahead with the proposed Indian Rivers Inter-link project. The LBA, signed in 1974, was not approved by the Indian parliament until 2015.[55] These factors contributed to a growing perception that Bangladesh had conceded more than what it received from India.[56]

Bangladesh's India-leaning foreign policy was based more on political considerations of the ruling BAL to ensure India's unqualified support to continue in power. India provided absolute support to the BAL even when the BAL's authoritarian bent was evident, and it had "assiduously subverted democratic norms and institutions."[57] The visit of Indian Foreign Secretary Sujatha Singh in 2013, ahead of the election that was boycotted by all opposition parties, and strong-arming the Jatiya Party led by H.M. Ershad to join was the height of India's open interjection into Bangladesh's domestic politics in support of the incumbent. On the other hand, India's ruling party leaders continued to allege that many Bangladeshis were entering India illegally and demonstrated disdain for Bangladeshis.[58] Although the Bangladesh government was unhappy with the enactment of National Registry of Citizenship (NRC) in Assam and passing of the Citizenship Amendment Act (CAA), its reaction was muted. The NRC, a list of citizens in Assam, was announced in August 2019, which is intended to identify the "illegal" individuals in the state. The ruling BJP insists that Bangladeshis illegally migrate to Assam and the NRC was meant to identify and expel them. CAA, passed in the parliament, allows the Indian government to give citizenship to the persecuted religious minorities from neighboring countries. However, Muslims are excluded from the list. Both are considered discriminatory.

China Makes Headway

While the relationship with India remained at the front and center of Bangladesh's international relations, China gradually made headway and transformed its relationship from an economic to a strategic partnership.[59] Beginning 2010, China started to make inroads to Bangladesh through massive investments and the Bangladesh-China relationship entered a new phase in recent years, exemplified by Bangladesh joining the Belt and Road Initiative (BRI) in 2016 and purchasing submarines.[60] Although Bangladesh's purchases of weapons from China was not new, as it had been the principal supplier since the mid-1970s, it reached a significant high between 2010 and 2019; during this period, about 75% of Bangladesh's weapons were supplied by China.[61] During a visit of Chinese President Xi Jinping, deals were signed between the two countries of Chinese investments to the tune of $38 billion.[62] In 2020, China offered Bangladeshi products tariff-free access to its market.

In 2018, even though Sheikh Hasina reassured India that "it need not to worry"[63] about Bangladesh's bonhomie with China, these developments did make India increasingly uncomfortable.[64] The COVID-19 pandemic provided an opportunity for China to accelerate its "vaccine diplomacy" and expand its influence in Bangladesh. When India failed to deliver the COVID-19 vaccines despite a commercial deal signed in 2020, Bangladesh turned to China. Bangladesh was relying exclusively on the vaccines produced in India; the decision to halt the supply created serious adverse public reactions. Bangladesh received vaccines from China in July 2021.

China has not been shy to demonstrate its growing power, as reflected in the request by the Chinese Defense Minister in April 2021 that Bangladesh should not join any military alliance outside the region,[65] and warned against joining the Quadrilateral Security Dialogue (Quad) or risk "substantial damage" to the relationship.[66] Although Bangladesh officially rebutted these Chinese pressures,[67] the Chinese government has not retracted its comments.

Despite such close relationships with China and India, Bangladesh has not received support from either of them in dealing with a major crisis it has been facing since 2017. Since August 2017, almost a million members of the Rohingya ethnic community, fleeing the genocide in Myanmar, have taken shelter in Bangladesh. Bangladesh's humanitarian gestures have received international applause but the hope of safe return of the refugees has faded. China, which remained the principal backer of the Myanmar military, the perpetrator of the genocide, continued to shield Myanmar from international sanctions. India, in a similar vein, has strengthened its relationship with Myanmar even after the military deposed the elected government on February 1, 2021. Bangladesh has signed an agreement with Myanmar about the repatriation of the refugees, ostensibly at the prodding of China, but little progress has been made in this regard.

Blatant Chinese warnings in 2021 came on the heels of the United States' growing interest in Bangladesh as a partner in its Indo-Pacific Strategy (IPS). Since 2010, the US-Bangladesh relationship has moved in a see-saw fashion. In 2010, when the Bangladesh government removed Nobel Laureate Professor Yunus from the helm of the Grameen Bank, the US government expressed its displeasure. The relationship was further strained in 2013–2014 on the question of the fairness of the election. The United States insisted on holding an inclusive election and the US Ambassador in Dhaka, Dan Mozena, tried to bring India on board,[68] but the BAL went ahead and held the election unilaterally. This remained a bone of contention between these two countries. On the other hand, since 2012, the two countries held several rounds of security and partnership dialogues and signed the Trade and Investment Cooperation Forum Agreement (TICFA) in 2013. In the wake of the growing militancy in Bangladesh, particularly after the attack on a cafe by Islamic State terrorists on July 1, 2016, security cooperation increased significantly.

Despite these cooperative efforts and increased trade relations, the United States paid little attention to Bangladesh from 2013 to 2019. It is widely believed in Bangladesh that the US has left India do its bidding. The US finally indicated an end to its strategic neglect in 2019, when it described Bangladesh as "an emerging partner" in the 2019 IPS document.[69] A series of events indicate that the US was trying to court Bangladesh to the emerging alliance. These include a call from then Defense Secretary Mark Esper in September 2020 to Bangladeshi Prime Minister Sheikh Hasina to discuss military cooperation and South and Central Asia affairs deputy assistant secretary Laura Stone's enthusiasm in September about working with Bangladesh under IPS.[70] These were followed by the visit of then US Deputy Secretary of State Stephan Biegun in October 2020. During the visit, Biegun described Bangladesh as the centerpiece of the IPS.[71] Bangladesh's response to the proposal was ambivalent[72] and it promised in November 2021 to make its position clear soon.[73] It is against this background that three US actions in late 2021 clearly indicated that US patience was wearing thin. First, Bangladesh was excluded from the Democracy Summit held on December 9–10, 2021.[74] Although it was well known that Bangladesh has had two consecutive controversial elections since 2014, the US had not been vocal against the ongoing democratic backsliding. Second, on December 10, the US Treasury Department imposed sanctions on Bangladesh's elite paramilitary force, the Rapid Action Battalion (RAB), as well as seven of its current and former officers for serious human rights violations.[75] The list of individuals includes current and former RAB chiefs, as well as four former Additional Director Generals of Operations. Additionally, the State Department imposed sanctions on two individuals, former RAB chief who now heads the national police and a former commanding officer of a RAB Unit.[76] Third, on December 1, 2021, the US sought Bangladesh's adherence to the Leahy Law, which governs the US funding for foreign security forces. It will require that Bangladesh ensures that US funding has not been used for forces or activities that have violated human rights.

These US actions have generated new tensions with Bangladesh. They have also demonstrated that Bangladesh is now in the midst of a tussle between the US and China as both are trying to expand their sphere of influence in the Asia-Pacific region. Some analysts are suggesting that this action may push the country "into the arms of Beijing."[77] But it is evident that the US is inclined to remain engaged instead of creating a rift. Its cooperation with various security entities such as the Anti-Terrorism Unit (ATU) and Counterterrorism and Transnational Crime Unit (CTTCU) has continued. For Bangladesh, maintaining trade and economic relationship with the US is imperative to maintain its current rate of economic growth.

Bangladesh's geographical location, that is sitting at the top of the Bay of Bengal littoral, provides it certain advantages as well as challenges.

Conclusions: The Path Forward[78]

The preceding discussion on Bangladesh's international relations shows that in the past 50 years, its foreign policy has witnessed continuity and change. The continuity of policies is evident between 1975 and 2009, despite changes in power from a military government to a civilian government and between elected political parties. As this chapter has demonstrated, in the early days of independence, the Mujib government chose to align with the Indo-Soviet axis for its support during the war of independence and the ideological orientation of the ruling Bangladesh Awami League.

At the height of the Cold War era, this alignment created a strained relationship with many Western nations, particularly with the United States. But with the change in state power, in 1975, the government of Ziaur Rahman (1977–1981) shifted Bangladesh's foreign policy orientation toward the West. The second military regime of H.M. Ershad (1982–1990) strengthened the relationship. The policy was followed by the governments of Khaleda Zia (1991–1996 and 2001–2006) and Sheikh Hasina in her first term (1996–2001). The first term of the Hasina regime fostered an increasingly warm relationship with India and maintained good relations with the United States. Differences between the US and India began to show after 2011 during Hasina's second term (2009–2014) as Bangladesh headed for an election in 2014. Hasina, in her third term (2014–2018), secured through a controversial election, strengthened political alliance and increased economic ties with India and continued to enjoy its unequivocal support. She, however, began to weigh her option of a closer relationship with China. Stronger relations with China and Russia, particularly the former, were nurtured as China adopted an assertive stance to increase its sphere of influence in South Asia. The United States' reliance on India for dealing with smaller states in South Asia, especially after 2001, created the space for China to step in. Domestic political developments, that is, the increasing authoritarian tendency of the Hasina government, has provided impetus for the regime to rely more on China.

This has offered challenges and opportunities to Bangladesh for charting its future direction in international relations. There are four possible options for the country: Maintaining the status quo, muddling through, changing course, or a radical realignment.

The status quo option will require minimum effort. It will involve maintaining its current policies of taking a limited role in the region and sustaining a close relationship with India, politically and economically. It will presuppose some walk-back from a closer relationship with China. This option will also mean limited openness in domestic politics, further restrictions on freedom of speech and doubling down of the authoritarian actions of the ruling party. However, this option has two challenges—regional and domestic. In terms of regional challenge, whether India is a match to counter the growing Chinese influence is an open question. How Bangladesh is willing to respond to the US strategy in Asia-Pacific will determine how Bangladesh will continue to chart its course. As for the domestic element, this option is increasingly becoming untenable for several reasons, especially due to the growing anti-Indian sentiment among Bangladeshis and the potential for the emergence of new dynamics in domestic politics.

The second option, muddling through, implies focusing on the newly emerging pattern of a precarious balancing act between US-China-India. While this will provide maximum flexibility, it will be devoid of a long-term strategy. The ad hoc nature will deter it from having a more institutionalized foreign policy. Muddling through policy runs the risk of becoming the battleground of China and the United States. The Biden administration's decision to highlight human rights and democracy has put Bangladesh under the spotlight. As such, even muddling through will require some adjustments.

Revising the course option requires looking beyond the region and utilizing Bangladesh's geostrategic and geopolitical advantages to pursue national interests. This option calls for a closer relationship with the West, particularly the United States, without being mediated through New Delhi. The foreign policy should not be viewed as making a choice between regional and/or global power; instead, long-term national interests should serve as the guide.

This is not to promote distance from influential countries but to adopt an equidistance policy and institutionalize the relationship through various cooperative arrangements on trade and security. This option will have domestic political course correction, pursuing inclusivity and protection of rights.

The radical realignment will be a complete departure from any previous situation. The realignment could be either with the Western world, particularly the United States, or alternatively, with China. Economic considerations and pragmatism will preclude a complete reliance on any particular power. Cooperation in other sectors, such as security, is already in place and has been strengthened in recent years. A dramatic shift toward China will create waves and will have implications for the country in global forums. Such a realignment may also impact domestic political structure. Besides, the geographical location of Bangladesh, being horseshoed by India, is a serious deterrent to such an alignment.

Each of these options has its prospects and challenges. Bangladesh will have to make its choice based on its national interests both in the short and long term, and demonstrate flexibility to adjust to the changing global and regional geopolitical dynamics.

Notes

1 Richard Sisson and Leo Rose, *War and Secession: Pakistan, India, and the Creation of Bangladesh,* (Berkeley: University of California Press, 1991); Srinath Raghavan, *1971: A Global History of the Creation of Bangladesh* (Cambridge: Harvard University Press, 2013).
2 Ishtiaq Hossain, "Bangladesh-India Relations: Issues and Problems," *Asian Survey* 21, no. 11 (1981): 1115–1128.
3 See comments of Abdus Samad Azad, the first foreign minister of Bangladesh, quoted in Iftikhar Ahmed Chowdhury, "Strategy of a Small Power in a Subsystem: Bangladesh's External Relations," *Australian Outlook,* 34, no. 1 (1990): 85–98.
4 Gary Bass, *The Blood Telegram: Nixon, Kissinger, and a Forgotten Genocide* (New York: Vintage, 2013).
5 Miriam Fendius Elman, "The Foreign Policies of Small States: Challenging Neorealism in Its Own Backyard," *British Journal of Political Science* 25, no. 2 (1995): 171–217; James D. Fearon, "Domestic Politics, Foreign Policy, and Theories of International Relations," *Annual Review of Political Science* 1, no. 1 (1998): 289–313.
6 Zaglul Haider, *The Changing Pattern of Bangladesh Foreign Policy: A Comparative Study of the Mujib and Zia Regimes* (Dhaka: The University Press Limited, 2006), 34.
7 V.K. Vinayaraj, "India as a Threat: Bangladeshi Perceptions," *South Asian Survey* 16, no. 1 (2009), 101–118.
8 S. Mahmud Ali, *Understanding Bangladesh* (New York: Columbia University Press, 2010), 105.
9 Ishtiaq Hossain, "Bangladesh-India Relations."
10 Smruti S. Pattanaik, "India's Neighbourhood Policy: Perceptions from Bangladesh," *Strategic Analysis* 35, no. 1 (2011), 71–87.
11 Ministry of External Affairs, Government of India, "Treaty of Peace, Friendship and Co-operation," August 9, 1971, https://mea.gov.in/bilateral-documents.htm?dtl/5139/Treaty+of.
12 Mohammad Sajjadur Rahman, "Bangladesh and Its Neighbors," in *Routledge Handbook of Contemporary Bangladesh*, eds. Ali Riaz and Mohammad Sajjadur Rahman (London: Routledge, 2016), 379.
13 Harun ur Rashid, *Bangladesh-India Relations: Living with a Big Neighbour* (Dhaka: A H Development Publishing House, 2010), 18.
14 Harun ur Rashid, the then Director General at the Bangladesh Foreign Ministry, mentioned of the Indian sentiment. See Harun ur Rashid, *Bangladesh-India Relations*, 20.
15 Vijay Sen Budhraj, "Moscow and the Birth of Bangladesh," *Asian Survey* 13, no. 5 (May 1973), 482–495.
16 Maidul Hasan, *Muldhara Ekattor (The Mainstream of 1971)* (Dhaka: University Press Limited, 1985).
17 Henry Tanner, "U.N.: Moscow Again Vetoes Truce Call," *The New York Times,* December 6, 1991, https://www.nytimes.com/1971/12/06/archives/un-moscow-again-vetoes-truce-call-u-n-deadlocked-on-peace-efforts-a.html.

18 "Sheik Mujib Off to Soviet For 5-Day Good Will Visit," *The New York Times*, March 1, 1972, https://www.nytimes.com/1972/03/01/archives/sheik-mujib-off-to-soviet-for-5day-goodwill-visit.html.

19 Harun ur Rashid, *Bangladesh Foreign Policy: Realities, Priorities and Challenges* (Dhaka: Academic Press and Publishers Library, 2005), 272.

20 Muhammad Abdul Halim, "Bangladesh Foreign Policy: A Review," in *Bangladesh: In the Threshold of the Twenty-first Century*, eds. Abdul Momin Chowdhury and Fakrul Alam (Dhaka: Asiatic Society, 2002), 585.

21 C. Van Hollen, "The Tilt Policy Revisited: Nixon-Kissinger Geopolitics and South Asia," in *The Regional Imperative: The Administration of US Foreign Policy Towards South Asian States Under Presidents Johnson and Nixon*, eds. L.I. Rudolph and S.H Rudolph (New Jersey, Humanities Press Inc, 1980), 421–450.

22 Thomas W. Oliver, *The United Nations in Bangladesh* (Princeton, NJ: Princeton University Press, 1978).

23 Dilara Chowdhury, Al Masud Hasanuzzaman, and T.S. Rahman, "Foreign Policy of Bangladesh: 1972–1996," in *Bangladesh at 25: An Analytical Discourse on Development*, eds. Abdul Bayes and Anu Muhammad (Dhaka: University Press Limited, 1998), 221.

24 See US Deputy Representative to the UN William Schaufele on June 10, 1972, *The Department of State Bulletin* 71, no. 1 (July 8, 1974): 73.

25 Memorandum of Conversation between Henry Kissinger and Chinese Ambassador to the UN, Hunag Hua, September 19, 1972; National Archives, Nixin Presidential Materials, NSC files, Box 850.

26 Robert Aiden, "China's First UN Veto Bars Bangladesh," *The New York Times*, August 26, 1972, https://www.nytimes.com/1972/08/26/archives/chinas-first-un-veto-bars-bangladesh-soviet-union-and-india-are.html.

27 Bangladesh recognized the North Vietnam-backed Provisional Revolutionary Government of the Republic of South Vietnam on February 11, 1973.

28 Amartya Sen, *Poverty and Famines: An Essay on Entitlement and Deprivation* (Oxford: OUP, 1983).

29 Rehman Sobhan, "Politics of Food and Famine in Bangladesh," *Economic and Political Weekly* 14, no. 48 (Dec. 1, 1979): 1973–1980.

30 Ali Riaz, *God Willing: The Politics of Islamism in Bangladesh* (Lanham, MD: Rowman and Littlefield, 2004).

31 Zaglul Haider, *The Changing Pattern of Bangladesh Foreign Policy: A Comparative Study of the Mujib and Zia Regimes* (Dhaka: The University Press Limited, 2006).

32 In September 2004, former State Department Coordinator for Counterterrorism Cofer Black stated that he was concerned over "the potential utilization of Bangladesh as a platform for international terrorism." Bruce Vaughn, "Islamist Extremism in Bangladesh," Congressional Research Service, January 31, 2007.

33 Sumit Ganguly, "The Rise of Islamist Militancy in Bangladesh," Special Report 171, Washington, DC: US Institute of Peace, August 2006.

34 Mohammad Abul Kawser and Md. Abdus Samad, "Political History of Farakka Barrage and Its Effects on Environment in Bangladesh," *Bandung Journal of Global South* 3, no. 16 (2016).

35 For background of the deal, its implementations and media coverage in 2015, see Muhammed Rashedul Hasan and Sheikh Mohammad Shafiul Islam, "Editorial Coverage on Implementation of Bangladesh–India Land Boundary Agreement: An Analysis of Six Dailies of Bangladesh and India," *Sage Open*, June, 2017.

36 Sanjoy Hazarika, "Bangladeshi Insurgents Say India Is Supporting Them," *The New York Times*, June 11, 1989.

37 Pranab Kumar Parua, *The Ganga: Water Use in the Indian Subcontinent* (Heidelberg: Springer, 2010), 145.

38 However, the transfer the Tin Bigha corridor to Bangladesh was delayed until 2001 due to objections from the Indian state of West Bengal, which is neighbor with Bangladesh.

39 For details of Chinese weapon supplies and military exchanges between 1977 and 1998, see John W. Garver, *Protracted Contest: Sino-Indian Rivalry in the Twentieth Century* (Seattle: University of Washington Press, 2001), 296–300.

40 Urvashi Aneja, China-Bangladesh Relationship: An Emerging Partnership? IPCS Special Report 33 (New Delhi: IPCS, November 2006), 6.

41 "China, Bangladesh Sign Landmark Defence Pact," *The Times of India*, December 25, 2002. https://timesofindia.indiatimes.com/china-bangladesh-sign-landmark-defence-pact/articleshow/32366373.cms.

42 Alamgir Mohiuddin, "The Government Has Ordered 18 Soviet Diplomats Expelled For...," *United Press India*, November 30, 1983, https://www.upi.com/Archives/1983/11/30/The-govenment-has-ordered-18-Soviet-diplomats-expelled-for/9240439016400/.

43 "Dhaka Expels Pakistani Diplomat," *BBC News*, December 15, 2000, http://news.bbc.co.uk/2/hi/south_asia/1072262.stm.

44 "Pakistani Diplomat Expelled from Dhaka," *Dawn*, February 4, 2015, https://www.dawn.com/news/1161488.

45 "Pakistan Expels Bangladeshi Diplomat amid Worsening 'Spy' Row," *Reuters*, January 7, 2016, https://www.reuters.com/article/us-bangladesh-pakistan-diplomacy/pakistan-expels-bangladeshi-diplomat-amid-worsening-spy-row-idUSKBN0UL0Z120160107.

46 "Bangladesh Prime Minister Shuns Pakistan Summit Invitation," *The Express Tribune*, November 13, 2012, https://tribune.com.pk/story/465004/bangladesh-prime-minister-shuns-pakistan-summit-invitation.

47 Shubhajit Roy and Yubaraj Ghimire, "SAARC Summit to be Called Off as Dhaka, Kabul and Thimphu Too Slam Islamabad," *The Indian Express*, September 29, 2016, https://indianexpress.com/article/india/india-news-india/dhaka-kabul-thimphu-too-blame-islamabad-saarc-summit-to-be-called-off-3054953/.

48 "Molla's Execution: Bangladesh's PM Condemns Pakistan's Stance," *The Express Tribune*, December 19, 2013, https://tribune.com.pk/story/647600/mollas-execution-bangladeshs-pm-condemns-pakistans-stance.

49 "Pakistan Condemns BD JI Chief's Execution," Dawn, May 12, 2016, https://www.dawn.com/news/1257796.

50 "Dhaka Approves New Pakistani High Commissioner to Bangladesh," *Arab News*, November 21, 2019, https://www.arabnews.pk/node/1587091/pakistan.

51 Baqir Sajjad Syed, "In a Rare Call to Hasina Imran Urges Closer Ties with Bangladesh," *Dawn*, July 23, 2020, https://www.dawn.com/news/1570633.

52 Pakistani Envoy Meets Bangladeshi PM in Sign of Warming Ties," *Aljazeera English*, December 4, 2020, https://www.aljazeera.com/news/2020/12/4/pakistani-envoy-meets-bangladeshi-pm-in-sign-of-warming-ties.

53 "Destinies of Our Peoples are Intertwined: Imran Khan Writes to PM Hasina," The Daily Star, March 25, 2021, https://www.thedailystar.net/world/south-asia/news/destinies-our-peoples-are-intertwined-imran-khan-writes-pm-hasina-2066757.

54 Between 2000 and 2017, at least 1133 Bangladeshis were killed, 1054 were injured, and 1341 were abducted by the BSF, according to human rights organization Odhikar, "Atrocities by Indian Border Security Force (BSF) against Bangladeshi Citizens," http://odhikar.org/wp-content/uploads/2018/01/Statistics_Border_2000-2017.pdf (accessed May 6, 2018). Official figures provided by the BGB claims 936 Bangladeshis were killed between 2001 and 2017 by the BSF and Indian nationals. "Why Border Killing Has Not Stopped," *Dhaka Tribune*, January 6, 2018, https://www.dhakatribune.com/bangladesh/2017/12/27/border-killing-not-stopped/ (accessed May 6, 2018).

55 Mahmood Hasan, "Land Boundary Agreement and Bangladesh-India Relations," *The Daily Star*, May 11, 2015.

56 Humayun Kabir, "Changing Relations between Bangladesh and India: Perception in Bangladesh," in *India and South Asia: Exploring Regional Perceptions*, ed. Vishal Chandra (New Delhi: IDSA and Pentagon Press, 2015), 380.

57 Pinak Ranjan Chakravarty, "Shadow of India, Hasina Government's Corruption, Repression of BNP Looms over Bangladesh Polls," *ORF Commentary*, September 9, 2018, https://www.orfonline.org/research/43844-shadow-of-india-hasina-governments-corruption-repression-of-bnp-looms-over-bangladesh-polls/.

58 "Illegal Immigrants are Like Termites, Will Throw Them Out if BJP Comes Back to Power: Amit Shah," *India Today*, April 11, 2019, https://www.indiatoday.in/elections/lok-sabha-2019/story/bjp-amit-shah-hindu-refugees-mamata-bannerjee-1499691-2019-04-11.

59 Christopher Finnigan, "Bangladesh-China Relations Have Metamorphosed into a Strategic Partnership," *LSE Blog*, June 20, 2019, https://blogs.lse.ac.uk/southasia/2019/06/20/bangladesh-china-relations-have-metamorphosed-into-a-strategic-partnership/.

60 "Bangladesh Buys Two Submarines from China," *The Times of India*, November 14, 2016, https://timesofindia.indiatimes.com/world/south-asia/bangladesh-buys-two-submarines-from-china/articleshow/55415904.cms.

61 Sumanth Samsani, "China-Bangladesh Strategic Linkages," *Observer Research Foundation*, May 11, 2021, https://www.orfonline.org/expert-speak/china-bangladesh-strategic-linkages/.

62 Sudha Ramachandran, "How Bangladesh Learned to Love the Belt and Road," *The Diplomat*, July 22, 2019, https://thediplomat.com/2019/07/how-bangladesh-learned-to-love-the-belt-and-road/.

63 Madhupurana Das, "India Need Not Worry about Bangladesh-China Ties: Sheikh Hasina," *The Economic Times*, February 23, 2018, https://economictimes.indiatimes.com/news/politics-and-nation/india-need-not-worry-about-bangladesh-china-ties-sheikh-hasina/articleshow/63037906.cms?utm_source=contentofinterest&utm_medium=text&utm_campaign=cppst.

64 Nayanima Basu, "China Takes Bangladesh into Its Embrace Now as Delhi-Dhaka Ties Go Downhill," *The Print*, July 31, 2020, https://theprint.in/diplomacy/china-takes-bangladesh-into-its-embrace-now-as-delhi-dhaka-ties-go-downhill/471769/.

65 "Bangladesh Should Oppose Powers from Outside the Region Forming 'Military Alliance' in South Asia: Chinese Defence Minister," *The Economic Times*, April 29, 2021, https://economictimes.indiatimes.com/news/defence/china-bangladesh-should-oppose-powers-from-outside-the-region-forming-military-alliance-in-south-asia-chinese-defence-minister/articleshow/82289339.cms?utm_source=contentofinterest&utm_medium=text&utm_campaign=cppst.

66 "China Warns of 'Damage' to Relations if Bangladesh Joins Quad Initiatives," *Radio Free Asia*, May 20, 2021, https://www.rfa.org/english/news/china/bangladesh-quad-05102021174758.html.

67 "We'll Decide Our Foreign Policy," *The Daily Star*, May 12, 2021.

68 "US-India Talks on Bangladesh Situation," *bdnews24.com*, October 23, 2013, https://bdnews24.com/bangladesh/2013/10/28/us-india-talks-on-bangladesh-situation.

69 "Indo-Pacific Strategy Report" (Washington, DC: Department of Defense, 2019), 21.

70 "US 'Excited to Work' with Bangladesh under IPS," *Prothom Alo English*, September 15, 2020, https://en.prothomalo.com/bangladesh/us-excited-to-work-with-bangladesh-under-ips.

71 "'Bangladesh Important in US Indo-Pacific Strategy': US Deputy Secretary," *South Asia Monitor*, October 15, 2020, https://www.southasiamonitor.org/bangladesh/bangladesh-important-us-indo-pacific-strategy-us-deputy-secretary.

72 Joyeeta Bhattacharjee, "Bangladesh: The Dilemma over the Indo-Pacific Strategy," Raisina Debates, *Observer Research Foundation*, November 10, 2020.

73 "Bangladesh to Make Its Position Clear over IPS: Foreign Secretary," *Prothom Alo English*, November 17, 2021, https://en.prothomalo.com/bangladesh/government/bangladesh-to-make-its-position-clear-over-ips-foreign-secretary.

74 "Bangladesh Not Invited to Biden's Democracy Summit," *The Business Standard*, November 24, 2021, https://www.tbsnews.net/world/bangladesh-not-invited-bidens-summit-democracy-333901.

75 US Department of Treasury, "Press Release" (Washington, DC, December 10, 2021), https://home.treasury.gov/news/press-releases/jy0526.

76 Anthony J. Blinken, "Press Statement: The United States Promotes Accountability for Human Rights Violations and Abuses," Department of State (Washington, DC, December 10, 2021), https://www.state.gov/the-united-states-promotes-accountability-for-human-rights-violations-and-abuses/.

77 "This Could Push Dhaka into the Arms of Beijing," *Prothom Alo English*, December 11, 2021, https://en.prothomalo.com/bangladesh/this-could-push-dhaka-into-the-arms-of-beijing.

78 This section is drawn on author's previous publication, "Geopolitics of the Pandemic: The Bangladesh Scene," Dhaka/Berlin: The Friedrich-Ebert-Stiftung, October 2021.

Bibliography

"Bangladesh Buys Two Submarines from China." *The Times of India*, November 14, 2016. https://timesofindia.indiatimes.com/world/south-asia/bangladesh-buys-two-submarines-from-china/articleshow/55415904.cms.

"'Bangladesh Important in US Indo-Pacific Strategy': US Deputy Secretary." *South Asia Monitor*, October 15, 2020. https://www.southasiamonitor.org/bangladesh/bangladesh-important-us-indo-pacific-strategy-us-deputy-secretary.

"Bangladesh Not Invited to Biden's Democracy Summit." *The Business Standard*, November 24, 2021. https://www.tbsnews.net/world/bangladesh-not-invited-bidens-summit-democracy-333901.

"Bangladesh Prime Minister Shuns Pakistan Summit Invitation." *The Express Tribune*, November 13, 2012. https://tribune.com.pk/story/465004/bangladesh-prime-minister-shuns-pakistan-summit-invitation.

"Bangladesh Should Oppose Powers from Outside the Region Forming 'Military Alliance' in South Asia: Chinese Defence Minister." *The Economic Times*, April 29, 2021. https://economictimes.indiatimes.com/news/defence/china-bangladesh-should-oppose-powers-from-outside-the-region-forming-military-alliance-in-south-asia-chinese-defence-minister/articleshow/82289339.cms?utm_source=contentofinterest&utm_medium=text&utm_campaign=cppst.

"Bangladesh to Make Its Position Clear over IPS: Foreign Secretary." *Prothom Alo English*, November 17, 2021. https://en.prothomalo.com/bangladesh/government/bangladesh-to-make-its-position-clear-over-ips-foreign-secretary.

"China Warns of 'Damage' to Relations if Bangladesh Joins Quad Initiatives." *Radio Free Asia*, May 20, 2021. https://www.rfa.org/english/news/china/bangladesh-quad-05102021174758.html.

"China, Bangladesh Sign Landmark Defence Pact." *The Times of India*, December 25, 2002. https://timesofindia.indiatimes.com/china-bangladesh-sign-landmark-defence-pact/articleshow/32366373.cms.

"Destinies of Our Peoples are Intertwined: Imran Khan Writes to PM Hasina." *The Daily Star*, March 25, 2021. https://www.thedailystar.net/world/south-asia/news/destinies-our-peoples-are-intertwined-imran-khan-writes-pm-hasina-2066757.

"Dhaka Approves New Pakistani High Commissioner to Bangladesh." *Arab News*, November 21, 2019. https://www.arabnews.pk/node/1587091/pakistan.

"Dhaka Expels Pakistani Diplomat." *BBC News*, December 15, 2000. http://news.bbc.co.uk/2/hi/south_asia/1072262.stm.

"Illegal Immigrants are Like Termites, Will Throw Them Out If BJP Comes Back to Power: Amit Shah." *India Today*, April 11, 2019. https://www.indiatoday.in/elections/lok-sabha-2019/story/bjp-amit-shah-hindu-refugees-mamata-bannerjee-1499691-2019-04-11.

"Indo-Pacific Strategy Report." Washington DC: Department of Defense, 2019.

"Molla's Execution: Bangladesh's PM Condemns Pakistan's Stance." *Express Tribune*, December 19, 2013. https://tribune.com.pk/story/647600/mollas-execution-bangladeshs-pm-condemns-pakistans-stance.

"Pakistan Condemns BD JI Chief's Execution." *Dawn*, May 12, 2016. https://www.dawn.com/news/1257796.

"Pakistan Expels Bangladeshi Diplomat amid Worsening 'Spy' Row." *Reuters*, January 7, 2016. https://www.reuters.com/article/us-bangladesh-pakistan-diplomacy/pakistan-expels-bangladeshi-diplomat-amid-worsening-spy-row-idUSKBN0UL0Z120160107.

"Pakistani Diplomat Expelled from Dhaka." *Dawn*, February 4, 2015. https://www.dawn.com/news/1161488.

"Pakistani Envoy Meets Bangladeshi PM in Sign of Warming Ties." *Aljazeera English*, December 4, 2020. https://www.aljazeera.com/news/2020/12/4/pakistani-envoy-meets-bangladeshi-pm-in-sign-of-warming-ties.

"Sheik Mujib Off to Soviet For 5-Day Good Will Visit." *The New York Times*, March 1, 1972. https://www.nytimes.com/1972/03/01/archives/sheik-mujib-off-to-soviet-for-5day-goodwill-visit.html.

"This Could Push Dhaka into the Arms of Beijing." *Prothom Alo English*, December 11, 2021. https://en.prothomalo.com/bangladesh/this-could-push-dhaka-into-the-arms-of-beijing.

"US 'Excited to Work' with Bangladesh under IPS." *Prothom Alo English*, September 15, 2020. https://en.prothomalo.com/bangladesh/us-excited-to-work-with-bangladesh-under-ips.

"US-India Talks on Bangladesh Situation." *bdnews24.com*, October 23, 2013. https://bdnews24.com/bangladesh/2013/10/28/us-india-talks-on-bangladesh-situation.

"We'll Decide Our Foreign Policy." *The Daily Star*, May 12, 2021.

"Why Border Killing Has Not Stopped." *Dhaka Tribune*, January 6, 2018. https://www.dhakatribune.com/bangladesh/2017/12/27/border-killing-not-stopped/ (accessed May 6, 2018).

Aiden, Robert. "China's First UN Veto Bars Bangladesh." *The New York Times*, August 26, 1972. https://www.nytimes.com/1972/08/26/archives/chinas-first-un-veto-bars-bangladesh-soviet-union-and-india-are.html.

Alamgir, Mohiuddin. "The Government Has Ordered 18 Soviet Diplomats Expelled For...." *United Press India*, November 30, 1983. https://www.upi.com/Archives/1983/11/30/The-govenment-has-ordered-18-Soviet-diplomats-expelled-for/9240439016400/.

Ali, S. Mahmud. *Understanding Bangladesh*. New York: Columbia University Press, 2010, 105.

Aneja, Urvashi. China-Bangladesh Relationship: An Emerging Partnership? *IPCS Special Report 33*. New Delhi: IPCS, November 2006.

Bass, Gary. *The Blood Telegram: Nixon, Kissinger, and a Forgotten Genocide*. New York: Vintage, 2013.

Basu, Nayanima. "China Takes Bangladesh into Its Embrace Now as Delhi-Dhaka Ties Go Downhill." *The Print*, July 31, 2020. https://theprint.in/diplomacy/china-takes-bangladesh-into-its-embrace-now-as-delhi-dhaka-ties-go-downhill/471769/.

Bhattacharjee, Joyeeta. "Bangladesh: The Dilemma over the Indo-Pacific Strategy." Raisina Debates, *Observer Research Foundation*, November 10, 2020.

Blinken, Anthony J. "Press Statement: The United States Promotes Accountability for Human Rights Violations and Abuses." Washington, DC: Department of State, December 10, 2021. https://www.state.gov/the-united-states-promotes-accountability-for-human-rights-violations-and-abuses/.

Budhraj, Vijay Sen. "Moscow and the Birth of Bangladesh." *Asian Survey* 13, no. 5 (May 1973): 482–495.

Chakravarty, Pinak Ranjan. "Shadow of India, Hasina Government's Corruption, Repression of BNP Looms over Bangladesh Polls." *ORF Commentary*, September 9, 2018. https://www.orfonline.org/research/43844-shadow-of-india-hasina-governments-corruption-repression-of-bnp-looms-over-bangladesh-polls/.

Chowdhury, Iftikhar Ahmed. "Strategy of a Small Power in a Subsystem: Bangladesh's External Relations." *Australian Outlook* 34, no. 1 (1990): 85–98.

Chowdhury, Dilara, Al Masud Hasanuzzaman, and T.S. Rahman. "Foreign Policy of Bangladesh: 1972–1996." In *Bangladesh at 25: An Analytical Discourse on Development*, edited by Abdul Bayes and Anu Muhammad, 217–252. Dhaka: University Press Limited, 1998.

Das, Madhupurana. "India Need Not Worry about Bangladesh-China Ties: Sheikh Hasina." *The Economic Times*, February 23, 2018. https://economictimes.indiatimes.com/news/politics-and-nation/india-need-not-worry-about-bangladesh-china-ties-sheikh-hasina/articleshow/63037906.cms?utm_source=contentofinterest&utm_medium=text&utm_campaign=cppst.

Elman, Miriam Fendius. "The Foreign Policies of Small States: Challenging Neorealism in Its Own Backyard." *British Journal of Political Science* 25, no. 2 (1995): 171–217.

Fearon, James D. "Domestic Politics, Foreign Policy, and Theories of International Relations." *Annual Review of Political Science* 1, no. 1 (1998): 289–313.

Finnigan, Christopher. "Bangladesh-China Relations Have Metamorphosed into a Strategic Partnership." *LSE Blog*, June 20, 2019. https://blogs.lse.ac.uk/southasia/2019/06/20/bangladesh-china-relations-have-metamorphosed-into-a-strategic-partnership/.

Ganguly, Šumit. "The Rise of Islamist Militancy in Bangladesh." Special Report 171, Washington DC: US Institute of Peace, August 2006.

Garver, John W. *Protracted Contest: Sino-Indian Rivalry in the Twentieth Century*. Seattle: University of Washington Press, 2001.

Haider, Zaglul. *The Changing Pattern of Bangladesh Foreign Policy: A Comparative Study of the Mujib and Zia Regimes*. Dhaka: The University Press Limited, 2006.

Halim, Muhammad Abdul. "Bangladesh Foreign Policy: A Review." In *Bangladesh: In the Threshold of the Twenty-First Century*, edited by Abdul Momin Chowdhury and Fakrul Alam. Dhaka: Asiatic Society, 2002.

Hasan, Mahmood. "Land Boundary Agreement and Bangladesh-India Relations." *The Daily Star*, May 11, 2015.

Hasan, Maidul. *Muldhara Ekattor (The Mainstream of 1971)*. Dhaka: University Press Limited, 1985.

Hasan, Muhammed Rashedul, and Sheikh Mohammad Shafiul Islam "Editorial Coverage on Implementation of Bangladesh–India Land Boundary Agreement: An Analysis of Six Dailies of Bangladesh and India." *Sage Open*, June 2017.

Hazarika, Sanjoy. "Bangladeshi Insurgents Say India Is Supporting Them." *The New York Times*, June 11, 1989.

Hollen, C. Van. "The Tilt Policy Revisited: Nixon-Kissinger Geopolitics and South Asia." In *The Regional Imperative: The Administration of US Foreign Policy Towards South Asian States Under Presidents Johnson and Nixon*, edited by Lloyd I. Rudolph and Suzanne H. Rudolph, 421–450. New Jersey, Humanities Press Inc, 1980.

Hossain, Ishtiaq. "Bangladesh-India Relations: Issues and Problems." *Asian Survey* 21, no. 11 (1981): 1115–1128.

Kabir, Humayun. "Changing Relations between Bangladesh and India: Perception in Bangladesh." In *India and South Asia: Exploring Regional Perceptions*, edited by Vishal Chandra, 29–45. New Delhi: IDSA and Pentagon Press, 2015.

Kawser, Mohammad Abul Md, and Abdus Samad. "Political History of Farakka Barrage and Its Effects on Environment in Bangladesh." *Bandung Journal of Global South* 3, no. 16 (2016). https://bandungjournal.springeropen.com/track/pdf/10.1186/s40728-015-0027-5.pdf

Ministry of External Affairs, Government of India. "Treaty of Peace, Friendship and Co-operation." August 9, 1971. https://mea.gov.in/bilateral-documents.htm?dtl/5139/Treaty+of.

Odhikar. "Atrocities by Indian Border Security Force (BSF) against Bangladeshi Citizens." http://odhikar.org/wp-content/uploads/2018/01/Statistics_Border_2000-2017.pdf (accessed May 6, 2018).

Oliver, Thomas W. *The United Nations in Bangladesh*. Princeton, NJ: Princeton University Press, 1978.

Parua, Pranab Kumar. *The Ganga: Water Use in the Indian Subcontinent*. Heidelberg: Springer, 2010.

Pattanaik, Smruti S. "India's Neighbourhood Policy: Perceptions from Bangladesh." *Strategic Analysis* 35, no. 1 (2011): 71–87.

Rahman, Mohammad Sajjadur. "Bangladesh and Its Neighbors." In *Routledge Handbook of Contemporary Bangladesh*, edited by Ali Riaz and Mohammad Sajjadur Rahman, 378–388. London: Routledge, 2016.

Ramachandran, Sudha. "How Bangladesh Learned to Love the Belt and Road." *The Diplomat*, July 22, 2019. https://thediplomat.com/2019/07/how-bangladesh-learned-to-love-the-belt-and-road/.

Rashid, Harun ur. *Bangladesh Foreign Policy: Realities, Priorities and Challenges*. Dhaka: Academic Press and Publishers Library, 2005.

Rashid, Harun ur. *Bangladesh-India Relations: Living with a Big Neighbour*. Dhaka: A H Development Publishing House, 2010.

Rehman Sobhan, Rehman. "Politics of Food and Famine in Bangladesh." *Economic and Political Weekly* 14, no. 48 (Dec. 1, 1979): 1973–1980.

Riaz, Ali. *God Willing: The Politics of Islamism in Bangladesh*. Lanham, MD: Rowman and Littlefield, 2004.

Roy, Shubhajit, and Yubaraj Ghimire. "SAARC Summit to be Called Off as Dhaka, Kabul and Thimphu Too Slam Islamabad." *The Indian Express*, September 29, 2016. https://indianexpress.com/article/india/india-news-india/dhaka-kabul-thimphu-too-blame-islamabad-saarc-summit-to-be-called-off-3054953/.

Sen, Amartya. *Poverty and Famines: An Essay on Entitlement and Deprivation*. Oxford: OUP, 1983.

Sisson, Richard, and Leo Rose. *War and Secession: Pakistan, India, and the Creation of Bangladesh*. Berkeley: University of California Press, 1991.

Raghavan, Srinath. *1971: A Global History of the Creation of Bangladesh*. Cambridge: Harvard University Press, 2013.

Sumanth, Samsani. "China-Bangladesh Strategic Linkages." *Observer Research Foundation*, May 11, 2021. https://www.orfonline.org/expert-speak/china-bangladesh-strategic-linkages/.

Syed, Baqir Sajjad. "In a Rare Call to Hasina Imran Urges Closer Ties with Bangladesh." *Dawn*, July 23, 2020. https://www.dawn.com/news/1570633.

Tanner, Henry. "U.N.: Moscow Again Vetoes Truce Call." *The New York Times*, December 6, 1991. https://www.nytimes.com/1971/12/06/archives/un-moscow-again-vetoes-truce-call-u-n-deadlocked-on-peace-efforts-a.html.

US Department of Treasury. "Press Release." Washington, DC, December 10, 2021. https://home.treasury.gov/news/press-releases/jy0526.

Vaughn, Bruce. "Islamist Extremism in Bangladesh." *Congressional Research Service*, January 31, 2007.

Vinayaraj, V.K. "India as a Threat: Bangladeshi Perceptions." *South Asian Survey* 16, no. 1 (2009): 101–118.

20

DOMESTIC POLITICS AND STRUCTURAL CONSTRAINTS

Pakistan and its South Asian Neighbors[1]

Ryan Brasher

Introduction

Structural accounts, rooted in realist international relations theory, prioritize asymmetric power relations and nuclear strategy as key external factors driving Pakistan's foreign policy behavior, particularly toward India.[2] Some practitioners, like Pakistan's former foreign minister Abdul Sattar, also argue that Pakistan pursues a calculated realist foreign policy strategy in South Asia. Its *realpolitik* is designed to forestall a putative existential threat from India and reoccurring territorial claims from Afghanistan, to push its claims on Kashmir, and to constructively engage its non-Indian neighbors in order to counter-balance India.[3] Culturalist approaches, on the other hand, seek explanations from Pakistan's domestic politics. Rizvi, for instance, suggests that Pakistan's foreign policy is guided by an ideology or strategic culture rooted in the country's Islamic identity: It seeks to foster cooperation among Muslim-majority countries, while also advocating for oppressed Muslim minorities around the globe. While this ideological orientation has led Pakistani policymakers to support Islamist militants in the region, it has also served to isolate it from its South Asian neighbors.[4] Christine Fair links Pakistan's strategic culture with its military, the dominant institution in the country. The military socializes its officer cadre into a set of beliefs, such as India as an existential threat, Pakistan's territorial deficiency without Kashmir, and the zero-sum nature of India-Pakistan relations, which close off cooperative avenues of conflict resolution and prioritize, among other tools, the cultivation of Islamic militants as proxies in Kashmir and elsewhere.[5]

But domestic political groups and institutions, particularly the military, are not simply sources of subjectivity, like ideology or strategic culture, that impinge on Pakistan achieving objective national interests. They are also rational actors whose domestic interests are externalized through foreign policy. This accords with the neo-classical realist approach, which departs from structural realism by accounting for the distorting effects of domestic politics, while still affirming the existence of objective interests. According to Rathbun, neo-classical realism can account for the short-term impact of misperceptions of real power capabilities, but it also explains how fragmented states dominated by parochial interests, including militaries that lack civilian control, do not act in accordance with their objective national interests, and thereby harm themselves in the long term.[6] In Pakistan, the military does not simply shape the country's strategic culture, it also has considerable economic interest in preserving its status

DOI: 10.4324/9781003246626-24

275

in Pakistan's political system: The military maintains a sprawling economic empire, with four major foundations running about 100 independent projects in manufacturing, banking and finance, education, and agriculture and landownership, which employ thousands of retired and active military personnel.[7]

In accordance with neo-classical realism, I argue that in Pakistan's relations with its South Asian neighbors, domestic actors and their own interests, particularly the military, often inadvertently hinder its pursuit of security. In order to extend this insight to bilateral relationships, I also draw from Putnam's two-level games framework. Two countries' decision to cooperate or not depends not only on top-level negotiations (level 1), but also on domestic audiences (level 2). For instance, moderate governments are more likely to find common ground for cooperation with each other, but they may face more difficulty in "ratifying" agreements due to domestic opposition. Hard-line governments, on the other hand, may stake out more exclusive claims, but are also more likely to implement any agreement, however limited, at home. Democratic countries with a number of institutional veto-players, or hybrid regimes with powerful non-elected institutions, may have greater difficulty in implementing agreements, while authoritarian states are insulated from domestic electoral pressures and may therefore find it easier to cooperate.[8]

In the following pages, I analyze how this interplay between structural conditions and domestic interests shape Pakistan's bilateral relations with its fellow South Asian Association for Regional Cooperation (SAARC) members. While SAARC was meant to improve regional multilateral cooperation, bilateral interaction continues to dominate international relations in the region.[9] Furthermore, major foreign policy speeches from the last two administrations indicate that Pakistan's policymakers have spent little time envisioning a comprehensive regional foreign policy for South Asia, beyond India, Afghanistan, and to a lesser extent Bangladesh.[10] Below I argue that Pakistan's perception of these three countries has often been filtered through domestic political considerations, and not simply driven by a rational interest-based approach, often to Pakistan's' own detriment. Regime type has been of particular importance in its relationship with India. Military governments have generally been more confrontational, but they also have had greater leeway to pursue negotiations. Civilian governments, on the other hand, are more willing to improve relations with India, but their efforts are viewed with skepticism by the military, which is not keen to weaken the country's adversarial perspective of India, particularly when it is not in control. In its policy toward Afghanistan, Pakistani leaders, encouraged by Pakistani religious parties, has struggled to maximize its influence in Kabul by promoting Islamist actors who do not seek to politicize an ethno-national identity potentially threatening to Pakistan's territorial integrity. The two-level game framework is particularly useful to understand Pakistan's fitful relationship with Bangladesh, with political changes in Bangladesh of special importance. By contrast, I show that Pakistan's relations with the other SAARC members have been much more cooperative, unhindered by domestic politics, albeit constrained due to Indian preponderance.

India

Pakistan's founding father, Muhammad Ali Jinnah, expected to have amicable relations with India, given their shared cultural and historical background as post-colonial states.[11] However, the dispute over the accession of Kashmir, claimed by both Pakistan and India, changed everything. The war of 1947–1948, precipitated by the indecisive Maharaja of Kashmir and an incursion of Pashtun tribesmen mobilized by Pakistan, left about two-thirds of Kashmir under Indian control, and one-third under Pakistani control.[12] Since then, Pakistan has been, by and large, the revisionist state seeking to change the status quo, while India has sought to defend it.[13]

The conflictual relationship is not simply propelled by historical grievances and structural forces, but also internal political dynamics. I argue that when Pakistan's military has been in power—or a civilian government closely aligned with the military—the potential for conflict has historically been higher. On the other hand, due to the military's greater ability to guarantee international cooperation, the potential for temporary rapprochement is potentially higher as well. When a civilian government with an independent power base has been in charge, the military's incentives to torpedo any potential entente increases: The ostensible Indian threat remains the military's biggest justification for its all-pervasive political and socio-economic footprint in the country.

Pakistan's relationship with India has witnessed some cooperative efforts, particularly through the Permanent Indus Commission, which has successfully adjudicated disputes related to water usage of the Indus River and its tributaries since 1960.[14] But on the whole the relationship has been mostly conflictual. Pakistan initiated the 1965 war in a gambit to cut off Kashmir from the rest of India, but military dictator Ayub Khan misperceived Indian resolve and military capacity due to motivated bias, and did not achieve his goals.[15] Pakistan's loss of East Pakistan in the war of 1971 ushered in an era of relative peace between the two countries largely due to India's massive military preponderance.[16] Because of its acquisition of nuclear capabilities, and the outbreak of the Kashmir insurgency in 1989, Pakistan began to pursue what Paul calls a "truncated asymmetric" strategy allowing it to match Indian power in the favorable Kashmir theater without risking a direct conflict that could lead to nuclear escalation.[17] While inter-state war was no longer a viable option, the chance of smaller skirmishes, from cross-border terrorist strikes to occasional exchange of artillery fire, greatly increased.[18]

The 1999 war represented somewhat of an overextension of this strategy: Chief of Army Staff Pervez Musharraf and a narrow coterie of generals ordered the occupation of several strategically important but remote mountain outposts across the line of control near Kargil, relying on the international community and particularly the US to stymie any forceful Indian response. However, a robust Indian military response and American pressure forced Pakistan into a humiliating withdrawal. Pakistan's civilian government under Nawaz Sharif in the 1990s was open to normalizing ties with India, partially because his political base had developed close ties to industrial and trading interests in central Punjab, and would benefit considerably from an expansion of trade with India.[19] The composite dialogue process between India and Pakistan was initiated by his government and Indian Prime Minister Vajpayee in 1998, culminating in the Lahore declaration of February 1999. Both countries committed to cooperation particularly in the area of nuclear armaments, but also pledged to work toward a solution in the Kashmir dispute.[20] However, the top military brass stayed away from the formal ceremony in Lahore, and in a pattern that would repeat itself a decade later in Mumbai, put a wrench in the peace process by initiating the Kargil war in May 1999, which led to a deterioration in civil-military relations and set the stage for Musharraf's military coup later that year.[21]

Insurgent attacks on civilian and military targets in Indian-held Kashmir saw a marked increase under Pakistan's last military dictator, Pervez Musharraf.[22] But his time in office was also characterized by unprecedented efforts to improve relations between the two countries, particularly when he sharply curtailed militant activity in Kashmir after several attempts on his life.[23] Musharraf restarted the composite dialogue process with India, signaling a willingness to shift from Pakistan's long-standing insistence on a Kashmiri plebiscite, and floated the idea of dividing Kashmiri regions between India and Pakistan, whilst placing others under a UN trusteeship. Indian Prime Minister Manmohan Singh demurred but offered the possibility of creating a movement-free zone for Kashmiris and possibly greater levels of Kashmiri autonomy. While the backchannel talks between both countries were at a promising stage in 2007, Musharraf's increasing political weakness at home, culminating in his departure from power in 2008, effectively put an end to the effort.[24]

The new elected civilian government under Zardari attempted to revive the peace process, but then the deadly terrorist attack in Mumbai occurred in November 2008, with all evidence pointing to Lashkar-e-Taiba (LeT), an extremist outfit with extensive links to Pakistan's intelligence apparatus. Manmohan Singh insisted that those responsible for the attack in Pakistan be prosecuted, but given the close relationship between LeT leader Hafez Saeed Muhammad and the military establishment, this was unlikely to happen.[25] When Nawaz Sharif was elected for a third term as prime minister in 2013, his government made another attempt to reach out to India after the election of Hindu nationalist Narendra Modi through their mutual friend, steel magnate Sajjan Jindal.[26] In a surprising move, Modi stopped by Lahore in December 2015, attending Nawaz Sharif's granddaughter's wedding at the latter's personal residence, and signaling a return to the composite dialogue process.[27]

However, institutional resistance to Sharif's informal diplomatic overture soon presented an insurmountable obstacle. Within days, a group of militants staged a complex attack on an Indian air force base in Pathankot, near the Pakistani border.[28] Later that year, 20 soldiers were killed in an Indian army brigade post near Uri in Jammu and Kashmir, the deadliest terrorist incident in over two decades, with LeT claiming responsibility.[29] The attack put an end to peace talks with Pakistan, and also led India to force SAARC members to boycott the scheduled 2016 Summit in Islamabad—no meeting has been held since. At home, Nawaz Sharif's government may have overplayed its hand by pushing the military to prosecute its erstwhile militant proxies. A leaked story about a mild confrontation between the PM's brother Shahbaz Sharif and the head of the Inter-Services Intelligence (ISI) in 2016 may have contributed to the end of his government's tenure in office in 2018.[30]

After the election of Imran Khan, the clear choice of the military establishment, the relationship initially turned sour quickly. In early 2019, over 40 Indian soldiers died when a suicide bomber targeted a military convoy near Pulwama in Kashmir. The Indian response established a new precedent: 12 Indian fighter jets crossed into Pakistan's airspace and targeted an alleged terrorist training camp near Balakot in Khyber Pakhtunkhwa (KPK) province. A tense two-day standoff ensued, with Pakistan crossing into Indian territory, while an Indian fighter pilot was shot down over Pakistani territory.[31] In August 2019, India abrogated Article 370 of its constitution, which had guaranteed a measure of autonomy for Jammu and Kashmir, and in response Pakistan downgraded its diplomatic ties with India, suspending cultural and trade relations at considerable cost to its own economy.[32] But Pakistan's military may again be seeking rapprochement. In a widely publicized speech in March 2021, chief of army staff Qamar Javed Bajwa spoke of Pakistan's strategic location in global international trade and the need for peaceful relations with its neighbors, particularly India, while remaining conspicuously silent on India's abrogation of Article 370 or Kashmiri self-determination.[33] While a promising overture, India's hard-line stance on Kashmir and the domestic interest of Pakistan's military establishment make any permanent entente unlikely.[34]

Bangladesh

Pakistan's relationship with Bangladesh had an ill-fated beginning. In the 1971 conflict that led to the separation of erstwhile East Pakistan, West Pakistani troops and their Islamist Bengali allies had engaged in a campaign of mass violence and terror termed "Operation Searchlight."[35] Pakistan's Hamoodur Rahman commission, set up to investigate the military handling of the conflict, admitted to the killing of 26,000 innocent civilians, although neutral sources argue that hundreds of thousands of civilians were killed, with up to 10 million refugees temporarily shifting to Indian Bengal. Bangladesh's new and unabashedly pro-Indian and anti-Pakistan leader, Mujibur Rehman, wanted to prosecute 1500 Pakistani POWS for war crimes, arrested over 100,000 suspected collaborators, and demanded an unconditional apology from Pakistan's leadership for war crimes committed in East Pakistan. Under the tripartite agreement of 1974, Mujib allowed all POWs to return, released over 30,000 people associated with Bangladesh's Jama'at-i-Islami (BJI), and declared a general amnesty for most pro-Pakistani elements. But Bangladesh still demanded a fair distribution of pre-1971 resources and wanted Pakistan to take about half a million Urdu-speaking "Bihari" Muslims who had come to East Pakistan after partition from northeastern India, but had largely supported West Pakistan in the 1971 war. Bhutto accepted just over 100,000 as part of the tripartite agreement, but would not consider any more than that. Furthermore, Bangladesh was not fully satisfied with Bhutto's deliberately vague apology, while Pakistan considered it to have been made under duress.[36]

The Pakistan-Bangladesh relationship did not really improve until the assassination of Mujib in 1975. The new military ruler, Ziaur Rehman, rehabilitated collaborationists of the 1971 war, exhibited greater openness toward the role of religion in public life, and sought to assert greater distance from India.[37] As a result, formal diplomatic relations between the two countries were established in early 1976, as potentially contentious issues were put aside by both countries, who now instead focused on reestablishing mutual trade. Cooperation became even easier after Zia ul-Haq's coup against Bhutto, as he shared Ziaur Rehman's Islamist, pro-American, and anti-Indian outlook. Zia ul-Haq was also willing to talk about repatriating Bihari refugees, pledging to take 250,000, of which over 50,000 moved to Pakistan by 1981.[38] Muhammad Ershad, who came to power in the coup of 1982, largely shared Ziaur Rehman's domestic and foreign policy preferences, even allowing the BJI to run in national elections after gradually restoring democracy in the late 1980s.[39]

Under Benazir Bhutto, Pakistan's stance on Bihari refugees hardened, as a large influx of Urdu-speakers would have bolstered her party's main rival in Sindh and exacerbated simmering tensions between Sindhi and Muhajir communities in Karachi. When Nawaz Sharif's Muslim League was in power, the government generally sounded a more hopeful tone, arguing that Pakistan should allow Biharis to come on "humanitarian grounds," even though they should not be considered Pakistani.[40] Relations remained cordial between the countries in the early 2000s, especially when the tenure of Khaleda Zia, the widow of Ziaur Rehman, coincided with Pervez Musharraf's military dictatorship. Both countries focused on deepening economic ties with each other, particularly in the textile industry, while Bangladesh avoided making any demands on Pakistan.[41] Musharraf, for his part, visited Bangladesh's war memorial in 2002 and expressed regret for the "excesses" of the 1971 war. It was the closest any Pakistani leader had ever come to apologizing for human rights violations in 1971.[42]

A major shift in mutual relations occurred in 2008, when the Awami League came to power with a two-thirds majority. The government under Mujibur Rehman's daughter, Sheikh Hasina, decided to establish an International Crimes Tribunal designed to prosecute war criminals from the 1971 war. The action was no doubt motivated by domestic political consideration, as most of the men put on trial were connected to the BJI, the main political ally of Khaleda Zia's BNP. In 2013, BJI leader Abdul Qader Mollah was sentenced for life, a verdict which was turned into a death sentence by the Supreme Court later that year. Bangladesh now also renewed demands for Pakistan to issue an apology for the events of 1971. Asif Ali Zardari's PPP government in Pakistan had little interest in interfering in a process aimed at weakening

Islamist forces in Bangladesh, but refused to issue an apology, to the chagrin of Sheikh Hasina.[43] The election of Nawaz Sharif in 2013 brought relations to the lowest point since the 1970s. In order to satisfy his conservative religious base, his party sponsored resolutions in the National Assembly as well as Punjab's provincial assembly condemning the war crimes trials in Bangladesh, which drew the Bangladeshi government's wrath, and resulted in large public protests in front of Pakistan's high commission in Dhaka. In 2015, Bangladesh declared a Pakistani consular diplomat *persona non grata* after accusing him of making connections with Islamic extremists on behalf of the ISI, Pakistan's main military intelligence agency, and the Pakistani government retaliated in kind. Political disagreements spilled over into economic relations as well, when Bengali officials and pundits blamed Pakistan for the devastating fire at the Rana Plaza textile plant in 2014.[44]

However, recent events have brought the two countries together again. In January 2020, Bangladesh was one of the first major International Cricket Council (ICC) countries to complete a cricket tour with a full strength team in Pakistan after an almost decade-long hiatus caused by the 2009 terrorist attack on the Sri Lankan team.[45] Then in July 2020, Imran Khan made a surprise call to Sheikh Hasina, congratulating Bangladesh on its upcoming 50th anniversary and expressing a desire to improve relations between the two countries.[46] In 2021, Sheikh Hasina made two high-profile visits to Pakistan's High Commission (embassy) in Dhaka, discussing the possibility of a sitting Prime Minister visiting Pakistan for the first time since 2006.

What might have brought about this change? First, the Awami League government's traditional warm ties with India have cooled off considerably in the wake of India's controversial anti-Muslim citizenship laws passed in 2019.[47] Secondly, the Awami League has consolidated political control in Bangladesh and seems to be moving toward a soft authoritarianism with a sufficiently cowed political opposition.[48] Greater insulation from electoral threats may therefore be mitigating the need for anti-Pakistani nationalist mobilization. And thirdly, Bangladesh has been developing friendlier relations with China, Pakistan's closest ally, with mutual trade increasing around 20-fold over the last 24 years, and Bangladesh becoming the second biggest recipient of Chinese military arms after Pakistan.[49] For now at least, Bangladesh's insistence on settling long-standing issues, first and foremost a formal public apology from Pakistan, may be on the backburner due to structural constraints presented by the actions of India and China, the region's two great powers.

Afghanistan

Pakistan's relationship with Afghanistan has been fraught from the very beginning. Afghanistan initially opposed the creation of Pakistan, as it viewed the colonial "Durand Line" frontier, which divided the Pashtun population, as illegitimate.[50] It has continued to make claims on all or parts of Pakistan's territory west of the Indus ever since. From 1953 to 1963, Prime Minister Daoud Khan pursued an irredentist policy, denouncing any Pakistani attempt to reduce the autonomy of Pashtuns in the Northwest Frontier Province and supporting anti-Pakistan activists in the country. The Pakistani government broke off diplomatic relations and closed transit trade on several occasions in response to cross-border raids by Afghan tribesmen.[51] While the bilateral relationship temporarily improved after Zahir Shah ousted him in 1963, Daoud came back to power in the 1973 coup and resumed pressing the Pashtunistan issue while also cultivating Pashtun and Baloch secessionist movements in Pakistan. Toward the end of his tenure, Daoud did seek to establish better relations with Pakistan in a series of direct talks, but the communist coup of 1978 put an end to this effort.[52]

Domestic Politics and Structural Constraints

Because of Daoud's hard-line nationalist policy in the 1970s, Zulfiqar Ali Bhutto decided to engage in a proactive effort to create a friendly regime in the country. He set up an "Afghan cell"—overseen by General Naseerullah Babar—that recruited Islamist anti-government activists, who promptly organized the first unsuccessful uprising against the Daoud regime in 1975. After the Soviet invasion of Afghanistan in 1979, the ISI coordinated Afghan resistance into seven groups in Peshawar, with massive assistance from the US. This was Pakistan's first chance to not only influence, but control, Afghanistan's future government, and decision-makers consistently favored Islamist figures with no interest in Pashtun nationalism. Gulbuddin Hekmatyar's Hizb-e-Islami emerged as an early favorite, given its close ties with Pakistan's Jama'at-i-Islami, which strongly supported military dictator Zia ul-Haq's regime in the early 1980s. As part of Zia's comprehensive Islamization campaign within Pakistan, he also had refugee children channeled into schools and madrasahs run by his favored groups, particularly those ascribing to the Deobandi school of thought.[53]

After the Soviet pullout in 1989, the chance to foster a broad-based peace process including both Afghan Communists and resistance fighters presented itself. But Pakistani policymakers were not interested in including former Communists in any future government, as they were considered pro-India, had harbored Baloch secessionists, and supported Pashtun nationalists in Pakistan. While the ISI's favored figure Gulbuddin Hekmatyar could not rally a critical mass of Afghans behind himself, his main rivals in charge of Kabul, Ahmed Shah Massoud and Burhanuddin Rabbani, were not as amenable to Pakistani influence and had already started developing ties with India. In 1994, however, Naseerullah Babar, now Benazir Bhutto's interior minister, encouraged his government to put its support behind the Taliban (he was known to refer to them as "my children"), which had roots in Pakistan's Deobandi religious schools and close connections with two Deobandi political parties, Fazlur Rahman's Jamiat Ulema-i-Islam and its more radical branch led by Sami ul-Haq. The Taliban took Kabul in 1996 and consolidated control over 90% of Afghanistan's territory by 1998. The ISI readjusted rather quickly when it became clear that Hekmatyar had been sidelined, but it is significant to note that the Taliban did not depend only on its relationship with the army but maintained connections with a diverse set of political and social actors within Pakistan.[54]

After the September 11 attacks and the US demand for full cooperation in its military operation in Afghanistan, Pakistan faced the difficult choice of turning against the Taliban, which had been a guarantee against encirclement by its Indian rival. Pakistan publicly agreed to withdraw official support from the Taliban and cooperate with the US military campaign in Afghanistan. But in private, Pakistan would express their reservations about the details of American demands.[55] In the end, Pakistan pursued a dual strategy toward the new regime in Afghanistan. On the one hand, it officially recognized the Karzai-led government, and even let Afghanistan join the SAARC as a full member. However, all of the Afghan political figures that had been invited to the Bonn process in 2001 were much more inclined toward India than Pakistan. As a result, Musharraf hedged his bets, abetted Taliban fighters fleeing Afghanistan, and tolerated the Taliban leadership in Balochistan as well as the Haqqani clan in North Waziristan.[56] Furthermore, the Musharraf government did not want to upset Islamist parties in the governing coalitions of both the Northwest Frontier Province (now KPK) and Balochistan at the time. But the influx of Taliban fighters and international militants greatly disrupted life in the border areas of Pakistan, leading to the rise of the Tehrik-i-Taliban Pakistan (TTP), the takeover by Taliban commanders of parts of the Federally Administered Tribal Areas (FATA) as well as Swat valley, while also fueling radicalism in other parts of the country.[57]

Afghanistan's leaders were torn in their response toward Pakistan's dual strategy. Karzai's government consistently criticized Pakistan for its continued support of the Taliban, while at the same time reaching out directly to Taliban leaders and rank-and-file members, seeking to draw them into the Afghan political process through the High Peace Council. Pakistan's military was not thrilled by these attempts, and put immense pressure on Taliban leaders and their families in Pakistan to ignore them.[58] Successive leaders of the National Directorate of Security (NDS), Afghanistan's intelligence agency, tried to turn the tables on Pakistan by fostering contacts among the TTP—a strategy that the US military deeply disapproved of when it became privy to it.[59] When Ashraf Ghani came into office in 2014, he tried to smooth over Kabul's relationship with Islamabad, even suggesting an official memorandum of understanding between the NDS and the ISI, a highly controversial initiative between two hostile agencies. But when this failed to change Pakistan's support for the Taliban, highlighted by a massive bomb blast in Kabul in August 2015, Ghani returned to Karzai's openly pro-Indian and anti-Pakistani rhetoric.[60]

The lightning takeover of Afghanistan by the Taliban in 2021 was facilitated by the agreement struck between the US and the Taliban under the Trump administration and confirmed by incoming president Biden. The talks served to delegitimize the Afghan government, ultimately pulling the rug from under its feet.[61] Many policymakers in Pakistan may view these events as a return on its long-term investment in the Taliban since 2001, much like its support of the mujahideen in the 1980s. Pakistan is the Taliban's most important ally and advocate, and relies on Pakistan's goodwill for commerce and trade.[62] Yet the Taliban is not as isolated as it was in the 1990s and maintains ties with Iran, Russia, and China, and even expressing openness toward normal relations with India.[63] A recent border skirmish with Pakistani forces related to the latter's border fence also indicate that it may not be as malleable to Pakistani interests as assumed.[64] Furthermore, there is considerable trepidation within Pakistan that a Taliban-controlled Afghanistan will once again lead to an uptick in radicalization within Pakistan itself. Pakistani decision-makers need to decide whether the short-term benefits of achieving its strategic goal of a friendly government in Kabul will not be outweighed by the long-term damage caused both to domestic Afghan and Pakistani politics.

The Other SAARC Members

Pakistan's relationship with Sri Lanka has been constructive, although Sri Lanka generally tries to avoid offending India. During the 1971 East Pakistan crisis, Sri Lankan allowed Pakistan's military planes to refuel under civilian guise, since India had closed its air space.[65] Pakistan also supplied military aid to Sri Lanka when it faced the beginnings of the Tamil insurgency in the early 1970s, but India also did the same, so this did not signal a realignment in Sri Lanka's foreign policy. The secession of Bangladesh did have a positive impact on Pakistan's trade relations with Sri Lanka, since it no longer had access to its traditional tea supply.[66] Pakistan made sure to support Sri Lanka in its fight with the LTTE, even when India was hesitant, particularly in the 2009 move to liquidate the insurgent organization. In turn, Pakistan has also requested training and support from Sri Lanka in its own counter-insurgency operations. A free-trade agreement exists between the two countries, although total trade remains modest.[67] Of particular interest is an unspoken agreement to remain silent on their respective domestic politics. Despite its advocacy on behalf of Muslim minorities in other countries, Imran Khan did not make any public remarks after communal riots targeted Sri Lankan Muslims in 2018 and 2019.[68] Pakistan appreciated Sri Lanka's measured response after its cricket team was targeted in a terrorist attack in Lahore in 2009, and the island nation gained even more sympathy within Pakistan when it became one of the first countries to engage in a cricket tour of Pakistan in 2017.[69] Similarly, after a Sri Lankan manager of a factory in Sialkot was brutally murdered by a mob accusing him of blasphemy in December 2021, the Sri Lankan government expressed its confidence in Imran Khan's government's response.[70] As in the case of Bangladesh, increasing Chinese economic influence within Sri Lanka may also serve to draw these two countries together.[71]

Pakistan has made little inroads with Nepal, which India sees firmly inside its own sphere of influence, recent Chinese inroads notwithstanding. Nepal officially remained neutral in the 1965 war, but it did allow its elite Gurkha troops to fight on the Indian side, as per their contractual obligation. Pakistan broke off relations with Nepal in 1972, when Nepal quickly moved to recognize Bangladesh. What trade had existed between the two countries had largely involved East Pakistan due to their close proximity. In 1980, Nepal sided with India and the USSR in the conflict in Afghanistan, further cementing the distance between the two countries.[72] In 2004, a short window of cooperation opened, as India and other Western powers sharply condemned Nepal's suspension of parliament and authoritarian crackdown on Maoist insurgents. While India froze defense supplies to Nepal, it appears that Nepal in turn looked to China and Pakistan to fill the void.[73] This four-year crisis concluded when the Nepalese government moved in a democratizing direction again and India resumed its weapons sales.[74] Yet another undeclared embargo of Nepal by India in 2015—ostensibly due to changes in Nepal's constitution—led to another falling out between the two neighbors.[75]

Pakistan's relationships with Bhutan and the Maldives are not extensive. Bhutan and Pakistan do not maintain diplomatic missions in each other's country, and India, which views Bhutan as a client state, remains suspicious of any attempt by Pakistan to deepen bilateral relations with Bhutan outside of SAARC.[76] Although the Maldives is majority-Muslim, it has traditionally been much closer to India than Pakistan. Scope for greater involvement with the Maldives opened with the controversial election of President Abdulla Yameen in 2013, who attempted to reorient his country away from India and toward China, and consequently also Pakistan.[77] In early 2018, a crisis ensued when exiled opposition leader Muhammad Nasheed called for Indian intervention in response to a declared state of emergency by the increasingly authoritarian Yameen.[78] After the elections in 2018, however, new president Solih announced a return to its traditional India-centric foreign policy.[79]

Conclusion

While Pakistani policymakers generally claim that they are acting in Pakistan's national interests in a difficult strategic environment, this overview suggests that in accordance with neo-classical realism, self-interested domestic political actors may by impeding the pursuit of its national interest. Domestic political dynamics push Pakistan toward confrontational behavior in its relationship with India, even though the country would benefit from bilateral stability and increased trade. Pakistan should have every interest in allying with Bangladesh to try and balance against Indian hegemony in South Asia, but it finds itself unable even to proffer a full apology for atrocities committed in 1971, a symbolic act without any tangible cost. In their never-ending quest to secure a friendly government in Afghanistan, Pakistani elites have repeatedly relied on political actors that have led to long-term negative consequences for both countries. Conversely, Pakistan's relationship with its more distant South Asian neighbors has generally been constructive, but limited by India's dominance. Increasing Chinese importance in the region may open avenues for Pakistan to project its influence, if political dynamics at home do not get in the way.

Notes

1 The author thanks Hania Khan, Amena Mehmood, and Uzair Gul for research assistance, and Melanie Brasher for proofreading the chapter.
2 See, for instance, Paul S. Kapur, "India and Pakistan's Unstable Peace," 127–152.
3 Abdul Sattar, *Pakistan's Foreign Policy, 1947–2009*," 271–272.
4 Hasan-Askari Rizvi, "Pakistan's Strategic Culture," 319–324.
5 Christine Fair, *Fighting to the End: The Pakistan Army's Way of War*.
6 Brian Rathbun, "A Rose by Any Other Name," 294–321.
7 Ayesha Siddiqa, *Military Inc.: Inside Pakistan's Military Economy*, 138–157.
8 Robert Putnam, "Diplomacy and Domestic Politics: The Logic of Two-Level Games," 427–460.
9 Faizal Yahya, "Pakistan, SAARC, and ASEAN Relations," 346–375. A cursory examination of major foreign policy statements by Pakistan's last two governments indicate that Pakistani policymakers have spent little time envisioning a comprehensive regional foreign policy for South Asia beyond India, Afghanistan, and to a lesser extent Bangladesh.
10 See for instance Sartaj Aziz, "Strategic Vision of Pakistan's Foreign Policy," and *Dawn*, "Read: Full text of Gen Bajwa's Speech at the Islamabad Security Dialogue."
11 Abdul Sattar, *Pakistan's Foreign Policy*, 12–14.
12 Šumit Ganguly, *The Crisis in Kashmir*, 8–13.
13 Šumit Ganguly, *Conflict Unending: India-Pakistan Tensions Since 1947*, 5–6.
14 Reeta Chowdhari Tremblay and Julian Schofield, "Institutional Causes of the India-Pakistan Rivalry," 225–248.
15 Šumit Ganguly, "Deterrence Failure Revisited: The Indo-Pakistani War of 1965," 77–93.
16 T.V. Paul, ed., *The India-Pakistan Conflict: An Enduring Rivalry*, 16.
17 Paul, *The India-Pakistan Conflict: An Enduring Rivalry*.
18 Kapur, "India and Pakistan's Unstable Peace," 143–147.
19 Owen Bennett-Jones, *Pakistan: Eye of the Storm*, 88–100.
20 Abdul Sattar, *Pakistan's Foreign Policy*, 293–297.
21 George Iype, "Pak Military Chiefs Boycott Wagah Welcome"; Steve Coll, "The Back Channel: India and Pakistan's Secret Kashmir Talks."
22 Total insurgent, civilian, and Indian security personnel deaths decreased from a high in the mid-1990s to 1998, and then increased again after Musharraf's accession to power. See "Jammu & Kashmir: Yearly Fatalities 2000-2021" and "Datasheet: Jammu & Kashmir: Fatalities Between 1988–2000."
23 Coll, "The Back Channel: India and Pakistan's Secret Kashmir Talks."
24 Abdul Sattar, *Pakistan's Foreign Policy*, 244–245; Coll, "The Back Channel: India and Pakistan's Secret Kashmir Talks."
25 Stephen Tankel, "Ten Years after Mumbai, the Group Responsible is Deadlier than Ever"; Coll, "The Back Channel: India and Pakistan's Secret Kashmir Talks."
26 Sachin Parashar, "Did Sajjan Jindal Help Set Up Pak Meet?"
27 Cyril Almeida, "The Nawaz and Modi Show."
28 Dexter Filkins, "The Pakistan Dystopia."
29 Aarti Tikoo Singh, "Lashkar-e-Taiba Claims Responsibility for Uri Terror Attack."
30 Cyril Almeida, "Exclusive: Act Against Militants or Face International Isolation, Civilians Tell Military."
31 T. Negeen Pegahi, "From Kargil to Pulwama: How Nuclear Crises Have Changed Over 20 Years," 149–161.
32 Mubarak Zeb Khan, "Pakistan Formally Suspends Trade with India."
33 *Dawn*, "Read: Full text of Gen Bajwa's Speech at the Islamabad Security Dialogue."
34 Ayesha Siddiqa, "Gen Bajwa Wanted a 'Paradigm Shift' with India, but Pakistan Military Isn't Ready."
35 Ashish Shukla, "Pakistan-Bangladesh Relations," 215–217.
36 Zahid Shahab Ahmed and Musharaf Zahoor, "Bangladesh-Pakistan Relations: Hostage to a Traumatic Past."
37 Harry Blair, "Party Overinstitutionalization, Contestation, and Democratic Degradation in Bangladesh," 98–117; Shukla, "Pakistan-Bangladesh Relations."
38 Minorities at Risk Project, "Chronology of Biharis in Bangladesh."

39 Blair, "Party Overinstitutionalization, Contestation, and Democratic Degradation in Bangladesh."
40 Shukla, "Pakistan-Bangladesh Relations"; Minorities at Risk Project, "Chronology of Biharis in Bangladesh."
41 Ahmed and Zahoor, "Bangladesh-Pakistan Relations: Hostage to a Traumatic Past," 43.
42 Shukla, "Pakistan-Bangladesh Relations," 225–226.
43 Shukla, "Pakistan-Bangladesh Relations," 228–231.
44 Ahmed and Zahoor, "Bangladesh-Pakistan Relations: Hostage to a Traumatic Past," 40–45; Shukla, "Pakistan-Bangladesh Relations," 227.
45 Staff Reporter, "Bangladesh Cricket Team Arrives in Lahore."
46 Baqir Sajjad Syed, "In Rare Call to Hasina, Imran Urges Closer Ties with Bangladesh."
47 Baqir Sajjad Syed, "Sheikh Hasina Desires Stronger Trade Ties Between Bangladesh, Pakistan."
48 Harry Blair, "The Bangladesh Paradox," 141–146.
49 The Observatory of Economic Complexity, "China and Bangladesh"; Pieter Wezeman, Alexandra Kuimova, and Semon Wiezeman, "Trends in International Arms Transfers, 2020."
50 Hafizullah Emadi, "Durand Line and Afghan-Pak Relations," 115–116.
51 Avinash Paliwal, "Pakistan-Afghanistan Relations since 2001: There are No Endgames," 194–195.
52 Mujtaba Razvi, "Pak-Afghan Relations since 1947: An Analysis," 34–50.
53 Khalid Nadiri, "Old Habits, New Consequences: Pakistan's Posture toward Afghanistan Since 2001," 133–137.
54 *Ibid.*, 137–139, 159–165.
55 Abdul Sattar, *Pakistan's Foreign Policy*, 207–209.
56 Paliwal, "Pakistan-Afghanistan Relations since 2001," 197–199.
57 Ryan Brasher and Šumit Ganguly, "Militant Islam in South Asia: Past Trajectories and Present Implications," 210–216; Rashid, "Pakistan and the Taliban," 79–89.
58 Paliwal, "Pakistan-Afghanistan Relations since 2001," 201–203.
59 Matthew Rosenberg, "Afghan Spy Chief Defies Labels, Usefully."
60 Paliwal, "Pakistan-Afghanistan Relations since 2001," 207–210.
61 Steve Coll and Adam Entous, "The Secret History of the Diplomatic Failure in Afghanistan."
62 Abbas Nasir, "Big Win, Bigger Challenges."
63 Rezaul Laskar, "Want Good India-Afghanistan Relations, Says Taliban Leader."
64 Ahmad Jibran, "Afghan Taliban Stop Pakistan Army from Fencing International Border."
65 Riaz Khokar and Asma Khalid, "Reviewing Pakistan-Sri Lanka Relations."
66 Sabiha Hasan, "Pakistan-Sri Lanka Relations," 110, 122.
67 Khokar and Khalid, "Reviewing Pakistan-Sri Lanka Relations."
68 Interview with Michael Kugelman, "Can Pakistan and Sri Lanka Find Common Ground beyond the Realm of Defense?"
69 Abdul Ghaffar, "Sri Lanka Team to Tour Pakistan in September in First Visit since 2009 Attack."
70 *Daily Mirror Online*, "Sialkot Incident Will Have No Impact on the Two Countries' Friendly Ties: SL High Commissioner."
71 Interview with Kugelman, 2018.
72 M.D. Dharamdasani, "India as a Factor in Pakistan-Nepal Relations," 16–24.
73 *Rediff News*, "China, Pak Pumping Arms into Nepal."
74 Manesh Chhibber, "Ending Four-Year Freeze, India to Supply Small Arms to Nepal."
75 Vishal Arora, "R.I.P., India's Influence in Nepal."
76 Ramtanu Maitra, "Pakistan's Bhutan Gambit Worries Delhi."
77 Reena Bhardwaj, "'New Cold War' Brewing in Indian Ocean, Says Expert."
78 Press Trust of India, "Maldives Crisis: Mohamed Nasheed Seeks India's Military and Diplomatic Intervention to End Ongoing Turmoil."
79 Mariyam Malsa, "President Solih Reaffirms India-First Policy."

Bibliography

Ahmed, Zahid Shahab, and Musharaf Zahoor. "Bangladesh-Pakistan Relations: Hostage to a Traumatic Past." *Commonwealth and Comparative Politics* 57, no.1 (2019): 31–51.

Almeida, Cyril. "Exclusive: Act Against Militants or Face International Isolation, Civilians Tell Military." *Dawn*, October 6, 2016. https://www.dawn.com/news/1288350/exclusive-act-against-militants-or-face-international-isolation-civilians-tell-military.

Almeida, Cyril. "The Nawaz and Modi Show." *Dawn*, December 27, 2015. https://www.dawn.com/news/1228835/the-nawaz-and-modi-show.

Arora, Vishal. "R.I.P., India's Influence in Nepal." *The Diplomat*, November 25, 2015. https://thediplomat.com/2015/11/r-i-p-indias-influence-in-nepal/.

Bennett-Jones, Owen. *Pakistan: Eye of the Storm*. New Haven: Yale University Press, 2002.

Bhardwaj, Reena. "'New Cold War' Brewing in Indian Ocean, Says Expert." *ANI*, February 23, 2018. https://www.aninews.in/news/world/asia/new-cold-war-brewing-in-indian-ocean-says-expert201802231307570001/.

Blair, Harry. "Party Overinstitutionalization, Contestation, and Democratic Degradation in Bangladesh." In *Routledge Handbook of South Asian Politics: India, Pakistan, Bangladesh, Sri Lanka, and Nepal*, edited by Paul Brass, 98–117. New York: Routledge, 2010.

Blair, Harry. "The Bangladesh Paradox." *Journal of Democracy* 31, no. 4 (2020): 138–150.

Brasher, Ryan, and Šumit Ganguly. "Militant Islam in South Asia: Past Trajectories and Present Implications." In *Afghanistan, Pakistan and Strategic Change*, edited by Joachim Krause, and Charles King Mallory, 213–230. London: Routledge, 2014.

Chhibber, Manesh. "Ending Four-Year Freeze, India to Supply Small Arms to Nepal." *The Indian Express*, December 23, 2009. https://indianexpress.com/article/news-archive/web/ending-fouryear-freeze-india-to-supply-small-arms-to-nepal/.

"China, Pak Pumping Arms into Nepal." *Rediff News*, January 23, 2006. https://www.rediff.com/news/2006/jan/22nepal.htm?print=true.

Coll, Steve, and Adam Entous. "The Secret History of the Diplomatic Failure in Afghanistan." *New Yorker*, December 10, 2021. https://www.newyorker.com/magazine/2021/12/20/the-secret-history-of-the-us-diplomatic-failure-in-afghanistan.

Coll, Steve. "The Back Channel: India and Pakistan's Secret Kashmir Talks." *New Yorker*, February 22, 2009. https://www.newyorker.com/magazine/2009/03/02/the-back-channel.

Dharamdasani, M. "India as a Factor in Pakistan-Nepal Relations." *Journal of Political Science* 1, no. 1 (1998): 16–24.

Emadi, Hafizullah. "Durand Line and Afghan-Pak Relations." *Economic and Political Weekly* 25, no. 28 (1990): 115–116.

Fair, Christine. *Fighting to the End: The Pakistan Army's Way of War*. Oxford: Oxford University Press, 2014.

Filkins, Dexter. "The Pakistan Dystopia." *New Yorker*, January 25, 2016. https://www.newyorker.com/news/news-desk/the-pakistani-dystopia?intcid=mod-latest.

Ganguly, Šumit. "Deterrence Failure Revisited: The Indo-Pakistani War of 1965." *The Journal of Strategic Studies* 13, no. 4 (1990): 77–93.

Ganguly, Šumit. *Conflict Unending: India-Pakistan Tensions since 1947*. New York: Columbia University Press, 2002.

Ganguly, Šumit. *The Crisis in Kashmir: Portents of War, Hopes of Peace*. Cambridge: Cambridge University Press, 1999.

Ghaffar, Abdul. "Sri Lanka Team to Tour Pakistan in September in First Visit since 2009 Attack." *Dawn*, August 14, 2017. https://www.dawn.com/news/1351507.

Hasan, Sabiha. "Pakistan-Sri Lanka Relations." *Pakistan Horizon* 38, no. 2 (1985): 104–128.

Iype, George. "Pak Military Chiefs Boycott Wagah Welcome." *Rediff on the Net*, February 20, 1999. https://www.rediff.com/news/1999/feb/20bus2.htm.

Jibran, Ahmad. "Afghan Taliban Stop Pakistan Army from Fencing International Border." *Reuters*, December 22, 2021. https://www.reuters.com/world/asia-pacific/afghan-taliban-stop-pakistan-army-fencing-international-border-2021-12-22/.

Kapur, S. Paul. "India and Pakistan's Unstable Peace: Why Nuclear South Asia is Not like Cold War Europe." *International Security* 30, no. 2 (2005): 127–152.

Khokar, Riaz, and Asma Khalid. "Reviewing Pakistan-Sri Lanka Relations." *South Asian Voices*, March 22, 2021. https://southasianvoices.org/reviewing-pakistan-sri-lanka-relations/.

Laskar, Rezaul. "Want Good India-Afghanistan Relations, Says Taliban Leader." *Hindustan Times*, August 30, 2021. https://www.hindustantimes.com/india-news/want-good-india-afghanistan-relations-says-taliban-leader-101630260163407.html.

Maitra, Ramtanu. "Pakistan's Bhutan Gambit Worries Delhi." *Asia Times Online Ltd*, November 25, 2004. https://web.archive.org/web/20120802001308/http:/atimes.com/atimes/South_Asia/FK25Df03.html.

Malsa, Mariyam. "President Solih Reaffirms India-First Policy." *The Edition*, June 8, 2019. https://edition.mv/news/10924.

Minorities at Risk Project. "Chronology of Biharis in Bangladesh." 2004. https://www.refworld.org/docid/469f3868c.html.

Nadiri, Khalid. "Old Habits, New Consequences: Pakistan's Posture toward Afghanistan since 2001." *International Security* 39, no. 2 (2014): 132–168.

Nasir, Abbas. "Big Win, Bigger Challenges." *Dawn*, September 19, 2021. https://www.dawn.com/news/1647179.

Paliwal, Avinash. "Pakistan-Afghanistan Relations since 2001: There are No Endgames." In *Pakistan at the Crossroads: Domestic Dynamics and External Pressures*, edited by Christophe Jaffrelot, 191–218. New York: Columbia University Press, 2016.

Parashar, Sachin. "Did Sajjan Jindal Help Set Up Pak Meet?" *The Times of India*, December 26, 2015. https://timesofindia.indiatimes.com/india/did-sajjan-jindal-help-set-up-pak-meet/articleshow/50328947.cms.

Paul, T.V., ed. *The India-Pakistan Conflict: An Enduring Rivalry*. Cambridge: Cambridge University Press, 2005.

Pegahi, T. Negeen. "From Kargil to Pulwama: How Nuclear Crises Have Changed Over 20 Years." *The Washington Quarterly* 42, no. 2 (2019): 149–161.

Press Trust of India. "Maldives Crisis: Mohamed Nasheed Seeks India's Military and Diplomatic Intervention to End Ongoing Turmoil." *Deccan Herald*, February 6, 2018. https://www.deccanherald.com/content/657989/nasheed-seeks-indian-military-intervention.html.

Putnam, Robert. "Diplomacy and Domestic Politics: The Logic of Two-Level Games." *International Organization* 42, no. 3 (1988): 427–460.

Rashid, Ahmed. "Pakistan and the Taliban." In *Fundamentalism Reborn? Afghanistan and the Taliban*, edited by William Maley, 72–89. New York: New York University Press, 1998.

Rathbun, Brian. "A Rose by Any Other Name: Neoclassical Realism as the Logical and Necessary Extension of Structural Realism." *Security Studies* 17, no. 2 (2008): 294–321.

Razvi, Mujtaba. "Pak-Afghan Relations since 1947: An Analysis." *Pakistan Horizon* 32, no. 4 (1979): 34–50.

"Read: Full text of Gen Bajwa's Speech at the Islamabad Security Dialogue." *Dawn*, March 18, 2021. https://www.dawn.com/news/1613207.

Rizvi, Hasan-Askari. "Pakistan's Strategic Culture." In *South Asia in 2020: Future Strategic Balances and Alliances*, edited by Michael Chambers, 305–328. Carlisle, PA: Strategic Studies Institute, 2002.

Rosenberg, Matthew. "Afghan Spy Chief Defies Labels, Usefully." *New York Times*, January 16, 2015. https://www.nytimes.com/2015/01/17/world/asia/afghan-spy-chief-defies-simple-label.html.

Sattar, Abdul. *Pakistan's Foreign Policy, 1947–2009: A Concise History*. Pakistan: Oxford University Press, 2010.

Shukla, Ashish. "Pakistan-Bangladesh Relations." *Himalayan and Central Asian Studies* 19, no. 1–2 (2015), 211–235.

"Sialkot Incident Will Have No Impact on the Two Countries' Friendly Ties: SL High Commissioner." *Daily Mirror Online*, December 6, 2021. https://www.dailymirror.lk/breaking_news/Sialkot-incident-will-have-no-impact-on-the-two-countries-friendly-ties-SL-high-commissioner/108-226287.

Siddiqa, Ayesha. "Gen Bajwa Wanted a 'Paradigm Shift' with India, but Pakistan Military Isn't Ready." *The Print*, April 5, 2021. https://theprint.in/opinion/gen-bajwa-wanted-a-paradigm-shift-with-india-but-pakistan-military-isnt-ready/633822/.

Siddiqa, Ayesha. *Military Inc.: Inside Pakistan's Military Economy*. London: Pluto Press, 2007.

Singh, Aarti Tikoo. "Lashkar-e-Taiba Claims Responsibility for Uri Terror Attack." *The Times of India*, October 25, 2016. https://timesofindia.indiatimes.com/india/Lashkar-claims-responsibility-for-Uri-terror-attack/articleshowprint/55047490.cms?null.

Staff Reporter. "Bangladesh Cricket Team Arrives in Lahore." *Dawn*, January 23, 2020. https://www.dawn.com/news/1529944/.

Syed, Baqir Sajjad. "In Rare Call to Hasina, Imran Urges Closer Ties with Bangladesh." *Dawn*, July 23, 2020. https://www.dawn.com/news/1570633/in-rare-call-to-hasina-imran-urges-closer-ties-with-bangladesh.

Syed, Baqir Sajjad. "Sheikh Hasina Desires Stronger Trade Ties Between Bangladesh, Pakistan." *Dawn*, October 26, 2021. https://www.dawn.com/news/1654016.

Tankel, Stephen. "Ten Years after Mumbai, the Group Responsible is Deadlier than Ever." *War on the Rocks*, November 26, 2018. https://warontherocks.com/2018/11/ten-years-after-mumbai-the-group-responsible-is-deadlier-than-ever/.

The Observatory of Economic Complexity. "China and Bangladesh." Accessed December 17, 2021. https://oec.world/en/profile/bilateral-country/chn/partner/bgd.

Tremblay, Reeta Chawdhuri, and Julian Schofield. "Institutional Causes of the India-Pakistan Rivalry." In *The India-Pakistan Conflict: An Enduring Rivalry*, edited by T.V. Paul, 225–248. Cambridge: Cambridge University Press, 2005.

Wezeman, Pieter, Alexandra Kuimova, and Semon Wezeman. "Trends in International Arms Transfers, 2020." *SIPRI Fact Sheet*, March 2021. https://sipri.org/sites/default/files/2021-03/fs_2103_at_2020.pdf.

Yahya, Faizal. "Pakistan, SAARC, and ASEAN Relations." *Contemporary Southeast Asia* 26, no. 2 (2004): 346–375.

Zeb Khan, Mubarak. "Pakistan Formally Suspends Trade with India." *Dawn*, August 10, 2019. https://www.dawn.com/news/1499076/pakistan-formally-suspends-trade-with-india.

21

INDIA'S RELATIONS WITH HER NEIGHBORS

Chris Ogden

As South Asia's dominant country, how India interacts with her neighbors is of a central significance to the region's stability and standing the world. The subcontinent's geostrategic position amplifies the importance of these relations, with South Asia acting as a bridge between East Asia and West Asia, while also providing geographical access northwards into Central Asia. Furthermore, the region borders the oil-rich Arabian Gulf, and physically dominates the Indian Ocean Region (IOR)—a crucial area for ensuring the energy and trade security of states not only within South Asia but encompassing numerous others in East Asia, Africa, and Europe. India's supremacy versus its immediate periphery is apparent across a range of hard power measures, be it regarding population size, gross domestic product (GDP), military capabilities, or territorial extent. Across all these dimensions, India dwarfs its neighbors both individually and collectively, and as India's first Prime Minister Jawaharlal Nehru resultantly advocated in a speech in 1947, "India, constituted as she is, cannot play a secondary part in the world."[1]

This chapter firstly examines the full spectrum of these dynamics, including the advantages and challenges that they present, as well as how they can be explored via International Relations theory. In its second section, it then investigates India's broad strategic aims toward its neighbors in South Asia, and the influence of the pre- and post-colonial periods upon them. The third section then considers the oscillating approaches that New Delhi has deployed and how these have shifted and evolved between India's political leaders and groupings until the present Modi government. The chapter's conclusions then sum up all of these perspectives.

Regional Dynamics

In terms of population, in 2020, India stood at 1,339 million versus 595 million combined for Pakistan, Bangladesh, Myanmar, Afghanistan, Nepal, Sri Lanka, Bhutan, and the Maldives.[2] Economically, in 2020, India accounted for over 75% of the region's GDP (PPP), which stood at $8,443 billion compared with $2,539 billion for her neighbors.[3] In terms of annual military spending, India also overshadows its neighbors with a budget that stood at $72.88 billion in 2020, while the rest of the region together spent $19.66 billion.[4] Such a disparity in military spending has been apparent in every year since 1947, which has compounded over time to now make India the region's premier military power. As we shall see, New Delhi

DOI: 10.4324/9781003246626-25

289

has periodically deployed this force toward its neighbors and—along with Pakistan—in 1998 developed a nuclear weapons capability. With a landmass of 3,287,263 square kilometers versus a total of 3,172,614 square kilometers for its neighbors combined,[5] India also physically dominates the region. India has both the region's longest land (13,888 kilometers) and sea (7,000 kilometers) borders. Importantly, and notwithstanding the offshore presence of Sri Lanka and the Maldives and the Afghanistan-Pakistan border, India is the only country in South Asia that is connected to *any* of the other countries in South Asia, which results in it being the region's natural fulcrum.

Moreover, India's position gives it a natural authority over the Indian Ocean Region (IOR), which is the world's third largest sea covering 70,560,000 square kilometers or 19.8% of the world's total area. The Indian landmass spearheads down into the IOR, which is also the world's most crucial maritime thoroughfare in terms of both trade security and energy security, accounting for 50% of world maritime trade, 50% of all container traffic, and 70% of the global trade in oil and gas in 2019.[6] These figures underscore the region's, and by extension India's, significance to the global economy. It is for this reason that Nehru summed up India's concerns in this regard when he stated that "'history has shown that whatever power controls the Indian Ocean has, in the first instance, India's sea borne trade at her mercy and, in the second, India's very independence itself.'"[7] In conjunction with her territorial dominance of South Asia, which makes India the region's major land-based economic thoroughfare, this positioning in the IOR furthermore serves to enhance the perception of India's regional centrality—and of it essentially being the region's hegemon—and it being encircled by a constellation of small satellite states.

Notwithstanding this objective and perceived dominance of its home region, India's positioning is on second sight much more nuanced and complex. As such, some factors central to New Delhi's regional supremacy bring additional challenges with them. This is apparent in terms of GDP per capita, whereby India's vast population (amid significant regional disparities) results in an annual figure of $6,100, which is far below that of Sri Lanka ($12,500), Bhutan ($10,900), and the Maldives ($13,000).[8] In addition, having the region's longest land and maritime borders effectively magnifies the threats posed to India not only by its assorted neighbors but also by non-traditional security hazards "in the guise of terrorists, separatists, insurgents, criminal organizations, political and religious activists, tribes, minorities, drug cartels, gangs, dissidents, computer hackers, and any wider groupings and associations that they may collectively form."[9] Moreover, India's overwhelming physical, economic, and military size innately makes it the primary—and expected—threat to her neighbors, especially given New Delhi's penchant to dissuade any interference from external actors in South Asia, as we shall see below. As shown elsewhere in this Handbook, such factors have also had a negative impact on the creation of any meaningful multilateral institutions, resulting in a less-than-well-integrated regional makeup.

As a result, for India, South Asia represents a combination of both strengths and weaknesses, whereby what appears as its natural domain is—for precisely the same factors—simultaneously beset by frictions and challenges concerning New Delhi's position and intentions. As such, despite being one of the fastest growing economic regions in the world, it is also one of the least integrated, and thus embodies a host of dichotomies concerning optimism and pessimism, security and insecurity, hope and fear. From this basis, Destradi's definition of a regional power as "a state which belongs to a region, disposes of superior power capabilities, and exercises an influence on regional neighbours"[10] captures well India's ability to dominate but not totally control South Asia, and is reflected in the policies of successive India's prime ministers. These leaders have sought to maintain India's preeminent position in the region regardless of wider dynamics in the international system or regional power balances. What has influenced how these dynamics are viewed has often been the attitude of different Indian leaders, from the active deterrence and use of force under Indira Gandhi, to the reciprocity and emergent pragmatism of I.K. Gujral, to a combination of these methods continued under Narendra Modi.

As such, in the last decade, the literature on India and her neighbors has focused upon the influence of the ideology of the Hindu nationalist *Bhartiya Janata Party* (BJP) upon India's relations with her neighbors. Often this has emphasized the presence of a more assertive and free-ranging streak in India's regional interactions that rests upon the combination of "military and diplomatic options,"[11] particularly toward Pakistan. Underpinning this arguably more comprehensive approach has been a focus upon mutually sustainable and reciprocal diplomacy and a desire for enhancing connectivity in terms of trade, infrastructure, and trust.[12] All these elements are frequently seen through the five themes of "Pancahmrit" that consist of *samman* (dignity and honor), *samvad* (greater engagement and dialogue), *samriddhi* (shared prosperity), *suraksha* (regional and global security), and *sanskriti evam sabhyata* (cultural and civilizational linkages).[13] Accompanying these beliefs has been a desire "to fulfil Bharat's global responsibilities as the world's most populous youth nation and largest democracy,"[14] which has particular significance in South Asia, given that India is arguably the region's only full-fledged democratic entity. It also has a final significance in that the BJP use the Hindi word Bharat rather than India, indicating their emphasis upon primarily representing Hindus, as shown by their *Hindutva* ideology and the desire for *Akhand Bharat* (undivided India).[15]

It is in this broad context of India's relations with her neighbors that any consideration of applicable theories from International Relations must be made. On face value, and given India's much higher military prowess, realist axioms that the "strong do what they have the power to do and the weak accept what they have to accept"[16] would appear to be highly applicable to the region, especially when bolstered by economic factors. However, given the disparities and tensions noted above concerning how India is regarded as the number one threat by those in the region, as well as—as we will see—the presence of significant levels of contestation and conflict between India and Pakistan, such a theoretical approach is somewhat undercut. In turn, theories relating to liberalism and institutionalism would emphasize how India's economic clout ought to create deep-seated interdependencies upon it throughout the region and result in the creation of binding (and stabilizing) multilateral regimes. Neither of these observations easily fits the South Asian context because of India's asymmetric power capabilities that place it far ahead of its neighbors. Many of these states also have little to offer India economically, and the ongoing specter of unwanted Indian dominance weakens any attempts at building meaningful regional institutions, as does the presence of China (and also the United States) that acts as an alternative to Indian influence (as most clearly shown vis-à-vis Pakistan).

From this basis, a constructivist approach that interconnects domestic identities, norms, and ideologies with foreign policy, and which stresses the importance of history and culture in the formation of these identities, appears to be most applicable. Such an approach provides the means to understanding the foundations of India's key bilateral and regional relations from the perspective of all the states involved. It also allows for an appreciation of the historical roots of India's policy toward South Asia, which we shall see dates in many ways to the colonial period, as well as how differing political identities [primarily from the Indian National Congress (INC) and the BJP] can produce different interpretations of threats and opportunities in the making of foreign policy. At its most useful, such a constructivist approach can be regarded as an ideational lens through which changes in regional and global power balances are to be best understood, and which thus enables a historically informed appreciation of this subject matter.

India's Strategic Aims

According to Destradi, India's main foreign policy goal in South Asia is "the idea of having a 'peaceful and tranquil periphery' ... (that) relate(s) to India's need to concentrate its resources on its own development without being hindered by instability emanating from neighbouring countries."[17] Such a goal belies India's status ambitions as it seeks to reemerge as a great power in international politics, which has been shared by Indian leaders since independence and who have mutually believed that India's strategic position and power potential are of both regional and global importance. Amassing economic power is the key fuel needed to drive such ambitions forward, which can be used in a number of ways to boost India's internal modernization, as well as converted into military, diplomatic, institutional, soft, and other forms of power. It also points to a degree of interdependence, whereby New Delhi "firmly believes that a stable and prosperous South Asia will contribute to India's own prosperity"[18] and can use economic advancement as a win-win mechanism for the region's wider security and wealth.

Such an aim harks back to the pre-colonial period when India accounted for between a third and quarter of all world trade,[19] and could be considered as a major pole in international affairs. From 200 BC until the 15th century, India's empire has gradually spread across and beyond South Asia, and whose "Indianization" was entirely peaceful and based on compassion and mutual exchange, not conquest and domination.[20] Combined with clear anti-colonial and anti-western sentiments, in an address in 1947, Nehru would hark back to such a time, noting that "it is fitting that India should play her part in this new phase of Asian development, ... far too long have we in Asia been petitioners in Western courts and chancelleries. That day must now belong to the past, ... we do not intend to be the playthings of others."[21] An amalgamation of these worldviews can be witnessed under the current BJP government, whereby succeeding economically continues to act as a springboard for India's global ambitions. As Modi stated in 2014, that would mean India "position(ing) itself in a leading role, rather than (as) just a balancing force, globally"[22] and maintaining full autonomy in its internal and external affairs.

As part of this aim, and as a way to assert its regional supremacy, New Delhi actively seeks to discourage any outside influences upon the region, as these alternative sources of power have the potential to debase both India's standing and influence. Similarly to other strategic aims relating to stability and status, this fear directly stems from the period of British imperialism, whereby "the memories of colonial rule contributed to a political culture which privileged the concept of national autonomy, ... (as) the desire to maintain the greatest possible independence in the conduct of India's foreign affairs ... pervaded the country."[23] India had been initially colonized in the 1700s by the East India Company, after a century during which the company had primarily focusing upon trade. As the Mughal Empire declined and the rival French East India Company rose in power, the British East India Company then expanded its territorial control to cover most of the Indian subcontinent. After widespread resentment of British rule led to a popular uprising culminating in the Indian Rebellion of 1857, the British East India Company's rule ended to be directly replaced by the British Crown, which continued to exploit India for its resource wealth and excellent strategic location. India and its capital Delhi then became the center of operations for the Asiatic conqueror as Britain used India's riches to simultaneously make herself a great power and take this status from India.

Once independence was achieved, the memory and "the resentment of imperial rule meant that Indian leaders wanted to avoid alliances with the existing western imperial powers and their close ally, the US."[24] In the earlier decades of the Cold War, this impulse resulted in New Delhi's strategic tilt toward the Soviet Union, and a general suspicion of any state becoming involved in India's immediate region or with any of her neighbors. It also drove a policy of territorial consolidation, with areas that became ambiguous under the 1947 Partition being either reclaimed (Hyderabad and Junagadh in 1947 and Sikkim in 1975) or imperial territories being taken back (Goa in 1961 from Portugal and Pondicherry in 1962 from France). More negatively, the colonial era demarcation of India's borders (mainly the Radcliffe Line and the McMahon Line) led to a series of ongoing border disputes, most seriously between India and Pakistan concerning Kashmir and between India and China concerning Arunachal Pradesh.

The legacy of colonial rule also—in a rather counterintuitive manner—confirmed India's geopolitical importance and the need to control the wider South Asian region. Such a mindset would permeate India's regional policy and included carrying on a tradition of having unequal treaty-based security arrangements with her smaller neighbors. Such arrangements would be set up with Bhutan (in 1949), Nepal (in 1950), Bangladesh (in 1972), and Sri Lanka (in 1987), and by demanding that India should be consulted in all foreign policy decisions, they gave New Delhi decisive influence over the internal and foreign affairs of these smaller South Asian countries. The colonial hangover also influenced attitudes toward the IOR, as policymakers sought to maintain India's influence across the "Curzonian Arc" that stretched from Aden on the east coast of Africa to Singapore on the IOR's eastern fringes. Such influence pertains to western colonizers having invaded India by sea, starting with the Portuguese in 1498, as well as a way—in the present era—to protect vital trade and energy routes. India's setting up of the tri-service Andaman and Nicobar Command in 2001 showed this lasting regional mindset.

Accompanying these inheritances was also a concerted effort by leaders in New Delhi to ensure that "India was more than just a product of British imperial design."[25] These included an emphasis upon India's civilizational basis but also a determination—through the Non-Aligned Movement—to champion "principles of sovereignty, territorial integrity and political independence of States, the rights of peoples to self-determination and non-intervention in matters which are essentially within the jurisdiction of states."[26] Known as "Panchsheel," they helped to project a particular Indian conception of international (and thus regional) affairs, which was also intended to protect India from unwanted external interference. India would also use these principles to extend its own anti-colonial success outwards, so as to encompass and help other entities seeking to end their imperial subjugations. Moreover, they also help us to pinpoint tensions within India's policy toward its neighbors in South Asia, whereby the promotion of such principles are often juxtaposed by a much deeper desire for asserting control.

Oscillating Approaches

As a result of these various strategic aims but also the myriad influences upon them, India's approach to its immediate neighbors has oscillated between her different leaders. In trying to conceptualize these undulations, Destradi's delineation of three types of policy that a regional power can pursue prove to be instructive concerning India and South Asia. These are: (a) imperialism based upon the threat and use of force; (b) practicing hegemonic strategies through the assertion of hard, intermediate or soft power; and (c) leadership, which centers upon enacting a "commonality of goals" between the leading power and its followers.[27] In many ways, the progression through these three types of policy can be seen as a general moderation of Indian foreign policy toward the region that has slowly eschewed—albeit not completely—deploying military power in favor of using more ideational factors such as a focus upon shared values and cultures. From this basis, during the Cold War period, there is arguably evidence that India pursued an imperial policy (while concurrently and vehemently denouncing colonialism). Once this conditioning reality in the international system was removed, New Delhi then appeared to switch to a more hegemonic—and seemingly benevolent—policy in the 1990s and early 2000s. Finally, under Narendra Modi, we can now see an attempt to pull the region's smaller states under the orbit of India's preeminent regional leadership as is apparent within grand narratives about ensuring regional stability through shared prosperity and development.

While the broad contours of this evolution toward the region *as a whole* appear to be applicable, the presence of continued antagonism between India and Pakistan also points to the continued and *simultaneous persistence* of all these approaches, making them act more as a *menu of possible policy choices*, rather than a set of clear-cut phases in New Delhi's behavior toward its region. It is also important to add that as India has become more powerful, especially economically after the slow, ongoing, and successful liberalization of her economy in the 1990s, the bandwidth underpinning these various policy choices has also increased. As such, New Delhi's expanding financial, military, and diplomatic prowess all serve as additional—and ever gestating—variables that influence and inform her regional strategic behavior. Changing global balances of power—most clearly Cold War frictions between the US and the Soviet Union giving way (after a denouement with the War on Terror) to competition between the US and China, as well as the advent of the Asian 21st century—now also shape India's conduct.

The Cold War and Beyond

Upon independence, India's most pressing strategic concern was to ensure the survival and autonomy of its newly sovereign state. Vulnerable not only materially, in that it had much of its natural resources and wealth systematically siphoned out of it over the preceding centuries, India was also vulnerable psychologically, as a result of a prolonged period of violent subjugation by an unwanted external power. As a result, achieving self-reliance in all its affairs—and by any means necessary—became a central mantra to create stability in its neighborhood. This attitude was immediately injected into its regional interactions, as we have already seen by India continuing a colonial-era mindset resting upon seeing the smaller states in South Asia as essentially protectorates that New Delhi had the right to control and marshal for its interests. In this way, Nehru's policy toward these states was "semi-imperial, denying them the very sovereignty that Indian recognised in all other nation states."[28] It also explicitly implied a clear hierarchy in the region whereby India was ranked higher than its other constituent members.

The use of force influenced New Delhi's perspective, which had been happy to use the Indian military to help reclaim the territories of Hyderabad and Junagadh in 1947 so as to aid India's territorial restoration and overall integrity. It would also feature as an early—and ultimately persistent—feature of India-Pakistan relations, primarily concerning the status of Kashmir, whose ownership would be contested from the creation of modern India and Pakistan onwards. As Cohen succinctly notes, the conflict over Kashmir "is as much a clash between identities, imagination and history as it is a conflict over territories, resources and peoples."[29] At its core, the contestation is emblematic of which national identity has legitimacy in the region—India's tolerant, all-inclusive and secular outlook, or Pakistan's more-narrow, Muslim-centric basis. Given that these identities are integral to the very essence of modern India and Pakistan, the status of Kashmir gained a zero-sum, all-or-nothing quality, meaning that it could not be conceded by either side. It is for these reasons that Nehru noted that "we have always regarded the Kashmir problem as symbolic for us, as it has far reaching consequences in India."[30]

India's Relations with Her Neighbors

More broadly, Pakistan is fearful of Indian hegemony in the region that would threaten its own national identity and as such is "the only South Asian state that has tried to resist Indian predominance through military and ideological means."[31] Magnified by the communal effects of Partition in 1947 that had seen 10 million people being resettled across the two new countries and had resulted in at least one million deaths, military conflict would come to punctuate India-Pakistan relations, resulting in direct wars in 1947–1948, 1965, 1971 (mainly centered upon East Pakistan), and 1999. Pakistan's use of insurgents in these conflicts also within Kashmir from 1989 onwards would furthermore underscore Pakistan as a source of instability in the region. Pakistan's acquisition of nuclear weapons, resulting in a nuclear test in 1998, only underscored this perspective, as did the strategic relationship with China dating from the mid-1960s. So close is this relationship, as based upon a shared concern to limit India's regional power, that it would produce mutual territorial, economic, and nuclear exchanges between Pakistan and China. This closeness deeply personified New Delhi's fear of unwanted external influence in South Asia and was augmented by close Pakistan-US ties during the Cold War that resulted in Islamabad receiving billions in US military aid, ostensibly to combat the Soviet Union in Afghanistan, but which could be used to alter the balance of power against India.

Nehru's daughter Indira Gandhi would enshrine the use of force—as both a means of deterrence and as a deployed foreign policy tool—through the "Indira Doctrine." The Doctrine was designed to primarily keep the Cold War superpowers out of South Asia but also allowed India to pursue an interventionist policy should interfering in a regional country be deemed necessary. Crucially, the Indira Doctrine declared that using military force was the core way to ensure the fulfillment of India's other strategic concerns toward South Asia relating to autonomy, stability, and prosperity. Reminiscent of the US's Monroe Doctrine dating from the 19th century, the exclusion of non-regional powers from South Asia served to augment India's regional hegemonic status and can be clearly regarded as an attempt by New Delhi to actively establish their own regional sphere of influence in international affairs. The Indira Doctrine would result in the frequent projection of military power by New Delhi toward India's neighbors, as well as ongoing efforts to continue preserving the IOR as being essentially an "India-only lake."

These projections included a bilateral peace-making operation in Nepal in 1950, as well as the threat of force during a trade dispute between the two sides in 1989–1990 that had also irked New Delhi due to Kathmandu's newfound spirit of independence in defense and foreign affairs. India would further use military force to liberate East Pakistan in 1971, leading to the formation of Bangladesh, which reduced the two-front threat from Pakistan and boosted India's claims to regional hegemony. New Delhi also successfully used military force in 1988 in the Maldives in order to prevent a military coup. The most notorious use of the Indian military relates to the 1987–1990 intervention in the Sri Lankan civil war that ended in abject failure and withdrawal, as well as 1,100 Indian deaths and 2,800 injuries.[32] In a variety of ways, such aggressive interventionism, although appearing to confirm and embolden India's supremacy in the region and among its neighbors, only added to their apprehension about Indian hegemony. Such an outlook would severely impact the South Asian Association for Regional Cooperation (SAARC), which was founded in 1985, and resulted in a deeply embedded fear among India's neighbors that the organization would undermine their political autonomy and sovereignty.

The end of the Cold War provided an opportunity for India to overcome the limitations of New Delhi's explicitly interventionist policy, as well as the impact that it had on regional perceptions toward India. By removing the fractious and dichotomous atmosphere of the previous decades, India's regional relations—as well as global diplomacy more generally—was able to profit from a post-Cold War peace dividend that emphasized mutually beneficial forms of interaction. For India, this meant the adoption of the far less belligerent and far more benevolent "Gujral Doctrine." While not detracting from New Delhi's ambitions to achieve and maintain its preeminent position in South Asia, the Doctrine reimagined India's relations with her neighbors and refashioned them away from being explicitly domineering to being implicitly dominant. The Doctrine rested upon five major new elements: (a) a willingness to grant India's neighbors concessions without expecting reciprocity; (b) instituting agreements based upon equality; (c) improving any negative perceptions of India being a threat to the region; (d) trying to see India's regional relations as not being wholly beholden to security issues with Pakistan; and (e) breaking India away from its South Asian myopia, thus allowing it to enhance its Asia-Pacific relations.[33]

Backing up on this new direction, in the 2000s, India renegotiated treaties with Nepal, Sri Lanka, and Bhutan that were more balanced, increased aid and investment to South Asian states, established Indian Council for Cultural Relations centers throughout the region and created the South Asian Free Trade Agreement (SAFTA) in 2004. The outlier in this regard remained Pakistan, whose relations did not always benefit from such measures. These efforts did, however, reflect the widening array of power sources in Indian foreign policy and New Delhi's combined use of trade, multilateralism, and increasing global standing to fashion a role as an Asian great power. In line with many established powers, ensuring regional stability and asserting regional hegemony was also seen as essential to becoming a power of global standing. It thus further reinforced the importance of South Asia, and New Delhi's relations with each of its neighbors, within the overall outlook, ambitions, and trajectory of Indian foreign policy, which moved from being solely "moralistic to ... slightly more realistic."[34]

Generation Modi

Reflective of India's great power ambitions but also New Delhi's continued quest for regional stability as a way to augment the state's development and modernization goals, when Narendra Modi entered office in 2014, he reached out to South Asia with a "neighborhood first" policy. As part of this policy, Modi invited all the South Asian heads of state to his swearing-in ceremony, enhanced regional connectivity via various infrastructure and technological innovations and visited then Pakistani Prime Minister Nawaz Sharif in Lahore on his birthday.[35] India under the BJP thus sought to continue "carving a benevolent face of India"[36] in South Asia that was based on creating mutually beneficial win-win scenarios, so as to engender a peaceful periphery and common economic development. The latter has become crucial to the BJP's domestic fortunes, therefore intertwining with its regional and international diplomacy, whereby Modi has "repeatedly emphasized the goal of promoting growth and employment generation as the fundamental criterion for a successful foreign policy."[37] Such policies reflect the driving ethos underpinning the five themes of "Pancahmrit." Modi has also recognized the need for the region to have a positive perception of India, noting in 2018 how "connectivity is vital. It does more than enhance trade and prosperity. It unites a region. ... (For connectivity) to succeed, we must not only build infrastructure, we must also build bridges of trust."[38]

Such intentions have, however, been tempered by core *Hindutva*-derived policies that often trumped having a purely benevolent regional outlook in contemporary Indian foreign policy. Protecting the *Hindu Rashtra* and achieving *Akhand Bharat* are both significant in this regard and translate into the greater sense of broken national unity that followed Partition, especially concerning the status of Kashmir. The BJP thus remain dedicated to protecting India's territorial integrity, as fuelled by the threats posed by western colonialism, Islam, Christianity, and capitalism,[39] and a belief that India and its neighboring states form one—culturally linked—nation. These viewpoints have underscored Modi's use of force against some of India's neighbors, including in 2015 when the Indian army launched a covert operation in Myanmar against separatists from Nagaland in India's north-east. In 2016, India also conducted a number of similar "surgical strikes" against militant bases in Pakistan. These actions highlighted how Indian foreign policy and regional diplomacy now rest upon a combination of military and diplomatic options, which Bajpai identifies as a "cooperation-defection dynamic previously largely absent from Indian foreign policy."[40] Notably, New Delhi has been "more forceful in its use of India's military capabilities, especially along the Himalayan border and also enacting stronger responses concerning any incursions by Chinese troops,"[41] such as those in June 2020.

In these ways, India's regional relations under the BJP confirm the presence of a menu of possible policy choices within Indian diplomacy that now acts as a malleable toolbox from which New Delhi can choose depending upon the task at hand. Such strategic flexibility and pragmatism is also evident in Modi's policy toward the IOR, which has included introducing the SAGAR (Security And Growth for All in the Region) initiative. Founded on the expanding presence of the Indian navy, SAGAR functions as a means of augmenting collaboration among India's neighboring states through increasing free trade, combating maritime issues like piracy and terrorism, and developing collective action mechanisms.[42] Building upon the work of his predecessors, Modi's India now strives to be a net security provider for the region, which has been aided by building a naval installation in the Seychelles, exporting indigenously produced Indian naval vessels to Mauritius, and the Indian Navy performing scores of port calls.[43] All of these actions help to create deeper interdependencies between India, South Asia, and the wider IOR, which in turn then assist in the protection of Indian interests and strategic autonomy, particularly versus an ever-more powerful and influential regional actor in the guise of China. Such a policy is also emboldened by—and compliments—closer India-US ties whereby "lining up a coalition against China is, indeed, perhaps the central objective of Modi's foreign policy."[44]

Conclusions: King of All But Master of None

Regardless of the time period under question, India has and will remain to be the most powerful and influential state within South Asia. Part of this dominance—in terms of its territory, population, and resultant economic potential—is largely circumstantial but another part of it is overwhelmingly due to the persistent attitude of India's leaders that India is *and must be* the region's most significant actor. Much of this attitude stems from historical experience, which through the objective of restoring India's glorious past as an unquestioned great power now clearly extends into the future as the guiding trajectory of contemporary Indian foreign policy. In this vein, Nehru's observation that "the burden of the past, the burden of both good and ill, is over-powering, and sometimes suffocating, more especially for those of us who belong to very ancient civilisations like those of India and China"[45] remains exceptionally pertinent, particularly in the context of China's concurrent modern return to international prominence. It is also applicable to continuing India's continued acquisition and accumulation of all sorts of powers—including military, institutional, and diplomatic—that further boost its status ambitions.

Such observations confirm how New Delhi's relationship with its region will continue to be influenced by the interplay between India's global interactions *outside of South Asia* and those with its immediate neighbors *within South Asia*. This interplay will continue to be beset by intrinsic and seemingly inalienable asymmetries between India and her bordering states. It is for this reason that Gupta has astutely argued that "the Indian elephant cannot transform itself into a mouse. If South Asia is to get itself out of the crippling binds of conflicts and cleavages, the six will have to accept the bigness of the seventh. And the seventh, that is India, will have to prove to the six that big can indeed be beautiful."[46] This dynamic will temper India's regional policy and how her leaders decide to use their ever-increasing power in global affairs, and ultimately whether they wish to pursue—returning to Destradi—a foreign policy based upon imperialistic, hegemonic, or community-centered impulses. While shared prosperity and development continue to be South Asia's great opportunity, the potentially destabilizing nature of balance of power politics between India, Pakistan, and China continues to be the persistent threat. Finding a pathway between these two dynamics will be India's continued challenge.

Notes

1 Quoted in Katherine Adeney and Andrew Wyatt, *Contemporary India* (Hampshire: Palgrave, 2010), 217.
2 CIA World Factbook, "Population – Country Comparison," *CIA*, November, 2021, https://www.cia.gov/the-world-factbook/field/population/country-comparison.
3 CIA World Factbook, "Real GDP (PPP) – Country Comparison," *CIA*, November, 2021, https://www.cia.gov/the-world-factbook/field/real-gdp-purchasing-power-parity/country-comparison.
4 "Military Expenditure," SIPRI, 2021, https://www.sipri.org/databases/milex.
5 CIA World Factbook, "Area – Country Comparison," *CIA*, November, 2021, https://www.cia.gov/the-world-factbook/field/area/country-comparison.
6 M.P. Muralidharan, "Economic and Strategic Importance of Sea in Modern Indian Context," *Indian Defence Review*, February 28, 2019, http://www.indiandefencereview.com/spotlights/economic-and-strategic-importance-of-sea-in-modern-indian-context/.
7 Quoted in Don Berlin, "The Rise of India and the Indian Ocean," *Journal of the Indian Ocean Region* 7, no. 1 (2011): 4.
8 CIA World Factbook, "Real GDP (PPP) Per Capita – Country Comparison," *CIA*, November 2021, https://www.cia.gov/the-world-factbook/field/real-gdp-per-capita/country-comparison.
9 Chris Ogden, *Indian National Security* (New Delhi: Oxford University Press, 2017), xviii.
10 Sandra Destradi, *Indian Foreign and Security Policy in South Asia: Regional Power Strategies* (London: Routledge, 2012), 5.
11 Raja Mohan quoted in Kanti Bajpai, "Narendra Modi's Pakistan and China Policy: Assertive Bilateral Diplomacy, Active Coalition Diplomacy," *International Affairs* 93, no. 1 (2017): 72.
12 Constantino Xavier, *Sambandh as Strategy: India's New Approach to Regional Connectivity* (Washington: Brookings Institution India Center, 2020).
13 Navtan Kumar, "BJP's Foreign Policy Based Upon 'Panchamrit' Principles," *The Sunday Guardian*, April 4, 2015, http://www.sunday-guardian.com/news/bjps-foreign-policy-based-on-panchamrit-principles.
14 BJP National Executive Resolution quoted in Kumar, "BJP's."
15 See Chris Ogden, *Hindu Nationalism and the Evolution of Contemporary Indian Security: Portents of Power* (New Delhi: Oxford University Press, 2014), 50–59.
16 Thucydides quoted Chris Ogden, *China & India: Asia's Emergent Great Powers* (Cambridge: Polity, 2017), 105.
17 Destradi, *Indian Foreign Policy*, 60.
18 "India and Neighbours," Ministry of External Affairs, 2017, http://mea.gov.in/india-and-neighbours.htm.
19 Angus Madisson, *The World Economy: Historical Statistics* (Paris: OECD Publishing, 2003), 261.
20 J.C. Van Leur, "On Early Asian Trade," in *Indonesian Trade and Society: Essays in Asian Social and Economic History*, ed. J.C. Van Leur (The Hague: W. van Hoeve Ltd, 1955), 357.

21 Quoted in Surjit Mansingh, *India's Search for Power: Indira Gandhi's Foreign Policy* (New Delhi: Sage Publications, 1984), 14.

22 Narendra Modi, "PM to Heads of Indian Missions," *Indian Press Information Bureau, Prime Minister's Office*, February 7, 2015, http://pib.nic.in/newsite/PrintRelease.aspx?relid=115241.

23 Šumit Ganguly and Manjeet S. Pardesi, "Explaining Sixty Years of India's Foreign Policy," *India Review* 8, no. 1 (2009): 5.

24 Adeney and Wyatt, *Contemporary*, 219.

25 Sinderpal Singh, "From Delhi to Bandung: Nehru, 'Indian-ness' and 'Pan-Asian-ness,'" *South Asia: Journal of South Asian Studies* 34, no. 1 (2011): 57.

26 Hennie Strydom, "The Non-Alignment Movement and the Reform of International Relations," *Max Plank Yearbook of United Nations Law* 11 (2007): 5.

27 Destradi, *Indian Foreign Policy*, 2.

28 Pratap Bhanu Mehta, "Still Under Nehru's Shadow? The Absence of Foreign Policy Frameworks in India," *India Review* 8, no. 3 (2008): 216.

29 Stephen P. Cohen, *India: Emergent Power* (Oxford: Oxford University Press, 2002), 213.

30 Quoted in Ashutosh Varshney, "Contested Meanings: India's National Identity, Hindu Nationalism, and the Politics of Anxiety," *Daedalus* 122, no. 3 (1993): 237.

31 Cohen, *India*, 229.

32 Devin T. Hagerty, "India's Regional Security Doctrine," *Asian Survey* 31, no. 4 (1991): 353–354.

33 Bhabani S. Gupta, "India in the 21st Century," *International Affairs* 73, no. 2 (1997): 308–309.

34 Jaswant Singh, *Defending India* (New Delhi: Palgrave Macmillan, 1998), 47.

35 Mohamed Zeeshan, "Has Modi Given UP on South Asian Cooperation?" *The Diplomat*, February 3, 2020, https://thediplomat.com/2020/02/has-modi-given-up-on-south-asian-cooperation/.

36 Pratip Chattopadhyay, "The Politics of India's Neighbourhood Policy in South Asia," *South Asian Survey* 18, no. 1 (2011): 101.

37 Rajiv Kumar, "The Role of Business in India's Foreign Policy," *India Review* 15, no. 1 (2016): 101.

38 Quoted in Xavier, *Sambandh*.

39 Walter Anderson and Shridhar Damle, *Messengers of Hindu Nationalism: How the RSS Reshaped India* (London: Hurst, 2019), 157.

40 Bajpai, "Modi's," 69.

41 Chris Ogden, "Tone Shift: India's Dominant Foreign Policy Aims under Modi," *Indian Politics and Policy* 1, no. 1 (2018): 13.

42 Shi Hongyuan, "The Indian Ocean Policy of the Modi Government," *China International Studies* 69, no. 2 (2018): 87–90.

43 Alyssa Ayres, *Our Time Has Come: How India Is Making Its Place in the World* (New York: Oxford University Press, 2020), 103–105.

44 Bajpai, "Modi's," 91.

45 Jawaharlal Nehru, *The Discovery of India* (New York: Oxford University Press, 1989), 36.

46 Bhabani Sen Gupta, "Tamil-Sinhala Conflict is Not India's Creation," *India Today*, April 30, 1984. https://www.indiatoday.in/magazine/guest-column/story/19840430-tamil-sinhala-conflict-is-not-india-creation-803002-1984-04-30.

Bibliography

Adeney, Katherine, and Andrew Wyatt. *Contemporary India*. Hampshire: Palgrave, 2010.

Anderson, Walter, and Shridhar Damle. *Messengers of Hindu Nationalism: How the RSS Reshaped India*. London: Hurst, 2019.

Ayres, Alyssa. *Our Time Has Come: How India Is Making Its Place in the World*. New York: Oxford University Press, 2020.

Bajpai, Kanti. "Narendra Modi's Pakistan and China Policy: Assertive Bilateral Diplomacy, Active Coalition Diplomacy." *International Affairs* 93, no. 1 (2017): 69–91.

Berlin, Don. "The Rise of India and the Indian Ocean." *Journal of the Indian Ocean Region* 7, no. 1 (2011): 1–31.

Chattopadhyay, Pratip. "The Politics of India's Neighbourhood Policy in South Asia." *South Asian Survey* 18, no. 1 (2011): 93–108.

CIA World Factbook. "Area – Country Comparison." *CIA*, November, 2021. https://www.cia.gov/the-world-factbook/field/area/country-comparison.

CIA World Factbook. "Population – Country Comparison." *CIA*, November, 2021. https://www.cia.gov/the-world-factbook/field/population/country-comparison.

CIA World Factbook. "Real GDP (PPP) – Country Comparison." *CIA*, November, 2021. https://www.cia.gov/the-world-factbook/field/real-gdp-purchasing-power-parity/country-comparison.

CIA World Factbook. "Real GDP (PPP) Per Capita – Country Comparison." *CIA*, November, 2021. https://www.cia.gov/the-world-factbook/field/real-gdp-per-capita/country-comparison.

Cohen, Stephen P. *India: Emergent Power*. Oxford: Oxford University Press, 2002.

Destradi, Sandra. *Indian Foreign and Security Policy in South Asia: Regional Power Strategies*. London: Routledge, 2012.

Ganguly, Šumit, and Manjeet S. Pardesi. "Explaining Sixty Years of India's Foreign Policy." *India Review* 8, no. 1 (2009): 4–19.

Gupta, Bhabani S. "India in the 21st Century." *International Affairs* 73, no. 2 (1997): 297–314.

Gupta, Bhabani Sen. "Tamil-Sinhala Conflict is Not India's Creation." *India Today*, April 30, 1984. https://www.indiatoday.in/magazine/guest-column/story/19840430-tamil-sinhala-conflict-is-not-india-creation-803002-1984-04-30.

Hagerty, Devin T. "India's Regional Security Doctrine." *Asian Survey* 31, no. 4 (1991): 351–363.

Hongyuan, Shi. "The Indian Ocean Policy of the Modi Government." *China International Studies* 69, no. 2 (2018): 86–112.

Kumar, Navtan. "BJP's Foreign Policy Based Upon 'Panchamrit' Principles." *The Sunday Guardian*, April 4, 2015. http://www.sunday-guardian.com/news/bjps-foreign-policy-based-on-panchamrit-principles.

Kumar, Rajiv. "The Role of Business in India's Foreign Policy." *India Review* 15, no. 1 (2016): 98–111.

Leur, J.C. Van. "On Early Asian Trade." In *Indonesian Trade and Society: Essays in Asian Social and Economic History*, edited by J.C. Van Leur, 350–362. The Hague: W. van Hoeve Ltd, 1955.

Madisson, Angus. *The World Economy: Historical Statistics*. Paris: OECD Publishing, 2003.

Mansingh, Surjit. *India's Search for Power: Indira Gandhi's Foreign Policy*. New Delhi: Sage Publications, 1984.

Mehta, Pratap Bhanu. "Still Under Nehru's Shadow? The Absence of Foreign Policy Frameworks in India." *India Review* 8, no. 3 (2008): 209–233.

"Military Expenditure." SIPRI, 2021. https://www.sipri.org/databases/milex.

Ministry of External Affairs. "India and Neighbours." *Ministry of External Affairs*, 2017. http://mea.gov.in/india-and-neighbours.htm.

Modi, Narendra. "PM to Heads of Indian Missions." *Indian Press Information Bureau, Prime Minister's Office*, February 7, 2015. http://pib.nic.in/newsite/PrintRelease.aspx?relid=115241.

Muralidharan, M.P. "Economic and Strategic Importance of Sea in Modern Indian Context." *Indian Defence Review*, 28 February, 2019. http://www.indiandefencereview.com/spotlights/economic-and-strategic-importance-of-sea-in-modern-indian-context/.

Nehru, Jawaharlal. *The Discovery of India*. New York: Oxford University Press, 1989.

Ogden, Chris. "Tone Shift: India's Dominant Foreign Policy Aims Under Modi." *Indian Politics and Policy* 1, no. 1 (2018): 3–23.

Ogden, Chris. *China & India: Asia's Emergent Great Powers*. Cambridge: Polity, 2017.

Ogden, Chris. *Hindu Nationalism and the Evolution of Contemporary Indian Security: Portents of Power*. New Delhi: Oxford University Press, 2014.

Ogden, Chris. *Indian National Security*. New Delhi: Oxford University Press, 2017.

Singh, Jaswant. *Defending India*. New Delhi: Palgrave Macmillan, 1998.

Singh, Sinderpal. "From Delhi to Bandung: Nehru, 'Indian-ness' and 'Pan-Asian-ness.'" *South Asia: Journal of South Asian Studies* 34, no. 1 (2011): 51–64.

Strydom, Hennie. "The Non-Alignment Movement and the Reform of International Relations." *Max Plank Yearbook of United Nations Law* 11 (2007): 1–46.

Varshney, Ashutosh. "Contested Meanings: India's National Identity, Hindu Nationalism, and the Politics of Anxiety." *Daedalus* 122, no. 3 (1993): 227–261.

Xavier, Constantino. *Sambandh as Strategy: India's New Approach to Regional Connectivity*. Washington: Brookings Institution India Center, 2020.

Zeeshan, Mohamed. "Has Modi Given UP on South Asian Cooperation?" *The Diplomat*, February 3, 2020. https://thediplomat.com/2020/02/has-modi-given-up-on-south-asian-cooperation/.

22

REINVENTING NON-ALIGNMENT IN SOUTH ASIA

The Foreign Policies of Nepal and the Maldives

Nicolas Blarel and Constantino Xavier

Introduction

From the end of the British Indian empire up to 2010, the South Asian region resembled a unipolar system with a highly unequal distribution of material capacities, and characterized by India as the sole pole and all other regional actors lagging behind.[1] The last decade, however, has seen a series of international changes with the increasing economic involvement of China in South Asia, in conjunction with domestic economic and political developments in most South Asian states. This chapter focuses on explaining the evolution of the foreign policies of two small South Asian states, Nepal and the Maldives. Up to the mid-2000s, both Nepal and the Maldives saw their external policies mainly constrained, if not dictated, by the decisions and actions of India. This chapter aims at two key questions related to the changing regional order: First, how has this Indian influence specifically shaped the foreign policies of both South Asian states? Second, how have the domestic and regional changes over the last 15 years, such as political reforms in both countries and the rise of China, led to any shift in the external behaviors of both Nepal and the Maldives?

To address these questions and to account for the continuities and transformations in the foreign policy approaches of Nepal and the Maldives over the last 70 years, this chapter will build on a series of theoretical approaches that varyingly highlight the shifting distribution of material power in the region, the configuration and role of institutions and economic interdependence, and the influence of domestic politics over the two states' foreign policy preferences. This chapter also focuses on these two states as they share historical and contemporary characteristics. Both countries have inherited institutional legacies of the British Indian empire that have subsequently shaped their interactions with India and other South Asian states. Both are second-tier states in the South Asian regional system dominated in all material indicators by India, and their low state capacities have made them particularly vulnerable to external influence. Over the last two decades, both states have also undergone a rapid transition in their domestic political systems, with the adoption of new constitutions in 2015 (Nepal) and 2008 (Maldives), which have provided greater power to competitive multiparty legislatures. Finally, both states have developed important economic and strategic ties with China over the last decade.

DOI: 10.4324/9781003246626-26

The remainder of this chapter is as follows. The first section briefly reviews existing theoretical arguments used to explain the foreign policy choices of small South Asian states. The two subsequent sections then build on these approaches to account for the evolution of the foreign policies of Nepal and the Maldives. Finally, a concluding section summarizes and compares the general findings of the chapters and suggests potential directions for the foreign policy orientation of both states.

Revisiting the Scholarship on South Asia's Small States' Foreign Policy Behavior

When accounting for the foreign policies of small South Asian states like Nepal and the Maldives, the dominant focus has long been on the realist paradigm. This contends that structural propensities of the South Asian regional system, such as capabilities asymmetry in favor of India, compel small South Asian states to either "balance" against or "bandwagon" with India in order to maximize their security and foreign policy autonomy.[2] Recent refinements of the "balancing" argument have noted that small South Asian states have engaged in a more subtle array of strategies to avoid direct confrontation with India and to develop more autonomous foreign policy approaches.[3] Within this realist scholarship, *strategic hedging* has been an oft-used concept to define small states' attempt to maintain some degree of strategic autonomy by balancing economic and security interests amid great power competition.[4] The evolving foreign policy positions of Nepal and the Maldives amid growing China-India rivalry in South Asia have been experimenting with this balancing behavior to increase their maneuvering ground.

By contrast, liberal institutionalists have held that regular and institutionalized interactions have lowered transaction costs and information asymmetries between South Asian states. According to this argument, the important power disparities in South Asia have incentivized small South Asian states to support the creation of the South Asian Association for Regional Cooperation (SAARC) in the 1980s. Efforts to develop trade agreements in the 1990s not only sought to formally and informally bind India through multilateral rules, norms, and procedures but also to develop previously limited trade ties among South Asian states.[5] India's shift to a liberalized economy and its faster growth rate since the early 1990s have also led small South Asian states to view India as an opportunity for trade and a source of investment rather than as a threat.[6] However, trade between each of the smaller states and India as well as the rest of the region has not increased significantly. South Asia thus remains one of the world's least politically and economically integrated regions, and it is, therefore, unclear to what extent the objectives and incentives toward regional cooperation have shaped the foreign policy of Nepal or the Maldives.[7]

Finally, building on another liberal argument stressing that domestic ideas, interests, and institutions influence state behavior by shaping state preferences, another line of scholarship has emphasized that changes in domestic politics have often correlated with shifts in foreign policy orientations in India or other South Asian states.[8] The focus is therefore on the evolving domestic political bargaining environment that enables or constrains the options of political elites and thereby ultimate foreign policy choices. Following this line of inquiry, this chapter also examines whether and how domestic political institutional and societal changes in Kathmandu and Malé have correlated with changes in foreign policy preferences.

In the following two sections, this chapter assesses which of these theoretical schools and varying emphases on material distribution of power, regional institutions and trade, and domestic politics, or a combination thereof, can best explain the external behaviors of Nepal and the Maldives.

Nepal's New Foreign Policy

Despite being South Asia's oldest independent state, Nepal has a long history of limited sovereignty and foreign policy dependence. Its landlocked situation in the Himalayas, at the crossroads of the Indian subcontinent and the Tibetan plateau, has compelled Nepal to adopt different balancing policies from the late 18th to the early 20th century, which have been described as a "strategy for survival."[9]

With India's independence in 1947, followed by the annexation of Tibet by the People's Republic of China (PRC), Nepal further lost strategic autonomy, entering a period of security and economic dependence on India. The India-China war of 1962 was followed by occasional Chinese economic assistance and diplomatic support for Nepal during political crises, yet these were never enough to impede Kathmandu's gravitation into New Delhi's sphere of influence.

From the 1960s until the 2000s, Nepal's foreign policy thus froze together with the postcolonial order in South Asia, under the rule of kings Mahendra (1956–1972) and Birendra (1972–2001). The country's external relations were then marked by three factors of continuity, two of which are at the structural level and one at the domestic.

First, Nepal remained in a position of structural dependence on India. Kathmandu's limited attempts to push against India's regional hegemony all failed, including proposals to declare Nepal a neutral "zone of peace" or by importing defense supplies from China to reduce its security dependence on India.[10]

Second, Nepal's foreign policy was constrained by the country's economic insulation and inability to foster regional linkages and institutions with other South Asian countries, fully dependent on transit trough India. In the 1980s, Kathmandu's early experiments with economic liberalization and its support to institutionalize regional cooperation through SAARC had limited success.[11]

The third line of continuity in Nepal's foreign policy related to the domestic stability and authoritarian order until the 2000s. Nepal's foreign policy was the prerogative of the monarch and a restricted elite, with a marginal group of democratic dissidents being either imprisoned or forced into exile.[12] Since the 2000s, however, Nepal's foreign policy has been witnessing a rapid transformation on all these three levels.

Exploring a More Permissive Regional Power Distribution

After having been frozen for decades, the India-centric distribution of power in South Asia began eroding in the late 2000s with the growing footprint of China and of other extra-regional actors. Nepal has turned into one of the main sites of friction between India and China's increasingly overlapping spheres of influence.[13] Less exposed to the concentration of power in New Delhi, Kathmandu has revived its old balancing strategies as a small state to regain autonomy, maximize its "transactional value," and recover its "geostrategic centrality."[14] From a structural realist perspective, Nepal's foreign policy preoccupation in balancing through extra-regional diversification reflects its priority to mitigate India's still predominant power in South Asia.

China assumes the most important role, especially after Nepal signed on to the Belt and Road Initiative (BRI) (2017) and was showered with loans and grants from Beijing to modernize its economy and deepen security cooperation. When faced with an informal economic blockade from India during the 2015 constitutional crisis, Kathmandu pushed for alternative trade routes with China, leading to a series of agreements to enhance trans-Himalayan connectivity and cross-border infrastructure.[15] Nepal–China bilateral trade subsequently surged and, in 2019, Xi Jinping became the first Chinese leader to visit Nepal in more than 20 years. In 2018, Nepal and China had held their first-ever military exercise and, in 2021, Nepal joined a Chinese-led initiative to deepen cooperation with South Asia, further riling India.[16]

Beyond China, Nepal's balancing strategy has also focused on diversifying relations beyond Asia, particularly by establishing new diplomatic relations with countries in Africa, Europe, and the Gulf regions. Kathmandu has also deepened ties with other global and regional powers, including Japan, the United Kingdom, the European Union, and Turkey. In 2017, it signed one of its largest developmental agreements with the United States, comprising a $500 million grant for its power and road sectors. Reflecting the geostrategic rationale of the deal, one analyst underlined that "Nepal needs a strong US presence to forestall the possibility of the country's fate being decided by (or between) its two giant neighbors."[17] In an increasingly competitive regional order, the main priority of Nepal's foreign policy has thus been to reduce its traditional dependence on India and maximize the benefits of a more permissive, competitive, and flexible regional order.

Economic Development through Regional Interdependence and Institutions

A second shift in Nepal's foreign policy relates to its economic modernization and investment in new cooperative institutions to deepen regional interdependence. Rather than extra-regional balancing, in which Kathmandu seeks alignment with China and others to reduce its reliance on India, this approach focuses on Nepal as an inter-regional economic link between its two giant neighbors. Sangeeta Thapliyal thus notes that this attempt to "redefine" Nepal's foreign policy puts "new emphasis on connectivity and economic development."[18] Targeting an average economic growth rate of 10%, Nepal aims to graduate from its least developed country status by 2022, achieve the Sustainable Development Goals and become a middle-income country by 2030.[19]

Nepal's foreign policy has thus sought to position the country as a trans-Himalayan hub or economic corridor. This attempts to maximize the country's strategic role through economic linkages between the Eurasian hinterland and the Indian subcontinent and Indian Ocean regions. During his 2018 visit to China, then Prime Minister K.P. Sharma Oli thus spoke of Nepal "as a bridge between our two neighbours" and the objective "to move from the state of a land-locked to a land-linked country through the development of adequate cross-border connectivity."[20] This geoeconomic vision is driven by an attempt to revive Nepal's historical role as a pivot state at the heart of trans-Himalayan commercial routes between the Indian and Chinese economies.

Kathmandu's emphasis on economic interdependence can also be observed from a liberal institutionalist perspective. As an alternative to SAARC, which remains stagnated since 2016 due to India-Pakistan hostilities, Nepal's foreign policy has persisted by reorienting its cooperative efforts. In 2018, it hosted the fourth summit for The Bay of Bengal Initiative for Multi-Sectoral Technical and Economic Cooperation (BIMSTEC). This seven-member regional organization includes Myanmar and Thailand and thus caters to Kathmandu's growing interest to connect eastwards with the Southeast Asian economies. The BBIN Initiative, also including Bangladesh, Bhutan, and India, has additionally played an important role to push for quadrilateral, sub-regional cooperation in the trade, transit, and energy sectors. Nepal has further developed ties with other regional institutions to deepen economic cooperation, including with the Asian Development Bank's South Asia Subregional Economic Cooperation (SASEC) and by joining the Asian Infrastructure and Investment Bank (AIIB) in 2016.

Adjusting to Democratic Transition and Political Competition

Nepal's contemporary foreign policy can also be explained by a third transformation relating to the domestic dimension of its recent political transition. This democratization process began in the 1990s but accelerated in the late 2000s.[21] Traditionally a quasi-monopoly of Nepali kings and elites until the 1990s, foreign policy-making has since then been influenced by an increasingly large number of competing interest groups.[22]

Especially after the establishment of its federal republic in 2008, followed by the 2015 constitution, Nepal's external alignments have been shaped by sharp political competition. With ten central governments in ten years amid complex coalition politics, now also at the provincial level, weak state capacity has further exposed Nepal's foreign policy to volatility and paralysis. [23] Political liberalization, partisan competition, and nationalist sentiments have had paradoxical effects on foreign policy, including a growing alignment with autocratic China and divergences with democratic partners such as India or the United States.[24]

The more striking example of the effects of democratization on foreign policy relates to a bilateral agreement signed with the United States, in 2017, for a USD $500 million grant to develop the power and road sectors. Despite being a purely developmental project, the Millennium Challenge Compact (MCC) was delayed repeatedly due to concerns about its relation to Washington's Indo-Pacific strategy and alleged military intent to counter China and curtail Nepal's foreign policy autonomy.[25] No other Nepali foreign policy issue has played such a politically salient and pernicious role in recent decades. The controversy about the MCC stands in stark contrast to Nepal's decision to sign on to China's BRI, also in 2017. There was no significant political criticism even after China failed to deliver on several BRI projects promised and, in 2021, intensified its interference in Nepal's politics.[26]

This holdup in an important development partnership with a democratic partner was the result of political competition, exposing foreign policy as an attractive ground for partisan mobilization. As observed by Tika Dhakal, the "current divisions over the MCC are partly a clamor for [political] opportunity, and are partly based on ideology," with political parties "using it as a tool to boost their nationalistic credentials and strengthen their political position.[27]

Maldives' Increasingly Contested Foreign Policy Orientation

The Maldives only gained complete independence from British rule in 1965.[28] The newly independent state was intrinsically vulnerable given its small land size (approximately 1,200 islands), population size, and GDP. It thereby depended on external support for its security and economic development. This led the Maldives to quickly establish diplomatic relations with India in 1965. India also viewed the security of former British Island protectorates as part of its historical legacy. As former Indian Foreign Secretary Shyam Saran wrote: "With respect to the island countries of Sri Lanka and the Maldives, India inherited the mandate of providing for their security as British power receded."[29] However, in spite of Indian designs and the prevailing material asymmetry, the Maldives did not bandwagon with India and initially tried to maintain a diversified and autonomous foreign policy, notably by establishing diplomatic ties with China in 1972.[30]

Following a liberal-institutionalist logic, the Maldives also applied in the 1970s to become the member of various multilateral fora such as the UN, the Commonwealth, the Non-Alignment Movement, and it was a founding member of the SAARC. The quest for foreign policy autonomy was one of the drivers for the Maldives to join these organizations and notably to support the creation of SAARC, as it could provide a means to partly check Delhi's hegemonic ambitions. Despite its structural fragility, the Maldives also resisted the use of its territory by any external power. It for instance rejected a proposal by the Soviet Union to lease one of its islands. Initially, the Maldives did not have any special strategic relationship with India and developed trade relations with most South Asian states, especially with Sri Lanka due to the geographical proximity.[31]

However, this attempt at maintaining some foreign policy autonomy came to an abrupt end after India sent paratroopers to assist then President Abdulla Gayoom fight back an attempted coup in 1988. The Maldives, under Gayoom (1978–2008), chose to build a friendly relationship with India. From 1991 onward, India became a net security provider for the Maldives after initiating the "Dosti" joint safeguard operation exercises. Since 2013, the Maldives has also been linked with India and Sri Lanka in the Trilateral Maritime Security Cooperation agreement.[32] Besides security ties, India has also provided significant economic aid and participated in several infrastructure programs in the Maldives since the 1990s. India also replaced Sri Lanka as the Maldives' closest bilateral trade partner. In parallel, Maldivian efforts to secure diplomatic support to address its security vulnerabilities did not lead to any substantive outcomes other than some UN General Assembly resolutions that offered only non-binding acknowledgments of the special vulnerabilities of small states like the Maldives. Yet, the closer alignment with India was never explicitly articulated as a strategy in order to leave some strategic space for the Maldives to develop ties with Pakistan and the Gulf states.

Growing Chinese Presence

The international situation for the Maldives drastically changed with the growing economic and financial involvement of China in South Asia. Both states established diplomatic ties in 1972, but Beijing only opened an embassy in Malé in 2011. Prior to the COVID pandemic, China provided up to a third of annual tourist arrivals in a state that depends heavily on its tourism industry.[33] China has also emerged over the last decade as the largest investor in the Maldives, notably in infrastructure projects such as the "China-Maldives Friendship Bridge" connecting the capital Malé and the nearby island of Hulhumale where the international airport, also built through Chinese support, is located.[34]

The airport deal was especially controversial as the then Waheed government abruptly cancelled the initial contract with Indian companies in 2012, invoking "technical, financial and legal" issues. The opposition claimed the cancelation occurred to appease anti-India elements of Waheed's political coalition and Delhi viewed this as signaling a shift toward China.[35] In 2014, the Maldives formally joined the Maritime Silk Road Initiative and then signed in 2017 a free trade agreement with China, becoming the second South Asian state to do so after Pakistan.[36] China also expanded its maritime presence in the Maldives through call of ports and investments in port development projects. In December 2017, China and the Maldives decided to set up a Joint Ocean Observation Station in 2018.

Given the longstanding military ties between the Maldives and India, Delhi expressed concerns about the port visits and the Joint Observation Station, which could have military applications. Furthermore, the Maldivian government requested in 2018 for India to terminate its military cooperation and to withdraw the two military helicopters support it had leased to Malé since 2013. India refused to recall the helicopters and personnel. India was reportedly warned by China not to intervene in this crisis, notably by sending 11 Chinese warships, including multiple destroyers and frigates.[37] This diplomatic crisis marked the lowest point in India-Maldives ties.

Some scholars have perceived the Maldives' embrace of Chinese investments as a typical example of strategic hedging behavior.[38] The competition between India and China gave the Maldives new options to overcome or at least mitigate the vulnerabilities stemming from its traditional asymmetric relationship with India as well as to extract new strategic dividends. The problem is that argument has almost exclusively focused on the bargaining or hedging strategies of the Maldives as a result of regional systemic factors and has therefore mainly overlooked the impact of domestic politics.

Democratization and Polarization

What is important to note is that the growing Chinese involvement in the Maldives happened alongside a transformative political phase at the national level. The first democratic elections were held in 2008, in which Mohamed Nasheed, leader of the Maldivian Democratic Party (MDP), defeated the traditionally pro-India Gayoom, who had been in power for 30 years. However, Nasheed was forced to resign in 2012, sparking a political crisis. Following international criticism, Nasheed's replacement, Mohammed Waheed Hassan, praised China for its non-interference while criticizing "other influential countries" for meddling in Maldivian affairs.[39] Following another election, Nasheed lost to the Progressive Party (PPM)'s Abdullah Yameen. While Nasheed had gradually improved economic ties with China, Yameen (2013–2018) broke with the Maldives' traditional deference toward Indian interests and openly encouraged further Chinese investments.[40]

This led the domestic political opposition, the MDP, to raise concerns that Maldives could fall into a "debt trap." Some estimates showed that overall Chinese debt was close to $3 billion, a considerable amount for a country whose GDP in 2017 was estimated at $4.9 billion.[41] Major Chinese infrastructure projects were considered to be pushing to this severe debt situation. In addition, Chinese companies were accused of seizing Maldivian land in the name of development assistance, a move that was facilitated by the Yameen government, which amended the constitution and land law in a rushed 48-hour parliamentary session to allow foreign ownership in 2015. This expedited process, which bypassed traditional constitutional reform channels of consultation, was interpreted by India and the Maldivian political opposition as evidence of a favor to Chinese companies that could acquire land and eventually set up military bases.[42]

As a result, as expected by traditional liberal arguments emphasizing the influence of societal interests and preferences over foreign policy, the increasingly politicized and polarized debate over China's influence in Maldivian politics decisively shaped the Maldives' foreign policy debate in the 2010s. Nasheed, who came to power following the first democratic elections in the history of Maldives in 2008, was seen to be close to India. Later, political actors with clear pro-China leanings, such as Mohammed Waheed Hassan (2012–2013) and Abdulla Yameen (2013–2018), emerged and pursued closer economic and political ties with Beijing despite claiming that the Maldives continued to follow an "India first" policy. From 2012 to 2018, the opposition parties, notably the MDP, accused the Yameen government of locking the Maldives into a situation of overreliance on Chinese investments.

The 2018 electoral defeat of Maldives President Yameen was another important illustration of a growing India-China proxy war between Maldivian political factions. Yameen's proximity to Beijing and allegations of corruption were reportedly critical to his defeat. The elections resulted in the unexpected landslide parliamentary victory of the opposition led by Ibrahim Mohamed Solih (MDP). The Solih government stated it would renegotiate debt repayments with China, threatened to halt Chinese projects (including the Joint Observatory), and asserted a reset of ties with India.[43] When it took power, the Solih government also accused the prior government of corruption and accepting kickbacks from Chinese contractors, notably in the context of the construction of the China-Maldives Friendship Bridge. Another highly publicized deal, the Free Trade Agreement was also reconsidered by the new government given its opposition to its terms not being beneficial to the Maldivian fishing industry.

The new government also signaled a recalibration of its foreign policy toward India, which India quickly welcomed. In November 2018, Indian Prime Minister Narendra Modi made a visit to the Maldives to attend Solih's swearing-in-ceremony. Solih's first overseas visit was also to India in December 2018. During the visit, Modi announced a US$1.4 billion loan to the Maldives to pay its debt to China. In a show of diplomatic support, India also backed the Maldives' membership of the Indian Ocean Rim Association. In 2019, Modi began his second term with a visit to the Maldives. Beyond the symbolical visits, India provided both funds (notably a US$800 million Line of Credit Agreement) and technical assistance to civic infrastructure projects, notably in the Greater Malé Connectivity Project. The two countries also signed an agreement to share White Shipping Information between the Indian Navy and the Maldives National Defence Force. In a 2020 visit, the External Affairs Minister S. Jaishankar announced a financial package of US$250 million to support the Maldives' efforts to fight against the COVID-19 pandemic and announced the start of a direct cargo ferry service between India and the Maldives. In a following 2021 visit, Jaishankar finalized an agreement to develop, support, and maintain a Maldives National Defence Force (MNDF) Coast Guard Harbour at Sifvaru (Uthuru Thila Falhu, or UTF).

However, the UTF agreement was criticized by the political opposition led by Yameen as putting the national sovereignty of the Maldives in danger. In 2020, the Maldives' opposition coalition of the Progressive Party of Maldives and the People's National Congress held a number of rallies across the island country to protest what they call "selling off the Maldives" to India, marking the escalation of an "India Out" campaign. The ruling MDP accused China of secretly funding the "India Out" campaign to stir up the Maldives' domestic politics, a charge that was denied by the Chinese ambassador.[44]

As a result, given these political pressures from the "India Out" campaign and the importance of existing Chinese investments and of Chinese tourism for the Maldives, the new Maldivian government did not completely cut ties with Beijing. In 2019, the Maldives' Foreign Minister mentioned to the Xinhua News Agency that heightened cooperation between China and the Maldives had been mutually beneficial and that China would remain an important economic partner for the Maldives. In September 2019, Solih visited Beijing where he discussed strengthening relations between the two countries. The Maldives then announced in 2020 that the Chinese government had agreed to partially suspend debt repayment for a period of four years.[45] It is also important to note that the Solih government also diversified further its strategic options by also developing closer ties with Japan and the US. The Maldives notably signed a military agreement with the US in September 2020 and Secretary of State Michael Pompeo visited Malé in October 2020.[46]

Conclusion

From their independence up to the mid-2000s, due to historical and institutional legacies of the British Indian empire and the prevailing material asymmetry, Nepal and the Maldives have had no other choice but to follow a bandwagoning strategy with the neighboring hegemon, India. While the two small South Asian states have been unable to advance an independent foreign policy agenda, its political elites have been dissatisfied with their underlying vulnerability to Indian influence. This led them to develop strategies to balance India's influence,

Reinventing Non-Alignment in South Asia

such as trying to develop economic and institutionalized ties with other South Asian states, notably through SAARC, or by courting extra-regional powers like China, albeit with little success until the 2000s.

The international situation for Nepal and the Maldives drastically changed with the growing economic and financial clout of China in South Asia. In the geopolitical competition with India in South Asia, China and its economic and financial resources have managed to weaken India's traditionally dominant influence. Over the last decade, our analysis shows that both Nepal and the Maldives have avoided balancing and bandwagoning in the classic realist sense and have often managed to "steer clear of making definite choices" between China and India.[47] Instead, the two South Asian states have frequently engaged in complex bargaining to gain economic assistance not only from the great powers in the region, China and India in particular, but also the US and Japan.

The case of Nepal shows how foreign policy behavior has adjusted to three factors, marking a departure on three dimensions, two structural and one domestic. First, Kathmandu has been exploring a more permissive regional environment through balancing and diversification in order to escape India's traditional predominance. Second, Nepal's changing foreign policy is also increasingly driven by a logic of economic interdependence that Kathmandu seeks to achieve by fostering cooperative institutions in South Asia, beyond just India and traditional organizations like SAARC. Finally, Nepal's foreign policy decisions have also been increasingly exposed to political instability and rapid democratization, with a growing set of interest groups and stakeholders.

Similarly, Maldivian foreign policy decisions seem to have been increasingly shaped by a combination of shifting geopolitical and domestic political factors. China's increasing involvement in the region and the opportunity to attract Chinese funds and tourists has pushed Maldivian political leaders to cultivate ties with Beijing while still respecting India's sensibilities. However, since 2012 and the controversial removal of Nasheed from office, political competition between the MDP and the PPM has increasingly become a struggle between pro-India and pro-China factions. As a result, heightened great power competition, coinciding with increasing political competition and polarization at home, has led to the electoral salience of strategic hedging decisions in the Maldivian context. Consequently, a return of the PPM to power in the next elections could be expected to favor a new pivot to China.

This chapter therefore demonstrates that a mix of structural and domestic political factors shape the foreign policies and hedging options of Nepal and the Maldives. Deviating from realist expectations, this chapter concludes that hedging does not automatically become a preferred strategy for small states in South Asia as fierce competition between the ruling government and the main opposition in both Nepal and the Maldives seem to have reduced any strategic leverage the leadership used to enjoy. An increasingly contested domestic political space has led in both cases to a proxy war with political parties closely aligning with one or the other great power patron. As such, it seems that a more adequate framework to understand the contemporary and future foreign policies of the two South Asian states is a two-level game approach, which takes both domestic politics and the evolving external environment into account to explain statesmen's decisions.[48] The upcoming elections in 2022 (Nepal) and 2023 (the Maldives), will therefore likely be decisive in determining the foreign policy direction these countries will take.

Notes

1 Šumit Ganguly, "India as a Regional Power: Opportunities and Constraints," in *Regional Powers and Contested Leadership*, eds. Hannes Ebert and Daniel Flemes (Germany: Palgrave MacMillan, 2018), 231–246.

2 Barry Buzan, "The South Asian Security Complex in a Decentring World Order: Reconsidering Regions and Powers Ten Years On," *International Studies* 48, no. 1 (2011): 1–19; Swarna Rajagopalan, "South Asia's Small States in World Politics," in *South Asia in World Politics*, ed. Devin. T. Hagerty (Lanham: Rowman & Littlefield, 2005), 89–112.

3 T.V. Paul, "When Balance of Power Meets Globalization: China, India and the Small States of South Asia," *Politics* 39, no. 1 (2019): 50–63.

4 Darren J. Lim and Rohan Mukherjee, "Hedging in South Asia: Balancing Economic and Security Interests amid Sino-Indian Competition," *International Relations of the Asia-Pacific* 19, no. 3 (2019): 493–522.

5 Bhumitra Chakma, *South Asian Regionalism: The Limits of Cooperation* (Bristol: Bristol University Press, 2020).

6 Sanjay Kathuria, *A Glass Half Full: The Promise of Regional Trade in South Asia* (Washington, DC: World Bank, 2018).

7 Riya Sinha and Niara Sareen, "India's Limited Trade Connectivity with South Asia," *Brookings India*, May 2020, https://www.brookings.edu/wp-content/uploads/2020/05/Trade-Policy-Brief.pdf.

8 Sandy Gordon, *India's Rise as an Asian Power: Nation, Neighbourhood, and Region* (Washington, DC: Georgetown University Press, 2014), 43–77.

9 Leo E. Rose, *Nepal: Strategy for Survival* (Berkeley: University of California Press, 1971).

10 Ramjee P. Parajulee, *The Democratic Transition in Nepal* (Lanham: Rowman & Littlefield, 2000).

11 S.D Muni, *India and Nepal: A Changing Relationship* (New Delhi: Konark, 1992).

12 B.P. Koirala, *Atmabrittanta: Late Life Recollections* (Lalitpur: Himal, 2001).

13 Constantino Xavier, "Across the Himalayas: China in India's Neighborhood," in *Routledge Handbook of China-India Relations* (England: Routledge; Taylor & Francis Group, 2020), 420–433.

14 Rupak Sapkota, "Nepal's Conundrum in the Indo-Pacific amidst the Emergence of the Great Power Rivalry," *International Relations* 56, no. 2 (2020): 115, 117.

15 Amish R. Mulmi, *All Roads Lead North* (London: Hurst Publishers, 2021).

16 Vijay Gokhale, "India's Fog of Misunderstanding Surrounding Nepal–China Relations," *Carnegie India*, October 4, 2021, https://carnegieindia.org/2021/10/04/india-s-fog-of-misunderstanding-surrounding-nepal-china-relations-pub-85416.

17 Biswas Baral, "Political Briefing: The US Failure on MCC Compact," *The Annapurna Express*, September 15, 2019, https://theannapurnaexpress.com/news/political-briefing-the-us-failure-on-mcc-compact-3619.

18 Sangeeta Thapliyal, "From 'Landlocked' to 'Land-linked': Changes in the Emphasis on Nepal's Foreign Policy," *Journal of the United Service Institution of India* CXLIX, no. 617 (2019), https://usiofindia.org/publication/usi-journal/from-landlocked-to-land-linked-changes-in-the-emphasis-on-nepals-foreign-policy/.

19 "Envisioning Nepal 2030: Proceedings of the International Seminar," *Asian Development Bank*, March 2016, https://www.adb.org/sites/default/files/publication/185557/envisioning-nepal-2030.pdf.

20 PTI, "Nepal Can Be Bridge Between India, China," *The Hindu*, June 23, 2018, https://www.thehindu.com/news/international/nepal-can-be-bridge-between-india-china/article24242061.ece.

21 Sebastian von Einsiedel, David M. Malone, and Suman Pradhan, eds., *Nepal in Transition: From People's War to Fragile Peace* (New York: Cambridge University Press, 2012).

22 Nischal Nath Pandey, "Charting a New Direction and Strategy in Nepal's Foreign Policy," *Journal of Foreign Affairs* 1, no. 1 (January 2021), https://www.nepjol.info/index.php/jofa/article/view/36250.

23 Pramod Jaiswal, "Foreign Policy Imperatives for Nepal," *The Annapurna Express*, April 1, 2018, https://theannapurnaexpress.com/news/foreign-policy-imperatives-for-nepal-208.

24 Lok Raj Baral, "Nepal's Foreign Policy Failure," *The Kathmandu Post*, June 23, 2021, https://kathmandupost.com/columns/2021/06/23/nepal-s-foreign-policy-failure.

25 Santosh Sharma Poudel, "Should Nepal Ratify the MCC Nepal Compact?" *The Diplomat*, October 11, 2021, https://thediplomat.com/2021/10/should-nepal-ratify-the-mcc-nepal-compact/.

26 Deep Pal, "China's Influence in South Asia: Vulnerabilities and Resilience in Four Countries," *Carnegie Endowment for International Peace*, October 13, 2021, https://carnegieendowment.org/2021/10/13/china-s-influence-in-south-asia-vulnerabilities-and-resilience-in-four-countries-pub-85552.

27 "Government is Morally Bound to Take Ownership of MCC Compact," *The Annapurna Express*, January 1, 2020, https://theannapurnaexpress.com/news/government-is-morally-bound-to-take-ownership-of-mcc-compact-2170.

28 However, the British maintained an air base on the island of Gan until 1976.

29 Shyam Saran, *How India Sees the World: Kautilya to the 21st century* (New Delhi: Juggernaut Books, 2017), 38.

30 Azim Zahir, "India–China Rivalry in the Indian Ocean: Emergence of a New Indo-Maldives Strategic Dynamic," *Journal of the Indian Ocean Region* 17, no. 1 (2021): 78–95.

31 Swarna Rajagopalan, "South Asia's Small States in World Politics," in *South Asia in World Politics*, ed. Devin T. Hagerty (Lanham, Md.: Rowman & Littlefield Publishers, 2005), 103.

32 Derek McDougall and Pradeep Taneja, "Sino-Indian Competition in the Indian Ocean Island Countries: The Scope for Small State Agency," *Journal of the Indian Ocean Region* 16, no. 2 (2020): 124–145.

33 Maldives Ministry of Tourism, "Statistics," 2019, https://www.tourism.gov.mv/en/statistics/dashboard.

34 Daniel Bosley, "Maldives Gives Airport Contract to Chinese Firm during Xi's Visit," *Reuters*, September 15, 2014, https://www.reuters.com/article/china-maldives-idINKBN0HA1TS 20140915.

35 Indrani Bagchi, "Anti-India Sentiments behind Maldives' Termination of GMR Contract?" *The Times of India*, November 29, 2012, http://timesofindia.indiatimes.com/articleshow/17418942. cms?from=mdr&utm_source=contentofinterest&utm_medium=text&utm_campaign=cppst.

36 "Why is the FTA between China and Maldives Important to India?" *Indian Express*, December 15, 2017, https://indianexpress.com/article/india/maldives-fta-india-china-4983730/.

37 Engen Tham, Ben Blanchard, and Jing Wang, "Chinese Warships Enter East Indian Ocean amid Maldives Tensions," *Reuters*, February 20, 2018, https://www.reuters.com/article/us-maldives-politics-china/chinese-warships-enter-east-indian-ocean-amid-maldives-tensions-idUSKCN1G40V9.

38 Darren J. Lim and Rohan Mukherjee, "Hedging in South Asia: Balancing Economic and Security Interests amid Sino-Indian Competition," *International Relations of the Asia-Pacific* 19, no. 3 (September 2019): 493–522, https://doi.org/10.1093/irap/lcz006.

39 *Ibid.*.

40 C. Raja Mohan, "China's Two-Ocean Strategy Puts India in a Pincer," *Foreign Policy*, January 4, 2022, https://foreignpolicy.com/2022/01/04/india-china-ocean-geopolitics-sri-lanka-maldives-comoros/.

41 Sanjeev Miglani, "After Building Spree, Just How Much Does the Maldives Owe China?" *Reuters*, November 23, 2018, https://www.reuters.com/article/us-maldives-politics-china-idUSKCN1NS1J2.

42 Shubhajit Roy, "Simply Put: For India, Islands of Disquiet in the Indian Ocean," *Indian Express*, August 10, 2015, https://indianexpress.com/article/explained/simply-put-for-india-islands-of-disquiet-in-the-indian-ocean/.

43 Simon Mundy and Kathrin Hille, "The Maldives Counts the Cost of Its Debts to China," *Financial Times*, February 11, 2019.

44 "Ambassador: China Will Not Get Dragged into 'Local Party Game," *Sunonline*, September 7, 2020, https://en.sun.mv/62826.

45 "China to Suspend Debt Repayment for Four Years: President Solih," *Maldives Today*, June 25, 2020, https://www.maldivestoday.com/post/China%20to%20suspend%20debt%20repayment%20 for%20four%20years:%20President%20Solih.

46 Amy Mackinnon, "Pompeo Courts the Maldives in Latest Bid to Check China's Influence," *Foreign Policy*, October 28, 2020, https://foreignpolicy.com/2020/10/28/pompeo-courts-maldives-embassy-defense-china-influence/; Meera Srinivasan, "Maldives to Receive Japanese Grant to Strengthen Coast Guard," *The Hindu*, November 22, 2020, http://thehindu.com/news/international/maldives-to-receive-japanese-grant-to-strengthen-coastguard/article33155784.ece.

47 Rajesh Basrur and T.V. Paul, eds., *India-China Maritime Competition: The Security Dilemma at Sea* (London: Routledge, 2019), 2.

48 Robert D. Putnam, "Diplomacy and Domestic Politics: The Logic of Two-Level Games," *International Organization* 42, no. 3 (1988): 427–460.

Bibliography

"Ambassador: China Will Not Get Dragged into 'Local Party Game.'" *Sunonline*, September 7, 2020. https://en.sun.mv/62826.

Bagchi, Indrani. "Anti-India Sentiments behind Maldives' Termination of GMR Contract?" *The Times of India*, November 29, 2012. http://timesofindia.indiatimes.com/articleshow/17418942. cms?from=mdr&utm_source=contentofinterest&utm_medium=text&utm_campaign=cppst 2012.

Baral, Biswas. "Political Briefing: The US Failure on MCC Compact." *The Annapurna Express*, September 15, 2019. https://theannapurnaexpress.com/news/political-briefing-the-us-failure-on-mcc-compact-3619.

Baral, Lok Raj. "Nepal's Foreign Policy Failure." *The Kathmandu Post*, June 23, 2021. https://kathmandupost.com/columns/2021/06/23/nepal-s-foreign-policy-failure.

Basrur, Rajesh, and T.V. Paul, eds. *India-China Maritime Competition: The Security Dilemma at Sea.* London: Routledge, 2019.

Bosley, Daniel. "Maldives Gives Airport Contract to Chinese Firm during Xi's Visit." *Reuters*, September 15, 2014. https://www.reuters.com/article/china-maldives-idINKBN0HA1TS 20140915.

Buzan, Barry. "The South Asian Security Complex in a Decentring World Order: Reconsidering Regions and Powers Ten Years On." *International Studies* 48, no. 1 (2011): 1–19.

Chakma, Bhumitra. *South Asian Regionalism: The Limits of Cooperation.* Bristol: Bristol University Press, 2020.

"China to Suspend Debt Repayment for Four Years: President Solih." *Maldives Today*, June 25, 2020. https://www.maldivestoday.com/post/China%20to%20suspend%20debt%20repayment%20 for%20four%20years:%20President%20Solih.

"Envisioning Nepal 2030: Proceedings of the International Seminar." *Asian Development Bank*, March 2016. https://www.adb.org/sites/default/files/publication/185557/envisioning-nepal-2030.pdf.

Ganguly, Šumit. "India as a Regional Power: Opportunities and Constraints." In *Regional Powers and Contested Leadership*, edited by Hannes Ebert, and Daniel Flemes, 231–246. Germany: Palgrave MacMillan, 2018.

Gokhale, Vijay. "India's Fog of Misunderstanding Surrounding Nepal–China Relations." *Carnegie India*, October 4, 2021. https://carnegieindia.org/2021/10/04/india-s-fog-of-misunderstanding-surrounding-nepal-china-relations-pub-85416.

Gordon, Sandy. *India's Rise as an Asian Power: Nation, Neighbourhood, and Region.* Washington, DC: Georgetown University Press, 2014.

"Government is Morally Bound to Take Ownership of MCC Compact." *The Annapurna Express*, January 1, 2020. https://theannapurnaexpress.com/news/government-is-morally-bound-to-take-ownership-of-mcc-compact-2170.

Jaiswal, Pramod. "Foreign Policy Imperatives for Nepal." *The Annapurna Express*, April 1, 2018. https://theannapurnaexpress.com/news/foreign-policy-imperatives-for-nepal-208.

Kathuria, Sanjay. *A Glass Half Full: The Promise of Regional Trade in South Asia.* Washington, DC: World Bank, 2018.

Koirala, B.P. *Atmabrittanta: Late Life Recollections.* Lalitpur: Himal, 2001.

Lim, Darren J., and Rohan Mukherjee. "Hedging in South Asia: Balancing Economic and Security Interests amid Sino-Indian Competition." *International Relations of the Asia-Pacific* 19, no. 3 (2019): 493–522.

Mackinnon, Amy. "Pompeo Courts the Maldives in Latest Bid to Check China's Influence." *Foreign Policy*, October 28, 2020. https://foreignpolicy.com/2020/10/28/pompeo-courts-maldives-embassy-defense-china-influence/.

Maldives Ministry of Tourism. "Statistics." 2019. https://www.tourism.gov.mv/en/statistics/dashboard.

McDougall, Derek, and Pradeep Taneja. "Sino-Indian Competition in the Indian Ocean Island Countries: The Scope for Small State Agency." *Journal of the Indian Ocean Region* 16, no. 2 (2020): 124–145.

Miglani, Sanjeev. "After Building Spree, Just How Much Does the Maldives Owe China?" *Reuters*, November 23, 2018. https://www.reuters.com/article/us-maldives-politics-china-idUSKCN1 NS1J2.

Mohan, C. Raja. "China's Two-Ocean Strategy Puts India in a Pincer." *Foreign Policy*, January 4, 2022. https://foreignpolicy.com/2022/01/04/india-china-ocean-geopolitics-sri-lanka-maldives-comoros/.

Mulmi, A.R. *All Roads Lead North*. London: Hurst Publishers, 2021.

Mundy, Simon, and Kathrin Hille. "The Maldives Counts the Cost of Its Debts to China." *Financial Times*, February 11, 2019.

Muni, S.D. *India and Nepal: A Changing Relationship*. New Delhi: Konark, 1992.

Pal, Deep. "China's Influence in South Asia: Vulnerabilities and Resilience in Four Countries." *Carnegie Endowment for International Peace*, October 13, 2021. https://carnegieendowment.org/2021/10/13/china-s-influence-in-south-asia-vulnerabilities-and-resilience-in-four-countries-pub-85552.

Pandey, Nischal Nath. "Charting a New Direction and Strategy in Nepal's Foreign Policy." *Journal of Foreign Affairs* 1, no. 1 (January 2021). https://www.nepjol.info/index.php/jofa/article/view/36250.

Parajulee, Ramjee P. *The Democratic Transition in Nepal*. Lanham: Rowman & Littlefield, 2000.

Paul, T.V. "When Balance of Power Meets Globalization: China, India and the Small States of South Asia." *Politics* 39, no. 1 (2019): 50–63.

Poudel, Santosh Sharma. "Should Nepal Ratify the MCC Nepal Compact?" *The Diplomat*, October 11, 2021. https://thediplomat.com/2021/10/should-nepal-ratify-the-mcc-nepal-compact/.

PTI. "Nepal Can Be Bridge Between India, China." *The Hindu*, June 23, 2018. https://www.thehindu.com/news/international/nepal-can-be-bridge-between-india-china/article24242061.ece.

Putnam, Robert D. "Diplomacy and Domestic Politics: The Logic of Two-Level Games." *International Organization* 42, no. 3 (1988): 427–460.

Rajagopalan, Swarna. "South Asia's Small States in World Politics." In *South Asia in World Politics*, edited by Devin T. Hagerty, 89–112. Lanham: Rowman & Littlefield, 2005.

Rose, Leo E. *Nepal: Strategy for Survival*. Berkeley: University of California Press, 1971.

Roy, Shubhajit. "Simply Put: For India, Islands of Disquiet in the Indian Ocean." *Indian Express*, August 10, 2015. https://indianexpress.com/article/explained/simply-put-for-india-islands-of-disquiet-in-the-indian-ocean/.

Sapkota, Rupak. "Nepal's Conundrum in the Indo-Pacific Amidst the Emergence of the Great Power Rivalry." *International Relations* 56, no. 2 (2020): 115–117.

Saran, Shyam. *How India Sees the World: Kautilya to the 21st Century*. New Delhi: Juggernaut Books, 2017.

Sebastian von, Einsiedel, David M. Malone, and Suman Pradhan, eds. *Nepal in Transition: From People's War to Fragile Peace*. New York: Cambridge University Press, 2012.

Sinha, Riya, and Niara Sareen. "India's Limited Trade Connectivity with South Asia." *Brookings India*, May 2020. https://www.brookings.edu/wp-content/uploads/2020/05/Trade-Policy-Brief.pdf.

Srinivasan, Meera. "Maldives to Receive Japanese Grant to Strengthen Coast Guard." *The Hindu*, November 22, 2020. http://thehindu.com/news/international/maldives-to-receive-japanese-grant-to-strengthen-coastguard/article33155784.ece.

Tham, Engen, Ben Blanchard, and Jing Wang. "Chinese Warships Enter East Indian Ocean Amid Maldives Tensions." *Reuters*, February 20, 2018. https://www.reuters.com/article/us-maldives-politics-china/chinese-warships-enter-east-indian-ocean-amid-maldives-tensions-id USKCN1G40V9.

Thapliyal, Sangeeta. "From 'Landlocked' to 'Land-linked': Changes in the Emphasis on Nepal's Foreign Policy." *Journal of the United Service Institution of India* CXLIX, no. 617 (2019). https://usiofindia.org/publication/usi-journal/from-landlocked-to-land-linked-changes-in-the-emphasis-on-nepals-foreign-policy/.

"Why is the FTA between China and Maldives Important to India?" *Indian Express*, December 15, 2017. https://indianexpress.com/article/india/maldives-fta-india-china-4983730/.

Xavier, Constantino. "Across the Himalayas: China in India's Neighborhood." In *Routledge Handbook of China-India Relations*. England: Routledge; Taylor & Francis Group, 2020.

Zahir, Azim. "India–China Rivalry in the Indian Ocean: Emergence of a New Indo-Maldives Strategic Dynamic." *Journal of the Indian Ocean Region* 17, no. 1 (2021): 78–95.

23

TRENDS IN US POLICY TOWARD SOUTH ASIA

Jeff Smith

Introduction

In recent years, arguably no region of the world has climbed the ranks of America's strategic priorities faster than South Asia and the Indian Ocean region. For much of the Cold War, South Asia was largely an afterthought for the US government, with Europe, the Middle East, and East Asia occupying the lion's share of America's strategic attention. Since the collapse of the USSR and the turn of the century, however, new geopolitical challenges and opportunities for the US have compelled a strategic reorientation toward South Asia and the Indian Ocean.

The growing importance of South Asia for the US is partly a consequence of the expanding demographic and economic heft of the region broadly, and India specifically. Now among the top five economies worldwide, India's rise, and the dramatic transformation of the India-US relationship, is reshaping the geopolitical map and opening new opportunities for deeper US engagement with the rest of the region.

It is also because developments in South Asia and the Indian Ocean are increasingly relevant to vital US national security interests, even after the US withdrawal from Afghanistan in late 2021 following a 20-year military involvement in the country. Today, China's expanding footprint in the region, the longstanding and nuclear-tinged India-Pakistan rivalry, and the threat of terrorism and extremism from Afghanistan and Pakistan continue to pose acute risks to US interests and regional stability.

As the China-US rivalry has increasingly assumed center-stage in US foreign policy debates, the US government views a rising India as a valuable strategic and democratic counterweight to China's growing power and influence. US policy toward the region is thus heavily influenced by the realist school of international relations theory and the desire to promote a favorable balance of power in the Indo-Pacific while mitigating the threat of terrorism from the region. America's ongoing commitment to promoting democracy and human rights in the region, however, suggests US policy is also influenced by strains of liberalism.

This chapter will examine the rising importance of South Asia and the Indian Ocean for the United States and key challenges, trends, and opportunities in US policy toward the region, with a focus on developments between 2010 and 2020.

314

DOI: 10.4324/9781003246626-27

Rising Tides: Demographics and Economics

South Asia is a remarkably diverse region, comprising the Hindu-majority states of India (population roughly 1.3 billion) and Nepal (30 million); the Muslim-majority states of Pakistan (230 million), Bangladesh (170 million), Afghanistan (33 million), and the Maldives (582,000); and the Buddhist-majority states of Sri Lanka (22 million) and Bhutan (756,000).[1]

Today, South Asia is home to nearly two trillion people, or almost one-in-every-four persons on earth. That represents a remarkable doubling of the regional population since 1980 and a quadrupling of the population since 1950.

If it hasn't already surpassed China as the most populous country in the world, India is expected to do so soon and is likely to enjoy a population near 1.5 billion people through mid-century. Meanwhile, Pakistan hosts one of the fastest-growing populations in the world at a time fertility rates are rapidly declining globally. From a population of roughly 220 million in 2020, the UN estimates Pakistan could count over 400 million inhabitants by 2050.[2]

As South Asia's population has grown, so too has its economic impact. India, whose nearly $3 trillion economy is now the world's fifth largest, remains the regional economic heavyweight and by far America's most important trading partner in the region. India is now among America's top 10 trading partners even as the US has become India's top trading partner overall. India-US bilateral goods trade eclipsed $90 billion in 2019 and total trade in goods and services reached a new record of $146 billion that year before declining to $122 billion in 2020 due in part to the COVID-19 pandemic.[3]

US goods trade with South Asia as a whole nearly doubled between 2010 and 2019, from $65 billion to $115 billion. Despite this considerable growth, in 2019 South Asia still accounted for less than 3% of total US external trade.[4] By comparison, US trade with Southeast Asia that year was nearly three times greater, at $300 billion, despite the region having only one-third of South Asia's population.

After India, America's economic relationships in the region are of only modest, if gradually rising, importance. Now with an over $300 billion economy, Bangladesh hosts one of the fastest-growing developing economies in the world. Nevertheless, in 2019 US goods trade with Bangladesh ($318 billion GDP) amounted to just $9 billion, ranking it as America's 46th largest goods trading partner. The same year, bilateral goods trade with Pakistan ($284 billion GDP) was $6.6 billion; Sri Lanka ($87 billion GDP) was $3.1 billion; Afghanistan ($19 billion GDP) was $800 million; Nepal ($30 billion GDP) was $200 million; and the Maldives ($6 billion GDP) was just over $60 million.[5]

Though ostensibly all free market economies, regional capitals have struggled to liberalize markets and remove barriers to trade and investment. Every economy in South Asia was designated as "mostly unfree" by the Heritage Foundation's 2021 Index of Economic Freedom.[6] The US currently has no free trade agreements with any of the countries in South Asia.[7] In recent years, both India and the US opted out of joining multilateral trade agreements like the Trans-Pacific Partnership (TPP) and Regional Comprehensive Economic Partnership (RCEP). Despite leader-level commitments in both capitals, and multiple rounds of negotiations, India and the US were unable to secure an even modest trade deal during the administration of President Donald Trump.

Strategic Challenges

If South Asia's economic importance to the US remains modest, it has assumed a much more prominent role on America's strategic horizons, presenting both significant challenges and opportunities that are reshaping US strategy toward the region. Among the key challenges confronting the US: Terrorism in the Afghanistan-Pakistan space, China's growing profile in the region, and the India-Pakistan rivalry, particularly over the disputed territory of Kashmir.

Terrorism and the War in Afghanistan

The risks of terrorism in South Asia remain acute. After a two-decade US war and reconstruction effort in Afghanistan following the September 11 terrorist attacks, a rapid military offensive brought the Taliban back to power in Kabul in August 2021 amid a chaotic US withdrawal from the country.

The US government has yet to formally recognize the Taliban government and has frozen Afghan government assets, citing concerns about the Taliban's gross human rights violations, repression of women and minorities, as well as its links to international terrorist groups like al Qaeda. In October 2021, the Biden administration assessed that al Qaeda and the Islamic State were both operating in Afghanistan and could generate the capability to attack the US in as soon as six months.[8]

Of additional concern is the prominent role the Haqqani Network is now playing in the Afghan government and the Taliban leadership structure. A longtime proxy of Pakistan's Inter-Services Intelligence (ISI), the Haqqani Network was responsible for many of the deadliest terrorist attacks on US and Afghan government targets during the war in Afghanistan and maintains close links with al Qaeda.[9]

Meanwhile, a wide variety of terrorist and extremist groups continue to operate from within Pakistan, many with the sanction and support of the ISI. Complicating matters, Pakistan now faces elevated security risks from the Pakistani Taliban and other anti-state extremist groups, whose attacks inside of Pakistan have increased since the fall of Kabul and risk destabilizing the nuclear-armed country even further.[10]

For now, it is unclear how the Taliban's takeover in Afghanistan might impact other regional flashpoints, including the ongoing dispute between India and Pakistan over Kashmir. Some experts are anticipating an uptick in militancy there as Pakistan seeks to redirect the activities of militant groups previously preoccupied with the war in Afghanistan.

Beyond the Afghanistan-Pakistan theater, India, Bangladesh, and the Maldives each face modest threats of domestic terrorism largely contained by the state but capable of surges of violence. Notably, Sri Lanka suffered its first major terrorist attack by an Islamist extremist group on Easter Day 2018, although to date it has proven an isolated incident.[11]

India-Pakistan Rivalry and Kashmir

Kashmir remains a dangerous flashpoint in the region. In recent years, the disputed territory—administered in part and claimed in whole by both India and Pakistan—has been the source of several volatile clashes between the two rivals, as both sides' appetite for risk and escalation seems to be growing.

Relations between the two rivals remain paralyzed by acrimony and mistrust. After an aborted attempt at a diplomatic thaw shortly after the election of Narendra Modi in 2014, in recent years the India-Pakistan relationship has retrenched to a more combative state, with diplomatic interactions substantially curtailed. Meanwhile, tensions along the Line of Control (LOC) in Kashmir have been elevated since 2016, when Pakistani-backed militants launched an attack on an Indian army base in Uri. The Indian military responded with a "surgical strike" on militant targets across the LOC in Pakistan-administered Kashmir.[12]

In 2019, India suffered the deadliest-ever single attack in Kashmir when 40 Indian soldiers were killed in a bombing in Pulwama that India claimed was orchestrated in Pakistan. Indian fighter jets responded with an attack on suspected terrorist training camps in Balakot, deep inside Pakistani territory, prompting a dogfight between Pakistani and Indian fighter jets the following day and the loss of at least one Indian fighter jet.[13] Periodic bouts of artillery shelling and exchanges of gunfire along the LOC in recent years have ensured it remains one of the most volatile disputed borders in the world.

The history of conflict, and the presence of nuclear weapons, ensures that the risk of a Pakistan-India conflict remains a persistent concern for the US government, even as it has moved away from efforts to actively mediate the dispute.

China's Entry into the Region

Arguably the most impactful trend reshaping the geopolitics of South Asia, and US strategy there, has been China's dramatic entry into the region. China has enjoyed strong political, economic, and military ties to Pakistan since the 1960s. It has served as Islamabad's patron at the UN Security Council and a key supplier of military equipment. It has aided the country's nuclear weapons program and provided billions of dollars in economic aid and investment. Those ties have only grown closer in recent years, particularly after Beijing announced its intention to invest tens of billions of dollars in a China-Pakistan Economic Corridor (CPEC) in 2015.

Beyond Pakistan, however, China's footprint in the region was until recently quite marginal, constrained by China's own limited ambitions and Beijing's longstanding rivalry with the region's traditional hegemon, India. That began to change in the late 2000s.

In late 2008, China began operating a regular, rotating anti-piracy naval task force in the Indian Ocean. In 2013 and 2014, it began routine nuclear and conventional submarine patrols in the Indian Ocean. In 2015, it opened its first naval base in the Indian Ocean at the Port of Doraleh in Djibouti and a Chinese entity assumed control of operations at Pakistan's Gwadar port.[14]

In the Maldives, Nepal, and Sri Lanka, China found three democracies in periods of turbulent political transitions or civil conflicts. Each carried some historical resentment toward India and a desire for Chinese investments. While China did bring capital and infrastructure to these countries, it also brought with it some commercially questionable and strategically suspicious initiatives. Its activities and investments in South Asia have since drawn charges of secrecy, corruption, and espionage while it has seemed to reinforce authoritarian instincts of regional leaders. Meanwhile, China's expanding military and diplomatic footprint in the region has fueled concerns about strategic encirclement in New Delhi, further aggravating the China-India rivalry.

However, arguably nothing has done more to sour China-India relations in recent years than the increasingly tense situation along their disputed border, the source of a brief but consequential war in 1962. A series of border crises at the Line of Actual Control (LAC) beginning in 2013 foreshadowed a substantial deterioration of ties under the governments of Indian Prime Minister Narendra Modi and Chinese Communist Party Chairman Xi Jinping.

Two unprecedented border crises—one on the Doklam Plateau (in the neighboring Himalayan state of Bhutan) in 2017,[15] and one in the Galwan Valley in 2020—plunged bilateral relations to new lows. The latter produced the first casualties from hostilities at the disputed border in over 40 years.[16] Meanwhile, in 2020, China announced new claims on territory in eastern Bhutan, and satellite images revealed the construction of Chinese villages inside both Bhutanese and Indian territory.[17]

Since the Galwan crisis, the Indian government has consistently signaled that diplomatic relations cannot be normalized without a withdrawal of Chinese forces to pre-crisis positions along the LAC. While the two sides did reach agreements to deescalate and withdraw forces to buffer zones at several contentious standoff sites along the border in Ladakh, to date, Beijing has shown no willingness to budge from forward positions at several other standoff sites.

The deteriorating situation at the LAC has provoked an unprecedented response in India, including: A significant military mobilization along the border; a sharp backlash in Indian public opinion toward China; the cancellation of several proposed Chinese investments and the banning of popular Chinese software applications; and an enhanced Indian willingness to expand strategic cooperation with the US and other Indo-Pacific democracies.

US Strategic Engagement with South Asia

Against the backdrop of these key security trends, US policy toward South Asia has undergone three key evolutions over the past decade. First, the US government has recast its "mental map" of the region, incorporating South Asia and the Indian Ocean into the new "Indo-Pacific."[18] Second, the US has "de-hyphenated" its approach to India and Pakistan and rebalanced engagement away from the latter toward the former. Finally, and partly as a consequence of this rebalancing, the US has witnessed a slow but gradual expansion of ties with the smaller states of South Asia.

Indo-Pacific

Despite America's growing interest in the region, the US government doesn't have a dedicated "South Asia strategy." Instead, during the administration of Donald J. Trump, the US government effectively merged South Asia and East Asia, the Indian Ocean and Western Pacific, into a super-theater known as the Indo-Pacific. This geographic reconstruction was joined by an evolution terminology and in America's strategic vision for the region, the "free and open Indo-Pacific." US strategy toward the region is thus guided by a series of interconnected interests, opportunities, challenges, and bilateral relationships couched within its broader vision for a free and open Indo-Pacific.

Although the concept originated in Japan in the mid-2000s—and was debated and adopted in Australia in the years to follow—the US government began formally shifting from the traditional "Asia-Pacific" to the "Indo-Pacific" terminology with the release of the White House National Security Strategy in December 2017.[19] As I argued in 2018:

> the "Indo-Pacific" attempts to elevate the importance of the maritime domain and encapsulate the geopolitical consequences of China pushing west and India pushing east, creating an expanding zone of competitive overlap and progressively binding the Indian and Pacific Oceans to each other and to overland strategic developments in South and East Asia.[20]

Though a creation of the Trump administration, the free and open Indo-Pacific framework was largely retained by the Biden administration.[21] While there have been slight variations, most permutations of the free and open Indo-Pacific include the following pillars: Peaceful dispute settlement; respect for the rules-based order and freedom of navigation; recognition of "ASEAN Centrality" and its role as convener of regional multilateral dialogues; support for US allies and strategic partners in the region; and support for responsible, transparent, high-standards infrastructure and economic initiatives.

In the years since the US adoption of the Indo-Pacific, the terminology has gained widespread popularity in the region. It is now commonly used not only by US partners and allies in the region like Australia, Japan, and India, but by Southeast Asian countries, including in their ASEAN Outlook for the Indo-Pacific.[22]

India-Pakistan Rebalancing

In the latter half of the 20th century, America's diplomatic engagement with the region was heavily weighted toward its strategic partnership with Pakistan, and the tactical cooperation they pursued against a common enemy, the Soviet Union. Meanwhile, the balance of power politics of the Cold War left India and the US geopolitically estranged. As the Pakistan-US partnership morphed into a China-Pakistan-US entente in the early 1970s, India pursued a defense treaty with the USSR on the eve of the Third Indo-Pakistan war of 1971.

The end of the Cold War, the 9/11 terrorist attacks, and the rise of China reshuffled the geopolitical chessboard, bringing the US military to Afghanistan, and rebalancing America's engagement with India and Pakistan. The war in Afghanistan opened a new chapter in Pakistan-US relations characterized by tactical cooperation and strategic mistrust. Throughout the course of the war, Pakistan's ISI was regularly charged by US officials with practicing a duplicitous double game. It was credibly accused of covertly providing support and safe haven to the Taliban and ISI allies like the Haqqani Network.

US frustration with this double game reached a tipping point in 2011 when al Qaeda leader and 9/11 mastermind Osama bin Laden was discovered in a Pakistani safe house less than one mile from a Pakistani military academy in Abbottabad, Pakistan. The US launched a secret nighttime raid that killed bin Laden, raising the level of mistrust and acrimony in an already dysfunctional relationship. Soon after, Pakistan evicted the US from a base it was using to launch drone strikes against terrorist targets.[23]

Pakistan-US relations were downgraded further during the administration of Donald Trump. On New Years' Day 2018, President Trump announced the US was suspending billions of dollars of aid to Pakistan, claiming: "The United States has foolishly given Pakistan more than 33 billion dollars in aid over the last 15 years, and they have given us nothing but lies and deceit."[24] Additionally, the Trump administration helped sponsor United Nations sanctions on terrorist groups operating in Pakistan and supported efforts to have Pakistan "grey-listed" by the Financial Action Task Force, an international terrorism finance watchdog.

Pakistan-US relations have remained comparatively frosty since the election of President Joe Biden, with President Biden reportedly refusing to communicate directly with Prime Minister Imran Khan and Pakistan declining an invitation to attend President Biden's December 2021 Summit for Democracy. Deputy Secretary of State Wendy Sherman visited Pakistan in October 2021 to discuss "the importance to holding the Taliban accountable to the commitments they have made." In India days earlier, she proclaimed: "We don't see ourselves building a broad relationship with Pakistan. And we have no interest in returning to the days of hyphenated India-Pakistan."[25]

Once considered partial to Pakistan in arbitrating bilateral disputes with India, the US government has been assuming a more neutral position in regional crises since the 1999 Kargil conflict. The US has largely dropped any pretense of involvement in mediating the Kashmir dispute and has become more vocal in signaling Islamabad's responsibility to rein in terrorist groups operating on Pakistani soil.

The souring of the Pakistan-US relationship has been mirrored by the consummation of the India-US strategic partnership. After decades of Cold War estrangement, the rapprochement began in earnest in 2005 with a ten-year defense partnership framework and a civil nuclear deal. Since 2008, India has purchased over $25 billion in US defense equipment, including aircraft engines, heavy transport aircraft, combat helicopters, anti-submarine warfare helicopters and airplanes, guided munitions, anti-ship missiles and torpedoes, surface-to-air missiles, advanced radar, and unmanned aerial vehicles.

Between 2016 and 2020, the two sides signed three important and once-contentious "foundational" military agreements, covering everything from logistics support to encrypted communications and geospatial intelligence sharing. In 2018, the Trump Administration issued a federal notification granting India Strategic Trade Authorization Tier 1 (STA-1), easing regulatory burdens for US high-tech defense and aerospace exports.[26] At each turn, the US government has emphasized the vital role India plays in America's vision for the Indo-Pacific.[27]

Finally, the burgeoning India-US partnership was pivotal in the revival of the "Quad" in November 2017, a strategic grouping joining Australia, India, Japan, and the US. Since that inaugural meeting, the Quad has been elevated to the foreign minister level and its agenda expanded. In 2020, the four countries re-launched quadrilateral naval exercises when Australia was welcomed to rejoin the India-Japan-US Malabar naval exercises, and in 2021, the Biden administration signaled its commitment to the Quad by hosting the first-ever leader-level Quad summit in Washington DC.[28]

Engagement with Other South Asian States

US engagement with South Asia remains heavily weighted toward India, Pakistan, and Afghanistan. While a crude metric, it is telling that no US president has ever visited Nepal, Sri Lanka, the Maldives, or Bhutan while in office. By contrast, there have been eight visits to India, eight to Afghanistan, five to Pakistan, and one to Bangladesh.[29] It is also telling that the last US president to visit Pakistan was George W. Bush in March 2006. Since then, there have been six presidential visits to Afghanistan and four to India.

Beyond the "big three," US defense relationships in the region remain limited. Since 2010, the US registered no arms sales to the Maldives or Bhutan and sold or gifted a small number of military platforms to Sri Lanka (two helicopters and one offshore patrol vessel), Nepal (two turboprop engines and one light helicopter), and Bangladesh (four aircraft engines, two offshore patrol vessels, and 50 second-hand armored personnel carriers).[30]

While defense ties remain marginal and presidential visits scarce, US diplomatic and economic cooperation with the rest of South Asia has been expanding slowly over the past decade, aided in part by the maturation of India-US ties.

Bhutan

The small Buddhist kingdom situated in the Himalayas has no formal diplomatic relationship with the US and largely defers to India on foreign policy and defense-related matters. In fact, Bhutan has a declared policy foregoing formal diplomatic relations with any of the five permanent members of the UN Security Council. Informal ties between Bhutan and the US nevertheless remain warm. Bhutan's permanent mission to the United Nations in New York enjoys consular jurisdiction in the US and America's ambassador to India serves as America's informal US diplomatic interlocutor with Bhutan, making periodic courtesy calls to Bhutan's capital, Thimphu, to meet the prime minister.[31]

Trends in US Policy toward South Asia

In 2015, US Secretary of State John Kerry met with Bhutan's prime minister on the sidelines of an international conference in India, touting the two countries' commitment to "supporting institutions and values that have brought peace and prosperity to the Indo-Pacific region and the world."[32] Bhutan receives USAID funds to support disaster management as well as energy security and clean energy access and State Department assistance to support STEM training and to counter human trafficking. Bhutan also sends military officers and officials to attend courses at a Pentagon-affiliated think tank in Hawaii.[33]

Bangladesh

Bangladesh, the eighth most populous country in the world with the fourth-largest Muslim population, has enjoyed favorable and gradually improving ties with the US over the past decade. The government led by Prime Minister Sheikh Hasina and her Awami League party since 2011 have moved to improve ties with the US, including enhancing counterterrorism cooperation. The two sides signed a Counterterrorism Cooperation Initiative in 2013 and Bangladesh participates in the State Department's Antiterrorism Assistance Program.[34]

Despite a mixed record domestically, including credible charges of election fraud and human rights violations, Washington has applauded several moves Dhaka has taken to prove itself a responsible actor on the international stage, including using international legal arbitration tools to settle a maritime boundary dispute with India in 2014. One year later, it signed a historic land border swap agreement with India.

More recently, Bangladesh has served as a refuge for over one million Muslim Rohingyas fleeing ethnic cleansing in neighboring Myanmar. In late 2016, attacks by the Burmese military against the Rohingya minority sparked a humanitarian crisis, the burden of which has largely fallen to Bangladesh and the network of refugee camps it has established to house hundreds of thousands of stateless victims.[35]

Maldives

The US enjoys stable diplomatic ties with the Maldives. In 2007, a referendum transformed the country's political system, heralding its first transition to genuine democratic elections the following year.

After a soft coup in 2012 ousted the country's first democratically elected president, Mohamed Nasheed, concerns mounted about democratic backsliding and the new government's embrace of China. The next two governments, led by presidents Mohamad Waheed and Abdullah Yameen, reoriented the Maldives away from its traditional patron, India, and toward China. They welcomed an influx of Chinese loans and investments that later drew charges of corruption, predatory lending, and undemocratic practices.

In 2018, President Yameen was upset by presidential candidate Ibrahim Mohamed Solih, an ally of former President Nasheed, whom the Trump Administration described as "a reform-oriented leader committed to rebuilding the country's democratic institutions."[36]

In a 2019 visit to the US, Maldivian Foreign Minister received a commitment of $10 million in economic support funds to financial management, rule of law, and civil society building. The US Treasury Department offered to provide Male "assistance on debt strategy and domestic debt management." Ongoing State Department initiatives in the Maldives include the promotion of civil society and women's economic empowerment and the preservation of marine ecosystems. A Department of Justice program provides legal advisor and criminal justice support and a Department of Treasury program assists the country with combating financial crimes.

Jeff Smith

Finally, in September 2020, the Maldives and the US signed a new "Framework for a Defense and Security Relationship," setting forth "both countries' intent to deepen engagement and cooperation in support of maintaining peace and security in the Indian Ocean."[37] The two sides also agreed to begin holding a new Defense and Security Dialogue.

Nepal

The US has historically enjoyed limited relations with the relatively small and poor Himalayan kingdom of Nepal. The country witnessed the end of a brutal Maoist domestic insurgency in 2006 and began a prolonged, oft-troubled transition to democracy replete with a new constitution enacted in 2015.

Nepal also suffered a devastating earthquake in 2015 that claimed over 8,000 Nepali lives. In response, the US government provided Nepal over $190 million in earthquake relief funds, assistance in reconstruction, and helped set up a new Disaster Management Authority in Kathmandu.[38] The US also established a rare, single-country trade preference program for Nepal, offering 77 Nepali products duty-free entry into the US until 2025.[39] USAID remains the largest bilateral donor in Nepal, and overall the US government has provided roughly $1.6 billion in aid since independence in 1951.

The US State Department articulates America's policy objectives in Nepal as centered on "helping Nepal build a peaceful, prosperous, resilient and democratic society...supporting a stable, democratic Nepal that respects the rule of law; promoting investor-friendly economic development; and improving disaster risk management systems."[40] In 2017, then head of US Pacific Command Adm. Harry Harris visited Nepal for a UN peacekeeping exercise.[41] The same year, the US Millennium Challenge Corporation signed a $500 million compact with Nepal investing in roads and power transmission projects.[42]

Nepal's foreign minister visited the US for bilateral discussions in 2018, stressing that "robust economic development is Nepal's highest priority." In 2019, INDOPACOM commander Phil Davidson met Nepal's prime minister and Army chief.[43] The US has also engaged Nepal in its Digital Connectivity and Cybersecurity Partnerships (DCCP) program.

One point of potential friction lies in China's expanding influence in Nepal, which has coincided with a crackdown on Tibetan refugees living in Nepal. Nepal hosts the second-largest Tibetan exile community after India and the flow of refugees fleeing Tibet through Nepal has fallen dramatically since Beijing began expanding its influence in the country. US lawmakers successfully warned Nepal against signing an extradition treaty with China in 2019, and a bill introduced in the Senate in 2019 encourages the Nepali government to "provide legal documentation to long-staying Tibetan residents in Nepal who fled a credible threat of persecution in Tibet."[44]

Sri Lanka

The island nation of Sri Lanka off India's southern coast was destabilized by a decades-long counterinsurgency conflict against the Tamil Tigers as well as a host of other separatist organizations. A terrorist group claiming to defend the rights of the country's Hindu Tamil minority, the Tigers led the world in suicide bombings from 1980 to 2003. A brutal but effective military offensive against the group in the late 2000s by President Mahinda Rajapaksa's government largely ended the conflict but produced accusations of human rights violations and corresponding sanctions by the US. Subsequently, President Rajapaksa oversaw a dramatic expansion of Chinese aid and investments in the country, including the construction of the controversial Hambantota Port.

Trends in US Policy toward South Asia

Sri Lanka-US ties improved substantially following 2015 national elections in which Rajapaksa was unseated by President Maithripala Sirisena. That year, Sri Lanka welcomed its first visit by a US Secretary of State in 30 years.

In 2017, a US aircraft carrier visited Sri Lanka for the first time in over three decades and Sri Lanka endorsed the US vision for a free and open Indo-Pacific."[45] In 2018, the US granted Colombo $39 million under the Bay of Bengal Initiative "to support Sri Lanka's coastal maritime radar system, to provide training and equipment for improved surveillance response and interdiction." Notably, in 2018 and 2019, the US Navy used Sri Lankan ports to resupply vessels in the Indian Ocean under a new government-to-government arrangement.[46]

The election of Gotabaya Rajapaksa, Mahinda's brother, as Sri Lanka's president in late 2019 slowed the momentum in Sri Lanka-US ties. The Rajapaksa government canceled a nearly-complete $480 million US Millennium Challenge Corporation Compact that would have funded infrastructure improvements in Sri Lanka.[47] Talks on a Sri Lanka-US status of forces agreement were also frozen with President Rajapaksa signaling a determination to again court Chinese investments.

Longstanding and ongoing US programs in Sri Lanka including mine-clearing initiatives, cultural preservation projects, disaster relief aid, counter-narcotics and counter-terrorism assistance, English-language training, and agriculture assistance. The US also remains the top destination for Sri Lankan exports.[48]

International Relations Theory and US Policy toward South Asia

The United States government has a variety of interconnected interests, challenges, and opportunities in South Asia. Arguably America's three preeminent policy concerns relate to (1) mitigating the risks of terrorism in the Afghanistan-Pakistan region; (2) strengthening strategic ties with India to promote a favorable balance of power in the region and a free and open Indo-Pacific and; (3) managing the risks of a nuclear conflict between India and Pakistan. As a result, realist theory and its emphasis on balance of power politics arguably serves as the most useful prism through which to view US policy toward South Asia.

There are, however, myriad other US interests and objectives in the region beyond or beneath these top national security priorities. The US government has myriad policy initiatives designed to promote capacity building and economic development, democracy and human rights, or political and religious freedom that are untethered from the US-China rivalry, the risks of nuclear conflict, or concerns about terrorism. This would suggest an influential strain of liberalism present in US policy toward South Asia.

However, this distinction is blurred by the fact that many of these initiatives are also consistent with a realist paradigm, advancing America's national security interests and liberal ideals simultaneously. Democratic countries that respect human rights historically make better partners and are less likely to act belligerently on the international stage. Economic development and liberalization creates new markets for US trade and investment and promotes stability. In many cases, ostensibly liberal pursuits advance realist objectives. Moreover, it is revealing that when these two come into conflict, realist priorities and national security imperatives often—though not always—take precedence.

Conclusion

The winds of change are sweeping South Asia in ways that are both encouraging and discouraging for US policy and regional stability.

In many ways, South Asia is growing more prosperous and peaceful. The toll and intensity of several domestic conflicts and insurgencies have diminished over the past decade-plus, including in Nepal (Maoists), Sri Lanka (Tamil Tigers), and India (Naxalites, Northeast, and Kashmir Insurgencies). With one glaring exception—the volatile India-Pakistan relationship—the risk of interstate conflict among South Asian states remains low. India and Bangladesh have set responsible precedents by resolving territorial disputes through negotiation and international arbitration. Economic growth has propelled hundreds of millions out of poverty, replete with access to health care and the digital economy.

Not all trends are positive, however. The threat of terrorism emanating from Afghanistan and Pakistan remains an acute concern for the US. Without direct access to the landlocked country, US counterterrorism options in Afghanistan are limited and the relationship with Pakistan remains strained. Similarly, the US government has few tools available for addressing the volatile situation along the Line of Control in Kashmir, cognizant that prior attempts at more active mediation by the US proved ineffective.

Though nearly all democracies in name, the US has articulated ongoing concerns about the health of democracy and human rights across the region. Afghanistan is now governed by terrorist groups aligned with al Qaeda. Pakistan's civilian government is subservient to a military and intelligence complex that uses terrorism as an extension of its foreign policy. Sri Lanka is ruled by a family widely accused of nepotism, human rights abuses, and autocratic instincts. Nepal, now ruled by former Maoist insurgents, appears stuck in perpetual political gridlock. The Maldives' young democracy has already been tested by at least one coup and confronts risks from rising Islamist extremism and Chinese debt. Bangladesh's last national election faced widespread accusations of fraud and the political opposition remains imprisoned. The Indian government has been accused of stoking Hindu nationalism and imposing an illiberal security crackdown in Kashmir.

China is casting a long shadow over the region. Just ten years ago, there were no Chinese submarines patrolling the Indian Ocean, no Chinese naval base in the Horn of Africa, and no China-Pakistan Economic Corridor or Chinese presence at Pakistani or Sri Lankan ports. Perhaps most important, the China-India border was relatively quiet. As all of that has changed, the China-India rivalry has bled into the political, economic, and geopolitical calculations of regional capitals, with the two engaged in an intensifying tug-of-war in battleground states like Nepal, Sri Lanka, Bhutan, and the Maldives. One consequence has been India's growing comfort with the US presence and activities in the region, with New Delhi now assenting to the US signing defense pacts with the Maldives or refueling naval vessels from Sri Lanka. Shared concerns about China have helped fuel expanded arms trade, elevated intelligence-sharing, and the completion of once-contentious military interoperability agreements.

For the US government, its own intensifying rivalry with China has become an animating force across numerous regional foreign policy initiatives, including in South Asia. The merging of South Asia and the Indian Ocean into the new "Indo-Pacific," the revival of the Quad, and the burgeoning India-US strategic partnership reflect US attempts to promote a regional balance of power more favorable to the Quad democracies and reveal the influence of realism on US policy in the region.

Notes

1 "List of the Populations of the World's Countries, Dependencies, and Territories," World Data Editors, Britannica, accessed January 11, 2022, https://www.britannica.com/topic/list-of-the-populations-of-the-worlds-countries-dependencies-and-territories-2156538.

2 United Nations, Department of Economic and Social Affairs, *World Population Prospects*, New York, 2019, https://reliefweb.int/sites/reliefweb.int/files/resources/WPP2019_Highlights.pdf.

3 Executive Office of the President, Office of the U.S. Trade Representative, "India," accessed January 12, 2022, https://ustr.gov/countries-regions/south-central-asia/india.

4 "United States Product Exports to South Asia, in U.S.$ Thousand 2010–2019," World Integrated Trade Solutions, accessed January 12, 2022, https://wits.worldbank.org/CountryProfile/en/Country/USA/StartYear/2010/EndYear/2019/TradeFlow/Export/Indicator/XPRT-TRD-VL/Partner/SAS/Product/all-groups.

5 Executive Office of the President, Office of the U.S. Trade Representative, "South & Central Asia," accessed January 12, 2022, https://ustr.gov/countries-regions/south-central-asia/.

6 2021 Index of Economic Freedom, Country Rankings, accessed January 12, 2022, https://www.heritage.org/index/ranking.

7 Executive Office of the President, Office of the U.S. Trade Representative, "Free Trade Agreements," accessed January 12, 2022, https://ustr.gov/trade-agreements/free-trade-agreements.

8 "Islamic State in Afghanistan Could be Able to Attack U.S. in Six Months—Pentagon Official," *Reuters*, October 26, 2021, https://www.reuters.com/world/islamic-state-afghanistan-could-be-able-attack-us-six-months-pentagon-official-2021-10-26/.

9 Jeff M. Smith, "The Haqqani Network: The New Kingmakers in Kabul," *War on the Rocks*, November 12, 2021, https://warontherocks.com/2021/11/the-haqqani-network-afghanistans-new-power-players/.

10 Abdul Sayed, "The Evolution and Future of Tehrik-e-Taliban Pakistan," Carnegie Endowment for International Peace, December 21, 2021, https://carnegieendowment.org/2021/12/21/evolution-and-future-of-tehrik-e-taliban-pakistan-pub-86051.

11 World Almanac of Islamism, "South Asia/ Sri Lanka," last updated August 16, 2020, https://almanac.afpc.org/almanac/countries/sri-lanka.

12 Nitin A. Gokhale, "The Inside Story of India's 2016 'Surgical Strikes,'" *The Diplomat*, September 23, 2017, https://thediplomat.com/2017/09/the-inside-story-of-indias-2016-surgical-strikes/.

13 Jeff M. Smith, "India and Pakistan: Living on Borrowed Time," The Heritage Foundation, March 11, 2019, https://www.heritage.org/middle-east/commentary/india-and-pakistan-living-borrowed-time.

14 Jeff M. Smith, "China-India Relations in the Modi-Xi Era," U.S.-China Economic and Security Review Commission, March 10, 2016, https://www.uscc.gov/sites/default/files/SMITH_Remarks%20031016.pdf.

15 Jeff M. Smith, "High Noon in the Himalayas: Behind the China-India Standoff at Doka La," *War on the Rocks*, July 13, 2017, https://warontherocks.com/2017/07/high-noon-in-the-himalayas-behind-the-china-india-standoff-at-doka-la/.

16 Jeff M. Smith, "China-India Border Crisis," *Indo-Pacific Perspectives*, 29–33, https://www.airuniversity.af.edu/Portals/10/JIPA/IndoPacificPerspectives/June%202021/07%20Smith.pdf.

17 John Pollock, "Bhutan and the Border Crisis with China," LSE South Asia Centre blog, July 19, 2021, https://blogs.lse.ac.uk/southasia/2021/07/19/bhutan-and-the-border-crisis-with-china/.

18 Jeff M. Smith, "Unpacking the Free and Open Indo-Pacific," *War on the Rocks*, March 14, 2018, https://warontherocks.com/2018/03/unpacking-the-free-and-open-indo-pacific/.

19 National Security Strategy of the United States of America, December 2017, https://trumpwhitehouse.archives.gov/wp-content/uploads/2017/12/NSS-Final-12-18-2017-0905.pdf.

20 Jeff M. Smith, "Unpacking the Free and Open Indo-Pacific," *War on the Rocks*, March 14, 2018, https://warontherocks.com/2018/03/unpacking-the-free-and-open-indo-pacific/.

21 U.S. Department of State, Office of the Spokesperson, Fact Sheet, "Secretary Blinken's Remarks on a Free and Open Indo-Pacific," December 13, 2021, https://www.state.gov/fact-sheet-secretary-blinkens-remarks-on-a-free-and-open-indo-pacific/.

22 "ASEAN Outlook on the Indo-Pacific," accessed January 18, 2022, https://asean.org/asean2020/wp-content/uploads/2021/01/ASEAN-Outlook-on-the-Indo-Pacific_FINAL_22062019.pdf.

23 Declan Walsh, "Pakistan Orders U.S. out of Drone Base," *The Guardian*, June 30, 2011, https://www.theguardian.com/world/2011/jun/30/pakistan-orders-us-out-drone-base.

24 Daniella Diaz, "Trump's First 2018 Tweet: Pakistan has 'Given Us Nothing but Lies & Deceit,'" *CNN Politics*, January 2, 2018, https://www.cnn.com/2018/01/01/politics/donald-trump-2018-pakistan/index.html.

25 Ayaz Gul, "U.S. Official Slams Taliban for Falling Short on Public Pledges," *VOA News*, October 8, 2021, https://www.voanews.com/a/us-diplomat-discusses-afghanistan-bilateral-ties-with-pakistan-leaders/6262799.html.

26 "India Third Asian Nation to Get STA-1 Status from US," *The Economic Times*, August 4, 2018, https://economictimes.indiatimes.com/news/defence/india-third-asian-nation-to-get-sta-1-status-from-us/articleshow/65266841.cms.

27 U.S. Department of State, Office of the Spokesperson, Fact Sheet, "The United States and India: Deepening our Strategic Partnership," July 27, 2021, https://www.state.gov/the-united-states-and-india-deepening-our-strategic-partnership/.

28 The White House, Statements and Releases, "Fact Sheet: Quad Leaders' Summit," September 24, 2021, https://www.whitehouse.gov/briefing-room/statements-releases/2021/09/24/fact-sheet-quad-leaders-summit/.

29 Office of the Historian, "Travels Abroad of the President," accessed January 18, 2022, https://history.state.gov/departmenthistory/travels/president.

30 Stockholm International Peace Research Institute, Trade Registers, accessed January 12, 2022, https://armstrade.sipri.org/armstrade/page/trade_register.php.

31 U.S. Embassy and Consulates in India, "Ambassador Kenneth I. Juster Visits Bhutan," May 17, 2018, https://in.usembassy.gov/ambjusterbhutan/.

32 "Kerry Greets Bhutan on its National Day," *Business Standard*, December 18, 2015, https://www.business-standard.com/article/pti-stories/kerry-greets-bhutan-on-its-national-day-115121800102_1.html.

33 U.S. Department of State, Bureau of South and Central Asian Affairs, Bilateral Relations Fact Sheet, "U.S. Relations with Bhutan," July 29, 2020, https://www.state.gov/u-s-relations-with-bhutan/.

34 Congressional Research Service, *Bangladesh and Bangladesh-U.S. Relations*, updated October 17, 2017, https://crsreports.congress.gov/product/pdf/R/R44094/6.

35 "Do More to Resolve Rohingya Crisis: UN Envoy in Bangladesh," *Aljazeera*, December 20, 2021, https://www.aljazeera.com/news/2021/12/20/rohingya-crisis-un-envoy-bangladesh.

36 U.S. Department of State, "A Free and Open Indo-Pacific: Advancing a Shared Vision," November 4, 2019, https://www.state.gov/wp-content/uploads/2019/11/Free-and-Open-Indo-Pacific-4Nov2019.pdf (accessed October 6, 2020).

37 U.S. Department of Defense, "The Maldives and U.S. Sign Defense Agreement," September 11, 2020, accessed October 8, 2020, https://www.defense.gov/Newsroom/Releases/Release/Article/2344512/the-maldives-and-us-sign-defense-agreement/.

38 U.S. Department of State, Bureau of South and Central Asian Affairs, Bilateral Relations Fact Sheet, "U.S. Relations with Nepal," July 29, 2020, https://www.state.gov/u-s-relations-with-nepal/.

39 Embassy of Nepal, "Nepal U.S. Relations," accessed January 12, 2022, https://us.nepalembassy.gov.np/nepal-us-relations/.

40 U.S. Department of State, "U.S. Relations with Nepal."

41 "U.S.–Nepal Security Cooperation," *VOA Editorials*, April 12, 2017, https://editorials.voa.gov/a/us-nepal-security-cooperation/3807166.html.

42 U.S. Department of State, "U.S. Relations with Nepal," July 29, 2020, https://www.state.gov/u-s-relations-with-nepal/.

43 "U.S. Indo-Pacific Admiral Philip S. Davidson Visits Nepal," *Nepali Sansar*, January 11, 2019, https://www.nepalisansar.com/world/us-indo-pacific-admiral-philip-s-davidson-visits-nepal/.

44 U.S. Congress, House, Foreign Affairs and Judiciary Committees; Senate, Committee on Foreign Relations, *Tibetan Policy and Support Act of 2019*, 116th Cong., 2019–2020, H.R. 4331, https://www.congress.gov/bill/116th-congress/house-bill/4331/text?format=txt&r=3&s=1.

45 "Joint Statement from the U.S. Department of State and the Ministry of Foreign Affairs of Sri Lanka on the Second U.S.–Sri Lanka Partnership Dialogue," U.S. Indo–Pacific Command, November 6, 2017, accessed January 30, 2019, http://www.pacom.mil/Media/News/News-Article-View/Article/1364170/joint-statement-from-the-us-department-of-state-and-the-ministry-of-foreign-aff/.

46 Jeff M. Smith, *Sri Lanka: A Test Case for the Free and Open Indo-Pacific Strategy*, The Heritage Foundation, March 14, 2019, https://www.heritage.org/asia/report/sri-lanka-test-case-the-free-and-open-indo-pacific-strategy.

47 U.S. Embassy in Sri Lanka, "Statement on Decision of Millennium Challenge Corporation Board," December 17, 2020, https://lk.usembassy.gov/statement-on-decision-of-millennium-challenge-corporation-board/

48 U.S. Department of State, Bureau of South and Central Asian Affairs, Bilateral Relations Fact Sheet, "U.S. Relations with Sri Lanka," July 27, 2020, https://www.state.gov/u-s-relations-with-sri-lanka/.

Bibliography

"ASEAN Outlook on the Indo-Pacific." Accessed January 18, 2022. https://asean.org/asean2020/wp-content/uploads/2021/01/ASEAN-Outlook-on-the-Indo-Pacific_FINAL_22062019.pdf.

"Do More to Resolve Rohingya Crisis: UN Envoy in Bangladesh." *Aljazeera*, December 20, 2021. https://www.aljazeera.com/news/2021/12/20/rohingya-crisis-un-envoy-bangladesh.

"India Third Asian Nation to Get STA-1 Status from US." *The Economic Times*, August 4, 2018. https://economictimes.indiatimes.com/news/defence/india-third-asian-nation-to-get-sta-1-status-from-us/articleshow/65266841.cms.

"Islamic State in Afghanistan Could be Able to Attack U.S. in Six Months—Pentagon Official." *Reuters*, October 26, 2021. https://www.reuters.com/world/islamic-state-afghanistan-could-be-able-attack-us-six-months-pentagon-official-2021-10-26/.

"Kerry Greets Bhutan on its National Day." *Business Standard*, December 18, 2015. https://www.business-standard.com/article/pti-stories/kerry-greets-bhutan-on-its-national-day-1151218 00102_1.html.

"U.S. Indo-Pacific Admiral Philip S. Davidson Visits Nepal." *Nepali Sansar*, January 11, 2019. https://www.nepalisansar.com/world/us-indo-pacific-admiral-philip-s-davidson-visits-nepal/.

Britannica. "List of the Populations of the World's Countries, Dependencies, and Territories." World Data Editors. Accessed January 11, 2022. https://www.britannica.com/topic/list-of-the-populations-of-the-worlds-countries-dependencies-and-territories-2156538.

Congressional Research Service. *Bangladesh and Bangladesh-U.S. Relations.* Updated October 17, 2017. https://crsreports.congress.gov/product/pdf/R/R44094/6.

Diaz, Daniella. "Trump's First 2018 Tweet: Pakistan has 'Given Us Nothing but Lies & Deceit.'" *CNN Politics*, January 2, 2018. https://www.cnn.com/2018/01/01/politics/donald-trump-2018-pakistan/index.html.

Embassy of Nepal. "Nepal U.S. Relations." Accessed January 12, 2022. https://us.nepalembassy.gov.np/nepal-us-relations/.

Executive Office of the President. Office of the U.S. Trade Representative. "India." https://ustr.gov/countries-regions/south-central-asia/india.

Executive Office of the President. Office of the U.S. Trade Representative. "Free Trade Agreements." Accessed January 12, 2022. https://ustr.gov/trade-agreements/free-trade-agreements.

Executive Office of the President. Office of the U.S. Trade Representative. "South & Central Asia." Accessed January 12, 2022. https://ustr.gov/countries-regions/south-central-asia/.

Gokhale, Nitin A. "The Inside Story of India's 2016 'Surgical Strikes.'" *The Diplomat*, September 23, 2017. https://thediplomat.com/2017/09/the-inside-story-of-indias-2016-surgical-strikes/.

Gul, Ayaz. "U.S. Official Slams Taliban for Falling Short on Public Pledges." *VOA News*, October 8, 2021. https://www.voanews.com/a/us-diplomat-discusses-afghanistan-bilateral-ties-with-pakistan-leaders/6262799.html.

Hamre, John J., and Rex Tillerson. "Defining Our Relationship with India for the Next Century: An Address by U.S. Secretary of State Rex Tillerson." Center for Strategic and International Studies, October 18, 2017. https://www.csis.org/analysis/defining-our-relationship-india-next-century-address-us-secretary-state-rex-tillerson.

Index of Economic Freedom. Country Rankings. Accessed January 12, 2022. https://www.heritage.org/index/ranking.

National Security Strategy of the United States of America. December 2017. https://trumpwhitehouse.archives.gov/wp-content/uploads/2017/12/NSS-Final-12-18-2017-0905.pdf.

Office of the Historian. "Travels Abroad of the President." Accessed January 18, 2022. https://history.state.gov/departmenthistory/travels/president.

Pollock, John. "Bhutan and the Border Crisis with China." LSE South Asia Centre blog, July 19, 2021. https://blogs.lse.ac.uk/southasia/2021/07/19/bhutan-and-the-border-crisis-with-china/.

Sayed, Abdul. "The Evolution and Future of Tehrik-e-Taliban Pakistan." Carnegie Endowment for International Peace, December 21, 2021. https://carnegieendowment.org/2021/12/21/evolution-and-future-of-tehrik-e-taliban-pakistan-pub-86051.

Smith, Jeff M. "China-India Border Crisis." *Indo-Pacific Perspectives*, 29–33. https://www.airuniversity.af.edu/Portals/10/JIPA/IndoPacificPerspectives/June%202021/07%20Smith.pdf.

Smith, Jeff M. "China-India Relations in the Modi-Xi Era." U.S.-China Economic and Security Review Commission, March 10, 2016. https://www.uscc.gov/sites/default/files/SMITH_Remarks%2003101016.pdf.

Smith, Jeff M. "High Noon in the Himalayas: Behind the China-India Standoff at Doka La." *War on the Rocks*, July 13, 2017. https://warontherocks.com/2017/07/high-noon-in-the-himalayas-behind-the-china-india-standoff-at-doka-la/.

Smith, Jeff M. "India and Pakistan: Living on Borrowed Time." The Heritage Foundation, March 11, 2019. https://www.heritage.org/middle-east/commentary/india-and-pakistan-living-borrowed-time.

Smith, Jeff M. "The Haqquani Network: The New Kingmakers in Kabul." *War on the Rocks*, November 12, 2021. https://warontherocks.com/2021/11/the-haqqani-network-afghanistans-new-power-players/.

Smith, Jeff M. *Sri Lanka: A Test Case for the Free and Open Indo-Pacific Strategy.* The Heritage Foundation, March 14, 2019. https://www.heritage.org/asia/report/sri-lanka-test-case-the-free-and-open-indo-pacific-strategy.

South Asia Terrorism Portal. "Yearly Fatalities." Jammu & Kashmir Datasheet. Accessed January 11, 2022. https://www.satp.org/datasheet-terrorist-attack/fatalities/india-jammukashmir.

Stockholm International Peace Research Institute. Trade Registers. Accessed January 12, 2022. https://armstrade.sipri.org/armstrade/page/trade_register.php.

The White House. "Fact Sheet: Quad Leaders' Summit." Statements and Releases. September 24, 2021. https://www.whitehouse.gov/briefing-room/statements-releases/2021/09/24/fact-sheet-quad-leaders-summit/.

U.S. Congress. House Foreign Affairs and Judiciary Committees; Senate Committee on Foreign Relations. *Tibetan Policy and Support Act of 2019.* 116th Cong., 2019–2020. H.R. 4331. https://www.congress.gov/bill/116th-congress/house-bill/4331/text?format=txt&r=3&s=1.

U.S. Department of Defense. "The Maldives and U.S. Sign Defense Agreement." September 11, 2020. Accessed October 8, 2020. https://www.defense.gov/Newsroom/Releases/Release/Article/2344512/the-maldives-and-us-sign-defense-agreement/.

U.S. Department of State. "U.S.-Maldives Cooperation." February 20, 2019. https://www.state.gov/u-s-maldives-cooperation/.

U.S. Department of State. *A Free and Open Indo-Pacific: Advancing a Shared Vision.* November 4, 2019. https://www.state.gov/wp-content/uploads/2019/11/Free-and-Open-Indo-Pacific-4Nov2019.pdf.

U.S. Department of State. Bureau of South and Eastern Asian Affairs. "U.S. Relations with Bangladesh." Bilateral Relations Fact Sheet. January 20, 2021. https://www.state.gov/u-s-relations-with-bangladesh/.

U.S. Department of State. Bureau of South and Central Asian Affairs. "U.S. Relations with Bhutan." Bilateral Relations Fact Sheet. July 29, 2020. https://www.state.gov/u-s-relations-with-bhutan/.

U.S. Department of State. Bureau of South and Central Asian Affairs. "U.S. Relations with Nepal." Bilateral Relations Fact Sheet. July 29, 2020. https://www.state.gov/u-s-relations-with-nepal/.

U.S. Department of State. Bureau of South and Central Asian Affairs. "U.S. Relations with Sri Lanka." Bilateral Relations Fact Sheet. July 27, 2020. https://www.state.gov/u-s-relations-with-sri-lanka/.

U.S. Department of State. Office of the Spokesperson. "Secretary Blinken's Remarks on a Free and Open Indo-Pacific." Fact Sheet. December 13, 2021. https://www.state.gov/fact-sheet-secretary-blinkens-remarks-on-a-free-and-open-indo-pacific/.

U.S. Department of State. Office of the Spokesperson. "The United States and India: Deepening our Strategic Partnership." Fact Sheet. July 27, 2021. https://www.state.gov/the-united-states-and-india-deepening-our-strategic-partnership/.

U.S. Embassy and Consulates in India. "Ambassador Kenneth I. Juster Visits Bhutan." May 17, 2018. https://in.usembassy.gov/ambjusterbhutan/.

U.S. Embassy in Sri Lanka. "Statement on Decision of Millennium Challenge Corporation Board." December 17, 2020. https://lk.usembassy.gov/statement-on-decision-of-millennium-challenge-corporation-board/.

U.S. Indo–Pacific Command. "Joint Statement from the U.S. Department of State and the Ministry of Foreign Affairs of Sri Lanka on the Second U.S.–Sri Lanka Partnership Dialogue." Office of the Spokesperson. November 6, 2017. Accessed January 30, 2019. http://www.pacom.mil/Media/News/News-Article-View/Article/1364170/joint-statement-from-the-us-department-of-state-and-the-ministry-of-foreign-aff/.

United Nations. *World Population Prospects*. Department of Economic and Social Affairs. New York, 2019. https://reliefweb.int/sites/reliefweb.int/files/resources/WPP2019_Highlights.pdf. Executive.

"U.S.–Nepal Security Cooperation." *VOA Editorials*, April 12, 2017. https://editorials.voa.gov/a/us-nepal-security-cooperation/3807166.html.

Walsh, Declan. "Pakistan Orders U.S. out of Drone Base." *The Guardian*, June 30, 2011. https://www.theguardian.com/world/2011/jun/30/pakistan-orders-us-out-drone-base.

World Almanac of Islamism. "South Asia/Sri Lanka." Last updated August 16, 2020. https://almanac.afpc.org/almanac/countries/sri-lanka.

World Integrated Trade Solutions. "United States Product Exports to South Asia, in U.S.$ Thousand 2010–2019." Accessed January 12, 2022. https://wits.worldbank.org/CountryProfile/en/Country/USA/StartYear/2010/EndYear/2019/TradeFlow/Export/Indicator/XPRT-TRD-VL/Partner/SAS/Product/all-groups.

24
CHINA AND SOUTH ASIA
Beijing Builds Influence

Andrew Scobell

Introduction

Since the 1990s, the People's Republic of China (hereafter "PRC" or "China") has emerged as the most important external power in South Asia. While the PRC has long been a factor in the international relations of South Asia, over the course of the past three decades, Beijing has emerged as the most significant out-of-region great power. China has already become the region's most important external power through its economic and military involvement and is poised to also become South Asia's most significant out-of-region great power diplomatically.

China is the most sizeable and substantial rising power both across the entire Asia-Pacific—or Indo-Pacific—and in the greater global arena. South Asia is but one of several pivotal venues in China's expansive neighborhood. Chinese growing power and influence have been most dramatic and evident in other regions of the Indo-Pacific whereas China's rising activism and involvement in South Asia has been less visible until the past decade or two. By virtue of growing comprehensive national power, heightened ambitions, and geographic proximity, Beijing appears destined to play an enhanced role in the international relations of South Asia.

History and Themes

Most scholarship on relations between China and South Asia focuses explicitly on Sino-Indian relations.[1] Even those studies that claim to examine China's interactions with the entire region tend to concentrate on relations between Beijing and New Delhi.[2] Another focal point in the academic analyses on the international relations of China and South Asia is the relationship between Beijing and Islamabad while other bilateral relationships get far less attention.[3] For example, almost no attention is paid to the small Himalayan states of Nepal and Bhutan.[4] Nevertheless, the former has "enough power to play an autonomous role between China and India,"[5] while the latter, the sole South Asian state without diplomatic relations with China, shrewdly navigated a shift from Indian protectorate (since 1949) to United Nations member state (since 1971).[6] More recently, Bhutan did gain attention in 2017 when the kingdom became the target of Chinese coercion as China and India faced off in the remote Doklam plateau, which is disputed territory claimed by both Beijing and Thimphu.

330

DOI: 10.4324/9781003246626-28

The dominant themes of the scholarship on China-South Asia relations have been a specific conflict, a particular era of confrontation, or the broader rubric of strategic rivalry. A key focal point for study has been the Sino-Indian border war of 1962 while multiple studies have examined Cold War and post-Cold War era tensions between China and India.[7] While there have been periods of comity and cooperation, notably in the 1950s and 1980s, these brighter chapters tend to be considered the exception rather than the rule.

The dominant theme of recent decades in studies of China's relations with South Asia has been interstate rivalry. The landmark volume in this vein is John Garver's *Protracted Contest*, which provides an in-depth analysis of the "deep and enduring geopolitical rivalry" between Beijing and New Delhi during the second half of the 20th century.[8] Garver "isolates and analyzes the conflictual element of ... [Sino-Indian] relations" in a thorough and comprehensive study that incorporates consideration of smaller South Asian states.[9] Volumes during the subsequent decades continue to frame China's relationship with India as an enduring rivalry.[10] Susan Shirk has described Sino-Indian relations as a "one-sided rivalry" as a way to depict the asymmetrical nature of strategic competition between Beijing and New Delhi.[11] While most Indians see the two countries locked in an ongoing peer or near-peer great power rivalry, most Chinese perceive India as not constituting serious strategic competition for China. Although many Indians recognize that the balance of hard power—economic and military—is significantly skewed in China's favor, most continue to perceive the two great powers as being on par with each other. By contrast, many Chinese consider India to be a tier below China—certainly not in the same league.[12]

China's relations with other states in South Asia have fluctuated from conflict to cooperation. China's most enduring cooperative bilateral relationship in the region, and indeed anywhere in the world, has been with Pakistan. Relations between Beijing and Islamabad have been characterized as an "axis," an "entente," and an "entente cordiale" underscoring the close-knit nature of bilateral ties.[13] Cooperation with Pakistan strengthened in the early 1960s as China's relations with India worsened and India developed a closer relationship with the Soviet Union just as Beijing's own relationship with Moscow deteriorated from a formal security alliance to outright conventional military confrontation and conflict on their common border to the very brink of nuclear war.

China has formed close relationships with the island states of Sri Lanka and the Maldives. After establishing full diplomatic ties with Colombo in 1957, Beijing developed cordial relations over subsequent decades. Economic activity has ramped up as China increased its trade, investments, and construction of infrastructure. Particular attention has focused on major port facilities and an airport at Hambantota. China has also sold an array of arms to Sri Lanka and increased its military engagement. The 2014 visit of a Song class submarine to Colombo underscored Beijing's geostrategic interest in the Indian Ocean region. The Maldives have also attracted China's interest in the 2010s. After gaining independence in 1965, the Maldives established diplomatic relations with China in 1972. Decades later, the Maldives opened an embassy in Beijing (in 2009) and China opened its embassy in Male two years later (in 2011). China is involved in several infrastructure projects, including an airport and a bridge. Moreover, hundreds of thousands of Chinese tourists have visited the Maldives in the last decade. There is also a security dimension to Sino-Maldives relations. This includes port visits by Chinese naval vessels and a 2017 agreement for Beijing to build an ocean observation facility on the northern island of Makunudhoo. While speculation swirls that China will establish a naval base in the Maldives, Beijing insists that this installation will be purely for civilian scientific purposes.[14]

Meanwhile, China's relationship with Bangladesh was tense in the early years of the latter's existence. Formerly part of Pakistan, Bangladesh attained independence in 1971 with Indian support. Initially Beijing was wary of Dhaka and until 1974 blocked its entry into the United Nations. But China's relations with Bangladesh have warmed considerably since the two countries established full diplomatic relations in 1976. Dhaka has become a significant market for Chinese weapons and Beijing is building an array of Bangladeshi infrastructure, including a railway project, a tunnel project, and a sewage treatment plant. Other scholarship, rather than focus on bilateral relationships, analyzes China's relations with the entire South Asian region, some of it very comprehensively.[15]

Recent Trends

The literature on China's relations with South Asia has elements of both continuity and change. On the former, research continues on enduring territorial disputes, with the major focus on bilateral disputes between China and India. One treatment of the Sino-Indian border dispute by Taylor Fravel stands out. Coverage of the Himalayan standoff over territory constitutes only a portion of *Strong Borders, Secure Nation*—the volume surveys all China's border disputes—but it stands as one of the most thorough, authoritative, and theoretically informed on the topic.[16]

Continuing albeit less scholarship focuses on ethnic unrest in the western Chinese border regions of Tibet and Xinjiang and among ethnic minorities—Tibetans and Uighurs—in the context of China's relations with South Asia. China's relations with South Asia are impacted by the presence in India of the Tibetan government-in-exile and the residence of the Tibetan spiritual (and temporal) leader the Dalai Lama since the Tibetan revolt of 1959. India is also home to more than one hundred thousand ethnic Tibetans—most of whom are refugees. Beijing perceives New Delhi to be at the very least sympathetic to the cause and at most grasping Tibet as a point of leverage and means to interfere in China's internal affairs. According to Mao Zedong, speaking in 1964 to a delegation from Nepal: "The major problem [in India-China relations] is ... the Tibet question."[17] The Tibet issue is not simply a dispute over territory but also a transnational ethno-religious one with potent identity politics at play for China, India, and the Tibetan diaspora.

China's relations with South Asia are also impacted by another transnational ethnic group—the Uyghurs, approximately a million of whom reside outside the borders of the PRC, mostly in Central Asia and Europe. Nevertheless, some Uyghurs reside in Afghanistan and Pakistan and have been active in insurgencies and extremist groups in these countries. Starting in the 1980s, ethnic Uyghurs studied at madrassas and trained in camps in Pakistan at a time when China's southwestern neighbor became Xinjiang's gateway to the world and a waystation for Chinese Muslims embarking on the hajj. By the 21st century, Beijing had become deeply concerned about Pakistan's role promoting religious extremism and militancy within western China.[18] China's massive infusion of Belt and Road Initiative (BRI) funds in Pakistan since the 2010s—dubbed the China-Pakistan Economic Corridor (CPEC)—is considered an investment in China's future. Beijing hopes that greater stability and prosperity in Pakistan stimulated by Chinese infrastructure projects in the country will in turn contribute to greater stability within neighboring Xinjiang.[19]

There have also been major changes in the China-South Asia relations literature. One change is a broadening from a narrow focus on traditional security issues, such as interstate war, to nontraditional security issues, such as terrorism and political economy. The shocking terrorist attacks in the United States on September 11, 2001, and other subsequent high-profile terrorist incidents in China, India, and Pakistan, which are invariably perceived by the government in the target state as the result of transnational networks facilitated or sponsored by hostile states, have expanded the scope of major studies of Beijing's relations with South Asia.[20] China's growing trade with and investment in South Asian states has also generated studies of China's economic relations with the region.[21]

Moreover, the China-South Asia relations literature on military matters has expanded from analyses of border clashes and confrontations—mostly between Chinese and Indian troops—to include bilateral military exercises—the majority being between the militaries of China and Pakistan. Military relations between Beijing and New Delhi have grown complex on the one hand, including violent and sometimes lethal hand-to-hand combat along their common disputed frontier,[22] while on the other hand including cooperation to conduct periodic bilateral counterterrorism and naval search and rescue drills.[23] China is also a significant supplier of weaponry and equipment to the militaries of Bangladesh and Pakistan.[24]

A second shift in the international relations of China and South Asia is from an exclusive focus on Sino-Indian continental competition to nuclear competition, to maritime competition, and to economic competition between China and India. Nuclear competition as an area of study leapt to the fore following the Indian and Pakistani nuclear tests of May 1998. But this development is not merely an India-Pakistan dynamic for two reasons. First, because China provided vital assistance to Pakistan's nuclear program and second, because India explicitly justified its acquisition of a nuclear arsenal as being to counter the threat from China.[25]

Maritime competition also emerged as an area of study as China expanded its commercial shipping tonnage and activism: Indeed, its seaborne trade in the Indo-Pacific and beyond grew and its consumption of petroleum imported from the Middle East and Africa increased. The result was increased traffic in the sea lanes crisscrossing the Indian Ocean and greater attention to the body of water by Beijing.[26] Lagging behind China's civilian maritime presence but nonetheless clearly discernible was the gradual growth in China's naval presence in the Indian Ocean. This presence includes not just deployments of People's Liberation Army Navy (PLAN) surface and subsurface vessels but also the growing number of visits by PLAN vessels to ports across the region signaling the emergence of a naval rivalry between Beijing and New Delhi.[27] This increased activity and increasing rivalry raise the specter of what several Indian analysts attending a seminar sponsored by a US-based international consultancy two decades ago dubbed an emerging Chinese "string of pearls"—naval bases or logistics hubs in countries around the rim of the Indian Ocean.[28] Following the establishment of China's first official overseas military base in the small Horn of African state of Djibouti in 2017, speculation has grown that China would establish additional naval bases with some of the most plausible locations being around the rim of the Indian Ocean, perhaps even in Pakistan.[29]

In addition, China's economic engagement and presence in South Asia has greatly expanded. The most high-profile dimension has been China's 2013 launch of paramount leader Xi Jinping's flagship foreign policy initiative, the Belt and Road Initiative (BRI), with a substantial focus on the subcontinent. Two further points merit mention. First, BRI has been dubbed "debt trap diplomacy" and depicted as a ploy by which Beijing deliberately seeks to ensnare developing countries in financial servitude and neocolonial dependency. A prominent case often cited is that of Sri Lanka and China's involvement in the port project at Hambantota. Second, BRI serves to on the one hand highlight the enduring great power rivalry between China and India while on the other hand underscoring the resilience of the long-standing cooperative relationship between China and Pakistan. In the wake of Beijing's highly ambitious global initiative to finance and build massive infrastructure projects, New Delhi distinguished itself as one of the small number of capitals to decline to participate in the BRI. In dramatic contrast, Pakistan became the largest single recipient of Belt and Road funds anywhere in the world—reportedly $46 billion dollars. Moreover, at least some projects were being built on disputed territory controlled by Pakistan but claimed by India.[30]

Two lacunae in the scholarship on China-South Asia relations are Afghanistan and multilateral fora. Largely absent from the literature—or at least receiving minimal attention—is China-Afghan relations. Although the two countries share a short 92-kilometer border and Afghanistan has been described as being "on the periphery of China's diplomacy,"[31] in recent decades, Kabul has loomed disproportionately large for Beijing. Afghanistan straddles the fault line between South and Central Asia and has proved to be an epicenter of regional instability and Islamic radicalism. Since the Soviet withdrawal from the country in 1989, China has taken a pragmatic and even-handed approach in dealing with the regime in power. While Beijing's direct influence in Afghanistan has been very limited, it can potentially exert influence indirectly thorough Pakistan. However, to date this mechanism has remained unexercised.[32]

A second gap in the scholarship has been China-South Asia multilateral interactions, whether in global or regional fora. Chinese involvement with the states of South Asia in the United Nations, for example, has received very little attention. Chinese participation in the South Asian Association for Regional Cooperation (SAARC) has garnered little attention—since 2005, China has held observer status in the regional organization.[33] Similarly, Indian and Pakistani involvement in the Shanghai Cooperation Organization has also received almost no attention since the two South Asian states were admitted to membership in 2017.

Theoretical Paradigms

The dominant theoretical approach to the study of China's international relations with South Asia is realism with multiple authors embracing the paradigm and invoking the security dilemma to explain the confrontational nature of relations between Beijing and New Delhi.[34] Most scholars have blended realism with other approaches. A number of scholars have emphasized geopolitics, either implicitly or explicitly.[35] Other studies have incorporated constructivism in their analyses and/or highlighted ideational factors.[36]

Future Trends

The current burgeoning rubric in the scholarship on China-South Asia relations is geopolitical rivalry, and this seems destined to remain prominent. There are several reasons for this. First, China's relations with most states, not just the United States but almost all great powers, including all but a handful of neighboring states in the Indo-Pacific, have deteriorated in recent years and all of them exhibit few signs of ameliorating any time soon. Notable exceptions are several states geographically proximate to China—Russia, North Korea, and Pakistan—that each currently enjoy cordial relations with China. Yet, of these three states—all of which happen to be nuclear powers—only Pakistan has maintained a consistently positive and cooperative relationship with China across many decades.

Second, a range of countries have strengthened and/or seem likely to strengthen their relationships and cooperation with other states or constellations of states to counter China's growing might and contentiousness. There are, of course, an array of US allies in the Indo-Pacific and beyond that have increasingly gauged China to be more powerful, more adversarial, and more threatening. As a result, these states look to balance by enhancing their cooperation with the United States and each other. Manifestations of this include a reinvigorated Quadrilateral Security Dialogue (aka "the Quad"), which includes Australia, India, Japan, and the United States, as well as the recently constituted AUKUS grouping of Australia, the United

China and South Asia

Kingdom, and the United States. Even the rise to prominence in recent years of an Indo-Pacific geostrategic construct in lieu of Asia-Pacific formulation signals a change in the way the United States and other states—including India, Japan, and Australia—conceive of the region and China's disposition within it. Hence, rivalry and geostrategic competition will almost certainly continue to dominate the literature in China-South Asia relations for the foreseeable future.

Another emerging trend in the literature on China-South Asia relations is nuclear dynamics.[37] The nuclear dimension looms larger and more ominously hence fueling greater concern about and attention to strategic stability on the subcontinent. Two strategic dyads present themselves and are inextricably linked: The most prominent India-Pakistan nuclear dyad and the more low-profile China-India nuclear dyad. It seems appropriate to speak of a Beijing-Islamabad-New Delhi strategic triangle because a change in the relationship between any two of the three vertices inevitably impacts the third. Moreover, South Asia constitutes "Exhibit A" in the contemporary study of the stability-instability paradox: Being the only region in the world where two nuclear power dyads have come to blows conventionally during the past three decades and the threat of nuclear escalation has seemed frighteningly plausible even while multiple political-military crises and conventional border confrontations have come and gone without escalating to nuclear usage.

Yet the future trajectory of China-South Asia relations is not preordained. While continuity with the past and current emerging trends are likely to persist, one can also anticipate discontinuities and disruptions. Brief consideration of four topics merits attention. First, China's considerable economic engagement with South Asia, while likely to persist in the foreseeable future, will also continue to face serious challenges and could conceivably flounder. Indeed, BRI projects have already confronted problems in multiple countries, notably in Pakistan and Sri Lanka. These problems could ultimately be rectified but it is possible that they will not and engender economic hardship. This in turn could foment social upheaval and generate political instability within countries. Furthermore, an implicit assumption of most scholars is that China's economy will continue to grow and Beijing's economic global activism will persist and even expand. Yet, it seems implausible that the Chinese economy will grow indefinitely. Indeed, retrenchment, recession, or extreme downturn are possible, and any one of these outcomes would certainly impact China's economic presence and posture in South Asia in predictable as well as unpredictable ways.

Second, China's relationship with its two most important partners in South Asia is impossible to predict going forward. Continuity seems most likely in Beijing's relations with both New Delhi and Islamabad. The former relationship will almost certainly continue to be contentious but relatively stable while the latter relationship will very probably remain cordial and cooperative. Yet, each could experience shocks and/or unexpected disruptions. Unforeseen circumstances could see a dramatic improvement in Sino-Indian relations, although a more plausible trajectory would be a more serious worsening of ties between Beijing-New Delhi. A deterioration in bilateral relations could be triggered by a future clash along their disputed border and escalate horizontally into a wider conventional conflict or vertically into a nuclear face-off. Meanwhile, China's enduring friendship in Pakistan could rupture, ignited by a dispute. While it seems likely that Sino-Pakistani relations will remain cordial and cooperative in the foreseeable future, this state of affairs should not be assumed.

Third, Afghanistan is likely to become more important as a factor in China's relations with South Asia. As noted above, Beijing considers Kabul important in its own right. The Taliban takeover of Afghanistan and the US pullout of Kabul in 2021, far from simplifying the situation on China's westernmost flank, had created new headaches and complications for Beijing.[38] But Beijing has indicated a readiness to work with the Afghan Taliban and

335

the Taliban leadership has signaled a willingness to engage with China. Afghanistan can serve as a reason for cooperation or conflict between China and multiple countries in South Asia. Most obviously, the country will impact China-Pakistan relations. Yet, Afghanistan will also figure in China's relations with India and other states of the region. At a minimum, South Asian capitals will closely monitor how China behaves vis-à-vis Afghanistan—whether Beijing is constructive and engaged, or aloof and absent, will influence how leaders in New Delhi, Dhaka, Colombo, and elsewhere perceive Beijing's engagement in the region.

Fourth, China's involvement with South Asia in multilateral fora is not easy to forecast. Beijing's interest and activism in multilateral organizations has significantly increased during the past two decades. While in the past, China's preference has been to use these platforms as umbrellas under which it can work bilaterally, as Beijing becomes more ambitious within existing multilateral organizations and its own multilateral creations, Chinese behavior may adjust accordingly.[39]

Conclusion

In recent decades, the PRC has built up its power and influence in South Asia to become the region's most significant out-of-area great power. Dominant themes across seven decades of international relations between China and South Asia are rivalry and confrontation with smoldering strategic competition between China and India front and center, while China's most enduring cooperative relationship remains with Pakistan. The scope of the rivalry between Beijing and New Delhi is simmering and has widened as interactions have increased and grown increasingly complex with burgeoning bilateral relations. Geopolitical realism, rooted in structural and ideational sources, best explains historical and contemporary developments.

The China-India rivalry appears at once "intractable and manageable."[40] Beijing and New Delhi have weathered previous crises and tensions, such as the aftermath of the 1998 Indian nuclear tests, which caught China and the rest of the world by surprise.[41] Nevertheless, areas of cooperation and mutual benefit such as "trade and mutual economic gains have not neutralized the security dilemma."[42] As a result, what Mark Frazier dubbed two decades ago "quiet competition"[43] has in recent years become more outspoken, rambunctious, and, at times, even lethal. In June 2020, the most serious border clash since the 1962 border war occurred in the Galwan Valley with at least 20 fatalities.[44]

While Beijing's attention to South Asia with likely remain centered on New Delhi and Islamabad, its regional aperture will continue to widen with Colombo, Dhaka, and other capitals figuring more prominently. The outlook for China's relations with South Asia is unclear, but the actual trajectory will likely see more Chinese influence that will generate divergent impulses, stimulating forces for both stability and instability in the region.

Notes

1 See, for example, John W. Garver, *Protracted Contest: Sino-Indian Rivalry in the Twentieth Century* (Seattle: University of Washington Press, 2001) and T.V. Paul, *The China-India Rivalry in the Globalization Era* (Washington, DC: Georgetown University Press, 2018).

2 See, for example, G.W. Chaudhury, *India, Pakistan, Bangladesh and the Major Powers* (New York: Free Press, 1975).

3 On Pakistan, see for example, Andrew Small, *China-Pakistan Axis: Asia's New Geopolitics* (New York: Oxford University Press, 2015) and Yaacov Vertzberger, *The Enduring Entente: Sino-Pakistan Relations, 1960–1980* (New York: Praeger, 1982).

China and South Asia

4 For some notable exceptions, see Surjit Mansingh, "China-Bhutan Relations," *China Report* 30, no. 2 (1994); Vijay Kumar, *India and Sri Lanka-China Relation (1948–1984)* (New Delhi: Uppal, 1986); T.R. Ghoble, *China-Nepal Relations and India* (New Delhi: Deep and Deep, 1991).

5 Garver, *Protracted Contest*, 138.

6 Garver, *Protracted Contest*, 180.

7 On the 1962 war, see, for example, Neville Maxwell, *China's India War* (Garden City: Anchor Books, 1972); Allen S. Whiting, *The Chinese Calculus of Deterrence* (Ann Arbor: University of Michigan Press, 1975); Cheng Feng and Larry M. Wortzel, "PLA Operational Principles and Limited War: The Sino-Indian War of 1962," in *Chinese Warfighting: The PLA Experience Since 1949*, eds. Mark A. Ryan, David M. Finkelstein, and Michael A. McDevitt (Armonk: M.E. Sharpe, 2003), 173–197; John W. Garver, "China's Decision for War in 1962," in *New Directions in the Study of Chinese Foreign Policy*, eds. Alastair Iain Johnston and Robert S. Ross (Princeton: Princeton University Press, 2006), 86–130. On the relationship during the Cold War, see Garver, *Protracted Contest*. See also Tanvi Madan, *Fateful Triangle: How China Shaped U.S.-Indian Relations during the Cold War* (Washington, DC: Brookings Institution Press, 2020). On the post-Cold War relationship, see Waheguru Pal Singh Sidhu and Jing-dong Yuan, *China and India: Cooperation or Conflict?* (Boulder: Lynne Rienner, 2003).

8 Quote in Garver, *Protracted Contest*, 4.

9 Quote in Garver, *Protracted Contest*, 4.

10 See, for example, Mohan Malik, *China and India: Great Power Rivals* (Boulder: First Forum, 2011) and Jeff M. Smith, *Cold Peace: Sino-Indian Rivalry in the Twenty-First Century* (Lanham: Lexington Books, 2013).

11 Susan Shirk, "One-Sided Rivalry: China's Perceptions and Policies toward India," in *The India-China Relationship: What America Needs to Know*, eds. Francine R. Frankel and Harry Harding (New York: Columbia University Press, 2004), 75–102.

12 See, for example, Shirk, "One-Sided Rivalry."

13 Small, *China-Pakistan Axis*; Vertzberger, *The Enduring Entente*; Garver, *Protracted Contest*, chapter 7.

14 "Beijing says Maldives Marine Observatory is Non-military," *Asia Times*, February 28, 2018, https://asiatimes.com/2018/02/beijing-says-maldives-marine-observatory-non-military/.

15 See, for example, Andrew Scobell et al., *At the Dawn of Belt and Road: China in the Developing World* (Santa Monica: RAND, 2018). Chapter 6 surveys China's involvement in South Asia.

16 M. Taylor Fravel, *Strong Borders, Secure Nation: Cooperation and Conflict in China's Territorial Disputes* (Princeton: Princeton University Press, 2008). Other significant contributions include Šumit Ganguly, "India and China: Border Issues, Domestic Integration and International Security," in *The India-China Relationship*, eds. Frankel and Harding, 103–133, and Mahesh Shankar, "Territory and China-India Competition," in *The China-India Rivalry in the Globalization Era*, ed. T.V. Paul (Washington, DC: Georgetown University Press, 2018), 27–54.

17 Mao's quote appears in Garver, *Protracted Contest*, 59.

18 Andrew Small, *The China-Pakistan Axis: Asia's New Geopolitics* (New York: Oxford University Press, 2015), 71.

19 Daniel Markey, *China's Western Horizon: Beijing and the New Geopolitics of Eurasia* (New York: Oxford University Press, 2020), 47.

20 See, for example, Small, *The China-Pakistan Axis*.

21 Scobell et al., *At the Dawn of Belt and Road*, chapter 6, and Matthew Castle, "Globalization's Impact: Trade and Investment on China-India Relations," in *The China-India Rivalry in the Globalization Era*, ed. T.V. Paul, 205–230.

22 USIP China-South Asia Senior Study Group, *China's Impact on South Asian Conflict Processes* (Washington, DC: United State Institute of Peace, 2020), 36.

23 Scobell et al., *At the Dawn of Belt and Road*, Table 6.2 on 141.

24 Scobell et al., *At the Dawn of Belt and Road*, 138.

25 On China's involvement in Pakistan's acquisition of a nuclear program, see Garver, *Protracted Contest*, 324–331; on China as an explicit rationale for India's pursuit of nuclear weapons, see Garver, *Protracted Contest*, 336–337.

26 Jingdong Yuan, "China and the Indian Ocean: New Departures in Regional Balancing," in *Deep Currents and Rising Tides: The Indian Ocean and International Security*, eds. John Garofano and Andrea J. Dew (Washington, DC: Georgetown University Press, 2013), 157–184.

27 James R. Holmes and Toshi Yoshihara, "Redlines for Sino-Indian Naval Rivalry," in *Deep Currents and Rising Tides*, eds. Garofano and Dew, 185–212.

28 Julia A. McDonald et al., *Energy Futures in Asia* (McLean: Booz Allen Hamilton, 2004) and Christopher Pehrson, *String of Pearls: Meeting the Challenge of China's Growing Influence across the Asian Littoral* (Carlisle Barracks: U.S. Army War College Strategic Studies Institute, 2006).

29 For analysis, see Isaac B. Kardon et al., *Gwadar: China's Potential Strategic Strongpoint in Pakistan* (Newport: U.S. Naval War College China Maritime Studies Institute, 2020).

30 Andrew Scobell, "Himalayan Standoff: Strategic Culture and the China-India Rivalry," in *China-India Rivalry in the Era of Globalization*, ed. T.V. Paul, 165–186, at 177.

31 Zhao Huasheng, *China and Afghanistan: China's Interests, Stances, and Perspectives* (Washington, DC: Center for Strategic and International Studies, 2012), p. 2.

32 Andrew Scobell, "China Ponders Post-2014 Afghanistan: Neither 'All in' Nor Bystander," *Asian Survey* 55, no. 2 (March/April 2015): 325–345.

33 For an exception, see Jagannath P. Panda, "China in SAARC: Evaluating the PRC's Institutional Engagement and Regional Designs," *China Report* 46, no. 3 (2010): 299–310.

34 See, for example, Garver, *Protracted Contest*, 16ff, and George J. Gilboy and Eric Heginbotham, *Chinese and Indian Strategic Behavior: Growing Power and Alarm* (New York: Cambridge University Press, 2013), 273ff.

35 Garver, *Protracted Contest*; Andrew Scobell et al., *China's Strategy toward South and Central Asia: The Empty Fortress* (Santa Monica: RAND, 2014); Small, *China-Pakistan Axis*; Markey, *China's Western Horizon*.

36 Andrew Scobell, "'Cult of Defense' and 'Great Power Dreams': Strategic Culture in Sino-Indian Relations," in *South Asia in 2020*, ed. Michael R. Chambers (Carlisle Barracks: U.S. Army War College Strategic Studies Institute, 2002), 329–360; Andrew Bingham Kennedy, *The International Ambitions of Mao and Nehru: National Efficacy Beliefs and the Making of Foreign Policy* (New York: Cambridge University Press, 2012); Gilboy and Heginbotham, *Chinese and Indian Strategic Behavior*; Jagannath Panda, *India-China Relations: Politics of Resources, Identity, and Authority in a Multipolar World Order* (New York: Routledge, 2017); Scobell, "Himalayan Standoff," in *China-India Rivalry in the Era of Globalization*, ed. T.V. Paul, 165–186; Xiaoyu Pu, "Status Concerns and the China-India Rivalry," in *The China-India Rivalry in the Era of Globalization*, ed. T.V. Paul, 55–74.

37 See, for example, Lowell Dittmer, ed., *South Asia's Nuclear Dilemma: India, Pakistan, and China* (Armonk: M.E. Sharpe, 2005); Vipin Narang, "Nuclear Deterrence in the China-India Dyad," in *The China-India Rivalry in the Globalization Era*, ed. T.V. Paul (Washington, DC: Georgetown University Press, 2018), 187–204; George Perkovich, "The Nuclear and Security Balance," in *The India-China Relationship: What the United States Needs to Know*, eds. Francine Frankel and Harry Harding (New York: Columbia University Press, 2004), 178–218.

38 Andrew Scobell, "China and the U.S. Exit from Afghanistan: Not a Zero-Sum Outcome," *Analysis and Commentary*, United States Institute of Peace, September 22, 2021, https://www.usip.org/publications/2021/09/china-and-us-exit-afghanistan-not-zero-sum-outcome.

39 Scott L. Kastner, Margaret M. Pearson, and Chad Rector, *China's Strategic Multilateralism: Investing in Global Governance* (New York: Cambridge University Press, 2018).

40 Mahesh Shankar, "Territory and China-India Competition," in *The China-India Rivalry in the Globalization Era*, ed. T.V. Paul, 27–54.

41 John W. Garver, "The Restoration of Sino-Indian Comity Following India's Nuclear Tests," *The China Quarterly* 168 (December 2001): 865–889.

42 Jonathan Holslag, *China and India: Prospects for Peace* (New York: Columbia University Press, 2010), 169.

43 Mark W. Frazier, "Quiet Competition and the Future of Sino-Indian Relations," in *The India-China Relationship*, eds. Frankel and Harding, 294–320.

44 Andrew Scobell and Šumit Ganguly, "China's Latest Tussle with India Could Lead to War," *The National Interest*, June 20, 2020, https://nationalinterest.org/feature/chinas-latest-tussle-india-could-lead-war-163111.

Bibliography

"Beijing says Maldives Marine Observatory is Non-Military." *Asia Times*, February 28, 2018. https://asiatimes.com/2018/02/beijing-says-maldives-marine-observatory-non-military/.

Castle, Matthew A. "Globalization's Impact: Trade and Investment in China-India Relations." In *China-India Rivalry in an Era of Globalization*, edited by T.V. Paul, 205–230. Washington, DC: Georgetown University Press, 2018.

Chaudhury, G.W. *India, Pakistan, Bangladesh and the Major Powers*. New York: Free Press, 1975.

Dittmer, Lowell, ed. *South Asia's Nuclear Dilemma: India, Pakistan, and China*. Armonk: M.E. Sharpe, 2005.

Feng, Cheng, and Larry M. Wortzel. "PLA Operational Principles and Limited War: The Sino-Indian War of 1962." In *Chinese Warfighting: The PLA Experience Since 1949*, edited by Mark A. Ryan, David M. Finkelstein, and Michael A. McDevitt, 173–197. Armonk: M.E. Sharpe, 2003.

Fravel, M. Taylor. *Strong Borders, Secure Nation: Cooperation and Conflict in China's Territorial Disputes*. Princeton: Princeton University Press, 2008.

Frazier, Mark. "Quiet Competition and the Future of Sino-Indian Relations." In *The India-China Relationship: What the United States Needs to Know*, edited by Francine R. Frankel and Harry Harding, 294–320. New York: Columbia University Press, 2004.

Ganguly, Šumit. "India and China: Border Issues, Domestic Integration and International Security." In *The India-China Relationship: What the United States Needs to Know*, edited by Francine R. Frankel and Harry Harding, 103–133. New York: Columbia University Press, 2004.

Garver, John W. "China's Decision for War in 1962." In *New Directions in the Study of Chinese Foreign Policy*, edited by Alastair Iain Johnston and Robert S. Ross, 86–130. Princeton: Princeton University Press, 2006.

Garver, John W. "The Restoration of Sino-Indian Comity Following India's Nuclear Tests." *China Quarterly* 168 (December 2001): 865–889.

Garver, John W. *Protracted Contest: Sino-Indian Rivalry in the Twentieth Century*. Seattle: University of Washington Press, 2001.

Ghoble, T.R. *China-Nepal Relations and India*. New Delhi: Deep and Deep, 1991.

Gilboy, George J., and Eric Heginbotham. *Chinese and Indian Strategic Behavior: Growing Power and Alarm*. New York: Cambridge University Press, 2013.

Holmes, James R., and Toshi Yoshihara. "Redlines for Sino-Indian Naval Rivalry." In *Deep Currents and Rising Tides: The Indian Ocean and International Security*, edited by John Garofano and Andrea J. Dew, 185–212. Washington, DC: Georgetown University Press, 2013.

Holslag, Jonathan. *China and India: Prospects for Peace*. New York: Columbia University Press, 2010.

Kardon, Isaac B., Conor M. Kennedy, and Peter M. Dutton. *Gwadar: China's Potential Strategic Strongpoint in Pakistan*. Newport: China Maritime Studies Institute, 2020.

Kastner, Scott L., Margaret M. Pearson, and Chad Rector. *China's Strategic Multilateralism: Investing in Global Governance*. New York: Cambridge University Press, 2018.

Kennedy, Andrew Bingham. *The International Ambitions of Mao and Nehru: National Efficacy Beliefs and the Making of Foreign Policy*. New York: Cambridge University Press, 2012.

Kumar, Vijay. *India and Sri Lanka-China Relation (1948-1984)*. New Delhi: Uppal, 1986.

Madan, Tanvi. *Fateful Triangle: How China Shaped U.S.-Indian Relations During the Cold War*. Washington, DC: Brookings Institution Press, 2020.

Malik, Mohan. *China and India: Great Power Rivals*. Boulder: First Forum Press, 2011.

Mansingh, Surjit. "China-Bhutan Relations." *China Report* 30, no. 2 (1994): 75–86.

Markey, Daniel. *China's Western Horizon: Beijing and the New Geopolitics of Eurasia*. New York: Oxford University Press, 2020.

Maxwell, Neville. *China's India War*. Garden City: Anchor Books, 1972.

McDonald, Juli A., Amy Donahue, and Bethany Danyulk. *Energy Futures in Asia*. McLean: Booz Allen Hamilton, 2004.

Narang, Vipin. "Nuclear Deterrence in the China-India Dyad." In *The China-India Rivalry in the Globalization Era*, edited by T.V. Paul, 187–204. Washington, DC: Georgetown University Press, 2018.

Panda, Jagannath P. "China in SAARC: Evaluating the PRC's Institutional Engagement and Regional Designs." *China Report* 46, no. 3 (2010): 299–310.

Panda, Jagannath P. *China-India Relations: Politics of Resources, Identity and Authority in a Multipolar World Order*. New York: Routledge, 2017.

Paul, T.V., ed. *The China-India Rivalry in the Globalization Era*. Washington, DC: Georgetown University Press, 2018.

Pehrson, Christopher. *String of Pearls: Meeting the Challenge of China's Growing Influence across the Asian Littoral*. Carlisle Barracks: U.S. Army War College Strategic Studies Institute, 2006.

Perkovich, George. "The Nuclear and Security Balance." In *The India-China Relationship: What the United States Needs to Know*, edited by Francine R. Frankel and Harry Harding, 178–218. New York: Columbia University Press, 2004.

Pu, Xiaoyu. "Status Concerns and the China-India Rivalry." In *The China-India Rivalry in the Globalization Era*, edited by T.V. Paul, 55–74. Washington, DC: Georgetown University Press, 2018.

Scobell, Andrew. "China and the U.S. Exit from Afghanistan: Not a Zero-Sum Outcome." *Analysis and Commentary*, United States Institute of Peace, September 22, 2021. https://www.usip.org/publications/2021/09/china-and-us-exit-afghanistan-not-zero-sum-outcome.

Scobell, Andrew. "'Cult of Defense' and 'Great Power Dreams': The Influence of Strategic Culture on China's Relationship with India." In *South Asia in 2020: Future Strategic Balances and Alliances*, edited by Michael R. Chambers, 329–360. Carlisle Barracks: U.S. Army War College Strategic Studies Institute, 2002.

Scobell, Andrew. "China Ponders Post-2014 Afghanistan: Neither 'All in' Nor Bystander." *Asian Survey* 55, no. 2 (March/April 2015): 325–345.

Scobell, Andrew. "Himalayan Standoff: Strategic Culture and the China-India Rivalry." In *The China-India Rivalry in the Globalization Era*, edited by T.V. Paul, 165–186. Washington, DC: Georgetown University Press, 2018.

Scobell, Andrew, and Šumit Ganguly. "China's Latest Tussle with India Could Lead to War." *The National Interest*, June 20, 2020. https://nationalinterest.org/feature/chinas-latest-tussle-india-could-lead-war-163111.

Scobell, Andrew, Bonny Lin, Howard J. Shatz, Michael Johnston, Larry Hanauer, Michael S. Chase, Astrid Struth Cevallos, Ivan W. Rassmussen, Arthur Chan, and Aaron Strong et al. *At the Dawn of Belt and Road: China in the Developing World*. Santa Monica: RAND, 2018.

Scobell, Andrew, Ely Ratner, and Michael Beckley. *China's Strategy toward South and Central Asia: The Empty Fortress*. Santa Monica: RAND, 2014.

Shankar, Mahesh. "Territory and China-India Competition." In *The China-India Rivalry in the Globalization Era*, edited by T.V. Paul, 27–54. Washington, DC: Georgetown University Press, 2018.

Shirk, Susan L. "One-Sided Rivalry: China's Perceptions and Policies toward India." In *The India-China Relationship: What the United States Needs to Know*, edited by Francine R. Frankel and Harry Harding, 75–102. New York: Columbia University Press, 2004.

Sidhu, Waheguru Pal Singh, and Jing-dong Yuan. *China and India: Cooperation or Conflict?* Boulder: Lynne Rienner, 2003.

Small, Andrew. *The China-Pakistan Axis: Asia's New Geopolitics*. New York: Oxford University Press, 2015.

Smith, Jeff M. *Cold Peace: Sino-Indian Rivalry in the Twenty-First Century*. Lanham: Lexington Books, 2013.

USIP China-South Asia Senior Study Group. *China's Influence on the Conflict Processes in South Asia*. Washington, DC: United States Institute of Peace, 2020.

Vertzberger, Yaacov. *The Enduring Entente: Sino-Pakistan Relations, 1960-1980*. New York: Praeger, 1982.

Whiting, Allen S. *The Chinese Calculus of Deterrence: India and Indochina*. Ann Arbor: University of Michigan Press, 1975.

Yuan, Jingdong. "China and the Indian Ocean: New Departures in Regional Balancing." In *Deep Currents and Rising Tides*, edited by John Garofano and Andrea J. Dew, 157–184. Washington, DC: Georgetown University Press, 2013.

Zhao, Huasheng. *China and Afghanistan: China's Interests, Stances, and Perspectives*. Washington, DC: Center for Strategic and International Studies, 2012.

25

RUSSIA AND SOUTH ASIA

Vidya Nadkarni

Moscow's abiding interest in South Asia is rooted in the region's proximity to Central Asia, which Russia has traditionally claimed as a sphere of influence.[1] Since the late 19th century, complex and dynamic intra- and inter-regional interactions have shaped imperial, Soviet, and post-Soviet Russia's calculation of strategic objectives in the geographical space occupied by Afghanistan, India, and Pakistan. While Moscow has maintained cordial ties with Bhutan, Sri Lanka, Bangladesh, the Maldives, and Nepal, none play a central role in Russia's South Asia strategy.[2] This chapter will focus on Russia's engagement with Afghanistan, India, and Pakistan.

The Regional and International Contexts

Regional geography and strategic factors frame the context for competition among intra-regional and external actors in South Asia.

As a regional power, India is geographically dominant, sharing maritime borders with Sri Lanka and the Maldives and land borders with all South Asian countries except Afghanistan. India's southern peninsula abuts three bodies of water: The Bay of Bengal to the east, the Arabian Sea to the west, and the eponymous Indian Ocean to the south. India's primary geographical disadvantage comes from Pakistan's denial of land access for trade through its territory to Afghanistan and thence to countries in Central Asia. Pakistan shares borders with India to the east, Afghanistan to the northwest, and Iran to the southwest and is separated from Tajikistan by the narrow Wakhan Corridor of Afghanistan. Pakistan's southern border fronts on the Arabian Sea giving Islamabad access to the Persian Gulf. Afghanistan is land-locked, with Pakistan to the southeast, Iran to the west and Turkmenistan, Uzbekistan, and Tajikistan to the north.

At the strategic level, several region-specific considerations are noteworthy. Enduring India-Pakistan and India-China rivalries juxtaposed with a Sino-Pakistan alliance since the early 1960s have influenced Russia's alignments with India and Afghanistan in South Asia. Long-standing and unresolved boundary delineations between India and Pakistan and Pakistan and Afghanistan have led New Delhi and Islamabad respectively to vie for a friendly government in Kabul. India-Afghanistan relations have historically been cordial until the mid-1990s installation of the Pakistan-sponsored Taliban government, which was returned

DOI: 10.4324/9781003246626-29

341

to power in September 2021. In the 1980s, radical Muslim groups began receiving state patronage in Pakistan and gained momentum in Afghanistan after the 1979 Soviet invasion, leading to concerns of spillover in India, Tajikistan, and Uzbekistan.[3] Russia, therefore, has a vested interest in maintaining influence in Afghanistan by working, when strategically feasible, with India and Pakistan.

Cold War dynamics superimposed external structural pressures on the region's fragile strategic ecosystem. The Soviet move to an Indo-centric policy emerged gradually over the course of the 1960s and early 1970s as Moscow sought to balance hostile ties with China and the United States. The 1979 invasion of Afghanistan introduced a direct Soviet presence in South Asia with significant regional and global ramifications that reverberated through the final decades of the 20th century. The end of the Cold War in the late 1980s coincided with the 1989 Soviet withdrawal from Afghanistan and was followed in 1991 by the implosion of the Soviet Union. These developments, for a time, reduced the Russian footprint in South Asia as Moscow was preoccupied with the monumental task of building a new Russia and reordering relations with the newly independent states of the former Union of Soviet Socialist Republics (USSR). In the last decade of the 20th century, the demise of the US-Soviet bipolar competition ushered in what Charles Krauthammer termed "the unipolar moment."[4] The 9/11 terrorist attacks in the United States plotted by al-Qaeda leaders who sheltered in Taliban-governed Afghanistan represented the opening salvo of the 21st century pulling Russia, which along with India had been supporting the anti-Taliban Northern Alliance, into aiding the unilateral US retaliatory war in October 2001.

A decade later, the concatenation of three developments—a protracted and inchoate US-China global power transition, a Russia-China alliance, and a globally resurgent Russia—have introduced strategic ambiguities in Moscow's South Asia policy. Unmoored from the certainties of Cold War geopolitics, Russian objectives are not reducible to a structural logic: Strategic hedging explains Moscow's simultaneous attempt to safeguard the "special and privileged" relationship with India while carving out space for meaningful ties with Pakistan. Russia's outreach to Islamabad stems from dual objectives: To blunt the effects of India's drift into the US orbit and to preserve and strengthen pathways for influence in Afghanistan.

The Historical Context

Against the background of a shifting kaleidoscope of external actors, security and geopolitical considerations have represented enduring factors in defining imperial/Soviet/Russian objectives in South Asia. The centrality of the Indo-Soviet relationship during the Cold War years was underpinned by Soviet largesse in the form of economic aid and a flourishing arms trade, which shored up India's defenses, creating a reservoir of trust that sustained the partnership through the turbulent end of the Cold War. Afghanistan was another important recipient of Soviet military and economic aid. Terrorism and nuclear proliferation, with its attendant implications for regional political instability and for the India-Pakistan conflict, emerged as specific concerns in the last decade of the 20th century and remain salient in the 21st century.

The 19th and Early 20th Centuries

In the 19th and early 20th centuries, geopolitical competition between imperial Russia and imperial Britain fueled a jockeying for influence in Afghanistan. This "Great Game" unfolded at the crossroads of Central and South Asia as the southwardly expanding Russian Empire encroached on Afghanistan and impinged on the northwestern edge of the British Indian

Empire, exposing the land route into the Indian subcontinent.[5] To keep the Russians from expanding further south, the British fought two wars in Afghanistan in the 19th century but were never able to hold the country.

Russia, meanwhile, annexed the oasis of Panjdeh south of the line that the British and Afghan King Abdur Rahman Khan had presumed to represent the reach of Afghan authority. Flustered by Khan's decision to cede this area to Russia, the British decided to neutralize the threat to their economically profitable Indian Empire.[6] Pivoting to diplomacy, they sought to secure the border between Afghanistan and British India and between Afghanistan and Russian Central Asia believing that "whatever was not held outright by the British or by the Afghan king was potentially open to annexation by the Russians."[7] The 1895 Russo-British Pamir Boundary Commission delineated the northern border of Afghanistan, creating the Wakhan Corridor to ensure discontiguity between the British and Russian Empires.

The Cold War

During the Cold War, the United States and the USSR, as ideological protagonists in a bipolar world, sought client states in South Asia in a global competition for influence. Pakistan joined the US-sponsored anti-communist security architecture in Asia, signing a Mutual Defense Agreement with the United States in 1954 and joining the Southeast Asia Treaty Organization (SEATO) and the Baghdad Pact (later renamed Central Treaty Organization— CENTO) in 1955.[8] To preserve foreign policy autonomy, India opted to remain non-aligned. Until the death of Stalin in October 1953, Soviet involvement in South Asia was limited.

Robert Donaldson notes that after Khrushchev's accession, a "qualitative change" occurred in Soviet policy toward India when the "diplomatic, economic, and cultural instrumentalities of the Soviet state" were directed to "build Indian support for the 'anti-imperialist' objectives of Soviet foreign policy."[9] Over the course of the 1960s, the USSR sought strong ties with India while engaging sporadically with Pakistan when strains emerged in the US-Pakistan alliance following President Kennedy's support of India in the 1962 Sino-Indian War and subsequent US promotion of democratic India's case in the economic development race against communist China.[10] Unwilling to oppose Beijing openly during the ideologically fractious Sino-Soviet split, Moscow vacillated between supporting India and China during the 1962 Sino-Indian War.[11]

In the 1950s and 1960s, Afghanistan, like India, charted a nonaligned path. Alam Payind, a noted expert on Afghan foreign policy, states that "more than any other political or economic issue," the "Pashtunistan question" and the related Pakistan-Afghanistan boundary dispute influenced Kabul's relationship with "the Soviet Union, Pakistan, India, and the United States."[12] Soviet engagement in Afghanistan began in 1953 when pro-Soviet General Mohammed Khan Daoud, cousin of King Zahir Shah, became prime minister and sought assistance from the USSR to support social reforms and to shore up the country's defenses against Pakistan, which was using US-supplied arms for political leverage in the Pashtunistan areas straddling their disputed border. Afghanistan also had to contend with the economic hardships resulting from the intermittent closure by Pakistan of their common border. Kabul thus welcomed the Soviet offer of economic aid in 1955 and military assistance in 1956.[13]

Extant literature of the period details the significant economic and military aid that the USSR funneled to India and Afghanistan.[14] By 1966, the USSR was the largest supplier of arms to the Afghan army, creating as one scholar noted, "a situation of total dependence of the Afghan Army on Soviet military supplies and logistical support."[15] Soviet arms sales to India began in 1955. By the end of the 1980s, a lucrative arms relationship served as the primary anchor of Indo-Soviet ties.[16]

Between the mid-1950s and the 1960s, Moscow sought to balance the challenges of its fraying alliance with China and its competition with the United States with an India-centric approach to South Asia. Soviet objectives in the region became more ambitious after Premier Kosygin's diplomatic success in mediating the 1965 India-Pakistan War, with the unveiling of a 1969 plan adumbrated by Brezhnev for a collective security system in Asia. While the ostensible aim was to check the intrusion of external powers, the unstated objective was to deepen Soviet influence in South Asia. Sensing an anti-China effort, Pakistan refused participation. New Delhi, while not publicly opposed, abjured interest in having any great power guaranteeing Asian security.[17]

By the early 1970s, the Soviet pursuit of détente with the United States and Beijing's adoption of conditional rapprochement with the United States using Pakistan's good offices raised concerns in the USSR of double containment and in India of encirclement, leading to the signing of the 1971 Indo-Soviet Treaty of Peace, Friendship, and Cooperation.[18] Afghanistan emerged as a Cold War battleground with the 1979 Soviet invasion undertaken to protect a beleaguered communist government in Kabul from an armed revolt of conservative Islamic and tribal leaders who had formed the guerrilla mujahedin movement in June 1978. The invasion raised alarm in Washington and drew the United States into a decade-long proxy war in the region. US arming of mujahedin rebels against the Soviet-backed government began as early as January 1980.[19] The Soviet withdrawal from Afghanistan in 1989 followed a protracted and politically unwinnable decade-long military struggle against the mujahedin.

The end of the Cold War in the late 1980s and the collapse of the USSR in 1991 set the stage for a series of realignments in South Asia. The liberal phase of Soviet/Russian policy spanned the 1989–1992 period when pro-Western Atlanticists sought to inject a more balanced Soviet/Russian approach toward India and Pakistan. India-Russia relations were propelled by inertial forces of mutual dependence that tied Russia's defense industry to the huge Indian appetite for Russian-sourced weapons. By 1993, as the rising influence of Eurasianists eclipsed the sway of the Atlanticists, Russia abandoned a pro-West focus to attend to the neglected, but important, relationship with India.[20] Indo-Soviet/Russian relations, which had been strained by difficult renegotiations over Soviet-era debt, were steadied during President Yeltsin's first visit to New Delhi in January 1993 and bilateral ties slowly improved. The arms trade, which had temporarily languished, resumed.

Preoccupied with managing a complex domestic transformation and buffeted by economic stringencies, Moscow paid scant attention to Afghanistan until the Taliban takeover. US support for the Afghan mujahedin from 1980 to 1989, funneled through Pakistan, had created an entrenched presence of such groups in the Pakistan-Afghanistan region. Pakistan used jihadist groups as proxies to foment instability in Kashmir and in Afghanistan. The decade of the 1990s opened with a rise in terrorist attacks in Indian-administered Kashmir by Pakistan-based militant Islamic groups tacitly and materially supported by the Pakistan Army's Inter-Services Intelligence (ISI).[21] India and Russia joined in the fight against terrorism signing two declarations in 1994: The first highlighted the challenges of political extremism and international terrorism; the second sketched multi-faceted ways to deepen bilateral cooperation.[22]

In 1996, the Pakistan-created Taliban, a predominantly Pashtun-led fundamentalist movement, took power in Kabul.[23] Recognized only by Pakistan, Saudi Arabia, and the United Arab Emirates, the Taliban's harsh and illiberal rule and offer of a haven for Osama bin Laden and al-Qaeda, his global jihadist network, left Afghanistan internationally isolated. In northern Afghanistan, alienated Uzbeks and Tajiks united against the Taliban in late 1996. Concerned about the spread of Islamic fundamentalism in India (via Pakistan) and in the

Russian sphere of interest in Tajikistan and Uzbekistan, New Delhi and Moscow cooperated to support the Northern Alliance, a loose coalition of anti-Taliban forces led by Buhranuddin Rabbani and Ahmad Shah Massoud. Indian and Russian concerns were heightened when two al-Qaeda operatives assassinated Massoud, a fierce and charismatic leader known as the "Lion of Panjshir." This assassination on September 9, 2001, earned bin Laden the gratitude of his Taliban hosts who felt honor-bound to protect him and refused Washington's demand for his surrender after his fateful decision two days later to launch a series of devastating terrorist attacks in the United States.

As the Cold War historical narrative indicates, three geopolitical trends framed Soviet involvement in South Asia. First, Sino-Soviet hostility and Soviet-American competition cemented a defensive Soviet alliance with India. Second, Soviet engagement with Pakistan was circumscribed by Islamabad's alliances with China and the United States and Moscow's concerns over Indian sensibilities. Third, Soviet interest in ensuring Afghanistan's neutrality in the East-West conflict forged a strong Soviet-Afghan relationship in the early period of the Cold War.[24] Later, Moscow's concerns centered on fundamentalist Muslim movements that might penetrate and destabilize the Muslim-majority republics of Soviet Central Asia.

The 21st Century

Two curtain raisers heralded the 21st century: India and Russia signed a strategic partnership agreement in 2000 that foregrounded defense and military-technological cooperation. In October 2001, the United States invaded Afghanistan. Over the course of the second decade of the century, even as India and Russia upgraded their relationship to a "special and privileged" partnership in 2010, fissures emerged between the two countries as New Delhi's strategic partnership with the United States deepened to confront the challenges posed by a globally assertive China.[25] India has been prioritized as an important partner in the Biden administration's Quadrilateral Security Dialogue.[26] Meanwhile, US-Russia estrangement has served to tighten the Sino-Russian alliance. China's deep pockets and its all-weather friendship with Pakistan have allowed Beijing to expand influence in Afghanistan. These twin developments propelled Moscow to seek engagement with Pakistan.[27] At the end of the second decade of the century, then, complex interlocking factors have led Russia to pursue a hedging strategy in South Asia.

After the al-Qaeda attacks in the United States, Russia ceded influence in Afghanistan to the United States, which inserted a direct military presence with a retaliatory war against the Taliban. As US objectives aligned with those of Russia and India, Washington found ready assistance from Moscow, which provided intelligence and logistical support for the war effort.[28] Thereafter, Russia remained sidelined in Afghanistan until 2006 when fraying US relations with Pakistan and Afghanistan opened opportunities for Moscow to enlarge its footprint in the region.[29]

Islamabad's indignation with US drone strikes in the Afghan-Pakistan region and US exasperation with Pakistan's covert support of the Taliban insurgency introduced wrinkles in the US-Pakistan relationship. Pakistan showed displeasure by periodically closing the Khyber Pass to Afghanistan-bound NATO supply trucks.[30] To bypass this intermittent logistical challenge, NATO finalized a military transit agreement with Russia in 2009 opening an alternative northern supply route into Afghanistan from Tajikistan.[31] This route served as an important lifeline to the Afghan Army and US–NATO forces when relations with Islamabad turned frostier after bin Laden was killed in a 2011 covert US operation. The US decision that year to purchase Russian arms with which the Afghan Army was familiar offered Moscow greater influence.[32] Additionally, Moscow was quick to support President Karzai's claim to victory in the 2009 election that was marred by allegations of fraud. Moscow simultaneously began engaging diplomatically with purported "moderate" Taliban elements.[33]

Russian foreign policy took an assertive turn in the second decade of the 21st century. First elected as president in 2000, Vladimir Putin returned in 2012 to a third term determined to reclaim Russia's rightful place as a great power by reviving military might and regaining global influence.[34] Russia's pivot to Asia followed two decades of unsuccessful attempts to fit into an "enlarged West." Moscow, as Trenin explains, cast its role as a "free non-Western agent, standing apart from united Europe and focused on building its own power base in the center of the continent—a Eurasian Union."[35]

In 2014, Moscow lifted a voluntary arms embargo against the sale of offensive weapons to Pakistan with an agreement for the delivery of assault helicopters. In 2016, Russia and Pakistan conducted the first bilateral joint military exercise in Cherat, Pakistan.[36] On the economic front, Russia has provided Pakistan with funding for energy infrastructure projects.[37] In making these inroads, however, Russia was at pains to signal to India that Moscow prizes its partnership with New Delhi. Moscow vetoed Pakistan's proposed location for the joint military exercises of Gilgit-Baltistan in Pakistan-administered Kashmir for fear of offending India. Moscow's energy investment projects in Pakistan likewise steer clear of the China-Pakistan Economic Corridor (a signature project in BRI—China's Belt-Road Initiative), which runs through Gilgit-Baltistan. Russia is also likely to refrain from arms sales of high-technology military hardware that might be viewed with disfavor in India.[38] Moscow's outreach to Pakistan stems from an interest in diversifying arms exports, maintaining another avenue for influence with the Taliban, and in gaining advantage in its asymmetrical partnership with China.

Russia's interests in Afghanistan are deep and abiding. After the election of pro-US President Ashraf Ghani in 2014, Moscow initiated contact with the Taliban, set up trilateral talks with China and Pakistan in 2016 focused on stabilizing Afghanistan and discussing counterterrorism strategies aimed at fighting back against the growing foothold in Afghanistan of the global Islamic State-Khorasan Province (ISKP), and at curbing the activities of the Islamic State of Uzbekistan and Islamic Jihad, which use northern Afghanistan as a base to expand their reach in Uzbekistan and Tajikistan.[39] Russia set up the Moscow Format as a multilateral framework for intra-Afghan dialogue to work toward a political compromise that would end the civil conflict in Afghanistan and in November 2018 invited a Taliban delegation for talks.[40] In 2019, Moscow set up the Troika Plus Group that included the United States, China, and Pakistan.[41]

With the Taliban government back in the saddle in September 2021, Afghanistan has once again become a battleground for geopolitical competition primarily between China and Russia. Moscow has worked with India and Pakistan to secure Russian interests in Afghanistan. While Russia welcomed Pakistan's participation in the Troika Plus talks, Moscow is wary of Islamabad's support of the Haqqani network and concerned over the appointment of Sirajuddin Haqqani as interior minister in the Taliban government. To ensure Russia's interests, Putin set into motion an agreement in May 2021 to create a joint air defense system with Tajikistan, giving Moscow control over Tajik air defenses and greater control over the Afghan-Tajik border.[42] New Delhi's wary insistence that the Taliban's claim of moderation was tactical had kept India on the sidelines of Moscow's confabulations on the Afghan question. On August 24, 2021, however, India and Russia established a permanent bilateral channel for consultations on Afghanistan. Reprising their 1990s coordination, National Security Advisor Ajit Doval met Secretary of Russia's Security Council Nikolai Patrushev in September to expand cooperation against terrorism and drug-trafficking, to cooperate in intelligence sharing, and to engage in post-conflict development as Moscow recognized the "grassroots-level public acceptance" of India in Afghanistan.[43]

The primary conundrum Moscow faces in South Asia is how to sustain Russia's prized strategic partnership with New Delhi and thereby safeguard its lucrative position as India's primary arms supplier while wooing Pakistan, India's rival in South Asia. Viewing Moscow's relationship with New Delhi solely through the filter of US-Russia estrangement, however, overlooks the larger import of the India-Russia nexus. Long-term portents for Moscow of the Sino-Russian alliance are inauspicious. Lagging far behind China in the size of its economy, Russia cannot match Beijing's investments in Afghanistan, Pakistan, and elsewhere in the developing world. Outlays under BRI, a massive infrastructure development program inaugurated in 2013, are estimated to reach $1.2 trillion by 2027.[44] While Putin's rather nebulous Greater Eurasian Partnership (GEP) Concept, announced in 2016, rhetorically exceeds the scope of Brezhnev's plan for an Asian Collective Security system, it cannot match the reach or deep pockets of BRI. GEP builds on Putin's 2015 Eurasian Economic Union (EAEU) plan for regional integration in the post-Soviet space. Putin's characterizations of GEP have been protean: In 2016, the partnership was stated to include EAEU, China, Pakistan, Iran, and post-Soviet states; in 2017, he noted that GEP would subsume BRI, EAEU, SCO (Shanghai Cooperation Organization), and ASEAN (Association of South-East Asian Nations).[45]

A more promising competitor to BRI is the International North-South Transport Corridor (INSTC). Initiated in 2000 by Russia, India, and Iran to link Mumbai to Moscow via Iran's Chabahar Port, INSTC is important because the 7,200 km sea-rail-road network would "reduce carriage cost between Russia and India by 30 percent and bring down the transit time from 40 days by more than half compared to the traditional Suez route, which is overloaded and more expensive."[46] Russia sees INSTC as an instrument for connectivity with the Persian Gulf states and via the Indian Ocean to states in Africa, as a boost to trade for EAEU member-states, and as a counter to rising Chinese economic influence. While geopolitical barriers in the form of US sanctions against Iran, Western sanctions against Russia, and conflicts among INSTC members have hampered progress, the first train departed from Helsinki, Finland, on June 21, 2021, with cargo bound for Nhava Sheva, India's largest container port in Navi Mumbai.[47] INSTC competes with other multilateral transport projects sponsored by BRI but unlike the latter, which is led by China, is developing more haphazardly.[48] Neither Russia nor India have the economic resources or the diplomatic heft to transform INSTC into a fully operational venture, which, if successful, would provide Russia easier access to the Gulf States and Africa, allow India to overcome the obstacles to land access to Central Asia, and open Afghanistan to trade via alternative land and ocean routes.

As a junior partner in the Sino-Russian alliance, India's strategic value to Russia in South Asia in the unfolding 21st century stems from Moscow's interest in hedging against a rising and revisionist China poised to displace Russian influence in South and Central Asia.

Conclusion: Theory and Prospects

Geopolitical and geostrategic objectives that are the primary drivers of Moscow's South Asia policy are best captured by realist theory.[49] Neorealism with its emphasis on systemic variables helps explain the Cold War-era Soviet concern with structurally driven competition with the United States that paved the path to a Soviet alignment with India and Afghanistan and the US tilt toward Pakistan.

While the Cold War was also ideologically driven, expectations of liberal international relations theories that states sharing similar values would be natural partners were confounded in South Asia where India and the United States remained alienated during the Cold War.[50] Pakistan's troubled democracy, which experienced frequent military coups, did not forestall a US-Pakistan alliance. As a monarchy, Afghanistan in the 1950s and 1960s introduced significant liberal reforms. During the turbulent 1970s, one-party rule under communist auspices was established in 1978. The form of the country's government, however, played scant role in the strategic game of Cold War politics. The choice to remain non-aligned in the Cold War conflict and spurn blandishments to join US-sponsored multilateral security organizations in Asia set the West against India and Afghanistan.

Ideology and values were not entirely irrelevant, however, because they served as post-facto justifications for policies based on strategic interests. Khrushchev reframed the anti-colonial and anti-Western underpinnings of the non-aligned movement by arguing that this bloc represented a vast "zone of peace" with which the Soviet Union could make common cause. Loathe to concede ground entirely to the USSR, the United States supported India and Afghanistan with economic aid and offered New Delhi military assistance during the 1962 war with China.

Structural drivers also explain how the transition from "tight" to "loose" bipolarity in the 1960s and strategic triangularity in the 1970s led successively to Sino-Soviet hostility, Sino-American rapprochement, and alliances respectively between China and Pakistan and the USSR and India.[51] These developments once again illustrate the secondary role of ideology and values as China and the USSR—two communist states—rended apart, fighting a border war in 1969, while China and the capitalist-democratic United States decided to engage in circumscribed cooperation for pragmatic reasons.

The end of the Cold War tellingly revealed the structural imperatives that had fashioned erstwhile alignments and alliances. President Gorbachev's new thinking in foreign policy abjured the straitjacket of Cold War shibboleths and introduced liberal elements in the Soviet world view. As Gorbachev recast Soviet national identity to serve universal interests, Sino-Soviet relations improved, and US-Soviet relations began to thaw. When the Soviet Union disintegrated, this liberalizing trend continued into the first year of the new Russian state. In South Asia, the impact of these shifts resulted in a temporarily attenuated relationship between India and the USSR/Russia. Constructivist ontology is useful in explaining how a shift in identity affected the Soviet/Russian foreign policy posture and definition of interests in South Asia where Moscow prioritized liberal goals of conflict resolution and nuclear non-proliferation by adopting "even-handedness" in relations with India and Pakistan respectively and ended the Soviet occupation of Afghanistan.

Stung by the loss of status as a global player after the Soviet implosion and facing resistance to its influence within a post-Soviet space helmed by fiercely nationalist leaders, Russia had to deal with the added insult to its prestige of NATO expansion to the country's western border. Abandoning a pro-West orientation, Moscow recalibrated by pivoting east to India and China. In the 21st century, structural factors once again influence Moscow's definition of the national interest. Gorbachev's liberal identity discourse was reformulated to emphasize a "new Russian exceptionalism."[52] President Putin advanced the narrative of a unique Russian civilization founded on Orthodoxy, traditional values, and a strong sense of nationalism to frame Russia's global return.[53] Classical realism that dips into individual-, state-, and system-level variables explains Putin's apotheosis as both an ideologue and a pragmatist.

Moscow's forays in the multilateral domain have been similarly guided by interest-driven motivations. The BRICS grouping (Brazil, Russia, India, China, and South Africa); the SCO of which Russia, China, Kazakhstan, Kyrgyzstan, Tajikistan, and Uzbekistan are members, along with India and Pakistan; and the expansive GEP have as their primary aim the promotion of a "polycentric" world in which Russia is a major global player.

In South Asia, a strengthening Indo-US strategic partnership, a fraught Pakistan-US relationship, and US withdrawal from Afghanistan on August 31, 2021, has introduced novel pressures on the "special and privileged" India-Russia partnership. Putin, the strategist, determined to play an instrumental role in Taliban-governed Afghanistan, sees Pakistan as an asset. Moscow has steadily deepened engagement with Islamabad since 2014 while continuing to nurture the relationship with India. For instance, Moscow, along with New Delhi, decided to withhold official recognition from the newly formed Taliban government in 2021 and to monitor the nascent opposition to the Taliban in northern Afghanistan. Strategic hedging characterizes Moscow's approach to South Asia during a period when the structural distribution of power is indeterminate, and a protracted global power transition is underway.

As an erstwhile British colony, India's armed forces at independence in 1947 were sourced with British-made weapons systems. The move to the Soviet Union as India's primary arms supplier resulted from British and American unwillingness to acquiesce to non-aligned India's demands for sophisticated weaponry and technology-sharing. Strategic and economic incentives therefore drew India and the USSR into an arms relationship. Moscow offered joint production under licensing agreements, transfer of technology, and affordable pricing. India's arms purchases, in turn, supported the Russian defense industrial complex. Over time, Soviet/Russian arms came to predominate in all branches of India's armed forces. One study has calculated that Russian weapons platforms constitute 85% of Indian military hardware creating a "lock-in effect" that will sustain the India-Russia partnership.[54] Despite concerns in Moscow that India's diversification of arms supplies will reduce Indian demand for Russian weapons platforms, the bilateral arms trade has continued robustly. India signed a $5.5 billion deal for the Russian S-400 defense system in 2018, with the first tranche of components delivered in December 2021, notwithstanding the threat of US sanctions. Arms sales, which remain the mainstay of a relationship that sprang from shared geostrategic objectives, will serve as a heavy anchor for the Indo-Russian partnership in the medium term, but if the relationship rests on an instrumentalized rather than a strategic foundation, strong ties may erode over time.

For now, Russia's long-nurtured partnership with India is militarily and strategically too important for Moscow to jeopardize. While the structural buttresses for Indo-Russian ties are not as sturdy as they were during the Cold War, three factors offer compelling reasons for the durability of this partnership: The arms nexus is mutually beneficial; India and Russia prize their strategic autonomy; the relationship with India serves as a hedge against China. In the 21st century, Russia will remain deeply engaged in South Asia. India and Afghanistan will continue to be the pivotal states engaging Moscow's interests. If Russia's outreach to Pakistan is cautiously incremental, the relationship with India will not be significantly prejudiced. Game changers would be an Indian pivot to an alliance with the United States or an unequivocal Russian embrace of Pakistan.

Notes

1 Afghanistan, Bangladesh, Bhutan, India, the Maldives, Nepal, Pakistan, and Sri Lanka are members of the South Asian Association for Regional Cooperation (SAARC) founded in 1985.
2 For instance, a book on South Asia by Russian experts focused solely on India, Pakistan, and Afghanistan. See Vyacheslav Belokrenitsky et al., *Iuzhnaia Aziia V Sovremennom Politicheskom Mire* [South Asia in the Contemporary Political World] (Queenston, ON: The Edwin Mellen Press, 2016).

3 Aarish Ullah Khan, *The Terrorist Threat and the Policy Response in Pakistan*, SIPRI Policy Paper no. 11 (Stockholm International Peace Research Institute, September 2005), 7–9, https://www.sipri.org/sites/default/files/files/PP/SIPRIPP11.pdf; and Graham Fuller, *Islamic Fundamentalism in Afghanistan: Its Character and Prospects* (Santa Monica, CA: RAND Corporation, 1991), https://www.rand.org/pubs/reports/R3970.html.

4 Charles Krauthammer, "The Unipolar Moment," *Foreign Affairs* 70, no. 1 (1990/1991): 23–33.

5 Edward Ingram, *The Beginning of the Great Game in Asia, 1828-1834* (Oxford: Clarendon Press, 1979).

6 William C. Rowe, "The Wakhan Corridor: Endgame of the Great Game," in *Borderlines and Borderlands: Political Oddities at the Edge of the Nation-State*, eds. Alexander C. Diener et al. (Lanham, MD: Rowman and Littlefield, 2010), 59–61.

7 Rowe, "The Wakhan Corridor: Endgame of the Great Game," 59.

8 Mohammed Ayub Khan, "The Pakistan-American Alliance: Stresses and Strains," *Foreign Affairs* 42, no. 2 (January 1964): 195–209.

9 Robert H. Donaldson, *Soviet Policy toward India: Ideology and Strategy* (Cambridge, MA: Harvard University Press, 1974), 151.

10 Zubeida Hasan, "Pakistan's Relations with the USSR in the 1960s," *The World Today* 25, no. 1 (January 1961): 27. See also Nick Cullather, "Hunger and Containment: How India Became 'Important' in US Cold War Strategy," *India Review* 6, no. 2 (April–June 2007): 59–90.

11 Vojtech Mastny, "The Soviet Union's Partnership with India," *Journal of Cold War Studies* 12, no. 3 (Summer 2010): 50–90.

12 Alam Payind, "Soviet-Afghan Relations: From Cooperation to Occupation," *International Journal of Middle East Studies* 21, no. 1 (February 1989): 110.

13 Payind, "Soviet-Afghan Relations," 111–113.

14 M.S. Noorzoy, "Long-Term Economic Relations between Afghanistan and the Soviet Union: An Interpretive Study," *International Journal of Middle East Studies* 17, no. 2 (May 1985): 159. On India, see Janos Horvath, "Economic Aid Flow from the USSR: A Recount of the First Fifteen Years," *Slavic Review* 29, no. 4 (December 1970): 616.

15 Noorzoy, "Long-Term Economic Relations," 160.

16 P.R. Chari, "Indo-Soviet Military Cooperation: A Review," *Asian Survey* 19, no. 3 (March 1979): 232; see also, Harsh V. Pant, "India and Russia: Convergence across Time," in *Indian Foreign Policy: An Overview*, ed. Harsh V. Pant (Manchester University Press: 2017), 57–59.

17 Donaldson, *Soviet Policy*, 210, 218–225.

18 For the text of the Indo-Soviet Treaty of Peace, Friendship, and Cooperation, see Donaldson, *Soviet Policy*, Appendix, 267–269. On the treaty, see Pant, "India and Russia," 52–54.

19 "Memorandum from the President's Assistant for National Security Affairs (Brzezinski) to President Carter," *Foreign Relations of the United States, 1977-80*, Volume XII, Afghanistan, Document 152 (January 9, 1980): 441, https://history.state.gov/historicaldocuments/frus1977-80v12/d10.

20 Graham Smith, "The Masks of Proteus: Russia, Geopolitical Shift, and the New Eurasianism," *Transactions of the Institute of British Geographers* 24, no. 4 (1999): 481–494.

21 Gurmeet Kanwal, "Proxy War in Kashmir: Jehad or State-sponsored Terrorism?" *Strategic Analysis* 23, no. 1 (April 1999): 55–83.

22 Vidya Nadkarni, *Strategic Partnerships in Asia: Balancing without Alliances* (London: Routledge, 2010), 86.

23 See Michael Collins Dunn, "Great Games and Small: Afghanistan, Tajikistan, and the New Geopolitics of Southwest Asia," *Middle East Policy* 5, no. 2 (May 1997): 146. For details on Pakistan's support to Taliban-led Afghanistan, see Bruce Riedel, "Pakistan, Taliban, and the Afghan Quagmire," Brookings Institution (August 24, 2013), https://www.brookings.edu/opinions/pakistan-taliban-and-the-afghan-quagmire/. For details on Pakistan's support for the Taliban from the 1990s to 2021, see Riedel, "Pakistan's Problematic Victory in Afghanistan," Brookings Institution (August 24, 2021), https://www.brookings.edu/blog/order-from-chaos/2021/08/24/pakistans-problematic-victory-in-afghanistan/.

24 Noorzoy, "Long-Term Economic Relations," 158–159.

25 Nadkarni, *Strategic Partnerships*, 89–95; Robert H. Donaldson and Vidya Nadkarni, *Foreign Policy of Russia: Changing Systems, Enduring Interests* (New York: Routledge, 2019): 350.

26 C. Raja Mohan, "AUKUS, the Quad, and India's Strategic Pivot," *Foreign Policy* (September 23, 2021).

Russia and South Asia

27 Tahir Amin, "Pakistan-Russia Relations and the Unfolding 'New Great Game' in South Asia," in *The Regional Security Puzzle around Afghanistan: Bordering Practices in Central Asia and Beyond*, ed. Helena Rytövuori-Apunen (Verlag Barbara Budrich: 2016), 191–206. See also, Ume Farwa, "Russia's Strategic Calculus in South Asia and Pakistan's Role," *Strategic Studies* 39, no. 2 (Summer 2019): 33–47.

28 Donaldson and Nadkarni, *Foreign Policy of Russia*, 385–386.

29 Donaldson and Nadkarni, *Foreign Policy of Russia*, 345.

30 Donaldson and Nadkarni, *Foreign Policy of Russia*, 345–346.

31 Donaldson and Nadkarni, *Foreign Policy of Russia*, 346.

32 Donaldson and Nadkarni, *Foreign Policy of Russia*, 346.

33 Donaldson and Nadkarni, *Foreign Policy of Russia*, 345.

34 Fyodor Lukyanov, "Putin's Foreign Policy: The Quest to Restore Russia's Rightful Place," *Foreign Affairs* 95, no. 3 (May/June 2016): 30–37; Dmitri Trenin, "The Revival of the Russian Military: How Moscow Reloaded," *Foreign Affairs* 95, no. 3 (May/June 2016): 23–29.

35 Dmitri Trenin, *Russia and the Rise of Asia* (Washington, D.C: Carnegie Endowment for International Peace, November 2013): 3

36 Donaldson and Nadkarni, *Foreign Policy of Russia*, 354–355.

37 Claudia Chia et al., "Russia-Pakistan Economic Relations: Energy Partnership and the China Factor," *ISAS Working Paper* no. 135 (October 2021), https://www.isas.nus.edu.sg/wp-content/uploads/2021/10/WP-351.pdf.

38 Study Paper, "Russia's Strategic Hedging in South Asia," European Foundation for South Asian Studies, Amsterdam (August 2019), https://www.efsas.org/publications/study-papers/russia's-strategic-hedging-in-south-asia/.

39 Samuel Ramani, "Balancing Ties, Russia Expands Cooperation with Both India and Pakistan," Middle East Institute (September 13, 2021), https://www.mei.edu/publications/balancing-ties-russia-expands-afghanistan-cooperation-both-india-and-pakistan.

40 Ramani, "Balancing Ties."

41 Ramani, "Balancing Ties."

42 Witold Rodkiewicz et al., "How Russia is Reacting to the Situation in Afghanistan," Centre for Eastern Studies, Warsaw, Poland (July 15, 2021), https://www.osw.waw.pl/en/publikacje/analyses/2021-07-15/how-russia-reacting-to-situation-afghanistan. See also, Ramani, "Balancing Ties."

43 Ramani, "Balancing Ties."

44 Andrew Chatzky et al., "China's Massive Belt-Road Initiative," *CFR Backgrounder* (New York: Council on Foreign Relations), last updated January 28, 2020, https://www.cfr.org/backgrounder/chinas-massive-belt-and-road-initiative.

45 Gaziza Shakhanova et al., "The Belt and Road Initiative and the Eurasian Economic Union: Exploring the 'Greater Eurasian Partnership,'" *Journal of Current Chinese Affairs* 49, no. 1 (2020): 34–35.

46 Nvard Chalikyan et al., "Geopolitics of the North-South Transit Corridor," *South Asian Voices*, Stimson Center (July 9, 2021), https://southasianvoices.org/geopolitics-of-the-north-south-transport-corridor/.

47 Ilham Karimli, "Freight Train Begins First Journey from Finland to India via North-South Corridor," *Caspian News*, June 25, 2021, https://caspiannews.com/news-detail/freight-train-begins-first-journey-from-finland-to-india-via-north-south-corridor-2021-6-24-0/.

48 Chalikyan, et al., "Geopolitics of the North-South Transit Corridor."

49 Allen Lynch, "The Realism of Russia's Foreign Policy," *Europe-Asia Studies* 53, no. 1 (January 2001): 7–31.

50 Dennis Kux, *India and the United States: Estranged Democracies, 1941–1991* (Washington, DC: National Defense University Press, 1992).

51 Chi Su, "The Strategic Triangle and China's Soviet Policy," in *China, the United States, and the Soviet Union: Tripolarity and Policy Making in the Cold War*, ed. Robert Ross (New York: M.E. Sharpe, 1993), 45–46.

52 Mark Galeotti et al., "Putin's Empire of the Mind," *Foreign Policy*, no. 206 (2014): 16–19.

53 Donaldson and Nadkarni, *The Foreign Policy of Russia*, 126–129.

54 Sameer Lalwani et al., "The Influence of Arms: Explaining the Durability of India-Russia Alignment," *Journal of Indo-Pacific Affairs* 4, no. 1 (2021): 3.

Bibliography

Amin, Tahir. "Pakistan-Russia Relations and the Unfolding 'New Great Game' in South Asia." In *The Regional Security Puzzle Around Afghanistan: Bordering Practices in Central Asia and Beyond*, edited by Helena Rytövuori-Apunen, 191–206. Leverkusen, Germany: Verlag Barbara Budrich, 2016. https://doi.org/10.2307/j.ctvbkjzm0.

Belokrenitsky, Vyacheslav, Vladimir Moscalenko, and Tatyana Shaumian. *Iuzhnaia Aziia V Sovremennom Politicheskom Mire [South Asia in the Contemporary Political World]*. Queenston, ON: The Edwin Mellen Press, 2016.

Chalikyan, Nvard, and Yeghia Tashjian. "Geopolitics of the North-South Transit Corridor." *South Asian Voices*, Stimson Center, July 9, 2021. https://southasianvoices.org/geopolitics-of-the-north-south-transport-corridor/.

Chari, P.R. "Indo-Soviet Military Cooperation: A Review." *Asian Survey* 19, no. 3 (March 1979): 230–244.

Chatzky, Andrew, and James McBride. "China's Massive Belt-Road Initiative." *CFR Backgrounder*. New York: Council on Foreign Relations, last updated January 28, 2020. https://www.cfr.org/backgrounder/chinas-massive-belt-and-road-initiative.

Chia, Claudia, and Zheng Haiqi. "Russia-Pakistan Economic Relations: Energy Partnership and the China Factor." ISAS Working Paper no. 135, October 2021. https://www.isas.nus.edu.sg/wp-content/uploads/2021/10/WP-351.pdf.

Cullather, Nick. "Hunger and Containment: How India Became 'Important' in US Cold War Strategy." *India Review* 6, no. 2 (April-June 2007): 59–90.

Donaldson, Robert H. *Soviet Policy toward India: Ideology and Strategy*. Cambridge, MA: Harvard University Press, 1974.

Donaldson, Robert H., and Vidya Nadkarni. *The Foreign Policy of Russia: Changing Systems, Enduring Interests*. New York: Routledge, 2019.

Dunn, Michael Collins. "Great Games and Small: Afghanistan, Tajikistan, and the New Geopolitics of Southwest Asia." *Middle East Policy* 5, no. 2 (May 1997): 142–149. https://doi.org/10.11111/j.1475.1997.tb00270.x.

Farwa, Ume. "Russia's Strategic Calculus in South Asia and Pakistan's Role." *Strategic Studies* 39, no. 2 (Summer 2019): 33–47.

Fuller, Graham. Islamic Fundamentalism in Afghanistan: Its Character and Prospects. Santa Monica, CA: RAND Corporation, 1991. https://www.rand.org/pubs/reports/R3970.html.

Galeotti, Mark, Andrew S. Bowen, and Andrew Zbihlyj. "Putin's Empire of the Mind." *Foreign Policy*, no. 206 (2014): 16–19.

Hasan, Zubeida. "Pakistan's Relations with the USSR in the 1960s." *The World Today* 25, no. 1 (January 1961): 26–35.

Horvath, Janos. "Economic Aid Flow from the USSR: A Recount of the First Fifteen Years." *Slavic Review* 29, no. 4 (December 1970): 613–632.

Ingram, Edward. *The Beginning of the Great Game in Asia, 1828–1834*. Oxford: Clarendon Press, 1979.

Kanwal, Gurmeet. "Proxy War in Kashmir: *Jehad* or State-Sponsored Terrorism?" *Strategic Analysis* 23, no. 1 (April 2008): 55–83. https://doi.org/10.1080/09700169908455030.

Karimli, Ilham. "Freight Train Begins First Journey from Finland to India via North-South Corridor." *Caspian News*, June 25, 2021. https://caspiannews.com/news-detail/freight-train-begins-first-journey-from-finland-to-india-via-north-south-corridor-2021-6-24-0/.

Khan, Aarish Ullah. *The Terrorist Threat and the Policy Response in Pakistan*. SIPRI Policy Paper no. 11. Stockholm International Peace Research Institute, September 2005, https://www.sipri.org/sites/default/files/files/PP/SIPRIPP11.pdf.

Khan, Mohammed Ayub. "The Pakistan-American Alliance: Stresses and Strains." *Foreign Affairs* 42, no. 2 (January 1964): 195–209.

Krauthammer, Charles. "The Unipolar Moment." *Foreign Affairs* 70, no. 1 (1990/1991): 23–33.

Kux, Dennis. *India and the United States: Estranged Democracies, 1941–1991*. Washington, DC: National Defense University Press, 1992.

Lalwani, Sameer, Frank O'Donnell, Tyler Sagerstrom, and Akriti Vasudeva. "The Influence of Arms: Explaining the Durability of India-Russia Alignment." *Journal of Indo-Pacific Affairs* 4, no. 1 (Special Issue, 2021): 2–41.

Lukyanov, Fyodor. "Putin's Foreign Policy: The Quest to Restore Russia's Rightful Place." *Foreign Affairs* 95, no. 3 (May/June 2016): 30–37.

Lynch, Allen. "The Realism of Russia's Foreign Policy." *Europe-Asia Studies* 53, no. 1 (January 2001): 7–31.

Mastny, Vojtech. "The Soviet Union's Partnership with India." *Journal of Cold War Studies* 12, no. 3 (Summer 2010): 50–90.

Memorandum from the President's Assistant for National Security Affairs (Brzezinski) to President Carter. *Foreign Relations of the United States, 1977–80*. Volume XII, Afghanistan, Document 152, January 9, 1980. https://history.state.gov/historicaldocuments/frus1977- 80v12/d10.

Mohan, C. Raja. "AUKUS, the Quad, and India's Strategic Pivot." *Foreign Policy*, September 23, 2021.

Nadkarni, Vidya. *Strategic Partnerships in Asia: Balancing Without Alliances*. London: Routledge, 2010.

Noorzoy, M.S. "Long-Term Economic Relations between Afghanistan and the Soviet Union: An Interpretive Study." *International Journal of Middle East Studies* 17, no. 2 (May 1985): 151–173.

Pant, Harsh V. "India and Russia: Convergence across Time." In *Indian Foreign Policy: An Overview*, edited by Harsh V. Pant, 50–63. Manchester: Manchester University Press, 2017.

Payind, Alam. "Soviet-Afghan Relations: From Cooperation to Occupation." *International Journal of Middle East Studies* 21, no. 1 (February 1989): 107–128.

Ramani, Samuel. "Balancing Ties, Russia Expands Cooperation with Both India and Pakistan." Middle East Institute, September 13, 2021. https://www.mei.edu/publications/balancing-ties-russia-expands-afghanistan-cooperation-both-india-and-pakistan.

Riedel, Bruce. "Pakistan, Taliban, and the Afghan Quagmire." Brookings Institution, August 24, 2013. https://www.brookings.edu/opinions/pakistan-taliban-and-the-afghan-quagmire/.

Riedel, Bruce. "Pakistan's Problematic Victory in Afghanistan." Brookings Institution, August 24, 2021. https://www.brookings.edu/blog/order-from-chaos/2021/08/24/pakistans-problematic-victory-in-afghanistan/.

Rodkiewicz, Witold, and Piotr Zochowski. "How Russia is Reacting to the Situation in Afghanistan." Centre for Eastern Studies, Warsaw, Poland, July 15, 2021. https://www.osw.waw.pl/en/publikacje/analyses/2021-07-15/how-russia-reacting-to-situation-afghanistan.

Rowe, William C. "The Wakhan Corridor: Endgame of the Great Game." In *Borderlines and Borderlands: Political Oddities at the Edge of the Nation-State*, edited by Alexander C. Diener and Joshua Hagen, 53–68. Lanham, MD: Rowman and Littlefield, 2010.

Shakhanova, Gaziza, and Jeremy Garlick. "The Belt and Road Initiative and the Eurasian Economic Union: Exploring the 'Greater Eurasian Partnership.'" *Journal of Current Chinese Affairs* 49, no. 1 (2020): 33–57. https://doi.org/10.1177/1868102620911666.

Smith, Graham. "The Masks of Proteus: Russia, Geopolitical Shift, and the New Eurasianism." *Transactions of the Institute of British Geographers* 24, no. 4 (1999): 481–494.

Study Paper. "Russia's Strategic Hedging in South Asia." European Foundation for South Asian Studies, Amsterdam, August 2019. https://www.efsas.org/publications/study-papers/russia's-strategic-hedging-in-south-asia.

Su, Chi. "The Strategic Triangle and China's Soviet Policy." In *China, the United States, and the Soviet Union: Tripolarity and Policy Making in the Cold War*, edited by Robert Ross, 39–61. Armonk, New York: M.E. Sharpe, 1993.

Telegram from the Embassy in Afghanistan to the Departments of State and Defense, the National Security Agency, and the United States Pacific Command. *Foreign Relations of the United States, 1977-80*, Volume XII, Afghanistan, Document 10, April 30, 1978, 19–21. https://history.state.gov/historicaldocuments/frus1977-80v12/d10.

Trenin, Dmitri. "The Revival of the Russian Military: How Moscow Reloaded." *Foreign Affairs* 95, no. 3 (May/June 2016): 23–29.

Trenin, Dmitri. *Russia and the Rise of Asia*. Washington, DC: Carnegie Endowment for International Peace, November 2013.

26

JAPAN'S RELATIONS WITH SOUTH ASIA

Monika Chansoria

Introduction

The subcontinent of South Asia remained peripheral as far as Japan's post-war "Asia vision" was concerned, especially in comparison to its far profounder engagement with East and Southeast Asia. During that period, South Asia professedly was the "other Asia" for Japan. A systemic dissection of the Asian continent into its many sub-regions, it was found that Japan's presence and influence in South Asia, be it economic, political, or strategic, came nowhere close to the effect it wielded in the other sub-regions. Despite its dense population of 1.97 billion, which makes up for 24.9% of the globe's humanity, South Asia's widespread poverty, limited industrialization, and inward-looking economic policies placed limits on Japan's economic and diplomatic penetration of the region.[1] Japan's limited influence in South Asia was also reflected in the inadequate attention it received in Japanese scholarship and media concerning Japan-Asia relations. For instance, a *Far Eastern Economic Review* article on the changing role of Japanese *sogo shosha* (Japan's prominent companies involved in trade and business) in Asia did not even mention South Asia.[2]

The three areas that remained particularly underdeveloped in Japan-South Asia ties were aid, trade, and investment-commercial ties. South Asia and the South Pacific constituted two sub-regions where Japan was not involved in any striking conflicts. Besides, both remained of lesser geo-economic status. Foreign policymaking in Japan leans toward being rather "reactive," principally responding to external developments and gravity. Since the post-war period, Japan and South Asian nations were best defined as distantly estranged Asian neighbors with a conventional view that Japan came to act only under heavy "external pressure" (*gaiatsu*). It remained the case that *gaiatsu* did, at times, play a critical role in bringing about key Japanese foreign policy initiatives to fruition.[3] Tokyo's post-war foreign policy between 1952 and 1973 followed a "separation of economics and politics" (*seikei bunri*) strategy, whereby it avoided involvement in almost all international issues. This phase, however, abruptly ended in late 1973 with the Organization of the Petroleum Exporting Countries' (OPEC) quadrupling of oil prices and the oil embargo by the Arab states. It was here when Japan arrived at comprehending that it was no longer possible to separate economics from politics, as a consequence of which came about its "comprehensive security" (*sogo anzen hosho*) strategy that involved active diplomatic involvement.[4]

354

DOI: 10.4324/9781003246626-30

Japan and South Asia: A Brief Historical Context

Rising from the ashes of 1945, Tokyo's exponential growth miracle rendered it an economic superpower enabling it to master a neo-mercantilist strategy that lasted from 1973 until 1990. The period saw Japan's foreign economic presence throughout the Third World (including South Asia) expand rapidly as Tokyo confronted a range of issues in its quest for diversified sources of markets, raw materials, cheap labor, and energy.[5] Japan's policy toward the Third World became a foundational strategy through which Tokyo employed foreign aid as a diplomatic tool to spread its influence across the Third World including South Asia. Interestingly, in February 1989, Thailand's Prime Minister Chatichai Choonhavan commented, "The world economic war is over, Japan has won."[6] That said, however, Japanese investments in South Asia were minuscule between 1979 and 1986, which could be gauged from the fact that it constituted less than 0.1% of its total foreign investments globally during the period, and less than 0.5% of its total investments in Asia.[7] Japan's interest in South Asia [particularly India] grew very gradually post-1991 following several high-profile investment missions, including one by officials from the Federation of Economic Organizations (*Keidanren*) and a first-ever visit by the Minister of International Trade and Industry (MITI) in 1995.[8]

The decade of the 1990s saw relations between the global economic power (Japan) and South Asia (particularly India) improve dramatically.[9] The primary factors behind this were Japan's ambition to reemerge as an international actor with former Premier Yasuhiro Nakasone's repeated call for the "internationalization of Japan." His successor, Noboru Takeshita, echoed that Japan needed to revive and widen the ambit of its ties with other nations, and not singularly deal with the West, including the US. This approach seemingly stemmed from the friction that Japan was experiencing with Washington and Europe over matters pertaining trade, tariffs, and investments, which were being seen as a serious challenge to Japan's economic growth. In its search for newer markets and partners, South Asia as a region emerged as a natural contender with its enormous size and potential.

The visits of successive PMs to South Asia, from Nakasone to Toshiki Kaifu in April 1990, only strengthened the view that "… peace and stability in Asia is a matter of great concern to Japan … the development of this region inhabited by … one fifth of all mankind, is in itself one of the major interests of the whole world …"[10] Kaifu further underscored that Japan would seek deepening of engagement on issues without limiting to agenda items on bilateral or Asian issues alone.[11] It was for these reasons that despite the fact that Japanese Premiers had previously visited the region in 1957, 1961, and 1984, the visit of Prime Minister Kaifu to four South Asian countries, namely India, Bangladesh, Pakistan, and Sri Lanka, became a landmark in the history of Japan-South Asia ties. By means of this visit, Japan sought to convey that after achieving an "Asian economic powerhouse" status, Tokyo's policy interests and approach, traditionally limited to East and Southeast Asia, were increasingly seeking a shift toward South Asia.

The subcontinent began assuming greater significance for Japan's economic and political interests from the fact that 70% of its oil imports from the Middle East came via sea crossing the Indian Ocean. It was thus in Japanese interests that regional security and stability be maintained by means of providing economic/development assistance. By this time, Japan had already established its credentials in so far as investment and aid across the Third World was concerned. South Asia, for its part too, was seeking Japan's technological, economic-development, and foreign aid assistance. Being a net creditor nation soon led to Japan becoming the leading individual donor of development for this region.[12] There was a convergence of Japan's overall regional politico-economic strategies with South Asia, in that, the region (especially and most notably, India) was pursuing an economic liberalization and deregulation agenda.

Further, South Asia began deriving benefits from Japan's economic and technological assistance and acknowledged the imperatives of its economic interdependence with Tokyo in view of the prevailing global economic realities. Economic assistance was an area where responsibility was[13] and continues to be shared widely by various ministries in Japan. The formation of the basic policy of Official Development Assistance (ODA) is made by the coordinated efforts of Japan's Ministries of Foreign Affairs and Finance, the Ministry of Economy, Trade and Industry (METI), and the Economic Planning Agency (EPA). Of this, influence of the METI remains most pronounced in terms of yen loans, with the Ministry of Foreign Affairs (MOFA) playing a decisive role in determining grant aid. The MOFA divided Japan's aid policy regime into four[14] different stages: Firstly, system development period (1954–1976); secondly, system expansion period (1977–1991); thirdly, policy and philosophy enhancement period (1992–2002); and finally, meeting the challenges of a new era (2003 onward).

Notably, the ODA's Charter of 1992 stipulates few principles of such political use.[15] In case of South Asia, official aid has been a more dominating feature of relations with Japan, given that the latter remains a top aid donor to most of the subcontinent's nations.

Despite the gradually ascending and reassuring graph of regional ties illustrated above, the end of the decade of the 1990s witnessed a steep decline and acrimony in Japan's ties with India and Pakistan in particular, following the nuclear tests conducted by both nations in May 1998 that led to the nuclearization of the subcontinent. Given Japan's commitment to the Nuclear Non-Proliferation Treaty, Japan's censure came in the form of an immediate freeze on all grant aid and subsequently on new yen loans.[16] Japan also became the first Organization for Economic Cooperation and Development (OECD) nation to impose a range of economic sanctions on both India and Pakistan.[17] That said, the India and Pakistan's nuclear tests inherently exposed certain limitations of Japan's post-Cold War foreign policy. Japan's aid diplomacy, its bids to initiate joint action in international forums, and attempts at mediation were largely ineffectual in case of South Asia's nuclear tests. The aid sanctions meant to punish failed, however, to achieve the intended results.[18] More so, then-Premier Hashimoto Ryutaro's diplomacy attempting to isolate India and Pakistan failed at yielding any tangible results for Japan's foreign policy[19] or gain traction for that matter. Subsequently, the period of 2000–2010 began witnessing a gradual thawing of ties between Japan and India—a distance long traveled since the time when during the mid-1960s, South Asia, including India, were omitted from what Japan considered "Asia."

This embrace seemingly mirrors the regional and global geopolitics and geo-strategy at play, which have been impacted by the strategic shifts in policy thinking and approaches occurring within Asia. Japan and India by now shared similar perceptions of the evolving environment in the region and the world at large; recognized their common commitment to democracy, human rights, and the rule of law for promoting stability and development in Asia and beyond; acknowledged common interest in the safety of sea lines of communications; committed to jointly fight against terrorism and recognized each other's counter-terrorism efforts; and sought to establish a "Strategic and Global Partnership" driven by converging long-term political, economic and strategic interests, aspirations, and concerns.[20]

Conceptual and Theoretical Framework

South Asia's evolution as a playing field in the Asian geostrategic landscape has transited multiple phases. Beginning essentially with being a reluctant player that achieved independence from many decades of British colonial rule following the end of World War II, it emerged as a region that houses the Indian Ocean—a lifeline water body connecting the Far East with the Atlantic. This added to the subcontinent's significance in a remodeled multipolar regional architecture. This chapter chronicles a blend of foreign policy approaches and strategies cited in the context of historical and current influences and motivations. The conceptual underpinnings of this chapter find roots in realism (*political realism* to be more precise) that prioritizes national interest and security. This notion is often tantamount with power politics to a large extent, including extended variables such as the drive for regional status, ambitions, and applied strategies including economic statecraft.[21] In the realist paradigm, security is based on the principle of balance of power, as state-centric approaches are placed in the traditional realist framework of security that essentially centers around the concept of power. South Asia's political realism exhibits its competitive and conflictual sides equally, especially in terms of the struggle for regional significance and power.[22]

From a Japanese perspective, while great powers often produce theories of international relations (IR), in the case of Japan, being a failed challenger to American hegemony in the past and having been embedded in the global governance system dominated by the US has inhibited theoretical advancement.[23] This, combined with the relatively weak tradition of positivistic hypothesis testing in social science and the relatively strong tradition of descriptive work have tended to discourage the development of a Japanese theory of IR.[24] For Japan, its style and form of integration holds three distinctive features that have developed step by step on a domestic, regional, and global scale. Japan's approach to IR theories, among other planes, needs to be identified and understood through the prism of *identity* as among a key concept.

Nishida Kitaro, in particular, has attempted to address the rather barbed issue of Japanese identity in IR as Japan juggles to fit in a space that lies somewhere between the East and the West. Nishida as an innate constructivist makes identity the thrust of his philosophy. He rejects Cartesian logic and adopts dialectic, in which a thesis and an antithesis coexist without forming a synthesis, thereby arguing that Japanese identity emerges through a coexistence of opposites, i.e., Eastern and Western. What is striking about Nishida's philosophy is his effort to make Japanese identity construction universally understood, as opposed to forming a parochial topic.[25] The Constructivist analysis of IR states that the notion of identity is ideational, shaped by complex factors such as history, way of life, values, and interests. This seems to be particularly useful for analysis in East Asia, which affects policy decisions particularly in Japan.

Meanwhile, Japan seeks to approach regional politics and statecraft through regional economic integration, another key concept of IR study that has been put to use in this study. This, when combined with sustainable development, places regional integration theories higher than state sovereignty as economist Hirano Yoshitaro has argued.[26] There are two competing ideological factors at work in Japan's approach to the regional economic integration theory. The first is the desire for historical rapprochement with Japan's neighbors in Asia based on the postwar Franco-German model. The other factor is a new nationalism in Japan, designated as the desire for greater "assertiveness" in foreign (especially Asian) affairs. This includes some resentment of Japan's continued military dependence on the United States and desire for a stronger Asian role in world affairs (if not Japanese dominance of that role). In the short term, Asian economic integration serves both ideologies.[27] It requires Asian neighbors to put the past relationship with Japan behind them in significant ways, reorients Japanese policy initiatives toward Asia (and away from the United States), and, finally, puts Japan in the position of being a vital player in the region.[28]

The classical theories on regionalism have focused on regional integration processes explained via geostrategic rationality, realism, and economic interdependence, and through traditional material factors such as security, economic flows, and geostrategic choices.[29] Substantively, Japan's IR has evolved to reach a stage of developing its own Japan-centric world order, where Japan is part of Asia, but somewhat separate from Asia.[30] Based on these concepts and theories, wherein identity, norms, and interaction of personalities remain vital components, the evolving equation and geostrategic dynamics between Japan and South Asia shall be evaluated, amid contesting systemic conditions and states' priorities to shape a future geopolitical and economic order of Asia. These processes could prospectively produce an alternative regional Asian dynamic.

"Confluence of the Two Seas" and Understanding of a Broader Asia: A Decade of Japan's Free and Open Indo-Pacific Framework

Originally a geographic concept comprising of the Indian Ocean and Pacific Ocean that shaped linkages between the United States and East Asia, it evolved into a geostrategic concept and strategy. When stretched till the Indian Ocean, it paved way for what more popularly has now come to be known by the new framework of the "Indo-Pacific." The origin of the term "Indo-Pacific" can be traced to the 1920s when German geopolitical scholar Karl Haushofer cited this term in his work, *Indopazifischen Raum*. In the contemporary context, Japan was among the first countries to begin using the phrase "Free and Open Indo-Pacific" in its official discourse and documents. And, the US government started to use the term "Indo-Pacific" under the Obama administration's rebalancing strategy toward Asia. The notion of the greater Indo-Pacific has eclipsed the spheres of influence limited to the Indian Ocean, East China Sea, South China Sea, and the Western Pacific. In this context, numerous policy statements coming from Japan have indicated that security issues in the Indian Ocean, Pacific Ocean, South China Sea, and East China Sea cannot be treated separately, or as standalone issues alone. At its heart, a strategic system can be understood as a set of geopolitical power relationships among nations where major changes in one part of the system affect what happens in the other parts.[31] Analyzing the past decade of politics and policies in Asia brings to the fore certain momentous developments that have redefined Asian geopolitics, expectedly impacting South Asia and the Indian Ocean Region (IOR). By 2030, Asia will contribute the majority of global growth,[32] thus underscoring its importance and that of the Indo-Pacific.

The US "pivot" and later "rebalance" in Asia was almost concurrently followed by former Japanese PM Shinzo Abe's proposed Indo-Pacific concept and strategic framework in 2012. When Abe penned his book *Utsukushii kuni e* (Towards a Beautiful Country) in 2006, he publicly advocated the concept of a "broader Asia" that constitutes nations in the Pacific and Indian Oceans. Abe appeared to have anticipated Asia's geostrategic future exclusively through the prism of political realism, and rightly so.[33] The concept of a "broader Asia" appears to have transcended geographical boundaries, with the Pacific and Indian Oceans' mergence becoming far more pronounced and evident than ever. In order to catch up with the reality of broader Asia, the Abe administration rehabilitated its focus on South Asia in general, and India in particular, within the ambit of Japan's *Free and Open Indo-Pacific Strategy* launched and pushed during his second tenure in December 2012. Abe's bid to forge this vision, in fact, began during his first term as Japan's PM, when he addressed the Indian Parliament in August 2007, wherein he quoted the famously authored work of Mughal prince Dara Shikoh's book *Majma-ul-Bahrain* (*Confluence of the Two Seas*, published in 1655). This book is said to have been the inspiration, foundation, and title of Abe's vision to nurture an open and transparent Indo-Pacific maritime zone as part of a broader Asia.[34]

Abe's focus on reviving Japan's economy in foreign policy could be gauged in an interview with *Foreign Affairs*, where he stated that, "When I served as Prime Minister last time, I failed to prioritize my agenda ... my second administration should prioritize turning around the Japanese economy."[35] The presence and engagement with South Asia have become vital pillars for Japan's *Free and Open Indo-Pacific Strategy*[36] in order to catch up with the reality of its broader Asia interpretation. It is also for Japan's own stability, prosperity, and engagement in the Indo-Pacific region at large, of which South Asia constitutes the core, geographically. The phrase "broad-based diplomacy in Asia" is often discussed and debated within Tokyo's policymaking circles. It is argued that the major challenge for Japan's go forward strategy in Asia would be devising novel ways that suggest engagement in economic areas and hedging in terms of security, instead of being a mere counterweight to China's rise and presence.[37] Security discussions in the South Asian context can be extremely complex given its internal security dynamics ranging from wars, internal conflicts, civil war, insurgencies, factionalism, hunger, disease, and repression.[38] Besides, low levels of intra-regional trade and political considerations often override the prospect of economic engagement. With security dependencies among regional nations remaining deeply intertwined with the impact of external players, the strategic setting of the subcontinent tends to remain fluid.

Japan's engagement with South Asia symbolizes acknowledgment of the economic and strategic dependence of developments across a much wider maritime region, wherein the Indian Ocean lies at its heart. The Indo-Pacific concept has been embraced with many nations enunciating their strategies and outlook for the region, witnessed by the creation of partnerships and mechanisms as opportunities, concerns, and stakes of these nations intersect with that of South Asia. Most prominently, the "Quad," constituting the United States, Australia, Japan, and India, remains bound being political democracies, market economies, and pluralistic societies. Integrated via common areas of interest and convergences to advance common goals, the Quad partners are committed to its shared commitment for maintaining a free, open, and inclusive Indo-Pacific by means of upholding a rules-based international order, underpinned by the rule of law, transparency, freedom and navigation in the international seas, respect for territorial integrity and sovereignty, and peaceful resolution of disputes.[39]

In this context, the IOR doubles up as a geopolitical and geo-economic nerve center that remains critical to the regional construct, and its primacy. To a large extent, the Indian Ocean has significantly replaced the Atlantic as the world's busiest and strategically most significant trade corridor.[40] Consequently, major East Asian economies, including Japan, have acute dependence on oil imports across the Indian Ocean from the Middle East and Africa. The region is often labeled as the artery that carries resources to fuel the growth of regional economies. However, on the flip side, dependence of this nature also becomes a strategic vulnerability that could well influence regional partnership-building and diplomatic relations. Investments in seaports across various locations in the IOR have critical strategic ramifications that shall likely shuffle security alignments regionally. This geostrategic graph of existential realities across the Indo-Pacific has rendered South Asia and the IOR critical for Japan's foreign policy and strategic interests. For this prioritized approach, Tokyo today seeks collaboration with its partners in South Asia to build their politico-economic capacities in order to render them capable of retaining and exercising autonomy, defend their interests, and identify common regional security challenges.

Development Aid, Assistance, and Foreign Policy Interests and Influence: The Japan-South Asia Case

While development assistance and aid, ideally, should be separated from foreign policy object-ives, the former tends to be driven in focusing on security concerns of developed nations in the politically fragile regions where aid is to be granted. Specifically, the geostrategic import-ance and vulnerabilities of South Asia make it almost impossible for a donor country to keep politics out of its development aid agenda to further the politico-diplomatic goals of the donor, along with ensuring the developmental objectives of recipient nations.[41] According to surveys of Japanese companies conducted in the past decade by the Foundation for Advanced Studies on International Development (FASID), the biggest problem when investing in South Asia remains its poor infrastructure. While the subcontinent has registered robust economic growth, yet, an equally assertive reality is its ratio of people living in absolute poverty (about 220 million) making up one-third of the world's total.[42] Thus arises a pressing need to address two major bottlenecks for future growth in the region: Insufficient physical and nonphysical infrastructure and inadequate human capital formation.[43] The areas in which Japan expected enhanced ODA expansion were centered on physical infrastructure such as power, roads, and ports, cited in that order. The weaker growth performance in South Asia coupled with its slower pace of urbanization have rendered the levels of current infrastructure provision and of human capital generally weaker and more unevenly distributed.[44] Any nation that is capable of exporting infrastructure systems is able to increase leverage on partner countries through support for infrastructure development and enhance regional influence.[45] Connectivity devel-opment through infrastructure building has crucial impacts on the economy and society in individual countries, as well as in the overall development of the broader region.[46] Japan's growing interest in supporting infrastructure development in South Asia complements its finding of a new source of economic growth in exporting infrastructure systems in Asia's emerging regions and economies, which can then serve as vital foreign policy tools.[47]

That said, Japan and its ODA policy has also come under criticism from the defense and security establishment owing to an excessive tendency to lend only for hardcore infrastructure-related projects alone.[48] There has been debate and criticism about Japan's ODA administra-tion being non-participatory, lacking a coherent national strategy, and disproportionate bias in favor of hard infrastructure and against soft infrastructure and social sector development.[49]

Japan's former Prime Minister Nobusuke Kishi, who served in office from January 1957 to July 1960, became the first-ever Japanese PM to visit New Delhi in 1957. It was during this visit that he launched Japan's first post-war ODA to India with the grant of international yen loans that Japan began to provide in 1958. From then, Japan has gone on to become India's largest bilateral lender and largest humanitarian assistance provider, both directly and indirectly, through multilateral agencies.[50] Japan's bilateral ODA to India grew from 1.7% in 2007 to 8.6% in 2008, shooting to 14.2% in 2016. Japan International Cooperation Agency (JICA)—the primary governmental agency that coordinates and delivers the bulk of Japan's ODA to developing countries—views the stability and development of South Asia as critical since it is a strategic region linking ASEAN with the Middle East and Africa. Developing economic foundations and improving connectivity especially in India, Bangladesh, and Sri Lanka, in line with relevant intergovernmental joint statements, JICA is implementing programs and projects that contribute to developing transport infrastructure (railways, roads, and ports) that are an essential element for sustainable growth. For improving connectivity in the region, JICA has formulated a national highway improvement project, which constitutes part of an international corridor program that will connect Northeast India with Bangladesh.

Besides, JICA has also completed a project to improve a mountainous section of Pakistan's National Highway 70, thus stimulating physical distribution between Afghanistan and Iran. Seen as an arm to further Japanese government's policies largely falling under the ambit of its *Free and Open Indo-Pacific* strategy and framework, JICA will remain further committed to promote intra- and inter-regional connectivity; enhancing industrial competitiveness, including improving the investment environment; ensuring peace, stability, and security; and above all, improving access to basic human needs.

Infrastructure Initiatives, Capacity-Building, and Sustainable Development in the Indian Ocean: Japan's Approach and Engagement in the Regional Maritime Security Environment

The Indian Ocean is the third-largest among the world's oceanic divisions woven together by trade routes. It commands control of major sea-lanes carrying half of the world's container ships, one-third of the world's bulk cargo traffic, and two-thirds of global oil shipments. South Asia constitutes the IOR's core sub-regions and is witness to nearly half of the world's trade passing through it. The region's size and diversity explain its geo-economic and consequent geopolitical significance. The IOR countries share similar challenges and opportunities by virtue of their strategic location, access to limitless unexploited maritime resources, vulnerability to natural disasters, political instability, and the looming shadow of a rising China that seeks to drive and establish an economic and politico-security dominant Asian architecture. In this backdrop, Indian Ocean as a strategic node becomes even more crucial, in that the power that shall likely dominate the Indian Ocean will eventually control entire Asia.[51] Given the severe diversity and differential between countries that are bound together by the Indian Ocean, the need to promote sustained growth and balanced development in the region through regional economic cooperation becomes far more pronounced.

Japan's policies and approach for operating in the IOR underwent a major transformation with the lifting of the ban on Japanese troops to enable its Self-Defense Forces in dispatching armed troops to Iraq in 1992.[52] Today, notably, nearly 40% of all Japan's Self-Defense Forces' missions have occurred in the IOR, and a half of Japanese ODA goes to the IOR countries.[53] While China's Belt and Road Initiative cuts across strategic ports in South Asia and the IOR, both economically and militarily,[54] Japan's presence and role in the Indian Ocean is qualitatively different from that of China. Tokyo tends to focus more on regional norms that depict and practice transparency, economic sustainability, sustainable development, and a rules-based order.[55] Japan's increasing interest and presence in the Indian Ocean also hinges on the critical reality of its dependency on energy supplies shipped across the Indian Ocean. Thus, securitization of the sea lanes of communication (SLOCs) from West Asia to Japan is a primary driver for the latter to build upon security and economic partnerships with potential strategic partners across the IOR.

Viewing through the prism of geopolitics of connectivity, South Asia presents itself, perhaps, as a connecting link with the other half of the Indo-Pacific. For Japan, it has become an indispensable subcontinent that shall serve in maintaining its status as a vital Asian player in the region. And thus, establishing a more than visible presence here has become a necessity for Tokyo. While India remains the cornerstone of Japan's South Asia policy and strategy, be it in the economic, political, military, and cultural spheres, the past decade has witnessed Tokyo taking a keen interest in deepening cooperation and engagement with other South Asian countries including Bangladesh, Nepal, and Sri Lanka. South Asia's significance for Japan has never been greater, in terms of strategy, policies, budgets, and attention with Japan joining multiple major port construction/renovation projects spread across South Asia and the IOR. In 2012, 83% of Japan's oil imports came from West Asia (through the Indian Ocean), rising from 70% during the 1980s.[56] Between 2011 and 2014, Japan imported 66.5% of its raw materials from the IOR.[57] From a meager 1.1% of Japanese foreign direct investment (FDI) in 1999, the IOR countries commanded 21.3% of Japanese FDI in 2014.[58] Besides, Japan's trade with IOR nations has shot up to $225 billion, and similar is the fate of energy reliance.[59]

The past decade saw Japan becoming a technologically advanced pillar and principal hub of infrastructure development in South Asia and the littoral countries in the IOR.[60] Japan's *Partnership for Quality Infrastructure Initiative*, first announced in 2015, involved infrastructure spending (over five years) of around $110 billion in Asia. A few significant Japan-sponsored ports infrastructure projects[61] in and around South Asia since 2016 include: Mumbai, India: Trans-harbor link ($2.2 billion); Matarbari, Bangladesh: Port and power station ($3.7 billion); Yangon, Myanmar: Container terminal ($200 million); and, Dawei, Myanmar: Port and special economic zone ($800 million).

Japan has provided yen-based loans to three key countries of the region—Bangladesh, Myanmar, and Sri Lanka—in order to develop deep seaports in Matarbari (which will be large enough to handle 50% of the country's cargo, thereby easing pressure on the Chittagong port), Dawei, and Trincomalee, respectively.[62] Japan's discussions for infrastructure investment with Sri Lanka in the key northeastern port of Trincomalee, the world's second-deepest natural harbor, will aid in securing its vital sea lanes used to import oil from West Asia.[63] By promoting entrepreneurship and collaborative infrastructure development in third-party countries, namely Sri Lanka, Myanmar, and Bangladesh, Japan is encouraging capacity-building and sustainable development and growth in and around South Asia. Moreover, Tokyo is a key trading partner for Nepal, accounting for a major portion of FDI in the Himalayan nation. Japan additionally is the largest bilateral ODA donor to Bangladesh, Bhutan, Maldives, and Sri Lanka. In so far as Pakistan is concerned, Tokyo undertakes a more than cautious approach, and has yet to make any significant inroads toward investment and engagement. Pakistan's perilous security environment acts as a deterrent for Japan to invest in it, more so as China remains Pakistan's principal benefactor and patron.

Propelling growth and investment through capacity-building, quality infrastructure projects slated to build institutional, industrial, and transport corridors in and via South Asia are a key avenue for Japan given its expertise in providing quality infrastructure and state-of-the-art technology. This shall simultaneously serve as a balancer in the regional maritime paradigm of the IOR. Perhaps, it is the apprehension of being outmaneuvered by China that has placed the theories of functional integration in the region to test. As economic activities in South Asia and the IOR expand, the maritime transport on its sea route will likely propel implementation of the *Blue Economy Strategy*, which brings together various sectors of ocean resources' sustainable use.[64] Being the world's foremost maritime nations with a long oceanic history, the sea has played a pivotal role in defining Japan's economy and its role in promoting a *Blue Economy* while harnessing ocean resources for economic growth.

Awareness of its immediate and extended geopolitical neighborhood is manifested in Tokyo's defense outlook and approach with major South Asian nations. Since 2018, India and Japan have initiated bilateral exercises between all three components of their defense forces. Upgrading this came the First India-Japan 2+2 Foreign and Defense Ministerial Meeting held in November 2019, which affirmed to further enhance Indo-Japanese "strategic depth of bilateral security and defense cooperation" in view of the developing security situation in the Indo-Pacific.[65] Moreover, Japanese Maritime Self-Defense Force (MSDF) deployment seeks more opportunities for Japanese vessels to visit ports in South Asia during voyages across the Indian Ocean. Japan seeks to play an active role in stabilizing the Indian Ocean and reinforcing a rules-based order in the engagement with key IOR states such as Myanmar, Bangladesh, and Sri Lanka through investments in infrastructure and capability-building, and an enhanced role for the Japanese Coast Guard.[66] Interestingly, between 2011 and 2015, Japan's MSDF vessels visited Sri Lankan ports on 22 occasions.[67] Moreover, Japan has also donated two patrol craft to the Sri Lankan Coast Guard (each vessel costing nearly $11 million).

Conclusion

Since the time South Asia along with other sub-regions came up on Japan's foreign policy radar, it started becoming increasingly clear that Tokyo's "Third World policy" will serve as a vital component of its overall comprehensive security thinking and approach.[68] From that period till date, the contemporary realist variables in decision-making in the realm of foreign policy have amplified that while economic symbiosis appears the ideal driver for states to adopt cooperative frameworks, the concurrently pressing and contesting geostrategic realities shall continue to invade upon any/all regional realignments, be it in South Asia or the Indian Ocean Region. Recalling Samuel Huntington's famous words when he said, "... the size of China's displacement of the world balance is such that the world must find a new balance within a few decades."[69] The power differential caused by Beijing's growth and push outside its borders, evidenced by imposing initiatives such as the Belt and Road Initiative, will be a significantly defining factor in determining future regional geostrategic permutations, the outcome of which shall bear an imprint on the future security design of South Asia in particular, and Asia at large.

Regional players will be pushed to make prudent choices based on national interests, while struggling to pursue a sovereign foreign policy path that best suits their respective security interests. Japan's present and future approach in South Asia shall seemingly be one that includes aiding its partner nations in the region by improving their infrastructure, which could ensure strategic independence, freedom, and maintenance of a critical regional power balance.[70] Despite the significance of Japanese aid to South Asia, the rationales and results of development cooperation activities that Japan has executed in the region have been underexplored.[71] It would further be reasonable to argue that Japan's foreign policy formulation for South Asia will likely position itself toward engaging with the latter deeply to achieve strategic deliverables. While a strategic and economic partnership between Japan and South Asia promises to hold optimum benefits ideally, there are various critical thresholds and extrinsic and intrinsic geostrategic factors at play in the subcontinent. While Tokyo is creating a roadmap to fashion its place and say in all affairs' South Asia, the latter seemingly is holding on to its own in a rapidly evolving strategic graph, the future of which shall impact upon entire Asia.

The concurrence of thought in Tokyo that in a world where it is no longer possible to separate economics from politics (*seikei bunri*), Japan's new comprehensive security (*sogo anzen hosho*) strategy should revolve more acutely around active politico-diplomatic involvement. Tokyo's policy interests and approach, traditionally limited to East and Southeast Asia prior to the Cold War, have increasingly shifted toward South Asia since. Tokyo has employed foreign aid as a diplomatic tool to spread its influence across the developing world, prominently in South Asia. One of the primary determinants behind this approach remains Japan's objective of reemerging as an active player in the Indo-Pacific region. Of this, South Asia as a region, with its enormous size and potential, will continue to serve as a natural contender for the major geostrategic and geo-economic interests of the whole world. South Asia's presence in

Japan's economic diplomacy and technological aid and assistance schematic will continue to capitalize, more critically, on strategic necessities, as the subcontinent hosts its competitive and conflictual facets of regional significance and power correspondingly.

Notes

1 William R. Nester, *Japan and the Third World: Patterns, Power, Prospects* (New York: St. Martin's Press, 1992), 271–274.
2 "Tokyo's Deal Makers," *Far Eastern Economic Review*, February 1, 1996, cited in Purnendra Jain, "Japan's Relations with South Asia," *Asian Survey* 37, no. 4 (April 1997): 340–352.
3 Tanaka Akihiko, "Domestic Politics and Foreign Policy," in *Japanese Foreign Policy Today: A Reader*, eds. Inoguchi Takashi and Purnendra Jain (New York: Palgrave Macmillan, 2000), 3–17.
4 Nester, *Japan and the Third World: Patterns, Power, Prospects*, 15.
5 *Ibid.*, 18.
6 Bruce Koppel and Michael Plummer, "Japan Ascendancy as a Foreign-Aid Power," *Asian Survey* 29, no. 11 (1989): 1043–1056.
7 *Ibid.*
8 Jain, "Japan's Relations with South Asia."
9 Badar Alam Iqbal, "Indo-Japanese Economic Relations in the 1990s," *India Quarterly* 52, no. 1/2 (January-June 1996), 39–72; also see Rajesh Mehta, "Indo-Japanese Trade: Recent Trends," RIS Discussion Papers, no. 12, May 2001.
10 Speech by PM Toshiki Kaifu, *Japan and South Asia: In Pursuit of Dialogue and Cooperation for Peace and Prosperity* (Parliament House, New Delhi, April 30, 1990).
11 *Ibid.*
12 Saburo Okita, "Japan's Quiet Strength," *Foreign Policy* 75 (Summer 1989), 128–145.
13 Purnendra Jain, "Japan and South Asia: Between Cooperation and Confrontation," in *Japanese Foreign Policy Today: A Reader*, eds. Inoguchi Takashi and Purnendra Jain (New York: Palgrave Macmillan, 2000), 266–282.
14 Japan Ministry of Foreign Affairs on ODA, available at https://www.mofa.go.jp/policy/oda/cooperation/anniv50/pamphlet/index.html.
15 Akihiko, "Domestic Politics and Foreign Policy."
16 "Nuclear Anxiety: The Allies; Japan Freezes Some Grants; Other Nations Seem Doubtful," *The New York Times*, May 14, 1998.
17 Jain, "Japan and South Asia: Between Cooperation and Confrontation."
18 *Ibid.*
19 *Ibid.*
20 "Joint Declaration on Security Cooperation between India and Japan," Ministry of External Affairs, India, October 22, 2008, https://www.mofa.go.jp/region/asia-paci/india/pmv0810/joint_d.html.
21 Roger D. Spegele, *Political Realism in International Theory* (Victoria: Cambridge University Press,1996); for related reading on the subject, see R. Harrison Wagner, *War and the State: The Theory of International Politics* (The University of Michigan Press, 2007).
22 The theoretical roots of South Asia as a sub-region in terms of its strategic thinking and orientation can be traced back in history to the end of 4th century BCE, when the Indian treatise *Arthashastra* (meaning the "Science of Material Gain" or the "Science of Polity")—a voluminous seminal masterpiece written in Sanskrit, delineating theories of statecraft, diplomacy, strategy, and prerequisites of politics and power—was penned by Kautilya. *Arthashastra* became a trailblazing document that contains a realist vision of politics. It is considered unique and defining in Indian literature (and erstwhile united South Asia) owing to the forthright advocacy of its cardinal virtue, *realpolitik*.
23 Takashi Inoguchi, "Why are There No Non-Western Theories of International Relations? The Case of Japan," in Barry Buzan and Amitav Acharya, eds., *Non-Western International Relations Theory: Perspectives on and beyond Asia*, (Oxon: Routledge, 2010).
24 *Ibid.*
25 Kitaro Nishida, *Intelligibility and the Philosophy of Nothingness: Three Philosophical Essays* (Honolulu: International Philosophical Research Association of Japan and East-West Center Press, 1958).
26 Inoguchi, "Why are There No Non-Western Theories of International Relations? The Case of Japan."

27 Adam S. Posen, "Japan's Distraction by Regional Economic Integration," State Department INR Roundtable on Northeast Asian Regional Economic Integration, Peterson Institute for International Economics, June 2002.

28 *Ibid.*

29 Sergio Caballero Santos, "Regional Integration Theories: The Suitability of a Constructivist Approach," Paper 383, *Session on Globalization and Governance*, IPSA-Chile, July 2009.

30 Inoguchi, "Why are There No Non-Western Theories of International Relations? The Case of Japan."

31 Rory Medcalf, "The Evolving Security Order in the Indo-Pacific," in *Indo-Pacific Maritime Security: Challenges and Cooperation*, ed. David Brewster (Canberra: National Security College, Crawford School of Public Policy, Australian National University, 2016), 7–11; also see Rory Medcalf, "The Indo-Pacific: What's in a Name?" *The American Interest* 9, no. 2 (November/December 2013), 58–66.

32 Praneeth Yendamuri and Zara Ingilizian, "In 2020 Asia Will Have the World's Largest GDP. Here's What That Means," World Economic Forum, December 20, 2019, https://www.weforum.org/agenda/2019/12/asia-economic-growth/.

33 Monika Chansoria, "Modi-Abe Personality Impacts Foreign Policy," *The Sunday Guardian*, September 20, 2014.

34 *Ibid.*

35 Shinzo Abe and Jonathan Tepperman, "Japan is Back: A Conversation with Shinzo Abe," *Foreign Affairs* 92, no. 4 (July/August 2013), 2–8.

36 Monika Chansoria, "Indo-Japanese Strategic Partnership: Scope and Future Avenues," Note de la FRS no. 17, September 19, 2017, https://www.frstrategie.org/en/publications/notes/indo-japanese-strategic-partnership-scope-future-avenues-2017; also see Monika Chansoria, "Japanese Investments are Instrumental to India's Act East Policy," *Asia Pacific Bulletin* 385, June 21, 2017.

37 Editorial, "Japan-India Ties Should Go Beyond Countering China," *The Japan Times*, October 30, 2018; more so, the author makes this argument based on her opinion and inferences following numerous discussions and interactions with senior officials in the Japanese Ministry of Foreign Affairs and the Cabinet Secretariat, Tokyo.

38 Sagarika Dutt et al., eds. *South Asian Security: 21st Century Discourses* (Oxon: Routledge, 2012).

39 V. Muraleedharan, "Remarks at International Workshop on 'Quad in the Indo-Pacific,'" transcript of speech delivered at Ministry of External Affairs, New Delhi, April 29, 2021, https://www.mea.gov.in/Speeches-Statements.htm?dtl/33828/Remarks_by_Shri_V_Muraleedharan_Minister_of_State_for_External_Affairs_at_International_Workshop_on_Quad_in_the_IndoPacific.

40 Justin Jones, "Submarines and Maritime Strategy – Part 1," *The Strategist*, January 29, 2013; and see page 13 of the Commonwealth of Australia's 2013 Defence White Paper: Ministry of Defence (Australia), Defense White Paper 2013, http://www.defence.gov.au/whitepaper/2013.

41 For details on the subject, see Antonio Estache, "Emerging Infrastructure Policy Issues in Developing Countries: A Survey of the Recent Economic Literature," POVNET Infrastructure Working Group Background Paper, November 2004, https://elibrary.worldbank.org/doi/abs/10.1596/1813-9450-3442; also see Stephen D. Jones, "Contribution of Infrastructure to Growth and Poverty Reduction in East Asia and the Pacific," Oxford Policy Management Background Paper, October 2004; and see Stephen Jones, "Infrastructure Challenges in East and South Asia," *IDS Bulletin* 37, no. 3 (May 2006), Institute of Development Studies, 29.

42 "Poverty and Shared Prosperity 2018: Piecing Together the Poverty Puzzle," World Bank, 2018, https://openknowledge.worldbank.org/bitstream/handle/10986/30418/9781464813306.pdf.

43 "JICA Annual Report 2020," Japan International Cooperation Agency, 2020, https://www.jica.go.jp/english/publications/reports/annual/2020/c8h0vm0000fc7q2b-att/2020_07.pdf.

44 *Ibid.*, p. 29.

45 Hidetaka Yoshimatsu, "New Dynamics in Sino-Japanese Rivalry: Sustaining Infrastructure Development in Asia," *Journal of Contemporary China* 27, no. 113 (2018): 721.

46 *Ibid.*, 720.

47 *Ibid.*

48 Hadi Soesastro, "Sustaining East Asia's Economic Dynamism: The Role of Aid," PRI-OECD Research Project, May 2004, https://www.oecd.org/gov/pcsd/31970823.pdf.

49 Masahiro Kawai and Shinji Takagi, "Japan's Official Development Assistance: Recent Issues and Future Directions," *Journal of International Development* 16 (2004): 255–280.

50 Sunil Chacko, "Japanese Investment to India: Possibilities and Constraints," *The Sunday Guardian*, May 2, 2020.
51 Press Release, "Chinese Navy is a Force that is here to Stay," *Press Trust of India*, January 10, 2019.
52 John Hartle, "The Normalization of Japanese Policy in the Indian Ocean Region," *Policy Report*, June 21, 2018.
53 Peter Wyckoff, "Making Waves: Japan and the Indian Ocean Region," The Stimson Center, May 1, 2017.
54 *Ibid.*
55 Hartle, "The Normalization of Japanese Policy in the Indian Ocean Region."
56 "Japan is the Second Largest Net Importer of Fossil Fuels in the World," US Energy Information Administration, November 7, 2013.
57 "Japan Import by Country and Region 2011-2015," World Bank, World Integrated Trade Solution, accessed March 23, 2022, https://wits.worldbank.org/CountryProfile/en/Country/JPN/Year/2015/TradeFlow/Import/Partner/all/Product/16.
58 "Trade and Investment Statistics," Japan External Trade Organization (JETRO), accessed March 23, 2022, https://www.jetro.go.jp/en/reports/statistics/.
59 *Ibid.*
60 Chansoria, "Indo-Japanese Strategic Partnership: Scope and Future Avenues," 2.
61 David Brewster, "Japan's Plans to Build a 'Free and Open' Indian Ocean," Lowy Institute, May 29, 2018, https://www.lowyinstitute.org/the-interpreter/japan-plans-build-free-and-open-indian-ocean; and see Hartle, "The Normalization of Japanese Policy in the Indian Ocean Region."
62 *Ibid.*
63 "Japan, Sri Lanka Exploring Port Infrastructure Deals to Counter Reliance on China," *The Japan Times*, August 26, 2016.
64 Cited in, "As Japan Makes Its Move in the Indian Ocean Power Play, What Will Be the Future of the Blue Economy?" Blue Economy Knowledge Center Seychelles, August 27, 2018, http://blueeconomyseychelles.org/item/130-japan-indian-ocean-blue-economy; also see "Why the World Ocean Summit is going to Japan in 2020," *The Economist*, August 22, 2019.
65 "First India-Japan 2+2 Foreign and Defence Ministerial Meeting," India's Ministry of External Affairs, November 30, 2019, https://mea.gov.in/bilateral-documents.htm?dtl/32131/Joint_Statement__First_IndiaJapan_2432_Foreign_and_Defence_Ministerial_Meeting.
66 Masanori Nishi, "The Role of Japan in Indian Ocean Security: A Japanese Perspective," in *Indo-Pacific Maritime Security: Challenges and Cooperation*, ed. David Brewster (Canberra: National Security College, Crawford School of Public Policy, Australian National University, 2016), 55–58.
67 Monika Chansoria, "Development of Sri Lanka's East Container Terminal Port: Japan & India's Regional Cooperation in South Asia Shaping Up," The Japan Institute of International Affairs, June 28, 2019, https://www.jiia-jic.jp/en/policybrief/pdf/PolicyBrief_Chansoria_190628.pdf.
68 Nester, *Japan and the Third World: Patterns, Power, Prospects*, p. 279.
69 Samuel P. Huntington, "The Clash of Civilizations," *Foreign Affairs* 72, no. 3 (Summer 1993), 22–49.
70 Monika Chansoria, "Washington and Tokyo's Old Alliance for a New Era: Changing Strategic Priorities and Expectations," *9Dashline*, May 28, 2021, https://www.9dashline.com/article/washington-and-tokyos-old-alliance-for-a-new-era-changing-strategic-priorities-and-expectations.
71 Sojin Shin, "Japan's Foreign Aid to South Asia: Addressing a Strategic Need," NUS–ISAS Working Paper no. 318, March 8, 2019, https://www.isas.nus.edu.sg/papers/318-japans-foreign-aid-to-south-asia-addressing-a-strategic-need/.

Bibliography

"As Japan Makes Its Move in the Indian Ocean Power Play, What Will Be the Future of the Blue Economy?" Blue Economy Knowledge Center Seychelles, August 27, 2018. http://blueeconomyseychelles.org/item/130-japan-indian-ocean-blue-economy.
"Chinese Navy is a Force that is Here to Stay." *Press Trust of India*, January 10, 2019.
"Japan, Sri Lanka Exploring Port Infrastructure Deals to Counter Reliance on China." *The Japan Times*, August 26, 2016.
"Japan-India Ties Should Go Beyond Countering China." *The Japan Times*, October 30, 2018.

"Nuclear Anxiety: The Allies; Japan Freezes Some Grants; Other Nations Seem Doubtful." *The New York Times*, May 14, 1998.

"Why the World Ocean Summit is going to Japan in 2020." *The Economist*, August 22, 2019.

Abe, Shinzo, and Jonathan Tepperman. "Japan Is Back: A Conversation with Shinzo Abe." *Foreign Affairs* 92, no. 4 (July/August 2013): 2–8.

Akihiko, Tanaka. "Domestic Politics and Foreign Policy." In *Japanese Foreign Policy Today: A Reader*, edited by Inoguchi Takashi and Purnendra Jain, 3–17. New York: Palgrave Macmillan, 2000.

Brewster, David. "Japan's Plans to Build a 'Free and Open' Indian Ocean." Lowy Institute, May 29, 2018. https://www.lowyinstitute.org/the-interpreter/japan-plans-build-free-and-open-indian-ocean.

Chacko, Sunil. "Japanese Investment to India: Possibilities and Constraints." *The Sunday Guardian*, May 2, 2020.

Chansoria, Monika. "Development of Sri Lanka's East Container Terminal Port: Japan & India's Regional Cooperation in South Asia Shaping Up." The Japan Institute of International Affairs, June 28, 2019. https://www.jiia-jic.jp/en/policybrief/pdf/PolicyBrief_Chansoria_190628.pdf.

Chansoria, Monika. "Indo-Japanese Strategic Partnership: Scope and Future Avenues." Note de la FRS no. 17, September 19, 2017. https://www.frstrategie.org/en/publications/notes/indo-japanese-strategic-partnership-scope-future-avenues-2017.

Chansoria, Monika. "Japanese Investments Are Instrumental to India's Act East Policy." *Asia Pacific Bulletin* 385 (June 21, 2017).

Chansoria, Monika. "Modi-Abe Personality Impacts Foreign Policy." The Sunday Guardian, September 20, 2014.

Monika, Chansoria. "Washington and Tokyo's Old Alliance for a New Era: Changing Strategic Priorities and Expectations." *9Dashline*, May 28, 2021. https://www.9dashline.com/article/washington-and-tokyos-old-alliance-for-a-new-era-changing-strategic-priorities-and-expectations.

Dutt, Sagarika, et al., eds. *South Asian Security: 21st Century Discourses*. Oxon: Routledge, 2012.

Estache, Antonio. "Emerging Infrastructure Policy Issues in Developing Countries: A Survey of the Recent Economic Literature." POVNET Infrastructure Working Group Background Paper, November 2004. https://elibrary.worldbank.org/doi/abs/10.1596/1813-9450-3442.

Hartle, John. "The Normalization of Japanese Policy in the Indian Ocean Region." *Policy Report*, June 21, 2018.

Huntington, Samuel P. "The Clash of Civilizations." *Foreign Affairs* 72, no. 3 (Summer 1993): 22–49.

Inoguchi, Takashi. "Why Are There No Non-Western Theories of International Relations? The Case of Japan." In *Non-Western International Relations Theory: Perspectives on and Beyond Asia*, edited by Barry Buzan and Amitav Acharya, 51–68. Oxon: Routledge, 2010.

Iqbal, Badar Alam. "Indo-Japanese Economic Relations in the 1990s." *India Quarterly* 52, no. 1/2 (January–June 1996): 39–72.

Jain, Purnendra. "Japan and South Asia: Between Cooperation and Confrontation." In *Japanese Foreign Policy Today: A Reader*, edited by Inoguchi Takashi and Purnendra Jain, 266–282. New York: Palgrave Macmillan, 2000.

Jain, Purnendra. "Japan's Relations with South Asia." *Asian Survey* 37, no. 4 (April 1997): 340–352.

Japan External Trade Organization (JETRO). "Trade and Investment Statistics." Accessed March 23, 2022. https://www.jetro.go.jp/en/reports/statistics/.

Japan International Cooperation Agency. "JICA Annual Report 2020." 2020. https://www.jica.go.jp/english/publications/reports/annual/2020/c8h0vm0000fc7q2b-att/2020_07.pdf.

Jones, Justin. "Submarines and Maritime Strategy – Part 1." The Strategist, January 29, 2013.

Jones, Stephen D. "Contribution of Infrastructure to Growth and Poverty Reduction in East Asia and the Pacific." *Oxford Policy Management Background Paper*, October 2004.

Jones, Stephen D. "Infrastructure Challenges in East and South Asia." *IDS Bulletin* 37, no. 3 (May 2006).

Kaifu, Toshiki. *Japan and South Asia: In Pursuit of Dialogue and Cooperation for Peace and Prosperity*. New Delhi: Parliament House, 1990.

Kautiliya. *The Arthashastra*. Translated by L.N. Rangarajan. New York: Penguin Books, 1987.

Kawai, Masahiro, and Shinji Takagi. "Japan's Official Development Assistance: Recent Issues and Future Directions." *Journal of International Development* 16 (2004): 255–280.

Koppel, Bruce, and Michael Plummer. "Japan Ascendancy as a Foreign-Aid Power." *Asian Survey* 29, no. 11 (1989): 1043–1056.

Medcalf, Rory. "The Evolving Security Order in the Indo-Pacific." In *Indo-Pacific Maritime Security: Challenges and Cooperation*, edited by David Brewster, 7–11. Canberra: National Security College, Crawford School of Public Policy, Australian National University, 2016.

Medcalf, Rory. "The Indo-Pacific: What's in a Name?" *The American Interest* 9, no. 2 (November/December 2013): 58–66.

Mehta, Rajesh. "Indo-Japanese Trade: Recent Trends." RIS Discussion Papers, no. 12, May 2001.

Ministry of Defence (Australia). Defense White Paper 2013, 2013. http://www.defence.gov.au/whitepaper/2013.

Ministry of External Affairs (India). "First India-Japan 2+2 Foreign and Defence Ministerial Meeting." November 30, 2019. https://mea.gov.in/bilateral-documents.htm?dtl/32131/Joint_Statement__First_IndiaJapan_2432_Foreign_and_Defence_Ministerial_Meeting.

Ministry of External Affairs (India). "Joint Declaration on Security Cooperation between India and Japan." October 22, 2008. https://www.mofa.go.jp/region/asia-paci/india/pmv0810/joint_d.html.

Muraleedharan, V. "Remarks at International Workshop on 'Quad in the Indo-Pacific.'" Transcript of speech delivered at Ministry of External Affairs, New Delhi, April 29, 2021. https://www.mea.gov.in/Speeches-Statements.htm?dtl/33828/Remarks_by_Shri_V_Muraleedharan_Minister_of_State_for_External_Affairs_at_International_Workshop_on_Quad_in_the_IndoPacific.

Nester, William R. *Japan and the Third World: Patterns, Power, Prospects*. New York: St. Martin's Press, 1992.

Nishi, Masanori. "The Role of Japan in Indian Ocean Security: A Japanese Perspective." In *Indo-Pacific Maritime Security: Challenges and Cooperation*, edited by David Brewster, 55–58. Canberra: National Security College: Crawford School of Public Policy, Australian National University, 2016.

Nishida, Kitaro Nishida. *Intelligibility and the Philosophy of Nothingness: Three Philosophical Essays*. Honolulu: International Philosophical Research Association of Japan and East-West Center Press, 1958.

Okita, Saburo. "Japan's Quiet Strength." *Foreign Policy* 75 (Summer 1989): 128–145.

Posen, Adam S. "Japan's Distraction by Regional Economic Integration." State Department INR Roundtable on Northeast Asian Regional Economic Integration, June 2002.

Santos, Sergio Caballero. "Regional Integration Theories: The Suitability of a Constructivist Approach." Paper 383, *Session on Globalization and Governance, IPSA-Chile*, July 2009.

Shin, Sojin. "Japan's Foreign Aid to South Asia: Addressing a Strategic Need." NUS-ISAS Working Paper no. 318, March 8, 2019. https://www.isas.nus.edu.sg/papers/318-japans-foreign-aid-to-south-asia-addressing-a-strategic-need/.

Soesastro, Hadi. "Sustaining East Asia's Economic Dynamism: The Role of Aid." PRI-OECD Research Project, May 2004. https://www.oecd.org/gov/pcsd/31970823.pdf.

Spegele, Roger D. *Political Realism in International Theory*. Victoria: Cambridge University Press, 1996.

U.S. Energy Information Agency. "Japan Is the Second Largest Net Importer of Fossil Fuels in the World." *US Energy Information Administration*, November 7, 2013.

Wagner, R. Harrison. *War and the State: The Theory of International Politics*. Ann Arbor, MI: The University of Michigan Press, 2007.

World Bank. "Japan Import by Country and Region 2011-2015." World Integrated Trade Solution. Accessed March 23, 2022. https://wits.worldbank.org/CountryProfile/en/Country/JPN/Year/2015/TradeFlow/Import/Partner/all/Product/16.

World Bank. "Poverty and Shared Prosperity 2018: Piecing Together the Poverty Puzzle." 2018. https://openknowledge.worldbank.org/bitstream/handle/10986/30418/9781464813306.pdf.

Wyckoff, Peter. "Making Waves: Japan and the Indian Ocean Region." The Stimson Center, May 1, 2017.

Yendamuri, Praneeth Yendamuri, and Zara Ingilizian. "In 2020 Asia Will Have the World's Largest GDP. Here's What That Means." World Economic Forum, December 20, 2019. https://www.weforum.org/agenda/2019/12/asia-economic-growth/.

Yoshiatsu, Hidetaka. "New Dynamics in Sino-Japanese Rivalry: Sustaining Infrastructure Development in Asia." *Journal of Contemporary China* 27, no. 113 (2018): 719–734.

27
THE UK AND SOUTH ASIA

David Scott

Introduction

A century ago and the present-day states of South Asia (Bangladesh, Bhutan, India, Maldives, Nepal, Pakistan, and Sri Lanka) were part of British India—the so-called jewel in the crown for London. Afghanistan, having avoided falling into the clutches of British India during the 19th century, followed its own path beyond the Khyber Pass. Following decolonization in 1947, and the UK's so-called withdrawal from East of Suez in the late 1960s, the UK's role in South Asia was low key. In terms of foreign policy, the South Asian states were low on London's horizons, and indeed vice versa.

What has been noticeable in the last decade is a newly re-awakened UK engagement with South Asia. Two events drove the UK's renewed focus. Firstly, in 2001, 9/11 saw attention homing in on Afghanistan, and consequent effects of jihadism across the region and back into the UK. Secondly, a focus on economic outreach to Asia under David Cameron's premiership, from 2010 to 2016, was matched by announcements by 2015 that the UK intended to pursue a *Return to East of Suez* security posture in the Indian Ocean,[1] with India the key security partner in South Asia. Thirdly, this economic outreach was significantly magnified by the UK withdrawal (Brexit) from the European Union (EU) in 2020. This has meant a search for new trade markets, with India pinpointed as particularly important to cultivate by *Global Britain*.[2] From both security and economic perspectives, India was a significant element in the UK *Tilt to the Indo-Pacific* proclaimed in 2021.[3]

The literature on this re-engagement is relatively underdeveloped, the topic somewhat neglected. The importance of the topic in international relations (IR) is that it involves a significant power (the UK) moving away from its previous setting with the European Union, and instead re-engaging with a particularly significant rising power (India). The importance of the topic in the regional context is that the UK was an important military presence in Afghanistan during the 21st century, and has focused on the importance of India in its current tilt to the Indo-Pacific. This tilt is now giving the UK a greater geopolitical and geo-economic presence in South Asia and its surrounding waters, alongside larger involved actors like China, the US, and of course India, with India in turn gaining further regional weight through this cooperation with the UK.

In terms of IR theories and frameworks, this chapter does not advocate or follow any one approach. Instead it goes "beyond paradigms" in advocating the "analytical eclecticism"

DOI: 10.4324/9781003246626-31

suggested by Rudra Sil and Peter Katzenstein for understanding world politics.[4] Nevertheless, there are some theories that seem of little relevance now for understanding the UK re-engagement with South Asia. Institutionalism and regionalism have little significance, given that the UK has exited from the European Union, where such theory has been forged, and instead is looking to South Asia, a region whose regional institution, the South Asian Association for Regional Cooperation (SAARC), is not a supranational body in the way that the EU is, and has been paralyzed since 2014 due to India-Pakistan divisions.

In this spirit of analytical eclecticism, there are several useful theories and frameworks to explain the UK re-engagement with South Asia. The UK re-orientation away from the EU, and its embrace of a Global Britain role, is partly a matter of national identity; here, Critical Geopolitics with its focus on a country's *position* in terms of hopes, fears, and images is in play. Traditional Geopolitics, in terms of a country's *position* in terms of location, is reflected in a UK drive for bigger relationships with India, precisely because of India's giant-sized presence in South Asia in size, population, and location. Geo-economics is also in play for the UK in terms of India's huge economic weight within South Asia, which makes India the essential economic partner for the UK to pursue. It is also in play in trade flows, where security of the SLOCs (Sea Lines of Communication) threatened by piracy in the Gulf of Aden, is a shared UK-India concern. A touch of geo-culture might be in play in UK worries over Islamist jihadism, worries which distance the UK from Pakistan and now Afghanistan, but bring the UK and India together. Normative theory would suggest greater (or easier) UK cooperation with India, as a fellow *democracy*, with Pakistan, Bangladesh, Sri Lanka, and most recently Afghanistan suffering various collapses of democracy. UK-India military cooperation also has an element of tacit balancing, which reflects a strategic logic of IR realism toward China.

With regard to London's re-engagement with South Asia, this chapter is divided into three parts. First is South Asia as a region. Second is the South Asian periphery surrounding India—namely, Afghanistan, Pakistan, Nepal, Bhutan, Sri Lanka, and the Maldives. Third is India, the heart of South Asia—the giant around which the other smaller states float, and the state in South Asia that UK foreign policy has particularly re-engaged with.

South Asia

Sadly, the SAARC has proved to be an ineffective regional framework of little interest to the UK government. The UK Department of International Development hosted comments in 2008 that "SAARC [....] has yet to take off and contribute toward the creation of a predictable and orderly regional environment."[5] Commentators noted in 2012 that, like other global powers, "the UK treats South Asia as a cluster of uneven states where the process of regional co-operation has faltered and failed," requiring bilateral rather than regional diplomacy by the UK.[6] SAARC continued to falter during the 2010s with a lapse of SAARC summits after 2014, following India's claims about Pakistan's complicity in the 2016 Uri terror attack by the Jaish-e-Mohammed group, a Kashmiri jihadist group based in Pakistan. Admittedly, the EU (of which the UK was a then member) gained Observer status with SAARC in 2006. However, there has been no indication of any intent by a post-Brexit UK to seek such status.

UK links with South Asia continue to be affected by the legacy of empire, migration, which has led to a significant South Asia-origin community in the UK.[7] The 2011 Census recorded the following numbers: British Indians as 1,451,862; British Pakistanis as 1,174,983, British Bangladeshis as 451,529, and British Sri Lankans (Sinhalese and Tamils) as 129,076. The electoral weight of the British Indian community has led to the Labour Party distancing itself from its overt earlier criticism of Indian policies over Kashmir.[8] Hindutva policies pushed in Modi's India have generated some concerns about the Hindu Right taking over various Hindu organizations in the UK, as well as concerns over the UK governmental reluctance to criticize Hindutva policies carried out in India.[9] Hindu-Muslim communal tensions in India can and have spilled back into such tensions in the UK. Within the British Indian community, there is a large Sikh component, some 420,196 in the 2011 Census. This has generated Sikh concerns about Hindutva policies in India disrupting communal harmony in the UK,[10] and concerns from India about pro-Khalistan (independent Sikh state) elements in the UK. Identity politics has become an issue in the UK South Asian community.[11] Questions of ethnic versus religious pulls are a shifting ambiguity for the South Asian communities.[12] Post 9/11 and the rise of al-Qaeda and ISIS, the question of Islamist radicalization among Pakistani and Bangladeshi communities in the UK blur the line between domestic and foreign policies.[13]

While South Asian residents in the UK voted in favor of Brexit, questions of post-Brexit immigration arrangements are a domestic political issue, but one with foreign policy implications and economic negotiations.[14] Whereas India's weight and desires for the UK to strike a free trade agreement with India have meant immigration blocks on India are being removed, those on Pakistan and Bangladesh are set to remain. It is no coincidence that moves in January 2022 by the UK to conclude economic trade talks with India were underpinned by relaxation of visa entry requirements for Indian workers.[15]

Some UK sympathies with the Tamil cause in Sri Lanka brought tensions with the victorious Sinhalese-dominated government, and of course heightening tensions between the Tamil and Sinhalese communities in the UK. UK readiness to support Bangladeshi independence in 1972 brought a chill in relations with Pakistan, from whom Bangladesh had broken away. Given their adversarial relationship, closer UK links with India generally brings a degree of distancing from Pakistan. The Pakistan Prime Minister Imran Khan cancelled his planned visit to London in July 2021, on account of the privileged *Roadmap 2030 for India-UK Future Relations* recently signed between the UK and India.[16] The UK drive for closer economic links and general Indo-Pacific security cooperation with India has led the UK government to subtly distance itself from Pakistan's criticisms of Indian actions in Kashmir.[17]

The South Asian Periphery (Afghanistan-Pakistan-Nepal-Bhutan-Bangladesh-Sri Lanka-Maldives)

UK foreign policy toward Afghanistan and Pakistan was summed up in 2010 by the Foreign and Commonwealth Office as being, in their opening point, that "Afghanistan and Pakistan are this Government's top priorities in Foreign Affairs," since "violent extremism in both countries poses a threat to UK interests."[18]

In Afghanistan, UK foreign policy revolved around support for the new Afghan governments of Karzai and then Ghani installed after the Taliban were toppled in 2001. Alongside this political support was UK participation in the US-led NATO International Security Assistance Force (ISAF) operation from 2001 to 2014, in which the UK operated in Helmand Province, providing 9500 troops for ISAF, as against the 78430 US troops. Some local success was enjoined by UK forces. The downside of this involvement, illustrating the "illusion" of significant autonomous UK role, was that the UK felt obliged to withdraw once the US had stated their intention in 2021 to withdraw their much larger forces.[19] The result was the reversal of UK policy in Afghanistan as the Taliban re-occupied Kabul in August 2021. The immediate response in the UK was the Afghan Citizens Resettlement Scheme announced in September 2021 to resettle up to 20,000 people from Afghanistan, with 5000 in the first year.

In Pakistan, the last decade saw delicate attempts by the UK to strengthen security cooperation, and thereby strengthen civilian government against jihadist groupings in Pakistan, partly to curb Taliban groups operating across the border back into Afghanistan, but also to counter jihadist groups operating in Pakistan from launching operations against the UK.[20] The UK's Counter Terrorism Strategy (CONTEST) stressed in 2009 how "most significant terrorist investigations in the UK have links to Pakistan and for this reason cooperation with Pakistan is critical to our delivery of CONTEST."[21] The UK counter-terrorism program with Pakistan, worth approximately £10 million in 2008/09, included assistance with forensics, crime scene management, crisis response, and civil aviation security, with further funding directed toward counter-narcotics projects. An Enhanced Strategic Dialogue (ESD) was announced in 2011 to facilitate greater intelligence sharing.

Nevertheless, the weakness of the civilian politicians versus the military and the ambiguous role of Pakistan's Inter-Services Intelligence (ISI) agency in aiding and abetting the Taliban in Afghanistan hampered such anti-terrorism cooperation between Pakistan and the UK. David Cameron caused great offence in Pakistan by his accusation in July 2010, when visiting India, that with specific regard to Pakistan, "we cannot tolerate in any sense the idea that this country is allowed to look both ways and is able, in any way, to promote the export of terror, whether to India or whether to Afghanistan or anywhere else in the world."[22] His comments caused uproar in Pakistan, with effigies of Cameron being burned in Karachi. Nevertheless, there was some weakening of Pakistan-generated terrorist activities in the UK, but with UK jihadism developing its own local roots.[23]

The UK Foreign Secretary William Hague may have proclaimed the importance of UK-Pakistan relations in 2011,[24] but initial high hopes[25] did not progress in the 2010s. The 2011 ESD mechanism has not, in retrospect, delivered very much. Imran Khan's advent to power in 2018 brought a new civilian leader to the fore in Pakistan with some previous UK links—for example, he had been married to Jemima Goldstein from 1995 to 2004 and was Chancellor of Bradford University from 2005 to 2016—but these UK links have born little fruit in his period in power.

Defense links between the two establishments remain cordial enough, but of secondary importance for both countries. There has been talk of UK soft power, values, and standards in play with Pakistani officer training at Sandhurst.[26] However, this has not stopped Pakistan's military from interfering in civilian politics, nor Pakistan's ISI from covertly assisting the Taliban and other jihadist groupings, nor Pakistan's increasingly close military alliance with China. The UK's co-sponsorship in April 2019 at the UN to designate Masood Azhar the head of Jaish-e-Mohammed as a *terrorist*, and thereby impose an assets freeze, was an uncomfortable move for Pakistan, based as Azhar was in Pakistan.

Bangladesh, under the secular leadership of Sheikh Hasina, and the UK have shared concerns about jihadist destabilization of Bangladesh and blowback into the UK. The Jammat-ul Mujahideen Bangladesh (JMB) was proscribed in the UK in July 2007 under the Terrorism Act. A formal Joint Working Group on counter-terrorism was set up in 2009, with sharing intelligence and training of law enforcers identified as areas to develop. Ironically, whereas the UK has been concerned about the spillover into the UK of Pakistan-based terrorists, with regard to Bangladesh, it has been the spillover of UK-based Bangladeshi jihadists back into Bangladesh that has been a concern for both governments.[27] Bangladesh refused to accept the ISIS jihadi bride Shahmima Begum as a Bangladeshi citizen after the UK stripped her of UK nationality in 2019.

Economically, the UK outreach to Pakistan and Bangladesh is modest, neither of them is very significant, and there is little appetite in the UK to negotiate free trade agreements with them. The Pakistan-UK Trade and Investment Roadmap agreed in 2012 had only limited impact. The agreement in September 2021 to set up a Working Party to formulate a strategy for strengthening bilateral ties in multiple spheres, including trade and investment, is indicative of the low level that it presently operates from.

In contrast, in recent years, various mechanisms have been set up with Bangladesh. An annual Strategic Dialogue was set up in 2018, the UK-Bangladesh Climate Partnership in January 2020, the UK-Bangladesh Trade and Investment Dialogue in February 2021, and Defense Dialogue mechanism in 2022. The UK offered support to Bangladesh's hosting of Rohingya refugees. Like trade, defense links between the UK and Bangladesh remain modest rather than substantial. Bangladesh's graduation from Least Developed Country to Middle Income Country suggests more potential in UK-Bangladesh links.[28]

Relations with Nepal are marginal, although the fate of the Gurkha pension rights has been a political issue of some domestic significance in the UK, helped by the media efforts of the actress Joanna Lumley. Bhutan's foreign relations are handled through India and so do not really register with the UK.

Sri Lanka has been of low importance in UK foreign policy. UK trade with Sri Lanka is modest, although the importance of Sri Lanka as a trade route point for UK trade flows across the Indian Ocean is significant. The active work of Tamil breakaway groups in the UK has been an irritant in Sri Lanka-UK relations, with the UK in turn wary of human rights abuses by the Mahinda administration when bringing the Tamil insurgency to an end in 2009. China's growing presence in Sri Lanka is unwelcome for the UK, and renders Chinese commentary on UK-China cooperation in Sri Lanka unrealistic.[29]

UK relations with the Maldives, a former colony, have been minimal. However, the Maldives has been drawn into the various *lawfare* issues over continuing UK hold over the Chagos archipelago, and with it the important UK/US base at Diego Garcia. The Maldives recognized UK sovereignty over the Chagos, when their 1992 Agreement drew up equidistant Exclusive Economic Zone lines between agreed baselines. The Maldives opted in 2017 and 2019 to vote at the UN against Mauritian claims over the Chagos archipelago.[30]

The South Asia Heartland (India)

The UK focus on South Asia has become primarily on India, reflecting India's dominance of size, population, economy, and location in South Asia as well as India's international rise.[31] Hence, David Cameron's comments in 2015 that "for years, the relationship between Britain and India was in some way imprisoned by the [colonial] past;" but that now the UK sought a new "21st century partnership."[32]

Under Cameron, the UK sought deeper economics-driven relations with India, with the relationship promoted to an "enhanced partnership" in 2010.[33] In his first official trip to India in 2010, Cameron told an Indian audience that "from the British perspective, it's clear why India matters. Most obviously, there is the dynamism of your economy."[34] On his second visit to India, Cameron famously told Indian audiences in 2013: "Yes, it's a partnership about business [....] and that's why I'm here; Britain wants to be your partner of choice."[35] The only trouble for the UK is that it was unlikely to be the partner of first choice for India. Indeed, the UK had fallen from being India's second largest trade partner in 1998–1999 to 17th in 2018–2019.

India featured quite prominently during the 2016 Brexit referendum debate. In an important statement for the *Vote Leave* campaign, which was also released in the Indian media, one of Cameron's minister's Priti Patel argued that "although the focus of the Conservative government on enhancing our relationship with India has led to an increase in trade since 2010, we could go further if we were not held back by the vested self-interests of the EU," and predicted that "voting to leave the European Union would be a massive boost to UK-India relations" opening up "new opportunities for the UK and India to [....] develop stronger trading links."[36] Brexit strengthened this economic imperative still further.[37] The House of Commons Foreign Affairs Committee noted "as the UK prepares to leave the EU, it is time to reset this relationship."[38]

With UK post-exit arrangements finally agreed by 2020, the UK has pushed an economic reset with India. The 10th UK-India Economic and Financial Dialogue, held in October 2020, was seen as a "landmark" moment by the UK government, with the announcement of a new UK-India Partnership on Infrastructure Policy and Financing as well as a new UK-India Sustainable Finance Forum to green the financial system.[39] Trade arrangements were pursued, with an Enhanced Trade Partnership announced in May 2021. Final-stage negotiations with India were formally initiated in January 2022. The UK government stressed the strategic significance of such a deal; "using trade to tilt toward the Indo-Pacific, a UK-India agreement would help put Global Britain at the heart of the Indo-Pacific region."[40]

Security cooperation with India has been a developing area for the UK and India. A UK-India Defense and International Security Partnership was announced in November 2015, upgraded to an Enhanced Defense Partnership in May 2021. The first tri-services exercise (KONKAN Shakti)—involving land, air, and naval forces—was run in October 2021.

Initially, security cooperation focused on common concerns over jihadist destabilization in Afghanistan, blowing back into India and the UK, together with common concerns over Pakistani softness toward terrorist groups operating out from Pakistan. In this vein, 2002 witnessed the setting up of the UK-India foreign ministry-led Joint Working Group (JWG) on Terrorism, and joint statements criticizing the work of jihadist groups based in Pakistan and indeed calling out Pakistan.[41] The UK has moved against Pakistan-based jihadist groups carrying out operations against India. In such vein, the Jaish-e-Mohammed group, fighting for liberation of Kashmir from India, was formally proscribed by the UK in March 2007 under the 2000 Terrorism Act. In 2015, during Modi's visit to the UK, the Pakistan-based Lashkar-e-Taiba (LeT) group, responsible for the November 2008 Mumbai terror attacks, was similarly designated and subjected to UK disruption of their financial and tactical support.

India and the UK signed a Defense Equipment Memorandum of Understanding (MoU) in 1997, which was renewed in 2007 and 2019. A few joint-ventures (JVs) and co-production agreements for the Indian military emerged in the 2010s—namely Agusta Westland with Tata Sons on the AW119 Koala utility helicopters, BAE Systems with Mahindra Defense on co-production of M777 howitzers, and with Hindustan Aeronautics for licensed production of Hawk advanced trainer aircraft. These were modest projects, with Russia, the US, and more recently France continuing to play a bigger part in Indian arms acquisitions.

Nevertheless, the UK is now pushing for bigger deals.[42] Projects currently on offer include joint development of jet engine technology and sixth-generation fighter jet technology that can be used in India's Advanced Medium Combat Aircraft (AMCA) currently under development.[43] In May 2021, an agreement was signed between Hindustan Aeronautics Limited and Rolls Royce to move aspects of the manufacturing of the MT30 Gas Turbine engine to India, the basis of the UK's Integrated Electric Propulsion system that powers the Queen Elizabeth Class Aircraft Carriers, as well as the UK's Type 23 frigate and Type 45 destroyers.[44]

UK maritime cooperation with India has continued to strengthen. This involves common concerns over security of SLOCs threatened by piracy in the Gulf of Aden, which brought parallel and mutually supportive ongoing deployments of UK and Indian naval units since

2009. There has been growing common concern over China's naval push across the Indo-Pacific,[45] on show with UK-India naval exercising in July 2021.[46]

KONKAN annual navy exercises were initiated in 2004, and have increased in strength. This was on show with the extended exercising of the UK Carrier Strike Group with the Indian Navy in the Bay of Bengal and then the Arabian Sea in 2021. April 2017 witnessed the signing of a White Shipping MoU, followed in March 2019 by the setting up of a Carrier Capability Partnership mechanism between the two navies. The UK has also offered designs of its Queen Elizabeth-class carrier for the development of India's third aircraft carrier. In June 2021 a UK liaison officer joined the Indian Navy's Information Fusion Centre for Indian Ocean Region.

However, while UK-India maritime cooperation has strengthened in the Indian Ocean, it remains hampered by the issue of Diego Garcia.[47] The UK has sought Indian help to leverage Mauritius, on show in Boris Johnson's trip to India as Foreign Secretary in January 2017.[48] However, this has been of little avail. At the UN, India has continued to vote with Mauritius against the UK, first in June 2017 in the General Assembly vote to ask for an advisory opinion on the Chagos archipelago, and second in the General Assembly Resolution in May 2019 calling for the UK to comply with the opinion to hand over the Chagos archipelago to Mauritius. India remains torn between the political-ethnic pull of post-colonial ties with Mauritius and the defense imperatives of working with the UK and US role at Diego Garcia as a military counter to China in the Indian Ocean. Diego Garcia remains an uncomfortable millstone around UK calls for a rules-based order in the Indo-Pacific.[49]

Cyber-security cooperation is another area for cooperation, given India's Information Technology (IT) strengths.[50] Cyber-dialogues between their Foreign Ministries have been running since 2012. In November 2015, both sides agreed to establish a Cyber Security Training Centre of Excellence, and a five-year framework agreement on various cyber cooperation areas was agreed in April 2018, to run through 2023.

UK-India links have undeniably strengthened, yet this has generated an asymmetric relationship. In economic terms, a declining UK is faced with a rising India, while in economic and security cooperation terms, India is more important for the UK than the UK is for India.

Looking Forward

On the regional front, it is unlikely that SAARC will provide much attraction for UK policymakers. However, there is an alternative, given the greater success of BIMSTEC, set up in 1997 as in effect SAARC without Pakistan and a bridge to Southeast Asia, which now embraces Bangladesh, India, Sri Lanka, Nepal, and Bhutan from South Asia and Thailand and Myanmar from Southeast Asia.[51] BIMSTEC might be a more effective South Asia vehicle for the UK to follow rather than SAARC.

With regard to Afghanistan, it remains to be seen how far the Afghan Resettlement Scheme will be sufficient, given the larger numbers in view. It also remains to be seen what relationship the UK reestablishes with an Afghanistan, as of September 2021, now under Taliban control, a signal defeat for UK policy objects of the previous two decades. This may weaken the importance of Pakistan in the UK calculus, which previously could be seen as a necessary state to cultivate for the success of Western operations in Afghanistan.

India though remains an increasingly important factor for the UK South Asia calculus, envisaged for the coming decade in the *2030 Roadmap for India-UK Future Relations* agreed by both governments in their May 2021 Summit. Similar distrust of a Taliban Afghanistan, of a jihadist-supporting Pakistan, of an aggressive China, and of piracy destabilizations of the sea lanes are all shared concerns that will continue to operate between the UK and India. With regard to India, a free trade agreement is envisaged for the end of 2022, and is reasonably likely. Military cooperation is likely to increase, including greater naval exercising as the UK deploys its carrier Strike Groups on a regular basis. Both navies' basing/facilities use at Duqm could be further integrated, and they could cooperate bilaterally on specific anti-piracy patrols off the Gulf of Aden rather than separately as is the current norm. Naval technology transfers and warship building, focusing on aircraft carrier capability, could be enhanced, e.g. INS Vishal, India's second scheduled indigenous aircraft carrier.[52] A Logistics Cooperation Agreement (LCA) is impending. This would give Indian access to the UK base at Bahrain, and the UK access to India's Andaman & Nicobar Islands. However, India will be unlikely to (openly) use the UK base at Diego Garcia, given India's already noted support for Mauritian claims over the Chagos Archipelago.

Potential problems include a slide of Modi's India's into an anti-democratic Hindutva box, thereby creating some normative (democracy) strains for the UK. The asymmetric nature of the UK-India relationship may be exacerbated still further by long-term economic damage by Brexit, although long-term Brexit-generated economic renewal for the UK would reduce the asymmetry.

Within South Asia IR, the UK will play a lesser role in the north-west of the subcontinent, given the UK withdrawal from Afghanistan and lack of immediate traction with Pakistan. The UK will play a larger role with the bulk of South Asia, namely India, where the UK provides useful assets for India across the political, economic, and military spectrum. However, there are limits to this UK re-engagement with South Asia, where the UK is likely to operate as a modest external middle ranking rather than a leading power presence within the IR of South Asia.

Notes

1 David Scott, "Britain Returns to the Indian Ocean?" *Round Table, Commonwealth Journal for International Affairs* 107, no. 3 (2018): 307–316, https://doi.org/10.1080/00358533.2018.1476096.
2 Frank O'Donnell, "The 'Global Britain' Concept and UK Policy toward India," *Written Evidence*, October 18, 2018, https://data.parliament.uk/writtenevidence/committeeevidence.svc/evidence-document/foreign-affairs-committee/global-britain-and-india/written/90899.pdf.
3 Harsh Pant and Tom Milford, "The UK Shifts to the Indo-Pacific: An Opportunity for India-UK Ties," *ORF Issue Brief* no. 444 (February 2021).
4 Rudra Sil and Peter Katzenstein, *Beyond Paradigms. Analytical Eclecticism in the Study of World Politics* (Palgrave Macmillan, Basingstoke, 2011).
5 Kripa Sridharan, "Regional Organizations and Conflict Management: Comparing ASEAN and SAARC," Department for International Development (London), January 1, 2008, https://assets.publishing.service.gov.uk/media/57a08bc040f0b652dd000e7c/wp33.2.pdf.
6 Muhammad Jabed, "British Interests in a 'Regionalised' South Asia," *South Asia* 35, no. 3 (2012): 726.
7 Judith Brown, "The Role of the Modern Diaspora in the UK–Indian Relationship," in *Reconnecting Britain and India: Ideas for an Enhanced Partnership*, ed. Jo Johnson and Rajiv Kumar (New Delhi: Academic Foundation, 2012), 165–170.
8 Patrick Wintour, "Kashmir: Labour Shifts Policy after Backlash by Indian-heritage Voters," *Guardian*, November 12, 2019, https://www.theguardian.com/politics/2019/nov/12/kashmir-labour-shifts-policy-after-backlash-by-indian-heritage-voters.
9 Amrit Wilson, "The New Strategies of Hindu Supremacists in Britain," *Byline Times*, December 9, 2021, https://bylinetimes.com/2021/12/09/the-new-strategies-of-hindu-supremacists-in-britain/.
10 Surji Dusanjh, and Manmagun Randhawa, "SCUK. 'Hindutva' Threat to UK Communal Harmony," *Press Release* (Sikh Council UK), February 17, 2021, https://sikhcouncil.co.uk/wp-content/uploads/2021/02/PR-Threat-to-UK-Communal-Harmony-17221-final.pdf.

11 Rahsaan Maxwell, "Muslims, South Asians and the British Mainstream: A National Identity Crisis?" *West European Politics* 29, no. 4 (2006): 736–756.

12 Eleanor Nesbitt, "British, Asian and Hindu: Identity, Self-narration and the Ethnographic Interview," *Journal of Beliefs and Values* 19, no. 2 (1998): 189–200; Jessica Jacobson, "Religion and Ethnicity: Dual and Alternative Sources of Identity among Young British Pakistanis," *Ethnic and Racial Studies* 20, no. 2 (1997): 238–256.

13 Shane Brighton, "British Muslims, Multiculturalism and UK Foreign Policy: 'Integration' and 'Cohesion' in and Beyond the State," *International Affairs* 83, no. 1 (2007): 1–17.

14 Asad Abbasi, "Why did South Asians Vote for Brexit?" *Blog* (LSE), November 2, 2016, https://blogs.lse.ac.uk/southasia/2016/11/02/why-did-south-asians-vote-for-Brexit/.

15 Naomi Canton, "Talks on Historic India-UK Trade Deal to Begin with Offer on UK Visas," *Times of India*, January 2, 2022, https://timesofindia.indiatimes.com/world/uk/talks-on-historic-india-uk-trade-deal-to-begin-with-offer-on-uk-visas-report/articleshow/88639538.cms.

16 ANI, "Pakistan PM Postpones UK Tour, Wanted Pact Similar to India," *NDTV*, June 22, 2021, https://www.timesnownews.com/international/article/speculations-as-pakistan-pm-imran-khans-uk-visit-is-postponed/774422.

17 Sanjay Suri, 'Nub Beyond Noise: Subtle Shift in UK Stance on Kashmir Signals India's Growing Importance," *News 18*, September 30, 2021, https://www.news18.com/news/opinion/the-nub-beyond-the-noise-subtle-shift-in-uk-stand-on-kashmir-signals-indias-growing-importance-4265138.html.

18 Foreign Affairs Committee (House of Commons), *The UK's Foreign Policy towards Afghanistan and Pakistan*, November 5, 2010, 3, https://publications.parliament.uk/pa/cm201011/cmselect/cmfaff/writev/afpak/afpak.pdf.

19 Michael Clarke, "Afghanistan and the UK's Illusion of Strategy," *Commentary* (RUSI), August 16, 2021, https://rusi.org/explore-our-research/publications/commentary/afghanistan-and-uks-illusion-strategy.

20 James Brandon, "The Pakistan Connection to the United Kingdom's Jihad Network," *Terrorism Monitor* 6, no. 4 (2008), https://jamestown.org/program/the-pakistan-connection-to-the-united-kingdoms-jihad-network/.

21 HMG, *The United Kingdom's Strategy for Countering International Terrorism* (Cm. 7547) (London: Her Majesty's Government, 2009), 100.

22 David Cameron, "British Prime Minister David Cameron's Speech at Infosys in India," July 28, 2010, https://www.gov.uk/government/news/british-prime-minister-david-camerons-speech-at-infosys-in-india.

23 Lewis Herrington, "British Islamic Extremist Terrorism: The Declining Significance of al-Qaeda and Pakistan," *International Affairs* 91, no. 1 (2015): 17–35.

24 William Hague, "Britain's Relationship with Pakistan is Here to Stay," September 27, 2011, https://www.gov.uk/government/speeches/britains-relationship-with-pakistan-is-here-to-stay.

25 Jack Goodman, "Why Pakistan is the Key to Britain's South Asian Renaissance," Foreign Policy Centre (London), June 4, 2014, https://fpc.org.uk/why-pakistan-is-the-key-to-britains-south-asian-renaissance/.

26 Mary Hunter, "Soft Power in International Military Relations: A UK-Pakistan Case Study," *Commentary* (RUSI), September 30, 2020, https://rusi.org/explore-our-research/publications/commentary/soft-power-international-military-relations-uk-pakistan-case-study.

27 Simon Tisdall and Anna Ridout, "British Jihadis in Bangladesh Fanning Flames of Extremism, Says Dhaka," *Guardian*, September 16, 2015, https://www.theguardian.com/world/2015/sep/16/british-jihadis-bangladesh-extremism-uk-isis-sheikh-hasina. Also "How Britain Exports Islamist Extremists to Bangladesh," *Economist*, September 21, 2019, https://www.economist.com/britain/2019/09/19/how-britain-exports-islamist-extremism-to-bangladesh.

28 Saleemul Huq and David Lewis, "What Should be the Future of UK-Bangladesh Relations after Aid? Exit DFID, Enter the Universities," *Blog* (LSE), July 13, 2018, https://blogs.lse.ac.uk/internationaldevelopment/2018/07/13/what-should-be-the-future-of-uk-bangladesh-relations-after-aid-exit-dfid-enter-the-universities/.

29 Jing Gu and Pei Chua, "Sri Lanka Case Study: Investigating Potential for Sri Lanka-China-UK Trilateral Cooperation" (Brighton: Institute of Development Studies Brighton, 2020).

30 Aishath Shaany, "Chagos Islands Dispute: Maldives Votes 'No' to End UK Control," May 23, 2019, https://raajje.mv/56700. Also Ahmed Mujuthaba and David Brewster, "Maldives Embroiled

in Mauritius-UK Tussle over Chagos," *The Interpreter* (Lowy Institute), December 8, 2021, https://www.lowyinstitute.org/the-interpreter/maldives-embroiled-mauritius-uk-tussle-over-chagos.

31 David Scott, "The Rise of India: UK Perspectives," *International Affairs* 93, no. 1 (2017): 165–188, https://doi.org/10.1093/ia/iiw007.

32 David Cameron, "Joint Press Conference," November 12, 2015, https://www.gov.uk/government/speeches/joint-press-conference-david-cameron-and-prime-minister-narendra-modi; Cameron, "UK–India: A 21st Century Partnership," in *Reconnecting Britain and India: Ideas for an Enhanced Partnership*, eds. Jo Johnson and Rajiv Kumar (New Delhi: Academic Foundation, 2012), 27.

33 House of Commons, Business and Enterprise Committee, *Waking Up to India: Developments in UK-India Economic Relations* (London: Stationary Office, 2008).

34 David Cameron, "A Stronger, Wider, Deeper Relationship," *The Hindu*, July 28, 2010, https://www.thehindu.com/opinion/lead/A-stronger-wider-deeper-relationship/article16213238.ece.

35 Cameron, "David Cameron's Speech at Unilever Offices in Mumbai," February 18, 2013, https://www.gov.uk/government/speeches/david-camerons-speech-at-unilever-offices-in-mumbai.

36 "Brexit will Give Massive Boost to India-UK Ties: Priti Patel," *Hindustan Times*, February 23, 2016, https://www.hindustantimes.com/world/Brexit-will-give-massive-boost-to-india-uk-ties-priti-patel/story-GQaiT2qRlpsiqXhp77buOM.html.

37 Frank O'Donnell, "British Engagement with India Following the EU Referendum," *Written Evidence*, July 2016, http://data.parliament.uk/writtenevidence/committeeevidence.svc/evidencedocument/foreign-affairscommittee/implications-of-leaving-the-eu-for-the-uks-role-in-the-world/written/35374.htm; Iulia Oehler-Şincai, "The Strategic Importance of the UK-India Partnership from the Brexit Perspective," *Revista de Economie Mondiala / The Journal of Global Economics* 9, no. 2 (2017): 36–48; Pramit Chaudhuri, "Brexit and India-UK Relations," in *India and the European Union in a Turbulent World*, ed. R. Jain (Singapore: Palgrave Macmillan, 2020), 91–107.

38 House of Commons, Foreign Affairs Committee, *Building Bridges: Reawakening UK-India Ties* (London: Stationary Office, 2019), 3.

39 British High Commission (New Delhi), "Finance Ministers Sunak and Sitharaman Hold Landmark Dialogue," October 28, 2020, https://www.gov.uk/government/news/finance-ministers-sunak-and-sitharaman-hold-landmark-dialogue.

40 Department of International Trade, *UK-India Free Trade Agreement. The UK's Strategic Approach*, January 13, 2022, www.gov.uk/government/publications/uk-approach-to-negotiating-a-free-trade-agreement-with-india. Also Alex Ellis [UK High Commissioner to India], "Ink India-Britain Free Trade, Unlock New Opportunity," *The Hindu*, February 3, 2022, https://www.pressreader.com/india/the-hindu/20220203/281913071512706, for economic and strategic reasons.

41 Rahul Roy-Chaudhury, "India-UK Counter-terrorism Cooperation: Convergences and Challenges," *Analysis* (IISS), January 2, 2020, https://www.iiss.org/blogs/analysis/2020/01/india-uk-counter-terrorism-cooperation.

42 ID Staff, "DefExpo 2020: DRDO Tech Impresses UK Minister, Joint R&D Projects Proposed," *Indus Dictum*, February 9, 2020, https://indusdictum.com/2020/02/09/defexpo-2020-drdo-tech-impresses-uk-minister-joint-rd-projects-proposed/. Also Gavin Thompson, "India-UK Military Ties: Huge Potential for Co-operations," Interview, *Financial Express*, January 15, 2021, https://www.financialexpress.com/defence/india-uk-military-ties-huge-potential-for-co-operation-says-uk-defence-adviser-to-india/2171444/.

43 PTI, "India, UK Agree on Technology Collaboration for Combat Aircraft," *Hindustan Times*, May 5, 2021, https://www.hindustantimes.com/india-news/india-uk-agree-on-technology-collaboration-for-combat-aircraft-101620172808260.html.

44 FP Staff, "India, UK to Discuss Technology to Create Electric Warships on Friday: How This Will Boost Indian Naval Power," *First Post*, October 22, 2021, https://www.firstpost.com/india/india-uk-to-discuss-technology-to-create-electric-warships-on-friday-how-this-will-boost-indian-naval-power-10074621.html.

45 Nayanima Basu, "Eye on China, Modi & Johnson Set 2030 Target for India-UK Comprehensive Strategic Partnership," *The Print*, May 4, 2021, https://theprint.in/diplomacy/eye-on-china-modi-johnson-set-2030-target-for-india-uk-comprehensive-strategic-partnership/652367/.

46 Rajat Pandit, "UK Carrier Group Conducts Exercise with India in Strategic Signal to China," *Times of India*, July 22, 2021, https://timesofindia.indiatimes.com/india/uk-carrier-group-conducts-exercise-with-india-in-strategic-signal-to-china/articleshow/84656682.cms; Pradip Sagar, "India,

UK Conduct Maritime Wargames with Eye on China," *The Week*, July 23, 2021, https://www.theweek.in/news/india/2021/07/23/india-uk-maritime-wargames-eye-on-china.html.

47 Samuel Bashfield, "Mauritian Sovereignty over Chagos Archipelago? Strategic Implications for Diego Garcia from UK-US Perspectives," *Journal of the Indian Ocean Region* 16, no. 2 (2020): 166–181, https://doi.org/10.1080/19480881.2020.1770949.

48 Prasun Sonwalker, "Britain and US Seek India's Assistance on Diego Garcia," *Hindustan Times*, January 19, 2017, https://www.hindustantimes.com/world-news/britain-and-us-seek-india-s-assistance-on-diego-garcia/story-thHY7JObIZETj2zIQ73DwL.html.

49 Peter Harris, "Want a Rules-Based Order for the Indo-Pacific? Start with Diego Garcia," *The Diplomat*, January 8, 2021, https://thediplomat.com/2021/01/want-a-rules-based-order-for-the-indo-pacific-start-with-diego-garcia/.

50 Rahul Roy-Chaudhury, "India-UK Cybersecurity Cooperation: The Way Forward," *Analysis* (IISS), November 22, 2019, https://www.iiss.org/blogs/analysis/2019/11/sasia-india-uk-cyber-security-cooperation.

51 Archishman Goswami, "BIMSTEC: Why Britain Should Increase Strategic Cooperation," *Britain's World* (Council on Geostrategy), January 20, 2022, https://www.geostrategy.org.uk/britains-world/bimstec-why-britain-should-increase-strategic-cooperation/.

52 Ajai Shukla, "UK Eager to Help India Design Second Indigenous Aircraft Carrier INS Vishal," *Business Standard*, February 7, 2020, https://www.business-standard.com/article/defence/uk-eager-to-help-india-design-second-indigenous-aircraft-carrier-ins-vishal-120020601976_1.html.

Bibliography

Abbasi, Asad. "Why did South Asians Vote for Brexit?" *Blog* (LSE), November 2, 2016. https://blogs.lse.ac.uk/southasia/2016/11/02/why-did-south-asians-vote-for-Brexit/.

ANI. "Pakistan PM Postpones UK Tour, Wanted Pact Similar to India." *NDTV*, June 22, 2021. https://www.timesnownews.com/international/article/speculations-as-pakistan-pm-imran-khans-uk-visit-is-postponed/774422.

Aryan, Javin. "The Next Chapter India-UK Defense Relationship." *Young Voices* (ORF), April 24, 2021. https://www.orfonline.org/expert-speak/the-next-chapter-in-india-uk-defence-relationship/.

Bashfield, Samuel. "Mauritian Sovereignty over Chagos Archipelago? Strategic Implications for Diego Garcia from UK-US Perspectives." *Journal of the Indian Ocean Region* 16, no. 2 (2020): 166–181. https://doi.org/10.1080/19480881.2020.1770949.

Basu, Nayanima. "Eye on China, Modi & Johnson set 2030 target for India-UK Comprehensive Strategic Partnership." *The Print*, May 4, 2021. https://theprint.in/diplomacy/eye-on-china-modi-johnson-set-2030-target-for-india-uk-comprehensive-strategic-partnership/652367/.

Brandon, James. "The Pakistan Connection to the United Kingdom's Jihad Network." *Terrorism Monitor* 6, no. 4 (2008). https://jamestown.org/program/the-pakistan-connection-to-the-united-kingdoms-jihad-network/.

Brighton, Shane. "British Muslims, Multiculturalism and UK Foreign Policy: 'Integration' and 'Cohesion' in and Beyond the State." *International Affairs* 83, no. 1 (2007): 1–17.

British High Commission (New Delhi). "Finance Ministers Sunak and Sitharaman Hold Landmark Dialogue." October 28, 2020. https://www.gov.uk/government/news/finance-ministers-sunak-and-sitharaman-hold-landmark-dialogue.

Brown, Judith. "The Role of the Modern Diaspora in the UK–Indian Relationship." In *Reconnecting Britain and India: Ideas for an Enhanced Partnership*, edited by Jo Johnson and Rajiv Kumar, 165–170. New Delhi: Academic Foundation, 2012.

Cameron, David. "Joint Press Conference." November 12, 2015. https://www.gov.uk/government/speeches/joint-press-conference-david-cameron-and-prime-minister-narendra-modi.

Cameron, David. "A Stronger, Wider, Deeper Relationship." *The Hindu*, July 28, 2010. https://www.thehindu.com/opinion/lead/A-stronger-wider-deeper-relationship/article16213238.ece.

Cameron, David. "British Prime Minister David Cameron's Speech at Infosys in India." July 28, 2010. https://www.gov.uk/government/news/british-prime-minister-david-camerons-speech-at-infosys-in-india.

Cameron, David. "David Cameron's Speech at Unilever Offices in Mumbai." February 18, 2013. https://www.gov.uk/government/speeches/david-camerons-speech-at-unilever-offices-in-mumbai.

Cameron, David. "UK–India: a 21st Century Partnership." In *Reconnecting Britain and India: Ideas for an Enhanced Partnership*, edited by Jo Johnson and Rajiv Kumar, 27. New Delhi: Academic Foundation, 2012.

Canton, Naomi. "Talks on Historic India-UK Trade Deal to Begin with Offer on UK visas." *Times of India*, January 2, 2022. https://timesofindia.indiatimes.com/world/uk/talks-on-historic-india-uk-trade-deal-to-begin-with-offer-on-uk-visas-report/articleshow/88639538.cms.

Chaudhuri, Pramit. "Brexit and India-UK Relations." In *India and the European Union in a Turbulent World*, edited by Rajendra Jain, 91–107. Singapore: Palgrave Macmillan, 2020.

Clarke, Michael. "Afghanistan and the UK's Illusion of Strategy." *Commentary* (RUSI), August 16, 2021. https://rusi.org/explore-our-research/publications/commentary/afghanistan-and-uks-illusion-strategy.

Department of International Trade. *UK-India Free Trade Agreement. The UK's Strategic Approach*, January 13, 2022. www.gov.uk/government/publications/uk-approach-to-negotiating-a-free-trade-agreement-with-india.

Dusanjh, Surjit, and Manmagun Randhawa. "'Hindutva' threat to UK Communal Harmony." *Press Release* (Sikh Council UK), February 17, 2021. https://sikhcouncil.co.uk/wp-content/uploads/2021/02/PR-Threat-to-UK-Communal-Harmony-17221-final.pdf.

"How Britain Exports Islamist Extremists to Bangladesh." *Economist*, September 21, 2019. https://www.economist.com/britain/2019/09/19/how-britain-exports-islamist-extremism-to-bangladesh.

Ellis, Alex. "Ink India-Britain Free Trade, Unlock New Opportunity." *The Hindu*, February 3, 2022. https://www.pressreader.com/india/the-hindu/20220203/281913071512706.

Foreign Affairs Committee (House of Commons). *The UK's Foreign Policy towards Afghanistan and Pakistan*. November 5, 2010. https://publications.parliament.uk/pa/cm201011/cmselect/cmfaff/writev/afpak/afpak.pdf.

FP Staff. "India, UK to Discuss Technology to Create Electric Warships on Friday: How This Will Boost Indian Naval Power." *First Post*, October 22, 2021. https://www.firstpost.com/india/india-uk-to-discuss-technology-to-create-electric-warships-on-friday-how-this-will-boost-indian-naval-power-10074621.html.

Goodman, Jack. "Why Pakistan is the Key to Britain's South Asian Renaissance." Foreign Policy Centre, June 4, 2014. https://fpc.org.uk/why-pakistan-is-the-key-to-britains-south-asian-renaissance/.

Goswami, Archishman. "BIMSTEC: Why Britain Should Increase Strategic Cooperation." *Britain's World* (Council on Geostrategy), January 20, 2022. https://www.geostrategy.org.uk/britains-world/bimstec-why-britain-should-increase-strategic-cooperation/.

Gu, Jing, and Pei Chua. *Sri Lanka Case Study: Investigating Potential for Sri Lanka-China-UK Trilateral Cooperation*. Brighton: Institute of Development Studies, 2020.

Hague, William. "Speech ('Britain's Relationship with Pakistan is Here to Stay')." September 27, 2011. https://www.gov.uk/government/speeches/britains-relationship-with-pakistan-is-here-to-stay.

Harris, Peter. "Want a Rules-Based Order for the Indo-Pacific? Start with Diego Garcia." *The Diplomat*, January 8, 2021. https://thediplomat.com/2021/01/want-a-rules-based-order-for-the-indo-pacific-start-with-diego-garcia/.

Herrington, Lewis. "British Islamic Extremist Terrorism: The Declining Significance of Al-Qaeda and Pakistan." *International Affairs* 91, no. 1 (2015): 17–35.

HMG. *2030 Roadmap for India-UK Future Relations*. May 4, 2021. https://www.gov.uk/government/publications/india-uk-virtual-summit-may-2021-roadmap-2030-for-a-comprehensive-strategic-partnership/2030-roadmap-for-india-uk-future-relations.

HMG. *The United Kingdom's Strategy for Countering International Terrorism*. Cm. 7547, March 2009. https://assets.publishing.service.gov.uk/government/uploads/system/uploads/attachment_data/file/228644/7547.pdf.

House of Commons. Business and Enterprise Committee. *Waking up to India: Developments in UK-India Economic Relations*. London: Stationary Office, 2008.

House of Commons. Foreign Affairs Committee. *Building Bridges: Reawakening UK-India Ties*. London: Stationary Office, 2019.

Hunter, Mary. "Soft Power in International Military Relations: A UK-Pakistan Case Study." *Commentary* (RUSI), September 30, 2020. https://rusi.org/explore-our-research/publications/commentary/soft-power-international-military-relations-uk-pakistan-case-study.

Huq, Saleem, and Lewis David. "What Should be the Future of UK-Bangladesh Relations After Aid? Exit DFID, Enter the Universities." *Blog* (LSE), July 13, 2018. https://blogs.lse.ac.uk/internatio naldevelopment/2018/07/13/what-should-be-the-future-of-uk-bangladesh-relations-after-aid-exit-dfid-enter-the-universities/.

ID Staff. "DefExpo 2020: DRDO Tech Impresses UK Minister, Joint R&D Projects Proposed." *Indus Dictum*, February 9, 2020. https://indusdictum.com/2020/02/09/defexpo-2020-drdo-tech-impresses-uk-minister-joint-rd-projects-proposed/.

Jabed, Muhammad. "British Interests in a 'Regionalised' South Asia." *South Asia* 35, no. 3 (2012): 726–752.

Jacobson, Jessica. "Religion and Ethnicity: Dual and Alternative Sources of Identity among Young British Pakistanis." *Ethnic and Racial Studies* 20, no. 2 (1997): 238–256.

Maxwell, Rahsaan. "Muslims, South Asians and the British Mainstream: A National Identity Crisis?" *West European Politics* 29, no. 4 (2006): 736–756.

Mujuthaba, Ahmed, and David Brewster. "Maldives Embroiled in Mauritius-UK Tussle Over Chagos." *The Interpreter* (Lowy Institute), December 8, 2021. https://www.lowyinstitute.org/the-interpreter/maldives-embroiled-mauritius-uk-tussle-over-chagos.

O'Donnell, Frank. "British Engagement with India following the EU Referendum." In *Written Evidence* (House of Commons, Foreign Affairs Committee), July 2016. http://data.parliament. uk/writtenevidence/committeeevidence.svc/evidencedocument/foreign-affairs-committee/implications-of-leaving-the-eu-for-the-uks-role-in-the-world/written/35374.htm.

O'Donnell, Frank. "The 'Global Britain' Concept and UK Policy toward India." In *Written Evidence* (Foreign Affairs Committee), October 18, 2018. https://data.parliament.uk/writtenevidence/committeeevidence.svc/evidencedocument/foreign-affairs-committee/global-britain-and-india/written/90899.pdf.

Oehler-Şincai, Iulia. "The Strategic Importance of the UK-India Partnership from the Brexit Perspective." *Revista de Economie Mondiala/The Journal of Global Economics* 9, no. 2 (2017): 36–48.

Pandit, Rajat. "UK Carrier Group Conducts Exercise with India in Strategic Signal to China." *Times of India*, July 22, 2021. https://timesofindia.indiatimes.com/india/uk-carrier-group-conducts-exercise-with-india-in-strategic-signal-to-china/articleshow/84656682.cms.

Pant, Harsh, and Tom Hilford. "The UK Shifts to the Indo-Pacific: An Opportunity for India-UK Ties." *ORF Issue Brief* no. 444 (February 2021), Observer Research Foundation.

Patel, Priti. "Brexit will Give Massive Boost to India-UK Ties: Priti Patel." *Hindustan Times*, February 23, 2016. https://www.hindustantimes.com/world/Brexit-will-give-massive-boost-to-india-uk-ties-priti-patel/story-GQaiT2qRlpsiqXhp77buOM.html.

PTI. "India, UK Agree on Technology Collaboration for Combat Aircraft." *Hindustan Times*, May 5, 2021. https://www.hindustantimes.com/india-news/india-uk-agree-on-technology-collaboration-for-combat-aircraft-101620172808260.html.

Roy-Chaudhury, Rahul. "India-UK Counter-terrorism Cooperation: Convergences and Challenges." *Analysis* (IISS), January 2, 2020. https://www.iiss.org/blogs/analysis/2020/01/india-uk-counter-terrorism-cooperation.

Roy-Chaudhury, Rahul. "India-UK Cybersecurity Cooperation: The Way Forward." *Analysis* (IISS), November 22, 2019. https://www.iiss.org/blogs/analysis/2019/11/sasia-india-uk-cyber-security-cooperation.

Sagar, Pradip. "India, UK Conduct Maritime Wargames with Eye on China." *The Week*, July 23, 2021. https://www.theweek.in/news/india/2021/07/23/india-uk-maritime-wargames-eye-on-china. html.

Scott, David. "Britain Returns to the Indian Ocean?" *Round Table. Commonwealth Journal for International Affairs* 107, no. 3 (2018): 307–316. https://doi.org/10.1080/00358533.2018.1476096.

Scott, David. "The Rise of India: UK Perspectives." *International Affairs* 93, no. 1 (2017): 165–188. https://doi.org/10.1093/ia/iiw007.

Shaany, Aishath. "Chagos Islands Dispute: Maldives Votes 'No' to End UK Control." May 23, 2019. https://raajje.mv/56700.

Shukla, Ajai. "UK Eager to Help India Design Second Indigenous Aircraft Carrier INS Vishal." *Business Standard*, February 7, 2020. https://www.business-standard.com/article/defence/uk-eager-to-help-india-design-second-indigenous-aircraft-carrier-ins-vishal-120020601976_1.html.

Sil, Rudra, and Peter Katzenstein. *Beyond Paradigms. Analytical Eclecticism in the Study of World Politics.* Basingstoke: Palgrave Macmillan, 2011.

Sonwalker, Prasun. "Britain and US Seek India's Assistance on Diego Garcia." *Hindustan Times*, January 19, 2017. https://www.hindustantimes.com/world-news/britain-and-us-seek-india-s-assistance-on-diego-garcia/story-thHY7JObIZETj2zIQ73DwL.html.

Sridharan, Kripa. "Regional Organizations and Conflict Management: Comparing ASEAN and SAARC." London: Department for International Development, January 1, 2008. https://assets.publishing.service.gov.uk/media/57a08bc040f0b652dd000e7c/wp33.2.pdf.

Suri, Sanjay. "Nub Beyond Noise: Subtle Shift in UK Stance on Kashmir Signals India's Growing Importance." *News 18*, September 30, 2021. https://www.news18.com/news/opinion/the-nub-beyond-the-noise-subtle-shift-in-uk-stand-on-kashmir-signals-indias-growing-importance-4265138.html.

Thompson, Gavin. "India-UK Military Ties: Huge Potential for Co-operations." Interview, *Financial Express*, January 15, 2021. https://www.financialexpress.com/defence/india-uk-military-ties-huge-potential-for-co-operation-says-uk-defence-adviser-to-india/2171444/.

Tisdall, Simon, and Anna Ridout. "British Jihadis in Bangladesh Fanning Flames of Extremism, Says Dhaka." *Guardian*, September 16, 2015. https://www.theguardian.com/world/2015/sep/16/british-jihadis-bangladesh-extremism-uk-isis-sheikh-hasina.

Wilson, Amrit. "The New Strategies of Hindu Supremacists in Britain." *Byline Times*, December 9, 2021. https://bylinetimes.com/2021/12/09/the-new-strategies-of-hindu-supremacists-in-britain/.

Wintour, Patrick. "Kashmir: Labour Shifts Policy after Backlash by Indian-heritage Voters." *Guardian*, November 12, 2019. https://www.theguardian.com/politics/2019/nov/12/kashmir-labour-shifts-policy-after-backlash-by-indian-heritage-voters.

Wyatt, Andrew. "India and the United Kingdom: Finding a New Equilibrium." In *Engaging the World: Indian Foreign Policy Since 1947*, edited by Šumit Ganguly, 225–244. New Delhi: Oxford University Press, 2016.

28

FRANCE AND SOUTH ASIA

Gilles Boquérat

Introduction

After the prospect of a Franco-Russian expedition to India was given up in the early 19th century, putting a final end to Napoleon's pretentions to oust the British East India Company from the subcontinent, France had to contend herself with the presence on Indian soil of just five "comptoirs" (establishments) and a few "loges" (trading posts).[1] After Independence, French foreign policy during the Fourth Republic (1946–1958) was largely focused on the alliance of the Western world against the Communist bloc and fighting liberation movements in Indochina and Northern Africa. South Asia was better left to the Anglo-Saxon powers: Its élite had often been educated in the United Kingdom, and India and Pakistan were members of the Commonwealth and maintained meaningful relations with the United States. If, after completing the decolonization process, Gaullist France claimed a proactive approach and an independent stance on world affairs, the subcontinent was one area where France, due to a lack of political and economic investments, did not have a specific policy. The European integration process, the balance of power on a global scale, the establishment of a working relationship with former colonies, and the Middle East powder keg were seen as more relevant issues, reducing the subcontinent to the periphery of French foreign policy. The Soviet invasion of Afghanistan, the pursuit of nuclear ambitions, and then a global security architecture in a state of flux after the end of the Cold War and the disbandment of barriers of alignment have led France to take greater interest in the region as it looks for partnerships to give credence to a global stature.

In this chapter, we will look at the original deficit of interest in the region, the reappraisal done at turn of the century, the geopolitical factors at play, and the constitutive and prospective elements of the strategic partnership with India conceived notably as a channel of influence in the Indo-Pacific. This chapter contends that the school of Realism most persuasively explains French conduct toward South Asia.[2] While Paris has engaged substantively with the most powerful South Asian states, it has had minimal relationships with the region's smaller countries. Within this pattern of French diplomacy, military support—especially in arms sales—has loomed large. Moreover, its engagement preferences have hewed closely to global power shifts, such as the US in strengthening ties with India as responses to the end of the Cold War and rise of China as a new Western competitor. In response to this contention,

DOI: 10.4324/9781003246626-32

Constructivist theorists might reiterate their traditional critique of Realism. This holds that Realist assumptions and policies (especially regarding global and relative power shifts as a predictor of state behavior and a military-first and self-help approach to security issues) should be viewed only as a set of intersubjective understandings between state leaders and strategic communities in the international system, rather than the logical response to the absence of a controlling world government. However, the Constructivist argument that Realism is not a universal logic and that France's Realist diplomatic perceptions could be replaced by an alternative set of intersubjective norms and practices does not necessarily invalidate the argument that French conduct toward South Asia most closely represents Realist expectations.[3] The liberal and critical theory schools are less persuasive theoretical alternatives; French engagement has neither prioritized security over economic trade, nor sought to reorient the regional definition and practice of security around that of the individual citizen rather than the state.[4]

The First Decades after 1947[5]

During for first few decades after the end of British rule, the attitude of France toward the subcontinent was sharply sum up in a diplomatic note written in 1979: "For reasons that have to do with our history (no South Asia policy even under the monarchy, militancy of the decolonized of the subcontinent against our colonization elsewhere in the world, lack of interest of our industrialists for a restricted market and treated as the preserve of the Anglo-Saxons), we are still almost absent from these countries with which we have not had until now any active and ongoing political dialogue (...) French visits to South Asia have remained rare and so far have done little to reduce the burden of commonplaces that confine France's interest in these countries to the level of exotic entertainment or charitable self-pity."[6] If Paris' engagement vis-à-vis South Asian countries was limited, there was nevertheless the aspiration to work toward the consolidation of their independence, through modest bilateral and multilateral economic assistance[7] and to support diplomatic initiatives favoring peaceful resolutions of disputes. In a Cold War environment, the objective was to make a contribution to the prevention of those countries falling in the enemy bloc; the sale of arms was also part of it, even if it was primarily a response to commercial opportunities.

In 1956, Pondicherry (now Puducherry) and other French establishments (Karikal, Mahé, Yanaon/Yanam) were transferred to India[8] and, in 1962, with the fourteenth amendment of the Constitution, incorporated as the ninth Union Territory. The colonial issue that had bogged down the bilateral relation was finally settled. Yet, it was not until January 1980, soon after the entry of Soviet tanks in Kabul and Indira Gandhi's return to power, that a French head of state, Valéry Giscard d'Estaing, officially visited India for the first time, 33 years after independence. Two French Premier Ministers had visited India earlier: Georges Pompidou in 1965 (he also went to Pakistan) and Jacques Chirac in January 1976, the first leading Western statesman to be in India after the declaration of the Emergency six months prior. A comment in the then recently launched *India Today* weekly magazine summed up bilateral relations as lacking substance: "Unlike the highly emotional relations with America, Britain and the Soviet Union, Indo-French relations over the last 25 years have largely run a quiet course least disturbed by public controversies. On international issues, they have agreed and often differed without leaving any ill will on either side."[9] In the 1950s, Nehru had been critical of the reluctance of French authorities to decolonize, and a strategic divide had existed between non-aligned India and France's participation in NATO. This divergence subsided somehow with De Gaulle's insistence on having independent positions on international issues and generated an affinity between the French and Indian quest for degrees of strategic autonomy in the middle of the Cold war. Yet, nuclear deterrence was an essential component of the policy of *grandeur* (greatness) intended by De Gaulle whereas non-aligned India was championing disarmament. In a memoir, the French president (1959–1969) asserted that "as champions of the balance of power, we have the best reasons to wish that, in the face of China, Hindustan assert her strength."[10] Still, Paris had striven to maintain an equidistance between the two subcontinental rivals and not to get unduly involved on the contentious Kashmir issue, beyond voting initially in favor of the original resolutions supporting the principle of a free and impartial plebiscite toward the settlement of the dispute and later on hoping for a fair solution through a direct agreement between the two countries.

In November 1982, it was the turn of François Mitterrand, the socialist President, to tour India. After winning the presidential elections the year before, he had appointed Claude Cheysson, known for his Third World sensitivities, as his minister for External Relations. The latter wasted no time in visiting Mexico, Algiers, and New Delhi, the three capitals bound to be the bridgehead for North-South cooperation. The initiative did not survive his departure from the ministry. Beyond sharing a will for a new world economic order, the bilateral relations remained constrained by Cold War rigidities, attitudes differing for instance on the Soviet presence in Afghanistan, the Vietnamese intervention in Cambodia, or nuclear disarmament. On the eve of coming to India for the second and last time, in February 1989, Mitterrand admitted that Franco-Indian relations were below expectations.[11] A major irritant for India during those years remained France's arms sales to Pakistan.

As with India after independence, the colonial question was hanging over the relations with Pakistan. Being one of the largest Muslim states, the concern was the possible condemnation in international fora of the French colonial rule in North Africa. The criticism remained muted; both countries were partners within Southeast Asia Treaty Organization and Pakistan looked for French support when the Kashmir issue was discussed at the UN. Pakistan's diplomatic position hardened after the insurrection in Algeria became an increasingly bloody conflict between the French armed forces and the independentists. It was too tempting for Islamabad to see a link with self-determination requested for Kashmir. And the settlement of the Algerian issue in 1962 was seen as a victory for the liberation forces and a lesson for nations suppressing independence movements. De Gaulle, deviating from American policies, whether in Southeast Asia or in the Middle East, attracted some interest, notably the critical stance taken vis-à-vis Israel, at a time when Pakistan itself was trying to look beyond its relation with Washington. Trying to catch up with the military assistance provided by the Soviet Union to India, Pakistani requests for arms poured in: Daphné submarines, Mirage III/V fighter planes, Puma helicopters, Breguet Atlantic maritime patrol aircraft, etc. Bilateral relations suffered a setback when Paris reneged on a 1976 agreement to supply Pakistan with a nuclear reprocessing plant following pressure from Washington, which considered the risk to be too high as it might help Pakistan to acquire a nuclear bomb.

There was an attempt to revive cooperation with the visit of François Mitterrand to Pakistan at the beginning of 1990—the first ever by a French head of State (and the only one to date)—after the return of democracy, but it was hampered by political instability and later by the military coup engineered by General Pervez Musharraf. Nevertheless, the arms business sustained bilateral relations. The Pakistan Air Force became the largest operator of Mirage aircraft outside France: Islamabad signed a deal in 1990 with the Australian government for 50 second-hand Mirage III, followed by a contract in 1996 for the acquisition of 40 refurbished Mirage III/V fighters previously owned by the French air force. The prospect of France selling Mirage-2000 to Pakistan (a more advanced version than those acquired by India in the mid-1980s) never materialized, much to the comfort of New Delhi.

A Transformative Shift

The turning point in Indo-French relations was 1998, when Paris acknowledged India's emergence in the wake of the post-Cold War reconfiguration of international relations. To remain a global power, France needed to develop strong connections within powerful institutions like the European Union or with emerging powers like India. Liberalization of the Indian economy and business prospects in an expanding market contributed to this reassessment.[12] In January, President Chirac, chief guest at the Republic Day Parade for the second time, declared that "France wishes to accompany the powerful march of an Asian giant."[13] On this occasion, India signed with France its first strategic partnership and five consultative mechanisms were set up before long. In May, India went ahead with five underground nuclear tests. Paris stood for a measured criticism (the new Indo-French High Committee on Defense had met barely a week before the tests) and did not support the sanctions route.[14] France was in fact the first major power to open a dialogue with India after the tests.[15] Within weeks, Brajesh Mishra was in Paris as special envoy of Prime Minister Atal Bihari Vajpayee. In October, the two sides opened a strategic dialogue at the level of National Security Advisors whose 35th edition took place in November 2021. Over time, the agenda expanded to include counter-terrorism, intelligence sharing, and cybersecurity issues, in addition to the original nuclear, space, and defense-related matters.

Gone were the days when Paris tried to maintain an even-handedness between the subcontinent's foes. France supported permanent membership for India in a reformed Security Council and advocated a multipolar world where India could become one of the poles of the prospective world order.[16] It was positively received by Indian leaders and diplomats, eager to see their country being recognized in its rightful place by the international community. If the rapprochement with the United States and the concern over the "usual suspects" (Pakistan and China) were logically assuming priority, Indo-French relations gathered momentum through regular high-level exchanges and a common concern for the faith in multilateralism, the threat of terrorism, and the defense of the rule of law. France, a maritime power with the largest exclusive economic zone thanks to its overseas departments and territories scattered all over the oceans, was keen to engage India located at the center of the eponymous ocean.[17] The 2013 White Paper on Defense and National Security reiterated French commitment, as a neighboring power in the Indian Ocean, to be a player in the security of the Indian Ocean and the Pacific. It required enhanced military capabilities enabling to take action, reinforced by the development of privileged relations with India seen as a partner and a country providing an element of stability in the subcontinent.[18] It was already a long time ago that the two navies were conducting joint naval exercise (first in 1983, and an annual occurrence called "Varuna" since 2001). The Garuda exercise between the two Air Forces (since 2003) and the Shakti exercise involving the land forces (since 2011) were to follow suit, and may also lead in the future to tri-service military exercise.

In January 2017, India and France signed a white shipping agreement (exchange of information on identity and movement of commercial merchant vessels) to shore up maritime domain awareness in the Indian Ocean Region (IOR) amid China's expanding naval forays in the area. When President Macron visited India in March 2018, a provision of reciprocal logistics support for their armed forces in each other's ports and bases in the IOR was agreed, in the spirit of the Logistics Exchange Memorandum of Agreement signed between India and the United States. The visit was also the occasion to adopt a "Joint Strategic Vision" for maintaining the safety of international sea lanes, countering maritime terrorism and piracy, and for greater coordination in regional/international fora in the IOR.[19] India's acceptance of France as a net security provider in the Indian Ocean was a far cry from the Cold War days when New Delhi was strongly opposed to the presence of external power fleets and considered French possessions as colonial leftovers. In 2020, the Indian Navy conducted for the first time a joint patrol with the French Navy from the Reunion Island. Seen together with another agreement to protect classified and protected information, and the willingness to enhance operational cooperation between the Indian and French counter-terrorism agencies, the concurrence is bound to deepen the cooperation in the strategic sphere.

Paris came also to back India's efforts at multilateral forums to counter the activities of Pakistan-based terror groups and individuals. During a visit to Mumbai in 2010, two years after the 26/11 attacks, President Sarkozy was to recall that it was "not acceptable for the world that terrorist attacks be planned or carried out by groups trained in Pakistan."[20] As a country itself targeted by terrorist actions at the national level, France co-sponsored in 2017 a proposal at the United Nations to designate Masood Azhar, leader of Jaish-e-Mohammed, as a global terrorist under the al-Qaeda Sanctions Committee 1267. Blocked by China, the initiative was renewed after the Pulwama terrorist strike of February 2019. The inability to demonstrate sufficient action against money laundering and terror financing led Pakistan to be grey-listed since June 2018 by the global watchdog, the Financial Action Task Force headquartered in France.[21] The Kashmir issue has been during the last decades essentially viewed through the prism of terrorism, a stand not to the liking of Pakistani rulers and diplomats who have repeatedly been trying to have India condemned for human rights violations in the valley.[22] Anti-terrorism cooperation and sharing of intelligence took increasing importance in the relations with Pakistan, as the country has been visited by Western jihadists and was neighboring Afghanistan where French forces were deployed as part of the international coalition (the deployment ended in 2014).[23]

Exchanges at a high level have been largely sporadic. The last visit of a head of State or government to France was Asif Ali Zardari, then president of Pakistan, in December 2012. Cooperation in the fields of defense, through major arms contracts, had been the driving force in the bilateral relations with Pakistan after France acquired the image of a reliable and independent partner. But this traditionally trusting relationship with the military elite was affected by the strengthening of the defense relationship with India and a cautious stance on military exports.[24] By the beginning of the millennium, France has foregone the opportunity to sell major weapons systems to Pakistan and its defense industry has focused on strong cooperation with India.

Nurturing the Defense Partnership with India

Arms transfers and military cooperation are inextricably linked to a close strategic partnership. In the 18th and early 19th centuries, French military officers shared their know-how with Indian princes. As a major arms producer, France took advantage after independence of the Indian desire not to be overly dependent on British supplies and later on Soviet equipment. During the Cold War, France was the third largest supplier of weapons to India, behind the Soviet Union and the United Kingdom, notably for the Indian Air Force as early as the 1950s. In October 1953, the first four Dassault MD-450 Ouragan, out of 60-odd units ordered the year before, landed at Air Force Station Ambala (Punjab). Rechristened "Toofani," the fighter bombers remained in service till 1967, in particular deployed during the military takeover of Goa in December 1961. In the meantime, India went for the subsonic Dassault Mystere IV in 1957; 104 warplanes were to be commissioned. They performed during the Indo-Pak 1965 war and finally made way in 1973 to more advanced Soviet fighters. Dassault Aviation returned to India with the Mirage-2000H in the mid-eighties as a strategic defensive countermeasure to Pakistan buying F-16 variants from the United States. Mirage-2000s, fitted with precision guided munitions, played a key role in blasting Pakistan Army bunkers in the Batalik and Drass heights during the 1999 Kargil war and when the IAF carried a strike against a terrorist camp in Khyber-Pakhtunkhwa in February 2019.[25] An agreement was signed in 2011 for the upgradation of 51 Mirage-2000H to Mirage 2000-5 standards.

When the IAF, confronted with a depleting number of squadrons, looked for a new generation of fighter aircrafts, Dassault was inevitably in contention with the multirole Rafale. Initially, the Congress-led government had opted to buy 126 Rafale aircraft, 108 of which were to be made in India by the state-owned Hindustan Aeronautics Ltd. (HAL). Failing to close the deal over pricing issues, it is Narendra Modi who in 2015 secured a deal to buy 36 warplanes (the intergovernmental agreement finalizing the sale was signed on September 2016). No arms deal goes without generating a controversy over the terms of the contract and this one was no exception, especially in the run-up to the 2019 general elections and after the Supreme Court dismissed in December 2018 all petitions filed against it. The Rafale jets are India's first major acquisition of fighter planes after the induction of the Russian Sukhoi SU-30 jets in the IAF in 1997. All 36 Rafale must be delivered by end-2022 to form two squadrons, one at AFS Ambala (Punjab) and the other at AFS Hasimara (West Bengal). The possibility of getting India-specific enhancements and using the Rafale, as with the Mirage 2000 before, in a nuclear strike role has been a significant factor in choosing the French fighter jet.[26] The Rafale will be equipped with MBDA's Meteor beyond visual range air-to-air missile with a strike range of 120–150 km, the 3000 km range "Scalp" cruise missiles and the Safran's Hammer air-to-ground missile with a strike range of 60 km. Dassault Aviation remains a contender for the putative tender for more than 100 medium multirole fighters, as well as offering to the Indian naval air arm the maritime variant of the Rafale to equip an aircraft carrier.

In the early 1960s, Hindustan Aeronautics Limited (HAL) entered an agreement with Sud-Aviation (later on Aerospatiale) to manufacture under license the light utility helicopter Alouette III. Renamed Chetak, more than 350 were to be produced in Bangalore. Toward the end of the 1970s, HAL would also see the licensed production of the multirole SA.315B Lama (Cheetah) helicopter. The upgraded versions of both helicopter types remain in service, with the Cheetah still conducting supply operations for the army formations deployed in the Himalayan region, like the 17,000 feet high Siachen Glacier. The French company Turbomeca has a long history of supplying engines to power India's indigenously developed (like the Dhruv) or license-built rotorcraft. Among other collaborative efforts with public sector undertakings, there is the production of the anti-tank guided missiles (ATGMs) by Bharat Dynamics Limited, starting with the SS.11 of Nord Aviation in the 1970s, soon followed by the Milan.[27] In 2005, India signed a $3.5 billion deal with France's DCN (name changed to DCNS in 2007, now Naval Group since 2017) to build six Scorpene conventional diesel-electric submarines with transfer of know-how at Mazagon Dock Limited in Mumbai (four have been so far commissioned in the Indian Navy). Naval Group and its subsidiary Naval Group India expect to remain a major partner for the Indian Navy in the follow-up project 75(I). With the intention of going beyond a client-supplier relation, French defense majors, like Thales and Safran, have set up joint ventures with Indian industrial actors, public as well as private, under the "Make in India" and "Atmanirbhar Bharat" campaigns, involving transfer of technology and joint development to bolster a wide range of advanced capabilities, like engine manufacturing, with also a view to export some of the equipment produced in third country markets.

In contrast, the military-industrial relationship with Pakistan has run out of steam. The last major arms contract signed with Pakistan was in 1994 with the sale and the technology transfer of three diesel-electric Agosta-90B-class-submarines, the last one commissioned in 2006. Their modernization, starting in 2016, was given to a Turkish company rather than to the French company (DCNS) that originally designed and built the submarines.[28] The Pakistan Air Force is the largest operators of Mirage III, and its ground-attack variant, Mirage 5, whose procurement was spread out from 1967 to 1982. After the United States suspended the delivery of F-16 in retaliation to the Pakistan nuclear program, a mid-life update of the Mirage started in the 1990s along with the acquisition of second-hand Mirage fighters from various countries (Australia, Belgium, Lebanon, Libya, and Spain) and even surplus Mirage 5F from the French Air Force. In 2020, the PAF acquired 36 Mirage 5 from Egypt to be refurbished before being pressed into service.

A Look at Structuring Cooperation

Besides being a military hardware supplier, other long-standing collaborations structuring the relationship have been in existence in the space and civil nuclear sectors dating back to the early days of India's quest for self-sufficiency in these fields and leading to agreements between national organizations. This is true between the Centre national d'études spatiales (CNES) and the Indian Space Research Organisation (ISRO) and its predecessor. CNES has, for instance, contributed its expertise in the production of small satellites, a sector in which India has specialized, and has also undertaken two joint missions "Megha-Tropiques" (2011) dedicated to atmospheric research and "Saral-Altika" (2013) on the study of ocean circulation. In August 2019, CNES and ISRO committed to developing and building a constellation of satellites carrying telecommunications and radar and optical remote-sensing instruments, constituting the first space-based system in the world capable of tracking ships continuously. The satellites will be operated jointly by France and India to monitor ships in the Indian Ocean. As of 2021, 25 Indian communication satellites of the INSAT series (telecommunications, meteorology) and GSAT (communications) has been placed in orbit by the European launcher Ariane from French Guiana. Indo-French space collaboration is to expand into space exploration and human space flight program (Gaganyaan mission).

Closely on the heels of independence, a scientific collaboration started with the French Commissariat à l'énergie atomique (CEA) and the Indian Atomic Energy Commission (AEC). It was suspended for a time after the "peaceful" nuclear explosion of May 1974, but in the early eighties, France took the place of the United States for the supply of enriched uranium—until 1993—to the Tarapur Atomic Power Station after Washington terminated the contract following its displeasure over the Pokhran atomic test. While New Delhi refuses to sign a non-proliferation treaty that it deemed to be discriminatory, Paris supported and welcomed India's accession to the multilateral export control regimes, whether it be the Missile Technology Control Regime (MTCR) in June 2016, the Wassenaar Arrangement in December 2017, or the Australia Group in January 2018. During Manmohan Singh's visit to Paris in September 2008, the two countries entered into an agreement on nuclear energy cooperation following the waiver given by the International Atomic Energy Agency and the Nuclear Suppliers' Group removing impediments to civil nuclear cooperation with the international community. It was followed by a framework agreement signed in December 2010 for the construction of two third-generation EPR nuclear reactors (and eventually six) of 1650 megawatts each in Jaitapur (Maharashtra), 400 km south of Mumbai. The project has been bogged down by legal obstacles over liability clauses and techno-commercial considerations between the two managing enterprises, the French firm EDF and National Power Corporation India Limited (NPCIL), but its realization is still seen as a low-carbon energy solution to meet the significant cut in CO_2 emissions that the Indian government has committed to achieve. To this end, France and India also jointly launched the International Solar Alliance initiative in 2015 at the 21st Conference of Parties of the United Nations Framework Convention on Climate Change (COP21).

Handling Relations with the Smaller Countries

With no significant colonial legacy in the subcontinent, Paris entertained for a long time a modest involvement with India and Pakistan; the more so with the smaller countries. Sri Lanka (then Ceylon) was the first country with which France established diplomatic relations in September 1948. It was important to keep the benevolent neutrality of Ceylon to allow the passage of French ships and planes carrying soldiers *en route* to Indochina where the battle raged against the Viet Minh. Especially so as Nehru's India was not forthcoming unlike the anti-communist John Kotelawala, the Ceylonese Prime Minister from 1953 to 1956. The Ceylonese leaders adopted a more critical stance as France was mired in the struggle against the national liberation movement in Algeria. But once it was settled, the shared desire not to be firmly attached to any of the rival blocs eased political relations, which nevertheless remained without much substance. In the name of the principle of freedom of navigation on the high seas, France abstained from the vote at the United Nations General Assembly in 1972 on the resolution presented by Colombo and aimed at making the Indian Ocean a "zone of peace." Paris could not ignore the civil war in the island as a number of Tamil migrants looked for political asylum (more than 50,000 have settled in metropolitan France). The Liberation Tigers of Tamil Eelam was listed by the European Union as a terrorist organization in 2006. Paris's role was essentially restricted to highlight human rights violations and to assist humanitarian actors. For instance, as the conflict was ending, the French foreign minister, Bernard Kouchner, went to the island in April 2009 along with the British Foreign Minister, David Miliband, to unsuccessfully obtain Sri Lanka's agreement to a cease-fire with Tamil rebels as well as the protection of civilians trapped on the war zone.

It is in 1949, through the channel of the embassy in New Delhi and that of Nepal in London, that diplomatic relations were established between France and the Hindu kingdom. Relations only really took shape after King Mahendra's official visit to Paris in October 1966, followed in 1967 by the opening of embassies in Paris and Kathmandu, the last of the P-5 to do it. Friendly relations were thus established, Kathmandu appreciating the policy of national independence and the French attitude toward the Third World. François Mitterrand paid a one-day visit to Nepal in May 1983, the only one by a French president to this day. The context was favorable: The socialist government had committed itself to increasing aid to Third World countries to 0.7% of France's gross domestic product (GDP). On this occasion, he expressed his sympathy for Nepal's proposition floated by King Birendra to be declared "zone of Peace" and vowed to use France's good relations with Nepal's major neighboring countries to encourage them to respect its sovereignty.

As for Bangladesh, France's stand in the UN when the Indo-Pakistan conflict was discussed at the end of 1971 was generally appreciated in Dhaka. The newest of the South Asia states was officially recognized in February 1972 and supplied with food assistance over the following years. It remains that the relationship with the smaller countries is largely guided by financial assistance, bilateral and multilateral, technical cooperation on development projects, notably those looked after by the *Agence française de développement*, cultural and academic engagement, the promotion of French language, and also modest economic exchanges.

In Afghanistan, situated on the margins of South Asia, France, because of its links with the royal family, exerted a privileged influence during King Amanullah's time (1919–1929), mainly within the framework of cultural conventions concluded with this country in the educational field and archaeological research. Eclipsed by the Second World War, this influence was largely competed after the war by the United States and the USSR, without however totally disappearing by relying on a French-speaking elite and the revival of the cultural links in the 1960s.[29] In May 1968, Georges Pompidou was the first French head of government to go to Afghanistan on an official visit. If there was an irritant factor, given the tense relations between Kabul and Islamabad, it was the French arms sales to Pakistan. After the communist takeover in 1978, the bilateral relations were frozen, only resuming after the fall of the Taliban regime in 2001. French forces were deployed in Afghanistan from late 2001, as part of the International Security Assistance Force (ISAF), carried out by NATO on a United Nations mandate and as a component of the "Operation Enduring Freedom," under US command, as part of the War on Terror. At the height of their involvement, French forces numbered nearly 4,000 men. The combat forces were withdrawn at the end of 2012, and two years later, the last French soldiers left the country.[30] After the withdrawal of the military presence, assistance to support the reconstruction and the economic, political, and social development was pursued until the second fall of Kabul to the Taliban.

Conclusion

From a claimed equidistance during the Cold War years that saw France entertaining good relations with Pakistan, allied to the Western camp and enlivened by defense ties, and a benign neglect of non-aligned India, Paris, in the following period, engineered a shift leading to put the emphasis on the strategic partnership with New Delhi and witnessing unremarkable relations with Islamabad. Cooperating with New Delhi resulted from the pragmatic analysis that India possessed a dynamism missing in crisis-laden Pakistan and a capacity to produce a multiplier effect on French projection in the Indo-Pacific through the deepening of a privileged defense relationship at strategic and operational levels.[31] It also opens the door to multilateral security efforts to preserve freedom of navigation at sea and in the air in a high-growth zone, for which France would like other European nations to participate. The announcement of the AUKUS in September 2021, clubbing together Australia, the United States, and the United Kingdom in a trilateral security partnership, has temporarily compromised the strategic dialogue between Paris, New Delhi, and Canberra held for the first time a year earlier at foreign secretary level for better coordination in the face of China's troubling ambitions. But, given also India's traditional reluctance to alliances, this could be a further impetus to expand a trust-based relationship and their strategic autonomy, while possibly looking for synergies with other countries for a rules-based Indo-Pacific order. Both countries maintain separately strategic partnerships with Indonesia, Japan, Singapore, and Vietnam and could jointly take multistakeholder cooperative initiatives. From an Indian perspective, a strong partnership with France could potentially increase its bargaining power with other major powers. After Brexit, France also has ambitions to be the primus inter pares of the EU nations in relation to New Delhi. While relations with India have followed an upswing trajectory, those with Pakistan have reached a historic low in 2020 with the lenient attitude of the authorities vis-à-vis anti-France protests by the extremists of the Tehreek-i-Labbaik Pakistan over the issue of "blasphemous caricatures." Pakistan's National Assembly and Senate took over in passing unanimous resolutions claiming that sentiments of Muslims have been hurt after President Macron recalled that freedom of expression was not restricted in France by the offence of blasphemy. The Prime Minister of Pakistan, Imran Khan, personally slamming the French president for the same, added to the erosion of confidence. The bilateral relations with the South Asian rivals are following divergent trajectories.

Notes

1 These trading posts represented an area of 285 hectares, compared to about 500 square kilometers for the establishments. The "loges" were formally retroceded to India soon after independence.
2 For further discussion of Realism and South Asia, see Chapter 1.
3 For further discussion of Constructivism and South Asia, see Chapter 3.
4 For further discussion on Liberalism and Critical Theory and South Asia, see Chapters 2 and 4 respectively.
5 For further reading on the period, see, Gilles Boquérat, "France's Political Interaction with India through the Quai d'Orsay Archives (1947-1972), in *India in the Mirror of Foreign Diplomatic Archives*, eds. Max-Jean Zins and Gilles Boquérat (New Delhi: Manohar, 2004), 11–31; Boquerat, "Les relations avec le Pakistan au regard des documents diplomatiques français (1947–1970)," *Revue d'Histoire Diplomatique* 131, no. 1 (2017): 53–64.
6 Note from the Asia-Oceania Division, Ministry of Foreign Affairs, October 26, 1979, file no. 212INVA/2429.
7 France joined in 1961 the Aid-to-India Consortium formed under the patronage of the World Bank in 1958. It also became a member of the Aid-to-Pakistan the same year.
8 The fifth French establishment, Chandernagor (Chandannagar), had already been restored to India in 1949.
9 Arun Kumar, "Economic Cooperation between India and France Given a New Dimension by French PM Jacques Chirac's Visit," *India Today*, January 31, 1976, https://www.indiatoday.in/magazine/indiascope/story/19760131-economic-cooperation-between-india-and-france-given-a-new-dimension-by-french-pm-jacques-chiracs-visit-819558-2015-03-31.
10 Charles de Gaulle, *Mémoires d'espoir, Le renouveau 1958-1962/ L'effort 1962* (Paris: Plon, 1970), 281.
11 Dileep Padgaokur and Vaiju Naravane, "France to Offer N-plant Aid," *The Times of India*, January 29, 1989, 1.
12 See Ministry of Commerce and Industry, "Quarterly Fact Sheet: Fact Sheet on Foreign Direct Investment (FDI) from April, 2000 to March, 2021," Department for Promotion of Industry and International Trade, accessed March 6, 2022, https://dpiit.gov.in/sites/default/files/FDI_Factsheet_March%2C21.pdf. Economic ties have long been a weak link in the chain of bilateral exchanges. An enhancement is noticeable, leaving room for further improvement. Regarding FDI equity inflows from March 2000 to April 2021, France comes fourth among EU countries, after the Netherland, UK, and Germany. More than 600 French companies have a presence in India. In the opposite direction, there are 200 Indian businesses operating in France. France accounted for only 1.3% of Indian imports in 2019–2020 (German exports to India are twice more) and 1.6% of Indian exports.
13 Jaques Chirac, "Discours de M. Jacques Chirac, President de la Republique, sur les fondements culturels et economiques d'un nouveau partenariat etre la France et l'Inde a New Dehli le 25 Janvier 1998," Office of the President of France, January 25, 1998, https://www.elysee.fr/front/pdf/elysee-module-8874-fr.pdf.
14 Paris associated itself with Security Council resolution 1172 of June 6, as well as with the minutes of the G-8 foreign ministers' meeting on June 12, in order to ask India—and Pakistan—to adopt a certain number of measures aimed at preventing any escalation of tensions and a nuclear arms race.
15 Rakesh Sood, former ambassador to France (2011–2013), "How Delhi and Paris Became Friends," Observer Research Foundation, August 27, 2019, https://www.orfonline.org/research/how-delhi-and-paris-became-friends-54811/. France conducted its last nuclear explosion in January 1996, when the other nuclear powers—except China—had already declared a moratorium by 1992.
16 A seminar was organized around this theme in New Delhi in February 2000. It was attended by Hubert Védrine, French foreign minister of the socialist government of Lionel Jospin (1997–2002) who made a name for himself in describing the then uncontested American supremacy as "hyperpower." See, *India and France in a Multipolar World, proceedings of the seminar*, CERI/CSH/IIC (New Delhi, Manohar), 2001.

17 France has overseas departments (Réunion, Mayotte) and territories (Terres australes et antarctiques françaises) in the Indian Ocean.

18 Ministry of Defence (France), "White Paper on Defence and National Security, 2013," April 29, 2013, https://www.defense.gouv.fr/english/dgris/defence-policy/white-paper-2013/white-paper-2013.

19 Along with India, France became a full member of the Indian Ocean Rim Association in 2020 and participates in the Indian Ocean Naval Symposium, whereas India has an observer status in the Indian Ocean Commission. There is a French liaison officer at the Indian Navy's Information Fusion Center—Indian Ocean Region (IFC-IOR)—established at Gurugram.

20 Nicolas Sarkozy, "Commemoration of the Mumbai Attacks," Embassy of France, December 6, 2010. The joint statement issued on the occasion of the state visit of Emmanuel Macron in 2018 also called upon all countries to work toward disrupting terrorist networks and their financing channels, and halting cross-border movement of terrorists like al-Qaeda, Daesh/ISIS, Jaish-e-Mohammed, Hizbul Mujahideen, Lashkar-e-Tayabba, https://in.ambafrance.org/Commemoration-of-the-Mumbai.

21 In April 2018, France hosted the first edition of the "No money for terror" conference to discuss ways and means to strengthen the efficiency of action against terrorism financing. India is to hold the third edition.

22 See, for instance, "Les relations Franco-Pakistanaises Bilan mitigé de la visite de Mme Bhutto à Paris," *Le Monde*, November 6, 1994, https://www.lemonde.fr/archives/article/1994/11/06/les-relations-franco-pakistanaises-bilan-mitige-de-la-visite-de-mme-bhutto-a-paris_3850124_1819218.html.

23 Mohammed Merah, a Franco-Algerian terrorist, responsible for killings in south-west of France in 2012, had gone to Pakistan the year before.

24 Manu Pubby, "India Inks Mirage Deal, France says No to Pak," *The Indian Express*, April 5, 2010, http://archive.indianexpress.com/news/india-inks-mirage-deal-france-says-no-to-pak/600042/. In 2010, France suspended the sale of electronic equipment and missiles for the Chinese JF-17 fighter aircraft manufactured in Pakistan, officially for fear that the technology could fall into Chinese hands and doubts over Pakistan's ability to pay for the systems. India has also been insisting that any advanced technologies should be kept out of reach of Pakistan.

25 See, for instance, Rahul Bedi, "Rafale Delivery Underlines France's 'Below Radar' Role as Key Source of Weapons for India," *The Wire*, July 30, 2020, https://thewire.in/security/rafale-delivery-underlines-frances-below-radar-role-as-key-source-of-weapons-for-india.

26 Sushant Singh, "Behind Rafale Deal: Their 'Strategic' Role in Delivery of Nuclear Weapons," *The Indian Express*, September 18, 2016, https://indianexpress.com/article/india/india-news-india/behind-rafale-deal-their-strategic-role-in-delivery-of-nuclear-weapons-3036852/.

27 "Defence Ministry Seals Deal with BDL to Acquire 4,690 Anti-Tank Guided Missiles," *The Hindu*, March 19, 2021, https://www.thehindu.com/news/national/defence-ministry-seals-deal-with-bdl-to-acquire-4690-anti-tank-guided-missiles/article34107796.ece. In March 2021, the defense ministry signed a deal with state-run Bharat Dynamics Limited (BDL) for supply of 4,960 MILAN-2T ATGMs for the Indian Army.

28 The Pakistan Navy had earlier acquired two Agosta-70 class submarines. In May 2002, 11 French engineers of the Direction des Constructions Navales (DCN) supervising the construction of two vessels (the first one, built in France, was delivered in 1999) were killed in a bomb attack in Karachi.

29 King Mohammed Zahir Shah (1933–1973) and President Mohammed Daoud Khan (1973–1978) received an education in France, whereas Ahmad Shah Massoud did his secondary education at the French Esteqlal High school in Kabul.

30 In 13 years of military engagement in Afghanistan, the French army has suffered 89 deaths and 700 injuries.

31 See Ministry of the Armed Forces (France), "France's Defense Strategy in the Indo-Pacific, 2019," Daniel K. Inouye Asia-Pacific Center for Security Studies, accessed March 6, 2022, https://apcss.org/wp-content/uploads/2020/02/France-Defence_Strategy_in_the_Indo-Pacific_2019.pdf.

Bibliography

"Defence Ministry Seals Deal with BDL to Acquire 4,690 Anti-Tank Guided Missiles." *The Hindu*, March 19, 2021. https://www.thehindu.com/news/national/defence-ministry-seals-deal-with-bdl-to-acquire-4690-anti-tank-guided-missiles/article34107796.ece.

"Les relations Franco-Pakistanaises Bilan mitigé de la visite de Mme Bhutto a Paris." *Le Monde*, November 6, 1994. https://www.lemonde.fr/archives/article/1994/11/06/les-relations-franco-pakistanaises-bilan-mitige-de-la-visite-de-mme-bhutto-a-paris_3850124_1819218.html.

Bedi, Rahul. "Rafale Delivery Underlines France's 'Below Radar' Role as Key Source of Weapons for India." *The Wire*, July 30, 2020. https://thewire.in/security/rafale-delivery-underlines-frances-below-radar-role-as-key-source-of-weapons-for-india.

Boquérat, Gilles. "France's Political Interaction with India through the Quai d'Orsay Archives (1947-1972)." In *India in the Mirror of Foreign Diplomatic Archives*, edited by Max-Jean Zins and Gilles Boquérat, 11–31. New Delhi: Manohar, 2004.

Boquérat, Gilles. "Les Relations avec le Pakistan au regard des Documents Diplomatiques Français (1947-1970)." *Revue d'Histoire Diplomatique* 131, no. 1 (2017): 53–64.

Chirac, Jacques. "Discours de M. Jacques Chirac, Président de la Republique, sur les fondements culturels et economiques d'un nouveau partenariat entre la France et l'Inde à New Delhi le 25 Janvier 1998." Office of the President of France, January 25, 1998. https://www.elysee.fr/front/pdf/elysee-module-8874-fr.pdf.

De Gaulle, Charles. *Mémoires d'espoir, Le Renouveau 1958–1962/L'effort 1962*. Paris: Plon, 1970.

India & France in a Multipolar World: Proceedings of the Seminar. New Delhi: Manohar, 2001.

Kumar, Arun. "Economic Cooperation between India and France Given a New Dimension by French PM Jacques Chirac's Visit." *India Today*, January 31, 1976. https://www.indiatoday.in/magazine/indiascope/story/19760131-economic-cooperation-between-india-and-france-given-a-new-dimension-by-french-pm-jacques-chiracs-visit-819558-2015-03-31.

Ministry of Commerce and Industry (India). "Quarterly Fact Sheet: Fact Sheet on Foreign Direct Investment (FDI) from April, 2000 to March, 2021." Department for Promotion of Industry and International Trade. Accessed March 6, 2022. https://dpiit.gov.in/sites/default/files/FDI_Factsheet_March%2C21.pdf.

Ministry of Defence (France). "White Paper on Defence and National Security, 2013." April 29, 2013. https://www.defense.gouv.fr/english/dgris/defence-policy/white-paper-2013/white-paper-2013.

Ministry of Foreign Affairs (France) Asia-Pacific Division – File No. 212INVA/2429. Ministry of Foreign Affairs, Diplomatic Archives.

Ministry of the Armed Forces (France). "France's Defense Strategy in the Indo-Pacific, 2019." Daniel K. Inouye Asia-Pacific Center for Security Studies. Accessed March 6, 2022. https://apcss.org/wp-content/uploads/2020/02/France-Defence_Strategy_in_the_Indo-Pacific_2019.pdf.

Padgaonkar, Dileep, and Vaiju Naravane. "France to Offer N-plant Aid." *The Times of India*, January 29, 1989.

Pubby, Manu. "India Inks Mirage Deal, France says No to Pak." *The Indian Express*, April 5, 2010. http://archive.indianexpress.com/news/india-inks-mirage-deal-france-says-no-to-pak/600042/.

Sarkozy, Nicolas. "Commemoration of the Mumbai Attacks." Embassy of France in India, December 6, 2010. https://in.ambafrance.org/Commemoration-of-the-Mumbai.

Singh, Sushant. "Behind Rafale Deal: Their 'Strategic' Role in Delivery of Nuclear Weapons." *The Indian Express*, September 18, 2016. https://indianexpress.com/article/india/india-news-india/behind-rafale-deal-their-strategic-role-in-delivery-of-nuclear-weapons-3036852/.

Sood, Rakesh. "How Delhi and Paris Became Friends." Observer Research Foundation, August 27, 2019. https://www.orfonline.org/research/how-delhi-and-paris-became-friends-54811/.

29

GERMANY'S SOUTH ASIA POLICY

Christian Wagner

Germany and South Asia in Historical Perspective

Relations between German scholars and the Indian subcontinent started long before the first modern German state was established in 1871. The first contacts go back to the early 16th century when representatives of German business houses were accompanying Vasco da Gama on his second journey to India. Missionary societies from Germany have been active in India since the early 18th century.[1] Economic relations flourished again in the 19th century when German exporters became the second largest trading partner for British India. The beginning of political relations dates back to 1886 when the first German consulate general opened in Calcutta.[2]

But the main cultural linkages that resonate until today were established in the early 19th century when German scholars systematized the languages of the subcontinent and established the field of Indology as a separate academic discipline. The Goethe-Institutes in India, which are the official cultural institutions of the Federal Republic of Germany/West Germany (FRG), are also housed in buildings named after Max Mueller, a famous German scholar at the University of Oxford in the 19th century, who never visited the Indian subcontinent.

The cultural linkages are also important in Germany's relations with other South Asian countries. Muhammad Iqbal, Pakistan's most famous poet and philosopher, studied in Heidelberg in the early 20th century, and Annemarie Schimmel, a highly reputed scholar of Islamic studies, has always been a prominent personality in Pakistan. In the interwar period between 1918 and 1939, the German government supported the modernization in Afghanistan in the educational field.

There have been long historical and cultural linkages between the German cultural sphere and the Indian subcontinent long before the modern nation states were established in Europe and South Asia. But these relations never translated into a special focus toward South Asia, neither after the creation of the FRG and the German Democratic Republic/East Germany (GDR) in 1949 nor after the reunification in 1990.

In the 1950s and 1960s, the FRG was integrated into the North Atlantic Treaty Organisation (NATO) and the emerging European community. The GDR saw its integration into the Warsaw Pact and its institutions. Because of their status, the two Germanys only had limited foreign policy options. But there was one area in which the West German government

DOI: 10.4324/9781003246626-33

395

under Chancellor Adenauer followed an independent foreign policy agenda. The preamble of the Basic Law of the FRG included the claim for the unification of Germany. Hence, it became important for the West German government that the GDR should not officially be recognized by other countries. The main point was the undemocratic character of the GDR, which was ruled by the Socialist Unity Party of Germany (SED). The so-called Hallstein-Doctrine became a leading principle of West Germany's foreign policy until 1969. It ended after Chancellor Willy Brandt and his coalition of the Social Democrats and the Liberal party took office in 1969. His *Ostpolitik* that led to treaties with the Soviet Union (1970), the GDR (1972), and other Eastern European countries ended the Hallstein-Doctrine. The question of recognition was also an important aspect in the early phases of West Germany's relations with South Asian countries.[3]

From Asia-Pacific to the Indo-Pacific: South Asia in Germany's Foreign Policy Concepts after 1990

The unification of Germany in October 1990 also brought new room for maneuver in international affairs. In the process of globalization, West German companies had already intensified its relations with Asia since the 1980s, especially with the rising economies in East and Southeast Asia.

The first Asia concept of the German government in 1993 highlighted the economic and political importance of East and Southeast Asia.[4] The concept helped to raise the awareness of Asia's importance for Germany's economic development. In the era of globalization, the focus was primarily on issues related to trade and economic development. The concept identified the main priority areas such as economy, scientific and technological cooperation, environment, and others. Security policy was only shortly mentioned at the end. The main instruments were dialogue formats by which European experiences like the EU and confidence-building measures (CBMs) of the Conference on Security and Co-operation (CSCE) could be promoted. South Asia was mainly represented by India and its growth potential after the economic liberalization of 1991.

The low political consideration for South Asia was also linked to developments in the academic sector. More and more scholars in the field of China and Southeast Asia studies had turned to social sciences in the 1980s. This increased the linkages between the academic world, political decision-makers, and the business community.[5] But similar developments did not take place in the field of South Asian Studies in Germany. Most chairs in Indology focused on their classical agenda; only in some universities, chairs for Modern Indology were established with a focus on modern languages and literature. Modern South Asian studies at that time were mainly done at the South Asia Institute at the University of Heidelberg and individual scholars at other universities.[6]

The Asia concept of the German Foreign Office of 2002 was formulated in the aftermath of the attacks of September 11, 2001, and the Western intervention in Afghanistan.[7] Developments in Asia were now seen in a different light. First, the new concept divided Asia into three sub-regions: East, Southeast, and South Asia. This differentiation recognized the different political and economic developments in the respective sub-regions. Second, security issues gained a much greater importance compared to 1993. This was not only linked to the developments in Afghanistan but also to the conflict between India and Pakistan and the civil wars in Sri Lanka and Nepal.

The central concerns of the South Asia concept were democracy, rule of law and human rights, peace and stability, Germany's economic interests, and environmental protection.[8]

In the following years, the German government supported conflict resolution and peace processes by various means. In Afghanistan, Germany supported the military intervention and became an important partner in the process of state-building. In Nepal and Sri Lanka, Germany supported multilateral peace approaches but also initiatives by non-governmental organizations (NGOs) for reconciliation. In bilateral relations, India remained Germany's top priority in South Asia.[9]

Germany's relations with South Asia intensified during the 2000s, but the region still received lesser political attention compared to East and Southeast Asia. China, East Asia, and the Association of South East Asians Nations (ASEAN) offered better economic opportunities for German industry, so that political relations with these regions expanded in a much larger way than with South Asia.

The Indo-Pacific guidelines of September 2020 opened a new chapter in Germany's relations with Asia.[10] The guidelines reflected the rise of China and its repercussions in Europe and Germany. So far China had predominantly been seen as an economic opportunity. But in early 2019, a report of the Federation of German Industries highlighted the growing concerns of German companies in China. In March 2019, the EU qualified China as a cooperation and negotiating partner, an economic competitor, and a systemic rival.[11] Hence, the guidelines signal an interesting geopolitical and geo-economic shift in Germany's foreign policy. So far, German governments had traditionally been reluctant to formulate its strategic interests. In contrast to this, the guidelines spelled out the geopolitical interests "peace and security," "diversifying and deepening relations," and "neither unipolar nor bipolar" structures. In the field of geo-economics, "open shipping routes," "open markets and free trade," and "digital transformation and connectivity" are identified as main interests, followed by the issues "protecting our planet" and "access to fact-based information."[12]

In continuation of previous concepts, the guidelines have a strong emphasis on regional organizations, with ASEAN at the center. South Asia is mentioned only four times; the South Asian Association for Regional Cooperation (SAARC) is mentioned only once. But the guidelines underline again India's strategic role for Germany's Indo-Pacific policy. It seems that South Asia as a region is losing further interest in Germany's foreign policy. The weak performance of SAARC and the lack of regional economic collaboration will shift the foreign policy focus to the respective bilateral relationships.

Bilateral Relations

India

India was among the first countries to recognize West Germany in March 1951. But in the beginning, the West German government of Chancellor Adenauer was critical about India. Jawaharlal Nehru, India's first prime minister, had strong rhetoric of "anti-imperialism," "anti-colonialism," and "anti-Americanism." His ideas of a reunited and de-militarized Germany were not acceptable for Adenauer, and the socialist tendencies of his government were seen in Bonn at least as indirect support for the Soviet Union.[13] Both countries had also diverging views on global and regional crises. With regard to Goa, the West German government supported Portugal, which was also a member of the NATO.[14] In Hungary, India was not willing to follow the Western protests against the intervention of the Soviet Union during the rebellion in 1956.

Relations between the FRG and India were complicated by two issues: The question of Germany's recognition and the relations between India and Pakistan. First, despite all differences, the Adenauer government saw India as an important international player with regard to the question of recognition. The two German states were recognized within their respective ideological blocs. But the Hallstein-Doctrine of 1955 was of special importance with regard to the larger international community. Here, India played an important role.

Nehru aimed for an international order for the newly independent countries in Africa and Asia beyond the bloc confrontation between the Soviet Union and the USA. Nehru, together with Nasser, Tito, and Sukarno, became one of the main architects of the Non-Aligned Movement (NAM) that was established in 1961 in Belgrade. The FRG was aware of India being an important voice in the NAM that could also influence the view of other countries in the question of recognition of Germany.[15]

The second issue was the position of the FRG vis-à-vis India's conflict with Pakistan over Kashmir. In order to achieve India's support on the question of recognition, the FRG should have been sympathetic with India's position vis-à-vis its conflict Pakistan. But Pakistan became a pro-Western ally when it became a founding member of Central Treaty Organisation (CENTO) in 1955. The Pakistan government received arms supplies from the United States and its western partners. The question of arms sales to Pakistan became a challenge for West Germany with regard to its relations with India and the issue of recognition. The Indian government was aware of West Germany's dilemma. In summer 1968, Prime Minister Indira Gandhi made it clear that she would recognize the GDR immediately should American tanks from Germany find their way to Pakistan.[16]

Even if India and the FRG would not necessarily agree on many international issues in the Cold War period, economic cooperation and development assistance laid the foundation for their bilateral relations. For India, West Germany became a much more attractive trading partner compared to the GDR.[17] The new instrument of development cooperation that started with India in 1958 was also a useful mechanism to open the Indian market for West German business. Important West German investments in India were for instance in modern industries like the steel plant in Rourkela and in higher education like in Indian Institute of Technology (IIT) in Madras. The FRG became one of India's most important capital investors, second only to the United States.[18] Nehru was also aware that the FRG was the more important economic partner to support India's economic modernization and development. At the summit in Brioni in 1956 with Tito and Nasser, Nehru prevented a declaration on the existence of two German states, which could have had a signaling effect for other countries.[19]

The GDR was in a weaker position. It had opened its first trade mission in India in 1954. But its newly established socialist planned economy faced many difficulties to comply with trade commitments toward other countries. In the case of India, trade figures were exaggerated, which also caused criticism in parliament. The trade mission in Bombay closed down; another one that was planned for Madras was never opened.[20] The GDR was a more active partner in the field of culture. Sometimes, East Germany also had the upper hand in the competition with West Germany. For instance in 1959, when GDR Prime Minister Grotewohl became the first German head of government to visit India.[21] But in their talks, Nehru declined Grotewohl's attempts to recognize the GDR or even to discuss the issue at the level of foreign ministers.[22]

New Delhi recognized the GDR only on October 8, 1972, in consultation with the FRG.[23] This development became possible after the new treaties between Bonn and East Berlin had come into effect, which were the outcome of Chancellor Willy Brandt's new *Ostpolitik*. After the question of recognition was no longer relevant, the political interest of West Germany toward India remained limited and was characterized until the end of the Cold War as "benign neglect."[24]

The end of the Cold War, the reunification of Germany, and India's economic reforms opened a new chapter in their bilateral relationship. India invited foreign direct investments, promoted technology transfer, and expanded its export industries in order to increase growth and to integrate into the global economy. Germany became India's most important trading partner within the EU. The Indian government started a special program for the German *Mittelstand* in order to attract technology transfer from mid-size companies, some of which are global technological champions. Already in 1956, the Indo-German Chamber of Commerce (IGCC) was set up in Mumbai. Today it is the largest chamber of commerce of German industries abroad. India twice was a partner country of the Hannover industrial fair, in 2006 and 2015, which signaled the country's high economic potential for German companies. Since the 1990s, both countries started to expand their academic and scientific cooperation, which today is one of the most important pillars. All major German universities and research institutions have opened programs with counterparts in India. One outcome was an increasing number of Indian students studying at German universities, which was over 25,000 in 2019/20.[25]

Development cooperation remained another important pillar in the bilateral relationship. India is the largest recipient of German official development assistance (ODA). In 2019, Germany gave more than 1.6 billion Euros to India for development cooperation. More than 90% was assigned to financial collaboration.[26] The focus of technical cooperation is now to support the transformation of India's economy in order to meet the Sustainable Development Goals (SDG) in 2030.

India also wanted a stronger engagement of Germany in the modernization of its armed forces. But for a long time, Germany remained a reluctant partner in the field of arms exports to India. In the inter-governmental consultations (IGC) of 2019, both sides agreed to deepen their security cooperation and to facilitate military exports to India.[27] This would also strengthen the Make in India initiative of the Modi government. But the future of the security cooperation between the two countries will depend on their respective domestic coalitions.

Both countries have also intensified their political cooperation since the 1990s. In May 2000, Germany and India signed a strategic partnership agreement. One common interest was to strengthen the multilateral system. India is an important player in the UN as a leading voice of the Global South and for the provision of peacekeeping forces. Germany is one of the most important donors of the UN. In the mid-2000s, both countries, together with Japan and Brazil, formed the Group of Four (G4) in order to push reforms in the UN including a new structure of the Security Council. The German government applied for membership in the International Solar Alliance (ISA) that was established by India and France in 2015. India on the other hand joined the Alliance for Multilateralism that was launched by Germany and France in 2019. In 2011, India and Germany agreed to establish IGC, which are undertaken on a biannual basis at cabinet level.[28] This also underlined the new quality of the bilateral relationship. The Indo-Pacific guidelines of 2020 have underlined again India's strategic role in Germany's foreign policy. India is regarded as a partner with whom Germany shares common values. This will be the basis to enhance the political and economic cooperation between the two countries.

There are also contentious areas in the bilateral relationship. The German government has raised its concerns about the increasing restrictions on NGOs in India. Moreover, Chancellor Merkel has also criticized the human rights situation in Jammu & Kashmir during the IGC in November 2019 in Delhi.

Pakistan

The relations of East and West Germany with Pakistan were very different after 1949. Because of its conflict with India over Kashmir, Pakistan established close military links with the United States, joined the South East Asia Treaty Organisation (SEATO) in 1954 and

CENTO in 1955. Because of this pro-Western orientation, the FRG was closer to Pakistan than the GDR. But Pakistan was also looking for arms sales from the FRG. This created a dilemma for West Germany because arms sales to Pakistan could have endangered its relations with India, which was a more important international partner with regard to the question of recognition. There have been some uncoordinated arms supplies to Pakistan in this period, which fortunately did not affect the relations of the FRG with India.[29] In 1961, the FRG also started development cooperation with Pakistan. For the GDR, it was more difficult to establish links with Pakistan. First because of Pakistan's pro-Western stance and secondly because the GDR supported the position of the Soviet Union on Kashmir which was in line with India.[30]

After 1990, Germany developed good relations with a focus on trade and development cooperation.[31] Germany belongs to Pakistan's top global trading partners and is the most important one in the European Union (EU). Pakistan is a major exporter of textiles and received special privileges for the European market with the Generalised Scheme of Preferences (GSP) Plus Status in 2014. Germany supported the initiative for the diversification of Pakistan's export industry.[32]

Collaboration in science and technology was also expanded. In 2017, the number of students from Pakistan enrolled at German universities rose to more than 5,000.[33] A German-Pakistan Chamber of Commerce and Industry (GPCCI) was set up to further increase economic ties between the two countries.[34] German truck manufacturers like MAN have used the economic opportunities of the growing Chinese investment under the China Pakistan Economic Corridor (CPEC) to set up new plants in Pakistan.[35]

In the years 2019 and 2020, Pakistan received a total of 109.1 million Euros of ODA. The main focus of German projects was in the fields of good governance, energy, and sustainable economic development.[36] The amount was significantly smaller than German contributions to India and Afghanistan. This also reflected the lower priority of Pakistan in Germany's foreign policy vis-à-vis the region.

The political cooperation with Pakistan at the international level remained limited compared to India. Pakistan opposed, together with countries like Italy and others, the G4 for reforming the United Nations. Germany was propagating bilateral dialogue between Pakistan and India, whereas Pakistan always aimed for a solution in the context of the UN resolutions.

Germany has also limited military cooperation with Pakistan. Arms exports are restricted because of Pakistan's conflict with India. The main military exports are engines for the modernization of the navy.[37] Germany and Pakistan have also intensified their cooperation in the fight against terrorism. In the mid-2000s, Islamists from Germany received military training in the tribal areas in Pakistan. Some of them were part of the Islamic Jihad Union and formed the so-called Sauerland-Gruppe, which was arrested in Germany before they could commit attacks.[38] Another sensitive area was the activities of A.Q. Khan, the father of Pakistan's nuclear bomb. He had studied in Berlin in 1961 before he moved to the Netherlands. Later his network also established linkages to German companies that provided dual-use equipment to Pakistan. In 2005, a German businessman was convicted because of his illegal dealings with the Khan network.[39]

Afghanistan

Relations with Afghanistan date back to 1915, when a German expedition reached Kabul and tried to convince the Emir to declare war against Russia and Great Britain. The Emir refused the idea, but the contacts between the two countries continued in the inter-war period with a focus on economic relations and education. In 1922, 40 Afghans were sent on a scholarship to Germany and an Afghan cultural institute was opened in Munich. In 1923, Germany opened a mission in Kabul, followed by a German-speaking school in 1924.[40]

The support of the Weimar Republic for the modernization of Afghanistan laid the basis for the bilateral relationship after the 1950s. The FRG supported higher education in Afghanistan and became one of Afghanistan's most important development donors in the 1970s.

It was only after the coup of April 1978 that the GDR gained a stronger role in Afghanistan. The GDR had been officially recognized in 1973, but East Berlin opened its first embassy in Kabul only in 1978.[41] After the Soviet invasion in 1979, the FRG stopped its development cooperation with Afghanistan. Because of its pro-Soviet government, Afghanistan developed closer links with the GDR during the 1980s.

After the attacks of 9/11, Germany also contributed troops to the International Security Assistance Force (ISAF). With the Petersberg Conference in December 2001, Germany signaled its long-term commitment for the reconstruction of Afghanistan. Until the withdrawal of the international troops in August 2021, Germany was one of the most important donors in Afghanistan. Germany supported capacity building of the Afghan police force, the education of girls and women, and the promotion of small and medium enterprises.

Germany's 20 years engagement in Afghanistan cost more than 17.3 billion Euros.[42] The largest part of more than 12.3 billion Euros was spent on ISAF, Operation Enduring Freedom (OEF), and the Resolute Support Mission (RSM). Fifty-nine German soldiers lost their lives, which was the biggest loss for the armed forces in foreign missions so far.

The takeover of the Taliban in August 2021 marked a watershed in the bilateral relationship. The Taliban government has made it clear that it wants to continue the development cooperation with Germany and other western donors. But it remains to be seen in how far Germany in cooperation with its western partners will be able to formulate a common policy toward the new regime.

Sri Lanka

Relations between West Germany and Ceylon/Sri Lanka started in 1953 when diplomatic ties were established. The relations were marred when the government of the socialist Sri Lanka Freedom Party (SLFP) under Prime Minister Sirimavo Bandaranaike recognized the GDR in 1970.[43] After the unification of Germany, the bilateral relationship was shaped by trade, tourism, and development cooperation. But the civil war in Sri Lanka and the growing number of Tamil refugees also affected the bilateral relationship since the 1990s. The Sri Lanka Tamil community is estimated to have around 50,000 members in Germany. Before the Liberation Tigers of Tamil Eelam (LTTE) were listed as a terrorist organization by the EU in 2006, the group had opened an office in Germany in order to support their armed struggle. After the listing, several LTTE members were arrested and convicted in Germany for membership in a foreign terrorist organization and other crimes. Germany supported international initiatives by the EU and Norway for a political solution. German NGOs like the Berghof-Foundation started various initiatives for peace-building. The collapse of the peace process both by the LTTE and the government after 2006 also curtailed the activities of international NGOs.[44]

After the end of the civil war in 2009, the bilateral relationship focused again on economic and development cooperation. Germany also supported the process of reconciliation after the civil war and has together with the EU voiced its concerns over the deterioration of human rights and the restrictions for civil society both in bilateral relations but also in the

Human Rights Council of the UN. The Indo-Pacific guidelines of 2020 underlined again the support for NGOs and human rights mechanisms also in Sri Lanka.[45]

Relations with Bangladesh and Nepal

West Germany and Nepal started their diplomatic relations in 1958. Development cooperation was the main area, with a focus on health, energy, and sustainable development. But Germany has also supported programs for democracy and reconciliation after the end of the civil war in 2006. Bilateral trade was around 50 million Euros in 2020. The first German-Nepal Business Forum was established in 2019 in Kathmandu in order to improve economic ties.[46] In 2020, the Ministry for Economic Cooperation and Development announced a new reform plan for 2030. One of its consequences is that development cooperation with Nepal, still among the least developed countries, will be stopped. This decision has led to various protests by civil society organizations in Germany.

West Germany was among the first European countries to recognize the new state of Bangladesh in 1972. In recent years, Bangladesh saw better social and economic development than India or Pakistan and became a middle income country in 2021.[47] Germany and the EU are main markets for Bangladesh's textile exports. But Germany's attention toward domestic development in the third largest country of South Asia is generally low.[48] The country only came into the limelight after the collapse of the Rana Plaza complex in 2013, which also affected German textile manufacturers, after major terrorist attacks like in 2016, or after the Rohingya crisis in Myanmar in 2017. But Bangladesh is regarded as an important player in the region. Berlin and Dhaka share a strong commitment for regional cooperation. It was ultimately the initiative of Bangladesh in the late 1970s that led to the creation of SAARC. Hence, it is not astonishing that the Indo-Pacific guidelines have identified the Bay of Bengal Initiative for Multi-Sectoral Technical and Economic Cooperation (BIMSTEC) as an important area for Germany's future engagement.[49]

The Regional Level

West Germany has always been an ardent supporter of regional cooperation because of its own positive experiences with the process of European integration. With its growing economic linkages to East and Southeast Asia, West German governments have also fostered development of regional organizations in Asia like the ASEAN. There were also great hopes for closer regional collaboration when SAARC was established in 1985. But in contrast to ASEAN, SAARC has never been able to overcome the fundamental differences among its members or to become a stable platform for CBMs. The India-Pakistan rivalry hampered the process of collaboration. Intra-regional trade remained low, and South Asia continued to be one of the least integrated regions in global comparison.

The EU started some initiatives for closer linkages with SAARC but they remained unsuccessful. Germany's interest to strengthen regional cooperation in South Asia was promoted by programs and initiatives of the different political party foundations. Since the 1990s, the Konrad Adenauer Foundation, the Friedrich Ebert Foundation, the Friedrich Naumann Foundation, and others have supported various regional initiatives between think-tanks, civil society organizations, media, parties, trade unions, and others in order to foster regional cooperation. The foundations are independent institutions but they are closely linked to the political parties that are represented in the German parliament. The budgets and programs

Prospects for Germany's South Asia Policy between the Asia-Pacific and the Indo-Pacific

of the foundations are funded mainly from the Ministry for Economic Cooperation and Development (BMZ) but also from the Foreign office and other ministries.

South Asia, understood as the SAARC region, never had a prominent role in Germany's foreign policy, especially when compared with East and Southeast Asia. Several reasons contributed to this development. First, the FRG and the GDR only had limited sovereignty between 1949 and 1990. Except for a few areas, their foreign policies were strongly influenced by Washington and Moscow. Second, Germany's foreign policy after 1990 had a strong focus on economics rather than on strategic issues. Hence, the focus in Asia was on East Asia with Japan, South Korea, and China and on Southeast Asia with its emerging economies and the success of ASEAN. Despite impressive growth rates of individual countries like India and Bangladesh, South Asia remained one of the least integrated regions economically, with little attraction for Germany.

The Indo-Pacific guidelines of 2020 have increased the relevance of the region, but it remains to be seen whether and to what extent South Asia will benefit from it or only individual countries like India. The guidelines highlight again Germany's strong commitment for regionalism, but most regional organizations, except for ASEAN, show only a weak performance. The new architecture of the Indo-Pacific seems to consist of different mini-lateral networks between middle powers. On the one hand, this will open new opportunities for collaboration between Germany and traditional partners like India. On the other hand, this may further weaken traditional instruments like regional cooperation.

At the same time, the idea of South Asia also seems to be undergoing far-reaching changes. Within the regional setup of SAARC, the de-coupling of India-Pakistan relations since 2016, the growing role of China especially in the aftermath of the pandemic, the continuing weakness of SAARC, and the emergence of new regional institutions like BIMSTEC foster a new geopolitical and geo-economic understanding of the region.[50] The emerging systemic rivalry between China and the US in the Indo-Pacific will also resonate in South Asia and will reinforce these developments. Hence, Germany's policy toward the countries of South Asia will continue to be shaped by larger geostrategic and geo-economic considerations, now of the Indo-Pacific, rather than by the characteristics of this sub-region.

Notes

1 Heike Liebau, *Die Quellen der Dänisch-Halleschen Mission in Tranquebar in deutschen Archiven. Ihre Bedeutung für die Indienforschung* (Berlin: Verlag das Arabische Buch, 1993); Erika Pabst and Thomas Müller-Bahlke, eds., *Quellenbestände der Indienmission 1700–1918 in Archiven des deutschsprachigen Raums* (Tübingen: Niemeyer, 2005).

2 Amit Das Gupta, *Handel, Hilfe, Hallstein-Doktrin. Die bundesdeutsche Südasienpolitik unter Adenauer und Erhard 1949 bis 1966* (Husum: Matthiesen-Verlag, 2004), 27.

3 Das Gupta, *Handel, Hilfe, Hallstein-Doktrin*, 186–192.

4 Deutscher Bundestag, *Asien-Konzept der Bundesregierung* (Berlin, 1993), accessed October 12, 2021, https://dip.bundestag.de/drucksache/asien-konzept-der-bundesregierung/124602.

5 Thomas Scharping, *Die sozialwissenschaftliche China-Forschung: Rückblick und Ausblick. Social Science Research on China: Review and Perspectives* (Cologne: China Studies Online, 2000). (Working papers on Chinese Politics, Economy and Society, No. 1).

6 Christian Wagner, *Die Bedeutung Südasiens in der Forschungs- und Universitätslandschaft der Bundesrepublik Deutschland: Eine Bestandsaufnahme* (Hamburg: Institut für Asienkunde, 2001).

7 Auswärtiges Amt, *Aufgaben der deutschen Außenpolitik. Südasien am Beginn des 21. Jahrhunderts* (Berlin, 2002) (mimeographed paper).

8 Auswärtiges Amt, *Aufgaben der deutschen Außenpolitik,* 6–11.

9 Auswärtiges Amt, *Aufgaben der deutschen Außenpolitik,* 8.

10 The Federal Government, *Policy Guidelines for the Indo-Pacific, Germany – Europe – Asia. Shaping the 21st Century together* (Berlin, 2020), accessed October 12, 2021, https://www.auswaertiges-amt. de/en/aussenpolitik/regionaleschwerpunkte/asien/german-government-policy-guidelines-indo-pacific/2380510.

11 European Commission, High Representative of the Union for Foreign Affairs and Security Policy, *EU-China – A Strategic Outlook*, Strasbourg, March 12, 2019, accessed October 12, 2021, https://ec. europa.eu/info/sites/default/files/communication-eu-china-a-strategic-outlook.pdf.

12 Federal Government, *Policy Guidelines*, 9–10.

13 Das Gupta, *Handel, Hilfe, Hallstein-Doktrin*, 89.

14 Das Gupta, *Handel, Hilfe, Hallstein-Doktrin*, 93.

15 Das Gupta, *Handel, Hilfe, Hallstein-Doktrin*, 199.

16 Das Gupta, *Handel, Hilfe, Hallstein-Doktrin*, 457.

17 Johannes H. Voigt, "Deutsch-indische Beziehungen im 20. Jahrhundert," *Indien in der Gegenwart (Indian Council for Cultural Relations)* 4, no. 4 (1999): 14.

18 Johannes H. Voigt, "Anerkennung oder Nicht-Anerkennung – das war die Frage Indien im deutsch-deutschen Kalten Krieg 1952-1972," in *Wechselwirkungen*, ed. Universität Stuttgart (Universität Stuttgart: Eigenverlag, 2001), 86.

19 Das Gupta, *Handel, Hilfe, Hallstein-Doktrin*, 460.

20 Das Gupta, *Handel, Hilfe, Hallstein-Doktrin*, 187.

21 Voigt, "Anerkennung oder Nicht-Anerkennung," 74.

22 Johannes H. Voigt, *Die Indienpolitik der DDR: von den Anfängen bis zur Anerkennung (1952–1972)* (Köln Weimar: Böhlau, 2008), 283–287.

23 Das Gupta, *Handel, Hilfe, Hallstein-Doktrin*, 457.

24 Dietmar Rothermund, "Die deutsch-indischen Beziehungen," in *Indien. Kultur, Geschichte, Politik, Wirtschaft, Umwelt. Eine Handbuch*, ed. Dietmar Rothermund (München: C.H. Beck, 1995), 474.

25 DAAD India, *Germany Welcomes Record Number of Indian Students*, accessed October 12, 2021, https://www.daad.in/en/2020/10/13/germany-welcomes-record-number-of-indian-students/#: ~:text=Die%20neuesten%20Zahlen%20veröffentlicht%20von,stiegen%20 um%204,3%25%20auf% 20411%2C601.

26 Federal Ministry for Economic Cooperation and Development, *India. An Important Partner in International Cooperation* (Berlin, 2021), accessed October 12, 2021, https://www.bmz.de/en/ countries/india.

27 Government of India, Ministry of External Affairs, *Joint Statement during the Visit of Chancellor of Germany to India*, November 1, 2019, accessed October 12, 2021, https://mea.gov.in/bilateral-documents.htm?dtl/31991/Joint+Statement+during+the+visit+of+Chancellor+of+Germany+ to+India.

28 The IGC at cabinet level are chaired by the German Chancellor and the Prime Minister of India.

29 Das Gupta, *Handel, Hilfe, Hallstein-Doktrin*, 455–456.

30 Alexander Benatar, "Die Beziehungen Zwischen Pakistan und der DDR bis 1973," accessed October 12, 2021, https://www.projekt-mida.de/reflexicon/die-beziehungen-zwischen-pakistan-und-der-ddr-bis-1973/.

31 Alfred Vestring, "Zum Stand der Deutsch-Pakistanischen Beziehungen," in *Pakistan. Zweite Heidelberger Südasiengespräche*, eds. Dieter Conrad and Wolfgang-Peter Zingel (Stuttgart: Franz Steiner Verlag, 1992) 150–153; Erich Riedler, "Relations between Germany and Pakistan," *Pakistan Horizon* 48, no. 4 (1995): 7–14.

32 Talat Mahmood, *Assessment of German-Pakistani Relations in Trade, Investment and Strategic Cooperation* (Berlin: WZB Social Science Center, 2014) (Discussion Paper No. 4).

33 Hassan Khan, "Pak-German Ties on an Upward Trajectory," *The Daily Times*, February, 21, 2017, accessed February, 22, 2017, http://dailytimes.com.pk/opinion/21-Feb-17/pak-german-ties-on-an-upward-trajectory.

34 "Businessmen Asked to Enhance Trade with Germany," *The Tribune*, August 10, 2017, accessed August 11, 2017, https://tribune.com.pk/story/1477828/businessmen-asked-enhance-trade-germany/.

35 Farhan Zaheer, "German Truck Maker MAN SE to Set Up Assembly Plant in Pakistan," *The Tribune*, March 2, accessed March 3, 2017, https://tribune.com.pk/story/1343204/german-truck-maker-man-se-set-assembly-plant-pakistan/.

36 Federal Ministry for Economic Cooperation and Development, *Pakistan. Influential Partner Country in South Asia* (Berlin 2021), accessed October 12, 2021, https://www.bmz.de/en/countries/pakistan.

37 Bonn International Center for Conversion (BICC), *Länderinformation Pakistan* (Bonn: 2021), 8.

38 Guido Steinberg, *German Jihad. On the Internationalization of Islamist Terrorism* (New York: Columbia University Press, 2013).

39 "German Found Guilty of Supplying Nuke Weapons Tech to Pakistan," Outlook, November 24, 2005, accessed October 12, 2021, https://www.outlookindia.com/newswire/story/german-found-guilty-of-supplying-nuke-weapons-tech-to-pakistan/337366.

40 Willi A. Boelcke, "Deutschlands Politische und Wirtschaftliche Beziehungen zu Afghanistan bis zum Zweiten Weltkrieg," *Tradition: Zeitschrift für Firmengeschichte und Unternehmerbiographie* 14, no. 3/4 (Juli 1969): 153–188; Ernst-Albrecht von Renesse, "Freundschaft Verpflichtet. Hundert Jahre Deutsch-Afghanische Beziehungen," in *Freundschaft verpflichtet*, ed. Evangelische Akademie Villigst, XXIX. Afghanistan-Tagung (Villigst: Evangelische Akademie, 2015), 2–17.

41 Thomas Ruttig, "Deutsch-Afghanische und DDR-Afghanische Beziehungen," October 22, 2016, accessed October 12, 2021, https://thruttig.wordpress.com/2016/10/22/deutsch-afghanische-und-ddr-afghanische-beziehungen/.

42 "Afghanistan-Einsatz Kostete Mehr als 17,3 Milliarden Euro," *ZEIT Online*, 5, October, 2021, accessed October 12, 2021, https://www.zeit.de/politik/ausland/2021-10/bundeswehr-afghanistan-einsatz-kosten-17-milliarden-deutschland?utm_referrer=https%3A%2F%2Fwww.google.com%2F.

43 Ulrich Kampe, "Schwerpunkte der Beziehungen Deutschland – Sri Lanka," in *Sri Lanka. Fünfte Heidelberger Südasiengespräche*, eds. Georg Berkemer and Tilman Frasch (Stuttgart: Franz Steiner Verlag, 1995), 133–137.

44 Oliver Walton, "Between War and the Liberal Peace: The Politics of NGO Peacebuilding in Sri Lanka," *International Peacekeeping* 19, no. 1 (2012): 19–34.

45 The Federal Government, *Policy Guidelines for the Indo-Pacific*, 43.

46 Federal Foreign Office, "Germany and Nepal: Bilateral Relations," September 23, 2021, accessed October 12, 2021, https://www.auswaertiges-amt.de/en/aussenpolitik/nepal/235712.

47 Barkat-e-Khuda, "How Bangladesh Transformed from Its Challenging Beginning into a Middle-Income Country," *The Daily Star*, June 3, 2021, accessed June 4, 2021, https://www.thedailystar.net/opinion/news/how-bangladesh-transformed-its-challenging-beginning-middle-income-country-2103713.

48 Norbert Holl, "Schwerpunkte Deutsch-Bangladeshischer Beziehungen," in *Bangladesh. Dritte Heidelberger Südasiengespräche*, eds. Dieter Conrad and Wolfgang-Peter Zingel (Stuttgart: Franz Steiner, 1994), 166–172.

49 The Federal Government, *Policy Guidelines for the Indo-Pacific*, 26.

50 Christian Wagner, *Rethinking South Asia. Scenarios for a Changing Geopolitical Landscape* (Berlin: Stiftung Wissenschaft und Politik, 2017) (SWP Comment 30, August).

Bibliography

"Afghanistan-Einsatz kostete mehr als 17,3 Milliarden Euro. "*ZEIT Online*, October 5, 2021. Accessed October 12, 2021. https://www.zeit.de/politik/ausland/2021-10/bundeswehr-afghanistan-einsatz-kosten-17-milliarden-deutschland?utm_referrer=https%3A%2F%2Fwww.google.com%2F.

"Businessmen Asked to Enhance Trade with Germany." *The Tribune*, August 10, 2017. Accessed August 11, 2017. https://tribune.com.pk/story/1477828/businessmen-asked-enhance-trade-germany/.

"German Found Guilty of Supplying Nuke Weapons Tech to Pakistan." *Outlook*, November 24, 2005. Accessed October 12, 2021. https://www.outlookindia.com/newswire/story/german-found-guilty-of-supplying-nuke-weapons-tech-to-pakistan/337366.

Auswärtiges, Amt. *Aufgaben der deutschen Außenpolitik. Südasien am Beginn des 21. Jahrhunderts*. Berlin: 2002. Mimeographed paper.

Barkat-e-Khuda. "How Bangladesh Transformed from Its Challenging Beginning into a Middle-Income Country." *The Daily Star*, June 3, 2021. https://www.thedailystar.net/opinion/news/how-bangladesh-transformed-its-challenging-beginning-middle-income-country-2103713.

Benatar, Alexander. "Die Beziehungen zwischen Pakistan und der DDR bis 1973." Accessed October 12, 2021. https://www.projekt-mida.de/reflexicon/die-beziehungen-zwischen-pakistan-und-der-ddr-bis-1973/.

Boelcke, Willi A. "Deutschlands Politische und Wirtschaftliche Beziehungen zu Afghanistan bis zum Zweiten Weltkrieg." *Tradition: Zeitschrift für Firmengeschichte und Unternehmerbiographie* 14, no. 3/4 (Juli 1969): 153–188.

Bonn International Center for Conversion (BICC). *Länderinformation Pakistan*. Bonn: Bonn International Center for Conversion, 2021.

Das Gupta, Amit. *Handel, Hilfe, Hallstein-Doktrin. Die bundesdeutsche Südasienpolitik unter Adenauer und Erhard 1949 bis 1966*. Husum: Matthiesen-Verlag, 2004.

Deutscher Bundestag. *Asien-Konzept der Bundesregierung*. Berlin 1993. Accessed October 12, 2021. https://dip.bundestag.de/drucksache/asien-konzept-der-bundesregierung/124602.

Federal Foreign Office. "Germany and Nepal: Bilateral Relations." September 23, 2021. Accessed October 12, 2021. https://www.auswaertiges-amt.de/en/aussenpolitik/nepal/235712.

Federal Ministry for Economic Cooperation and Development. "India. An Important Partner in International Cooperation." Berlin. Accessed October 12, 2021. https://www.bmz.de/en/countries/india.

Federal Ministry for Economic Cooperation and Development. "Pakistan. Influential Partner Country in South Asia." Berlin. Accessed October 12, 2021. https://www.bmz.de/en/countries/pakistan.

Government of India, Ministry of External Affairs. "Joint Statement during the Visit of Chancellor of Germany to India." November 1, 2019. Accessed October 2021. https://mea.gov.in/bilateral-documents.htm?dtl/31991/Joint+Statement+during+the+visit+of+Chancellor+of+Germany+to+India.

Hassan, Khan. "Pak-German Ties on an Upward Trajectory." *The Daily Times*, February 21, 2017. Accessed February 22, 2017. http://dailytimes.com.pk/opinion/21-Feb-17/pak-german-ties-on-an-upward-trajectory.

Holl, Norbert. "Schwerpunkte Deutsch-Bangladeshischer Beziehungen." In *Bangladesh. Dritte Heidelberger Südasiengespräche*, edited by Dieter Conrad and Wolfgang-Peter Zingel, 166–172. Stuttgart: Franz Steiner Verlag, 1994.

Kampe, Ulrich. "Schwerpunkte der Beziehungen Deutschland – Sri Lanka." In *Sri Lanka. Fünfte Heidelberger Südasiengespräche*, edited by Georg Berkemer and Tilman Frasch, 133–137. Stuttgart: Franz Steiner Verlag, 1995.

Liebau, Heike. *Die Quellen der Dänisch-Halleschen Mission in Tranquebar in deutschen Archiven. Ihre Bedeutung für die Indienforschung*. Berlin: Verlag das Arabische Buch, 1993.

Mahmood, Talat. *Assessment of German-Pakistani Relations in Trade, Investment and Strategic Cooperation*. Berlin: WZB Social Science Center, 2014. Discussion Paper No. 4.

Pabst, Erika, and Thomas Müller-Bahlke, eds. *Quellenbestände der Indienmission 1700–1918 in Archiven des deutschsprachigen Raums*. Tübingen: Niemeyer, 2005.

Riedler, Erich. "Relations between Germany and Pakistan." *Pakistan Horizon* 48, no. 4 (1995): 7–14.

Rothermund, Dietmar. "Die deutsch-indischen Beziehungen." In *Indien. Kultur, Geschichte, Politik, Wirtschaft, Umwelt. Eine Handbuch*, edited by Dietmar Rothermund, 472–482. München: C.H. Beck, 1995.

Ruttig, Thomas. "Deutsch-Afghanische und DDR-Afghanische Beziehungen." October 22, 2016. Accessed October 12, 2021. https://thruttig.wordpress.com/2016/10/22/deutsch-afghanische-und-ddr-afghanische-beziehungen/.

Scharping, Thomas. *Die sozialwissenschaftliche China-Forschung: Rückblick und Ausblick. Social Science Research on China: Review and Perspectives*. Cologne: China Studies Online, 2000. Working papers on Chinese Politics, Economy and Society, No. 1.

Steinberg, Guido. *German Jihad. On the Internationalization of Islamist Terrorism*. New York: Columbia University Press, 2013.

The Federal Government. *Policy Guidelines for the Indo-Pacific, Germany – Europe – Asia. Shaping the 21st Century Together*. Berlin, 2020. Accessed October 12, 2021. https://www.auswaertiges-amt.de/en/aussenpolitik/regionaleschwerpunkte/asien/german-government-policy-guidelines-indo-pacific/2380510.

Vestring, Alfred. "Zum Stand der deutsch-pakistanischen Beziehungen." In *Pakistan. Zweite Heidelberger Südasiengespräche*, edited by Dieter Conrad and Wolfgang-Peter Zingel, 150–153. Stuttgart: Franz Steiner Verlag, 1992.

Voigt, Johannes H. "Anerkennung oder Nicht-Anerkennung – das war die Frage Indien im deutsch-deutschen Kalten Krieg 1952-1972." In *Wechselwirkungen*, edited by Universität Stuttgart, 71–87. Universität Stuttgart: Eigenverlag, 2001.

Voigt, Johannes H. "Deutsch-Indische Beziehungen Im 20. Jahrhundert." *Indien in Der Gegenwart, (Indian Council for Cultural Relations)* 4, no. 4 (1999): 11–28.

Voigt, Johannes H. *Die Indienpolitik der DDR: von den Anfängen bis zur Anerkennung (1952–1972)*. Köln Weimar: Böhlau, 2008.

Von Renesse, Ernst-Albrecht. "Freundschaft verpflichtet. Hundert Jahre deutsch-afghanische Beziehungen." In *Freundschaft erpflichtet*, edited by Evangelische Akademie Villigst. XXIX. Afghanistan-Tagung, 2–17. Villigst: Evangelische Akademie, 2015.

Wagner, Christian. *Rethinking South Asia. Scenarios for a Changing Geopolitical Landscape*. Berlin: Stiftung Wissenschaft und Politik, 2017 (Comment 30, August).

Wagner, Christian. *Die Bedeutung Südasiens in der Forschungs- und Universitätslandschaft der Bundesrepublik Deutschland: Eine Bestandsaufnahme*. Hamburg: Institut für Asienkunde, 2001.

Walton, Oliver. "Between War and the Liberal Peace: The Politics of NGO Peacebuilding in Sri Lanka." *International Peacekeeping* 19, no. 1 (2012): 19–34.

Zaheer, Farhan. "German Truck Maker MAN SE to Set Up Assembly Plant in Pakistan." *The Tribune*, March 2, 2017. Accessed March 3, 2017. https://tribune.com.pk/story/1343204/german-truck-maker-man-se-set-assembly-plant-pakistan/.

PART IV

CROSS-CUTTING REGIONAL ISSUES

30

THE POLITICS OF CLIMATE CHANGE IN SOUTH ASIA

Dhanasree Jayaram[1]

Introduction

Despite the global nature of the climate change problem, regions have emerged as pivotal stakeholders in global climate governance. Regional organizations such as the European Union (EU), the African Union (AU), and the Association of Southeast Asian Nations (ASEAN) have introduced climate action strategies, which are tied to the international climate regime governed primarily by the United Nations Framework Convention on Climate Change (UNFCCC). South Asia also has regionally oriented climate change-related policies, streamlined through either regional organizations such as the South Asian Association for Regional Cooperation (SAARC) or other bilateral/minilateral mechanisms such as India-Bangladesh cooperation on climate change in the Sundarbans. In addition, since 2000s, the South Asian countries (Afghanistan, Bangladesh, Bhutan, India, Maldives, Nepal, Pakistan, and Sri Lanka) have introduced several climate mitigation and adaptation policies domestically. These policies are not only a response to domestic vulnerabilities, but they are also linked with international climate policy.[2]

The South Asian countries share geographical and socio-economic similarities that tend to homogenize climate vulnerabilities such as extreme weather events, health hazards, water stress, sea level rise, etc. across the region. Many vulnerabilities are transboundary in nature, whether it pertains to the Hindu Kush Himalayan region or the Indian Ocean region. However, these similarities have not yet led to a comprehensive regional strategy, except in a few cases such as disaster management due to geopolitical fault-lines, differing perceptions of these vulnerabilities, and economic imperatives. While India is seen as a laggard by its neighboring countries on promoting regional climate cooperation, countries such as Bangladesh and the Maldives, owing to the existential nature of the threat (as perceived by them), are vociferous champions of climate action on international platforms.[3]

Against this background, this chapter discusses the climate change-related challenges faced by the South Asian countries and the policies that governments have adopted to address the likely effects of climate change. It additionally looks at the "regional" (transnational) climate initiatives by focusing on regional organizations. It uses the concept of "regionalism" to analyze the evolving dynamics of regional climate cooperation as well as interlinkages between the domestic, regional, and international realms pertaining to climate governance.

DOI: 10.4324/9781003246626-35

Importantly, the chapter also draws parallels between the policies introduced by individual countries in South Asia and the challenges faced by them to implement them. Without over-emphasizing the geopolitical dimension of regional cooperation, it attempts to provide a more nuanced view of politics of climate change in the South Asian context—by focusing on shared problems, causes for cooperation and fragmentation, and the interactions between the three levels of analysis—domestic, regional, and international.

The framework of regionalism tends to bring in elements of major International Relations theories such as realism, liberalism, constructivism, and critical theory while explaining cooperation and conflict within regions. In the South Asian case, the struggle between a shared consciousness (owing to colonial history, pluralistic cultures, etc.) and state-centric power politics (geopolitical rivalries, balance of power, etc.) is evident. However, the conventional constructivist approach (state-centric) that helps understand and explain the behavior of states in the region based on the context—characterized by their history, culture, politics, society, and economy—best suits the issue of climate change. Ideas and identities are critical to notions of regionalism, and in the case of South Asia, these concepts are central to explaining climate change policies of all states as they have shaped the climate policy agenda—by influencing perceptions around climate change solutions, rationale for climate action, choice of actors to be involved in climate action, as well as norms built on regional climate cooperation.

Regionalism and Climate Change Cooperation

A region is traditionally considered a geographical space with common characteristics that can be grouped as an identifiable unit. Regions are characterized by territorial, military, economic, and cultural variables.[4] While state-centric notions tend to dominate the characterization of regions, with the emergence of "new regionalism," non-state actors have also become important drivers of regionalization—defined as "the actual process of increasing exchange, contact and coordination, and so on within a given region"[5]—thereby highlighting the role of ideologies, identities, and social interactions (not just economic benefits of regional integration).[6] Regionalism, which is defined as "a programme, an ideology, or a situation where there exists a clear idea of a region, a set of goals and values associated with a specific project that an identifiable group of actors wish to realize,"[7] is considered an integral part of governance-related literature. As international organizations struggle to grapple with a "wicked problem" like climate change, regional organizations are also expected to share the responsibility of global climate governance—by imbibing the values and principles that are propagated by international agreements such as the Kyoto Protocol and Paris Agreement.

The evolution of literature on regionalism over the past five decades has given rise to several narratives with respect to the conceptual/theoretical, analytical, and disciplinary prisms.[8] From an organizational perspective, regionalism manifests mostly in the form of a regional organization, based on the existence of "formal agreement among governments," "diplomatic forums," and "bureaucracy."[9] Regional organizations are formed for various purposes, including for promoting collective welfare, economic growth, and sustainable development; creating or protecting a specific collective identity; and bolstering the bargaining positions of the member countries on international platforms or with third parties.[10]

The failure of the global institutions and organizations in tackling climate change has also raised the significance of regional organizations as possible alternatives for steering climate governance. Many a time, the interests of smaller and less developed nations are ignored on the global decision-making scene, and these tend to get accommodated within a regional organization's objectives. It is known to work more effectively in terms of augmenting capacity to deal with the emerging challenges by prioritizing the region's problems. At the same time, climate change can no longer be addressed at the national and/or subnational levels alone either. The transboundary nature of climate change ties it to foreign policy of the nation states, making it imperative for them to engage in regional and international climate cooperation.[11]

South Asia, as a "region," has high levels of interdependence as far as climate change-related concerns and their broader repercussions are concerned. One of the oft-employed frameworks in the environmental cooperation discourse is the regional scale of analysis. It is believed that environmental cooperation is more plausible and tangible at the regional level than at the global one due to greater "ecological interdependence" in the former in comparison to the latter.[12] The existing literature also focuses on individual regional organizations such as the EU, AU, ASEAN, and SAARC and analyze their responses (and their effectiveness) to climate change.[13] In the case of South Asia, regional climate cooperation has been marred by the lack of "mutual trust and interest," as "local and national interests" are given precedence over regional ones. This is regarded as the reason for the lack of motivation to meet or update the existing climate goals.[14]

Climate Change-related Challenges in South Asia

The diversity of the physical landscape of South Asia presents a mammoth challenge to the countries of the region when it comes to impacts of climate change. From glacial melt in the Himalayas to rising sea levels in the Indian Ocean, and from floods in the Indo-Gangetic plains to droughts in the Deccan Plateau (India), the range of climate change impacts are enormous in the region. Even the report released by the Intergovernmental Panel on Climate Change (IPCC) in 2021 can be read as a wake-up call to the region. According to the report, South Asia is most likely to face the worst effects of rising land surface temperatures and sea surface temperatures, unpredictable monsoonal patterns, intensifying extreme weather events like cyclones, rising sea levels, and glacial recession among others in the future.[15] These effects have multifarious implications, especially in terms of water, food, health, livelihood security, and so on.

The climate change impacts affect various sectors negatively. Agriculture is arguably the most vulnerable sector. The agricultural sector in the region is already being affected by reduced yields and crop failures due to degradation and loss of arable lands and damage to livestock, saltwater intrusion, and reduced water sources for irrigation, among others. The majority of rivers in South Asia are transboundary and originate in the Tibetan Plateau. The Indus basin's (shared by India, Pakistan, Afghanistan, and China) dependence on glacial and snow melt for its water flow, particularly during the dry season, is the highest.[16] The rivers of this basin are the lifeline of one of the world's largest agricultural belts. This has direct implications for livelihood and food security. According to a study, "approximately 9 percent of wheat production, 15 percent of rice, 28 percent of cotton, and 17 percent of sugarcane annually, can be attributed to meltwater from glaciers and snow."[17]

Sea level rise is linked with coastal erosion, saltwater intrusion, storm surges, and even effects on the fisheries sector as it directly affects the coastal fishing communities. According to estimates, the rate of rise in the sea level has doubled from 1.4 mm every year in the 20th century to 3.6 mm per year during 2006–2015.[18] South Asian countries such as Bangladesh, India, the Maldives, Pakistan, and Sri Lanka have considerably long coastlines that are affected by this phenomenon. This region could therefore experience forced relocations of almost 63 million people, especially in the low-lying areas, as rising sea levels are detrimental to their livelihoods and survival.[19] Besides, some of the large coastal cities of the region including

Mumbai, Karachi, Colombo, Kolkata, and Chennai could face serious consequences, due to impacts on resources, industry, populations, and infrastructure.[20]

Climate change influences displacement and migratory patterns in the region, such as displacement due to disasters, migration from coastal regions to interior areas, rural-to-urban migration, etc. According to the World Bank, "in South Asia, internal climate migrants could number over 40 million, representing up to 1.8 percent of the region's total population."[21] In addition to visibly increasing trends of internal migration and forced displacement due to disasters and other effects of climate change in recent years, international migration is also influenced by climate change. For instance, people in Nepal engaged in agricultural and livestock sectors and affected by climate change-related disasters migrate seasonally to India. This practice is more common among subsistence farmers who own small tracts of land and have less resources to cope with climate change-related shocks.[22]

Human health is yet another sector that is affected by climate change. The rise in the number and frequency of cyclones, heatwaves, floods, and droughts affects human health in adverse ways. The lack of safe drinking water and sanitation is often linked with climate change-related disasters, which leads to waterborne diseases such as cholera, typhoid, and diarrhea. Heatwaves in India and Pakistan have been held responsible for a rising number of deaths, respiratory and cardiovascular diseases, and psychological stress, thereby also negatively affecting economic growth owing primarily to the considerable reduction in working hours in extreme heat conditions.[23]

Climate Change Policies in South Asian Countries

To start with, a land-locked country in the South Asian region, Afghanistan has been undergoing severe political turmoil that affects its ability to cope with the severe effects of climate change. Unlike other countries in the regions, Afghanistan has not developed a national climate change policy, although it developed the Afghanistan Climate Change Strategy and Action Plan that has not been translated into policy. Some of the policies that relate to climate change concerns include: Afghanistan National Development Strategy (2008) and National Environmental Action Plan (2009). Since Afghanistan is threatened by desertification and various other issues, it has over a period of time prioritized the need for adaptation, which is addressed through a combined document—National Adaptation Programme of Action for Climate Change and National Capacity Needs Self-Assessment for Global Environmental Management.[24] Despite the political and economic challenges, Afghanistan submitted its first Nationally Determined Contribution (NDC) in 2016 and pledged to reduce its greenhouse gas (GHG) emissions by 13.6% by 2030, conditional upon international support. However, the political dynamics after the takeover of Kabul by the Taliban and persisting instabilities in the country make it hard to carry out the plans and projects designed to tackle climate change.

Bangladesh is one of the earliest countries in the region to come up with a National Adaptation Plan of Action back in 2005 itself due to the extreme climate vulnerabilities faced by it. Since then, the country has implemented various climate change policies such as the Bangladesh Climate Change Strategy and Action Plan (BCCSAP), under which activities funded by the Bangladesh Climate Change Trust Fund and Bangladesh Climate Change Resilience Fund have been carried out. Due to its specific vulnerabilities, it invests immensely in coastal protection, forest management, renewable energy, and so on, through policies such as the 100-year Bangladesh Delta Plan 2100.[25] Bangladesh became the Chair of the Climate Vulnerable Forum (CVF) for the second time and assumed the Presidency of the Vulnerable

20 Group of Financial Ministers in 2020. Apart from building resilience by rehabilitating displaced populations, the country is also focusing on distributing clean cooking stoves to people to reduce GHG emissions. It invests around 6–7% of its annual budget on climate adaptation measures.[26] However, this will not be enough for it to protect its vulnerable populations as the impacts of climate change worsen in the future.

Bhutan, being a least developed country, is particularly vulnerable to climate change as it lacks the necessary resources to deal with challenges posed by climate change. Bhutan was among the first countries to pledge carbon neutrality in 2009. Because of its low emissions as compared to its estimated sequestration capacity, Bhutan is considered a net sink of GHGs.[27] Before releasing the 2020 Climate Change Policy, Bhutan introduced the National Strategy and Action Plan for Low Carbon Development in 2012 and several other policies that underline the need for achieving high energy efficiency in different sectors, mainly industrial, residential, and tertiary sectors, and using renewable energy to generate a major proportion of the electricity needs.[28] Bhutan is one of the world's least contributors to global emissions. However, its National Adaptation Plan faces several challenges including the lack of data, investments, institutional capacity, inter-sector coordination, rigorous monitoring and review, and so on.[29]

In India's case, as far as climate change is concerned, the country has adopted an executive policy-based approach and therefore no significant legislation has yet been passed to deal with climate change. The National Action Plan on Climate Change (NAPCC) 2008 is the most crucial executive policy that introduces several missions, including solar, energy efficiency, sustainable agriculture, Himalayan ecosystems, etc.[30] Climate change-related policies targeted at forestry, electricity, electric mobility, urban housing, etc. have also been introduced since 2010. India has committed to achieve net-zero emissions target by 2070 and reach non-fossil energy capacity of 500 GW by 2030.[31] However, India's commitments to reduce emissions largely depend on climate finance from international financial institutions and industrialized countries, as reiterated by India even at the 2021 Glasgow Climate Summit. Besides, there are various structural limitations such as the lack of institutional/agency coordination as well as monitoring and review, rising energy demand and coal dependence, inadequate investments in adaptation, and limited devolution of powers to local governments in climate change-related issues, among others that inhibit effective and timely implementation of various policies.[32]

The Maldives, being a low-lying country and composed of several islands, faces an existential threat from climate change. It has played an important role in the climate change negotiations that led to the adoption of the UNFCCC and was also the first country to sign the Kyoto Protocol. Like other South Asian countries, the Maldives also launched its National Adaptation Program for Action (NAPA) formulation process in early 2000s with the aim of enhancing the resilience of the country's population and ecosystems. Another major policy introduced by the country was the Maldives Climate Change Policy Framework (2015) with the goal of ensuring financing for adaptation, promoting low-emissions development schemes, building resilient infrastructure and communities, etc.[33] In the Maldives, according to studies, the execution of climate change-related policies is harder due to relatively low capacities of the public sector and local governments, as compared to the national government. Capacity-building is therefore key to the achievement of the Maldives' climate policy goals. The country's middle income status also makes it heavily reliant on external sources to finance climate resilience-related projects. The Foreign Minister also stated, "For small states it is not easy. By the time the financing is obtained, we may be underwater."[34]

Nepal began to address climate change through its periodic plans in the 2000s, despite being one of the least contributors of GHGs.[35] In 2010, Nepal submitted its NAPA to the UNFCCC and adopted Local Adaptation Plan for Action (LAPA) to advance bottom-up adaptation mechanisms at the domestic level. In 2011, Nepal introduced its Climate Change Policy. As a country that was still reeling under the effects of a decade-long civil war and had not sufficiently achieved human development standards, it was imperative for Nepal to balance its priorities and lay emphasis on a low-carbon development path, climate-resilient socio-economic development, climate justice, and sustainable development.[36] Many of Nepal's initiatives have not so far taken off effectively as the processes for implementing them were long. Nepal's second NDC submission to the UNFCCC lays out strong ambitions, especially in the area of forest conservation. It has significantly made advances in reducing deforestation. Similarly, Nepal has also been able to decentralize climate governance and forest management by delegating responsibilities to local governments, communities, and groups, such as Village Development Committees and municipalities in local adaptation programs. However, Nepal's GHG emissions are expected to further rise in the future—to the tune of 31–36% by 2030, in comparison to 2016 levels.[37] The country requires further financial and technological support to implement more stringent policies to achieve its climate action targets.

Pakistan is also one of the most climate-vulnerable countries to climate change in the region. Banking on the legislative measure of Climate Change Act (2017), Pakistan strives to fulfill its international obligations on climate action by introducing and implementing appropriate mitigation and adaptation programs. Pakistan has also introduced a series of policies targeting power, energy, forestry, agricultural, and disaster risk reduction sectors. The larger emphasis is laid on prevention of degradation of natural resources, mitigation of emissions from highly polluting sectors such as transportation and industry, conservation of energy, expansion of renewable energy, ecological restoration of degraded lands and afforestation, promotion of climate-resilient crop production for enhanced food security, etc.[38] Pakistan's coal consumption has tripled since 2015 and is likely to increase in the future too. However, the share of renewable energy has also increased from 0.25% in 2015 to 5% in 2020.[39] Nevertheless, like other South Asian countries, the lack of institutional capacity and resources continue to hamper Pakistan's climate policies. In addition, political instability also contributes to an incoherent approach toward climate action.

Sri Lanka, despite being a low carbon emitting country, remains highly vulnerable to the impacts of climate change. Sri Lanka adopted the National Climate Change Policy in 2012 that employs the framework of sustainable development to address climate mitigation and adaptation.[40] Its National Adaptation Plan (2016–2025) was adopted in 2016 and is focused on agriculture, transportation, coastal and marine areas, health, biodiversity, energy, and tourism, among others. As a developing country, Sri Lanka is also conscious of its development imperatives and has therefore put greater emphasis on the adoption of environment-friendly technologies with co-benefits of emissions reduction and socio-economic development. Climate action and disaster risk reduction are in particular integrated into various policies.[41] Under the Paris Agreement, Sri Lanka has declared a net-zero target—to go carbon neutral by 2060. It has also agreed to not add any more coal-based power plants and increase forest cover by 32% by the end of 2030.[42] However, many analysts have identified the lack of institutional capacity and coordination along with the lack of technology and tools in sectors such as coastal management, ecosystem management, etc. that come in the way of effective climate action.[43]

Challenges to Regional Climate Change Cooperation in South Asia

One of the most important regional organizations in South Asia, SAARC, was founded in 1985 with the goal of advancing economic and social welfare of the people residing in the South Asian countries. Environmental and climate change-related concerns have featured in

SAARC's agenda since the beginning. With the introduction of the SAARC Plan of Action on Climate Change in 2008 and 2010 Thimphu statement on climate change, SAARC recognized the need for a regional approach to tackling climate change. Regional projects became central to SAARC's action plan on climate change. Various regional centers have been established by SAARC, acknowledging various aspects of climate change and its impacts, such as SAARC Disaster Risk Management Centre (SDMC) that would provide advice on policy and capacity-building, including research, development, training, and learning. While there has been some movement in the direction of exchanging information and sharing local experiences, due to the ineffectiveness of SAARC as a regional organization, many initiatives could not be sustained for too long.[44] Moreover, since no SAARC summit has been held since 2014 (other than the virtual meeting held in 2020 on COVID-19), the existing initiatives have failed to produce tangible results.

The Bengal Initiative for Multi-Sectoral Technological and Economic Cooperation (BIMSTEC) is another regional organization that consists of South Asian countries (among others): Bangladesh, Bhutan, India, Nepal, and Sri Lanka. The Bay of Bengal region is extremely vulnerable to extreme weather events with frequent cyclones that bring about massive destruction. Climate change became one of the focus areas of BIMSTEC at the 14th Senior Officials meeting held in Myanmar in 2009. At the 15th session held in Nepal, it concluded that it would be imperative for the BIMSTEC countries to cooperate on climate change at all levels—national, regional, and international—in light of the grave challenges posed by it and the growing momentum in terms of showing solidarity with the Paris Agreement. Yet, there has been little progress in stepping up climate change cooperation through information sharing using remote-sensing satellites for disaster management, agriculture, etc. This is another regional organization that has not been able to meet its envisaged goals due to delays in implementation and a reactive approach to climate change (mainly disaster management).[45] In fact, despite being seen as an alternative to SAARC, BIMSTEC has held only four summits until 2021.

There are other intergovernmental organizations in the region that are also involved in climate change cooperation—spurred by non-state actors that tie to the rise of new regionalism in South Asia. For example, the International Centre for Integrated Mountain Development (ICIMOD) is an "established international and regional academic, experiential, and understanding organization" that serves the Hindu-Kush Himalayas' (HKH) eight regional member states including Afghanistan, Bangladesh, Bhutan, China, India, Myanmar, Nepal, and Pakistan.[46] The ICIMOD represents the mountain societies of South or Southern Asia and was founded in Nepal in 1983. It brings together governments, governmental agencies, scientific organizations, donors, non-governmental organizations, and civil society organizations to secure the future of the people and ecosystems of the HKH region. It provides technical (capacity-building) assistance to countries in the region to implement climate mitigation and adaptation strategies.

Despite shared problems and opportunities, differences in perceptions around climate change-related challenges are a key impediment to cooperation on crucial issues such as disasters, water security, food security, migration, health and well-being, among others. As is the case with regional cooperation, it is not necessary that the existence of common or even comparable problems can lead to cooperation. This is applicable in South Asia wherein priorities in agenda-setting based on the varied nature of vulnerabilities, disparities in economies, external factors (such as finance), differing perceptions of the costs of climate action, and geopolitical tensions hinder effective collaboration over a longer period of time. One could argue that regional disparities in income, growth, human development, and poverty pose fundamental obstacles to regional cooperation in South Asia since these issues scuttle resource pooling and equal stakeholder participation in solutions. For example, the perceived vulnerabilities of the Maldives and Bangladesh are considered far more existential in comparison to the other countries in the region due to the low-lying nature of vast tracts of land in these countries.[47] Hence, these countries tend to focus on strengthening their national-level climate change policies rather than exploring resource pooling opportunities.

One could argue that the tension between the regional and the national perspectives is a significant obstacle to regional cooperation, as also stated in the SAARC Action Plan on Climate Change, which aims to "provide the impetus for a regional-level action plan on climate change through national-level activities."[48] This goal emphasizes how the progress of regional plans is largely dependent on progress in the member states' climate action. If countries lag behind nationally, the momentum for regional action could reduce. In fact, the SAARC Action Plan also seeks to develop a common understanding among the South Asian countries regarding their negotiating positions at the international level. However, this has so far not materialized due to the lack of regional coordination—clearly reflecting the interconnectedness between the domestic, regional, and the international.

All the countries in South Asia belong to lower-middle-income and middle-income economy categories, according to World Bank data. Even in such a scenario, the economically stronger country (India in this case) could be expected to deliver more in terms of regional cooperation. India is considered a major emerging economy due to the relative vastness of its economy, population, and resource base. Yet, to expect a group of lower-middle-income and middle-income economies to cooperate and share the costs of climate action would be unreasonable, as these countries have all reiterated that their climate action is contingent on international support. This pushes regional cooperation to the backburner while placing the agenda for international climate cooperation on the forefront.

South Asia is also one of the least integrated regions of the world—economically, politically, or in other realms.[49] Long-standing territorial conflicts and geopolitical rivalries in the region have always acted as a barrier to regional cooperation and ineffectiveness of regional organizations. While India-Pakistan equations are often cited as the primary cause for the lack of regional cooperation, other relationships such as India-Nepal relations and Bangladesh-Pakistan relations have also been strained. One also cannot rule out the perception or misperception of India as a regional hegemon by its neighbors as a cause for concern. India's Minister of External Affairs of the Government of India, S. Jaishankar said, "Regionalism has taken root in every part of the world. We have lagged behind; it is because South Asia does not have the typical commerce and connectivity that other areas do." It is this "disconnection" between India and its neighbors that the region has not been able to overcome so far, which has been exacerbated by the growing Chinese presence in the South Asian countries.[50] For India though, regional cooperation is seen as an essential ingredient of its global positioning and rise, because a country's approach to issues at the regional level tends to determine how it approaches it at the global level.[51] Therefore, it is imperative for India to expand its focus on regional climate cooperation to lend greater legitimacy to its envisioned image of a global climate leader or responsible climate leader at the international level.

A Case for South Asian Climate Regionalism

South Asia, despite being one of the world's most climate-vulnerable regions, remains fragmented in its climate change response. Regionalism and regionalizing trends in South Asia have so far shown little promise, but that does not imply that there are no opportunities to scale up regional cooperation. As the climate crisis worsens, the demand for more ambitious climate action is expected to rise across South Asia. An ecoregional or bioregional approach that transcends political boundaries and focuses on sustaining ecosystems (instead of the utility of nature resources) could potentially bring together the South Asian countries to deal with shared ecogeographical features such as the Himalayas, rivers, Sundarbans, Indian Ocean, etc.[52] Similarly, the fact that all the countries in the region are still developing, there are opportunities for designing a context-based framework of development regionalism, based on climate change vulnerabilities and sustainability standards. Increasingly, developmental gains made by the region's countries are being eroded by climate change impacts. As South Asia pushes the agenda of connectivity and trade through regional mechanisms, climate change could be integrated into the planning and implementation processes.

At all levels of governance, climate change continues to be less prioritized, which contributes to a fragmented response. More exclusive climate change-related policies, laws, institutions, and knowledge mechanisms would strengthen the national-level response. This could then provide greater impetus to a coordinated regional approach to building climate-resilient economies that could offer significant benefits in areas such as river basin management, agricultural development, renewable energy expansion, insurance schemes, etc. However, as specified in the chapter, the international realm is critical to the national-level climate policy-making process, primarily due to the South Asian countries' dependence on climate finance from the industrialized countries. Hence, climate change response necessitates a multi-level governance framework that coalesces competing and converging interests of countries within a region such as South Asia. Hence, rightfully, as seen in the case of the SAARC Action Plan on Climate Change, both the national and international realms are indispensable to a regional approach to climate change.

Notes

1 Acknowledgments: The author would like to thank Ms. Priyanka Jaiswal, postgraduate student in the Department of Geopolitics and International Relations, Manipal Academy of Higher Education, for her immense support in collating literature and data to write this chapter.

2 Baniateilang Majaw, *Climate Change in South Asia: Politics, Policies and the SAARC* (Abingdon: Routledge, 2020).

3 Dhanasree Jayaram, "Climate Diplomacy and South Asia: Is there Room for Cooperation?" *India Foundation Journal* 7, no. 4 (July–August 2019): 58.

4 Raimo Väyrynen, "Regionalism: Old and New," *International Studies Review* 5, no. 1 (March 2003): 27.

5 Helge Hveem, "The Regional Project in Global Governance," in *Theories of New Regionalism*, eds. Fredrik Söderbaum and Timothy M. Shaw (London: Palgrave Macmillan, 2003), 83.

6 Costa Filippo Buranelli and Aliya Tskhay, "Regionalism," *Oxford Research Encyclopedia of International Studies*, August 28, 2019.

7 Hveem, "The Regional Project," 83.

8 Fredrik Söderbaum, *Rethinking Regionalism* (London: Macmillan Education, 2016).

9 Joseph S. Nye, *Peace in Parts: Integration and Conflict in Regional Organization* (Lanham: University Press of America, 1987), 5.

10 Hveem, "The Regional Project," 82.

11 F. Korthals Altes, "New Paths to International Environmental Cooperation," *Advisory Council on International Affairs*, March 2013, https://www.hydrology.nl/images/docs/alg/2013.07.11_AIV84_ENG.pdf.

12 Ken Conca and Geoffrey D. Dabelko, *Environmental Peacemaking* (Washington, DC.: Woodrow Wilson Center Press, 2003), 13.

13 Eva-Karin Gardell and Bertjan Verbeek, "Key Actors in the Management of Crises: International and Regional Organizations," *Oxford Research Encyclopedia of Politics*, December 22, 2021.

14 Habib Zafarullah and Ahmed Shafiqul Huque, "Climate Change, Regulatory Policies and Regional Cooperation in South Asia," *Public Administration and Policy* 21, no. 1 (2018): 31.

15 Intergovernmental Panel on Climate Change, *Climate Change 2021: The Physical Science Basis. Contribution of Working Group I to the Sixth Assessment Report of the Intergovernmental Panel on Climate Change* (Cambridge: Cambridge University Press, 2021), https://www.ipcc.ch/report/ar6/wg1/downloads/report/IPCC_AR6_WGI_Full_Report_smaller.pdf.

16 H. Biemans, et al., "Importance of Snow and Glacier Meltwater for Agriculture on the Indo-Gangetic Plain," *Nature Sustainability* 2, no. 7 (2019): 594.

17 Biemans, "Importance of Snow," 596.

18 Rebecca Lindsey, "Climate Change: Global Sea Level," *National Oceanic and Atmospheric Administration*, August 14, 2020, https://www.climate.gov/news-features/understanding-climate/climate-change-global-sea-level.

19 Megan Rowling, "Climate Change Could Create 63 Million Migrants in South Asia by 2050," *Reuters*, December 18, 2020, https://www.reuters.com/article/usclimate-change-migration-southasia-tr-idUSKBN28S1WV.

20 Dhanasree Jayaram, "Climate Fragility Risk Brief: South Asia," *adelphi*, November 12, 2019, https://climate-security-expert-network.org/sites/climate-security-expert-network.com/files/documents/csen_climate_fragility_risk_brief_-_south_asia_0.pdf.

21 Kanta Kumari Rigaud, et al., "Groundswell: Preparing for Internal Climate Migration," World Bank, March 19, 2018, http://hdl.handle.net/10986/29461.

22 Yograj Gautam, "Seasonal Migration and Livelihood Resilience in the Face of Climate Change in Nepal," *Mountain Research and Development* 37, no. 4 (2017): 443–444.

23 Banalata Sen, et al., "Climate Change: Health Effects and Response in South Asia," *BMJ* (November 2017): 1–4.

24 Asian Development Bank, *Climate Change, Coming Soon to a Court near You: National Climate Change Legal Frameworks in Asia and the Pacific* (Manila: Asian Development Bank, December 2020), 45–51.

25 Ministry of Environment, Forest and Climate Change, "Nationally Determined Contributions (NDCs) 2021," Government of Bangladesh, 2021, https://www4.unfccc.int/sites/ndcstaging/PublishedDocuments/Bangladesh%20First/NDC_submission_20210826revised.pdf.

26 Ministry of Environment, Forest and Climate Change, "Nationally Determined Contributions."

27 National Environment Commission, "Climate Change Policy of the Kingdom of Bhutan," Royal Government of Bhutan, 2020, 1, https://www.gnhc.gov.bt/en/wp-content/uploads/2020/02/Climate-Change-Policy.pdf.

28 Dorji Yangka, Vanessa Rauland, and Peter Newman, "Carbon Neutral Policy in Action: The Case of Bhutan," *Climate Policy* 19, no. 6 (2018): 672–673.

29 Marion Davis and Lailai Li, "Understanding the Policy Contexts for Mainstreaming Climate Change in Bhutan and Nepal: A Synthesis," Regional Climate Change Adaptation Knowledge Platform for Asia, Stockholm
Environment Institute, 2013, https://mediamanager.sei.org/documents/Publications/Climate/akp-understanding-policy-contexts-bhutan-nepal-synthesis.pdf.

30 Prime Minister's Council on Climate Change, "National Action Plan on Climate Change," Government of India, 2008, https://archivepmo.nic.in/drmanmohansingh/climate_change_english.pdf.

31 Soumya Sarkar, "India Breathes Life into Glasgow Climate Summit by Net-Zero Commitment," *Mongabay*, November 4, 2021, https://india.mongabay.com/2021/11/india-breathes-life-into-glasgow-climate-summit-by-net-zero-and-panchamrit/.

32 Parul Kumar and Abhayraj Naik, "India's Domestic Climate Policy Is Fragmented and Lacks Clarity," *Economic and Political Weekly*, February 27, 2019, https://www.epw.in/engage/article/indias-domestic-climate-policy-fragmented-lacks-clarity.

33 Amjad Abdulla, Ahmad Waheed, Ali Shareef, Mareer Mohamed Husny, Mohamed Asif, and Zammath Khaleel, "Climate Change Policy Framework," Maldives: Ministry of Environment and Energy, 2015, http://extwprlegs1.fao.org/docs/pdf/mdv172920.pdf.

34 Alasdair Pal and Devjyot Ghoshal, "'We Can't Wait': Maldives Desperate for Funds as Islands Risk Going Under," *Reuters*, January 17, 2020, https://www.reuters.com/article/us-climate-change-maldives-idUSKBN1ZG0XS.

35 Luni Piya, Keshav Lall Maharajan, and Niraj Prakash Josh, "Climate Change in Nepal: Policy and Programs," in *Socio-Economic Issues of Climate Change: A Livelihood Analysis from Nepal*, eds. Luni Piya, Keshav Lall Maharajan, and Niraj Prakash Joshi (Singapore: Springer Nature, 2019), 35–36.

36 Nanki Kaur, "Climate Change Planning in Nepal," *Green Growth Best Practice*, 2014, https://www.greengrowthknowledge.org/sites/default/files/downloads/best-practices/GGBP%20Case%20Study%20Series_Nepal_Climate%20Change%20Planning.pdf.

37 Hannah Ritchie, "Where in the World Do People Have the Highest CO2 Emissions from Flying?" *Our World in Data*, September 24, 2021. https://ourworldindata.org/carbon-footprint-flying.

38 Senate Secretariat, "Pakistan Climate Change Act, 2017," Government of Pakistan, March 31, 2017, http://extwprlegs1.fao.org/docs/pdf/pak172391.pdf.

39 Government of Pakistan, *Updated Nationally Determined Contributions 2021*, United Nations Framework Convention on Climate Change, 2021, https://www4.unfccc.int/sites/ndcstaging/PublishedDocuments/Pakistan%20First/Pakistan%20Updated%20NDC%202021.pdf.

40 Ministry of Environment, "The National Climate Change Policy of Sri Lanka," Government of Sri Lanka, 2021, http://www.climatechange.lk/CCS%20Policy/Climate_Change_Policy_English.pdf.

41 Vindya Hewawasam and Kenichi Matsui, "Historical Development of Climate Change Policies and the Climate Change Secretariat in Sri Lanka," *Environmental Science & Policy* 101 (2019): 255–261.

42 Sri Lanka UN-REDD Programme, "Sri Lanka's Forest Reference Level submission to the UNFCCC," United Nations Framework Convention on Climate Change, July 2017, https://redd.unfccc.int/files/sl_frl_modified_submission_november_2017.pdf.

43 Vositha Wijenayake, et al., "Policy Gaps and Needs Analysis for the Implementation of NDCs on Adaptation and Loss and Damage in Bangladesh, Nepal, and Sri Lanka," *APN Science Bulletin*, December 15, 2020, https://www.apn-gcr.org/bulletin/article/policy-gaps-and-needs-analysis-for-the-implementation-of-ndcs-on-adaptation-and-loss-and-damage-in-bangladesh-nepal-and-sri-lanka/.

44 Md Saidul Islam and Edson Kieu, "Tackling Regional Climate Change Impacts and Food Security Issues: A Critical Analysis across ASEAN, PIF, and SAARC," *Sustainability* 12, no. 3 (2020): 883.

45 Aparna Roy, "BIMSTEC and Climate Change: Setting a Common Agenda," Observer Research Foundation, December 31, 2019, https://www.orfonline.org/research/bimstec-climate-change-setting-common-agenda/.

46 "Who We Are," International Centre for Integrated Mountain Development, accessed December 15, 2021, https://www.icimod.org/who-we-are/.

47 A.K.M. Nazrul Islam, Salma Sultan, and Afroz. "Climate Change and South Asia: What Makes the Region Most Vulnerable?" *Research Papers in Economics*, January 2009, https://ideas.repec.org/p/pra/mprapa/21875.html.

48 Bishal Thapa, "Thimphu Statement on Climate Change a Mere Rhetoric," South Asia Watch on Trade, Economics and Environment, 2013, http://www.sawtee.org/publications/Policy-Brief-28.pdf.

49 Riya Sinha and Niara Sareen, "India's Limited Trade Connectivity with South Asia," *Brookings*, May 26, 2020. https://www.brookings.edu/research/indias-limited-trade-connectivity-with-south-asia/.

50 Constantino Xavier, "Interview: On India's Neighbourhood, Regional Institutions and Delhi's Policy Space," *Brookings*, June 9, 2020, https://www.brookings.edu/blog/up-front/2020/06/09/interview-on-indias-neighbourhood-regional-institutions-and-delhis-policy-space/.

51 K. Yhome and Tridivesh Singh Maini, "India's Evolving Approach to Regionalism: SAARC and Beyond," *Rising Powers Quarterly* 2, no. 3 (August 2017): 147–165, https://risingpowersproject.com/indias-evolving-approach-to-regionalism-saarc-and-beyond/.

52 Rajni Bakshi, "Bioregions: India's Strategic Imperative," Gateway House, December 12, 2017, https://www.gatewayhouse.in/bioregions-a-strategic-imperative/.

References

Abdulla, Amjad, Ahmad Waheed, Ali Shareef, Mareer Mohamed Husny, Mohamed Asif, and Zammath Khaleel. "Climate Change Policy Framework." Maldives: Ministry of Environment and Energy, 2015. http://extwprlegs1.fao.org/docs/pdf/mdv172920.pdf.

Altes, F. Korthals. "New Paths to International Environmental Cooperation." Advisory Council on International Affairs, March 2013. https://www.hydrology.nl/images/docs/alg/2013.07.11_AIV84_ENG.pdf.

Asian Development Bank. *Climate Change, Coming Soon to a Court near You: National Climate Change Legal Frameworks in Asia and the Pacific.* Manila: Asian Development Bank, December 2020. https://www.adb.org/sites/default/files/publication/659966/national-climate-change-legal-frameworks.pdf.

Bakshi, Rajni. "Bioregions: India's Strategic Imperative." Gateway House, December 12, 2017. https://www.gatewayhouse.in/bioregions-a-strategic-imperative/.

Biemans, H., C. Siderius, A.F. Lutz, S. Nepal, B. Ahmad, T. Hassan, W. von Bloh, R.R. Wijngaard, P. Wester, A.B. Shrestha, and W.W. Immerzeel. "Importance of Snow and Glacier Meltwater for Agriculture on the Indo-Gangetic Plain." *Nature Sustainability* 2, no. 7 (2019): 594–601. https://doi.org/10.1038/s41893-019-0305-3.

Buranelli, Costa Filippo, and Aliya Tskhay. "Regionalism." Oxford Research Encyclopedia of International Studies, August 28, 2019. https://doi.org/10.1093/acrefore/9780190846626.013.517.

Conca, Ken, and Geoffrey D. Dabelko. *Environmental Peacemaking.* Washington, DC: Woodrow Wilson Center Press, 2003.

Davis, Marion, and Lailai Li. "Understanding the Policy Contexts for Mainstreaming Climate Change in Bhutan and Nepal: A Synthesis." Regional Climate Change Adaptation Knowledge Platform for Asia, Stockholm Environment Institute, 2013. https://mediamanager.sei.org/documents/Publications/Climate/akp-understanding-policy-contexts-bhutan-nepal-synthesis.pdf.

Gardell, Eva-Karin, and Bertjan Verbeek. "Key Actors in the Management of Crises: International and Regional Organizations." *Oxford Research Encyclopedia of Politics*, December 22, 2021. https://doi.org/10.1093/acrefore/9780190228637.013.1499.

Gautam, Yograj. "Seasonal Migration and Livelihood Resilience in the Face of Climate Change in Nepal." *Mountain Research and Development* 37, no. 4 (2017): 436–445. https://doi.org/10.1659/mrd-journal-d-17-00035.1.

Government of Pakistan. *Updated Nationally Determined Contributions 2021.* United Nations Framework Convention on Climate Change, 2021. https://www4.unfccc.int/sites/ndcstaging/PublishedDocuments/Pakistan%20First/Pakistan%20Updated%20NDC%202021.pdf.

Hewawasam, Vindya, and Kenichi Matsui. "Historical Development of Climate Change Policies and the Climate Change Secretariat in Sri Lanka." *Environmental Science & Policy* 101 (2019): 255–261. https://doi.org/10.1016/j.envsci.2019.09.001.

Hveem, Helge. "The Regional Project in Global Governance." In *Theories of New Regionalism*, edited by Fredrik Söderbaum and Timothy M. Shaw, 81–98. London: Palgrave Macmillan, 2003.

Intergovernmental Panel on Climate Change. *Climate Change 2021: The Physical Science Basis. Contribution of Working Group I to the Sixth Assessment Report of the Intergovernmental Panel on Climate Change.* Cambridge: Cambridge University Press, 2021. https://www.ipcc.ch/report/ar6/wg1/downloads/report/IPCC_AR6_WGI_Full_Report_smaller.pdf.

International Centre for Integrated Mountain Development. "Who We Are." Accessed December 15, 2021. https://www.icimod.org/who-we-are/.

Islam, Md Saidul, and Edson Kieu. "Tackling Regional Climate Change Impacts and Food Security Issues: A Critical Analysis across ASEAN, PIF, and SAARC." *Sustainability* 12, no. 3 (2020): 883. https://doi.org/10.3390/su12030883.

Islam, A.K.M. Nazrul, and Salma Sultan, and Afroz. "Climate Change and South Asia: What Makes the Region Most Vulnerable?" *Research Papers in Economics*, January 2009. https://ideas.repec.org/p/pra/mprapa/21875.html.

Jayaram, Dhanasree. "Climate Diplomacy and South Asia: Is There Room for Cooperation?" *India Foundation Journal* 7, no. 4 (July–August 2019): 58–67.

Jayaram, Dhanasree. "Climate Fragility Risk Brief: South Asia." *adelphi*, November 12, 2019. https://climate-security-expert-network.org/sites/climate-security-expert-network.com/files/documents/csen_climate_fragility_risk_brief_-_south_asia_0.pdf.

Kaur, Nanki. "Climate Change Planning in Nepal." *Green Growth Best Practice*, 2014. https://www.greengrowthknowledge.org/sites/default/files/downloads/best-practices/GGBP%20Case%20Study%20Series_Nepal_Climate%20Change%20Planning.pdf.

Kumar, Parul, and Abhayraj Naik. "India's Domestic Climate Policy Is Fragmented and Lacks Clarity." *Economic and Political Weekly*, February 27, 2019. https://www.epw.in/engage/article/indias-domestic-climate-policy-fragmented-lacks-clarity.

Lindsey, Rebecca. "Climate Change: Global Sea Level." National Oceanic and Atmospheric Administration, August 14, 2020. https://www.climate.gov/news-features/understanding-climate/climate-change-global-sea-level.

Majaw, Baniateilang. *Climate Change in South Asia: Politics, Policies and the SAARC*. Abingdon: Routledge, 2020.

Ministry of Environment, Forest and Climate Change. "Nationally Determined Contributions (NDCs) 2021." Government of Bangladesh, 2021. https://www4.unfccc.int/sites/ndcstaging/PublishedDocuments/Bangladesh%20First/NDC_submission_20210826revised.pdf.

Ministry of Environment. "The National Climate Change Policy of Sri Lanka." Government of Sri Lanka, 2021. http://www.climatechange.lk/CCS%20Policy/Climate_Change_Policy_English.pdf.

National Environment Commission. "Climate Change Policy of the Kingdom of Bhutan." Royal Government of Bhutan, 2020. https://www.gnhc.gov.bt/en/wp-content/uploads/2020/02/Climate-Change-Policy.pdf.

Nye, Joseph S. *Peace in Parts: Integration and Conflict in Regional Organization*. Lanham: University Press of America, 1987.

Pal, Alasdair, and Devjyot Ghoshal. "'We Can't Wait': Maldives Desperate for Funds as Islands Risk Going Under." *Reuters*, January 17, 2020. https://www.reuters.com/article/us-climate-change-maldives-idUSKBN1ZG0XS.

Piya, Luni, Keshav Lall Maharajan, and Niraj Prakash Josh. "Climate Change in Nepal: Policy and Programs." In *Socio-Economic Issues of Climate Change: A Livelihood Analysis from Nepal*, edited by Luni Piya, Keshav Lall Maharajan, and Niraj Prakash Joshi, 35–51. Singapore: Springer Nature, 2019.

Prime Minister's Council on Climate Change. "National Action Plan on Climate Change." Government of India, 2008. https://archivepmo.nic.in/drmanmohansingh/climate_change_english.pdf.

Rigaud, Kanta Kumari, Alex de Sherbinin, Bryan Jones, Jonas Bergmann, Viviane Clement, Kayly Ober, and Jacob Schewe, et al. "Groundswell: Preparing for Internal Climate Migration." World Bank, March 19, 2018. http://hdl.handle.net/10986/29461.

Ritchie, Hannah. "Where in the World Do People Have the Highest CO2 Emissions from Flying?" *Our World in Data*, September 24, 2021. https://ourworldindata.org/carbon-footprint-flying.

Rowling, Megan. "Climate Change Could Create 63 Million Migrants in South Asia by 2050." *Reuters*, December 18, 2020. https://www.reuters.com/article/usclimate-change-migration-southasia-tr-idUSKBN28S1WV.

Roy, Aparna. "BIMSTEC and Climate Change: Setting a Common Agenda." Observer Research Foundation, December 31, 2019. https://www.orfonline.org/research/bimstec-climate-change-setting-common-agenda/.

Sarkar, Soumya. "India Breathes Life into Glasgow Climate Summit by Net-Zero Commitment." *Mongabay*, November 4, 2021. https://india.mongabay.com/2021/11/india-breathes-life-into-glasgow-climate-summit-by-net-zero-and-panchamrit/.

Sen, Banalata, Meghnath Dhimal, Aishath Thimna Latheef, and Upasona Ghosh. "Climate Change: Health Effects and Response in South Asia." *BMJ* (November 2017): 1–4. https://doi.org/10.1136/bmj.j5117.

Senate Secretariat. "Pakistan Climate Change Act, 2017." Government of Pakistan, March 31, 2017. http://extwprlegs1.fao.org/docs/pdf/pak172391.pdf.

Sinha, Riya, and Niara Sareen. "India's Limited Trade Connectivity with South Asia." *Brookings*, May 26, 2020. https://www.brookings.edu/research/indias-limited-trade-connectivity-with-south-asia/.

Söderbaum, Fredrik. *Rethinking Regionalism*. London: Macmillan Education, 2016.

Sri Lanka UN-REDD Programme. "Sri Lanka's Forest Reference Level submission to the UNFCCC." United Nations Framework Convention on Climate Change, July 2017. https://redd.unfccc.int/files/sl_frl_modified_submission_november_2017.pdf.

Thapa, Bishal. "Thimphu Statement on Climate Change a Mere Rhetoric." South Asia Watch on Trade, Economics and Environment, 2013. http://www.sawtee.org/publications/Policy-Brief-28.pdf.

Väyrynen, Raimo. "Regionalism: Old and New." *International Studies Review* 5, no. 1 (March 2003): 25–51. https://doi.org/10.1111/1521-9488.501002.

Wijenayake, Vositha Dennis Mombauer, Prabin Man Singh, and Mohammed Nadiruzzaman. "Policy Gaps and Needs Analysis for the Implementation of NDCs on Adaptation and Loss and Damage in Bangladesh, Nepal, and Sri Lanka." *APN Science Bulletin*, December 15, 2020. https://www.apn-gcr.org/bulletin/article/policy-gaps-and-needs-analysis-for-the-implementation-of-ndcs-on-adaptation-and-loss-and-damage-in-bangladesh-nepal-and-sri-lanka/.

Xavier, Constantino. "Interview: On India's Neighbourhood, Regional Institutions and Delhi's Policy Space." *Brookings*, June 9, 2020. https://www.brookings.edu/blog/up-front/2020/06/09/interview-on-indias-neighbourhood-regional-institutions-and-delhis-policy-space/.

Yangka, Dorji, Vanessa Rauland, and Peter Newman. "Carbon Neutral Policy in Action: The Case of Bhutan." *Climate Policy* 19, no. 6 (2018): 672–687. https://doi.org/10.1080/14693062.2018.1551187.

Yhome, K., and Tridivesh Singh Maini. "India's Evolving Approach to Regionalism: SAARC and Beyond." *Rising Powers Quarterly* 2, no. 3 (August 2017): 147–165. https://risingpowersproject.com/indias-evolving-approach-to-regionalism-saarc-and-beyond/.

Zafarullah, Habib, and Ahmed Shafiqul Huque. "Climate Change, Regulatory Policies and Regional Cooperation in South Asia." *Public Administration and Policy* 21, no. 1 (2018): 22–35. https://doi.org/10.1108/pap-06-2018-001.

31

POLYCENTRIC VERSUS STATE-LED RESPONSES TO THE COVID-19 PANDEMIC

Dinsha Mistree

Introduction

The COVID-19 pandemic is likely to be recorded as the most devastating event to afflict South Asia since the end of colonization. Millions of people have already lost their lives. Many others will experience long-lasting health effects. Additionally, the economic destruction wrought by the pandemic has upended livelihoods across the income spectrum. In the face of such calamity, pundits around the world have suggested that we will have to adjust to a "new normal."

For scholars of public administration and international relations, however, the governance response to the COVID-19 pandemic in South Asia is anything but new. Harkening back to earlier generations where most processes of development—including governance over infectious disease and public health—were firmly controlled by state-led processes, it is important to recognize how the South Asian response to the COVID-19 pandemic resembles this older model of governance. Across the region, country leaders sidelined technical experts and foreign advisors, sometimes even restructuring institutions such that all major decisions—including technical decisions—would be controlled by state leaders.

This reversion to state-led processes for responding to the COVID-19 pandemic is somewhat surprising. For much of the past four decades, scholars have documented how policymaking in public health and infectious disease has been extensively shaped by actors that are external to the state machinery. International entities like the World Health Organization (WHO), the Global Fund to Fight AIDS, Tuberculosis, and Malaria (the Global Fund), the World Bank, and the Bill and Melinda Gates Foundation have separately and collectively spent billions of dollars on infectious disease in the South Asian region. Although these entities have had mixed success in fighting infectious disease, the states of South Asia have historically turned to them as partners for guidance, coordination, and policy execution. At the same time, these international entities have shown a willingness to circumvent central governments by partnering with state and local governments or non-government organizations (NGOs) and the private sector. Because of the emergence of these international entities, public health and infectious disease in South Asia over the past two decades fits a pattern of "polycentric governance," whereby the state and a multitude of non-state entities work on the same development projects.[1]

DOI: 10.4324/9781003246626-36

425

As state-led governance over public health and infectious disease has given way to a system of polycentric governance across the region, it is also worth recognizing how state institutions have transformed in recent years. International entities including the US Centers for Disease Control and Prevention (US CDC) have deployed considerable resources to reform public health institutions within states in the region. By embedding trained public health experts within state machinery—and by sometimes building entire state institutions from scratch—these foreign entities have sought to develop a network of transnational technical expertise that could internally inform and shape states' approaches to public health and infectious disease. Such epistemic networks have been influential in a number of other technical domains and seemed to be influential in addressing South Asian epidemics over the past ten years.

Then the COVID-19 pandemic hit. Models of "polycentric governance" and epistemic transnational networks faltered as technical experts and foreign entities were sidelined across the region.[2] In India, Narendra Modi quickly moved to orient the main thrust of the pandemic response through the Prime Minister's Office. For Sri Lanka, the military played outsized roles in policymaking and execution. In Bangladesh, Sheikh Hasina's government controlled the pandemic response, opting to implement few countermeasures. Perhaps the sole example of polycentric governance in the region comes from Pakistan where the military and the civilian government relied heavily on the WHO for designing and implementing a COVID-19 response.

The ramifications of a state-led response to the COVID-19 pandemic are real and important. From a practitioner perspective, foreign organizations and technical experts who seek to alter the response to future disease outbreaks must recognize the primacy of the state system: Outside entities and other transnational epistemic networks are unlikely to play a determinative role in public health policymaking without first achieving a greater degree of political buy-in. Merely building institutions within a state is not likely to be enough. Foreign entities and technical experts must be prepared to engage with political processes in order to ensure relevance and policy influence.

For scholars of international relations, the COVID-19 pandemic highlights the importance—and perhaps even the primacy—of the state during times of crisis. Perhaps more than any other sphere of governance, the management of public health and infectious disease has come to be controlled by well-funded foreign entities like the WHO, the Gates Foundation, and the US CDC, along with networks of transnational experts. In the presence of such entities and networks, according to theories derived from the Liberal paradigm, the state should have become more of an executor than a locus of decision-making. Foreign entities and experts should have been making decisions. This did not happen, possibly because these entities and experts simply expected political actors to approach them for assistance. But domestic political actors did not wait around and instead crafted policy without much technical guidance.

As a result, even though non-state entities and epistemic networks have historically played powerful roles in combating infectious disease and public health—in line with conventional views of Liberalism—the politics of this pandemic seems to follow what realist theorists would suggest.[3] With the onset of the crisis, non-state entities were marginalized. Looking for direction, citizens seemed to turn to their state leaders instead of experts. Leaders in democratic states like India and Sri Lanka suspended the ordinary functioning of their governments, just like what we observe in more authoritarian states like Bangladesh. The states of South Asia not only took control over their processes of pandemic response, but they responded in more or less the same ways regardless of the structures of their domestic institutions.

The rest of this chapter is structured as follows. In the next section, I trace a brief history of governance of infectious disease in the South Asian region. I then document the nascent scholarship on the politics and response of the COVID-19 pandemic. For the most part, individual states have been handling their own responses, although it is important to note that limited international coordination has taken place on the matter of vaccine development and distribution (i.e., vaccine diplomacy). Taken together, these developments during the COVID-19 pandemic suggest that states are likely to remain the central node for responding to infectious diseases and other health emergencies. Foreign entities and technical experts need to identify how best to politically engage in these kinds of state-led processes.

A Brief History of Infectious Disease in South Asia

Broadly speaking, the challenge of infectious disease can be divided into two types, both of which necessitate different public health approaches. There are epidemics that public health officials seek to control when outbreaks occur. These forms of infectious disease include challenges like plague, cholera, smallpox, and the present COVID-19 pandemic. Apart from these outbreak diseases, infectious disease experts also work to address more endemic challenges like malaria and typhoid. During the colonial era, the British built institutions across South Asia to address and control both forms of infectious disease. For both epidemic and endemic diseases—the thrust of a field that would come to be known as tropical medicine—British public health officials designed new institutions and practices mostly from scratch.[4]

Almost from the beginning of the East India Company, medical personnel were assigned to ships traveling to India; by 1650, major factories in India were required to be staffed by British medical personnel. In 1763, the British created the Bengal Medical Service, followed by similar services in the Madras and Bombay Presidencies. Soon, these bureaucracies also developed broader oversight as they formed medical boards in charge of licensing and developing general medical policy in the respective presidencies. With the centralization of power following the 1857 uprising and the end of the East India Company, the Government of India created an Indian Medical Service (IMS). The IMS, like other senior colonial services, was almost exclusively staffed by Europeans and primarily focused on serving the military and the administrative needs of the colonial state.[5] Initial research was often conducted using captive populations, specifically those worked in the military and in prisons.[6] From these studies, the British colonial enterprise often framed public health and sanitation as disciplinary matters to be imposed through force if necessary.[7]

Ultimately, however, the British were selective in using force to enact public health measures on the general public, particularly after the 1857 uprising.[8] After all, the principal aim of the British colonial enterprise—and British efforts for regulating public health—was to extract as much as possible at the lowest cost. Unpopular policies like compulsory vaccinations, quarantines, and sanitary regulations in temples could contribute to political instability, and so during outbreaks of cholera and smallpox in the 19th century, the British refused to introduce such public health measures. One major test took place when the Bombay plague epidemic gripped the city from 1896 to 1905. In 1897, the colonial administration granted massive powers to the government with the passage of the Epidemic Diseases Act.[9] This Act enabled the government to take any measures deemed necessary to combat the outbreak of an infectious disease. But even when armed with the powers to shut down the city, the British exercised these powers selectively, mostly targeting Bombay's poorest neighborhoods where political resistance would have been marginal.[10]

By the early part of the 20th century, the British Empire was developing an extensive set of institutions to tackle infectious disease in India. Considerable investments were made in urban sanitation. Medical colleges and universities in India frequently offered programs in tropical medicine. Hospitals across the country focused on providing basic public health, particularly in urban areas. The Government also created several standalone institutions including the Central Malaria Bureau in 1909 and the Indian Research Fund Association in 1911.[11]

The groundwork laid by the British would shape infectious disease responses long after the British left. When the British left South Asia in 1947, they bequeathed a slew of universities and hospitals across the region. The Indian Medical Service was disbanded soon after Independence, but standalone institutions created under the British were repurposed. The Central Malaria Bureau, for instance, eventually became India's National Centre for Disease Control (NCDC). In a similar vein, the Indian Research Fund Association would become the Indian Council for Medical Research. In former British colonies like India, Pakistan, and Sri Lanka, the Epidemic Diseases Act of 1897 was never amended and remained in force long after each of these countries declared independence. It remains the main law for addressing epidemics in India.[12]

Following the departure of the British, the leaders of South Asia charted mostly statist policies of development, which also spilled over into public health and infectious disease. During the 1950s and 1960s, the states of South Asia played a determinative role in almost all aspects of infectious disease governance. Foreign philanthropies like the Ford and Rockefeller Foundations, as well as foreign governments and international bodies like the World Bank, mostly sought to support state capacity building in ways that South Asian states requested. Consider the establishment of the All India Institute of Medical Sciences (AIIMS), what is today recognized as India's leading medical center. The initial vision of AIIMS was crafted in 1946 by a health and survey development committee chaired by Joseph Bhore.[13] Following Indian Independence in 1947, Prime Minister Jawaharlal Nehru and his then Health Minister, Rajkumari Amrit Kaur, sought out financial support for AIIMS, eventually receiving several grants provided by the Government of New Zealand in accordance with the Colombo Plan, along with some minor financial support and technical training offered by the Rockefeller Foundation.[14] In 1956, Parliament passed the AIIMS Act, putting AIIMS squarely under the control of the central government.[15] Even though they had footed the costs for AIIMS and were concerned about its lack of starting autonomy, the Government of New Zealand and the Rockefeller Foundation did not formally complain or threaten to pull out of the project.[16]

Two important changes took place in the late 1970s and early 1980s. First, statist approaches to development began to fall out of favor. International development experts rapidly shifted from supporting efforts to help states determine their development priorities to a worldview where states were seen as the problem. Developing states needed to have narrow roles while actors in the non-governmental sectors designed and implemented policy. This ideological repositioning would come to be known as the Washington Consensus and contributed to a radical shift in international health policy engagement. Additionally, in the mid-1970s, the WHO became much more powerful in developing and executing infectious disease policy. Despite being founded in 1947, the budget and aims of the WHO had remained modest for most of its early years. In the 1950s and early 1960s, the WHO had experienced limited success in its global campaigns against tuberculosis, malaria, and smallpox. With small budgets, the WHO provided a few experts to a given developing country or outbreak situation. State institutions would still bear the primary responsibility for designing and executing public health policy.

Things started to change in the late 1960s, when a new disease surveillance method showed great promise in containing and controlling smallpox. Over the 1970s, the WHO would eliminate smallpox, the first disease ever eradicated by human effort. On the heels of this success, the WHO announced that it would pursue a "Health for All" approach, whereby the organization's intended focus would be on securing the health and well-being of people, rather than serving its constituent states. In the 1980s, outside groups began to heavily fund the WHO's efforts, including its campaign to combat the spread of HIV/AIDS and its Global Polio Eradication Initiative.[17] With considerable resources at its disposal, the WHO could expand its bench of experts. It could also hire its own implementation teams without relying on governments in developing countries. This radically changed the governance of infectious diseases in developing countries. From the 1990s to the 2010s, the WHO has mirrored other international organizations in decentralizing decision-making by including more civil society organizations and other stakeholders in their processes.

Also, it is important to recognize that the WHO is just one in a constellation of international and global institutions that focuses on infectious disease. Other prominent international institutions include the World Bank, the Global Fund, and other agencies affiliated with the UN such as UNICEF. Each of these organizations are well-endowed, providing them the flexibility to circumvent typical state processes if they so choose. Consider the Global Fund, which was formed in 2002 to fight AIDS, tuberculosis, and malaria. By 2022, the Global Fund will have spent more than 60 billion USD in this fight, a staggering amount of money that provides the ability to circumvent state apparatuses when it so chooses.[18]

Apart from international institutions, philanthropies like the Gates Foundation have also been active funders and policymakers in South Asian public health and infectious disease. Although other philanthropies like the Ford Foundation and the Rockefeller Foundation have operated in the public health space for decades prior to the Gates Foundation, the Gates Foundation operates at an unprecedented scale and size. The Gates Foundation began its efforts in South Asia in 2003 when it launched a $100 million HIV prevention initiative in India.[19] In 2020, the Gates Foundation spent more than $3.5 billion on public health challenges—much of which was concentrated in India and South Asia—in addition to making $250 million contribution to the Global Fund. To provide a sense of scale, the Ford Foundation has spent $500 million in total on all of its missions over the past 60 years across India, Nepal, and Sri Lanka combined.[20]

With its ample resources, the Gates Foundation has been able to operate with a considerable level of autonomy. Although the Gates Foundation officially seeks to collaborate and coordinate with central governments in South Asia, it has proven just as willing to circumvent central governments by partnering with state governments or by working directly with NGOs and the private sector. Although global philanthropies like the Gates Foundation do not always marginalize the central governments, they are often able to choose how they engage with states in the region.[21] Governance of public health and infectious disease has evolved from being state-led to being polycentric in nature.

As this evolution was taking place, state machineries themselves were being transformed. Across the South Asian region, the US CDC and the World Bank either overhauled state institutions or created new institutions to detect and trace infectious disease. For instance, in India, the US CDC overhauled the NCDC in 2009, providing resources and technical guidance leading to the formation of India's Epidemic Intelligence Services and regular frontline health worker training programs.[22] The US CDC also helped the NCDC develop its flagship program, the Integrated Disease Surveillance Program (IDSP), a decentralized mechanism to collate weekly disease surveillance data from across India on approximately 30 diseases.[23]

By developing training programs and embedding technically trained personnel within these countries' infectious disease institutions, the US CDC was building a transnational network that could steer policy. At least on paper, it is hard to overstate the importance of the NCDC—and by proxy the US CDC—for managing epidemics and pandemics in India. Because the IDSP serves as "the backbone for disease surveillance and detection of early warning signs," the NCDC is supposed to play a leading policymaking role in the event of an infectious disease crisis like a pandemic.[24] According to the guidelines of India's Disaster Management Act, the central government is supposed to establish a control room jointly operated by the NCDC and the Ministry of Health and Family Welfare. Robust epistemic communities and transnational networks are supposed to be able to steer policy, and the US CDC had enjoyed a considerable level of success in coordinating responses to various epidemics across South Asia during the 2010s.

To summarize, the governance of public health and infectious disease in South Asia has radically evolved. Following their independence from the British, the states of South Asia kept colonial-era public health laws and institutions in place. In the decades after independence, states almost completely controlled the governance of public health and infectious disease. Due to limited resources and an ideological belief in state capacity, foreign entities sought to support health projects identified by central government leaders. With the growth of the WHO and other international and global public health institutions in the 1980s—along with the emergence of the Washington Consensus—South Asian states' monopolies over public health and infectious disease governance became compromised. In the 2000s, the activities of the Gates Foundation further transformed this space. By the time the COVID-19 pandemic emerged, states were just one of many actors operating in the public health and infectious disease space. Governance of public health and infectious disease has evolved from being state-led to being polycentric in nature. Additionally, foreign entities like the US CDC developed strong ties with various state institutions. By developing epistemic communities and transnational networks, the US CDC was in a strong position to influence central government policymaking in a number of South Asian countries.

The COVID-19 Pandemic: A Case of International Experts in Estrangement

The first officially confirmed victim of COVID-19 fell sick on December 8, 2019 in Wuhan, China. South Asia would soon begin to detect COVID-19 cases. Nepal recorded its first case of COVID-19 on January 23, 2019 from a man traveling back from China.[25] This was followed by Sri Lanka's first case being reported on January 27, 2019, when a tourist from China tested positive.[26] Soon thereafter, India recorded its first case of COVID-19 on January 30, 2020, in the Thrissur District of Kerala, whose state government had proactively begun testing all arrivals from China.[27] Pakistan's first two cases of COVID-19 were detected on February 26, 2020, when two travelers from Iran tested positive for the virus.[28] Bangladesh's first cases were linked to travelers arriving from Italy.[29]

Although Sri Lanka and the Indian state of Kerala had been proactive in testing travelers, other South Asian central governments took few preventative measures. The situation changed in mid-March 2020, when all states across the region suddenly announced stringent national lockdowns. The effects of these lockdowns reverberated across the region. Migrant workers in the Middle East were forced to return to their home countries of Pakistan, India, Bangladesh, and Sri Lanka.[30] In India, the national lockdown triggered one of the largest internal migrations in history as tens of millions of workers left cities to return to their villages. Although lockdowns and quarantines have historically been used for other

Polycentric versus State-Led Responses to the COVID-19 Pandemic

non-health-related purposes, the official purpose of a lockdown is usually to stanch an out-break when it gets to the point that it might overwhelm a health system while planning for the next steps. Typically, public health responders should develop other measures like a con-tact tracing program or a coordinated public health campaign. Instead, India's leaders took the exact opposite approach. By mid-March, the NCDC's IDSP had detected 110 confirmed cases from 13 states across India. According to whistleblowers, the NCDC's IDSP was banned from releasing or collecting data related to COVID-19, and states were instead instructed to send their records directly to the Ministry of Health and Family Welfare.[31]

Despite being legally expected to coordinate the central government's operations room during a pandemic, the NCDC was also separated from COVID-19-related policymaking. Instead, the Prime Minister's Office established a set of ad hoc bodies known as Empowered Groups. These Empowered Groups were dominated by favored generalist bureaucrats drawn from the ranks of the Indian Administrative Service. IAS officers headed ten of the eleven original Empowered Groups, with only one Empowered Group led by a medical doctor.[32] Of the 66 members in the six reconstituted Empowered Groups, 39 were IAS officers, all of whom were closely tied to the prime minister.[33]

India's track record on vaccines is also revealing. Pfizer and Moderna vaccines were not made available to Indian citizens, despite being donated to the country through COVAX. After negotiating with Pfizer and Moderna for most of 2021, the government initially delayed providing use authorizations and then decided not to grant basic liability protections to the companies. At a time when Indian citizens were desperate for vaccines, the govern-ment charted an anti-public health course in order to favor the manufacture of domestically produced vaccines.

Taken together, India's overall policymaking structure during the COVID-19 pandemic has been one that pulls loyalists to the fore while technical expertise remains on the periphery. Few experts serve on the PMO's Empowered Groups, while the NCDC and other important government institutions have been excluded from making major decisions.[34] Furthermore, despite decades of investment and involvement in infectious disease, foreign entities like the WHO and the Gates Foundation do not seem to be playing relevant roles in COVID-19 policymaking.[35]

Within the South Asian region, India provides perhaps the most extreme example of the sidelining of foreign and technical expertise, but government leaders in other states also displayed statist tendencies. In Sri Lanka, for instance, the two main committees tasked with leading the COVID-19 response are headed by the Army chief and by President Mahinda Rajapaksa's brother, who also supports the army. Civil society and outside technical advisors were mostly not involved.[36] Also, because Sri Lanka maintains a robust domestic health infra-structure, hardened over several rounds of emergencies including war and tsunamis, Sri Lanka did not have to rely on outsiders. Because the military and police have played central roles in policy decision-making, and since the state has mostly been able to use its own infrastructure without relying on parallel structures for implementation, Sri Lankan scholars have written that the country's COVID-19 response is also following a "statist" approach.[37]

A similar account emerges from Bangladesh, where Prime Minister Sheikh Hasina and her political and military advisors have made most decisions regarding the pandemic response. Under her leadership, Bangladesh has charted a less stringent and more economically friendly course than other countries in South Asia. Although Sheikh Hasina initially utilized the army to enforce a national lockdown (termed a "general holiday"), enforcement was lack-luster and inconsistent. In April 2020, more than 100,000 Bangladeshis gathered for the funeral of a religious leader in defiance of the lockdown. Once the lockdown period ended in

May 2020, the country moved quickly to resume economic activity and normalize conditions. Unlike other countries, Bangladesh resumed public transportation and in-person government schooling by the autumn of 2020. In March 2021, Bangladesh decided to celebrate the Golden Jubilee of the country and the centenary of Sheikh Mujibur Rahman despite the upward trend of the infections and deaths. In the summer of 2021, Bangladesh again issued lockdown decrees following a wave of infections brought on by the Delta variant, but once again, these lockdowns were inconsistently enforced. Despite warnings from experts, no new preventive measures were taken and the country's health care system was ultimately overwhelmed.[38] One bright spot—and a notable exception to the statist model of Bangladesh's COVID-19 response—came from Building Resources Across Communities (BRAC), one of the largest NGOs in the world that also happens to be based in Bangladesh. BRAC utilized tens of thousands of its staff to distribute masks and teach social distancing practices, resulting in a demonstrably better outcome in the villages in which BRAC engaged.[39]

Across the South Asian region, state-led responses to the COVID-19 pandemic frequently sidelined outside institutions and experts. More often than not, these statist responses were dominated by country leaders who used the pandemic to further other political objectives. Perhaps the most surprising exception to this trend comes from Pakistan, where in March 2020, Prime Minister Imran Khan created a National Command and Operation Center composed of leaders from the military, members of Khan's cabinet, provincial leaders from different political parties, and domestic and foreign health experts. In addition to technical experts, the Pakistani government leaned heavily on the WHO in designing its COVID-19 response. In April 2020, Pakistan launched a COVID-19 Response Plan that had been drafted by the WHO and attracted almost 600 million USD from outside donors.[40] On the ground, tens of thousands of WHO community health workers who had been deployed as part of an anti-polio campaign were redirected to conduct surveillance, contact tracing, and care for COVID-19 patients. To be sure, the military was also heavily involved in implementation. They were tasked with implementing smart lockdowns, while a tracking tool developed by Pakistan's Inter-Services Intelligence (ISI) has been used to conduct contact tracing. Pakistan's response to the COVID-19 pandemic is perhaps the only real example of polycentric governance in the region.

Summary

For the past two decades, foreign entities like the WHO and the Gates Foundation have played an outsized role in the governance of public health and infectious disease across South Asia, in addition to much of the rest of the developing world. Additionally, transnational networks of public health officials, epidemiologists, doctors, and scholars seemed to have formed strong epistemic communities, oftentimes shaping policymaking and execution in this space. When the COVID-19 pandemic emerged, however, these foreign entities and transnational networks of experts were mostly estranged from the policymaking process. Instead, South Asia experienced largely state-led responses to the COVID-19 pandemic. As is documented in this chapter, decision-making was consolidated in the Prime Minister's Office in India; for Sri Lanka, decision-making rested with Rajapaksa and the leaders of the military; in Bangladesh, Sheikh Hasina and her advisors charted an economy-friendly response to the COVID-19 pandemic. Of the principal states of South Asia, only Pakistan relied on a foreign entity—the WHO—for guidance and implementation.

Although not addressed in this chapter, the states of South Asia displayed little interest in bilateral or regional multilateral coordination in response to the COVID-19 pandemic.

The only seemingly salient issue in most bilateral negotiations dealing with the COVID-19 pandemic involved vaccine sourcing, with India encouraging its neighbors to acquire Indian-manufactured vaccines. Prior to the wave of infections brought on by the Delta variant, India also engaged in "vaccine diplomacy" by pledging to donate massive amounts of vaccines to some of its neighboring countries. This program was suspended with India's deadly Delta variant wave and only restarted in the latter part of 2021. Multilateral engagement was also muted. At the suggestion of Narendra Modi, the South Asian Association for Regional Cooperation (SAARC) developed a modest—if mostly symbolic—COVID-19 Emergency Fund.[41] Apart from this effort, SAARC has not played much of a role in coordinating responses to the pandemic. Ultimately, the states of South Asia confronted the COVID-19 pandemic on their own, eschewing foreign entities and technical guidance.

As South Asia continues to struggle with the COVID-19 pandemic, it is likely that states will continue to chart their own courses without accepting much foreign or technical guidance. As a region that faces a constant struggle against both endemic and epidemic disease, it remains to be seen how the COVID-19 pandemic will affect governance of public health and infectious disease in the future. On the one hand, the COVID-19 experience could prove to be a blip and systems of polycentric governance could resume in the future. Alternatively, state leaders in South Asia might recognize the critical political dimension of public health and infectious disease and build out their own capabilities by internally designing their emergency response plans and infectious disease monitoring systems.

Foreign entities like the WHO and the Gates Foundation, along with other technical experts, must consider how and why they were squeezed out of the policymaking process in most states of South Asia. The circumstances suggested that they should have had unimpeded access, and yet, despite decades of spending massive amounts of money, building out strong networks of technical experts, and implanting entire infectious disease agencies across South Asia, it is important to recognize that technical experts failed to shape the regional COVID-19 response. In the future, organizations and experts who work in public health and infectious disease must identify how to engage in political processes such that their input is taken into account. To source this political clout, these organizations and experts may have to engage in activities that they ordinarily seek to avoid, such as running mass publicity campaigns to source public support or cooperating with reluctant politicians and military leaders. Without such efforts to engage in political processes, South Asia will be ill-prepared to respond to future infectious disease challenges.

Notes

1 Lieberman describes how the presence of groups like the Gates Foundation and the Global Fund had created a system of polycentric governance over public health and infectious disease in South Africa. See Evan S. Lieberman, "The Perils of Polycentric Governance of Infectious Disease in South Africa," *Social Science and Medicine* 73 (2011): 676–684. The original concept of polycentric governance comes from Vincent Ostrom, Charles M. Tiebout, and Robert Warren, "The Organization of Government in Metropolitan Areas: A Theoretical Inquiry," *The American Political Science Review* 55, no. 4 (1961): 831–842.

2 Likewise, Peter Haas and others have described how epistemic communities—specifically transnational networks of technical experts—are often able to take control of technical political processes. Technical fields like public health and epidemiology should be dominated by epistemic communities. See Peter M. Haas, "Epistemic Communities and International Policy Coordination," *International Organization* 46, no. 1 (1992): 1–35.

3 For a useful summary of realism versus neoliberalism, see Robert Jervis, "Realism, Neoliberalism, and Cooperation: Understanding the Debate," *International Security* 24, no. 1 (1999): 42–63. It must

also be noted that a model of polycentric governance relies on the rejection of realism since non-state entities are seen as exercising power that could be against the state's interests, as has been the case at times with public health and infectious disease governance in South Asia.

4 India and its civilizations and empires had long contended with infectious diseases. There are accounts of epidemics dating back to the 1300s, when a Moroccan traveler named Ibn Battuta wrote about an infectious disease afflicting southeast India. Accounts of epidemics became more frequent with the establishment of Portuguese colonies in the 16th century, a rise that is often attributed to increased intrastate commerce and trade. For the most part, sanitation and public health practices that India's precolonial states pursued were not incorporated during the era of colonization. See Mark Harrison, *Contagion: How Commerce Has Spread Disease* (New Haven: Yale University Press, 2012), 5–7.

5 David Arnold, *Colonizing the Body: State Medicine and Epidemic Disease in Nineteenth-Century India* (Berkeley: University of California Press, 1993), 57–61.

6 David Arnold, "Crisis and Contradiction in Indian Public Health," in *The History of Public Health and the Modern State*, ed. Dorothy Porter (Amsterdam: Brill Publishing, 1994), 335–355, 339.

7 Arnold, *Colonizing the Body*.

8 Arnold, "Crisis and Contradiction in Indian Public Health," 341–342.

9 The 1897 Act was passed in response to a number of infectious disease issues as epidemics had become commonplace in India during the latter decades of the 19th century. For its history, along with a more critical view of the Act, see Parikshit Goyal, "The Epidemic Diseases Act, 1897 Needs an Urgent Overhaul," *Economic and Political Weekly* 55, no. 45 (November 7, 2020).

10 Prashant Kidambi, "'An Infection of Locality': Plague, Pythogenesis and the Poor in Bombay, c. 1896–1905," *Urban History* 31, no. 2 (2004): 249–267.

11 Muhammad Umair Mushtaq, "Public Health in British India: A Brief Account of the History of Medical Services and Disease Prevention in Colonial India," *Indian Journal of Community Medicine* 34, no. 1 (2009): 6–14.

12 Goyal, "The Epidemic Diseases Act, 1897 Needs an Urgent Overhaul."

13 The Rockefeller Foundation was involved in making sure that AIIMS was put on the Bhore Committee's agenda, and they offered some funds and technical training, but they ultimately played a minor role in advising or institution-building. See Shirish N. Kavadi, "Autonomy vs. Ministerial Control in AIIMS: A Tussle Born in the 1950s," *Economic and Political Weekly* 41, no. 27/28 (July 8, 2006): 2967–2969.

14 The Colombo Plan was not specifically about public health; instead, the purpose of the Colombo Plan was to discourage the spread of communism in South and Southeast Asia. See Dinsha Mistree, *Understanding Meritocracy* (Ph.D. Dissertation), Princeton University, 2015.

15 The Institute Committee would become the main governing body of AIIMS. Fifteen out of its 17 members would be selected directly by the central government. The other two members were the vice-chancellor of Delhi University (who would be nominated by a semi-independent committee and confirmed by the central government) and the director of the Institute, who would be selected by the Committee itself. Additionally, the central government reserved the right to review and overturn anything passed by the Governing Body, which would be the main executive body of the Institute. The Governing Body would be chaired by the Minister of Health and would have a majority of government appointees. Government control in the administrative ranks came at the expense of technical ability: as of 2015, the Governing Body had 11 members, only five of whom had medical degrees. See Mistree, *Understanding Meritocracy*.

16 Even though the Rockefeller Foundation did not lodge any formal or public complaints, Marshall Balfour, the Associate Director of the Foundation in India, kept careful notes that were critical of the direction of AIIMS. Balfour ultimately concluded that "although the AIIMS is an autonomous body which can accept grants from any sources the real fact is that the ministry does control the institute and its governing body in the final analysis." See Marshall Balfour, "Balfour Note," *Rockefeller Foundation Archives* Record Group 1.2, Series 464 A, Box 37, Folder 307, March 18, 1958.

17 The US Government, as well as several private sector organizations, helped launch the WHO's Special Programme on AIDS. The Global Polio Eradication Initiative came about in 1988, following Rotary International's centennial campaign that raised 100 million USD to initiate the effort. See Kelley Lee and Jennifer Fang, *Historical Dictionary of the World Health Organization* (Lanham, MD: Rowman and Littlefield, 2013).

Polycentric versus State-Led Responses to the COVID-19 Pandemic

18 Global Fund, *Financials*, https://www.theglobalfund.org/en/financials/ (accessed December 31, 2021).

19 See the Gates Foundation, *India*, https://www.gatesfoundation.org/our-work/places/india (accessed December 31, 2021).

20 See the Ford Foundation, *India, Nepal and Sri Lanka*, https://www.fordfoundation.org/our-work-around-the-world/india-nepal-and-sri-lanka/ (accessed December 31, 2021).

21 Manjarai Mahajan, "Philanthropy and the Nation-State in Global Health: The Gates Foundation in India," *Global Public Health* 13, no. 10 (2017): 1357–1368.

22 Director General of Health Services, *National Centre for Disease Control Booklet* (New Delhi: Government of India, 2018), https://ncdc.gov.in/linkimages/NCDC%20Booklet.pdf (accessed December 31, 2021).

23 CDC, *CDC India Anniversary Report* (2021), https://www.cdc.gov/globalhealth/countries/india/anniversary-report/pdf/India-Anniversary-Report.pdf (accessed January 14, 2022).

24 NDMA, *National Disaster Management Guidelines: Management of Biological Disasters* (New Delhi: Government of India, 2008), https://nidm.gov.in/pdf/guidelines/new/biological_disasters.pdf (accessed December 31, 2021).

25 A. Bastola et al., "The First 2019 Novel Coronavirus Case in Nepal," *Lancet Infectious Disease* 20, no. 3 (2020): 279–280.

26 Malji, "The COVID-19 Pandemic and Deepening Marginalization in Sri Lanka."

27 M.A. Andrews, et al., "First Confirmed Case of COVID-19 Infection in India: A Case Report," *Indian Journal of Medical Research* 151, no. 5 (May 2020): 490–492.

28 Ayaz Gul, "Pakistan Detects First Coronavirus Cases, Links to Iran Outbreak," *Voice of America*, February 26, 2020, https://www.voanews.com/a/science-health_coronavirus-outbreak_pakistan-detects-first-coronavirus-cases-links-iran-outbreak/6184888.html (accessed January 15, 2022).

29 Ruma Paul, "Bangladesh Confirms its First Three Cases of Coronavirus," *Reuters*, March 8, 2020, https://www.reuters.com/article/us-health-coronavirus-bangladesh/bangladesh-confirms-its-first-three-cases-of-coronavirus-idUSKBN20V0FS (accessed January 15, 2022).

30 On the plight of Indian immigrants working in the Middle East, see Nicolas Blarel, "Fallout from the Pandemic: The Experience of Indian Diasporas in the Gulf States," in *The COVID-19 Pandemic in South Asia*, eds. Šumit Ganguly and Dinsha Mistree (New York: Routledge Press, forthcoming).

31 Vidya Krishnan, "Epidemiologists Say India's Centre for Disease Control Withheld COVID-19 Data since Pandemic Began," *The Caravan*, May 11, 2020, https://caravanmagazine.in/health/epidemiologists-say-india-centre-disease-control-withheld-covid-19-data-since-pandemic-began (accessed December 31, 2021).

32 The original 11 Empowered Groups were consolidated into six Empowered Groups on September 11, 2020. Like the original Empowered Groups, the membership of the six reconstituted groups was mostly drawn from the IAS, with few subject matter experts. Of the six reconstituted groups, five are headed by IAS officers. For a complete membership list of the original Empowered Groups, see Ministry of Home Affairs Order No. 40-3/2020-DM-I(A) (dated March 29, 2020), https://www.mha.gov.in/sites/default/files/MHA%20Order%20on%20%20Disaster%20Management%20Act%202005.pdf. For the membership of the reconstituted groups, see Ministry of Home Affairs Order No. 40-3/2020-DM-I(A) (dated September 11, 2020), https://www.ndmindia.nic.in/images/gallery/Reconstitution%20of%20Empowered%20Group.pdf.

33 Several senior IAS officers in the Empowered Groups were formerly in the Modi-led Gujarat state government, including V. Thiruppugazh, Bharat Lal, and A.K. Sharma. See also Moushumi Das Gupta, "Loyalty and Performance: Why Modi Appointed Trusted Men to Helm Crucial Ministries amid Covid," *The Print*, April 28, 2020. https://theprint.in/india/governance/loyalty-and-performance-why-modi-appointed-trusted-men-to-helm-crucial-ministries-amid-covid/410195/. Also see The National Herald Web Desk, "Gujarat Cadre Officers Call the Shots in Modi Government," *The National Herald*, October 6, 2018, https://www.nationalheraldindia.com/india/gujarat-cadre-officers-call-the-shots-in-modi-government.

34 Vidya Krishnan and Sarah Nabia, "The Indian Government Used the Pandemic as a Political Image and Failed to Save Lives," *The Caravan*, September 14, 2021, https://caravanmagazine.in/health/the-indian-government-used-the-pandemic-to-craft-a-political-image (accessed January 15, 2022).

35 Although the central government has squeezed out experts, some state governments still seem to be formulating policy in close coordination with various infectious disease bodies, especially

Kerala. See Šumit Ganguly and Dinsha Mistree, "Fragile India, Strong India: Why Some States Handled COVID-19 Better than Others," *Foreign Policy*, May 28, 2021, https://foreignpolicy.com/2021/05/28/fragile-india-strong-india/ (accessed January 1, 2022).

36 The government and the army have also used the COVID-19 pandemic as an opportunity to marginalize political opponents and minorities. See Andrea Malji, "The COVID-19 Pandemic and Deepening Marginalization in Sri Lanka," in *The COVID-19 Pandemic in South Asia*, eds. Šumit Ganguly and Dinsha Mistree (New York: Routledge Press, forthcoming).

37 Kalinga Silva, "Identity, Infection, and Fear: A Preliminary Analysis of COVID-19 Drivers and Responses in Sri Lanka," *International Center for Ethnic Studies* (2020), 19.

38 Nazmul Ahasan and Jenny Lei Ravelo, "Bangladesh Battles Third Wave of COVID-19," *Devex*, July 14, 2021, https://www.devex.com/news/bangladesh-battles-third-wave-of-COVID-19-100340 (accessed January 1, 2022).

39 Jason Abaluck, et al., "Impact of Community Masking on COVID-19: A Cluster-Randomized Trial in Bangladesh," *Science*, forthcoming.

40 WHO, "COVID-19 in Pakistan: WHO Fighting Tirelessly against the Odds," https://www.who.int/news-room/feature-stories/detail/covid-19-in-pakistan-who-fighting-tirelessly-against-the-odds (accessed January 1, 2022).

41 Narendra Modi, "PM Interacts with SAARC Leaders to Combat COVID-19 in the Region," March 15, 2020, https://www.narendramodi.in/prime-minister-narendra-modi-s-interaction-with-saarc-leaders-on-fighting-coronavirus-548793 (accessed January 15, 2022).

Bibliography

Abaluck, Jason, Laura Kwong, Ashley Styczynski, Ashraful Haque, Alamgir Kabir, Ellen Bates-Jeffreys, Emily Crawford, Jade Benjamin-Chung, Shabib Raihan, Shadman Rahman, Salim Benhachmi, Neeti Bintee, Peter Winch, Maqsud Hossain, Hasan Reza, Abdullah Jaber, Shawkee Momen, Aura Rahman, Faika Banti, Tahrima Huq, Stephen Luby, and Ahmed Mobarak. "Impact of Community Masking on COVID-19: A Cluster-Randomized Trial in Bangladesh." *Science*, 375, no. 6577 (2021).

Ahasan, Nazmul, and Jenny Ravelo. "Bangladesh Battles Third Wave of COVID-19." *Devex*, July 14, 2021. Accessed January 1, 2022. https://www.devex.com/news/bangladesh-battles-third-wave-of-COVID-19-100340.

Andrews, M., Binu Areekal, K. Rajesh, Jijith Krishnan, R. Suryakala, Biju Krishnan, C. Muraly, and P. Santosh. "First Confirmed Case of COVID-19 Infection in India: A Case Report." *Indian Journal of Medical Research* 151, no. 5 (May 2020): 490–492.

Arnold, David. "Crisis and Contradiction in Indian Public Health." In *The History of Public Health and the Modern State*, edited by Dorothy Porter. Amsterdam: Brill Publishing, 1994.

Arnold, David. *Colonizing the Body: State Medicine and Epidemic Disease in Nineteenth-Century India*. Berkeley: University of California Press, 1993.

Balfour, Marshall. "Balfour Note." *Rockefeller Foundation Archives* Record Group 1.2, Series 464 A, Box 37, Folder 307. March 18, 1958.

Bastola, A., R. Sah, A.J. Rodriguez-Morales, B.K. Lal, R. Jha, H.C. Ojha, B. Shrestha, D.K.W. Chu, L.L.M. Poon, A. Costello, K. Morita, and B.D. Pandey. "The First 2019 Novel Coronavirus Case in Nepal." *Lancet Infectious Diseases* 20, no. 3 (2020): 279–280.

Blarel, Nicolas. "Fallout from the Pandemic: The Experience of Indian Diasporas in the Gulf States." In *The COVID-19 Pandemic in South Asia*, edited by Šumit Ganguly and Dinsha Mistree. New York: Routledge, 2022.

CDC. *CDC India Anniversary Report*. 2021. Accessed January 14, 2022. https://www.cdc.gov/globalhealth/countries/india/anniversary-report/pdf/India-Anniversary-Report.pdf.

Das Gupta, Moushomi. "Loyalty and Performance: Why Modi Appointed Trusted Men to Helm Crucial Ministries Amid Covid." *The Print*, April 28, 2020. https://theprint.in/india/governance/loyalty-and-performance-why-modi-appointed-trusted-men-to-helm-crucial-ministries-amid-covid/410195/.

Director General of Health Services. *National Centre for Disease Control Booklet*. New Delhi: Government of India, 2018. Accessed December 31, 2021. https://ncdc.gov.in/linkimages/NCDC%20Booklet.pdf.

Ford Foundation. *India, Nepal and Sri Lanka*. Accessed December 31, 2021. https://www.fordfoundation.org/our-work-around-the-world/india-nepal-and-sri-lanka/.

Ganguly, Šumit, and Dinsha Mistree. "Fragile India, Strong India: Why Some States Handled COVID-19 Better Than Others." *Foreign Policy*, May 28, 2021. Accessed January 1, 2022. https://foreignpolicy.com/2021/05/28/fragile-india-strong-india/.

Gates Foundation. *India*. Accessed December 31, 2021. https://www.gatesfoundation.org/our-work/places/india.

Goyal, Parikshit. "The Epidemic Diseases Act, 1897 Needs an Urgent Overhaul." *Economic and Political Weekly* 55, no. 45 (November 7, 2020).

Gul, Ayaz. "Pakistan Detects First Coronavirus Cases, Links to Iran Outbreak." *Voice of America*, February 26, 2020. Accessed January 15, 2022. https://www.voanews.com/a/science-health_coronavirus-outbreak_pakistan-detects-first-coronavirus-cases-links-iran-outbreak/6184888.html.

Haas, Peter. "Epistemic Communities and International Policy Coordination." *International Organization* 46, no. 1 (1992): 1–35.

Harrison, Mark. *Contagion: How Commerce Has Spread Disease*. New Haven: Yale University Press, 2012.

Jervis, Robert. "Realism, Neoliberalism, and Cooperation: Understanding the Debate." *International Security* 24, no. 1 (1999): 42–63.

Kavadi, Shirish. "Autonomy vs. Ministerial Control in AIIMS: A Tussle Born in the 1950s." *Economic and Political Weekly* 41, no. 27/28 (July 8, 2006): 2967–2969.

Kidambi, Prashant. "'An Infection of Locality': Plague, Pythogenesis and the Poor in Bombay, c. 1896-1905." *Urban History* 31, no. 2 (2004): 249–267.

Krishnan, Vidya. "Epidemiologists Say India's Centre for Disease Control Withheld COVID-19 Data since Pandemic Began." *The Caravan*, May 11, 2020. Accessed December 31, 2021. https://caravanmagazine.in/health/epidemiologists-say-india-centre-disease-control-withheld-covid-19-data-since-pandemic-began.

Krishnan, Vidya, and Sarah Nabia. "The Indian Government Used the Pandemic as a Political Image and Failed to Save Lives." *The Caravan*, September 14, 2021. Accessed January 15, 2022. https://caravanmagazine.in/health/the-indian-government-used-the-pandemic-to-craft-a-political-image.

Lee, Kelley, and Jennifer Fang. *Historical Dictionary of the World Health Organization*. Lanham, MD: Rowman and Littlefield, 2013.

Lieberman, Evan. "The Perils of Polycentric Governance of Infectious Disease in South Africa." *Social Science and Medicine* 73 (2011): 676–684.

Malji, Andrea. "The COVID-19 Pandemic and Deepening Marginalization in Sri Lanka." In *The COVID-19 Pandemic in South Asia*, edited by Šumit Ganguly and Dinsha Mistree. New York: Routledge Press, forthcoming.

Mahajan, Manjarai. "Philanthropy and the Nation-State in Global Health: The Gates Foundation in India." *Global Public Health* 13, no. 10 (2017): 1357–1368.

Ministry of Home Affairs Order No. 40-3/2020-DM-I(A). Dated September 11, 2020. https://www.ndmindia.nic.in/images/gallery/Reconstitution%20of%20Empowered%20Group.pdf.

Ministry of Home Affairs Order No. 40-3/2020-DM-I(A). Dated March 29, 2020. https://www.mha.gov.in/sites/default/files/MHA%20Order%20on%20%20Disaster%20Management%20Act%20 2005.pdf.

Mistree, Dinsha. *Understanding Meritocracy* (Ph.D. Dissertation). Princeton University, 2015.

Modi, Narendra. "PM Interacts with SAARC Leaders to Combat COVID-19 in the Region." March 15, 2020. Accessed January 15, 2022. https://www.narendramodi.in/prime-minister-narendra-modi-s-interaction-with-saarc-leaders-on-fighting-coronavirus-548793.

Mushtaq, Muhammad. "Public Health in British India: A Brief Account of the History of Medical Services and Disease Prevention in Colonial India." *Indian Journal of Community Medicine* 34, no. 1 (2009).

National Herald Web Desk. "Gujarat Cadre Officers Call the Shots in Modi Government." *The National Herald*, October 6, 2018. https://www.nationalheraldindia.com/india/gujarat-cadre-officers-call-the-shots-in-modi-government.

NDMA. *National Disaster Management Guidelines: Management of Biological Disasters*. New Delhi: Government of India, 2008. Accessed December 31, 2021. https://nidm.gov.in/pdf/guidelines/new/biological_disasters.pdf.

Ostrom, Vincent, Charles Tiebout, and Robert Warren. "The Organization of Government in Metropolitan Areas: A Theoretical Inquiry." *The American Political Science Review* 55, no. 4 (1961): 831–842.

Paul, Ruma. "Bangladesh Confirms its First Three Cases of Coronavirus." *Reuters*, March 8, 2020. Accessed January 15, 2022. https://www.reuters.com/article/us-health-coronavirus-bangladesh/bangladesh-confirms-its-first-three-cases-of-coronavirus-idUSKBN20V0FS.

Silva, Kalinga. "Identity, Infection, and Fear: A Preliminary Analysis of COVID-19 Drivers and Responses in Sri Lanka." *International Center for Ethnic Studies*. 2020.

Slaughter, Anne Marie. *A New World Order*. Princeton, NJ: Princeton University Press, 2004.

WHO. "COVID-19 in Pakistan: WHO Fighting Tirelessly against the Odds." Accessed January 1, 2022. https://www.who.int/news-room/feature-stories/detail/covid-19-in-pakistan-who-fighting-tirelessly-against-the-odds.

32
REFUGEES AND MIGRATION IN SOUTH ASIA

Kavita R. Khory

The arrival of massive numbers of migrants on European shores in 2015, followed by an unprecedented rise in asylum seekers and refugees globally, widespread displacement and disruption brought on by climate change, and, most recently, the global lockdown precipitated by the COVID-19 pandemic have drawn renewed attention to the challenges and opportunities of international migration. While the interests and actions of Western governments are often at the forefront of policy debates on many forms of migration, countries in South Asia have long wrestled with some of the most significant population movements in history, catastrophic climate events, and internally displaced persons.

At the same time, South Asia today is a major point of origin for labor migration, and according to some estimates, the highest number of emigrants in the world are from India. In 2020, nearly 18 million Indians were living abroad.[1] Approximately, 44 million people from South Asia live outside their country of origin, which gives South Asia the distinction of being the region with the largest number of emigrants in the world. It is also among the highest recipients of remittances. Migration, most of all, cannot be separated from public debates in South Asia on national identity and citizenship, the trade-offs between development and protecting the environment, and human rights and security—issues that have grown more urgent during the pandemic, which has further exposed the precarious lives of many migrants and refugees around the world.

This chapter examines the migrations and refugee movements that have profoundly shaped South Asia's history and political economy. Although scholars of migration are rightly paying greater attention to internal migration and displacement, including climate-induced migration, we will be focusing principally on cross-border migrations in and from South Asia. Despite shared histories and cultural affinities, each country's experience with migration is distinctive, marked by vastly different geographies, demographics, economies, and strategic priorities.

We begin with a brief overview of the relevance of International Relations (IR) theories for the study of migration and highlight major themes in recent scholarship on "forced" and "voluntary" migration in South Asia—a region marked by contested borders and geopolitical conflicts. We then look at important examples of voluntary and forced migration, such as: Labor migration from colonial times to the more recent circular migration of low- or semi-skilled workers to the Gulf Cooperation Council (GCC) countries;[2] the migration of highly skilled

DOI: 10.4324/9781003246626-37

439

workers and professionals to advanced economies; the feminization of labor migration; and finally, forcible displacement and refugee movements, stemming from the Partition of the subcontinent in 1947 to the Bangladesh war of independence in 1971, and protracted conflicts in Sri Lanka, Afghanistan, and Myanmar. For purposes of analytical clarity, we distinguish forced migration from voluntary movements, although in practice there is significant overlap between the two categories. As politically contested concepts, neither forced nor voluntary migration fully captures the dynamic nature of migration or the lived experiences of migrants themselves.

Throughout we ask: What are the social, economic, and political forces driving temporary and permanent migration in South Asia? How do new patterns of migration impact South Asian states and societies, which have substantial émigré populations yet also serve as transit points and destinations? How effective are different mechanisms, adopted by South Asian governments, in "managing" and "controlling" migration? How do global norms and institutions inform and shape national policies? What are the implications of migration for sovereignty and citizenship, including the engagement of diaspora populations?

IR Theories, Themes, and Approaches

Situated at the intersection of domestic politics and foreign policy, migration, as a distinctive, multidisciplinary field of study, did not receive much attention from IR theorists until the waning years of the Cold War. Previously dismissed as "low politics," scholars began to look more carefully, first, at forms and patterns of migration in relation to globalization and the ongoing transformation of the global economy, and second, the implications of human mobility for sovereignty and security. Neither globalization nor the securitization of migration is of recent origin, yet both have reinforced the importance of migration for the study and practice of IR, with varying consequences for migrants and refugees.

Major IR theories—realism, liberalism, constructivism, and critical theories such as post-colonial, decolonial, and feminist—advance our understanding of migration trends and policies in different ways, depending on the levels of analysis and assumptions about the structure of the international system, the power and interests of states, and the importance of identities, cultural norms, and transnational networks in global politics. Lacking a unified theory, much of the scholarship on migration is informed by a combination of theories and approaches in IR, as well as other disciplinary frameworks. To give one example, liberalism or an international political economy (IPE) perspective is useful for understanding structural shifts in the global economy while also shedding light on the preferences and policies of the "migration state" in navigating tensions between markets and rights in liberal democracies.[3] More recently, scholars like Fiona Adamson and Gerasimos Tsourapas have refined and extended the concept of the migration state from Western democracies to the global South, applying it to "developmental" or "neoliberal" models of migration management, which have been adopted by countries in South Asia.[4] Again, as we see in South Asia, state interests and power, typically the focus of realists, do not operate independently of discourses of national identity, public diplomacy, and soft power—topics more familiar to constructivists. Post-colonial and decolonial approaches, which, until recently, were mostly ignored in the IR literature, inform the work of a number of scholars who study the hierarchies of power and how issues of race, gender, and class function in relation to migration in South Asia. Similarly, feminist scholars further our understanding of the feminization of migration—a relatively recent development in South Asia.

The literature on migration in South Asia engages many of the topics and themes that broadly animate the study of global migration, for example: Labor mobility and development, "securitizing" immigration, diaspora communities, citizenship and integration, climate-induced displacement, and the management of mass and mixed migrations. Leaving aside different disciplinary or theoretical perspectives, scholars of South Asian migration offer valuable insights into the historical and contemporary experiences and practices of non-European states and non-state actors, which have been neglected in the study of migration and policy, especially at the international level. Scholars and policymakers in the global South, more broadly, have questioned the application of norms and conventions, formulated chiefly for and by a post-World War II Europe, to a region like South Asia with its particular colonial histories and legacies.[5] Partha Ghosh, Ranabir Samaddar, and Pia Oberoi, for example, question the relevance of global migration and refugee regimes, which do not take into account the postcolonial state, or allow for different interpretations and local practices of "responsibility" and "care." They argue for broadening existing definitions of forced migration and developing a wider range of administrative and judicial measures for protecting refugees and stateless persons, such as Rohingyas in Bangladesh and India.[6]

In addition to stressing the importance of global and regional perspectives, several scholars of South Asian migration have moved beyond colonial and Cold War conceptions of regions by engaging explicitly with transnational and global approaches to migration. Instead of looking at global migration from the perspective of the transatlantic slave trade or South to North movements, historians like Sunil Amrith have challenged static, bounded definitions of borders and cultures by showing how trade routes, migrations, and cultural contacts across the Bay of Bengal have long connected India, Sri Lanka, and Bangladesh with Malaysia, Thailand, and Indonesia.[7]

Throughout modern history, population movements, displacement, and refugees have been intrinsic to the formation of new states. South Asia is no exception, as the Partition of the Indian subcontinent in 1947 led to one of the largest and most violent population transfers in the world. Yet Partition and its aftermath, except for passing references, rarely appear in studies of global refugee movements after the World War II, which set the stage for the 1951 Refugee Convention and the 1967 Protocol affirming the rights of refugees and the responsibility of states to protect them.[8] In addition to standard accounts of the political developments leading up to and after Partition, a younger generation of historians, anthropologists, and feminist scholars have written eloquently about ordinary people who experienced firsthand the partitioning of India and its devastating consequences. In doing so, they broaden our understanding of Partition and its connections with contemporary examples of cross-border migrations in South Asia, complex movements that do not fit neatly into binary categories like voluntary and forced migration.[9]

Scholars and policymakers have begun to look more holistically at the refugee experience in South Asia, including the role of international organizations and non-state actors in coordinating relief aid and assistance, and the economies of refugee camps. Stressing the individual and collective agency of refugees and displaced persons further complicates conventional narratives of forced migration and its implications for states and societies.[10] As examples from Bangladesh and Pakistan, among others, suggest, self-advocacy can be empowering for refugees trying to access health care, education, and employment in refugee camps and local communities.[11]

Contentious debates over the social, political, and legal status of migrants, asylum seekers, and refugees are closely tied to issues of national identity and citizenship. The perennial question of who qualifies as a citizen became more urgent after Partition, particularly in policy debates on refugee resettlement and its place in the nationalist projects of India and Pakistan.[12] Some scholars have called for broadening the definition of citizenship in South

Asian countries, citing the marked differences between legal and formal conceptions of citizenship and the lived experiences of migrants in post-colonial societies, while others are looking more closely at the increasingly restrictive and arbitrary policies and the criteria for acquiring citizenship—a trend extending well beyond South Asia.[13] Citizenship—in theory and practice—is a work-in-progress, contested, politicized, and manipulated more so than ever. The most recent example being the Indian Citizenship Amendment Act in 2019, which fast-tracked citizenship for migrants of all faiths from neighboring countries in South Asia with the exception of Muslims.

Citizenship is an equally contested concept in relation to South Asian diasporas, as governments, which had once neglected their émigré populations, have been increasingly turning to diasporas for promoting economic development at "home" while leveraging their cultural capital and political power in countries of settlement. Though globalization and neoliberalism explain to some extent the reversal in government policies toward diasporas, nationalism and foreign policy have played an equally important role in redefining the scope of diaspora-state relations.[14] Diasporas, in turn, have been calling for dual citizenship, or more flexible forms of citizenship that would allow them to access the rights and privileges generally reserved for citizens, including political participation and voting. A number of scholars have focused almost exclusively on the importance of diasporas for development, paying particular attention to those who have settled in the West,[15] while others have turned their attention toward Asia and the Middle East, following historical patterns of settlement and the formation of diaspora communities.[16] Overall, the literature on South Asian diasporas, particularly at the elite level, leans heavily toward Indian migrants, with fewer studies of diaspora communities whose origins lie elsewhere in the region.[17]

Migration Trends Post-1947

Colonial patterns of labor migration in South Asia were instrumental in forming the region's political economy, its demography, and territorial boundaries. Beginning in the 1830s, the British recruited indentured labor from Bengal, Bihar, and Tamil Nadu to work on plantations across the British Empire. Migration, in turn, led to sizable numbers of Indians settling in South Africa, the Caribbean, Malaysia, Myanmar, and Sri Lanka, among other places.[18] The British also imported labor from Bengal and Nepal to work in the tea plantations and coal mines of Assam. Labor migration did not occur in a political or administrative vacuum. Colonial classifications of religion, race, caste, and ethnicity followed British subjects, leading to escalating social and political tensions along the lines of religion, ethnicity, and class during British rule and long after its demise. Indeed, disputes over citizenship in Assam, the exclusion of Indian Tamils from Sri Lankan citizenship, and, most recently, the statelessness of Rohingya can be seen as the legacies of colonial policies and practices.

Migrations from South Asia followed different trajectories after World War II. Massive demands for labor created by the post-war reconstruction of European countries attracted semi-skilled labor as well as skilled workers and professionals from South Asia, with many going to the UK at the time. Elimination of racial and national-origin quotas by the US, Canadian, and Australian governments in the 1960s and 1970s offered additional choices and opportunities for migrants with a broad range of skills. Further incentives in the form of educational exchange programs, recruitment of students and professionals, particularly by US institutions and firms, the introduction of short-term visas, and family reunification programs encouraged even larger numbers of migrants from South Asia to move to high-income countries temporarily or to settle permanently.

Although migration from South Asia today is global in scope, one of the most notable trends from the 1970s onwards is the expansion and growth of labor migration to GCC countries, which have become prime destinations for migrant labor and a major source of remittances for South Asian states. GCC economies, in turn, have grown heavily reliant on the labor of South Asians, low- and semi-skilled workers, and professionals. Below we look at high-skill and professional migration, as well as labor migration, specifically to the Gulf countries, and consider the implications of both strands for countries in South Asia.

High-skill and Professional Migration

Migrants with specialized knowledge, training, and skills can be of benefit to both countries of origin and settlement. At the same time, they may demand higher levels of engagement and access, commensurate with their perceived status, occupation, and wealth. In spite of vast differences among high skilled migrants from South Asia, from countries of origin to financial capabilities and relationships with home and host states, we can see how public attitudes and polices toward an elite segment of migrants have evolved over time, driven by global economic trends, increasing connectivity through travel and technology, and the rise of diasporas as prominent non-state actors in international politics.

After having taken a more or less "hands off" approach to populations settled abroad under colonialism, governments in South Asia began paying greater attention to them as globalization intensified and neoliberalism became the dominant paradigm after the Cold War. With low economic growth and severe balance of payment crises calling into question the viability of state-led development models, not to mention the pressure from international financial institutions and funding agencies to adopt market-based economic reforms and structural adjustment measures, governments sought additional sources of revenue and investment. Educated and well established, medical professionals, scientists, titans of industry, writers, artists, and philanthropists became targets of opportunity for governments seeking capital investments and knowledge and technology transfers in a highly competitive global economy.

Mobilizing diaspora wealth and knowledge is complicated and calls for a range of incentives and high levels of reciprocity, which in themselves do not guarantee success. The interests and objectives of migrants may not necessarily align with those government officials or private citizens in countries of origin or settlement, leading to missed opportunities and disappointments. In South Asia, the results have been mixed, even within states, with some areas benefitting more so than others, depending on local and national politics, investment opportunities, labor market conditions, and public opinion. Governments have been setting up new agencies to cultivate the support of emigrant communities and leverage it more effectively. The Ministry of Overseas Indian Affairs, which later merged with the Ministry of External Affairs, was set up specifically for this purpose. In 2013, Pakistan established the Ministry of Overseas Pakistanis and Human Resources Development in 2013 for similar reasons.

By all measures, India has been the most successful in mobilizing the collective power of emigrants, including second- and third-generations, who are often more committed to "homeland" projects than their parents or grandparents. Information, technology, and off-shore outsourcing are among the major beneficiaries of the synergy between young tech-savvy workers and Indian multinationals, such as WIPRO, and their counterparts abroad.

In addition to material resources, governments increasingly are looking to diasporas as social and cultural ambassadors, instruments of soft power aimed at enhancing a state's prestige and status and promoting its national identity. Frequently cited examples include the CEOs of top American companies (Alphabet, IBM, Microsoft, Adobe, and Twitter) who are of Indian origin and Prime Minister Modi's highly orchestrated rallies in London, Sydney, New York, and Houston, major metropolitan areas with sizable numbers of Indian immigrants and BJP supporters, which have become occasions for showcasing India's growing power and prestige, not to mention marketing Modi's own "brand" to global audiences.

Labor Migrations

While there is a long history of labor migration between South Asia and the Persian Gulf region, the rising demand for labor in the 1970s was driven in large part by an increase in oil prices in the early 1970s, major investments in construction and infrastructure by GCC governments, and an acute shortage of local labor to power the building boom. The need for semi-skilled and skilled labor intensified after the departure of Palestinian and Yemini workers from Saudi Arabia and other Gulf countries following the first Persian Gulf War in 1991.[19] Labor migration to the GCC, in contrast to other destinations, is most often temporary, contractual, and subject to stringent restrictions that severely curtail workers' rights.[20]

India sends the largest number of migrants to GCC countries, followed by Pakistan and Bangladesh. In South Asia, like elsewhere, some regions and provinces have become major hubs for labor migration, resulting in a concentration in specific locations of income and investments from remittances. In India, Kerala and Tamil Nadu were the top two sources of migrant labor in the 1990s, although Uttar Pradesh and Bihar have recently caught up, with the largest number of workers from these two states going to Saudi Arabia.[21] Similarly, in Pakistan, a majority of workers going to the GCC countries are from two provinces, Punjab and Khyber Pakhtunkhwa (KP), with fewer benefits accruing to Sindh or Balochistan from the South Asia-Gulf migration corridor. The number of labor migrants from Nepal is relatively lower, while the largest number of female migrants from South Asia is of Sri Lankan origin.

When weighing the pros and cons of labor migration, some argue that immigration deprives countries of human capital and creates greater inequality. Others believe that it stimulates growth, promotes human development and social transformation, and improves living conditions for households and communities. Oftentimes, the costs and benefits of migration for states and societies are debated along the lines of "brain drain" vs "brain gain," which rarely take into account the unseen costs and calculations for individuals and families when considering migration.

Overall, labor migration, despite its drawbacks, is seen as benefitting low- and middle-income countries like Sri Lanka, Bangladesh, Pakistan, and India. First, it reduces poverty in households and communities by providing employment and remittances, which are a major source of foreign exchange and direct investment, leading to better outcomes in education, nutrition, and healthcare. In 2021, India was the top recipient of global remittances in a region where remittances are the dominant source of foreign exchange, three times as large as all other sources of foreign direct investment.[22] The relationship between migration and development, however, is rarely straightforward, as development can alleviate the pressures to immigrate, but also facilitate the process, as additional resources become available. Poverty is often cited as a major driver of outward migration, yet extreme poverty reduces the likelihood of international migration, which requires some measure of resources to pull off.[23]

Second, labor migration can mitigate demographic pressures, especially under conditions of low job growth. The "youth bulge" is particularly challenging for South Asia, as almost half of its population of 1.8 billion is under the age of 24. In areas where there is a labor surplus, along with limited employment opportunities and severe constraints on economic and social advancement, migration is viewed as a "household livelihood strategy" for generating employment and expanding sources of income.[24]

Third, in addition to anticipated economic gains, migration is known to alter individual and familial expectations, social mores, and cultural practices as a result of the "social remittances" that accrue from immigration.[25] The payoff, however, is likely to be mixed. Migration, for example, can advance gender norms and women's empowerment while also destabilizing familiar household roles, relationships, and kinship structures. The responsibilities and status of women are likely to shift when they become the de facto household heads in the absence of men who have migrated abroad. When women migrate, regardless of the benefits, it is equally likely to trigger changes among families and caregivers as they adjust to new realities.

The growing feminization of labor migration in and out of South Asia reflects global trends. The highest number of women migrants comes from Sri Lanka, where women make up nearly half of all migrants. Even as their numbers have been increasing steadily, women migrants have not been as visible as men, and are often unaccounted for in official data and records for three reasons: One, they tend to work in informal sectors including private households, which have proved to be less-than-scrupulous in their recruitment and employment practices; two, not all governments in South Asia disaggregate migration data along gender lines; and three, as governments of Sri Lanka and other South Asian counties have tightened restrictions on women traveling to the Gulf countries for domestic work, women have opted to travel on tourist visas or via third countries, thereby avoiding government scrutiny and recordkeeping.[26] While many women from South Asia have gone to GCC countries, they are also migrating to Malaysia, Singapore, and other Southeast Asian states, mostly as domestic and healthcare workers. In addition to socio-economic, political, or environmental factors motivating migration, social networks and families play an important role in supporting and enabling the migration of women from South Asia to the Gulf countries.[27]

Labor migration from South Asia, like other forms of migration, is neither cost- nor risk-free. On the contrary, the intangible costs of temporary or permanent emigration—long separations from families and support systems, exploitation by recruiters and employers, and gender-based violence—remind us of the vexed choices that individuals and families must make every step of the way. The high price of migration begins, first, with recruiters who charge enormous fees for arranging documents, travel, and employment contracts, which can deplete migrants' savings, or worse still, leave them with substantial debts that turn their contracts into a form of servitude.

Second, the exploitation and discriminatory treatment of workers continues in destination countries. In the GCC, for example, the *kafala* or sponsorship system gives private employers and companies enormous power over workers' immigration status and employment, depriving them of fundaments rights and protections. Additionally, contracts are often ignored, salaries delayed, and employment terminated without compensation.[28] Though there are efforts underway to reform the *kafala* system because of international pressure, these have been mostly ad hoc and piecemeal. Third, the precarity of migrant labor is heightened by weak regulatory frameworks and oversight in both countries of origin and destination, not to mention inadequate support for workers' rights by governments who hesitate to intercede even on behalf of their own citizens abroad for fear of disrupting highly lucrative labor markets. Already, there is some worry that the shift toward employing local workers, particularly in Saudi Arabia, may affect future labor recruitment from South Asia. So far there is little evidence to suggest that Saudi Arabia or other GCC countries will be able to replace foreign labor with their own workers in the near term.

While largely avoiding public criticism of the labor practices of GCC countries, governments in South Asia have introduced a series of measures aimed at better regulating recruitment, reducing fees and the cost of ancillary services either at the source or through government-sponsored loans, requiring employers to pay travel and visa costs up front, and even going so far as to set minimum wages, as the Sri Lankan government did for women recruited for domestic work in the United Arab Emirates. Governments are also working on reducing the high costs of foreign exchange transfers, which can easily deplete workers' wages. Transferring funds through unofficial channels, though less expensive for migrants, is not always reliable and reduces state revenues. Governments are developing resource centers and centralized databases, such as India's "eMigrate" system, to promote greater transparency and provide timely information and assistance to prospective migrants in local languages. Though the results have been mixed, India, Pakistan, and Bangladesh are providing pre-departure training programs and strengthening diplomatic and consular services to aid and protect citizens abroad during emergencies—an area of particular concern for labor migrants, especially women.[29]

The protection of female domestic workers has become a particularly thorny issue for governments in South Asia. On the one hand, officials in India, Bangladesh, and Nepal have been praised for imposing strict conditions, including minimum age limits, on women seeking domestic work abroad, particularly in the Gulf states. Activists and advocates for women's rights, on the other hand, accuse governments of adopting "patriarchal" policies that fail to take into account the particular circumstances of women migrants, thereby forcing them to work with unregulated recruiters and leaving them vulnerable to further exploitation.[30]

Labor migration in South Asia is governed by a patchwork of rules, regulations, institutions, and agencies. Most South Asian states did not begin crafting formal legislation and policies for governing labor migration until the 1980s when labor migration to the Gulf countries became a serious business. Even with national policies in place, it is not always clear as to whether the federal government or provinces and states have primary responsibility for emigrant labor including recruitment, training, and resettlement upon return. While there is considerable variation among countries in South Asia, ministries and agencies set up to regulate and manage labor migration often do not have the capacity or resources to perform vital functions, and poor coordination between different agencies is a chronic problem.[31] In some cases, existing regulations have not kept pace with recent developments in the area of migrant rights, or the challenges facing emigrant workers, their families, and communities following the global lockdown during the COVID-19 pandemic, which left states in South Asia scrambling to support and repatriate workers trapped abroad.[32]

Despite shared concerns about irregular migration and human trafficking, South Asia lacks a cross-border framework and structures for governing intraregional migration, an issue that is further complicated by insufficient data on migration within the region. Cross-border migration is either permitted or restricted according to the status of bilateral relations, long-standing geopolitical conflicts, and security concerns. India's borders with Pakistan, for instance, remain tightly controlled and highly militarized. The ongoing construction of a 4,000 km fence on the Bangladesh-India border has severely limited seasonal migration and cut off trade and exchange between towns and villages on both sides of the border. Nepali citizens, for the most part, are allowed to work and travel freely across the border with India under a bilateral agreement, similar to one between India and Bhutan. Looking more broadly at regional and multilateral efforts, the South Asian Association for Regional Cooperation (SAARC), for instance, has agreed upon conventions for preventing and combating human trafficking, but it lacks authority over its member states and there is no appetite for collective action.

Other joint initiatives for improving standards for labor recruitment and employment, such as the 2003 Colombo Process, supported by the International Organization for Migration (IOM), and the Abu Dhabi Dialogue formed in 2008, serve a largely consultative function, sharing information and promoting cooperation between countries of labor origin and destination. In lieu of multilateral frameworks, governments like India have opted for bilateral agreements or MoUs with individual GCC countries to ensure fair and safe working conditions for its citizens under the host country's labor laws. Though an important step toward protecting workers' rights, these types of agreements are often non-binding and apply only to those migrants who have secured employment through official channels, thereby excluding a good number of workers who obtain jobs through informal networks.[33]

Refugees and Asylum Seekers

Refugees, driven from their homes by the wars in Syria, Iraq, and Afghanistan, have captured the most attention in recent years, as many have sought safety and security in Europe, often with devastating consequences. Aside from occasional graphic accounts of lives lost at sea, the focus is mostly on the experiences of European states and citizens, which not only obscures the horrors of war and the experiences of refugees themselves, but also ignores the fact that the vast number of refugees in the world remain in the global South, most often in places that are in close proximity to their own countries. According to the United Nations High Commissioner for Refugees (UNHCR), out of 82.4 million people forcibly displaced in the world, 86% are hosted in developing countries and 73% remain in neighboring countries.[34]

As of the end of 2019, there were nearly 3.6 million refugees in southern Asia, including Iran. Nearly 2.7 million refugees are from Afghanistan, constituting, after Syrians and Venezuelans, the third largest refugee population in the world, divided mostly between Pakistan and Iran. In 2020, Bangladesh hosted over 900,000 Rohingya refugees from Myanmar.[35] Despite the protracted refugee crises,[36] and the region's history of refugee movements, no South Asian country, except for Afghanistan, has signed the 1951 Refugee Convention or the 1967 Protocol, citing, among other reasons, the Convention's narrow focus on Europe after World War II and the lack of provisions for burden-sharing, even as India and Pakistan were dealing with the aftermath of Partition, which left nearly one million dead and an additional 20 million displaced across the subcontinent.[37]

The story of refugees in postcolonial South Asia and the task of resettling them begins with the violent partition of the subcontinent and the forcible displacement that followed. Hastily drawn borders, disputed by India, Pakistan, Afghanistan, and China, disrupted familiar and routine border crossings, leaving entire communities in legal limbo as officials tried to determine who was a citizen or a refugee in the newly constituted states—issues that South Asians continue to wrestle with 75 years after Partition. The next refugee crisis in South Asia was precipitated by the civil war in East Pakistan, leading to the creation of Bangladesh in 1971. In nine months, 10 million refugees crossed into the Indian states of West Bengal, Assam, and Tripura. Although the refugees received a mixed reception in India, proximity to the border, ethnic affinity, and sympathy for the Bengali cause provided a temporary haven for Bengalis fleeing from the Pakistani military.[38] Unlike other protracted refugee situations in South Asia, most of the refugees returned to the new state of Bangladesh shortly after the India-Pakistan war was over.

Sri Lankan Tamil refugees, who have now been in India 30 years or more, present a different set of challenges for the federal government as well as the Tamil Nadu state government. Sri Lankan Tamil refugees began arriving in 1983, as the conflict between Tamils and the Sri Lankan government escalated into a full-blown secessionist movement that was supported by India. In the mid-1990s, there were over 200,000 refugees in Tamil Nadu. Although the civil war in Sri Lanka ended in 2009, as of July 2021, there were approximately 93,000 Tamils of Sri Lankan origin still living in Tamil Nadu, with more than half the population continuing to live in refugee camps.[39] In addition to India, Sri Lankan Tamils have received asylum in Norway and Canada, which hosts the largest Sri Lankan Tamil population outside of Sri Lanka.

The first of the Afghan refugees began arriving in the KP province of Pakistan soon after a military coup against the Daud government in 1978. The number of refugees grew rapidly after the Soviet invasion of Afghanistan in 1979, with additional refugees arriving at different times—during the Soviet withdrawal in 1988–1989, the Taliban takeover of the country in 1996, and the US invasion in 2001. Although refugees remain in camps in KP and Balochistan, where some have lived for over four decades, many more are dispersed throughout Pakistan, having settled in major urban centers like Karachi. At the request of Pakistan's government, UNHCR at various times has facilitated the repatriation of Afghan refugees, often against the wishes of refugees, many of whom have never lived in or even visited Afghanistan. Officially, 1.4 million Afghan refugees reside in Pakistan, while another million or so live in the country without formal documents.[40] Even with the growing number of internally displaced persons (IDPs) in Afghanistan leading up to and immediately after the US exit from Afghanistan, the number of refugees crossing into Pakistan and Iran remained relatively low.

The refugee crisis in Bangladesh is among the most severe in the world, worsened by demographic pressures and resource constraints, which have become even more acute as a result of climate change and environmental degradation. Though Rohingyas have been entering Bangladesh in significant numbers from 1978 onwards, the vast majority fled from Myanmar in 2017 following the mass killings perpetrated by Myanmar's military and with the complicity of civilian leaders. Persecuted for decades and denied fundamental rights, Rohingyas remain a stateless people, who do not even meet the legal definition of a refugee, and although they are entitled to the same status and protections as refugees, these are rarely accorded to them. Rohingyas have not fared much better in India, Malaysia, or Saudi Arabia, which also host smaller populations.[41]

The impact of refugees on host countries and societies depends on a number of factors, among them, the duration and nature of the conflict and its spill over across borders, the interests and involvement of the host state and/or international and non-state actors in the conflict, state capacity, and public opinion. As examples in South Asia and elsewhere show, refugees can instigate or worsen tensions in host societies, even in cases where refugees and local populations share ethnic, linguistic, and cultural affinities. Whether it is Tamil Nadu, KP, or Cox's Bazar in Bangladesh, sympathy and support for refugees can sour quickly if they are perceived as "overstaying their welcome," creating friction among local communities, upsetting the demographic "balance," or competing for scarce resources including jobs, healthcare, and education.

In Tamil Nadu, public opinion quickly turned against Sri Lankan Tamil insurgents after the assassination of former Prime Minister Rajiv Gandhi by a Sri Lankan Tamil suicide bomber in Chennai in 1991. Similarly, Afghan refugees are accused of importing into Pakistan a "Kalashnikov culture"—a potent combination of weapons and drugs used to finance wars in Afghanistan, first against the Russians and later against US forces. In both cases, the Indian and Pakistani governments experienced a "blowback effect," the unintended consequences of supporting insurgents for advancing their own geopolitical goals. And as the two governments learned, civil wars and separatist movements, once they spill over, prove difficult to contain, even in cases where the host state has provided substantial material and moral support to insurgents.

Refugees can find themselves in even more precarious situations after the immediate threat has passed. They are exploited by smugglers and traffickers, abused by government officials, and often left to their own devices, without adequate aid or legal assistance. Although refugees, even without official documents, find ways of navigating local economies and bureaucracies, many find it difficult to access government and private services without legal status and documentation. The involvement of international organizations like the UNHCR in registering asylum seekers and refugees might provide temporary support for vulnerable populations, but it does not guarantee a favorable outcome as the ultimate authority to grant refugee status rests with the state. The issue of citizenship for refugees who have lived outside of their home countries for decades remains a vexing one for countries in South Asia. For example, second- and third-generation Afghan refugees do not qualify for citizenship even though they were born and raised in Pakistan. A proposal by Prime Minister Imran Khan in 2018 to grant citizenship to children of Afghan refugees was shot down by opposition parties over demographic and security concerns. The disputes over citizenship for Bengalis who have lived in India for generations echo similar anti-immigrant sentiments.

In the absence of a national or regional framework for protecting asylum seekers and refugees, governments in South Asia have favored ad hoc policies and administrative arrangements for handling refugees, depending on their strategic interests, domestic politics, and, occasionally, international pressure. India, for example, has treated various refugee populations differently based on a combination of immediate and long-term foreign policy goals and pressure from domestic constituencies. It has welcomed Tibetan refugees while mostly rejecting Rohingyas. Having supported pro-democracy activists from Myanmar in the past, the central government is no longer allowing refugees from Myanmar to enter the country, although it has not been able to prevent the Mizoram state government from sheltering refugees after the latest military coup in Myanmar.[42]

Unlike most other regions, South Asia lacks any kind of multilateral framework for refugee protection, which leaves individual states to work out bilateral arrangements, sometimes involving the UNHCR or other international organizations. Examples include Bangladesh and Myanmar, Pakistan and Afghanistan, and India and Sri Lanka. After steadfastly refusing the sign either the 1951 Convention or the 1967 Protocol, South Asian states have now signed on to the Global Compact for Refugees, which is a non-binding agreement.

Conclusion

As South Asia demonstrates, migration is no longer ignored or dismissed as an issue of "low politics." Because of its complexity and connections with a wide range of policy areas, including public health and the environment, migration has risen to the top of the agenda for policymakers. Like pandemics and climate change, migration cannot be easily controlled or deterred by building more walls or installing sophisticated surveillance technologies. Regional states and societies, meanwhile, must contend with a global economy still shadowed by the COVID-19 pandemic and its impact on low- and middle-income countries. Though many of the contract workers employed in the GCC and elsewhere lost their jobs and were forced to return home, overall remittances to South Asia increased by more than 5% in 2020. The long-term effects of the pandemic have yet to be determined, although it seems unlikely that it will trigger a more permanent disruption in labor migration from South Asia.

Governments today face increasing demands for social justice and equal rights, even as nativist and anti-immigrant movements, mobilized in some cases by public officials, have been flourishing in South Asia. The issue of housing and resourcing refugee populations in light of diminishing international support remains a challenge for Pakistan and Bangladesh, and to some extent, India as well. Regularizing refugee status is one option, although the pushback is likely to be significant. Repatriation under present conditions would violate the principle of non-refoulement.

Geopolitical rivalries and conflicts have long stymied regional cooperation and multilateral solutions to common problems involving different forms of migration, forced displacement, and human trafficking. As climate change intensifies and public policy falls short, we are more likely to see forcible displacement and/or the adoption of migration as a mitigation strategy. Most migration related to climate change in South Asia is domestic, although it could lead to more cross-border migration in the future. Climate change, even if it does not directly induce migration, weakens state capacity, as it puts additional pressure on states and societies, while further undermining the security and well-being of migrants and refugees.

Notes

1 "At 18 Million, India Has the World's Largest Diaspora Population," *The Economic Times*, January 15, 2021, https://economictimes.indiatimes.com/nri/migrate/at-18-million-india-has-the-worlds-largest-diaspora-population/articleshow/80290768.cms?from=mdr.

2 Established in 1981, the Gulf Cooperation Council for the Arab States of the Persian Gulf includes Saudi Arabia, Kuwait, the United Arab Emirates, Qatar, Bahrain, and Oman.

3 See, for example, James F. Hollifield, "Migration and International Relations," in *The Oxford Handbook of the Politics of International Migration*, eds. Marc R. Rosenblum and Daniel J. Tichenor (New York: Oxford University Press, 2012), 357–360.

4 Fiona B. Adamson and Gerasimos Tsourapas, "The Migration State in the Global South: Nationalizing, Developmental and Neoliberal Models of Migration Management," *International Migration Review* 54, no. 3 (2020): 853–882.

5 Partha Ghosh, *Migrants, Refugees and the Stateless in South Asia* (New Delhi: Sage Publications India, 2016), xii.

6 Ghosh, *Migrants, Refugees and the Stateless in South Asia*, xii–xiii; Ranabir Samaddar, "Power and Responsibility at the Margins: The Case of India in the Global Refugee Regime," *Refuge* 33, no. 1 (March 2017): 41–43; and Pia Oberoi, *Exiles and Belonging: Refugees and State Policies in South Asia* (New York: Oxford University Press, 2006), 12–18.

7 Sunil S. Amrith, *Crossing the Bay of Bengal: The Furies of Nature and the Fortunes of Migrants* (Cambridge, MA: Harvard University Press, 2013).

8 Ian Talbot and Shinder Thandi, eds., *Punjabi Colonial, and Post-Colonial Migration* (Karachi: Oxford University Press, 2004).

9 See, for example, Vazira Zamindar, *The Long Partition and the Making of Modern South Asia: Refugees, Boundaries, Histories* (New York: Columbia University Press, 2007); Urvashi Butalia, *The Other Side of Silence: Voices from the Partition of India* (Durham, NC: Duke University Press, 2000); and Mahbubar Rahman and Willem van Schendel, "'I Am Not a Refugee': Rethinking Partition Migration," *Modern Asian Studies* 37, no. 3 (July 2003): 581–583.

10 Navine Murshid, *The Politics of Refugees in South Asia: Identity, Resistance, Manipulation* (New York: Routledge, 2014), 13–14, 121–124, and Calcutta Research Group, *Voices of the Internally Displaced in South Asia* (Kolkata: 2006).

11 IOM (UN Migration), "Community Advocates Inspire Positive Change across Rohingya Refugee Camps," *The Storyterller*, April 16, 2021, https://storyteller.iom.int/stories/community-advocates-inspire-positive-change-across-rohingya-refugee-camps. See also Shinga Bahadur Khadka, "Social Mobilisation in IDP Camps in Pakistan," *Forced Migration Review* 34 (February 2010).

12 Samaddar, "Power and Responsibility in the Margins," 44.

13 Ranabiir Samaddar, *The Postcolonial Age of Migration* (New York: Routledge, 2020), xi–xii; Kamal Sadiq, *Paper Citizens: How Illegal Immigrants Acquire Citizenship in Developing Countries* (New York: Oxford University Press, 2009), 8.

14 Itty Abraham, *How India Became Territorial: Foreign Policy, Diasporas, Geopolitics* (Stanford, CA: Stanford University Press, 2014), 106.

Refugees and Migration in South Asia

15 Devesh Kapur, *Diaspora, Development, and Democracy: The Domestic Impact of International Migration from India* (Princeton, NJ: Princeton University Press, 2010); Daniel Naujoks, *Migration, Citizenship, and Development: Diasporic Membership Policies and Overseas Indians in the United States* (New Delhi: Oxford University Press, 2013).

16 Sunil Amrith, *Migration and Diaspora in Modern Asia* (New York: Cambridge University Press, 2011).

17 See, for instance, Adil Najam, *Portrait of a Giving Community: Philanthropy by the Pakistani-American Diaspora* (Cambridge, MA: Harvard University Press, 2006) and Virinder S. Kalra, ed., *Pakistani Diasporas: Culture, Conflict, and Change* (Karachi: Oxford University Press, 2009).

18 Abraham, *How India Became Territorial*, 78.

19 Prakash C. Jain and Ginu Zacharia Oomen, *South Asian Migration to Gulf Countries: History, Politics, Development* (New York: Routledge, 2016), 4.

20 Ravi Srivastava and Arvind Kumar Pandey, *Internal and International Migration in South Asia: Drivers, Interlinkage and Policy Issues* (New Delhi: UNESCO, 2017), 17.

21 S.K. Sasikumar, "Indian Labor Migration to the Gulf: Recent Trends, the Regulatory Environment and New Evidences on Migration Costs," *Productivity* 60, no. 2 (2019): 113.

22 World Bank Group-KNOMAD, "Recovery: Covid-19 Crisis through a Migration Lens," *Migration and Development Brief 35* (Washington, D.C.: World Bank, 2021), 56.

23 Nicholas Van Hear, Oliver Bakewell, and Kay Long, "Push-Pull Plus: Reconsidering the Drivers of Migration," *Journal of Ethnic and Migration Studies* 44, no. 6 (2018): 929.

24 G.M. Arif, Shujaat Farooq, and Nasir Iqbal, "Labor Migration from Pakistan to Gulf Countries: An Investigation of Regional Disparities in Outflows of Workers, Remittances and Poverty," in *Asianization of Migrant Workers in the Gulf Countries*, eds. S.I. Rajan and G.Z. Oommen (Singapore: Springer Nature, 2020), 196.

25 Hein de Haas, Stephen Castles, and Mark J. Miller, *The Age of Migration: International Population Movements in the Modern World*, 6th ed. (London: Red Globe Press, 2020), 345–346.

26 Madhuka Sanjaya Wickramarachchi, "Sri Lanka—GCC Temporary Economic Migration Corridor and the Circular Migration of Female Domestic Workers," *International Journal of Scientific and Research Publications* 10, no. 10 (2020): 25.

27 Srivastava and Pandey, "Internal and International Migration in South Asia," 20.

28 Ginu Zacharia Oomen, "South Asian Migration to the GCC Countries: Emerging Trends and Challenges," in *South Asian Migration to Gulf Countries*, 33.

29 Srivastava and Pandey, "Internal and International Migration in South Asia," 43–44.

30 Garima Maheshwari, "Migration Policy and Politics in India," *Economic and Political Weekly* 53, no. 28 (2018): 29.

31 Santosh Adhikari, Fred Gale, and Joanne Vince, "Labor Migration Management in South Asia Region," 4th International Conference on Public Policy, Concordia University, Canada (June 2019), 4.

32 Themrise Khan, "Labor Migration Governance in Pakistan: Protecting Pakistan's Overseas Labor Migrants," *LSE*, June 3, 2020, https://blogs.lse.ac.uk/southasia/2020/06/03/labour-migration-governance-in-pakistan-protecting-pakistans-overseas-labour-migrants/.

33 Sameena Hameed, "India's Labour Agreements with the Gulf Cooperation Council Countries: An Assessment," *International Studies* (2021): 12.

34 UNHCR, "Global Trends: Forced Displacement in 2020" (December 2020), https://www.unhcr.org/flagship-reports/globaltrends/.

35 International Organization for Migration, "Migration Data in Southern Asia," *Migration Data Portal*, June 2021, https://www.migrationdataportal.org/regional-data-overview/southern-asia.

36 According to UNHCR, a protracted refugee situation is "one in which 25,000 or more refugees from the same nationality have been in exile for at least five consecutive years in a given host country." UNHCR, *Global Trends: Forced Displacement in 2020* (June 2021), 20.

37 Sreya Sen, "Understanding India's Refusal to Accede to the 1959 Refugee Convention: Context and Critique," *Refugee Review* (May 28, 2015).

38 Murshid, *The Politics of Refugees in South Asia*, 56–58.

39 Dennis S. Jessudasan, "Survey Planned to Ascertain How Many Sri Lankan Tamils Want Indian Citizenship," *The Hindu*, January 4, 2022.

40 Zuha Siddiqui, "For Afghan Refugees, Pakistan is a Nightmare, but Also Home," *Foreign Policy*, May 9, 2019, https://foreignpolicy.com/2019/05/09/for-afghan-refugees-pakistan-is-a-nightmare-but-also-home/.

41 Amal de Chickera, "Stateless and Persecuted: What's Next for Rohingya?" *Migration Information Source*, March 18, 2021, https://www.migrationpolicy.org/article/stateless-persecuted-rohingya.
42 Prachi Raj, "Understanding Citizenship and Refugee Status in India," *Economic & Political Weekly* 55, no. 23 (June 6, 2020).

Bibliography

Abraham, Itty. *How India Became Territorial: Foreign Policy, Diaspora, Geopolitics*. Stanford, CA: Stanford University Press, 2014.

Adamson, Fiona B., and Gerasimos Tsourapas. "The Migration State in the Global South: Nationalizing, Developmental and Neoliberal Models of Migration Management." *International Migration Review* 54, no. 3 (2020): 853–882.

Adhikari, Santosh, Fred Gale, and Joanna Vince. "Labor Migration Management in South Asian Region." 4th International Conference on Public Policy. Concordia University, Canada (June 2014).

Amrith, Sunil. *Crossing the Bay of Bengal: The Furies of Nature and the Fortunes of Migrants*. Cambridge, MA: Harvard University Press, 2013.

Amrith, Sunil. *Migration and Diaspora in Asia*. New York: Cambridge University Press, 2011.

Arif, G.M., Shujaat Farooq, and Nasir Iqbal. "Labor Migration from Pakistan to the Gulf Countries: An Investigation of Regional Disparities in Outflows of Workers, Remittances and Poverty." In *Asianization of Migrant Workers in the Gulf Countries*, edited by S.I. Rajan and G.Z. Oommen, 189–217.Singapore: Springer Nature, 2020.

Butalia, Urvaishi. *The Other Side of Silence: Voices from the Partition of India*. Durham, NC: Duke University Press, 2000.

de Chikera, Amal. "Stateless and Persecuted: What's Next for Rohingyas?" *Migration Information Source*, March 18, 2021. https://www.migrationpolicy.org/article/stateless-persecuted-rohingya.

de Haas, Hein, Stephen Castles, and Mark J. Miller. *The Age of Migration: International Population Movements in the Modern World*. 6th ed. London: Red Globe Press, 2020.

Ghosh, Partha S. *Migrants, Refugees and the Stateless in South Asia*. New Delhi: Sage Publications India, 2016.

Hameed, Sameena. "India's Labor Agreements with the Gulf Cooperation Council Countries: An Assessment." *International Studies* 58, no. 4 (2021): 442–465.

Hollifield, James F., and Daniel Tichenor. "Migration and International Relations." In *The Oxford Handbook of the Politics of International Migration*, edited by Marc R. Rosenblum, 345–379. New York: Oxford University Press, 2012.

International Organization for Migration (UN Migration). "Community Advocates Inspire Positive Change Across Rohingya Refugee Camps." April 16, 2021. https://storyteller.iom.int/stories/community-advocates-inspire-positive-change-across-rohingya-refugee-camps.

International Organization for Migration. "Migration Data in Southern Asia." *Migration Data Portal*, June 2021. https://www.migrationdataportal.org/regional-data-overview/southern-asia.

Jain, Prakash C., and Ginu Zacharia Oommen, eds. *South Asian Migration to Gulf Countries: History, Policies, Development*. New York: Routledge, 2016.

Kapur, Divesh. *Diaspora, Development, and Democracy: The Domestic Impact of International Migration from India*. Princeton, NJ: Princeton University Press, 2010.

Khadka, Shinga Bahadur. "Social Mobilisation in IDP Camps in Pakistan." *Forced Migration Review* 34 (February 2010).

Khan, Themrise. "Labor Migration Governance in Pakistan: Protecting Pakistan's Overseas Labor Migrants." *LSE*, June 3, 2020. https://blogs.lse.ac.uk/southasia/2020/06/03/labour-migration-governance-in-pakistan-protecting-pakistans-overseas-labour-migrants/.

Maheshwari, Garima. "Migration Policy and Politics in India." *Economic and Political Weekly* 53, no. 28 (July 14, 2018): 28–30.

Murshid, Navine. *The Politics of Refugees in South Asia: Identity, Resistance, Manipulation*. New York: Routledge, 2014.

Rahman, Mahbubar, and Willem van Schendel. "'I Am Not a Refugee:' Rethinking Partition Migration." *Modern Asian Studies* 37, no. 3 (July 2003): 551–584.

Raj, Prachi. "Understanding Citizenship and Refugees' Status in India." *Economic and Political Weekly* 55, no. 23 (June 6, 2020).

Samadar, Ranabir. "Power and Responsibility at the Margins: The Case of India in the Global Refugee Regime." *Refuge* 33, no. 1 (March 2017): 42–51.

Samaddar, Ranabir. *The Postcolonial Age of Migration.* New York: Routledge, 2020.

Sasikumar, S.K. "Indian Labor Migration to the Gulf: Recent Trends, the Regulatory Environment and New Evidences on Migration Costs." *Productivity* 60, no. 2 (July-September 2019): 111–125.

Sen, Sreya. "Understanding India's Refusal to Accede to the 1959 Refugee Convention: Context and Critique." *Refugee Review*, May 28, 2015.

Srivastava, Ravi, and Arvind Kumar Pandey. *Internal and International Migration in South Asia: Drivers, Interlinkage and Policy Issues.* New Delhi: UNESCO, 2017.

Talbot, Ian, and Shinder Thandi, eds. *Punjab: Colonial and Post-Colonial Migration.* Karachi: Oxford University Press, 2004.

UNHCR. *Global Trends: Forced Displacement in 2020.* June 2021.

Van, Nicholas Hear, Oliver Bakewell, and Katy Long. "Push-Pull Plus: Reconsidering the Drivers of Migration." *Journal of Ethnic and Migration Studies* 44, no. 6 (2018): 927–944.

Wickramarachchi, Madhuka Sanjaya. "Sri Lanka – GCC Temporary Economic Migration Corridor and the Circular Migration of Female Domestic Workers." *International Journal of Scientific and Research Publications* 10, no. 10 (October 2020): 118–128.

Zamindar, Vazira. *The Long Partition and the Making of Modern South Asia: Refugees, Boundaries, Histories.* New York: Columbia University Press, 2007.

33

SPACE PROGRAMS, POLICIES, AND DIPLOMACY IN SOUTH ASIA

Ajey Lele

South Asia is a region marred by political unrest, and there are issues related to mass poverty, hunger, and health. Various states in the region are found making sincere efforts to overcome many of the fallacies, which are found hindering its growth. Technological backwardness is another area of concern. There is realization that science and technology have an important role toward nation-building, and there is a need to invest more in this sector. Space science and technologies is one arena that states in the region understand has a major role for growth. This chapter debates on the approach of South Asian nations toward factoring space technologies in their socioeconomic and geopolitical calculus.

The Context

The human quest for space could be said to have begun with the launch of the first satellite, called Sputnik during 1957 by the Soviet Union. This was the Cold War era, and any technological achievements were viewed with strategic biases. The US launched its first satellite in 1958. Subsequently, in 1961, Yuri Gagarin (Soviet Cosmonaut) became the first human to visit the space. Finally, this technology supremacy of the Soviet Union was challenged by the US by sending the first man to the Moon (Apollo 11 mission, 1969). Various South Asian states during that period were mostly endeavoring to evolve as independent states and were far away from the Cold War-era technology superiority politics. But surprisingly, states like India and Pakistan were cognizant of the advantages of space technologies for the society, and 1960s was the period when the interest of these states in the domain of space technologies was becoming visible.

The world is witnessing significant growth in the overall space activities of various nation-states in the 21st century. Particularly, post 2010, there has been a major boost to activities in the outer space with some private agencies undertaking satellite developments and launches. During the last decade or so, a few states have established some important programs. NASA has launched a revolutionary new space observatory, the James Webb Space Telescope. While the work has begun toward the Artemis program, a United States-led international program for the return of humans to the Moon. China has formally commissioned its BeiDou-3 global satellite positioning system. It has also started constructing the Tiangong space station. China and Russia have put forward a roadmap for a joint moon base called the International Lunar Research Station; Russia has conducted an anti-satellite test (ASAT) leading to debris

454

DOI: 10.4324/9781003246626-38

creation. In the South Asian context, India has undertaken Moon and Mars missions and has established its own regional navigational system. The 2019 Indian ASAT test did create some geopolitical ripples, but being almost debris-less, this test did not receive major criticism. While other South Asian states have started increasing their investments in the space domain, their focus remains limited to launching satellites required for earth observations and commutations. They do not have any indigenous technology structure to support any expansion for their space programs and would mainly depend on international assistance.

At the global level, it appears that the involvement of private sector is going to increase in the future, and space tourism sector would flourish significantly. Also, major players like the US, Russia, and China would try to establish their own space alliances by asking friendly states to join them for future missions to Moon and other planets. Subsequently, such groupings could even emerge as pressure groups, while deciding any rule-based mechanism for conducting activities in the space. The major point of debate likely to emerge in the future is about the ownership of space resources and the mineral rights on asteroids and other planets. Without clarity on these issues, in South Asia, India is unlikely to join any US- or Russia-supported space groups, at least in the near future. However, other states in the region could be lured by the big powers to join them by offering them assistance with their space programs.

Space Landscape

Space technologies are fairly beneficial to resolve various difficulties posed by the general characteristics of the South Asian region, which include challenging geography, inclement weather, poverty, high population density, and geopolitics. Pakistan began its journey with the establishment of Space and Upper Atmosphere Research Commission (SUPARCO) on September 16, 1961. This agency began functioning from 1964. The Indian Space Research Organisation (ISRO) came into existence on August 15, 1969, while the Bangladesh Space Research and Remote Sensing Organization (SPARRSO) was founded in 1980. The interest of other South Asian states started becoming evident only in the 21st century. The Sri Lanka Space Agency (SLSA) was established in 2010.[1] While Afghanistan, Nepal, Bhutan, and the Maldives are yet to establish official state-sponsored space agencies, they have some agencies or sections in the government or in the private sector that are dealing with space technologies and satellites.

Investments in space domain cannot be divorced from the overall interests of the states in the scientific domain. As per the 2021 Scientific Index-Country Rankings, India ranks 20th in the world, while Pakistan is 40th and Bangladesh is 83rd. The remaining states have less than average rankings.[2] There are a few global rating agencies that identify India somewhere between fifth to seventh positions in the space domain.

South Asian investments in the space domain are minuscule in global comparison. Just to get a broad indication, the figures of satellite holdings could be looked at. According to Union of Concerned Scientists (UCS), which keeps a record of operational satellites, globally there are 3,372 satellites that are active as on January 1, 2021. Amongst them, India has around 50 operational satellites and Pakistan has five. For the remaining states in South Asia, the figure for active satellites ranges from 0 to 1. For the sake of comparison in monetary terms, the budgets of the most successful global space agency and the most successful South Asian space agency could be taken into account. As per the available figures, the budget of the US space agency NASA for fiscal year (FY) 2021 is US$23.3 billion, while the budget of India's space department (which includes ISRO and some other agencies) for the financial year 2021–2022 is around US$1.9 billion. Pakistan, as another important South Asian investor in the space domain, has a budget of US$46 million (2021–2022). It is important to have these realities in the backdrop before attempting any critical assessment of South Asia's space agenda.

Afghanistan, Nepal, and Bhutan could be viewed as the northern and eastern peripheral states of South Asia, while Sri Lanka and Maldives are the island nations of the region. All these states are smaller in size, population, and scientific and financial resources in comparison with the remaining states like India, Pakistan, and Bangladesh. Geographically, Sri Lanka is located at 7° North latitude and Maldives is located at 4° North latitude. This closeness to the equator makes these states suitable for developing a launch station and undertaking satellite launches.[3]

Before discussing space programs of various South Asian states, it is important to situate the two main space programs of the region, namely Pakistan and India, in the strategic realm of the region. Since independence, India and Pakistan have fought four wars[4] till date. For the last 75 years, India and Pakistan have been at loggerheads owing to the Kashmir problem and unresolved boundary disputes. Both are nuclear weapon states and have dynamic missile programs. India has also conducted[5] an anti-satellite test (ASAT).[6] Broadly, technologies like nuclear, missiles, and space get identified as strategic technologies. Obviously, space programs of both these states are viewed with strategic bias. It is important to note that the investments in space domain for both these powers had begun much before they had started investing in nuclear weapons and missile technologies. However, in the present context, such assessment is unavoidable. It is also important to mention that owing to their nuclear polices, space agencies of India and Pakistan were put under the sanctions by the US and other states. For some decades, these agencies were not in a position to have any international technology collaborations and no technology transfer from major space players happened. India converted the sanctions regime into an opportunity and made good progress toward indigenous space technologies.

The space domain did emerge as an environment for superpower competition during the Cold War period. Today, a larger number of states have begun developing space programs for social, scientific, and strategic reasons. It is argued that techno–nationalism even today remains a powerful motivator for space exploration.[7] This could be true (partially) in the South Asian context too. How do South Asian states actually view the space domain? Is it a sphere for international influence or for societal use or both? Are nationalism and power dynamics associated with it? Would space power theory be useful in describing, explaining, and predicting how South Asian states can best derive utility, balance investments, and reduce risks in their interactions with the cosmos?[8] Possibly, it could be a tall order to judge the investments of all South Asian states through the prism of space power dynamics. India and Pakistan could be the notable exceptions, where the notion of space power needs critical assessment. For all this, there is a need to learn about space policies and diplomatic and strategic initiations of the states in the region. Before that, it is important to put some useful details about the origin and progress of space programs of various South Asian states.

Space Polices

For many decades, there has been a debate about why should poorer states invest into costly technologies like space, when they are yet to address the basic issues like hunger, joblessness, sanitation, and clean drinking water. However, actually these technologies have significant relevance for the socioeconomic development and hence such apprehensions are baseless. South Asian states understand that the domain of space, which mainly during the 20th century was the sole domain of the wealthiest developed states, is now assessable for the rest of the world too. There is a realization that economically backward states need to invest in these technologies since they could help assist them in progressing toward prosperity. It is important to look at the space policies of South Asian states against this backdrop.

The region of South Asia has its own contradictions. India is the only prominent player in the region that is technologically and economically strong. Possibly, for other states, may be with the exception of Pakistan, space programs are yet to become part of the national strategies and policies, which strive to strengthen their international status, security, and economic benefits.[9] At present, smaller states in South Asia are just beginning their journey in the space domain. They understand the importance of space for social and technological development. Weather inputs are of much use since many of these states have significant dependence on agriculture. These states are active participants in the UN program for developing satellites.

During the 1970s and 1980s, India had very limited resources; still it spent large amounts of money on a sophisticated space program. The Indian state pursued a policy of using high technology to solve the country's social and economic problems, and at the same time to strengthen its international position. Satellite-aided communications, educational programs, meteorology, and resources survey and management were (are) the priority areas.[10]

Over the years, an increasing number of smaller and rising middle powers have been found to add indigenous space capabilities to their list of national priorities. Mostly, these capabilities are fulfilled by building or purchasing the required infrastructure. States are keen to use their space programs for contributing to their comprehensive national power. They also look at space programs as an instrument to help improve their national economies by raising the level of science and technology and generating high-tech jobs, and also serve national security concerns through military security, intelligence gathering, and diplomacy.[11] In South Asia, India is the only space-faring state and its policy appears to be congruent with such a view. Interestingly, India is yet to finalize its 2017 draft of Space Activities Bill. India needs to formulate and enact Space Legislation quickly.

India invests in space technologies for socioeconomic purposes. Still, on March 27, 2019 (Mission Shakti), India conducted an anti-satellite weapon test. What could be the rationale behind this move? India has always been against space weaponization. It appears that India is responding to what is happening in the surroundings. China is known to be doing major investments in the counterspace arena[12] and had conducted an ASAT in 2007. Also, India was keen to ensure that the history of nuclear non-proliferation negotiations does not get repeated in the space domain. The Nuclear Non-proliferation Treaty (NPT) is essentially about a group of five nuclear weapons states coming together and deciding the policies for the rest of the world. The NPT allows only five states in the world to hold nuclear weapons and treats the rest of the world as secondary citizens. India wants to ensure that such situation does not get repeated in the space domain. India knows that it needs to remain prepared to handle the challenges of space warfare and is working toward evolving its military space policy accordingly.

Pakistan's security-related challenges are mostly India-centric. Pakistan normally looks for parity with India in various strategic sectors. Particularly, space is one area where it is just not able to match the technological superiority of ISRO. Also, it understands that India being an ASAT power, the value of Pakistan's nuclear power architecture stands diminished. Space technologies are also part of China-Pakistan Economic Corridor (CPEC) cooperation. More importantly, Pakistan is the first country outside China to use BeiDou Navigation Satellite System (BDS) for its military. Overall, Pakistan's space policy is tilted toward assistance from China.

Apart from India and Pakistan, other South Asian states are yet to fully establish their policies in the space domain. One obvious reason for this is the lack of financial and technological capabilities. However, this is not to say that the states have actually no plans for the future. Their approach appears to try to get all possible assistance from the global players to evolve their space programs. They are found putting some amount of state funding and are also encouraging the private sector to participate toward evolving a space program. Some of them are also found using the available assets to their advantage. Like these states do understand the relevance of owning an orbital slot for the positioning of satellites in the Geosynchronous Earth Orbit (GEO). Such slots are allotted by the International Telecommunications Union (ITU) and get recognized as prime, and scarce, real estate.[13] Due to the lack of capacity, states like Afghanistan, Bhutan, and Nepal are not able to use the slots allotted to them yet. But they understand that the agency that would help them put satellites in these slots would also benefit in terms of data gathering for itself. They are likely to use these slots as a barging chip. Generally, over the next few years, these states are expected to evolve their policies based on the nature of space assets they are able to pull in for the purpose of socioeconomic development.

South Asian Space Programs

Pakistan

Pakistan's space program has a long history. SUPARCO, which is headquartered at Karachi, implements the space policy of Pakistan since the 1960s. This agency was established by the Space Research Council (SRC), whose president is the prime minister of Pakistan. Pakistan started their space program with the launching of sounding rockets. In collaboration with NASA and the US Air Force, Pakistan launched its first rocket Rehbar-1 in June 1962, thus becoming the third state in Asia, after Japan and Israel. During the early 1960s, it was only the 10th country in the world with a successful sounding rocket program. Unfortunately, Pakistan could not consolidate on this timely entry in the domain of space.[14] SUPARCO's progress has been far below expectations all these years.

There are multiple reasons for Pakistan's very limited progress in the space sector. Financial limitations and political apathy are the possible reasons for this. Also, the way scientific leadership had dominated the nuclear sector (Dr Abdul Qadeer Khan), possibly there was no strong personality in the space domain to make politicians aware about its necessity. Moreover, the process of overall development in the country as such was sluggish; obviously there was an insufficient demand for satellite data during the 1970s. This limited SUPARCO's ambitions to think big. For some time now, its core area of focus has been remote sensing and communications.[15] SUPARCO had established its indigenous National Remote Sensing Centre in 1980, called RESACENT, which is based in Karachi. This is a modern facility for digital interpretation and analysis of remotely sensed data.[16] During the 1980s, SUPARCO was getting relevant information, particularly meteorological inputs and remote sensing information in real time from sources like LANDSAT, SPOT, and NOAA, and the required ground station was established at Islamabad. During this period, SUPARCO could be said to have developed its expertise toward establishment of ground infrastructure for data reception.

The biggest space project planned by Pakistan was the launch of its own communication satellite named Paksat. However, during his visit to SUPARCO in 1984, the then President Zia-ul-Haq announced a sudden end of this project because of budgetary constraints. This led many scientists to leave the organization.[17] All this forced the remaining scientists to devote time toward developing microwave components and assemblies, especially antennae of different diameters and types, low-noise amplifiers, and down converters for a large number of ground terminals, such as television receive-only (TVRO) terminals, for the reception of

TV signals from the satellites. There idea was to offer the benefits of satellite technologies to villages. During the 1970s/1980s, some 70% of the population of Pakistan was living in rural areas comprising over 50,000 villages.[18] However, the state was not able to reach such a vast population owing to a total lack of communication facilities.

On July 16, 1990, Pakistan launched its first experimental satellite, BADR-1, with the help of China. This was Pakistan's first indigenously developed satellite. The year 1993 was to witness the next (similar) launch; however, SUPARCO could launch the second experimental satellite, BADR-B, only on December 10, 2001. In between, Pakistan had purchased a communication satellite from Boeing which was already available in space. Table 33.1 (below) gives details of various satellites launched by Pakistan so far.

In 2011, with the launch of Paksat-1R, Pakistan announced a 30-year plan for SUPARCO called "Vision 2040." As per this space vision, Pakistan proposes to launch five GEO and six LEO satellites by 2040. Also, there was an announcement made on October 25, 2018, that Pakistan is going to send an astronaut into space in 2022 with the help of China. The long-term plan also includes a proposal to build its own launcher and become self-reliant by 2040.[19] The Space Program 2040, which later came to be known as Space Vision 2047, is known to be a program meant for peaceful purposes. Interestingly, the mission statement of Pakistan's Space Vision 2047 considers "space as a strategic sector, exploit all aspects of space science, technology, and its applications for national wellbeing and national security."[20] During the last few years, Pakistan has been able to make some progress in the space domain. However, it appears that there is going to be increasing dependence on China in the future. At present, China is mainly catering to both satellite manufacturing and launch requirements of Pakistan.

Table 33.1 Details of Various Satellites Launched by Pakistan so Far

Name of satellite	Type	Launch agency	Date	Remarks
Badr-1	52 kg, LEO	China	July 16, 1990	SUPARCO with Surrey University
PAKSAT 1	3000 kg, geostationary	US Was launched for Indonesia as its original customer, but then leased to Pakistan	Feb. 1, 1996	Built and owned by the Boeing Company
BADR B	68.5 kg, LEO, first E/O satellite	Russia	Dec. 10, 2001	SUPARCO with Rutherford Laboratory
PAKSAT 1R	5115 kg, geostationary	China	Aug. 11, 2011	Made in China
ICUBE 1	1 kg satellite in LEO	Russia	Nov. 21, 2013	Built in Pakistan
AsiaSat 4 became Paksat-MM 1	4137 kg, geostationary	US (Boeing)	April 12, 2003 March 2018	In 2018, leased to SUPARCO
PAKTES 1A	300 kg, LEO remote sensing	China	July 9, 2018	Technology evaluation satellite, SUPARCO
PRESS 1	LEO	China	July 9, 2018	China's first optical remote sensing satellite sold to Pakistan

India

India launched its first sounding rocket on November 21, 1963. This launch took place from a location called Thumba, a small fishing village in the southern parts of India (Kerala). Thumba was selected since the geomagnetic equator passes through Thumba.[21] The sounding rocket launch was assisted by the US space agency NASA. From this simple beginning, India has come a long way over the years and now even has successful Moon and Mars programs.

As an agency to cater to India's space interests, in 1962, the Indian National Committee for Space Research (INCOSPAR) was established, which subsequently developed into the ISRO in 1969. This was followed by the establishment of the Department of Space (DoS) and space commission, which are headed by the Prime Minister of India. Over the years, ISRO has established itself as one of the leading space organizations globally. India now has several space research centers and autonomous institutions for remote sensing, astronomy, astrophysics, atmospheric sciences, and space sciences.[22]

Two scientists deserve credit for conceptualizing and executing India's space vision in the early years. They are Dr. Vikram Sarabhai (August 12, 1919–December 30, 1971) and Prof. Satish Dhawan (September 25, 1920–January 3, 2002). It was Dr. Sarabhai who gave the original vision that was implemented, modified, and expanded upon by Prof. Dhawan. In simple terms, the articulated vision then was "to use space for socioeconomic development," which continues to remain relevant.

India launched its first satellite in 1975 with the assistance from the erstwhile USSR. India became a spacefaring state in 1980 by launching indigenously developed satellite from the Indian rocket. Since then, India has made significant progress. Till date India has sent a range of satellites to different orbits. Particularly, to launch satellites into the GEO, India is required to take assistance from other agencies; however, this dependence is decreasing with India having developed its own heavy satellite launch vehicle for geostationary orbit. India's space journey has spanned 46 years now, and from 1975 to 2021, over 120 satellites[23] have been sent into orbit.

ISRO has a successful launch vehicle program. Its first vehicle during the 1980s to carry satellites into the space was SLV-3. The next vehicle for ISRO was the Augmented Satellite Launch Vehicle (ASLV), which was followed by the Polar Satellite Launch Vehicle (PSLV) and the Geosynchronous Satellite Launch Vehicle (GSLV).[24] PSLV has been the most successful vehicle for ISRO, and it has been used even for undertaking Moon and Mars missions. ISRO took time to establish its GSLV program. This was owing to the absence of cryogenic engine technology. ISRO was to get this technology from Russia during the early 1990s. However, the US told (coerced) the Russians that the deal could be inconsistent with the Missile Technology Control Regime (MTCR) arrangement and hence technology transfer was denied. Also, US sanctions were imposed on Russian and Indian space groups.[25] Subsequently, ISRO took almost two decades to indigenize this technology and now it has different variants of GSLV (Mark I, II, and III) available. At present, ISRO is developing semi-cryogenic engine technology so that it can carry satellites weighing 4–6 tons into the geostationary orbit.[26] Presently, keeping an eye on the future commercial market for launch of small satellites, ISRO is developing a Small Satellite Launch Vehicle (or SSLV). The first SSLV is expected to be developed by 2022.

Over the years, ISRO has acquired good capabilities to build very complex and world-class satellites for remote sensing, weather, and communications. ISRO has also developed navigation, astronomy, and various categories of small satellites.

Around the 1980s, ISRO had conceptualized two major projects for societal development: The Indian Remote Sensing Satellite system (IRS) and the Indian National Satellite system (INSAT). Particularly, INSAT was a unique experiment, where a single satellite was designed and developed for undertaking multiple tasks. It was a multipurpose system consisting of telecommunication, meteorological, and TV broadcasting elements. It was the world's first geostationary satellite system to combine these three elements together.[27] During the 1980s, India was not in a position to afford single-purpose satellites, and hence decided to design a multipurpose satellite. At present, India has around 50 operational satellites[28] that are used for different roles like remote-sensing, weather, commutations, and navigation. India's earth observations satellites (remote-sensing) have best imaging capabilities with sub-metric resolution, which is at par with the best in the world. India has also established its regional navigation program called the Indian Regional Navigation Satellite System, with an operational name of NavIC. This system provides accurate real-time positioning and timing services. It covers India and a region extending 1,500 km around it,[29] with plans for further extension.

India also has a well-articulated Deep Space agenda. India's first Moon mission, Chandrayaan-1 (2008–2009), was an important success. This mission was instrumental toward the discovery of water on the Moon. The second lunar mission encountered delays, given uncertainties in Russia, which was assisting India with a rover and lander system for this mission. Subsequently, India undertook this mission with an indigenously designed and developed rover and lander system. This mission was launched in July 2019. However, it was a partial success since the Moon landing was a failure. The orbiter launched during this mission is providing good observations of the Moon's surface.[30] India's first mission to Mars, Mars Orbiter Mission (MOM), has been a great success (2003–2004). India proposes to undertake its first human space mission by 2022. This mission has got delayed owing to the COVID-19 crisis. The only Indian to visit space so far has been Wg Cdr Rakesh Sharma, a former Indian Air Force pilot. He flew aboard Soyuz T-11 on April 3, 1984, as part of the Soviet Interkosmos program.[31]

To cater to India's commercial interest in the space domain, two agencies were established: The Antrix Corporation Limited (ANTRIX) in 1992 and NewSpace India Limited (NSIL) in 2019. Today, India's overall space agenda is also ably supported by public sector organizations like Hindustan Aeronautics Limited (HAL) and various private industries. Their involvement is more as a manufacturer and assembler at sub-system level. India has begun the process of establishing a full-grown ecosystem for private space industry. The government is pushing space reforms in a big way. It is expected that in the near future, most of the commercial launches that are presently undertaken by ISRO would be carried out by the private industry. On October 11, 2021, a few Indian private industries established an agency called Indian Space Association (ISpA), which is expected to supplement the government's efforts toward making the Indian space industry a major contributor to the global space business. However, India has a long way to go, and at present, the Indian space industry has only around 2% share of the $360 billion global market. Till date the total number of customer satellites from foreign countries placed into orbit by ISRO is 342 satellites from 34 countries.[32]

Bangladesh

In 1972, Bangladesh established the Space and Atmospheric Research Centre (SARC) at the Bangladesh Atomic Energy Commission. Already, there was an Automatic Picture Transmission (APT) ground station working on the premises of the atomic energy center. By 1980, various such agencies were merged together and SPARRSO (Bangladesh Space

Research and Remote Sensing Organisation), a multi-sectoral research and development agency of the Government of Bangladesh under the ministry of defense, was established. This agency has technical capabilities, trained manpower, and allied facilities for receiving, processing, analyzing, archiving, and utilizing aerial photographs and satellite data. The main focus is on imagery analysis. For this purpose, data is received from meteorological satellites like NOAA of US and GMS (Geostationary Meteorological Satellite) of Japan. The received data is used for day-to-day weather forecasting and agro-climatic environmental monitoring, as well as in water resource studies.[33]

Japan conducts a UN program called the Joint Global Multi-Nation Birds Satellite (BIRDS) project, which supports non-spacefaring countries to build their first satellite. Under this program, Bangladesh had developed its first satellite called BRAC Onnesha, a nanosatellite (CubeSat). It was launched by SpaceX on June 3, 2017. The first geostationary communications satellite for Bangladesh, Bangabandhu Satellite-1, was launched by SpaceX on May 11, 2018.[34] It is expected that Bangladesh is getting ready to launch its second satellite, Bangabandhu Satellite-2, by 2023. Apart from the US, Bangladesh has good relations in the space domain with various other states, including China, Russia, and Japan.

Sri Lanka

Sri Lanka's first communication satellite (SupremeSAT-1) was launched on November 22, 2012, from China. The satellite is partly owned by a private company, SupremeSAT. This project is a joint venture with two Chinese companies, China Great Wall Industry Corporation (CGWIC) and Sino Satellite Communications Company Ltd. The project included the construction of a satellite Content Management Station and a Space Academy at Kandy (now operational). Presently, the state-of-the-art teleport at Pallekele-Kandy is providing a broad range of uplink and downlink services from a secure and strategically located position in the Indian Ocean.[35] The company was to deliver SupremeSAT-2 with China's help in 2018. The project has been kept on hold due to poor market conditions.

Before the private agency entering the space domain, the Sri Lankan state was working toward the launch of an earth observation satellite. In 2009, the Sri Lanka Space Agency (SLASA) signed a Memorandum of Understanding (MoU) with Surrey Satellite Technology Ltd. (SSTL), a British company. As per this MoU, SSTL was to launch an earth observation satellite for Sri Lanka and was also expected to help in designing Sri Lanka's communications satellite. However, nothing much is known about this idea.

A satellite called Raavana-1 was launched on April 18, 2019, by the US under the BIRDS satellite launch program. This project is a UN initiative to help countries launch their first satellites. Raavana-1 is Sri Lanka's first cube research satellite and has been designed and developed by two Sri Lankan youth while studying space engineering in Japan.[36]

Afghanistan

The United States Armed Forces completed their withdrawal from Afghanistan on August 30, 2021, marking the end of the two-decade-old war in Afghanistan. This has brought the terrorist organization Taliban to power, and it is really not known how various governmental agencies are working currently. Afghanistan has not much of a history of making investments in the space domain. Possibly, US agencies could have been making the required data available for use in Afghanistan during the last two decades.

Space Programs, Policies, and Diplomacy in South Asia

In 2014, the government of Afghanistan managed to purchase a satellite. They had purchased an already operational satellite for use. A French telecommunications satellite, Eutelsat W2M, was launched in 2008 for a 15-year mission. This satellite was developed and manufactured by ISRO for satellite operator Eutelsat under the ISRO-EADS Astrium alliance. This satellite was also known by names such as Eutelsat 48B, Eutelsat 28B, and Eutelsat 48D. Finally, it was sold to Afghanistan (2014) and got renamed as Afghansat 1. The satellite was redeployed from 28.5° to 48° east.[37] This satellite is supporting a wide range of services including broadcasting, mobile telephony, and providing access to Information and Communication Technology and broadcast services. For war-ridden Afghanistan, such a satellite is of great importance for connectivity, particularly in unserved areas. Finally, one Afghanistan national has visited space, in 1988. Their only cosmonaut is Abdul Ahad Mohmand, who was part of three-person Soyuz crew for a nine-day mission to Russia's Mir space station.

Nepal and Bhutan

Nepal and Bhutan have developed satellites under the UN-supported BIRDS project. Japan's Kyushu Institute of Technology is spearheading this project. Nepal has launched its first satellite called NepaliSat-1 in April 2019. In June 2018, Bhutan launched BHUTAN-1, the first Bhutanese nanosatellite. This satellite was built during Kyushu Institute of Technology's program and was launched into orbit aboard the SpaceX mission. Bhutan is also proposing to establish its own space agency in the near future.

Nepal has launched its first PocketQube picosatellite developed by ORION Space with a mass of less than 250 grams on January 13, 2022 from Falcon 9. This satellite is called Nepal-PQ1 (SanoSat-1) and scientists from Nepal are working on this project. The satellite would be launched from SpaceX's Falcon 9 rocket.[38]

Nepal Telecommunication Authority (NTA) is proposing to launch a communications satellite by 2022 and is seeking professional advice for this project. They are keen to determine whether it will be more feasible to rent a satellite or launch a satellite. So far, nine international companies from China, India, UK, France, Singapore, UAE, and Germany have submitted Expressions of Interest for consultancy services.[39] NTA's decision is awaited.

Maldives

The mission for the Institute for Global Success (IGS)[40] is to develop a new breed of leaders, engineers, and scientists in the Maldives. IGS is proposing to establish the space program for the Maldives. It even wants to train local astronauts, equip them with the tools necessary to conduct world-class scientific research, and create a platform to build and launch spacecrafts. In collaboration with the KFS Space Foundation of the United Kingdom, there is a proposal to build the prototype satellite to research about the weather and climate changes that are happening in the world. Presently, under this first-ever project for space sector in the Maldives, 12 local students are expected to be trained for the world's first Nano-Satellite Engineering Professional certification.[41]

Space Diplomacy

Science diplomacy is an important tool for bilateral and multilateral collaboration. Science diplomacy is about the use of scientific collaborations amongst the states to deal with common problems faced and build constructive international partnerships. This allows every country to avoid the burden of reinventing the wheel every time for technology development.

Science diplomacy has a long history as a facilitator to promote scientific discourse that unites researchers across borders notwithstanding political oppositions among nations. The operation of the South Asian University,[42] which has a major component for scientific research, is a good example of science diplomacy's successes in South Asia.[43] The countries in the region have also shown enthusiasm for collaboration in fighting the COVID-19 pandemic. This health diplomacy has an important element of science associated with it. Space is also emerging as an important component for regional collaboration.

In South Asia, the moral obligation is on India to share the benefits of space technologies and engage the neighbors constructively. Indian scientists had suggested the idea of a SAARC satellite way back in 1995 to celebrate the 10th anniversary of the setting up of SAARC satellite. This was suggested on the eve of the eighth SAARC summit (New Delhi, May 1995).[44] However, the idea remained dormant. Finally, the South Asia Satellite (GSAT-9) was launched on May 5, 2017. Pakistan was not ready to become part of this project. Hence the satellite could not be called a SAARC satellite. Except Pakistan, all other South Asian states are part of this project, which has been spearheaded by ISRO. GSAT-9 is a geostationary communications and meteorological satellite. It helps in commutations and television broadcasting and in collection of weather data. The satellite also provides crucial information for undertaking tele-medicine, tele-education and banking services and provides all required assistance in this regard. India has also made available the ground infrastructure to the member countries for real-time data reception. In addition, India is keen to provide the navigational assistance to its neighbors with its regional navigational network (NavIC).

Presently, India is involved in space diplomacy at various other non-regional forums too, for example, the BRICS (Russia, India, Brazil, China, and South Africa) space arrangement. These five states are presently working toward establishing a network of remote-sensing satellites to help deal with global challenges such as climate change, natural disasters, and environmental deterioration.[45] At the same time, the Asian power politics is found impacting the space sector too. The Asia-Pacific Space Cooperation Organization (APSCO), which is an inter-governmental organization headquartered in Beijing, has avoided to collaborate with the two important regional space players, Japan and India.

Investments by most of the South Asian states are very limited in the domain of space. However, the presence of India in the region should make them much more comfortable. Smaller states can get the various benefits of space technologies by collaborating with India. For India, its expertise in the space domain offers a good opportunity for a proactive regional diplomacy.

Space Arms Control

Arms control agreements follow a complementary approach to enhance stability, augment deterrence, and avoid any possible arms race.[46] Thus, it is worth checking whether arms control can play a useful role in mitigating potential threats in space. The concept of space arms control is not new and has been debated since the Cold War period. The 1967 multilateral Outer Space Treaty (OST) prohibits the stationing of weapons of mass destruction (WMDs) in orbit. There are few other mechanisms like Moon treaty and START nuclear arms control agreement, which directly or indirectly prohibit any intentional interference with space-based systems.[47] Since space arms control is a key part of space diplomacy, it is important to appreciate the South Asian positions in this regard.

Military technologies, which are strategic in nature, are normally viewed as instruments that a state could use to secure its interests through deterrence. Keeping the China threat in mind, India has undertaken an ASAT test. However, India has made it clear that India is against the weaponization of space. India is party to various international treaties relating to outer space and supports various international efforts to reinforce safety and security of space-based assets. India is of the firm opinion that any global mechanism on space aspects should emerge as a rule-based and legally binding mechanism.[48] Other states in the region are also signatories to OST and various other space mechanisms. Many of them are found keenly participating in various UN-supported and other multilateral activities associated with space security. Sri Lanka was part of the UN-appointed Group of Governmental Experts (GGE, 2011–13) on Transparency and Confidence-building Measures (TCBMs) in Outer Space. South Asian states are also committed to the UN-sponsored "no first placement of weapons in outer space," and many of them have been part of developing a draft resolution[49] in this regard.

In South Asia, India and Pakistan are nuclear weapons states and have their own views in respect of treaty measures like the NPT and other associated arms control measures. However, in the domain of space, normally there appears to be a consensus amongst the states in the region on aspects associated with space arms control. More so, since these states (except India and to some extent Pakistan) do not have the ability to develop any counter-space technologies, it is expected they would continue arguing against the weaponization of space.

In Closing

South Asia is a classic case where only one country, India, is dominating the space realm and has earned a global reputation for its competence. India needs to ensure that the smaller states in the region do not get anxious owing to their standing. States are investing in space for assisting the society as a whole.

The region is marred with various challenges related to climate change and natural disasters. Also, states in the region suffer from poverty, hunger, and unemployment. Space technologies could offer some answers to such challenges and assist in the process of development. The commercial value of space technologies is increasing very rapidly. India is emerging as an important space commercial hub, and other states could also think of commercial involvement based on their strengths, like Sri Lanka could plan for the development of satellite launch pad to offer commercial launching services.

Actually, space could offer an opportunity to overcome the differences on earth. It has been observed that the states like the US and Russia, which have major geopolitical differences, do not carry much of their acrimony in the space domain and are actually found collaborating in some fields. There is much to learn for India and Pakistan from this. South Asia needs to put forward a joint view on space security.

India is arguably the most important space power in the region. It exercises this power in a constructive way, as indicated by its pioneering of the South Asia Satellite. Space is offering a soft power status to India. However, owing to the fissures in its relationship with India, Pakistan is keeping away from developing any harmonious relationship in the space domain. Pakistan understands the strategic relevance of space technologies. They have very limited capabilities in the strategic domain of space. Hence, in order to offset this disadvantage, it is tilting more toward China for getting assistance in the space domain.

Notes

1 Institute of Aeronautics and Space, "Space Agencies," accessed October 14, 2021, https://www.iae.cta.br/prospecta/1d_space_agencies.html.

2 "Top Countries in World 2022," AD Scientific Index, accessed December 28, 2021, https://www.adscientificindex.com/country-ranking/.

3 Locations close to the equator offer the best sites for rocket launches. The rockets are required to be launched in easterly direction so as to maximize the use of earth's rotational speed and these launches provide the necessary orientation for arriving at a geostationary orbit.

4 There were four major wars: The first Kashmir War (October 1947), 1965 and 1971 (Bangladesh Liberation War) and the 1999 Kargil war.

5 Narendra Modi, "Speech by Prime Minister on 'Mission Shakti', India's Anti-Satellite Missile test conducted on 27 March, 2019," Ministry of External Affairs (India), March 27, 2019, https://mea.gov.in/Speeches-Statements.htm?dtl/31180/Speech+by+Prime+Minister+on+Mission+Shakti+27+March+2019.

6 ASATs are the capabilities aimed at intentionally destroying or disabling satellites. They are two types of ASATs: kinetic and non-kinetic. Kinetic ASATs involve physically striking (say by using missile) a satellite in order to destroy it. A non-kinetic ASAT can use nonphysical means to disable or destroy a satellite like jamming or cyber-attack. For more details, refer Daniel Porras, "Towards ASAT Test Guidelines," United Nations Institute for Disarmament Research, May 17, 2018, https://www.unidir.org/publication/towards-asat-test-guidelines.

7 Joan Johnson-Freese, "How Does IR Relate to Space Exploration in the 21st Century?" *E-IR*, July 19, 2013, https://www.e-ir.info/2013/07/19/how-does-ir-relate-to-space-exploration-in-the-21st-century/.

8 P.L. Hays, "Spacepower Theory," in *Handbook of Space Security*, eds. K.U. Schrogl, P. Hays, J. Robinson, D. Moura, and C. Giannopapa (New York: Springer), 57–79.

9 Agnieszka Lukaszczyk, "Space Policy – What Is It and Why Do Emerging Space States Need It?" Paper Presented at the *International Astronautical Conference*, Cape Town, South Africa, 2011, https://swfound.org/media/50812/al%20iac%202011%20sp.%20policy%20in%20emrg.%20sp.pdf.

10 Stephan F. von Weick, "India's Space Policy: A Developing Country in the 'Space Club,'" *Space Policy* 3, no. 4 (November 1987): 326.

11 Robert C. Harding, *Space Policy in Developing Countries* (Routledge: New York, 2013), 8.

12 UNIDIR, Counterspace Capabilities, August 2018, https://www.unidir.org/files/medias/pdfs/counterspace-capabilities-backgrounder-eng-0-771.pdf.

13 Louis de Gouyon Matignon, "Orbital Slots and Space Congestion," *Space Legal Issues*, June 8, 2019, https://www.spacelegalissues.com/orbital-slots-and-space-congestion/.

14 Gulraiz Iqbal, "The Fall and Rise of Pakistan's Space Ambitions," *South Asian Voices*, September 11, 2020, https://southasianvoices.org/the-fall-and-rise-of-pakistans-space-ambitions/.

15 Miqdad Mehdi and Jinyuan Su, "Pakistan Space Programme and International Cooperation: History and Prospects," *Space Policy* 47 (February 2019): 175–180.

16 Iqbal, "The Fall and Rise of Pakistan's Space Ambitions."

17 Mehdi and Su, "Pakistan Space Programme and International Cooperation: History and Prospects."

18 Salim Mehmud, "Pakistan's Space Programme," *Space Policy* 5, no. 3 (August 1989): 222.

19 Miqdad Mehdi and Jinyuan Su, "Pakistan Space Program and International Cooperation: History and Prospects."

20 Misbah Arif, "Let's Take To the Skies and Beyond," *Daily Times*, July 16, 2018, https://dailytimes.com.pk/268167/lets-take-to-the-skies-and-beyond/.

21 S.K. Das, *Touching Lives: The Little Known Triumphs of the Indian Space Programme* (Penguin Books: New Delhi, 2007), 1.

22 "Facts on India's Space Research and List of Research Centres in India," *India Today*, October 19, 2021, https://www.indiatoday.in/education-today/gk-current-affairs/story/facts-on-india-s-space-research-and-list-of-space-research-centres-in-india-1866683-2021-10-19.

23 Arfa Javaid, "List of Indian Satellites (1975-2021)," July 29, 2021, https://www.jagranjosh.com/general-knowledge/list-of-indian-satellites-1624957731-1.

24 S. Krishnamurthy, ed., "India's Launch Vehicle Programme," *Space India*, July–Sept 1997, 8–12.

25 "US Sanctions Imposed on Russian, Indian Space Groups," Federation of American Scientists, May 11, 1992, https://nuke.fas.org/control/mtcr/news/920511-227224.htm.

26 M. Ramesh, "ISRO Moves On, Gears Up to Test Semi-Cryogenic Engine in Ukraine," *The Hindu Business Line*, September 19, 2019, https://www.thehindubusinessline.com/news/science/isro-moves-on-gears-up-to-test-semi-cryogenic-engine-in-ukraine/article29451601.ece.

27 A. Baskaran, "Competence Building in Complex Systems in the Developing Countries: The Case of Satellite Building in India," *Technovation* 21 (2001): 109–121.

28 M.P. Sidharth, "India has 49 Satellites in Earth's Orbit, Four More Ready for Launch, says Senior ISRO Official," *Zee News*, September 18, 2020, https://zeenews.india.com/india/india-has-49-satellites-in-earths-orbit-four-more-ready-for-launch-says-senior-isro-official-2310561.html.

29 Department of Space (India), "Indian Regional Navigation Satellite System (IRNSS): NavIC," Indian Space Research Organization, accessed December 5, 2021, https://www.isro.gov.in/irnss-programme.

30 Sohini Ghosh and Amitabh Sinha, "Explained: What Chandrayaan-2 has sent," *Indian Express*, September 10, 2021, https://indianexpress.com/article/explained/isro-chandrayaan-2-mission-to-the-moon-water-molecule-7499795/.

31 Dinakar Peri, "Indian Pilots to Return to Russia Soon for Customised Space Suits," *The Hindu*, August 29, 2021, https://www.thehindu.com/sci-tech/science/indian-pilots-to-return-to-russia-soon-for-customised-space-suits/article36158300.ece.

32 Department of Space (India), "PSLV-C51, The First Dedicated Launch by NSIL, Successfully Launches Amazonia-1 and 18 Co-passenger Satellites from Sriharikota," Indian Space Research Organization, February 28, 2021, https://www.isro.gov.in/update/28-feb-2021/pslv-c51-first-dedicated-launch-nsil-successfully-launches-amazonia-1-and-18-co.

33 "SPARRSO," *Banglapedia: National Encyclopedia of Bangladesh*, June 18, 2021, https://en.banglapedia.org/index.php?title=SPARRSO.

34 Gunter D. Krebs, "Bird B, BTN, G, J, JPN, LKA, M, MYS, N, NPL, PHL (BRAC Onnesha, Bhutan 1, GhanaSat 1, Toki, Uguisu, Raavana 1, Mazaalai, UiTMSAT 1, EduSat 1, NepaliSat 1, Maya 1)," Gunter's Space Page, accessed December 28, 2021, https://space.skyrocket.de/doc_sdat/bird.htm.

35 Ajey Lele, "China to Launch Satellite for Sri Lanka: India's Missed Opportunity?" IDSA Comment, November 16, 2012, https://idsa.in/idsacomments/ChinatoLaunchSatelliteforSriLankaIndiasMissedOpportunity_alele_161112; "China Launches Sri Lanka's First Satellite as India Watches Ties Grow," *Reuters*, November 27, 2012, https://www.reuters.com/article/us-srilanka-satellite-china-idUSBRE8AQ0HO20121127.

36 "Sri Lanka Joins Global Space Age with First Cube Research Satellite," *Sputnik News*, June 17, 2019, https://sputniknews.com/20190617/srilanka-launches-first-satellite-1075912624.html.

37 Ajey Lele, "India Launches a South Asia Satellite," May 8, 2017, https://www.thespacereview.com/article/3233/1.

38 Timothy Aryal, "One Small Step: First Made-in-Nepal Picosatellite to be launched into Space in 2020," *Kathmandu Post*, February 1, 2019, https://kathmandupost.com/art-entertainment/2019/02/01/one-small-step-for-nepal.

39 Raju Banskota, "Finally, Nepal to get own satellite," *Nepal Times*, January 31, 2021, https://www.nepalitimes.com/latest/finally-nepal-to-get-own-satellite/.

40 IGS was created (2019) to develop a new breed of leaders who are committed to reach their full potential and achieve world-class success.

41 Fathmath Zunaam, "Maldives to Build its First Prototype Satellite," *Times of Addu*, April 24, 2021, https://timesofaddu.com/2021/04/24/maldives-to-build-its-first-prototype-satellite/; "KSF Space Foundation Signs MOU with Maldives to Build the First Universal Satellite," *Satnews*, October 30, 2020, https://news.satnews.com/2020/10/30/ksf-space-foundation-signs-mou-with-maldives-to-build-the-first-university-satellite/.

42 South Asian University (SAU, since 2010) is an international university established by the eight member nations of South Asian Association for Regional Co-operation (SAARC).

43 Uttam Babu Shrestha and Anindita Bhadra, "Science in South Asia," *Science* 364, no. 6447 (June 28, 2019), https://www.science.org/doi/10.1126/science.aay4475.

44 P.J. Lavakare, "India and the SAARC Satellite," *Current Science* 108, no. 1 (January 10, 2015): 15.

45 "BRICS to Set Up Remote-Sensing Satellite Network," *Space Daily*, August 19, 2021, https://www.spacedaily.com/reports/BRICS_to_set_up_remote_sensing_satellite_network_999.html.

46 John Lauder, Frank G. Klotz, and William Courtney, "How to Avoid a Space Arms Race," Rand Corporation, October 26, 2020, https://www.rand.org/blog/2020/10/how-to-avoid-a-space-arms-race.html.

47 Julie Dahlitz, "Arms Control in Outer Space," *The World Today* 38, no. 4 (April 1982): 154–155.

48 D.B. Venkatesh Varma, "Statement by Mr D. B. Venkatesh Verma, Indian Ambassador to the Conference on Disarmament at the UNDIR space security conference, Geneva," Ministry of External Affairs (India), April 28, 2016, http://meaindia.nic.in/cdgeneva/?4870?000.

49 United Nations, "No First Placement of Weapons in Outer Space: Draft Resolution," United Nations Digital Library, December 9, 2016, https://digitallibrary.un.org/record/845371?ln=en.

Bibliography

"BRICS to Set Up Remote-Sensing Satellite Network." *Space Daily*, August 19, 2021. https://www.spacedaily.com/reports/BRICS_to_set_up_remote_sensing_satellite_network_999.html.

"China Launches Sri Lanka's First Satellite as India Watches Ties Grow." *Reuters*, November 27, 2012. https://www.reuters.com/article/us-srilanka-satellite-china-idUSBRE8AQ0HO20121127.

"Counterspace Capabilities." United Nations Institute for Disarmament Research, August 2018. https://www.unidir.org/files/medias/pdfs/counterspace-capabilities-backgrounder-eng-0-771.pdf.

"Facts on India's Space Research and List of Research Centres in India." *India Today*, October 19, 2021. https://www.indiatoday.in/education-today/gk-current-affairs/story/facts-on-india-s-space-research-and-list-of-space-research-centres-in-india-1866683-2021-10-19.

"KSF Space Foundation Signs MOU with Maldives to build the First Universal Satellite." *Satnews*, October 30, 2020. https://news.satnews.com/2020/10/30/ksf-space-foundation-signs-mou-with-maldives-to-build-the-first-university-satellite/.

"Space Agencies." Institute of Aeronautics and Space. Accessed October 14, 2021. https://www.iae.cta.br/prospecta/1d_space_agencies.html.

"SPARRSO." *Banglapedia: National Enclyclopedia of Bangladesh*, June 18, 2021. https://en.banglapedia.org/index.php?title=SPARRSO.

"Sri Lanka Joins Global Space Age with First Cube Research Satellite." *Sputnik News*, June 17, 2019. https://sputniknews.com/20190617/srilanka-launches-first-satellite-1075912624.html.

"Top Countries in World 2022." AD Scientific Index. Accessed December 28, 2021. https://www.adscientificindex.com/country-ranking/.

"US Sanctions Imposed on Russian, Indian Space Groups." Federation of American Scientists, May 11, 1992. https://nuke.fas.org/control/mtcr/news/920511-227224.htm.

Arif, Misbah. "Let's take to the skies and beyond." *Daily Times*, July 16, 2018. https://dailytimes.com.pk/268167/lets-take-to-the-skies-and-beyond/.

Aryal, Timothy. "One Small Step: First Made-in-Nepal Picosatellite to be launched into Space in 2020." *Kathmandu Post*, February 1, 2019. https://kathmandupost.com/art-entertainment/2019/02/01/one-small-step-for-nepal.

Banskota, Raju. "Finally, Nepal to Get Own Satellite." *Nepal Times*, January 31, 2021. https://www.nepalitimes.com/latest/finally-nepal-to-get-own-satellite/.

Baskaran, A. "Competence Building in Complex Systems in the Developing Countries: The Case of Satellite Building in India." *Technovation* 21 (2001): 109–121.

Dahlitz, Julie. "Arms Control in Outer Space." *The World Today* 38, no. 4 (April 1982): 154–155.

Das, S.K. *Touching Lives: The Little Known Triumphs of the Indian Space Programme*. New Delhi: Penguin Books, 2007.

Department of Space (India). "Indian Regional Navigation Satellite System (IRNSS): NavIC." Indian Space Research Organization. Accessed December 5, 2021. https://www.isro.gov.in/irnss-programme.

Department of Space (India). "PSLV-C51, the First Dedicated Launch by NSIL, Successfully Launches Amazonia-1 and 18 Co-passenger Satellites from Sriharikota." Indian Space Research Organization, Feb 28, 2021. https://www.isro.gov.in/update/28-feb-2021/pslv-c51-first-dedicated-launch-nsil-successfully-launches-amazonia-1-and-18-co.

Ghosh, Sohini Ghosh, and Amitabh Sinha. "Explained: What Chandrayaan-2 has sent." *Indian Express*, September 10, 2021. https://indianexpress.com/article/explained/isro-chandrayaan-2-mission-to-the-moon-water-molecule-7499795/.

Harding, Robert C. *Space Policy in Developing Countries*. New York: Routledge, 2013.

Hays, P.L. "Spacepower Theory." In *Handbook of Space Security*, edited by K.U. Schrogl, P. Hays, J. Robinson, D. Moura, and C. Giannopapa, 57–79. New York: Springer, 2015.

Iqbal, Gulraiz Iqbal. "The Fall and Rise of Pakistan's Space Ambitions." *South Asian Voices*, September 11, 2020. https://southasianvoices.org/the-fall-and-rise-of-pakistans-space-ambitions/.

Javaid, Arfa. "List of Indian Satellites (1975-2021)." July 29, 2021. https://www.jagranjosh.com/general-knowledge/list-of-indian-satellites-1624957731-1.

Johnson-Freese, Joan. "How Does IR Relate to Space Exploration in the 21st Century?" *E-IR*, July 19, 2013. https://www.e-ir.info/2013/07/19/how-does-ir-relate-to-space-exploration-in-the-21st-century/.

Krebs, Gunter D. Krebs. "Bird B, BTN, G, J, JPN, LKA, M, MYS, N, NPL, PHL (BRAC Onnesha, Bhutan 1, GhanaSat 1, Toki, Uguisu, Raavana 1, Mazaalai, UiTMSAT 1, EduSat 1, NepaliSat 1, Maya 1)." Gunter's Space Page. Accessed December 28, 2021. https://space.skyrocket.de/doc_sdat/bird.htm.

Krishnamurthy, S., ed. "India's Launch Vehicle Programme." *Space India*, July–Sept 1997, 8–12.

Lauder, John, Frank G. Klotz, and William Courtney. "How to Avoid a Space Arms Race." Rand Corporation, October 26, 2020. https://www.rand.org/blog/2020/10/how-to-avoid-a-space-arms-race.html.

Lavakare, P.J. "India and the SAARC Satellite." *Current Science* 108, no. 1 (January 10, 2015): 15–16.

Lele, Ajey. "China to Launch Satellite for Sri Lanka: India's Missed Opportunity?" IDSA Comment, November 16, 2012. https://idsa.in/idsacomments/ChinatoLaunchSatelliteforSriLankaIndiasMissedOpportunity_alele_161112.

Lele, Ajey. "India Launches a South Asia Satellite." May 8, 2017. https://www.thespacereview.com/article/3233/1.

Lukaszczyk, Agnieszka. "Space Policy – What Is It and Why Do Emerging Space States Need It?" Paper presented at the *International Astronautical Conference*, Cape Town, South Africa, 2011. https://swfound.org/media/50812/al%20iac%202011%20sp.%20policy%20in%20emrg.%20sp.pdf.

Matignon, Louis de Gouyon. "Orbital Slots and Space Congestion." *Space Legal Issues*, June 8, 2019. https://www.spacelegalissues.com/orbital-slots-and-space-congestion/.

Mehdi, Miqdad, and Jinyuan Su. "Pakistan Space Programme and International Cooperation: History and Prospects." *Space Policy* 47 (February 2019): 175–180.

Mehmud, Salim. "Pakistan's Space Programme." *Space Policy* 5, no. 3 (August 1989): 217–226.

Modi, Narendra. "Speech by Prime Minister on 'Mission Shakti', India's Anti-Satellite Missile Test Conducted on 27 March, 2019." Ministry of External Affairs (India), March 27, 2019. https://mea.gov.in/Speeches-Statements.htm?dtl/31180/Speech+by+Prime+Minister+on+Mission+Shakti+27+March+2019.

Peri, Dinakar. "Indian Pilots to Return to Russia Soon for Customised Space Suits." *The Hindu*, August 29, 2021. https://www.thehindu.com/sci-tech/science/indian-pilots-to-return-to-russia-soon-for-customised-space-suits/article36158300.ece.

Porras, Daniel. "Towards ASAT Test Guidelines." United Nations Institute for Disarmament Research, May 17, 2018. https://www.unidir.org/publication/towards-asat-test-guidelines.

Ramesh, M. "ISRO Moves On, Gears Up to Test Semi-Cryogenic Engine in Ukraine." *The Hindu Business Line*, September 19, 2019. https://www.thehindubusinessline.com/news/science/isro-moves-on-gears-up-to-test-semi-cryogenic-engine-in-ukraine/article29451601.ece.

Shrestha, Uttam Babu, and Anindita Bhadra. "Science in South Asia." *Science* 364, no. 6447 (June 28, 2019). https://www.science.org/doi/10.1126/science.aay4475.

Sidharth, M.P. "India has 49 Satellites in Earth's orbit, Four More Ready for Launch, says Senior ISRO Official." *Zee News*, September 18, 2020. https://zeenews.india.com/india/india-has-49-satellites-in-earths-orbit-four-more-ready-for-launch-says-senior-isro-official-2310561.html.

United Nations. "No First Placement of Weapons in Outer Space: Draft Resolution." United Nations Digital Library, December 9, 2016. https://digitallibrary.un.org/record/845371?ln=en.

Varma, D.B. Venkatesh. "Statement by Mr D. B. Venkatesh Verma, Indian Ambassador to the Conference on Disarmament at the UNDIR space security conference, Geneva." Ministry of External Affairs (India), April 28, 2016. http://meaindia.nic.in/cdgeneva/?4870?000.

Weick, Von, and F. Stephan "India's Space Policy: A Developing Country in the 'Space Club.'" *Space Policy* 3, no. 4 (November 1987): 326–334.

Zunaam, Fathmath. "Maldives to Build Its First Prototype Satellite." *Times of Addu*, April 24, 2021. https://timesofaddu.com/2021/04/24/maldives-to-build-its-first-prototype-satellite/.

34

REGIONAL TRADE AND INVESTMENT IN SOUTH ASIA

Surupa Gupta

Economists consider international trade and cross-border investments key tools in economic development. The experience of fast-paced growth and economic development in East and Southeast Asia during the second half of the 20th century, a process labeled as the East Asian Miracle by the World Bank, provided strong support to this insight. The miracle, however, eluded the South Asian region, which continued to see high levels of poverty and low levels of growth during most of the 20th century. Relatedly, these economies also experienced low levels of trade and investment. The region's economic trajectory began to change after India liberalized its economy in 1991, continuing the liberalizing trend that other countries in the region, notably Bangladesh and Sri Lanka, had begun earlier. The rapid economic growth that resulted from such liberalization lifted millions out of poverty. While poverty alleviation is an important end goal in itself for each of the countries in the region, higher growth offers other benefits as well. Higher growth provides the opportunity to create reserves that countries can tap into during crisis or to build infrastructure for infrastructure and to provide for other development. For an emerging power such as India, such growth affords it the capacity to play a dominant political and economic role in the region. Smaller countries also benefit from having more options to tap into for trade and investment ties and to secure funding for much-needed development of infrastructure and connectivity. There are clear implications for international relations of the region and particularly for the strategic goals and ambitions of competing regional hegemons such as China and India as well as for other major actors such as the United States, European Union, Japan, and Australia. Besides the strategic angle, a set of more liberal economic policies will continue to make the region an attractive destination for foreign investment and trade, providing opportunities for other countries to take advantage of its large and expanding market.

This chapter posits that liberalization of barriers to trade and investment in the region has led to greater prosperity in the region, reflected in higher growth rates and per capita incomes and reduction in the number of citizens living under national poverty levels. The discussion also makes it clear that political leaders have initiated policy reform leading to removal of such barriers when they have realized that previously adopted import substitution industrialization models have limited effectiveness in delivering growth and economic development. International market conditions and international institutions such as the International Monetary Fund and the World Bank have also played a role in encouraging

470

DOI: 10.4324/9781003246626-39

such liberalization. However, it is important to point out that these institutions have varying levels of influence on the countries of the region. At the international level, major power competition has also played a role in approaches to and attitudes toward economic liberalization. The discussion further points to domestic political factors that limit such opening up: Domestic interest groups, for example, have pushed back against opening up. In the section that follows, the chapter provides a brief background to the adoption of liberal economic policies in the region. A discussion of the specific details of trade and investment liberalization in the major countries in the region follows. The subsequent section discusses the limits of trade and investment liberalization in South Asia. The final section discusses the political economy factors that have shaped these developments. The chapter ends with some conclusions. The discussion is framed within the liberal perspective in international relations, which argues that states are better off when they adopt market liberalization policies and engage in regimes that encourage market integration at both the global and the regional level.

Post-independence Adoption of Import Substitution Industrialization Models

Three of the eight countries in the region—India, Pakistan, and Sri Lanka—gained independence from British colonial rule in 1947–1948. Bangladesh was formed in 1971 when the territory of East Pakistan seceded from Pakistan. The Partition of India in 1947 and the redrawing of maps into India on the one hand and East and West Pakistan on the other interrupted age-old transportation links and severed connected markets. After independence, India grew increasingly protectionist over time, raising tariffs and preventing ownership of firms by domestic and foreign private investors in many sectors. After adopting liberal economic policies post-independence, Pakistan's economic policies also took a turn toward autarky in the 1970s. Newly formed Bangladesh adopted an economic model involving state planning. With its plantation-based economy, Sri Lanka remained engaged in and dependent on international trade but its economic development model also relied on a large public sector and elaborate restrictions on imports until the 1970s, when it undertook a liberalization program. A brief discussion of each of these experiences follows.

In India, ownership of enterprise was regulated early on through the Industrial Policy Resolutions of 1948 and 1956, and many sectors, particularly those occupying the commanding heights of the economy, were placed within the public sector. Entry of foreign investment as well as engagement with international trade did not face restrictions in the initial years.[1] However, this began to change in the 1960s, and by the mid-1970s, import duties increased, trade in several goods were restricted for various reasons, the government put caps on the extent to which private sector units could grow, and foreign corporations could only own minority stakes in their Indian affiliates. In India's case, the decision to allow the public sector to occupy key industries emerged from a combination of reasons. The legacy of colonial rule, and its origins in foreign investment, had left a level of wariness about inviting foreign capital. The Soviet Union's apparent success in building a strong, planned, industrial economy made the model attractive to Indian leaders. The Indian private sector was not interested in leading the industrialization and modernization program that Jawaharlal Nehru, India's first Prime Minister, and other nationalist leaders envisaged. The decision to adopt a state-led import-substituting industrialization model emerged as a product of these factors.[2] Subsequently, India's turn toward more autarkic policies with respect to trade and foreign investment emerged from economic considerations such as adverse and persistent balance of payments issues and a political turn toward populism during the 1970s.

Pakistan adopted a relatively more liberal set of economic policies in the immediate post-independence period but eventually turned to what came to be known as Islamic socialism in the 1970s—a set of populist economic policies that then Prime Minister Zulfikar Ali Bhutto initiated in response to the rising dissatisfaction with post-independence capitalist policies that raised the specter of class conflict and also to rebuild Pakistan's identity after the loss of territory in the 1971 war that gave rise to the new state of Bangladesh.[3] Bangladesh's own turn toward interventionist economic policies involving state planning and a central role of the public sector were a response to pre-independence oligarchic and capitalist policies pursued by the Pakistan government. This was also the path its new leadership decided to follow to attain its goals for economic development and growth with redistribution. State ownership of industry, i.e., the state's ownership of industrial assets increased from 34% in 1970 to 92% in 1972.[4] Finally, in case of Sri Lanka, a somewhat statist model was a legacy of British colonial rule and was strengthened under the post-independence leadership as the country faced a severe economic crisis that was rooted in the dynamics of international commodity markets.[5] Sri Lanka was the first to liberalize trade in the 1970s and was followed by Bangladesh, Pakistan, and India later. The closed nature of these economies limited both the volume of international trade and the inflow of foreign investments.

Trade and Investment Reforms 1970s–1990s

The 1970s and 1980s signaled a change in the economic policy orientation of these countries. Sri Lanka led the way by ushering in market-oriented economic policies after the 1977 elections brought the conservative United National Party to power.[6] During the 1980s, Pakistan and Bangladesh undertook structural adjustment programs. Bangladesh undertook liberal reforms gradually, beginning in the late 1970s and continuing through subsequent decades. The policy initiatives were geared toward strengthening the private sector and creating an enabling environment for them, liberalizing trade and exchange rate regimes, and reforming the public sector.[7] After moving in the direction of import substitution, Pakistan undertook structural adjustment programs in the 1980s and adopted similar liberal measures. The Indian economic policy establishment also began to rethink the country's economic development model and began to liberalize cautiously in the early 1980s. India took its major turn toward adopting liberal trade and investment policies in 1991 in response to a severe balance of payments crisis. The government abandoned the regulated economic framework it had adopted in the 1950s through the 1970s, opening up sectors hitherto reserved for the public sector to domestic and foreign private investors. This section discusses these liberalization episodes in some detail.

Although Indian policymakers stemmed the tide toward increasing autarky in the 1980s, the attempt to liberalize trade and investment did not go far during that decade. Although India undertook a round of trade and investment liberalization in the mid-1980s under Rajiv Gandhi, these were stalled due to pressures from interest groups and from within the ruling party.[8] In 1990–1991, India faced a balance of payments crisis that continued to worsen till the threat of India defaulting on its external payments, for the first time in its history, became a real possibility in June 1991.

The crisis was a long time coming. The import liberalization in the 1980s had increased the pressure on foreign exchange. In 1990, in the wake of the Gulf War, India was hit by higher energy prices. At the same time, India had to airlift its citizens who worked in the region and the resultant drying up of remittances exacerbated the balance of payments crisis.[9]

Regional Trade and Investment in South Asia

Having nearly exhausted its capacity to borrow non-emergency funds from the International Monetary Fund, the government sold gold to cover its payments obligations.

In July 1991, a newly elected Congress government led by the late P.V. Narasimha Rao announced several policy changes in trade and investment, signaling an end to the era of inward-looking, interventionist economic policies. To boost exports, the government devalued the rupee by 18% against the dollar. It took a number of initiatives to encourage exports and reduced regulations and the number of licensing controls on trade. For example, it was now easier for exporters to import capital goods as well as intermediate products for further processing and export. In subsequent years, the government continued to reduce tariff on all goods. Average applied tariffs fell from a high of 80.85% in 1990 to 8.88% in 2010 before rising to 10.21% in 2019.[10] Tariffs in manufacturing fell more steeply during this period than tariffs in agricultural products.

Investments, including from foreign sources, were also liberalized in 1991. The government deregulated several sectors to make industry more efficient and competitive. Sectors previously reserved for production in the public sector were now opened up to participation by the private sector. Most notably, industrial licensing, a central feature of India's industrial policies since 1948, was abolished for all except 18 sectors, in which it was maintained for strategic and environmental reasons. Restrictions on firm growth were removed, allowing Indian firms to grow and become competitive in international markets. Foreign investors were allowed majority equity holdings, reversing an earlier decision when their holdings were capped at 40%. In subsequent years, successive governments from different parties have continued to open up sectors. Net inflows of foreign direct investment (FDI) increased from around a quarter billion dollars in 1990 to $50.6 billion in 2019.[11]

Collectively, these reforms and the reorientation of economic policies in a more liberal direction led to an increase in India's GDP growth rate from an average of 4.1% per year between 1950 and 1991 to a more robust 6.3% per year between 1992 and 2019 (calculation based on data from the World Bank). The proportion of the population living under the national poverty line fell from 45.3% in 1993 to 22% in 2011. India's per capita income increased from $367 in 1990 to $2100 in 2019.[12]

Sri Lanka was the first of the South Asian countries to reform its trade and investment policies, orienting it in a liberal direction. Given its small domestic market and its reliance on exports for earnings, opening up to trade and investment made sense for Sri Lanka. Sri Lanka had always relied on export of tea, rubber, and coconut to earn all its foreign exchange, but that earning allowed it to not only buy all the food it needed but also establish a welfare state and, in time, put in place aspects of import substitution industrialization. By the 1970s, its terms of trade had deteriorated to such a point that the export earnings were not adequate to pay for the food, the welfarism, and the public sector that had grown during the first two decades after independence. The subsequent liberalization measures were based on an export-led growth model. The government offered incentives to foreign and domestic capital, devalued the currency, relaxed import controls, and committed to tariff reduction. To encourage private foreign and domestic capital's engagement in industrial activity and, in particular, in export-oriented sectors, the government rationalized the tax structure. It abolished import licensing, removed public sector monopolies on imports, and eliminated import quotas. An Export Development Board was established to encourage exports.[13] In 1990, Sri Lanka's average tariff stood at 26.38%. Subsequently, it came down to 7.87% in 2015 but since then has more than doubled to 16.38% in 2019.[14]

Subsequently, manufacturing saw high growth, though much of it was concentrated in the garment industry. Its modest 5% growth rate facilitated its transition to the World Bank's middle income country category by 1997—the first major South Asian economy to do so.[15] However, its average growth rate remained modest, averaging 4.76% during 1977–2019. While poverty went down initially after the reforms, by the government's own admission there was little progress in poverty reduction during the 1990s. The government adopted a new policy framework for poverty reduction in 2000, and subsequently, poverty, according to the World Bank's benchmark, has come down from 22.7% to 4.1% between 2002 and 2016. Sri Lanka's per capita income increased from $463 in 1990 to $3852 in 2019.[16]

Bangladesh's post-independence economic policies were autarkic and relied on public sector and government intervention in the economy. The trade regime was highly restricted, with high tariff and non-tariff barriers and an overvalued exchange rate. The government pursued a policy of import substitution industrialization, seeking to create a protected domestic market for its own manufacturing sector. As it became clear over time that the statist model was unable to deliver growth and poverty reduction, the Bangladesh government began to liberalize its economy in the late 1970s by restructuring the public sector and building a strong private sector. The announcement of the New Industrial Policy in 1982 indicated Bangladesh's transition in a liberal direction. Subsequently, a structural adjustment program initiated in 1987 led to wide-ranging policy reforms that addressed trade, industrial, monetary, fiscal and exchange rate policies, in addition to recommending privatization of public sector enterprises and opening up further to FDI. The Bangladesh government sought to open up all but seven sectors to private sector participation. Hundreds of public sector units were sold to private buyers.[17]

In trade, the government adopted an explicit export-led growth strategy to replace earlier attempts at import substitution. It included across-the-board reduction in tariffs, elimination of duty on imported inputs, financial assistance for non-traditional exports, tax rebates on income from exports, cheaper import of capital, and rationalization of exchange rates. The government also simplified imports, reducing the number of tariff rates, eliminating import quotas, and simplifying procedures. Replacing a complex tariff structure that was in place till the mid-1980s and that featured rates as high as 200% on luxury items, the government initiated a tariff structure where the highest tariffs were on finished products and could be as high as 45% while tariffs on intermediate products, raw materials, and machinery were capped at 30%, 15%, and 7.5% respectively.[18] This new structure brought the average applied tariff down from 105.36% in 1989 to 27.52% in 1998 and further to 12.19% in 2019. These reforms collectively made Bangladesh an attractive destination for ready-made garment manufacturing and attracted FDI into this sector. The net inflow of FDI, just over $3 million in 1990, went up to $2.8 billion, before falling to $1.9 billion in 2019.[19] Besides ready-made garments, FDI has now entered in sectors such as power, food, and banking.

As trade and investment have gone up, they have driven Bangladesh's GDP growth rate, which has registered an average of 6% per year since 2000.[20] Its poverty rate at national poverty line fell from 48.9% in 2000 to 24.3% in 2016.[21] Its per capita income went up from $306 in 1990 to $1855 in 2019. Remarkably, according to World Bank classification, Bangladesh transitioned from a low-income economy to a lower-middle-income economy in 2015. Further, its growth rate puts it on a trajectory to graduate from the United Nations Least Developed Countries list in 2026.

Pakistan also began its economic reform process in 1988 in response to an economic crisis. The government adopted an orthodox structural adjustment program recommended by the International Monetary Fund and the World Bank. In addition to import liberalization, the program relied on a reduction of the budget deficit, increasing taxes, changes in prices of food and energy products, and an accompanying reduction in subsidies. The government began liberalizing trade in 1989–1990 by replacing restrictions and other non-tariff barriers with tariffs. It reduced the highest tariff level from 225% to 100%.[22] However, Pakistan's pace of tariff reforms was slower: While India's average tariff rate fell from 94% in 1991–1992 to 40.2% in 1997–1998 and Bangladesh's fell from 73.6% to 33.2% during that period, Pakistan reduced its average tariffs from 61% in 1992 to 51% in 1995 and then to 47% in 1998. Since then, Pakistan's average tariffs have dramatically come down to 12.58% in 2019.[23]

Pakistan allows 100% FDI in most industries barring a few strategic sectors such as arms, ammunitions, airlines, banking, and print and electronic media. Beginning in the late 1990s, and continuing in the early 2000s, the government of Pakistan was also successful in raising savings and reducing expenditures, managing domestic and external debt, and increasing public investment.[24] For a period after this, FDI increased dramatically, from $308 million in 2000 to $5.59 billion in 2007 before falling equally dramatically to $859 million in 2012. Since then, it has increased again to $2.23 billion in 2019. Pakistan's growth rate has not been as impressive during the last couple of decades as its South Asian neighbors: The average GDP growth in Pakistan has been fluctuating between a low of 1.7% and a high of 7.54%, averaging at 4.16% over 1990–2019 (calculation based on World Bank data). However, the poverty rate has reduced from a high of 64.3% in 2001 to 21.9% in 2018. Its per capita income has gone up from $371 in 1990 to $1288 in 2019.[25]

The remaining four countries in South Asia—Afghanistan, Bhutan, Maldives, and Nepal—are diverse and defy easy classification. Bhutan and Nepal are landlocked countries that are highly dependent on trade with India. Nepal has been going through several political milestones during the last couple of decades, and that has moderated its economic performance. Afghanistan's economic performance has similarly been limited by political and security factors during the last four decades. Maldives is a tiny but relatively more prosperous island nation that defies comparison with other South Asian countries.

Bhutan's economic policy is guided by its philosophy of focusing on Gross National Happiness (GNH).[26] The sale of hydroelectricity to India and tourism are the sources of its foreign exchange earnings. The government has invested revenue from these sources to develop human capital and provided service delivery and access to education and health. While the country has enormous trade potential in mineral exports, the government's policy is to manage growth in mining and exports consistent with its overall focus on GNH.[27]

Nepal has been going through a major political transition during the last three decades. A protracted internal conflict (1995–2006) involving Maoist rebels and government forces, the end of the monarchy in 2008, and the adoption of a new constitution in 2015 have been milestones in this transition. While Nepal liberalized its trade and investment regime through structural adjustment programs recommended by the IMF and the World Bank, its complicated political journey does not allow us to draw definite conclusions about the impact of liberalization. In 2004, it joined the World Trade Organization and has signed bilateral trade agreements with 17 countries.[28] Its tariffs came down from an average of 21.67% in 1998 to 14.36% in 1999 and then to 11.82% in 2013. In 2019, the average tariff increased dramatically to 20.2%.[29] Its average GDP growth rate increased from 3% per year between 1961 and 1989 to 4.6% per year between 1990 and 2019. Its per capita income increased from $191 in 1990 to $1194 in 2019.[30] While it has not met all the requirements for doing so—its per capita income is below the threshold for such a milestone—it is close to graduating out of the UN list of Least Developed Countries.[31]

Over the last four decades, Afghanistan has witnessed several conflicts: The Soviet invasion and exit, the takeover by Taliban, the US invasion in 2001, and its withdrawal and subsequent takeover by Taliban again chronicle a complicated history. Under the circumstances, even during the US intervention in Afghanistan, trade and investment have been minimal; GDP growth has fluctuated wildly, per capital income at $494 (2019) remains low, and the percentage of people living under the national poverty line has increased from 33.7% in 2007 to 54.5% in 2016.[32]

Maldives has been the most open of all the South Asian states. It has also had the highest GDP per capita—$10561 in 2019—and a well-developed infrastructure.[33] As a small island country, its earnings rely mostly on tourism, fishery, and construction, and as such, the economy is highly integrated with the outside world.

Challenges to Further Progress

The discussion thus far has demonstrated the progress this region has made in opening up to trade and investment. It has also shown how such efforts have contributed to growth and development in the region. However, the progress is far from adequate. Even though almost the entire region has become more integrated with the rest of the global economy, during the last five years, the region's major economies have also seen an increasing tendency to adopt protectionist trade policies. Second, while the countries in the region have increased their integration with the rest of the world, the region itself remains at a low level of integration. Third, while greater openness has raised incomes and lifted millions out of poverty, poverty rates still remain high in South Asia.

Tariffs in South Asian countries have come down from their historic highs associated with a period of import substitution policy. However, almost all countries still have average tariffs that are higher than comparable countries in Southeast Asia. The average tariffs in South Asia in 2016 were 13.6%, while the world average was less than half of it at 6.3%.[34] In addition, countries have shown a tendency to increase tariffs in recent years: Both India and Pakistan are guilty of this as are others in the region. Additionally, even where tariffs are not a problem, non-tariff and para-tariff barriers restrict the trade potential of the countries in the region. While non-tariff measures—rules and standards taken to protect non-trade concerns—are legitimate instruments for protecting consumer, environmental, and other interests, lack of transparency and unnecessary obfuscation in those measures can work as non-tariff barriers to trade. Taneja demonstrates how current standards such as labeling requirements can impose unnecessary costs on exporters and can lead to discriminatory trade practices that discourage the growth of trade.[35]

The World Bank identifies South Asia as the least integrated region in the world. Intraregional trade constitutes 50% of total trade in East Asia and 22% of total trade in Sub-Saharan Africa, while in South Asia, the percentage hovers around 5%. This means that while the states in the region have opened up to trade and investment with the rest of the world, they have not opened up their borders to each other and realized possible gains from intraregional trade to the extent possible. Economists estimate that opening up to intraregional trade could nearly triple the value of trade, currently at $23 billion to $67 billion.[36]

One way to achieve such intraregional integration is through a regional trade agreement. Following the establishment of the South Asian Association for Regional Cooperation in 1985, the countries established a South Asian Free Trade Area (SAFTA). This agreement, established in 2006, was based on a relatively low level of ambition with respect to trade liberalization. Member countries maintained long sensitive lists of products in which there is no liberalization. Bangladesh and Sri Lanka maintain almost 45% of their imports from other SAFTA members in their list of sensitive items on which no tariff negotiations are carried out. Additionally, members maintain high para-tariffs, which are taxes on imports and yet do not fall under measures that are subject to trade liberalization. If para-tariffs are included in tariff calculations, Bangladesh's average tariff for 2016–2017 would have been 25.6%, almost doubling the 13.63% average tariff rate. Sri Lanka also imposes a large number of para-tariffs.[37] The lack of trade between India and Pakistan also limits the extent to which trade in the region can increase. India and Pakistan are the two largest countries in the region and trade liberalization between them would increase intraregional trade both through increasing volumes and by enabling the setting up of regional value chains in textiles and garments, automobiles, and auto parts.

A protracted conflict between India and Pakistan has precluded progress in further trade liberalization under SAFTA. India has sought to build on the potential of regional market integration by reviving the sub-regional initiative called the Bay of Bengal Initiative for Multisectoral Technical and Economic Cooperation involving South Asian countries to the east and south (Bangladesh, Bhutan, Nepal, and Sri Lanka) as well as Myanmar and Thailand. It not only would allow the South Asian member countries to intensify integration while avoiding the thorny security issues that limit liberalization efforts involving both India and Pakistan, but it would also create a link to Southeast Asia through Myanmar and Thailand. Within South Asia, other bilateral efforts such as the India-Sri Lanka Free Trade Agreement (ISLFTA) and the multi-country effort such as Bangladesh-Bhutan-India-Nepal (BBIN) initiative also seeks to build trade and connectivity instead of letting the SAFTA process slow everyone down. Besides trying to create sub-regional groups, countries in the region have also engaged with those outside it to develop both strategic and economic relations. China has taken advantage of this situation to engage them both bilaterally and through its Belt and Road Initiative.

Admittedly, none of these subregional and bilateral efforts have been easy. Other than the ISLFTA, none have yielded many fruits thus far. However, there is more willingness to negotiate in these subregional forums. In 2016, the Modi government in India highlighted the BIMSTEC process by bringing all the leaders of the group to the BRICS meeting that India hosted that year.[38] BIMSTEC has started to negotiate a free trade agreement among its members. The member governments are also cooperating on creating air, road, maritime, and electronic connectivity within the subgroup, creating infrastructure that will facilitate movement of goods and services. Another notable effort to increase intraregional trade has been India's offer of duty-free quota-free access to its markets for all least developed countries.[39] Within the region, only Maldives, Pakistan and Sri Lanka do not fall in that category but Sri Lanka has access to the Indian market through the ISLFTA. Finally, the successful ratification of the Trade Facilitation Agreement negotiated under the World Trade Organization will likely facilitate trade within the region. Under this agreement, World Trade Organization (WTO) member countries including those in South Asia have committed to reducing bureaucratic and procedural complexity associated with trade. While the actual implementation of trade facilitation measures is a recent phenomenon, its likely impact on the cost of engaging in trade, particularly in developing countries, is expected to increase trade volumes and incomes.[40]

Barriers to investment in the region also remain high, and investment is limited by several factors. First, even though most countries have taken significant steps to liberalize policies and improve other aspects of their investment climate, restrictive policies remain. India sought to open up retail services to foreign investment but pushback from both small traders and large Indian conglomerates with an interest in retail kept the reforms incomplete. Second, even where sectors can attract 100% foreign investment in one sector, policy challenges in related sectors limit the attractiveness of investment. One such example is the food processing sector in India, which has a huge potential for growth. The Indian government's policies allow 100% foreign ownership of firms in that sector but policies in the farm sector and in agricultural marketing limit foreign firms' interest in investing. Another example is Pakistan, where in most sectors, 100% foreign ownership of firms is allowed, but foreign investment remains low. Diverse factors such as chronic energy shortages, issues with overall security and, relatedly, the high cost of doing business place constraints on larger flow of investments.[41]

Finally, poverty remains high and the COVID-19 pandemic highlighted the fragility of development in the region. Notwithstanding the substantial fall in poverty in the region, other than Sub-Saharan Africa, South Asia still has the largest number of poor people. While smaller countries such as Bhutan, Maldives, and Sri Lanka have poverty rates in single digits, the larger countries in the region, Bangladesh, India and Pakistan have 22–25% of citizens living under their national poverty levels. The region also scores high on the measure of multidimensional poverty: A measure that looks at access to health, education, and standard of living and complements the income-based poverty measures used by the World Bank.[42] These measures point toward the fragility of the progress the region has made in addressing issues of poverty and economic development. The COVID-19 pandemic demonstrated how quickly the life of the working poor can unravel: When countries such as India imposed lockdowns, the unfortunate plight of thousands of working poor—mainly migratory workers—became clear.[43] In all countries except Bangladesh, per capita income declined as a result of the pandemic.[44]

International Relations of Trade and Investment in South Asia

The discussion above demonstrates that at the international level, both security and economic considerations have driven developments in trade and investment in the region. The turn toward market-oriented development during the 1980s contributed to the direction of economic policies in South Asia during that decade and after. Second, states in the region were able to take advantage of global markets to fuel growth within their borders. Third, the politics of foreign aid has shaped the perception of these countries. Finally, the strategic competition in South Asia and Asia-Pacific has shaped both attitudes toward trade.

The turn away from import substitution industrialization in the 1970s–1990s was consistent with the international trend toward adoption of neoclassical economic policy by developing countries across Latin America and Asia. While in case of smaller countries, the guidance to adopt such policies came from institutions such as the International Monetary Fund and the World Bank, in case of larger countries such as India, the prescriptions for change were largely home-grown.[45] Most countries in the region continued to liberalize their economies, albeit slowly; however, recent trends have been in favor of moving toward more protectionist policies. While this is also a global trend, this has several sources.

Global markets have created opportunities for countries in the region: Sri Lanka and Bangladesh, for example, have inserted themselves in the global supply chains for apparel and have benefited from trade liberalization. India has taken advantage of the developed world's need for information technology-related services, pharmaceuticals, and others goods and services.

Third, the rise of China has shaped opportunities for Pakistan as well as the smaller countries of the region. Pakistan has developed its ties with China and entered into agreement with China to develop infrastructure under the China Pakistan Economic Corridor. Most of the smaller countries have also reached out to China to help them develop their infrastructure. In this regard, Sri Lanka's experience with developing the Hambantota port and the Maldives' experience with building a highway between the capital and its international airport are instructive: Both left the countries deeply in debt. India's inability to help with infrastructure building and the United States and other Western states' conditionalities for such help are partly the reason why the smaller countries have relied on China.

Fourth, strategic considerations have also slowed down the pace of regional integration. In this regard, the most important factor is the protracted conflict between India and Pakistan. The deep distrust between the two countries stand in the way of progress in trade liberalization, building supply chains and infrastructure connectivity in the region. It has also encouraged the efforts, particularly on India's part, in creating sub-regional groupings for cooperation on trade and investment.

Finally, strategic competition between China and India has been an important factor in shaping India's approach toward trade. In India, concerns regarding China have led to a rethinking of economic policy under Modi. This has resulted in a focus away from trade liberalization and, in fact, has led to increasing tariffs. On the one hand, India has walked away from a mega-regional trade agreement, the Regional Comprehensive Economic Partnership, in part because of China's dominance in it. On the other hand, India has focused on strengthening ties with the smaller countries through sub-regional groupings such as BIMSTEC and BBIN. It has also led to a sharp focus on attracting foreign investment.

Conclusion

South Asian countries, like others, have used trade and investment as pathways to growth and development. Unlike East and Southeast Asian countries, they mostly began this process toward the late 1980s in response to economic crises. Both domestic and international-level factors have shaped their approach to these issues. At the domestic level, interest politics and the states' autonomous developmental goals are important factors in explaining trade and investment policy choices. At the international level, dominant ideas and international institutional pressure, global markets as well as strategic considerations and the politics of foreign aid have been crucial factors in shaping choices.

The countries in the region will need to revisit their economic policies and seek newer trade partners even as they build a more robust free trade infrastructure within South Asia. The COVID-19 pandemic has demonstrated the need to strengthen trade and investment linkages and the need to build regional value chains. India will need to play a leadership role in getting others in the region to cooperate. A focus on trade and investment by itself will limit the ability to improve citizens' lives: It needs to be complemented by efforts to improve human development indicators including access to education and health.

Notes

1 Arvind Panagariya, *India: The Emerging Giant* (New York: Oxford University Press, 2008), 26–29.
2 Under import-substituting industrialization, states imposed high tariff barriers on imports in order to offer protection to newly emerging domestic firms, so that the latter are not forced to compete with more established firms. The goal was to diversify the newly independent state's industrial base.
3 William Richter, "The Political Dynamics of Islamic Resurgence in Pakistan," *Asian Survey* 19, no. 6 (June 1979): 549–555.
4 Syed Serajul Islam, "The Role of the State in the Economic Development of Bangladesh during the Mujib Regime," *The Journal of Developing Areas* 19 (January 1985): 189.
5 Ronald Herring, "Economic Liberalization of Policies in Sri Lanka," *Economic and Political Weekly* 22, no. 8 (February 21, 1987): 325–326.

6 *Ibid.*

7 Fahimul Quadir, "The Political Economy of Pro-Market Reforms in Bangladesh: Regime Consolidation through Economic Liberalization?" *Contemporary South Asia* 9, no. 2 (2000).

8 Atul Kohli, "Politics of Economic Liberalization in India," *World Development* 17, no. 3 (March 1989): 305–328.

9 Department of Economic Affairs, *Economic Survey, 1991–92A* (New Delhi: Government of India, 1992), 6–10.

10 World Bank, *Data Bank*, https://databank.worldbank.org, accessed January 25, 2022. All data on tariff, GDP, per capita income, and foreign direct investment inflows are from this source.

11 World Bank, *Data Bank*, https://databank.worldbank.org, accessed January 25, 2022.

12 *Ibid.*

13 Sriyani Dias, "Economic Liberalization and the Development of Manufacturing in Sri Lanka," *Asian Survey* 31, no. 7 (July 1991): 614–615.

14 World Bank, *Data Bank*, https://databank.worldbank.org, accessed January 25, 2022.

15 Neranjana Gunetilleke, "A Note on the Sri Lankan Experience on Poverty Reduction," *The Pakistan Development Review* 39, no. 4 (Winter 2000): 1193.

16 World Bank, *Data Bank*.

17 Mohammad A. Hossain and Mohammad Alauddin, "Trade Liberalization in Bangladesh: The Process and Its Impact on Macro Variables Particularly Export Expansion," *The Journal of Developing Areas* 39, no. 1 (Fall 2005): 128–132,

18 *Ibid.*

19 World Bank, *Data Bank*, https://databank.worldbank.org, accessed January 25, 2022.

20 Shahid Yusuf, "Bangladesh: Growth Miracle or Mirage?" Center for Global Development, June 16, 2021.

21 World Bank, *Data Bank*.

22 Tilat Anwar, "Structural Adjustment and Poverty: The Case of Pakistan," *The Pakistan Development Review* 35, no. 4 (Winter 1996): 911–926.

23 World Bank, *Data Bank*, https://databank.worldbank.org, accessed January 25, 2022.

24 Matthew McCartney, *Pakistan – The Political Economy of Growth, Stagnation and the State, 1951–2009* (New York: Routledge, 2011), ch. 8.

25 World Bank, *Data Bank*, https://databank.worldbank.org, accessed January 25, 2022.

26 Gross National Happiness, a term first used by Bhutan's King Jigme Singye Wangchuk in 1972, looks at the economic performance of a country from a more holistic point of view—instead of looking only at the growth in gross national product, it takes into account sustainability of its development model and the impact the latter has on non-economic indicators of well-being. See, for example, University of Oxford, "Oxford Poverty and Human Development Initiative," https://ophi.org.uk/policy/gross-national-happiness-index/, accessed February 10, 2022.

27 Government of Bhutan, "Mineral Development Policy (Draft)," https://www.gnhc.gov.bt/en/wp-content/uploads/2017/05/Mineral-Development-Policy.pdf.

28 US Department of Commerce, "Nepal – Country Commercial Guide: Trade Agreements," https://www.trade.gov/country-commercial-guides/nepal-trade-agreements.

29 World Bank, *Data Bank*, https://databank.worldbank.org, accessed January 25, 2022.

30 *Ibid.*

31 Government of Nepal, "Nepal's Statement on LDC Graduation for 2021 Triennial Review," https://www.un.org/development/desa/dpad/wp-content/uploads/sites/45/Nepal-2021-CDP-Plenary.pdf.

32 World Bank, *Data Bank*, https://databank.worldbank.org, accessed January 25, 2022.

33 *Ibid.*

34 Sanjay Kathuria and Priya Mathur, "Overview," in *A Glass Half Full: The Promise of Regional Trade in South Asia*, ed. Sanjay Kathuria (Washington, DC: World Bank, 2018), 13.

35 Nisha Taneja, "A Granular Approach to Addressing Nontariff Barriers: India's Trade with Bangladesh and Nepal," in Sanjay Kathuria, *A Glass Half Full*, 105–138.

36 Kathuria and Mathur, 7.

37 Sanjay Kathuria and Priya Mathur, "South Asia: A Work in Progress," in *A Glass Half Full*, 39–40.

38 BRICS stands for Brazil, Russia, India, China, and South Africa and is a grouping of emerging economies that have engaged in some collective action on economic and other issues.

39 "India to Provide Duty-Free Access to Products from LDCs," *Economic Times*, March 23, 2010, https://economictimes.indiatimes.com/news/economy/foreign-trade/india-to-provide-duty-free-access-to-products-from-ldcs/articleshow/5715399.cms?from=mdr.

40 "Bangladesh Enters Era of Paperless Trade from Today," The Daily Star, February 20, 2021, https://www.thedailystar.net/business/news/bangladesh-enters-era-paperless-trade-today-2047925.

41 World Trade Organization, "Pakistan: Trade Policy Review," 9, https://www.wto.org/english/tratop_e/tpr_e/tp411_e.htm.

42 The World Bank uses a $1.90 per day income threshold to classify people as poor. It uses the $3.20 per day measure to classify working poor.

43 "Covid 19 Impact: Fearing Lockdowns, Migrant Workers Flee Big Cities across India," *Indian Express*, April 20, 2021, https://indianexpress.com/article/india/migrant-exodus-covid-19-india-7282861/.

44 This observation is based on data from the World Bank.

45 Praveen K. Chaudhry, Vijay L. Kelkar and Vikash Yadav, "The Evolution of 'Homegrown Conditionality' in India: IMF Relations," *The Journal of Development Studies*, 40, no. 6, (August 2004): 59–81.

Bibliography

"Bangladesh Enters Era of Paperless Trade from Today." *The Daily Star*, February 20, 2021. https://www.thedailystar.net/business/news/bangladesh-enters-era-paperless-trade-today-2047925.

"Covid 19 Impact: Fearing Lockdowns, Migrant Workers Flee Big Cities across India." *Indian Express*, April 20, 2021. https://indianexpress.com/article/india/migrant-exodus-covid-19-india-7282861/.

"India to Provide Duty-Free Access to Products from LDCs." *Economic Times*, March 23, 2010. https://economictimes.indiatimes.com/news/economy/foreign-trade/india-to-provide-duty-free-access-to-products-from-ldcs/articleshow/5715399.cms?from=mdr.

Anwar, Tilat. "Structural Adjustment and Poverty: The Case of Pakistan." *The Pakistan Development Review* 35, no. 4 (Winter 1996).

Department of Economic Affairs. *Economic Survey, 1991–92A*. New Delhi: Government of India, 1992.

Dias, Sriyani. "Economic Liberalization and the Development of Manufacturing in Sri Lanka." *Asian Survey* 31, no. 7 (July 1991).

Government of Bhutan. "Mineral Development Policy (Draft)." https://www.gnhc.gov.bt/en/wp-content/uploads/2017/05/Mineral-Development-Policy.pdf.

Government of Nepal. "Nepal's Statement on LDC Graduation for 2021 Triennial Review." https://www.un.org/development/desa/dpad/wp-content/uploads/sites/45/Nepal-2021-CDP-Plenary.pdf.

Gunetilleke, Neranjana. "A Note on the Sri Lankan Experience on Poverty Reduction." *The Pakistan Development Review* 39, no. 4 (Winter 2000).

Herring, Ronald. "Economic Liberalization of Policies in Sri Lanka." *Economic and Political Weekly* 22, no. 8 (February 21, 1987).

Hossain, Mohammad A., and Mohammad Alauddin. "Trade Liberalization in Bangladesh: The Process and Its Impact on Macro Variables Particularly Export Expansion." *The Journal of Developing Areas* 39, no. 1 (Fall 2005).

Islam, Syed Serajul. "The Role of the State in the Economic Development of Bangladesh during the Mujib Regime." *The Journal of Developing Areas* 19 (January 1985).

Kathuria, Sanjay, and Priya Mathur. "Overview." In *A Glass Half Full: The Promise of Regional Trade in South Asia*, edited by Sanjay Kathuria. Washington, DC: World Bank, 2018.

Kohli, Atul. "Politics of Economic Liberalization in India." *World Development* 17, no. 3 (March 1989).

McCartney, Matthew. *Pakistan – The Political Economy of Growth, Stagnation and the State, 1951–2009*. New York: Routledge, 2011.

Panagariya, Arvind. *India: the Emerging Giant*. New York: Oxford University Press, 2008.

Quadir, Fahimul. "The Political Economy of Pro-Market Reforms in Bangladesh: Regime Consolidation through Economic Liberalization?" *Contemporary South Asia* 9, no. 2 (2000).

Richter, William. "The Political Dynamics of Islamic Resurgence in Pakistan." *Asian Survey* 19, no. 6 (June 1979).

Taneja, Nisha. "A Granular Approach to Addressing Nontariff Barriers: India's Trade with Bangladesh and Nepal." In *A Glass Half Full: The Promise of Regional Trade in South Asia*, edited by Sanjay Kathuria. Washington, DC: World Bank, 2018.

US Department of Commerce. "Nepal – Country Commercial Guide: Trade Agreements." https://www.trade.gov/country-commercial-guides/nepal-trade-agreements

World Bank. *Data Bank*. Washington DC: World Bank, 2022. https://databank.worldbank.org.

World Trade Organization. "Pakistan: Trade Policy Review." p. 9. https://www.wto.org/english/tratop_e/tpr_e/tp411_e.htm.

Yusuf, Shahid. "Bangladesh: Growth Miracle or Mirage?" Center for Global Development, June 16 2021. https://www.cgdev.org/blog/bangladesh-growth-miracle-or-mirage.

INDEX

Note: Page references in *italics* denote figures, in **bold** tables and with "n" endnotes.

9/11 terrorist attacks *see* September 11, 2001
attacks
21st Conference of Parties of the United Nations
Framework Convention on Climate Change
(COP21) 390
"26/11" complex attack *see* Mumbai terror
attacks (2008)
*2030 Roadmap for India-UK Future
Relations* 375

Abdullah, Farooq 164
Abe, Shinzo 358–359
Abu Dhabi Dialogue 447
Adamson, Fiona 440
Adenauer, Konrad 396, 397–398
Afghan crisis 47
Afghanistan 10, 371–373; American withdrawal
from 1, 3, 54, 314; cybersecurity 219;
economic crisis in 54; and Germany 400–401;
National Directorate of Security (NDS) 282;
political ideologies 21–23; refugees from 200;
regime types 25–26, 239; regional dynamics
240; regional relations 232, 233–240;
relations with Bangladesh 236; relations with
Bhutan 236; relations with India 231–232,
234–235, 237–238; relations with Maldives
236; relations with Nepal 236; relations with
Pakistan 10, 231–232, 234–235, 237–238,
280–282; relations with South Asia 231–241;
relations with Sri Lanka 236, 252; Soviet
invasion of 49, 281, 342; space program of
462–463; stability in 239–240; takeover by
Taliban in 2021 282; Taliban rule in 3–4,
40, 146–147, 239; Tehrik-e-Taliban 2; trade
volume 237; US war in 12, 145; *see also* Taliban

Afghanistan-Pakistan Action Plan for Peace and
Solidarity (APAPPS) 235
Afghanistan-Pakistan Transit Trade Agreement
(APTTA) 235
Afghan Resettlement Scheme 375
Afghan Taliban *see* Taliban
African Union (AU) 411, 413
Agence française de développement 391
Agni missiles 122–123
Agusta Westland 374
Ahmar, Moonis 51
Ahmed, Zulafqar 37
Akali Dal 159, 164
Akhand Bharat (undivided India) 291, 296
Al Emarah 218
Alliance for Multilateralism 399
al-Qaida (AQ) 142, 143, 146, 150, 163, 316, 344,
371; *see also* terrorism
Amanullah, King of Afghanistan 391
Anandpur Sahib Resolution 164
Andersson, Ruben 167
Annan, Kofi 201
Antarctic Treaty 70
anti-Americanism 397
anti-colonialism 397
anti-imperialism 397
anti-satellite test (ASAT) 454–457, 465
Antrix Corporation Limited (ANTRIX) 461
AQ Khan proliferation network 118
Arthashastra (Kautilya) 7
Article 370 of the Constitution (India): described
168n15; scrapping 111, 146
Ashkenaze, Kerry 167
Asian Infrastructure and Investment Bank
(AIIB) 304

Index

Asia-Pacific Space Cooperation Organization (APSCO) 464

Association of South East Asians Nations (ASEAN) 347, 360, 397, 402, 411, 413

asylum seekers 447–449

Atatürk, Kemal 160

Atlantic Council of the United States 188

Atmakuri, Archana 246

"Atmanirbhar Bharat" campaign 388

Atmar, Mohammed Haneef 235, 237

Attanayake, Chulanee 246

authoritarianism 21, 24; political 49; soft 280; and South Asia 51–53

Awami League 52, 162

Ayoob, Mohammed 205

Azhar, Masood 372, 387

Babar, Naseerullah 281

Babur 1B cruise missiles 178

Bachelet, Michelle 248

BAE Systems 374

Baghdad Pact 343; *see also* Central Treaty Organization (CENTO)

Bajpai, Kanti 297

Bajwa, Qamar Javed 278

Balakot air strikes 110–111, 135, 137–138, 145

balance of power (BoP) 35; politics 93, 95–97, 298, 319, 323; regional 7

Ballistic Missile Defence (BMD) 117

BALUSA Group 187

Bandaranaike, S.W.R.D. 250, 401

Bandung conference 246

Bangla Bhai 162

Bangladesh 3, 258–259, 371–373; during 2009-2021 264–265; Bangladesh-Pakistan relations 263–264; and China 262–263, 265–266; Counterterrorism Cooperation Initiative 321; cybersecurity 219; democracies 25; and Germany 402; governance failure 203; and identity clashes 37–38; in Indo-Soviet Axis 259–261; Jamaat-e-Islami 162; "Look East" policy 263; in midst of a tug-of-war 264–265; and Muslim Rohingyas 321; and Pakistan 278–280; path forward 266–268; refugees hosted by 200; regime types 25; relations with Afghanistan 236; and Soviet Union 258; space program of 461–462; and Sri Lanka 249–250; and U.S. 321; War of Independence 249, 258; westward shift: 1979–2009 261–262

Bangladesh Atomic Energy Commission 461

Bangladesh Awami League (BAL) 259, 261, 267

Bangladesh-Bhutan-India-Nepal (BBIN) initiative 304, 477, 479

Bangladesh Climate Change Resilience Fund 414

Bangladesh Climate Change Strategy and Action Plan (BCCSAP) 414

Bangladesh Climate Change Trust Fund 414

Bangladesh Nationalist Party (BNP) 261

Bangladesh-Pakistan relations 263–264

Bangladesh Space Research and Remote Sensing Organization (SPARRSO) 455

Bangladesh War 96, 118, 249, 440

Baruah, Sanjib 166

Basu, Ipshita 165

Batchelder, Scott 167

Bay of Bengal Initiative for Multi-Sectoral Technical and Economic Cooperation (BIMSTEC) 27, 215, 218, 240, 304, 375, 402–403, 417, 477, 479

BBIN initiative 27

BeiDou global navigation satellite system (GNSS) 218

Belt and Road Initiative (BRI) 1, 27, 217, 265, 303, 332–333, 346–347, 361, 363

Bhabha, Homi 116, 118

Bhabha Atomic Research Center (BARC) 119, 124

Bharatiya Janata Party (BJP) 36, 108, 124, 166, 262, 291

Bharatiya Jans Sangh 124

Bhindranwale, Jarnail Singh 164

Bhore, Joseph 428

Bhutan 4, 371–373; GNH 475; governance failure 203; National Strategy and Action Plan for Low Carbon Development 415; norm creation 38; political ideologies 21–23; relations with Afghanistan 236; space program of 463; and Sri Lanka 251; and U.S. 320–321

Bhutanisation 38

Bhutto, Benazir 279, 281

Bhutto, Zulfiqar Ali 13, 130, 131, 160, 263, 281, 472

Biden, Joe 232, 319

Biegun, Stephan 266

Bill and Melinda Gates Foundation 425–426, 429, 431, 433

bin Laden, Osama 319, 344–345

Birendra, king of Nepal 303, 390

Blue Economy Strategy 362

Boxer Rebellion 92

BRAC 432

Brahmos supersonic cruise missile 178

Brandt, Willy 200, 396, 398

Brasstacks crisis 132

Brexit 369, 371, 373–374, 391

BRICS (Brazil, Russia, India, China, and South Africa) 70, 348, 464

British East India Company 292, 383

British imperialism 292

Brundtland, Gro Harlem 200

Burton, John 184

Index

Bush, George W. 320
Buzan, Barry 8
Byman, Daniel 147

Cameron, David 369, 372, 373
capitalism 297
Carranza, Mario 37
cause-effect ideas 34
Central Intelligence Agency (CIA) 94
Central Malaria Bureau, India 428
Central Treaty Organization (CENTO) 343, 398, 400; *see also* Baghdad Pact
Centre national d'études spatiales (CNES) 389
Chacko, Priya 36
Chandra, Uday 165
Chao Track 186
Chatterjee, Partha 50
Chatterjee, Shibashis 37–38
Cheysson, Claude 385
China 1–2; and Bangladesh 262–263, 265–266; Belt and Road Initiative (BRI) 332–333, 346–347, 361; cyber espionage 213; entry into South Asia 317–318; future trends 334–336; history and themes 330–332; Indian military doctrines toward 175; investment in South Asian countries 12; Japanese invasion of 93; Ladakh incursion 2; and Maldives 306–307; nuclear assistance to Pakistan 96; and Pakistan relations 13, 84; recent trends 332–334; and South Asia 330–336; theoretical paradigms 334; UN Security Council seat 12–13
China Great Wall Industry Corporation (CGWIC) 462
China-Maldives Friendship Bridge 306, 308
China-Pakistan Economic Corridor (CPEC) 27, 84, 235, 317, 324, 332, 346, 400, 457, 478
Chinese Muslims 332
Chirac, Jacques 384, 386
Chittagong Hill Tracts (CHT) 162, 205
Choonhavan, Chatichai 355
Chowdhary, Rekha 166
Christianity 297
CHT Peace Accord 162
citizenship 205–206
Citizenship (Amendment) Act 2019 (India) 204
Citizenship Amendment Act (CAA) 264
CIVICUS 204
civilizational exceptionalism 36
climate change 204; challenges in South Asia 413–414; and displacement 414; and migratory patterns 414; policies in South Asian countries 414–416; regional cooperation 416–418; regionalism and climate change cooperation 412–413; South Asian climate regionalism 418–419
Clinton, Hillary 145

Cohen, Stephen P. 294
Cold Start 109, 135–136, 174, 176
Cold War 8, 11, 14, 69, 245, 247, 259, 292, 314, 319, 383, 440; bipolarity 246; bipolar world order 258; and India 294–296; rigidities 385; and Russia 343–345
Colombo Plan 251, 428
Colombo Powers Conference (1954) 246
colonialism, Western 297
communism 21, 247
Comprehensive Test Ban Treaty 97, 118
Computer Emergency Response Teams (CERT)/Computer Incident Response Teams (CIRT) 215–216
Conciliation Resources 187
Conference on Security and Co-operation (CSCE) 396
conflict resolution dialogues 186
conflict transformation 186
Congress System 56n37
constitutional legitimacy 37
constitutive norms 34
Constructivism 2, 32–41, 80, 245, 440; as interpretive meta-theory 32; and South Asian IR 35–40; as theory of IR 32; variants of 34
contested identities 36
The Cooperative Monitoring Center 187
Copeland, Dale 8
cosmopolitan ethics 47
Council for Strategic Defence Research (CDSR) 186
counterinsurgencies (COIN): overview 158–159; in South Asia 158–167
counterinsurgency constitutionalism 166
counter-terrorism: agencies 387; in South Asia 142–151; UK, program with Pakistan 372
COVID-19 pandemic 1, 3, 70, 265, 306, 308, 315, 439, 446, 449, 464, 478, 479; death in South Asian region 4; infectious disease in South Asia 427–430; international experts in estrangement 430–432; poverty in South Asian region 197
Cox, Robert 47
Critical Constructivism 34
critical theory 2, 245, 440; approaches to international relations 172; approaches to South Asian IR 46–54; regional/international context 47–48
Cuban Missile Crisis 95
Cunningham, David E. 147
"Curzonian Arc" 293
cyberattacks 3, 216, 219–220; in Asia-Pacific region 213; by Russia 214; *see also* cybersecurity
Cyber Crime Code 218

Index

cyber instability: approaches to cybersecurity 218–220; drivers of 216–218; in South Asia 215–220

cyber power 214

cybersecurity 213; economic dimension of 218–219; incidents in South Asia 217; in South Asia **216**; South Asian approaches to 218–220

cyberspace: activities by Russia 213–214; defined 214; sovereign 219–220; theory of 214–215

Dalai Lama 94, 99, 332

Dara Shikoh (Mughal prince) 358

Dassault 388

Davidson, Phil 322

deep strategic culture 66, 68–70; pursuit of status 69–70; strategic autonomy 68–69

Defence Research and Development Organisation (DRDO) 119, 124

De Gaulle, Charles 384–385

democracy: Bangladesh 25; Maldives 25; Nepal 25; and South Asia 51–53; Sri Lanka 25

De Silva, Shakthi 246

d'Estaing, Valéry Giscard 384

Destradi, Sandra 290, 292, 293, 298

Dhakal, Tika 305

Dhirragu 217

Digital Silk Road (DSR) 217

digital technologies 213

Doklam Crisis 98

domestic politics 70, 267; Bangladesh 264; and India-Pakistan rivalry 110–112; Maldives' 49; and structural constraints 275–283; *see also* politics

Donaldson, Robert 343

Doval, Ajit 346

DPRK 213

Draft Nuclear Doctrine (1999) 121

Durand Line 234

Easter Sunday bombings 252

East India Company 292, 427

economic development: and Nepal 304; through regional institutions 304; through regional interdependence 304

Epidemic Diseases Act 427

Ershad, Hussain Mohammed 261–264, 267, 269

Esper, Mark 266

Eurasian Economic Union (EAEU) plan, 2015 347

European imperialism 21

European Union (EU) 26, 369–370, 386, 400, 411, 413; Generalised Scheme of Preferences Plus (GSP+) program 248; membership 26

Fair, C. Christine 82, 87, 167, 275

Far Eastern Economic Review 354

Federally Administered Tribal Areas (FATA) 281

Federation of Economic Organizations *(Keidanren)* 355

Federation of German Industries 397

Federation of Indian Chambers of Commerce and Industry 188

Federation of Pakistan Chambers of Commerce and Industry 188

Financial Action Task Force (FATF) 86, 151

Finnemore, Martha 34

First Gulf War 261

forced displacement 198–199

Ford Foundation 428–429

Foreign Affairs 359

Foundation for Advanced Studies on International Development (FASID) 360

Fourth Republic (1946–1958) 383

France: and Afghan Taliban government 4; defense partnership with India 387–389; first decades after 1947 384–385; handling relations with smaller countries 390–391; relationship with Pakistan 4; and South Asia 383–392; structuring cooperation 389–390; transformative shift 386–387

Franco-Russian expedition to India 383

Fravel, Taylor 332

Frazier, Mark 336

French Commissariat à l'énergie atomique (CEA) 389

French East India Company 292

Frey, Karsten 123

Friedrich Ebert Foundation 402

Friedrich Naumann Foundation 402

Gagarin, Yuri 454

Galwan Valley crisis 317–318, 336

Gamage, Rajni Nayanthara 246

Gandhi, Indira 65, 67, 69, 112, 118, 164, 259, 262, 291, 295, 384

Gandhi, Rajiv 97, 118–119, 164, 251, 448, 472

Ganges Water Sharing Treaty 262

Ganguly, Šumit 51, 82–83, 163

Garver, John 331

Gautama Buddha 251

Gayner, Gillian 165

Gayoom, Abdulla 306–307

geography: and Realism 10–11; South Asia's 10–11

geopolitics 51

Gerasimov, Valery 214

German-Pakistan Chamber of Commerce and Industry (GPCCI) 400

Germany/West Germany: and Afghanistan 400–401; from Asia-Pacific to Indo-Pacific 396–397; and Bangladesh 402; bilateral relations 397–402; and Ceylon/Sri Lanka 401–402; foreign policy concepts after 1990 396–397; and India 397–399; Indo-Pacific

policy 397; and Nepal 402; and Pakistan 399–400; regional level 402–403; and South Asia in historical perspective 395–396
Ghani, Ashraf 218, 235, 282
Ghosh, Partha 441
Glasgow Climate Summit 415
Global Britain 369
Global Compact for Refugees 449
Global Fund to Fight AIDS, Tuberculosis, and Malaria (the Global Fund) 425, 429
globalization 396, 440
Global Polio Eradication Initiative 429
Goethe-Institutes in India 395
Goldstein, Jemima 372
Gorbachev, Mikhail 97, 348
Gordon, Sandy 55n9, 64
governance failure 203–204; Afghanistan 203; Bangladesh 203; Bhutan 203; India 203; Myanmar 203; Pakistan 203; Sri Lanka 203; Taliban 203
Grameen Bank 265
Gramsci, Antonio 47
Gray, Colin 63, 80
Greater Eurasian Partnership (GEP) Concept 347
Green Revolution 163
gross domestic product (GDP) 38
gross national happiness (GNH) 38, 475
Gujral, I.K. 291
"Gujral Doctrine" 296
Gulf Cooperation Council (GCC) countries 439, 443, 444–447
Gunasekara, Sandya Nishanthi 246
Gyalo Thondup 94

Habermas, Jurgen 47
Haggard, Stephan 20
Hague, William 372
Haidari, Mohammad Ashraf 236
Hallstein-Doctrine of 1955 396, 398
Hamid, Faiz 79
Haq, Mahbub ul 200–201
Haq, Sami ul 281
Haqqani, Sirajuddin 346
Haqqani Network 146, 316, 319
Harris, Harry 247, 322
Hasangani, Sandunika 38
Hasina, Sheikh 261, 279, 280, 426
Haushofer, Karl 358
Heart of Asia-Istanbul Process 235
Hekmatyar, Gulbuddin 281
Heritage Foundation's 2021 Index of Economic Freedom 315
high-skill migration 443–444
Hindu Rashtra 22, 296
Hindustan Aeronautics Limited (HAL) 374, 388, 461
Hindutva ideology 291

Hizb-e-Islami 281
horizontal proliferation 132
Huang Hua 96
human development 201
human security: citizenship 205–206; climate change 204; discourse on 200–202; governance failure 203–204; poverty in South Asia 197; in South Asia 197–206; structural inequalities 202–203
Huntington, Samuel 363

IBSA 70
ideas: and Constructivism 34, 38–40; defined 34; types of 34
identity 35–38; contested 36; and ethnic conflicts in South Asia 37–38; and India-Pakistan relations 36–37; socio-cognitive 36
ideologies 34
imperialism: British 292; European 21
import substitution industrialization 471–472, 478
India 1–2, 289–298; alliance with Soviet Union 11–12, 96; Chandrayaan-1 461; Citizenship (Amendment) Act 2019 204; and Cold War 294–296; Deep Space agenda 461; defense partnership with France 387–389; Dravidian movement 38; economy and COVID-19 pandemic 3; Epidemic Diseases Act of 1897 428; focus on internal balancing 12–13; Franco-Russian expedition to 383; Generation Modi 296–297; and Germany 397–399; Hindu supremacism in 2; Hindutva policies in 370–371; Industrial Policy Resolutions of 1948 and 1956 471; Mars Orbiter Mission (MOM) 461; material superiority 10; military forces 9; Non-Aligned Movement 293; nuclear tests of May 1998 333; oscillating approaches 293–297; Pakistan enmity with 48–49; Personal Data Protection Bill 220; political ideologies 21–23; regime types 24; regional dynamics 289–291; regional leadership efforts of 15; relations with Afghanistan 231–232, 234–235, 237–238; relations with Pakistan 276–278; relations with Sri Lanka 250–251; *Roadmap 2030 for India-UK Future Relations* 371; space program of 460–461; strategic aims 292–293; and UK 373–375; war of 1947–1948 276
India-Bangladesh relationship 262
India-China war of 1962 303
India-Japan-US Malabar naval exercises 320
Indian Air Force 119
Indian Army Land Warfare Doctrine 174
Indian Atomic Energy Commission (AEC) 389
Indian Atomic Energy Establishment (IAET) 117
Indian Citizenship Amendment Act (2019) 442
Indian Council for Medical Research 428
Indian Medical Service (IMS) 427, 428

Index

Indian military doctrines 170–179; limited war 172–173; overview 170–171; precision-guided munitions (PGMs) 177–178; technological transformation 177–178; toward China 175; toward Pakistan 173–175

Indian National Committee for Space Research (INCOSPAR) 460

Indian National Congress (INC) 259, 291

Indian National Satellite system (INSAT) 461

Indian nuclear weapons program 116–125; ballistic missile program 121; history of 117–118; Intermediate Range Ballistic Missiles 122; and international relations 123–124; origins 117–118; overview 116–117; reserved arsenal (1989–1999) 118–120; responsible arsenal (1998–2008) 120–121; resurgent arsenal (2008-) 122–123

Indian Ocean: capacity-building in 361–363; infrastructure initiatives in 361–363; *Return to East of Suez* security posture in 369; sustainable development in 361–363; as Zone of Peace 247

Indian Ocean Region (IOR) 289–290, 358, 359, 361–362, 386, 411

Indian Ocean Rim Association (IORA) 39–40, 308

Indian Rebellion of 1857 292

Indian Remote Sensing Satellite system (IRS) 461

Indian Research Fund Association 428

Indian Space Association (ISpA) 461

Indian Space Research Organisation (ISRO) 389, 455, 457, 460–461, 463

Indian strategic culture: caste system 64; contemporary 65–66; employment of force 66–67; intervention 66–67; myths and clarifications 64–65; nuclear restraint 67–68; overview 63–64

"India Out" campaign 49

India-Pakistan rebalancing 319–320

India-Pakistan rivalry 2, 53, 104–112; Balakot strikes 110–111; and domestic politics 110–112; explaining 105–107; and Kashmir 316–317; and nuclear weapons 107–108; origins of 104–105; overview 104; since 1990s 107–112; and terrorism 108–109; *see also* India; Pakistan

India-Pakistan war (1965) 11, 13, 81, 95, 96, 344

India-Pakistan war (1971) 13, 49, 81, 83, 132

India-Sri Lanka Free Trade Agreement (ISLFTA) 477

India Strategic Trade Authorization Tier 1 (STA-1) 320

India Today 384

IndigoZebra 217

"Indira Doctrine" 295

Indo-German Chamber of Commerce (IGCC) 399

Indo-Pacific 318–319

Indo-Pak Youth Forum for Peace 187

Indopazifischen Raum (Haushofer) 358

Indo-Soviet Treaty of 1971 259, 344

Indo-US Civilian Nuclear Agreement 121

Institute for Global Success (IGS), Maldives 463

insurgencies: onset of 159–165; overview 158–159; persistence of **165**, 165–166

"integrated battle group" (IBG) 173–174

Intercontinental Range Ballistic Missiles (ICBMs) 117

Intergovernmental Panel on Climate Change (IPCC) 413

International Atomic Energy Agency (IAEA) 117

International Centre for Integrated Mountain Development (ICIMOD) 417

International Commission on Intervention and State Sovereignty 201

International Cricket Council (ICC) 280

International Crimes Tribunal (ICT) 162

International Institute for Strategic Studies (IISS) 187

International Monetary Fund 470, 473, 474–475, 478

International North-South Transit Corridor (INSTC) 240, 347

International Organization for Migration (IOM) 447

international politics: global systemic variables 11–12; regional variables 9–11; South Asia 9–12; *see also* politics

international relations (IR): constructivist approaches to South Asian 32–41; and Indian nuclear weapons program 123–124; and India-Pakistan military posturing 32–41; liberal approaches to South Asian 20–27; Realist approaches to South Asian 15; South Asia 3, 8–9; of trade and investment in South Asia 478–479

International Security Assistance Force (ISAF) 391, 401

International Solar Alliance (ISA) 399

International Telecommunications Union (ITU) 458

interpretive meta-theory 32

Inter-Services Intelligence (ISI) 79, 144, 278, 280, 316, 319, 344, 372

investment liberalization 470–471

Iqbal, Muhammad 22, 395

ISIS 2, 371–372; *see also* terrorism

ISIS-K 3

Islam 82, 297; fundamentalist 49; Maldives conversion to 21

Islamic Jihad Union 400

Islamic State (IS) 142, 143, 146–147, 163, 316; *see also* terrorism

488

Index

Jaggrata Muslim Janata Bangladesh (JMJB) 162
Jaipur Literature Festival 187
Jaishankar, S. 102n53, 308, 418
Jaish-e-Mohammed 111, 145, 374, 387
Jamaat-e-Islami Bangladesh 25, 160, 162–163, 262, 279, 281
James Webb Space Telescope 454
Jamiat Ulema-i-Islam 281
Jammat-ul Mujahideen Bangladesh (JMB) 372
Japan: and assistance 360–361; capacity-building 361–363; conceptual and theoretical framework 356–358; and development aid 360–361; foreign policy interests/influence 360–361; *Free and Open Indo-Pacific* strategy and framework 358–359, 361; historical context 355–356; infrastructure initiatives 361–363; Ministry of Economy, Trade and Industry 355–356; Ministry of Foreign Affairs 356; and Nuclear Non-Proliferation Treaty 356; Official Development Assistance 356, 360; *Partnership for Quality Infrastructure Initiative* 362; and regional maritime security environment 361–363; relations with South Asia 354–364; *seikei bunri* strategy 354; and sustainable development 361–363
Japanese Maritime Self-Defense Force (MSDF) 362–363
Japanese *sogo shosha* 354
Japan International Cooperation Agency (JICA) 360–361
Jaschik, Kevin 39
Jatiyo Rakhi Bahini (JRB) 259
Jayasekera, P.V.J. 246
Jayewardene, J.R. 251
Jervis, Robert 246
Jharkhand Mukti Morcha (JMM) 164–165
Jindal, Sajjan 278
Jinnah, Muhammad Ali 22, 160–161, 167n6, 276
Johnson, Boris 375
Johnston, Alastair Iain 80–81

kafala system 445
Kaifu, Toshiki 355
Kaila, Heidi 166
Kampani, Gaurav 119, 122
Kamra, Lipika 166
Kant, Immanuel 23
Kargil War (1999) 49, 108, 121, 122, 133–134, 178, 277, 319
Karzai, Hamid 232, 252, 281–282, 346
Kashmir: and India-Pakistan rivalry 105, 106; India-Pakistan rivalry and 316–317; insurgency 164; as Muslim-majority state 106; Pakistan claims on 130; *see also* India-Pakistan rivalry
Kashmir Study Group 187
Katzenstein, Peter 370
Kaufmann, Chaim 161–162

Kaur, Rajkumari Amrit 428
Kautilya 7, 65
Kaviraj, Sudipta 54n1
Keen, David 167
Kelegama, Saman 246
Kennedy, John F. 343
Kerry, John 321
KFS Space Foundation 463
Khalistan 164, 167
Khan, Abdul Qadeer 131, 400, 458
Khan, Abdur Rahman 343
Khan, Ayub 161, 277
Khan, Daoud 280–281
Khan, Feroz Hassan 84
Khan, Ijaz 86
Khan, Imran 251, 263, 278, 280, 282, 319, 371, 392, 449
Khan, Mohammed Daoud 280–281, 343, 392n29
Khan, Yasmin 159
Khan, Zafrullah 113n9
Khrushchev, Nikita 343, 348
Kishi, Nobusuke 360
Kissinger, Henry 3
Kitaro, Nishida 357
Konrad Adenauer Foundation 402
Korean War 93
Kotelawala, John 390
Kothari, Rajini 56n37
Kouchner, Bernard 390
Krauthammer, Charles 342
Kreps, Sarah E. 147
Kristensen, Hans M. 40
Kyoto Protocol 412

labor migrations 444–447
Ladakh Crisis 98
Lahore Literary Festival 187
Lal Masjid 160
Lalwani, Sameer P. 165
Land Boundary Agreement (LBA) 262, 264
Language Martyrs Day 161
Lantis, Jeffrey S. 86
Lashkar-e-Tayyiba 83, 145, 278
Lavoy, Peter R. 83, 84
Lazarus Group 217
Leites, Nathan 80
Lhasa Revolt 94–95
liberalism 2, 46–47, 54, 245, 246, 426, 440; international institutions 26–27; regime types 23–26; societal actors 23–26; and South Asian international relations 20–27
Liberation Tigers of Tamil Eelam (LTTE) 23, 38, 48, 248, 251, 252, 282, 390, 401; *see also* Sri Lanka
Linklater, Andrew 47
Lumley, Joanna 373

Index

Macron, Emmanuel 386, 392, 393n20
Mahatma Gandhi National Rural Employment
  Guarantee Scheme 166
Mahayana 251
Mahendra, king of Nepal 303, 390
Mahindra Defense 374
Majma-ul-Bahrain (Confluence of the Two Seas)
  (Dara Shikoh) 358
Make in India initiative 388, 399
Maldives 4, 371–373; Chinese presence in
  306–307; conversion to Islam 21; democracies
  25; democratization and polarization 307–308;
  domestic politics 49; foreign policy of 302,
  305–308; "Framework for a Defense and
  Security Relationship" 322; "India Out"
  campaign 308; National Adaptation Program
  for Action (NAPA) 415; political ideologies
  21–22; relations with Afghanistan 236;
  relations with Sri Lanka 249; space program of
  463; and U.S. 321–322
Maldives Climate Change Policy Framework 415
Maley, William 40
Malik, Yasin 164
Maoist insurgencies 164
Mao Zedong 332
Maritime Silk Road Initiative 306
"martial race" doctrine 160
Massoud, Ahmed Shah 281, 345, 393n29
Maududi, Abul 160
migration: high-skill 443–444; International
  Relations (IR) theories 440–442; labor
  444–447; professional 443–444; refugees
  and asylum seekers 447–449; themes and
  approaches 440–442; trends post-1947
  442–443
Miliband, David 390
military doctrines *see* Indian military doctrines;
  Pakistani military doctrines
military technologies 464–465
Millennium Challenge Compact (MCC) 305
Mir, Mohm Amin 37
Mishra, Brajesh 386
Missile Technology Control Regime 70
missionary societies 395
Mitterrand, François 385, 390
Moderna 431
Modi, Narendra 36, 98, 110–112, 145, 278, 291,
  292, 294, 296–297, 308, 316–317, 371, 374,
  388, 399, 426, 433, 444
Mohmand, Abdul Ahad 463
Mollah, Abdul Quader 162–163, 263, 279
Monroe Doctrine 295
Montville, Joseph 185
Moon treaty 464
Mostofa, Shafi Md 162
Mozena, Dan 265
Mueller, Max 395

Mughal Empire 292
Muhammad, Hafez Saeed 278
mujahideen 144
multialignment 69
Multiple Independent Reentry Vehicle (MIRV)
  117
Mumbai terror attacks (2008) 49, 108–109,
  133–134, 145, 387
Musharraf, Pervez 83, 145, 277–278, 281, 385
Myanmar 265, 297, 321, 362–363; Bamar ethnic
  majority in 38; governance failure 203;
  Rohingya exodus from 203, 402, 447–449
mythmakers 83

Naga National Council (NNC) 159
Nakasone, Yasuhiro 355
NASA 454–455, 458, 460
Naseemullah, Adnan 166
Nasheed, Mohamed 283, 307, 309, 321
Nasser, Gamal Abdel 398
nationalism 37, 50; Hindu 22, 36, 110, 324;
  Muslim 22, 160; Pakistani 82; Pashtun 281;
  Sinhala 2; territorial 37
National Power Corporation India Limited
  (NPCIL) 390
National Registry of Citizenship (NRC) 264
National Security Adviser (NSA) 218
nation-building: politics of 50; and South Asia 50
NCDC 429–431
Neemrana Dialogue 186
Nehru, Jawaharlal 24, 65, 67, 69, 93, 112, 116,
  289–290, 292, 294–295, 384, 397, 398, 428,
  471
neo-classical realism 276
"neo-neo" approaches 32
Neorealism 37, 84
Nepal 4, 13, 371–373; and Belt and Road
  Initiative (BRI) 303, 305; democracies
  25; and democratic transition 305; Digital
  Connectivity and Cybersecurity Partnerships
  program 322; economic development of 304;
  foreign policy behavior 302; and Germany
  402; new foreign policy 303–305; and political
  competition 305; political ideologies 21–22;
  and regional power distribution 303–304;
  relations with Afghanistan 236; space program
  of 463; and Sri Lanka 251; and U.S. 322
Nepal Telecom Breach 217
Nepal Telecommunication Authority (NTA) 463
NewSpace India Limited (NSIL) 461
Nizami, Motiur Rahman 263
Non-Aligned Movement (NAM) 27, 65, 68, 293,
  305, 398
non-governmental organizations (NGOs) 397,
  425, 432
normative beliefs 34
norms 38–40; categories of 34; defined 34

490

Index

North Atlantic Treaty Organisation (NATO) 345, 348, 384, 391, 395, 397

Northern Alliance 146, 234, 342, 345

NotPetya 215

Nuclear Command Authority (NCA) 121

Nuclear Non-Proliferation Treaty (NPT) 97, 118, 356, 457, 465

Nuclear Proliferation Treaty 79

nuclear restraint: doctrine of "minimum deterrence" 67; Indian strategic culture 67–68; No First Use (NFU) 67–68

nuclear strategy of no-first-use (NFU) 117

nuclear submarines (SSBNs) 117

nuclear weapons 108–112; and India-Pakistan rivalry 84, 107–108; *see also* Indian nuclear weapons program; Pakistani nuclear weapons program

Oberoi, Pia 441

Ogata, Sadako 201

Oli, K.P. Sharma 304

Onuf, Nicholas G. 32

Open-ended Working Group (OEWG) format 219

operational code 80

Operation Bluestar 164

Operation Brasstacks 132

Operation Enduring Freedom (OEF) 401

"Operation Enduring Freedom" 391

"Operation Searchlight" 278

Opium Wars 92

Organisation of Islamic Cooperation CERT (OIC-CERT) 216

Organization for Economic Cooperation and Development (OECD) 356

Organization of Islamic Conference (OIC) 260

Organization of Islamic Cooperation 27

Organization of the Petroleum Exporting Countries' (OPEC) 354

Orredoo 217

Ostpolitik (Brandt) 396, 398

Ottawa Dialogue 186–187

Outer Space Treaty (OST) 464

Pakistan 1–2, 275–283, 371–373; balancing against India 15; and Bangladesh 278–280; and China relations 13, 84; Climate Change Act (2017) 416; Cybersecurity Policy 219; economic crisis in 54; enmity with India 48–49; Epidemic Diseases Act of 1897 428; FATF's pressure on 86; and Germany 399–400; governance failure 203; government support of militant groups 142, 143, **144**, 144–146; Hamoodur Rahman Commission 278; importance in South Asia 3; and India 276–278; Indian military doctrines toward

173–175; Inter-Services Intelligence (ISI) 278, 280, 316, 319, 344, 372; material capacity 13; military forces 9; mutual defense agreement with the US 11–12; National Cybersecurity Policy 2021 220; nuclear tests of May 1998 333; and other SAARC members 282–283; Permanent Indus Commission 277; political ideologies 21–23; refugees hosted by 200; regime types 24–25; relationship with France 4; relationship with United Kingdom 4; relations with Afghanistan 231–232, 234–235, 237–238, 280–282; right-wing Islamist politics 49; satellites launched by **459**; space program of 458–459, **459**; and Sri Lanka 250–251; support for Taliban 145–146; surgical strikes by India 49; territorial disputes over Kashmir 48; war of 1947–1948 276

Pakistan Army Green Book 176

Pakistani military doctrines 170–179; deterrence-by-denial concept 175–177; overview 170–171; precision-guided munitions (PGMs) 177–178; Quid Pro Quo Plus concept 176, 177; technological transformation 177–178

The Pakistan-India Peoples' Forum for Peace and Democracy (PIPFPD) 187

Pakistani nuclear weapons program: effects on security policy and regional stability 133–137; future regional security 137–139; global nuclear dynamics 137–139; motivations 131–133; origins 131–133; overview 130

Pakistani Taliban 145, 159

Pakistan-Occupied Kashmir (POK) 105

Pakistan's strategic culture: beliefs 82; and creation of Pakistan 81; impact on policies 82–85; overview 79–80; religiously motivated militant groups 83; subcultures 85–87

Palme, Olof 200

Panchsheel 94

Paris Agreement 412, 416, 417

Parkes, Aidan 84, 88

Pashtun nationalism 281

Pashtun Tahafuz Movement (PTM) 235

Patel, Priti 373

Patrushev, Nikolai 346

Paul, T.V. 277

peaceful nuclear explosion (PNE) 116, 132

Peoples Liberation Army Navy (PLAN) 3, 4

People's Republic of China (PRC) *see* China

Perkovich, George 116

Persian Gulf War 444

Pfizer 431

plausible deniability 147

polar powers 11–12; behavior in South Asia 14–15

policy entrepreneur 39

policy prescription ideas 34

political authoritarianism 49

Index

political ideologies: Afghanistan 21–23; Bhutan 21–23; India 21–23; Maldives 21–22; Nepal 21–22; Pakistan 21–23; *see also* ideologies

politics: balance of power (BoP) 93, 95–97, 298, 319, 323; of climate change in South Asia 411–419; of nation-building 50; *see also* domestic politics

Pompeo, Michael 308

Pompidou, Georges 384, 391

Posen, Adam S. 161

poverty 454–455, 474–476, 478; endemic 3; and outward migration 444; in South Asia 197, *198*

power: cyber 214; soft 214

Pralay conventional ballistic missile 177–178

Prasad, Ravi Shankar 219

precision-guided munitions (PGMs) 177–178

prescriptive norms 34

Pressler Amendment 86, 132

principal-agent theory 142; and Afghan Taliban regime's behavior 149–150; challenges of 147–148; overview 147–148; and Pakistan 148–149; and state sponsorship in South Asia 148–150

Prithvi missiles 122–123

professional migration 443–444

Protracted Contest (Garver) 331

proximity, and Realism 10–11

The Public Law 480 260

Pugwash Conferences on Science and World Affairs 187

Pulwama-Balakot conflict 1, 108–109, 171, 387

Putin, Vladimir 346; Eurasian Economic Union plan of 2015 347; Greater Eurasian Partnership Concept 347

Quadrilateral Security Dialogue (Quad) 70, 265, 320, 324, 334, 345, 359

quasi-violence 165

Raajje Online 217

Rabbani, Burhanuddin 281, 345

Rahman, Fazlur 281

Rahman, Sheikh Mujibur 258–259, 261, 262, 432

Rahman, Ziaur 259, 261–263, 267, 279

Rajapaksa, Gotabaya 323

Rajapaksa, Mahinda 252, 322–323

Rao, P.V. Narasimha 473

Rathbun, Brian 275

Realism 2, 7–8, 46, 54, 245, 383–384, 440; and bipolarity 14; and geography 10–11; and proximity 10–11; and South Asian international relations 8–9

realpolitik 21, 64, 275

Recorded Future 217

refugees 447–449; from Afghanistan 200; hosted by Bangladesh 200; hosted by Pakistan 200; hosted in 2020 **200**; *see also* migration

regime types: Afghanistan 25–26; Bangladesh 25; India 24; liberalism 23–26; Pakistan 24–25; Sri Lanka 25

regional climate change cooperation, South Asia 416–418

Regional Comprehensive Economic Partnership (RCEP) 315

regional distribution of power 9–10

regionalism: and climate change cooperation 412–413; defined 412

regional trade and investment: challenges 476–478; import substitution industrialization models 471–472; international relations of trade and investment 478–479; in South Asia 470–479; trade and investment reforms 472–476

regional variables: geography 10–11; international politics 9–11; proximity effects 10–11; regional distribution of power 9–10

regulative norms 34

Rehman, Mujibur 279

reserved arsenal 117, 118–120

Resolute Support Mission (RSM) 401

responsible arsenal 117, 120–121

resurgent arsenal 117, 122–123

Return to East of Suez security posture in Indian Ocean 369

Rietig, Katharina 39

Rizvi, Hasan-Askari 82, 87, 275

Roadmap 2030 for India-UK Future Relations 371

Rockefeller Foundation 428–429

Rubber-Rice barter agreement 247

Russia 4; 19th and early 20th centuries 342–343; 21st century 345–347; Cold War 343–345; cyberspace activities 213–214; historical context 342; regional and international contexts 341–342; and South Asia 341–349; sponsored cyberattacks 213; theory and prospects 347–349; *see also* Soviet Union

Russo-British Pamir Boundary Commission 343

Ryutaro, Hashimoto 356

SAGAR (Security And Growth for All in the Region) initiative 297

Salehyan, Idean 147, 148

Samaddar, Ranabir 441

Sandia National Laboratory 187

Sarabhai, Vikram 118

Saran, Shyam 120, 305

Sarkozy, Nicolas 387, 393n20

Sattar, Abdul 275

Sauerland-Gruppe 400

Schelling, Thomas C. 172

Schimmel, Annemarie 395

science diplomacy 463–464

Index

SCO (Shanghai Cooperation Organization) 347, 348–349

Scott, David 39

Security Dilemma of a Small State (Werake and Jayasekera) 246

security seekers 81

Seeds of Peace 187

Sen, Amartya 200, 201

Senaratne, Bhagya 246

Sepoy Mutiny of 1857 158

September 11, 2001 attacks 281, 316, 319, 332, 342, 396; *see also* terrorism

Seventeen Point Agreement 94

Seventeenth Mountain Strike Corps 175

Shah, Amit 110, 113n30

Shah, Aqil 85, 87

Shah, Reza 160

Shah, Zahir 280

Shahbag movement 163

Shahmima Begum 372

Shanghai Cooperation Organization 27, 70, 235, 334

Sharif, Nawaz 277–278, 296

Sharma, Rakesh 461

Shastri, Lal Bahadur 117–118

Sherman, Wendy 319

Shirk, Susan 331

Sikh insurgency 163

Sikkink, Kathryn 34

Sil, Rudra 370

Singh, Manmohan 277–278

Singh, Sujatha 264

Singh, Swaran 250

Singhal, Saurabh 166

Sinhalese culture 23

Sino-Indian rivalry 92–99; asymmetry and rising tensions 98–99; balance-of-power politics (1962–1988) 95–97; China on India's status 92; cooperation amidst tensions (1988–2008) 97–98; phase 1 (run-up to 1962) 93–95; as strategic rivalry 92

Sino-Indian War 11, 14, 93, 95, 343

Sino Satellite Communications Company Ltd. 462

Sirisena, Maithripala 323

Siroky, David 148

Skrede Gleditsch, Kristian 147

Smith, David O. 82, 83

Snyder, Jack 80

Social Constructivism 34

socio-cognitive identities 36

soft power 214

Solih, Ibrahim Mohamed 307–308, 321

South Asia 245–253, 370–371; Afghanistan relations with 231–241; and China 317–318, 330–336; climate change policies in 414–416; climate change-related challenges in 413–414;

coining of term 46; connectivity in **216**; counterinsurgencies in 158–167; counter-terrorism in 142–151; cyber instability in 215–220; cybersecurity in **216**; demographics and economics 315; and France 383–392; gender indicators for **199**; and Germany's foreign policy 396–397; history 48–50; human security in 197–206; imbalance of power in 13–14; India-Pakistan rivalry and Kashmir 316–317; insurgencies in 158–167; internal displacement in **200**; international politics 9–12; international relations 3, 8–9, 478–479; Islamist actors 2; Japan's relations with 354–364; non-alignment in 301–309; polar power behavior in 14–15; politics of climate change in 411–419; refugees and migration in 439–450; regional climate change cooperation in 416–418; regional trade and investment in 470–479; and Russia 341–349; small states' foreign policy behavior 302; space programs 458–463; Sri Lanka's relations with 252–253; stability-instability paradox 134–135; strategic challenges 315–318; terrorism in 142–151; UK and 369–376; US goods trade with 315; US policy toward 314–324; US strategic engagement 318–323; *see also specific countries*

South Asia Alliance for Poverty Eradication 202

South Asia Free Trade Area 26

South Asian Association for Regional Cooperation (SAARC) 26–27, 39–40, 188, 215, 218, 234, 245, 252, 262, 276, 281, 295, 302, 304, 305–306, 309, 334, 370, 375, 397, 402, 411, 413, 446, 476; Action Plan on Climate Change 418–419; COVID-19 Emergency Fund 433; Disaster Risk Management Centre (SDMC) 417; Members 282–283; Plan of Action on Climate Change 417; satellite 464

South Asian Free Trade Area (SAFTA) 296, 476–477

South Asian Voices 187

South Asia Subregional Economic Cooperation (SASEC) 304

South Asia Terrorism Portal (SATP) 160

Southeast Asian Treaty Organization (SEATO) 93, 343, 385, 399

sovereign cyberspace 219–220

Soviet Union: and Afghanistan 23; Asian Collective Security Proposal 96; and Bangladesh 258; India alliance with 11–12, 14, 96; Interkosmos program 461; invasion of Afghanistan 49, 281, 342; and strategic culture 80; *see also* Russia

space: arms control 464–465; diplomacy 463–464; landscape 455–456; polices 456–458

Space and Upper Atmosphere Research Commission (SUPARCO) 455, 458–459

Index

space programs: Afghanistan 462–463; Bangladesh 461–462; Bhutan 463; India 460–461; Maldives 463; Nepal 463; Pakistan 458–459, **459**; in South Asia 458–463; Sri Lanka 462

Sputnik 454

Sri Lanka 13–14, 159, 245–253, 371–373; and Bangladesh 249–250; Bay of Bengal Initiative 323; and Bhutan 251; brief empirical history 247–248; democracies 25; Epidemic Diseases Act of 1897 428; four theoretical schools 245–246; and Germany 401–402; governance failure 203; international relations and religious division 22–23; major changes in past decade 248–249; and Maldives 249; National Adaptation Plan (2016–2025) 416; National Climate Change Policy 416; and Nepal 251; and Pakistan 250–251; regime types 25; relationships within South Asia 249; relations with Afghanistan 236, 252; relations with India 3, 250–251; relations with South Asia 252–253; Sinhala nationalism 2; Sinhalese culture 23; Sinhalese-Muslim riots 38; space program of 462; subfield of small states 246–247; and U.S. 322–323

Sri Lankan Civil War 38

Sri Lanka Space Agency (SLSA) 455, 462

stability-instability paradox 134–135

Stalin, Joseph 343

START nuclear arms control agreement 464

Stone, Laura 266

strategic culture: deep (*see* deep strategic culture); defined 80; theorizing 80–81

Strategic Forces Command (SFC) 121, 123

strategic hedging 302

strategic rivalries 92–99

strategic subcultures 85–87

Strong Borders, Secure Nation (Fravel) 332

structural inequalities 202–203

Subrahmanyam, K. 118

subterranean nuclear explosion for peaceful purposes (SNEPP) 117–118

Sukarno (Former President of Indonesia) 398

Surrey Satellite Technology Ltd. (SSTL) 462

sustainable development 361–363

Sustainable Development Goals (SDG) 304, 399

Takeshita, Noboru 355

Taliban 49, 79, 83, 281, 282, 316, 319, 335–336, 375, 391, 475; Haqqani Network 235; Pakistan support for 145–146; rule in Afghanistan 3–4, 40, 146–147; support for militant groups 142

Tallinn Manual 215, 219

Tanham, George 64

Tannenwald, Nina 34

Tata Sons 374

Tehrik-i-Taliban Pakistan (TTP) 2, 3, 25, 87, 159, 160, 281

terrorism: confronting, in new nuclear context 109–110; and India-Pakistan rivalry 108–109; Mumbai attacks (2006 and 2008) 49, 108–109, 133–134, 145, 387; Pulwama attack (2019) 1, 108–109, 171; in South Asia 142–151; US-designated terrorist organizations 142, **143**

Thapliyal, Sangeeta 304

Theravada 251

Theys, Sarina 38, 39

Third Indo-Pakistan war of 1971 319

Tiananmen Square massacre 97

Tibet: Lhasa Revolt 94–95; PLA's invasion of eastern 92, 93–94; revolt of 1959 332

Tito, Josip Broz 398

Track Three dialogues 185–186

Track Two Diplomacy: impact on conflict 189; India-Pakistan case 186–188; and IR theory 185; levels of 185; local ownership 190; "multi-track" approach 191; and opinion 190; overview 184–186; security/foreign policy-oriented dialogues 189; support for dialogues 188–189; sustainability 188

Trade and Investment Cooperation Forum Agreement (TICFA) 266

trade and investment reforms 1970s–1990s 472–476

Trans-Pacific Partnership (TPP) 315

Treaty of Friendship, Co-operation and Peace 259

Trump, Donald J. 86, 99, 315, 318, 319

Tsourapas, Gerasimos 440

Tuteja, Divya 166

"Two Nation Theory" 22

UIDAI 217

UK-Bangladesh Climate Partnership 373

UK-Bangladesh Trade and Investment Dialogue 373

UK-India Defense and International Security Partnership 374

UK-India Economic and Financial Dialogue 374

UK-India Sustainable Finance Forum 374

UNICEF 429

Union of Concerned Scientists (UCS) 455

unipolarity 14

United Kingdom (UK): and Afghan Taliban government 4; Counter Terrorism Strategy (CONTEST) 372; and India 373–375; relationship with Pakistan 4; *Roadmap 2030 for India-UK Future Relations* 371; and South Asia 369–376; South Asian periphery (Afghanistan-Pakistan-Nepal-Bhutan-Bangladesh-Sri Lanka-Maldives) 371–373; Terrorism Act 372, 374; *Tilt to the Indo-Pacific* 369

Index

United Nations (UN) 21, 215, 259, 305, 334, 429; Climate Change Conference (COP26) 204; General Assembly 262, 306, 390; Human Rights Council 402; Joint Global Multi-Nation Birds Satellite (BIRDS) 462; Least Developed Countries list 474; Office Human Rights High Commission 49

United Nations Conference on Trade and Development (UNCTAD) 218

United Nations Development Programme (UNDP) 201; Human Development Report 201; introduction of human security 201

United Nations Framework Convention on Climate Change (UNFCCC) 411, 415–416

United Nations High Commissioner for Refugees (UNHCR) 200, 447–449

United States (US): "Atoms for Peace" program 132; and Bangladesh 321; and Bhutan 320–321; and China 317–318; demographics and economics 315; "Framework for a Defense and Security Relationship" 322; goods trade with South Asia 315; and India-Pakistan rebalancing 319–320; on India-Pakistan rivalry and Kashmir 316–317; and Indo-Pacific region 318–319; and Maldives 321–322; and Nepal 322; Pakistan mutual defense agreement with 11–12; role in nuclear risk reduction in South Asia 137–138; and South Asia strategy 1; and Sri Lanka 322–323; strategic challenges 315–318; strategic engagement with South Asia 318–323; terrorism and the War in Afghanistan 316; toward South Asia, trends in 314–324; war in Afghanistan 12, 145; withdrawal from Afghanistan 1, 3, 54, 314

UN Security Council 260, 317, 320

Uri terrorist attack 137

USAID 321

US Battle Act 247

US Centers for Disease Control and Prevention (US CDC) 426, 429–430

US-designated terrorist organizations: in Afghanistan 142, **143**; in Pakistan 142, **143**

US Millennium Challenge Corporation 322, 323

US State Department 46, 322

Utsukushii kuni e (Abe) 358

Vajpayee, Atal Bihari 67, 120, 277, 386

Vasco da Gama 395

Vote Leave campaign 373

Wæver, Ole 8

Wahabi Sunni 49

Waheed Hassan, Mohammed 306, 307, 321

Walt, Stephen 7

Waltzian Structural Realism 10–11

Wang Gungwu 102n53

WannaCry 215

War on Terror 294, 391

Warsaw Pact 395

"war systems" theory 167

Washington Consensus 430

Wassenaar Arrangement 70

Waterman, Alex 166

Wendt, Alexander 33

Werake, Mahinda 246

Western colonialism 297

women: economic empowerment 321, 445; migrants 445; in South Asia 197–198; and Sri Lankan government 446; and Taliban's national norms 40, 316

Women in Security, Conflict Management and Peace (WISCOMP) 187

Wood, Reed M. 148

World Bank 26, 202, 414, 425, 428, 429, 470, 473–475, 476, 478

World Health Organization (WHO) 425, 426, 428–430, 432–433; Global Polio Eradication Initiative 429; "Health for All" approach 429

World of Our Making (Onuf) 32

World Order Models Project 200

World Trade Organization (WTO) 475, 477

World War II 356, 441, 442, 447

Xi Jinping 98, 265, 304, 317, 333

Xinhua News Agency 308

Yameen, Abdullah 283, 307

Yeltsin, Boris 344

Yoshitaro, Hirano 357

Youth for Peace 187

Yunus, Muhammad 265

Zahir Shah, King of Afghanistan 343

Zardari, Asif Ali 278, 279, 387

Zia, Khaleda 261, 263

Zia-ul-Haq, Muhammad 144, 279, 281, 458